THE FACTS ON FILE
COMPANION TO

BRITISH POETRY

BEFORE 1600

MICHELLE M. SAUER

Facts On File
An imprint of Infobase Publishing

The Facts On File Companion to British Poetry before 1600

Facts On File, Inc.
An imprint of Infobase Publishing
132 West 31st Street
New York NY 10001

Library of Congress Cataloging-in-Publication Data

The Facts on File companion to British poetry before 1600 / [edited by] Michelle M. Sauer.
    p. cm. — (Companion to literature)
  "The Facts On File Companion to British Poetry before 1600 is part of a four-volume set on British poetry from the beginnings to the present."
  Includes bibliographical references and index.
  ISBN 978-0-8160-6360-4 (acid-free paper) 1. English poetry. I. Sauer, Michelle M., 1972– II. Facts on File, Inc. III. Title: Companion to British poetry before 1600.
  PR1175.F19 2008
  821—dc22 2007024865

Facts On File books are available at special discounts when purchased in bulk quantities for businesses, associations, institutions, or sales promotions. Please call our Special Sales Department in New York at (212) 967-8800 or (800) 322-8755.

You can find Facts On File on the World Wide Web at http://www.factsonfile.com

Text design adapted by Annie O'Donnell
Cover design by Salvatore Luongo

Printed in the United States of America

VB Hermitage 10 9 8 7 6 5 4 3 2 1

This book is printed on acid-free paper and contains 30 percent postconsumer recycled content.

CONTENTS

INTRODUCTION

HOW TO USE THIS BOOK

The Facts On File Companion to British Poetry before 1600 is part of a four-volume set on British poetry from its beginning to the present. This particular volume covers poetry written during the Anglo-Saxon, Middle English, and early Renaissance (Tudor) literary periods in the area traditionally referred to as the British Isles, which includes England, Ireland, Scotland, and Wales.

Today's Great Britain includes Wales, Scotland, England, and Northern Ireland. The Republic of Ireland has been independent since 1921. The issue of what, exactly, makes up "British literature" is a complicated one. Certainly, the first "British" people were Celtic in origin, and the word itself derives from the people who populated a region that is now in northern France (Brittany). After the Germanic invasions (traditional date 449 C.E.), the Angles and Saxons melded into a singular culture that pushed the Celtic Britons into the further reaches of Wales, Cornwall, and Scotland. As they expanded outward, the Anglo-Saxons tended to absorb the native culture; thus, Arthur—originally Welsh in origin—became an Anglo-Saxon hero. Certainly, the Anglo-Saxons, and, later, the English, embarked upon campaigns of military conquest against the various Celtic peoples and over the years subjugated Wales, Ireland, and Scotland. By the time James Stuart took the throne as James I in 1603, he was styled King of England, Scotland, and Ireland (Wales, as an annexed principal-ity, was not part of the monarchial title). In essence, English culture was one of colonization, starting with the original Germanic invasions.

Recent criticism has striven to present Ireland and Irish literature within the context of postcolonial studies, and these ideas have been extended to Welsh and Scottish literary productions too. Despite being problematic, however, the term *British* is the one used most often, if just for convenience sake. Part of the difficulty with the discussion also stems from differences in viewing terms from an American standpoint versus an English, Irish, Welsh, or Scottish one. Universities in the United Kingdom and the Republic of Ireland tend to separate English studies from Celtic studies; however, that same separation is rarer in American colleges and universities. In fact, one of the traditional staples of the American curriculum is the "British literature survey," which generally includes Celtic contexts. Thus, *British literature* is a loosely used term in the United States, without any overt politically disruptive intent. This is not an excuse, per se, but rather more of an explanation, and one that certainly warrants further discussion. In the meantime, however, the reality is that the Celtic literatures are often grouped under the heading "British." Although not an ideal solution, I suggest that it is preferable to excluding the literature altogether, or to grouping it under the title "English" literature. Even "literature written in English" is exclusionary, especially in the medieval and Renaissance eras, when so much literary production took place in

iv

Latin, Anglo-Norman, Welsh, Middle Scots, and other languages. I hope, then, that I can be forgiven the term *British,* especially in regards to the multilingual fluidity of the medieval era alongside a fervent desire not to make any political gaffes.

Entries cover the poems and poets most often taught in high school and college classrooms and the concepts most important to understanding the poetry of the period. The approach throughout is to combine current critical approaches with more traditional methods, providing a balanced framework and presenting works in the context of their time. Entries are self-contained and relatively jargon-free. Although primarily aimed at a student audience, this book is also designed to benefit teachers, librarians, and general readers who love poetry.

Entries on individual poems provide an overview or summary of the text and a discussion of the style or genre of the work. Difficult terms are glossed, and historical and literary context is provided where appropriate and necessary. The standard or most common interpretation of the work is usually presented, in addition to an overview of critical debates and current trends. Biographical entries provide information about the author's life and work in general. Historical entries cover significant events relevant to the creation, distribution, and inspiration of pre-1600 poetry (e.g., the Norman Conquest). Thematic entries provide background discussion on important areas, such as the classical tradition, while entries on poetic terms important to the period clarify entry content and provide relevant examples drawn from works included in volume. There are a few non-British writers, such as Ovid and Virgil, included if they had a profound impact on British poetry. The appendix includes a bibliography and a brief glossary of general poetic terms.

EDITORIAL CONVENTIONS

Many scholars have contributed to this encyclopedia, but I strove to achieve conformity of content and style, if not complete uniformity. All entries feature the contributor's name at the end of the entry. Unsigned entries were written by the volume editor.

For the most part, spelling has been regularized to modern standards: for example, the poets' names are given as *Sidney* (not *Sydney*) and *Spenser* (not *Spencer*) consistently throughout the volume. However, if the standard medieval or early modern spelling of a work does not interfere with understanding, it has usually been retained (e.g., Spenser's poem is *The Shepheard's Calender,* not *The Shepherd's Calender*).

Some of the finest poetry of the period is in the form of the sonnet, and many sonnets appeared as part of larger works called *sonnet sequences.* In this volume, major sonnet sequences, such as Sidney's *Astrophil and Stella,* are discussed generally in overview entries under the title of the sequence, with individual coverage of the most commonly read and important sonnets given in subsections just below the overview entry. (Shakespeare's untitled sequence appears under the editorially given name *Shakespeare's Sonnets.*) This same convention holds true for other longer works that are frequently excerpted (e.g., *Piers Plowman*). There are two major exceptions to this practice. The individual "tales" of Chaucer's *Canterbury Tales* appear as unique entries, alphabetized under the name of their titles (for example, "The Pardoner's Tale" appears under *P*), as do the individual lays (*lais*) in Marie de France's collection. These works are often taught as individual pieces rather than as part of a greater whole, and it seemed more useful to categorize them as such in this book. As well, since the prologues and epilogues are usually taught with each individual Canterbury Tale, those discussions are assumed throughout.

Unless otherwise indicated, the standard editions for works are used. *The Riverside Chaucer* (Houghton-Mifflin, 1987) and *The Riverside Shakespeare* (Houghton-Mifflin, 1997) can be assumed for all relevant entries. For entries on major sonnet sequences and other longer works, the main editions and critical works used for each entry on a particular sonnet appear at the end of the overview entry. Any further reading lists appearing in individual sonnet entries reflect additional sources.

Where necessary, dates are written as B.C.E. (Before the Common Era) or C.E. (Common Era). Derogatory terminology (e.g., *pagan* instead of *pre-Christian* or *non-Christian*) and disparaging nicknames (e.g., "Bloody Mary" Tudor) are not used. The terms *Renaissance* and *early modern* are used interchangeably throughout this work. Scholars continue to debate the correctness of each term, and both are commonly employed. In order to clarify some of the issues, I have included an entry on the idea of "early modern v. Renaissance."

POEMS AND POETS INCLUDED

In choosing works and writers to include in this book, I consulted with all the major anthologies of literature of the period, including the Norton, Longman, Broadview, and Blackwell. I also consulted several high school texts. Space constraints prevented the inclusion of everything one would wish; nonetheless, all the works and poets that students are likely to encounter are included here. The inclusion of Irish, Scottish, and Welsh literature has become standard classroom practice, and most anthologies today include so-called companion pieces or Celtic contexts, which are also often available as supplemental reading in electronic form, on sites dedicated to a specific classroom anthology.

It was particularly difficult to decide which Tudor works to include, as the sheer volume of poetry of that period is staggering. Medieval choices proved only slightly less tricky, and these were further complicated by the availability of translations. Most instructors teach Chaucer in the original Middle English, as well as some of the later authors, such as Lydgate and Hoccleve, the Scottish Chaucerian works, and medieval lyrics. However, earlier works—especially the Anglo-Saxon, Welsh, and Irish texts—are almost wholly dependent on modern English versions being available for student consumption, and, therefore, some readily available texts displaced others that are less accessible. At the same time, however, some early Middle English pieces that were crucial to the development of the vernacular tradition (such as *Handlyng Synne*) warranted inclusion. Overall, I believe all of the included texts provide essential insight into this period of literature.

Finally, personal inclination and modern politics dictate that women poets and woman-centered texts be fairly represented. I have striven, therefore, to represent women authors fairly. Among the complications of studying the medieval period is the lack of identifiable authors. As a medievalist, I have long lamented the tendency for anthologies to prioritize those works that can be attributed to a named author, thus poten-

tially excluding a great deal of female-oriented texts. Moreover, many named female medieval authors wrote in prose, not poetry, and thus lie beyond the boundaries of this volume.

PRE-1600 POETRY OF THE BRITISH AND CELTIC WORLD: A BRIEF OVERVIEW

This book covers the medieval and early Renaissance periods of British and Celtic poetry. For purposes of this volume, the Celtic texts are grouped within the appropriate "medieval" or "Renaissance" category, without further division. In English literature, however, the medieval time period can be further broken down into the Old English period and the Middle English period, with some scholars suggesting a third distinct division, the Anglo-Norman period. The Old English period runs roughly from 700 C.E. to 1066 C.E., the date of the Norman Conquest. The Anglo-Norman period, then, covers the immediate post-conquest time, or 1066–1154, when English went "underground," ending with King Stephen's death. The Middle English period traditionally ends with the death of King Richard III at Bosworth Field in 1485.

The early Renaissance is technically the Tudor era, named after the period's ruling dynasty. After Richard III's death, Henry Tudor ascended the throne as King Henry VII. He was followed by his second son, who became King Henry VIII (1509–1547), who in turn was followed by each of his three children: Edward VI (1547–1553), Mary I (1553–1558), and Elizabeth I (1558–1603). When Elizabeth died, the son of her cousin Mary, Queen of Scots, James Stuart, ascended the throne as the first monarch of the new Stuart dynasty.

OLD ENGLISH POETRY AT A GLANCE

The 30,000 lines of surviving Old English poetry are collected, for the most part, in four manuscripts: The Exeter Book, the Vercelli manuscript, the Junius manuscript, and the Nowell Codex (also known as Cotton Vittelius A.xv). These are all anthologies of texts collected after they were written, not assembled for a specific purpose. No texts describing the art of poetry survive from the Old English period. Scholars, however, have been able to piece together a general view of Old English meter. The basic rhyme scheme was alliteration (repeated initial consonant sounds), a system that relies upon the quantity of vowels, syllabic alteration, and prosody (rhythm). In 1885, Eduard Sievers outlined five distinct alliterative patterns within Old English verse. His research continues to be accepted today, particularly because each of his permutations can be found in all of the older Germanic languages. Old English verse lines are divided into half-lines by a caesura, or pause. Each half-line has two stressed syllables. The first stressed syllable of the second half-line alliterates with one or both of the stressed syllables of the first half-line; the second stressed syllable of the second half-line need not alliterate.

English and Celtic literature had its beginnings in the oral tradition. Singers and storytellers held powerful positions at court and were considered the memory keepers of the people: Anglo-Saxon *scops*, Irish *filis*, Welsh bards, and Scottish *makars*. Some, such as Taliesin, a sixth-century Welsh poet, are identified in their work. Four Old English poets are named specifically within the works they produced: Cædmon, Bede, Alfred, and Cynewulf. Some remain a mystery outside of what has been discovered from their work. For example, there was obviously a *scop* named Deor about whom the poem of the same name was composed, but nothing is known of him aside from the information in the poem itself. Of course the vast majority of Old English and Celtic poets remain anonymous.

This rich tradition of oral-formulaic literature left its mark on written poetry. It is likely, for instance, that a poet was accompanied by a harp, perhaps being plucked during the caesuras. Old English poems are marked by mnemonic devices such as repeated key phrases and descriptors (e.g., in *Beowulf,* the phrase "Beowulf maþelode, bearn Ecgþeow," "Beowulf, son of Ecgtheow, spoke"), as well as digressions—stories that enhance the central tale but also impart the history of a people. Because of this oral tradition, many of the surviving poems were likely composed before they were finally written down. The Celtic works derived from a long history, and many were not written down until the 12th century. A similar oral tradition is found within the Anglo-Saxon world, though a few more examples

remain. *Beowulf* is the only surviving full-length Old English epic that survives, but several examples of heroic poetry—battle poetry—survive, including *The Battle of Maldon, The Battle of Brunanburh, The Fight at Finnsburh, Widsith,* and *Waldere.* Though epic and martial poetry present serious subject matter, there are occasional bouts of lightheartedness. A poetic device commonly used within Old English poetry is the *litotes,* or dramatic understatement employed for comic or ironic effect. These understatements appear with regularity in *Beowulf* and battle poems and occasionally in other types of poems, especially elegies and religious verse.

The elegy was the other major form of pre-Christian poetry written in Old English. An elegy, or poetic lament for the passing of someone dear, can be extended to the whole of society as well. Both *The Wanderer* and *The Seafarer,* for instance, relate the tale of the passing of the Anglo-Saxon warrior culture as well as an individual's story. "The Ruin" is an elegy about seeing a destroyed city, possibly Bath. Sometimes these poems are referred to as "epic songs," especially when the lament becomes all-encompassing, shifting the focus outward toward society.

Lyrics present personal and emotional poetry—laments, complaints, and even love poetry. Several of them, including "The Wife's Lament," "The Husband's Message," and "Wulf and Eadwacer," straddle the line between elegy and lyric, as they are about loss and exile but not specifically about death and changing fortune. There is no set stanzaic form for the lyrics, which use an alliterative scheme.

Riddles, in which the subject is described in ambiguous terms, reveal the Anglo-Saxon fascination with word play. Indeed, true Anglo-Saxon heroes were expected to be almost as good with words as they were with weapons. In Old English poetry, "boasting" is used to establish the identity and battle record of the hero, as well as serving as a promise of deeds yet to come. There are two main types of boast: the *gilph* (about past deeds) and the *beot* (tall tales; uncertain outcome). Other poetic elements that demonstrate this intrigue with manipulating words include the epithet (renaming) and the kenning (metaphorical rephrasing). All of these, however, reveal something entirely different about Old English itself—the lexicon (word bank) was limited, and although it expanded through various means (loanwords, compounds, affixes, etc.), that expansion was slow. Related to the riddles are a number of charms found scattered throughout various Old English texts. These are generally pre-Christian in nature and serve a mystical purpose.

As the society shifted towards Christianity, a new type of poet, the monastic writer, emerged, though these, too, were generally unknown. Some of these religious poems include poetic paraphrases of Old Testament texts (Genesis, Exodus, and Daniel), Guthlac A and B (two versions), Judith, Christ and Satan, and The Fates of the Apostles, among several others. An assortment of Psalms, creeds, prayers, and hymns also survives. Cynewulf, author of the Old English poems *Juliana, Elene, Fates of the Apostles,* and *Ascension,* signed his poems using a runic signature—his name spelled in Futhark—hidden in the manner of an acrostic. Other than his name, however, very little is actually known about Cynewulf. The poems were composed in the 8th or 9th century and signal a shift in Old English poetry from heroic or martial verse to meditative devotional pieces. Still, the biblical themes are presented in manners similar to the Anglo-Saxon heroic poems. The dream vision poem *Dream of the Rood,* for instance, blends Christian mysticism with Germanic heroism in a successful manner. A similar occurrence can be found in "Resignation," an elegy about sin and forgiveness.

Finally, some poetry was composed in Latin or was composed in imitation of a classical form. Of particular relevance are the physiologius poems, which are adaptations from the Latin bestiary tradition, including "The Phoenix," "The Partridge," "The Whale," and "The Panther." As well, there is a surviving translation/adaptation of Boethius's *Consolation of Philosophy,* generally attributed to Alfred the Great.

MIDDLE ENGLISH POETRY AT A GLANCE

With the Norman Conquest in 1066, English literature was irrevocably changed, as was the English language. William the Conqueror and his followers spoke Norman French, and as they replaced the existing Anglo-Saxon nobility, French became the language of court and commerce. English was driven underground. A mournful poem found in the Worcester Cathedral Library, MS 174, records this passing: "many of the teachers are being destroyed and the people forthwith." As the language changed, the Old English verse forms died out too.

Literature survived in three languages: Anglo-Norman, the emerging Middle English, and Latin. The earliest poems in Middle English tended to be awkward and rough but ably demonstrate linguistic shifts. For example, *The Ormulum,* a vernacular work of the middle-to-late 12th century, while poetically lacking, is of tremendous importance to orthographers and grammarians. This massive work—20,000 lines of exegetical homilies on Christ—contains numerous authorial attempts to regularize spelling and grammar. Works such as this, in addition to the *Anglo-Saxon Chronicle,* which continued into the 12th century, show the linguistic adjustments brought on by the spread of Norman French.

Thematically, the shift is away from epic and elegy and toward romance and lyric. Still, the earliest romances often relied on vestiges of the Old English martial style. For example, one of the first is Layamon's *Brut,* based on Wace's *Roman de Brut* (1155), which was written in Anglo-Norman. Both were composed in England and based on Geoffrey of Monmouth's Latin prose work *Historia Regum Britanniae* (*History of the Kings of Britain;* ca. 1130–36). In each of these, the kings of Britain descend from Brutus, Aeneas's grandson, and thus trace their lineage back to Troy. The country, Britain, is named after Brutus, and no distinction is made between the Celtic Britons (the "British") and the Germanic Anglo-Saxons (the "English"); thus, Arthur, once a Welsh prince and enemy of the Saxons, becomes one of the English people's greatest heroes.

Romances recorded knightly adventures ("quests") and honorable deeds, occasionally with a subordinate element of love. Their main focus was chivalry, although later romances show the impact of the idea of courtly love. These poems recorded the idealized version of the upper-class life: hunting, battles, defending ladies, feasting, reading, playing chess, and other such leisure activities. A more traditional division includes the following: the Matter of Britain (Arthur and his knights); the Matter of England (English and Germanic heroes); the Matter of France (Charlemagne); the Matter of Greece and Rome (Alexander the Great and the Trojan War). Each of these provided subject matter for numerous tales of adventure and delight and, occasionally, for moral instruction.

Marie de France, a late 12th-century woman living in England who wrote in Norman French, composed a series of *lais* (minstrels' tales) as well as a number of fables and a life of St. Brendan. At around the same time, translations of Chrétien de Troyes's French Arthurian romances, *Erec et Enide, Cligès, Yvain, Lancelot,* and *Perceval* (the first Grail quest story), both changed the "Matter of Britain" from legend into literature, and also spread the popularity of the Arthur story. Early English romances, such as *King Horn* (ca. 1225), *Floris and Blancheflour* (early 13th century), *Havelok the Dane* (ca. 1300), were not as complex as the French ones, although some, such as *Sir Orfeo* (ca. 1330), showed development and depth. These early Middle English works, however, served to reestablish the vernacular as a language worthy of reading and writing. As romances grew more popular, the conventions of courtly love, outlined in the 12th century by the French writer Andreas Capellanus, permeated the culture alongside the ideals of chivalry.

English writing revived fully in English after 1360 and flowered during the reign of Richard II (1372–99). Ricardian poetry often focused on confession and redemption, a theme aided, no doubt, by the ravages of the Black Death (1348–50), during which more than one-third of Europe's population died. Lyrics and religious verse dominated, although a few Arthurian verse romances surfaced, including the stanzaic *Morte d'Arthur* and the alliterative *Morte d'Arthur.*

The newly emergent Middle English language was not as adaptable to alliterative verse, although the 14th century witnessed a revival thereof in an adapted form. Aside from the alliterative *Morte d' Arthur,* the so-called 14th-century alliterative revival encompassed such poems as *Sir Gawain and the Green Knight,* an Arthurian romance that combines spiritual and chivalric values into a complex poem about redemption. The *Gawain*-poet also wrote several other poems—*Pearl, Purity (Cleanness),* and *Patience*—in

this alliterative style. Another well-kn[own] this era is William Langland's *Piers Pl[owman],* alliterative dream vision about the d[ecay of the?] world and concern with salvation.

The best-known poet of the late 14th century is by far Geoffrey Chaucer, often called the "father of English poetry." Chaucer wrote in numerous genres, including the ballade, lyric, dream vision, fable, fabliau, hagiography, romance, and others. His career culminated with the composition of the unfinished *Canterbury Tales,* perhaps the greatest collection of stories ever produced in English. This frame narrative examines the social and religious milieu of the 14th century in a lively poetic manner and served to firmly (re)establish the vernacular as a language worthy of great poetic achievement. Chaucer's friend and contemporary John Gower wrote in all three major languages of the day—Latin, French, and Middle English, and while his achievement was perhaps not as great as Chaucer's, he, too, amply demonstrated the flexibility of English verse and the ability of the English imagination.

Debate poems, such as *The Owl and the Nightingale* (early 13th century) gained some popularity but were soon eclipsed by the rise of the lyric. Lyrics grew from ballads, servant songs, hymns, Christmas carols, and the like. They can be divided into two categories—secular and sacred. Secular ones tended to be bawdy, rowdy, and lively. Religious lyrics focused on the mysteries of religion, especially the Virgin Mary and Christ's life. The vast majority of these lyrics are anonymous. Spiritual verse, aside from lyrics, include mystic poems by hermits such as Richard Rolle (ca. 1300–49) and various anonymous hagiographies, especially of virgin martyr-saints. Most shared the common goals of educating the unlearned to become closer to God, though a few are more explicitly didactic.

Satiric poems, such as the *Land of Cokaygne* (late 13th century) were rare but usually well written. However, a form of social satire, the *fabliau* (bawdy tale), grew quite popular in the 14th century and later. Another form of satire is found in the beast fable, found in adaptations of Aesop's fables but also in other forms, such as Chaucer's "The Nun's Priest's Tale."

The 15th century witnessed a distinct falling off in English verse and was dominated by the so-called

English Chaucerians, such as Thomas Hoccleve and John Lydgate. Both wrote in Middle English and in a variety of genres, including the complaint, lyric, and narrative. Similarly, the French noble Charles d'Orléans could almost be dubbed a French Chaucerian for his reliance upon the English poet for inspiration for verses that he composed in both French and English while a captive in the Tower of London.

Celtic poetry from this era tends to be nationalistic. For instance, John Barbour's *Bruce* (ca. 1375) is a long (14,000 lines) heroic poem that combines chronicle and romance to celebrate the life, reign, and victories of Robert I the Bruce. Other Scottish poets from the 15th century, including Robert Henryson, Gavin Douglas, William Dunbar, and even James I of Scotland, are often grouped together under the heading "Scottish Chaucerians," though this is somewhat of a misnomer. These Celts did not strive to imitate Chaucer so much as to embody his spirit in a non-English manner.

The Book of Leinster (ca. 1100) contains many early Irish poems, legends, and geographical details. It also records battles fought, and, perhaps most significantly, it preserves some of the great Ulster cycle (tales of the hero Cú Chulainn), including the *Táin Bó Cúalnge* (*Cattle Raid of Cooley*). As well, the only copy of *Togail Troi,* an Irish adaptation of tales of the destruction of Troy, is found here too. Later Irish poetry, like that of its companion lands, collapsed toward chronicle, romance, and lyric.

One of the greatest Welsh poets, Dafydd ap Gwilym, dates to this era, as he flourished in the 14th century. Dafydd drew his inspiration from Continental and traditional Welsh sources but avoided, for the most part, English ones. Although he lived in a time of relative peace, Welsh nationalism was strong; indeed, by 1400, Owen Glyn Dwr had fomented an uprising that was quickly demolished. In addition to Dafydd, a number of lesser poets were also active, demonstrating that the great Welsh poetic tradition continued unabated, if altered.

TUDOR ERA POETRY

The Middle English era ends with the close of the 15th century, not so much because Henry VII ascended the throne, but rather because of the advent of the printing press and the first stirrings of the Reformation. When the first printed English book appeared in 1476, English had been transformed into a form not too different than present-day English, except orthographically. Printing helped to spread a literary standard under the Tudors. The "King's [Queen's] English" was eventually disseminated by such centrally issued works as the Book of Common Prayer (1549, 1552, 1559) and the Authorized Version of the Bible (1611).

Lyric poetry dominated the Tudor era. The most significant development was the refinement of the sonnet, a 14-line lyric poem that had been perfected in 14th-century Italy by Petrarch. Courtier-poets Henry Howard, earl of Surrey, and Sir Thomas Wyatt adapted the form to English, and its popularity exploded. Sonnet sequences, series of sonnets linked together by theme and content, quickly became the fashion. Sonnets depended upon a number of conventions, including a redefinition of courtly love, conceits (unique metaphorical comparisons), paradox, and other such linguistic tensions, which reflected the tension found at the heart of most sonnets—disdain for the poet by the beloved. Sonnets became so important as a mark of true poetic skill that it became essential that every aspiring author write them. William Shakespeare, for instance, best known as the "playwright of the people," established himself by composing a sonnet sequence and solidified his patronage by writing long narrative poems such as *The Rape of Lucrece* (ca. 1590).

Though arguably the most popular poetry, sonnets were not the only development found in the Tudor age. Poets experimented with a variety of forms, including the strambotto, epanodes, sapphics, quantitative verses, and quatorzains. Musical poetry grew in distinction during the Tudor era, encouraged by the thriving university culture as well as court culture. Henry VIII was known to compose songs and ballads, and, according to traditional folklore, wrote the still-popular tune "Greensleeves." John Dowland and Thomas Campion were masters of the ayre (lute song) and madrigal, but numerous others tried their hand at them. Poets such as Sir Philip Sidney also adapted traditionally musical poetry (e.g., the villanelle and canzone) to nonmusical settings.

Classical literature provided a great deal of inspiration during the Tudor age, providing models for the reinvention of traditional forms such the pastoral and the eclogue. Pastoral poetry was widespread and became adapted to fit other literary genres as well, resulting in pastoral drama, and pastoral sonnet sequences, although superb pieces, such as Christopher Marlowe's "The Passionate Shepherd to His Love" (before 1592) and the various responses to it, were also popular. Long narrative poetry made a comeback, especially in the form of the epyllion (minor epic), such as Marlowe's *Hero and Leander.* Eclogues, pastorals, and their accompanying themes were adapted by the sonneteers too. Some of the finest versions of this can be found in Richard Barnfield's works, including *The Affectionate Shepherd* (1594), although more traditional forms were also found, such as Edmund Spenser's series of eclogues, *The Shepheard's Calender* (1579). Poetic translations of Ovid and Virgil allowed easier access to Latin works, as well as resulting in unique poetry. The prevalence of classical forms also inspired new versions of quantitative verse and the return of the epic in the form of Spenser's *The Faerie Queene* (1595).

Irish literature became less influential in England as Ireland was firmly subsumed under the English Crown. Writers like Spenser, who were born in England but spent their adult life in Ireland, became the dominant voices. Scotland, however, retained its own distinct voice. A great deal of Scottish poetry from this time survives in the form of the popular ballad. As well, the Scottish monarchs Mary, Queen of Scots, and her son, James VI (later James I of England), were both accomplished writers in a number of genres, including poetry.

Finally, devotional poetry in the Tudor era is complicated. The Reformation irrevocably changed the world—politically, socially, intellectually, and literarily, as well as spiritually. Poetry became the medium for celebrating the Protestant cause and for showing support for other Protestant powers in Europe. Poetry also became the language of the court, especially during the reign of Queen Elizabeth I, who demanded that her courtiers speak using the language of courtly love. Poetry also became a way of upholding one's beliefs: Anne Askew, the Protestant martyr, and Robert Southwell, the Jesuit martyr, for instance, both wrote poetry about their faith during their incarceration. The Protestant emphasis on personal devotional reading, especially of the Bible, merged with the political dimensions and the growing interest in translation, resulted in numerous adaptations of the biblical psalms. In particular, *The Whole Book of Psalms Collected Into English Meter* (Sternhold and Hopkins, 1562) became the most popular book of poetry printed in English, going through almost 500 editions within 150 years. However, this was not the only version of the psalms. Another well-known version is the *Sidneian Psalms* (1599), a poetic adaptation/translation begun by Sir Philip Sidney and completed by his sister, Mary Sidney Herbert, countess of Pembroke. As well, the first sonnet sequence in English, *Meditations of a Penitent Sinner* (1560), written by Anne Lock, consists of 26 sonnets considering Psalm 51.

While these verse forms—the sonnet, the sonnet sequence, and the lyric—would continue in popularity throughout the 17th century, the onset of the English Civil War and the establishment of the Commonwealth (1642–1660) saw a distinct shift in religious sentiments, to be sure, but also in political and social expectations. Literature and poetry changed with the government, and the lighthearted courtly love of the Tudor era became exchanged for heavier lyric poetry or frenzied *carpe diem* motif poems from the Cavalier poets. The increasing emphases on empire and the New World also irrevocably altered the view of English identity, a change also reflected in the literature.

THE FUTURE OF PRE-1600 POETRY

It might sound odd to discuss the future of pre-1600 poetry some 400 years after its end; however, there remains a great deal of work to be done in this area. Many manuscripts in which vernacular writing survived have been overlooked, neglected, or ignored. During the Reformation and after, some manuscripts were burned, shredded, or otherwise destroyed. Still others have been hidden away and lost—even today, manuscripts are being found. For instance, *Sir Gawain and the Green Knight* was not printed until 1839, 300 years after its composition, and the *Book of Margery Kempe* (ca. late 14th–early 15th century), a prose spiritual autobiography, was not discovered until 1934. Printed texts do not necessarily fare much better. For example, there are a number of sonnet sequences that exist but have not been edited, updated, or critically analyzed (e.g., Richard Linche's *Diella,* 1596; William Percy's *Sonnets to the Fairest Coelia,* 1593; William Smith's *Chloris,* 1596). All in all, a great deal of literature from the pre-1600 era remains to be discovered and explored. Perhaps this book will provide a glimpse of the adventure that awaits.

ACKNOWLEDGMENTS

This project was infinitely rewarding, and I have seen positive effects on my teaching already. First, my thanks must go to the contributors who lent time, energy, and expertise to this volume. It was gratifying to work with so many scholars across the world.

I would also like to extend my appreciation to my editor, Jeff Soloway, for his forbearance and insight. As well, I appreciate the technical assistance provided by my student, Deborah Ringham, who particularly aided me with organization and tracking down entries. I should also thank the Minot State University grant program for the award that provided student assistance.

There are two individuals without whom this project could not have been completed. The first is my former student, Melissa Harris, who served as my "editorial assistant" and plied the computer keyboard on my behalf, patiently formatting and reformatting. It was rewarding to work with another perfectionist! Finally, I owe a sincere debt of gratitude to my spouse, Adam Bures, for his love and support—as well as for his editorial assistance. He is the only person I trusted in that regard, and that trust was well placed.

Michelle M. Sauer

JOURNAL
ABBREVIATIONS

A

ACCENTUAL VERSE Rhythm deriving from stress falling or not falling on a syllable, rather than on the length (quantity) of a syllable, is said to be accentual. Old English poetry, as in *BEOWULF* or *The DREAM OF THE ROOD,* is rigorously accentual. Its line has four stresses, bound by ALLITERATION, admitting a variable, although not unlimited, number of unstressed syllables. Accentual syllabic verse, which emerged in the later Middle Ages under French influence, uses a strictly controlled pattern of stressed and unstressed syllables to define the line.

The terminology of Greco-Roman quantitative verse has been adapted to describe accentual syllabic verse's metrical pattern or "feet" of stressed and unstressed syllables. A line will be composed of a given number of the same foot. For example, a great deal of 16th-century English poetry is written in pentameter (five feet) or hexameter (six feet) lines. The most common metrical feet are trochee (two syllables with the stress on the first [happy]), iamb (two syllables with the stress on the second [delight]), dactyl (three syllables with the stress on the first [merrily]), anapest (three syllables with the stress on the last [cavalier]). The spondee (two stressed syllables [heartbreak]) and Pyrrhic (two unstressed syllables [in the]) may be introduced for variation.

Helen Conrad-O'Briain

ACROSTIC An acrostic is a poem more concerned with wordplay than with any specific rhyme or

rhythm. In an acrostic poem, certain letters—usually the first in the line—form a name, word, or message that relates to the subject of the poem. Acrostics have a venerable history; at least two appear in the Bible. They were also popular among early Christians and monks, as well as with later poets. CYNEWULF signed his poems using runes that formed an acrostic.

See also DAVIES, SIR JOHN.

"ADAM LAY BOUND" ANONYMOUS (15th century) This eight-line lyric, extant in a single 15th-century manuscript, testifies to the cult of the Virgin Mary in the late Middle Ages. The anonymous author tells a story through the lyric: Adam and all humanity were once damned to hell because of Adam's disobedience, but the Virgin Mary gave birth to Christ, who offers the opportunity for salvation. The poet's true focus concerns not Adam and his act of disobedience but, rather, Mary's crucial role in the process of salvation. The poem ultimately celebrates Mary's appearance in history, proclaiming it a good thing that Adam took the forbidden fruit.

The poem begins on a seemingly grim note, referring to Adam's confinement in hell for 4,000 years or more: "Adam lay ybounden, bounden in a bond" (l. 1). The "bond" points to the new contract with God that Adam initiated when he ate the forbidden fruit. The verse form, however, with its trochaic and anapestic elements (see ACCENTUAL VERSE) establishes an almost jaunty rhythm. Even reference to what should be a long period of time comes out as something less than the torture of the damned: "Four thousand winter thoughte he not too long" (l. 2), as if Adam might have chosen to remain longer in such bondage. The 4,000-year duration refers to the scheme of world ages popularized by Augustine of Hippo, which said that humans who lived in the five world ages before Christ were damned for all eternity, although Christ not only offered men and women the possibility of salvation in the sixth age but also "harrowed" hell, releasing the virtuous "heathens"—including, notably, Adam and Eve.

Recent criticism of the lyric has emphasized the poem's versification and its musicality rather than its doctrinal issues. The middle portion of the lyric is dominated by the "apple," which the poet mentions five times. The first two mentions, in line 3, emphasize Adam's sin and priestly recording of the deed ("As clerkes finden writen in hire book [l. 4]) and the sin's deadly consequences. The second two references to the apple, in line 5, celebrate that sin as the event that allows Mary to become "hevene qwene" (l. 8). The lyric offers a late medieval English version of the "fortunate fall" from the *Exultet* of the Easter liturgy: It was a good thing that the first Adam fell because his fall created the conditions for the new Adam, Christ, born of the Virgin Mary. The Middle English poet even confers a special status on the moment of the apple's selection: "Blessed be the time that apple taken was" (l. 7). Blessing the time of Adam's disobedience seems to anticipate and allude to the angel's greeting to Mary in Luke 1.42: "Blessed art thou among women, and blessed is the fruit of thy womb." The lyric's final line proclaims that, because of Adam's sin and Mary's elevation to heaven, "we" all may "singen *Deo Gratias*" (l. 8). The poem has threatened to break into song from the opening verses, and the conclusion lyrically glorifies Mary's triumph by calling upon all people to sing "Thanks be to God."

See also MIDDLE ENGLISH LYRICS AND BALLADS, MIDDLE ENGLISH POETRY, VIRGIN LYRICS.

FURTHER READING
Duncan, Thomas G. "The Text and Verse Form of Adam Lay I-Bowndyn." *RES* New Series 38, no. 150 (1987): 215–221.

Manning, Stephen. *Wisdom and Number: Toward a Critical Appraisal of the Middle English Religious Lyric.* Lincoln: University of Nebraska Press, 1962.

Woolf, Rosemary. *The English Religious Lyric in the Middle Ages.* Oxford: Clarendon, 1968.

James M. Dean

"ADMONITION, BY THE AUTHOR, THE" ISABELLA WHITNEY (1567)

This poem was included in ISABELLA WHITNEY's first book of poetry, *The Copy of a Letter,* published in 1563. The first poem in this book, "I. W. TO HER UNCONSTANT LOVER," is a letter from a woman to a lover who has been unfaithful to her. The second poem is an admonition or warning to other women not to trust men's flattery. As critics have often noted, these poems may not be autobiographical; nevertheless, the use of the phrase *by the Author* in the title suggests that we should imagine that Whitney is the speaker, and that she is speaking as a betrayed woman advising other women on how to avoid such betrayals. She begins by addressing young women who feel "raging love" boiling in their hearts (l. 3) and who generally do not receive advice. She cautions women to beware of men's flattery, and she compares this flattery to the songs of mermaids, who have beautiful voices they use to lure sailors to their deaths. She also warns women that some men will pretend to cry in order to get their sympathy, and she reminds women that men have learned this trick from OVID's *The Art of Love.* These poems, which teach men how to seduce women, were often used in the English Renaissance to teach men and boys the art of rhetoric, or persuasion.

Whitney complains that less trickery than is taught in Ovid would suffice to deceive women, but then she cleverly appropriates Ovid's poems for her own purposes, using examples from Ovid's *Heroides* and his *Metamorphoses* to warn women not to be overly trusting. She recites the story of Scylla, who betrayed her father and stole the lock of hair that made him invincible in order to give it to the man she loved (who then betrayed her). She writes about Oenone, a nymph loved and abandoned by Paris before he was with Helen of Troy. Next is Phyllis's tale—she killed herself when her lover abandoned her and was then transformed into a tree.

Finally, Whitney tells the story of Hero, a woman who, unlike the other women cited in the poem, measured her man before she trusted him. Though she knew Leander loved her, Hero tested him by making him swim across the sea to her each night. In this way, he proved himself trustworthy. He also eventually drowned. Hero mourned him, but in spite of this tragic ending, Whitney suggests that it is better to "try before ye trust" (l. 87). There are few men like Leander, she claims, and she cautions women to be like a fish that carefully tests food in case it conceals a hook. By citing examples from Ovid's poems, Whitney provides the young women who are her audience with the same sort of information that men were given by Ovid. While men were taught how to seduce women, Whitney instructs women how to avoid deceitful men.

See also HERO AND LEANDER.

FURTHER READING

Bell, Ilona. "Women in the Lyric Dialogue of Courtship: Whitney's *Admonition to al yong Gentilwomen* and Donne's 'The Legacie.'" In *Representing Women in Renaissance England,* edited by Claude J. Summers and Ted-Larry Pebworth, 76–92. Columbia: University of Missouri Press, 1997.

Donna C. Woodford

"AGINCOURT CAROL, THE" ANONYMOUS (1415)

"The Agincourt Carol," written after Henry V's triumphal return from France, celebrates the king's victories at Harfleur and Agincourt during the HUNDRED YEARS' WAR. The events are altered from historical truth so that the triumphal aspects of the campaign may recount the king's rightful claim to French lands.

The BURDEN, "Deo gracias anglia / redde pro victoria," (Give thanks to God, England, for victory) occurs twice, once at the beginning and then after stanza 1, where it is labeled *Chorus.* The burden, having the quality of a doxology, is recalled at the end of each stanza with the words *Deo gracias,* a phrase that simulataneously recalls two events: the actual battle and the welcoming ceremonies upon Henry's return, where the words *Deo gracias* were placed on a victory banner.

Critical attention has focused on the religious aspects of this CAROL. For instance, the repetition of the phrase *Yahweh of Hosts is his name* is part of the hymnic structure of judgment, reminiscent of a pledge to God. The same emphasis can be seen in the CAROL'S REFRAIN, where England, as a nation, is being called on to affirm God's power and chosen minister, and to give God credit for the victory, which is reinforced with the verb *redde* (return). The doxology, the controlling structure of the poem, contrasts with the nationalistic impulses observable in the words of warlike savagery, strength, and compassionate justice.

The Carol's STANZAS recall the 1415 campaign itself. Stanza 1 provides a general introduction; stanza 2, the siege at Harfleur; stanzas 3 and 4, the battle of Agincourt; stanza 5, the return to London; and stanza 6, generalized thanksgiving for victory. Stanza 3 in the Bodleian Library's manuscript is placed after stanza 6, thus emphasizing the defeat of the French at Agincourt. Placing the elimination of French pride at Agincourt as the last words to be sung or heard would have particular memorial appeal as it would linger in the minds of all as the most significant aspect of the campaign.

The first stanza serves as an introduction and summation of the 1415 campaign. Normandy was particularly important to Henry V (reigned 1413–22). Since the time of William the Conqueror, Normandy had been regarded as an important link to the Norman control of England, and now, with the balance of power reversed, it was England that was claiming the right to Norman soil. The carol writer is particularly keen to portray Henry's campaign as being one of CHIVALRY and righteousness (l. 2); the king's position was moderate, and accounts show that he was particularly concerned with reining in the potentially abusive activities of his soldiers.

With the second stanza, the carol recounts the experience at Harfleur, especially the siege. Harfleur was important because of its location at the mouth of the Seine River, making it a key point of entry in Henry's original plan of attack on Paris. In celebrating the victory, no mention is made of the heavy losses that altered Henry's campaign strategy; instead, the strength of the attack became the focus of the recounting of the event, and its recording both in CHRONICLE and in song is raised to the legendary.

Stanza 3 recalls the 150-mile trek of Henry's forces across northern France and the crossing of the Somme at an unguarded place amid the threat of attack from the French forces. The battle at Agincourt is commemorated in the fourth stanza. The carol writer, building on the images of corporate strength, celebrates Henry's warlike masculinity. The "grace of god" (l. 15) is the power behind the battle, which results in the twofold victory of a single battle and an entire campaign that cripples French power, for which the singers again return thanks to God with "Deo gracias."

The carol closes in the last stanza with a prayerful petition for providential protection for the king, "His peple, & alle his well-wyllynge" (l. 22), a phrase that probably was also intended to include those singing the carol at some historical distance from the event. The protection is requested so that the "merth" of the celebration may continue.

"The Agincourt Carol" provided the growing cult of Henry V in the 15th century with a text to remember the legendary victory in France. The carol underlines English legitimacy on national and international fronts through the performance of hymnic justice. God fights with and through the English in this act of political propaganda and nostalgia that reassigns to the events of 1415 the status of a personal, regal, and divine victory.

FURTHER READING

Crenshaw, James L. *Hymnic Affirmation of Divine Justice*: *The Doxologies of Amos and Related Texts in the Old Testament.* Missoula, Mont.: Scholars Press, 1975.

Greene, Richard Leighton, ed. *The Early English Carol.* Oxford: Clarendon Press, 1935.

Hibbert, Christopher. *Agincourt.* Moreton-in-Marsh, U.K.: Windrush Press, 1995.

Jacob, E. F. Jacob. *Henry V and the Invasion of France.* London: Hodder/Stoughton, 1947.

Robbins, Rossell Hope. "Notes to Agincourt Carol." In *Historical Poems of the Fourteenth and Fifteenth Century.* New York: Columbia University Press, 1959, 296–297.

Daniel F. Pigg

"ALAS SO ALL THINGS NOW DO HOLD THEIR PEACE . . ." ("A COMPLAINT BY NIGHT OF THE LOVER NOT BELOVED")

HENRY HOWARD, EARL OF SURREY (1557) This poem, along with all of Surrey's surviving lyric poetry, was published posthumously in the collection *Songes and Sonnettes* (TOTTEL'S MISCELLANY) in 1557 under the title "A Complaint by Night of the Lover Not Beloved." It is unusual among Surrey's SONNETS for the simplicity of its rhyme scheme: *abab, abab, abab, cc.* It is an adaptation of PETRARCH's Sonnet 164, and for the first half, it follows the original quite closely. The first QUATRAIN and line encompass a loose translation of lines 522 and following of book 4 of *The Aeneid,* wherein Dido, queen of Carthage, laments Aeneas, a Trojan warrior. This is accomplished through syntax and rooted in the early modern TRANSLATION TRADITION. Though the poem is an adaptation of Petrarch, its originality comes from its psychological investigation of the desiring subject following line 6. Using Petrarch as a starting point, Surrey investigates the absence of the beloved's image as the cause of the subject's suffering.

Line 1 sets up the thematic dialectic between the first and last words of the line, in accordance with classical rhetorical precepts, and is dominated by the ellipsis following "Alas." Lines 3, 4, and 5 all invert the syntax, sometimes placing the verb at the end of the phrase "the stars about doth bring" (l. 4); sometimes creating intentionally artificial constructions—the air singing in line 3, for example; and sometimes using CHIASMUS and onomatopoeia to indicate the serenity of the scene (l. 5).

Only in line 6 does the poem turn to the interior turmoil of the desiring subject as contrasting the peaceful exterior world. That the sonnet's VOLTA occurs in line 6, signaled by the second "alas!," is not extraordinary as the conventions of the English sonnet were still being created, and the Petrarchan original also changes at this point. The volta signals an investigation of the ways in which love "doth wring" the subject to extremes of emotion—"I weep and sing / In joy and woe." Love presents to the desiring subject the object of his desire "before my face" (l. 7), but it is not until the final couplet that we learn the cause of the subject's despair. Though he is presented with images of the object of his desire, he must "live and lack the thing should rid my pain" (l. 14).

See also SURREY, HENRY HOWARD, EARL OF.

Andrew Bretz

ALBA   The term *alba,* or "dawn song," comes from the Occitan regions of southern France. The verse form varies, but the subject matter involves lovers who have spent the night together reluctantly having to part at dawn. The tone resembles a LAMENT, the lovers wishing the night would continue forever. Some poems involve an appeal to the lover to awaken, and many incorporate a warning from a watchman who has guarded the lovers from spies and other interruptions during the night. The origins of the alba can be traced to the late 10th century, although classical precedents exist, but the first surviving Occitan text is Guiraut de Bornelh's "Reis glorios" (Glorious sun) from the late 12th century. In Folc de Marseilla (d. 1231), the form is even adapted to a religious purpose in "Vers Dieus, el vostre nom et de Sancta Maria." Though technically the alba is a subset to the AUBADE, the two terms are often used interchangeably.

FURTHER READING

Dronke, Peter. *The Medieval Lyric.* 3rd ed. Cambridge: D.S. Brewer, 1996.

Van Vleck, Amelia E. "The Lyric Texts." In *A Handbook of the Troubadours,* edited by F. R. P. Akehurst and Judith M. Davis, 21–60. Berkeley: University of California Press, 1995.

Carol E. Harding

ALDHELM (640?–ca. 709)   Very little is known about Aldhelm except that he studied at Canterbury under Archbishop Theodore and the abbot Hadrian and later served as abbot at Malmesbury and bishop of Sherborne. However, many of Aldhelm's works still exist, and they provide important evidence for studying the beginnings of recorded poetry and prose in England. Aldhelm wrote in a complicated linguistic style called hermeneutical Latin, though many speculate he also wrote Old English poetry that has been lost.

Aldhelm wrote many different kinds of texts, including riddles, treatises on the art of metrics, religious lyric poems, letters, charters, and poetic and prosaic versions of a text called the *De virginitate* (*On Virginity*). Aldhelm's riddles were perhaps the most popular of his writings. Covering numerous topics from cats to

women giving birth, they are composed in Anglo-Latin hexameters. Stylistically, the texts are short and mysterious. His writings on metrics, particularly *De metris* (*On Meters*) and *De pedum regulis* (*On the Rules of Feet*), outline in great detail the proper ways for poets to construct their verse and demonstrate the study of metrics to be both an art and a science. All of these works—the riddles and the two metrical treatises—are found in a lengthy letter from Aldhelm to Acircius, which can be dated sometime between 685 and 705.

See also ANGLO-SAXON RIDDLES, EXETER BOOK.

FURTHER READING

Lapidge, Michael, and James L. Rosier, trans. *Aldhelm: The Poetic Works.* Woodbridge, Suffolk, U.K.: D.S. Brewer, 1985.

Orchard, Andy. *The Poetic Art of Aldhelm.* Cambridge Studies in Anglo-Saxon England 8. Cambridge: Cambridge University Press, 1994.

Joshua R. Eyler

ALEXANDRINE   A 12-syllable line of verse written in iambic hexameter, in which each line of six feet has two syllables with an unstressed syllable followed by a stressed syllable. An alternate pattern features a short syllable followed by a long syllable. The form originated in French heroic verse. A prominent English example is found in EDMUND SPENSER's *The Faerie Queene,* in which eight lines of iambic pentameter are followed by an alexandrine.

ALFRED THE GREAT (AELFRED THE GREAT) (849–899)   The fifth and youngest son of Ethelwulf of Wessex and his wife Osburga of the Jutes, Alfred assumed the throne in 871 after the death of his brother, Aethelred. He had spent his youth in Kent, learning literature and philosophy alongside the warrior arts.

Alfred's first action was to buy peace from the Vikings. This peace was short-lived, and he spent the next several years engaged in guerilla-style battles, finally retaking London in 886, upon which he declared himself "King of the English." Alfred also forged the Danelaw (common boundary) with his former enemy, Guthrum. Politically astute, he reformed the legal code, established both standing and reserve units of the army, and created the first English navy. By 897, he had established a system of *burhs* (boroughs) across Wessex and halted the Viking advance.

Alfred was also an accomplished scholar. He helped reestablish monasteries demolished by the Vikings and founded a court school to educate noble children. He vigorously promoted the use of the VERNACULAR, making English the official language of the court. He also personally translated a number of works from their Latin original into Old English, including BOETHIUS's *The CONSOLATION OF PHILOSOPHY,* Bede's *Ecclesiastical History of the English People,* and Pope Gregory the Great's *Dialogues* and *Pastoral Care* (for which he also wrote a metrical preface). He also authorized the writing of the *ANGLO-SAXON CHRONICLE* in the late 9th century, requiring that many copies be made and distributed.

Alfred died at Wantage on October 26, 899. He was buried at Hyde Abbey, where his remains stayed until the Dissolution of the Monasteries.

See also METERS OF BOETHIUS, METRICAL PREFACE TO THE *PASTORAL CARE.*

FURTHER READING
Turk, Milton Haight, ed. *The Legal Code of Ælfred the Great.* 1893. Reprint, Clark, N.J.: Lawbook Exchange, 2004.

"ALISOUN" ("ALYSOUN") ANONYMOUS (1340)
This playful love poem is one of the many fine medieval English lyrics found, in London's British Museum (MS Harley 2253), in a 13th-century manuscript. "Alisoun" has received a great deal of scholarly attention both for its formal qualities and for the way the poet responds to the traditions of medieval love poetry.

Striking features of the verses in "Alisoun" include strong ALLITERATION and the rhythm created by varying three or four stresses per line. Both contribute to the rapid pace of the poem and to the effect hinted at in the first lines of the poem—that of a lover singing like a bird in the springtime. The poem also has a complex rhyme scheme that links together the STANZAs and keeps up this smooth and rapid flow. The first stanza begins *abab, bbbc, dddc,* and the remaining three stanzas follow this pattern, with the last four lines of each stanza making up the repeated REFRAIN.

"Alisoun" begins with a reference to springtime and love, a trope common in medieval love poetry. From this discussion of the renewal of nature and life, the speaker moves directly to his love-longing for the fairest of all women, his Alisoun. Following the pattern prescribed by the tradition of medieval love poetry, the poet then discusses the lady's physical beauty in the second stanza, and the third stanza describes the speaker's sleeplessness and torment—his LOVESICKNESS because of his longing for the lady. In the final stanza, the speaker worries that someone else may take away his lady, and he begs her to listen to his plea.

A number of scholars have explored the relationship between "Alisoun" and the tradition of medieval love poetry by examining the poem's connections to GEOFFREY CHAUCER. Though there is no clear evidence that Chaucer knew the lyric, he was certainly familiar with this type of poem. The first lines of "Alisoun" clearly draw upon the same tropes as the opening lines of *The CANTERBURY TALES.* Further, Chaucer gives the heroines of two of his tales the name Alisoun. The Alison of "The MILLER'S PROLOGUE AND TALE" seems very like the Alisoun of the lyric—a beautiful woman who excites men's passions. The Wife of Bath, also named Alisoun, is an older version of the same character type. Chaucer was not necessarily borrowing directly from the lyric, however. The name Alisoun or Alysoun, including variations on the name Alice, was commonly given to middle-class female characters in Middle English literature. That observation has lead to interpretations of the poem "Alisoun" that examine how the poet adapted the conventions of COURTLY LOVE for a bourgeois lady.

Recent critical trends have also explored issues of gender and sexuality in this poem. Alisoun is presented as an object of male desire; the attributes catalogued by the speaker are physical in nature and serve primarily to attest to her sexual desirability. We learn specifically about her "browe broune, hire eye blake," the fairness of her hair, the whiteness of her neck, and her "middel smal ant wel ymake" [small waist and fine shape] (ll. 13–16). More explicitly sexual is the phrase "Geynest vnder gore" (l. 37), meaning "fairest under clothing," which unmistakably refers to Alisoun's genitalia. Recent critics have discussed "Alisoun" in terms of the speaker and reader as voyeur. Nevertheless, although

Alisoun is presented as an object of sexual desire, she is also endowed with her own power in the poem. She has not yet acquiesced to the speaker's requests, and the speaker himself notes that there is no man in the world so clever that he can tell all of her excellence. While this may be read as a commentary on the extent of Alisoun's good qualities, it can also be read as a comment that no man may recount these qualities because none has been able to be sexually intimate with her. Alisoun retains her own mystery, and with it, her own power.

See also MIDDLE ENGLISH LYRICS AND BALLADS.

FURTHER READING

Brook, G. L., ed. *The Harley Lyrics*. Manchester, U.K.: Manchester University Press, 1948.

Fein, Susanna, ed. *Studies in the Harley Manuscript*. Kalamazoo, Mich.: Medieval Institute Publications, 2000.

Stemmler, Theo. "An Interpretation of *Alysoun*." In *Chaucer and Middle English Studies in Honor of Rossell Hope Robbins*, edited by Beryl Rowland, 111–118. Kent, Ohio: Kent State University Press, 1974.

Kathryn C. Wymer

ALLEGORY Allegory, in the broadest sense, refers to any figurative, or secondary, meanings that exist simultaneously with the literal, or primary, meaning of a text. The term's etymology from the Greek words *allos* (other) and *agoreuien* (to speak openly) reflects this definition and suggests why allegory has had so controversial a history. Speaking or writing allegorically allows one to make public declarations while concealing certain ideas from some part of the audience. Thus, allegory functions as the perfect vehicle for expressing political, theological, or other ideas not intended for general consumption.

Unlike related rhetorical forms such as irony, sarcasm, and enigma, where the secondary meaning corrupts or contradicts the primary one, in allegory the two levels are generally congruous with each other. In fact, the characters and actions on the literal level provide the hints by which readers are enabled to discover the allegorical meanings. For example, in the morality play *Everyman* (1500), the title character's name provides a hint that his experiences apply literally to him but figuratively to all people.

In addition to the broad definition, by the early modern era (see EARLY MODERN V. RENAISSANCE), allegory had acquired a number of specific and significant connotations, which for clarity's sake have been organized into three categories: rhetorical figure, interpretive scheme, and narrative text. While dividing allegory in this manner simplifies the process of understanding the uses of the term, it should be kept in mind that in practice the categories tend to overlap.

Understanding allegory as a rhetorical figure requires a turn to the rhetorical handbooks of the CLASSICAL TRADITION, where figures were discussed for their value as devices to enliven a speech. Starting with Quintilian's *Institutes oratorio* (Principles of Oration), allegory tended to be defined as a kind of extended metaphor, differing from it only in duration. Allegory might continue through an entire oration or poem, whereas metaphor is typically restricted to a line or short sentence. To illustrate this point, Quintilian offers as an example of allegory Horace's *Odes* (l. 14) where the state is compared to a ship sailing on a stormy sea. While classical rhetoric placed significant value on allegory's ornamental value, some rhetoricians noted that allegory could also influence ideas being expressed, an observation that later writers would exploit in various ways. Direct evidence that the influence of classical rhetoric extended through the early modern period can be seen in the fact that English rhetorical handbooks, including those by Thomas Wilson (*Arte of Rhetoric*) and Henry Peacham (*Garden of Eloquence*), and related works such as George Puttenham's guide to writing poetry (ARTE OF ENGLISH POESIE) generally do little more than repeat ideas developed by Quintilian or Cicero. Perhaps the most original aspect of early modern treatments of allegory is in the increased emphasis they give to the pleasure writers have in creating allegories and that readers take in unraveling them.

The history of allegorical interpretation (*allegoresis*), like that of allegory as rhetorical figure, reaches back into the classical world, where scholars used it to reinterpret significant earlier texts, most notably Homer's great EPICs, in ways that showed those texts' relevance to contemporary events. Late in the first century, Origen, a Christian scholar in Alexandria, combined this classical tradition with the Jewish interpretive tradition called midrash to form a systematic method for interpreting the Old Testament scriptures in which different levels of meaning could be discerned. While different interpreters in the late-classical and medieval periods argued over how many levels of meaning exist—St. Augustine, for example, generally speaks of two levels—the fourfold method of interpretation became the best-known example of this allegorical system. Somewhat confusingly, the second level in this scheme is called the allegorical level, while the third level is called the moral (tropological) level and the fourth the anagogic (eschatological) level (see ANAGOGY). The clearest and most famous example of this method appears in Dante's "Letter to Can Grande Della Scala," where he provides an interpretation of the Israelites' exodus from Egypt: "If we look only at the letter, this signifies that the children of Israel went out of Egypt in the time of Moses; if we look at the allegory, it signifies our redemption through Christ; if we look at the moral sense, it signifies the turning of the soul from the sorrow and misery of sin to a state of grace; if we look at the anagogical sense, it signifies the passage of the blessed soul from the slavery of this corruption to the freedom of eternal glory." While interpreters using the fourfold method have applied it to most scriptures in the Old Testament, very few yield distinctly different readings on all four levels.

While early theologians such as Augustine and Origen, and poets like Dante claimed Paul's injunction that "the Letter killeth, while the spirit saveth" legitimized the search for hidden or mysterious senses of scriptural passages, the practice was always controversial. For instance, William Tyndale, an early translator of the Bible, warned, "if thou leave the literal sense, thou canst not but go out of the way." While Tyndale's concern lay solely with the interpretation of scripture, the same caution has been called for in the interpretation of secular texts, despite there being no sure method for knowing if an interpretation has gone astray. The most that can be safely said is that allegorical interpretation requires a balance between the verbal and historical context established by the text and the historical situation of the individual reader. The consistency of interpretation between the literal and figurative levels of the text provides the only test of the soundness of allegorical interpretations. If the figurative meaning imputed to the text remains compatible with the literal level over the entire text, then the allegorical reading is valid. However, if conflicts emerge, the allegorical reading should be abandoned.

The most famous allegorical narratives, Dante's *Divine Comedy* and EDMUND SPENSER's *The FAERIE QUEENE,* represent the culmination of the rhetorical and interpretive forms of allegory. From the rhetorical tradition, narrative allegory takes the use of continued metaphors to delight readers, and from the interpretive tradition there is the potential for a reader's engagement with such a text to be instructive. The centrality of Dante's and Spenser's texts in the genre of allegorical narratives rests on a number of factors, not the least of which is artistry, but it also includes their connection to external, explanatory documents. Spenser's case concerns his *Faerie Queene* and its dedicatory letter to SIR WALTER RALEIGH. In this document, Spenser discusses both his authorial intention, which "is to fashion a gentleman or noble person in vertuous and gentle discipline," and his method for doing so, the "continued Allegory, or darke CONCEIT." The central allegorical device in each book of the poem is a knight who becomes perfected in a virtue. For example, in the first book he presents, Spenser says "Redcrosse, in whome I expresse Holynes," in the second he presents "Sir Guyon, in whome I sette forth Temperaunce," and so on. Each of his knights faces a set of tasks and challenges, the successful completion of which strengthens their possession of the virtue they represent. In defending his decision to use allegory to achieve his ends, Spenser acknowledges that the dark conceit is a "Methode [that . . .] will seeme displeasaunt" to some of his readers who "had rather have good discipline delivered plainly in way of precepts, or sermoned at large, as they use," but he defends his choice on the grounds that telling readers how to behave is less effective than showing them how to act.

While Spenser's and Dante's works hold a central place in the canon of allegorical narratives because of the external materials that have provided such valuable insights into the allegorical method, such materials are not essential for a work to be considered an allegorical text. What is essential is that the text engages the reader in a process of sustained interpretation. Allegorical works use a variety of means to help engage readers in such interpretive processes, means ranging from the generic conventional opening of a DREAM VISION, in which a narrator solicits the reader's help in understanding a dream, to the use of PERSONIFICATION, where inanimate objects and/or abstractions are represented as human beings with the ability to speak and act.

See also EXEGESIS, MIDDLE ENGLISH POETRY.

FURTHER READING

Fletcher, Angus. *Allegory: The Theory of a Symbolic Mode.* Ithaca, N.Y.: Cornell University Press, 1964.

Lewis, C. S. *The Allegory of Love: A Study in Medieval Tradition.* 1936. Reprint, Oxford and New York: Oxford University Press, 1968.

Todorov, Tzvetan. *Theories of the Symbol,* translated by Catherine Porter. Ithaca, N.Y.: Cornell, University Press, 1982.

Tuve, Rosemond. *Allegorical Imagery: Some Medieval Books and Their Posterity.* Princeton: Princeton University Press, 1966.

J. Hunter Morgan

ALLITERATION

ALLITERATION Alliteration occurs when a consonant is repeated in words that are next to or near each other. In English, typically, alliteration happens at the beginning of words that are part of a single line of verse. It may also appear in the stressed syllables within words, across two or more lines of a verse paragraph, and in various kinds of prose. Because alliteration produces a conspicuous, if brief, consonantal echo, it is best understood as a sound effect rather than a rhyme.

Scholars consider alliteration to be among the most ancient of metrical devices. The earliest poems were spoken or sung and therefore, if of any length, were difficult to recall. As a mnemonic device, alliteration enabled poets and listeners to better remember what they had performed and heard. Besides enabling language to be repeated more accurately, alliteration imposed order on spoken words and, by so doing, gave speech some of its earliest formal patterns. Listeners (and later readers) learned to treat instances of alliteration with greater attention than the more irregular utterances of everyday language. Alliteration thus helped to make poetry and prose more stylized over time.

Old English poetry had alliteration as its formal basis. Its poets divided a line of verse by inserting a CAESURA, or significant pause, at about the line's mid-

point. Alliterative consonants spanned the resulting HALF-LINES, typically by emphasizing a consonant of one or two of the stressed syllables. By the latter half of the 14th century, an ALLITERATIVE REVIVAL arose. Responding to Old English versification and opposing continental poetry, MIDDLE ENGLISH POETRY both used alliteration and varied it. As poets investigated alliterative possibilities, the best and often densest poetry of the period resulted. Indeed, major poems on the order of *PIERS PLOWMAN* and *SIR GAWAIN AND THE GREEN KNIGHT* expanded how alliteration could be imagined.

By the early Renaissance, alliteration had changed from an organizing principle to a less frequently used poetic device. *SHAKESPEARE'S SONNETS*, with their more sporadic but still-strategic use of alliteration, best demonstrate this change. For instance, the first QUATRAIN of Sonnet 30 treats the memories of lost love and dead friends by repeating, famously, the *s* and *w* consonants in lines 1 and 4, respectively. The repetition in "woes," "wail," and "waste" (l. 4) concludes the first portion of the poem by foregrounding an onomatopoetic of lament.

FURTHER READING

Cable, Thomas. *The English Alliterative Tradition.* Philadelphia: University of Pennsylvania Press, 1991.

Larry I. Shillock

ALLITERATIVE REVIVAL (ca. 1350–1400)

There is little agreement about the so-called alliterative revival. What it is, why it happened, and, indeed, whether it happened at all are all up for debate. Nevertheless, in the last half of the 14th century a number of nonrhyming, alliterative poems were written, most of them originating from north and northwest England. Although these poems vary greatly in terms of meter, rhyme, and generic form, they have in common their use of ALLITERATION, a poetic device in which two or more words begin with the same sound. The opening line of *PIERS PLOWMAN* serves as a good example: "In a somer seson, whan softe was the sonne" (l. 1). This group of poems is often referred to as a *revival* because alliteration is a basic form in Old English poetry.

Traditionally, scholars have differentiated between so-called formal (or classical) alliterative poems and informal alliterative poems. Formal poems have an alliterative pattern of *aa, ax,* meaning that each line of verse contains four stresses, the first three of which are alliterated, as in this opening line from *The Wars of Alexander,* where the initial "b" sound is repeated "this barne quen he borne was, as me the boke tellis" (l. 1). Formal alliterative poetry tends to have a more elevated style, as seen in alliterative ROMANCES such as *SIR GAWAIN AND THE GREEN KNIGHT* and the *Morte Arthure.* Poems in this group also include the alliterative *ST. ERKENWALD, CLEANNESS, Patience, The Destruction of Troy, The Siege of Jerusaleum, Winner and Waster, The Parliament of the Three Ages,* and *William of Palerne.* Informal alliterative poetry has a much less regularized rhyme and meter scheme and more variation it its alliteration. Many of these texts were written in the south midlands of England and examine contemporary religious and social life. Poems in this group include *Piers Plowman* and texts inspired by *Piers Plowman,* such as *MUM AND THE SOTHSEGGER* and *PIERCE THE PLOUGHMAN'S CREDE.*

Little is known about how these texts were produced and who produced them. Most are preserved in only one copy, with the exception of *The Siege of Jerusalem* and *Piers Plowman.* In addition, the majority of these manuscripts date not from the time of their composition in the 14th century, but rather from the 15th and in some cases the 16th and 17th centuries. Even less is known about the audience of these poems, although most scholars today believe the lesser clergy and nobility were the intended audiences.

Given these difficulties, why speak of an "alliterative revival" at all? The term developed in part in an effort to explain a mystery. *The BRUT,* which was composed at the end of the 12th century, is the last alliterative, non-rhyming poem written before the alliterative revival began in the mid-14th century. Thus, there seems to have been a 100-year period, from approximately 1250 to 1350, when no alliterative poetry was written, followed by a flurry of activity for about 50 years, at which time the form again waned (although it remained popular in Scotland for much of the 15th century).

As noted above, the term *revival* suggests that Middle English alliterative poetry hearkens to Anglo-Saxon verse forms. Not only is alliteration characteristic of Anglo-Saxon poetry, but the poems of the alliterative revival often use Old English or Old Norse words, which rarely appear in nonalliterative Middle English poetry. Therefore, at first glance these poems seem to be quite self-consciously modeling themselves on their Anglo-Saxon predecessors. Although there is comparatively little written Anglo-Saxon poetry extant, some scholars have argued that these older forms were preserved through oral tradition, citing as evidence the scenes of public storytelling in noble households that sometimes appear in these poems. One explanation offered for the revival of alliterative verse is that in the mid-14th century the influence of ANGLO-NORMAN was waning and poets were looking for a literary language to replace it. Others have suggested that the poets of this period turned to alliterative verse in an effort to develop a poetic style that was distinctly English in order to break away from French, which had shaped literature and culture since the NORMAN CONQUEST in 1066.

However, there are a number of difficulties with this thesis. While late medieval, alliterative poetry shares similarities with its Anglo-Saxon counterpart, it has a different meter and style. In addition, while Old English, Old Norse, and even Scandinavian words appear in 14th-century alliterative poetry, there are also a number of new, contemporary words used in the poems, many of which relate to clothing, hunting, siege warfare, and armor. Nor do we have evidence that Anglo-Saxon alliterative verse was preserved in oral culture. Even if it was, there are two aspects of Middle English alliterative poetry that make it unlikely that it was inspired by an oral tradition. First, the poems tend to be very bookish, often citing textual sources for their stories. This device could certainly be a convention (just as a scene of public recitation could be a convention, rather than reflective of actual practice), but many of these texts are translations of French or Latin sources. Second, some of the poems are very long. Ten alliterative poems are 1,000–7,000 lines, and *The Destruction of Troy* a daunting 14,000 lines. These lengths do not invite memorization and oral recitation. Others have suggested that alliterative verse was passed down to 14th-century writers not through oral tradition but, rather, through texts that are now lost to us. According to this theory, there is continuity in the composition of alliterative verse, rather than disruption in the form of a 100-year gap. It has been proposed that missing manuscripts could have been preserved in monastic libraries in Southwest England. Indeed, a manuscript of the *The Siege of Jerusalem* has been linked to the priory at Bolton, Yorkshire. The manuscripts' delicate nature suggests there are missing manuscripts that, if found, would provide important clues about the development of Middle English alliterative poetry. However, given the limited number of extant and available manuscripts, it is difficult to draw firm conclusions about the composition and preservation of these poems.

Some scholars have suggested abandoning the term *alliterative revival* altogether, since there is a great deal of alliterative prose and poetry that encompasses the period 1250–1350. Little of it is of the formal style (nonrhyming, with the *aa, ax* alliteration pattern) and therefore it has been dismissed as unrelated to its mid-14th-century predecessor (although, paradoxically, some who dismiss these precursors also, in turn, argue that they are a source for the mid-14th-century form). Others are disturbed by the nationalistic assumptions behind the idea of a "revival" that challenges French language and culture, and see this theory as more a reflection of modern politics than of 14th-century literary practice. Recently, one scholar has suggested that this diverse group of poems is connected by broader thematic interests, including an examination of the complicated relationship between the past and the present, an engagement with pressing social and cultural issues, a suspicion of romantic love, a reliance on Latinate sources, and an authoritative and confident narrative voice.

See also GAWAIN-POET.

FURTHER READING

Chism, Christine. *Alliterative Revivals.* Philadelphia: University of Pennsylvania Press, 2002.

Turville-Petre, Thorlac. *Alliterative Poetry of the Later Middle Ages: An Anthology.* Washington: Catholic University Press; Padstow, Cornwall: TJ Press, 1989.

Zimmerman, Harold C. "Continuity and Innovation: Scholarship on the Middle English Alliterative Revival." *Jahrbuch für Internationale Germanistik* 35, no. 1 (2003): 107–123.

Diane Cady

AMORETTI (OVERVIEW) EDMUND SPENSER (1595) EDMUND SPENSER's Petrarchan SONNET SEQUENCE *Amoretti* was one of his later works, published in 1595, the year after his marriage to Elizabeth Boyle, the only partially imaginary inspiration for the piece. It consists of a dedication, introductory poem, 89 SONNETs, and four shorter pieces detailing Cupid's intervention in the love experience. The sonnets follow a male lover's seemingly conventional pursuit of his female beloved, culminating in a disappointment and followed by a four-part poem labeled *anacreontics* (sexual love). The anacreontics present very conventional portraits of the relationship between Cupid and the lover, drawn from Marot, Tasso, Theocritus, Alciati, and two MADRIGALS. However, *Amoretti* was published along with a very different EPIC poem, *EPITHALAMION*, following the triumph of the lover's wedding day with his beloved, from his predawn preparations through the evening and day and into the early hours of the next morning, so readers of the combined work need not feel their disappointment for long. In fact, *Amoretti* (Italian for Cupids) both incorporates and violates the conventions for the lover's sonnet sequence common in the 16th century and in *Epithalamion* (Greek term for a wedding song), which traditionally celebrated the wedding of kings or nobility, and is told from the perspective of an observer, not the lover himself.

Amoretti and *Epithalamion* were published in 1595, shortly before the expanded *FAERIE QUEENE*, books 1–6 (1596). Spenser's own progress through this larger work is noted in Sonnet 80 (fit for the handmaid of the Faerie Queene), giving rise to one interpretation of the *Amoretti* as poems about being a poet. The earliest critics of this work, other poets, tended to focus on certain pieces as the core of their interpretation. Some went so far as to recommend that certain sonnets be discarded; in one case, 18 of the 89 sonnets were considered worthless imitations, and in another it was recommended that the anacreontics be ignored. *Amoretti*'s measure is taken in relation to Italian precursors such as Dante's *La Vita Nuova* and English ones such as SIR PHILIP SIDNEY's *ASTROPHIL AND STELLA*, and it has been found wanting. But more recent critics have looked for the logic of the entire piece and explicated it in terms of representations of human and supernatural time, the progress of proper Christian love in marriage, the demonstration of poetic virtuosity, and even the poet Spenser's means of achieving a distinction that would make up for his less-than-noble birth.

The sequence has received much attention, both on its own and in relation to Spenser's poetic ambitions, as well as in relation to the classical-poetic revival of England in the latter part of the 16th century. His exploration of Italianate poetic forms mirrored that of Sidney, SIR WALTER RALEIGH, and others of his age who sought to invest English literature with a loftier aesthetic. Thus, *Amoretti* compares with other sonnet sequences—most of which were originally circulated in manuscript, not published, form—in incorporating courtly love conventions of the lover pursuing and spurned by his beloved. He alternately praises and chases her, and he valorizes her beauty, chastity, virtue, and even, in several different sonnets, her "cruel paine" (vanity), a convention of this sonnet form. Earlier critics of Spenser's work virtually dismissed it for these conventionalities. It has also been variously interpreted as "merely autobiographical" in terms of the actually passage of time, from just before Lent up to the poet's wedding day of June 11, 1594, and also as a demonstration of Spenser's expertise with the sonnet form as well as his rising aesthetic and social status. Some critics see the collection as a lyric gesture toward the old aristocracy and a narrative one toward the emerging nascent capitalism, or an acknowledgement that Spenser's rising star in Ireland presented an alternative center to the Elizabethan court in England. Another recent interpretation sees the sequence as representative of the poet's own inability to reconcile his desire to belong to the nobility with his dependence on a new social and economic order for his education, his wealth, and ultimately his social position.

In order for these more recent economic and social analyses of *Amoretti* to take place, however, some basic interpretation of the work had to be in place; this includes such analysis as that of the conventions and their violations, the time progression, the derivation from Petrarchan forms, the allusions, and the illustrations of the Cupid emblem. For example, while it is clear there are autobiographical elements in the work—it is addressed to Elizabeth Boyle, Spenser's second wife, references in some sonnets a time sequence that corresponds to a period just before Spenser and Boyle were married, and contains references to his newly won Irish estate in Kilcolman, Munster—the poetic form is at least as significant.

Although *Amoretti* follows the conventions of the Elizabethan sonnet sequence—the fruitless pursuit of a cold, cruel, superior beloved, etc.—each of these conventions is undermined in some way. For example, in Sonnet 15, in describing her superiority to precious commodities such as rubies, pearls, and ivory, and the merchants who seek them Spenser also derides the merchants' useless efforts, thereby lowering both the value of his object of comparison and the goods to which he compares her. While he pays lip service to the "cruel fair" convention, Spenser also suggests a confidence in the ultimate success. For Spenser, the pride that causes his beloved to scorn his advances is also a mark of her distinction and individuality. Moreover, conventionally, and like WILLIAM SHAKESPEARE, Spenser uses his sonnets to suggest the use of poetry to counteract the mutability of life.

From conventional Elizabethan love lyric to representation of the poet's virtuosity to emblem of nascent capitalism, it is clear that *Amoretti* rivals *The Faerie Queene* as one of Spenser's lasting accomplishments, regardless of the obvious fact that Spenser himself used the piece to, in a sense, market himself and his larger work-in-progress.

See also ITALIAN (PETRARCHAN) SONNET.

FURTHER READING

Bernard, John D. "Spenserian Pastoral and the *Amoretti*." *ELH* 47, no. 3 (1980): 419–432.

Brown, Ted. "Metapoetry in Edmund Spenser's *Amoretti*." *PQ* 82, no. 4 (2003): 401–417.

Dunlop, Alexander. "The Unity of Spenser's *Amoretti*." In *Silent Poetry: Essays in Numerological Analysis,* edited by Alastair Fowler, 153–169. London: Routledge, 1970.

Hadfield, Andrew, ed. *The Cambridge Companion to Spenser.* Cambridge: Cambridge University Press, 2001.

Hamilton, A. C., ed. *The Spenser Encyclopedia.* Toronto: University of Toronto Press, 1990.

Heiatt, A. Kent. "A Numerical Key for Spenser's 'Amoretti' and Guyon in the House of Mammon." *The Yearbook of English Studies* 5, no. 3 (1973): 14–27.

Johnson, William C. *Spenser's Amoretti: Analogies of Love.* Lewisburg, Ohio: Bucknell University Press, 1990.

Klaske, Carol V. "Spenser's *Amoretti and Epithalamion* of 1595: Structure, Genre, Numerology." In *ELR* 8 (1978): 271–295.

Lever, J. W. "The *Amoretti*." In *The Elizabethan Love Sonnet*. London: Methuen, 1956, 99–136.

Maclean, Hugh. *Edmund Spenser's Poetry*. New York: Norton, 1968.

———, and Anne Lake Prescott, eds. *Edmund Spenser's Poetry*. New York: Norton, 1993.

Martz, Louis. "The *Amoretti* 'Most Goodly Temperature.'" In *Form and Convention in the Poetry of Edmund Spenser,* edited by W. Nelson, 146–168. New York: Columbia University Press, 1961.

Montrose, Louis A. "The Elizabethan Subject in the Spenserian Text." In *Literary Theory/Renaissance Texts,* edited by Patricia Parker and David Quint, 303–340. Baltimore: Johns Hopkins University Press, 1986.

Spenser, Edmund. *The Yale Edition of the Shorter Poems of Edmund Spenser,* edited by William A. Oram. *et al.* New Haven, Conn.: Yale University Press, 1989.

Warley, Christopher. "'So Plenty Makes Me Poore': Ireland, Capitalism, and Class in Spenser's *Amoretti* and *Epithalamion*." *ELH* 63, no. 9 (2002): 567–598.

Janice M. Bogstad

Amoretti: Sonnet 1 ("Happy ye leaves when as those lilly hands") EDMUND SPENSER (ca. 1595)

As the first SONNET in EDMUND SPENSER'S SONNET SEQUENCE, this opening sally addresses the work holistically and introduces the audience to the Lady who is the inspiration. The "happy leaues" (leaves, e.g., pages) addressed in the first line are successively identified with the poetic work, which will hopefully be read by the Lady in question. The hands and eyes of the beloved are first addressed—hands to hold the pages and eyes to read its contents. Thus, recurrent themes are established at the outset, in addition to what is generally considered to be the overall thematic concern, the mutability of life and, by extension, a woman's physical beauty. There is also a bid for immortality in the written work. Likewise established is the reversal of the usual patriarchal relationship between the lordly man and otherwise submissive woman, a reversal that characterizes the love-sonnet form. The early lines establish the Lady's control over the fate of the written work, culminating in the assertion that it is written for her: "seeke her to please alone" (l. 13). The poet's words demonstrate a guise of humility, that the Lady will "deigne to sometimes to look" (l. 6). However, some critics make the equation between the Lady who is conventionally invoked and any reader of the text who can satisfy the poet's stated desire to please the reader as his loftiest goal. Thus, each ENCOMIUM to the Lady is one to the reader, and each gesture of humility by the author is a valorization of his work.

Each of the three QUATRAINS also juxtaposes two lines detailing the Lady's lofty act of noticing the poetic lines with responses characterizing their author's humble efforts to create these "captive lines" written with "sorrows" and "teares" and, in the third quatrain, a soul that "long lacked foode." Yet the many references to the value of the written work are reinforced with the two lines of the sonnet calling attention to the aforementioned book with the physical "leaues" on which it is printed, lines in which the sentiments are encoded and rhymes which make up the craft of the poem (l. 13).

Most explications of the *Amoretti* refer to a conventional love-sonnet progression through the stages of a lover's courtship, focusing either on a calendar of days before the actual wedding on June 11, 1594, which is immortalized in Spenser's EPITHALAMION, or on the constancy of the Lady's pride and the volatility of the speaker's reaction; however, this first sonnet also foregrounds its contrivance. The object of the sequence is clearly the creation of a written work, as well as a demonstration of the poet's ability to do so. As several critics have pointed out, *Amoretti*'s sonnet sequence is about writing poetry and Sonnet 1, along with Sonnets 33 and 80 (see below), which allude to the poet's completion of Book 6 of *The FAERIE QUEENE,* firmly established that desire.

See also *AMORETTI* (OVERVIEW).

FURTHER READING
Judson, A. C. "*Amoretti,* Sonnet I." *MLN* 58, no. 7 (1943): 548–550.

Janice M. Bogstad

Amoretti: Sonnet 4 ("New yeare forth looking out of Janus gate") EDMUND SPENSER (1595)

Sonnet 4 of *Amoretti* is at once humorous and profane, underscoring the inevitable consummation of courtship with marriage and the marriage bed. EDMUND SPENSER's SONNET SEQUENCE loosely follows the liturgical calendar, with the 21 sonnets referencing January—ordinary time—and the courtship phase of his relationship. Thus, Sonnet 4, which employs simple rhyme and sexual imagery, is meant to woo.

Spenser combines imagery, metaphor, and personification as "New yeare forth looking out of Janus gate" (l. 1) calls "Fresh love" (l. 6) from sleep and bids the lady to "Prepare your selfe new love to entertaine" (l. 14); with the approach of spring, the lady is encouraged to be open to new love. That "New yeare" looks through Janus's gate is not trivial; Janus, keeper of gates and god of harmony in the Roman tradition, indicates that as the new year unfolds, it brings with it new life and harmony, ideal circumstances in which to foster a relationship. Spenser's natural world is dominated by masculine forms—New yeare, Janus, Fresh love (Cupid), and spring. In this context, the solitary female element, Earth (l. 11) is told to prepare herself for "lusty spring" (l. 9) in a fashion that mirrors the arranged marriages of the era. Her preparation takes on a ritualistic aspect reminiscent of a bride's preparation for her wedding as she is instructed to adorn herself and to prepare her dowry "with divers colord flower / To deck hir selfe, and her faire mantle weave" (ll. 11–12).

In describing the lady of the poem as "you faire flowre" (l. 13), Spenser aligns her with Earth, and the sexual undertones triumph: "Lusty spring now in his timely howre, / Is ready to come forth him [Cupid] to receive" (ll. 9–10). The employment of terms such as *wanton wings* and *darts of deadly power* (l. 8) also underscores the male sexuality prevalent within this sonnet. Spenser is clear about his intention to court and capture his lady, and there is no doubt that there will be a consummation of this love. Furthermore, the feminine, and by association the lady, has no voice in this poem, as is customary in Renaissance society and the natural world. As Earth is fertile and receives spring in the New Year without fuss or question, so should the lady receive her intended lord.

See also *AMORETTI* (OVERVIEW), SONNET.

M. A. Elmes

Amoretti: Sonnet 13 ("In that proud port, which her so goodly graceth") EDMUND SPENSER **(1595)** Sonnet 13 is more characteristic of EDMUND SPENSER's *Amoretti* than it is remarkable. Each QUATRAIN elicits the trope (figure of speech) of contrast that we find in many of the others, the second recurrent trope being a list. Here the contrast is between the Lady's pride and lofty aims that look toward the heavens and her acknowledgement of earthly ties. The contrast in the first quatrain is between lines 2 and 3, where the lady's face rises to the skies but her eyes embrace the earth; the second quatrain is an exercise in asserting earthy humility; the third has a 1–2 couplet looking to the divine and a 3–4 couplet decrying earthly imagery such as "drossy slime." In deliberately using words considered archaic even in his own time ("drossy slime"), Spenser achieved an atmosphere of age and mystery. Sonnet 13 is surrounded by sonnets characterized by such lexical choices and tropes of opposition, perhaps reinforcing the reading that *Amoretti* is a sort of "tour de force" performance for Spenser.

While often overlooked in early critiques of the SONNET SEQUENCE, Sonnet 13 has received more attention in recent decades as an example of Neoplatonism, intimating that the divine may be achieved at the expense of the physical. Only the SONNET's conclusion wrests it from that philosophical dichotomy between base body and elevated mind or spirit, for in the last two lines, the narrator links return to the earth, to the body, and to the attentions of the poet-lover with his somewhat arrogant claim that his writing will facilitate her ascent to both spiritual and physical bliss. "To looke on me, such lowlinesse shall make you lofty be" (ll. 13–14). This invocation has also been offered as a suggestion that looking at the entire *Amoretti* will produce a kind of elevation, the look being at the work rather than at the narrator and the looker being the reader rather than the lady. This sort of metapoetic (unconventional imagery) interpretation requires separating the subject and object of the internal narrative (lover speaking to his beloved lady) from the subject of the work itself as a demonstration of authorial versatility.

See also *AMORETTI* (OVERVIEW).

Janice M. Bogstad

Amoretti: Sonnet 15 ("Ye tradefull Merchants, that with weary toyle") EDMUND SPENSER (1595)
In Sonnet 15 from EDMUND SPENSER's *Amoretti*, the speaker praises his Lady's beauty extravagantly, asking merchants why they look all over the world to buy precious beautiful things when all the world's riches may be found right here in the person of his beloved. Twelve lines of Sonnet 15 are a conventional catalogue of the lady's beauty, a BLAZON, but the COUPLET establishes the lady's mind to be "that which fairest is," for it is "adornd with vertues manifold" (ll. 13–14).

Unlike most English SONNET SEQUENCES, the poems in *Amoretti* are not addressed to an unobtainable mistress, but to Elizabeth Boyle, the woman Spenser hoped to—and eventually did—marry. While some of the sonnets were probably written before the two became involved, the couplet of Sonnet 15 indicates the speaker has a more comprehensive experience of the woman's mental qualities beyond her superficial appearance. This knowledge raises *Amoretti* 15 above the level of a conventional blazon, and the lady above the level of a simple love object. This SONNET is largely indebted to Sonnet 32 of Philippe Desportes' *Les Amours des Diana* (*The Loves of Diana*); however, Desportes' sonnet is entirely a blazon, with no references to the lady's mind or personality. He creates the occasion for his blazon by asking merchants why they search the world for treasure when here they will find all that Africa could offer. Spenser has taken over the scenario and the strategy, but he has carried the result beyond the physical.

Spenser's characteristic STANZA form—*abab, bcbc, cdcd, ee*—permits him to evade the usual restrictions of the sonnet, and, logically, it reads most clearly as SESTET, sestet, couplet; syntactically, as QUATRAIN, couplet, sestet, couplet. The first quatrain sets the scene by asking why the "tradefull Merchants" (l. 1) work so hard to obtain rare and beautiful treasures from all around the world. "[B]oth the Indias" (l. 3) encompasses the entire commercial world, since the East Indias refer to the Malay Archipelago and the West Indias to the lands in the Caribbean. Beginning in line 5, the speaker claims his beloved is more beautiful than anything to be found in the entire world; within the genre of sonnets, such HYPERBOLE is conventional. His inventory fol-

lows a strict pattern. Each valued item is presented in a clause that omits the verb phrase *you seek;* thus: "If [you seek] Saphyres, loe her eies be Saphyres plaine" (l. 7). These are not similes; in fact, they are barely comparisons. Her eyes are not as blue as sapphires; they are sapphires. Only in line 10 does the poet substitute "weene" (think) for "be"; this is the single place where he acknowledges the metaphoric character of his beloved's treasures. Otherwise, the speaker's beloved "doth in her selfe containe / All this worlds riches" (ll. 5–6) very literally; six precious materials—sapphires, rubies, pearls, ivory, gold, and silver—compose this woman's head and hands, the only features the poet describes.

The couplet indicates that what makes this woman special and most beautiful to the poet—her mind—remains private and exclusive. This is signaled in the sonnet by the doubled use of "but" in two distinctive senses: "But that which fairest is, but few behold" (l. 13). The first "but" is a conjunction, the second a modifying intensifier, synonymous with "only." Although everyone can see the woman's eyes, hair, lips, hands, etc., only a few can know her well enough to be acquainted with her mind "adornd with vertues manifold" (l. 14). Another feature of this intimate detail is the way the poet expresses it: While the speaker details six features, not one virtue is named. The woman's face and hands are public territory; anyone privileged to see her can observe her beauty. Only someone further honored by her acquaintance, however, can appreciate the quality of her mind.

See also *AMORETTI* (OVERVIEW).

Marjory E. Lange

Amoretti: Sonnet 22 ("This holy season fit to fast and pray") EDMUND SPENSER (1595)   One of the "little love poems" dedicated to Elizabeth Boyle, EDMUND SPENSER's wife, the poem details the second year of their courtship. As part of the structural time scheme inherent in the overall *Amoretti* sequence, this poem is set during the Lenten season, the period of fasting and penitence that begins with Ash Wednesday and ends with Easter ("This holy season fit to fast and pray," l. 1). The poet compares his devotion to his beloved with his religious devotion, elevating her to "my sweet Saynt" (l. 4), following in the style of Italian and French love lyrics and SONNETS. Instead of comparing her to a goddess, as is common in other English sonnets and the Italian predecessors, Spenser keeps the focus on the woman's spiritual beauty, a concept that he continues in *EPITHALAMION* (the marriage poem) and expands upon in his EPIC poem *The FAERIE QUEEN*.

The poem uses the ITALIAN (PETRARCHAN) SONNET form, setting the situation up in the OCTAVE, although it employs the Spenserian sonnet rhyme scheme. During the holy season of Lent, men's attention should be focused on their devotion; therefore, the speaker seeks some appropriate way to give service to his "Saynt," who is his beloved and the object of his devotion. Instead of residing in a church, this saint's image resides in a temple located in the speaker's mind, so that day and night he can attend to her just as the priests attend to the statues of the saints found in churches. By setting up this comparison, the speaker clearly conflates religious and secular love.

After setting up this ideal picture of the beloved, the turn of the SESTET takes the speaker down a non-Christian path with a higher form of sacrifice. He announces a plan to build for her, the source of his happiness, an altar that will "appease" (l. 9) her anger, with the implication that the only reason for her "ire" (l. 10) is his love for her; on that altar his heart will be sacrificed, burnt by the flames of "pure and chaste desire" (l. 12). If the beloved, who is now referred to as "goddess" (l. 13), accepts this offering, it will be one of her most precious mementos. The imagery found here in the sestet is more traditionally associated with the Petrarchan convention from which Spenser is writing. The archaic spelling he uses in the sequence allows a play on words of heart with "hart" in line 11, which continues with dearest and "deerest" in line 14 to expand the possible interpretations of the sestet from a figurative to a literal sacrifice.

See also *AMORETTI* (OVERVIEW).

Peggy J. Huey

Amoretti: Sonnet 30 ("My love is lyke to iyse, and I to fyre") EDMUND SPENSER (1595)

One of the many SONNETS on the lover's pain, Sonnet 30 of EDMUND SPENSER's *Amoretti* is tempered by a humorous turn of phrase, playing with poetic convention as well as with natural order. It may also be classified as one of the "cruell fayre" sonnets so characteristic of this poetic form and the COURTLY LOVE tradition. In this case, the CONCEITS are organized around the contrast between ice (or iyse) and fire, a Petrarchan cliché taken to extremes: common contrast rendered absurd through repetition. "My Love is lyke to iyse and I to fyre" (l. 1) begins the poem, so we have contrasting opposites at first glance. Simultaneously, these symbolize constancy in the Lady and volatility in the lover as the narrative progresses through paradox as well as opposites. The major focus of all three quatrains is a common theme of the suffering, here represented in the various aspects of fire: "hot desire" (l. 3), "boyling sweat" (l. 7), and the power to melt, all of which have no effect upon the Lady's "sencelesse cold" (l. 11).

Unlike the usual celebration of the lover's mortal and senseless suffering, this sonnet ends with the celebration of a mystery. The lover's hot desire cannot melt the Lady's cold, and his intensified burning only hardens it more. The contrasts are so extensively pursued that the oppositional qualities of ice and fire are reevaluated, as well as their conceit within the whole range of love poetry. Instead of a means to arouse sympathy for the lover, the unusual relationship between ice and fire becomes a valorization of love itself. Love is elevated because it "can alter all the course of kynd" (l. 14) and, by extension, overcome the natural forces. Ordinarily, fire would melt ice not harden it, but the force of love creates an unnatural situation.

The humor mentioned above is in this paradox, which violates both the natural order and the expected convention of the love-sonnet. Most commentary on this sonnet focuses on the conventional phrases rather than their unconventional resolution of love's transcendence, but recent criticism has explored these twists. In particular, a religious reading suggests the contrast between divine fire and human ice: The cold soul is hardened by God, for whom all things are possible. Other critics have called attention to the contrived language, the archaic spellings and diction strongly represented here, especially "desyre," "iyse," and "fyre." Most question whether or not the practice contributes to the sonnet's effectiveness.

See also *AMORETTI* (OVERVIEW), ITALIAN (PETRARCHAN) SONNET.

Janice M. Bogstad

Amoretti: Sonnet 37 ("What guyle is this, that those her golden tresses") EDMUND SPENSER (1595)

Coming as it does within a group of SONNETS about the manipulations of eyes and ears (35–37 focus on sight, 39–40 on seeing the lady's smile, 38 on hearing, 43 on silence or speaking), this sonnet from EDMUND SPENSER's *Amoretti* explores metaphors of worth and sight, described, as usual, from the perspective of the lover. Sonnet 37 presents the deceptive appearance of interchangeability between a "golden snare" (l. 6) and the lady's hair, as if the author were trying out yet another in a long list of rhetorical strategies. The CONCEIT is that the lady's hairnet of gold and her golden hair appear to be so cleverly intertwined that one cannot be distinguished from the other by sight alone. The wordplay between golden hair and net of gold, and the net as a "golden snare" (l. 6) in which the lover can be "entangled" at that same time he is seduced by gold, is itself attributed to the lady's guile and craftiness rather than to some accident of nature. He is snared, entrapped, caught, and enfolded in her net. This metaphor of deceit also produces an intermingling of values in that gold has concrete value, whereas the lady's hair has only metaphorical power—but before it, the lover is powerless. Thus, the expected convention of COURTLY LOVE poetry—powerless lover v. powerful lady—is reinforced.

Some critics have argued that the author builds up this image through allusions to the lady's power, vanity, and disdain, only to finally valorize her seeming cruelty as properly modest behavior. This ultimately frustrates the convention and even, for some critics, turns it into the preface for the joys of church-sanctioned Christian love.

See also *AMORETTI* (OVERVIEW).

Janice M. Bogstad

Amoretti: Sonnet 46 ("When my abode's prefixed time is spent") EDMUND SPENSER (1595)

This SONNET pits the lady's strength against that of "heauen [heaven's] most hideous stormes" (l. 3). The lover must choose between obeying the lady's attraction and observing the will of the heavens, "willing me against her will to stay" (l. 4). He concludes that the lady's will is stronger, but asks the heavens to cease pulling at him, since he cannot affect her behavior: "Enough it is for one man to sustaine, the stormes, which she along on me doth raine" (l. 13). He establishes firmly both his loyalty to the lady and his own weakness—he cannot bear the "wrack" coming from both parties. His lady is more accessible than the heavens, so he implores them to show the mercy she will not. This poetic gesture has been variously interpreted as acknowledging their superiority (thus he needs their mercy) or foregrounding their irrelevance (thus he does not care). Is he acknowledging the inferior, human status of both himself and the lady, or pinpointing the unfairness of the heavens in expecting him to fight on two fields of battle at once? Most critics argue the latter as another form of humility and the former as a kind of pride that begins to equate lover and lady.

See also *AMORETTI* (OVERVIEW); SPENSER, EDMUND.

Janice M. Bogstad

Amoretti: Sonnet 54 ("Of this worlds Theatre in which we stay") EDMUND SPENSER (1595)

Seemingly one of the more conventional of *Amoretti*'s SONNETS, Sonnet 54 has, until recently, received little attention. The three QUATRAINS repeatedly oppose the lover's volatile emotions to the calm, unmoving constancy of his Lady, to the extent that he ends by calling her a "sencelesse stone." The first quatrain contrasts their demeanor. She is a cold spectator to a pageant and he the player in that scene. The second addresses his volatility, from heights of joy and mirth to depths of sorrow, and the third her indifference. The extended metaphor of the quatrains is that of a theatre performance, one in which the lover is the performer and the beloved the only important, and usually indifferent, audience. His emotions are the highs and lows of comedy or tragedy; hers are barely perceptible, and only as mocking or laughter. She responds to his emotions as if they were a display for her amusement.

Within the framework of a poetic reading, critics assert that the lover is demonstrating the knowledge that he, or both of them, plays a part in a familiar drama. His is the part of the suffering lover and his Lady's that of the hard-hearted observer. Some have gone so far as to interpret the entire sonnet as a self-reflexive presentation of performance and artistry, that his volatility is a mere varied attempt to get a reaction, not a display of true emotion. In other words, there are two lover and two lady personae, those who play the ITALIAN (PETRARCHAN) SONNET roles and those who transcend them with a sophisticated understanding of the play of words and roles. And in playing a part, the narrator may speak of suffering, but is also comfortable in the assurance that his suit will succeed.

See also *AMORETTI* (OVERVIEW); SPENSER, EDMUND.

Janice M. Bogstad

Amoretti: Sonnet 62 ("The weary yeare his race now having run") EDMUND SPENSER (1595)   Sonnet 62 from EDMUND SPENSER's *Amoretti* celebrates the commencement of the new year. In many ways, the poem reads as a typical "New Year's resolution": full of optimism, hope, and plans for personal betterment. Lines 1–4 describe the transition from the old "weary" year to the new year. With the image of the "shew of morning" in line 3, the speaker brings the larger idea of the new year into focus by minimizing it to the span of a single day; thus, the sunrise, the start of a new day, is a metaphor for the start of a new year. In lines 5–8, the speaker asks that with the new weather there be a new attitude, a reformation of behavior. The image of the sun is again conveyed in lines 9–12; this time, the new year is figured as the sun shining after a storm. The metaphor here is based on a conditional: If we amend our behavior, as the speaker calls for us to do in the previous lines, then the "glooming world" with its "stormes" will calm down, and the clouds will "tymely cleare away"—in short, our new year will be better than our last year. However, a reformed outlook is not the only path to a happier year; in the final COUPLET, the speaker changes the subject specifically to love, which he states also has the power to "chaunge old yeares annoy to new delight."

The SONNET's rhyme scheme conforms to Spenser's trademark form: three quatrains rhyming *abab, bcbc, cdcd;* and a final couplet rhyming *ee.* Often considered the most difficult form in the English language, the Spenserian sonnet complicates the traditional ENGLISH SONNET form by employing a series of "couplet links" between quatrains. By interweaving the quatrains, the sonnet reduces the stress on the final couplet to resolve the foregoing argument, observation, or question. Consequently, the speaker begins to resolve his argument in line 9. This structure reveals how the entire sonnet is composed as a conditional statement, which essentially asserts the following: If we refresh ourselves with the renewal of the year, then our year will be better than the last. In the final couplet, love functions as the mode through which we may replenish ourselves with the new year.

Criticism of the poem has centered mainly on the interpretation of the date it is celebrating. Most critics agree that the New Year to which the poems refers is the one beginning on March 25, the date of Gabriel's annunciation to Mary, rather than the one noted in Elizabethan almanacs, which starts on January 1. Detractors of this theory assert that such a date would place the sonnet cycle during the season of Lent, which was not an appropriate time for wooing (since weddings could not be performed during Lent). However, proponents of the Lenten date indicate that the phrase *chaunge eek our mynds* (l. 6) is extracted from a prayer proper to Lent from the Geneva Bible meaning "to change the mind," "to be converted," or "to repent." Moreover, the religious undertones of the sonnet, as well as of the entire SONNET SEQUENCE, confirms the poem's theological meaning. For example, the frequent images of sunlight, and specifically the line "into the glooming world his gladsome ray" (l. 10), refer to biblical passages such as the following from John 12.46: "I am come a light into the darkened worlde." Aside from this dominant critical debate, many critics opt to read the poem biographically, viewing the first-person plural pronouns *us* and *we* as references to Spenser and his future wife, Elizabeth Boyle.

See also *AMORETTI* (OVERVIEW).

Melissa Femino

Amoretti: **Sonnet 64 ("Comming to kisse her lyps—such grace I found")** EDMUND SPENSER **(1595)** In Sonnet 64 of EDMUND SPENSER's *Amoretti*, time and action are suspended. In this ekphrastic moment (see EKPHRASIS), as the two lovers remain poised and about to kiss, the speaker gives his reader a poetic description of his love. Using the conventional method of the BLAZON, each part of the Lady's body—her lips, her cheeks, her eyes, her bosom, her neck, her breast, and even her nipples—is compared to a flower from a luxurious garden. These comparisons are not based on sight, however; they are based on smell.

Employing the standard Spenserian rhyme scheme of *abab, bcbc, cdcd, ee,* the poem is constructed as two complete syntactic units. In the first sentence, the speaker describes the moment of action, which is never fully achieved: his movement toward his lover's lips. The second sentence is composed of a series of similes.

Using floral imagery to symbolize femininity is a conventional literary technique, but Spenser's blazon is unusual because it depends solely upon olfactory imagery. The flowers the speaker uses to describe this fragrant woman are significant. Roses, a bed of strawberries, lilies (often represents female virginity), "Iessemynes" (jasmine), and columbines are all fairly standard metaphors for love and beauty, but gillyflowers, *bellamoures,* and *pincks* are a little less obvious. Gillyflowers, though traditionally thought of as a plant with flowers scented like cloves, can have a secondary meaning as well. The first part of the word, *gill,* is defined in the OED as "a giddy young woman" (l. 4). This, combined with the word *flower,* becomes a word that denotes something like "a giddy young woman's flower." The same compound structure is used in the reference to *bellamoures.* The word seems to be a composite of two foreign words: the Italian *bel* (beautiful) and the French *amour* (love). Some critics have contended that these are not flowers at all but loving glances. They base their reading on the word's close relationship to another word derived from Italian, *belgards* (*bel* plus *guardo,* which means "looks"—beautiful glances). This reading makes sense since *bellamoures* are used to describe her eyebrows; thus, the lady's gaze is emphasized. *Pincks* could refer to the general name of the species *Dianthus* (pink), which has variegated sweet-smelling flowers. The use of this image to describe the lady's eyes is appropriate since *dianthus* means "double-flowering."

In terms of the sequence of the entire *Amoretti* cycle, the poem takes place on March 27, the Wednesday before Easter. Reading the sonnet in regard to its structural placement, some critics view the kiss upon which the entire poem is based as a CONCEIT that corresponds to the biblical topos of Judas's kiss, by which he betrayed Jesus (recounted in the gospel proper to the Wednesday before Easter: Luke 22.1–71). Further evidence of this link between the poem and the passage from Luke is that the betrayal takes place in the Garden of Gethsemane. If read this way, by delaying the kiss in the poem, the speaker may be delaying Judas's betrayal and, subsequently, Jesus's suffering.

See also *AMORETTI* (OVERVIEW).

Melissa Femino

Amoretti: **Sonnet 65 ("The doubt which ye misdeeme, fayre love, is vaine")** EDMUND SPENSER **(1595)** Constructed as an argument, Sonnet 65 of *Amoretti* follows the traditional discourse of a Petrarchan lovers' debate, with the male speaker as a passive wooer and his love as the coy woman. The poem's argument centers on the speaker's attempts to alleviate any fears his love may have about losing her freedom in marriage—an understandable concern for any independent-minded woman in 16th-century England. Married women relinquished all financial and personal freedoms to their husbands. That the speaker needs to address this issue says much about the woman whom he is addressing. If she is concerned with her independence, then she must be fairly independent already. The speaker, who acknowledges her independence, wants to capture her nonetheless. Repeated images of bonds, bounds, bands, and cages demonstrate this. His intent is to demonstrate that her bondage will not be an unpleasant one if she enters into it willingly and gently: As he writes, "the gentle birde feeles no captivity / within her cage, but singes and feeds her fill" (ll. 7–8). The anagram implicit in EDMUND SPENSER's spelling of "birde" as bride, if scrambled correctly, seems to strengthen the idea that he is addressing his future wife.

What proceeds after these initial statements is a loving description of marriage. The first two quatrains play with the word *bond* from the phrase *bonds of marriage*—punning on *bonds* as "bondage" and then moving to the word *bands* in the next four lines. These lines are both an affirmation and a contradiction of common Petrarchan CONCEIT. The captive lover is a traditional feature of Petrarchan love poetry, as is the poet's argument that the lady will paradoxically gain more liberty once captured than if she remains unfettered by the bonds of love. However, Spenser's use of the conceit is different: He places this idea within the context of marriage rather than an affair or a platonic relationship. Most Petrarchan lovers sing to women who are unattainable: those of higher social classes or those who are already married.

The placement of the poem within the structure of the SONNET SEQUENCE adds yet another caveat to Spenser's use of Petrarchan conceits. The poem takes place on March 28, the Thursday before Easter (Maundy Thursday). This day celebrated the institution of the new covenant, sealed by the Resurrection. The day was associated with marriage in Spenser's time through the common reading of Psalm 128, which was often read at evening prayers on that day; it was also read during the marriage service. Spenser's application of post-Reformation covenantal thought to a Petrarchan poem about marriage is a clear departure from the traditional use of the form by 16th-century English poets.

See also *AMORETTI* (OVERVIEW), ITALIAN (PETRARCHAN) SONNET.

Melissa Femino

Amoretti: Sonnet 66 ("To all those happy blessings which ye have") EDMUND SPENSER (1595)

In some ways, Sonnet 66 of EDMUND SPENSER's *Amoretti* is a continuance of the argument for marriage that was offered in the previous SONNET. The speaker describes his fiancée in the most exalted terms; about himself he uses the most humble and self-deprecating terms, describing himself as something that is made even baser through his comparison to her. "To all those happy blessings which ye have,   this one disparagement they to you gave, / that ye your love lent to so meane a one" (ll. 3–4). It is not until the final COUPLET

that the argument for marriage is made, though marriage itself is alluded to in many of the previous lines.

The final argument is again based on his unworthiness and on her perfection. He begins by writing, "for now your light doth more it self dilate, / and in my darknesse greater doth appeare" (ll. 11–12). Thus, he is not merely arguing that she should marry, but that she should marry him; with him, she will be even more perfect, more so than if she married "a princes pere" (l. 10). The couplet then offers the main thesis of his poem: "Yet since your light hath once enlumind me, / with my reflex yours shall encreased be" (ll. 13–14). These lines suggest a reciprocal relationship. The speaker is telling his future bride that she is more brilliant with him than she would be without him because he reflects her light. He is a foil for her luminosity.

Although this poem functions as another facet in the speaker's ultimate plan to get this woman to marry him, its placement in the larger structure of the SONNET SEQUENCE—as taking place on Good Friday, March 29—suggests that there may be a second subject, or addressee, in the poem: Jesus. Read this way, the poem is the speaker's contemplation on the nature of Jesus' sacrifice and on humanity's unworthiness of it. The reciprocal relationship alluded to in the final couplet, then, could be the poetic image of that sacrifice: the idea that Jesus became Christ by first becoming human ("ye stoup unto so lowly [a] state" (l. 12)) and then dying as a human.

See also *AMORETTI* (OVERVIEW).

Melissa Femino

Amoretti: Sonnet 67 ("Lyke as a huntsman after weary chace") EDMUND SPENSER (1595)

Hunting imagery dominates Sonnet 67. In the first few lines, the hunting simile—"Lyke as a huntsman"—is converted to a metaphor with a pun on the word *deare* (l. 7), and it remains consistent throughout the poem, which continues to play extensively with puns on venery (dear / deer, hart / heart). The OCTAVE describes an active hunt (the "chace"), while the SESTET concentrates upon the capture of the "deare."

Hunting metaphors are common in the love poetry of 16th-century England. However, in his SONNET, EDMUND SPENSER adapts this traditional device and modifies it. Although the poem begins with an image of a hunter, the main subject of the first complete sentence of the poem is the "gentle deare," which does not appear until line 7. Read this way, the hunter and the speaker are the syntactic objects of the deer, and the lines are constructed around one very long simile in which the deer is compared to the "huntsman." Thus, the opening lines may be restated as "the deer, like a hunter tired from the hunt, returns to a brook to quench her thirst." Because the deer is equated with the hunter, the woman of Spenser's poem—figured as the deer—is afforded more agency (personal power) than is traditionally given to hunted women in other poems that employ this CONCEIT. The deer / dear of Spenser's poem is in charge: She wants to be caught. Such a reading would answer the speaker's bewilderment in the final COUPLET: "Strange thing me seemd to see a beast so wyld, / so goodly wonne with her owne will beguiled" (ll. 13–14). He is bewildered because he does not know that it was he who was being hunted all along.

Spenser's unique use of these motifs is proper to the poem's position within the *Amoretti* cycle. Set on the evening before Easter, March 30, the poem speaks to the ancient liturgical tradition associated with that date: the procession of the catechumens to the front of the church to be baptized while Psalm 42, a psalm of spring, was sung. Sonnet 67 echoes this psalm with its opening construction of "Lyke as" (l. 1) and with its images of "thirst" and a "brooke" (l. 8). Moreover, the idea of the willful prey alludes not only to the catechumens' willing movement to baptism—which is a symbolic death—but also to the willing movement of Christ to his own slaughter.

See also *AMORETTI* (OVERVIEW).

Melissa Femino

Amoretti: Sonnet 68 (Easter Sonnet, "Most glorious Lord of lyfe, that on this day") EDMUND SPENSER (1595)

Sonnet 68 of EDMUND SPENSER's *Amoretti* is also known as the Easter Sonnet. Paired with Sonnet 22 (said to invoke Ash Wednesday in the Christian calendar), it is central to autobiographical, numerological, religious, and calendar / real-time interpretations of the SONNET SEQUENCE. Moreover, the number of SONNETS between 22 and 68 equals the number of days

between Ash Wednesday and Easter in 1594, the year of Spenser's marriage. Thus, the calendar and autobiographical interpretations are compelling, despite the contrived nature of such an interpretation.

The religious content of the work is also emergent in this poem, as Spenser links the progress of his courtship with Elizabeth Boyle to the holiness of Christian (specifically Protestant) matrimony. Love within matrimony becomes the way men and women can most closely approach the love of God. For example, Spenser addresses his remarks to the Lord in the three QUATRAINS, only turning to his lady love in the COUPLET. In fact, while it is clear that he addresses his Lady at the end, asking that their love for one another should imitate what the "Lord us taught," the earthly sentiment between man and woman can easily be conflated with that between humans and heavenly Lord. In this vein, the tension between mutable human life and love, and between the eternity of the Lord's life and love, is demonstrated in each of the first three lines, which reference resurrection and eternal life alongside the potential for the lover and his Lady to "entertayne" (l. 12) each other. This particular sonnet is thus noted for the clarity with which differentiates eternal from human love, and human capacity from the divine.

The otherworldly aspect of this stanza is offset by its presence between Sonnet 67, which makes use of hunting imagery, and Sonnet 69, which invokes warriors and conquest. It is as if the author were trying a range of imagery to define his relationship to the object of his affection rather than establishing the Lord's love as its only "worthy" measure (l. 9). Some critics have used this STANZA to highlight the tension throughout the poem between the Neoplatonic philosophy of transcendence (in which human love leads us to divine love) and acknowledgement of human limitations, for human life is "lyke" but not equal to the divine.

See also *AMORETTI* (OVERVIEW).

Janice M. Bogstad

Amoretti: Sonnet 74 ("Most happy letters fram'd by skilfull trade") EDMUND SPENSER (1595)

This poem details the second year of the courtship between EDMUND SPENSER and Elizabeth Boyle. It uses the linked QUATRAIN pattern of the

Spenserian sonnet and blends the poet's love for the three Elizabeths in his life: his mother, his queen, and his beloved.

The speaker begins the first quatrain with a PAEAN to the letters that make up the name of Elizabeth, because three women bearing that name have made him happy, giving him gifts "of body, fortune and of mind" (l. 4). The second quatrain announces that the first gift came from his mother, who gave him life, while the second gift came from the queen, who has honored him and given him riches. The third quatrain is dedicated to his beloved, who has raised his spirit out of the dust of his widowhood; therefore, of all the people alive, she is most deserving of his praise and glorifying. The final COUPLET, then, hopes that the three Elizabeths might live forever for giving him those graces.

See also *AMORETTI* (OVERVIEW).

Peggy J. Huey

Amoretti: Sonnet 75 ("One day I wrote her name upon the strand") EDMUND SPENSER (1595)

This SONNET, like the previous one in *Amoretti*, addresses the courtship between EDMUND SPENSER and Elizabeth Boyle. The rhyme scheme follows the linked quatrain pattern of the Spenserian sonnet, and thematically it plays with the familiar CONCEIT of immortality.

The speaker begins the OCTAVE by setting a scene at the beach one day, when he writes his beloved's name in the sand; however, as is to be expected, the waves come in and wash the name away. So once again, he writes the name upon the sand, and once again, the waves come in and wash it away. The beloved chastises him for his vanity that would allow him vainly to attempt to immortalize in this manner someone such as she, who is mortal, and who eventually will be wiped out of all memory, just as her name has been erased from the beach. In the SESTET, however, the speaker protests the beloved's self-deprecating assessment of the situation, claiming that she shall live forever because his verses will make her name famous, and her virtues will make her eternal. Their love will live on to be renewed in the afterlife when death has subdued their world.

See also *AMORETTI* (OVERVIEW).

Peggy J. Huey

Amoretti: Sonnet 79 ("Men call you fayre, and you doe credit it") EDMUND SPENSER (1595)

Another of the SONNETS from *Amoretti* detailing the second year of the courtship between EDMUND SPENSER and Elizabeth Boyle, this poem follows the standard Spenserian sonnet form. The critical consensus is that this poem blends Christian and Neoplatonic terms to express the poet's vision of the force and meaning of love.

The OCTAVE begins with the speaker observing that men have told his beloved that she is fair, and she believes them because she can look in the mirror and see her beauty. However, the truly fair person has a gentle wit and a virtuous mind, two qualities that are much more deserving of this poet's praise. Others may be fair now, but time will change that as they lose those looks; the only thing that is permanent is that which outlasts the flesh, which is revealed in the SESTET. True beauty is divine, coming from heaven, from the "fayre Spirit" (l. 11) that is the source of perfection. Beauty is within; everything else fades with time just as flowers fade.

See also *AMORETTI* (OVERVIEW).

Peggy J. Huey

Amoretti: Sonnet 80 ("After so long a race as I have run") EDMUND SPENSER (1595)

Like Sonnet 33, Sonnet 80, which is often featured in critiques of *Amoretti* that highlight its poetic achievement, contains direct references to EDMUND SPENSER's ongoing project in honor of Queen ELIZABETH I,—that is, *The FAERIE QUEEN*. He opens the sonnet by referring to the "long race"—the narrator's pursuit of his elusive Lady. However, Sonnet 80 mostly references the many years the author has spent on what was to become his magnum opus. The first three of a projected 12 books of *The Faerie Queene* were published in 1590 to great acclaim. In this context, in Sonnet 80 Spenser announces the completion of a total of six books. He then ends the sonnet by identifying the whole SONNET SEQUENCE as "handmayd" of the Faerie Queene, citing the book by name. (The edition including books 1–6 was published the next year, 1596). It is only with the third QUATRAIN that Spenser readdresses the matter at hand, having also somewhat trivialized it as "pleasant mew," a form of leisurely entertainment to give him a break from the longer work.

Acknowledging the multiple narrative paths in this sonnet, critics have praised Spenser's mastery in simultaneously referring to his other work; alluding to the fact that his Lady and his Queene are both named Elizabeth; and noting that, at least in the sense of her minor nobility, his Elizabeth is a handmaid to Queen Elizabeth just as this *Amoretti* is a sort of handmaid to *The Faerie Queene,* a minor work in which he hones his poetic skills. He simultaneously elevates his Lady by intimating that association with her will help him to "gather to myself new breath awhile" in order to complete his other, more momentous poetic work. She thus becomes the minor muse and inspiration of this piece, which allows him to later do justice to Queen Elizabeth.

Others have extended this interpretation to claims of a metapoetic intent for the entire sequence to be a demonstration on the part of the poet, Spenser, of his versatility and accomplishment. Sonnet 80 reveals the whole to be part of a career path to the status of poet laureate that he charts for himself, a way of claiming aesthetic ground that will grant him a measure of nobility he can never attain on the basis of birth or social station. This minor work advertises the major one, in anticipation of its completion and its success. Regardless of the autobiographical, aesthetic, or social frame given its intertextual references, this sonnet projects a meaning that breaks the love-story narrative of the whole sequence, making it stand as both triumph and symptom of the poet's work.

See also AMORETTI (OVERVIEW).

Janice M. Bogstad

AMPLIFICATION Amplification is the deliberate repetition of words or phrases in a poem in order to create a mood, indicate emphasis, or heighten tension. Unlike ANAPHORA, amplification may be accomplished through the use of synonyms. An excellent example can be found in Surrey's "SET ME WHEREAS THE SONNE DOTH PERCHE THE GRENE."

See also SURREY, HENRY HOWARD, EARL OF.

ANAGOGY This is a poetic technique wherein scriptural EXEGESIS or other mystical interpretive tools are used to demonstrate allusions to or connections with heaven or the afterlife.

ANAPHORA Anaphora is a poetic device in which successive lines begin with the same word or phrase. Though similar to AMPLIFICATION, anaphora insists on the exact same phrasing, not simply synonyms.

ANDREAS CAPELLANUS (ANDRÉ THE CHAPLAIN) (late 12th century) Andreas Capellanus is the author of one of the most influential medieval works, *The ART OF COURTLY LOVE.* Little is known about Andreas's life. He resided at the court of Count Henry of Champagne, in Troyes (northwestern France), during the second half of the 12th century. He was most likely chaplain to Henry's wife, Countess Marie, daughter of Eleanor of Aquitaine.

See also COURTLY LOVE, LOVESICKNESS.

FURTHER READING
Cherchi, Paolo. *Andreas and the Ambiguity of Courtly Love.* Toronto: University of Toronto Press, 1994.

"AND WILT THOU LEAVE ME THUS" SIR THOMAS WYATT (ca. 1535) Never published in SIR THOMAS WYATT's lifetime, this poem is preserved in one manuscript, a poetic miscellany of the coterie around Anne Boleyn, which dates it to around the mid-1530s. This manuscript's verse shows a group of authors not only interested in writing pleasing COURTLY LOVE poetry but also commenting on the poetic form. Wyatt's poem is critical of the subject position of the speaking, courtly lover, as he places himself abjectly before the object of his desire.

The traditional servant-mistress relationship is established in the initial line, with the object of desire as the active party and the speaker appearing passive, offering only a weak protest: [. . .] "Blame / Of all my greffe and grame" (ll. 3–4). When the opening question is repeated at the end of the STANZA, the speaker offers a response on the part of the silent and occluded mistress: "Say nay, Say nay!" (l. 6). This question and suggested response is repeated throughout the other stanzas with the effect of the speaker appearing more and more abject each time it is repeated.

The second and third stanzas focus the attention of the poem on the speaker's actions and emotional state. In the second stanza, the speaker emphatically declares that his love has been faithful "In welthe and woo" (l.

9), and in the third stanza, he reinforces his steadfastness, as he would not leave "Nother for payn nor smart" (l. 16). These descriptions increase the undignified, self-piteous subject positioning of the speaker, and both conclude with the question and suggested response for the silent mistress. There is no attempt at psychological introspection here—no justification for the love of the mistress—only a helpless servant-speaker in the face of his mistress.

The fourth stanza refocuses the poem's attention on the mistress and her lack of pity for the abject lover. The cruel mistress is given all the power, while the speaker places himself in a position of utter impotence, again offering the refused suggested response of "Say nay, Say nay!" (l. 24). Introspectively, Wyatt has established the utter undesirability of being the courtly lover.

See also "THEY FLEE FROM ME."

Andrew Bretz

ANEIRIN   See Y GODODDIN.

ANGLO-NORMAN

Anglo-Norman is the French dialect that took root among the cultured classes in England after the NORMAN CONQUEST and lasted in various forms until the mid-15th century. The term is also used to describe texts written in French during the same period for English patrons or by authors in England. In 1066, William the Conqueror—then duke of Normandy—invaded England and successfully claimed its throne. As Normans increasingly replaced Anglo-Saxons in powerful institutional positions, French became the language of politics and of the elite. Over time, Anglo-Norman steadily replaced Latin for legal, clerical, commercial, and administrative purposes. It was also spoken at the royal court. Consequently, cultured English people sought to learn the language because of its newfound prestige and practicality.

There is some debate about the extent to which Anglo-Norman was spoken or understood by the general public, but the current scholarly consensus holds that most of the population during these years spoke only English. Nevertheless, since the French dialect was considered far more refined than English, Anglo-

Norman quickly became the preferred VERNACULAR of poets and clerics. The new dialect was embraced as a literary language and produced a significant and lasting impact. By the late 14th century, English had absorbed about 10,000 French words into the language, many of which endure.

After a few centuries of use, Anglo-Norman lost linguistic ground in England. In 1337, the English king Edward III (reigned 1327–77) attempted to claim the recently vacated French throne and provoked the HUNDRED YEARS WAR (1337–1453). The diplomacy engendered by the conflict bolstered the prestige of continental French, which began to take the place of the less standardized Anglo-Norman. As a literary language, however, Anglo-Norman was almost entirely replaced by English by the end of the 14th century. Henry IV (reigned 1399–1413), the first of the Lancastrian kings, became the first monarch in over 300 years to make English the predominant language at court. By the middle of the 15th century, most of the upper echelons of English society had rejected the French dialect. Anglo-Norman eventually disappeared from England altogether, but it left permanent traces in the English language.

See also ANGLO-NORMAN POETRY.

FURTHER READING

Calin, William. *The French Tradition and the Literature of Medieval England.* Toronto, Buffalo, and London: University of Toronto Press, 1994.

Crane, Susan. "Anglo-Norman Cultures in England." In *The Cambridge History of Medieval English Literature,* edited by David Wallace, 35–60. Cambridge: Cambridge University Press, 1999.

Anne Salo

ANGLO-NORMAN POETRY

After the NORMAN CONQUEST, William the Conqueror filled his court with advisers from home, and the French dialect ANGLO-NORMAN became the court, administrative, and literary language of England. Critics have suggested that many of the highborn Normans who immigrated to England over the next three centuries may have felt the need to distinguish themselves from their Norman siblings still living on the continent, and that, as a consequence of their PATRONAGE, CHRONICLES, ROMANCES, and hagiographies (see HAGIOGRAPHY)—all of which tend to ennoble the present by linking it to an illustrious past—became the first popular genres of Anglo-Norman literature in England. The increasing demand for literary production inspired many writers to become bilingual, and they borrowed freely from French texts. This trend continued well into the 15th century, when the court of Henry IV (reigned 1399–1413) increased its use of English, which had begun to emerge as a poetic language in its own right. On the whole, aristocratic patronage is credited with having produced much of the Anglo-Norman poetry that still survives today.

The earliest extant Anglo-Norman poem dates to the first part of the 12th century, when William's son Henry I (reigned 1100–35) was in power. *The Voyage of St. Brendan* (ca. 1106) recounts legendary episodes from the life of St. Brendan and tells of a fantastic voyage filled with great adventure. The poem was likely commissioned by Henry's first wife and composed by a Benedictine monk. It appears to be the oldest surviving example of a poem written in rhyming COUPLETs with eight syllables to a line. This structure is significant because later romances adopted the same form; the Anglo-Norman romance *Tristan,* for example, follows this format. *Tristan* (ca. 1170), one of the most famous romances, was written by Thomas d'Anglettere during the rule of Henry II (1154–89).

Many 12th-century poets writing in Anglo-Norman name female patrons. WACE's famous ROMAN DE BRUT (1155), which narrates a legendary history of the founding of Britain, dates to Henry II's rule, and the author may have given the work as a gift to Henry's queen, Eleanor of Aquitaine. Women authors, too, composed notable poetry from this period. The *Life of St. Catherine* (ca. 1175), for example, was written by the nun Clemence of Barking, and MARIE DE FRANCE is famous for her 12 short stories (*lais* [see LAY]) composed in Anglo-Norman verse. Her *lais* (ca. 1170) were so popular that two of them were later translated into Middle English.

Critics have pointed out that Anglo-Norman occupied a unique linguistic position throughout its life in England: It was both a cultured language of privilege and an appropriate medium for women writers, for whom a romance VERNACULAR was considered more suitable than the more learned Latin.

The early 13th century saw a dramatic increase in the production of Anglo-Norman spiritual writings. The Fourth Lateran Council (1215), which established the requirement of Christian confession once a year, had a particularly significant impact. Manuals and treatises—designed to edify both the laity and the clerics who would be hearing their confessions—proliferated. It was not until the later part of the 14th century however, that the last great achievement of Anglo-Norman poetry appeared. JOHN GOWER, whose literary career spanned the rule of three monarchs—Edward III (1327–77), Richard II (1377–99), and Henry IV (1399–1413)—addressed the problem of human sin in the *Mirour de l'Omme* (ca. 1376–79), which he wrote in octosyllabic STANZAs of 12 lines each. *Mirour* was the last significant work in French verse to be written by an English author. Though the dialect persisted into the 15th century, after the rule of Henry IV, it was used almost exclusively as an administrative language, rather than a poetic one.

FURTHER READING

Calin, William. *The French Tradition and the Literature of Medieval England.* Toronto, Buffalo, and London: University of Toronto Press, 1994.

Crane, Susan. "Anglo-Norman Cultures in England." In *The Cambridge History of Medieval English Literature,* edited by David Wallace. 35–60. Cambridge: Cambridge University Press, 1999.

Legge, M. Dominica. *Anglo-Norman Literature & Its Background.* London: Oxford University Press, 1963.

Anne Salo

ANGLO-SAXON CHRONICLE (9th–12th centuries)

Begun by ALFRED THE GREAT in the 890s, the *Anglo-Saxon Chronicle* records the history of the Anglo-Saxon settlement in England. Alfred ordered that the CHRONICLE be copied and distributed to monasteries and priories, and that it be updated frequently. Nine manuscript copies survive. Three provide continued coverage after the NORMAN CONQUEST, with the last entry being dated 1154. All nine are composed in Old English, though one contains translations of the chronicle into Latin, and one displays evidence of early Middle English. Each chronicle began as an exact copy of the "original" but then was updated independently. The result is varying descriptions of "national" and world events—as well as careful records of local events not otherwise noted. The *Anglo-Saxon Chronicle* provides important records of history, as well as of the shifts in English linguistics. Moreover, the *Chronicles* are an important step in establishing the presence of the VERNACULAR, as well as in the development of historiography.

FURTHER READING

Bredehoft, Thomas A. *Textual Histories: Readings in the Anglo-Saxon Chronicle.* Toronto: University of Toronto Press, 2001.

Savage, Anne. *The Anglo-Saxon Chronicles.* New York: Barnes & Noble, 2000.

ANGLO-SAXON POETRY The first poetry in English was written in a form of the language usually referred to as Old English, sometimes referred to as Anglo-Saxon. Old English was spoken in England for centuries and is represented by a large body of literature. Though prose works account for the great majority of that literature, a substantial amount of Old English poetry survives as well. The earliest datable piece of Anglo-Saxon poetry is "CÆDMON'S HYMN," a nine-line Christian poem of praise to God, which can be dated to around 670 C.E. The end of the Anglo-Saxon period is traditionally placed at 1066, the date of the NORMAN CONQUEST of England, but Anglo-Saxon poems continued to be written well into the early years of the 12th century.

Our knowledge of Anglo-Saxon poetry is limited to the works that have survived in manuscript form. It is, of course, impossible to know how much Anglo-Saxon poetry may have been written and lost, and how much may have been circulated orally and never written down, but approximately 30,000 lines of Old English poetry remain, 10 percent of which are found in one poem, the EPIC *BEOWULF.* Most of the major Anglo-Saxon poems are found in four manuscripts, which are usually referred to as the EXETER BOOK (Exeter Cathedral Chapter Library MS 3501), the Vercelli Book (Vercelli Cathedral Library, MS CXVII), the Junius manuscript (Oxford Bodleian Library, MS Junius 11), and the Nowell Codex (London British Library, MS COTTON VITELLIUS A.XV). Although most Anglo-Saxon poetry is anonymous, a few named authors are known. Cædmon, the seventh-century author of "Cædmon's

Hymn," is described by the Venerable Bede as the author of many Christian poems, though only the one poem apparently remains. An eighth-century poet by the name of CYNEWULF has been identified as the author of four poems: *Juliana* and *Christ II,* which are found in the Exeter Book, and *Elene* and *Fates of the Apostles,* in the Vercelli Book. ALFRED THE GREAT is believed to be the author of a poetic paraphrase of BOETHIUS's *The CONSOLATION OF PHILOSOPHY,* usually referred to as METERS OF BOETHIUS, and the METRICAL PREFACE TO PASTORAL CARE. The Anglo-Latin author ALDHELM is described in medieval sources as having written poetry in Anglo-Saxon, but none of his works have survived.

Each line of Anglo-Saxon verse is usually divided into two HALF-LINES, separated by a pause, or CAESURA. Each half-line contains two accented syllables and a varying number of unaccented syllables. The principal formal element in the verse is ALLITERATION, which generally is used to link the two half-lines together. Stylistically, Anglo-Saxon poetry makes use of many of the same devices found in later poems, including metaphor, simile, and APOSTROPHE. Two techniques are particularly common in Anglo-Saxon poetry: KENNINGS (compound words) and variation (renaming the same person or object multiple times in one passage of the poem, using a different word or phrase each time; also known as epithesis).

Although Anglo-Saxon poetry deals with a relatively wide range of subjects, scholars have traditionally divided the corpus into a few broad categories. Secular heroic poems, such as *Beowulf,* account for a fairly small portion of Anglo-Saxon poetry overall, though the general popularity of this type of verse has garnered it a disproportionate level of attention from readers and scholars. Religious poems, especially hagiographies (saints' lives) are much more common in Anglo-Saxon verse, though at times the lines between secular and religious do become blurred. Some Anglo-Saxon poems, for example, recount the lives or deeds of important figures in biblical or church history, but they do so using some of the conventions and language developed in secular heroic verse and are the forerunners of ROMANCE. As a further example, the two Old English poems on the life of the seventh-century martyr St. Guthlac (often referred to as *Guthlac A* and *Guthlac B*) found in the

Exeter Book contain descriptions of Guthlac's battles with heathens and struggles against attacks by demons.

Several Anglo-Saxon religious poems, with titles such as *Genesis A & B, Exodus,* and *Daniel,* consist of paraphrases of books of the Bible, while others, like "Cædmon's Hymn" and the well-known *The DREAM OF THE ROOD,* appear to be entirely original compositions. A large number of Anglo-Saxon poems are neither heroic nor religious in content, however. ANGLO-SAXON RIDDLES, CHARMS, maxims, and occasional poems tend to be much briefer than the works discussed above but do demonstrate the wide variety of Anglo-Saxon poetry.

See also HAGIOGRAPHY.

FURTHER READING

Godden, Malcolm, and Michael Lapidge, eds. *The Cambridge Companion to Old English Literature.* Cambridge: Cambridge University Press, 1991.
Greenfield, Stanley, and Daniel Calder. *A New Critical History of Old English Literature.* New York: New York University Press, 1986.

William H. Smith

ANGLO-SAXON RIDDLES (WISDOM POETRY, GNOMIC VERSE)

A riddle asks a question or describes a concept and challenges the listener to identify it; the terms used seem obscure until the answer is known. Anglo-Saxon riddles ask questions about familiar objects or animals in terms that often suggest paradox. In Anglo-Saxon England, the tradition of riddling begins with several eighth-century Latin collections written in imitation of earlier Continental models. Old English riddles appear as elements in poetic and prose texts such as *Apollonius of Tyre* and the *Dialogues of Solomon and Saturn,* as well as in other freestanding forms.

The majority of Old English riddles are poems of around 10 or 15 lines and are preserved in the EXETER BOOK, which contains three different groups of riddles, 90 in total, though scholars think the collection may have originally consisted of 100 riddles.

Latin collections typically provide solutions for the riddles they contain, but the Exeter Book collection does not, so readers are left to attempt to discern the answers. The Exeter Book riddles typically describe a common thing or an animal in the context of human life. Several riddles describe an ox or its leather in various terms; in one of these (#10), the living creature plunders the land while its dead form serves men. The ox plows fields; its skin can be used for a wineskin, a floor covering, or cord, among other things.

In Riddle 45, the riddler obscures the bookworm's origins by saying the moth eats words (rather than the books in which they are written). The text is full of double meanings: WYRD, typically translated as "fate," may pun on "speech" or "sentence," while *cwide* may mean "that which is chewed" as well as "speech." Like other Old English poetry, riddles in verse contain ALLITERATION and repetition, or the use of several words referring to the same idea.

Several Old English riddles have double meanings that allow for a sexual subtext hidden behind an innocent solution. One, solved innocently as "onion," describes a thing very useful to women, standing upright in a bed and shaggy with hair below, that a peasant's daughter grips firmly so that her eye becomes wet.

See also ANGLO-SAXON POETRY.

FURTHER READING

Wilcox, Jonathan. "'Tell Me What I Am': The Old English Riddles." In *Readings in Medieval Texts: Interpreting Old and Middle English Literature,* edited by David Johnson and Elaine Treharne, 46–59. Oxford and New York: Oxford University Press, 2005.
Williamson, Craig. *The Old English Riddles of the Exeter Book.* Chapel Hill, N.C.: Duke University Press, 1977.

Heide Estes

ANTITHESIS

A common rhetorical device used in love poetry and the SONNET tradition, antithesis involves contrasting ideas and/or parallel arguments within words, clauses, or sentences. This common device is found throughout many SONNET SEQUENCES, finding particular favor within the works of SIR PHILIP SIDNEY and WILLIAM SHAKESPEARE. For example, in Sonnet 23 from *SHAKESPEARE'S SONNETS,* the first QUATRAIN depends on antithesis to explain the narrator. Sustained antithesis became known as Petrarchan paradox.

APOSTROPHE

From the Greek *apostrephein,* "to turn away," an apostrophe is a poetic device in which an inanimate, absent, or imaginary person—or a personified abstraction—is directly addressed. For example, in the first line of SIR PHILIP SIDNEY's Sonnet 31 from ASTROPHIL AND STELLA—"With how sad steps, O Moon, thou climb'st the sky!"—the speaker addresses the moon as a fellow sufferer.

See also PERSONIFICATION.

ARCADIA

Arcadia is an idyllic rural location in the Peloponnese (southern Greece) known for its remote, unspoiled location. Used first by the Roman poet VIRGIL in his adaptation of the *Eclogues* and subsequently by a long line of English writers, the name *Arcadia* came to represent a peaceful rural environment where humans lived in harmony with nature—a haven from the complexities and corruption of urban life. Thus, it became the customary setting for PASTORALS, a rustic paradise governed only by the gods, the seasons, and the cycles of life. Idealized shepherds and farmers inhabit it—free from concerns, well-dressed, and well-fed. Copious amounts of leisure time allow them to compose music and poetry, debate philosophy, and engage in lusty pursuits.

See also ECLOGUES; LOCUS AMOENUS; "PASSIONATE SHEPHERD TO HIS LOVE, THE."

FURTHER READING
Gifford, Terry. *Pastoral: The New Idiom.* London: Routledge, 1999.

J. A. White

ARTHUR *king of Britain*

King Arthur is widely known throughout history and literature since many tales have been written about Arthur and his Knights of the Round Table—especially those concerning Lancelot and Gawain; Guinevere; Arthur's famous sword, Excalibur; and his majestic palace, Camelot. These tales, filled with some of the most appealing characters in literature, have had an enormous impact on Western culture from the beginnings of Britain to the present day. But the question over whether Arthur was truly a historical figure remains hotly debated in current scholarship. Records from the presumed Arthurian period are so scarce that, like the battle and characters of Troy, it remains difficult to discern whether or not the tales of ARTHURIAN LITERATURE have any historical validity. At present, however, critics are divided, and there are generally two opposing schools of thought concerning the historical Arthur: those who believe Arthur indeed existed and those who hold that Arthur serves as some kind of romantic, national symbolic figure.

If Arthur did exist, he lived sometime between the years of 450 and 550 C.E. The first historical mention of Arthur appears in *Historia Brittonum,* around 800 C.E., in which he is depicted as a fierce warlord. Some 150 years later, there are two mentions of Arthur in *Annales Cambriae* (*The Annals of Wales*), stating that an Arthur was victorious at the Battle of Badon, where he carried the cross of Jesus Christ on his shoulders for three days, and that at the Battle of Camlann, both Arthur and his son Mordred died. What became of this Arthur and what other deeds are attributed to him remain unknown; however, Geoffrey of Monmouth continued the story of King Arthur in his 1136 work *Historia Regum Britanniae* (*History of the Kings of Britain*). Geoffrey claims that he discovered an old manuscript containing citations for his stories, although critics dismiss this as a literary convention.

Whether Geoffrey created these accounts or wrote from fact, he certainly cemented Arthur's place in the lore of Britain. Arthur became a symbol of national spirit and a paragon of virtue and justice for medieval kings and laymen. Other stories of Arthur followed, most notably *ROMAN DE BRUT,* the ANGLO-NORMAN poem by WACE, and Sir Thomas Malory's Prose work *Morte d'Arthur,* both of which were largely based on Geoffrey's work. *Roman de Brut* introduced a new element in the Arthurian legend that would spawn even more stories, the Knights of the Round Table, which spurred the publication of various Welsh ROMANCEs with Arthur as the main character. These early works in turn influenced other writers, such as Chrétien de Troyes and the unknown author of *SIR GAWAIN AND THE GREEN KNIGHT,* to publish longer and more involved romances concerning Arthur and his knights. Both works introduced a variety of other knights—Chrétien's *Lancelot* and the *GAWAIN*-POET's Gawain, to name a few—and both centered on the ties between chivalric attitudes and courtly life.

However, it was Malory's *Morte d'Arthur,* a combination of extent tales, which became the major source of what most people know about the story of Arthur today. Malory combined stories that had been written to produce a large work focusing on tragedy and CHIVALRY. He broke his account of Arthur into eight books, each covering important points in the romance. Malory begins with Arthur's birth as the son of Uther Pendragon and the chaste Igrayne, and moves to his crowning. Additionally, the account covers the invasion of France and Rome, the story of Tristan and Isolde, and a version of the Holy Grail. *Morte d'Arthur* also includes the infamous love affair of Lancelot and Guinevere and accounts of knights such as Gareth and Gawain. In the final death scene, Arthur kills Mordred but is struck with Mordred's poison sword, and a group of women in black take Arthur away to parts unknown.

While Malory's tale is not the greatest literary work or even a feasible representation of an historical Arthur, until the 18th century it remained the foremost depiction of the Arthurian legend. Part of the reason for the paucity in Arthurian legend was that by the time of the Renaissance, Geoffrey's history of Arthur had been so widely disputed that most historians and literary authors neglected to include Arthur in any works of the time. Consequently, this scholarly stalemate resulted in his being dropped from favor in literature for a time. Nevertheless, Arthur did continue to make minor appearances. In fiction, he appears in EDMUND SPENSER's *The FAERIE QUEENE,* but only as a minor character. He resurfaced in numerous poems for a time during the Gothic period of the late 18th and early 19th century, but until the publication of Alfred Lord Tennyson's *The Idylls of the King,* he continued to remain largely ignored in fiction as well as history. In the 19th century, however, as Victorians struggled to find meaning and national unity in the midst of the Industrial Revolution, Tennyson's Arthur again represented all the romantic glories of Britain.

The trend to envision Arthur either historically or romantically continues into the 21st century. He appears in various places in pop culture, and there have been several cinematic portrayals of Arthur on film: *Camelot* (1967) and *Excalibur* (1981) are among the romanticized Arthur movies; *First Knight* (1995) and *King Arthur* (2004) focus more on a historical Arthur. While it remains debatable whether the historical King Arthur existed and whether the tales of his exploits involve historical accuracy or romantic representations, it is clear that Arthur continues to represent an ideology of noble ideals and chivalric COURTLY LOVE.

FURTHER READING

Bryden, Inga. *Reinventing King Arthur: The Arthurian Legends in Victorian Culture.* Burlington, Vt.: Ashgate, 2005.

Finke, Laurie A., and Martin B. Shichtman. *King Arthur and the Myth of History.* Gainesville: University Press of Florida, 2004.

Sklar, Elizabeth S., and Donald L. Hoffman, eds. *King Arthur in Popular Culture.* Jefferson, N.C.: McFarland, 2002.

Michael Modarelli

ARTHURIAN LITERATURE   After the Romans left in 410 C.E., Britain was subject to invasions and attacks by various continental races, thus necessitating a national hero to help create a sense of identity. King ARTHUR filled that role. He is first mentioned as a leader who fights against the Germanic invaders; later, he becomes a king who changes the course of history. The earliest references to Arthur can be found in Latin CHRONICLES (Nennius's *Historia Brittonum,* the *Annales Cambriae,* Gildas's *De excidio et conquestu Britanniae*).

Early in the 12th century, Geoffrey of Monmouth took these references and expanded them with the aid of Celtic stories, such as Adomnán's life of the Irish saint Columba, when writing his chronicle of the kings of Britain. The account of Arthur is the climax of the work, occupying a third of its length. He established the descent of Britain from Troy and raised Arthur to the status of a powerful heroic king. Geoffrey's audience was the new ANGLO-NORMAN aristocracy, and he wanted to link them to the Celts, demonstrating that they were the legitimate rulers of England. By 1155, there were two adaptations in French: *L'Estoire des Engles* by Geoffrey Gaimar and WACE's verse *ROMAN DE BRUT.* Wace was from Jersey and basically made the history more rational. He redefined Arthur as a chivalric hero (see CHIVALRY). LAYAMON, a man of Norse-Irish descent, chose to write in Middle English and to use the native tradition of alliterative verse (see ALLITERATION), combined with rhyming COUPLETS. Layamon's

BRUT (1189–99) has a strong Welsh overtone and a sense of the supernatural; his Arthur is a fierce warrior-king. Clearly, Layamon's goal was to establish the Englishness of both Arthur and the land.

Geoffrey of Monmouth and Layamon drew upon Celtic, especially Welsh, accounts of Arthur, which depicted him as an ideal soldier and a hero. Arthur is alluded to in many early Welsh poems, such as *Y Gododdin,* a mixture of military realism and heroic ideology; "Canu Aneirin"; and three poems from *The Black Book of Carmarthen,* one of which names his followers. "Preiddeu Annwn" in *The Book of Taliesin* relates how the poet accompanied Arthur to the otherworld to get the magic cauldron called the Head of Annufn. Three other poems in the collection refer to widespread legends, as do many Welsh Triads (catalogues of heroic and romantic materials that serve as mnemonics for storytellers). The *Mabinogin* contains the tale *"Culwch ac Olwen,"* in which Arthur is depicted as a king of a well-known court with an established reputation for valor. This prose is the first to take a common folktale and put it in an Arthurian context, illustrating Arthur's early popularity. Arthur is also depicted not as an active warrior but, rather, as a king whose court is a center for other knights, giving Arthur symbolic stature. Both these trends are developed in later works from all cultures.

In early hagiographies of British saints (see HAGIOGRAPHY), Arthur is a *rex tyrannus,* a king who terrorizes the church and is defeated by saintly heroes. These texts reflect a collision of Celtic and Anglo-Norman cultures, ultimately prioritizing the values of the church over secular power. In the *Life of St Cadoc,* written ca. 1075, Arthur is a petty tyrant. In the *Life of St Gildas,* he is portrayed as the king of the whole of Britain. Guinevere is carried off by Melwas and imprisoned, and Arthur finds her after a year of searching. In the *Life of St Carantac,* Arthur is a drunk who keeps spilling his cups.

An influential version of the Arthur legend was created by Chrétien de Troyes. Taking his lead from Wace, he wrote five verse ROMANCEs between 1160 and 1190, transforming the Arthur material into elegant tales of CHIVALRY and COURTLY LOVE. These were prized by audiences who had a newly acquired belief that human emotion is important for inspiring noble behavior. Chrétien was the first to develop roles for Lancelot and Percival, who, together with Tristan, became the most important figures in French and continental texts thereafter. The English redactors changed the emphasis of his romances, concentrating on war and chivalry rather than courtly love. An important English adaptation of his *Yvain* is *Ywain and Gawain.*

MARIE DE FRANCE, writing in England from ca. 1160 to ca. 1180, popularized the genre of Breton *lais* (LAYS). Her *lais* have an air of simplicity and elegance, and two are connected with Arthur. A charming example is "LANVAL," which was reworked on four occasions, once by Thomas Chestre. This is a tale of wish fulfillment, with Arthur depicted as a *roi fainéant* (do nothing king), fronting a court pervaded by false values, sexual corruption, and injustice. It examines the oppositions of public/private, masculinity/femininity, court/forest, and the knight/king relationship.

Sometime between 1215 and 1230, the Vulgate Cycle (or Lancelot-Grail Cycle) was compiled under the influence of Cistercian teaching. These works gathered all the stories concerning Arthur and his court into one vast, chronological cycle. It takes its lead from Chrétien de Troyes, and consists of the 13th century works *Lancelot, Queste del Saint Graal, Le Morte le Roi Artu,* and the later prequels of *Estoire del Saint Graal* and *Estoire de Merlin.* The Tristan legend was added as *Le Roman de Tristan de Leonais,* ca. 1225–35, and *Suite de Merlin* (ca. 1230–40) completed the cycle with an expanded role for Merlin. In this cycle, Lancelot has a greater role than Arthur, with his courtesy, prowess, and honor underpinned. His failure to win the Grail is perceived as the folly of secular chivalry. This set the course for subsequent French Arthurian works, which all tend to focus on chivalric love, and the Germanic tradition, which highlights the Grail, Percival, and the need for piety.

In English works, Gawain remains Arthur's foremost knight, having on the whole a greater role than Arthur himself. Another popular figure is Merlin. Highlighted by Geoffrey of Monmouth, he has four romances almost entirely devoted to him in Middle English: *Of Arthour and Merlin* (1250–1300), Lovelich's *Merlin* (ca. 1430), the prose *Merlin* (ca. 1450), and the prose

Joseph of Arimathea (ca. 1500). *Of Arthour and Merlin* is based on *Estoire de Merlin* but is more concerned with action sequences than internal struggles. Lovelich's *Merlin* is slavishly based on the same Latin romance with which he had difficulties in adapting. Another such legendary figure is Joseph of Arimathea, supposed guardian of the Grail.

By 1191, Glastonbury Abbey had declared itself as Avalon, the resting place of Arthur, and also adopted Joseph as its founder. This caused renewed English interest in this figure. A surviving text about Joseph— *Estoire del Saint Graal* by Henry Lovelich in 1450— highlights Joseph rather than Arthur, but still links the Holy Grail firmly to the end of the Arthurian world.

Lancelot never really attained great prominence in Britain due to the continued dominance of Gawain. Only three romances, inspired by the French tradition, have him as chief protagonist: *Stanzaic Morte Arthure, Lancelot of the Laik* (1482–1500), and *Sir Lancelot du Lac. Lancelot of the Laik* opens with a spring setting and dream, describing how Lancelot fights both for and against Arthur and has a fateful affair with Guinevere. Gawain is Lancelot's foil, and the poem elaborates on their achievements and bonds. *Sir Lancelot du Lake* is a late BALLAD that tells of Lancelot's encounter with Sir Tarquin. The *Stanzaic Morte Arthure* is a kind of tragedy derived from the *La Mort le Roi Artu,* which teaches that even those who exhibit individual greatness are still imperfect. In this poem, Lancelot is perceived as a valiant knight, while Gawain is a peacemaker and friend of Lancelot's. Arthur is subordinated to both, making a series of ill-advised decisions and shifting allegiance from Gawain to Lancelot, rising to prominence only in the final catastrophe.

Again in the tragic vein, the *Alliterative Morte Arthure* (late 14th century) highlights the inadequacies of chivalry and the problems of territorial expansion. In line with native tradition, Arthur is a noble heroic king who wins many victories and amasses lands. At this point he dreams of FORTUNE's wheel, with eight of the nine worthies and himself at its pinnacle. This portends his end in a climatic battle caused by his son Mordred's treachery. It is a dramatic fall, and Arthur's pride, based on his initial successes, constitutes his tragic flaw. None of the figures in this poem are entirely good or evil. In addition, the romance reflects the political situation in England of the time and raises the possibility of what happens when lawlessness goes unchecked during the absence of the king.

Romances focusing on Gawain dominate Arthurian literature in medieval Britain. He is the epitome of chivalry and courtesy, against whom all must measure themselves. In SIR GAWAIN AND THE GREEN KNIGHT, Arthur and his court are merely the setting for Gawain's quest, symbolizing the prioritizing of chivalry over piety. Other Gawain literature emphasizes its Celtic roots.

The Tudor monarchs took the tradition of Arthur and, from it, created a lineage for themselves in order to validate their regime, as did earlier rulers. EDMUND SPENSER, the most archetypal of Renaissance writers, uses Arthur to glorify ELIZABETH I in his poetic masterpiece *The FAERIE QUEENE.* Arthur is a prince searching for the awe-inspiring Gloriana.

Analysis of Arthurian literature was initially dominated by surveys that tried to establish the historical Arthur and the Celtic origins of the subsequent legends and texts. Other criticism tended to favor the French texts over those in Middle English, which were regarded as derivative and provincial. Recent scholarship, however, has endeavored to show how successive groups, individuals, and societies appropriated Arthurian material and reinterpreted it to validate differing ideological, social, and political needs. Other critics have chosen to trace a specific theme from one text to another. Most scholars today share a belief that there is a pool of elements that have grown up to form the basis of Arthurian literature alongside varying genres, and that these interpenetrate each other, defying simple classifications or even temporal and cultural boundaries.

FURTHER READING

Barron, W. R. J., ed. *The Arthur of the English: The Arthurian Legend in Medieval English Life and Literature.* Cardiff: University of Wales Press, 1999.

Lacy, N. J., ed. *The New Arthurian Encyclopedia.* New York/London: Garland, 1991.

Morris, Rosemary. *The Character of King Arthur in Medieval Romance.* Oxford: D.S. Brewer, 1982.

Pearsall, Derek. *Arthurian Romance: A Short Introduction.* Oxford: Blackwell, 2003.

Wilhelm, James J., ed. *The Romance of Arthur: An Anthology of Medieval Texts in Translation.* New York and London: Garland, 1994.

Bonnie S. Millar

ART OF COURTLY LOVE, THE ANDREAS CAPELLANUS (ca. 1184–86)

ANDREAS CAPELLANUS achieved fame by composing a Latin treatise on love (ca. 1184–86) entitled *Liber de arte honeste amandi et reprobatione inhonesti amantis* (*Book of the Art of Loving Nobly and the Reprobation of Dishonourable Love*). It is commonly referred to as *The Art of Courtly Love.* Inspired by OVID and the poetry of the Provençal troubadours, Andreas explores the practices associated with what the French philologist Gaston Paris referred to as "COURTLY LOVE" (*amour courtois*): a refined love, occurring exclusively outside of marriage and, in general, among courtly societies. (The phrase *courtly love* was coined by Paris; in Old French and MIDDLE ENGLISH, *fin' amors* and *trwe love* were much more common terms.)

The work of Andreas Capellanus was translated into Old French, Catalan, Italian, and German. It became one of the most influential works of the Middle Ages— almost every ROMANCE, for instance, relies on its principles of courtly love. It also greatly influenced medieval vernacular literature aside from romances, including Guillaume de Lorris and Jean de Meun's *Romance of the Rose* and CHAUCER's *TROILUS AND CRISEYDE,* among many other works.

Andreas dedicates his treatise to a noble, although probably fictitious, friend, Walter. He divides the study into three parts. In Book One, he provides a series of definitions with etymologies: "'Love' [*amor*] is derived from the word 'hook' [*amar*], which signifies 'capture' or 'be captured.' For he who loves is caught in the chains of desire and wishes to catch another with his hook." The love described by Andreas is explicitly Ovidian and sexual in nature: It is an "inborn suffering derived from the sight of and excessive meditation upon the beauty of the opposite sex, which causes each one to wish above all things the embraces of the other." Nonetheless, love elevates the lover's character and is capable of making "an ugly and rude person shine with all beauty, knows how to endow with nobility even one of humble birth, can even lend humility to the

proud." According to Andreas, the male partner must initiate the love affair by revealing his feelings and asking for the lady's affection. She, in turn, may choose to accept or deny her suitor. The woman maintains considerable power over her admirer, who must do her bidding whether or not she agrees to return his love.

In Book Two, Andreas outlines how love may be retained by providing his reader with 31 rules. These include statements about the conditions in which love will flourish and about how a lover should behave; for example: "marriage is no real excuse for not loving" (Rule 1); "boys do not love until they arrive at the age of maturity" (Rule 6); "love is always a stranger in the home of avarice" (Rule 10); "good character alone makes a man worthy of love" (Rule 18); "he whom the thought of love vexes eats and sleeps very little" (Rule 23); and "love can deny nothing to love" (Rule 26). In accepting and applying these rules, the lover will prove worthy of his lady.

Book Three, entitled "A Rejection of Love," stands in stark opposition to the preceding sections, although it, too, draws upon Ovid, in particular, his *Remedia Amoris* (*Remedies of Love*). Here, Andreas explains why courtly love ought not to be practiced, especially by Christians. This conclusion has caused much debate: Did Andreas add his rejection because he was a Chaplain and faced repercussions from the church? Or is his entire treatise a parody of courtly love and its negative influences?

See also CHIVALRY, LOVESICKNESS.

FURTHER READING
Allen, Peter L. "Ars Amandi, Ars Legendi: Love Poetry and Literary Theory in Ovid, Andreas Capellanus, and Jean de Meun." *Exemplaria* 1, no. 1 (1989): 181–205.

Andreas Capellanus. *The Art of Courtly Love.* Translated by John Jay Parry. New York: Columbia University Press, 1990.

Williams, Andrew. "Clerics and Courtly Love in Andreas Capellanus' *The Art of Courtly Love* and Chaucer's *Canterbury Tales.*" *Revista Alicantina de Estudios Ingleses* 3 (1990): 127–136.

K. Sarah-Jane Murray

ART OF ENGLISH POESIE (ARTE OF ENGLISH POESY) GEORGE PUTTENHAM (1569)

According to George Puttenham, presumptive author

of *The Art of English Poesie,* Sir THOMAS WYATT and HENRY HOWARD, EARL OF SURREY, went to Italy and brought back the verse forms that make them "the first reformers of our English meter and stile" (49). The introduction of these new Italian forms, in turn, necessitated the flurry of Renaissance poetry manuals by GEORGE GASCOIGNE, SAMUEL DANIEL, Charles Webb, Sir PHILIP SIDNEY, and Puttenham, among others.

Book I, "Of Poets and Poesie," contains a remarkably credible history of poetry in Greek, Latin, and English. All subjects, including science and law, were written in verse in primitive times, and the types of poetry number in the dozens. Because it is decorated with versification and figures of speech, poetry is a more persuasive and melodious form of language and is very much given to structure and accuracy. The countless examples of dignities and promotions given to poets throughout history, and the numerous examples of royal poets, show up the ignorance of Renaissance courtiers who suppress their poetry or publish under a pseudonym.

In Book II, "Of Proportion Poetical," Puttenham compares metrical form to arithmetical, geometrical, and musical pattern. He adduces five points to English verse structure: The "Staffe," the "Measure," "Concord or Symphony," "Situation," and "Figure." The *staffe,* or STANZA, is four to 10 lines that join without intermission and finish all of the sentences thereof. Each length of the stanza suits a poetic tone and genre. Each is overlaid by a closed rhyme scheme. This latter, termed "band" (65) or "enterlacement" (70), is of primary concern to Puttenham. He views English as having solely a syllabic system of measure (meter). The length of lines may alternate in patterns that support the rhyme scheme and, so, increase the band. Syllabic length is a factor, but accentuation is not. "Concord, called Symphonie or rime" (76) is an accommodation made for the lack of metrical feet in English versification. The matching of line lengths, rhymed at the end, in symmetrical patterns, is a further accommodation. Puttenham includes a number of graphs to illustrate the variety of rhyme schemes and line-length patterns, or situation. Proportion in figure is the composition of stanzas in graphic forms ranging from the rhombus to the spire.

Book III, "Of Ornament," which comprises a full half of the *Arte,* is a catalog of figures of speech. Puttenham believes that language, since it is inherently artificial, not natural, is suitable for the added artifice of figures. Figures give more "pithe and substance, subtilitie, quicknesse, efficacie or moderation, in this or that sort tuning and tempring them by amplification, abridgement, opening, closing, enforcing, meekening or otherwise disposing them to the best purpose" (134). This definition is followed by a catalog of the various figures of speech, which Puttenham analyzes. His book concludes with a lengthy analysis of "decency," and the artificial and natural dimensions of language.

Robert Einarsson

ASKEW, ANNE   See "BALLAD WHICH ASKEW MADE AND SANG WHEN IN NEWGATE, A."

ASSONANCE   Assonance occurs when vowel sounds are repeated in words that are next to or near each other. The sounds may be identical or similar, but in all cases the vowels will be accented. Scholars often call assonance *vocalic rhyme,* since it is more of a sound effect than a rhyme proper: the words *sit* and *bit* rhyme, but *sit* and *bin* reflect assonance. The reader's expectation that a rhyme may occur, especially within a line of poetry, enables poets to produce varied effects via assonance. For instance, a number of poems from the 14th-century ALLITERATIVE REVIVAL employ assonance and ALLITERATION simultaneously, with striking results.

Larry T. Shillock

"ASSYRIANS' KING IN PEACE WITH FOUL DESIRE, THE" HENRY HOWARD, EARL OF SURREY (1557)   This SONNET was first published in *TOTTEL'S MISCELLANY,* 10 years after the execution of HENRY HOWARD, EARL OF SURREY. This angry and critical poem is deeply imbedded in its own time.

Surrey was born into a well-established and powerful family, the Howards. As he matured, he saw himself as a champion of tradition and as an enemy of those he saw as newly made, many of whom had become close advisers to HENRY VIII during the latter part of his reign and who were, to Surrey's way of thinking, corrupting the king. During his short life, Surrey sometimes fell afoul of the king and his advisers and was jailed more than once. It is no wonder, therefore, that many critics have understood this poem as an implicit criticism of Henry VIII, though we have no direct evidence to support this conjecture.

The poem's rhyme scheme is that of the ENGLISH SONNET; however, unlike the vast majority of Surrey's other sonnets, which deal with amatory themes, this poem's theme is civic. The speaker is disgusted by the unnamed king's lack of self-control, the unnamed king being King Sardanapalus, a legendary king of Assyria whom earlier authors such as JOHN GOWER and JOHN LYDGATE had used as an EXEMPLUM of degenerate kingship. Throughout the poem, Surrey masterfully uses antithesis, a common Renaissance rhetorical figure, to illuminate the degeneracy of this king. For example, the opening QUATRAIN contrasts corrupted peace (ll. 1–2) with dignified war (ll. 3–4). The Assyrians' king has yielded to sloth, living "in peace with foul desire" (l. 1), and has shown no interest in nobly defining himself through "martial art" (l. 4). This personal irresponsibility is significant because Renaissance theories of kingship identified the king's personal body with the body politic. If the king permitted his body to degenerate through irresponsible living, the body politic would inevitably follow suit.

The second quatrain employs an even more tightly focused antithetical structure. On each side of the four lines' CAESURAS, Surrey places contrasting images: swords and kisses (l. 5); the king's "lady's side" and his "targe [his shield]" (l. 6), "glutton feasts" and "soldier's fare" (l. 7), and finally contrasting the weight of the king's helmet to "a garland's charge [weight]" (l. 8). The quatrain also manages to appeal to all five senses: Not only do we clearly see all that the speaker describes, we also hear the "dint of swords," feel the "lady's side," taste the "glutton feasts," and smell the king's garland.

The final quatrain again employs an antithetical structure, this time making more explicit what the second quatrain implied: The king has become dangerously effeminate. He "scace [scarcely]" retains "the name of manhood" (l. 9), because he has permitted himself to be "Drenched in sloth and womanish delight" (l. 10). His less than manly approach to living (read less than Stoical) has left him "Feeble of sprite, impatient of pain" (l. 11) and as a result he has "lost his honor and his right" (l. 12). The couplet finishes on an ironical note, given that only by means of suicide does the king "show some manful deed" (l. 14).

Surrey has been called the quintessential courtier-poet because he was not only a nobleman of great intelligence and learning, he was also a man of action, who, when on good terms with Henry VIII, led the king's troops into battle against the French and served on numerous occasions as Henry's personal ambassador to other monarchs. In short, he lived a dutiful life—the absolute antithesis of the life lived by the Assyrians' king.

FURTHER READING

Session, William A. *Henry Howard, Earl of Surrey*. Twayne's English Authors Series. Boston: G.K. Hall, 1986.

Kantorowicz, Ernst. *The King's Two Bodies: A Study in Mediaeval Political Theory*. Princeton, N.J.: Princeton University Press, 1957.

Surrey, Henry Howard, earl of. *Henry Howard, Earl of Surrey: Selected Poems*. Edited by Dennis Keane. New York: Routledge, 2003.

Richard J. Erable

ASTROPHIL AND STELLA (OVERVIEW)
SIR PHILIP SIDNEY (ca. 1582) SIR PHILIP SIDNEY's *Astrophil and Stella*, a monument of English Renaissance verse, is considered the first complete SONNET SEQUENCE in English. Though its exact date of composition is unknown, the poems are thought to have been written in the early 1580s, and the sequence was first published in 1591. Publisher Thomas Newman released two editions of the poems during this year: The first was unauthorized, based on a circulating manuscript, and the second was reportedly based on a manuscript provided by the Sidney family. What has become the authorized and authoritative version appeared in the 1598 printing of *The Countess of Pembroke's Arcadia*. The 1591 edition excluded Sidney's Sonnet 37, the 11th Song, and portions of the Eighth Song, placing them at the end of the sonnets, while the 1598 edition distributes the songs throughout the text. The substance and ordering of the 1598 edition is

taken among scholars to be authoritative since its publication was overseen by MARY SIDNEY HERBERT, COUNTESS OF PEMBROKE, the poet's sister and editor.

Scholarly debates abound concerning efforts to ascribe a set plot to *Astrophil and Stella,* and little agreement exists on how to interpret the sequence's structure. Nonetheless, a narrative does emerge. The series contains a total of 119 poems: 108 SONNETS in either iambic pentameter and iambic hexameter, all of which are variations on the ENGLISH SONNET and ITALIAN (PETRARCHAN) SONNET forms; and 11 "songs" of varying prosody. With the exception of the Eighth Song, which is written in the third person, the speaker of the poems is Astrophil ("star-lover") who is in love with Stella ("star").

The first 35 poems introduce Stella and meditate on Astrophil's love for her. Sonnet 36 is the first poem that addresses Stella directly and initiates a series of poems that attempt to obtain her affections. Sonnet 37, the Fifth Song, and the Eighth Song hint that Stella could already be married, which may explain her refusal of Astrophil's advances. Nonetheless, by Sonnet 69, Stella agrees to a virtuous reciprocal love for Astrophil. Astrophil breaches his promise to love her chastely in the Second Song, stealing a kiss from Stella as she sleeps and incurring her anger. Astrophil continues to struggle with his strong physical desire for Stella, again seeking consummation in the Fourth Song. Stella's anger only cools in the Eighth Song as the couple reconciles and she departs. The remainder of the series bemoans the lady's absence, ending with a final meditation on Astrophil's continued loneliness and despair.

Astrophil and Stella has had a significant influence on the development of English poetry, in part because of Sidney's approach to the dominant poetic influence of the day: Petrarchism, the legacy of the 14th-century Italian poet PETRARCH. Sidney's response to the mode of writing prescribed by Petrarchism introduced a new era of poetic production in England. Unlike earlier English Petrarchists, like SIR THOMAS WYATT and HENRY HOWARD, EARL OF SURREY, Sidney did not directly translate Petrarch's poems. Yet *Astrophil and Stella* is highly Petrarchan and is widely held responsible for sparking the so-called sonnet craze of the 1590s. Sidney was so strongly identified with Petrarchism that a contemporary called him "our English Petrarke." The poems in the sequence are spoken by Astrophil to his beloved Stella. As is typical of Petrarchan poetry, Astrophil loves Stella ardently and pursues her despite her tenacious rebuffs. The uncomplicated resemblance of this series to Petrarch's *Rime Sparse* ends here.

Astrophil and Stella has been admired since its publication because of Sidney's effort to reinterpret, rather than merely reflect, Petrarchan paradigms. The primary relationship that Sidney's sequence describes differs provocatively from the typical Petrarchan love relationship. Sidney's Stella does not have the combination of blond hair and blue eyes, of the typical Petrarchan mistress. Though Stella's hair is blond, her eyes are black. This seemingly minor detail invokes a new vision of the beloved, separating her from preconceived notions about how the beloved, and even the lover, should be described in verse. Thus, Sidney sets the stage for a very different courtship.

Unlike the typical Petrarchan beloved who is admired chastely from afar, Astrophil struggles openly with physical desire, and his relationship with Stella does have a physical component. Stella is married and is certainly both worshipped and unreachable through much of the series, but Sidney innovates by maintaining a close physical proximity between lover and beloved. In the Second Song, Astrophil kisses Stella as she sleeps, an act that approaches violence and is incommensurate with the distance of the typical Petrarchan beloved. In the Fourth Song, he seeks consummation of their now reciprocal affection, asking "Take me to thee, and thee to me," to which Stella responds, "No, no, no, no, my Deare, let be." Though Stella obviously refuses Astrophil's advances, it is more typical of Petrarchan verse to avoid such overt entreaties for physical love.

Even the resolution of this sonnet sequence both approaches and avoids Petrarchan influence. Petrarch's Laura finally dies, becoming absolutely unattainable. His sequence then turns to a more virtuous meditation on spiritual love. While Astrophil also fails to win Stella, her life continues and Astrophil even looks, though briefly, to other women for solace (Sonnet 106). Although other poets of the day used Petrarchan conventions to discuss physical love, notably Sir Thomas Wyatt in "THEY FLEE FROM ME," Sidney is the first to so fully address desire in love.

The language of the sequence further reveals Sidney's difficult relationship with the Petrarchan influence. While the circumstances portrayed in the sequence do have original aspects, the language Sidney uses to describe them often makes use of Petrarchan tropes, including, among others, the oxymoron of the "cruel fair," which identifies the lady as beautiful but cruelly dismissive of his love; frequent use of the BLAZON, a part-by-part description of the beloved; and the highly Petrarchan notion that the lady's eyes can pierce the lover's heart. On the other hand, Sidney also uses *Astrophil and Stella* to cultivate his own signature literary devices. Sidney's speaker famously calls for poetic originality in the first line of Sonnet 1: "Foole, said my muse to me, looke in thy heart and write" (l. 14).

The sequence is very witty, and Sidney typically ends his sonnets with a pithy final COUPLET which often subverts or reframes the poem that precedes it. As many critics have noted, it is the very tension between Petrarchism and originality that make the sequence both difficult to read and compelling. The version of Petrarchan love Sidney presents in *Astrophil and Stella* both broadened and altered the type of influence Petrarchan verse had on Renaissance poets and has contributed to the slipperiness of this term in contemporary criticism.

Astrophil and Stella has been consistently read and revered since its publication, yet critical interpretations of the series vary widely. One major line of critical debate concerns the sequence's biographical elements. From the 19th century to the middle of the 20th century, *Astrophil and Stella* was considered primarily a portrayal in verse of Philip Sidney's thwarted love affair with Penelope Devereux, the oldest daughter of the earl of Essex. There is evidence to suggest that the earl wished Penelope to marry Sidney; however, she married Lord Rich in 1581. Puns on *rich* throughout the series, the most provocative perhaps being Sonnet 24, have been taken as textual support for this hypothesis, as has Stella's implied married status. Today the solely autobiographical interpretation of the sequence is increasingly rare; many contempo-

rary critics downplay it, while some argue that the historical evidence for a romantic liaison between the two is virtually nonexistent.

Recent criticism has also produced numerous other approaches to understanding the sequence. The tension in the series between Sidney's devout Protestantism and the primarily secular, even bodily or worldly, goals of the Petrarchan love lyric has received much scholarly attention. The structure of the sequence has also been variously interpreted. Do the poems, read in sequence, tell a coherent story? Or do they only reveal a tenuous narrative with each sonnet as a discrete part? Sidney's poems have additionally been brought into discussions about 16th-century concepts of the self. To this end, more recent criticism has even compared Sidney's poems to other types of artistic production and the material culture of the English Renaissance. Notably, the scholar Patricia Fumerton has explored how Sidney's sonnets relate to miniature portraits in their efforts to both conceal and reveal their subjects' internal experiences.

The continued interest scholars and students have shown in *Astrophil and Stella* and its complex discourse of love attests to the strong influence Sidney's poetry has had both on English literature and on contemporary concepts of how love can be represented through language.

FURTHER READING

Cooper, Sherod M., Jr. *The Sonnets of Astrophil and Stella: A Stylistic Study.* The Hague: Mouton, 1968.

Duncan-Jones, Katherine. *Sir Philip Sidney.* Oxford and New York: Oxford University Press, 1989.

Ferry, Anne. *The 'Inwar' Language: Sonnets of Wyatt, Sidney, Shakespeare, and Donne.* Chicago and London: University of Chicago Press, 1983.

Fumerton, Patricia. "'Secret' Arts: Elizabethan Miniatures and Sonnets." In *Representing the English Renaissance,* edited by Stephen Greenblatt. 57–97. Berkeley: University of California Press, 1988.

Hamilton, A. C. *Sir Philip Sidney: A Study of His Life and Works.* Cambridge: Cambridge University Press, 1977.

———. "Sidney's *Astrophil and Stella* as a Sonnet Sequence." *ELH* 36, no. 1 (1969): 59–87.

Herman, Peter C., ed. *Sir Philip Sidney's An Apology for Poetry and Astrophil and Stella: Texts and Contexts.* Glen Allen, Va.: College Publishing, 2001.

Kalstone, David. "Sir Philip Sidney and 'Poore *Petrarchs Long Deceased Woes.'"* In *Sir Philip Sidney: An Anthology of Modern Criticism,* edited by Dennis Kay. 21–32. Oxford: Clarendon Press, 1987.

Kay, Dennis, ed. *Sir Philip Sidney: An Anthology of Modern Criticism.* Oxford: Oxford University Press, 1988.

Nelson, Lowry Jr. "The Matter of Rime: Sonnets of Sidney, Daniel, and Shakespeare." In *Poetic Traditions of the English Renaissance,* edited by Maynard Mack and George de Forest Lord, 123–142. New Haven, Conn., and London: Yale University Press, 1982.

Peterson, Douglas L. *The English Lyric from Wyatt to Donne: A History of the Plain and Eloquent Styles.* Princeton, N.J.: Princeton University Press, 1967.

Ringler, William A., ed. *The Poems of Sir Philip Sidney.* Oxford: Clarendon, 1962.

Roche, Thomas P., Jr. *Petrarch and the English Sonnet Sequences.* New York: AMS Press, 1989.

Spiller, Michael R. G. *The Development of the Sonnet. An Introduction.* London and New York: Routledge, 1992.

Stillinger, Jack. "The Biographical Problem of *Astrophil and Stella*." In *Essential Articles for the Study of Sir Philip Sidney,* edited by Arthur F. Kinney. 617–639. Hamden, Conn.: Archon, 1986.

Tuve, Rosamond. *Elizabethan and Metaphysical Imagery: Renaissance Poetic and Twentieth-Century Critics.* Chicago: University of Chicago Press, 1947.

Waller, Gary. *English Poetry of the Sixteenth Century.* London/New York: Longman, 1993.

Margaret M. Simon

Astrophil and Stella; Sonnet 1 ("Loving in truth, and fain in verse my love to show") SIR PHILIP SIDNEY (ca. 1582)

Sonnet 1 of *Astrophil and Stella,* which reflects SIR PHILIP SIDNEY's authorial concerns about joining the formidable SONNET SEQUENCE tradition, serves an important in function: Through it, Sidney makes the genre his own.

The poem begins with a declaration of Astrophil's love, held in his heart but (as of yet) unknown to Stella. The entire sequence is aimed at obtaining "grace" (l. 4) by offering Stella the pleasure of his pain (l. 2). Astrophil seeks "fit words to paint the blackest face of woe" (l. 5), thereby placing himself in the traditional Petrarchan position as supplicant. Desperately, Astrophil examines "others' leaves" (poetry, l. 8) for inspiration. Unfortunately, as the last six lines of the poem indicate, the words do not come easily, and invention remains unresponsive. Astrophil bites his "truant" pen and "beat[s] himself" for not being able to perform better (l. 13), and the "blows [of] stepdame Study" (l. 14) fail, leaving other "feet" [poetry] useless. However, the "Muse," a figure representing poetic inspiration, interrupts and instructs him to look into his heart and simply write what he finds there. Thus the poem turns from the need to write to the external authorities offering proper models, and then to the surer guidance of the poet's own heart.

As the first poem in one of the most important sequences written in England, this SONNET is enormously significant in its own right, not least because it clearly states Sidney's own objectives in writing his sonnets. When he says that he is truly in love and struggling for words to fit that love, he means to be taken seriously. At the same time, these opening lines also draw explicit attention to Sidney's relationship with his sources, including his predecessors PETRARCH, SIR THOMAS WYATT, and HENRY HOWARD, EARL OF SURREY. Moreover, Sidney is referencing contemporary sonnets, suggesting that his sequence will be the outflow of his heart rather than an invention contextualized within a well-established genre.

Critical approaches to the poem focus on the sonnet tradition and its philosophical complexities, particularly in regard to Petrarch. Since Astrophil says that others' writing is unfit for his needs and that the rhetoric of the form is stale, critics often examine how (and if) Sidney is doing anything new, as he claims. The poem can also be read as the first salvo in a seduction or as an exploration of the relationship between the sexes, since the entire series of sonnets is written to achieve an erotic aim. Recent work in studying the early modern passions is likely to offer new insights into the love, pity, and spite that play such a large role in this dramatic opening statement.

See also *ASTROPHIL AND STELLA* (OVERVIEW).

FURTHER READING
Lanham, Richard A. "*Astrophil and Stella*: Pure and Impure Persuasion." *ELR* 2, no. 1 (1972): 100–115.

Christopher A. Hill

He then concludes, "[It is] yet true that I must Stella love" (l. 14).

See also ASTROPHIL AND STELLA (OVERVIEW), ITALIAN (PETRARCHAN) SONNET, SONNET SEQUENCE.

Kerri Lynn Allen

Astrophil and Stella: Sonnet 7 ("When Nature made her chief work, Stella's eyes") SIR PHILIP SIDNEY (ca. 1582)

Sonnet 7, like a number of others in *Astrophil and Stella*, combines features from both the ITALIAN (PETRARCHAN) SONNET tradition and the ENGLISH SONNET form. Its rhyme scheme—*abba, abba, cdcd, ee*—more closely follows the Italian form of OCTAVE and SESTET, but the concluding rhyming COUPLET is more typical of the English tradition.

This SONNET deviates from the standard by celebrating the beauty of black—or, rather, Stella's ability to overcome black and still be beautiful. This contrast is introduced immediately: "When Nature made her chief work, Stella's eyes, / In color black, why wrapped she beams so bright?" (ll. 1–2). Darkness obscures sight—and thus beauty—so the speaker is both distressed and confused. To resolve this dilemma, he turns to art: "Would she [Nature] in beamy black, like painter wise, / frame dantiest luster, mixed of shades and light?" (ll. 3–4). The 15th century witnessed the development of a new school of painting, chiaroscuro, favored by Michelangelo Caravaggio and Rembrandt. This style of painting accentuates beauty by representing only light and shade, relying on varying and complex plays of light and dark to convey what varying shades of colors do in other works.

If artistry was not Nature's intent, however, the speaker must find another solution. Perhaps, he muses, Nature ". . . that sober hue devise, / In object best to knit and strength our sight" (ll. 5–6). In this case, Nature is doing the speaker a favor. If Stella's eyes were not dimmed at least a little, he would be so blinded that he could not appreciate their beauty. Thus, Stella must be diminished so the speaker can flourish, but with his capacities intact, he can recreate her.

Not content with either of these options, the speaker proposes a third: "Or would she her miraculous power show, / that whereas black seems beauty's contrary, she even in black doth make all beauties flow?" (ll. 9–11). The traditional English standard of beauty included a fair complexion, blue eyes, and blond hair—the opposite of black. Darkness was unattractive and potentially evil; why would Nature burden Stella in such a manner? The apparent question answers itself, however. Nature, it seems, is merely showing off her power by rendering Stella the finest creation, even though she has a touch of darkness. The feminine Nature has applied her cosmetics properly, so that Stella's beauty is enhanced, tying all the possibilities together: Painting and writing, like cosmetics, can create and preserve beauty, but can also change it.

The final three lines demonstrate the effectiveness of Nature's work, as the speaker insists that Nature has darkened Stella's eyes in mourning "to honor all their deaths, who for her bleed" (l. 14). In vying for her love, many have fallen. This image is particularly intriguing. In medieval and Renaissance belief, sight was the initial step to love (or lust)—a penetrative look. Stella's gaze, therefore, has pierced many a man, leaving them to die. Again, the inherent pun may refer to *la petit morte* (the little death)—the belief that each time a man ejaculated, he lost some of his life's essence (sperm), thereby reducing his lifespan. In this case, Stella's beauty has inspired the "deaths" of many men, perhaps through masturbation or nocturnal emissions. As these activities usually occur in darkness, the blackness imposed by Nature serves a greater purpose—fulfillment.

See also ASTROPHIL AND STELLA (OVERVIEW), SHAKESPEARE'S SONNETS: SONNET 127 AND SONNET 129.

Astrophil and Stella: Sonnet 10 ("Reason, in faith thou art well served, that still") SIR PHILIP SIDNEY (ca. 1582)

In Sonnet 10, Astrophil addresses "Reason," and the poem draws on a typical Neoplatonic dialectical opposition between reason and passion. The last two lines express the classical and Renaissance moral philosophical paradox that the faculty of reason is supposed to rule over the passions in the soul. Yet in this sonnet, Reason abandons its rule of the soul in order to serve the object of Astrophil's passion, Stella. Sonnet 10 is written in the ITALIAN (PETRARCHAN) SONNET style that SIR PHILIP SID-

NEY frequently used in *Astrophil and Stella*. Although the turn occurs at line 9, as is usual in Italian sonnets, the forceful COUPLET at the end of this poem is reminiscent of the ENGLISH SONNET form that Shakespeare preferred.

Astrophil introduces his paradox in the first QUATRAIN, although this is not obvious until the end of the poem. He tells Reason that even though Reason would prefer to fight against the "sence" (Astrophil's five senses, through which he experiences Stella) and "love" that Astrophil prefers, Reason will find its principles obeyed all the same. In the remainder of the OCTAVE, Astrophil suggests employments more fruitful for Reason than attempting to subdue his passion. He uses an ANAPHORA to tell Reason what it ought to do: it should "clime the Muses' hill, / Or reach the fruite of Nature's choisest tree, / Or seeke heavn's course, or heavn's inside to see" (ll. 3–5). The Muses' "hill," usually Mount Parnassus, is the source for poetic inspiration. The fruit of Nature's tree refers to seeking patterns in Nature to be emulated, and seeking heaven's course alludes to cosmological speculations as well as to the fact that "Stella" means "star," and "Astrophil" star-lover. Astrophil concludes his octet with the relatively gentle admonition that Reason should "leave love to will" (l. 8).

In line 9, the sonnet's initial turn, Astrophil returns to his claim that Reason wants to fight against both love and the delight Astrophil takes in his senses when he is around Stella. Reason is a sword fighter who gives "wounds of dispraise" with "sword of wit" (l. 10), but whose "cunning fence"—that is, artful fencing skill—will be foiled by the blows delivered by "Stella's rayes" (ll. 11–12). Here Sidney probably puns on the word *foyle* (l. 11), using it as a verb but also referring to the fencing foil.

The couplet extends the fencing metaphor and constrains it to an obviously courtly sporting combat, asserting that after it has been struck by Stella's rays, Reason itself kneels in submission and offers its services to prove the necessity of loving Stella. Astrophil uses a CHIASMUS—"By reason good, good reason [Stella] to love" (ll. 13–14)—to illustrate Reason's reversal of its former argument against love. Thus, reason is well "serv'd," as Astrophil asserts in line 1, by being taught by Stella's beauty and virtue that to love Stella is ultimately reasonable.

See also ASTROPHIL AND STELLA (OVERVIEW).

Joel B. Davis

Astrophil and Stella: Sonnet 15 ("You that do search for every purling spring") SIR PHILIP SIDNEY (ca. 1582)

Sonnet 15 returns to the admonition against insincere imitation that characterizes Sonnets 1 and 6. It is written in iambic pentameter and follows the ITALIAN (PETRARCHAN) SONNET form. Here, lines 9 and 10 form a COUPLET that sums up the OCTAVE, so that the poet's rhyme scheme for the SESTET (*cdcd, ee*) becomes *ccdeed*. Likewise, the VOLTA (turn) we expect in line 9 is delayed until line 12, where it is marked by the adversative *but*.

In the octave, Astrophil lists the faulty practices of imitative poets. In the first quatrain, he speaks of their practices figuratively, suggesting that they seek every "spring" that flows from Mount Parnassus, the mythological home of the Muses, (inspiration) and "wring" their poetics from every flower, "not sweet perhaps," that grows nearby (ll. 2–4). Thus, not only are imitative poets too busy looking for models to imitate, they also imitate poor models—the flowers that are not sweet. When Astrophil expands his criticism to include the sins of ALLITERATION and poor imitation of Petrarchan CONCEITS, he alliterates as he mocks alliteration, characterizing it as "running in ratling rowes" (l. 6). He then mocks the use of Petrarchan imagery as "poore *Petrarch*'s long-deceased woes" and "new-borne sighes and denisened wit" (ll. 8–9). "Denisend wit" is a controversial phrase in the poem. It has been variously printed as "devised wit" and "wit disguised," but the most authoritative manuscripts contain "denisend wit," so critics have taken line 8 to mean that the wits of imitators of PETRARCH are inhabited with nothing more than sighs.

The first half of the sestet completes the thought of the octave. Astrophil tells imitative poets, "You take wrong waies," and he warns them that "stolne goods"—that is, the ideas, imagery, and techniques they borrow from other poets—are eventually recognized as unoriginal. He then goes in to make inspirational suggestions. On one hand, the advice is what we would expect, for he tells lesser poets to look at Stella and then begin to write (l. 14). Like the typical poet-lover, Astrophil protests that his beloved is the fairest and most inspiring beloved of all. But on the other hand, Astrophil does not exactly say that admiring Stella will make his listener into a better poet. Instead, he says that if such a poet want to "nurse" his "name . . . at fullest breasts of Fame," he should fix his gaze on Stella (ll. 12–13). Stella is a means to fame, not necessarily to good poetry. This reference resonates with the imagery of Parnassus and Petrarch (the Italian poet whose style and imagery heavily influenced 16th-century lyric poetry). But at the same time, it reveals that Astrophil has been playing a game in seeming to oppose insincere imitation against sincere inspiration: instead, he opposes poor poetry that deserves its oblivion to better poetry that earns fame by taking Stella as its object.

See also *Astrophil and Stella* (overview); Sidney, Sir Philip; sonnet.

FURTHER READING

Coldiron, A. E. B. "Sidney, Watson, and the 'Wrong Ways' to Renaissance Lyric Poetics." In *Renaissance Papers,* edited by Trevor Howard-Hill and Philip Rollinson, 49–62. Columbia, S.C.: Camden House Press, 1997.

Joel B. Davis

Astrophil and Stella: **Sonnet 16 ("In nature apt to like when I did see")** Sir Philip Sidney (ca. 1582)   Sonnet 16 is unusual in that, rather than maintaining a pose of sincerity that is subtly undermined by the terms in which he expresses it, Astrophil here narrates his conversion from being one who merely believes he loves into a true lover. It follows the Italian (Petrarchan) sonnet form in that its first two quatrains constitute a coherent octave, rhymed *abbaabba*. The turn, where Astrophil tells us of truly falling in love, occurs at line 9, so that the last part of the sonnet may be taken as a coherent sestet, rhyming *cdcdee*. Sonnet 16 also marks a shift in the sonnet sequence itself. Though there is some variance in their themes, the first 15 sonnets emphasize the difference between Astrophil's claim to sincerity and his criticism of other, more imitative poets. Sonnet 16, in contrast, begins Astrophil's long account of his own follies.

The first quatrain is an apostrophe to love in which Astrophil expresses the shallowness of his initial infatuations in unflattering terms that evoke a cool and avaricious assessment. Before he saw Stella, he compared "beauties"—a word that primarily denotes beautiful women but also suggests different kinds of beauty itself—to the measurement of the purity of gold. Thus, the beauties he has seen "were of manie Carrets fine" (l. 2): relatively refined and pure gold. These beauties convinced Astrophil that he was "full" of love (ll. 3–4). The second quatrain continues the apostrophe, explaining that Astrophil did not feel in himself the "flames" of love that others claimed to feel, and that he denigrated these others' expressions as a "whine" over a mere "pinne's hurt" (ll. 6–7). In line 8 he says he based his judgment on his own as-yet shallow experience of love.

In the third quatrain, Astrophil ceases his address to Love and speaks about love instead, characterizing his dalliance as playing "with this young Lyon" (l. 9). In this image, he alludes to a fable in which a shepherd brings home a lion cub, thinking to make it a pet. When the lion matures, it destroys the shepherd's flocks, an action that is subsequently compared to the devastation of Troy wrought by Paris's love for Helen. Thus, Astrophil hints at the destructive power that he himself will find in love. He questions whether his eyes were "curst or blest" (l. 10) when they first beheld Stella, which caused him to fall in love truly; in this, he exploits the fascination with paradox that characterizes 16th-century love poetry, and particularly Petrarchan love poetry. Astrophil compares himself to a schoolboy in the end of the quatrain, claiming that, having seen Stella, he "speld" (which means both learned and written out—like this very poem, in fact) a "new lesson" (l. 12).

The couplet extends the metaphor of Astrophil-as-schoolboy, as he explains to us that he has "learn'd Love right" now that he has seen Stella (l. 13). Astrophil's conclusion invokes much darker imagery and implies that he has fallen from a state of innocence. He asserts that one who has learned of love by an experience like his own is like one who "by being poisond doth poison know" (l. 14). Poison is used as a metaphor for corruption and sin, an image derived from the story of Adam and Eve, with Astrophil's knowledge of love being congruous with Adam's knowledge of good and evil.

See also ASTROPHIL AND STELLA (OVERVIEW); SIDNEY, SIR PHILIP.

FURTHER READING

Richards, Jennifer. "Philip Sidney, Mary Sidney, and Protestant Poetics." *Sidney Newsletter & Journal* 14, no. 1 (1996): 28–37.

Joel B. Davis

Astrophil and Stella: **Sonnet 18 ("With what sharp checks I in myself am shent")** SIR PHILIP SIDNEY **(ca. 1582)** This SONNET is the first in the *Astrophil and Stella* SONNET SEQUENCE that takes full advantage of the contrastive possibilities of the terminal COUPLET, projecting the object of desire as oppositional to an entire set of inherited values. The opening OCTAVE of this ITALIAN (PETRARCHAN) SONNET is also deeply invested in the oppositional dialectic of desire. Throughout the poem, three sets of opposites (reason–passion, natural position–artful indolence, wealth–bankruptcy) are combined to describe, through negation, the rightful place of the desiring subject. The speaker is "banckrout" (l. 3) and "unable quite to pay even Nature's rent" (l. 5) because "my wealth I have most idly spent" (l. 8)—a condition not unknown to the young aristocrats of the day. It is "Reason's audite" (l. 2) that demonstrates that the speaker's natural, aristocratic, and ultimately desirable position has been pawned. This form of rational introspection into the speaker's failure to live up to his inherited expectations leads to a kind of self-loathing at the end of the octave.

The expected VOLTA between the octave and the SESTET never comes as the litany of self-abuse continues. The rhyme of the intellectual "toyes" (l. 9) the speaker creates—his poetry with "vaine annoyes" (l. 11)—is reminiscent of SIR PHILIP SIDNEY's own suggestions that his writings *Arcadia* and the *DEFENSE OF POESY* were trifles and ink-wasting. The indolence and loss of purpose is concluded and surpassed in line 12 with a suggestion of the speaker's own damnation: "I see my course to lose my self doth bend." In the loss of his "self," the speaker implies the loss of his own soul, which is against nature and reason.

The COUPLET turns on the rest of the poem, framing Stella and the inherited values of an aristocratic culture as mutually incompatible. The speaker recognizes that his actions are denying him his "birthright" (l. 6), yet he is not as saddened by that as by the fact that he cannot lose more "for Stella's sake" (l. 14). The repeated "no" midway through the couplet turns the speaker's love for Stella into desire for greater sorrow, thus pitting Petrarchan self-loathing against a uniquely English heritage of aristocratic birthright and the loss of wealth.

See also ASTROPHIL AND STELLA (OVERVIEW).

Melissa A. Elmes

Astrophil and Stella: **Sonnet 20 ("Fly, fly, my friends, I have my death-wound, fly")** SIR PHILIP SIDNEY **(ca. 1582)** This SONNET reflects the viewpoint of a soldier who has just received a mortal wound. The first OCTAVE begins with the narrator telling his friends to fly for he has received his "death wound" (l. 1). A "muth'ring boy" (l. 2) lay in ambush "like a thief" and assailed the narrator, the "wrongful prey" (l. 4). The concluding SESTET details the narrator's naïve approach to the place of ambush—enjoying the "prospect" (l. 10), yet unaware that his assailant lay in wait. The narrator's serenity is broken when he sees his attacker move with "lightening grace" and fire at him. The final line concludes with the narrator feeling the bullet hitting his heart.

The sonnet displays a number of Renaissance conventions. One is the horror of the advent of modern warfare (the narrator is shot from ambush, not slain in hand-to-hand combat). Another is the development of an elaborate CONCEIT by which the entire sonnet could be seen as an ALLEGORY for an individual falling in love: The unsuspecting narrator is pierced in the heart by a bullet from an unexpected source, just as the hapless Astrophil was ambushed by the waiting Stella, who struck his heart with love.

See also ASTROPHIL AND STELLA (OVERVIEW); SIDNEY, SIR PHILIP,

FURTHER READING

Borris, Kenneth. *Allegory and Epic in English Renaissance Literature: Heroic Form in Sidney, Spenser, and Milton*. Cambridge: Cambridge University Press, 2000.

Joseph Becker

Astrophil and Stella: **Sonnet 21** ("Your words, my friend—right healthful caustics—blame") Sir Philip Sidney (ca. 1582)   In Sonnet 21, Astrophil responds to a friend who has admonished him against writing love poetry. The theme is one of critical self-examination in which Astrophil's poems serve as evidence that he has wasted his abilities on "coltish gyres" (l. 6) rather than having bent them to more serious and virtuous pursuits. The SONNET is written in IAMBIC PENTAMETER and follows the ITALIAN (PETRARCHAN) SONNET form.

The opening OCTAVE recounts the arguments of Astrophil's well-meaning friend, and it contrasts the friend's words against Astrophil's poetry. The interlocutor has offered advice, which Astrophil compares to medicine ("healthful caustiks") intended to illustrate how love has "marde" his "young minde" (l. 2), a point further emphasized by the three consecutive stresses that slow down line two and give it a sense of moral gravity. The second half of the OCTAVE turns more serious, linking Astrophil's failure to reform himself morally (after having read Plato) to his failure to fulfill "nobler desires" and "great expectation" (ll. 7–8). In these lines, and continuing through line 11 (the first half of the SESTET), Sonnet 21 seems to allude in very general terms to some aspects of SIR PHILIP SIDNEY's own life: By 1582–83, when Sidney was likely composing *Astrophil and Stella,* he had gained no important office at the court of Queen ELIZABETH I. In 1579, various political setbacks, stemming mostly from arguments with other courtiers (e.g. the Earl of Oxford), likely resulted in the question that ends the first half of the sestet: "If now the May of my yeares much decline, / What can be hoped my harvest time will be?" This certainly seems to suggest the series of Sidney's failures.

The conclusion of the poem characteristically contradicts the standard: After conceding the wisdom of the interlocutor's advice and alluding obliquely to Sidney's own tribulations, Astrophil returns to his fictional world and demands "Hath this world ought so faire as *Stella* is?" Thus, by returning to the theme of Stella's beauty, the poem subverts its own autobiographical intimations and trumps all the conventional judgments offered by the friend.

See also *ASTROPHIL AND STELLA* (OVERVIEW).

Joel B. Davis

Astrophil and Stella: **Sonnet 23** ("The curious wits, seeing dull pensiuenesse") Sir Philip Sidney (ca. 1582)   In Sonnet 23, Astrophil takes his reader aside for a moment, pointing out all the ways that "the curious wits" (l.1) misread his moods, before he turns, in a dramatic APOSTROPHE to those who watch him, to declare his love for Stella. It is the first in a series of SONNETs that directly address the atmosphere of courtly suspicion and gossip where Astrophil imagines his poems are interpreted; the others are Sonnets 27, 28, 54, and 104.

Like most of the sonnets of *Astrophil and Stella,* Sonnet 23 is written in iambic pentameter and follows the ITALIAN (PETRARCHAN) SONNET form. In the opening OCTAVE, Astrophil admits that his own eyes reveal a "dull pensiveness" (ll. 1–2), but he suggests that the "curious wits" that surround him speculate about his motives inaccurately, "with idle paines, and missing ayme" (l. 4). He offers us an ambiguity in the third line, "Whence those same fumes of melancholy arise," which may refer either to his own eyes or to the "curious wits" who observe him. Melancholy itself is a fashionable humor at court: In SIR PHILIP SIDNEY's time, those who affected melancholy were given to playing with language extravagantly and drawing out intricate metaphors (also called CONCEITS).

The second half of the octave explains that some observers of Astrophil believe he is being excessively studious (ll. 5–6), while other observers noting his service to the "Prince" believe he takes the courtier's role of counselor too seriously, and that he attempts to give political advice to correct errors of his "state" (l. 8). Although neither of these interpretations of Astrophil's behavior relates directly to Sidney's own life, they nevertheless hint at Sidney's studious and serious nature, his position as a courtier, and his advocacy of the militant policies that Queen ELIZABETH I did not wish to pursue (especially in the Netherlands).

The closing SESTET begins by naming even harsher judges of Astrophil's behavior, who see him caught up in "ambition's rage" (l. 9), frustrated with his own lack of advancement, and thus scheming to get ahead at court. In the second half of the sestet, Astrophil suddenly turns to those he imagines have been whispering about him, and he exclaims "O fooles, or over-wise"

(l. 12), as if he were unable to determine whether they overanalyze his actions or merely fail to understand him. Against the harshness of the "ambition's rage" with which his severest critics charge him, Astrophil offers a wistful note: ". . . alas, the race / Of all my thoughts hath neither stop nor start, / But only Stella's eyes and Stella's hart" (ll. 12–14). Here the "race of all my thoughts" is an admission that Astrophil is indeed constantly thinking, which resonates with the "dull pensiveness" of line 1 and the image of "my young braine captiv'd" in line 11. But Astrophil deflects all suspicions with his characteristic flourish, declaring that he thinks only of his beloved's eyes and heart.

See also ASTROPHIL AND STELLA (OVERVIEW).

FURTHER READING

Jones, Ann Rosalind, and Peter Stallybrass. "The Politics of *Astrophil and Stella.*" *SEL* 24 (1984): 53–68.

Joel B. Davis

***Astrophil and Stella*: Sonnet 27 ("Because I oft, in dark abstracted guide")** SIR PHILIP SIDNEY (ca. 1582) In Sonnet 27, Astrophil complains to his reader that his solitariness and quietness are misinterpreted and spun into unflattering rumors by his courtly rivals, a theme he takes up in Sonnets 23, 28, 54, and 104 as well. Sonnet 27 is in Sidney's preferred ITALIAN (PETRARCHAN) SONNET form, with a very clear turn at line 9 marking the separation of the OCTAVE from the SESTET.

The octave contrasts Astrophil's "darke abstracted guise," in which he seems "most alone in greatest companie," against the rivals "that would make speech of speech arise"—that is, Astrophil's rivals like to talk about what other people *say* rather than anything more substantial (ll. 1–4). Astrophil's withdrawal from courtly gossip has been understood as one important step toward developing a way of speaking about inward, private experience, contrasting it against outward, public experience.

The second half of the octave explains the rumors being spread about Astrophil; "bubbling pride," which is compared to "poison," has lodged in his "swelling breast" (ll. 6–7). "Bubbling" and "swelling" connote motion, like the rumor that "flies," again in contrast to

Astrophil's static pose. Moreover, Astrophil explains that he is said to "Fawne" on himself in narcissistic self-love, which was considered a particularly scandalous and effeminate vice among Elizabethans (l. 8).

At the VOLTA, Astrophil responds to the rumors with what initially appears to be an admission of his own self-absorption; when he looks into the mirror he sees an even "worse fault, ambition" (l. 11). Astrophil confesses that he often passes over his "best friends . . . unseene, unheard" (ll. 12–13). Here, Sidney is ambiguous as to whether it is Astrophil himself who is unseen and unheard or whether he fails to see and hear his friends. The syntax supports either reading, and we can suppose that Astrophil wants us to take it both ways. The fact that either Astrophil or his friends, or both, are unseen and unheard underscores the theme of inwardness in the poem: Something about interior lives cannot be captured and made visible to us on the printed page. Language can only admit existence; it can never fully explain it. Ultimately, Astrophil links this hidden experience to his thoughts, which he says aim toward the "highest place" (again, playing on the theme of his self-confessed "ambition")—that is, "Stella's grace" (ll. 13–14).

While "*Stella*'s grace" ostensibly means getting on her good side and winning her love, the word *grace* also has strong overtones in Protestant theology. The Calvinist doctrine of election states that one cannot enter heaven on the merits of one's good deeds; only God's "grace" can "elect" the saved. Like Calvinists then, Astrophil undergoes self-examination (ll. 9–10) to determine whether or not he has earned grace and become one of the elect. However, Astrophil's quest is an erotic one, not spiritual, so it is only Stella who can provide salvation.

See also ASTROPHIL AND STELLA (OVERVIEW); SIDNEY, SIR PHILIP; SONNET.

Joel B. Davis

***Astrophil and Stella*: Sonnet 28 ("You that with allegory's curious frame")** SIR PHILIP SIDNEY (ca. 1582) In Sonnet 28, Astrophil addresses those who discuss his behavior directly. In the OCTAVE, Astrophil asks those who read and interpret his poetry, either figuratively or allegorically, to desist. He compares his poems to children, and, extending this metaphor, he asks his audience not to make his "children" into "changelings." Changelings are the offspring of fairies, left in the place of human children, whom the fairies would take for their own uses. In Sonnet 28, "changelings" are misinterpretations and over-readings of Astrophil's "children." His poems, he insists, have no meanings deeper than their obvious declaration of love for Stella. He is not seeking "brazen fame," only Stella's affections; she is the "Princesse of Beautie" (l. 6). Waxing political, Astrophil notes that for Stella, submitting to love would be difficult, since "Nations count it shame" to do so (l. 8). Renaissance political theory held that rulers should follow reason rather than the passions. Stella, as ruler, is controlled by reason; Astrophil is not.

The SESTET does not make the characteristic VOLTA. Instead, Astrophil continues to insist that the SONNET was not written for the sake of "eloquence," nor was it written in pursuit of a deeper philosophical goal. Literary critics, however, do not take Astrophil's claims at face value. Some critics emphasize the poem's self-conscious interest in the so-called plain style of rhetoric. Another school of critics find Platonic philosophy at work in this sonnet, reading it as Astrophil's admission that he is aware of the Platonic ideal of love but unable to grasp it fully.

Astrophil himself protests that "in pure simplicitie" his poems only reflect the "flames" of love that burn in his own heart (l. 12). However, the final line of the poem undermines Astrophil's protestations of innocence. He confesses that there is, after all, an "art" in the poem. When he says that *"Love"* is "reading" this art to him, he seems to mean that he has learned the art of his poetry from Love itself (l. 14). For modern critics, the question is—which "love"? On one hand, it could be platonic love; on the other hand, it could be ordinary erotic love. Both possibilities remain open.

See also *ASTROPHIL AND STELLA* (OVERVIEW); SIDNEY, SIR PHILIP.

Joel B. Davis

Astrophil and Stella: Sonnet 31 ("With how sad steps, O Moon, thou climb'st the skies") SIR PHILIP SIDNEY (ca. 1582)   As Sonnet 31 opens, the speaker, Astrophil, sees the melancholic moon and

addresses it familiarly, deciding that, like him, it suffers from LOVESICKNESS. He goes on to muse about Cupid's role in the moon's lovesickness—has the "busy archer" managed to shoot the moon with one of his arrows? Astrophil decides that it is so, and thus the moon must be lovesick. He is so experienced at being in love that he can take one look at the moon's face and read the longing written there. Since he and the moon are in a similar position, Astrophil wonders if games of love are handled the same way in the heavens as they are on earth: Are those who are consumed with love treated like fools? Are heavenly women as disdainful as earthly women? Do they recognize virtue when they see it?

Sonnet 31 is a fairly standard ITALIAN (PETRARCHAN) SONNET in form and theme. In the OCTAVE, the speaker personifies the moon, addressing it in an APOSTROPHE: "With how sad steps, O moon, thou climb'st the skies!" (l. 1). He observes the sadness of the moon and believes that it, too, is experiencing the woe of unrequited love. In assuming that the moon, an element of nature, shares the same feelings as he does, the speaker has fallen victim to the pathetic fallacy, which is one byproduct of PERSONIFICATION. He also sets himself up as an experienced lover who can identify love at any distance based solely on appearances.

In the SESTET, the speaker rhetorically questions the moon about the capricious nature of beautiful women. Rhetorical questions serve to reveal the speaker's feelings about his own situation while presumably talking about someone else's circumstances. In this way, he is distanced from the powerful emotions that threaten to overwhelm him.

Throughout the poem, the repeated word *love* serves both as a reminder of the subject at hand and also as a metaphorical prison. While the idea of love is implied in the first four lines, the term is first used outright in line 5. As the poem moves toward its conclusion, the word becomes used repeatedly in various forms, as different parts of speech, and it fulfills a number of grammatical functions. It is part of an adjectival compound ("long-with-love-acquainted eyes," l. 5), an object of a preposition ("of love," l. 6), a piece of a possessive ("a lover's case," l. 6), a noun ("constant love," l. 10), a verb and an infinitive verb ("Do they above love to be loved . . . ," l. 12), and as part of a plural noun and nominative structure ("those lovers scorn whom that love doth possess?" l. 13). Love is subject and object, active and passive, singular and manifold. Love is intrinsically intertwined with all of Astrophil's thoughts and deeds, and as such is inescapable. He has constructed his own confinement.

Most of the critical controversy surrounding the poem is focused on the rhetorical questions in the sestet, particularly the final question: "Do they call virtue there ungratefulness?" (l. 14) There are two basic approaches. The first group believes that the question reads, "Do heavenly ladies call their lovers' virtue ungratefulness?" The second holds the position that the question reads, "Do heavenly ladies call their own ungratefulness virtue?" The first school of thought is more widely accepted. This interpretation is based primarily on the COURT CULTURE that influenced the SONNET tradition. Through the use of rhetorical questions, the speaker points out the absurdity of his position. In early modern COURTLY LOVE games, male lovers were supposed to be utterly and completely devoted to their lady, focusing on her and her alone with a single-minded, passionate determination. Astrophil laments that his unflagging love has been called unintelligent by Stella, as he asks the moon, "Is constant love deemed there but want of wit?" (l. 10). Yet she is truly the one who is acting irrationally, since she wants to be loved but then mocks the person who loves her. Further, she terms his virtue in the face of no response "ungrateful ness." Again, the speaker complains that the ladies look down on what they should actually hold dear.

The second school of thought relies on the rhetorical idea of paromologia, conceeding one point in orer to gain the advantage. The speaker has carefully constructed his opponent's position, but then dramatically reverses the positions, undercutting his opponent all the more. In this case, the speaker, who has been complaining about the heavenly ladies, unexpectedly asks these same selfish women to comment on their own behavior, which smacks of superiority. Thus, he has provided them with a rather painful example of their rudeness, perhaps in the hope that they will gain some self-knowledge. At the least, the proud "virtuous" beauties should have gained something unanticipated to consider.

These positions are complicated somewhat by the mythological connotations contained within the sonnet. In the first reading, the speaker undercuts his position in choosing to address the moon. In classical mythology, the moon is associated with Diana, the virgin goddess known for her changeable nature, who viciously guards her chastity. That Astrophil assumes the moon has been shot by Cupid seems impossible, as she should be immune to his arrows of love. Furthermore, as the goddess of the hunt, Diana is an archer in her own right and able to shoot her own arrows of justice. Therefore, for Astrophil to ask the moon to see his point is useless, as the moon has never been and can never be lovesick, as he is. In this case, the virginal moon would indeed consider his dogged determination to love the unwilling lady as "ungratefulness." If the moon is directly aligned with Stella, however, the mythological associations uphold the second reading. Stella, like the moon, is cold, remote, fickle, and untouched. In this case, Astrophil is virtuous not only because of his constancy but also because he restrains himself sexually. He reminds her that such self-control is painful, emotionally and perhaps physically, and deserves compassion and approval. Instead of being considerate of his plight, Stella instead unreasonably charges her lover with being ungrateful. She believes she is being reasonable and kind simply by allowing Astrophil to serve her, and she insists that he should be content with what he has. Since he is not truly satisfied merely by enslaving himself, he is then compelled to point out her folly.

Other critics have employed psychoanalytic approaches in interpreting Sonnet 31. As a poem about sublimation, not fulfillment, it is preoccupied with the psychological status of male lovers. It is clear from the outset that the speaker is bitter toward women and society. Because of social conventions, he is trapped into devotedly serving one woman despite her cold disdain. The sarcasm employed by the speaker betrays his true feelings about the state of affairs. By speaking to the moon and imbuing it with human characteristics and feelings, the speaker has displaced his own emotions. Displacement results in emotional distance; this is considered by psychoanalysts to be a defense mechanism used to stave off depression, but actually resulting in repression. This distancing is made apparent in the sestet, where the speaker can only employ rhetorical questions to reveal his inner self. However, his turmoil and frustration are clearly conveyed even through these queries.

In terms of Sigmund Freud's tripartite structure of the human psyche, the woman, who has continued to fend off her would-be lover's physical attentions, serves in the capacity of the superego, keeping the male id (libido) in check. In the Freudian scheme, every human's mind consists of three parts: the id, the ego, and the superego. The id is comprised of the base, instinctual desires; the superego reflects the rules of society and functions as a restraint for the id, which continually attempts to take over. These psychic battles take place within the ego, which is the middle realm. Although the woman/superego can sometimes prevail, and the speaker/id will humbly withdraw, in Sonnet 31 the speaker/id seems to be winning the struggle, and his bitter reproach is an attempt to assail her remote calm. Which will prevail? The sonnet does not provide an answer.

See also *ASTROPHIL AND STELLA* (OVERVIEW); SIDNEY, SIR PHILIP; SONNET SEQUENCE.

FURTHER READING

Daalder, Joost. "Sidney's *Astrophil and Stella* 31." *Explicator* 49, no. 3 (1991): 135–136.

Stull, William. "Antanaclasis in *Astrophil and Stella* 31." *ANQ* 20, nos. 1–2 (1981): 3–6.

Astrophil and Stella: **Sonnet 33 ("I might— unhappy word—O me, I might")** SIR PHILIP SIDNEY **(ca. 1582)** In Sonnet 33, SIR PHILIP SIDNEY employs images of heaven and hell, abduction and romance, theft and fortune, and day and night to convey the contradictory nature of Astrophil's feelings for Stella. Although the rhyme scheme generally follows the ENGLISH SONNET form, Sidney creates a series of unrhymed pairs of lines within this greater scheme to contain his paradoxical images. He begins this pattern immediately: "I might—unhappy word!—oh me, I might / And then would not, or could not, see my bliss" (ll. 1–2), juxtaposing the words *unhappy* and *bliss*. The next two lines compare "infernal night" (l. 3) to "heav'nly day" (l. 4), and a few lines later, images of robbery and FORTUNE are intertwined: "No force, no fraud, robbed thee of thy

delight, / Nor fortune of thy fortune author is" (ll. 7–8). The pattern culminates in the final line, where Astrophil paradoxically laments, "That I had been more foolish— or more wise!" (l. 14). The series of oppositional images demonstrate Astrophil's confused state of mind as he attempts to explain his feelings for Stella.

Astrophil speaks to his heart concerning his current state, resulting in uncertainty about his previous conviction that his love for Stella is good. The personified heart is told to "rent thyself, thou dost thyself but right" (l. 5). Astrophil then declares, "No lovely Paris made thy Helen his" (l. 6). The love affair between Paris and Helen—created by the gods—is juxtaposed with Astrophil's own state, and he soon concludes that "to myself myself did give the blow" (l. 9). He has willfully chosen to love Stella; *he* has created his situation, not fate. Now, however, he feels he has done himself (and his heart) a disservice; indeed, it seems almost as though he mourns the passing of his carefree days before this love began, and he curses the wittiness that has led him to this point: "While too much wit, forsooth, so troubled me / That I respects for both our sakes must show" (ll. 10–11). Astrophil feels himself ensnared by his behavior and apologetic toward his unsuspecting heart, which now suffers as a result of his choice.

Still, despite his misgivings, Astrophil maintains that his love for Stella brings a fairness and beauty to life that he had not expected upon entering into the situation; he ". . . Could not by rising morn foresee / How fair a day was near" (ll. 12–13), even as he wrestles with his conflicting feelings. Astrophil does not himself know what to make of his love for Stella, and remains in a state of emotional turmoil. Astrophil lived in darkness until Stella brought him daylight, but living ignorant of love also allowed him to live without confusion. Would it, perhaps, have been better to have remained in darkness? Astrophil wonders.

See also *ASTROPHIL AND STELLA* (OVERVIEW); SIDNEY, SIR PHILIP; SONNET,

Melissa A. Elmes

Astrophil and Stella: **Sonnet 34 ("Come, let me write. 'And to what end?' To ease")** SIR PHILIP SIDNEY **(ca. 1582)** This SONNET deals with the motivations of poets and the ability of literature to both express and ease emotion. Sonnet 34 marks a change in tactic for the long-suffering Astrophil, since he has now realized that Stella is married to another and chooses to remain chaste. Thus, the opening lines portray writing poetry as supreme self-indulgence: "'And to what end?' To ease / A burthened hart" (ll. 1–2), especially when the possibility of wooing the object of desire is now gone forever, recalling the Petrarchan theme of the ability of words to soothe.

At the beginning of the second quatrain, SIR PHILIP SIDNEY alludes to Aristotle, an author he was later to write about in his *DEFENSE OF POESY,* going on to question the place of fame in poetry and what "wise men" (l. 7) will think of his poem. He discounts the censure of others by claiming that if they think his words "fond ware" (l. 7) or foolish trifles, then they are "close" (l. 8), or emotionally incapable of understanding his verse. He acknowledges the difficulty of feeling emotional pain yet not being able to express it: "What harder thing then smart, and not to speake?" (l. 10), alluding to the confessional aspect of poetry, especially love poetry. The VOLTA in next line then privileges the confessional over poetic conventions—"With wit my wit is mard" (l. 12)—and returns the poem to a single voice.

The final lines argue that the real reason for the poem and any publication of the poem is not to achieve fame; rather, it is so that "perhaps some find / Stella's great powrs" (ll. 13–14). Seemingly generous, this sentiment is actually quite selfish, as Astrophil desires to showcase Stella and his talents, thus confirming the indulgent aspect of sonnet writing.

See also *ASTROPHIL AND STELLA* (OVERVIEW).

Andrew Bretz

Astrophil and Stella: Sonnet 37 ("My mouth doth water, and my breast doth swell") SIR PHILIP SIDNEY (ca. 1582)   A variation of the ITALIAN (PETRARCHAN) SONNET, the rhyme scheme in Sonnet 37 follows an OCTAVE and SESTET rhyme pattern of *abbaabba, cdcdee.* The poem itself, however, exhibits an additional variation—a syntactical and semantic one that is an aberration within the SONNET tradition. This poem is unique in that it uses the first quatrain to announce a riddle, which then evolves over the next 10 lines.

Sonnet 37 is also significant because it is the first poem in *Astrophil and Stella* that actually refers to Penelope Devereux Rich, the model for Stella. SIR PHILIP SIDNEY here demonstrates that the abject lover is not as powerless as he might appear; indeed, he has power over the beloved because he writes (names) her. Sometimes the naming is not very flattering. For example, as he describes his tongue's role in the creative process, "Rich" rhymes with "itch" (l. 2). Puns on the name *Rich* appear throughout the sonnet, reducing the beloved to material goods (commodification). She is the property of another man, and the lover is an upstart for pursuing her through his poems.

Sonnet 37 also uses images associated with pregnancy (for example, swollen breasts) to talk humorously about giving birth to his poetry. In this case, he gives birth to a poem in the form of a riddle for the court, the intended audience of the work, making this one of the few poems in the sequence whose intended audience is not the beloved. Though pregnancy is a female attribute, Sidney successfully appropriates the image for his own masculine purpose, and then proves to be more fertile than biological women, as he produces numerous poems.

See also *ASTROPHIL AND STELLA* (OVERVIEW).

FURTHER READING
Fienberg, Nona. "The Emergence of Stella in *Astrophil and Stella.*" *SEL* 25, no. 1 (1985): 5–19.

Peggy J. Huey

Astrophil and Stella: Sonnet 39 ("Come sleep! O sleep the certain knot of peace") SIR PHILIP SIDNEY (ca. 1582)   Sonnet 39 deals with a typical Petrarchan subject: the lover's sleeplessness due to his pining for the beloved. Opening with a PAEAN to personified sleep—"Come sleep! O sleep the certain knot of peace" (l. 1)—the speaker then details the advantages of sleeping; it is the state that brings peace, provides a resting place for wit, eases pain, and provides wealth to a poor man and release to a prisoner. Another request, "with shield of proof shield me from out the prease [group]" (l. 5), relies on wordplay. Using *shield* first as a noun and then as a verb, the speaker asks to be protected from the throng of darts thrown by

Despair. Eventually he proposes an incentive: ". . . smooth pillows, sweetest bed, / a chamber deaf to noise and blind to light" (ll. 9–10)—the gifts conventionally offered to Morpheus, god of sleep, so he can rest his "weary head" (l. 11). If his request is denied, then the only life left in him will be Stella's image. Sidney's bribe is wholly dependent on his social class, as common people would not have had access to an unshared bed in a dark quiet room with clean, smooth sheets.

See also *ASTROPHIL AND STELLA* (OVERVIEW), LOVE-SICKNESS.

Peggy J. Huey

Astrophil and Stella: Sonnet 41 ("Having this day my horse, my hand, my lance") SIR PHILIP SIDNEY (ca. 1582)

Like several other SONNETs in *Astrophil and Stella,* the rhyme scheme in Sonnet 41 follows an OCTAVE and SESTET pattern of *abbaabba, cdcdee,* while the narrative sense more closely resembles the ENGLISH SONNET form, with the final three lines providing resolution. It is directly autobiographical and historically contextualized.

Taking place during a tournament in May 1581 that was held to entertain commissioners from France, the speaker begins by setting the stage. During the tournament, he guided his horse, his hand, and his lance so well that all who were present judged him the tournament's winner. Public opinion decides that his skill in these arts of war comes from various sources, each reflecting the observer's own partiality, such as the speaker's instinctive ability on a horse (according to the horsemen) and his innate strength (according to the popular view). More precise observers praise the skill that the speaker's experiences in other combats have provided, while some credit his good luck, or Nature, as in natural innate sources. A final possibility is his heredity, because his father, grandfather, and maternal uncles, the earls of Leicester and Warwick, had frequently participated in tournaments. However, according to the speaker, all of these options are incorrect. "The true cause" (l. 12) of his success in the tournament is the fact that Stella was watching; her presence and "the beams" (l. 14) from the eyes in "her heavenly face" (l. 13) gave him all of the power he needed in order to win.

See also *ASTROPHIL AND STELLA* (OVERVIEW).

FURTHER READING
De Grazia, Margreta. "Lost Potential in Grammar and Nature: Sidney's *Astrophil and Stella.*" *SLE* 21, no. 1 (1981): 21–35.

Peggy J. Huey

Astrophil and Stella: Sonnet 45 ("Stella oft sees the very face of woe") SIR PHILIP SIDNEY (ca. 1582)

Sonnet 45 further explores how poetry can arouse the reader's emotions. Specifically, Astrophil comes to understand that poetry about his love might cause Stella to pity him more than his physical presence can. Astrophil claims that Stella looks at him and knows that he is truly sad, but she cannot pity him even though his love for her is the reason for his sorrow. Stella is instead moved to pity by a tale—a "fable" (l. 5)—of tragic love. This fictional tale of "Lovers never knowne" (l. 6) moves Stella more deeply than Astrophil's own real love for her. Astrophil expresses concern that fiction has more capacity to inspire emotion than does reality. He suspects that "Fancy drawne by imag'd things" (l. 9) is more emotive than "servants wracke," or the real suffering of a lover (l. 11). Though the servant's endurance "honor brings," it does not bring the grace and pity Stella gives to the fictional lovers. Indeed, Stella is so deeply affected by the lover's tale that it penetrates her heart ("her breast," l. 7), causing her to cry.

The way SIR PHILIP SIDNEY describes Stella's tears suggests that she is full of strong emotion. He writes of her response to the love story, "Pitie thereof gate in her breast such place, / That from that sea deriv'd teares spring did flow" (ll. 6–7)—that is, her heart contains a sea of tears. The power of the lovers' story releases a spring of tears from this sea, a sea to which Astrophil cannot gain access. Astrophil ends the SONNET by addressing Stella directly and begging her to look at him as a fictional character taking part in "some sad tragedie" (l. 13). He suggests that by seeing him as a fictional character, Stella might pity his suffering as she pitied that of the lovers in the fable.

This poem is an elaboration of the concerns introduced in the first poem of the SONNET SEQUENCE. The language of the first three lines of Sonnet 45 parallels lines in the first sonnet. In Sonnet 1, Astrophil sets forth a plan to win Stella's pity. He begins by seeking "fit words to paint the blackest face of woe" (l. 5). In Sonnet 45, it is clear that Astrophil has succeeded in painting this woeful picture when he says that Stella has seen "the verie face of wo / Painted in [his] beclowded stormie face" (ll. 1–2). Seeing his sadness does not, however, have the effect on Stella that Astrophil intends. She "cannot skill to pitie [his] disgrace" (l. 3). Sidney's use of the word *skill* suggests that perhaps Stella is to blame for her lack of sensitivity to Astrophil's plight. She is somehow deficient in emotional skill, and her knowledge of his sadness does not "pity win" (l. 4) as he hopes it will in Sonnet 1. As noted, Astrophil describes the fictional lovers who win Stella's pity as "Fancy drawne by imag'd things" and "false" (l. 9). Though he subtly indicts Stella for preferring the fictional to the real, Astrophil's love for her is so strong that he cannot help but attempt to win her by making himself into the fiction he condemns.

Thus, the power the fictional lovers have over Stella's emotions challenges the type of inspiration that Astrophil says he will rely on to win her in Sonnet 1. At the start of the sequence, Astrophil disavows outside inspiration for his poetry. He intends to "looke in [his] heart and write" (l. 14). In Sonnet 45, however, while Astrophil looks into his own heart for words to inspire Stella's pity, Stella is instead moved by stories about other lovers. This means that in order to win Stella's pity, Astrophil must try a new approach. Astrophil entreats Stella: "Then thinke my deare, that you in me do reed / Of Lovers ruine some sad Tragedie" (ll. 12–13). In asking that she see him as a fictional character, however, he creates a paradox. In order to have Stella's pity, he must give up all hope of having her, since in pitying "the tale of him" she will not see him as a real lover. This standard ITALIAN (PETRARCHAN) SONNET ends with the line "I am not I, pitie the tale of me" (l. 14), a paradoxical statement that suggests Astrophil's very status as a unified subject is at risk in this poem. Such compromised subjectivity is typical of speakers in Petrarchan verse, in which the lover is often metamorphosed, or changed, by his interactions with the beloved. In this poem, however, Sidney suggests that Astrophil himself, not Stella, is in control of his transformation.

The language Sidney uses in this sonnet augments the complicated view of poetry's power Sidney develops both in *Astrophil and Stella* and DEFENSE OF POESY. Initially Stella "sees" in Astrophil "the verie face of wo" (l. 1). By the end of the sonnet, however, Astrophil asks her to "reed" (l. 12) him. Written description seems privileged over visual representation. The "wo" which Stella sees "Painted in [Astrophil's] beclowded stormie face" does not move her as the written tale of other lovers. Yet the source of Astrophil's frustration with Stella may not just be that she is swayed by fiction, but that she is swayed by someone else's fiction, not Astrophil's. He suddenly realizes that, as a reader of poetry Stella may choose what she wants to read and she has not chosen his poems. He hopes that by creating distance between the "real" Astrophil and the fictional one, Stella will come to prefer his verse. This is ironic since many critics argue that Sidney has done the same thing: He has made himself into the fictional Astrophil in order to convey his love to Penelope Devereux (Stella) through the sonnet sequence.

See also ASTROPHIL AND STELLA (OVERVIEW).

Margaret R. Simon

Astrophil and Stella: Sonnet 47 ("What, have I thus betrayed my liberty?") SIR PHILIP SIDNEY (ca. 1582)

This SONNET details Astrophil's sufferings at the hands of his beloved Stella who treats him like a slave ("In my free side, or am I borne a slaue," l. 3). He ponders what has become of his liberty, and feels as if his "free side" has been branded by Stella's glance. Confused, he ponders the meaning of Stella's "yoke of tyranny" (l. 4) over his heart. In the ensuing lines, Astrophil bemoans his lack of reward despite his "long faith" (l. 7) in Stella, which has reduced him to "the scorn of beggary" (emotional poverty; l. 8). Astrophil spends the concluding SESTET seeking to break free of Stella's emotional slavery. However, when he sees her approach, his resolve melts away, and, despite his emotional torment, he allows himself to continue in bondage. The poem vividly displays Astrophil's emotional struggle, indecision, and ultimate helplessness.

See also ASTROPHIL AND STELLA (OVERVIEW), LOVESICKNESS.

Joseph Becker

Astrophil and Stella: **Sonnet 49 ("I on my horse, and Love on me doth try") SIR PHILIP SIDNEY (ca. 1582)** In Sonnet 49, Astrophil compares his mastery over a horse to love's mastery over him. SIR PHILIP SIDNEY was familiar with equestrianism: He participated in tilts at court on several occasions between 1574 and 1584. At the same time, the CONCEIT that Love rides the lover as an equestrian rides a horse is a conventional Petrarchan one.

The first quatrain sets up Astrophil's comparison through a CHIASMUS in line three, where Astrophil tells us that he is "a horseman to [his] horse, a horse to *Love*." Placing the word *horse* in the middle of the chiasmus is consistent with the "great chain of being" of Renaissance cosmography, in which humanity stands in the middle of a chain connecting the divine (Love as a god) to the animal world (the horse). Thus, when Astrophil refers to himself as a beast in line four, it is with reference to humanity's position between the gods and the beasts, partaking partly in both. The word *descrie* means both to observe and to reveal, so that Astrophil both observes his own faults or wrongs and reveals them to us in his poetry.

The last four lines of the OCTAVE as well as the first three of the SESTET extend the metaphor by which Love "rides" Astrophil like a horse. The humility that love has stirred in Astrophil is compared to reins. Love's "raines" are connected to the bit that fits in the horse's mouth, by which the rider controls the "Reverence." In line 7, Astrophil makes a pun on a "guilt boss" on the bit. A boss is a decorative knob on the bit; a gilt boss has been gilded, usually in gold. Here, gilt is spelled "guilt"—fear and guilt restrain Astrophil's passions. Moreover, the boss on Astrophil's metaphorical bit is gilt not with gold but with "Hope," illustrating the relationship among fear, hope, and guilt in the unrequited lover: The hope of having a sexual encounter attracts the lover, but this hope conceals the guilt the lover feels at the possibility of sexually defiling his pure beloved. Astrophil's "Will" is figured as the whip or "Wand," spurring on his desire. "Fancie," which Astrophil figures as the saddle, compares to fantasy—Astrophil's fulfillment.

Critics have read this SONNET as a platonic ALLEGORY of love, noting that in Plato's *Phaedrus* the soul is com-pared to a two-horse chariot driven by a charioteer, and certainly both Sidney and Petrarch were familiar with Plato. As well, Astrophil relates that he takes "delight" in being ridden by Love, similar to the way Plato describes human progress toward enlightenment—from loving base objects to preferring rarified things. Other critics see the poem as Astrophil's moral and psychological descent from reason into animal passion.

See also *ASTROPHIL AND STELLA* (OVERVIEW).

FURTHER READING

Lovejoy, Arthur O. *The Great Chain of Being: A Study of the History of an Idea.* Cambridge, Mass.: Harvard University Press, 1936.

Joel B. Davis

Astrophil and Stella: **Sonnet 52 ("A strife is grown between Virtue and Love") SIR PHILIP SIDNEY (ca. 1582)** In Sonnet 52, Astrophil humorously imagines the struggle between erotic desire and moral injunctions against fulfilling it as a legal case between the personified figures of *Love* and "Vertue" (Virtue). Though this is an ITALIAN (PETRARCHAN) SONNET in form, the VOLTA unmistakably occurs not between the OCTAVE and the SESTET at line 9, but rather in the witty COUPLET at the end.

The first two lines outline the whole of the metaphorical lawsuit: both Virtue and Love lay claim to Stella, as if she were an object or, perhaps, a prized servant. In the rest of the first QUATRAIN, Love claims that because Stella's "eyes" and "lips" are sexually attractive, they wear his "badge" as a servant wears the livery of his master. The second quatrain sets out the grounds of Virtue's claim to Stella. Virtue's argument is that the real Stella is not her mere body but, instead, "that vertuous soule" (l. 7). Though Virtue admits that Stella's "outside" is beautiful and that it attracts "our hearts," he maintains that Stella's outer beauty is not her essence. In the first part of the sestet, Astrophil sums up Virtue's case, once again admitting that although Stella's "beauty" and her "grace" belong to Love, nevertheless Love may not claim a place in Stella's "selfe," again meaning her soul.

The second part of the sestet is an APOSTROPHE in which Astrophil turns to address Love directly. Here he reveals to us that he has taken Love's side in the suit, and he admits that "this demurre" puts an end or a "stay" to the suit. A *demurrer* is a legal term that refers to a strategy wherein an attorney admits the facts of his opponent's case—that Stella is beautiful—but argues that these facts entitle the opponent to no legal relief.

Astrophil seems on the verge of admitting defeat when, in the final couplet, he adds a final condition to the concession to Virtue. Virtue may have Stella's "selfe," he says, only if Virtue will grant to Love and to Astrophil "that body" of Stella's. This witty reversal typifies Astrophil's stance throughout the whole of *Astrophil and Stella*: He recognizes that his erotic desire conflicts with virtue, but he cannot help voicing its needs—as he does more famously in the final line of Sonnet 71. Sonnet 52 has been called an anti-Platonic SONNET for this reason. It is philosophically analytical in assigning qualities to the opposing categories of Love (Stella's eyes, lips, and whole body) and Virtue (her soul). However, Platonic philosophy holds that, once we analyze a situation and understand the claims of virtue, we will want to conduct ourselves virtuously. Astrophil deliberately mocks Platonic philosophy here, clearly demonstrating that he understands the notion of virtue and its demands, but insisting nevertheless on Stella's "faire outside" for his erotic pleasure.

See also ASTROPHIL AND STELLA (OVERVIEW); SIDNEY, SIR PHILIP.

Joel B. Davis

Astrophil and Stella: Sonnet 53 ("In martial sports I had my cunning tried") SIR PHILIP SIDNEY (ca. 1582)

Sonnet 53 is thought to have been written soon after Penelope Devereux (Stella) married SIR PHILIP SIDNEY's rival, Lord Rich. In this SONNET, Astrophil acknowledges his prior focus on "martial sports" (l. 1) and acknowledges that he wears "Mars' livery" (l. 6). Despite this warlike attitude, he also displays a wry awareness of the role of love in a person's life. Astrophil declares himself a "slave" to Cupid (l. 5), who must do as he is told—namely look away from the "martial" field, away from the masculine games of war, to "spie" Stella standing by a window, watching (l. 8). Sidney here stresses Stella's transformative power as she "makes the window send forth light" (l. 8). The

earth "quakes," and Astrophil is so "dazzled" (l. 10) by her appearance that he "forgets to rule" and "forgets to fight" (l. 11). The exterior world is lost to him as he gazes upon her: No "trumpets sound . . . nor friendly cries" (l. 12) penetrate his senses. "Her blush" (l. 14) serves not only to facilitate Astrophil's return to normalcy but also illustrates Stella's awareness of Astrophil's obvious love interest in her.

Sidney's use of dialogue within the sonnet was a departure from sonnet conventions, but it heightens the sense of immediacy: When Cupid addresses Astrophil as "Sir Fool" (l. 7), it adds reality to the poem and breaks up the cadence, providing a sensory jolt prior to Astrophil's stupor.

See also ASTROPHIL AND STELLA (OVERVIEW).

Leslie J. Ormandy

Astrophil and Stella: Sonnet 54 ("Because I breathe not love to everyone") SIR PHILIP SIDNEY (ca. 1582)

In Sonnet 54, Astrophil returns to the theme of what is said about him at court, but unlike sonnets 27 and 28, here Astrophil discusses the gossip of "courtly Nymphs" (the ladies of the court) rather than that of his rivals (l. 5). The SONNET is written in iambic pentameter and follows the ITALIAN (PETRARCHAN) SONNET form. The first quatrain tells the aspects of Astrophil's behavior that elicit rumors, and the second quatrain tells us what the rumors are, so that the OCTAVE forms a single complex sentence explaining a cause and an effect. The entire sonnet has a political edge as well as an erotic one, for the political language of the Elizabethan court is very much the language of love. ELIZABETH I wanted her courtiers to act as suitors for a lady's favors when they sought advancement.

The first cause for the rumors is that Astrophil does not speak of love to everyone at court. Astrophil claims not to play the role of the lover, stating that he does not wear "set colours" (black was especially fashionable in the late Elizabethan court because it signified melancholy, a lover's affliction similar to LOVESICKNESS), nor does he covet locks of the beloved's hair (an affectation common to Petrarchan poetic imagery). The ladies expect male courtiers to play the role of lovers, bearing "*Love's* standard" in their speech, as Astrophil puts it, but because Astrophil refuses to play the lover, the ladies say that Astrophil cannot love. In political terms, this is effectively to say that he cannot gain the queen's favor—that he is both politically and sexually impotent.

At the sonnet's VOLTA, beginning with line 9, Astrophil poses as a man content to hear such things said about him. As long as his beloved Stella knows what he really thinks, he does not care what others think of him. In line 11, he turns to address the ladies directly, admonishing them that true love lies "in the hart" (l. 12) rather than in outward affectations. Astrophil implicitly compares himself to a silent ("Dumbe") swan (l. 13), while he unflatteringly compares other courtiers who speak the language of love to "chatring" magpies, which sets up the end of this increasingly self-righteous little sermon: He argues that only those who "quake to say they love" are true lovers (l. 14).

Because of its anti-Petrarchan appearance and its claims to distinguish the mere ornaments of love from the real thing, this sonnet has been taken as an important precursor to 17th-century love poetry, especially that of John Donne. The irony is, of course, that Astrophil has actually been very talkative indeed. This sonnet stands in the middle of a SONNET SEQUENCE—108 in total—all about Astrophil's love, and so it is difficult to take his claims not to play the lover very seriously. As so often happens in *Astrophil and Stella,* Astrophil presents us with a witty and rational argument, only to subvert it in the end by revealing how taken with passion he really is.

See also *ASTROPHIL AND STELLA* (OVERVIEW); SIDNEY, SIR PHILIP.

Joel B. Davis

Astrophil and Stella: Sonnet 56 ("Fie, school of Patience, fie, your lesson is") SIR PHILIP SIDNEY (ca. 1582)

Sonnet 56 is an APOSTROPHE to the figure of Patience, personified as a schoolmaster. Astrophil plays the part of the reluctant student, and Stella is the book. SIR PHILIP SIDNEY uses the ITALIAN (PETRARCHAN) SONNET form here, and while we find the expected turn at the beginning of line 9, Astrophil adds the final twist to his argument in the last three lines (the last half of the SESTET). Most of the critical attention to the poem

focuses on its rhyme, which is seen to be rather strained, and on the fact that in the first QUATRAIN of *Astrophil and Stella,* the positions of this sonnet and Sonnet 55 have been reversed.

In the first half of the OCTAVE, Astrophil complains that the lesson Patience teaches is too long to be memorized—to be learned "without booke"—and asserts that he cannot remember the whole thing—Patience's "large precepts"—because he has not seen his book for an entire week (ll. 2, 4). In the second half of the octave, Astrophil reveals that his book is actually Stella's face. Stella's face bears fair "letters" that, when Astrophil reads them, "teach vertue" (ll. 5–6). Astrophil essentially tells his schoolmaster, Patience, that he possesses patience when he can see Stella's face, but to hear the lesson without seeing Stella is more than he can tolerate, or "brooke." He then rather arrogantly suggests that even when he listens to Patience, he takes its advice like that of a well-meaning but misinformed or dull-witted friend.

Astrophil begins the sestet by repeating his previous point. He poses it as a rhetorical question: Now that he can no longer see Stella (*want* here means "lack," so that Astrophil is saying he lacks the sight of Stella before him), he asks, can Patience seriously believe that Astrophil would heed his advice? Patience's counsel is "cold stuff," in which can be found only a "phlegmatick" delight. Of the FOUR HUMORS, phlegm was thought to be the cold and moist humor in Renaissance natural philosophy, what we might call a "wet blanket" thrown on Astrophil's passion—the "fire" of the last line.

In the end, we can see Astrophil most impatiently stamping his foot, telling the schoolmaster Patience that if he wants to do some good for his pupil, he must make Stella return and listen to his expressions of love patiently herself. Part of the genius of this poem is the childish tone it evokes: Astrophil begins chiding with "Fy . . . Fy" in the first line; he uses "What" as an interjection to begin two increasingly aggressive rhetorical questions in lines 3 and 10; he brazenly admits that he does not take Patience seriously; and finally he suggests that it is Stella who should have patience, not himself. Thus, we get the impression of a very impatient schoolboy refusing to learn, and Astrophil, while appearing clever, also appears in an unflattering light.

See also *ASTROPHIL AND STELLA* (OVERVIEW).

Joel B. Davis

Astrophil and Stella: Sonnet 60 ("When my good Angel guides me to the place") SIR PHILIP SIDNEY (ca. 1582)

Sonnet 60 describes the effects of Astrophil's effort in Sonnet 45 to make himself a fictional character, thereby encouraging Stella to love and pity his image, not himself. Discussing Stella in the third person, Astrophil begins by describing in typical Petrarchan terms his pleasure in Stella's presence. Yet as he sees Stella, he must realize that she takes no pleasure in his presence. Her eyes deliver fierce looks of disdain. When he is away from her, however, Stella laments and pities him in his absence. He is trapped in a paradoxical situation: In order to have Stella's love, he must forego her presence; if he is to have her presence, she will not love him. As in Sonnet 45, he can only win her pity through his own absence from her.

This ITALIAN (PETRARCHAN) SONNET introduces sadness and dejection on the part of Astrophil that lasts through the end of the sequence. This shift is made particularly poignant by the relative levity of the previous sonnet. Sonnet 59 is a fairly lighthearted CONCEIT of the lover competing with his lady's lapdog. This somewhat congenial domestic scene of Astrophil vying with Stella and her dog is abruptly replaced in Sonnet 60 by Astrophil languishing far from his beloved. He gazes up, pining "all my good I do in Stella see" (l. 2), while she, in response to his gaze, "throwes only down on [him] / Thundred disdaines and lightnings of disgrace" (ll. 3–4). The phrase *all my good* complicates the first QUATRAIN. It might mean that the lover uses Stella's presence to manifest his own goodness, a narcissistic maneuver common in Petrarchan verse. Although such poems seem to be in praise of a beloved, often the speaker uses his beloved as proof of his own worth. The fact that Astrophil loves Stella says less about her worthiness than about his excellent taste in loving her. She is, however, blind to the goodness in Astrophil that she reflects. There is a gap between Astrophil's perception of himself and what Stella sees. His presence before her

inspires her scorn. It is equally plausible that *all my good* refers more generally to the good qualities he recognizes and appreciates in Stella. Stella's response to Astrophil's gaze is itself notable because it introduces the notion that love and presence are incompatible. This incompatibility pervades Sonnet 60 and recurs throughout the rest of the SONNET SEQUENCE.

The second quatrain answers the first. If the first suggests that presence cannot lead to love, the second suggests that absence can. As soon as Astrophil is made to "fall from her site, then sweetly she / With words, wherein the Muses's treasures be, / Shewes love and pitie to [his] absent case" (ll. 6–8). Stella herself becomes a poet, her voice carrying the "Muses's treasures" (l. 7). She is inspired by the Muses of classical mythology who preside over poetry and the other arts. Her words of pity, however, require her lover's absence, which suggests that she refashions the absent Astrophil into an at least partially imagined lover whose case she wishes to plead. She has taken the advice Astrophil provides her in Sonnet 45 and has begun to "pity the tale" of him. (l. 14). Thus, the poem intimates, Stella engages in the same idealized "presencing" of Astrophil as he does of her in almost every poem.

Stella's paradoxical behavior makes Astrophil confused, and he expresses this confusion through oxymoron, a figure commonly used to express the torment of unrequited love in Petrarchan verse. He finds he cannot looke into / The ground of this fierce Love and lovely hate" (ll. 10–11). This CHIASMUS presents the lack of logic Astrophil perceives at Stella's inability to love him while he stands before her, though she can love him when he is out of view. The illogical situation leads the language of the poem into confusion as well. SIR PHILIP SIDNEY conveys this confusion by again using oxymoron and chiasmus: "Then some good body tell me how I do, / Whose presence, absence, absence presence is; / Blist in my curse, and cursed in my blisse" (ll. 12–14). For Astrophil, his presence before the lady means his absence in her affections and vice versa. He is thus blessed by her love when he is cursed by not being near her, and cursed by her scorn when he stands blissfully before her.

The symmetrical paradox of presence and absence created in these three lines suggest a broader shift in how the language of individual poems contribute to the movement of the series as a whole. In the first poem of *Astrophil and Stella,* Sidney displays not only faith in his ability to "look into [his] heart and write" (l. 14) but also a faith in predictable causal chains. He predicts, "Pleasure might cause her reade, reading might make her know, / Knowledge might pitie winne, and pitie grace obtain" (ll. 2–4). The forward progression from the lady's pleasure to her pity and ultimately to graciousness to the lover so clearly mapped in the first sonnet devolves in Sonnet 60 into a cycle of presence-as-absence, absence-as-presence. Astrophil's concern about the source of his poetic inspiration in Sonnet 1 is quickly solved by the last line of the poem. He will look into his heart and write. In Sonnet 60, however, frustration resides in the incompatibility of love and presence. By ending with two consecutive oxymorons, the poem leaves the reader and Astrophil with no resolution to his untenable situation.

See also *ASTROPHIL AND STELLA* (OVERVIEW).

Margaret M. Simon

Astrophil and Stella: Sonnet 61 ("Oft with true sighs, oft with uncalled tears") SIR PHILIP SIDNEY (ca. 1582)

Sonnet 61 signals the oncoming end of the relationship between Astrophil and Stella. In form and style, it indicates a break from the action of the first two-thirds of the cycle and summarizes what the reader may expect from this point on in terms of the subject and function of the poems.

Like the previous sonnets in *Astrophil and Stella,* Sonnet 61 makes use of simple, masculine rhyme, but in other aspects it differs greatly, thus signaling the changes ahead. Semantic upheaval, indicated through simultaneous revelations of Stella's expectations from a lover—"That who indeed infelt affection bears, / So captives to his saint both soul and sense / That, wholly hers, all selfness he forbears" (ll. 5–7)—and indications of her feelings for Astrophil's love—"Now since her chaste mind hates this love in me" (l. 9)—send mixed messages about love and poetry. The SONNET's structure further reflects this juxtaposition, as it follows nei-

ther the ITALIAN (PETRARCHAN) SONNET form nor the ENGLISH SONNET form. Though divided into OCTAVE and SESTET, the ending rhyme scheme is *eefggf* in place of the hopeful final COUPLETs found in the earlier sonnets. Astrophil and Stella are effectively separated, semantically and metrically, and the status quo has been altered to an unrecognizable form. Further instability is indicated through the replacement of IAMBIC PENTAMETER with a more strident spondaic rhythm (e.g., "Oft with true sighs, oft with uncallèd tears," l. 1), indicating finality through an authoritative voice that makes no promises as it delivers an ultimatum to the lover. The shifts in rhythm create a metrical variance within the poem that adds to the overall feeling of instability Sidney is trying to impose.

The metaphorical language employed in Sonnet 61 furthers this sense of defeat. Initially, the poet describes a final physical and emotional assault attempted by Astrophil—"I Stella's eyes assail, invade her ears" (l. 3)—but that is quickly thwarted by Stella: "But this at last is her sweet-breathed defence" (l. 4). Astrophil quickly realizes that he has lost the war. He will no longer delude himself into believing he has a chance, for Stella refuses to see his love as true. Turning from words of war to those of a medical treatment, Astrophil appeals to "Doctor Cupid," (l. 12) intending to make a clean break from this erstwhile love.

See also *ASTROPHIL AND STELLA* (OVERVIEW); SIDNEY, SIR PHILIP.

Melissa A. Elmes

Astrophil and Stella: Sonnet 63 ("O grammer-rules, O now your vertues show") SIR PHILIP SIDNEY (ca. 1582)

Sonnet 63, one of the lighter SONNETs in *Astrophil and Stella,* is an academically sophisticated and amusing quibble, relying on the reader's understanding of the conventions of Latin grammar as well as those of love. It amounts to a comic PAEAN sung in triumph, only qualified in the last lines. Astrophil has asked Stella for the thing desired "which she ever denies" (l. 6), and she has answered, "No, No" (l. 8). The speaker pounces upon her double negative and asserts that she has, by grammar's rule that a double negative makes a positive, really granted his request.

During the 16th century, a double negative in English only emphasized the negative, although in Latin, two negatives did make a positive statement. Thus, for a contemporary of SIR PHILIP SIDNEY's, the sonnet's victory is a sophistry—the speaker pretends to win by rules that do not apply.

Structurally, this is an ITALIAN (PETRARCHAN) SONNET. In the OCTAVE, Astrophil invokes "Grammer" (l. 1), urging a display of the power of the rules (the "vertues"); children read with "awfull" eyes—that is, with eyes filled with awe for the power of grammar—and so may Stella (young Dove) recognize the true meaning her words convey when they are viewed grammatically. The rest of the octave describes Astrophil's humble petition ("with eyes most low") of his powerful desire ("with heart most high," l. 5) and Stella's reaction. Sidney's diction and syntax in line 6 create ambiguity— "She lightning *Love,* displaying *Venus'* skies"—and anticipate Astrophil's interpretation of Stella's "No, No" in line 7, even while they literally describe Stella's blush: Venus is the evening star, visible in the rose-hued sunset. Astrophil recognizes that Stella means to emphasize her negative when he says she spoke twice in case with only one "no" she might not be heard (l. 8). The first quatrain in this Italian sonnet is bounded by the repeated "vertues," first Grammer's, then Stella's. As Grammer's rules will demonstrate the truth of Stella's words, so Stella's own integrity ("vertue," l. 4) will make her acknowledge the validity of Astrophil's interpretation, despite her intent to the contrary.

The SESTET begins with Astrophil invoking his muse to sing praises and appealing to heaven not to envy him in his triumph. Heaven and Grammer both should, he asserts, recognize and confirm with him that, by repeating her "no," Stella has, by all the rules, said "yes" to his desire, because a double negative equals a positive. The use of ANAPHORA, repeating "Grammer" with a verb or noun, in the sestet, act like a triumphant dance. When he tells his muse to sing *"Io paean,"* Astrophil alludes to OVID's *Ars Amatoria,* quoting a phrase from a passage where that poet expresses his joy that the mistress he has sought has fallen into his hands at last. This reference to a popular and available parallel underscores the nature of Astrophil's triumph: It is both learned and conventional.

The irony of Astrophil's triumph can be seen in the poet's choice of modifier for (the unnamed) Stella: "young Dove" (l. 3) aligns her closely to "children" (l. 2). The poet executes a subtle critique of his speaker's delight in Stella's error of speech, ruefully recognizing her innocence. The sonnet's conclusion deconstructs itself at the hands of its author. Its structure, based on the two invocations and repeated confidence in the power of grammar, provides the strongest interpretive element, and as grammar fails, so does Astrophil.

Sonnet 63 is tightly structured, painstakingly argued, cocky, and full of sophisticated fun at the expense of all love's sincerity and serious understanding. Its place within *Astrophil and Stella,* between a sonnet in which Stella urges Astrophil to anchor himself to a virtuous course of action, and the First Song, which praises Stella's beauties and virtues, reinforces its confident tone.

See also ASTROPHIL AND STELLA (OVERVIEW).

Marjory E. Lange

***Astrophil and Stella*: Sonnet 64 ("No more, my deare, no more these counsels trie")** SIR PHILIP SIDNEY (ca. 1582)   Sonnet 64 is a particularly good example of SIR PHILIP SIDNEY's dual purpose of telling the lovers' story and also of expressing English manners and mores. In this poem, Astrophil presents his case to Stella through the employment of a variety of images, all of which are intended to demonstrate his willingness to humble himself in order to retain her affections. He begins conventionally enough, asking her to desist in her constant refusal: "No more, my dear, no more these counsels trie; / O give my passions leave to run their race" (ll. 1–2). Then, in a cascading series of lines, each punctuated by a semicolon, he seems unable to restrain his emotions, begging her to "Let FORTUNE lay on me her worst disgrace; / Let folk o'ercharged with brain against me cry; / Let cloud bedim my face, break in my eye" (ll. 3–6), finishing the six-line outburst with the emphatic plea "But do not will me from my love to fly!" (l. 8). Directly following this impassioned request, Astrophil seems to gain control of himself and turns to a more rational approach, claiming simple humanity—"I do not envy Aristotle's wit, / Nor do aspire to Caesar's bleeding fame; / Nor aught do care though some above me sit" (ll. 9–11)—before giving rein to his hurt feelings by petulantly deeming Stella the possessor of a "cruel heart" (l. 13) and stating that "Thou art my Wit, and thou my Virtue art" (l. 14).

This poem is deceptively simple. Written in perfect IAMBIC PENTAMETER and in the ENGLISH SONNET form, Sonnet 64 is comprised of simple-rhyme, end-stopped lines, and it makes liberal use of repetition, ALLITERATION, and PERSONIFICATION. Because of this highly conventional use of poetic techniques, the poem appears to be a straightforward appeal from scorned lover to his beloved. In actuality, this SONNET pushes the genre to its limits in terms of structure and subject matter.

The organization of Astrophil's argument—from the calm, conventional literary request for mercy and understanding, to the tempestuous outburst in lines 3–8, to the return to rational discourse, and finally to the stingingly vindictive final COUPLET with its undertones of blame—indicates at once supreme literary control in terms of organization and punctuation, as well as unsuppressed emotion. Within this structure, Sidney employs a rich understanding of the nuances of language; in the same fashion as a master painter, he uses subtle literary brushstrokes to deepen the emotional character of the overall work. The use of the lowercase d in "my dear" (l. 1) underscores the uncertainty with which Astrophil makes his plea: He is not sure of this woman, and so he does not call her "my Dear" in confidence, but rather "my dear" in uncertainty. The choice of the phrase give my passions leave to run their race (l. 2) indicates that he sees a "finish line" to their relationship and gives voice to his emotional state; he has no more control over his passions than he would the entries in a horse race. The mention of Aristotle and Caesar at once heralds a return to rational, ordered thinking.

Further examination of this poem shows that it is a repository for "all things English," encompassing many subjects and cultural aspects that were popular at the time. The idea of Fortune, personified as it is in line 2, was prevalent in 16th-century England, when the world seemed to be changing so quickly with the rise of the merchant class and the ability of individuals to create a fortune through the new commercial atmosphere brought about by trade and industry. The mention of "folk o'ercharged with brain" in line 4 speaks to the power of the educated upper class and the court-influenced admiration of intellect, while Aristotle and Caesar recall the CLASSICAL TRADITION. Further, the use of sports terminology such as run its race and course sprinkled throughout this sonnet gives voice to the popularity of pleasure riding in the upper classes, and the recurrent use of the term wit speaks to the rising interest in writing and writers during this time.

Sonnet 64 admirably demonstrates the possibilities of the genre. Through masterful control of language and skillful manipulation of form, Sidney is able to indicate not only the feelings of Astrophil but also the world in which he exists. Astrophil is making his final efforts and calls on everything he has experienced and everything he knows in order to salvage this relationship. Through his openly vulnerable plea, he becomes mortal and sympathetic.

See also ASTROPHIL AND STELLA (OVERVIEW).

Melissa A. Elmes

Astrophil and Stella: Sonnet 69 ("O joy, too high for my low style to show") SIR PHILIP SIDNEY (ca. 1582)   In Sonnet 69, Astrophil basks in Stella's promise of love, singing a triumphant PAEAN. In his delight at Stella's capitulation, he almost ignores her constraint—that she gives her heart only as long as he remains on a virtuous course—dismissing it with the comment that all kings have to make some concessions ("covenants," l. 14) in order to take power.

This poem is deliberately simpler than most of the Astrophil and Stella SONNETs; the reader's attention is called immediately to the "low stile" (l. 1), which Astrophil complains is all he is capable of producing. Only the association of virtue with power raises Sonnet 69 above what is otherwise a fairly conventional accumulation of images and tone. Astrophil is being called to responsible living; the love he desires has been promised only contingently upon his course of action. In this poem, it remains unsure whether he sees the "covenant" (l. 14) as something he will need to live up to or renegotiate—or if he will simply try to ignore its restrictions. The conflict between desire and virtue is fundamental to Sir Philip Sidney's *Astrophil and Stella*; it underlies many of his occasions for poetry. For the time being, however, Astrophil wants simply to rejoice in being granted the monarchy of Stella's heart. The last three lines foretell of the sonnets to follow, which explore the role of poetry in joy and the constraints virtue places on a lover's desires.

The images Sidney has heaped on the OCTAVE of this ITALIAN (PETRARCHAN) SONNET are images of change, growth, and fluidity. Astrophil speaks of the "Oceans of delight" flowing within him, and asks to "powre" (pour) himself upon the friend who has stood by him through all the miseries leading up to this moment (ll. 4–6). Winter has given way to an amazing spring. All of these images appear to contradict the speaker complaining that he lacks the "high stile" to celebrate appropriately. The entire octave is built of APOSTRO-PHES: In turn, Astrophil calls upon personified joy, bliss, envy, and his friend, each to contribute appropriately to his delightful mood of conquest.

The SESTET turns on images of monarchy: Stella has promised (given "with words") the rule of her heart to Astrophil (l. 10); he can say she is his: "I, I, I may say, that she is mine" (l. 11), and the repetition of the *I* illustrates his dawning awareness that it is, indeed, *he* and no other to whom this power over his beloved's heart has been given. The conventional SYNECDOCHE of heart for the whole of Stella's love allows Astrophil to become monarch of her through her love for him. Only in the last three lines does he acknowledge the stipulation Stella imposes; he rules her heart only "while vertuous course I take" (l. 13), a condition he brushes off by shrugging "No kings be crown'd, but they some covenants make" (l. 14). For this sonnet, Astrophil is more impressed with the power over her heart Stella has given him than with the fact of love.

See also *Astrophil and Stella* (OVERVIEW).

Marjory E. Lange

Astrophil and Stella: Sonnet 71 ("Who will in fairest book of Nature know") Sir Philip Sidney (ca. 1582)

Using a variation of the ITALIAN (PETRARCHAN) SONNET, the rhyme scheme in Sonnet 71 follows an OCTAVE and SESTET pattern of *abbaabba, cdcdee*. However, the sense of the poem is closer to the

ENGLISH SONNET form of three QUATRAINS and a COUPLET, with a significant variation that creates conflict between the rhyme scheme and the syntax of the poem: The final line of the third quatrain works with the closing couplet to provide the resolution of the situation set up in the initial 11 lines.

The speaker begins by stating to a general audience that anyone who wants to know how Virtue and beauty can coexist in Nature should turn to Stella, whose "fair lines . . . true goodness show" (l. 4). These "lines" can refer either to the lines (as in a drawing) that create the image that is Stella, or to the lines of text in the book of Nature that is Stella, making her a poem in that book that provides instruction through delight. In the lines that are Stella, the reader will find vices overthrown by sweet reason instead of "rude force" (l. 6), when the light of reason from the sun shining in her eyes scares away the owls that are emblematic of various vices. The sestet then turns the speaker's attention to Stella herself, who, "not content to be Perfection's heir" (l. 9), tries to push all who admire her good qualities toward manifesting those qualities themselves. The speaker concludes by acknowledging that Stella's beauty encourages his heart to love her, her Virtue keeps the focus on proper acknowledgement of that love, and his Desire cries out for more in their relationship. The sestet introduces Platonic concepts of perfection (which include nonsexual love), but the final line undercuts these as amorous passion searches its "food" (l. 11)— the beloved's love. The speaker is thereby distracted by Desire and cannot enjoy reading Virtue in the book that is Stella. In this way, Astrophil uses what is referred to as moral sophistry, a misleadingly sound argument, to present his true desire. Reason and logic do not allow him to extinguish his desire for this woman, which represents the poet's departure from the Petrarchan convention of a chaste and an ideal love.

See also *Astrophil and Stella* (OVERVIEW).

FURTHER READING

Scanlon, James J. "Sidney's *Astrophil and Stella*: 'See What It Is to Love' Sensually!" *SEL* 16, no. 1 (1976): 65–74.

Peggy J. Huey

Astrophil and Stella: Sonnet 72 ("Desire, though thou my old companion art") SIR PHILIP SIDNEY (ca. 1582)

In this SONNET, Astrophil addresses "Desire" (l. 1), which causes him difficulty in discerning the differences between his erotic attraction and his platonic love for Stella. Personifying his erotic impulse as "Venus" (l. 5), Astrophil emphasizes that platonic love (which he calls "Dian" [l. 5]—that is, Diana, the virgin Greco-Roman goddess) is the foundation upon which erotic love rests (l. 5). He then proclaims that he will turn to "Virtue" and allow it to be his guide along with "Service" and "Honor" (l. 6). As the poem draws to a conclusion in the SESTET, Astrophil states that he will rely on care and faith (l. 11), which Stella has left him, to sustain him as he dismisses Desire. Nonetheless, the sonnet concludes with Astrophil's acknowledgment that Desire's banishment is tenuous and with his uncertainty that it will remain so.

By opening with an allusion from the CLASSICAL TRADITION combined with PERSONIFICATION, the poem operates on a richly textured symbolic level, integrating the poem's present with that of its author's cultural heritage. The sonnet also uses the dichotomy of the two states to represent the divided loyalties of the heart and mind, which in turn can be viewed as symbolic of the maze of sociopolitical alliances of the Tudor court.

See also *ASTROPHIL AND STELLA* (OVERVIEW); COURT CULTURE; SIDNEY, SIR PHILIP.

Joseph Becker

Astrophil and Stella: Sonnet 74 ("I never drank of Aganippe well") SIR PHILIP SIDNEY (ca. 1582)

Though it contains, essentially, a concluding COUPLET, Sonnet 74 follows the ITALIAN (PETRARCHAN) SONNET form overall, both in rhyme scheme (*abab, abab, cdcd, ee*) and narrative, with the OCTAVE setting up the situation and the SESTET resolving it. In this case, the situation is about writing poetry.

The ambiguous first line initiates the self-reflection: "I never drank of Aganippe well" (l. 1), which culminates in Astrophil's declaration, "Poor layman I, for sacred rites unfit" (l. 4). If "well" in line 1 is a noun, then the speaker claims that the Muses have never been kind to him because he has never drunk from their sacred well at the foot of Mt. Parnassus, rendering him unfit to receive inspiration. If *well* is an adverb, however, the sense is that the speaker has visited Aganippe and drunk from the well, but he was judged unfit to receive the Muses' inspiration. Swearing the most binding oath possible, "by blackest brook of hell" (the river Styx, l. 7), the speaker insists that he has never been a "pick-purse of another's wit" (l. 8)—all his ideas are his own. This is likely a direct response to accusations that SIR PHILIP SIDNEY imitated Thomas Watson's SONNET SEQUENCE *Hekatompathia* (1582).

The sestet begins in a rather self-laudatory manner: "How falls it then that with so smooth an ease/ my thoughts I speak, and what I speak doth flow / in verse, and that my verse best wits doth please?" (ll. 9–11) Without divine inspiration or thievery, the speaker is clearly a superior poet, as his contemporaries agree. After a brief, somewhat coy, exchange, he reveals the secret—he speaks so well because he *has* been inspired—by "Stella's kiss" (l. 14).

See also *ASTROPHIL AND STELLA* (OVERVIEW); SIDNEY, SIR PHILIP.

FURTHER READING

Coldiron, A. E. B. "Sidney, Watson, and the 'Wrong Ways' to Renaissance Lyric Poetry." In *Renaissance Papers 1997*, edited by T. H. Howard-Hill and Philip Rollinson, 49–62. Columbia, S.C.: Camden House, 1997.

Peggy J. Huey

Astrophil and Stella: Sonnet 81 ("O kiss, which dost those ruddy gems impart") SIR PHILIP SIDNEY (ca. 1582)

In SIR PHILIP SIDNEY's Sonnet 81, Astrophil uses extravagant praise of her kisses to convince the blushing Stella to silence him by kissing him again. The tone of this ITALIAN (PETRARCHAN) SONNET is physically passionate and ironic, as the poet turns a conventional—and inconsequential—moment into an occasion for a humorous reaction expressed in wordplay.

The OCTAVE is an extended APOSTROPHE addressing the kiss from Stella's lips. This continues the movement from Sonnet 79, also an apostrophe to the kiss, and Sonnet 80, which begins and ends *at* Stella's lip. The first four lines employ asyndeton (leaving out conjunctions) to good effect. With this technique, Astrophil describes the kiss as gems, fruits of newfound paradise, breathing all bliss, sweetening the heart, in order to conclude that it teaches lips a "nobler exercise"—a list that increases the poem's energetic tension with each phrase. This kiss provides his mouth with a nobler use than speech—or writing poetry, although *nobler* is pointedly ironic.

In the next QUATRAIN, Astrophil moves from asyndeton to direct PERSONIFICATION of an experience, longing to "paint" the kiss as a concrete object for all people to see, even if he could only approximate the reality, and even though a kiss is "only Nature's art" (l. 6). This desire puts him at odds with Stella, who forbids his praise of her kisses: She would be known for better things ("higher seated praise," l. 10), says Astrophil, speaking for her. He then cries that his burning heart make this commanded silence impossible. If she wants him silent, he says, then she must stop his mouth by kissing him again. Once Stella's objection has been presented, the full irony of kissing as a "nobler" activity (l. 4) becomes evident.

Wordplays grow thick in the last three lines, contributing irony and humor to the trivial situation. Most potent is the double entendre in Astrophil's assertion that "I, mad with delight, want wit to cease" (l. 13). *Want* can mean either "desire" or "lack;" here both meanings apply. Astrophil says that he lacks the wit to cease his praises of her kisses, and, simultaneously, that he wants his wit to cease altogether so he can simply enjoy the kisses—both conditions caused by the madness of delight generated by those kisses themselves.

In addition to the personification, asyndeton, and double entendres, Sidney controls the energy of this SONNET by limiting the variety in diction. In the octave, repetitions of *kisse* and *gemmes,* and *kisse* and *soules,* produce a pattern that emphasizes the speaker's desired direction. In the sestet, each of the two opposing positions starts with *but*—"But she forbids" (l. 9) and "But my heart burnes" (l. 11)—leading Astrophil to tell Stella she must stop his mouth "with still still kissing me," the doubled "still" playing on the word's two senses of "silence" and "always." The sestet links back to the octave by means of "faine": Astrophil "faine would . . . paint thee [the kiss]" (l. 7), and he claims that Stella

"faine would have me peace." In addition, there are several synonyms for *stop* in the SESTET, each with its own value and playful quality: *silent, peace, cease, stop,* and *still.* By employing such a variety of words to express a single issue after having so strictly limited the vocabulary of the first 10 lines, Astrophil emphasizes the impossibility of his silence—in a sonnet.

See also *ASTROPHIL AND STELLA* (OVERVIEW).

Marjory E. Lange

Astrophil and Stella: Sonnet 86 ("Alas, whence came this change of lookes? If I") SIR PHILIP SIDNEY (ca. 1582)   In SIR PHILIP SIDNEY's climatic Sonnet 86, Astrophil suffers the consequences of the kiss he stole from the sleeping Stella in the Second Song. The series of SONNETS and songs following the Second Song and culminating in the Fourth Song show Astrophil rejoicing over his stolen kiss and the poetic inspiration this illicit caress has aroused. By Sonnet 86, Stella has learned of this unsolicited kiss—most likely through reading Astrophil's poetry. In this sonnet, Stella slaps Astrophil, in a clear rejection of his advances.

In the first QUATRAIN, Astrophil notices Stella's "change of lookes." He contends that if he has done something to warrant this change, then his "own conscience" would be "self condemning," and therefore Stella would not need to punish him. Astrophil continues to refute the validity of Stella's change in the second quatrain by claiming both his soul and love for Stella are as pure as "spotless ermine," a reference to the white fur used to adorn Renaissance clothing and a popular symbol for chastity in Renaissance art and literature. In the third quatrain, Stella slaps him, and Astrophil begs, "O ease your hand" (l. 9). Throughout Stella's escalating reactions, Astrophil continues to maintain that her judgment is not based on any justifiable "faults" (ll. 9–10). In the final COUPLET, Astrophil claims that far worse than her physical retribution is the pain he sees in Stella's "blessed eyes," where "one's heaven become his hell" (l. 14).

As the only single sonnet in the sequence flanked by two songs, Sonnet 86 structurally functions as a fulcrum between Astrophil's previous manic poetic highs and his quick decline into anger and despair. In the

Fifth Song, he calls Stella everything from a murderer to a tyrant to a devil. While the form of Sonnet 86 follows the ENGLISH SONNET structure—three quatrains followed by a final couplet—the content shows Astrophil's struggle with Petrarchan themes, such as the idealization of the beloved. In Astrophil's eyes, Stella is not a model of virtue at this point because her change in temperament seems uncalled-for and she resorts to violence; instead, Astrophil positions himself as pure of soul because Stella is "his sole object of felicity" (l. 7). Astrophil's distinction between body and soul are also Petrarchan, reflecting the Christian struggle between the pure soul and the impure body. The lover seeks to use the virtue of the female beloved as inspiration to overcome the corrupt body, allowing his pure soul a closer connection to God. The final line of the sonnet, when Astrophil paradoxically connects Stella's heaven with his hell, further illustrates this Petrarchan duality.

In Sonnet 86, Stella's ongoing cruelty in not returning Astrophil's love—and her escalating anger in this sonnet in particular—causes Astrophil's continuous suffering. As in earlier sonnets, Astrophil compares himself to a slave and Stella to his master (l. 9). The question that arises from this power construction is whether or not Stella has complete control over Astrophil—or if Astrophil chooses to relinquish his power to her. Is Astrophil a masochist who derives his pleasure from self-imposed suffering by intentionally choosing a beloved who will not reciprocate his love? If he is a masochist, then the slap becomes a symbolic act of consummation making the sonnet more Ovidian than Petrarchan in that, that physical, not spiritual, connection is the ultimate goal. If Stella represents either the married Penelope Devereux or Queen ELIZABETH I, as some speculate, then *Astrophil and Stella* in general and Sonnet 86 in particular become Sidney's way to negotiate his own agency (personal power) and pleasure in a court ruled by a woman.

See also ASTROPHIL AND STELLA (OVERVIEW).

Lauri S. Dietz

Astrophil and Stella: Sonnet 87 ("When I was forced from Stella ever dear") SIR PHILIP SIDNEY (ca. 1582)

Sonnet 87 bewails the separation of Astrophil from Stella. Astrophil is "forst from *Stella*" (l.

1) by "iron lawes of duty" (l. 4). His only relief from his own anguish is the recognition that Stella, too, is grieving. When he hears her sighs and sad words and sees tears in her eyes, he suffers along with her, but he also rejoices in these evidences of her love for him. He finds himself in a paradoxical situation: Losing her is "th' effect most bitter" (l. 12); the cause of her grief (loving him) seems sweet. He would have been vexed by it if he had not already been vexed by the situation itself.

Sonnet 87 follows the ITALIAN (PETRARCHAN) SONNET structure. The OCTAVE presents the lovers' separation and Astrophil's observations of Stella's reactions to it. Sidney parallels the patterns of repetition in the two QUATRAINS of the octave to underscore the lovers' unity even in this division. In the first quatrain, Stella's name repeats three times (the only times it appears in the SONNET). SIR PHILIP SIDNEY exercises a rough rhythm to underscore Astrophil's grief. Instead of IAMBIC PENTAMETER, the second line scans as trochee, trochee, iamb, trochee, iamb. This strategy emphasizes each noun, and although it maintains the pentameter, the rhythm is forced into the chaos of mourning that Astrophil feels for himself and observes in Stella.

The second quatrain describes what Astrophil sees Stella undergoing. The phrases *I found* (l. 5) or *I saw* (ll. 6–7) appear in nearly the same feet as *Stella* in the previous quatrain. Astrophil finds that she suffers ("did smart," l. 5) with him; he sees tears in her eyes, sees sighs in the opening of her lips, and hears his own sorrow in her words.

The pattern of experiences in the octave repeats in the SESTET. In the sestet's first three lines, Astrophil reacts to what he observed of Stella's reactions: "I wept" because of her tears ("pearles scattered," l. 9), "I sighd," and "[I] wailed" (l. 10). But the sestet introduces an extra dimension of emotion: as well as grieving, Astrophil swims in joy (l. 11) because, for him, the signs of Stella's grieving measure the depth of her love (l. 11). The CHIASMUS in line 14 emphasizes the paradoxical nature of Astrophil's suffering—that is, in effect, he would have been vexed if he were not already vexed.

In context, this sonnet appears after Songs 5–9, the longest break in the entire SONNET SEQUENCE. Although there is no consistent narrative throughout *Astrophil* and Stella, Sonnet 87 recognizes a break in the lovers' relationship in dramatic fashion.

See also ASTROPHIL AND STELLA (OVERVIEW).

Marjory E. Lange

Astrophil and Stella: Sonnet 89 ("Now that of absence the most irksome night") SIR PHILIP SIDNEY (1582) Sonnet 89 is thought to have been composed during the summer of 1582, soon after Penelope Devereux (Stella) married Sidney's rival, Lord Rich; thus, Astrophil loses Stella. Because of this devastating loss, Sonnet 89 breaks many metrical rules. Sidney uses the same two words—*night* and *day*—for each line's end rhyme. Interestingly, the words occur an equal number of times, as Astrophil laments the "absence" (l. 1) of his "Stella's eyes" (l. 3), which provided the necessary light to his emotional world. The constant repetition of the two opposing forces destabilizes the reader, as Sidney moves the positive "day" into an unfamiliar negative in which it contains no light but is merely the absence of darkness. Day brings no comfort to this suffering lover—but neither does the night. Still, Astrophil overcomes day with its "darkest shade" (l. 2), and without Stella there will be no lifting of the darkness even when day arrives. Instead the new day lasts too long and leaves the abandoned lover longing for the covering comfort of "long-stayed night" (l. 6). Night brings no solace, bearing instead a horrible "silence" (l. 8) that is as unendurable as the "darkness of his day" (l. 10). In the absence of the stabilizing influence of his love for Stella, Astrophil is now "living in blackest winter night," (l. 13) even while his soul suffers the hellish agony of remembrance of the "flame" of his summer's impassioned "day" (l. 14).

See also ASTROPHIL AND STELLA (OVERVIEW); SIDNEY, SIR PHILIP; SONNET.

Leslie J. Ormandy

Astrophil and Stella: Sonnet 90 ("Stella, thinke not that I by verse seeke fame") SIR PHILIP SIDNEY (ca. 1582) Sonnet 90 of *Astrophil and Stella,* like several earlier poems in the SONNET SEQUENCE (1, 3, 6, 15, and 74), reflects on the act of writing poetry, serving as a reminder to Astrophil that he writes not only *of*

Stella and her love but *for* her, too; she is both audience and content.

This ITALIAN (PETRARCHAN) SONNET is built on a foundation of negative statements, of denials: each of the five phrases—"thinke not" (l. 1); "Nor so ambitious I" (l. 5); "In truth I sweare, I wish not" (l. 7); "ne if I would" (l. 9); and "For nothing from my wit or will doth flow" (l. 12)—introduces a different nuance of the poetic creative experience. In addition, there are subsidiary denials, all of which together lead steadily toward the conclusion that Astrophil claims he is interpreting the love that flows through him, not creating it.

The SONNET also addresses fame garnered through writing. In the first four lines, the speaker states that he has never sought fame; one audience—Stella—is enough ("If thou praise not, all other praise is shame," l. 4). The only fame he seeks, implicitly, is that of being known for loving Stella. In a crescendo of verbs—*seek, hope, love, live*—Astrophil places himself in relation to Stella as her faithful lover. He goes so far as to claim that he "live[s] but for thee" (l. 2). The next six lines deal with ambition. Here there is no mention of Stella; the speaker repudiates the name of poet on the grounds that he cannot call himself a poet on account of "the plumes from others' wings I take" (l. 11). This sentiment echoes both Sonnet 1 and SIR PHILIP SIDNEY's arguments in his DEFENSE OF POESY, where the poet is specifically defined as a "maker," one who does not borrow from nature—or other poets—but creates from within his own mind.

The last three lines clarify that Astrophil's poetry comes from Stella's beauty and his own love (ll. 13–14), which is a very different situation than borrowing "others leaves" (Sonnet 1, 1.7). He gives to Stella's beauty the full credit for providing all his words as well as the impetus for writing them down. What makes this sonnet stand out is the poet-lover's self-defensive tone; the series of negatives acts to undermine the strength of the poet's argument, defending before there has been any attack.

See also ASTROPHIL AND STELLA (OVERVIEW), SYNECDOCHE.

Marjory E. Lange

***Astrophil and Stella*: Sonnet 91 ("Stella, while now by Honour's cruell might")** Sir Philip Sidney (ca. 1582) Sonnet 91 builds on a controlling metaphor that Stella is Astrophil's sun, so that without her he remains in darkness, except for those other women whose features momentarily light his night with their beauty. Astrophil, concerned lest Stella think him unfaithful in his love for her, seeks to assure her that these others only please him because he sees her in them, and that is what moves him.

This Italian (Petrarchan) sonnet begins its octave with an oxymoron, "honour's cruell might" (l. 1), highlighting Astrophil's state of mind and the inversion of values that passionate love produces. Absence from Stella, like night or a veil, creates a darkness that grieves him. The second half of the octave treats other women as synecdoches for Stella; Astrophil says that he sees them as if they were candles (compared to Stella's sun). In a parody of the blazon, elements of individual women—the hair, hands, cheeks, lips, or eyes—illuminate his darkness slightly. The metaphor of eyes as "seeing jets, blacke, but in blacknesse bright" (l. 8) focuses the image both in its alliteration and in the oxymoron of black brightness.

In the sestet, Astrophil admits these beauties please his eyes, but only because "of you they models be" (l. 10). He extends the simile to claim that these women's features are "wood-globes of glistring skies" (l. 11); that is, they are like wooden models of astral bodies, resembling them in form but reflecting only some tiny portion of the original's light. The sonnet's conclusion offers to reassure Stella: Astrophil does not love these women even if it looks that way, even if "they seeme my hart to move" (l. 13). He loves them for what they reflect of Stella, "you in them" (l. 14).

Astrophil addresses Stella throughout this sonnet. Naturally, such apostrophes occur more frequently in sonnets when the two lovers are separated than when/where they are together, when he is more likely to talk about her. Astrophil bridges her absence by invoking her name. The conceit that Stella is the original and all other beautiful women merely copies or reflections of her reappears in Song 11 (ll. 21–25). By the end of Sonnet 91, Stella has emerged as an archetype for things that are fundamentally incomparable.

See also *Astrophil and Stella* (overview); Sidney, Sir Philip.

Marjory E. Lange

***Astrophil and Stella*: Sonnet 94 ("Grief, find the words; for thou hast made my brain")** Sir Philip Sidney (ca. 1582) In Sir Philip Sidney's Sonnet 94, Astrophil relinquishes the responsibility for writing sonnets. He addresses personified Grief in an extended apostrophe, first complaining that he is unable to write because his grief is so great and telling Grief to complain on his behalf—to write his poetry, in fact. The entire sonnet is hyperbolic (overblown or exaggerated), but the eventual destination is a piece of self-criticism: The speaker recognizes that he is grieving excessively.

The octave of this Italian (Petrarchan) sonnet orders Grief to "find the words" (l. 1) to write because Astrophil's brain has become darkened by the misty vapors rising from grief's "heavy mould" (l. 2). This metaphor compares grief to a swamp from which noxious fogs rise, blinding Astrophil so that he cannot even see what is making him suffer. Grief, he says, is able to complain (l. 5); being the source of the pain Astrophil suffers, Grief must do the writing. In these lines, Astrophil first acknowledges the severity of his grieving: He suffers the sickness of grief even though "harbengers of death lodge there in his braine" (l. 8). The speaker recognizes how out of control he really is, and he tries to turn the responsibility for poetry over to Grief, the more balanced of the two. The sestet develops this conceit by suggesting that Grief has reason to complain on his own behalf, since the association with Astrophil makes him "more wretched" than he would be otherwise.

This sonnet has more than the usual number of variants among the manuscript and early printed editions, attesting to its many difficulties of syntax and diction. Line 9, for instance, occurs in four completely different versions. Thus, although the general meaning and overall sentiment are extraordinarily clear, the details of this sonnet remain more obscure than many, which emphasize Astrophil's condition and point. The convoluted syntax contrasts with an unusually smooth rhythm.

Only the fifth line has any breaks in the IAMBIC PENTAMETER rhythm, as Astrophil intensifies Grief's presence by doubling the direct address: "Do thou then (for thou canst) do thou complaine." Triple repetitions of "thou" forces the reader's attention to remain focused on Grief, away from both the speaker and from Stella, who is never mentioned, even implicitly. Addressing Grief so relentlessly allows Astrophil to create some distance between himself and the intensity of his emotion. Even though he claims to be unable to envision his own pain (l. 4), the underlying strategy of Sonnet 94 separates speaker from feeling. We can see just how exaggerated the grief has become.

In addition to the twisted syntax, Sidney uses AMPLIFICATION—meticulous repetitions of certain words both for emphasis and for contrast. The last three lines reinforce Astrophil's sense of being a "wretch" by juxtaposing it with Grief's "wretchedness" twice.

Contextually, Sonnet 94 follows the wild anguish of the careless, unintentional injury, insult, or upset dealt to Stella in Sonnet 93. It can be argued that the intense despair in Sonnet 94 represents the nadir of *Astrophil and Stella* as a whole. If so, the speaker's dawning awareness of the disproportion of his grief marks the beginning of the upswing that finds its fulfillment in Sonnets 107 and 108. Hyperbole and apostrophe together create a sonnet whose very extremeness provides the rationale for a return to a more reasonable poetic presence.

See also *ASTROPHIL AND STELLA* (OVERVIEW).

Marjory E. Lange

Astrophil and Stella: Sonnet 104 ("Enuious wits, what hath bene mine offence") SIR PHILIP SIDNEY (ca. 1582)

Relying on a conversational tone, Sonnet 104 addresses the observers following Astrophil's sorrow. The first part of the OCTAVE of this ITALIAN (PETRARCHAN) SONNET paints a vivid picture of Astrophil being covertly watched by "enuious wits" (l. 1) who note everything that might indicate what he is feeling. Wondering what he has done to deserve such treatment, he alleges they act as if they envy his "sorrowe's eloquence" (l. 4), an ambivalent phrase that simultaneously stresses the speaker's self-deprecating sorrowful mood and his self-praising ability to write about it. In the second half of the octave, Astrophil asks his enemies if it is not enough that he is so separated from Stella that "scarce any sparke / Of comfort" (ll. 6–7) can reach him where he is, "thence, thence, thrice-repeated thence" (ll. 5–6) from her. The ENJAMBMENT of the first two "thence"s makes the distance described all the greater, and strengthens the uncertainty of where Astrophil actually is. Although he speaks of a "dungeon darke" (l. 7) and "rigrows exile" (l. 8), clearly the poem is set at the court, so his distance from his beloved is not geographic so much as symbolic, and the envious wits are contributors to this separation.

The SESTET exemplifies Astrophil's COMPLAINT. Using the parenthetical phrase in line 11, SIR PHILIP SIDNEY slyly has Astrophil interpret his own actions in the same multivalent way as his detractors have been doing: He is "glad" (l. 11) that he can look through a window that is "happy" (l. 9) because Stella looked out of it at some point. But it does not matter what he does, because the envious wits take note of every word—every gesture—and pull from it "hid meaning" (l. 13) that he loves Stella. Fools, he says in the last line—who denies it? The irony in the last lines is that there is no hidden meaning; the "morall notes" (l. 12)—that is, allegorical interpretations—are really the literal meaning, and the unsympathetic observers in the court have inadvertently provided Astrophil with assistance.

See also *ASTROPHIL AND STELLA* (OVERVIEW).

Leslie J. Ormandy

Astrophil and Stella: Eleventh Song ("'Who is it that this dark night'") SIR PHILIP SIDNEY (ca. 1582)

The eleventh Song is the last of the songs inserted among the SONNETs in *Astrophil and Stella*, appearing between Sonnets 104 and 105. It takes the form of a dialogue; each of the 11 five-line stanzas is divided so that Stella speaks the first two lines and Astrophil the remaining three. Written in trochaic tetrameters, each STANZA's first, third, and fifth lines have feminine endings, while the second and fourth lines end in the masculine form. The rhyme scheme is *ababa*. Song 11 asserts Astrophil's continuing faithful love for Stella against every doubt presented.

The first two stanzas identify speakers and situation. Stella opens by asking who stands in the dark beneath her window, complaining; Astrophil answers it is the one who, exiled from her, refuses any other light. She replies by asking if he has not fallen out of love with her yet, to which Astrophil insists that the only change she will ever see in him is to ruin. A COMPLAINT is a recognized category of love poetry; by naming it specifically, Stella recognizes what Astrophil's presence indicates.

In the middle five stanzas, Stella explores the depth and basis for Astrophil's love: absence, time's passage, and new beauties will dim her in his eyes; reason and all that he has suffered will argue against her. First she suggests that since they can no longer see one another, his feelings will die. He agrees, ironically, that absence might help, but qualifies himself by adding it could help only if he could be absent from himself, since his heart is irrevocably bound to hers. She continues her argument by asserting that time passing will make his pain easier, but he retorts that time can only work in accordance with the subject's nature, offering as example the turtledove, who, traditionally, was believed to mate for life. You will see new beautiful women, protests Stella. They will seem only like saints' paintings, imperfect images of your perfection, Astrophil replies. Stella shifts her ground to Astrophil's own personality: Your reason will insist that you stop loving me, she says. Astrophil rejoins that his love for her is founded precisely in his reason; it is not merely dependent upon her beauty. Her final protest is that all the wrongs he has borne on account of his love for her will finally force him to stop loving. He insists that the more troubles that come to shake love, the more deeply it roots itself.

The last pair of stanzas provide the only possible way to break the impasse. The lovers are interrupted: Stella thinks she hears someone listening and is afraid to be caught speaking with Astrophil. He agrees to leave, but only because he does not want to endanger her, and he assures her that his soul remains with her. She, heatedly, tells him to go, now, before Argus's eyes see him. Astrophil complains that the greatest injustice in the whole miserable situation is that he must run away from louts.

Sidney uses three devices to place the song's lovers and their situation into the tradition. First, Stella is located physically above Astrophil, inside a guarded space; Astrophil must stand below, bemoaning their separation outside. Second, Astrophil compares himself to the biblically and classically faithful turtledove, a popular emblem of lifelong fidelity. Finally, Stella refers to her watchers metaphorically as Argus, the mythical 100-eyed creature set by Hera to guard Io (one of Zeus's mortal mistresses) from his further advances. Argus could be relied on to see any intruder, since some of his 100 eyes were always open. The implication is that no matter how faithfully Astrophil loves, he cannot compete successfully against the combined barriers of the gulf imposed by enclosed space and wardens. The dialogue format and the length allow the poet to develop a more extended narrative than is possible within a SONNET.

See also *ASTROPHIL AND STELLA* (OVERVIEW); EMBLEM; SIDNEY, SIR PHILIP.

Marjory E. Lange

Astrophil and Stella: Sonnet 106 ("O absent presence, Stella is not here") SIR PHILIP SIDNEY (ca. 1582)

In Sonnet 106, Astrophil continues to mourn Stella's final departure from him—a wretched state that began in Sonnet 87. Second to last in the SONNET SEQUENCE, Sonnet 106 marks Astrophil's final and unsuccessful efforts to accept Stella's absence and to look for a new lover.

The poem is a variation on the ITALIAN (PETRARCHAN) SONNET and begins as an APOSTROPHE to "hope." The first QUATRAIN begins with an oxymoron: absent presence. Stella is present in Astrophil's thoughts but physically absent. He blames his misery on hope, which he asserts has deceived him into believing that Stella might return. The "Orphane place" (l. 3) he inhabits emphasizes that he is alone, without her. The phrase also resonates provocatively with Orpheus, the poet-musician who similarly seeks to reclaim his absent beloved and whose hope is finally dashed by his own error. Astrophil, too, has erred, losing Stella when he breaks his promise to love her chastely. He goes on to ask Hope where Stella is, asserting that Hope had promised Astrophil that his "famist," or hungry, eyes would be sated with the sight of Stella. Reference to his eyes as the needy agents in this SONNET continues the strong emphasis on the role of vision in love in *Astrophil and Stella*. The second quatrain reveals that Hope has vanished, disgraced at its failure to procure Stella's return. Astrophil laments this loss, for without hope, his isolation is total.

The SESTET introduces a dramatic turn from interior contemplation to exterior experience, as Astrophil seeks out other women to fill the void left by Stella. He imagines that he might speak with these ladies and be charmed by their conversation. This, he implies, could supplant his love for Stella, invoking a new object of affection. He says these ladies might "Make in my heavy mould new thoughts to grow" (l. 11). Here the word *mould* means "body," which gives a decidedly physical, as opposed to intellectual or spiritual, aspect to his desire for these other ladies. Likewise, the verb *grow* emphasizes the lustful aspect of Astrophil's attempt to meet other women. But with reference to the "store of faire Ladies" he meets, Astrophil may not be totally sincere. To suggest that he has a large supply of women renders these ladies generic and makes it seem unlikely that Astrophil, who has spent 117 sonnets and songs focusing on one specific beloved, would so quickly change his course for the company of many.

This insincerity is confirmed later in the sestet as Astrophil turns scornfully from these other women, invoking a metaphor to explain his aversion to such an enterprise. He likens himself to a recently wounded man whose friend blithely encourages him to forget his pain and be merry. Sidney's use of a physical wound as the metaphor for Astrophil's sorrow again emphasizes the prominence of the body and desire in the sequence. Stella's absence has affected him as profoundly as a physical injury. And, like a physical injury, his recovery will take time; his recovery, indeed, exceeds the bounds of the SONNET SEQUENCE.

In Sonnet 106, Astrophil faces a choice between looking to the outside world for solace or continuing to focus his despair inward; the public and private are at odds. In confronting Astrophil with the specter of other lovers, the sonnet attempts a closure that the sequence ultimately rejects: Astrophil will not end the sequence by redirecting his affections to someone else. Instead he turns inward, preferring to nurse his wounds privately.

See also ASTROPHIL AND STELLA (OVERVIEW).

Margaret M. Simon

Astrophil and Stella: Sonnet 107 ("Stella, since thou so right a princesse art") SIR PHILIP SIDNEY (ca. 1582)

Sonnet 107 marks a shift in tone and purpose from the despair and sorrow in the poems that precede it. Here, Astrophil, using metaphors of public service, proposes either to conquer his passion for Stella, or at least to sublimate it by using it to fuel some other endeavor. He addresses her first as "Princesse" (l. 1), then as "Queene" (l. 9), acknowledging her power over him, but asks her to let him have a time of peace from loving her and, more, to aid him in his "great cause" (l. 8). Unless this happens, he fears that others will be able to condemn Stella for Astrophil's weakness.

The opening of this ITALIAN (PETRARCHAN) SONNET immediately establishes Stella's right to rule Astrophil, as do many of the poems in this sequence. Astrophil unstintingly admits that "all the powers which life bestowes in me" (l. 2) are under Stella's aegis. Because she is his ruler, Astrophil says, before he can undertake any work (l. 3), he must have both Stella's approval and her support. The second half of the OCTAVE offers the only release from the images of power and regime: Astrophil addresses Stella, imploringly, as "Sweete" (l. 5). He begs her to let him stop loving her ("give respite to my hart," l. 5), admitting that he cannot control his passion on his own: ". . . my hart, / Which pants as though it still should leape to thee" (ll. 5–6). At this point in the narrative of the love relationship, Astrophil has no expectation of success, but that does not stop him from being sexually and emotionally involved with Stella in his imagination. Astrophil's excitement and commitment to his new course of action can be seen syntactically: There is no complete stop until line 11 (a colon was very "light" punctuation during the 16th century). Eagerly, Astrophil urges his monarch to send him out to employ his experience, "use" and talents, "art" in the "great cause" of turning his personal passion into some appropriate and legitimate service

(l. 8). The word *Lieftenancy* (l. 7) assures readers that Stella is still the motive for all of Astrophil's actions; what has changed is the nature and sphere of those accomplishments.

What Astrophil does not say is that this is what Stella has sought all along. Instead, in Sonnet 107, Astrophil makes the situation look like his own idea, and he implores Stella for permission to do what she has been urging him to do. In many ways, Sonnet 107 answers Sonnet 69, not least because in the earlier SONNET Astrophil was given the "monarchie" of Stella's "high heart" (l. 10), and in Sonnet 107 he repeatedly affirms her command over him. The final irony of Sonnet 107 comes in the last three lines, when Astrophil hints that if he is not allowed to take up some greater work, it will be Stella's perceived fault: "On servants' shame oft Maister's blame doth sit" (l. 12). The wheedling tone of line 5's "Sweete" now fulfills its purpose. Astrophil does not want his faithful loving to be scorned because it resulted in nothing more than the passionate outpourings of an unsuccessful suitor. However, by accepting his own responsibility for his change in attitude, he reverses his fortune and his love endeavor succeeds.

See also *ASTROPHIL AND STELLA* (OVERVIEW); SIDNEY, SIR PHILIP.

Marjory E. Lange

Astrophil and Stella: Sonnet 108 ("When Sorrow—using mine own fire's might") SIR PHILIP SIDNEY (ca. 1582)

This, the last SONNET of SIR PHILIP SIDNEY's *Astrophil and Stella,* is weighted heavily with alchemical imagery, references to metals, and the refining, annealing processes of transformation. The speaker, Astrophil, acknowledges that his love for Stella remains simultaneously his joy and his only ongoing frustration. This admission ends the entire *Astrophil and Stella* SONNET SEQUENCE utilizing a very Petrarchan strategy, the paradox that the joys and dissatisfactions of love are inextricably interwoven.

This ITALIAN (PETRARCHAN) SONNET begins with Astrophil describing himself as burdened by the molten lead of sorrow, melted in the heat of his own passion ("mine owne fier's might," l. 1) within his heart's furnace ("my boyling brest," l. 2). This burden is leaden, heavy, grey—and destructively hot. Into this darkness, however, shines the light of his joy that is his beloved Stella, who is not named in Sonnet 108.

The second part of the OCTAVE and first part of the SESTET illustrate what happens to Astrophil when, empowered by thought of Stella (the one who "breeds my delight," l. 5), he tries to fly to her comfort ("my yong soule flutters to thee his nest" (l. 6). Despair, who is with him all the time, cuts his wings, wraps him in darkness, and forces him to admit that one who is imprisoned (within "iron doores," l. 11) by despair cannot possibly appreciate the sun itself ("*Phoebus'* gold," l. 10). Astrophil's only solution is to declare that just as Stella is the only joy that can alleviate his woes, so she also provides the only "annoy" (l. 14) destroying his joy. The key to the last three lines is the parenthetical alas—"So strangely (alas) thy workes in me prevaile" (l. 12)—because it reinforces Astrophil's ambivalence about his whole situation. In Sonnet 108, he recognizes that he can never win the satisfaction of union with Stella, but neither can he escape the way her "workes" master ("prevaile [in]") him (ll. 13–14).

Sonnet 108 depends on alchemical images. Alchemy was the process by which baser metals could, presumably, be transformed into gold using various chemical reactions, principally extreme heat and pressure. Here, Astrophil is both the alchemist and the location where transformational operations take place; Stella becomes both the gold being sought and the agent of the change. The distance between base "lead" (l. 2) and "*Phoebus'* gold" (l. 10) establishes the extremity of change Astrophil longs to experience in his love for—and from—Stella. The "darke fornace" (l. 3) of his "boyling brest" (l. 2) becomes the vessel wherein the transformation might take place. Sorrow, personified (see PERSONIFICATION), provides the lead needed to begin the reaction and initiates the process of transformation. Representing himself as a "yong soule" and Stella as his "nest" (l. 6) thickens Astrophil's imagery by adding a child/mother relationship to the images of alchemy. Using *nest* as METONYMY for mother, and combining the attributes of a soul with those of a young bird, the poet inserts a separate pattern of transformation into his metallurgic one. Later in the sonnet, Stella's "workes" (another alchemical term) are both the alchemical changes detailed in Sonnet 108 and the entire pattern of achievement and loss Astrophil has undergone in the previous 107 sonnets and 11 songs. Although this sonnet ends the sequence, there is no real conclusion, no closure for Astrophil or the reader. This inconclusive end is another typical Petrarchan trope—the lover trapped in love but aware he will never achieve its gratifications.

As late as the 1960s, many scholars were dissatisfied with this sonnet as the end to the sequence. In fact, early editions appended Sonnets 31 ("Thou blind man's marke") and 32 ("Leave me, O love") from *CERTAIN SONNETS* to provide a more fitting outcome to Astrophil's progress through the course of love. However, there is no historical evidence to support any but Sonnet 108 to end the sequence.

See also *ASTROPHIL AND STELLA* (OVERVIEW).

FURTHER READING
Cain, Jeffrey P. "Sidney's *Astrophil and Stella,* Sonnet 108." *Explicator* 52, no. 1 (1993): 12–16.
Murphy, Karl. "The 109th and 110th Sonnets of *Astrophil and Stella.*" *PQ* (1955): 349–352.

Marjory E. Lange

"AS YOU CAME FROM THE HOLY LAND" SIR WALTER RALEIGH (ca. 1580?–1593?)
"As You Came from the Holy Land" is a brief poem attributed to SIR WALTER RALEIGH. Like most of Raleigh's poetry, it serves as a tribute and COMPLAINT to Queen ELIZABETH I, "Who like a queen, like a nymph, did appear" (l. 15). The poem shares Raleigh's recurrent theme of a suitor abandoned by his love. In this case his love has ventured on pilgrimage and no longer loves him, for he is old: "Love likes not the falling fruit / From the withered tree" (ll. 27–28). The date of the poem is unknown, but it was probably written in the 1580s or early 1590s, during the height of Raleigh's career in Elizabeth's court. The authorship of the poem is also unclear, and while attributed to Raleigh in various compilations after his death, there are no early manuscripts to prove authorship.

FURTHER READING
May, Steven W. *Sir Walter Raleigh.* Boston: Twayne Publishers, 1989.

Catherine Ann Perkins

AUBADE   The aubade branched out from the ALBA (lament of lovers parting at dawn) tradition. Though the terms are sometimes used interchangeably, the aubade developed into a broader category of dawn or morning poems, including poems designed to greet the dawn, celebrate the dawn, or simply express a morning-time love. The aubade has no standard verse format. GEOFFREY CHAUCER's *TROILUS AND CRISEYDE* contains several aubades—for example: "And day they gonnen to despise al newe, / Callyng it traitour, enuyous, and worse" (*T&C,* 3.1699–1700).

Carol E. Harding

AUREATION   From the Latin *aureus* for "gold," aureation is the practice of making language "golden" through the use of elaborate vocabulary and intricate syntax, the result of which is a grandiloquent and ornate poetic diction. Some of the English poets of the 15th century, particularly JOHN LYDGATE and Stephen Hawes (fl. 1502–1521), and many of the SCOTTISH CHAUCERIANS, including ROBERT HENRYSON, WILLIAM DUNBAR, and GAVIN DOUGLAS, favored aureate diction and wrote using ornamental language full of VERNACULAR coinages of Latin words.

FURTHER READING
Nichols, Pierrepont H. "Lydgate's Influence on the Aureate Terms of the Scottish Chaucerians." *PMLA* 47 (1932): 318–322.
Pearsall, Derek. "The English Chaucerians." In *Chaucer and Chaucerians,* edited by D. S. Brewer, 201–239. London: Nelson, 1966.

Mark DiCicco

AYRE (LUTE SONG)   Also known as an art song or lute song, an ayre was a poem composed specifically for voices accompanied by a lute.

See also *BOOKE OF AYRES, A;* "COME AWAY, COME SWEET LOVE"; DOWLAND, JOHN.

FURTHER READING
Fischlin, Daniel. *In Small Proportions: A Poetics of the English Ayre 1596–1622.* Detroit: Wayne State University Press, 1998.

B

BALLAD (FOLK BALLADS) Ballads, also known as folk ballads, or popular ballads, were composed to be sung. Unlike the similar CAROL, however, ballads were based on legends or traditions from the local area and were commonly passed down orally between generations. Thus, the medieval and Elizabethan ballads extant today are only one version of many that once existed. Ballads typically depict dramatic situations, are told either by an omniscient narrator or through dialogue, and often begin the tale in media res.

The ballad has no set form, but typically falls into four-line STANZAS rhyming *abcb*. There are more than 300 extant English and Scottish ballads, which fall into five general categories: romantic ("BARBARA ALLEN"), nautical ("Henry Martin"), historic ("The BONNY EARL OF MURRAY"), heroic (the ROBIN HOOD BALLADS), and supernatural ("The Wife of Usher's Well"). The first, and still most comprehensive, collection of ballads was compiled by Francis James Child in the 19th century (*English and Scottish Popular Ballads*).

See also BALLAD STANZA, BORDER BALLADS, MIDDLE ENGLISH LYRICS AND BALLADS.

FURTHER READING
Child, Francis James, ed. *The English and Scottish Popular Ballads.* 5 vols. 1802. Reprint, New York: Dover Publications, 1965.

BALLAD See BALLAD (FOLK BALLADS), BALLAD STANZA, BORDER BALLADS, MIDDLE ENGLISH LYRICS AND BALLADS, ROBIN HOOD BALLADS.

BALLADE A ballade is a poem with three STANZAS of seven, eight, or 10 lines, an ENVOI, amd a REFRAIN. The lines are generally in either iambic tetrameter or IAMBIC PENTAMETER and rhyme. Traditionally, the envoi was addressed to the poet's patron.

The eight-line ballade is most standard. The 10-line ballade is sometimes called the ballade supreme and is predominantly a French verse form. The seven-line ballade is also known as the ballade royal. It consists of four stanzas of RHYME ROYAL verse, all following the same pattern, all using the same refrain, and having no envoi.

The most well-known writer of ballades is François Villon (1431–1465?). GEOFFREY CHAUCER wrote several ballades, including the envoi-less "To Rosemunde." In the 16th century, Sir PHILIP SIDNEY experimented with the form, as did EDMUND SPENSER, among others.

See also ENVOI.

"BALLAD ON THE MARRIAGE OF PHILIP AND MARY, A" JOHN HEYWOOD **(1554)** The dramatist, musician, and poet John Heywood (ca. 1497–ca. 1580) was on the payroll of the Tudor royal family for a number of decades. He was particularly favored by MARY I (queen of England), and during her reign of 1553–58, the anti-Protestant Heywood enjoyed considerable PATRONAGE and prestige.

Published as a stand-alone text in 1554, "A Ballad on the Marriage of Philip and Mary" is a brief and piquant expression of Heywood's loyalty to the Catholic, Marian regime. The format of the poem seems simple: It contains 12 seven-line STANZAs in *ababbcc* rhyme; the lines are almost all in regular tetrameter. The poem is more complex than it appears initially. It fits into several differing genres and takes advantage of strong aesthetic effects. The poem is an ALLEGORY depicting the controversial marriage between Mary and the Catholic king of Spain, Philip II. It is a BEAST FABLE because it describes the improbable union of a proud eagle and a disciplined lion—the eagle signifying Spain, the lion England. The poem can also be called an epithalamium—a political and romantic ode—because it celebrates a contemporary marriage in a eulogistic manner. More simply, it can be called a BALLAD because Heywood's original text identifies it as such; it conveys a basic narrative and could conceivably be sung.

The poem begins with a description of the Spanish "birde" being drawn to Mary, the living embodiment of the "red and whight" Tudor rose. The object of the eagle's affection is Mary, who embodies the leonine boldness of England. Mary is not a wild lion but a "lamblike lion feminyne." Although strong and secure in her association with English puissance, the queen is meek and mild, feminine. There is a great match, because in Philip we have a "kinglie king" and in Mary we have a "queenelie queene": "lyke to lyke here matched is," announces the celebratory verse. Heywood uses ANAPHORA to stress the royal couple's compatibility: Several lines at the start of stanza 6 are exclamations of joy that begin with the claim that the couple is "so meete [fit] a matche." Five successive one-line comments in stanza 8 describe the marital union's virtues; each line begins with the word "Suche." Sparing use of ALLITERATION heightens the intensity of satisfaction that English subjects should feel—"what matche may match more mete then this" (l. 35).

Ultimately, Heywood's "Ballad on the Marriage" works as pro-state, pro-status quo propaganda, providing an artistic instance of pro-Catholicism, its own complex elaborateness reflecting the complicated political situation.

FURTHER READING

Farmer, John S., ed. *The Proverbs, Epigrams, and Miscellanies of John Heywood*. Guildford, U.K.: Charles W. Traylen, 1986.

Fisher, Joshua B. "'He is Turned a Ballad-Maker': Broadside Appropriations in Early Modern England." *Early Modern Literary Studies* 9, no. 2 (2003). Available online. URL: http://www.shu.ac.uk/emls/09–2/fishball.html. Downloaded on January 21, 2008.

Kevin de Ornellas

BALLAD STANZA Although there is no absolute format set for BALLADS, many share a common form. This standard, which has become known as the ballad STANZA, is a QUATRAIN with the rhyme scheme *abcb*, alternating four-stress and three-stress lines.

See also BALLAD (FOLK BALLADS), BORDER BALLADS, MIDDLE ENGLISH LYRICS AND BALLADS, ROBIN HOOD BALLADS.

"BALLAD WHICH ASKEW MADE AND SANG WHEN IN NEWGATE, A" ANNE ASKEW (1546)

Anne Askew (1521–1546) married a Catholic member of the gentry but converted to Protestantism and left her husband. Questioned numerous times for heresy, she was burned at the stake on July 16, 1546.

Besides being a prominent figure in the English Reformation, Askew is a notable presence in early modern literature. She wrote two spiritual autobiographies while imprisoned: *The First Examynacyon* and *The Lattre Examynacyon*. Her writings portray the state of doctrinal struggles in the mid-16th century as well as the importance of biblical learning for women.

"A Ballad Which Askew Made and Sang When in Newgate" appears at the end of *The Lattre Examynacyon*. It is divided into three sections of four STANZAs each, corresponding to faith, hope, and charity. In the first section, the narrator compares herself with an "armed knight," protected by a shield of faith, ready to face the battlefield of the world. In the second section, hope causes the narrator to rejoice because Christ will fight with her and for her. Her hope in Christ is limitless before her enemies' unending "spight." In the final section on the theme of charity, the narrator recalls that "cruel wit" has swallowed up "rightwisness," or justice; nevertheless, she prays for her oppressors, displaying Christ-like charity.

This BALLAD reinforces not only the Protestant ideal that true faith lies within the Bible, but also illustrates the nationalist trend prompting a belief in an English Church. In particular, Askew's comparison of faith to a beset ship (stanza 9) recalls the Protestant view that the church (ship) needed reforms (storms) to restore it to the true faith (anchor).

FURTHER READING

Beilin, Elaine, ed. *The Examinations of Anne Askew.* Oxford: Oxford University Press, 1996.

McQuade, Paula. "'Except that they had offended the Lawe': Gender and Jurisprudence in *The Examinations of Anne Askew.*" *Literature & History* 3, no. 2 (1994): 1–14.

R. L. Smith

"BARBARA ALLEN" ("BARBARA ALLAN")

ANONYMOUS (ca. 14th century)   Many versions of this very popular folk BALLAD exist under a few different titles. One source says that there are 92 variations, but they all share a common storyline: Barbara Allen is called to deathbed of a young man who is dying of love for her. She leaves him, and on her way home she hears the bell tolling his death. In most, but not all, versions, she then herself dies of love, as though in this way she and he are at last united.

The vitality of the ballad over the centuries suggests the romantic power of the notion that men and women will really die for love (although few of them do); this is an extension of the LOVESICKNESS ideal. Like most other folk ballads, the tale's grim climax is presented with little or no exposition or buildup.

The song certainly has its roots before 1600, although the first explicit reference of it is found in Samuel Pepys' diary in 1666. The variety of locations named (Scarlet Town, the West Country, and Reading Town, among others), the variety of names given the dying man (Sir John Graeme, Jemmy Grove, Willie Grove, etc.), and the variety of reactions to the situation by Barbara Allen suggest the revisionist workings of a long oral tradition.

Three commonly studied versions come from Francis Child's *The English and Scottish Popular Ballads,* and the varying titles show different emphases: "Bonny Barbara Allan," "Barbara Allen's Cruelty," and "Barbara Allan," although all convey a sense of bleakness.

In the first version, "Bonny Barbara Allen," the setting is "the west country" in autumn—"in and about the Martinmas time / when the green leaves were a falling" (ll. 1–2). Young Sir John Graeme seems to have been cursed by Barbara, who, when called to his bedside, reproaches him for slighting her when toasting others. It is not at all clear what she has done to him, or whether this is just Divine Providence dealing rough justice, but "he turnd his face unto the wall" and dies (ll. 23–24). Barbara rises "slowly, slowly," returns home, and announces to her mother, "My love has died for me to-day, I'll die for him to-morrow" (ll. 39–40).

In "Barbara Allen's Cruelty," the setting is Scarlet Town in "the merry month of May" (l. 5). When Barbara is called to the unnamed young man's deathbed, she shows no sympathy for him, saying, "If on your death-bed you be lying, / What is that to Barbara Allen" (ll. 30–31). The ringing death knell seems to mock Barbara Allen, calling her unworthy, and when she sees the young man's corpse, she laughs. However, this reaction must have indicated some very emotional reaction to his death, for she dies herself shortly thereafter, repenting that she "did deny him" (l. 63).

"Lammas time / When the woods grow green and yellow" (ll. 1–2) is the setting for "Barbara Allan." The unnamed "wooer" comes "out of the West" and unlike the other versions, he actively woos Barbara for three full stanzas (2–4), asking her to come see his fields and boats. She apparently rejects his offers, and stanza 5 finds him dying in bed. He confesses he is dying "all for the love of thee, My bonny Barbara Allan" (ll. 36–37). Her only remark is: "Och hone, och hone, He's dead and gone, / For the love of Barbara Allan!" (ll. 40–41). Not clearly regretful, there is no indication that she will die of lovesickness herself.

See also MIDDLE ENGLISH LYRICS AND BALLADS.

FURTHER READING

Kolinski, Mieczyslaw. "'Barbara Allen': Tonal Versus Melodic Structure." *Ethnomusicology* 12 (1968): 1–73, 208–218.

McCarthy William, Bernard. "'Barbara Allen' and 'The Gypsy Laddie': Single Rhyme Ballads in the Child Corpus." In *The Flowering Thorn: International Ballad Studies,* edited by Thomas A. McKean, 143–154. Logan: Utah State University Press, 2003.

Eric P. Furuseth

BARBOUR, JOHN (ca. 1320–1395)

John Barbour was a MIDDLE SCOTS poet best known for his historical work *The BRUCE.* Like many of his contemporaries, very little is known about Barbour's life other than that he held the important post of archdeacon of Aberdeen (one of the most important and wealthy cities in medieval Scotland), beginning in 1357, and remained in that office until he died. Although no records attest to his education, most scholars believe he was educated at Oxford.

The Bruce, written in octosyllabic COUPLETs, is for the most part a factual poem that celebrates the life of ROBERT I THE BRUCE and the war between the Scottish and the English. Although the poem is historically based, Barbour weaves components of other popular medieval genres into his verse, notably ROMANCE. In the poem, Bruce is a chivalric hero who surpasses all of his knights and opponents. Later medieval historians would consider Barbour's work more as a CHRONICLE of history and the authoritative voice on Bruce's life than as a piece of poetic value. Indeed, there is still much work to be done evaluating Barbour as a poet and not simply a historian.

Barbour finished his poem around 1376, only about 50 years after the death of his subject. The proximity of the events to his writings allowed him access to such sources as surviving veterans and a largely unchanged landscape where the events took place. Records show that Barbour received payment and a pension from the king, Robert II, who possibly commissioned the work.

Several other works have been attributed to Barbour, but none have been fully proven to be his. These include a poem on the siege of Troy which is in the same meter as *The Bruce* and a Scottish translation of some French poems called *The Buik of Alexander,* but *The Bruce* has truly been Barbour's legacy, and it influenced, among others, BLIND HARY's EPIC poem, *The WALLACE.*

FURTHER READING

Goldstein, R. James. *The Matter of Scotland: Historical Narrative in Medieval Scotland.* Lincoln: University of Nebraska Press, 1993.

McDiarmid, M. P., and J. Stevenson, eds. *Barbour's Bruce.* 3 vols. Edinburgh: Scottish Text Society, 1980–85.

Jennifer N. Brown

BARCLAY, ALEXANDER (ca. 1475–1552)

Alexander Barclay is credited with being the first poet to write English PASTORALS. Little is known with certainty regarding Barclay's life, and many scholars turn to his writings to obtain information on his life and experiences. Some believe he was born in Scotland around 1475. He enjoyed a brief literary career, during which he produced poems, translations, and a French textbook. While many of his writings are translations, Barclay's writing style retained the character of the original work, encompassing his own ideas about English society. He was among the first writers to benefit from a wider circulation of his works as a result of the printing press. Consequently, Barclay had an important role in introducing Continental literature to the English public.

Barclay is typically seen as a transitional figure between late medieval and early Renaissance verse. He lived during the earliest part of the Tudor Dynasty (1485–1547), and his verse picks up on some of the newer elements of the early modern period; he believed he was writing something new. Scholarly appraisals of Barclay's works have been exceptionally critical about his poetic abilities. Some of his best known works are *The Castell of Labour* (1503), *Ship of Fools* (1509), and *Certayne Eglogues* (ECLOGUES; printed in various parts from 1514, but reprinted in 1570 in complete form). *The Castell of Labour* is a medieval ALLEGORY, filled with PERSONIFICATION, about the nature of working for a living and its problems. *Ship of Fools,* accompanied by an elaborate woodcut, refutes medieval notions of scholasticism, medicine, and witchcraft, and presents itself as a translation of a Latin poem by Jacob Locher. This may be the earliest example of the loose translation that was to become normative in English translation in the later Renaissance and the attempt to update the translated poem with contemporary English references.

Without question, Barclay's *Certayne Eglogues* merited the attention of his day and today. Written in COUPLETs, the poems are a loose translation of Mantuan, with original interpolations. Pastoral poetry as a locus for political commentary under the veiled images of a pastoral world of shepherds thus became the norm for the Renaissance pastoral. EDMUND SPENSER is a direct inheritor of this tradition in his SHEPHEARDES CALENDER. In the prologue to *Certayne Eglogues,* Barclay notes that his poetry will consider topics such as courtly misery, the exploits of Venus, true love, false love, avarice and its effects, virtue praised, and war deplored, in addition to other matters. The emphasis on virtue is very important in Barclay's verse; he is an ardent moralist. In his fourth eclogue, the dialogue between Codrus (a rich person, relatively speaking) and Minalcas (a poor poet) considers that simply attaching one's self to a wealthy lord will bring happiness. In fact, Minalcas rejects the advice of his friend because wealthy patrons are less interested in poetry, more attuned to sensual pleasures, and more rooted in vice. Minaclas even rejects his wealthy friend Codrus on account of his own self-interest.

See also PATRONAGE.

FURTHER READING

Cooper, Helen. *Pastoral: Medieval into Renaissance.* Cambridge: D.S. Brewer, 1977.

Lewis, C. S. *English Literature in the Sixteenth Century.* London: Oxford University Press, 1954.

Daniel F. Pigg

BARNFIELD, RICHARD (1574–1620/1627)

Richard Barnfield was baptized on June 13, 1574, at Norbury, Staffordshire, at the family church of his parents, Richard Barnfield, Sr., and Maria Skrymsher. In 1581, his mother died while giving birth to a daughter, so the remainder of his childhood was supervised by his unmarried aunt, Elizabeth Skrymsher. Barnfield was educated at Brasenose College, Oxford University, where he met other budding poets of his day, including MICHAEL DRAYTON. After earning his B.A. in 1592, Barnfield began preparations for his master's studies, but he left the university rather abruptly without continuing his education.

Soon after leaving college, Barnfield moved to London, where he continued to associate with other poets and authors. Besides Drayton, Barnfield knew Thomas Watson, Francis Meres, and EDMUND SPENSER. He also developed a close friendship with WILLIAM SHAKESPEARE. While in London, his literary career took off at a rapid pace, and he quickly became one of a number of rising stars.

In 1594, Barnfield published—anonymously—his first major work, *The Affectionate Shepherd.* The piece is a reworking of VIRGIL's second ECLOGUE and is written in the classical homoerotic PASTORAL style. The two-book poem, dedicated to Lady Penelope [Devereux] Rich, celebrates the love of the shepherd Daphnis for a boy named Ganymede, who rejects him in favor of a woman. The poem caused quite a sensation, and Barnfield was forced to defend his homoerotic verse in the preface to his next work, the PANEGYRIC volume CYNTHIA WITH CERTAIN SONNETS which itself was dedicated in familiar terms to William Stanley, earl of Derby. This extraordinary long poem is written entirely in Spenserian SONNET form and celebrates Queen ELIZABETH I. It also continues to outline the competition for Ganymede's affections.

By 1598, Barnfield was being hailed by his contemporaries as one of the best pastoral writers. That year also saw the publication of his long poem *The Encomium of Lady Pecunia,* which satirized the power of money. However, this poem, and the successive ones, did not receive the high praise his previous work had. Disheartened, Barnfield faded from the scene.

For many years, critics believed that Barnfield retired to the country, married a woman named Eliza (the subject of one of his odes), and settled into bucolic country life. His will lists Richard Barnfield, supposedly his son, and his cousin Elinor Skrymsher as his executors, leading to the conclusion that he was a widower at the time of his death. More recently, however, scholars have begun to question this idyllic scene. There is no evidence of Barnfield's supposed marriage, and the will in question may have been his father's. Indeed, new evidence has shown that Barnfield was twice disinherited by his father in favor of a younger brother. Many now believe that the poet's fictitious marriage was created by early biographers to cover up Barnfield's homosexuality, and that instead of living quietly in the country as a country gentleman, he was really exiled in disgrace.

By the 19th century, Barnfield's reputation was beginning to deteriorate rapidly, as Victorian critics increasingly dismissed him as "perverse," a trend that continued through the 20th century, at least to some degree. More recently, however, Barnfield has been hailed as a "gay champion," a brave pioneer writing homosexual verse. Still other reassessments have astutely fitted Barnfield's work into the pastoral tradition. The most recent research blends these latter responses, and criticism of Barnfield's works has become increasingly sensitive and appreciative.

See also CYNTHIA WITH CERTAIN SONNETS; ENCOMIUM.

FURTHER READING

Giantvalley, Scott. "Barnfield, Drayton, and Marlowe: Homoeroticism and Homosexuality in Elizabethan Literature." *Pacific Coast Philology* 16 (1981): 9–24.

Klawitter, George, ed. *Richard Barnfield: The Complete Poems.* Selinsgrove, Pa.: Susquehanna University Press, 2001.

Worrall, Andrew. "Richard Barnfield: A New Biography." *N&Q* 39 (1992): 370–371.

"BATTLE OF ARGOED LLWYFAIN, THE" TALIESIN (late sixth century) This poem, contained in the *Book of Taliesin,* is one of the oldest poems in Welsh. It recounts a mid-sixth century battle between Owain mab Urien, son of the king of Rheged, and the men of Bernicia under Fflamddwyn (Firebrand), possibly the Anglian king Theodric. Owain taunts the "fourfold hosts of Fflamddwyn," all of whom Owain defeats and slaughters, demonstrating his prowess as a speaker and a warrior. The poet uses the historic present to make the battle feel real as the two leaders yell insults at each other. Owain incites his men into a battle frenzy from which they emerge victorious. Even the ravens are pleased, as they end up covered in gore from their grisly meals. Bards often accompanied battle parties so they would be able to provide immediate and living monuments to the leader's deeds, so this may be an eyewitness account.

See also TALIESIN; "WAR-BAND'S RETURN, THE."

FURTHER READING

Koch, John, and John Carey. *The Celtic Heroic Age.* Malden, Mass.: Celtic Studies Publishing, 2003.

Bradford Lee Eden

BATTLE OF MALDON, THE ANONYMOUS
(991) *The Battle of Maldon* describes an engagement between English and Danish Viking forces that took place on the River Blackwater three miles south of Maldon, Essex, on August 10 or 11, 991. Though the poem details a historical defeat, *The Battle of Maldon*'s importance comes not from its celebration of how the English forces fought, but rather how they died. The text epitomizes the medieval heroic code, resulting in a moral victory for the English forces.

Little is known of the anonymous author, though it has long been surmised that the poet may have been a witness to or participant in the battle itself, or was familiar with someone who was. The poem's accuracy of events has been little questioned, and while it is probable that the poem exaggerates events, the battle probably took place as was recorded. The poem survived in only one manuscript, which was destroyed by fire in 1731, though fortunately a copy had been made a few years prior. It falls into the heroic genre and tradition of ANGLO-SAXON POETRY, though it is not typical of that genre. First, it celebrates a defeat, and not a victory; second, the poem's description of the battle is atypical of similar works, such as *The Battle of Brunanburh*. The poem also has some metrical irregularities and utilizes patterns of rhyme and rhythm not typically found in classical heroic-tradition works; nonetheless, its subject is very heroic in matter, though there is also an element of ELEGY to it as well.

The poem, which is missing a few lines at both its beginning and end, commences with BYRTHNOTH, the leader of the English force, marshalling his men and issuing instructions in how to best defend the land from the Vikings. The Vikings have come to demand danegeld, or tribute in the form of gold, in exchange for not attacking the English. Byrthnoth has no intention of paying them, and conflict ensues. However, the English have the Vikings bottled up on a causeway, which prevents the full Viking force from attacking. Limited to small assaults, it seems likely that the Vikings will grow frustrated and eventually leave.

This is when the Danes resort to guile. They ask permission of Byrthnoth to cross the river, and the English general allows them. He does so because of his OFERMOD, a word that is often translated into meaning "too much honor" or "too much pride." It is unclear exactly what the poet is referring to here; it may be that the poet is criticizing Byrthnoth, who is arrogant enough to believe that his English force might prove victorious against a much larger Danish army. Or it could be that the poet believes that Byrthnoth has made a foolish if honorable decision to engage the Vikings; Byrthnoth's sense of military fairness may lead him to believe that keeping the Danes bottled up against the coast does not give them a "sporting chance" and was thus an affront to the English general's honor. Recently, critics have argued that if Byrthnoth had not allowed the Danes to cross, they would have probably sailed up the coast and attacked a town or monastery that had little or no defenses at all, leaving a civilian population to be slaughtered by the Vikings. In this case, Byrthnoth does the honorable act in engaging the Vikings because he alone has the opportunity to thwart their raids on the English coast.

Regardless of what *ofermod* entails, the poem is clear that this is a tactical, if not foolish, error on Byrthnoth's part. While the battle is close at first, the Danes have superior numbers and are better trained soldiers, and soon the battle swings in their favor. Then Byrthnoth falls. In a glorious and bloody scene, the poet describes Byrthnoth's death at the hands of the invaders by sword and spear-point. As he falls, Byrthnoth thanks God his creator and commends his soul into heaven before he expires.

Seeing the death of their leader, a few of the English forces flee, but several of the veterans step forward, proclaiming their ancestry and honor, as was typical in Old English poetry, urging the English forces to keep fighting; however, as each man rushes into battle, he is cut down by the opposing forces. Finally, an old retainer named Bryhtwold strides forward and speaks: "The bolder be each heart, / Each spirit sterner, valor more, now that our strength is less!" His exhortation to continue fighting even in the face of hopeless odds is the epitome of the heroic code.

Because of the missing lines, the poem lacks a conclusion, though it is recorded that the English lost the battle. The loss at Maldon was the first of numerous similar defeats, and in 1016, Canute the Great was crowned as king of England, solidifying the Danish conquest of England. Despite this, though, *The Battle of Maldon* remained a tremendously important piece of English battle poesy, symbolizing the epitome of the heroic code and offering a moral victory when an actual one could not be had.

FURTHER READING

Clark, George. "The Hero of Maldon: Vir Pius et Strenuus." *Speculum* 54, no. 2 (1979): 257–282.

Gordon, E. V., ed. *The Battle of Maldon*. London: Metheun Educational Ltd., 1937.

Holland, Kevin Crossley, and Bruce Mitchell. *The Battle of Maldon and Other Old English Poems*. New York: St. Martin's Press, 1966.

North, Richard. "Getting to Know the General in *The Battle of Maldon*." *Medium Aevum* 60, no. 1 (1991): 1–15.

Michael Cornelius

BEAST FABLE   Beast fables are a variety of FABLE in which animals are used to convey a certain moral lesson or truth. In beast fables, the main characters are animals and birds that are personified, taking on the characteristics of humans, such as speaking to each other. More than just simple children's tales, beast fables seek to impart a moral lesson and are often didactic in tone, demonstrating to the reader, through the antics of the animal characters, examples of the consequences certain behaviors or errors in judgment can cause. These stories are written in both poetry and prose.

Perhaps the most widely known—and one of the earliest—examples of beast fables are *Aesop's Fables*. ROBERT HENRYSON adapted these later in his MORALL FABILLIS OF ESOPE THE PHRYGIAN. MARIE DE FRANCE also adapted a collection of 103 fables, translated from Henry Beauclerc under the title of *Ysopet*.

Beast fables are usually relatively short tales; long beast fables are known as beast EPICS. The beast epic shares all of the qualities of the beast fable but is usually lengthy and involves more characters shaping a more complex story (or stories) than the shorter fables. A famous example of a beast epic is the tradition of REYNARD LITERATURE. Again, these occur in both poetry and prose.

GEOFFREY CHAUCER adapted a tale from this tradition for "The NUN'S PRIEST'S TALE." Chaucer's use of the beast fable differs from more traditional treatments of the genre. Most of his tale focuses on logic, reasoning, and dialogue rather than on narrative, action, and adventure. Overall, Chaucer's tale emphasizes philosophical and ideological ideas over moral or instructive ones.

See also MIDDLE ENGLISH POETRY, PERSONIFICATION.

FURTHER READING

Henderson, Arnold Clayton. "Medieval Beasts and Modern Cages: The Making of Meaning in Fables and Bestiaries." PMLA 97, no. 1 (1982): 40–49.

Erin N. Mount

BEHEADING GAME The folk motif of the beheading game is used to test a warrior's honor. In later ROMANCES, it became a test of knightly virtues and a measure of the warrior's CHIVALRIC OATHS. The game serves as a reminder that the surety of a man's word is worth as much as his physical prowess.

Though the most famous example of the beheading game is found in SIR GAWAIN AND THE GREEN KNIGHT, numerous European examples predate it. For instance, a ninth-century Irish EPIC features two occurrences of the game in which the hero CÚ CHULAINN emerges triumphant. Continental ARTHURIAN LITERATURE also features the game—in The Book of Carados (Le Livre de Carados) and Percival (Perlesvaus)—as do three additional Middle English Arthurian works involving Gawain: Sir Gawain and the Carl of Carlisle, The Turk and Gawain, and The Green Knight.

Andrew Bethune

BEOWULF ANONYMOUS (ca. 1000) Beowulf, a poem of 3,182 lines written in the West Saxon dialect of Old English, is preserved on folio 132r–201v (official foliation) of the British Library manuscript COTTON VITELLIUS A.XV, written around the year 1000. The unusual subject matter of the poem has made its dating an arena of fierce (and ultimately irresolvable) controversy. The poem is set in Scandinavia and deals principally with the Danes, Swedes, and Geats. For this reason, a dating before the first Viking incursions, which began at the end of the eighth century, long held sway. This was challenged in the early 1980s by a claim that the poem dated from the reign of King Canute (reigned 1016–35), but there is also considerable support for locating it to mid-10th-century East Anglia.

The poem opens with a prologue (ll. 1–52) that describes the reign of Scyld Scefing of Denmark and his descendants. Scyld was found washed up on the shore, but he became a mighty monarch and subjugated all the surrounding peoples to his authority. For this the poet characterizes him as a good king (l. 12) and continues with the observation that God sent Scyld a son, Beowulf (not the hero of this poem), as a comfort to the people. This son, too, prospers as a young man should do if he is to be supported by his people later on in time of war (ll. 20–24). Scyld's magnificent funeral is described. He is placed with great wealth on a ship and returned to the sea from whence he came (ll. 26–52).

The poem proper begins with an account of the Danish Beowulf, his son Healfdene, and his grandson Hrothgar, who also becomes a famous warrior. At the height of his power, Hrothgar builds the world's greatest mead-hall, named Heorot, and the feasting and gift-giving begins. At this point, the poet breaks in and says that it will not be long before the hall burns down as the result of dynastic feuding (ll. 83–85). Moreover, a fearsome creature hiding in the darkness, Grendel, is upset by all this merry-making. He visits the hall at night, eats 15 warriors on the spot, and carries off another 15. Grendel ravages Heorot for 12 years while Hrothgar and his warriors stand helpless. In a perverse way, Grendel becomes one of Hrothgar's hall thanes (retainers) (l. 142), but he does not play by the rules, for he refuses to pay WERGILD for the men he has killed (ll. 154–158).

While Hrothgar broods on his sorrows, news travels widely. One of the thanes of King Hygelac of the Geats (people in southwestern Sweden), the strongest man in the world of his time, hears of the tragedy, and travels to Denmark. Challenged at the doors of the hall, the Geat finally reveals his name: Beowulf. He asks for permission to see Hrothgar, who, as it turns out, had rescued Ecgtheow, Beowulf's father, by paying wergild for him. Summoned before Hrothgar, Beowulf says he has been sent by his people and asks permission to cleanse Heorot of Grendel, which task he pledges to carry out with his bare hands (ll. 435–440). Beowulf is welcomed, and at the ensuing banquet, Unferth, one of Hrothgar's councilors, challenges him. He has heard reports that Breca bested Beowulf in a swimming contest. Beowulf scornfully sets the record straight and then throws the challenge back in Unferth's face, reminding him that Grendel would not be such a problem if Unferth's words matched his deeds. The company laughs, and Hrothgar's queen, Wealhtheow, fills their cups. The banquet ends, and all depart for safer quarters except the Geats, who bed down in the hall's entrance.

Grendel, meanwhile departs for Heorot and, arriving at the hall, immediately seizes one of the Geats and devours him on the spot. Then he steps forward and encounters Beowulf. A mighty struggle follows, which ends when Beowulf tears off Grendel's arm before he flees. In the morning, all follow a blood-stained trail out to the mere (lake) where Grendel has his home, and they praise Beowulf as peerless. On the way, the SCOP tells stories of Sigmund, his nephew Fitela, a dragon fight, and the terrible king, Heremod (who reigned before Scyld Scefing) (ll. 874–915). Hrothgar thanks God both for the end of his troubles and for sending Beowulf, whom he will love as a son. Another banquet is prepared, and Beowulf receives splendid gifts. The scop tells the story of the Dane, Hnæf. While visiting his sister, Hildeburh—who was married to Finn, king of the Frisians—as a peaceweaver, Hnæf was killed, as was Finn's son, and though a truce was patched together, the Danes attacked in the spring, killing Finn and taking Hildeburh (ll. 1068–1159). After this recital, Wealtheow again pours drinks, but she also reminds Hrothgar that he already has two sons.

That night, Grendel's mother seeks revenge by carrying off one of the senior Danes. In the morning, Hrothgar challenges Beowulf to deal with her ("seek her out if you dare," l. 1379). Beowulf readily accepts the challenge and heads off to Grendel's mere. This time he is fully armed, and Unferth loans him a hafted sword called Hrunting. All of this is just as well, for when Beowulf gets to the bottom of the mere, he has a much more difficult time with Grendel's mother than he had with Grendel. Hrunting turns out to be useless. As Beowulf lies trapped under Grendel's mother, he sees a weapon on the wall made by giants. He gets free, wields it, kills Grendel's mother, and then cuts off Grendel's head. The monstrous blood causes the blade to melt, so Beowulf returns to the surface with the hilt and Grendel's head to find that, except for his Geatish companions, all have left, thinking him dead.

Beowulf returns to Heorot, where the evening banquet is already underway, with the head and the hilt for Hrothgar. As he hands them over, the poet reminds us that Hrothgar was the "best of those kings of the world who have distributed treasure in Denmark" (ll. 1684–87). Hrothgar responds in a long speech that is sometimes termed "Hrothgar's sermon" (ll. 1700–84). He thanks Beowulf for having helped the Danes, unlike Heremod, who abandoned them. Hrothgar warns Beowulf to take heed: God sometimes allows a man to achieve everything until "the whole world goes according to his desires" (ll. 1738–39). Then a portion of disdain (*oferhygd*, l. 1740; the word is an exact synonym of *OFERMOD*) begins to grow in Beowulf, and nothing seems sufficient; he is pointedly warned not to heed *oferhygd*. For the present, he may glory in his strength, but eight different possibilities are listed by which death may overwhelm him. Hrothgar continues by reminding his audience what happened to him after 50 years of successful rule, and he thanks God (not Beowulf) that he has lived to see his misery at an end. He then charges Beowulf to join in the feasting, and Beowulf does so. Hrunting is returned to Unferth, and Beowulf asks permission to return to Geatland. This is granted, but not before Beowulf is given further magnificent gifts.

The Geats return home, and Beowulf comes to Hygelac's court, where the queen, Hygd, is introduced with the story of Thryth (or Modthryth as she is also called), the imperious princess who kills the men who even dare look at her. Finally she is married to Offa, who puts an end to this kind of behavior, and Thryth becomes a model queen (ll. 1931–62). Hygelac is full of curiosity to hear about Beowulf's exploits. In his response, Beowulf discusses numerous matters for the first time, such as introducing Hrothgar's daughter, Freawaru, who has been betrothed to Ingeld, ruler of the Heathobards. Beowulf does not think this will work out, and the reason he gives echoes the narrative of Hnæf and Finn that was told earlier: The enmity between the two groups is too deep and bitter for a peace-weaver to be able to bridge it. Beowulf tells about his encounters with Grendel and Grendel's mother, and he displays the treasures that Hrothgar had given him, which he in turn gives to Hygelac. For this, Hygelac rewards him with precious weapons and a large grant of land.

The kingdom passes into Beowulf's hand (ll. 2207–08), and he rules 50 years. At this point someone disturbs the treasure guarded by a dragon, who responds enraged with an attack on the Geats (ll. 2210–20).

The section of the manuscript that describes the history, acquisition, and robbing of the dragon's hoard is severely damaged. Many speculate that the dragon, like others in Germanic myth, was originally a man who changed into a dragon because of greed. The tale resumes as the dragon burns down Beowulf's hall (ll. 2325–27). Beowulf has an iron shield made and prepares to meet this threat. He ignores Hrothgar's example to put matters in God's hands. Furthermore, the poet says he "disdained" (*oferhogode*, l. 2345, the verbal form of the *oferhygd* he was warned about earlier) to go with a troop because he had done this sort of thing alone before when he cleansed Heorot (ll. 2348–54). Beowulf does take a troop of 12 men with him, but they are to keep their distance.

This time the fight does not go well. The dragon attacks with fire, and Beowulf has to retreat. One of the men standing by, Wiglaf, cannot bear this and rushes to help him. Together they kill the dragon, but Beowulf is mortally wounded. He laments that he has no son (ll. 2729–32) and sends Wiglaf to examine the treasure and show him some of it. When Wiglaf returns, Beowulf thanks God for the treasure he is now able to leave to his people (ll. 2791–90), gives instructions for where his barrow is to be built, bids Wiglaf farewell, and dies.

The retainers now cautiously approach and are given a tongue-lashing by Wiglaf (ll. 2864–91). The news is carried to the people, and the messenger adds to the report his fears that the Geats will now be subject to the depredations of both the Franks and the Swedes (ll. 2910–3007). The treasure is loaded onto a wagon and taken to the place where Beowulf's barrow is to be. Beowulf's funeral pyre is lit, and it is watched by a Geatish woman who is apprehensive about the future, fearing the impending hostilities because for her it will mean humiliation and captivity (ll. 3150–55). The poem ends with the Geats mourning their lord and praising him for being the mildest of individuals and the most courteous, the most gracious to his people and the most eager for fame (ll. 3178–82).

Exactly how to interpret the final word, *lofgeornost*—and with it the poem—is a matter of some controversy. Is it to be understood positively, or does it have the negative connotations that characterize its usage elsewhere in Old English, where it has overtones of boasting and vainglory? It can be argued that the word is appropriate for the young Beowulf when he is making a name for himself, but it is inappropriate when he becomes a king. The poem asks Beowulf's behavior as king to be compared with that of Hrothgar, a king whose behavior is exemplary, who trusts in God and not in his own might. It is this very Christian portrayal of Hrothgar and the way it permeates the poem that is perhaps the strongest argument for a late dating. For this reason, the poem is not a heroic poem or an EPIC in any conventional way, and this helps account for what many have noted as the elegiac tone of the verse, especially in the last third of the poem.

The scholarship on *Beowulf* is enormous and so heterogeneous that there is no possible way to characterize it in general. The most influential essay ever written on the poem, and one that remains the starting point for all modern criticism, is J. R. R. Tolkien's 1937 "Beowulf: The Monsters and the Critics." Tolkien's essay insists upon seeing the poem as a complete and coherent unit that needs to be evaluated as a whole in its present form and not atomized in the search for materials on extraneous matters such as Germanic pre-Christian religion. The codicology, or study of the original manuscript, of the *Beowulf* text has been another area involving basic research. The most prominent of those working in this area has been Kevin Kiernan, whose 1981 book *Beowulf and the Beowulf Manuscript* (New Brunswick, N.J.: Rutgers University Press) initiated the controversy on dating, which continues to reverberate into the present. Even more controversial have been readings of the dragon as being the metamorphosis of the evil Danish king, Heremod. Other readings have examined the audience (or audiences) of the poem, as well as the meter, rhyme, and other poetic conventions.

More recently, studies have concentrated on the poem's women, carefully examining present and absent women in the poem, contextualizing it within Germanic culture. Power relations are an important concept here as well. Other recent scholarship has undertaken phenomenological and/or psychoanalytic approaches with varying degrees of success. More adroit, perhaps, are new anthropological approaches, which look at the "Germanic" Beowulf as a construct. Other important approaches have examined the poem as a performed text rather than an object to be read and studied. All of these views prove the endurance of what is often called the first English epic.

See also *BEOWULF*-POET, OLD NORSE/ICELANDIC EDDAS AND SAGAS.

FURTHER READING

Bjork, Robert E., and John D. Niles, eds. *A Beowulf Handbook*. Lincoln: University of Nebraska Press, 1997.

Damico, Helen. Beowulf's *Wealhtheow and the Valkyrie Tradition*. Madison: University of Wisconsin Press, 1984.

Hill, John M. *The Cultural World in Beowulf*. Toronto: University of Toronto Press, 1995.

Mitchell, Bruce, and Fred C. Robinson, eds. *"Beowulf": An Edition with Relevant Shorter Texts*. Rev. ed. Oxford: Blackwell, 2006.

Niles, John D. *Beowulf: The Poem and its Tradition*. Cambridge, Mass.: Harvard University Press, 1983.

Overing, Gillian R. *Language, Sign, and Gender in Beowulf*. Carbondale and Edwardsville: Southern Illinois University Press, 1990.

Shippey, T. A., and Andreas Haarder, eds. *Beowulf: The Critical Heritage*. London: Routledge, 1998.

Shaun F. D. Hughes

BEOWULF*-POET The *Beowulf*-poet is the anonymous author of the English EPIC *BEOWULF*. The question of authorship of the poem *Beowulf* is to a significant degree also connected with the vexed questions of date, audience, and provenance. However, a few issues may be outlined.

The first set of issues involves asking whether the poet is a single writer or whether the poem is the result of multiple composers. Criticism of the poem has vacillated to a great degree between these two views. At the beginning of modern *Beowulf* criticism, many attempted to locate a specific poet or at least a tradition in which that poet worked. Such attempts were based on the belief that the poem was written not long after the death of Hygelac (ca. 521) and that it was written during a time of high learning in Anglo-Saxon England. Thus, an author who lived sometime in the second half of the seventh century was suggested, whether Caedmon or one of his companions north of the Humber; someone in Theodore's Canterbury; or ALDHELM of Malmesbury, south of the river. In reaction against this view, there is what has come to be called the ballad theory—that is, the poem was not composed by a single person but rather, like a ballad or oral epic, was composed, retold, added to, and subtracted from in every performance until someone wrote down a performance, perhaps at the instigation of a king, lord, or other nobleman.

The result of these two competing theories was a synthesis of them. There was an "author," but at the end of a long process of oral composition. This author gave the poem its current shape and Christian overlay. Other theorists suggested a reviser of a Danish original, and there are similar attempts to mediate between the two poles of interpretation.

Since 1900, some form of a single-author theory has held the majority of the field. The question then turns on whether the poet was a Christian skaldic (Scandinavian) singer of tales, and so probably a layperson, or, rather, a learned cleric steeped in both Christian and pre-Christian traditions. However, the Christian elements in the poem, as well as the fact that throughout the Anglo-Saxon period the best opportunities for writing occurred in the context of the cloister, strongly suggest a clerical environment. Further, many have pointed out the familiarity the poet seems to have with Christian Latin sources, further indicating a clerical author.

See also ANGLO-SAXON POETRY, COTTON VITELLIUS A.XV.

FURTHER READING

Bjork, Robert E., and John D. Niles, eds. *A Beowulf Handbook* Lincoln: University of Nebraska Press, 1997.

Mitchell, Bruce, and Fred C. Robinson, eds. *Beowulf: An Edition with Relevant Shorter Texts*. Oxford: Blackwell Publishing, 1998.

Orchard, Andy. *A Critical Companion to Beowulf*. Cambridge: D.S. Brewer, 2003.

Larry Swain

BEVIS OF HAMPTON Anonymous (1320s)   A
Middle English ROMANCE, extant in varying forms in six
manuscripts, *Bevis of Hampton* is most closely related to
the ANGLO-NORMAN *Boeuve de Haumtone*. The story,
with some variations, runs thus: After his father, Guy
of Southampton, is murdered by his mother's lover,
Bevis is sold to SARACEN merchants, who carry him off
to the land of Ermonye in the East. Here, Bevis is raised
among the Saracens, establishes himself as a knight
through feats of bravery, and has Josian, the king's
daughter, fall in love with him. After being imprisoned
for seven years, escaping, rescuing Josian from an
unwilling arranged marriage, and acquiring a marvellous horse and a giant servant, Bevis and his new wife
flee to Cologne, where Josian is baptized. Afterward,
Bevis returns to reclaim his patrimony in England
before being forced once more into exile in the East.
Eventually, after the birth of two sons, a period of separation from Josian, and an eventual reunion, Bevis
wins back his English lands once more for one of his
sons, marries the other off to the daughter of King
Edgar of England, and conquers and converts the kingdom of Mombraunt in the East for himself, where both
he and Josian die after many years of happy marriage.

Recent critical approaches to the romance have
emphasized its articulation of national and cultural
identity. Like many medieval romances, *Bevis* defines
English identity through a contrast with the racial, religious, and cultural other: the Saracens. However, *Bevis*
himself is constructed as a curiously hybridized figure.
English and Christian, but raised in the East, married
to a Saracen convert, and returning to live in the East
rather than England. As such, the romance questions
the processes of medieval cultural identity, asking
whether Christian knights can remain culturally unaf-
fected by the Saracens with whom they have contact,
especially those knights who live for extended periods
in the lands of the East.

FURTHER READING

Calking, Siobhan Bly. *Saracens and the Making of English
   Identity*. New York, N.Y.: Routledge, 2005.
Rouse, Robert Allen. *The Idea of Anglo-Saxon England in Mid-
   dle English Romance*. Cambridge, UK: D.S. Brewer, 2005.

Robert Allen Rouse

BIBLICAL ALLUSIONS   An allusion is a reference to a generally well-known literary text, event, or
person that the author leaves unexplained but expects
his/her readers to know and understand. In English literature of the premodern period, both the Bible and
the CLASSICAL TRADITION provide a large storehouse of
possible allusions that authors of the period frequently
drew upon to enrich their own writings. Any part of
the Bible was "fair game" for reference, but the Creation and Fall of humanity, Genesis and Exodus, the
Incarnation and Passion, and the Apocalypse provided
the most common ones. As such, Adam and Christ are
typological partners, as are Isaac and Christ, Eve and
Mary, and so forth. Certainly others make an appearance, but the chief biblical allusions derive from the
liturgical year and the essential catechetical story.

See also EXEGESIS, HAGIOGRAPHY, VIRGIN LYRICS.

Larry J. Swain

"BIRTH OF ROBIN HOOD, THE" ANONY-
MOUS (1681–1684)   At times also referred to as
"Robin Hood's Birth, Breeding, Valour, and Marriage,"
this later ROBIN HOOD BALLAD is one in which we start
to see a change in the character of Robin Hood. The
poem is 220 lines long and arranged into 55 four-line
STANZAs rhyming *abcb*. There are three surviving versions of this ballad. In each, the title character has
begun to be gentrified.

This poem begins with the introduction of Robin of
Locksley, Nottinghamshire. His father was a forester,
and his mother (named Joan) was a niece to Guy of
Warwick and sister to Gamwell of Gamwell Hall. The
main narrative involves Robin and his mother traveling
on Christmas Eve to visit her brother Gamwell. When
they arrive, the feast resembles the royal banquets of
SIR GAWAIN AND THE GREEN KNIGHT and not of the secre-
tive and illegal forest feasts Robin and his men organized as a result of poaching. As the feast continues,
Robin is told by his uncle that he shall inherit his land
when he dies, and Robin agrees, but only if Little John
can be his page.

Robin then leaves the hall to venture into Sherwood
Forest, where a group of yeomen are living, apparently
under his watch. While there, Robin encounters Clo-

rinda, "queen of the shepherds." The two venture into the forest, whereupon she shoots a buck with her bow and arrow. Robin is smitten and wants to marry Clorinda at once; however, she is due at Titbury for a feast. Robin, Clorinda, Little John, and assorted yeomen go together to Titbury, but they are ambushed on the way. Robin kills five men at once, and then all go to the Titbury Christmas fair, where people are singing ballads and dancing. Robin and Clorinda are married by the parson, and the poem ends with a prayer for the king, that he "may get children, and they may get more, / To govern and do us some good" (ll. 219–220).

This poem highlights the turning point between the yeoman Robin Hood, who tricks the established aristocracy and ruling classes, and the Robin Hood who is of noble pedigree. At the close of *The Birth of Robin Hood*, it is clear that the gentrification of the outlaw here has made him a respected individual. Some scholars have seen this as a bit problematic: How can an outlaw hero, one who purports to know and fight for the less fortunate, originate from the very estate that seeks to dominate and oppress the less fortunate? Others have researched the clash between city life and rural life, especially the growing trend toward urbanization. Another area of interest to scholars is the character of Gamwell. *The Birth of Robin Hood* opens with a genealogy, so to speak, of English outlaws, all of whom were featured in their own narratives or included at length in a Robin Hood ballad. Of those named, only Gamwell, Robin's uncle, does not have an existing narrative; perhaps at one point there was a Gamwell outlaw narrative(s).

See also *GEST OF ROBYN HODE, A.*

FURTHER READING

Robin Hood's Birth, Breeding, Valour, and Marriage. Robin Hood and Other Outlaw Tales, TEAMS Middle English Text Series, edited by Stephen Knight and Thomas Ohlgren, 527–540. Kalamazoo, Mich.: Medieval Institute Publications, 2000.

Knight, Stephen. *Robin Hood: A Mythic Biography.* Ithaca, N.Y., and London: Cornell University Press, 2003.

Alexander L. Kaufman

"BISCLAVRET" MARIE DE FRANCE (late 12th century) The fourth of the 12 Breton *lais* of MARIE DE FRANCE, "Bisclavret" (titled in Norman French "Garwuf," or "The Werewolf," the narrator tells us) is preserved complete in one ANGLO-NORMAN manuscript. Typical of Marie's *lais* (see LAY), love is a central thematic element of the poem, yet in "Bisclavret" a base sexual relationship stands in stark contrast to the exemplary, dutiful love between a king and one of his loyal lords.

In Brittany, in northwestern France, a noble lord who is "a fine, handsome knight" (l. 17) is loved by neighbors and is very close to his king. He is married to an estimable woman who is content in all but the fact that her husband regularly disappears for three days midweek. When nagged and pressed by his wife, he admits that he becomes a werewolf, living in the woods off his hunted prey and going about unclothed. After extracting from her husband where he hides his clothes when transformed, the wife hastily offers herself to another knight who has loved her for years (and for whom she feels no love) in the hope of engaging his services. Having been told the exact route to the hiding place, the knight steals the lord's clothes, rendering him trapped in his werewolf form.

Out hunting one day, the king's hounds chase the werewolf, Bisclavret, only to see the werewolf beg on the king's stirrups for mercy. Recognizing that the beast possesses "understanding and sense" (l. 157), the king calls off his hounds and hunters and pardons the werewolf, who becomes a favorite at court. His noble behavior remains consistent until at a feast of all the king's lords and barons, he savagely attacks the evil knight who stole his clothes and who is now married to his wife. Here again, reason is key, as members of the court stay the king from punishing the beast and explain that since he has never harmed anyone before, he must surely have some grudge against the knight whom he therefore justifiably attacked. Mollified, the king spares the beast a second time.

Hearing that the king will pass near her home on a progress one day, the wife dresses herself in her finest clothes to meet him, only to be attacked by Bisclavret, who tears her nose from her face. Rather than punish the beast, the court decides that, again, Bisclavret must have had some just cause for the attack, and, under torture, the wife reveals his true identity and the deception she and her knight lover have committed.

Bisclavret's clothes are fetched. After a knight explains to the king that the beast has "great shame" (l. 288), he is left alone in a bedchamber to put on his clothes and be transformed back into a man. Upon re-entering the chamber, the king finds his beloved knight Bisclavret asleep on the bed; they embrace and kiss, rejoicing at being reunited. The wife and her knight are banished; many of the women of their lineage are born noseless (*esnasees*).

Tales of lycanthropy—the phenomenon of humans being transformed into werewolves—were popular in Europe from classical antiquity forward. Both the *Natural History* of Pliny the Elder (23–79 C.E.) and the *Satyricon* of Petronius (27–66 C.E.) contain accounts of lycanthropy, and there are numerous examples from the Middle Ages. In Marie de France's "Bisclavret," the emphasis on the beast's rational behavior, his fealty to the king, and the love the king bears him in both his human and werewolf form is particularly significant. The poem is an interesting and early example of an examination of the nature and origin of nobility and the tension that exists between nobility of blood and nobility of character. Both the wife and her lover are of a social standing that demands comportment according to established chivalric norms, yet their actions betray those norms—she willingly enters into an adulterous relationship with a knight for whom she feels no love; he betrays a lord and, by extension, his king.

The poem also invites a *demande d'amours,* or "question of love" of the sort popular in 12th-century literature of the court: Can the wife be blamed for not wanting to stay with a man who becomes a werewolf three days of the week? Here Marie leaves no doubt as to the answer to which readers should come. In Bisclavret's reasonable behavior, the court sees a startling nobility of character that leads them to defend the beast when it attacks the knight and to torture the wife when the beast has torn off her nose. In the end, the only love consistent and laudable in the poem is that between the king and Bisclavret, his loyal knight, and the wife and knight's fate is to have some of their offspring born noseless, leaving them marked with a physical deformity that signifies the unchivalrous nature of their ancestors and the base and flawed sexual love through which they were conceived.

Recent criticism of "Bisclavret" has focused on a number of tensions evident in the poem. We are told at the opening that werewolves are savages that kill men, yet the only violence the beast in the poem demonstrates are his (apparently justified) attacks on his wife and her lover. Other critical works examine the relationship between the king and Bisclavret in his werewolf and human form, positing analogous chivalric relationships in other of the *lais,* while queer readings suggest that homosocial (and perhaps homosexual) relationships are privileged. Feminist critics have examined the violence done to the wife, including her abandonment, torture, and nose-slicing.

FURTHER READING

Holten, Kathryn I. "Metamorphosis and Language in the Lay of *Bisclavret.*" In *Quest of Marie de France, a Twelfth-Century Poet,* edited by Chantal A. Maréchal, 193–211. Lewiston, N.Y.: Mellen, 1992.

Marie de France. *Lais.* Edited by Alfred Ewert. Oxford: Blackwell, 1960.

———. *The Lais of Marie de France.* Edited and translated by Robert Hanning and Joan Ferrante. Durham: Labyrinth Press, 1978.

Pappa, Joseph. "The Bewildering Bounded/Bounding Bisclavret, or Lycanthropy, Lieges, and Lotta Leeway in Marie de France." *Crossings: A Counter Disciplinary Journal* 4 (2000): 117–143.

Andrew Bethune

BLACK DEATH (1347–1351)

BLACK DEATH (1347–1351) This pestilence of massive proportions ravaged Europe in the late 1340s, reaching England in 1348 or 1349. A similar plague was reported in the Middle East, suggesting that both may have been part of a pandemic attack. It lasted two years, and by the time it was over, between one-third and one-half of Europe's population had died. Subsequent outbreaks of the plague occurred in nearly every generation for more than 300 years (the 1665 Great Plague of London is generally considered to have been the last major occurrence in England). The population level of England, which later suffered further reductions from new visitations of pestilence, did not return to its pre-1348 height for two centuries or more.

The plague took three forms: bubonic, septicemic, and pneumonic. The bubonic (from the buboes, or swellings, that appeared on the necks and armpits of victims) was the most common, probably because it had a slightly longer incubation period than the other forms and so was more easily carried from one place to another. All three were routinely fatal, and the septicemic form, in which the skin blackened as blood coagulated throughout the body, had a nearly 100% mortality rate and killed its victims in as little as a day.

The Black Death, as the first occurrence of the plague came to be called later (at the time, it was referred to simply as "the Great Mortality"), horrified those who witnessed its effects. Seemingly healthy people died within days or even hours.

Few religious or secular institutions were able to function. Communication between different parts of the countryside was exceedingly scarce. Contemporary accounts most often held that the plague was a divine punishment. WILLIAM LANGLAND wrote in PIERS PLOWMAN that "thise pestilences were for pure synne," while the chronicler Henry Knighton called the 1349 plague "God's . . . marvelous remedy" for the decadent lifestyle of the noble and merchant classes.

The plague's survivors found themselves in a much-changed world. Laborers, plentiful and comparatively powerless before 1348, suddenly became scarce. Edward III and his successor, Richard II, issued a series of labor laws, beginning with the 1351 Statute of Laborers, designed to buttress preplague pay scales and tenancy agreements. The changed circumstances of the peasant class, however, made this unenforceable. Employers competed for laborers, who felt they had the upper hand. Social unrest resulted in incidents such as the PEASANT'S REVOLT.

The culture of England after 1350 was somewhat darker than it had been. Saints' cults and the trade in relics grew, as the pardoner in GEOFFREY CHAUCER'S "THE PARDONER'S PROLOGUE AND TALE" demonstrates. Architecture became more austere, with few of the adornments that characterized buildings of the 13th and early 14th centuries. The arts reflected a heightened sense of the inevitability of death, with increased use of cadaver images on tombs and church windows, while the popularity of poems such as *Danse Macabre* (dance of death) and *Disputacione betwyx the Body and the Wormes* gives testament to the morbid fascination plague survivors had for the dead.

See also "LITANY IN TIME OF PLAGUE, A"; HUNDRED YEARS WAR; PEASANTS' REVOLT.

FURTHER READING

Hatcher, John. "England in the Aftermath of the Black Death." *Past and Present* 144 (1994): 1–35.

Ormod, W. M., and P. G. Lindley, eds. *The Black Death in England.* Stamford: Watkins, 1996.

Platt, Colin. *King Death: The Black Death and its Aftermath in Late Medieval England.* Toronto: University of Toronto Press, 1996.

John P. Sexton

"BLAME NOT MY LUTE" SIR THOMAS WYATT (ca. 1535)

Despite the title, this poem does not portray the poet as a man inspired to poetry by his lady's disdain. Instead, this lyric is addressed to a lady who has blamed the poet's lute for reporting her infidelity and broken its strings in her anger. The poet, however, asks her not to blame his instrument: "And though the songs which I indite / Do quit thy change with rightful spite, / Blame not my lute" (ll. 19–21). He goes on to argue that it is not the lute's fault because he is its master, and, in fact, the lady has no one to blame but herself: "Then since that by thine own desert / My songs do tell how true thou art, / Blame not my lute" (ll. 26–28). Although the speaker chastises the lady, it is a gentle rebuke. He reminds her just as the lute is but the poet's instrument, so, too, is the poet the instrument of truth. He must record the truth about the lady, and any spite she feels is only felt through her own design.

The poem's recipient remains unidentified. Since court poetry was meant to be performed and not published, the intended addressee might only have identified herself by the details in the lyric or by a meaningful glance from the poet, and similarly only revealed herself through a blush: "And if perchance this foolish rhyme / Do make thee blush at any time, / Blame not my lute" (ll. 40–42).

The game of COURTLY LOVE depended on the servility of the lover and his need to publicize that enslavement in verse. This poem illustrates SIR THOMAS WYATT's plain style as well as his ethical exploration of the courtly love scenario. Instead of humbly submitting to the lady's punishment, Wyatt will—must—speak the truth. He rejects the servile position that the game of love demands, and instead demands that she also live up to the truth.

See also COURT CULTURE.

FURTHER READING
Estrin, Barbara L. *Laura: Uncovering Gender and Genre in Wyatt, Donne, and Marvell.* Durham, N.C.: Duke University Press, 1994.

BLANK VERSE
Blank verse is unrhymed IAMBIC PENTAMETER, a base line of five poetic feet where each foot consists of an unstressed syllable followed by a stressed syllable. Because of the prevailing movement from unstressed to stressed, the rhythm is classified as ascending. Occasionally, iambs with other poetic feet are substituted, without exceeding the 10 total syllables per line, to complement the content of the line. Blank verse was most commonly used for writing English EPICS and dramatic works during the latter half of the 16th century and the first half of the 17th century, but it also was important within the SONNET tradition.

HENRY HOWARD, EARL OF SURREY, developed English blank verse in his translation of books 2 and 4 of VIRGIL's *Aeneid*, first published in *TOTTEL'S MISCELLANY* (1557). He adapted blank verse from the Italians' unrhymed *endecasillabo,* a poetic line consisting of 11 syllables (*versi sciolti,* or "verse freed from rhyme"). Thomas Norton and Thomas Sackville are credited with being the first to adopt Surrey's blank verse for the stage in *Gorboduc* (1561), though it was CHRISTOPHER MARLOWE who popularized it. Playwrights favored blank verse because it closely follows conversational speaking patterns in English.

Lauri S. Dietz

BLAZON (BLASON, *BLASON ANATOMIQUE*)
A blazon is a poetic technique in which a woman, often the "beloved" in a SONNET or love lyric, is described in terms of individual body parts and not as a collective whole. These descriptions are elaborate, ornate, and eroticized. In this way, the "real" woman disappears, and her image is reconstructed according to the male poet's point of view, resulting in the (re)creation of an idealized woman who thus becomes his "possession." This is particularly important in SONNET SEQUENCES, as the beloved was generally unattainable otherwise. EDMUND SPENSER's Sonnet 64 from *AMORETTI* demonstrates this technique, comparing each feature of the woman to a flower.

The blazon was often parodied, as in SIR PHILIP SIDNEY's Sonnet 91 from *ASTROPHIL AND STELLA,* wherein portions from a variety of women are employed to stave off darkness. Another variation was the antiblazon, an example of which is WILLIAM SHAKESPEARE's Sonnet 130. In an antiblazon, an individual woman is fragmented, but this division is done to describe reality, not to create (or sustain) an idealized portrait. Instances of the blazon being used to describe male bodies were unusual until the 20th century.

Officially, the *blason anatomique* did not become a poetic genre until the 16th century, but the technique was based on the iconic representations found within medieval heraldry. Heraldic devices represented the entire family, or, in some cases, knightly qualities (e.g., the pentangle in *SIR GAWAIN AND THE GREEN KNIGHT*). Precursors to the more formal blazon tradition can also be found in medieval poetry. For instance, GEOFFREY CHAUCER's portrait of the Prioress in the GENERAL PROLOGUE TO THE *CANTERBURY TALES,* which corresponds to the romance tradition, mentions "eyen grey," "coral lips," and so forth.

See also COURTLY LOVE; *RAPE OF LUCRECE, THE.*

FURTHER READING
Miller, James I. "How to See Through Women: Medieval Blazons and the Male Gaze." In *The Centre and Its Compass,* edited by Robert A. Taylor et al., 367–388. Kalamazoo, MI: Western Michigan University Press, 1993.

Sawdy, Jonathan. *The Body Emblazoned: Dissection and the Human Body in Renaissance Culture.* London: Routledge, 1995.

Stout, John. "Le Blason Contemporain: On Women Poets' Objectifying of the Male Body." *Romance Studies* 21, no. 1 (2003): 53–69.

Vickers, Nancy. "'The Blazon of Sweet Beauty's Best': Shakespeare's *Lucrece.*" In *Shakespeare and the Question of Theory,* edited by Patricia Parker and Geoffrey Hartman, 95–115. New York: Methuen, 1985.

BLIND HARY (HENRY THE MINSTREL) (1440–1493)
Blind Hary's regional origin; whether

Hary was his name, surname, or simply a nickname; and the dates of his birth and death all remain conjectural. *The Accounts of the Lord High Treasurer of Scotland* report that there were payments made to him for performances at court between 1473 and 1492, but these sporadic references only attest that he was not a regular court poet. Textual evidence from his work *The Wallace* suggests that he was well read in VERNACULAR, French, and classical literature, so it is likely that he attended a university. Blind Hary's detailed and vivid account of battles, military tactics, and scenery indicate that he might have had a military background; had traveled through Scotland, England, and France; and was probably not blind by birth. Ideologically, Hary's political sympathies lay with James III's brother, Alexander, duke of Albany and earl of March, whose policies of matrimonial alliances with the English did not please everybody. WILLIAM DUNBAR's allusion to Hary in "Timor Mortis Conturbat Me" (1505) and John Mair's in *Historia Majoris Britanniae* (1518) demonstrate that he had acquired a reputation as a poet not long after his death.

Sergi Mainer

"BLUDY SERK, THE" ROBERT HENRYSON (1460)

One of the minor poems attributed to ROBERT HENRYSON, "The Bludy Serk" is a simple ALLEGORY of 120 lines, comprising a tale whose meaning is highlighted for the reader in a moral. It tells the story of a king whose daughter is abducted by a giant. Imprisoned in a "deip dungeon," she suffers while the king searches for a champion capable of defeating her captor. A knight fights and succeeds, but is left mortally wounded. Dying, he asks the lady to take his bloody shirt, remembering it and him when other suitors come to woo her. She refuses all others. The final STANZA of the tale anticipates the moral in identifying her fidelity as the duty which humanity owes to Christ, who died "For sinfull manis saik" (l. 94).

The king is identified with the Holy Trinity, the lady with the human soul, and the giant with Lucifer. The knight is Christ, whose death redeemed humanity from the "pit" of Hell, and pious meditation on this sacrifice emerges as a duty that will preserve the believer from the temptation of sin, represented by the wooers. The theme of Christ as lover-knight is common in medieval literature. However, Henryson's treatment is distinctive, highlighting the ROMANCE elements present in the narrative by adopting the simple style and meter of the BALLAD (see BALLAD STANZA). Moreover, Henryson's method here resembles that of his *MORALL FABILLIS OF ESOPE THE PHRYGIAN,* since the relationship between tale and moral is more complex than the formal division between the two would suggest. Rather than being separate, the content of the tale foreshadows the moral—for example, in the emphasis placed on the depth of the dungeon, and on the resemblance between the giant's fingernails and "ane hellis cruk."

FURTHER READING

Schweitzer, Edward C. "The Allegory of Robert Henryson's 'The Bludy Serk.'" *Studies in Scottish Literature* 15 (1980): 165–174.

Elizabeth Elliott

BOB-AND-WHEEL

The bob-and-wheel is a metrical pattern found predominately in alliterative poetry, especially that of the *GAWAIN*-POET and other 14th-century ROMANCEs. The bob-and-wheel pattern is found at the close of STANZAS. Five lines in total, it begins with the bob, a short line, generally only two or three syllables in length, which contains one stressed syllable preceded by one or two unstressed syllables. This line is followed by a QUATRAIN called the wheel. Together, the rhyme scheme is *ababa.*

The bob both echoes the ALLITERATION of the first part of the stanza and completes the concluding TAIL RHYME. As such, it functions as a linguistic link within each stanza that connects the competing rhyme schemes into a holistic pattern. Alternatively, the bob-and-wheel pattern may be used as a BURDEN, though this is uncommon.

See also ALLITERATIVE REVIVAL, *SIR GAWAIN AND THE GREEN KNIGHT.*

BOCCACCIO, GIOVANNI (1313–1375)

Giovanni Boccaccio spent his formative years at court in Naples, where he wrote several courtly ROMANCEs, one of the most influential being *Teseida, o delle nozze* d'Emilia (*Theseid, or on the nuptials of Emily*). However, it was after his return to Florence that he composed his masterpiece, the *Decameron*. Begun in the late 1340s, it is a FRAME NARRATIVE comprising 100 tales told by seven women and three men who have fled to the country seeking refuge from the plague (see BLACK DEATH). Though the stories vary widely, the collection as a whole presents humans overcoming changing fortunes and inevitable tribulations using their wit and skill (*ingegno*).

About 1350, Boccaccio met PETRARCH (Francesco Petrarca), which had a profound impact on him. Afterward, Boccaccio wrote predominantly in Latin, turning away from the Italian VERNACULAR that he had favored before. In these later years, he produced an encyclopedic account of the gods, *Genealogia gentilium deorum* (*Genealogy of the Gentile Gods*), as well as two compendious catalogues of famous men and women, *De casibus virorum illustrium* and the *De mulieribus claris*.

Boccaccio's influence in England is most profoundly felt in the work of GEOFFREY CHAUCER, and subsequent use of Boccaccio owes a great deal to Chaucer's translations and transmission of his work. For instance, the opening tale of *The CANTERBURY TALES,* told by the Knight, is derived from the *Teseida*. Book 7 of the *Teseida* is used again for the representation of the temple of Venus in *The PARLIAMENT OF FOWLS*. *Filostrato,* which features the story of Troilus and Cressida, inspired numerous adaptations, including ones by Chaucer, ROBERT HENRYSON, and WILLIAM SHAKESPEARE. The *Decameron* provides direct analogues for "The REEVE'S TALE," "The Clerk's Tale," "The Merchant's Tale," "The Franklin's Tale," and "The Shipman's Tale," and it has connections with "The MAN OF LAW'S TALE," "The PARDONER'S TALE," and "The MILLER'S PROLOGUE AND TALE." In the 15th century, JOHN LYDGATE made use of Boccaccio's work as well, as his *The FALL OF PRINCES* is indebted to the *De casibus* via French translation.

FURTHER READING

Bergin, Thomas G. *Boccaccio*. New York: Viking, 1981.
Wallace, David. *Chaucer and the Early Writings of Boccaccio*. Cambridge: D.S. Brewer, 1985.

K. P. Clarke

BOETHIUS (ANICIUS MANLIUS SEVERINUS BOETHIUS) (480–525)

Anicius Manlius Severinus Boethius was born in Rome to a politically influential family. Orphaned at a young age, he was raised in the household of Symmachus, a well-known aristocrat of the time, and eventually he married Rusticiana, Symmachus's daughter, with whom he had two sons.

Boethius is often dubbed the last of the ancients and first of the scholastics, reflecting his pivotal position between classical Greek and Roman traditions and those of the medieval period. He became consul in 510 and by 520 was *magister officiorum* to Theodoric the Great. He was accused of treason in 523 and was eventually executed. His guilt or innocence in regard to the charges remains controversial to this day. While in prison, Boethius wrote *The CONSOLATION OF PHILOSOPHY,* which, although largely ignored at the time, became a highly influential work throughout the medieval period and was later translated by ALFRED THE GREAT, GEOFFREY CHAUCER, and Queen ELIZABETH I.

See also FORTUNE, *METERS OF BOETHIUS*.

Lisa L. Borden-King

"BONNIE GEORGE CAMPBELL" ("BONNIE JAMES CAMPBELL") ANONYMOUS (15th century)

In its various versions, "Bonnie George Campbell" reflects a relatively common theme of tragic folk BALLADS: the death of a handsome young hero and the resulting sadness for his loved ones. The concentrated power of this ballad is typical of the genre. Bonnie George—or Bonnie James—Campbell rides off boldly. His horse, still saddled and bridled, then returns without him, and his family must consider him dead. Poignantly, we feel their grief. Whether the "bonnie" (handsome) hero rode to war or not is subject to the version of the song being considered and its interpretation.

In *The English and Scottish Popular Ballads,* Francis Child includes four versions of the song (labeled A, B, C, and D), of which the C version of the ballad is the best known. It begins "Hie upon Hielands, / and laigh upon Tay, / Bonnie George Campbell / rode out on a day" (ll. 1–4). This version apparently grew out of the idea that Bonnie George was going to war. Later editors added the lines "A plume in his helmet, / a sword at his knee," (l. 10) leaving little doubt that Bonnie George is prepared for battle. In other versions, however, Bonnie George/James simply goes riding.

The opening of the song conjures up the rugged highlands and scenic rivers of Scotland. The ballad is written in an evocative Scots dialect. The archaic quality of the language is part of its appeal to later generations who are taken back to the feudal world of the Highland clans.

"Bonnie George Campbell" probably dates from the late 1500s. Some critics have suggested that it refers to the 1594 Battle of Glenlivet, in which cousins Alexander Campbell and John Campbell died fighting for the cause of Protestantism with 10,000 Highlanders against a well-trained army of 2,000 fighting for Catholicism; however, there is no hint of religion in the ballad.

The ballad also highlights the traditions of Scotland. The beauty of the Highlands is an appropriate background for the heroes produced by the land, supporting the English belief that the clans were medieval or feudal in their chivalry and martial virtue. The heroic sense is heightened when combined with the ballad's rich, plaintive minor-key melody, the most popular of the different musical versions. In various versions, we find the wife pregnant with the child Bonnie George will never see; a loving mother mourning her fine son; and the fields that bloom again every year ironically juxtaposed with the fact that Bonnie George Campbell will never, never return.

Eric P. Furuseth

"BONNY EARL OF MURRAY, THE"
ANONYMOUS (16th century) A popular Scottish folk BALLAD that valorizes the rivalry between James Stewart, earl of Murray (or Moray) and the earl of Huntly. The conflict peaked in 1592, when Huntly murdered Murray, whom he believed to be conspiring with the earl of Bothwell against King JAMES VI (later James I). Murray's castle was torched, and Huntly was caught in Fife and executed. Huntly's actions were widely condemned, though the Crown did not punish him. The ballad diverges from history as it assigns to James a speech explicitly berating Huntly, perhaps in an attempt

to keep it from being declared treasonous. It also includes erroneous apocrypha about Murray being the queen's lover and next in line for the throne.

The first STANZA of this ballad is the source of the term *mondegreen* (misheard lyric). In popular culture, lines 3 and 4 ("They have slain the Earl of Murray, / And they layd him on the green") were long thought to be "They have slain the Earl of Murray, and Lady Mondegreen."

See also BORDER BALLADS, "LORD RANDAL."

FURTHER READING
Ives, Edward D. *The Bonny Earl of Murray: The Intersections of Folklore and History.* Champagne: University of Illinois Press, 1997.

BOOKE OF AYRES, A THOMAS CAMPION
(1601) THOMAS CAMPION's *A Book of Ayres,* which contains 21 lyrics for a single voice accompanied by the lute, reflects a new emphasis on the clarity of the words in songs. This work stands in stark in contrast to the MADRIGAL tradition, where the lyrics were often obscured by overlapping parts and multiple notes on individual syllables. The book is a collection of individual, self-contained poems which feature a wide range of personae and themes, and which demonstrate Campion's dexterity in both music and verse. Campion's poems were published as a collaboration effort with Philip Rosseter, a professional lutenist, who added another 21 AYRES of his own.

Most of the poems in *A Booke of Ayres* deal with themes of love. They range from songs of wooing and conquest ("I CARE NOT FOR THESE LADIES") to those dealing with loss and thwarted love ("WHEN TO HER LUTE CORINNA SINGS"). Some, like "My Love Hath Vowed," take on a female persona. Several of the songs draw inspiration from classical sources. For instance, in "MY SWEETEST LESBIA," the first STANZA is a loose translation of a poem by Catullus (ca. 84–54 B.C.). The final lyric in Campion's collection, "Come, Let Us Sound," turns to a divine theme and is a paraphrase of Psalm 19 from the Bible. This seriousness is also foreshadowed by the 18th song, "The Man of Life Upright," which advocates a withdrawal from worldly affairs. Other than this, the poems do not appear to have even a loose relation to each other. Thus, there is no sense of an overarching theme or development of a narrative.

Campion defends his form and subject matter in his preface to the collection. He describes the ayre as the musical equivalent of the EPIGRAM—that is, pithy, brief, and witty—and asserts that both forms achieve "their chiefe perfection when they are short and well seasoned." He admits that amorous, lighthearted songs, like his ayres, are often seen as less worthy than such serious or divine forms as the motet (a religiously themed unaccompanied part song), but he asserts that such apparently frivolous material still has its share of "Art and pleasure." Indeed, Campion is anxious to emphasize the effort and level of skill that goes into creating such brief poems. He argues that in such a condensed form, the poet has little to hide behind, and thus an ayre "requires so much the more invention to make it please."

The ayres are strophic poems. They all include at least two STANZAS, and each stanza repeats the meter and rhythm of the first. This enables the poems to be set to the same music for each stanza. Campion's music often features internal repeats, where the same music is used for more than one line, and this economy of material enhances the songs. His skillful musical arrangements effectively erase any metrical irregularities. The musical repetition also enables him to meditate on his CONCEITS and to develop his themes in a unified way.

See also STROPHE.

FURTHER READING

Davis, Walter R. *The Works of Thomas Campion*. London: Faber, 1969.

Lindley, David. *Thomas Campion*. Leiden: Brill, 1986.

Susan L. Anderson

BOOK OF THE DUCHESS, THE GEOFFREY CHAUCER (ca. 1368–1372)

The Book of the Duchess is the first major work by GEOFFREY CHAUCER, who wrote it sometime during the years 1368–72. Written in octosyllabic COUPLETS, the 1,335-line poem is a veritable mosaic of several genres—including ALLEGORY, DREAM VISION, ELEGY, and ROMANCE—infused with themes of love, loss, and consolation. It was most likely written as an occasional poem (a poem written to commemorate an event) commemorating the death of Blanche, duchess of Lancaster and wife of John of Gaunt; she perished from the BLACK DEATH on September 12, 1368. Gaunt had been Chaucer's patron since the late 1350s, and it is possible that the annuity the duke issued to Chaucer in 1374 was payment for writing *The Book of the Duchess*.

Because it has been so pervasively presumed that *The Book of the Duchess* was written as both an elegy to Blanche and a consolation for Gaunt, most readers have assumed that its principal characters are allegorized figures modeled on real-life personages—that is, the Black Knight represents John of Gaunt, White represents Blanche of Lancaster, and the unnamed male Narrator represents Chaucer. Also prominent within the poem are the intertextual connections between these three characters of Chaucer's invention and those he borrows from other sources—namely Ceys and Alcyone, the protagonists of a "romaunce" (l. 48), derived from OVID's *Metamorphoses*, which the Narrator reads prior to his dream vision. Many critics have suggested that rather than elegizing Blanche explicitly and addressing John of Gaunt directly, Chaucer instead elected to portray the fictional Black Knight eulogizing White/Blanche within the Narrator's vision—a scenario anticipated by the Narrator's bedtime reading, wherein Alcyone mourns the death of Seys.

Chaucer refers to *The Book of the Duchess* in two of his other major works. In the prologue to LEGEND OF GOOD WOMEN, Queen Alceste includes "the Deeth of Blaunche the Duchesse" in a list of the male Narrator's writings (l. 410) and in the (in)famous Retraction to *The CANTERBURY TALES*, Chaucer's narrator mentions "the book of the Duchesse" (l. 1087) in a repentant catalogue of his own writings. Thus, though none of the four known manuscripts of the text name Chaucer, a 15th-century source, JOHN LYDGATE's *Fall of Princes*, attests to Chaucer's authorship.

Though influenced by VIRGIL, OVID, and BOETHIUS, *The Book of the Duchess* remains primarily indebted to Middle French literature. The insomniac Narrator and the poem's dream-vision frame parallel Jean Froissart's *Le Paradys d'Amours* (*The Paradise of Love*, ca. 1369) a dream vision that in turn was influenced by the writings of Guillaume de Machaut, including his *Le Dit de la fonteinne amoureuse* (Story of the amorous fountain), which also retells the Ovidian Seys and Alcyone story.

Of pivotal significance, however, is the French *Roman de la Rose* (Romance of the Rose), of which a partial English translation has been attributed to Chaucer.

The Book of the Duchess does not feature a conventional guide figure. Instead, the poem begins by bringing the narrator's central dilemma to the forefront—he is a "melancolye" (l. 23) insomniac whose numbing sadness and unnatural ("agynes kynde," l. 26) condition have brought him to the brink of death. Though the source/cause for his near-death circumstance is not named, he conveniently provides his own self-diagnosis: "I holde it be a sicknesse / That I have suffred this eight yeer" (ll. 36–37). He goes so far as to suggest that "there is phisicien but oon / That may me hele" (ll. 39–40) but immediately adds "that is don. . . . Our first mater is good to kepe" (ll. 40–43). Thus, the Narrator acknowledges that there is an individual who can heal him, but he then refuses to name or even describe that person. Instead, the narrator bids his servant "reche [him] a book / A romaunce" (ll. 47–48) to read.

This tale is a truncation from Ovid's *Metamorphoses* and recounts the story of King Seys and Queen Alcyone: Seys is drowned at sea, and Alcyone, not knowing what has happened, laments intensely over his disappearance. Alcyone pledges herself to Juno, begging the goddess to send her a dream in which the fate of Seys will be revealed to her. Juno sends a messenger to Morpheus, the god of Sleep, who then, as per Juno's instructions, "crepe[s] into the body" of the dead king (l. 144) and speaks to Alcyone through the corpse to inform her that Seys is dead. Seys/Morpheus advises Alcyone that though temporal "blysse" is temporary and fleeting, holding on to sorrow is not a viable alternative. Alcyone's response, as recorded by the narrator, is telling: "With that hir eyen up she casteth / And saw noght. 'Allas!' quod she for sorwe, / And deyede within the thridde morwe" (ll. 212–214).

The narrator empathizes with Alcyone, whose sorrow and unknowingness reflect his own position at the beginning of the poem; however, when he recognizes the chance to tell his audience what she said while in her state of anguish, he chooses to silence her. Explaining his reasoning for doing so, he submits this excuse, which becomes all too familiar throughout Chaucer's oeuvre: "I may not telle yow now; / Hyt were to longe

for to dwelle" (ll. 216–217). In this instance, the narrator withholds information about a female character in favor of returning the focus of his narrative back to himself, saying: "My first matere I wil yow telle, / Wherfore I have told this thyng / Of Alcione and Seys the kyng" (ll. 218–220). Though for the next 70 lines, the narrator explains how "this thyng" has saved his life. Subsequent readers of this Ovidian episode have been far less appreciative. Feminist critics have taken the figure of the poet to task for silencing and exploiting Alcyone in his appropriation of a fictional female experience. Alcyone awakens from her dream vision, sees nothing, and dies; by contrast, the Chaucerian narrator who reads her story presumably awakens from his dream, recovers from his sleepless melancholy, picks up his pen, and moves on with his life and career as a poet.

In the next section of the poem, the narrator further laments his sleeplessness, although still asleep. Lines 291–343 capture the Narrator's surroundings in the dream world with acute aural and visual details. It is a sunny day in May, and the narrator is awakened within his dream by small birds, only to find himself "in [his] bed al naked" (l. 293). Significantly, the walls of this space are decorated with scenes from "the story of Troye" (l. 326) and painted with "bothe text and glose, / Of al the Romaunce of the Rose" (334). Blurring the boundaries between inside and outside, birdsongs resonate throughout the room and "bryghte bemes" (l. 337) of sunlight pour through the windows and onto the narrator's bed.

The next section describes the hunt in conventional garden imagery (ll. 344–443). Hearing "an hunte blowe" (l. 345), the narrator moves outdoors, mounts a horse, and rides off into the surrounding forest. Upon encountering a young man with a hound, he learns that the hunting party is with the ancient Roman "emperour Octovyen" (l. 368). Together, the Narrator and the lad travel until they meet up with the hunters, who forfeit their sport when their quarry—the "hert" (l. 381), or male red deer—outsmarts them and disappears. Now on foot, the Narrator walks through the forest and is approached by a lost "whelp" (l. 389). He follows the puppy deeper into the woods, traipsing through the shadows cast by the gigantic trees, until he finally becomes aware of "a man in blak" (l. 445) who is standing with his back to "an ook, an huge tree" (l. 447).

It takes over 100 lines for the Narrator to describe the Black Knight (ll. 444–559). As he voyeuristically gazes at (and into) the Knight's body, he infers that the "man" is a virtually beardless, but "wel-farynge knyght" (l. 452) of about 24 years old. Like the Narrator and Alcyone, the Black Knight is suffering in a state of acute sorrow that the Narrator labels as unnatural, thereby aligning himself with the man's condition. By eavesdropping on the Black Knight's love plaint, delivered as an unmelodious LAY, the Narrator discovers the Knight's love, his "lady bryght" (l. 477), has died—or, rather, this is the information that the Knight unmistakably discloses, and which the Narrator, for ambiguous and ultimately unknowable reasons, somehow forgets, or pretends to forget, as soon as he records it.

The Narrator eventually steps out of the shadows and approaches the Knight. As the two engage in a cordial and courtly conversation, the Narrator notices "how goodly spak thys knyght, / as hit had be another wyght" (ll. 529–530), and feminist readers have since noted that the Black Knight speaks like a woman and occupies a position filled elsewhere in medieval romances by fairy ladies. When the Narrator brings up the appropriately manly topic of the hunt, the Black Knight admits that he does not care about hunting—his mind is elsewhere. The Narrator acknowledges the Black Knight's sorrow and offers to listen to his companion's story and do whatever he can to "make [him] hool" (l. 553). From the Black Knight's monologue that follows, the audience learns more about him and the lady he loved and lost than is ever revealed about the Narrator and the unnamed object of his desire.

Lines 560–709 are spent explicating the Black Knight's sorrow. After a lengthy diatribe about all that is backward and unnatural about his existence, the Black Knight says the figure responsible for his sorrowful state is FORTUNE, an immortal female figure whom he describes disparagingly as a "trayteresse fals and ful of gyle . . . I lynke hyr to the scorpioun" (ll. 620, 636). The Black Knight's condemnation of Fortune says more about his character than hers: He played a metaphorical game of chess with her, lost his queen, and lost the game. Many critics have scrutinized this use of the chess metaphor, which Chaucer gleaned from his French sources and apparently did not understand. The Black Knight is an inept player and a sore loser: in one breath he condemns Fortune for defeating him, and in another exonerates her, saying he would have done exactly the same thing if he had been in her position (ll. 675–676).

Lines 710–757 take a comic turn, as the Narrator tries to tell his companion that his life is not as bad as it seems, and he subtly insults the Black Knight by implying that he is behaving like the irrational, suicidal women of literary tradition who have been abandoned by their lovers. According to the Narrator, only a fool would kill himself over a woman. In his own defense, the Black Knight suggests that the Narrator does not know what he is talking about, insisting: "I have lost more than thow wenest" (l. 744). The Black Knight proceeds to take charge of the conversation, and in lines 758–1311, he explains how he dedicated himself to the service of love, and how he fell in love with a "fair and bryght" lady called "White" (ll. 948, 950). The Black Knight recounts how he wooed White—loving her in secret, making a first supplication to her and being rejected, and making a second supplication a year later, which she accepts (ll. 1144–1297). All of this love talk is punctuated by humorous banter between the bumbling Narrator and the defensive Black Knight, leaving White's words noticeably out of the conversation. In fact, the one line attributed to White, "'Nay'" (l. 1243), is actually a paraphrase of her initial response to the Black Knight, who says he can only restate "the grete / Of hir answere" (ll. 1242–1243). The Black Knight, like the Narrator, silences the woman.

In the final 35 lines, the Narrator, for ambiguous reasons, forces the Black Knight to divulge the source of his sorrow: White "ys ded" (l. 1309). Afterward, the dream abruptly ends, and the narrator wakes to find himself in bed with his book about Seys and Alcyone in hand. The urgency of his near-fatal insomnia is replaced by incongruous carelessness. Waxing laconic about his unusual dream, he decides to someday translate it into "ryme" (l. 1332).

Most dream visions include an obligatory post-dream exposition in which the Dreamer reveals what special insight he or she has gained. Chaucer's text, however, noticeably omits any such explanation about just what made the Narrator's dream so "inwardly sweet" and therefore calls the very genre and purpose of his dream vision into question. Moreover, many romances and love visions tell the story of a man who seeks the love of a woman—but in this case, the courtly lady is dead.

The fictive White, like the actual Blanche, does not appear as a living and speaking subject in Chaucer's text. Instead, her character is reconstructed through a discourse between two men, the Narrator and the Black Knight, prompting feminist and gender critics to wonder if anyone—the narrator, Chaucer, John of Gaunt—is actually in pain and sorrow over the duchess's death. The tale has less to do with Blanche than it does with the men involved, revealing their relationships and alliances. Thus, its primary concern is the development of male textual and (hetero)sexual identity, not marriage or mourning.

FURTHER READING

Hansen, Elaine Tuttle. *Chaucer and the Fictions of Gender.* Berkeley: University of California Press, 1992.

Hendershot, Cyndy. "Male Subjectivity, *Fin Amor,* and Melancholia in *The Book of the Duchess." Mediaevalia* 21 (1996): 1–26.

Horowitz, Deborah. "An Aesthetic of Permeability: Three Transcapes of the *Book of the Duchess." Chaucer Review* 39 (2005): 259–279.

Margherita, Gayle. "Originary Fantasies and Chaucer's *Book of the Duchess.*" In *Feminist Approaches to the Body in Medieval Literature.* Edited by Linda Lomperis and Sarah Stanbury, 116–141. New Cultural Studies. Philadelphia: University of Pennsylvania Press, 1993.

Christopher D. Lozensky

BORDER BALLADS (15th and 16th centuries)

"The Border" refers to the border area between England and Scotland, geographically isolated and subject to centuries of conflict, allowing the development of an historical and cultural autonomy. As such, border ballads reflect the area in which they developed—riding, raiding, feuding, treachery, foray, and rescue. Many contain a supernatural element. Very few of these BALLADS contain allusions to the political events of their times.

These ballads are distinctive for their spareness. The simplicity of language and syntax goes hand in hand with the extreme economy of expression, accompanied by great evocative power in the choice of place names. This stylistic choice is connected with the intended audience: Ballads were generally recited, or more frequently sung, by minstrels who accompanied themselves with a musical instrument, generally playing modal, monodic, and homophonic tunes. These regional characteristics and the historical circumstances in which the ballads were performed link them to medieval ROMANCES.

See also BALLAD (FOLK BALLADS); "LORD RANDAL"; *TWA CORBIES, THE.*

FURTHER READING

Reed, James. *The Border Ballads.* London: Athlone, 1973.

Alessandra Petrina

BRETON *LAI* See LAY.

"BRING US IN GOOD ALE" ANONYMOUS (mid-15th century)

This drinking song, loosely dated to the time of Henry VI (1421–71), is connected with the Christmas season through its melody—a speeded-up version of the Christmas CAROL "Nowell, Nowell, Nowell"—and by connection to the Christmas custom of wassailing (from *wassail,* "good health"). In this festive activity, merry revelers go from house to house, singing and drinking.

The opening and chorus of the song celebrate excess, repeating: "Bring us good ale, and bring us in good ale, / For our blessed lady's sake, bring us in good ale." However, no one is interested in food. The revelers create mock excuses for why they cannot have any: Brown bread is "made of bran," bacon is "passing fat," mutton is "often lean," and, eggs have "many shells." The food list goes on and on and, obviously, lends itself well to additions and revisions by witty wassailers, recreatings a Christmas feast through words.

FURTHER READING

Rickert, Edith. *Ancient English Christmas Carols: 1400–1700.* London: Chatto/Windus, 1914.

Eric P. Furuseth

BRUCE, THE (THE BRUS) JOHN BARBOUR (ca.
1376)   *The Bruce,* JOHN BARBOUR's only surviving text,
stands as the first preserved literary work in Scots literature. Its importance is twofold, both as a literary
work of art and as a historical account of the life and
deeds of ROBERT I THE BRUCE. Containing about 12,000
verses, the poem was originally divided into 150 long
paragraphs or sections; it subsequently was divided
intto 20 books.

Historical evidence places Barbour's lifetime sometime around 1320–1395. When King Robert II, grandson of Robert I, commissioned him to write *The Bruce,*
Barbour was archdeacon of Aberdeen. Through the
example of Robert Bruce as a *speculum principis* (MIRROR
OF PRINCES genre), it was the main political intention of
this ROMANCE to encourage the nobles at Robert II's
court to support their monarch at a time when royal
authority was frail. As opposed to the other late medieval makars (poets), the Scottish Chaucerian tradition
did not exert any influence on Barbour's narrative.

Ideologically, the exercise of good kingship and
Scotland's national freedom are at the core of *The Bruce.*
Robert the Bruce's first intervention expounds the con-
ceptualizations of kingship and nation: "'Sir,' said he
[Robert the Bruce], 'I do not wish to have this Kingdom unless it falls to me by right" (1.157–159). God is
the only one with the authority to determine who the
rightful king of Scots should be. The Bruce implicitly
refuses Edward's role as an arbiter for the Scottish succession and advocates the autonomy of the realm and
its sovereign against any foreign threat such as of
Edward I. Continuing on, the Bruce alludes to the old
ancestry of rulers in Scotland, which legitimizes the
above-mentioned autonomy: ". . . I shall hold at [my
Kingdom] free . . . as my ancestors did before me"
(1.61, 63). Thus, his first words establish the hero's
principles for the adequate government of the country,
based on divine, legal, and ethnic premises.

National freedom has been traditionally considered
to be central to Barbour's general tenets. He introduces
this issue through a debate on the relativity of freedom
(1. 223–274) and the need to have a king who guaran-
tees both national and personal liberties within the
constraints of the feudal system. The author also dis-
credits Bruce's rivals to the Scottish throne, Edward de
Balliol and John Comyn, since they are willing to submit to Edward I in exchange for personal promotion
(1. 168–178 and 1. 557–581, respectively). In *The
Bruce*'s ideological project, there is room for individual
ambitions, but the collective national good must always
be prioritized.

Balliol's treason relates to the betrayals of the Nine
Worthies (nine historical figures seen as the embodiment of CHIVALRY: Hector, Alexander the Great, Julius
Caesar, Joshua, David, Judas, Macabeus, King ARTHUR,
Charlemagne, and Godfrey of Bullion). First, Barbour
alludes to Troy (1.521–526), then to "Alexander ye
conqueroure," who was "dystroyit throw pwsoune"
(1.529–535), followed by Julius Caesar (1.537–548)
and Arthur (1.549–560). This serves to match Bruce's
prowess with that of the heroes mentioned, marking
him the Tenth Worthy. Barbour's construction of his
hero emanates from both medieval and classical traditions, creating not only a unique hero different from
other medieval warriors, but also a new and distinctive
way of composing heroic literature in the VERNACULAR.

James Douglas, the second most important hero in
the narrative, is also constructed as an ideal knight.
Barbour projects an image of Douglas defined both by
EPIC virtues and romance traits. The amalgamation of
both traditions is devised to accomplish a paramount
objective: A deed of chivalry no longer serves personal
ambitions but also must contribute to the epic—and
national—cause.

Consistent with this idea, Barbour openly criticizes
Edward Bruce, Robert's brother, for his excessively
knightly conduct. Before Bannockburn, Edward's conduct is exemplary. Afterward, however, his chivalrous
ambitions increase disproportionately until his death
in battle against Ireland. His foolhardiness prompts
both his death and the collapse of Scottish aspirations
to liberate—or simply conquer—Ireland. This helps
Barbour to justify those instances where patriotic prag-
matism leads the Scots into unchivalric behavior. The
authorial control of the narrative anticipates a possible
negative response on the audience's part and, at the
same time, manipulates their reaction.

Another similar, later passage involves Randolph,
Robert the Bruce's nephew. Randolph complains about
the use of guerrilla warfare, believing the Scots should

confront the English in "playne fechting" (open fighting, 9.750). Randolph does not comprehend the Scottish reality yet, though Bruce does. Eventually, however, Randolph sees the truth. Barbour designed this situation to justify guerrilla tactics before his courtly audience, assuring them that the national liberty of Scotland is more important than chivalrous war.

Barbour subverts literary convention by attaching a great deal of importance to the lower social classes. Both the commoners and the nobility suffer from the English oppression in the same manner, and the Bruce must earn everyone's respect. In book 2, the peasants initially opt not to follow Bruce, but Barbour does not condemn their conduct (2.503–510). He implies that this is an understandable demeanour, since Bruce cannot now fulfil the duty to protect his subjects. Later, upon Bruce's return to Scotland, the people are too frightened of the English to collaborate with him (5.123–132), and Barbour understands their behavior once more. Bruce must show that he is a proper national leader who can take care of his subjects before they pay fealty to him. Once they accept him, however, the peasants prove helpful; indeed, it is their intervention in the Battle of Bannockburn that secures victory (13.225–264). Thus, in the climax of the romance, Barbour destabilizes the chivalric code by this displacement of roles. On doing this, the author emphasizes the importance of every single Scot, regardless of their social status.

The martially centered focus of the narrative does not allow for the development of COURTLY LOVE. Idealized, courteous scenes are little more than incidental because of the minimal presence of female characters. Robert the Bruce's well-known extramarital affairs are mentioned in passing (5.543–546), where his mistresses are given a practical rather than amorous role since they are labeled as informers. Not even Bruce's relationship with his wife Elizabeth gets much attention; she is referred to as the "quen(e)" without any further individualization. From the moment the English kidnap her (4.39) until she is freed again (13.693–697), she disappears from the narrative; her husband does not give her a single thought. By removing women, Barbour redefines courtesy in The Bruce to confirm Bruce's ideological purpose.

Barbour redefines courtesy not as social exchanges between the upper classes as a marker of their status, but rather as interclass communication, challenging late medieval literary and societal conventions. The Bruce displays the same courtesy with the few female characters no matter their class. In 16.270–296, the Bruce stops his army's advance to help a laundress to give birth. The poet could have regarded the king's demeanor as an act of mercy toward a commoner or transformed the laundress into a helpless lady; instead, he explicitly underlines Bruce's chivalry: "Yis wes a full gret curtasy" (16.293). This is a very rare example of how courtesy is transferred to an interclass exchange between a nobleman and a commoner. By subverting this literary convention, Barbour constructs Bruce as a people's king with an egalitarian behavior toward all Scots.

Bruce's death follows the archetypal model for kings and rulers in late medieval literature. In book 20, Scotland and England sign a treaty in which England recognizes Robert I's sovereignty and the independence of the country (20.55–58). After the monarch's death, the vassals' devotion and grief permeate the narrative (20.263–268). The Bruce secures his way into paradise by going on a crusade even after perishing when Douglas takes his heart to Spain to fight the Arabs. As a Christ-like figure, by symbolically rising from the dead, the king of Scots consummates the holy enterprise of confronting the heathen.

See also SCOTTISH CHAUCERIANS.

FURTHER READING

Ebin, L. A. "John Barbour's *Bruce*: Poetry, History and Propaganda." *Studies in Scottish Literature* 9 (1971–72): 218–242.

Goldstein, R. J. *The Matter of Scotland.* Lincoln and London: University of Nebraska Press, 1993.

Kliman, B. W. "The Idea of Chivalry in Barbour's *Bruce.*" *Studies in Scottish Literature* 35 (1973): 477–508.

Sergi Mainer

BRUSSELS CROSS (11th century) A reliquary (relic case) now housed in the Cathedral of Sts. Michael and Gudule in Brussels, Belgium, the badly damaged wooden cross, once covered in silver and jewels, bears an inscription, in FUTHARK runes, resembling lines from *The Dream of the Rood*, a DREAM VISION written in the West Saxon dialect of OLD ENGLISH.

The craftsman Drahmal (whose name is carved in the plate) constructed the cross in England, probably in the early 11th century. Besides the poem, the cross features a dedication: "To Ælfric from his brothers, Æthelmær and Æthelwold." Numerous attempts to identify the three brothers have proved unsuccessful, and the cross remains something of a mystery.

See also RUTHWELL CROSS.

FURTHER READING

d'Ardenne, Salvina. "The Old English Inscription on the Brussels Cross." *English Studies* 21 (1939): 145–164, 271–272.

BRUT, THE LAYAMON (ca. 1155)

LAYAMON's *The Brut* is a verse CHRONICLE of the history of England from the time of its alleged founding by the legendary Brutus, great-grandson of the Trojan hero Aeneas, until the last British king. Included in its contents is the reign of King ARTHUR.

The Brut comprises more than 16,000 lines of alliterative verse divided into HALF-LINES. It survives in two manuscripts, both dating to the later 13th century. Contrary to other renditions of early Britain, *The Brut* strips away most of the lavish aristocratic settings, focusing instead on the plight of ordinary people. This, coupled with its VERNACULAR composition, may indicate that its intended audience was nonaristocratic. On the other hand, the sheer cost of producing a manuscript of such length suggests wealthy PATRONAGE, and most of the aristocracy were bilingual.

After the NORMAN CONQUEST, there was a renewed interest in the history of Britain, leading to the proliferation of chronicles, both verse and prose. For his poem, Layamon used source material from the Venerable Bede's *Ecclesiastical History of the English People* (*Historia Ecclesiastica*), the ANGLO-SAXON CHRONICLE, Geoffrey of Monmouth's *History of the Kings of Britain* (*Historia Regum Britanniae*), and the *ROMAN DE BRUT*, by the Jersey poet WACE in the ANGLO-NORMAN language. *The Brut* is an important poem as it is the first work to cast the mythical history of England into the vernacular, and one of the few major pieces written in English during the immediate postconquest period.

See also ALLITERATION.

FURTHER READING

Allen, Rosamund. "The Implied Audience of Layamon's *Brut.*" In *The Text and Tradition of Layamon's Brut,* edited by Françoise Le Saux, 136–137. Cambridge: D.S. Brewer, 1994.

Stanley, E. G. "Layamon's Antiquarian Sentiments." *Medium Aevum* 38 (1969): 23–37.

David A. Roberts

BURDEN

A burden is a verse line in a CAROL(E) or hymn that signals the beginning and/or end of a STANZA. In function, it closely resembles a REFRAIN.

"BURNING BABE, THE" ROBERT SOUTHWELL (1595)

The most famous poem by the English Roman Catholic writer ROBERT SOUTHWELL is a Christmas vision. The poet stands shivering outdoors on a snowy winter's night when, suddenly, his chest feels warm (ll. 1–4). He looks up in fear to see if he is near a fire and sees the vision of a baby burning. The baby is weeping, he sees, but the tears only kindle the fire. The babe explains that he is sad because people have not come to warm themselves in the flame (ll. 5–8). Then, in a series of metaphors, he says his breast is a furnace where sinful souls are heated like metals (ll. 9–12). This operation is for their good, he adds, for, once melted, the souls will be bathed in his blood. Having said this, he vanishes, but the words are sufficiently pointed to remind the poet that it is Christmas Day (ll. 13–16).

"The Burning Babe" is written in FOURTEENERS 14 syllable lines of iambic verse. In all, there are eight rhymed COUPLETS, the first seven of which form a single period, or sentence, with semicolons after lines 6 and 12. The final couplet forms a second sentence, in which the vision vanishes and the poet identifies it as a reminder of Christmas.

The poem is most difficult where it becomes most interesting, with the series of metaphors equating the Christ child with fires of purgatory—the Roman Catholic place of preparation where souls are purged of their sins and prepared for entrance into Heaven. It is disturbingly far away from the sentimental verse of Christmas cards precisely because it reminds us that Jesus and Christ are the same at all times. Indeed, the fire is fueled by "wounding thornes" (l. 9), a reminder that the Crucifixion is already present at the moment of incarnation.

Southwell's furnace recalls the fiery furnace in Daniel 3, where a mysterious figure appears and saves the faithful, a figure that Christians took to be Christ. There may also be an echo of Isaiah 48:10: "Behold, I have refined thee, but not with silver; I have chosen thee in the furnace of affliction." Another apocalyptic echo is of Revelation 7:14: "These are they which came out of great tribulation, and have washed their robes, and made them white in the blood of the Lamb."

Southwell shows a general familiarity with the apparatus of chemistry, including the furnace, the fuel, and the chemical wash, or "bath." Similar language was used for the alchemical process; indeed, the mercurial wash used on the raw matter, after it had been "mortified," was often called blood. The parallels are accidental, however. Like other Jesuit authors, Southwell never suggested that Christ was present in a furnace, only that he could be symbolized by one.

Southwell was a Catholic missionary to Protestant England at a time when such activity was considered treasonable and punishable by a terrible public execution. His poetry has appealed especially to English Catholics who see hints of Southwell's own martyrdom in 1595 in the babe's suffering.

FURTHER READING

Baynham, Matthew. "The Burning Babe and Robert Southwell." *N&Q* 50, no. 1 (2003): 55–56.

McDonald, James H., and Nancy Pollard Brown, eds. *The Poems of Robert Southwell.* Oxford: Clarendon Press, 1967.

Pilarz, Scott R. *Robert Southwell and the Mission of Literature, 1561–1595: Writing Reconciliation.* Burlington, Vt.: Ashgate, 2004.

Thomas Willard

C

"CÆDMON'S HYMN" CÆDMON (seventh century) Generally considered the oldest poem written in English, "Cædmon's Hymn" is found in some 17 manuscripts dating from as early as the eighth century, which is remarkable for an Anglo-Saxon poem. "Cædmon's Hymn" owes its relative popularity to its parent work: the poem is reproduced as part of the Venerable Bede's *Historia Ecclesiastica Gentis Anglorum* (*Ecclesiastical History of the English People,* 731). Bede's work—and the poem itself—was written originally in Latin, however, the Old English poem is written outside the lined margins of the Latin text and in a smaller hand.

Bede tells the full story of the origins of "Cædmon's Hymn" in his *Historia* (4.24), dating the events to approximately 680. Cædmon, a cowherd serving the abbey of Whitby in Northumbria, was at a feast as a harp was passed from guest to guest, each reciting a poem when the harp came his way. Before the harp reached him, Cædmon, afraid to sing, left and returned to his shed. There he slept and dreamed of a heavenly visitor who prompted him to sing of the biblical Creation story. He returned and sang, and when the others heard Cædmon's song, they took him to the abbess, who welcomed Cædmon into the abbey. There he continued to compose biblical poetry. Some scholars thus assign other poems to him, or at least to a "school of Cædmon."

In addition to its antiquity, the poem is remarkable for bringing together two different traditions: It expresses Judeo-Christian content in a Germanic poetic form. The poem is not only written in Germanic verse (four-beat lines marked by ALLITERATION) but in a Germanic style, with multiple names for God: *metod* (creator), *dryhten* (lord, with martial overtones), *scieppend* (shaper), and *frea* (lord). Other appositives for God are more poetically expressed as KENNINGS; God is *heofon-rices weard* ("the keeper of the heavenly kingdom"), *wuldor-fæder* ("the glorious father"), and *mann-cynnes weard* ("the keeper of humankind"). Such variation of expression reflects the multiple perspectives the Germanic Anglo-Saxons had on the Christian God, and thereby offers significant insight into the reception and acceptance of Christianity among the newly converted Anglo-Saxons.

See also ANGLO-SAXON POETRY.

FURTHER READING

Bede. *Bede's Ecclesiastical History of the English People.* Edited by Bertram Colgrave and R. B. Mynors. Oxford: Clarendon Press, 1969.
"Cædmon's Hymn." In *Eight Old English Poems,* 3rd ed., edited by R. D. Fulk and John C. Pope, 3–4, 49–58. New York: Norton, 2001.
Scragg, Donald C. "The Nature of Old English Verse." In *The Cambridge Companion to Old English Literature,* edited by Malcolm Godden and Michael Lapidge, 55–70. Cambridge: Cambridge University Press, 1991.

Alexander M. Bruce

CAELICA SIR FULKE GREVILLE, BARON BROOKE (1576–1628) *Caelica* ("heavenly one") is frequently described as a SONNET SEQUENCE. However, although individual groupings of poems, recurrent preoccupations, and favored addressees are certainly perceptible, it might best be considered as an anthology of private responses to the brittle world of Elizabethan and Jacobean COURT CULTURE, to contemporaneous love poetry, and to more theological and philosophical issues and anxieties. *Caelica* comprises 109 poems, only 41 of which are 14-line SONNETs. Where he does employ the QUATORZAIN form, SIR FULKE GREVILLE adopts the ENGLISH SONNET style consisting of three QUATRAINs and a concluding COUPLET, though he increasingly develops the sonnet SESTET into the six-line STANZA form favored throughout his later verse treatises. *Caelica* was published posthumously in 1633.

The first 75 poems have been dated to between 1576 and 1587, and on several occasions they imitate or respond to SIR PHILIP SIDNEY's *ASTROPHIL AND STELLA*, though Greville is more explicitly skeptical toward the commonplaces of amorous verse. For instance, Caelica's conventional golden tresses are revealed to be a wig (Sonnet 58), and the agent of love, Cupid, is repeatedly scorned as being deceitful, inconstant, and a mere idol (Sonnet 62). *Caelica*'s first movement features many poems addressed to beloved figures named Myra, Cynthia, and Caelica, though there is little consistent characterization or biographical allusion. Each seems to be representative more of individual instances of worldly love and physical desire.

Caelica contains two other sets of sonnets in addition to the amorous ones. Greville's political sonnets (Sonnets 76–81, ca. 1587–1603) offer personal meditations on ambition, court favoritism, and the nature of tyranny, issues he interrogates further in his contemporaneous closet dramas *Mustapha* and *Alaham*. Greville's religious and philosophical meditations (Sonnets 82 and 85–109, ca. 1604–28) revisit such preoccupations as idolatry and worldly inconstancy but, more importantly, explore the implications of humanity's fallen nature, progressively realizing the soul's state of desolation and recasting absence in cosmic terms as a separation from divine grace, and demonstrating how faculty of reason makes sense of evil and sin.

Often admired for its suggestion of unmediated intimacy, verbal clarity, and directness of expression, Greville's poetry is held up as an exemplar of the "plain" style of early modern English verse. Relatively few poems self-consciously address the writing process itself (see, however, Sonnets 22 and 24), and Greville's wariness of duplicitous Petrarchan love games is reflected in his own writing and increasing unwillingness to allow language and metaphor to obscure the process of self-examination enacted and exhibited in his poetry.

In addition to addressing links between *Caelica* and individual lyrics of Greville's contemporaries, critics have attempted to explain the shift between the more worldly interests of the earlier poetry and the serious tone of the later, often suggesting that the change occurred following Sidney's death in 1586, when Greville experienced a deepening religious conviction or "conversion." Others trace the switch to the death of Queen ELIZABETH I. The Elizabethan court valued amorous verse as an expression of social, economic, and political ambition, whereas the Jacobean court favored philosophy. Recent critics are increasingly wary of characterizing "early" or "late" Greville, their work revealing that rigid divisions between secular and religious issues and language fail to adequately describe Greville's complex conception of the role of earthly faculties and institutions in God's divine scheme.

FURTHER READING

Rees, Joan. *Fulke Greville, Lord Brooke.* London: Routledge, 1971.

Vincent, Helen. "'Syon Lies Waste': Secularity, Skepticism and Religion in *Caelica*." *Sidney Journal* 19 (2001): 63–84.

Waswo, Richard. *The Fatal Mirror: Themes and Techniques in the Poetry of Fulke Greville.* Charlottesville: University of Virginia Press, 1972.

Matthew Woodcock

CAESURA   From the Latin, meaning "cut," a caesura is a stop or pause in the line of verse. When a caesura splits a line into HALF LINES, such as those prevalent in ANGLO-SAXON POETRY, it is called a medial caesura.

CAMPION, THOMAS (1567–1620)   Born and raised in London, Thomas Campion was educated at Peterhouse, Cambridge University, before returning to London to study law at Gray's Inn in 1586. Shortly thereafter, he accompanied the earl of Essex in a campaign against France, during which time a set of five of his poems were appended to an edition of SIR PHILIP SIDNEY's *ASTROPHIL AND STELLA*. Campion published his first book of Latin poetry, *Poemata*, in 1595, and shortly thereafter he began work on *A BOOKE OF AYRES*, though it would not be published until 1601. The following year, Campion wrote a poetics entitled *Observations in the Art of English Poesie*, which especially addressed rhyme and meter. Sometime between 1602 and 1606, Campion earned a doctor of medicine degree; however, his literary career continued at James I's court. Particularly known for his knowledge of music and dance, Campion composed court masques, musical compositions, MADRIGALs and a learned treatise on music theory. He died on March 1, 1620, leaving his entire estate to Philip Rosseter, with whom he had collaborated on many works, including *A Booke of Ayres*.

See also CANZONE, "I CARE NOT FOR THESE LADIES," "MY SWEETEST LESBIA," "WHEN TO HER LUTE CORINNA SINGS."

FURTHER READING

Rydingm, Erik S. *In Harmony Framed: Musical Humanism, Thomas Campion, and the Two Daniels*. Kirksville, Mo.: Sixteenth Century Journal Publishers, 1993.

Wilson, Christopher. *Words and Notes Coupled Lovingly Together: Thomas Campion, A Critical Study*. New York: Garland, 1989.

CANTERBURY TALES, THE (OVERVIEW)

GEOFFREY CHAUCER (ca. 1385–1400) GEOFFREY CHAUCER's most famous work, *The Canterbury Tales*, is a FRAME NARRATIVE piece that reflects the stories told by a motley group of pilgrims on their way to Canterbury Cathedral. It begins with a General Prologue that describes the Pilgrims and the context, followed by a number of Tales. The plan as outlined by the Host in the General Prologue calls for a total of four tales per Pilgrim; two told on the way to Canterbury, and two told on the way back. However, Chaucer died before even one full set of Tales could be written. He also never arranged the Tales in any particular order, leaving it to modern editors to reconstruct possible arrangements. Generally, editors divide *The Canterbury Tales* into 10 fragments based on implicit links between

Tales, and other internal clues, as few explicit references to Chaucer's intended organization exist. The most commonly accepted order is:

Fragment 1(A)	General Prologue, Knight, Miller, Reeve, Cook
Fragment 2 (B^1)	Man of Law
Fragment 3 (D)	Wife of Bath, Friar, Summoner
Fragment 4 (E)	Clerk, Merchant
Fragment 5 (F)	Squire, Franklin
Fragment 6 (C)	Physician, Pardoner
Fragment 7 (B^2)	Shipman, Prioress, Sir Thopas, Melibee, Monk, Nun's Priest
Fragment 8 (G)	Second Nun, Canon's Yeoman
Fragment 9 (H)	Manciple
Fragment 10 (I)	Parson

Some scholars put Fragment 8 (G) before Fragment 6 (C), while others break up Fragments 4 and 5 and redistribute those Tales among other subsections. The Chaucer Society added the alphabetical designations, based on the earliest accepted edition by Walter Skeat.

The setting of *The Canterbury Tales* is in motion. The pilgrims meet at the Tabard, an inn in Southwark, which is across the Thames from the actual City of London. All plan to travel to Canterbury Cathedral in Kent, a county south of London, to visit the shrine housing the relics of St. Thomas à Becket. A pilgrimage was, for medieval Christians, a journey undertaken to improve one's faith, to seek spiritual assistance from the saints, and as a measure of penance in reparation for one's sins. Few of Chaucer's Pilgrims, however, particularly appear to be on a pious journey of faith (the Parson is a notable exception, and several other Pilgrims without descriptions may be). The Tales are full of secular mirth, sex, and other sins, and the Pilgrims themselves are variously drunk, lecherous, deviant, deceptive, and so forth, although a few are relatively decorous.

Overall, these men and women represent a wide representation of medieval society and various professions. Chaucer is remembered, with reason, as the first writer to accurately depict the various social classes interacting in a single frame on a relatively even level. He is quite careful, also, to match the Tales and their tellers, sometimes startlingly so, often building upon descriptions begun in the General Prologue. Some contain references to other Tales, while others contain explicit debates between Pilgrims. Unlike many other frame narratives, then, Chaucer's individual Tales cannot be fully appreciated outside the context of the entire work, although they can certainly be enjoyed individually.

The Canterbury Tales features a variety of genres: FABLIAU, BEAST FABLE, ROMANCE, HAGIOGRAPHY, Breton *lai* (LAY), sermon, FABLE, confession, autobiography, Virgin miracle, and SATIRE among others. For his sources and inspiration, Chaucer turned to a variety of texts, from Classical to contemporary. Major analogues for the Tales as a whole include: OVID's *Metamorphoses,* BOCCACCIO's *Decameron,* BOETHIUS's *The CONSOLATION OF PHILOSOPHY,* John Bromyard's *Summa praedicantium,* Dante's *Divine Comedy, The Distichs of Cato,* JOHN GOWER's *CONFESSIO AMANTIS,* St. Jerome's *Adversus Jovinianum,* and the *Roman de la Rose,* as well as the Bible. Scholars continue to debate whether or not Chaucer had these in front of him as he wrote or recalled hearing or reading parts of these texts. As well, many Tales have unique sources, and some appear to be Chaucer's own invention.

Structurally, *The Canterbury Tales* is an interlocking linear frame narrative. The General Prologue provides the setup: It introduces the Pilgrims and suggests an order for the Tales. The Miller quickly violates this outline by interrupting the proceedings and telling his Tale after the Knight's, disregarding social rank. However, as this interruption is clearly by Chaucer's design, it does not disrupt the linear progression. The accepted order of tales also reflects a series of loose themes, although some general themes can be found throughout the collection. These general themes include a concern with the immediate historical context of the late-14th century: human desire (in multiple senses), the nature of love and friendship, and the role of FORTUNE. Perhaps the most famous subdivision of tales is the so-called Marriage Group, a topic suggested by the Wife of Bath. It includes "The WIFE OF BATH'S TALE," "The MAN OF LAW'S TALE," "The Clerk's Tale," "The Merchant's Tale," and "The FRANKLIN'S TALE," and it cuts across several of the accepted fragments.

The first fragment consists of "The Knight's Tale," "The MILLER'S PROLOGUE AND TALE," "The REEVE'S PROLOGUE AND TALE," and the fragment of "The Cook's Prologue and Tale." "The Knight's Tale," a chivalric romance concerned with COURTLY LOVE and war, matters of the aristocracy, and Boethian philosophy, begins *The Canterbury Tales.* The rest of the fragment is a series of fabliaux, bawdy tales that offset the Knight's elevated style. By deliberately disrupting the social order and allowing the coarse middle-class Tales to overcome the stately aristocratic one, Chaucer displays a concern with the changing social and economic structures of the late 14th century. That the Tales get increasingly more vulgar, however, demonstrates that too much social freedom can result in amoral chaos.

The second fragment consists solely of the Man of Law's Introduction, Prologue, Tale, and Epilogue. The complicated astronomical calculations at the beginning indicate this tale is told on April 18 at 10:00 A.M. It is based on an ANGLO-NORMAN story by Nicholas Trivet and John Gower's version of that, found in the *Confessio Amantis.* Alternately termed a secular hagiography or a romance, this Tale is lengthy and complicated, and it features numerous reversals of Fortune. The epilogue features the typical interruption found in other prologues and epilogues, but the manuscripts vary as to which Pilgrim interrupts—the Squire, the Summoner, or the Shipman. Internal evidence points to the reassignment of both "The Man of Law's Tale" and the following Tale.

The third fragment includes "The Wife of Bath's Prologue" and "The Wife of Bath's Tale," "The Friar's Prologue and Tale," and "The Summoner's Tale." There is no explicit link between Fragments 2 and 3; however, the subject matter implicitly suggests a "quiting" (an offset)—the Man of Law's ideal woman being offset by voracious women (the Wife and her characters). "The Friar's Tale," however, does not concern relations between the sexes; rather, it is an EXEMPLUM about the corruption of the ecclesiastical courts. The Summoner, at whom the Friar's tale was directed, retaliates with a tale about a long-winded hypocritical Friar that is part fabliau and part satire.

The fourth fragment consists of "The Clerk's Prologue," "The Clerk's Tale," "The Merchant's Prologue,"

"The Merchant's Tale," and "The Merchant's Epilogue." Both of these tales concern marriage, one an idealized portrait in which man is completely dominant and woman completely submissive, and the other a fabliau-style tale about an old husband with a young wife that follows romance conventions and incorporates numerous poetic devices. Internal references link these two tales together into a set, with "The Merchant's Tale" serving as a foil for "The Clerk's Tale."

The fifth fragment consists of "The Squire's Introduction," "The Squire's Tale," "The Franklin's Prologue," and "The Franklin's Tale." The Squire relates a romance, but this is a different romance than told by the Knight. Gone is Boethian philosophy and stilted discourse; included is high sentiment and fantastic, supernatural events. This tale is left unfinished. The Franklin interrupts the Squire at an opportune moment, leading many scholars to believe "The Squire's Tale" remains unfinished on purpose. "The Franklin's Tale" itself is a Breton *lai,* a type of short supernatural romance, usually based on Celtic antecedents. This tale takes up the subject of wedlock once again, exploring a marriage based on love and mutual respect.

Fragment 6 is composed of "The Physician's Tale," "The Pardoner's Introduction," "The Pardoner's Prologue," and "The PARDONER'S TALE." "The Physician's Tale" has been called an exercise in pathos by many critics; it derives from the Roman tradition. Ultimately, it illustrates shame and the public punishment of sin, just as its companion piece, "The Pardoner's Tale," aptly demonstrates guilt and the internal punishment of sin.

The seventh fragment covers a number of tales: "The Shipman's Tale," "The PRIORESS'S TALE," "The Prioress's Prologue," "The Prologue of Sir Thopas," "The Tale of Sir Thopas," "The Tale of Melibee," "The Monk's Prologue," "The Monk's Tale," "The Nun's Priest's Prologue," "The NUN'S PRIEST'S TALE," and "The Nun's Priest's Epilogue." "The Shipman's Tale" is considered Chaucer's earliest fabliau, and the tale was probably first assigned to the Wife of Bath. It is followed by the violently anti-Semitic Prioress's tale, which plays with popular devotional literature of the time.

Two prose tales are next. Chaucer the Pilgrim—the narrator persona inserted into the Pilgrimage by the author—tells the first, "The Tale of Sir Thopas." Despite his naïve appearance, the narrator relates a slightly bawdy minstrel romance. Minstrel romances were shorter than standard ones and specifically designed for oral presentation, with frequent asides to the audience. Topically, they are adventure tales characterized by rough meter and crude formulas. Chaucer's version, however, is a parody. Chaucer also tells Melibee's Tale after Sir Thopas's Tale has been interrupted by the Host. It is a long allegorical treatise couched as a discussion between Melibee and Prudence covering a number of moral and political issues. Some scholars believe this Tale is told in Chaucer's own voice, rather than by his narrator persona.

"The Monk's Tale" follows. Most scholars believe this Tale was composed prior to when work was begun on *The Canterbury Tales* proper. Described as a collection of tragedies, "The Monk's Tale" is designed to illustrate the workings of Fortune in a manner similar to JOHN LYDGATE's *The FALL OF PRINCES.* Fragment 7 concludes with the "The Nun's Priest's Tale," Chaucer's only beast fable, which draws on the tradition of REYNARD LITERATURE alongside courtly discourse. Thoroughly entertaining, this Tale nonetheless provides a number of morals for improving one's life.

The eighth fragment comprises "The Second Nun's Prologue," "The Second Nun's Tale," "The Canon's Yeoman's Prologue," and "The Canon's Yeoman's Tale." Both the tales, as well as "The Second Nun's Prologue," are thought to have been composed for another occasion but then inserted into the overall collection. "The Canon's Yeoman's Prologue," however, was composed strictly for *The Canterbury Tales* and provides a more complete introduction to a Pilgrim only briefly described in the General Prologue. "The Second Nun's Prologue" is an exercise in etymology, while "The Second Nun's Tale" is a hagiography of St. Cecilia, a virgin martyr. She is a powerfully active character, unlike many of Chaucer's other women. "The Canon's Yeoman's Tale" is a two-part occupational satire about the trickery of alchemists and a greedy canon. The two Tales incorporate the language of science and pseudo-science but ultimately reject both in favor of faith.

Fragment 9 consists solely of "The Manciple's Prologue" and "The Manciple's Tale." This Tale is a fable based on a story from Ovid—the story of Phoebus and the crow, a tale-telling bird. Ultimately it becomes a warning about the dangers of telling tales, "wheither they been false or trewe" (9.360).

The final division, Fragment 10, includes "The Parson's Prologue" and "The Parson's Tale," along with "Chaucer's Retraction." "The Parson's Tale" is clearly meant to end the collection, whether or not Chaucer intended to expand it later. It is a penitential tract that includes an examination of conscience and an overview of the SEVEN DEADLY SINS. Coming where it does, it serves as a reminder to the other pilgrims of their purpose for traveling to Canterbury. The Retraction follows, and is a traditional apology for Chaucer's lifetime of writing, not just *The Canterbury Tales*. Ultimately it concludes that salvation is more important than literature, a standard medieval perspective.

There are a total of 83 manuscripts that contain some portion of *The Canterbury Tales*—55 with the complete collection of tales (or intentions thereof) and 28 with one or more individual tales. There are also six early printed versions, the earliest of which is the 1478 edition by WILLIAM CAXTON. He printed a second version in 1484, claiming in the preface to have revised the text based on a manuscript supplied by a reader. The other four editions, dating to the late 15th and early 16th centuries, were printed by Richard Pynson (1492 and 1526), WYNKYN DE WORDE (1498), and William Thynne (1532). Various references in wills, letters, and catalogues imply the existence of a number of other copies, both in manuscript and early printed form, all now lost.

Of all the manuscripts, the earliest is MS Peniarth 392D, National Library of Wales, dubbed the "Hengwrt manuscript." Copied around the time of Chaucer's death, it is considered the most authoritative copy of the materials it contains. The same scribe produced the beautiful and complete Ellesmere manuscript (Ellesmere 26 9 C, Huntington Library, San Marino, California), which sets out the most accepted order of the Tales. The popularity of *The Canterbury Tales* has resulted in a multitude of editions and translations, dating as early as 1492.

Scholarship concerning *The Canterbury Tales* is vast. As is typical in literary scholarship, early studies tended to focus on textual variants, manuscript issues, structural concerns, linguistic puzzles, and so forth. Also of concern was connecting details of Chaucer's life with his work. Genre studies and examinations of poetic devices (e.g., irony, narrative, morals, and so on) followed, as did a spate of exegetic approaches (see EXEGESIS). These works provide a solid background to any student of Chaucer. Other studies have examined the social and historical contexts of Chaucer's works, placing them within contemporary events. Marxist critics have investigated the economic contexts surrounding *The Canterbury Tales*'s production and reception, as well as the economic structures within individual tales (e.g., the exchange of money for sex or similar favors). Feminist, gender, and queer theories have dominated the last decade or so of Chaucer scholarship, providing insight into areas not previously explored in depth.

See also GENERAL PROLOGUE TO THE CANTERBURY TALES.

FURTHER READING

Editions, Manuscript Studies, & Sources

Benson, Larry D. *The Riverside Chaucer*. 3rd ed. Boston: Houghton Mifflin, 1988.

Bryan, W. R., and Germaine Dempster, eds. *Sources and Analogues of Chaucer's* Canterbury Tales. Chicago: University of Chicago Press, 1941.

Donaldson, E. Talbot, ed. *Chaucer's Poetry: An Anthology for the Modern Reader*. 2nd ed. Glenview, Ill.: Scott Foresman, 1975.

Manly, John M., and Edith Rickert, eds. *The Text of* The Canterbury Tales, *Studied on the Basis of All Known Manuscripts*. 8 vols. Lewiston, N.Y.: Edwin Mellen, 1940.

Miller, Robert P., ed. *Chaucer: Sources and Backgrounds*. New York: Oxford University Press, 1977.

Robinson, F. N., ed. *The Works of Geoffrey Chaucer*. 2nd ed. Boston: Houghton Mifflin, 1957.

Pratt, Robert A., ed. *The Tales of Canterbury*. Boston: Houghton Mifflin, 1974.

Skeat, Walter, ed. *The Complete Works of Geoffrey Chaucer*. 6 vols. 1894. Supplementary volume, 1897.

Critical Studies

Allen, Valerie, and Ares Axiotis, ed. *Chaucer: Contemporary Critical Essays*. New York: Palgrave, 1997.

Beidler, Peter. *Masculinities in Chaucer*. Cambridge: Cambridge University Press, 1998.

Boitani, Piero, and Jill Mann, eds. *The Cambridge Chaucer Companion*. Cambridge: Cambridge University Press, 1986.

Brewer, Derek. *A New Introduction to Chaucer*. 2nd ed. London: Routledge, 1998.

———, ed. *Chaucer: The Critical Heritage*. Vol. 1, 1385–1837. Vol. 2, 1837–1933. London: Routledge, 1978.

Burnley, David. *A Guide to Chaucer's Language*. Stillwater: University of Oklahoma Press, 1983.

Cooper, Helen. *The Structure of The Canterbury Tales*. London and Athens: University of Georgia Press, 1983.

———. *Oxford Guides to Chaucer: The Canterbury Tales*. 2nd ed. Oxford: Oxford University Press, 1999.

Curry, Walter Clyde. *Chaucer and the Medieval Sciences*. 2nd ed. New York: Barnes & Noble, 1960.

Dinshaw, Carolyn. *Chaucer's Sexual Politics*. Madison: University of Wisconsin Press, 1989.

Hansen, Elaine Tuttle. *Chaucer and the Fictions of Gender*. Berkeley: University of California Press, 1992.

Mann, Jill. *Chaucer and Medieval Estates Satire*. Cambridge: Cambridge University Press, 1973.

Patterson, Lee. *Chaucer and the Subject of History*. Madison: University of Wisconsin Press, 1991.

Pearsall, Derek. *The Life of Geoffrey Chaucer*. Oxford: Oxford University Press, 1992.

Phillips, Helen. *An Introduction to The Canterbury Tales*. London: Palgrave, 2000.

Strohm, Paul. *Social Chaucer*. Cambridge, Mass.: Harvard University Press, 1989.

CANTO   From the Latin *cantus,* "song," this is a major division of a lengthy poem. First used by Dante for his *Divine Comedy,* it was introduced to English writing by EDMUND SPENSER in *The FAERIE QUEENE.*

See also STANZA.

CANZONE   Originally an Italian lyric poem consisting of five or six STANZAs and an ENVOI, the canzone came to include polyphonic songs and lyrics that derived from this form but resembled MADRIGALs. In English literature, THOMAS CAMPION was a master of the canzone.

"CAREFUL COMPLAINT BY THE UNFORTUNATE AUTHOR, A" ISABELLA WHITNEY (1573)

This poem was published in ISABELLA WHITNEY's second book of poetry, *A Sweet Nosegay.* It is the first of a set of three poems in which the poet engages in a literary conversation with "T. B." who was probably Whitney's friend, Thomas Berrie. In this COMPLAINT, Whitney bemoans her current misfortunes, which include, among other things, the loss of her position as a maid, and her lack of money and a job. It is part of an exchange between Whitney and T. B. couched as epistolary poems. In this Whitney is following in the tradition of OVID's *Heroides,* which also comprises verse epistles, as well as imitating in print the upper-class practice of circulating manuscripts of poems among friends.

In "A Careful Complaint," Whitney addresses Dido, the queen of Carthage who was abandoned by her lover, Aeneas, and who killed herself in despair. Whitney tells Dido to stop crying and to give up her sorrows, implying that she, Whitney, has a greater right to complain. Then she retracts her previous command and tells Dido instead to continue crying, but to cry for Whitney. She acknowledges that Aeneas mistreated Dido by abandoning her, but she claims that her own misfortunes are far greater since FORTUNE has turned against her, has deprived her of her health, and wants her dead. She tells Dido that if she (Dido) had not succumbed to the desire to kill herself, then she might have been happy again. Dido could have forgotten about Aeneas after he left, since fire only burns while it has fuel, and annoying things cease to be annoying once they are gone. Whitney, on the other hand, cannot escape from her grief and pain since it will not abandon her.

Whitney concludes the poem by asking death to come quickly and asking the three Fates to end her life and her troubles. This last request may be exaggerated. Modern critics have noted that early modern women writers often used impending death as an excuse for publishing their work. Despite the stigma associated with publication, a woman who thought she was near death might be forgiven for writing (and publishing) instructions or ideas that she wanted to survive her. Thus, Whitney's use of Dido, who committed suicide, becomes all the more poignant. Other critics have addressed the gendered implications of Whitney, comparing "Dame Fortune" to Aeneas.

See also "WILL AND TESTAMENT."

FURTHER READING
Wall, Wendy. "Isabella Whitney and the Female Legacy." *ELH* 58, no. 1 (1991): 35–62.

Donna C. Woodford

CAROL (CAROLE)

CAROL (CAROLE) The carol is a medieval verse form commonly associated with religious, especially Christmas, songs, but also connected to dancing. They are distinguished by having a REFRAIN or BURDEN, which opens the piece and is repeated after every STANZA. The verse form varies with respect to line length and meter, but is consistent within a single poem. The STANZA lines—commonly four—generally share a single rhyme, run *abcb,* or fall *aaab*[*b*], with the second *b* belonging to the refrain. In structure, the carol is related to the BALLAD, the RONDEAU, and the VIRELAI, also designed for performance and reliant upon refrains.

Roughly 500 medieval English carols survive, most from the 15th century, though the form existed earlier both in England and France. In Middle English contexts, the term *carol* is often connected directly to dance. In SIR GAWAIN AND THE GREEN KNIGHT, for instance, the term appears five times, each time connected to dancing. The association with Christmas may be traced to John Audelay, a monk who wrote a number of lyrics explicitly labeled "carals" and devoted to Christmas. This has led to some scholarly debate as to which texts are truly carols. For instance, "The CHERRY TREE CAROL" is about Christmas and dependent on its refrain, but its legendary theme connects it with the ballad tradition as well. Similarly, "The AGINCOURT CAROL" is not about Christmas—rather, it celebrates Henry V's victory over the French in 1415—but follows the other parameters of the genre. The form decreased in popularity after the 15th century, though another carol, "The Holly and the Ivy," has often been attributed to King HENRY VIII.

See also "BRING US IN GOOD ALE," MIDDLE ENGLISH LYRICS AND BALLADS.

FURTHER READING

Gray, Douglas. "Fifteenth-Century Lyrics and Carols." In *Nation, Court, and Culture: New Essays in Fifteenth-Century Poetry,* edited by Helen Cooney, 168–183. Dublin: Four Courts, 2001.

Greene, Richard L., ed. *The Early English Carols.* 2nd ed. Oxford: Clarendon Press, 1977.

Keyte, Hugh, and Andrew Parrot. *The New Oxford Book of Carols.* Oxford: Oxford University Press, 1992.

Carol E. Harding and Michelle M. Sauer

CARPE DIEM

CARPE DIEM Latin for "seize the day," the phrase is taken from the Roman poet Horace's *Odes.* Carpe diem became one of the standard motifs in the early modern era, particularly in erotic verse. In such poems, the speaker urges a woman, usually a virgin, to enjoy life's immediate pleasures (sex) instead of wasting time. The lyric "COME AWAY, COME SWEET LOVE" is one such example. It was also popular in the PASTORAL tradition—for example, in CHRISTOPHER MARLOWE's "The PASSIONATE SHEPHERD TO HIS LOVE" and ROBERT HENRYSON's *ROBENE AND MAKYNE,* both of which feature seductions. Finally, some poets used the carpe diem tradition to focus on mortality and the fleeting sense of earthly beauty (e.g., *The FAERIE QUEENE*: "Gather therefore the Rose, whilst yet is prime," 2.12.74–75).

CASKET LETTERS (OVERVIEW) SONNETS MARY, QUEEN OF SCOTS (before 1568)

CASKET LETTERS (OVERVIEW) SONNETS MARY, QUEEN OF SCOTS (before 1568) MARY, QUEEN OF SCOTS is one of the most iconographic figures in Scottish culture. Only recently, however, has Mary's poetry been seriously considered on a literary basis rather than as historical documents. At the heart of Mary's poetry lie the 11 SONNETS and SESTET, originally composed in French, Mary's first language, and printed in the so-called *Casket Letters,* allegedly addressed to James Hepburn, the earl of Bothwell. Critics have been divided over the sonnets' authenticity. In 1571, they were printed in a work of anti-Marian propaganda (*Detectioun of the duings* [doings] *of Marie Quene of Scotts*), where they are presented as evidence of Mary's involvement in the murder of her second husband, Henry Darnley. Her critics claimed she penned the letters and sonnets before being imprisoned. The sonnets' discovery sealed her downfall, leading to 19 years' imprisonment and her execution in 1587.

Critics are also divided over the question of whether the sonnets should be read as separate items, as a SONNET SEQUENCE, or as one continuous poem. The choice is rendered more difficult as the original *Casket Letters* do not survive; therefore, the resulting arrangement may be the work of Mary's persecutors. Despite this, the majority of scholars tend towards reading them as a sequence.

Mary's sonnets, like any other contrived poetic sequence, constitute a "fiction," though just what kind is also debatable. If the *Casket Letters* are the work of her detractors, then by the manipulation of the queen's voice, a level of ironic fictitiousness is introduced. If they are Mary's private reflections, does she consciously adopt a literary persona, or are the sonnets personal, and never intended to be read by the public?

In the sonnets, Mary asserts herself as a constant lover, who is ardent, truthful, and passionate. An important consideration is Mary's continual adaptation and reversal of conventional gender roles as found in ITALIAN (PETRARCHAN) SONNETS. In this light, critics have fruitfully explored the tensions between Mary's poetry and her role as queen of Scotland. Every poem is also political; as the publication of the *Casket Letters* clearly showed, the queen could not afford the luxury of private self-referential speech.

FURTHER READING

Bell, Robin, ed. and trans. *Bittersweet Within My Heart: The Collected Poems of Mary, Queen of Scots*. London: Pavilion, 1992.

Dunnigan, Sarah M. *Eros and Poetry at the Court of Mary Queen of Scots and James VI*. Basingstoke, U.K.: Palgrave Macmillan, 2002.

Herman, Peter C., ed. *Reading Monarch's Writing: The Poetry of Henry VIII, Mary Stuart, Elizabeth I, and James VI/I*. Tempe: Arizona Center for Medieval and Renaissance Studies, 2002.

Sebastiaan Verweij

Casket Letters: Sonnet 1 ("O goddis haue of me compassioun," "O Dieux ayez de moy compassion") MARY, QUEEN OF SCOTS (before 1568)

The first poem in the *Casket Letters* SONNET SEQUENCE, "O goddis haue of me compassioun," has as its theme "constancie." Reversing conventional gender roles, the female speaker casts herself as desiring subject (rather than the object of desire) and lists the various sacrifices she is prepared to make to win her love: "she will give up her funds, reconcile with her enemies, put aside fame and morality, and she will renounce the world" (ll. 9–12). The poem culminates in the ultimate sacrifice: "I will die to let him forwart alone" (l. 13). This image is a standard convention: In countless sonnets, innumerable lovers die metaphorical deaths at the hands of their uncaring paramours. Typically, how-

ever, as the speaker is male, this death also metaphorically refers to the shortening of their lives through ejaculation. Mary's continued gender role reversal implies a sexual attraction to her beloved, considered atypical for a woman.

See also MARY, QUEEN OF SCOTS; SONNET.

Sebastiaan Verweij

Casket Letters: Sonnet 2 ("In his hands and in his full power," "Entre ses mains & en son plein") MARY, QUEEN OF SCOTS (before 1568)

As in the sonnet preceding this one, Mary aims to persuade Bothwell of her constancy and her "faythfulnes." She does so in seemingly contradictory rhetorical terms, offering to utterly subject herself to his will, but also promising to actively intervene to prove her worth: "In his handis and in his full power, / I put my sonne, my honour, and my lyif, / My contry, my subiects, my soule al subdewit" (ll. 1–3). The speaker is prepared to surrender everything—son, queenship, and soul—to her beloved, a seemingly passive action. This is at odds with both the historical MARY, QUEEN OF SCOTS, and the constructed one. In the SONNETS, Mary assumes the active male role of seducer, a role reversal alluded to in the final quatrain: "That he sall know my constancie without fiction, / Not by my weping, or faynit [feigned] obedience, / Als others haue done: but by vther experience" (ll. 12–14). Not employing conventional female wiles—"weping," "obedience"—she suggestively offers "vther experience," a term that implies sexuality. After promising Bothwell the world, Mary sets herself up as sexual creature, in need of his attention, and with a clear-cut plan to get what she wants.

Sebastiaan Verweij

Casket Letters: Sonnet 3 ("And now she begins to see," "Et maintenant elle commence à voir") MARY, QUEEN OF SCOTS (before 1568)

The third SONNET of the *Casket Letters* creates a love triangle by introducing an unnamed "sche" who lacks all of Mary's positive qualities but receives all of the beloved's attention. This woman is Lady Jean Gordon, Bothwell's wife.

Jean, who "wald fayne deceiue my loue" (l. 4), is an example of all that MARY, QUEEN OF SCOTS, disdains.

She is untruthful, opportunist, frigid, and insensitive. In particular, Mary contrasts Jean's deceptiveness with her own constancy. Since the insipid Jean cannot conceive any persuasive arguments to win Bothwell on her own, she resorts to "writtinges and paintit learning" that were "borrowit from sum feate [fitting] authour" (ll. 5, 7)—she plagiarizes. Everything Jean says is suspect: "all hyr payntit wordis, / Hyr teares, hyr plaintes [are] full of dissimulation" (ll. 9–10). By contrast, Mary offers "constancie without fiction" (Sonnet 2, l. 12). Though Mary rightly points out that lies cannot communicate true love, Bothwell's failure to notice Jean's dissimulation reduces Mary's power.

Sebastiaan Verweij

Casket Letters: Sonnet 4 ("You believe her— alas—I perceive it too well," "Vous la croyez, las! Trop je l'apperçoy") Mary, Queen of Scots (before 1568) Another SONNET directly addressing the beloved, and complaining about his wife, this poem imagines many allegations made against the speaker, and passionately argues against them.

Mary, Queen of Scots, fears her beloved thinks of her as untrustworthy ("I see that you esteeme me light," l. 5); wavering in her affections ("And doost suspect [my hart] without any appearing cause," l. 7); perhaps undedicated and capricious ("You suspect that vther loue transporteth me / You thinke my wordes be but wind," ll. 10–11); and, finally and importantly, lacking wisdom, insight, and intelligence ("You imagine me an woman without jugement," l. 13). Judgment is crucial here, as it carries a wide range of connotations. Also, the speaker previously accused her beloved's (Bothwell's) wife (Jean Gordon) of "euill jugement" (evil judgment), meaning in this case the inability to know her husband, and to serve him truthfully and well. Scholars suggest a pun resides in line 9: "You do nat knaw the loue I beare to you." Mary may have known she was pregnant by Bothwell at least by June 1567, so this "loue" may be Bothwell's child.

Mary ends her sonnet unambiguously: After listing all possible misunderstandings she finds that "all that encreaseth my burning" (l. 14). Bothwell believing Jean's false allegations does not set Mary back but, rather, urges her on. Again, there is a double entendre: "Encreaseth" may refer to the pregnancy alluded to earlier, as pregnant women were often called "increasing." However, Mary also casts herself in the male role of wooer, urging the beloved to notice her "burning," or sexual desire. Throughout the "Casket sonnets" Mary adopts and reverses the conventional gender roles as found in ITALIAN (PETRARCHAN) SONNETS. In this light, critics have fruitfully explored the tensions between Mary's poetry and her role as queen of Scots.

Sebastiaan Verweij

CASSANDRA See CYNTHIA, WITH CERTAIN SONNETS.

CAXTON, WILLIAM (ca. 1422–1491) *printer* Very little is known about the early years of the man who first brought the printing press to England. William Caxton was born in Kent, and there is a 1438 record for his entry as an apprentice in the Mercer's Company of London. The nature of his apprenticeship suggests that he probably came from a successful merchant family. By the early 1450s, he was traveling regularly between England and the Low Countries (modern Belgium, Luxembourg, and Netherlands) on business, and by the early 1460s he had settled down as a merchant in Bruges. From roughly 1465 to 1470, he was governor of the fraternity of English merchants in Bruges.

Caxton may have already been dealing in manuscripts as part of his luxury trade during his time in Bruges, but in 1471 he moved to Cologne and expanded his business into the production and trade of printed books. He also acquired a printing press and learned the trade. By the end of the following year, Caxton returned with his printing press to Bruges, where he began publishing his own English translations of popular French books. Around the beginning of 1474, he printed *History of Troy,* the first book printed in English.

In 1476, Caxton moved back to England, setting up his press in the precincts of Westminster Abbey at the sign of the Red Pale. In close proximity to the court and government, he had a ready audience for his work. Soon afterward, he printed GEOFFREY CHAUCER's *The*

CANTERBURY TALES (1478). Being in England made it easier for Caxton to acquire texts already written in English. Although he occasionally published in Latin, his output was almost entirely in English, and he published a wide variety of poetry and prose on historical, religious, and chivalric subjects. Having easy access to English texts written and translated by others enabled Caxton to increase the volume of his business, but he also remained involved in writing and literary production. He continued to translate some works himself, edited others, and famously wrote his own prologues and epilogues for many of the works that came through his press.

William Caxton died in 1491. His legacy is a significant one. Caxton's introduction of the printing press to England, his pioneering efforts to make English literary texts available in the new medium of print, his sensitivity to literary fashions, and his own prologues, epilogues, and translations all make him an important figure in the history of English literature and to the VERNACULAR tradition. However, in his own lifetime, it is likely that Caxton saw himself primarily as a merchant who rightly perceived the trade of printed books in English as a profitable business venture.

See also PYNSON, RICHARD; WORDE, WYNKYN DE.

FURTHER READING

Blake, N. F. *William Caxton and English Literary Culture.* London: Hambledone Press, 1991.

Painter, George D. *William Caxton, A Biography.* New York: G. Putnam's Sons, 1977.

Christina M. Carlson

CERTAIN SONNETS (OVERVIEW) SIR PHILIP SIDNEY (ca. 1581) A self-selected 32-poem

collection, most of which was completed by 1581, *Certain Sonnets* comprises 27 original poems and five translations from Latin, Spanish, and Italian. It is a miscellany of forms such as sapphics (a form using four unrhymed lines with the first three in trochaic pentameter), songs, quantitative verses (meter of Classical Greek and Latin poetry that measures the length of time required to pronounce syllables), QUATORZAINS, and so forth. The collection also includes eight poems based on contemporary tunes (e.g., an English consort

song, MADRIGALS, villanelles). In particular, the tune used for Sonnet 23 ("Who hath his fancy pleased") is from the thematically syntactical "Wilhelmus van Nassouwe," the Dutch national anthem, from which SIR PHILIP SIDNEY also borrowed the syllabic structure and rhyme pattern. Sonnet 3 ("The fire to see my wrongs for anger burneth") and Sonnet 4 ("The nightingale, as soon as April bringeth") are both based on the Italian song "Non credo già che più infelice amante" (I do not believe there is a more unhappy lover). Sonnet 26 uses the tune and syllabic structure of the madrigal, "No, no, no, no, giammai non cangerò" (No, no, no, no, never will I change). Sonnets 12–14 are translations from Horace, Catullus, and Seneca, while Sonnets 28 and 29 are translations from Montemayor's *Diana.* Sonnet 16a is actually a SONNET by Sidney's friend Edward Dyer (1543–1607).

The first sonnet in this collection presents a series of internally opposed or oxymoronic statements—for example, "since, shunning pain, I ease can never find" (l. 1) or "since heart in chilling fear with ice is warmed" (l. 7)—and ends in the final COUPLET with a yielding to the pain and servitude of love ("Thou art my lord, and I thy vowed slave," l. 14). The phrasing and movement of the sonnet is Petrarchan. As an opening poem, though, it is formulaic. Sonnet 2 draws out the idea of a capricious and willful Love making an example of his subject, who attempts to resist his (Love's) power while Love "resolved to make me pattern of his might / like foe, whose wits inclined to deadly spite, / would often kill, to breed more feeling pain" (ll. 2–4).

Sonnet 3 ("The fire to see my wrongs for anger burneth") is a song Amphialus has performed for the imprisoned Philoclea by pretending to present it for the benefit of Anaxius in the new ARCADIA (*The Countess of Pembroke's Arcadia,* book 3, chapter 15). The next poem, Sonnet 4, is also written to the same tune; however, this sonnet focuses on the classic subject from OVID's *Metamorphosis* of Philomela, metamorphosed into a nightingale, after her rape by her brother-in-law Tereus. The poem equates raping and being raped with "wanting" and "too much having," alleging that being raped is simply having too much love and that the pain of love and desire is sadder than being raped: "But I, who daily craving / Cannot have to content me, / Have more cause to lament me, / Since wanting is more woe than too much having" (ll. 17–20).

A subset of sonnets are included on the subject of "his lady's face in pain": Sonnets 8 ("The scourge of life, and death's extreme disgrace"), 9 ("Woe, woe to me, on me return the smart"), 10 ("Thou Pain, the only guest of loathed constraint"), and 11 ("And have I heard her say, 'O cruel Pain!'"). Sonnet 9 is a BLAZON of his beloved: "Her eyes, whom chance doth never move" (l. 5), "Her breath, which makes a sour answer sweet" (l. 6), "Her milken breasts" (l. 7), and "her aye well-stepping feet" (l. 8).

The popular song, Sonnet 30, begins in glee that Love is dead—"Ring out your bells, let mourning shows be spread, / For love is dead" (ll. 1–2) and "From them that use men thus: / Good lord, deliver us" (ll. 9–10)—only to end with anger: "Alas, I live: rage hath this error bred; / Love is not dead, but sleepeth / In her unmatched mind, / Where she his counsel keepeth / Till due desert she find" (ll. 31–36), moving from pleased to saddened to angered to the final plea of "Good lord deliver us."

The collection ends on a resigned note: rejecting love and desiring to move the mind (ll. 1–4) to higher things; rejecting love's enslavement but seeing a kind of death (ll. 13–14) in that and yet opening up to an eternal love that will not rust or fade. The final poem is followed by the Latin inscription *Splendidis longum valedico nugis* (I bid a long farewell to splendid trifles [his poems]). Fortunately, Sidney did not completely abandon such trifles.

See also *ASTROPHIL AND STELLA* (OVERVIEW); HERBERT, MARY SIDNEY, COUNTESS OF PEMBROKE; ITALIAN (PETRARCHAN) SONNET; SONNET SEQUENCE.

FURTHER READING

Duncan-Jones, Katherine. *Sir Philip Sidney.* Oxford and New York: Oxford University Press, 1989.

Fabry, Frank J. "Sidney's Verse Adaptations to Two Sixteenth-Century Italian Art Songs." *Renaissance Quarterly* 23, no. 3 (1970): 237–255.

Marquis, Paul A. "Rereading Sidney's *Certain Sonnets.*" *Renaissance Studies* 8, no. 1 (1994): 65–75.

Ringler, William A., ed. *The Poems of Sir Philip Sidney.* Oxford: Clarendon Press, 1962.

Sidney, Philip (Sir). *Poems of Sir Philip Sidney.* Edited by W. A. Ringler. Oxford: Oxford University Press, 1962.

———. *Sir Philip Sidney.* Edited by Katherine Duncan-Jones. Oxford: Oxford University Press, 1973.

Warkentin, Germaine. "Sidney's *Certain Sonnets*: Speculations on the Evolution of the Text." *The Library* 2, no. 1 (1980): 430–444.

Christine Gilmore

Certain Sonnets 31: "Thou Blind Man's Mark" SIR PHILIP SIDNEY (ca. 1581)

This SONNET steps away from ENGLISH SONNET form and instead follows Continental sonnet traditions. Composed of an OCTAVE and SESTET, *Certain Sonnets* 31 experiments with an unusual rhyme scheme (*ababbaba, bccbcc*) that uses only three end-rhymes and risks stiltedness. Some might prefer the term QUATORZAIN for Sonnet 31 because of the unorthodox rhyme scheme, which appears in no other poems in SIR PHILIP SIDNEY's *Certain Sonnets.* However, this sonnet employs other conventions of the form. It has 14 rhymed lines, and the octave details a problem, while the sestet resolves the problem.

The octave describes the poet in an emotional and self-critical state, as if he were pointing at himself in the mirror and seeing his own weakness and inclination toward fancifulness and pursuit of love, leaving him "fond fancie's scum" (l. 2). In the course of this self-flagellation, the poet characterizes himself as a blind man's abused target, a fool's contrivance, and "dregs of scattred thought" (ll. 1–2). He has squandered his intelligence to pursue fancy: "Desire, desire I have too dearly bought" (l. 5), he cries, and the result is a "mangled mind" (l. 6) that should "to higher things prepare" (l. 8). As the son of Sir Henry Sidney, an administrator for Queen ELIZABETH I who served as both lord president of the Marches of Wales and lord deputy of Ireland, and, for a time, as heir to Robert Dudley, earl of Leicester, Sidney had great expectations for himself—and so did others, in England and on the Continent.

The traditional VOLTA opens the sestet. The poet moves from self-flagellation to a refusal to see himself as completely defeated, asserting that fancy has worked in vain to ruin him, making him aspire to idle and worthless things. Moving out of his despair, the poet insists that efforts to destroy him are in vain. Fancy has incited only smoke; he has not been burned or destroyed: "In vaine thou kindlest all thy smokie fire" (l. 11). These lines show growth as the poet construes his struggles as a battle between himself and fancy (i.e., both fancifulness and an amorous inclination). In the final three lines of the sonnet, the poet recommits to a new life shaped around virtue's lesson (ll. 12–14). This teaches him to keep his own counsel and to stifle desire—"Desiring nought but how to kill desire" (l. 14)—thus changing direction from the pursuit of the fanciful to the achievement of higher things.

See also CERTAIN SONNETS (OVERVIEW).

Christine Gilmore

Certain Sonnets 32: "Leave me, O Love" SIR PHILIP SIDNEY (1581)

In this poem from SIR PHILIP SIDNEY's Certain Sonnets, the speaker rejects human, temporal, impermanent love in favor of eternal love— the love for and of God. It is the most explicitly Christian, as well as the most specifically biblical of all Sidney's SONNETS. Thematically, it completes the collection because it complements part of the first sonnet, which reads: "I yeeld, ô Love, unto thy loathed yoke . . ." (Certain Sonnets 1.9). Sidney redefines love's "yoke," and shifts his speaker's allegiance from the lord of [courtly] love to the Lord of all Love.

Sidney rarely uses explicit references to any source texts, so specific references to the gospel and psalms passages mark this sonnet as unique among his secular writings, putting it more in line with the Psalms that Sidney translated with his sister, MARY SIDNEY HERBERT, COUNTESS OF PEMBROKE (1561–1621), and with the general Protestant cast of his overall literary and political character. This sonnet produces a mood not typical of Sidney's writing; it is absent in the SONNET SEQUENCE ASTROPHIL AND STELLA, in the two versions of the Arcadia, and rare in his prose works.

Structurally, Sonnet 32 is a variation of the ENGLISH SONNET; it has three quatrains, each with its own pair of rhyme sounds, and an ending COUPLET. The structural logic, however, reads better as an ITALIAN (PETRARCHAN) SONNET—that is, as two quatrains making an OCTAVE with a SESTET, since the couplet completes, rather than contrasts with, the preceding four lines. Unlike a typical English sonnet, Sidney utilizes an interlocking rhyme scheme of abab, cdcd, dd, and all the rhymes are

masculine (accented). This sonnet shows Sidney at his mature best. The iambic pentameter is consistent, and its rhythms are emphasized by the ALLITERATION used only in the first quatrain; other devices are employed in the remaining 10 lines.

As the sonnet opens, the speaker commands the impermanent, mortal love that reaches "but to dust" (l. 1) to leave him, and urges his mind to reach up for more elevated, important, and permanent heavenly love. Sidney alludes to Matthew 6:19–20, contrasting that which moth and rust consume—all material possessions and human affections—with that which neither moth nor rust can consume—heaven and divine love. Fleeting, mortal, ephemeral things give only momentary joy or satisfaction.

In the second quatrain, the speaker urges himself to pull in the sun of his personality ("beames"), to become humble, to yield his power, pride, and talent to "that sweet yoke, where lasting freedoms be" (l. 6). This image owes its power to Matthew, chapter 11, where Jesus urges his followers to take up the yoke of following him, calling it a light, easy burden. The last two lines of the STANZA reflect a psalm verse that says humans see light in God's light (Ps. 36.9).

In the final six lines, the speaker urges himself to hold tightly to the light of salvation that can guide the living person through the course of mortal life to a happy conclusion in heaven. The speaker condemns any who "slide." Since each "comes of heavn'ly breath," it is a principal human obligation to reject the claims of impermanent things in favor of "Eternall Love." The speaker concludes by asking eternal love to maintain its life in him.

Critics have been quick to pick up on this tonal shift. A great deal of scholarship contextualizes this sonnet within the burgeoning Protestant state as well as Sidney's own troubled political career. As well, it can be connected to the SIDNEIAN PSALMES begun by Sidney and finished by his sister after his death.

See also CERTAIN SONNETS (OVERVIEW).

Marjory E. Lange

CHARLES D'ORLÉANS See FORTUNES STABILNES.

CHARMS

CHARMS Anglo-Saxon charms were short texts containing recipes for curing or preventing a variety of maladies, both physical and mental. Among the hundreds of medicinal recipes in the Old English extant today, dozens contain some form of incantation or other verbal element, often from the liturgy, such as reciting the Pater Noster (Our Father) three times, and of these, about 12 contain a poetic element. These verbal pieces are known as charms.

Critics tend to study the metrical charms in relation to culture and anthropology instead of poetry. Nevertheless, the metrical charms are the most studied of the charms, perhaps leaving the false impression that most charms contained metrical incantations.

The metrical charms appear in various manuscripts dating from as early as the 10th and 11th centuries, though they are probably older. Some have argued that non-Christian elements in the charms (such as a reference to the Earth Mother in the "For Unfruitful Land" charm and a reference to Woden in the "Nine Herbs Charm") indicate that some of the charms date from the pre-Christian era. After the NORMAN CONQUEST of 1066, the Anglo-Saxon charms fell into disuse.

The users of the charms would have been medical practitioners called *leeches;* thus, the texts containing the charms are sometimes called *leechbooks.* Often leeches appear to have been connected with monasteries, and they may have been monks themselves; other leeches were probably private practitioners. Contrary to the popular image, leeches tended to rely on salves and poultices with certain herbal and animal ingredients to effect a cure rather than using parasitic leeches to suck out the blood.

Some of the charms show evidence of oral transmission. For example, two of the metrical charms for the loss of cattle appear to be different versions of the same charm, with a little three-line poem about Christ's birth in Bethlehem appearing in each with only slight differences in wording. The longer metrical charms seem to have garnered the most critical attention, especially "For Unfruitful Land" (also known as the "Acerbot charm"), the "Nine Herbs Charm," and "Against a Sudden Stitch."

The designation *charms* to mean medicinal remedies with an oral component is a completely modern distinction. The charms themselves appear in leechbooks filled with hundreds of remedies, or else in the flyleaves and margins of other manuscripts. For the most part, the modern separation of the Anglo-Saxon metrical charms is more the result of early scholarship equating the charms with magic and witchcraft rather than with early medicine. The most recent scholarship has therefore tended to move away from earlier depictions of the charms as magic and has instead focused on the efficacy of the charms themselves. Furthermore, recent editions of the charms have tended to focus on charms in their manuscript contexts, rather than by recategorizing them according to modern conceptions.

See also ANGLO-SAXON POETRY.

FURTHER READING

Jolly, Karen Louise. *Popular Religion in Late Saxon England: Elf Charms in Context.* Chapel Hill: University of North Carolina Press, 1996.

Pettit, Edward. *Anglo-Saxon Remedies, Charms, and Prayers from British Library MS Harley 585. The Lacnunga.* 2 vols. Lewiston, N.Y.: Edwin Mellen Press, 2001.

Pollington, Stephen. *Leechcraft: Early English Charms, Plant Lore, and Healing.* Norfolk: Anglo-Saxon Books, 2000.

Richard Scott Nokes

CHAUCER, GEOFFREY (ca. 1343–1400)

Geoffrey Chaucer was born in London in the early 1340s. His parents, John Chaucer, a vintner, and Agnes de Copton, were merchant class but comfortably wealthy. Chaucer likely received a good education at a local school, as his later writings demonstrate knowledge of Latin, Italian, and French among other things. By 1357, young Geoffrey had become a page in the household of Lionel, earl of Ulster and later duke of Clarence. In 1359–60, he served under Edward III during the HUNDRED YEARS' WAR and was captured by the French. After his ransom, he returned to Lionel's household. By 1366, he was married to Philippa Roet, a lady-in-waiting to Queen Philippa and sister to John of Gaunt's third wife. Together they had two sons, and perhaps two daughters.

Chaucer was frequently employed as a diplomat during the 1370s, visiting Italy at least twice. He also served as comptroller of customs in London (1374–86). Upon vacating this post, he moved to Kent, was appointed justice of the peace, and was elected to Parliament; Philippa died around 1387. Chaucer returned to London by 1389, when he was appointed clerk of the king's works (1389–91). He dabbled in administrative affairs afterwards, but never again achieved an important position. He died on October 25, 1400, and is buried in Westminster Abbey in what has become known as Poet's Corner.

Besides the above, there are only a few other facts known about Chaucer. He was sued for nonpayment of debts on several occasions, robbed at least once, and fined for beating a friar. Around 1380, a woman named Cecilia Chaumpaigne accused him of *raptus* (varyingly rape or abduction), but Chaucer paid 10 pounds to avoid legal action. Whether or not he was guilty remains unknown.

Chaucer's greatest achievement is the popularizing of the VERNACULAR. All of his works are written in the London dialect of Middle English. Scholars traditionally divide Chaucer's literary endeavors into three periods: the French period, the Italian period, and *The CANTERBURY TALES*. The first period dates up to 1370 and includes *The BOOK OF THE DUCHESS* and a partial translation of the *Roman de la Rose*. The Italian period (up to 1387) is indebted to Chaucer's travels and to the works of Dante and BOCCACCIO. These poems include *The HOUSE OF FAME, The PARLIAMENT OF FOWLS, The LEGEND OF GOOD WOMEN, Troilus and Criseyde,* and a translation of BOETHIUS's *The CONSOLATION OF PHILOSOPHY*. In writing *Troilus and Criseyde,* Chaucer perfected the poetic form known as RHYME ROYAL, which is sometimes referred to as CHAUCERIAN STANZA. Similarly, *The Legend of Good Women* introduces the HEROIC COUPLET to English poetry.

After Chaucer's return to London, he began working on *The Canterbury Tales*. Left unfinished at his death, it is a FRAME NARRATIVE poem that relates stories told by pilgrims on their way to Canterbury Cathedral. This famed work displays a diverse picture of 14th-century English life, and it is deservedly commended for its vivid characterization and adroit poetic techniques.

See also *GENERAL PROLOGUE TO THE CANTERBURY TALES*.

FURTHER READING

Boitani, Piero, and Jill Mann, eds. *The Cambridge Chaucer Companion*. Cambridge: Cambridge University Press, 1986.

Ellis, Steve. *Chaucer*. Plymouth, Northcote House, 1996.

Pearsall, Derek. *The Life of Geoffrey Chaucer*. Oxford and New York: Oxford University Press, 1992.

CHAUCERIAN STANZA See RHYME ROYAL.

"CHERRY-TREE CAROL, THE" ANONYMOUS (ca. 13th century)

There is no surviving medieval manuscript containing the text of "The Cherry-Tree Carol"; however, it is generally accepted to have been composed during the 13th century, alongside other popular CAROLS. As a result, there are four varying sets of lyrics that modern editors can choose from.

The basic narrative of this nativity carol is the same in all versions: Joseph and Mary are walking through a garden when the pregnant Mary asks Joseph to pick her some cherries. The aged Joseph angrily tells her to ask the one who impregnated her for some fruit. Upon hearing this response, Mary's baby (Jesus), still inside the womb, commands a cherry tree to bow down for his mother. Joseph immediately repents his harsh words upon witnessing the miracle. Two basic variants of prophetic STANZAs then follow: the now-born babe sits on Mary's knee, telling of his death and resurrection, or an angel appears to Joseph and foretells the circumstances of Jesus' birth.

The carol has a number of medieval literary analogues attesting to its early origins. Its closest analogue is chapter 20 of the apocryphal Gospel of Pseudo-Matthew, which enjoyed widespread popularity in the Middle Ages. The incident described there, however, takes place after Jesus' birth during the family's flight to Egypt and has Mary wishing for the fruit of a palm tree. Joseph responds that the tree is too high to climb, and thus Jesus commands it to bow down so they can gather the fruit. The 15th-century narrative poem *The Childhood of Jesus* also recounts this version of the story. However, the 15th-century N-Town Nativity play includes the incident as set forth in the carol. Some critics also consider the garden scene in GEOFFREY CHAUCER's "The Merchant's Tale" a parodic analogue of the carol. There, the foolish old knight January, in an ironic reversal of Joseph's skepticism, is easily deceived (and cuckolded) by his young wife May's desire for the fruit of a pear tree.

Musicologists disagree as to whether this folk song should be categorized as a carol or an early ballad. Its Nativity setting seemingly aligns it with the carol tradition. However, others point out that it does not include a REFRAIN, as most carols do, and exhibits some of the narrative techniques that typify later ballads.

See also VIRGIN LYRICS.

FURTHER READING

Rosenberg, Bruce A. "The 'Cherry-Tree Carol' and The Merchant's Tale." *The Chaucer Review* 5, no. 4 (1971): 264–276.

Royston, Pamela L. "'The Cherry-Tree Carol': Its Sources and Analogues." *Folklore Forum* 15, no. 1 (Winter 1982): 1–16.

SOUND RECORDINGS

Anonymous 4. "The Cherry Tree Carol." On *Wolcum Yule: Celtic and British Songs and Carols.* Harmonia Mundi, 2003.

Cambridge Singers. "The Cherry-Tree Carol." Arranged by David Willcocks. On *Christmas Night: Carols of the Nativity.* Collegium Records, 1987.

Lori A. Wallach

CHESTRE, THOMAS   See SIR LAUNFAL.

"CHEVREFOIL" ("THE HONEYSUCKLE")

MARIE DE FRANCE (late 12th century)   This 118-line poem, written in octosyllabic COUPLETS, is the shortest of MARIE DE FRANCE's *lais,* short poems or songs Marie adapted from the Breton *lai* tradition (see LAY). The preferred manuscript of Marie's *lais* is Harley 978 in the British Library, which is the only manuscript to contain all 12 *lais.*

"Chevrefoil" concentrates on a brief moment in the larger story of the legendary lovers Tristan and Iseult. It is generally assumed that Marie's audience would be familiar with the crucial crisis in the lovers' relationship: Tristan, nephew and knight of King Mark of Cornwall, has fallen in love with Mark's wife, Queen Iseult, who reciprocates Tristan's love. Marie's poem briefly alludes to the dismal fate the two lovers will have to endure, but the primary focus is on a brief moment of joy (with its full sexual connotation) amid their trials. The shortest of Marie's *lais,* "Chevrefoil" is widely regarded as one of her finest.

Marie characteristically opens the *lai* by calling attention to the poem as a work of artistic creation.

Then, after quickly mentioning that Tristan and Iseult are destined for suffering and death, Marie provides a bit of background to bring us up to the present of the story. Tristan, having been exiled as a result of his betrayal of King Mark, has subjected himself to dangers, including death, as will happen with faithful lovers who cannot attain their desires. Unable to remain apart from Iseult, Tristan returns to Cornwall; he spends the day in the forest so as not to be seen, and finds shelter with some peasants that night. Tristan learns from the peasants that Mark's knights are supposed to return to court, as is the queen; he is happy because he will get a glimpse of her going past.

On the day when Mark's entourage goes by, Tristan carves his name into a piece of hazelwood and waits to see if the queen will spot it. When Iseult rides by, she does indeed see the message and orders her retinue to stop so that she may rest. Iseult enters the woods, finds Tristan, and they experience great joy (*joie*) with each other. Iseult suggests that Tristan will be reconciled with Mark, and then the lovers tearfully depart, Tristan going to Wales to await word from the king. An accomplished harp player, Tristan composes a *lai* to memorialize the joy he experienced with Iseult.

Some literal problems of interpretation complicate this seemingly simple lay. First, the message that Tristan carves to signal his beloved is, according to lines 53–54, his name, but lines 61–78 suggest that there may be a much longer message regarding Tristan's and Iseult's feelings for one another. These lines, whether intended to be Tristan's own words or Marie's commentary, compare the two lovers to a hazel and a honeysuckle: The honeysuckle wraps itself around the hazel, and if the two are separated, they both perish. The section concludes with a famous couplet: "my love, so is it with us: neither you without me, nor I without you [can live]" (ll. 77–78). There has been significant debate over whether the hazel stick contains Tristan's name alone, whether the couplet is also to be included, or whether the lengthier sentiment regarding the hazel and honeysuckle is to be considered part of the writing. Perhaps Tristan's name is a sign, which Iseult is able to interpret as implying the deeper message. Or the lovers may have met at a prior time and exchanged words that will allow Iseult to understand the full import of Tristan's brief inscription. It has also been suggested that Tristan used OGHAM, a runic writing that would be much shorter and could contain a lengthy communication in a brief space.

A similar confusion exists at the end of "Chevrefoil," when Tristan creates his own *lai*. Marie's lines could be read to suggest that Tristan's song is the one that she is repeating, or it could be seen as a separate *lai* (untold) within the present one.

On a thematic level, the central crux involves Marie's stance with regard to the two lovers' transitory experience of pleasure in the woods. Is she highlighting, as the *lai*'s limited scope would seem to suggest, the ability of Tristan and Iseult to have this dedication to each other, this core of commitment and love, despite their pain? Or is one to understand precisely the opposite significance: that the joys of earthly passion are ephemeral and, while the lovers achieve immediate satisfaction, their devotion will lead to sorrow and even destruction?

Communication is the other prominent thematic concern. "Chevrefoil" not only calls attention to its own communicative role as poetry, but within the tale Tristan inscribes language first on the hazel stick and then in the song he composes. Just as the brief episode related in "Chevrefoil" opens onto a wider plot outside of the story, so, too, could Tristan's short message on the hazel stick be said to represent a deeper set of meanings. Viewed from one perspective, Marie could be charting the limitations of representation (just as she may be proposing the limitations of earthly love.) From another angle, Marie may be valorizing the power of language to convey, in a reduced form, the essential character of thoughts and feelings. In particular, scholars have paid attention to Marie's concern with the truth (*la verité*) at the commencement and conclusion of the poem.

Even Marie's attention to titles speaks of this synechdochal relationship between language and what it attempts to convey. The word *chevrefoil* refers to the *lai* itself; to the honeysuckle; and (presumably) to what the honeysuckle connotes metaphorically, both Iseult and her inseparable contribution to the love affair. Interestingly enough, Iseult is not mentioned by name in the poem (she is called simply "the queen"), and so the notion of *chevrefoil* again points to an absence, just as Tristan's writing speaks concisely of something to be more fully revealed in Iseult's heart, and just as the *lai* briefly communicates a much fuller experience.

See also COURTLY LOVE, SYNEDOCHE.

FURTHER READING

Cagnon, Maurice. "Chevrefeuil and the Ogamic Tradition." *Romania* 91 (1970): 183–155.

McCash, June Hall. "'Ensemble poënt bien durer': Time and Timelessness in the *Chevrefoil* of Marie de France." *Arthuriana* 9, no. 4 (1999): 32–44.

Reed, Thomas L., Jr. "Glossing the Hazel: Authority, Intention, and Interpretation in Marie de France's Tristan, 'Chevrefoil.' *Exemplaria* 7, no. 1 (1995): 99–143.

John Kerr

CHIASMUS Chiasmus is a figure of speech that relies on either semantic or syntactic reverse parallelism. Syntactically, the grammatical structures in one clause are mirrored in a second. Semantically, the rhetorical elements of an argument are reversed in order to create emphasis. The figure takes its name from the Greek letter *chi* (Φ), and *chiasmus* is literally a "placing crossways."

The device is used in both medieval and Renaissance literature. In Old English poetry, chiasmus is usually dependent on syntactical structure. BEOWULF illustrates this: "I shall undertake noble courage or my end day in this meadhall abide" (ll. 636–637). The structure of clause A (before the "or") has a subject-verb-object (SVO) structure. By contrast, clause B's structure is object-verb, OV, with an unstated subject, thus reversing the order and intensifying clause A.

MIDDLE ENGLISH POETRY and early modern poetry tend toward semantic chiasmus, where the clause is reversed in parallel. GEOFFREY CHAUCER's *The BOOK OF THE DUCHESS* demonstrates this: "For I am sorwe and sorwe is I. For I am sorrow and sorrow is I" (l. 595). Similarly, Sonnet 87 from SIR PHILIP SIDNEY's *ASTROPHIL AND STELLA* demonstrates this as well: "I *would have been* vexed if I *were not already* vexed" (l. 14).

Larry J. Swain

CHIVALRIC OATHS Chivalric oaths were a common poetic device of medieval ROMANCES, CHRONICLES, and EPICS. The swearing of oaths, in the chivalric sense, was always a sacred ritual act, a vow undertaken before and in the name of God; the sacredness of the vow placed a heavier burden on the Christian knight than did any secular oath or promise he might have made. The swearing of oaths was also a part of secular judicial practice and, in that manner, came to be incorporated into the chivalric literature of the Middle Ages and Renaissance. Chivalric oaths came in a variety of forms: They were statements of duty sworn to someone, as in ARTHURIAN LITERATURE, where the knights swear loyalty to King ARTHUR; they were sworn against someone, as in the *Song of Roland,* in which Roland swears to make the SARACENs suffer for every Frank who is killed; or they were personal vows of intent, as in *SIR GAWAIN AND THE GREEN KNIGHT,* in which the knightly hero vows to accept the Green Knight's challenge.

The oaths or vows of CHIVALRY have their origins in the Germanic warrior ethos, in which oaths and heroic boasting (and the two were closely linked) were an integral part of the warrior culture; and as such, oaths also played an integral part in warrior literature. Even before the codes of chivalry were articulated (beginning in the 12th century), Anglo-Saxon literature was filled with tales of warriors swearing oaths, promises of brave deeds to come, and vows of loyalty to chief and tribe. The swearing of oaths in ANGLO-SAXON POETRY, such as *JUDITH* or *The BATTLE OF MALDON,* provided a way for poets to convey the extent to which warfare, and the obligations it placed on the warrior class, held the society together. The swearing of oaths, particularly before or during a battle, created a communal identity for the oath-takers. The use of oaths, either prechivalry or chivalric proper, reinforced the warrior culture as the ideal social order. It was also a way for characters to establish social boundaries between the oath-taker and the oath-giver, while Renaissance poets added another layer to the oaths. In the great age of PATRONAGE, they often dedicated their works to specific (albeit sometimes unnamed) patrons, which were often written as oaths in poetic form, echoing the chivalric oaths that sometimes appeared within the works in question.

See also ANGLO-SAXON POETRY.

FURTHER READING

Keen, Maurice. *Chivalry.* New Haven, Conn.: Yale University Press, 1984, 1987.

Candace Gregory-Abbott

CHIVALRY   The simplest meaning of the term *chivalry* refers to the idealized conduct of war in the high-to-late Middle Ages (ca. 1100–1500). Chivalry can be as basic as heavily armed cavalry battling against each other or as sophisticated as philosophical theories about how war should be conducted. In its later, more sophisticated uses, it came to also be associated with a code of social behavior during that same time period. These are only two of the many concepts associated with chivalry. In both of these meanings, the term was wholly linked with the aristocratic class of the High Middle Ages.

In English literature, *chivalry* refers to the mounted noble warrior, the knight; his code of conduct (on and off the battlefield); and how the knight relates to his class, his king, and the object of his affection, his "lady." In its most Christianized form, chivalry carried with it high expectations of virtuous and noble behavior on behalf of God, the church, and those the church marked as worthy of protection. It emphasized the Christian virtues of generosity, loyalty, honesty, bravery, and spiritual purity (which are frequently exhibited by physical chastity). It was always more ideal than real. This ideal remained a staple of English culture throughout the Renaissance and later, and although the culture of commerce and trade eventually became the norm, chivalry was revived in the Victorian period as the epitome of noble, Christian behavior.

In terms of literature, chivalry was a staple of the medieval EPIC and ROMANCE genres. During the Renaissance, it was transformed into an elegiac, nostalgic genre that looked back to a medieval past that had never been as real as the writers might have wished. Chivalry was more real in the literature of the Middle Ages and Renaissance than it ever was in life: It represented life as it should have been. Chivalry and English medieval literature intersect at three points: literature that borrows from the culture of chivalry (as a mode of warfare, particularly in the epics); literature that in turn gives shape to the aristocratic social culture that surrounded the medieval warriors (as in the romances); and literature that encompasses handbooks, or guides, to chivalrous behavior in a more specific manner (in the code books and the courtesy texts of the late Middle Ages). During the Renaissance, chivalry was a way of redefining the past, as well as a way of criticizing contemporary morals and behavior.

As used in poems, chivalry can be both defining and distracting. At times, the rituals of chivalry seem to be little more than plot devices: All the ritual of the knighting (or "dubbing") ceremonies, such as confession and vigil, bathing and robing, girding with a sword, and the swearing of vows, are used to drive the narrative along and provide solemn breaks in the action, a way of resting between battles. Yet these rituals also help to define the characters and establish the parameters of their potential actions within the narrative, in that they define who the characters are and who they are supposed to be in terms of class and background.

The culture of chivalry, like the word itself, has its origins in France, and many English chivalric texts were translations or adaptations of French works. Although designed for secular entertainment, these poems were still viewed by the nobility as prescriptive texts on behavior and morality. The first romances in England appeared after the NORMAN CONQUEST and were a product of the newly formed ANGLO-NORMAN culture. Some of the earliest were versions of the *chansons de geste* (songs of great deeds) of Charlemagne and were written in French for the French-speaking Anglo-Norman nobility now ruling England. However, the Anglo-Norman versions and their later English redactions were more than mere copies. By the 13th century, native Middle English romances began appearing, such as *Richard Coeur de Lion* (ca. 1290), which portrays the king as a celebrated English hero.

The Crusades provided much of the backdrop for these romances. While in reality the Crusades were an outpouring of religiously motivated carnage and political greed, in literature they became the defining period of chivalrous behavior, when the knightly warrior put his military training to the noble purpose of purging the Holy Land of infidels. The tropes of crusading literature—vows; rescuing, wooing, and leaving behind of comely maidens; voyage and pilgrimage; defending Christian pilgrims from infidel brutality; delivering Jerusalem; miraculous victories and martyr-like defeats—became staples of chivalric literature. Even classical material was refashioned into chivalrous tales;

GEOFFREY CHAUCER's *Troilus and Criseyde* (ca. 1381) expands upon its Continental sources to depict Troilus as a chivalrous knight trying to protect his lady.

Nowhere is this more apparent than in ARTHURIAN LITERATURE, in which knights go forth on quests that resemble crusades and encounter numerous opportunities to display their chivalrous natures and boundless bravery. Gawain was one of the most popular of the chivalrous heroes, and in the 15th century there was a veritable cottage industry now called the Gawain cycle—*The Turke and Gowin, The Marriage of Sir Gawaine,* and *The Grene Knight,* to name a few.

Perhaps no English work of the later Middle Ages encapsulates the concept of chivalry as much as Sir Thomas Malory's prose epic *Morte d'Arthur* (1469). Malory drew on several traditional renderings of the Arthurian material, such as the alliterative *Morte Arthure,* c. 1400. In a single text he manages to create a chivalrous world in which knights and their class act according to the ideals of noble behavior; yet at the same time, Malory is writing a lament for a culture that had, by then, already ceased to be. Elements of chivalry that are found in Malory include the quest, combat between knights, pilgrimage, the rescuing of women and the weak, loyalty to lord and fellow knights, acts of generosity, and vigorous battle scenes.

Roughly contemporary with Malory, Sir John Writhe's *Garter Book* (ca. 1488) and WILLIAM CAXTON's English translation of Ramon Lull's *Book of the Ordre of Chyualry,* two popular handbooks to chivalry. Unfortunately, by the time these texts appeared in English, real military and social behavior had long left chivalry behind. Chivalrous handbooks such as this, which were original to England, or copies of earlier military texts (such as Vegetius's *De Re Militari,* which was translated into English in the 15th century) were popular for the same reasons Malory was: They looked back to a more idyllic time that never was, yet seemed so recent.

Chivalric romances continued to be popular in the Renaissance, as evidenced by the 1485 printing of Malory's *Morte d'Arthur,* which was reprinted by WYNKYN DE WORDE and RICHARD PYNSON in the late 15th and early 16th centuries. Renaissance poets were slightly apologetic about their interest in the romances: For all that they were popular with audiences, writers seemed to find them embarrassingly archaic and condemned them for celebrating violence. Some Protestants also objected to the glorification of Catholicism presented in the medieval romances. Yet the chivalric elements, such as the celebration of generosity, fidelity, piety, appealed to 16th- and 17th-century writers and audiences alike. Translations of Spanish romances and chivalric handbooks were particularly popular.

Renaissance romances were self-conscious reminiscences on the past. EDMUND SPENSER's *The FAERIE QUEENE* (1590–96), for example, resurrects a surreal landscape of epic battles and virtuous knights challenged by temptations of many kinds. That *The Faerie Queene* is an allegory only serves to emphasize the otherworldliness and unreality of the chivalric elements. SIR PHILIP SIDNEY's *Arcadia* is an even more traditional version of a chivalric romance.

See also ARTHUR; CHIVALRIC OATHS; *SIR GAWAIN AND THE GREEN KNIGHT*.

FURTHER READING

Aers, David. "'In Arthurus day': Community, Virtue, and Individual Identity in *Sir Gawain and the Green Knight*." In *Community, Gender, and Individual Identity: English Writing 1360–1430*. London/New York: Routledge, 1988.

Field, Rosalind. "Romance in England, 1066–1400." In *The Cambridge History of Medieval English Literature*, edited by David Wallace, 152–176. Cambridge: Cambridge University Press, 1999.

Keen, Maurice. *Chivalry*. New Haven, Conn.: Yale University Press, 1984, 1987.

Lyons, Faith. "Aspects of the Knighting Ceremony." In *The Medieval Alexander Legend and Romance Epic*, edited by Peter Noble, Lucie Polak, and Claire Isoz, 125–130. New York: Kraus International, 1982.

Ramsey, Lee. *Chivalric Romances: Popular Literature in Medieval England*. Bloomington: Indiana University Press, 1983.

Candace Gregory-Abbott

CHRONICLE An early form of historical writing, possibly associated with the *annales* of Latin classical literature, the chronicle may consist simply of a record of past events that sometimes mixes fact and legendary fiction (especially when the record stretches back for a long period of time) or registers the passing of the years by showing the annual changes in magistracies or computing from the years in a king's reign. Chronicles are written in both verse and prose. If they deal with events year by year, they are generally called *annals*; chronicles tend to be more rhetorically polished, but the two terms overlap.

Chronicles were very popular throughout medieval and early modern European literature, especially in Britain, as attested by the surviving number of manuscripts (nine pre-1400 C.E.; more than 100 dated 1400–75). Many chroniclers combined the duties of secretary, councilor, diplomatic envoy, and historian, and their activity was closely connected to royal or church policy, even if they were not directly employed by the Crown or by the ecclesiastical authority. Chronicles can also be read as a useful instrument for political propaganda, and as such they met particular favor in the late 15th and early 16th centuries.

Among the most famous examples of the genre, we can cite the *ANGLO-SAXON CHRONICLE*, begun in the ninth century and continued until 1154. Other well-known examples include John Trevisa's *Polychronicon* and John Capgrave's *Chronicle of England*, relating English history until the year 1417. Some scholars consider texts such as JOHN BARBOUR's *The BRUCE* (1375) among chronicles as well. Perhaps the most famous chronicle is Raphael Holinshed's *Chronicles of England, Scotland and Ireland* (1577–87), from which WILLIAM SHAKESPEARE drew much of his source material for his history plays.

FURTHER READING

Hay, Denys. *Annalists and Historians: Western Historiography from the Eighth to the Eighteenth Centuries*. London: Methuen, 1977.

Alessandra Petrina

CLASSICAL TRADITION Allusions to and incorporation of the themes, characters, and motifs of classical Greek or Roman literature in medieval English literature were limited to three primary areas: the Trojan War (Matter of Troy), the stories of Alexander the Great, and the founding of Rome (Matter of Rome). All three areas were sometimes grouped together under the general term, the "Matter of Antiquity." Until GEOF-FREY CHAUCER and JOHN GOWER, who wrote in the 14th and 15th centuries, most English texts that contained classical allusions were translations of Latin or continental French, Italian, or German texts. Most of this material was Christianized, if not in the Latin or Continental source material, then in the English. Because so many of the source texts were from the Continent, classical allusions in medieval English literature served as a way for English literature to associate itself both with the Greek and Roman past as well as Continental literatures (thus granting to literature in English a kind of double authority). Until the 14th century, there was a general sense that Continental literature (particularly French) was more sophisticated than English literature, thus making that association all the more necessary. Drawing on Latin or French texts validated English literature. In addition, the classical source material simply provided a familiar stock of characters and plots (such as the often-retold Troilus and Cressida story) that could be manipulated for many and varied purposes.

During the Renaissance, there was a dramatic increase in the number and variety of classical allusions as more classical texts were rediscovered and studied and humanism became influential. Yet Renaissance English literature continued to focus on the Matters of Troy, Alexander, and Rome, and poets devoted a great deal of energy to translations of classical texts. However, Renaissance writers turned directly to the Greek and Latin sources instead of the Continental versions.

Most classical allusions in medieval and Renaissance literature are found in ROMANCES, particularly in verse romances; there were, however, notable exceptions. The Matter of Troy makes an early and significant appearance in Geoffrey of Monmouth's *History of the Kings of Britain* (ca. 1138) and in LAYAMON's *The Brut* (ca. 1200). In both of these works, a direct connection was drawn between the kings of Britain (including the mythic King ARTHUR, who makes an early appearance in Geoffrey) and the royal family of Troy. Exiled, the nobility of Troy (in the person of Brut, a descendent of Aeneas) wandered onto the British Isles and colonized them. For Geoffrey and Layamon, creating an association between the British and the Trojans brought a veneer of respectability to the history of England as well as historical significance and a heroic, mythical "reality." The Matter of Troy is the one area of classical allusion in which English literature was most original and innovative, even if the source material was the usual continental or classical texts. In the Matter of Troy, medieval English literature moved beyond mere translation into invention of new legends.

The Matter of Troy continued to make substantial appearances in English throughout the 14th and 15th century, such as Chaucer's version of *Troilus and Criseyde* (1381); Gower's CONFESSIO AMANTIS (begun 1386; it includes other Greek myths as well as the Trojan material); and the alliterative *Destruction of Troy* (1400), which drew heavily and closely on a Latin text by Guido delle Colonne, *Historia destructionis Troiae* (Historical destruction of Troy). Colonne's text also provided the source for JOHN LYDGATE's *Troy Book* (ca. 1412–20) and *Siege of Thebes* (ca. 1421–22). The destruction of Troy by the Greeks was also referred to in SIR GAWAIN AND THE GREEN KNIGHT (late 14th century). As with all of the Matter of Antiquity, the Trojan stories were reinvented as lessons in Christian moral values and as an opportunity to criticize unjust rulers without referring directly to contemporary figures. However, because of the attribution of the founding of Britain to the heroes of Troy, the Matter of Troy moved beyond classical allusion into the creation of an English national identity.

During the Renaissance, the Matter of Troy continued to be popular, most notably in the works of WILLIAM SHAKESPEARE, including his own version of *Troilus and Cressida* (1603), and SIR PHILIP SIDNEY's *Arcadia* (1580). In contrast to the Middle Ages, though, in the 16th and 17th centuries, the Matter of Troy was viewed primarily as source material for plots and characters, and the connection between Trojan and English royalty was either ignored or challenged by other myths of origin, which tended to separate the English from continental identities.

As with the Matter of Troy, legends about Alexander the Great were retold, expanded upon, and Christianized. The various Alexander romances, most of which were first written on the Continent and then translated into English, also incorporated chivalrous elements. Perhaps the earliest English adaptation of the Alexander story is in the *Kyng Alisaunder* romance of ca. 1330. The inspiration for this text was an ANGLO-NORMAN romance. Typical of the romance genre, it elaborates upon the basic Alexander conquest story to incorporate marvels and elaborate battle sequences. Alexander makes a brief appearance in Ranulph Higdon's *Polychronicon* of 1362, which also includes more substantial Matter of Rome material, with references to Roman writers such as Josephus and Seneca. The *Polychronicon* was translated into English in 1385–87 by John of Trevisa and again in the 15th century by an unknown author.

Two fragmentary Alexander tales, known as *Alexander A* and *Alexander B,* were probably written in the late 14th century. The B fragment incorporates one of the standard medieval interpolations into the Alexander legend, a letter reputedly from Alexander to King Dindimus of Brahmin. The alliterative *Wars of Alexander* might be called the culmination of the Matter of Alexander; the poem dates from the late 14th or early 15th century. As with its predecessors, the *Wars of Alexander* is essentially a translation of a Continental Latin source—in this case, the 10th century *Historia de Preliis* by Leo of Naples.

A dramatic shift in the number and scope of classical allusions occurred with the rediscovery and revival of interest in Greek and Roman authors during the late 15th and throughout the 16th century. This is most notable in the proliferation in references to the Matter of Rome, which is directly tied to VIRGIL and OVID, the two most significant Roman authors for medieval and Renaissance English literature. Virgil's *Aeneid* and *Eclogues* were widely known, and various annotated versions in Latin, as well as commentaries on these texts, circulated in medieval England. Roman mythology, drawn from these texts, was a particularly fruitful source of characters and plots. However, the historical characters of Rome were also popular in the late Middle Ages and the Renaissance.

In terms of literature in English, Chaucer's *The LEGEND OF GOOD WOMEN* and Gower's *Confessio Amantis* draw heavily on the writings of Ovid, particularly his epistles and the *Amores*; the latter was itself translated into English by CHRISTOPHER MARLOWE (1580). Shakespeare's *Titus Andronicus* (1594) makes Ovid's *Metamorphoses* into a prop as well as invoking the poem in its own lines. There were many other important translations of classical texts in the 15th and 16th centuries, which provided more classical material for writers to incorporate into English literary creations. Around 1460, Benedict Burgh translated Cato's *Distichs,* which had been an influential text in its original Latin. The *Aeneid* was translated in 1513 by GAVIN DOUGLAS, and in 1573 by Thomas Phaer, and Virgil is cited directly by many authors of both the Middle Ages and the Renaissance. EDMUND SPENSER refers to Virgil as both his predecessor and his model in PASTORAL poetry in *THE SHEPHEARDES CALENDER* (1579), and one of Marlowe's earliest plays was *Dido, Queen of Carthage* (1586). The FABLES of Aesop, via Latin and French translations, were also popular in this period; WILLIAM CAXTON translated them from the French in 1484, and other versions appeared in English in the late 16th century, most notably, perhaps, by ROBERT HENRYSON.

Original works from this material include the *Seven Sages of Rome* (1470) and John Lydgate's *Secrees of olde Philisoffres,* which was completed by Benedict Burgh (1450). The latter was a translation of the *Secreta Secretorum,* a text on politics and the role of the prince which was widely thought to have been written by Aristotle, and which influenced numerous medieval treatises on government, including THOMAS HOCCLEVE's *Regiment of Princes* (1412). With the Matter of Rome, Renaissance literature once again (as with the Matter of Troy) moved beyond using the classical sources for literary purposes and returned to using it for didactic purposes. Roman models were particularly common in the plethora of Renaissance political treatises and manuals of governance.

FURTHER READING

Boitani, Piero, ed. *The European Tragedy of Troilus.* Oxford: Clarendon Press, 1989.

James, Heather. *Shakespeare's Troy: Drama, Politics, and the Translation of Empire.* Cambridge: University Press, 1997.

Noble, Peter, Lucie Polak, and Claire Isoz, eds. *The Medieval Alexander Legend and Romance Epic.* New York: Kraus International Publications, 1982.

Pearsall, Derek. *Old English and Middle English Poetry.* London: Routledge/Kegan Paul, 1977.

Wallace, David, ed. *The Cambridge History of Medieval English Literature.* Cambridge: University Press, 1999.

Candace Gregory-Abbott

CLEANNESS (PURITY) Anonymous (14th century)

Preserved in MS Cotton Nero A.x in the British Library, *Cleanness* survives along with three other poems (*PEARL, Patience,* and *SIR GAWAIN AND THE GREEN KNIGHT*) assumed to be written by the same poet. It is part of the ALLITERATIVE REVIVAL. While the *GAWAIN*-POET's other poems follow strict stanzaic structures, *Cleanness* is different. It is not divided into evident STANZAS (although many editors have done this for clarity), nor does the narration follow a very clear organization.

The poem's homiletic style is clear to all its readers, however. *Cleanness* consists mainly of exempla (see EXEMPLUM), a series of retold biblical stories that, for the most part, illustrate *unclean* or sinful behavior. There are three major exempla that illustrate God's vengeance on sinners: Noah's flood, the destruction of Sodom and Gomorrah, and Belshazzar's feast. These are surrounded by shorter ones, such as the fall of Lucifer and the biblical story of Lot. The *exempla* are set up chronologically, demonstrating the scope of human sins and God's response to them. The poet leads his readers through these stories as moral guide, teaching about God's abhorrence of uncleanness and the virtues of "purity" (another title given to this poem). Ultimately, the exempla are simply retellings of the biblical stories; however, in the poet's masterful hands they are given shape and emotion absent from their original form and read as if they are original stories, detailed and emotional. They serve their purpose as warnings against sin but also hold the reader's genuine interest in the process.

Cleanness opens with an introductory section praising "clannesse" as a virtue. This state of purity leads to God's greatest rewards: "If thay in clannes be clos, thay cleche gret mede" (l. 12). The introductory section closes with the parable of the Wedding Feast (Matthew 22:1–14), in which a noble man finally fills the feast hall but then expels a man dressed in rags for not showing proper respect. Similarly, humans garb themselves in sin instead of purity and cleanness, but they still try to enter the kingdom of heaven. This analogy of the kingdom of heaven to an earthly court is one that the poet also draws on in *Pearl*.

Next, the first exemplum, the fall of Lucifer, is introduced. This is followed by another short one, the fall of Adam. These two set up the first major story of sin and God's retribution, Noah's flood, showing God's vengeance in chronological order. The exemplum of the flood follows these first two to give context to God's rage at the world and the sins within it. The poet provides a vivid description of the sinful behavior that prompts God's actions, citing the people's reveling in "filth of the flesh," describing how they evily worked contrary to nature to slake their filthy, unnatural lusts. Moreover, devils consorted with them, spurring the people to greater acts of depravity (ll. 265–272). The uncleanness is clearly sexual—immoral acts against nature and devils coupling with human women.

God's flood will exterminate humanity, except for the good Noah and his family. The end of this first major section shows God telling Noah he will not enact the same kind of sweeping vengeance again and the poet reminding the audience that no one is without sin, which should be washed away and cleansed.

Two minor exempla also precede the second major one. First is the Old Testament story of God's visit to Abraham and Sarah, which results in the conception of Isaac. This is followed by the second short *exemplum,* the story of Lot and his disobedient wife, which is interspersed with the section's major exemplum, that of the destruction of Sodom and Gomorrah.

The poet describes the sexual sinfulness that permeates through the cities of Sodom and Gomorrah, resulting in God's decision to destroy them. Some critics have argued that the episode speaks to sexual uncleanness generally, but the passages seem to imply that only homosexual activity is unclean. The poet explains the horrors of Sodom where men couple in "female fashion:" "Uch male mas his mach a man as hymselven, / And fylter folyly in fere on femmales wyse" [tangle sinfully in fear of feminine ways] (ll. 695–696). This is contrary to God's own plan (the poet continues), of mutual heterosexual love as a kind of paradise (ll. 703–705). Most surprisingly, the poet continues by saying that this need not be limited to the state of marriage in order to be pure; however, this position underscores the sinfulness of homosexual coupling. To rid these cities of their sins, God wreaks his vengeance and reduces them to ashes.

The third part follows a slightly different structure than the first two, with one of the minor exempla integrated into the major one, instead of both leading up to its climax. These three are also more integrated stories than the *exempla* in the previous two sections. Beginning with the biblical story of Nebuchadnezzar, the poet describes how he sacked Jerusalem, seized its sacred vessels and held it captive.

The major exemplum is the story of Belshazzar, who defiled sacred vessels and then ignored the (literal) writing on the wall and Daniel's interpretation thereof. Belshazzar is killed. The story is allegorized for the readers, with the vessels representing the defiled human body, again reinforcing the notion that cleanness is necessary for salvation.

The poet intended this three-part structure to be the driving force of this sermon-like poem, as evidenced by the conclusion: "Thus upon thrynne wyses I haf yow thro schewed / That unclannes tocleves in corage [heart] dere" (ll. 1805–6). Three clear examples of uncleanness were presented; thus, "clannes" is God's "comfort." Although the structure of the poem does follow chronologically, it has been a point of intense study and scholarship. The poem is homiletic and adheres at least somewhat closely to the structure of a sermon, but it departs from it in some significant ways. Normally, a medieval sermon would build up to some sort of climax, but here God's punishments are lessened in time. The worst vengeance is Noah's flood, where the entire earth is punished for its sins, while Belshazzar's fate is his alone. Others argue that the poem's shape is informed by the poet's role as moral instructor and guide, leading his readers through illustrative examples to support his theoretical claims.

Most of the poem's meaning hinges on the word *clene* and its opposite, *fylth,* both of which have several connotations in Middle English. The adjective certainly does mean "clean" in the modern sense—physically washed—but it also means pure, complete, bright, and innocent, among other meanings. The word *clene* is interspersed with other similes, such as *pure,* as well as words like *courteous,* which play on the image of God

as king in his court of heaven. *Fylth* also has many meanings in Middle English, and scholarly debate over the poet's use of the word hinges on whether or not it has a predominantly sexual connotation.

Critics have also disagreed on the poem's tone. On the one hand, many argue that it is a largely negative, decrying humanity's sins. Indeed, at points it seems that the poem's given title should be *Uncleanness,* because this is really the only subject matter the poet discusses. Other scholars have pointed out that in the exempla, the poet has shown remarkable sympathy for the sinners, highlighting their very human characteristics and failings and providing hope for the reader.

FURTHER READING

Anderson, J. J. *Sir Gawain and the Green Knight, Pearl, Cleanness, Patience: Everyman Edition.* Rutland, Vt.: Charles E. Tuttle, 1999.

Andrew, Malcolm, and Ronald Waldron, eds. *The Poems of the Pearl Manuscript.* Exeter, U.K.: University of Exeter Press, 1999.

Clark, S. L. "The Significance of Thresholds in the Pearl-Poet's *Purity.*" *Interpretations* 12 (1980): 114–127.

Keiser, Elizabeth. *Courtly Desire and Medieval Homophobia: The Legitimation of Sexual Pleasure in "Cleanness" and Its Contexts.* New Haven, Conn.: Yale University Press, 1997.

Vantuono, William. "A Triple-Three Structure for *Cleanness.*" *Manuscripta* 28 (1984): 26–37.

Jennifer N. Brown

"COME AWAY, COME SWEET LOVE" JOHN DOWLAND (1597)

This lyric was set to music by the lutenist JOHN DOWLAND in his enormously popular *First Booke of Songs or Ayres* in 1597 and was reprinted in the 1600 miscellany *England's Helicon.* As an AUBADE welcoming the advent of morning, the song departs from the melancholy tone that characterizes most of Dowland's early lute songs, instead bearing a sense of CARPE DIEM: Each STANZA opens with the REFRAIN "Come away, come sweet love" and attempts to persuade the poet's beloved to seize the day and give in to his sexual advances.

The first stanza links love to the earth and air, portraying it as natural and joyful. The poet seeks to "mixe our soules in mutuall blisse" (1.7), referring somewhat flippantly to an ideal of Neoplatonism—sexual love as a divine meeting of souls. This playful tone continues in the second stanza, where the poet, hoping to entertain his mistress in the "grove" of love, declares they will spend their time "Flying, dying, in desire" (2.9), making use of the common Elizabethan pun on death as sexual ecstasy.

The third stanza makes the poem's most obvious appeal to the carpe diem argument, exhorting the beloved not to waste her beauty. In declaring that beauty "should rise, / Like to the naked morne" (3.2–3), the poet also alludes to the mythical birth of Venus, who in legend rose naked from the sea near Cyprus, an impression strengthened by the reference to "Cyprian flowers." The poet, after flattering his mistress with this comparison to Venus, finally admonishes her with the reproach of pride. Nonetheless, this remains lighthearted, in keeping with the rest of the poem.

The poet's sense of urgency is emphasized by the internal rhymes of line 9 of each stanza (and line 6 of the second stanza). It is given added impetus and energy by the alternating iambic and trochaic meter, which also provides Dowland with a rhythmically interesting lyric for his music.

See also AYRE.

FURTHER READING
Doughtie, Edward. *Lyrics from English Airs*. Cambridge, Mass.: Harvard University Press, 1970.

Susan L. Anderson

COMITATUS
Tacitus, the Roman historian, coined this term—from the Latin for company, or armed group—to describe members of an Anglo-Saxon king's personal retinue. Germanic tribes were led by chieftains ("kings") who kept their warriors' loyalties by providing booty from raids. In return, the warriors protected their king at all costs and swore never to abandon him. Breaking this bond is a serious breach of the warrior code. For instance, Beowulf's comitatus abandons him during the fight with the dragon (see *BEOWULF*). Similarly, comitatus flees in *The BATTLE OF MALDON*. In both cases, this forsaking of duty symbolizes the imminent destruction of Anglo Saxon society.

See also "WANDERER, THE"; "WAR-BAND'S RETURN, THE."

COMPLAINT
A poetic complaint focuses on a speaker complaining about his/her condition; as a subset of the LAMENT, the complaint is distinguished from the larger set by its tendency to request or seek a remedy for the condition under discussion. With no fixed verse form, the complaint's common topics include unrequited love, injustice, misfortune, and general undeserved misery. GEOFFREY CHAUCER's canon, for example, includes five poems titled complaints, including one parody, "The COMPLAINT OF CHAUCER TO HIS PURSE." Complaints are often intertwined with longer texts, as in "The FRANKLIN'S TALE" when Dorigen complains about her dishonorable situation. WILLIAM SHAKESPEARE's poem *A LOVER'S COMPLAINT* also features a female speaker facing dishonor.

FURTHER READING
Peter, John Desmond. *Complaint and Satire in Early English Literature*. Oxford: Clarendon, 1956.
Van Dyke, Carolynn. "'To Whom Shul We Compleyn?': The Poetics of Agency in Chaucer's Complaints." *Style* 31, no. 3 (1997): 370–390.

Carol E. Harding

"COMPLAINT OF CHAUCER TO HIS PURSE, THE" GEOFFREY CHAUCER (ca. 1400)
Unlike most of Chaucer's work, "The Complaint of Chaucer to his Purse" can be dated relatively precisely, probably sometime between late 1399 and Chaucer's death the following year. It is a 26-line ballade containing three STANZAS and a final five-line ENVOI rhyming *aabba*, in iambic pentameter.

The poem is a parody of the traditional COMPLAINT genre popular during the Middle Ages. In this case, the narrator pleads to his purse to "Be heavy again, or else I must die" (ll. 7, 14, 21). The poem uses standard language from lovers' complaints, calling the purse his "lady dere" (l. 5) and pleading "unto your mercy" (l. 6) and "unto your curtesye" (l. 20). The threat of death in each REFRAIN is also traditional of complaint poetry.

The envoi appears in only five of the poem's 11 manuscripts. It changes the poem from a parodic complaint to a begging poem, for these lines ask the "conquerour of Brutes Albyon" (l. 22)—Henry IV—to be mindful of the narrator's "supplicacion" (l. 26), indicating a plea for money.

FURTHER READING

Davenport, W. A. *Chaucer: Complaint and Narrative.* Cambridge: D.S. Brewer, 1988.

Yeager, R. F. "Chaucer's 'To His Purse': Begging, or Begging Off?" *Viator* 36 (2005): 373–414.

Michael W. George

CONCEIT   A conceit is a complex, extended poetic metaphor comparing disparate objects or ideas. Adapted from the Italian *concetto,* or "concept," the term was first used in the early Renaissance to describe a particularly imaginative turn of wit. This is a conscious elaborate and lengthy poetic comparison of two dissimilar images—particularly one that draws on extensive knowledge of philosophy and the sciences as a basis for its rhetorical power. PETRARCH is credited with defining the conceit.

The Petrarchan conceit was used in love poetry to express either the physical characteristics of the speaker's mistress or the tortured nature of the relationship between the speaker and his beloved. For example, SIR THOMAS WYATT, in "WHOSO LIST TO HUNT," compares his beloved to a fleet-footed deer—one wearing a diamond-encrusted collar engraved with the words *noli me tangere* (do not touch me), "for Caesar's I am . . ." (l. 13). Wyatt uses this conceit to express his bitterness at the paradoxical situation: He has grown weary of pursuing an unattainable woman, yet he has insisted on joining the chase, even though her emotional and physical remoteness has been clear for all to see. A comparison between a woman and a deer is not unusual, but the collar and its message add an unexpected complexity to the comparison.

See also SONNET.

J. A. White

CONFESSIO AMANTIS (THE LOVER'S CONFESSION) JOHN GOWER (1390–1393) JOHN GOWER first dedicated this massive English poem to King Richard II in 1390, but he published it again at least twice, in somewhat revised forms, by June 1393. An unusually large number of manuscript copies survive (48, excluding fragments), mostly from the 15th century. Many are of a very high quality and have illustrations.

Comprising well over 33,000 lines in English octosyllabic COUPLETS, the *Confessio Amantis* (*The Lover's Confession*) begins with a prologue that reflects on the value of books for preserving the memory of great people and announces Gower's intention to adopt a "middel weie" and write "Somwhat of lust, somwhat of lore" (l. 17, 19)—that is, he will write both for pleasure and for profit. In earlier versions of the poem, the dedication to Richard II follows next. Gower goes on to lament the vices of contemporary society, according to the conventions of medieval estates SATIRE, a send-up of the THREE ESTATES, which he had used earlier in his *Mirour de l'Omme* and *Vox Clamantis*. Next, he identifies social division as the cause of human suffering, basing his argument on the Babylonian king Nebuchadnezzar's dream. The prologue concludes with a plea for "An other such as Arion" (l. 1054), the mythological figure whose music could tame wild beasts and end human strife.

The poem itself is divided into eight books. Book 1 begins with an admission of defeat: Since the poet cannot resolve all the world's problems, he announces that he will change course and write about something less "strange"—namely, love. Gower describes love in a series of commonplaces, which betray the male perspective that dominates the poem. Love is experienced by every species and is lawless: No man can rule himself in love—rather, it rules him. Because love is blind and acts according to chance and not reason, there can be no certainty in love, "And thus fulofte men beginne, / That if thei wisten what it mente, / Thei wolde change al here entente" (1.58–60).

The narrator says that he will illustrate this principle using his own experience as an example, and when he transforms himself from a moralist into the lover, "Amans," the narrative that frames the vast bulk of the poem begins. Walking through the woods one day in May, the lover comes across a level clearing, and there he calls upon Cupid and Venus to complain that they have shown him no "pite" in his suit toward his lady. The deities appear. Cupid strikes the lover in the heart with a fiery arrow and departs, but Venus gives him audience. When the lover pleads for relief of his suffering on the basis that he is her faithful servant, Venus frowns and accuses him of "faiterie"—that is, false pretense. Venus ends the interview by charging Amans to undergo a pseudo-sacramental confession: "Unto my prest, which comth anon [immediately], / I woll thou telle it on and on, / Bothe all thi thoght and al thi werk" (1.193–95).

Venus's priest, Genius, an allegorical figure (see ALLEGORY) traditionally associated with Nature and with the animal instinct for procreation, duly arrives to hear Amans's confession. Modeled roughly on the sacramental confession of the church, the confession devotes a great deal of space to Genius's instruction of Amans—far more, in fact, than it does to Amans's account of his own conduct. Genius's instruction will have two main thrusts, as he himself states: Because he is a servant of Venus, he will speak (and question Amans) about love; because he is a priest, he will speak (and inquire) about virtue and vice. Genius instructs mainly through narrative and tells about 150 stories in all, taking them from various sources, including the works of OVID, ROMANCES told in the VERNACULAR, encyclopedic works, and EXEMPLUM collections. The stories range widely in length and complexity, from exempla of a few lines to the 2,700-line Apollonius of Tyre romance that fills most of book 8.

Gower organizes the confession according to the SEVEN DEADLY SINS, devoting the first six books to Pride, Envy, Wrath, Sloth, Avarice, and Gluttony, respectively, and further analyzing each of these sins according to their subspecies. No book gives a systematic analysis of the seventh sin, Lust, because amatory sins are dealt with in all the books. The unpredictable juxtapositions of Christian and amatory doctrines keep the lessons varied. For example, in book 1, Genius illustrates Surquiderie, by which he means lofty, contemptuous pride, with the Tale of Capaneus and with the Trump of Death; he then shows how this sin applies to love in the Tale of Narcissus, who was so proud of his own beauty that he thought no woman worthy of him. But Genius does not always do this. Sometimes he makes the application to love first; sometimes he omits one or the other entirely. Further, Genius applies the various sins to love in different ways. He applies Drunkenness (a species of Gluttony) to love metaphorically, making it an occasion to consider "Love-Drunkenness;" but he does not do this with Envy, which remains Envy whether in or out of an amatory context.

Genius also varies the structure of the confession by occasionally setting aside the seven deadly sins altogether. Amans contributes variety to the poem as well, since his answers to Genius's questions about his conduct range from flat denials to elaborate confessions of guilt to brazen wishes that he might find an opportunity to commit the sin. Usually, though not always, Genius concludes his analyses of the cardinal sins with a description of their "remedies," the virtues corresponding to them (e.g., the remedy for Pride is humility).

Before taking up the first sin, Pride, Genius begins book 1 with a discussion of the senses as the gates through which things enter the heart. The section raises interesting questions about moral agency. The Tale of Acteon shows the senses to be so susceptible to sin that humanity's condition appears almost hopeless. Seeing Diana naked, Acteon commits "mislok" [evil looking] and must pay by dying terribly. But the companion story, Perseus and the Gorgons, suggests that, however perilous humanity's condition may be, it is possible to resist sin. After treating sight and hearing, Genius abandons his discussion of the five senses and takes up Pride by telling the Tale of Florent, a version of the loathly lady story also told by GEOFFREY CHAUCER's Wife of Bath in The CANTERBURY TALES. The book ends with the Three Questions, in which a girl humbles the wisdom of her father and the king.

Book 2 features two important stories. First, the 1,000-line Tale of Constance, which Chaucer retells as "the MAN OF LAW'S TALE," illustrates Detraction (i.e., backbiting) and shows how Constance's virtuous suffering overcomes the ill effects of sin and fosters conversions to Christianity. The final story of the book, the Tale of Constantine and Silvester, similarly features dramatic reversal, resolution of social conflict, and conversion, bringing together the Book's themes and illustrating Envy's remedy, Charity.

Book 3 offers a version of the Ovidian Tale of Canace and Machaire, famous for treating brother-sister incest uncensoriously. Genius's main interest in the story concerns the frenzied "Malencolie" (melancholy) of the children's father, Eolus, who forces his daughter to commit suicide when he learns she is pregnant. Also noteworthy in this book is the condemnation of war, which comes within Genius's discussion of Homicide.

Book 4 is exceptional for its comparative lack of interest in its sin, Sloth. The forcefulness with which it condemns Sloth in love produces some strange and beautiful results, for example in the Tale of Rosiphelee, which excoriates idleness in love. Among the many stories in this book taken from Ovid are Pygmaleon and the Statue and the Tale of Iphis—two tales, which, remarkably, use starkly non-Christian metamorphoses to encourage steadfast prayer for love.

The noteworthy stories of book 5, on Avarice, include the Tale of Jason and Medea, which examines the sin of false witness in love, and the Tale of Tereus, which examines "Ravine" (rape). The book also includes a long digression, for which Gower has been strongly criticized, on the history of religion, most of which concerns the execrable beliefs found in Greek mythology.

Book 6, on Gluttony, denounces drunkenness and delicacy. Penitential tradition already associated these sins with sexual misconduct, so Genius does not have to stretch far to consider the amatory versions of these sins. The book ends with an account of Sorcery, which ecclesiastical writers sometimes associated with Gluttony. Finally, the Tale of Nectanabus, in which the sorcerer of that name uses magic to seduce King Philip's queen, Olympias, and fathers Alexander (the Great) on her, sets up an adroit transition to book 7. Since Nectanabus was not only Alexander's father but also his tutor, the story reminds Amans of the conqueror's other famous tutor, Aristotle, and he begs Genius to expound on the noble "Scole" of Aristotle. In book 7, the obliging Genius gives a popular account of Aristotle's teachings, dividing them into "Theorique," "Rhetorique," and "Practique." This book, which of all the books in the *Confessio* shows the strongest affinity to the mirrors of princes genre, ends with a discussion of Chastity, which Genius calls "The fifte point . . . of Policie" (7.4208–9). This theme transitions into book 8, which considers the antithesis of Chastity—Incest. The story of Apollonius of Tyre dominates this book. The hero, Apollonius, reveals a king's incestuous relationship with his daughter, whose hand he had been seeking. The king, Antiochus, pursues Apollonius, who escapes, goes into hiding, and eventually meets the woman he will marry. Several misadventures befall

them, but through everything they hold on to steadfast love.

Despite the pro-love stance Genius has shown earlier, at the end of the confession he tells Amans that it is "time to withdrawe" (8.2133). Amans replies that he cannot change his love, and the confession seems to have had no effect. He renews his COMPLAINT to Cupid and Venus, this time in the form of a "lettre" in 12 STANZAS done as RHYME ROYAL. Venus returns and makes clear for the first time that Amans is old, accusing him of "feign[ing] a yong corage" (8.2405) and alluding to his impotence. After Venus urges him to "make a beau retret" from love (8.2416), Amans faints. In a vision he sees companies of famous lovers, young and old, who come to dispute both sides of Amans's case. After Cupid and Venus confer together, the blind god of love gropes toward Amans and pulls out his fiery dart. Venus applies ointment to Amans's wounds and shows him his aging face in a mirror. She gives him a pair of black beads inscribed *por reposer* (for repose, 8.2907) and, addressing him not as Amans but as "John Gower," commands him to follow love no more, but to "preie hierafter for the pes" [peace] (8.2913) and follow "vertu moral" (8.2925). When Venus bids him "Adieu," Amans/John Gower reflects on what she has said and smiles. He returns home, resolved to obey what he has been instructed. The final section of the poem revisits the estates satire of the prologue, and concludes by rejecting erotic love in favor of charity.

Although Chaucer and others had written courtly literature in English before him, Latin and French had greater prestige at this time, and it is remarkable that Gower wrote a work on such a scale in English. Because Latin was the language of learning, Gower lent his poem a learned aura by adding a Latin device akin to those in medieval academic books. The form consists of two main parts, both of which were almost certainly written by Gower. Short poems in elegiac style, ranging from four to 12 lines, are inset before every new section of the English text to introduce the sections' themes. In addition, marginal glosses in prose summarize the argument of the main text.

A key debate surrounding the interpretation of the *Confessio* concerns the degree to which the poem constitutes a unified whole. Some critics have emphasized

Amans's "retret" from earthly love as the imperative to which the entire poem leads; with this view, we must understand Genius ironically whenever he advocates erotic love as a moral necessity. Other critics argue that Genius's advocacy of erotic love always has chaste marriage in view. The poem consistently promotes chaste, married love up until Amans's "retret," which should be seen as no more than a pious epilogue. Different versions of these arguments account for the poem's political interests in different ways. Other scholars deny that the unity of the work can withstand close scrutiny, arguing variously that Gower intended his readers only to read selectively, or else that Gower failed to carry out his ambitions for a large-scale, unified work.

The immediate and lasting success of the *Confessio Amantis* is attested to, not only by the number of early copies extant but also by laudatory assessments of the work by various writers from the 15th to the 17th centuries. It was quickly translated into Portuguese and Spanish, and WILLIAM SHAKESPEARE brought Gower onto the stage in *Pericles* (1607?), using Gower's Apollonius of Tyre as a source and also using "Gower" as narrator.

Several 20th-century assessments have argued for the aesthetic merit of the *Confessio* on many different levels. In the last 50 years, scholarship has made great progress in placing Gower's work within medieval literary traditions, especially in its relationships to the Boethian tradition of philosophical consolation, the vernacular French tradition subsequent to the 13th-century *Romance of the Rose,* and the MIRRORS FOR PRINCES genre. As well, the poem's connections to both Richard II and Henry IV make it highly relevant to the study of political rhetoric at this time. Several recent arguments have stressed the close relationship between erotic and political discourses, and the *Confessio* figures largely in these accounts. Gower's many stories involving the victimization of women by rape, seduction, and other forms of violence are attracting feminist readings. Finally, the manuscripts themselves, which contain evidence of the reading practices of the poem's first readers, continue to generate interest for studies in the history of reading.

See also CONSOLATION OF PHILOSOPHY, THE.

FURTHER READING
Echard, Siân, ed. *A Companion to Gower.* Cambridge: D.S. Brewer, 2004.

Nicholson, Peter. *Love and Ethics in Gower's Confessio Amantis.* Ann Arbor: University of Michigan Press, 2005.

Simpson, James. *Sciences and the Self in Medieval Poetry: Alan of Lille's Anticlaudianus and John Gower's Confessio Amantis.* Cambridge: Cambridge University Press, 1995.

Watt, Diane. *Amoral Gower: Language, Sex, and Politics.* Minneapolis: University of Minnesota Press, 2003.

T. M. N. McCabe

CONSOLATIO (CONSOLATION)   Comfort and consolation are frequent literary subjects. There are several different types of consolation, from the general comfort offered in some works in the ELEGY genre to the specific genre of the didactic *consolatio.* Old English elegiac examples include "The WANDERER," "DEOR," and "Resignation." These poems bemoan exile and loss but contain sections of consolation that enable the poet to continue on. As didactic poetry, the consolation involves a series of stock arguments delivered by a "wise one" and addressed to the afflicted person in order to encourage a change of view.

In the early sixth century, a Christian Roman consul, BOETHIUS, wrote the most influential of work this genre, *The CONSOLATION OF PHILOSOPHY.* Boethius combined the *consolatio* tradition of the classical period—which focused on instruction in virtuous conduct, often through dreams or ancestors—with the Christian apocalyptic vision. In this new hybrid, a divine or heavenly figure imparts knowledge and wisdom to the recipient.

See also METERS OF BOETHIUS.

FURTHER READING
Boethius. *The Consolation of Philosophy.* Translated by P. G. Walsh. Oxford World's Classics. Oxford: Oxford University Press, 2000.

Chadwick, Henry. *Boethius: The Consolations of Music, Logic, Theology, and Philosophy.* Oxford: Clarendon Press, 1990.

Larry J. Swain

CONSOLATION OF PHILOSOPHY, THE
BOETHIUS (ca. 523 C.E.)   *The Consolation of Philosophy* is a complex work that connects Greek and Roman thought to the medieval period and had significant

influence throughout the medieval times on writers such as Thomas Aquinas, GEOFFREY CHAUCER, Dante, and GIOVANNI BOCCACCIO. The work has been translated numerous times and into many languages. Chaucer's translation, entitled *Boece,* used only prose, rather than alternating prose and poetic forms. Queen ELIZABETH I also translated *The Consolation of Philosophy,* perhaps as an intellectual exercise or possibly to seek her own consolation at a difficult period in her life. Regardless of the reasons for the numerous translations and references, the impact of *The Consolation* remains beyond question.

BOETHIUS wrote *The Consolation of Philosophy* while imprisoned and facing execution for an apparently unfounded charge of treason against Emperor Theodoric. *The Consolation* is prosimetric in style—that is, it alternates verse and prose—and sets forth a conversation between Boethius and Lady Philosophy concerning the poet's ill fortune, the problem of evil in the world, and the existence of free will.

Book 1 begins with a verse in which Boethius bemoans his current ill fortune and sorrowful state. Lady Philosophy enters and casts the muses from his room, indicating that Boethius has "forgotten himself" but will be able to remember himself again if he is able to return to wisdom. Lady Philosophy promises to "remove the obscurity of deceitful affections" so that Boethius may "behold the splendour of true light."

In book 2, Lady Philosophy sets forth a critique of Boethius's current state of affairs. She concludes that FORTUNE, which has smiled mightily on Boethius, is necessarily fleeting and inconstant. Furthermore, she states, riches, prosperity, fame, glory, pleasure, and power are not the source of true happiness.

Book 3 turns to a discussion of true happiness. Lady Philosophy spends the first half of this book describing why no "temporal thing" can achieve or even contribute to true happiness. Perfect goodness and unity are identical and identified in God, who is perfect goodness, unity, and blessedness. Lady Philosophy then asserts that God cannot do evil and, that being the case, evil itself is nothing.

The assertion that God cannot do evil brings Boethius to articulate his "chief sorrow," which is that evil appears to both exist and to exist unpunished. Book 4 focuses on the question of why God permits evil. In order to address this question, Lady Philosophy distinguishes between Fate and Providence. Fate is the changeable and temporal order of things, whereas Providence is the unmovable and simple form of God's understanding. At the end of book 4, Lady Philosophy concludes that everything that seems evil is in fact intended to exercise, correct, or punish.

Book 5 begins with Boethius asking whether or not in the view of Lady Philosophy there is such a thing as chance. She replies that some actions appear as chance but are in fact guided by Providence. Boethius then asks if human beings have free will. Lady Philosophy replies that those who use reason have judgment, and we are free to the degree that we are in possession of reason. Boethius remains unsatisfied and asks for a fuller accounting to reconcile God's foreknowledge with human free will. In the end, Lady Philosophy asserts that foreknowledge is not a necessity from the divine perspective, as God does not reside in a temporal universe. In the same manner that a human being may observe an action and that observation does not "cause" the action, God exists in a "never fading instant," a constant present, and thus foresight does not imply necessity and free will exists from a temporal, human perspective. *The Consolation of Philosophy* ends with an exhortation to pursue virtue and avoid evil since we all live in the sight of a Judge who "beholdeth all things."

Many commentators have wondered why Boethius, to all appearances a Christian, would turn to the non-Christian representation of Lady Philosophy at the end of his life. Some have found in this fact reason to question his religious orientation; others have seen in the work an attempt to illustrate the compatibility of reason and faith within religion. Still others have argued that Lady Philosophy fails to respond to Boethius's final question about free will, and then provides a weak consolation to Boethius, implying through silence the primacy of faith. In the end, *The Consolation of Philosophy* resists simplistic interpretation, as is perhaps fitting for a work occupying such a pivotal position between ancient and medieval times.

FURTHER READING

Chadwick, Henry. *Boethius: The Consolations of Music, Logic, Theology, and Philosophy.* New York: Oxford University Press, 1981.

Marenbon, John. *Boethius.* New York: Oxford University Press, 2003.

Lisa L. Borden-King

CONSTABLE, HENRY (1562–1613)

Henry Constable earned a B.A. from Cambridge in 1580. He then served briefly as an English secret agent until being accused of treason due to his Roman Catholic faith. Spurned and bitter, Constable became an agent for the pope and the king of France. He was captured and sent to the TOWER OF LONDON in 1601/2, where he remained until 1604. Upon his release, Constable returned to France. He died in Liège in 1613.

Many scholars believe Constable's poetry crucial to the development of the SONNET tradition, having a particularly strong influence on WILLIAM SHAKESPEARE. Constable's SONNET SEQUENCE *Diana,* published in 1592, relies on the PETRARCHan tradition but is also indebted to contemporary French poetry (particularly that of Desportes). The result is a unique fusion of cultures. Constable's sonnets are often considered to be measured responses to beauty, rich with images of fire, color, and nature. Rapture is also a central concern of Constable's work, which includes *Spiritual Sonnets,* a PASTORAL version of *Venus and Adonis* presented as a CANZONE; the song "Diaphenia"; and four sonnets dedicated to the soul of SIR PHILIP SIDNEY, which were attached to an edition of his *DEFENSE OF POESY.*

See also "TO ST. MARY MAGDALEN."

FURTHER READING
Grundy, Joan, ed. *The Poems of Henry Constable.* Liverpool. U.K.: Liverpool University Press, 1960.

CONTEMPT FOR THE WORLD (CONTEMPTUS MUNDI)

Contempt for the world, or the *contemptus mundi,* is a tradition and a literary theme that originated in Latin religious writing but became a significant presence within VERNACULAR poetry. The name *contemptus mundi* is derived from the conjunction of the Latin terms *contemno,* meaning "to disdain" or "to hold in scorn," and *mundus,* denoting "the world." Originally, the form explored the dilemma faced by the Christian living in the world. On the one hand, the world was to be esteemed as God's creation, but on the other it was held as suspect because it was the zone humans were cast into following Adam and Eve's Fall from Grace. Contempt for the world eventually came to be a mainstay of the MIDDLE ENGLISH penitential lyric, exhorting the sinner into shame and contrition.

The *contemptus mundi* focuses on particular themes, typically the moral and physical decrepitude of man, the fickleness of FORTUNE, and the corruption of the flesh. These phenomena were inevitably traced back to Adam and Eve's disloyalty to God and the transmission of Original Sin to their descendants. In Old English poetry, "The WANDERER" and "The SEAFARER" are examples of this concept. A famous, but lost, Middle English example is GEOFFREY CHAUCER's claimed translation of Pope Innocent III's *De miseria humanae conditionis* (On the Misery of the Human Condition).

Expressions of the *contemptus mundi* include the UBI SUNT (literally, "where are they?" in Latin), the *timor mortis* (fear of death), and the memento mori (reminder of death). The first takes the form of a rhetorical style of questioning, which serves to expose the transience of created things. The *timor mortis* extends a meditation on the sobering aspects of death. The memento mori, meanwhile, warns of the inevitability of death and the decay of the human body. This motif is aptly illustrated in "ERTHE TOC OF THE ERTHE WITH WOH."

See also MIDDLE ENGLISH LYRICS AND BALLADS; "OLD MAN'S PRAYER, AN."

FURTHER READING
Delumeau, Jean. *Sin and Fear: The Emergence of a Western Guilt Culture, 13th–18th Centuries.* Translated by Eric Nicholson. New York: St. Martin's Press, 1990.

Innocent III. *On the Misery of the Human Condition (De miseria humanae conditionis).* Translated by M. M. Dietz. Indianapolis: Bobbs-Merrill, 1969.

Robin Gilbank

CORONA

In the 16th century, a corona (from the Latin for "crown") was a SONNET SEQUENCE featuring interlocking SONNETS—the last line in one sonnet becomes the first line in the following sonnet and so forth. The final line in the entire sequence then repeats the first line of the first sonnet, completing the circle. The result is a crown of glory for the poet and a crown of love for the beloved. Corona sonnets were often shorter sonnet sequences that served as introductions to longer sequences, or even to prose works.

"CORPUS CHRISTI CAROL" ANONYMOUS (before 1504)

The "Corpus Christi Carol" was found in a MANUSCRIPT that dates to 1504, but it was likely composed earlier. The short narrative describes a bed hung with gold raiment situated within a hall draped in purple. A knight is lying on the bed, bleeding from numerous wounds. A maiden kneels next to him, weeping. Beside her is a stone marker on which the words *Corpus Christi* ("body of Christ") are inscribed.

A CAROL denotes a poem intended for singing and dancing, though critics continue to debate whether the carol is liturgical or secular in origin. The BURDEN, which is repeated after each STANZA, was danced by a group, while the verses were sung and danced by a leader. In the unique case of the "Corpus Christi Carol," the burden begins the poem. Because of its two-line stanza, this carol has also been associated with the folk song and ballad traditions.

Scholars have noted the artfulness of this carol's form, discussing the REFRAIN, rhythm, ALLITERATION, ANAPHORA, CAESURA, and alternating adverbial phrases. Later versions lose the rhythm of the dance song while retaining some of its imagery. Interpretation of this poem—described by critics variously as "strange," "haunting," and "most mysterious and moving"—varies widely. Readings that associate this carol with Christ's Passion cast Christ as the poem's knight and Mary as the maid in a static "snapshot" in which the reader finds no Resurrection. The poem becomes a verbal pieta, communicating visions of mourning.

Liturgical readings of the carol suggest that it leads the reader to the Eucharist. Such readings align the inscribed stone with inscribed altarpieces, while noting that the colors red and purple have been associated with altar decorations and vestments. At least one reader has associated the poem with both Christmas and Good Friday by considering the relationship of the burden, here read as Mary's lullaby, to the rest of the poem. Either Mary sings the lullaby at the Nativity, foreshadowing Christ's death, or she sings it at Christ's death while remembering his birth.

Many readers refer to the Arthurian allusions in this carol and suggest that it invokes the Fisher King and the Holy Grail myth. Such readings occasionally place Mary as the "may" and often see Christ as either the "mak" or the knight. The stone inscribed *Corpus Christi* could refer either to the wounded knight or to the remedy for the wounded knight, as in the Fisher King tradition. The carol has also yielded numerous secular readings. One surprising and popular reading presents the speaker and weeping maid as Catherine of Aragon, who mourns with a lover's lament ("lullay") for her "mak" HENRY VIII. He has been borne away by the falcon, a heraldic badge for Anne Boleyn, Henry's second wife. In this reading, Christ's wounds continually bleed from Henry's heresy, and the "purple and pall" refer not to liturgical vestments but to a regal and wealthy secular hall.

Despite the interpretive cacophony surrounding this carol, most readings do agree that the poem contains both Celtic and Christian elements. Also, most readers praise the postponement of realization and the poem's deliberate steps into the setting before it reveals the final discovery of the stone to illuminate the earlier part of the poem, of which the burden reminds one at all times.

FURTHER READING

Greene, Richard Leighton. "The Meaning of the Corpus Christi Carol." *Medium Aevum* 29, no. 1 (1960): 10–21.

Karolyn Kinane

COTTON VITELLIUS A.XV (NOWELL CODEX, *BEOWULF* MANUSCRIPT) (ca. 800–1000)

The EPIC poem *BEOWULF* survives in a single manuscript housed in the British Library. Like many others, it originally belonged to Sir Robert Cotton, a 17th-century collector.

Cotton catalogued his manuscripts using a unique system: Each bookshelf in his library had the bust of a different Roman emperor atop it. The letters of the alphabet denoted which row, and the number indicated the book. Thus the *Beowulf* manuscript was on the Vitellius shelf, on the first (A) row, and was the 15th book in. Cotton bound the original manuscript together with an unrelated one. A 1731 fire in Cotton's library severely damaged the manuscript, which was scorched along the edges. Luckily, a Danish scholar had hired a scribe to make a complete transcription of it before the fire. The first edition of *Beowulf* based on Vitellius A.xv appeared in 1815 and relied on this transcription. Attempts to preserve the manuscript from further degradation in 1845 resulted in the loss of hundreds of letters, many of which are difficult to recover due to rebinding and so forth. Beginning in 1982, the manuscript has been the subject of an ongoing electronic project intended to preserve digitally what may disintegrate naturally.

Scholars date the manuscript anywhere from the eighth through the 11th centuries. However, this does not, necessarily date the poem to the same time frame, as it may have been written down long after its composition. Some scholars believe the late date because of parallels to the Blickling Homilies (11th-century sermons) and orthographic styles, while others believe the excessive praise of the Norse society's values indicate a much earlier date.

See also *BEOWULF-POET*.

COUPLET

COUPLET A couplet comprises two successive lines of verse that usually share the same rhythm, meter, and semantic message; thus, couplets are self-contained, complete poetic units. It is a simple and elegant poetic expression. In the 16th century, couplets became particularly crucial as they often ended SONNETS, completing the thought or narrative. There are a number of variations built upon couplets, including HEROIC COUPLETS (iambic pentameter), ALEXANDRINE couplets (iambic hexameter), and elegiac couplets (dactylic hexameter/dactylic pentameter). The latter were used by Greek poets for small-scale epics and by Romans for love poetry (e.g., OVID's *Amores*).

See also ENGLISH SONNET.

COURT CULTURE (TUDOR COURT CULTURE) (1485–1603)

COURT CULTURE (TUDOR COURT CULTURE) (1485–1603) Life at the Tudor court provided ample opportunity for engagement in literary, musical, and theatrical pastimes during the reigns of the five monarchs who bore the surname: Henry VII, HENRY VIII, Edward VI, MARY I, and ELIZABETH I. Economics, religion, and politics played equal parts in court behavior along with the individual personalities of the monarchs who reigned over it. The House of Tudor controlled the throne of England for 118 years, from 1485 to 1603. With Henry VIII and Elizabeth I combining to reign for 83 of those years, their influence on court life and the legacy they left are the most well-documented, though the other monarchs certainly played a part in shaping the culture of the Tudor court.

Upon his father's death, Henry VIII ascended to the throne at the age of 18. He and his queen, Catherine of Aragon quickly gathered around them courtiers who shared their love for music, performance, and poetry. Henry played several instruments, composed music, wrote poetry, and performed in courtly masques. He and his male courtiers once surprised the queen and her ladies when they appeared unannounced as Robin Hood and his band of Merry Men. The members of Henry's court were expected to participate in all that he enjoyed, and the court of the 1510s and 1520s was filled with music and poetry. Many times these artistic events were linked to what is called the game of COURTLY LOVE. Unlike a real romantic engagement, courtly love was intended as a show of formal, noncommitted affection, though at times it led to a more significant attraction and relationship. Single and married courtiers alike played the game, showering each other with love poetry, music, and gifts. Those at court during the time of these games of courtly love included the poets SIR THOMAS WYATT; JOHN SKELTON; and HENRY HOWARD, EARL OF SURREY.

As the early imprisonment of Surrey indicates, and a later one confirms, life at the Tudor court was not all merriment, poetry, and dancing; at times it was also perilous and precarious. The duke of Buckingham—father to Elizabeth Stafford Howard and grandfather to the earl of Surrey—was executed for treason around the same time Skelton was composing *GARLAND OF LAUREL*. Henry's subsequent financial, marital, and religious troubles also made the court a dangerous place. Henry expected complete, unquestioning support from those around him and became petulant and vengeful when it was not forthcoming. Officers of state were executed as easily as commoners. Sometime lord chancellor SIR THOMAS MORE, for instance, was beheaded for refusing to accept Protestantism.

After Henry's death in 1547, his nine-year-old son, Edward, became king. Though Edward VI was often ill, his court remained similar to his father's, offering entertainment and merriment alongside peril. Edward's own uncle, the duke of Somerset, who had been named his protector upon Henry VIII's death, was eventually executed. Despite the political and religious upheaval that went on around him, Edward had a troupe of actors retained at court, and, like his father, maintained a deep love for pageantry.

Mary I became queen upon the death of her younger sibling Edward in 1553. A devotee of music with fervent religious beliefs, the queen knew how to use pageantry to her advantage, beginning with an amazing show of spectacle for her coronation. Throughout the first few years of her reign, spectacle entertainments were quite popular at the Marian court. Musicians also continued to be in favor, including Thomas Tallis, who had originally performed for Henry VIII's court. Tallis's accomplishments as a musician and courtier should not be overlooked as he served under not only Henry VIII, Edward VI, and Mary, but also under Elizabeth I.

When Elizabeth came to the throne in 1558, she inherited a country in religious turmoil, financial distress, and political danger. Life at her court would prove perilous to some as the queen put down rebellion and rebuilt the country's wealth and power. However, she too enjoyed music, dancing, theater, and poetry. Her court was constantly moving from one royal residence to another or to the country homes of the ranking nobles, who often provided elaborate entertainments for their queen. Elizabeth immediately chose to ban religious drama, a deliberate attempt to erase the years of religious strife her predecessors had wrought by first leaving the Roman Catholic Church, then returning to it, then leaving it again. Elizabeth's banning of sacred drama was one of the factors that precipitated the great secular theater of the period.

Elizabeth I was also an accomplished dancer and musician, and her love of the arts provided an atmosphere in which different genres could flourish, both in her court and throughout England. Thus, lutenists such as THOMAS CAMPION coexisted with poets such as EDMUND SPENSER. Elizabeth ensured that the court was the center of the English artistic world, attended by poets such as SIR PHILIP SIDNEY and SIR WALTER RALEIGH. Sidney was considered a jewel of the court, and he wrote poems that illuminated the life of both queen and court, notably Sonnet 9 from his ASTROPHIL AND STELLA. Though the poem's overarching theme is one of love found and lost, the story it tells conveys a strong sense of the Elizabethan court. Also at court was Philip's sister, MARY SIDNEY HERBERT, countess of Pembroke, who was one of the earliest female poets.

Sir Walter Raleigh was a soldier, a courtier, an entrepreneur, and an explorer. These diverse aspects of his life in part contributed to a body of poetic works of varied forms and substance, and to a rounded view of the English court. He illustrated the court's liking for pomp and circumstance just as clearly as he showed that he shared the queen's love for farce.

Perhaps most intriguing was the "virgin queen's" insistence on continuing the game of courtly love within her court. Elizabeth chose "favorites" from among the many men who attended her—such as Robert Devereux, earl of Essex—with whom she carried on overt flirtations. It is likely that she slept with some of these men—the epithet "virgin queen" refers to her unmarried state, not her sexual experience. She also insisted that even peers who were not among her "favorites" treat her as if they were her ardent admirer, casting her in the role of the "cruel fair" woman so prevalent in the poets' SONNET SEQUENCES. This was a two-sided, dangerous game to play, and some men ended up in the TOWER OF LONDON merely for marrying without Elizabeth's permission.

See also PATRONAGE.

FURTHER READING

Anglo, Sydney. *Spectacle, Pageantry, and Early Tudor Policy.* 2nd ed. New York: Oxford University Press, 1997.

Dutton, Ralph. *English Court Life: From Henry VII to George II.* London: B. T. Batsford Ltd., 1963.

Elton, G. R. *England under the Tudors.* 3rd ed. London/New York: Routledge, 1991.

Kimberly Tony Korol

COURTLY LOVE Gaston Paris coined the term *courtly love* (*amour courtois*) in the late 19th century in reference to the curious dynamics of Lancelot and Guinevere's relationship in ARTHURIAN LITERATURE. In essence, courtly love refers to a highly stylized, ideal form of love, closely related to the "refined love" (*fin'* *amor*) of the troubadours, which focused on the poet's devotion to an unattainable lady of equal or higher rank. This concept is known as *amor de lohn* (distant love, or love from far away). At the end of the 12th century, ANDREAS CAPELLANUS composed a Latin treatise commonly known as *The Art of Courtly Love* (ca. 1184–86). According to Andreas, the love of a lady can ennoble a man's character and enable him to accomplish great deeds: "[T]he man in love becomes accustomed to performing many services gracefully for everyone" (book 1, ch. 4). Courtly love could only exist outside of marriage, and its code dictated that the man must initiate the love affair by pledging himself to a woman and by submitting to her desires. The lady, meanwhile, had the power to accept or reject her suitor, although he would continue to serve her faithfully, regardless of her decision. Thus, the courtly love relationship mirrored the FEUDAL OATHS sworn between a knight and his liegelord. Recent critical analysis has demonstrated the homosocial, if not homosexual, intent behind the "love triangles," whereby the competition between the lover-knight and the husband supersedes the desire either has for the woman.

The adulterous nature of courtly love stood in direct contrast to the church's teachings on adultery, but many scholars believe that the prevalence of arranged marriages required outlets for the expressions of romantic love denied within the context of marriage. Generally, courtly love was considered an idealized state and an achievable one, though consummation was not strictly excluded. It was, of course, reserved strictly for nobility and became tied to CHIVALRY.

PETRARCH borrowed from these conventions, leading to the revitalized cult of courtly love celebrated by the early modern writers of SONNETs. Renaissance courtly love relied more heavily on chaste or platonic love, although quite often the desire for (or intention of) consummation is expressed, without hope of fulfillment. Queen ELIZABETH I admired the ideals of courtly love so much that she insisted the rhetoric of her courtiers be expressed in amorous terms, resulting in the politicization of courtly love during the Tudor age.

Modern critics have explored the boundaries of courtly love, and a number have linked it to masochism. In particular, the early modern version features an abject lover suffering mightily at the hands of his "cruel fair" lady, who delights in his torment. Medieval courtly love, more dependent on formal interrelationships, tokens, and exchanges, is more closely aligned with fetishism.

See also LOVESICKNESS.

FURTHER READING

Andreas Capellanus. *The Art of Courtly Love.* Translated by John Jay Parry. New York: Columbia University Press, 1960.

Ferrante, Joan M., George D. Economou, and Frederick Goldin, eds. *In Pursuit of Perfection: Courtly Love in Medieval Literature.* Port Washington, N.Y.: Kennikat Press, 1975.

Paris, Gaston. "Etudes sur les romans de la Table Ronde: *Lancelot du Lac.*" *Romania* 12 (1883): 459–534.

Porter, Pamela. *Courtly Love in Medieval Manuscripts.* Toronto: University of Toronto Press, 2003.

K. Sarah-Jane Murray, Hannah Zdansky, and
Michelle M. Sauer

CROWLEY, ROBERT (ca. 1518–ca. 1588)

Robert Crowley was probably born in Tetbury, Gloucestershire. He entered Magdalen College, Oxford, in 1534, received his BA in 1540, and became a fellow of the college in 1542. Crowley most likely converted to Protestantism while at Oxford. Leaving Magdalen in 1544, he returned to Gloucestershire and became a tutor. Two years later, he moved to London and began publishing political poems and pamphlets. Among many others, he penned a response to the burning of Anne Askew, the Protestant martyr. Crowley spent most of 1549 translating and composing *The Psalter of David,* becoming the first to translate the entire Book of Psalms into English. In 1550, he edited three editions of WILLIAM LANGLAND's *The Vision of PIERS PLOWMAN.* He temporarily fled England when MARY I took the throne, but returned to become vicar of St. Giles Cripplegate. Crowley died on June 18, 1588.

See also "BALLAD WHICH ASKEW MADE AND SANG WHEN IN NEWGATE, A"; "OF UNSACIABLE PURCHASERS."

FURTHER READING

King, John. *English Reformation Literature.* Princeton, N.J.: Princeton University Press, 1982.

Martin, J. W. *Religious Radicals in Tudor England.* London and Ronceverte: The Hambledon Press, 1989.

A. Wade Razzi

"CROWNED KING, THE" ANONYMOUS (1415)

A poem in the alliterative PIERS PLOWMAN TRADITION, "The Crowned King" is often viewed as political propaganda. Such a designation, however, fails to recognize the subtle political theory that underlies the poem—one that places it in line with the practical political theory of the prologue of *PIERS PLOWMAN*. Knights, clergy, and the peasantry have obligations to their king—an image of the divine "Crowned King," referenced in the poem as Christ—although the poem is more focused on the obligations of the earthly and yet unnamed king, Henry V. It is set on the eve of Corpus Christi (May 29, 1415) and uses the form of a DREAM VISION, in which the poet overhears a kneeling cleric giving words that hover between advice and warning to the king.

The first 42 lines of the poem set up the historical frame, the dream vision, and the attitude of the poet toward his subject. The opening features the poet on a high hill and looking down on a "dale deppest of othre" (l. 32) containing a great and diverse multitude of people. Though this seems to echo the opening imagery of *Piers Plowman,* the location is used only to situate his dream, rather than to place theological implications on the landscape. In the midst of this scene, the poet/dreamer believes he hears the king requesting "A soleyn subsidie" ("solemn subsidy," l. 36) in order to fund his wars in France. Those who are able to pay are supposed to bear the taxation burden for the poor, at least in theory. The poet engages in the king's shortsighted and potentially exploitative vision, rather than sounding a rallying cry of patriotism.

The remainder of the poem, lines 43–144, provides counsel to the king that initially seems motivated by the request for the "soleyn subsidie" (l. 36) but becomes more far ranging in thought. Described as the "sawes [wisdom] of Salomon" (l. 44), the advice assumes the position of an authoritative discourse on the medieval community. In the position of justice, the king is to "justifie the trouthe" (l. 53) and to rule with reason, again echoing imagery from *Piers Plowman* about the king, who requires the aid of Conscience and Reason to govern correctly. As the chief minister of justice, the king should be particularly fair to the labor force since he enjoys the riches from their work.

"The Crowned King" is not, however, a poem of social protest. The king is not condemned for his luxury, but rather is counseled to remember its source. Working with his nobles in Parliament is seen as an act of strength as it brings together community support and empowerment. Further, the king is exhorted to "Be kende to thi clergi and comfort the pouere: / Cherissh thy champyons and chief men of armes" (ll. 93–94). Love is the uniting force of this community, yet the speaking cleric knows that the rule of arms is important; thus, the best wielder of arms should be appointed to the position of "marchall" (l. 102). Strong knights along with a wise counselor/philosopher are also important to good, stable rule. A wise king should avoid being covetous and should instead reward his people. The poet is keenly aware of the vulnerable but important position of the poor in the social order. The cleric recommends the king follow the example of Christ, the "crowned kyng" (l. 141), who always acted out of care and compassion, even in suffering. The poem then concludes with a wish for Christ's kingdom, where there is "Prosperite and pees" (l. 144), perhaps in contrast to the contemporary situation of war with France.

Contextualized within the Corpus Christi tradition, "The Crowned King" at first appearance seems to be an almost doctrinaire statement of the king's two bodies—just as Corpus Christi celebrates Jesus' two bodies—divine and incarnated. More subtly, the poem takes the form of wise counsel to suggest to the king the simultaneously strong position he can hold and the dependent position he also occupies. Bound together by love, a typically Langlandian notion, the medieval community will thrive if the king listens to his people. Such a poem seems almost ironically addressed to Henry V, a popular and compassionate ruler. It may also be seen as a keen observation on the impact of the HUNDRED YEARS WAR.

See also ALLITERATIVE REVIVAL.

FURTHER READING

Barr, Helen. *Signes and Sothe: Language in the Piers Plowman Tradition.* Cambridge: D.S. Brewer, 1994.

Lawton, David. "Middle English Alliterative Poetry: An Introduction." In *Middle English Alliterative Poetry and Its Literary Tradition,* edited by David Lawton, 1–20. Cambridge: D.S. Brewer, 1982.

Daniel F. Pigg

CÚ CHULAINN (SÉTANTA) (first century C.E.)

Cú Chulainn, who supposedly dates to the first century, is considered the greatest hero of Irish mythology. Born Setanta, he earned the name Cú Chulainn (Hound of Chulainn) at an early age by killing a fierce watchdog and then taking its place. At the age of seven, he took up arms in accordance with a Druid prophesy. His battle prowess was legendary, made even more so when he trained with the witch woman Scáthach, who taught him how to use the *gáe bulg,* a "blood-singing" spear, thrown with the foot, that was almost impossible to overcome.

As is typical with EPIC heroes, many of Cú Chulainn's adventures involved supernatural creatures. In one such tale, Cú Roí, king of Munster and a sorcerer, appeared to Cú Chulainn and two companions in disguise and challenged them to the BEHEADING GAME. After accepting the challenge, Cú Chulainn's friends beheaded the stranger, who subsequently picked up his head and left. The two friends then fled, while Cú Chulainn remained. Cú Roí spared his life and declared him honorable. This central story would be echoed centuries later in SIR GAWAIN AND THE GREEN KNIGHT.

Cú Chulainn was exceptionally handsome and had numerous lovers. However, he married only one woman, Emer. She patiently ignored his infidelities for the most part. Occasionally, however, Cú Chulainn would be overcome by love (instead of lust), and then Emer would grow petulant.

Cú Chulainn was killed after breaking the *geas* (magical condition) laid upon him by Druids and becoming spiritually weakened. Lugaid, son of Cú Roí, killed his charioteer, his horse, and then, finally, Cú Chulainn himself. Emer died of grief soon afterward. According to tradition, the couple are buried in one grave, marked with an OGHAM stone.

See also EARLY IRISH SAGAS.

CYNTHIA, WITH CERTAIN SONNETS (OVERVIEW) RICHARD BARNFIELD (1595)

As the result of recent research and a more complex understanding of human sexuality, RICHARD BARNFIELD's reputation has had the most radical reappraisal of all 16th-century poets. Earlier critics such as C. S. Lewis were often dismissive of Barnfield, based on an overt expression of same-sex desire, an element that was also observed in the 16th century. *The Affectionate Shepherd* (1594), for example, presented the often homoerotic love complaints of Daphnis for Ganymede, following the CLASSICAL TRADITION of male-male desire.

Barnfield's *Cynthia* reflects the established tradition of the PASTORAL, but the 20 SONNETS in this SONNET SEQUENCE also unmistakably represent same-sex desire that remains unrequited. Some critics insist that the poems represent only male friendship, which was valued above married heterosexual love. Attempts to dismiss the poems as representing male-male desire, however, are no longer the norm.

The published volume of 1595 includes *Cynthia, Certain Sonnets,* "An Ode," and *Cassandra. Cynthia,* written in a form that seems most clearly allied with the medieval DREAM VISION, is a poem of praise for Queen ELIZABETH I. In the poem, Barnfield shows his debt to EDMUND SPENSER's STANZA format. The rising of Cynthia, the moon, calls the pageant of gods and goddesses to appear in a beautiful place to which the dreamer/poet/recorder is directed. In this scene, the judgment of Paris to determine the fairest among Venus, Pallas Athena, and Minerva, with each promising to bestow good upon Paris, is itself put on trial. His decision to select Venus is appealed before the court of Jupiter, who, rather than overturning the verdict, pronounces the failings of each participant in light of one who is greater than them all.

Referred to as the "Fayrie Queene" (l. 144), a code word for Queen Elizabeth also observed in Spenser's *The FAERIE QUEENE,* this ruler exceeds all and serves as one to right wrongs herself. Jupiter orders a pearl to be sent to this "second Judith" (l. 161), a seeming anomaly that fuses both Greek and Hebrew traditions. Mercury is summoned to deliver the gem to Elizabeth, and the poem ends with the dreamer awakened by the rising of the sun. The dreamer/poet, deeply affected by the beauty of this vision, "gan almost weep" (l. 171).

Without a break, the 1595 collection continues with the 20 sonnets. Barnfield developed a new rhyme scheme for his sonnets (*abba, cddc, effe, gg*) but generally follows the ENGLISH SONNET structure. Classical allusions abound in the poems, which are set in the typical conventions of the love sonnet: the alienated and sometimes despondent seeker, Daphnis; the scornful, or at least indifferent, Ganymede; a BLAZON to Ganymede's beauty; and dialogues and monologues to resolve the unrequited love. The poems range from the philosophical to the sensual, at times quite graphic with sexual innuendo, and reverberate with the depth of emotional expression of desire.

Following the sonnets are "An Ode" and *Cassandra*. In "An Ode," the central feature of which is an overheard COMPLAINT of Daphnis concerning the scornful Ganymede, the poet/speaker, an observer, notes that in Daphnis's heart the word *Eliza* is written (l. 92). "An Ode" thus combines the world imaged in the sonnets with the world of *Cynthia*. *Cassandra* also has a stanza in praise of Queen Elizabeth I (ll. 217–222); here the poet asks for pardon for not being able to praise "Eliza" correctly, almost as an aside. The poem itself follows the prophetess Cassandra's fate during the Trojan War. Both blessed and cursed by the gift of prophesy that no one believes, the powerless Cassandra eventually commits suicide. It is an expression of amorous, heterosexual desire that stands in contrast to the other poems in this 1595 collection.

Cynthia, with Certain Sonnets (1595) is indeed a varied collection, featuring a range of poetic genres and subjects. The themes of passionate desire, whether heterosexual or homosexual, and nationalism enshrined in Queen Elizabeth make this collection unique in English poetry.

FURTHER READING

Barnfield, Richard. *The Complete Poems*. Edited by George Klawitter. Selinsgrove, Pa.: Susquehanna University Press, 1990.

Borris, Kenneth, and George Klawitter, eds. *The Affectionate Shepherd: Celebrating Richard Barnfield*. Selinsgrove, Pa.: Susquehanna University Press, 2001.

Bray Alan. *Homosexuality in Renaissance England*. New York: Columbia University Press, 1995.

Hicks-Jenkins, Clive. *The Affectionate Shepheard*. Llandogo, England: Old Stile Press, 1998.

———. *Sonnets by Richard Barnfield*. Llandogo, England: Old Stile Press, 2001.

Worrall, Andrew. "Richard Barnfield: A New Biography." *N&Q* 39 (1992): 370–371.

Daniel F. Pigg

Cynthia, with Certain Sonnets: Sonnet 1 ("Sporting at fancie, setting light by love") RICHARD BARNFIELD (1595)

Sonnet 1, "Sporting at fancie, setting light by love," written in RICHARD BARNFIELD's unique rhyme scheme (*abba, cddc, effe, gg*) combines elements of both ITALIAN (PETRARCHAN) SONNET and ENGLISH SONNET forms and uses imagery typical of the SONNET originating with PETRARCH and popularized in England by SIR THOMAS WYATT and HENRY HOWARD, EARL OF SURREY. Composed with an elaborate irony that confuses thief and victim, the sonnet shows that the speaker, Daphnis, has been complicit in the loss of his heart to the "theefe" (Ganymede). It has been taken, and he desired that it be taken. The poem depicts a kind of allegorical struggle in the speaker between the forces of reason and conscience. Reason is typically the faculty that promotes the judgment of ideas, and conscience provides a kind of moral check against actions that are performed. The "beauty" (l. 5) of Ganymede has brought about the loss of Daphnis's heart, yet there are no images of outward physical violence in the act of theft. Neither conscience as judge or "twelve Reasons" (l. 9) as the jury can convict Ganymede of the theft. The eyes are the avenue through which the theft has occurred, a typical site for the loss of the heart originating with the medieval tradition of COURTLY LOVE.

Rather than judgment being given against the "theefe," it is given against the speaker in the final COUPLET with "in teares still to be drowned, / When his faire forehead with disdain is frowned" (ll. 13–14). The conclusion is a typical convention of the sonnet in which the lady's scorn brings pain to the male speaker. Of course, here that convention is shifted seamlessly to two male lovers. Daphnis is ultimately responsible for the loss of his own heart.

See also ALLEGORY; *CYNTHIA, WITH CERTAIN SONNETS* (OVERVIEW).

Daniel F. Pigg

Cynthia, with Certain Sonnets: Sonnet 5 ("It is reported of fair Thetis' son") RICHARD BARNFIELD (1595)   Sonnet 5 develops the imagery of the Trojan War. In it, the speaker, Daphnis, is wounded by Ganymede's eyes, which are full of desire. At the beginning of the SONNET, Achilles is praised for his ". . . CHIVALRY, / His noble minde and magnanimity" (ll. 2–3), and by extension these qualities are projected onto Ganymede. The poem records the tradition that only the person who is wounded by Achilles' spear could be healed by a second touch of that "speares rust" (l. 8). The speaker, Daphnis, understands his fate to be like that of the person wounded by Achillles. The spear is equated with the "piercing eie" (l. 10) of Ganymede, but the "remedy" (l. 11) and how to find it remain unclear. Here the speaker seems to be playing the part of the coy lover, adopting at times both masculine and feminine qualities, as was common in RICHARD BARNFIELD's verse.

The poem's final COUPLET of the poem takes on a kind of teasing quality. The speaker says, "Then if thou hast a minde still to annoy me, / Kill me with kisses, if thou wilt destroy me" (ll. 13–14). The effect of "annoy" and "destroy" is highly significant because it connects the concepts of pain and pleasure. Given that the sonnet connects pain and pleasure together with the use of the imagery of war and healing, it seems only appropriate that the poet closes the poem with the bittersweet connections of that characteristic oxymoron. As in Sonnet 1, the speaker seems to desire the fulfillment of that connected pain and pleasure, "I know not how" (l. 12). Here the speaker seems to be playing as much with the minds of his audience as with Ganymede.

See also CLASSICAL TRADITION; *CYNTHIA, WITH CERTAIN SONNETS* (OVERVIEW).

Daniel F. Pigg

Cynthia, with Certain Sonnets: Sonnet 9 ("Diana—on a time—walking the wood") RICHARD BARNFIELD (1595)   Sonnet 9 develops a rich mythology for the origin of Ganymede that combines both elements represented by Diana, the goddess of chastity, and Venus, the goddess of love; the pairing of the two reveals important aspects of Ganymede's nature. According to the myth, Diana "Chanc't for to pricke her

foote against a thorne" (l. 4), and Venus was able to collect the drops of blood into a crystal vial. Venus, taking Diana's blood and snow from Rhodope (a mountain in Greece), creates "A lovely creature, brighter than the Dey" (l. 12). The combination of Diana and Venus is important here, for it conjoins desire and the tempering of desire at the same time. The image is one of chaste desire, an oxymoron intended to reveal important aspects of a creature fashioned by Venus. The poet is careful here of his historical allegory because it would have been less likely that Diana, connected with chastity, would produce such a child. Venus, combining elements of the human body and the ephemeral nature of snow, creates an image of beauty.

In the SONNET's final COUPLET, Venus takes the male child, has him "christened in faire Paphos shrine" (l. 13), and gives him the name Ganymede, a name of divine origin, according to the poem. According to legend, Ganymede, the son of King Tros, possessed great beauty. He was supposedly acting as a shepherd boy when Apollo abducted him. The intent of the poem is to show his divine origin and also to provide a rationalized view of his mixed qualities of passion and restraint.

See also CLASSICAL TRADITION; *CYNTHIA, WITH CERTAIN SONNETS* (OVERVIEW).

Cynthia, with Certain Sonnets: Sonnet 11 ("Sighing, and sadly sitting by my love") RICHARD BARNFIELD (1595)   Unlike many of the SONNETS in which Daphnis is speaking in a monologue to himself, Sonnet 11 contains a dialogue between Daphnis and Ganymede who are seated beside each other. Daphnis's sadness is apparent, so Ganymede inquires about its source. In a veiled reference, Daphnis credits his sadness to love and its incompleteness. Given that the poem employs an enigma in interpretation, Ganymede asks, "And what is she (quoth he) whom thou do'st love?" (l. 9). Whether Ganymede is being coy here or the poet is playing with the pronoun *she* to distinguish his poetry from that of other sonnet writers, the effect is clear.

A momentary interpretive problem is introduced that can only be solved with a rather dramatic revelation. Daphnis provides a mirror for Ganymede to look into as the source of love's problem, but it is apparently covered with a piece of cloth so as to heighten the effect of the revelation of truth. The mirror is itself a very frequent image in Renaissance literature (see, for example, *The* MIRROR FOR MAGISTRATES and WILLIAM SHAKESPEARE's *Richard II*). In each case, the mirror is a teaching device whose usage reveals facts that could not be revealed in any other way.

Holding the mirror, Ganymede "taking off the cover, / He straight perceav'd himselfe to be my Lover" (ll. 13–14). In this sonnet, Ganymede is not overtly disdainful of Daphnis's affection, but he seems to be unaware of both its reality and its depth until he himself appears in the mirror. If we accept the notion that mirrors to do not lie, then Ganymede has been brought to truth in a direct way.

See also BARNFIELD, RICHARD; *CYNTHIA, WITH CERTAIN SONNETS* (OVERVIEW).

Daniel F. Pigg

Cynthia, with Certain Sonnets: Sonnet 13 ("Speak, Echo, tell; how may I call my love?") RICHARD BARNFIELD (1595)

Sonnet 13, based on the classical myth of Echo and Narcissus, shows the growing futility that Daphnis experiences in his pursuit of Ganymede. In the myth, Echo desires to speak her love to the beautiful Narcissus, who seems overly self-important, but because Hera has placed a curse on her, Echo can only repeat what has been said to her. She wastes away on account of a broken heart. In invoking this myth, Daphnis questions, "how may I call my love? (l. 1). The stars find their place of delight in the heavens; gems are admired by those who receive them. Like Echo, however, Daphnis is not able to find words to praise Ganymede's hair. Even beauty itself does not have a name or word to describe it. In a brief allegory, the "Faire virgine-Rose" (l. 10) covers the "milke-white Lilly" (l. 11), an image that speaks to the intimacy of the two lovers. The image, however, seems restrained by the description.

In the final COUPLET, Daphnis says, "And blushing oft for shame, when he hath kist thee, / He vades away, and thou raing'st where it list thee" (ll. 13–14). The reference here fuses the notions of Echo and Narcissus

and Daphnis and Ganymede, both represented in the sonnets as failed lovers. Typical of the sonnet tradition, RICHARD BARNFIELD uses language to show the limitations of language in conveying meaning. The lack of communication leads to futility and shame.

See also CLASSICAL TRADITION; *CYNTHIA, WITH CERTAIN SONNETS* (OVERVIEW).

Daniel F. Pigg

Cynthia, with Certain Sonnets: Sonnet 14 ("Here, hold this glove—this milk-white cheverel glove") RICHARD BARNFIELD (1595)

If Sonnet 13 is in some measure about the failure of language, then Sonnet 14 is about the embedded playfulness of language in revealing a truth of love. The SONNET picks up on a traditional notion of a glove as a token of love and honor, but it employs the image as a pretense for conveying a stronger message: *glove* turns into *love*.

The poem itself provides instructions for wearing the glove and an explanation of its meaning. Daphnis begins the poem with "Here" (l. 1), obviously intended to have the accompanying Ganymede pay particular attention to this rare gift, not "quaintly over-wrought" (l. 2), nor "deckt with golden spangs" (l. 3). In contrast, it is described as "wholesome" (l. 4), a fitting tribute to Ganymede, at least according to the giver's understanding of him. In the unfolding drama imagined in this sonnet, Ganymede is apparently about to put the glove on his hand when Daphnis says "Ah no" (l. 5), so that it can be placed over Ganymede's heart as a token of the joining of hearts. Anticipating a less than favorable response from Ganymede in wearing the glove, Daphnis tells him that "If thou from glove do'st take away the g, / Then glove is love: and so I send it thee" (ll. 13–14). The glove becomes the tangible sign of love, a token of affection dating from the medieval romance. For Daphnis, the glove becomes a symbol of his love, and at the same time, it becomes a representation of the true virtues of Ganymede because it is not overly decorated, yet it is hardly plain. In a sense, it is a kind of golden mean between the extremes of plainness and gaudiness. It is a true token of love.

See also BARNFIELD, RICHARD; *CYNTHIA, WITH CERTAIN SONNETS* (OVERVIEW).

Daniel F. Pigg

Cynthia, with Certain Sonnets: **Sonnet 17 ("Cherry-lipped Adonis in his snowy shape")** RICHARD BARNFIELD (1595) Sonnet 17 uses as the major structuring device a convention typical of the SONNET tradition; the BLAZON. Drawing on imagery from the Song of Songs in the Hebrew Bible, the blazon is a catalog of the physical features—typically the face—of the beloved as a way of praising. WILLIAM SHAKESPEARE and EDMUND SPENSER use this form to praise their ladies; Shakespeare uses it with modifications to praise the LOVELY BOY of his sonnets. RICHARD BARNFIELD's use of the tradition is more descriptive and sensual than any other poet of the period. Adonis, celebrated in Shakespeare's *VENUS AND ADONIS* for his considerable beauty, fails to reach the excellence of Ganymede. Daphnis catalogs his "delicate soft limbs" (l. 5), his "lips ripe strawberries" (l. 9), his mouth as a "Hive" (l. 10), and his tongue as "a hony-combe" (l. 10). His teeth are like "pure Pearle in blushing Correll set" (l. 12). The poet speaker even considers writing on Ganymede's "faire front" (l. 3), perhaps the only time a writer contemplates writing an act of praise upon the literal body as a way of cataloging the beauty of that body.

In what is clearly a very sensual moment for Daphnis, he concludes his poem with "how can such a body sinne-procuring, / Be slow to love, and quick to hate, enduring? (ll. 13–14). In a rare moment in his sonnets, Barnfield ventures into a discussion of "sin," a rather perplexing thought given the views of same-sex desire in his day in religious and legal circles, documented in recent scholarship. The body itself is said here to be the physical force drawing Daphnis to him, and that desire seems to be worth the possible theological challenges, if only Ganymede were receptive. Daphnis seems perplexed by the attraction and repulsion that he experiences from the person whose physical body is the reason for that desire in the first instance.

See also *CYNTHIA, WITH CERTAIN SONNETS* (OVERVIEW).

Daniel F. Pigg

Cynthia, with Certain Sonnets: **Sonnet 19 ("Ah no; nor I myself: though my pure love")** RICH-

ARD BARNFIELD (1595) Fidelity in love on the part of the Daphnis in Sonnet 19 elevates what is physical desire to the love of a divine being, a reference to Sonnet 9. Beginning with what seems to be an abbreviated conversation—"Ah no" and "nor I my selfe" (l. 1)—the speaker bespeaks his fidelity in "pure love" (l. 1) to last until his death, perhaps wishing that this depth of love would move Ganymede. Quickly, however, Daphnis notes that Ganymede's divine status should not make him oblivious to the possibility of love. Even in a divine heart, "loves fire" (l. 7) can be felt. Enumerating the reasons for his love, the speaker celebrates beauty and the loss of his soul to Ganymede.

Since RICHARD BARNFIELD has used language and letters playfully throughout the SONNET SEQUENCE, he has Daphnis to say "Even so of all the vowels, I and U, / Are dearest unto me, as doth ensue" (ll. 13–14). It is as if the letters themselves become emblems of the affection that represent them. Sometimes vowels in words are separated by consonants. Daphnis envisions a world where the two letters—the two of them—can be together.

See also *CYNTHIA, WITH CERTAIN SONNETS* (OVERVIEW).

Daniel F. Pigg

CYWYDD Considered the most important metrical form of medieval Welsh poetry, the cywydd was the favorite meter of the Poets of the Nobility and continues to be used today. Cywydd is composed of seven-syllable lines arranged in rhyming COUPLETs, one ending with a stressed syllable and the other with an unstressed syllable (masculine/ feminine pattern). There is no set number of couplets employed. A variation of cywydd had the odd-numbered lines rhyme with the middle of the even-numbered lines, and the even-numbered lines rhyme with each other. This formula works best with interlocked couplets. The poems of DAFYDD AP GWILYM sometimes display cywydd.

See also WELSH WOMEN POETS, POETS OF THE PRINCES AND POETS OF THE NOBILITY.

DAFYDD AP GWILYM (fl. 14th century)

Dafydd ap Gwilym is generally recognized as Wales's greatest medieval poet. The handful of datable references in Dafydd's work all refer to events in or close to the 1340s, so it is likely that he flourished then. It is uncertain when he died, though many believe he died of the plague around 1350. He may have been the son of Gwilym Gam and was possibly descended from minor gentry in mid-Wales. His home is usually named as Brogynin, near the modern village of Penrhyn-Coch. He also had links to Dyfed in southwest Wales, and his uncle, Llywelyn ap Gwilym, was the steward in the castle at Newcastle Emlyn. Dafydd wrote a heartfelt ELEGY following Llywelyn's murder, in which he names his uncle his "tutor." There is no evidence that Llywelyn ap Gwilym was a poet himself, but his court was likely to have been a cosmopolitan place and probably had an influence on Dafydd. Dafydd's main patron was Ifor Hael, a wealthy landowner for whom he composed several poems. Most of Dafydd's corpus, however, comprises love poetry, nature poetry, or some combination thereof.

More than 400 poems are attributed to Dafydd ap Gwilym in various manuscripts, but it is uncertain how many of these he actually composed, as his popularity meant that poems written by others would be attributed to him in order to achieve greater circulation. Modern scholarship suggests that 154 of these poems are his work, while 177 are considered apocrypha. Dafydd's popularity stems from the fact that as well as being an accomplished poet in the strict Welsh meters, there is a complexity in his vision, and his personality is central to his work. He wrote mainly in the CYWYDD form, making it widely recognizable and popular.

Dafydd is often described as a love poet. He also wrote poems on nature and intertwined the two themes: He is at his best describing love trysts in the glade or sending a bird as a messenger to his love. This was a new development in the traditional Welsh poetic tradition, and Dafydd may have been influenced by newer themes found on the continent; indeed, his poetry is often compared to that of the troubadours in Aquitaine. He also refers to OVID as a poet of love. It is uncertain, however, how he was influenced by these poets, as there is no evidence that Dafydd ap Gwilym visited the Continent—or even England.

As a poet of nature, Dafydd appeared to be particularly interested in birds. He often personalized them, and in several poems he chose them as love messengers. For instance, in "The Gull" ("Yr Wylan"), Dafydd uses a guessing-game technique at the start of the poem to describe the gull; in fact, the bulk of the poem is descriptive, and the message itself is a brief afterthought. Dafydd's contribution to the genre was to put the love messenger before the message, or even before the girl. His love poetry was often directed toward his various girlfriends. He had two main loves in Ceredigion (today's Cardiganshire): Morfudd, who was married and often difficult to pin down, and Dyddgu, a noblewoman whom he appeared to worship from a distance. Morfudd, described as fair-haired and temperamental, features in over 35 poems that reflect different stages of her life. Dafydd's poem about her old age is especially masterful and moving.

Nature also features prominently in Dafydd's poetry, usually in combination with love or religion, and only rarely on its own. In Dafydd's work, nature is used to enhance his experiences of love or, occasionally, to hinder him in his pursuit of love trysts. Sometimes this has led to his being termed a "summer poet." However, Dafydd's poetry is wide-ranging and masterful on many levels, and it is paradoxical in nature: part of the native Welsh tradition, yet seemingly influenced by foreign ideas; comprised of experimental poetic forms, yet reflective of the traditional meters; lighthearted and humorous, yet insightful and astute. A nature poet in love with love, Dafydd ap Gwilym is very difficult to pin down, and perhaps this is part of his enduring charm.

See also "TROUBLE IN A TAVERN."

FURTHER READING

Bromwich, Rachel. *Aspects of the Poetry of Dafydd ap Gwilym. Collected Papers.* Cardiff: University of Wales Press, 1986.
———. *Dafydd ap Gwilym: A Selection of Poems.* Llandysul, Wales: Gomer Press, 1993.
Edwards, Huw Meirion. *Dafydd ap Gwilym: Influences and Analogues.* Oxford: Oxford University Press, 1996.
Fulton, Helen. *Selections from the Dafydd ap Gwilym Apocrypha.* Llandysul, Wales: Gomer Press, 1996.
Parry, Thomas, ed. *Gwaith Dafydd ap Gwilym.* Cardiff: University of Wales Press, 1952.
Thomas, Gwyn, trans. *Dafydd ap Gwilym: His Poems.* Cardiff: University of Wales Press, 2001

Sara Flin Roberts

DANIEL, SAMUEL (ca. 1562–1619)

Born in either Somerset or Wiltshire, Samuel Daniel entered Magdalen Hall, Oxford University, on November 17, 1581, leaving three years later without taking a degree. In 1585, he published *The Worthy Tract of Paulus Jovius,* a translation of Paolo Giovo's book of impresas (a combination of enigmatic pictures and accompanying mottos), *Dialogo dell'imprese militari et amorose* (1555). Daniel's translation marks the first exposure England had to French and Italian EMBLEM books. *DELIA,* a SONNET SEQUENCE, was clandestinely published alongside SIR PHILIP SIDNEY'S *ASTROPHIL AND STELLA* and then republished with the Sidney family's consent. Daniel then came under the PATRONAGE of MARY SIDNEY HERBERT, countess of Pembroke, publishing *Cleopatra* (1594), a Senecan closet drama, as a companion piece to the countess's translation of Robert Garnier's *Marc-Antoine.*

By 1593, Charles Blount, Lord Mountjoy, had befriended Daniel, and he became the poet's new patron. Daniel appropriately dedicated his works to Mountjoy, such as *The Poetical Essays* (1599), which include "Musophilus, or a Defence of All Learning"; and "A Letter from Octavia." He continued writing, and by 1604, he was working under the patronage of Queen Anne, wife of JAMES VI/I. Daniel primarily wrote plays and masques for the queen, including *The Queen's Arcadia* (1605), the first PASTORAL drama in English. He spent the last few years of his life on a prose history of England, of which he published the *First Part of the History of England* (1612) and later the *Collection of the History of England* (1618). For many years, he was remembered as a historian rather than as a poet. Daniel was buried on October 14, 1619, at Beckington in Somerset.

See also EKPHRASIS.

FURTHER READING

Rees, Joan. *Samuel Daniel: A Critical and Biographical Study.* Liverpool, U.K.: Liverpool University Press, 1964.
Seronsky, Cecil. *Samuel Daniel.* New York: Twayne Publishers, 1967.

Josie Panzuto

DARK LADY

This title refers to the mistress in *SHAKESPEARE'S SONNETS.* She becomes the particular focus of Sonnets 127–154. Scholars have dubbed the mistress the Dark Lady, though WILLIAM SHAKESPEARE only calls her "dark" once, in Sonnet 147. The poems devoted to her feature highly sexualized language and are the most discordant passions of the SONNETs. Some scholars believe that the Dark Lady is married to a man whose name is Will, that she is pursued by Will the poet, and that she is also sought after by a third Will, a friend of the poet. Other scholars have linked her to Mary Fitton, a noted beauty of the Tudor court (see COURT CULTURE).

Shakespeare's Fair Young Man or LOVELY BOY becomes the subject of desire for the Dark Lady, too, and the poet feels increasingly alienated as the Dark Lady "steals" the Fair Young Man from him. In Sonnet 154, the poet speculates about their disappearance. For the poet, the Dark Lady becomes the occasion for fiction making; she becomes the emblem of unchecked desire, passion, and frustration, but also a symbol of mystery.

FURTHER READING

Pequigney, Joseph. *Such Is My Love: A Study of Shakespeare's Sonnets*. Chicago: University of Chicago Press, 1985.

Daniel F. Pigg

DAVIES, SIR JOHN (1569–1626)   Sir John

Davies was born on April 16, 1569. He entered school at Winchester in 1580 and Queen's College, Oxford, in 1585. He left a year and a half later to read law at New Inn and then Middle Temple, where he remained. Davies was disbarred in 1598 for brawling but reinstated in 1601. After this, he had a very successful legal career.

Davies's first major work, *Orchestra, or a Poem of Dancing,* was dismissed as a "frivolous poem" by many of his contemporaries. GULLINGE SONNETS, a SATIRE mocking Petrarchan conventions, followed. His next undertaking, *Nosce Teipsum (Know Thyself)*, was a philosophical piece. By this time, Davies had succeeded in impressing Queen ELIZABETH I. His next major work, *Hymns to Astrea,* was a series of ACROSTIC poems spelling out "Elizabeth Regina" that earned him royal gratitude.

Davies's success continued after JAMES VI ascended the throne as James I, since the king particularly enjoyed *Nosce Teipsum.* Later in 1603, Davies was knighted and appointed solicitor general of Ireland. His success continued, culminating in his being appointed lord chief justice of England. Unfortunately, however, he died on December 8, 1626, one day before assuming office.

DEFENSE OF POESY, THE SIR PHILIP SIDNEY

(ca. 1579–1584)   This text revitalized the tradition of defenses of (or apologies for) poetry against the Greek philosopher Plato's attack, as well as contemporary attacks on poetry and art. *The Defense of Poesy* is arguably SIR PHILIP SIDNEY's most influential work. It highlights a quality of art that is the nub of Plato's criticism of the poet—distrust of the artist's power to move people.

Ever since Plato proposed to banish artists from his ideal state in *The Republic*—owing to their misrepresentation of "the nature of gods and heroes" (*The Republic,* book 2) and, as well, to their ability to sway not only public opinion but also conceptions of ideal and acceptable behavior while presenting poor models of godly behavior—philosophers, artists, and literary critics have attempted to justify artists' inclusion in republics, ideal or otherwise. Sidney's defense joins those of Coluccio Salutati, GEORGE GASCOIGNE, Richard Puttenham, THOMAS CAMPION, and others.

Plato's first criticism is that the poet must interpret the actions of the gods as "good and just, and [ensure] that sufferers [of the gods' actions] were benefited by being punished" (*The Republic,* book 2). Plato makes art an instrument to be used by the state to control its citizens. He was particularly concerned because many poetic texts were used as teaching materials and thus presented impiety and immorality as acceptable. He outlines three laws that should bind those who would write or speak of gods—that the gods are perfectly good, unchangeable, and truthful. He then states that these three principles are contested by their representation in art. The poets, Plato contends, represent the gods as evil, changeable, and deceitful, and such representations threaten a social order based on the good, the perfect (the changeless), and the truthful.

A second criticism of poets is that "they have said that unjust men are often happy, and just men wretched, that wrong-doing pays if you can avoid being found out, and that justice is what is good for someone else but is to your own disadvantage" (*The Republic,* book 3). A third criticism concerns another form of representation: The poet puts himself into the character of another. Plato supposes that the reader also does this; thus, the reader deviates from his own character for that of another (possibly morally) suspect character. Plato's fourth criticism of the poet is his lack of primary knowledge. Poets deal in deferred knowledge and vicarious experience without recognizing it as having a second-rate relationship to the truth, to actual knowledge. Poets represent, imitate, and mimic the world. Such representations are already imitations; thus no truth inheres in them.

As a consequence of Plato's criticism, translations and other paraphrases from the scriptures, even post-Reformation, come headed with apologias that justify their existence for the edification of readers. The poet as creator must clarify the intentions of his work and show its usefulness to society. Furthermore, Plato's criticism presents a double problem for the poet. By linking poetry to what is useful, the poet must then delineate the usefulness of his or her work, thereby opening it up to the full range of Plato's other criticisms.

In *Defense of Poesy*, Sidney's first response to the premise that poets are liars is to claim that "the poet, he nothing affirms, and therefore never lieth." To dignify his art, he turns to Aristotle's claim that poetry is a "more philosophical and more serious thing than history; poetry tends to speak of universals, history of particulars" (Aristotle, *Poetics* 3.2.351b5–10). That is, history speaks of what happened and poetry of what ought to.

In his somewhat contradictory efforts to reestablish the authority of poetry, Sidney begins by disavowing it as his chosen profession, calling it "my unelected vocation." Through this awkward mechanism, Sidney exchanges the poet's passive role of inspired observer, one who reflects on gods, for the active role of man of action (soldier) and man of influence (statesman and courtier). Sidney's posturing as an "author" relieved of the stigma of "poet" enables him to speak powerfully on poetry's behalf as an objective observer, even while he argues against unjust characterizations.

Second, Sidney proclaims poetry the chosen base of authority for historians, the repository of classical knowledge, and the repository of the culture of other countries and civilizations. Moreover, Sidney bestows the poet with divinity, calling the poet "diviner, foreseer, or prophet." Third, he makes the poet a super-divinity (or, at least, supernatural), a maker almost beyond his Maker:

Only the poet, disdaining to be tied to any such subjection, lifted up with the vigour of his own invention, doth grow in effect another nature, in making things either better than nature bringeth forth, or, quite anew, for such as never were in nature.

After setting the poet above Nature, Sidney must distinguish the poet as maker from God as Maker, for the poet does not make a "real" world. Rather, the poet's art is not in the work but in the idea. The characterization of the poet as free-ranging "only in the Zodiac of his own wit" (l. 182) encapsulates the uncontainability, the independence of poets.

Sidney avers that "the skill of each artificer standeth in that idea or fore-conceit of the work, and not in the work itself." The conceptual skill of the poet is what obliges him to the Maker, who is the ultimate authority. Sidney asks us to

give right honour to the heavenly Maker of that maker, who having made man to His own likeness, set him beyond and over all the works of that second nature: which in nothing he showeth so much as in poetry, when with the force of a divine breath he bringeth things forth surpassing her doings.

Sidney's argument shifts and conceives of poetry as imitation, as mimesis, or deliberate mimicry inspired by desire. The poet's work has become a faculty, a technique in service of an end.

Next, Sidney attempts to give poetry authority by yoking it to utility, especially through the power of poetry to teach. Sidney delineates three main reasons: One, poetry imitates the "unconceivable excellencies of God"; two, poetry deals "with matters philosophical, either moral, . . . natural, . . . astronomical, . . . or historical"; three, poets partake in "the divine consideration of what may be and should be." Sidney asserts that poets imitate to teach and to delight, borrowing freely from the world, but only doing so to expand, not usurp.

Ultimately, *Defense of Poesy* attempts to support the poet's efforts and ennoble them by focusing on the utility of the poet to the state and denigrating "his other competitors." Of his "principal challengers," Sidney finds the moral philosophers—with their "sullen gravity" and their "contempt of outward things; with books in hands against glory"—and, as well, the historians—whose "old mouse-eaten records" serve to impose themselves "upon other histories, whose greatest authorities are built upon the notable foundation of hearsay" and who are "better acquainted with a thousand years ago than with the present age"—to be many rungs below poets. Sidney's valuation is that "one giveth the precept, and the other the example." The philosopher gives the precept and the historian the exemplum, but the poet "performs" both tasks, giving precepts and exempla.

In Sidney's *Defense,* poesy's principal concern is to present speaking pictures that do not merely expound a precept or offer examples from history; rather, these speaking pictures present what ought to be "shunned" or "followed." Hence, they are akin to the prescriptive moral tracts that were as much concerned with political circumstances as with moral context. Ultimately, Sidney's *Defense* is concerned with establishing the poet-humanist within the state while elevating his art by virtue of "necessary consequences" on personal conduct in the heroic and dramatic arts.

In *Defense of Poesy,* Sir Philip Sidney attempts to reestablish the authority of poetry in a distinctly sociopolitical fashion in order for its structures to command obedience and to have "necessary consequences." Authority itself is usually secured by either a transcendental concept, such as religion, or a phenomenological concept, such as a monarchy, or by an abstract but defined domain. To endow poetry with authority, Sidney had not only to overturn traditional hierarchies that figured the poet as a deceitful aesthete—unaware of the source of his knowledge—against the historian and moral philosopher, but also to reendow words with secular weight. ELIZABETH I demanded loyalty and service in a courtly rhetoric that subsumed the language of courtship and CHIVALRY (based in deferred and enforced self-governance of desire). It did not tolerate any instruction or counsel that implied a usurpation of royal power and prerogative. In the *Defense of Poesy,* what Sidney offers instead is a counter to the queen.

FURTHER READING

Arendt, Hannah. *Between Past and Future: Eight Exercises in Political Thought.* New York: Penguin, 1961.

Plato. *The Republic.* 2nd ed. Translated by Desmond Lee. New York and London: Penguin, 1974.

Sidney, Sir Philip. "The Defense of Poesy." In *Sir Philip Sidney,* edited by Katherine Duncan-Jones, 212–250. Oxford: Oxford University Press, 1989.

Christine Gilmore

DELIA (OVERVIEW) SAMUEL DANIEL (1592)

Delia was first published in 1591 and appeared in a volume of poetry containing 28 of SAMUEL DANIEL's SONNETS and a stolen quarto of SIR PHILIP SIDNEY's SONNET SEQUENCE, *ASTROPHIL AND STELLA.* Sidney had been dead for five years, and the Sidney family was understandly affronted by this unauthorized printing; consequently, the volume was withdrawn. Nevertheless, Daniel was not held accountable, and a year later he republished *Delia* with *A Complaint of Rosamond,* dedicating it to Sidney's sister, MARY SIDNEY HERBERT, countess of Pembroke, in attempt to secure her PATRONAGE. Scholars have suggested that the first clandestine printing was a tactical maneuver on Daniel's part because he chose the same printer for the reprint, thus negating his previous claim of embarassment.

Daniel uses the ENGLISH SONNET pattern for his sonnets. At one point, a CORONA occurs as each last line of the COUPLET begins the first line of the next quatrain. Daniel also adopts the structure of the Spenserian sonnet for five of his poems, which would suggest, as scholars note, that throughout the numerous revisions of *Delia,* Daniels was privy to EDMUND SPENSER's *AMORETTI* (1595). As well, critics have identified Sonnets 9, 15, 29, 30 as translations or adaptations of Philippe Desportes' sonnets to *Diane* (1573), Sonnets 18 and 22 as borrowed from *L'Olive* (1549–50) by Joachim du Bellay, Sonnet 16 from PETRARCH, and Sonnet 31 from Torquato Tasso. Other sources cited by critics include Luigi Tansillo and Giovanni Battista Guarini. Despite the fact that he paraphrased from his sources, the end result is original work. *Delia* adopts Petrarchan CONCEITS; however, unlike other sonnet sequences, it does not follow a dramatic progression but instead is rhetorical in form. As well, *Delia* alludes to mythology, but as one critic notes, there is an essential difference between prior and contemporary references to myths in love poetry. Daniel inserts his allusions as psychological experiences rather than as miniature narratives, thereby constructing a character's emotional state.

Delia deals with the passionate and artless love of a poet-speaker who is seemingly more interested in gaining his beloved's love than in poetic renown. Delia is often depicted as a frowning lady with eyes as bright as stars, as cruel as she is fair. The poet-speaker, on the other hand, protests his sincerity and frequently refers to "limning" (painting) as being a means to counterfeit emotion, unlike his own expressions of woe for not being able to secure Delia's love. Interestingly, the final sonnet of the sequence ends with a seemingly coy, "I say no more, I feare I said too much"; however, given that Daniel revised *Delia* six times over a period of 10 years, it is not surprising that there is some confusion in the poet-speaker's self representation (Sonnet 55, l. 14).

Of the 28 sonnets from the first unauthorized printing, only 22 were included in the official 1592 edition dedicated to the countess of Pembroke, which comprised 50 sonnets. The sequence was augmented by five sonnets in the 1594 printing, and 18 of the 55 were reused. In the 1595 and 1598 printings, there were changes made, and the last printing in 1601 saw the greatest number of revisions made.

Delia provokes critical curiosity for two major reasons. First, this sonnet sequence was written soon after the period in Daniel's life about which critics know least, 1586–92. Second, there is dissent about who Delia might have really been. Two major theories exist: Delia lived by the Avon River and was upper-class (Sonnet 53); or, Delia is Mary Sidney. More recently, critics have suggested that Delia was completely fictional, which allowed Daniels freedom for his many revisions. Whatever the case, overall *Delia* boasts some of the most eloquent and passionate love poetry of the period.

FURTHER READING

Donow, Herbert S. *A Concordance to the Sonnet Sequences of Daniel, Drayton, Shakespeare, Sidney, and Spenser.* London and Amsterdam: Feffer & Simons, 1969.

Goldman, Lloyd. "Samuel Daniel's *Delia* and the Emblem Tradition." *JEGP* 67 (1968): 49–63.

Rees, Joan. *Samuel Daniel: A Critical and Biographical Study.* Liverpool, U.K.: Liverpool University Press, 1964.

Schaar, Claes. *An Elizabethan Sonnet Problem: Shakespeare's Sonnets, Daniel's Delia, and their Literary Background.* Lund, Sweden: Gleerup, 1960.

Seronsky, Cecil. *Samuel Daniel.* New York: Twayne, 1967.

Svensson, Lars-Hakan. *Silent Art: Rhetorical and Thematic Patterns in Samuel Daniel's Delia.* Lund, Sweden: Gleerup, 1980.

Josie Panzuto

Delia: Sonnet 6 ("Fair is my love, and cruel as she's fair") SAMUEL DANIEL (1592)

Delia's character is depicted in Sonnet 6 of SAMUEL DANIEL's SONNET SEQUENCE. The poet pauses and reflects on a number of contrasts found within Delia's character and between the poet-speaker and his beloved. The first QUATRAIN opens with a standard CONCEIT: "Fayre is my love, and cruell as sh'is fayre," evoking the emotion the speaker feels for Delia alongside the notion of Delia as his love (l. 1). This is a problematic opening, but it is probably intentional. The poet directs the reader's gaze from himself to Delia and then back to himself as the abject lover in the SONNET. A number of contrasts are drawn between cruelty and the many 16th-century definitions of *fair*: physically beautiful; of the female sex; a form of respectful address; blonde; untainted. Notably, "faire" as coupled with cruelty suggests that SAMUEL DANIEL was also using the word with the meaning "just." The sonnet draws more contrasts between her "sunny" eyes and "frownes" which her forehead "shades" (l. 2) by playing with the order in which her positive qualities appear. The first and fourth lines of the first quatrain list a negative quality first, followed by a positive one, while the second and third lines reverse that order.

In the second quatrain, the poet-speaker elaborates on Delia's exemplary attributes, and she becomes "Sacred on earth, design'd a Saint aboue," and thus the unattainable (l. 8). In the third quatrain, the poet reveals what makes Delia a union of opposites: the melding of "Chastitie and Beautie" (l. 9). The two qualities cannot coexist, according to the speaker, and his rhyming COUPLET wishes that she had been only chaste, so that his "Muse" would not have been tempted and his outpourings of emotion could have remained private.

Critics note that Sonnet 6 shares affinities with the Song of Songs from the Bible's Book of Solomon (4.7), and with Petrarch's sonnets 165 and 297 from the *Canzoniere*; however, Daniel contrasts beauty and chastity, rather than beauty and honesty. Importantly, scholars also note that the word *unkinde* in line 13 not only points to Delia's unfavorable attitude toward the speaker but also to her pitilessness—a quality incongruent with sanctity. Overall, this sonnet is firmly ensconced within the tradition because it highlights the poet's dismay at finding his beloved so beautiful and yet so impossibly out of reach.

See also *DELIA* (OVERVIEW).

Josie Panzuto

Delia: Sonnet 33 ("When men shall find thy flower, thy glory pass") SAMUEL DANIEL (1592)

In SAMUEL DANIEL's *Delia* (1592), Sonnet 33 forms the penultimate link in the second CORONA-style group of SONNETs (ll. 31–34). The speaker of this poem softens the message imparted by the CARPE DIEM motif in Sonnet 31 and promises Delia, his beloved, a "miracle"—he will love her even more than he already does when she is old and grey (l. 9). Sonnets 31 and 32 deal specifically with Delia at the height of her youth. Sonnet 33, however, situates her in the future, "When men shall finde thy flowre, thy glory passe" (l. 1). Within the first quatrain, the speaker envisages a Delia who sits with "carefull brow" before a mirror and realizes that her bloom or "glory" has faded (ll. 1–2 respectively). Presumably, Delia's brow is not only pensive but also expresses mournfulness, and sadness. The *Oxford English Dictionary* cites this obsolete meaning of *carefull* as appearing for the first time in Daniel's *Complaint of Rosamond*, published alongside *Delia* in 1592.

By the second quatrain, Delia is no longer alone before the mirror. She is joined by the speaker's promise of love, or "faith," which, paradoxically, has not died down with time and Delia's aging but has continued, steadfastly and inversely, to her repulsion of him, to "waxe, when thou art in thy wayning" (l. 8). The third quatrain bears the most rhetorical weight because the poet further develops the idea in the second quatrain, that the speaker's love has continued through time, and that even without heat, his love has continued to burn. Importantly, the miracle his love has

achieved is "That fire can burne, when all the matter's spent" (l. 10). Sonnet 33 decidedly moves away from the immediate concerns of the carpe diem motif and focalizes love onto a grander, cosmic level. What is miraculous about the speaker's love is that while in the second quatrain it "waxes" as the moon with his beloved's "wayning" youth, by the third quatrain, his love defies the laws of physics and continues to burn even without fuel (l. 8). It is only then that the speaker wishes Delia would "repent" her actions (ll. 12–13). Her repentance, however, does not suggest retribution to the speaker, nor a felicitous ending. The poem's rhyming COUPLET with its season CONCEIT—"When Winter snowes vppon thy golden heares"—leaves the reader, Delia, and the speaker to gaze upon old age (l. 14). This last line links Sonnet 33 to Sonnet 34.

Like most of the *Delia* sonnets, Sonnet 33 deploys the same structure as the Elizabethan sonnet with its three quatrains, rhyming couplet, and rhyming scheme. Additionally, it calls attention to the carpe diem motif, and to Petrarchan conceits with the description of blond hair as "golden heares" (l. 14). Critics have noticed shared affinities between WILLIAM SHAKESPEARE's Sonnet 2, "When forty winters shall besiege thy brow," but debates on poetic influence remain inconclusive. The accepted source of this sonnet is Sonnet 77 from Torquato Tasso's *Rime* (1567).

See also *DELIA* (OVERVIEW), ENGLISH SONNET.

Josie Panzuto

Delia: Sonnet 45 ("Care-charmer Sleep, son of the sable Night") SAMUEL DANIEL (1592)

One of SAMUEL DANIEL's best-known SONNETs from *Delia* (1592), Sonnet 45 begins with an APOSTROPHE and stock epithet for sleep in "Care-charmer sleepe" (l. 1). The speaker in this sonnet is tormented by his love for Delia. At night, his mind fashions dreams wherein he is happy with his beloved; upon waking up from his false dreams, he realizes that his love for her remains unrequited. Prayer-like, the first quatrain of this sonnet qualifies sleep as "sonne of Sable night;" and "brother to Death" and asks that it rouse him into a state of forgetful awakeness (ll. 1–2). The two quatrains are drawn closer together rhetorically as the last sentence of the first QUATRAIN flows into the first sentence of the second quatrain with an ENJAMBMENT. Punning on "morne" (l. 5), the speaker asks that it soon be morning and suggests that it will also be a time of *mourning* because he will no longer be able to dream happily of Delia. "Morne" is a variant spelling of the verb *to mourne* and the abbreviated poetic form of *morning*.

In the second quatrain, the speaker's regrets over a thoughtlessly spent youth echo Sonnet 5 in *Delia* in which the speaker says, "Whilst youth and error led my wandring minde, / And set my thoughts in heedeles [heedless] waies to range: / All unawares a Goddess chaste I finde" (ll. 1–3). In Sonnet 45, these words are repeated within the context of sleep, thereby insinuating that the speaker's "ill-aduentered youth" was sleep, and his maturity, years later, awareness. The lover's sleeplessness—a conventional Petrarchan theme—is thus further complicated by this parallel.

Because the speaker's dreams, regardless of how pleasant they are to him, are lies, he supplicates that they "cease . . . th'ymagery of our day desires" (l. 9). His nighttime dreams only serve to remind him, when day arrives, that Delia has not accepted his love. Dreams are also instrumental, however, in shaping his plans for the future, as is suggested by "To modell foorth the passions of the morrow" (l. 10). The third quatrain implies that his daytime reveries shape his thoughts at night and that the following morning, his memory reminds him more fully of Delia's absence. Caught between trying to escape the harshness of reality and the ethereality of dreaming, the speaker concludes this sonnet with a deathlike wish that he continue to sleep so that he "neuer vvake, to feel the dayes disdayne" (l. 14).

Unlike most of the sonnets in *Delia*, Sonnet 45 does not follow the Elizabethan (ENGLISH SONNET) rhyme scheme, nor does it follow generic sonnet conventions. The linked first and second quatrains suggest greater unity between the ideas that unfold in those first eight lines. Critics have noted a reference to the myth of Ixion and his grasping of clouds in the rhyming COUPLET; mythological allusions abound throughout *Delia*. More generally, Sonnet 45 is known for its pace, and

successful depiction of the contrasts between night and day.

See also *DELIA* (OVERVIEW).

Josie Panzuto

"DEOR" ANONYMOUS (before 1072) This 42-line lyrical poem is found in the EXETER BOOK alongside other elegies. Often classified as generally heroic, it is varyingly referred to as a CONSOLATIO, a LAMENT, and an UBI SUNT poem. The poem is comprised of six STANZAS, each of which ends with a REFRAIN: "This too shall pass." In line 37, the poet names himself—Deor.

Deor is a professional who expects his audience to be familiar with the general stories he references. Each of these touches on tragic events and responses to them. The first stanza encapsulates the story of Wayland, a skilled artisan imprisoned by King Nithad, who wreaks his revenge by killing Nithad's sons, raping his daughter, and then escaping. Stanza 2 continues this tale from the perspective of Beadohild, Nithad's daughter, pregnant from her rape. The third stanza is about the doomed lovers Geat and Maethild. The fourth declares Theodoric the bane of many. The fifth stanza depicts Eormenric as a cruel tyrant. Finally, the sixth addresses the general suffering of human existence. Turning personal, the poet identifies himself and bemoans his loss of status: Once a respected court poet, he was turned out by his lord.

These stories are taken from a variety of sources, including the OLD NORSE/ICELANDIC EDDAS AND SAGAS, although the names have been anglicized. Most criticism of the poem focuses on the historical connections or on the role of the SCOP (old English band), as well as the oral poetic tradition. However, some recent feminist criticism has investigated the poem's contents in light of women's power or lack thereof.

See also ELEGY, *WIDSITH*.

FUTHER READING
Alexander, Michael, trans. *The Earliest English Poems*. New York: Penguin, 1992.

Krapp, George Philip, and Elliott Dobbie van Kirk, eds. *The Exeter Book*. New York: Columbia University Press, 1966.

"DE PRINCIPE BONO ET MALO" SIR THOMAS MORE (1516)

This poem, like most of SIR THOMAS MORE'S EPIGRAMS, is composed in elegaic COUPLETS and is a response to the question, "What makes a good ruler?" This short composition offers a thought-provoking suggestion: A good ruler is like the guard dog that protects the sheep, and a bad ruler is like the wolf that preys on them.

Some scholars find likening the king to a dog shocking, but More's language recalls that of Christ's "I am the Good Shepherd" speech in John 10. The good king is obedient to the shepherd and takes nothing from the sheep, and a bad king is ravenous and self-interested like the wolf. Only behavior toward the flock distinguishes the two since both are canine and have similar appearances. In this contrast lies the sting of the epigram: The power of a ruler comes from God, not from brute strength or from the people. This power is manifested in obedience and selflessness, not in the exercise of might. Similarly, kingship is not an excuse for excess. A good king's rule is beneficial to his people.

FURTHER READING

Grace, Damian. "Thomas More's *Epigrammata*: Political Theory in a Poetic Idiom." *Parergon* 3 (1985): 115–129.

Miller, Clarence H., et al., eds. *The Complete Works of St. Thomas More. Vol. 3, Part II: Latin Poems*. New Haven, Conn., and London: Yale University Press, 1984.

Karen Rae Keck

"DESCRIPTIONS OF THE CONTRARIOUS PASSIONS IN A LOVER"

See "I FIND NO PEACE AND ALL MY HARD WORK IS DONE."

"DIVERS DOTH USE" SIR THOMAS WYATT (ca. 1535)

"Divers doth use" is one of many poems written by SIR THOMAS WYATT that appeared in *TOTTEL'S MISCELLANY*, so the date of composition is unknown. It follows Wyatt's preferred rhyme scheme—*abba, abba, cddc, ee*—and is Petrarchan in its setup. This SONNET, which describes a man whose lover has jilted him, begins with a catalogue of ways to handle grief. Some men, he explains, "mourn and wail" when their beloveds go through a change of heart in order to "pease their painful woe" (l. 4). Other men, however, choose to complain about the deceptive and fickle women who have broken their hearts. At the ninth line, the course of the poem changes through the use of a VOLTA, and the speaker begins to contrast other men's coping mechanisms with his own. He plainly states that he refuses to be sad, to "wail" or "lament," nor will he even say that his lady is false. He says that instead he will let his loss of favor pass and will believe that it is "of kind / That often change doth please a woman's mind" (ll. 13–14). This is similar to the regret expressed in "THEY FLEE FROM ME."

Readers can easily understand the content of Wyatt's poem. One thing to understand, however, is that while his characterization of female nature fits with traditional Petrarchan poetry—a man who pursues an unresponsive female—Wyatt confronts the typical reaction of the rejected lover. In the OCTAVE, he describes the typical Petrarchan lover pining after his beloved with lamentations and sorrowful wails, and the scorned lover who rails against his love; but in the SESTET, Wyatt describes how he refuses to cry over and insult his former lady. He chooses instead to blame this fickleness on female nature. Feminist critics have pointed out that although Wyatt presents a more realistic view of love, he continues to blame all the problems on women.

See also ITALIAN (PETRARCHAN) SONNET.

FURTHER READING

McCanles, Michael. "Love and Power in the Poetry of Sir Thomas Wyatt." *MLQ* 29, no. 2 (1968): 145–160.

Thomson, Patricia. *Sir Thomas Wyatt and His Background*. Stanford, Calif.: Stanford University Press, 1964.

Kerri Lynn Allen

"DOUBT OF FUTURE FOES, THE" ELIZABETH I (ca. 1571)

This poem was most likely written by Queen ELIZABETH I as a response to arrival of her cousin, MARY, QUEEN OF SCOTS, in Protestant England in 1568. The Roman Catholic Mary was very unpopular with her predominantly Protestant subjects. This unpopularity increased when it was discovered that she probably conspired with her lover, the earl of Bothwell, to murder her husband, Henry Darnley. Mary fled to England in order to save her life, but since it was thought that she had conspired to overthrow Elizabeth's rule and reestablish Roman Catholicism as the state religion, the queen of England was pressed by her advisers to execute Mary, for murder if nothing else. Elizabeth did not wish to execute her cousin, not because of family ties but because she feared setting a precedent for executing monarchs that could eventually be used against her. As a compromise, she had Mary confined to various estates in the country as Elizabeth herself had been confined before she was queen. Mary continued to conspire against her cousin, however, and when the plots against her became too egregious, Elizabeth was forced to agree to Mary's execution in 1587.

The poem concerns Queen Elizabeth's meditations back and forth between the threats to her person and her realm and her desire to meet these threats and maintain peace in her realm. The poem consists of eight, four-line STANZAS whose second and fourth lines rhyme. There is a final phrase unattached to a stanza that ends the poem. In the first stanza, the speaker worries about the "doubt" or the "dread" caused by "future foes" (l. 1) who have "exiled" her "present joy" (l, 2). Much of the language in this poem is that of monarchy and government, and exile was a punishment usually given to a noble who was a threat or an annoyance to a prince. Here the foe is not exiled, but the speaker feels that all her joy has been banished by the foe. The foe also seems to have set "snares," or traps, that threaten the queen, though her "wit" (l. 3) helps her to avoid them by warning her of their existence.

Stanza 2 continues this worrying as the queen points out that "falsehood now doth flow" (l. 5) in her kingdom and the "faith" of her subjects "ebbs" (l. 6), or recedes, like the tide. This should not be happening if "reason ruled" (l. 7) or the web of the kingdom were woven with "wit" (l. 8), or intellect. Elizabeth could be referring to herself as the person who is not ruling with reason or wit, as she refers to herself as being governed by wit in stanza 1. Or, she could be alluding to a lack of wisdom, as well as faith, among her subjects or courtiers that allows them to doubt that things will end happily.

The third stanza considers the "aspiring minds" (l. 10) of potential traitors that conceive of "joys untried" (l. 9), which they hope to experience by treasonous action. However, they may soon "repent" (l. 11) of those thoughts—and perhaps actions—when the "winds" (l. 12) of politics change. Stanza 4 continues in this manner by stating that what these potential traitors envisioned as the "top," or summit, of what they "supposed" to be their "hope" (l. 13) may "shortly" (l. 16) turn out to be the "root," or base ground, of what they "rue" (l. 16), or regret. The fourth stanza again reflects upon the contrast between good and bad subjects and how truth will always reveal falsehood. The potential traitors essentially cannot see straight: Their eyes are "dazzled" by "pride" (l. 17) and blinded by "ambition" (l. 18). It is important to remember that pride was the first of the SEVEN DEADLY SINS; it was the sin of Lucifer, whose pride allowed him to develop the ambition to overthrow God and take God's place. These unidentified subjects, like Lucifer, seek to overthrow their legitimate queen. However, their eyes "Shall be unsealed by worthy wights," or people (l. 19), who discover falsehood by "foresight" (l. 20)—literally, "looking ahead." This stanza is also incorporates an image from falconry in the "unsealed" eyes. Captured adult falcons or hawks were tamed by having their eyes sewn shut—or sealed—for a period of time. Being blind, the birds had to trust their handler for food. After a while, their eyes were unsealed—the stitches removed—and they could see again in a better way; they had come to "see" their handler meant them no harm.

The "daughter of debate" (l. 21) in stanza 6 is Mary of Scotland, who, like a farmer, "sows" discord in Elizabeth's kingdom. The "aye" in line 22 would mean something like "for sure"; it is also a sound pun on the blind "eyes" in stanza 5. But even though Mary may sow discord, she will not "reap" her crop because the "former rule" (l. 23), Elizabeth's, has taught the country to know peace, and it would shun the discord Mary would bring. While in the earlier stanzas Elizabeth may have worried about how her people would react to Mary's arrival, in the last stanzas she indicates that she is fearless in protecting her realm from traitors and invaders.

In stanza 7, Elizabeth indicates that she will not allow any "banished wight" (l. 25)—as Mary was from

Scotland—to land at England's ports. Elizabeth will also not allow invasion by "seditious sects" (l. 27), a reference to Roman Catholicism—seditious because the Pope had excommunicated Elizabeth and declared that any potential murderer would not be committing a mortal sin to kill her.

In the last stanza, we learn that Elizabeth's sword of state may be rusty from lack of use because her reign has not previously been threatened. She will not hesitate to use it, however, to "pull their tops who seek such change" (l. 31). "Pull" is probably a misprint for "poll," a practice by which the tops of trees were cut off to keep them from growing too tall. Elizabeth will not hesitate to lop the heads off anyone who thinks he or she can stand above the queen. The last Latin line, "Vivat Regina," means "Long live the queen"—Elizabeth's hope and, perhaps, her threat.

FURTHER READING

Elizabeth I. *Elizabeth I. Collected Works*. Edited by Leah S. Marcus, Janel Mueller, and Mary Beth Rise. Chicago and London: University of Chicago Press, 2000.

Hopkins, Lisa. *Writing Renaissance Queens: Texts by and about Elizabeth I and Mary, Queen of Scots*. Newark, Del.: Associated University Presses, 2002.

Theodora A. Jankowski

DOUGLAS, GAVIN (ca. 1474–1522)

Gavin Douglas was the third son of the fifth earl of Angus. He matriculated at St. Andrews University in 1489 and took a master's degree in 1494. Upon reaching his majority in 1496, he took holy orders, which was not uncommon for younger sons of nobility. Douglas moved up the ecclesiastical ladder from the deanery of Dunkeld to the provost of St. Giles (1503) and then to the bishopric of Dunkeld (1516). He died of the plague in September 1522 at the London home of Cardinal Wolsey while attempting to win support for the archbishopric of Edinburgh.

Along with several of his fellow MIDDLE SCOTS poets, Douglas is often considered one of the SCOTTISH CHAUCERIANS. However, of this group, Douglas was the first to refer to his language not as "Inglis" but as "Scottis." He sought to legitimize the VERNACULAR—in this case the Scottish vernacular—as a worthy vehicle for poetry.

Among other pieces, Douglas wrote a DREAM VISION, *Palice of Honour*, (ca. 1501–13) and may be the author of the minor poem *King Hart* (ca. 1500) as well. However, he is best known for his *Eneados*, which he completed on July 22, 1513. It was the first and only complete translation of VIRGIL's *Aeneid* until John Dryden's in 1700. Because he added the glosses of Servius Maurus Honoratus, the fourth-century grammarian, and Jodocus Badius Ascensius, the printer and scholar, as well as his own ideas about Virgil's text, this work is an important contribution to the TRANSLATION TRADITION.

Douglas's powerful use of his own culture, homeland, and literary dialect helped to establish and preserve Scotland's linguistic freedom from the political power of England and the cultural force of the English language.

FURTHER READING

Bawcutt, Priscilla. *Gavin Douglas: A Critical Study*. Edinburgh: University of Edinburgh Press, 1976.

———. *The Shorter Poems of Gavin Douglas*. Edinburgh: The Scottish Text Society, 2003.

Douglas, Gavin. *Eneados*. Edited David F. C. Coldwell. 4 vols. Scottish Text Society. Edinburgh: William Blackwood, 1957–64.

Mark DiCicco

DOWLAND, JOHN (1563–1626)

As a young man, John Dowland spent several years in Paris serving as clerk to the English ambassadors. During this time, he converted to Roman Catholicism. Returning to England, Dowland married and, in 1588, was admitted to Christ Church, Oxford, where he earned a bachelor's degree in music. His reputation grew, as did his commissions; however, the coveted post of court lutenist eluded him, as ELIZABETH I was reluctant to appoint a Catholic to any post. In 1594, Dowland departed for Rome, seeking education, experience, and further commissions. He became very well known and was respected across Europe. Ironically, upon his return to England after 1606, he found his own people disdainful of his music. In 1612, a weary Dowland was finally granted his wish and named a "King's lute." He died 14 years later.

Dowland composed a number of AYRES, predominantly for voice and lute, and was one of the instigators of the genre, and composed MADRIGALS as well. He was also the first person to earn a bachelor's degree in music from Oxford and Cambridge.

See also "COME AWAY, COME SWEET LOVE."

FURTHER READING

Fischlin, Daniel T. "'The Highest Key of Passion': Inexpressibility and Metaphors of Self in John Dowland's the *First Booke of Songs or Ayres*." *Journal of the Lute Society of America* 20 & 21 (1987): 46–86.

Pilkington, Michael. *Campion, Dowland, and the Lutenist Songwriters*. Bloomington: Indiana University Press, 1989.

DOWRICHE, ANNE EDGECUMBE (1550–1638)

Anne Dowriche was raised in Cornwall but moved to Exeter after her marriage. She was a staunch Protestant who fervently believed in a multinational Catholic conspiracy. Little else is known about her life, although her family was quite prominent. Her grandfather, Sir Richard Edgecumbe, was a country gentleman. Her brother, Pearse Edgecumbe, to whom she addressed the preface of her poem *The FRENCH HISTORY,* served as a member of Parliament for six terms. Her first husband, the Rev. Hugh Dowriche, associated with those active in arguing for Puritan-like reforms to the English Church during the reign of Queen ELIZABETH I.

Dowriche wrote in an age that severely restricted women's participation in public debate. Her only other surviving published works are some verses included with Hugh Dowriche's *The Jaylors Conversion* (1596), titled "Verses written by a gentlewoman upon *The Jaylors Conversion*," and signed by "AD." These exhort the faithful to endure suffering patiently, since "The rod that doth correct our life, / And sinfull waies reproue, / Is said to be a certain signe, / Of Gods eternal loue."

See also TUDOR WOMEN WRITERS.

FURTHER READING

Beilin, Elaine. "'Some Freely Spake Their Mind': Resistance in Anne Dowriche's *French Historie*." In *Women Writing and the Reproduction of Culture in Tudor and Stuart Britain,* edited by Mary Burke, Jane Donawerth, Linda Dove, and Karen Nelson, 119–140. Syracuse, N.Y.: Syracuse University Press, 2000.

Lysbeth Em Benkert

DRAYTON, MICHAEL (1563–1631)

Michael Drayton was born in Hartshill, England, to Christopher and Margerie Drayton. During his youth, he became page to Sir Henry Goodeere, who later became his patron and funded Drayton's education. The close association with Goodeere and his family had great influence on Drayton, and many believe Goodeere's daughter, Anne, became the inspiration for his SONNET SEQUENCES.

Drayton published his poetry from 1591 to 1630. He is often remembered for revising his previous works and publishing them under a different name. His first published work was *Harmonie of the Church* (1591). Drayton's later works were influenced by EDMUND SPENSER, especially in his PASTORAL series *IDEA THE SHEPHEARDS GARLAND*. In 1594, he published *IDEAS MIRROUR,* sometimes referred to as *Amours*. *England's Heroical Epistles* (1597) has been considered one of Drayton's finest works. He also wrote one play, *The First Part of Sir John Oldcastle*. His other works include: "Ode to the Virginian Voyage"; *Nymphidia, the Court of the Fairy*; and *The Muses' Elizium*.

Michael Drayton is critically admired for his pastorals and odes, and his literary works greatly influenced his contemporaries. Drayton died on December 2, 1631, and is buried in Poet's Corner in Westminster Abbey.

See also QUATORZAIN.

FURTHER READING

Elton, Oliver M.A. *Michael Drayton. A Critical Study*. New York: Russel & Russel, 1966.

Dianne Walbeck

DREAM OF THE ROOD, THE ANONYMOUS (10th century)

The Dream of the Rood, 156 lines written in the West Saxon dialect of Old English, is preserved on fol. 104v–106r of the Vercelli Book, a late 10th-century codex. No precise date for the poem is possible. Notably, excerpts of the poem are preserved in two additional locations. Several lines (ll. 39–42, 44–49, 56–59, 62–64) are engraved in runes on the sides of a large ornamental cross constructed ca. 730–50 and housed at Ruthwell, Dumfriesshire, Scotland (the RUTHWELL CROSS). As well, an inscription echoing ll. 44, 42a, and 48b are stamped on metal strips attached to the BRUSSELS CROSS, an 11th-century processional cross and reliquary.

The Dream of the Rood is a *visio* (Latin for dream), though some consider it a DREAM VISION. It is noteworthy for its use of the rhetorical figure prosopopoeia, in which an inanimate object (the Cross) is given voice. The poem also displays a skillful use of juxtaposition, paradox, and metaphor. The dreamer opens by recounting a dream in which he sees a glorious cross in the air, wound with beams of light. The dreamer immediately introduces one of the many paradoxes which are a feature of his poetic style: the Cross has five jewels on the crossbar (recalling Christ's five wounds); thus, it is not at all the gallows of a wicked person. The phrase *an angel of the Lord* identifies the Cross with Christ. The victorious tree is glorious, but the narrator is stained with sin. Even though the cross is decorated with gold and gems, the dreamer is able to see through to the former struggle of the sufferers (Christ and the Cross); he sees the moisture on the right side (the Water of Baptism and the Blood of the Eucharist, which flowed from Christ's right side). As the dreamer contemplates this vision, which oscillates between a gloriously adorned object and the instrument of the Crucifixion, he hears the Cross speak (ll. 27–121).

The Cross opens with its own history (ll. 27–33). Enemies cut it down at the edge of a wood and fashioned it into something on which to punish criminals. They carried it on their shoulders and set it up on a hill. The Crucifixion narrative follows (ll. 33–56). The Cross sees Christ, as a warrior hero, hastening toward it. The Cross as a good retainer wishes to protect his Lord, but on this occasion it dares not disobey Christ's command. It could have cut down all the enemies, but it stands fast. The young hero ascends the Cross, which trembles at the touch but dares not bend to the ground. People drive nails through the Cross and Christ, and both are smeared with the blood from Christ's side. The world grows dark. The Lord sends forth his spirit. All creation weeps. Christ is on the Cross.

The Cross sees people coming for the Prince, and it bends down to assist the Deposition (removal of Christ's body). In the sight of the Cross, they prepare a tomb and bewail Christ's passing in a song of sorrow. The

corpse grows cold (ll. 57–69). People cut down the Cross and its companions and bury them in a deep pit where afterward friends will find them and decorate them in gold and silver (ll. 70–77).

The Cross now addresses the dreamer, "his dear hero," and in a set of three paradoxes, explains the importance of the Cross for humanity, an importance confirmed by the Lord of Glory and his mother, Mary (ll. 78–94). The poem, which identified the Cross with Christ, now makes a link with Mary (the Crucifixion and the Annunciation are both supposed to have taken place on the same date).

Once again addressed as "my dear hero," the dreamer is exhorted to narrate this vision of the Cross: the Crucifixion, the Resurrection, and the Ascension. Christ will return on the Day of Judgment to judge all according to their merits (ll. 95–114), and the Cross ends its narration with three points (ll. 115–21): The Day of Judgment will cause fear; those who carry the Cross in their hearts need not fear; the Cross shows the way to the kingdom of heaven.

The response of the dreamer is prayer with *elne mycle* (great strength), the same phrase used to describe Christ approaching the Cross (l. 34), and the Cross as it bows down for the Deposition. Like Christ in the tomb (l. 69), he is with *mæte weorode* (a small troop, i.e., alone) (l. 124). The dreamer will devote himself to devout contemplation of the Cross. His daily hope is that the Cross will come to fetch him and carry him physically (as the Cross once carried Christ) into the joys of heaven. The final section of the poem is a prayer (ll. 144–156) to his friend Christ affirming the central mysteries of the Christian faith—the Crucifixion, Resurrection, and Ascension.

The Dream of the Road is especially noteworthy for its identification of Christ as a Germanic hero, like Beowulf (see BEOWULF). Christ approaches the Cross without fear, removes his own clothes, and ascends the rood. He calls upon his COMITATUS to remember and then rewards them with the gold of eternal life. Some critics have examined the idea of "volunteerism" within this poem: The Cross presents itself as a loyal retainer, but it also takes Christ's Passion upon itself, becoming a surrogate. Others have seen it as related to the development of the monastic tradition, as an invitation to "bloodless martyrdom." Recent scholarship emphasizes the liturgical features of the poet's thought, connecting it to the physical artifacts on which it appears.

See also FURTHARK ALPHABET.

FURTHER READING

Ó Carragáin, Éamonn. *Ritual and the Rood: Liturgical Images and the Old English Poems of the Dream of the Rood Tradition.* London: British Library, 2005.

Swanton, Michael, ed. *The Dream of the Rood.* Exeter, U.K.: University of Exeter Press, 1996.

Shaun F. D. Hughes

DREAM VISION In dream vision poems, a troubled narrator falls asleep, often by running water, dreams, and wakes to write his dream down. The earliest English dream vision is *The DREAM OF THE ROOD*; however, the genre reached its zenith much later. From the late 14th century up until the early 16th century, large numbers of poems were written with this format, and examples are found among the most important works of the three greatest poets of the late 14th century. These include WILLIAM LANGLAND's *PIERS PLOWMAN*, *PEARL*, and GEOFFREY CHAUCER's four dream poems: *The BOOK OF THE DUCHESS, The HOUSE OF FAME, The PARLIAMENT OF FOWLS,* and *The LEGEND OF GOOD WOMEN,* as well as his partial translation of the influential French dream poem *Le Roman de la rose (The Romance of the Rose).*

From the 14th century onward, the dream vision tended to consist of an ideal, often symbolic, landscape in which the dreamer encounters an authoritative figure, from whom he/she learns some religious or secular doctrine. The phase of the poem before the dreamer has fallen asleep often includes a very precise and detailed description of the dreamer's circumstances in the real world. For example, at the beginning of *The House of Fame,* Chaucer tells us that it is the "tenthe day now of Decembre," and in *Pearl* details of place and date are carefully delineated. These details offer a sense that the poet is describing something that really happened. They offer verisimilitude but also invest the dream with possible allegorical significance: These details may be personally resonant for the dreamer, or they may represent an important and perhaps divinely

ordered conjunction. The setting is usually a natural one, such as a garden, and it is usually spring or summer. One of the versions of *Piers Plowman,* for instance, opens with a description of the soft summer sunshine, while in Chaucer's *Legend of Good Women,* it is spring. In particular it is May, when flowers bloom and birds sing, glad that winter is over and that they have escaped the hunter; in defiance of the fowler, they croon lovesongs to each other. Similarly, the narrator of *Wynnere and Wastoure* (14th century) wanders in bright sunlight along the bank of a stream near a wood by a meadow at the beginning of his adventure. Along with the time of year, the landscape is often a LOCUS AMOENUS, a paradise of woods, streams, and flowers.

Although "paradise" is a typical dream-vision setting, there is an alternative setting in which the dreamer falls asleep—the bedroom. For instance, in Chaucer's early dream poem, *The Book of the Duchess,* the narrator, unable to sleep, calls for a book "To rede and drive the night away" and then falls asleep alone, separated from social activity. Sometimes the dreamer can seem to be on the brink of death. Langland's narrator has grown weary of the world; the dreamer in *The Book of the Duchess* fears his own death. The solitude and insomnia express the dreamer's mental and emotional condition. The beginning of the dream finds the dreamer preoccupied and anxious, though he or she is not always able to articulate the cause of the anxiety. The PEARL-POET (see GAWAIN-POET) is in grief for his infant daughter, but the causes of the sufferings of Chaucer's dreamers are not always clear. The narrators are thus in a highly receptive state at the moment of transition between the waking world and the dream state, and the dream allows for confrontation with the self and its preoccupations and for a process of self-realization to take place.

Once asleep, the dreamer usually finds himself or herself in a changed landscape, populated by figures of authority, such as Holy Church in *Piers Plowman.* Before the onset of the dream, the narrator seems to be floundering in a world bereft of meaning; in the dream, his or her actions seem to be full of significance, sometimes even allegorical significance. The dreamer relinquishes personal control and submits to the influence of powers beyond him. It is then that the dreamer sees sights and visions that offer new levels of understanding. Occasionally these include visions that give the impression of being dreams within dreams.

Dream visions end with the dreamer's awakening into reality. This reality, however, is marked by reflection on the content and meaning of the dream and the resolution to write it down—that is, to create the text that the reader has before them. At this point, the author can debate the dream's validity. Sometimes the dreamer awakes more unhappy and confused than before the dream, though this is not common.

Given the longevity of the dream visions format and its popularity among medieval poets, scholars have questioned whether dream vision poems constitute an independent literary genre. The particular conventions that are associated with it suggest to some critics that it may be seen as a separate genre. Other scholars have argued, however, that dream poems did not constitute a separate category of love narratives and that many of the characteristics that are associated with dream poems are also found in poems about love which did not adopt the dream form. Certainly, there are examples of poems that appear to make use of the conventions of dream poetry, but in which no one actually falls asleep and dreams. For example, the 15th-century poem *The Flower and the Leaf* is set in an idealized landscape and includes an authoritative guide who explains the allegorical significance of much of the action to the narrator. However, it includes no explicit mention of a dream.

The dream was a useful device for framing narratives. Describing a dream engages the audience through the use of a common experience and invites interpretation. Many scholars have noted the overlay of classical dream theory into medieval perceptions, with the result being hybrid dream logic. The dream mechanism also allows the author to disclaim responsibility for what follows. At the same time, the form allows the inclusion of memorable images and invokes the authoritative tradition of visionary literature. One of the hallmarks of dream poems is their fully realized sense of their own existence as poems. The poems have self-conscious narrators, and the action is made up of their experiences.

It has been suggested by some scholars that the dream framework functioned as a device for indicating an altered state of consciousness, providing an instrument of analysis and evaluation that enabled poets to explore the roots of the self and of society. It has been noted that dreams, by their nature, can express a sense of fragmentation, a loss of continuity between the self and the outside world since they operate by juxtaposition, distortion, displacement, condensation, and seeming incoherence. Recently, scholars have argued that the dream format was used by English poets in the second half of the 14th century to express alienation, a sense of lost authority or a search for connections.

See also ALLEGORY, MIDDLE ENGLISH POETRY.

FURTHER READING

Brown, Peter, ed. *Reading Dreams: The Interpretation of Dreams from Chaucer to Shakespeare.* Oxford: Oxford University Press, 1999.

Spearing, A. C. *Medieval Dream-Poetry.* Cambridge: Cambridge University Press, 1976.

Louise Sylvester

DUNBAR, WILLIAM (CA. 1460–1520)

Like many of the MIDDLE SCOTS poets, William Dunbar was not well known during his life. His reputation grew considerably in the 18th and 19th centuries, particularly because he was championed by Sir Walter Scott. Like his counterparts, Dunbar was heavily influenced by GEOFFREY CHAUCER and is known for his mastery of IAMBIC PENTAMETER, but he also wrote alliterative verse in his career (see ALLITERATION). Dunbar's poetry shows that he was also influenced by his Middle Scots compatriot, ROBERT HENRYSON, as well as by contemporary French poetry.

Very little is known about Dunbar's life other than that he was probably a student at St. Andrews and that he was certainly a court poet; almost all of his poetry was written in the period between 1500 and 1513, which coincides with James IV's reign. His death is referred to in Sir David Lindsay's poem *Testament of the Papyngo.* While many contemporary poets inserted autobiographical details into their poetry, Dunbar only seldom gave any personal information, making him perhaps the most enigmatic of the four major Middle Scots poets. Of all of these *makars,* or "makers," Dunbar was the most stylistically and generically versatile, and this may be because his court patrons demanded the subject and style of his poems. His three poems that have received the most critical attention are *The Thrissil and the Rois* (a poem in honor of James IV and Margaret Tudor written in 1503), *Goldyn Targe,* and *Dance of the Sevin Deidly Synnis.* However, the remainder of his canon is steadily gaining more attention, particularly his two longest poems (despite the fact that Dunbar is mostly a poet of shorter pieces): *The Flyting with Kennedie* (a quarrel poem of 550 lines, sometimes entitled *The Flyting of Dunbar and Kennedie*) and *Tretis of the Tua Mariit Wemen and the Wedo* (an ambitious work of 530 lines). In addition, the scope of Dunbar's canon is ever-changing. Some poems, which have been attributed to him in the past, are no longer considered his work, and others have been more recently discovered as probably Dunbar's.

Dunbar has also been credited, probably erroneously, with the first reference to the New World in a piece of English literature. In his poem *This Waverand Warldis Wretchidnes*, he refers to the "new fund Yle." More recently, historians and critics have argued that the "new fund Yle" is not America at all, but rather Newfoundland.

Dunbar is classified as one of the SCOTTISH CHAUCERIANS, and Chaucer's influence on him is apparent as he specifically cites the Englishman in two of his poems—"LAMENT FOR THE MAKARIS" and *Goldyn Targe*—as "the noble Chaucer" and the "reverend Chaucere"

respectively. Indeed, 18th- and 19th-century criticism of the poet focused mainly on the Chaucerian allusions and imitations in Dunbar's writings, and it is clear that the humor and bawdiness that often characterize some of Chaucer's writing can also be seen in much of Dunbar's. In addition, like Chaucer, Dunbar is a master at incorporating different voices and speakers into his work. However, the 20th century brought new focus to Dunbar criticism, turning away from his Chaucerian influence to his Scottish roots.

By the end of the 20th century, Dunbar had been studied at length for his "Scottishness" and how this manifests itself in his poetry. For example, in his poem "Lament for the Makaris," Dunbar discusses 24 different deceased English and Scottish poets whom he has considered influential in his own work, including Chaucer, JOHN GOWER, and JOHN LYDGATE. The term he coins there, the *makars,* has long been a synonym for Middle Scots poets.

See also FLYTING.

FURTHER READING

Mapstone, Sally, ed. *William Dunbar, "The Nobill Poyet".* *Essays in Honor of Priscilla Bawcutt.* East Linton, Scotland: Tuckwell, 2001.

Reiss, Edmund. *William Dunbar.* Boston: Twayne, 1979.

Tasioulas, Jackie, ed. *The Makars: The Poems of Henryson, Dunbar, and Douglas.* Edinburgh: Canongate, 2000.

Jennifer N. Brown

E

EARLY IRISH SAGAS (ca. fourth century)

Whether oral-literary or literary-oral in source, Early Irish EPIC literature remains a neglected genre. Irish story lore derives from a very ancient pan-Celtic heroic tradition: some scholars would place its earliest development as far back as the Iron Age (third century B. C.E.). During the medieval period, many of these heroic narratives were committed to manuscript in Old and Middle Irish. At the same time (10th–12th centuries), medieval professional poets organized hundreds of tales according to their titles and contents: "Destructions," "Cattle Raids," "Wooings," "Elopements," "Voyages," "Adventure Journeys," "Expeditions," "Visions," and "Love Tales." The most studied—and perhaps the most influential—stories are from the so-called Heroic Cycle, which is a modern name. The Ulster Cycle, as it is also named, recounts, in prose and in verse, exploits of heroes in prehistoric northeastern Ireland, a region famous for its legendary king Conchobar; his palace, Emain Macha; his Red Branch knights; and their extraordinary champion and central, precocious figure, Cú CHULAINN ("The Hound of Culainn").

The ninth-century narrative of "Mac Dathó's Pig" is likely the oldest "fore-tale." These are prefatory stories giving plot and motivations, culminating in the climactic *Táin Bó Cúailgne,* or Cattle Raid of Cooley, in which Cú Chulainn plays a key role. Culturally free (mostly) of Christian influence, the lively and entertaining *Scéla Mucce Meic Dathó* (Story of Mac Dathó's Pig) is embellished by boasting, contention over the hero's portion

and points of honor, and headhunting. It tells of a communal warrior feast given by Mac Dathó during which, one after the other, Ulstermen and rival Connachtmen claim the right to divide an enormous pig (to secure the champion's portion). When Conall Cernach (another heroic Ulster warrior) takes the best part for himself in victory, a bloody and violent skirmish ensues, and the Connacht party is put to flight in defeat.

Similarly, *Fled Bricrenn* (Bricriu's Feast, ca. eighth century) also involves contention—among three heroes, including Cú Chulainn—over the hero's portion and climaxes with a beheading. But the tale encompasses a humorous and sophisticated (though misogynistic) scenario in which the women of Ulster compete in a foot race for the sake of arbitration. Three separate companies of warrior's wives, led by Cú Chulainn's own spouse, Emer, are told separately by "the poisoned-tongued" host, Bricriu, that the one who enters the banquet hall first will be queen of the whole province. While running, the women raise their robes up to their buttocks in their effort to reach the hall first. Even though Emer wins the race, a vicious scuffle breaks out and further mediation follows, proving unquestionably Cú Chulainn's fearlessness and preeminence.

Cés Ulad, or *Noínden Ulad* ("The Pangs of Ulster," also known as "The Debility of the Ulstermen") attempts to explain, with topographical reference to Emain Macha ("the twins of Macha," the royal seat), why Cú Chulainn's youthful warrior services were needed when the Connacht queen and king and army invaded Ulster to capture the famed Black-Brown Bull (Donn Cuailgne). All grown males are subject to a mysterious and periodically recurring affliction because of a curse by the pregnant Macha, whom Conchobar had forced to race against the king's horses. Macha, about to give birth, appealed to the crowd to no avail, so she cursed them as she ran, then victoriously delivered twins at the finish line. At this point, she proclaimed that all Ulstermen would endure the same painful labor debility in times of greatest challenge. Cú Chulainn is immune because he is too young or too much of an outsider or latecomer to be overcome. The deeper meaning of the story, first written down in the mid-12th century, is much disputed.

Evil, trouble, and internecine strife caused by a woman, Deirdriu, lies at the heart of *Longas Macc n-Uisnig* (Exile of the Sons of Uisliu, ca. eighth–ninth centuries), another poetic explanatory narrative leading up to *Táin Bó Cúailgne*. This compelling and very modern love story combines coercion, obsession, defiance, revenge, betrayal, murder, and suicide. Deirdriu begins as a concubine for King Conchobar and ends her own life after a year-long fasting vigil while mourning the demise of her lover, Noísiu. When Deirdriu falls ominously in love with the boy, he and his brothers are forced to flee Ulster with her to escape the wrath of Conchobar. The king treacherously arranges their return, has the exiled band slain, and takes Deirdriu back for himself. In retaliation, the three protectors of the company—Fergus, Dubthach, and Cormac (Conchobar's son), along with 3,000 others—abandon Ulster and join forces with rivals in Connacht, King Ailill and his notorious spouse, Medb. This explains their presence in the opposite camp during the action of *Táin Bó Cúailgne*.

Heroic boasting, chariot fighting, and cattle raiding form the backdrop to Ireland's great medieval masterpiece of fantastic storytelling, the *Táin Bó Cúailgne* (Cattle Raid of Cooley), which dates from the seventh to ninth century. While societal traits present include the practice of fosterage and, as noted in the Deirdriu story, the taking of sureties or warrantors, logical plot unity and continuity is missing. Given an unusual epic style that ranges from brisk to florid, some critics would say that the *Táin*'s obscureties and imperfections merely call attention to other flaws, such as incidents of violent mutilation and direct references to bodily matters.

Yet the attractive adventure grips the reader, as it must have enchanted medieval listeners. Once the mustered Connacht armies arrive in Ulster to steal the bull, it falls to the youthful but fierce Cú Chulainn to hold them back single-handedly. The hero is even forced to meet kin in combat—both his foster father and his beloved foster brother, Fer Diad. Though he ultimately fails in his attempt to forestall the aims of Ailill, Medb, and their cohorts, Cú Chulainn's illustrious and relentless performance, patience, and persistence irresistibly overshadow the poem's anticlimax. The legendary rivalry of the White Bull of Medb and the Black Brown Bull of Cooley results in their cosmic battle—and a victory for the Bull of Cooley.

See also BEHEADING GAME, OGHAM.

FURTHER READING

Bitel, Lisa M. *Land of Women: Tales of Sex and Gender from Early Ireland.* Ithaca, N.Y., and London: Cornell University Press, 1996.

Caerwyn-Williams, J. E., and Patrick K. Ford. *The Irish Literary Tradition.* Cardiff: University of Wales Press, 1992.

Dillon, Myles, and Nora K. Chadwick. *The Celtic Realms.* London: Weidenfeld/Nicolson, 1967. Reprint, London: Phoenix Press, 2000.

McCone, Kim. *Pagan Past and Christian Present in Early Irish Literature.* Maynooth, Ireland: An Sagart, 1991.

The Táin. Translated by Thomas Kinsella. Oxford and New York: Oxford University Press, 1969.

Raymond J. Cormier

EARLY IRISH VERSE   In Early Irish society, the *fili* (poet) was often the best-educated and influential member of the tribe. *Filis* served as minstrels and entertainers but were also apprenticed and trained in verse forms and oral history. In this respect, *filis* were also closely connected with the religious and legal aspects of society. Their use of praise and SATIRE helped determine the ruler's status. Other duties included storyteller, counselor, eulogizer, and seer. In these respects, *filis* were much like SCOPs, skalds (ancient Scandinavian poets), and bards.

Between the eighth and 12th centuries, the oral tradition merged with a writing system that allowed Irish verse to be recorded. The introduction of Christianity provided the impetus to write down preexisting poems and to record Christian-related poetry and verse. The earliest Irish poetry was alliterative; this was often used for recitation of genealogies, prophecies, and eulogies well into the Middle Irish period. Some of the oldest Irish poetry preserved uses seven syllables with a trisyllabic final word; in fact, this type of ALLITERATION was used as a mnemonic device for the legal system. The meters of early Irish verse had a complicated system of ASSONANCE, consonance, alliteration, and internal and end rhymes, and they were based primarily on syllable count. Seven-syllable lines were the most common, and end rhymes might be formed by alternating lines or by COUPLETS. QUATRAINS were the most common form used.

There has also been a good deal of research on the relationships between Early Irish, English, and Welsh poetry. In particular, connections can be made within the traditions of penitential literature, elegiac poetry, and eremitic (hermits') prayer. As well, Early Irish verse, with both its pre-Christian and Christian-related topics, not only thrived in Ireland but spread throughout the Continent, as shown by its survival in the manuscripts of numerous Continental monasteries associated with Irish missionaries.

See also ELEGY.

FURTHER READING

Fowler, Barbara Hughes, ed. and trans. *Medieval Irish Lyrics*. Notre Dame, Ind.: University of Notre Dame Press, 2000.

Lehmann, Ruth P. M., ed. and trans. *Early Irish Verse*. Austin: University of Texas Press, 1982.

Murphy, Gerard, ed. *Early Irish Lyrics: Eighth to Twelfth Century*. Oxford: Clarendon Press, 1956.

Bradford Lee Eden

EARLY MODERN V. RENAISSANCE The

term *Renaissance* (or *Renascence*) literally means "rebirth." In the context of cultural studies (history, literature, fine arts, religion, sociology, etc.), the term applies to the time immediately after the Middle Ages. More specifically, it refers to the rebirth of the CLASSI-CAL TRADITION that triggered a new enthusiasm for scholarly and artistic pursuits during this era. However, the term *Renaissance* is grounded in a particular, long-term historical theory that has often been challenged by scholars.

In the original theory, the medieval period in Europe was considered a low point in all facets of civilization. Feudalism, the prevailing system of government, relegated ownership of virtually all the land to an elite few—the aristocrats, many of whom also controlled large numbers of serfs. The hierarchy of the Christian church exercised its power over all of Western Europe, making canon law as powerful as civil law. Literacy rates were low, and few "literary" works were written in the VERNACULAR. The fine arts almost exclusively reflected religious patronage, and the rules of painting followed the two-dimensional format of iconography. This view is, of course, a gross simplification of the realities of medieval Europe as we now understand them, but the basic course of development from the Middle Ages to the Renaissance depends on such simplification. The Renaissance (which is seen as beginning in the 14th century in Italy and the early 16th century in England) was perceived as an enlightened period that eliminated the primitivism of the medieval period; reintroduced "lost" concepts of art, government, and philosophy prevalent in classical Greece and Rome; and paved the way for the Enlightenment of the 18th century, and, eventually, its further development into modernism.

The importance of the Renaissance to this scheme of continuing human development and improvement was first articulated by the 19th-century German historian Jacob Burckhardt in 1860. His work, *The Civilization of the Renaissance in Italy*, begins with an examination of the state (government) as "a Work of Art" (Part 1) and points out how the "republics" that developed in various Italian city-states were culturally superior to the rule of despotic feudal lords during the medieval period. This "republican" form of government presumably developed from the actual and theoretical systems of rule in classical Greece and pre-Augustan Rome. Burckhardt sees the "Revival of Antiquity" (Part 3) as necessary for the development of Renaissance humanism, history, education, ethics, and literature overall.

But his major concern is the "Development of the Individual" (Part 2)—including, briefly, women—and the "Discovery of the World and of Man" (Part 4). Clearly Burckhardt's work continues the narrative of perfection encoded within the narrative of the development of medieval into Renaissance culture. His argument focuses on the development of *man* (as opposed to woman): "Man became a spiritual *individual*, and recognized himself as such" (121). Such individuality led to the discovery of new worlds and to the development of "artists who created new and perfect works in all branches of the arts, and who also made the greatest impression as men" (125). Burckhardt also claims that the Renaissance allowed upper-class women to be educated the same as men and to be "regarded as equal to men" (280), though he mitigates this view by stating that "women had no thought of the public; their function was to influence distinguished men, and to moderate male impulse and caprice" (281).

The Renaissance man was no longer a person submerged in familial, political, and religious loyalties; he was now an *individual* unfettered by state or religious loyalties, able to reveal personal preferences for an educated life guided by classical writings. He could, if he wished, use the example of classical literature to become a writer, use newly rediscovered classical statues or theories on perspective to become an artist, or use his newly developed confidence as an individual to become an explorer. While many of the ideas outlined here are certainly true, the extreme focus on the individual—specifically the upper-class male individual—by scholars like Burckhardt present a very one-sided view of an extremely complex period in European history. That is why many scholars of the English Renaissance prefer to use the term *early modern* to refer to their period of study.

First to question the traditional view of the Renaissance were Marxist and feminist critics. The Marxists pointed out that Burckhardt was simply following the "great man" theory of history, a reading that focused on the deeds and accomplishments of upper-class men: the discoveries of Christopher Columbus and Sir Francis Drake; the art of Leonardo da Vinci or Michaelangelo; the writings of Dante or PETRARCH. Marxists wished to investigate the histories of labor and laborers, especially as they related to the "class struggle" and its economic effect on society. Feminist scholars such as Joan Kelly-Gadol, concerned with Burckhardt's focus on upper-class men, pointed out that the development of the Renaissance state also led to the development of the concepts of "public" and "private," where women were usually relegated to the "private" (or home) space and were not permitted a role in "public" society.

Once Marxist and feminist critics began to question the use of the term *Renaissance* as an all-encompassing marker of a very important period of English cultural history, other critics followed, notably New Historicists and Cultural Materialists. These critics pointed out that the period from about 1500 to 1699 was certainly a high point in the development of English language and literature, producing such writers as SIR THOMAS WYATT, SIR PHILIP SIDNEY, EDMUND SPENSER, WILLIAM SHAKESPEARE, Ben Jonson, John Donne, Sir Francis Bacon, the translators of the King James Bible, and so on. The development of a vital, national literature is only one aspect of this dramatic change, however. Consistent and successful English attacks on Spanish treasure ships returning home from the new world as well as the later defeat of the SPANISH ARMADA gave England the power and reputation to control the seas. Further increases in the English wool trade led to the beginning of English dominance of world trade—in Europe, the New World, and India. The small country with a previously feudal/agricultural economy was changing to a capitalist/imperialist one. Such a change led to both fabulous increases in wealth for some citizens and descent into grinding poverty for others. England's embrace of the Protestant Reformation led not only to the dissolution of the monasteries—and a consequent restructuring of the social order—but also to a restructuring of government at home and political relationships abroad. ELIZABETH I's rule also seemed to allow more questioning of the role of women within this rapidly changing society.

The use of the term *early modern,* then, suggests that the user will be more open to considering the vast array of changes undergone by England in the period formerly referred to strictly as the English Renaissance. This is not to deny that critics who use the term *early modern* may, to some extent, regard some individuals as "great," as benefiting from the interaction of change agents swirling about England in the period from 1500 to 1699. But even if they lean in that direction, they would still be aware of the fact that the English Renaissance did not solely or suddenly give birth to a group of very talented men. Early modern critics are aware that a collection of vastly differing incidents led to very profound changes in all aspects of English political, social, literary, cultural, and economic life, and these changes taken together were what led England to move out of medieval feudalism and begin to create the social, political, and economic structures that would eventually produce the realities of 20th- and 21st-century life.

FURTHER READING

Burckhardt, Jacob. *The Civilization of the Renaissance in Italy.* Translated by S. G. C. Middlemore. 1860. Reprint, New York: New American Library, 1961.

Engels, Fredrick. *The Origin of the Family, Private Property, and the State. . . .* Translated by Alec West. New York: International, 1972.

Ferguson, Margaret W., Maureen Quilligan, and Nancy J. Vickers, eds. *Rewriting the Renaissance: The Discourses of Sexual Difference in Early Modern Europe.* Chicago: University of Chicago Press, 1986.

Howard, Jean E. "The New Historicism in Renaissance Studies." *ELR* 16 (1986): 13–43.

Jankowski, Theodora A. "Historicizing and Legitimating Capitalism": Thomas Heywood's *Edward IV* and *If You Know Not Me, You Know Nobody. Medieval and Renaissance Drama in England* 7 (1995): 305–337.

Kelly-Gadol, Joan. "Did Women Have a Renaissance?" In *Becoming Visible: Women in Euopean History,* edited by Renate Bridenthal and Claudia Koonz, 137–164. 3rd ed. Boston: Houghton, Mifflin, 1998.

Theodora A. Jankowski

ECLOGUE In classical literature, an eclogue is a poem covering bucolic themes that takes the form of a dialogue between shepherds. Eclogues often feature a subgenre, such as an ELEGY or a ROMANCE. The most well-known, and in the 16th century the most widely imitated, work in this genre is VIRGIL's *Eclogues*—on which, for instance, EDMUND SPENSER based his *SHEP-*

HEARDES CALENDER. During that same period, however, eclogues also came to include most poems following the PASTORAL tradition.

EKPHRASIS (ECPHRASIS) Ekphrasis—from the Greek *ek* [out] and *phrasis* [speak], or "to speak out"—is a narrative element that brings vivid images to the mind's eye. Ancient rhetoricians defined ekphrasis broadly to include any lively description that enhanced a verbal argument, but the meaning of the word has gradually become more specific, and now it is most commonly defined as the verbal description of visual art. Because it replicates the experience of "seeing" for the reader, ekphrasis has traditionally been used as the prime example of the poet's ability to mimic and even surpass the visual artist. Ekphrasis calls attention to the relationship between words and images and to the ways that literary texts and the visual arts influence one another.

Some ekphrastic examples include Sonnet 64 from *AMORETTI* by EDMUND SPENSER and the extended account of the wall pictures that depict the fall of Troy in WILLIAM SHAKESPEARE's *The RAPE OF LUCRECE.* Additionally, scholars have been investigating the works of SAMUEL DANIEL in connection to portraiture.

See also EMBLEM.

FURTHER READING

Heffernan, James. *Museum of Words: The Poetics of Ekphrasis from Homer to Ashbery.* Chicago and London: University of Chicago Press, 1993.

Webb, Ruth. "Ekphrasis Ancient and Modern: The Invention of a Genre." *Word and Image* 15 (1999): 7–18.

Rebecca Olson

ELEGY In the CLASSICAL TRADITION, elegies were defined by their meter—called elegiac COUPLETs or distich couplets, comprised of a dactylic hexameter followed by a pentameter—and not by their subject matter. Thus, they were sometimes composed on love, war, or politics. In the English tradition, however, an elegy is a poetic genre of lament for a deceased (or otherwise permanently lost) person, or, occasionally, a lost culture or way of life. For instance, "The WANDERER" is an Old English elegy in which a warrior mourns the loss of his lord, but the narrator in "The RUIN" mourns unknown people and their culture. The 16th century witnessed the development of the PASTORAL elegy, a lament for something or someone that was good. EDMUND SPENSER's poem about SIR PHILIP SIDNEY, *Astrophel* (1586), is sometimes considered the first one.

See also EXETER BOOK; *SEAFARER, THE*; "WIFE'S LAMENT, THE."

FURTHER READING

Guy-Bray, Stephen. *Homoerotic Space: The Poetics of Loss in Renaissance Literature.* Toronto: University of Toronto Press, 2002.

Leech, Mark. *The Anglo-Saxon Elegies.* Chippenham, U.K.: Pipers' Ash, 2004.

"ELIDUC" ("GUILDELUEC AND GUILLIADUN") MARIE DE FRANCE (ca. 1170) "Eliduc" is the longest and the last of MARIE DE FRANCE's *Les Lais.* It is composed in octosyllabic COUPLETS.

Eliduc, the title character, is a Breton knight married to a noble and wise lady named Guildeluec. Unfairly dismissed from court, Eliduc sails to Britain to make his fortune. He becomes the champion of a local king and, in doing so, wins the affection of the princess Guilliadun. Though he remains faithful, Eliduc cannot resist loving her back.

Recalled to Brittany, Eliduc is disconsolate, worrying everyone. He returns to Britain and helps Guilliadun sneak away to his ship. A huge storm blows up, causing a sailor to accuse Eliduc of earning God's wrath through his adultery. Guilliadun, who does not know about Eliduc's wife, falls into a coma.

Once in Brittany, Eliduc lays Guilliadun on the altar of a forest chapel. He visits her every morning, which arouses his wife's suspicions. She follows him one day and discovers the girl lying unspoiled in the chapel. Realizing Eliduc loves the girl and not her, Guildeluec mourns. However, observing a weasel resurrecting its mate with a special herb, she generously procures it and revives Guilliadun. She then calls Eliduc and retires to a convent. Eliduc and Guilliadun are married and live happily for many years until they, too, enter the religious life.

Numerous critics have pointed out that Guildeluec's selfless devotion to her husband's happiness stands in stark contrast to Eliduc's selfish pursuit of advancement and COURTLY LOVE. Eliduc further faces conflicting obligations in both love and feudal service—to two lords and two ladies. Some have explored the potential to "upgrade": Guildeluec is merely "noble and wise," whereas Guilliadun is the daughter of a king, so Eliduc's choice is socially justifiable. Similarly, Guildeluec is so virtuous that only God is truly worthy of her love. Recently, critics have explored the possibility that this *lai* (LAI) reflects the teachings of Bernard of Clairvaux (1090–1153)—that courtly passion can provide the first step toward loving God.

FURTHER READING

Kinoshita, Sharon. "Two for the Price of One: Courtly Love and Serial Polygamy in the Lais of Marie de France." *Arthuriana* 8, no. 2 (1998): 33–55.

Potkay, Monica Brzezinski. "The Limits of Romantic Allegory in Marie de France's *Eliduc." Medieval Perspectives* 9 (1994): 135–145.

Matthieu Boyd

ELIZABETH I (1533–1603) *queen of England*

Ruler of England for 45 years, Elizabeth had a profound effect on literature produced while she was queen. A writer herself, her personal literary production is primarily letters and speeches written for various political purposes such as addressing Parliament or negotiating with foreign powers. She also wrote at least 15 poems. The stability of her long reign and her emphasis on courtly behavior that included the ability to write creatively contributed to the immense literary production of this period, some of which focused on her.

Elizabeth was born to HENRY VIII and Anne Boleyn, his second wife. At birth, Elizabeth disappointed her parents because she was not male, so she was not considered able to succeed Henry as sovereign and lived in the shadow of her older half sister, Mary Tudor, later MARY I, daughter of Henry and his first wife, Catherine of Aragon. Henry demanded an act of succession from Parliament that allowed his older and then his younger daughter to inherit the throne if he should fail to provide a legitimate son. Approximately two years after Elizabeth's birth, Anne Boleyn was tried on charges of adulterous treason and beheaded. Henry then married Jane Seymour, by whom he had a son, Edward, who displaced Mary and Elizabeth as Henry's heir. However, all accounts indicate that Elizabeth and Edward enjoyed a cordial relationship, particularly under the Protestant influence of Henry's sixth wife, Catherine Parr.

With Edward, Elizabeth studied under Roger Ascham and William Grindal. She learned to read, write, and speak Latin, English, French, Italian, Spanish, and some Greek. Although Elizabeth's relationships with her siblings were cordial, they changed significantly when Edward, and then Mary, became England's rulers. King Edward VI was only 10 years old at his ascension, so his two uncles—first Edward Seymour, duke of Somerset, then John Dudley, duke of Northumberland—became regents. While Edward lived, Elizabeth continued her education and practiced her Protestant religion, while Somerset and Northumberland strove to make a politically advantageous marriage for her.

Edward died of tuberculosis at 16, leaving no clear successor. Northumberland attempted to place his daughter-in-law, Lady Jane Grey, on the throne. Henry VIII's act of succession was still in place, however, so, Jane Grey was deposed after nine days. In 1553, Mary Tudor ascended the throne and had Parliament declare her birth legitimate.

Under Mary, Elizabeth's life was increasingly jeopardized because the queen's sister represented both personal and political threats. Henry VIII's affection for Elizabeth's mother had caused Henry's divorce from Catherine of Aragon and had made England into a Protestant nation. Mary, however, was a devout Roman Catholic. As Mary's reign continued and she was unable to eradicate Protestantism or to produce an heir (she married Philip II of Spain in July 1554), Elizabeth became an increasing political threat. Elizabeth had the same claim to the succession as Mary, so resentful Protestants wanted her crowned queen. To counter any such plots, Mary demanded that Elizabeth publicly attend mass. Although Elizabeth refused initially, she eventually appeared to comply. Mary, however, eventually suspected Elizabeth of joining Protestant plots to depose her and had her sister imprisoned in the TOWER OF LONDON and examined for treason, then moved and guarded at Woodstock, and then at Hatfield in an effort to keep Elizabeth and others from conspiring against her. While imprisoned, Elizabeth continued to study and to write, scratching a poem on the window at Woodstock ("Written with a Diamond"). Regardless of Mary's suspicions, Elizabeth was never proven to have engaged in any plots to replace the queen. In 1558, Mary died without issue, and Elizabeth became queen at age 24.

As queen, Elizabeth faced several great challenges. She had to determine national religious practice; to decide which, if any, of her suitors to marry; to negotiate a foreign policy that kept England from the threat of war, especially with Catholic nations that might support MARY, QUEEN OF SCOTS in her effort to claim the English crown; and to maintain order within her own borders. Because each of these courses had national ramifications, these decisions provided material for writers of various texts, from peers to playwrights.

A Protestant, Elizabeth returned England to Protestant religious practice. This move, while popular at home, made England a target for Catholic nations abroad. To keep English Catholics from joining with these powers, Elizabeth imposed restrictions on them. She made hearing or saying mass a punishable offense and banned Catholic pamphlets written to discredit her and to foment rebellion. To prevent Catholic nations from declaring war, Elizabeth also used her position as the greatest marriage prize in Europe to keep suitors (including Philip II of Spain) dangling. As long as they believed that they might marry Elizabeth and thereby gain control of England, they hesitated to invade outright. The tensions between Roman Catholicism and Protestantism influenced many writers, including WILLIAM SHAKESPEARE and EDMUND SPENSER.

Elizabeth's persistent unmarried status became a focus of both national concern and international relations. Many of her letters and speeches, and the literary output of those who sought her PATRONAGE, focused on her position as an unwed queen, although she often used kingly language when speaking of herself. Elizabeth repeatedly characterized herself as a prince, as espoused to her country, or as a benevolent queen/mother to her subjects/children. Her authority allowed her to demand continued use of the language and behavior of COURTLY LOVE with very real political consequences. Of her hopeful courtiers, she had two English favorites: Robert Dudley, master of the horse and later earl of Leicester; and Robert Devereux, earl of Essex. But she did not marry either.

Until her early 40s, Elizabeth was able to keep everyone guessing whether she would marry or remain single. Her suitors' literary output—primarily letters—reflects their uncertainty. Some believed that she would never marry; others hoped that she would marry and bear children. She thus remained a central female figure of poetry written in her court. In her own poetry, notably "ON MONSIEUR'S DEPARTURE," she herself plays with elements of the courtly love tradition, particularly the images of burning ice and freezing fire. In this poem, she is the one who must allow others to suspect that she hates, while internally she feels differently. Of the poetry written to her, the best-developed example of the courtly love theme is EDMUND SPENSER's *The FAERIE QUEENE,* a poem that features Elizabeth in many guises: She appears as the Fairie Queen, Belphoebe, Diana, and Cynthia, among others. Each character maintains her virginity, and each one is an object of desire. Elizabeth also played this role in dramatic entertainments that occurred during the travels that she took through the country. Writers often cast her as herself or as the goddess Diana. In each case, she remained the "virgin queen."

Elizabeth also encouraged a sense of nationalistic pride that was closely associated with Protestantism. She faced two Roman Catholic threats: Mary, Queen of Scots, and Philip II, king of Spain. As Elizabeth's northern neighbor and cousin, Mary presented a problem: She was not only Catholic, she was closely connected to France, a Roman Catholic force. Mary's geographical and genealogical proximity also made her the focus of Catholic subjects who hoped to replace Elizabeth with a monarch legitimized by the pope. Because of her foolish political-personal decisions, however, Mary eventually found herself letting her heart rule her head, and she fled Scotland for England. Although she hoped Elizabeth would be hospitable, Mary was captured and held until her repeated plots against the English queen forced her execution in 1587.

Like Mary, Philip II also constituted a Catholic threat. As the war between the Protestant Netherlands and Philip intensified, the Protestants begged for Elizabeth's support, which she reluctantly gave. Frustrated by Elizabeth's refusal to return to Roman Catholicism, Philip planned a naval assault, which ended with the defeat of the SPANISH ARMADA in 1588. A Catholic nation had attempted invasion, thereby escalating the religious animosity. Pamphleteers used this episode as God-given material, and writers at and for the court and other audiences made stronger references to the conflict between the two religious systems.

Within her own borders, Elizabeth also had to maintain order. She successfully negotiated periods of famine and starvation and several outbreaks of the plague, and she variously expressed dissatisfaction with the carefully regulated social order. She used censorship to ensure that any work printed for public consumption presented her and England in a positive light and did not express views that contradicted those of the state. The master of the revels rigorously scrutinized any text for public consumption, and the stationers' register listed printers and the texts they printed. For this reason, writers could only obliquely refer to contemporary events. Those writers who dared to defy the censors were imprisoned and branded. Despite such controls, a wide variety of events merited glancing references—for example, the war in Ireland, English support of Protestants in the Netherlands, and continued exploration of the New World. Although the identity of her successor became a more pressing issue, Elizabeth refused to give any name. When she died, she whispered James Stuart's name to her attendants, indicating that she had chosen him to succeed her (see JAMES VI/I).

As a long-lived queen, Elizabeth provided the stability writers needed to produce a wide variety of literary works. Her court promoted English nationalism and built on the tradition of courtly love. While much of this literature centered on Elizabeth's virginity, she also possessed political and monetary power. Thus, a nobleman who wanted to advance at court wrote and offered poems to Elizabeth. Even those poets who were not peers wrote her poetry. These poems touched on issues important to the writer, and in them, Elizabeth often appeared as a major character. However the poet described her, he hoped that she found his depiction of her pleasant enough that she might give him money or a court appointment from which the writer and his family might enjoy additional income. Most of this literary output did not achieve the hoped-for results. Instead, many writers found that Elizabeth accepted these poems and made grateful noises, but money or preferment did not follow. Noblemen and women in her court, however, offered patronage to writers, including William Shakespeare, Ben Jonson, and others. Many texts, directly or indirectly, address social concerns, although some works simply show the writer's various talents. Writers who dared to depict Elizabeth in less positive language were treated as traitors, and their work was destroyed. Despite strict controls of printed or performed texts, Elizabethan writers produced a large body of work, much of which revolves around Elizabeth and her court.

See also COURT CULTURE; "DOUBT OF FUTURE FOES, THE"; "WHEN I WAS FAIR AND YOUNG"; "WRITTEN ON A WINDOW FRAME [OR WALL] AT WOODSTOCK" AND "WRITTEN WITH A DIAMOND."

FURTHER READING

Neale, J. E. *Queen Elizabeth*. Chicago: Academy Chicago Publishers, 1992.
Plowden, Alison. *Danger to Elizabeth*: *The Catholics under Elizabeth I*. Phoenix Mill/Stroud, Gloucestershire: Sutton Publishing Ltd., 1999.
———. *Elizabeth Regina*: *The Age of Triumph, 1558–1603*. Phoenix Mill, Thrupp, and Stroud, Gloucestershire, U.K.: Sutton Publishing Ltd., 2000.
———. *Marriage with My Kingdom*: *The Courtships of Elizabeth I*. Phoenix Mill and Stroud, Gloucestershire, U.K.: Sutton Publishing Ltd., 1999.
———. *The Young Elizabeth*: *The First Twenty-Five Years of Elizabeth I*. Rev. Ed. Phoenix Mill and Stroud, Gloucestershire, U.K.: Sutton Publishing Ltd., 1999.
Ridley, Jasper. *Elizabeth I*: *The Shrewdness of Virtue*. New York: Fromm International Publishing Company, 1989.
Weir, Alison. *The Life of Elizabeth I*. New York: Ballantine Books, 1998.

Martha Kalnin Diede

ELIZABETHAN SONNET   See ENGLISH SONNET.

EMBLEM   The Renaissance emblem was a genre where the text and image were melded into "speaking

pictures" or "silent parables." An emblem poem is dependent on its image as much as its words. The Italian writer Andrea Alciati (1492–1550) is credited with producing the first emblem book, as well as with creating the term *emblem*.

Each emblem has three parts: the *inscriptio* (motto printed above the picture), the *pictura* (the [allegorical] picture), and the *subscriptio* (prose or verse below the image which explains the moral application). All three parts had to be included in order for the emblem to be complete. As a whole, the emblem becomes a function of "wit," as it was termed in the early modern era, whereby the mind imposed connections on signifiers, or understood the inherent meanings revealed through art.

Pure *word emblems* are verbal structures in which words convey both picture and meaning, especially as a unifying element in poetry. These poems tend to be SONNETS and EPIGRAMS, the former because the common OCTAVE/SESTET division encourages a natural division into "pictorial" and "interpretation" sections, the latter because the form lends itself to wittiness and moralizing.

See also ALLEGORY, EKPHRASIS.

FURTHER READING

Bath, Michael. *Speaking Pictures*: *English Emblem Books and Renaissance Culture*. London: Longman, 1994.
Daly, Peter M. *Literature in the Light of the Emblem*: *Structural Parallels between the Emblem and Literature in the Sixteenth and Seventeenth Centuries*. Toronto: University of Toronto Press, 1979.

ENCOMIUM   Derived from the Greek *enkōmion*—a speech celebrating a victor—an encomium is a formal tribute expressing praise and warm affection, if addressed to a person, and enthusiastic approval if directed toward an object or event. The term is often used interchangeably with PANEGYRIC.

See also PAEAN.

ENGLISH CHAUCERIANS   This is the name given to a group of 15th-century English writers and associated texts written after GEOFFREY CHAUCER's death. These writings reflect Chaucerian form, content, tone, vocabulary, and style. A number of them even cite Chaucer directly, as both source and inspiration. This

group includes JOHN LYDGATE, THOMAS HOCCLEVE, Benedict Burgh (d. ca. 1483), George Ashby (d. 1537), Henry Bradshaw (d. 1513), George Ripley (15th century), Thomas Norton (1532–1584), and Osbern Bokenam (1393–ca. 1447). The texts (and thus their anonymous authors) include the so-called Chaucerian Apocrypha: The TALE OF GAMELYN, The Tale of Beryn (The Second Merchant's Tale), La Belle Dame sans Merci, The Cuckoo and the Nightingale, The Assembly of Ladies, The Flower and Leaf, and The Court of Love. These last group of texts include a number of DREAM VISIONS. Some scholars also consider several texts within the PIERS PLOWMAN TRADITION to be the work of English Chaucerians, and originally a number of those works were erroneously attributed to Chaucer. There is also some debate as to whether or not JOHN GOWER should be included in this group, since he was Chaucer's direct contemporary, not a follower, and a well-known author in his own right. The northern writers influenced by Chaucer are generally referred to as the SCOTTISH CHAUCERIANS. Differences can be found between the two groups, particularly in political stance and language usage.

The influence of Chaucer on English poetry of all dialects, especially immediately after his demise, is unprecedented and clearly demonstrates his importance within the VERNACULAR tradition, in addition to solidifying his place within the English literary canon.

FURTHER READING

Brewer, D. S., ed. Chaucer and Chaucerians: Critical Studies in Middle English Literature. London: Nelson, 1966.

Forni, Kathleen. The Chaucerian Apocrypha: A Counterfeit Canon. Gainesville: University Press of Florida, 2001.

ENGLISH SONNET (SHAKESPEAREAN SONNET, ELIZABETHAN SONNET) A

variation of the SONNET (14-line poem) found in the English literary tradition, the English sonnet was developed by SIR THOMAS WYATT and HENRY HOWARD, EARL OF SURREY. Because of WILLIAM SHAKESPEARE's popularity, this form is sometimes called the Shakespearean sonnet; it has also been called the Elizabethan sonnet after Queen ELIZABETH I.

The English sonnet exhibits four divisions of verse instead of the two sections commonly found in ITALIAN (PETRARCHAN) SONNETS: three quatrains and a concluding rhyming COUPLET. The quatrains may have differing rhyme schemes, but the most common one is *abab, cdcd, efef, gg.* Typically in this form, the narrative background begins in the first quatrain and is explained in the second. The third quatrain usually begins with a VOLTA, or turn, in which the story shifts, with the couplet providing a "summing up" at the end. Scholars suggest that this form was easily adapted to drama, a development found in early modern theatre.

ENJAMBMENT

Enjambment is a term describing the prosody (rhythm) of poetry, in which the meaning and the structure of a line runs into the following line. Often used in poetry composed of COUPLETS, it also became an important device used in SONNETS. For instance, in Sonnet 104 from ASTROPHIL AND STELLA, SIR PHILIP SIDNEY creates a sense of distance from his beloved through enjambment. In Sonnet 45 from DELIA, SAMUEL DANIEL links the first two quatrains through enjambment, extending the pun on *mourn* and *morn,* and drawing the reader into the poet's dream.

ENVOI (ENVOY)

From the Middle French word *envoy,* "to send," an envoi is the final part of a poem wherein the poet addresses the person to whom the poem is directed; it often contains a moral interpretation. Originally part of the French troubadour tradition, English poetry increasingly used the envoi after the 14th century. GEOFFREY CHAUCER's *Troilus and Criseyde* contains an envoi at the end in which he directs his "litel boke" to be subject to Poetry and kiss the footprints of VIRGIL, OVID, Homer, Lucan, and Statius. Two of Chaucer's shorter lyrics—"ENVOY TO SCOGAN" and "ENVOY TO BUKTON"—apparently use *envoy* in the sense of "message," but they also incorporate the taut moral aspect of traditional envois. JOHN LYDGATE and THOMAS HOCCLEVE also used envois in a number of their poems, such as at the end of Lydgate's *Troy Book* and in Hoccleve's *Regiment of Princes.* Another example of the envoi can be found at the close of *The KINGIS QUAIR* by JAMES I, king of Scotland. During the Renaissance, envois became a part of the SONNET tradition, and many individual poems as well as SONNET SEQUENCES feature elegant envois.

See also FALL OF PRINCES, THE; SESTINA.

K. P. Clarke

"ENVOY TO BUKTON" ("LENVOY DE CHAUCER A BUKTON") Geoffrey Chaucer

(1396) Chaucer's envoy (ENVOI), or verse letter, to Bukton is a short poem surviving in a single manuscript (where it is called "Lenvoy de Chaucer a Bukton"). There is some question as to who "Bukton" was: One candidate is Sir Robert Bukton, squire to Queen Anne and later to Richard II; the other, more likely, candidate is Sir Peter Bukton of Holdernesse, steward to the earl of Derby, future King Henry IV. The poem is in the conventional French lyric form of a ballade and consists of three eight-line STANZAS with a final eight-line envoy, or address to Bukton. Like Chaucer's "ENVOY TO SCOGAN," this poem probably owes much to the tradition of verse epistles dating back to the Latin satirist Horace. Certainly the tone of Chaucer's poem is gently satiric, like that of Horace.

"Envoy to Bukton" is a mock-serious condemnation of marriage, warning Bukton against his impending wedding with a good deal of lighthearted raillery. Marriage, the poem's speaker says, is folly or "dotage" (l. 8). It is for the "Unwys" (l. 27) or else for a "doted fool" (l. 13). It is a kind of hellish bondage, the "chayne / Of Sathanas, on which he gnaweth evere" (ll. 9–10), and a man should take his cue from Satan, who would never willingly be bound again if he were ever able to break out of his bonds. Only a fool would rather be chained up than free. A man who marries is his "wyves thrall" (l. 20), and would be better off to be taken prisoner in Frisia than caught in the trap of marriage. The speaker ends by advising Bukton to read *The WIFE OF BATH'S TALE* if he wants an authority on marriage, and then he prays that Bukton may live his life in freedom, for it is "ful hard" to be bound.

At least this is what the speaker seems to be saying. But part of Chaucer's wit and jesting tone in this poem stems from his deliberately slippery language. He begins the poem with an anecdote about Pilate's question to Christ, "What is truth?" Chaucer interprets Christ's failure to answer to mean "No man is al trew, I gesse" (l. 4). Of course, the poet's "gesse" about Christ's meaning is completely wrong, but he goes on to apply that conclusion to his own situation: He has promised to speak of the sorrow and woe in marriage, he says, but now claims that he must go back on his word. He

doesn't dare say anything bad about marriage, he says, for fear he'll fall into the trap again himself. He follows this up by declaring that he will *not* say that marriage is the chain of Satan. He then alludes to St. Paul's words in 1 Corinthians 7.9, that it is better to marry than to burn, and then goes on to twist Paul's words in 1 Cor. 7.27–28 to emphasize the "bondage" and "tribulation" that Paul mentions as a part of marriage. The poet follows up the authority of St. Paul by an allusion to the fictional authority of the Wife of Bath. Thus Chaucer technically never says anything bad about marriage nor directly condemns it. He tells us what he will not say and alludes to authorities, one of which he misinterprets and the other of which is his own fictional creation. The "Envoy to Bukton" thus becomes an exercise in how to say something without actually saying it.

The poem seems clearly to have been written after the death of Chaucer's wife in 1387, since he implies that he is unmarried. The allusion to the Wife of Bath suggests that "Envoy to Bukton" must have been written after the composition of "The Wife of Bath's Prologue," and at a time when that prologue was well known. But an allusion to the Frisians may be the most direct clue to the date of "Bukton," since it is known that an expedition was undertaken against the Frisians in 1396. The chronicler Jean Froissart mentions that the Frisians had a reputation for brutality toward prisoners, whom they would kill rather than ransom, which explains the allusion in the poem.

Most early scholarship on "Envoy to Bukton" was concerned with establishing the identity of Bukton. More recently, this kind of scholarship has considered who made up Chaucer's audience and what his short poems show us about his role in society. Other recent criticism has focused on the poem's speaker: Some see the narrator as displaying a dissolute nature, while others believe the whole poem is simply a game. Other recent discussions have cited the poem as an example of writing about the unreliability of language in the search for truth, a theme related to the late medieval philosophical concept of nominalism.

The "Envoy to Bukton" may well cause us to wonder just what Chaucer's own views on marriage were, but the poem really does not give us a clue. It is clearly not a serious text, and Chaucer playfully says nothing that can be taken unequivocally. The poem is a topical piece that is best looked upon as an exercise in comic irony.

See also SATIRE.

FURTHER READING

Bertolet, Craig E. "Chaucer's Envoys and the Poet-Diplomat." *Chaucer Review* 33 (1998): 66–89.

Braddy, Haldeen. "Sir Peter and the Envoy to Bukton." *PQ* 14 (1935): 368–370.

Chance, Jane. "Chaucerian Irony in the Verse Epistles 'Wordes unto Adam,' 'Lenvoy a Scogan,' and 'Lenvoy a Bukton.'" *PLL* 21 (1985): 115–128.

Lowes, John Livingston. "The Date of the *Envoy to Bukton*." *MLN* 27 (1912): 45–48.

Ruud, Jay. *"Many a Song and Many a Leccherous Lay"*: *Tradition and Individuality in Chaucer's Lyric Poetry.* New York: Garland, 1992.

Jay Ruud

"ENVOY TO SCOGAN" ("LENVOY DE CHAUCER A SCOGAN") GEOFFREY CHAUCER (1393)

GEOFFREY CHAUCER's "Envoy to Scogan" is a short poem in seven STANZAS of RYME ROYAL verse, the last of which is an envoy (ENVOI) directly addressed to Henry Scogan. Scogan was Chaucer's friend and fellow poet, who was to become tutor to the four sons of Henry IV and author of a poem called *A Moral Ballade* in which he quotes from Chaucer's short poem "Gentillesse" while discussing the nature of true nobility. Chaucer's envoy takes the form of a verse letter to Scogan, after the gently satiric manner of the Roman poet Horace, in which Chaucer apparently asks Scogan to put in a good word for him at the court. The poem is relatively late in Chaucer's career, most likely after 1391, when the poet lived away from the court. There were heavy rains around Michaelmas in the year 1393, which might suggest the poem belongs to that year.

The poem survives in three manuscripts, where it is called "Lenvoy de Chaucer a Scogan." It begins with a mock-serious lament that the laws of heaven have been broken, and Venus herself is weeping so abundantly that she has caused the recent deluge in England, threatening to drown the world—all because Scogan has given up the love of his lady. Scogan's scorning of love is dangerous, Chaucer insists, and he fears that Love will take vengeance not only on Scogan but on all of those who, like him and Chaucer, are old and "rounde of shap" (l. 31), so that they will receive no reward for all their labor. To Scogan's imagined response, "Lo, olde Grisel lyst to ryme and playe" (l. 35)—that is, the old man (Chaucer) likes to rhyme and play—Chaucer responds that he is past all that, that his muse is sleeping and rusting in his sheath, implying that, perhaps, he has, like Scogan, also given up on love—or at least on love poetry.

The final stanza of the poem, the envoi, has caused a great deal of critical commentary. Here Chaucer asks Scogan, kneeling at the head of the stream of grace, to remember Chaucer, forgotten in a solitary wilderness. Think on "Tullius kyndenesse," he tells Scogan, and mention his friend where it will prove most fruitful. The stream's head is apparently Windsor, while the solitary wilderness may be Greenwich, where Chaucer was living after 1390 when he was appointed deputy forester of Petherton. The reference to Tullius is not completely clear, though most likely it refers to Cicero's treatise on friendship, *De Amicitia*. Cicero emphasizes that friendship should be based on mutual love and not the expectation of profit, and that one should befriend others similar to oneself. Chaucer may be implying that Scogan's relationship with his lady did not follow Cicero's advice, but that his friendship with Chaucer himself is a more natural relationship. Ironically, of course, Chaucer seems to be ignoring Cicero's advice by asking to profit from Scogan's friendship. It is the kind of irony that Chaucer seems to have enjoyed a great deal.

See also "ENVOY TO BUKTON," SATIRE.

FURTHER READING

Minnis, A. J., V. J. Scattergood, and J. J. Smith. *Oxford Guides to Chaucer: The Shorter Poems.* Oxford: Clarendon Press, 1995.

Ruud, Jay. *"Many a Song and Many a Leccherous Lay"*: *Tradition and Individuality in Chaucer's Lyric Poetry.* New York: Garland, 1992.

Jay Ruud

EPIC

An epic poem is a long narrative piece focusing on the story of one or more heroic characters. Epic poets strive to craft serious and elevated poems that express the values of their culture. Thus, epics often interweave the formation or lionization of a particular culture or nation into the narrative of their characters. Besides a heroic focus, other important classical conventions include epic similes, lengthy catalogues of characters or things, a plot beginning in medias res (in the middle of things), a journey to the underworld, and a statement of the epic theme. BEOWULF is the earliest extant English epic, and while critics debate how well it fulfills the classical idea of the epic, the poem fulfills many of the criteria. For example, the poem begins with an extended recapitulation of Scyld Scefing and his heroic lineage, Beowulf appears in the midst of the uproar over Grendel's attacks, and he descends into the mere.

In his DEFENSE OF POESY (ca. 1580), SIR PHILIP SIDNEY begins to fashion the epic as an important genre to create. Epic, he claims, is "the best and most accomplished kind of poetry." A contemporary work, The FAERIE QUEENE (1590 and 1596), is an accomplished exemplar because its author was an accomplished student of classical and continental epic. EDWARD SPENSER is not a pure epic poet, but he uses a number of the aforementioned epic conventions. For example, each of The FAERIE QUEENE's six books states a different epic theme, there is a catalogue of the descendants and exploits of Brutus (the ostensible founder of Britain), and the lady Duessa descends into hell.

See also CLASSICAL TRADITION, EPYLLION.

FURTHER READING

Tillyard, E. M. W. The English Epic and Its Background. New York: Oxford University Press, 1954.

Craig T. Fehrman

EPIGRAM

EPIGRAM The epigram—a short, sharp, topical poem that often ends with a twist—was a popular medium for Tudor satirists. In one or two STANZAS, usually in rhymed iambic pentameter, epigrammatists would, as the titles of their collections claimed, expose "the abuses of our tyme, which may and ought to be put away" or create pithy, pleasant, and profitable verses for "the expert readers of quicke capacitie." Easily memorized and often viciously funny, epigrams could be a powerful verbal weapon for a middle-class

wit to deploy against those with more social or economic power. Epigrams are also a rich source of information about the objects of their disdain: actors, prostitutes, drunkards, shrews, rival poets, and the socially pretentious. Collections of epigrams, often grouped in "centuries," or units of 100, remained popular until the June 1599 ecclesiastical ban on satire.

See also COURT CULTURE, SATIRE.

FURTHER READING

Hudson, Hoyt H. The Epigram in the English Renaissance. Princeton, N.J.: Princeton University Press, 1947.

Catherine Loomis

"EPITAPHE ON SIR PHILIP SIDNEY, AN" JAMES VI, KING OF SCOTLAND (1587)

SIR PHILIP SIDNEY was killed in battle in 1586, inspiring the composition of King James VI's SONNET, which was both politically inspired and personally motivated. The poem features a distinctively Scottish interlaced rhyme scheme (abab, bcbc, cdcd, ee). Politically, it demonstrates James's commitment to melding English and Scottish interests, although the question of who would succeed the English queen ELIZABETH I was still in the future. Personally, it indicates James's respect for a great poet.

The first QUATRAIN conventionally asks a trio of gods to "bewail" (l. 8) Sidney's death: Mars, god of war; Minerva, goddess of wisdom and the arts; and Apollo, Sidney's divine patron and god of poetry. The second quatrain connects Apollo to Parnassus (a mountain near Delphi, Greece) and "the sisters that theron doe dwell" (l. 5). These are the nine Muses, conventionally associated with poetic inspiration, now called on to grieve the loss of one of their most inspired subjects. The third quatrain and closing COUPLET suggest Sidney's widespread fame will live on in his own works as well as James' commemoration.

See also JAMES VI/I.

FURTHER READING

Craigie, James, ed. The Poems of James VI of Scotland. 2 vols. Edinburgh: Scottish Text Society, 1955–58.

Westcott, Allan F., ed. New Poems by James I of England. 1911. Reprint, New York: AMS Press, 1966.

Sebastiaan Verweij

EPITHALAMION EDMUND SPENSER (1594)

Written in 1594 as a celebration of his own nuptials to Elizabeth Boyle and published a year later, EDMUND SPENSER's *Epithalamion* follows the basic tenets of its classical predecessors. The poem begins before dawn, follows the bride on her wedding day (which is also the summer solstice), and ends with nighttime felicitations of the bridal bed and prayers for fertility.

The poem insists that the festive day is a day outside of the mundane: "The joyfulst day that ever sunne did see" (l. 16). The longest day of the year is a triumph for the sun and the couple. It is set apart from time and simultaneously participates in it by banding oppositions into one—day and night and man and woman. The polarities also engender the poem's structure. There are (including the ENVOI) 24 STANZAS paralleling the 24 hours of the day as it passes from predawn to night. It has been noted that there is a shift from positive to negative as day turns into night.

There also is a varying rhyme scheme, but each stanza, with the exception of the last, is linked through the REFRAIN of an "Eccho" that the speaker demands "ring." This links to the ringing of the solstice bells. However, the ring imagery is not limited to the aural: Wedding bands, garlands, ring dances, and the revolution of the heavens also serve to link the stanzas together.

The poem marks time to protect itself from the erosion of memory: "This day is holy; doe ye write it downe / That ye forever it remember it may" (ll. 263–264). Although the speaker, the groom, is impatient, "for this time it ill ordained was, / To choose the longest day in all the yeare, / And shortest night, when longer fitter weare" (ll. 270–272), the conjunction of the wedding day and the summer solstice establishes a natural connection between the natural rhythm of the calendar year and the artificiality of human rituals: childbirth. Additionally, a child conceived on the evening of the summer solstice and carried for the expected nine months would be born in March—a Lenten month culminating in the Christian celebration of the ultimate triumph of light over dark with Christ's death and resurrection.

The poem insists on this inextricable nature of the human and the cosmic. For example, the wedding is dependent on the movement of the muses, the poem, and the bride herself. All are linked to the movement of the sun and the hours. The movement of the human is notably mirrored by, and therefore linked to, the heavenly.

Similarly, the poem takes a position between the classical and popular. The setting is a village celebration in the Irish countryside, attended by muses, deities, and local rustics, and thereby fully encompasses the actual landscape (Ireland) and the limitless geography of the gods and goddesses. Spenser reconciles the evocation of the Christian and the non-Christian in typical Renaissance fashion by easily linking one with the other. The solstice is the "day the sunne is in his chiefest hight, / With Barnaby the bright" (ll. 265–266) and the pagan customs are still very much evident despite the dedication of the day to St. Barnabas, and the Christian wedding. For example, in accordance with solstice custom, the young men of the town ring bells, light bonfires, and dance and sing about them to make the day wear away for the coming of night. The solstice rituals help mark time on the longest day of the year in its symbolic passage of birth, life, death, and rebirth. Likewise, the wedding and the celebratory feast afterward help to mark time and to celebrate a rite of transition from one state to another—virginity to connubial, and hopefully fruitful, bliss. This celebration is marked by music, an artful lay.

The double meaning of the word *lay* (the noun meaning "a song" and the verb meaning "to lay down") marks the ingenious transition from music to silence in stanza 17, when "day is doen, and night is nighing fast" (l. 298). The speaker's former commands for song are replaced by invocations for silence: "But let the night be calm and quietsome" (l. 326). He asks the attending damsels to "lay" the bride in her nuptial bed (ll. 302–308) and then commands them to "leave my love alone, / And likewise your former lay to sing: / The woods no more shal answere, nor your echo ring" (ll. 312–314). The word *lay* in both its contexts marks the transition from the music of the day, the virginal bed, into the silence of the night, the marriage bed. The transition is complete, and the speaker asks, "Send us the timely fruit of this same night" (l. 404).

Through the allusions to festivity and its numerological structure, *Epithalamion* is richly endowed with an added dimension. It participates in, and simultaneously evokes, a dynamic temporal symbolism. This helps to frame the poem's representation of marriage and offspring as security against the mutability of time.

FURTHER READING

Dasenbrock, Reed Way. "The Petrarchan Context of Spenser's *Amoretti*." *PMLA* 100, no. 1 (1985): 38–50.

Hieatt, A. Kent. *Short Time's Endless Monument.* New York: Columbia University Press, 1960.

Laroque, François. *Shakespeare's Festive World.* Translated by Janet Lloyd. Cambridge: Cambridge University Press, 1991.

Maia Adamina

EPYLLION (MINOR EPIC)

The Elizabethan minor EPIC was generally divided into two groupings: the epyllion, or minor epic "proper," which has topics related to classical mythology; and the historical COMPLAINT. Both are related to CHRONICLES. Epyllions take OVID's *Metamorphoses* for their inspiration and often relate narratives about sexual consummation. Historical complaints tend to focus on a female protagonist who confronts seduction and/or rape and death. Generally, however, epyllions feature elevated characters (e.g., divine or noble), mythological connections, and a sense of the supernatural, coupled with exalted versification.

The epyllion enjoyed a brief spate of popularity during the close of the Elizabethan era. CHRISTOPHER MARLOWE's *HERO AND LEANDER* and WILLIAM SHAKESPEARE's *VENUS AND ADONIS* both fall into this genre.

FURTHER READING

Hulse, Clark. *Metapmorphic Verse: The Elizabethan Minor Epic.* Princeton, N.J.: Princeton University Press, 1981.

Miller, Paul W. "The Elizabethan Minor Epic." *Studies in Philology* 55 (1958): 31–38.

"ERTHE TOC OF THE ERTHE WITH WOH" ("EARTH UPON EARTH") ANONYMOUS (14th century)

"Erthe toc of the Erthe with woh" is a family of MIDDLE ENGLISH LYRICS, the earliest version of which is believed to be a single-STANZA lyric of four meters. It is in essence a rhyming gloss on the words spoken by God to Adam in Genesis 3.19: "Remember Man that thou art dust and to dust thou shalt return." This scripture also formed part of the medieval liturgy for Ash Wednesday, the day on which Christians were exhorted to remember their mortality. Each of the subsequent adaptations of "Erthe toc of the Erthe with woh" retains a distinctly ironic flavor intended to stir the reader to penitence upon the realization of his vile origins and the brevity of this life. "Erthe" is one of the most enduring literary examples of the memento mori (reminder of death). Forms of the poem frequently appear in medieval commonplace books or in the surplus leaves at the beginning or end of manuscripts, as well as on tombstones as a popular epitaph.

The early lyric repeats the words *erthe* and *erthene* a dozen times, exploiting its multiple received meanings. Humans, Adam's progeny, originate in the "erthe." Through marrying and accumulating worldly goods, they draw more "erthe" to themselves, and by producing children, they bring forth further "erthe." Finally, in death they are laid in the grave—an "erthene through"—and, following the Scripture, "erthe" has been returned to its original matter. Overall, the poem offers a brief, satirical view of human life, well suited to eliciting penitence.

See also CONTEMPT FOR THE WORLD.

FURTHER READING

Duncan, Thomas G., ed. *A Companion to the Middle English Lyric.* Woodbridge, Suffolk, U.K.: D.S. Brewer, 2005.

———. *Medieval English Lyrics: 1200–1400.* Harmondsworth, Middlesex, U.K.: Penguin, 1995.

Murray, Hilda M., ed. *The Middle English Poem, Erthe upon Erthe. Printed from Twenty-Four Manuscripts.* Early English Text Society/Old Series 141. London: Oxford University Press, 1911.

Robin Gilbank

ESTATES SATIRE   See SATIRE, THREE ESTATES.

"EVEN NOW THAT CARE" MARY SIDNEY HERBERT, COUNTESS OF PEMBROKE (1599)

"Even now that Care" by MARY SIDNEY HERBERT, countess of Pembroke, appears in a sole version, in a presentation copy of the SIDNEAN PSALMS. Written in IAMBIC PENTAMETER using an *abab, bcbc* pattern, this poem, dedicating the *Sidnean psalms* to Queen ELIZABETH I, describes the construction of the *Psalter* as well as Elizabeth's rule and her connection to the Protestant scriptures. The biblical Psalms were attributed to the Old Testament's King David, an attribution that enhanced their appropriateness for a monarch. Indeed, Herbert's dedication of the *Sidnean Psalms* to Elizabeth falls perfectly into a lengthy tradition of Tudor piety, and Herbert herself underscores the connection between David and Elizabeth in the poem when she says, "A King should onely to a Queene bee sent" (l. 53). Herbert relies on this association between David and Elizabeth throughout the poem, drawing lengthy comparisons between his life and hers.

"Even now that Care" maintains a gracious and highly complimentary tone throughout its 12 STANZAS. The cares mentioned in the first line draw attention to Elizabeth's heavy burdens of state, but the second stanza metaphorically lightens the weight of the queen's responsibilities by drawing attention to her accomplishments and her God-given gifts, as well as her endurance: "To others toile, is Exercise to thee" (l. 16). To Elizabeth, work—which might include reading the *Psalms*—is but a trifling exercise.

Interestingly, "Even now that Care" differs from other dedicatory poems in its lack of references to Elizabeth's beauty or to mythological figures. Instead, Herbert tenders a higher compliment: She orients the poem around Elizabeth's political accomplishments as well as her relationship to Protestantism, praising actual accomplishments instead of fantastic adventures. Thus, the queen's real accomplishments are raised to the level of biblical heroism. The poem also contains subtle reminders of Elizabeth's role as effective guardian of Protestantism; part of her ruler's burden is to "dispose / What Europe acts in theise most active times" (ll. 7–8), suggesting that she is a guardian of Protestantism abroad as well as in England.

Early in the poem, Herbert acknowledges the dual authorship of the *Psalms*, noting that "Which once in two, now in one Subject goe, / the poorer left, the richer reft awaye" (ll. 21–22). SIR PHILIP SIDNEY had begun the work, but Mary Sidney Herbert was actually responsible for the bulk of the translation, as her brother died having completed only Psalms 1–43. Herbert expresses her grief for her brother's death as well as her own determination to finish the work: "hee did

warpe, I weav'd this webb to end" (l. 27). Herbert's comparison of the *Psalter* to a cloth or a piece of clothing allows her to commend her own translation, as she notes that the Psalms have often worn worse—or been translated in inferior versions.

Much of the poem, unsurprisingly, consists of praise for the duration and extent of Elizabeth's rule. As queen, Elizabeth controls "two hemispheres" (l. 75), suggestive of both her inherited throne and the power she wields in the New World. Elizabeth's dominion over men also merits mention. Herbert observes that:

> Kings on a Queene enforst their states to lay;
> Main-lands for Empire waiting on an Ile;
> Men drawne by worth a woman to obey;
> One moving all, herself unmov'd the while
> (ll. 81–84)

Despite her sex, Elizabeth rules at the center of the world, and perhaps the universe, as the image of Elizabeth "unmov'd" suggests the Elizabethan concept of the *primum mobile*, or prime mover, responsible for the revolution of the heavens, but not itself moved. The poem ends with the hope that Elizabeth will continue to live and thrive far beyond her peers, until she rivals "Judas Faithful King" (l. 94), David. Herbert ultimately encourages Elizabeth to do "more then hee" (l. 95) and to "Sing what God doth, and doo What men may sing" (l. 96). Elizabeth not only parallels David's life and rule, but ultimately exceeds it—and is, finally, a deserving recipient of David's Psalms.

See also "TO THE THRICE-SACRED QUEEN ELIZABETH."

FURTHER READING
Hannay, Margaret P., Noel J. Kinnamon, and Michael G. Brennan, eds. *The Collected Works of Mary Sidney Herbert, Countess of Pembroke*. 2 vols. Oxford: Clarendon Press, 1998.

Hannay, Margaret P. *Philip's Phoenix: Mary Sidney, Countess of Pembroke*. Oxford: Oxford University Press, 1990.

———. *Silent But for the Word: Tudor Women as Patrons, Translators, and Writers of Religious Works*. Kent, Ohio: Kent State University Press, 1985.

EXEGESIS Exegesis, the science of biblical interpretation, was heavily influenced in Europe by early

Christian theologians such as Gregory the Great and Augustine of Hippo. At times closely related to ALLEGORY, medieval Christian exegesis was often marked by the express attempt to situate all biblical content in its proper relationship to Jesus Christ. This "typological" approach would describe, for example, an Old Testament story, such as the Hebrew Exodus from Egypt, as a prefiguration of Christ's sacrifice, which liberated all people from enslavement to sin. Such systems are called the "Allegory of the Theologians." The most widely cited type of theologians' allegory, though by no means the only exegetical approach, is known as the *quadriga,* or the fourfold system of exegesis. Through this interpretive framework, biblical passages were revealed to have not one but four "senses" of meaning: literal, allegorical, tropological, and anagogical. A Latin COUPLET often used in medieval schools clarifies: *Littera gesta docet, quid credas allegoria, / Moralis quid agas, quo tendas anagogia* (The literal teaches the deeds, the allegorical what to believe, the moral what to do, and the anagoge what to strive for). Such interpretation addresses the act of reading Scripture and its proper application to the individual life, both morally and in shaping one's eschatological outlook.

See also BIBLICAL ALLUSIONS.

FURTHER READING

McAuliffe, Jane Dammen, Barry D. Walfish, and Joseph W. Goering, eds. *With Reverence for the Word: Scriptural Exegesis in Judaism, Christianity, and Islam.* Oxford: Oxford University Press, 2003.

Muller, Richard A., and John L. Thompson, eds. *Biblical Interpretation in the Era of the Reformation.* Grand Rapids, Mich.: W. B. Eerdmans, 1996.

Lydia Newell

EXEMPLUM In its simplest form, an exemplum (pl. exempla) is any narrative used to illustrate a point. In medieval literature, however, the *exemplum* more frequently refers to an example provided to teach some truth, illustrate a religious principle, or convey a moral lesson in sermons and didactic religious literature. Pope Gregory the Great (540–604 C.E.) promoted the use of exempla for moral instruction. Peter the Deacon, Gregory's interlocutor in the *Dialogues,* remarks in the preface that many people respond better to virtuous

examples than to godly sermons, a tactic Gregory utilizes in his *Homiliae.* Although Gregory himself employed exempla in his sermons and encouraged their use, their popularity did not become firmly entrenched until the beginning of the 13th century when preaching friars traveled throughout western Europe. During this time, many religious figures advocated using exempla to maintain the interest of their mostly uneducated audience.

By far the most frequent use of exempla comes in the forms of FABLES, parables, tales, anecdotes, and hagiographies (see HAGIOGRAPHY). Exempla can be either positive or negative. Positive exempla serve as models of behavior, while negative exempla effectively demonstrate the consequences of wrong thinking or actions. As the popularity of the exemplum spread throughout the Middle Ages, many preachers turned to collections such as the *Vitae Patrum,* the *Alphabetum Narrationum,* the *Alphabetum Exemplorum,* the *Legenda Aurea* of Jacobus de Voragine, the *Gesta Romanorum,* and Jacques de Vitry's *Exempla* for their sources. The exemplum continued to be a powerful rhetorical tool from the 13th to 15th centuries; however, its effectiveness began to decline as more and more preachers utilized it strictly for humorous purposes. Notable detractors such as Dante, John Wycliffe, and Erasmus castigated the use of exempla to produce humor in church and contributed to the decline in popularity of the exemplum among preachers, but its use was never completely eradicated and continues today. A famous literary example of an exemplum is GEOFFREY CHAUCER's "The PARDONER'S TALE.

Clinton Atchley

EXETER BOOK (*CODEX EXONIENSIS, LIBER EXONIENSIS*) (before 1072) Exeter, Cathedral Chapter Library, MS 3501—the formal name of the Exeter Book—is one of the significant surviving four manuscripts containing Old English (Anglo-Saxon) poetry along with the Vercelli Book, the Junius Manuscript, and MS COTTON VITELLIUS A.XV. It was a gift to the cathedral from Leofric, the first bishop of Exeter (d. 1072). He moved the Episcopal see from Crediton to Exeter in 1050, and may have taken the manuscript with him at that time. The codex (volume of a manuscript) was written sometime between 960 and 980 C.E. by one scribe; however, the date cannot be confirmed. All we know for certain is that Leofric's will mentions "one large book in English, concerning various matters, written in verse," and that the bishop died in 1072. This means that all the materials in the Exeter Book were composed before that date.

The Exeter Book is large. Each of the folios (pages) measures 12.5 inches by 8.6 inches, which is slightly larger than a standard sheet of copy paper. It is a plain volume, containing only a few line drawings and no illuminations (colored and/or decorated drawings) or ornamentation. However, each poem begins with an oversized initial capital, and the remainder of each first line is written in small capitals. The text has had a checkered past. At one point, it was used as a cutting board. It has large knife slashes on the first page, and where two particularly deep ones converge, a large triangle of vellum is missing. The book was also used as a beer stand and has a mug ring on the eighth folio; consequently, there are brown ale stains on that folio and the following two. Several of the leaves are missing, although the cause of their disappearance is unknown. Eight additional leaves were bound into the beginning of the manuscript prior to the early modern (Renaissance) era, but these are not the original folios. In fact, one of these pieces is Leofric's donation list. However, the most severe damage has been done to the final 14 folios of the manuscript. On these, a long diagonal burn destroyed a large portion of the text.

The Exeter Book contains some of the most famous pieces of ANGLO-SAXON POETRY, including the great elegies, "The WANDERER," "The SEAFARER," and "The WIFE'S LAMENT." It also contains the majority of the surviving clever ANGLO-SAXON RIDDLES (96 in total), as well as the physiologius poems (animal poems) "The Panther," "The Whale," "The Partridge," and "The Phoenix." Several of the gnomic verses (*Maxims I*) appear, too. The other texts include: *Christ A, B, C* (also known as *Advent Lyrics, Ascension,* and *Judgment*); *Guthlac A, B; Azarias; Juliana; The Gifts of Men; Precepts; Vainglory;* WIDSITH; *The Fortunes of Men; The Order of the World; The Riming Poem; Soul and Body II;* "DEOR"; "WULF AND EADWACER"; *Judgement I & II;* "Resignation"; *Descent into Hell; Alms-Giving; Pharaoh; The Lord's Prayer; Homiletic Fragment;* "The Husband's Message"; and "The RUIN." None of these poems has a title in the manuscript; all are modern conventions. The contents of the Exeter Book represent one-sixth of the surviving Old English corpus. Two of the poems, "Juliana" and "Ascension," (Christ A), are signed with an ACROSTIC forming the name of the enigmatic poet CYNEWULF in the FUTHARK ALPHABET.

Unfortunately, we do not know much else about the composition of the Exeter Book or its scribe. We are left, instead, with questions, especially about the order of the texts: Did the scribe put them in the order of an original example? Did he or she recopy the texts in their current order? Did he copy them at random as acquired? These questions will most likely remain unanswered. Nevertheless, the Exeter Book is an amazing monument to the early days of English literature.

FURTHER READING

Conner, Patrick W. *Anglo-Saxon Exeter: A Tenth-Century Cultural History.* Studies in Anglo Saxon History 4. Woodbridge, Suffolk, U.K.: Boydell Press, 1993.

Muir, Bernard J., ed. *The Exeter Anthology of Old English Poetry: An Edition of Exeter Dean and Chapter MS 3501.* 2 vols. Exeter: University of Exeter Press, 1994. Revised 2000.

F

FABLE A fable is a story in either verse or prose designed to convey a moral or lesson. PERSONIFICATION is a common device used within fables, as animals and objects are often the main characters. The most famous collection of fables was written by Aesop. Fables were common in the Middle Ages. Both MARIE DE FRANCE and ROBERT HENRYSON wrote a series of fables based on Aesop's work. Another famous fable is GEOFFREY CHAUCER's "The Nun's Priest's Tale," a BEAST FABLE following the adventures of a fox and a cock.

See also MORALL FABILLIS OF ESOPE THE PHRYGIAN, THE; REYNARD LITERATURE.

FABLIAU The term *fabliau* (pl. *fabliaux*) refers to a comic tale that was especially popular in the Norman and Picardy regions of France during the 13th century. Generally, the fabliau is a short comical or satirical tale written in verse and usually composed in octosyllabic COUPLETS, the standard meter of courtly ROMANCE. It is often considered to be a more realistic version of its counterpart, the romance, and typically subverts the ideals of courtly literature. Fabliaux dramatize the ribaldries of lower- and middle-class human characters that are purportedly too raucous and obscene for courtly convention to divulge. They are designed primarily to entertain—usually with bawdy humor ridiculing the (im)piety of the clergy, the stupidity of cuckolded husbands (often older men married to a younger wives), or the insatiable sexual appetites of women. Characteristically, each fabliau focuses on a single, brief, episode and its immediate (and humorous) consequences. The fabliaux were not intended for private reading, but rather for public performance by professional jongleurs (literally "jugglers" of words). They often feature love triangles that mirror the ones found in romances—a jealous and incapable husband, a lecherous wife, and a randy cleric are ingredients in one of the more common scenarios.

The fabliau style is vigorous, yet simple and straightforward, relying on bodily humor. Fabliaux are marked by their irreverence—their snubbing of the dictates of religion, the virtues, and the snobbery of the aristocracy. Although not all fabliaux are sexually obscene or explicitly bawdy, crudeness is a fabliau characteristic, and many feature rude words (e.g., *queynte* [cunt], cock, etc.). Some fabliaux feature "gentle" euphemisms for sexual acts (e.g., broaching the cask, feeding the pig, polishing the ring, etc.). Fabliaux are also distinctive for their rather cynical treatment of women—particularly for featuring transgressive behavior by women—and for vengeance schemes based on sex, both of which contribute to their characteristic misogynist outlook. A number of scholars have noted that fabliaux have their own ironic sense of justice. The endings, which often come as a surprise, have nonetheless been carefully set up throughout the story. In this way, the ending seems artistically fitting and appropriate. Finally, another common source of humor is the portrayal of decidedly *un*courteous characters trying to adopt stereotypically courteous manners. The fabliaux feature socially ambitious bourgeois merchants and artisans, and as such, many are also merciless on social climbers.

Approximately 150 *fabliaux* have survived, most averaging around 250 lines. During the 12th and 13th centuries, the fabliau flourished in France, and its popularity continued in England. The two most well-known fabliaux in Middle English are "The MILLER'S TALE," which is thought to borrow from *De Bérangier au lonc cul,* and (to a slightly lesser extent) "The REEVE'S TALE," both written by GEOFFREY CHAUCER as part of *The CANTERBURY TALES.* "The Shipman's Tale," "Summoner's Tale," and fragmentary "Cook's Tale" also exhibit fabliau characteristics.

While fabliaux are often said to lack the moralizing principles characteristic of FABLES, they do generally feature a dubious brand of "fabliau justice," according to which the unruly protagonists are indubitably punished for their baser motivations and physiological shortcomings. Nowhere is this more apparent than in "The Miller's Tale," in which jealous John the Carpenter, his infamously unchaste wife Alisoun, and her illicit suitors—an Oxford clerk called "hende Nicolas" (I, 3199) and his would-be rival, a foppish parish clerk named Absolon—all receive their comeuppance by the end of the tale.

See also MIDDLE ENGLISH POETRY; "MILLER'S TALE, THE."

FURTHER READING

Bloch, R. Howard. *The Scandal of the Fabliaux.* Chicago: University of Chicago Press, 1986.

Cooke, Thomas D. *The Old French and Chaucerian Fabliaux: A Study of Their Comic Climax.* Columbia: University of Missouri, 1978.

Cooke, Thomas D., and Benjamin L. Honeycutt, eds. *The Humor of the Fabliaux: A Collection of Critical Essays.* Columbia: University of Missouri Press, 1974.

Pearcy, Roy. "Investigations into the Principles of Fabliau Structure." *Genre* 9 (1976): 345–378.

Michelle M. Sauer, Jamie Gianoutsos, and
Christopher D. Lozensky

FAERIE QUEENE, THE (OVERVIEW)
EDMUND SPENSER (1590, 1596) According to the Renaissance idea of a poetic career, EDMUND SPENSER'S EPIC poem, which he dedicated to "the most high, mightie and magnificent empresse renowned for pietie, vertue, and all gratious government Elizabeth" (ELIZABETH I), marked his transition from a novice to a master poet. This idea derived largely from VIRGIL'S (70–19 B.C.E.) poetic career. Virgil became the inspiration for a number of Renaissance poets, both because of his artistic success and because his career exemplified the successful union of poetry and national destiny. Given the emerging nationalism of the Renaissance, many poets—especially Spenser, whom his contemporaries called "the English Virgil"—modeled their careers after Virgil's. This pattern of modeling is called the *cursus Virgilii,* the Virgilian course, as explained in a four-line proem (preface) appended to 16th-century editions of the *Aeneid.* There, Virgil describes how he began with the "shepherd's slender pipe" (PASTORAL poetry, his *Eclogues*), proceeded to the "farmlands" (his didactic *Georgics*), and finally arrived at the "sterner stuff of Mars" (epic poetry, his *Aeneid*).

Spenser uses similar language in the proem to Book 1 of *The Faerie Queene:* "Lo I the man, whose Muse whilome did maske, / As time her taught in lowly Shepheards weeds, / Am now enforst a far unfitter taske, / For trumpets sterne to chaunge mine Oaten reeds." In the Renaissance, a poet's move from pastoral to epic could only be achieved after sufficient artistic maturity, which at this point Spenser had achieved. By the time the first three books of *The Faerie Queene* were published (1590), Spenser had already made a name for himself as a great poet with *The SHEPHEARDES CALENDER* (1579), and by the time the last three books were published (1596), he had further distinguished himself with the publication of his collection of short poems called *Complaints* (1591) and his SONNET SEQUENCE entitled *AMORETTI* (1595).

When *The Faerie Queene* was first published in 1590, there were a series of items printed at the end of the volume that would later become the epic's prefatory matter. Spenser's epic may be organized into five distinct categories: There are the six complete books; seven commendatory verses; 17 dedicatory sonnets; the "Letter to Raleigh" ("A Letter of the Authors expounding his whole intention in the course of this work: which for that it giveth great light to the reader, for the better understanding is hereunto annexed," addressed to SIR WALTER RALEIGH); and the seventh book, which is often merely referred to as the Mutabilitie Cantos. Critics typically separate Book 7 from the other six books because it differs in many ways from its precursors. Read as the last published book of the epic and viewed as another stage on the way to the 12th book (promised in Spenser's "Letter to Raleigh"), its relation to the previous books is problematic, largely because its composition seems to have been an afterthought and largely unfinished. Though poetically the Mutabilitie Cantos recall other parts of *The Faerie Queene,* they are almost always read apart from the rest of the poem.

Commendatory and dedicatory verses were common in early modern works: Both types of verse served to advertise the work through praise and strategic "name-dropping." Commendatory verses were usually contributed by friends or colleagues of the author who would write short poems of tribute for the work. Their commendations acted as seals of approval and as recommendations for future discriminating readers. Dedicatory verses were submitted by the author, who offered his or her work for the approval of an actual or prospective patron in the hopes of being suitably rewarded; in return, the writer provided the patron a degree of fame—a tribute to the patron's munificence that would always be connected to the work. Normally works were dedicated to one person, and though Spenser's epic is dedicated principally to Queen Elizabeth I, his poem is remarkable for its number of subsidiary dedications—16 of them to both influential political figures such as Lord Burghley and Sir Francis Walsingham, and to poets such as Edward de Vere and MARY SIDNEY HERBERT, countess of Pembroke, and one to all the ladies of the court. In his dedicatory verses, Spenser appeals to those who might be expected to favor a work like *The Faerie Queene,* but their relationship to Elizabeth was also an important factor; most of the addressees were those who could advance Spenser's cause with her. Though he needed the support of lesser patrons, he clearly hoped also to impress the queen and win some recompense for glorifying her in his poem, a factor that should always inform one's reading of the epic.

In his "Letter to Raleigh," Spenser identifies the primary goal of his work: "the generall end therefore of all the booke is to fashion a gentleman or noble person in virtuous and gentle discipline." To achieve this end, he notes his choice of King ARTHUR as his model for personal excellence: "I labour to pourtraict in Arthure, before he was king, the image of a brave knight, perfected in the twelve private morall vertues, as Aristotle hath devised, the which is the purpose of these first twelve bookes." Critics have often wondered what became of Spenser's original plan to write 12 books, and whether the final result was caused by his early death or by a change of heart. Moreover, from the beginning, Spenser seems to have neglected his original intention of basing each book on an Aristotelian virtue. In the end, each of *The Faerie Queen*'s six complete books focuses on a religious and/or chivalric virtue. Book 1 is the book of Holiness, Book 2 is the book of Temperance, Book 3 is the book of Chastity, Book 4 is the book of Friendship, Book 5 is the book of Justice, and Book 6 is the book of Courtesy.

The poem is classified as an epic; Spenser explicitly remarks that he is following in the footsteps of Homer with his *Odyssey* and *Illiad,* and of Virgil with his *Aeneid* (Letter to Raleigh). However, *The Faerie Queene* contains a number of artistic elements that make its genre classification problematic.

Spenser's incorporation of romantic elements drawn from medieval, biblical, and classical sources is one point of contention. Primarily evident in his use of motifs—quest patterns, fighting for the honor of a lady, the supernatural—but also in his inclusion of certain characters such as the dragon and especially Arthur, Spenser's blending of epic and ROMANCE has led a number of critics to describe *The Faerie Queene* as a romantic epic. Another anomaly is that the poem's principal artistic device is ALLEGORY, which is not typically considered an epic convention. This device corresponds most appropriately with the poem's didactic intention to "fashion" a noble gentleman. Like FABLES and parables, the characters, setting, and other types of symbols within allegories convey both literal and figurative meanings; however, allegory differs from fables and parables by including in its narrative conspicuous directions for interpretation (for example, Spenser's naming the serpent "Errour" in Book 1, canto 1, line 18 [1.1.18]). Because the narrative is written with a specific interpretation in mind, many critics view the allegory as one-dimensional. Spenser addresses this issue in his "Letter to Raleigh": "Sir knowing how doubtfully all Allegories may be construed, and this booke of mine, which I have entitled the Faery Queene, being a continued Allegory, or darke conceit, I have thought good aswell for avoyding of gealous opinions and misconstructions, as also for your better light in reading thereof." Given this comment, we may view Spenser's use of allegory not so much as a way to classify the poem but as a way to read the poem.

The Faerie Queene begins with "The Legende of the Knight of Red Crosse," or Redcrosse—so called from the red cross he bears on his shield. (He is eventually named as St. George in Book 1, Canto 2, lines 11–12). Redcrosse's quest, defined as a whole, is most immediately understood as an allegory of the making of a Protestant saint. Characteristic of Spenser's knights, Redcrosse is untested at the beginning of the book—an incomplete representation of his virtue. As an individual, Redcrosse is a Christian everyman; his journey to holiness is archetypal in that it explores the challenges every human being goes through on his or her path to spiritual wholeness. Central to his quest for holiness is his need to learn to distinguish falsity from truth—to see clearly. His worst foes are the sorcerer Archimago (Latin, "arch image-maker") and the duplicitous Duessa (Latin, "to be two"), who work toward his destruction through guile, duplicity, and false appearances—making evil seem good, foulness beautiful, and vice versa. Before Redcrosse can complete his quest, he must learn how to see through such deceptions.

Redcrosse's companion, Una (Latin, "oneness"), whose name implies singleness and unity, stands in opposition to the duality and deception of Redcrosse's archenemies. Their duplicity illustrates the disjunction between truth and outward appearance that marks the worldly existence of the errant Christian. Most of Redcrosse's problems stem from this. The book even begins in the Wandering Wood, where dwells Errour, a half-woman, half-snake monster. Redcrosse's triumph over Errour, his first battle, does not armor him against the more insidious confusions forced on him when Archimago

makes a dream that challenges Una's chastity. Deceived by false appearances and overcome by jealousy and disappointment, Redcrosse deserts Una. In consequence of this act and his inability to see the reality beneath the surface, evident by his continued dalliance with Duessa, Redcrosse lands in the House of Pride. Enervated by his time there, he is unable to fight off Orgoglio, who enslaves him (canto 8). After his rescue by Prince Arthur, reschooling in the House of Holiness, and restoration to Una, Redcrosse is ready to face Sin: the dragon who has kept Una's parents exiled from Eden and captive in a brazen tower.

As a Christian allegory, the myth of Eden dominates Book 1. Redcrosse's mission, given to him by Gloriana (the queen of fairie-land) herself, is to release Una's parents from their imprisonment. They are the king and queen of Eden, Adam and Eve, and to liberate them is to restore Eden. Moreover, the book's central dilemma is Redcrosse's inability to distinguish truth from falseness, a dilemma traceable to Eve's inability to recognize good or evil in Eden. Book 1 also reminds us that our postlapsarian existence brings spiritual blindness. On the level of historical allegory, the book is speaking to the religious division between Catholics and Protestants within Elizabethan society. According to Spenser's theology, near the beginning of Christianity, Redcrosse (who is sometimes read as the personification of England) and Una (who is often read as the personification of the Protestant church) were "one." But under the influence of Augustine and later medieval Catholicism, England betrayed its ancient religion and deviated into the arms of Una's double, Duessa, an image of Catholicism. The betrothal of Redcrosse to Una marks England's return to the true Christian church.

After Book 1, religion no longer dominates poetically. In Book 2, "the Booke of Temperance," the impetus is humanism: the study of humanity with an emphasis on education as the path to human perfection. The central concern of the book is to analyze moral life and human nature, and to reconcile one to the other. The book begins with the reappearance of Archimago, who has escaped his captors and has woven his web of deception over the young knight of temperance, Guyon (taken from the Arthurian legend, elsewhere known as Gawain). Guyon, hearing the plaintive tale of Redcrosse's alleged sexual assault on the "virgin" Duessa, hastily runs off to avenge her. In his rashness, he charges into the fray, leaving behind his traveling companion and mentor, the Palmer. Thus begins the tale of a knight who needs to be schooled in the chivalric virtue of temperance.

Unlike Redcrosse and Prince Arthur, Guyon is not a historical or legendary figure; however, he is not simply an abstract virtue, either. Guyon is a character whose temptations and adventures demonstrate the nature and practice of his virtue. Like Redcrosse and the other knights of the epic, Guyon is an incomplete representation of his virtue and thus needs to be tested and reschooled at some point in the book. Because he is untested and imperfect, he relies on his companions—specifically the Palmer who represents human reason—to guide him. Parted from the Palmer, Guyon lacks the intuitive recognition of good and evil that reason provides, and he is susceptible to error, misjudgments, and rash behavior. This is what happens to Guyon throughout the book. Aside from his personal failings, we are also presented with varying forms and degrees of extreme behavior from the minor characters in the book. The tableau of human passions range from passion and concupiscence (Mordant, Amavia, and Ruddymane) to rage (Pyrochles), sexual jealousy (Phedon), sloth (Phaedria), and greed (Mammon). These excesses culminate in the presentation of the Bower of Bliss (canto 12)—a place of false beauty that is the domain of the enchantress Acrasia (the archenemy of Guyon). In penetrating to the heart of the Bower of Bliss and destroying it, Guyon frees human nature and the senses from the excesses of lust and indolence.

Allegorically, Book 2 is the portrait of a young man learning to master the disorder of his nature—to balance his emotions. However, to possess the virtue of temperance, he needs to practice it until it becomes second nature. After a number of experiences, Guyon changes from an untried beginner to someone alert in self-discipline. With the Bower of Bliss, he reaches maturity both as a character and as a representation of his virtue.

Book 3 presents the virtue of chastity, which transitions nicely from the second book since in the CLASSI-CAL TRADITION, chastity was a branch of temperance. However, Book 3 differs from the other five books in two ways. First, it features a female knight, Britomart, whose name combines *Briton* with *martial* (appropriately, Merlin's prophecy links her progeny to Elizabeth I). Second, the book deviates from Spenser's narrative plan (as outlined in his Letter to Raleigh) to depict each quest as bestowed upon a knight by the Faerie Queen, the completion of which would demonstrate the ideal nature of the virtue. This is not the way the narrative unfolds in Book 3. When we are introduced to Britomart, she has not even seen the Faerie Queen. She is in search of Artegall (the hero of Book 5) and has accidentally met with Guyon, Arthur, and his squire Timias. She has also come across another knight, Redcrosse, whom she saves from battle with six other knights. In Canto 2, via her conversation with Redcrosse, we learn that she is seeking "revenge" against Artegall, who has done her "foule dishonour"—that is, he has smitten her heart. At the end of canto 3, Redcrosse departs, never to be heard from again in the poem.

When reading Book 3, one must always remember that Spenser is writing his work primarily for Queen Elizabeth. Frequently, the speaker interjects comments on how men have ignored the feats of women in martial affairs and how there have been many examples of great female warriors and counselors (canto 2); naturally, these comments would appeal to and please an independent, politically minded queen. However, such a consideration raises a number of issues since throughout the book, Britomart is mistaken for a man (which, according to the so-called sumptuary laws of Elizabethan society, would be considered an aberration). Moreover, throughout the book, love and marriage are revered and praised as forces that motivate men and women to be great and brave—yet Elizabeth never married. Typical to our experiences with the rest of the epic, we constantly find ourselves asking whether Spenser is criticizing the queen at the same moments in which he seems to praise her.

Another interesting feature of Book 3 is that it has two endings. In the end, Britomart must reclaim one of the four heroines of the book from the element of fire, and cantos 11–12 comprise the story of Britomart's single-handed rescue of Amoret from the house of Busirane. In the 1590 conclusion, Scudamour (betrothed to Amoret) is reunited with his bride. In the 1596 conclusion, this reunion is deferred because when Britomart and Amoret come out of the house, Scudamour is not there, having left for help because he feared a mishap had befallen Britomart inside the house. With the original ending, Spenser concludes the book triumphantly and resolutely; with the 1596 version, he projects further complications to the adventures of Scudamour and Amoret, complications that would continue in Book 4 (and to some extent in Book 5).

In the proem to Book 4, Spenser defends himself from the charges made against the 1590 edition that his depictions of love lead youths to folly. Consequently, Book 4, "the book of Friendship," is often read as a continuation of, or at least a response to, Book 3. An episode-by-episode comparison between them shows a running analogy between the legends for sexual and social love, which exhibit similar internal contiguities. Book 4 is not merely similar to Book 3, but connected with it as its continuation. Unlike the other books, however, Book 4 does not center on the adventures of one knight; the book is titled as "Contayning the Legend of Cambel and Telamond, or Friendship," but it features a plurality of heroic protagonists. Many critics define it as a tale told by storytelling in that Book 4 is not the story of one character but the stories of many characters. Its unifying quality lies in that every story revolves around the philosophical inquiry of love and friendship, marriage and loneliness. Book 4 also marks the beginning of the last half of Spenser's epic. Characteristic of this half, the book ends less resolutely than the first three (evident in the 1596 ending of Book 3): The adventures are often interrupted or finished inconclusively.

Book 5 represents this trend most especially. "The Legend of Justice" has been for many modern readers the least-liked book of Spenser's epic. Part of the repulsion is due to its historical allegory, which is a justification of England's imperialism over Ireland. The central knight of the book, Artegall, does not come from history, legend, or mythology; he is Spenser's creation and is traditionally thought to be the fictional representation of Lord Grey de Wilton (to whom Spenser

was secretary in Ireland). Lord Grey was a staunch believer in the inherent barbarity of the Irish, and he wished to pursue a religious war in Ireland to stamp out Catholicism, which he believed to be the source of Irish wickedness. He believed the only way to implement a Protestant order in Ireland was to convert the people "by the sword" (much like Artegall's philosophy for meting out justice at 5.3.20). The Irish, represented in the poem by giants, tyrants, and scattered dishonorable knights and villagers, stand as the greatest threat to justice. These allegorical, destructive forces in Book 5 can only be combated by a knight who is as dangerous as the "villains" themselves: Sir Artegall, the knight of justice. With Artegall is Talus, the inhuman "yron man" who represents the English army under Grey's command.

Drawing from the poetic theory of Sir Philip Sidney (that poetry presents a "golden" world), Spenser demonstrates in Book 5 his vision of what England's foreign policy "should have been." Evidently, Spenser agreed with Grey that the only way the Irish could be reformed was "by the sword," which is exactly the manner in which Artegall executes justice (consequently, what was not supported in Britain is supported in Faerie land). Talus is endowed with superior strength, and to complete his role as the unfeeling executioner, he is inhuman and unmoved by human emotion or reason. In the final episode of the book, Artegall meets his archenemy Grantorto (Italian, "great wrong"), who seems to be the representation of all the corruptive forces in 16th-century Ireland: the rebels, the Catholic Church, and even the savagery of the Irish. This representation is implied by the fact that Grantorto's crime is the unlawful imprisonment of Irena, which means "Ireland" (the feminine form of the Greek word *eirene*). In the rescue scene that ensues, the colonial dream is played out and the "white lie" of the colonists is given credence. Irena, the "damsel in distress" and the figuration of Ireland, is saved from impending doom by Artegall and Talus, or Lord Grey and the English imperial army. After Grantorto is killed, Artegall and Talus begin to reform the commonwealth, but they are called back to Faerie Court before they can complete the reformation. As they return, they meet with Envy, Detraction, and the

Blatant Beast, who abuse them verbally, and Envy's serpent stings Artegall. Talus offers to chastise them, but Artegall restrains him and rides on, ignoring their taunts and slanders. This scene mirrors what occurred in July 1582 when, after years of disapproval, Elizabeth I recalled Lord Grey from Ireland because of his excessively cruel methods of dealing with the Irish. Such a presentation of Artegall and Talus suggests that Spenser was censuring Elizabeth's treatment of her own officers.

Though the repetitive violence and agenda pushing Book 5 make it aesthetically dull, Spenser redeems himself with Book 6, the "Legende of Courtesie," which is often considered the most aesthetically successful book. The pastoral world it creates contrasts sharply with the harshness of the world in Book 5. In terms of the poem's narrative structure and philosophy, the world of courtesy is regarded as dependent on the world of justice: Only after justice has been implemented can peace and beauty flourish. Yet this is not say that the world of Book 6 is without conflict; it merely presents conflict in a different way. In "The Booke of Courtesie," Spenser links the chivalric mode, in which knights ride out to battle adversaries in a hostile world, with the pastoral mode, which idealizes the natural world as majestic and regenerative. Its pastoral character is evident not only in the book's narrative structure but also in the inclusion of figures from folk legend such as a noble savage, a baby caught in the jaws of a bear, a pack of cannibals, and a band of brigands, among others. Although the central episodes feature a number of characters, the book as a whole is concerned with Calidore's pursuit of the Blatant Beast (which first appeared at the end of Book 5), a ferocious doglike creature that slanders innocent people. Rumor and slander are, appropriately, the major threats to courtesy.

Characteristic of the second half of Spenser's epic, Book 6 ends irresolutely. Broadly, we may characterize the first half of the poem as reformist, forward-looking, and optimistic, and the second half as rueful, retrospective, and pessimistic. For example, in Book 1, Redcrosse recovers Eden, but in Book 6, it is unclear whether Calidore saves or destroys ARCADIA. Perhaps this change occurs because of the nature of the virtues being represented. The first half of the epic is concerned with private virtues related to the proper conduct of the individual: holiness, temperance, and chastity. The second half deals with social or public virtues related to the interaction of the individual with others in friendship, justice, and courtesy. Perhaps, in the end, private virtues are easier to perfect.

Composition of *The Faerie Queene* occupied Edmund Spenser for most of his life. Due to the author's sudden death in 1599, several issues are left to be resolved, and what would have been the rest of his masterpiece must largely be left up to the reader's imagination. Yet during his lifetime, Spenser's hard work was rewarded, as the poem found political favor with Elizabeth I, was consequently very successful, and earned him a pension of 50 pounds a year for life.

Because of the elaborate structure of *The Faerie Queene,* citations are sometimes difficult. In general, scholars cite the book, canto, and line, sometimes including the stanza within a canto (eg., 1.2.14–15 or 1.2.1.14–15). If these items are noted earlier in a sentence, the line numbers alone are sufficient.

See also CHIVALRY.

FURTHER READING

Alpers, Paul. *The Poetry of The Faerie Queene.* Princeton, N.J.: Princeton University Press, 1967.

Freeman, Rosemary. *The Faerie Queene: A Companion for Readers.* Berkeley: University of California Press, 1970.

Hamilton, A. C. *The Structure of Allegory in the Faerie Queene.* Oxford: Oxford University Press, 1961.

Heale, Elizabeth. *The Faerie Queene: A Reader's Guide.* Cambridge: Cambridge University Press, 1987.

Hough, Graham. *A Preface to the Faerie Queene.* New York: Norton, 1963.

Kane, Sean. *Spenser's Moral Allegory.* Toronto: University of Toronto Press, 1989.

Wells, Robin Headlam. *Spenser's "Faerie Queene" and the Cult of Elizabeth.* London and Canberra: Croon Helm; Totowa, New Jersey: Barnes & Noble, 1983.

Melissa Femino

The Faerie Queene: Book 1 EDMUND SPENSER (1590)

EDMUND SPENSER explained in a letter to SIR WALTER RALEIGH that the context of his EPIC tale, *The Faerie Queene,* was that the Faerie Queen was holding a 12-day feast, and that each of these days was marked by the beginning of a quest by a different hero. The first of these heroes was a "tall clownishe yonge man" who took the quest of a maiden named Una. The knight was known only by his shield, which bore a red cross. This knight, known as Redcrosse, symbolized holiness and was revealed later in the book as St. George, the patron saint of England.

Like the other books of *The Faerie Queene,* Book 1 is divided into 12 cantos and a proem (preface).

In Canto 1, Redcrosse appears, famously "pricking on the plaine" (l. 1) and accompanying a lady. The knight is holiness personified; the lady, Una (truth), is symbolic of the one true Protestant church. A storm causes them to seek shelter in a forest, but it turns out to be the Wandering Wood, where the monstrous Error dwells. Una attempts to warn Redcrosse, but he ventures into Error's den regardless and is attacked. He defends himself, strangles Error, and leaves her body for her offspring to feed on, after which they swell with blood and burst. Holiness overcomes Error, and her spawn self-destruct.

After escaping from Error's den, the adventurers meet a hermit, the magician Archimago (arch-image) in disguise, who offers them lodging in his hermitage. While they sleep, Archimago conjures a legion of sprites to assist his mischief. One he sends to Morpheus, the god of sleep, to fetch a false dream to Redcrosse claiming his lady is false. Of the second sprite, he fashions a false Una, who attempts to seduce Redcrosse.

In Canto 2, Redcrosse, who was able to resist the false Una in Canto 1, here loses faith and abandons the real Una when he sees her "sport" with another. He flees into the forest, and Una must wander on alone. Redcrosse encounters Sansfoy (faithlessness) a pagan knight accompanied by his lady. The knights joust, and Redcrosse emerges victorious: holiness quickly conquers faithlessness. Sansfoy leaves behind his lover, Duessa (duplicity), who symbolizes the falsity of the Catholic church. Duessa pleads for safety under a false name (Fidessa, "fidelity"), and Redcrosse agrees to accompany and protect her. She leads him into a shady bower, where Redcrosse learns from a wounded tree the story of his transformation by Duessa. Redcrosse listens but does not realize the tree is referring to his

new lady, and she distracts him before he can figure it out. The two embrace in the woods, as holiness succumbs to the lure of the false church.

Canto 3 returns to Una, now alone in the forest, vulnerable and afraid. A raging lion charges with intent on devouring her, but he senses her virtue, and by the time he reaches her, instead of eating her, he kisses her and licks her like a devoted dog, and then becomes devoted companion. They find a damsel, Abessa (absence, or lack of attendance to church details), and follow her home to lodge with her and her mother, Corceca (blind heart). The two women hide in fear of the lion, and when Kirkrapine (church robber) comes in the night to visit his paramour (the absence that Abessa represents allows Kirkrapine to steal, and he brings his plunder to her), the lion kills him.

When Una departs the next morning, Archimago catches up with her, disguised as Redcrosse. She is overjoyed, but it is short-lived as Sansloy (lawlessness), Sansfoy's brother, attacks and bests the magician with a single blow. Sansloy then removes his opponent's helmet. When he discovers Archimago instead of Redcrosse, Sansloy then claims Una. The lion tries to defend her, but Sansloy runs it through and takes her away. Human lawlessness confounds the strength of natural law.

In Canto 4, Duessa leads Redcrosse to the House of Pride, where he becomes acquainted with the SEVEN DEADLY SINS. He meets Lucifera, the mistress of the beautiful but illicit house, who symbolizes Pride, and six of her counselors, the other sins of Sloth, Gluttony, Lechery, Avarice, Envy, and Wrath, each with symbolic mounts and accessories. Duessa is welcomed into this unholy congregation, and with her, Redcrosse. Redcrosse is recognized, rightly this time, by another of Sansfoy's avenging brothers, Sansjoy (joylessness), who immediately challenges him to a duel.

Canto 5 opens with the duel between Sansjoy and Redcrosse, which is long and fierce, but ultimately Redcrosse prevails. Duessa entreats him not to kill Sansjoy, but Redcrosse, his pride and bloodlust heightened by his surroundings, attempts to deliver a deathblow. Duessa causes a mist to conceal Sansjoy, preventing Redcrosse from following through, and later she spirits the wounded knight away to the underworld to be healed. While she is gone on this errand, Redcrosse, warned by a dwarf of the immense dungeons in Pride's house, steals away before she returns.

In Canto 6, Sansloy attempts to defile Una, who shrieks in fear and disgust. Her cries are heard by a troop of fauns and satyrs, who frighten away Sansloy and take Una with them to their woodland village. They are enraptured by Una and begin worshipping her. She discourages this as idolatry, and they respond only by shifting their adoration to her donkey instead. Satyrane, a half-human and half-satyr knight arrives and, compelled by Una's virtue much like the lion was, swears to protect and defend her. He gets her out of the satyrs' village and helps her track Redcrosse. They find Archimago, now dressed as a pilgrim, who reports that Redcrosse has been killed by Sansloy. His directions lead them to Sansloy, whom Satyrane immediately challenges, and while they fight, Una flees, followed by Archimago.

In Canto 7, Redcrosse continues through the forest. Duessa tracks him down and chastises him for leaving her. They make up and make love, and in his weakened state, Redcrosse is attacked by Orgoglio the giant. Duessa intercedes before Redcrosse is killed and offers herself as paramour to the victor. Redcrosse is imprisoned in Orgoglio's dungeon, and Duessa is enthroned and given a magnificent mount, symbolizing the whore of Babylon seated on the seven-headed beast of the apocalypse. Redcrosse's dwarf escapes from the dungeon, finds Una, and reports what has happened. In the forest, Una meets Prince Arthur, who agrees to champion her against Orgoglio. This is the first appearance of ARTHUR, the young knight who will become the great King Arthur and who, in *The Faerie Queene*, will quest after the Faerie Queen herself.

In Canto 8, Arthur fights Orgoglio and quickly gets the upper hand by slicing off the giant's left arm. Duessa leaps to Orgoglio's aid, but Arthur then attacks Duessa's beast, and when Orgoglio returns to the fight, Arthur dismembers him, cutting him down one limb at a time, like pruning a tree. When he falls, Orgoglio's body puffs out a huge gust of air, as though his size was all due just to a lot of hot air. Arthur leaves Duessa in his squire's charge and is led by blind Ignaro (ignorance) into the castle to find Redcrosse. When Red-

crosse emerges, weakened by sin, Una receives him and begins his retraining by first allowing Duessa to live, but on condition that her true form be revealed. Duessa, stripped of her scarlet robe, is foul, misshapen, and disgusting, and Redcrosse finally sees through her false appearance.

In Canto 9, Arthur continues to accompany Una and Redcrosse, telling them of his history and his quest for the Faerie Queen, and he and Redcrosse swear oaths of friendship and support. They exchange gifts and part ways. Redcrosse and Una are soon distracted by a terror-stricken knight with a noose around his neck. This knight describes his recent encounter with Despair, whom Redcrosse resolves to challenge. Despair lives in a cave strewn with corpses, including the still-bleeding body of his latest victim, and he does his best to persuade Redcrosse that his sins are sufficient to warrant death; Redcrosse should die now rather than sin further, omitting mention of God's mercy. Una stops Redcrosse from stabbing himself and takes him away; he has sunk as low as possible now, and the strength of holiness must be built back up before he faces the dragon.

Canto 10 witnesses Una's rehabilitation of Redcrosse, which takes place at the House of Holiness, a parallel construction to Pride's house from Canto 4. The same type of characters are present: The porter, Humility, leads the travelers in through a straight and narrow path, as opposed to Idleness's broad path at the House of Pride. This house is owned by Dame Caelia (heavenly) and her three daughters, Fidelia, Speranza, and Charissa (faith, hope, and charity). Redcrosse is taught, confessed, and strengthened through a series of allegorical encounters culminating in a vision of the New Jerusalem. Contemplation reminds him that his quest is earthly, and he may not choose to abandon it to go to heaven before his time.

In Canto 11, Una leads her refreshed hero to his battle with the dragon besieging her parents' castle. Redcrosse attacks the dragon on the first day and wounds its wing. The dragon responds by roasting him in his armor until he falls into the Well of Life. The knight of holiness is strengthened, then, by the water of baptism, and he returns the next day to fight again. This time the dragon stings Redcrosse, and while the knight gets in some good blows, slashing at the dragons's head and chopping off its tail, he is knocked down under the Tree of Life, where, in a symbolic gesture of communion, Redcrosse is healed, strengthened again, and ready for a third battle. On the third day, the dragon tries to eat the knight, but Redcrosse runs his spear in to the dragon's mouth, causing its death.

Finally, in Canto 12, after the dragon is defeated, Una's parents and their subjects come out and rejoice. They return to the palace, where Redcrosse and Una are betrothed, the wedding set for a time after Redcrosse finishes his six-year tour of duty for the Faerie Queen. While they organize the details, Archimago, dressed as a messenger, arrives and claims that Redcrosse is already bound to Duessa. By Una's counsel, Archimago is revealed and imprisoned. The tale ends as Redcrosse returns to fulfill his duty to the Faerie Queen, while Una waits for his return.

Critics have drawn attention in Book 1 to Spenser's use of BIBLICAL ALLUSIONS, and often praise it as being The Faerie Queene's most satisfying book from a narrative perspective. Specifically, the book has been linked to the Book of Genesis, as critics have seen Redcrosse's story as a resolution of the Eden story, with Una's parents as Adam and Eve and the dragon as Satan. Feminist criticism has explored the presentation of female characters, generally concluding that they reinforce the stereotypical perspectives of women as lustful and duplicitous. Una is pure, of course, but Redcrosse has difficulty accepting that. Postcolonial critics have examined the traces of colonialism as well as the presentation of the monstrous and the grotesque.

See also ALLEGORY; CHIVALRY; FAERIE QUEENE, THE (OVERVIEW).

Alison Baker

The Faerie Queene: Book 2 EDMUND SPENSER (1590)

Book 2 of The Faerie Queene tells the story of Sir Guyon (wrestler), the knight of temperance. The double meaning of the title, "Contayning The Legend of Sir Gvyon, or Of Temperance," suggests that EDMUND SPENSER had fun playing with the titles of his books in this EPIC work. Does the book tell the tale of the "legend" of temperance, or does it tell about the "legend" of Guyon?

Book 2 tells the tale of a knight who ostensibly has dedicated himself to his assigned virtue, but who eventually falls victim to emotional release. The proem begs the reader unfamiliar with Faerie Land not to make fun of the poem's tales, pointing out that nobody had heard of Virginia and Peru a few years earlier. As the book begins, Archimago (arch image) has just escaped from his imprisonment and become intent upon causing problems for the Redcrosse Knight. Archimago meets Sir Guyon and his squire, the Palmer (pilgrim), and tells them about a virgin whom a knight attacked. Archimago offers to lead the two travelers to the knight with a red cross on his shield to seek revenge. Guyon, the Palmer, and Archimago meet a damsel (Duessa in disguise) and she tells them Redcrosse ravished her. The party then meets Redcrosse (holiness), but Guyon decides he cannot attack a knight with a cross on his shield, and the two become friends.

Sir Guyon and the Palmer continue on their journey and meet a damsel named Amavia (suffer), who plunges a knife in her chest as they approach her. They soon discover that she holds a newborn baby in her arms and that she lies by the body of her dead husband, Mordant. Amavia tells the story of how an evil enchantress named Acrasia had seduced her husband into her Bower of Bliss, where she offers men sexual enticements and ultimately turns them into beasts. Mordant had managed to free himself from the enchantment, but Acrasia (incontinence) then poisoned him.

Guyon tries to save Amavia, but she dies in his arms. Guyon takes the baby, Ruddymane, and tries to wash the blood off his body but cannot. Guyon (who now has lost his horse) and the Palmer continue on their journey and come across a castle inhabited by three beautiful sisters. The middle sister, Medina, accepts the travelers, and they soon find that two knights, Sir Huddibras (foolhardiness) and Sansloy (lawlessness), stand courting the youngest (Perissa) and the oldest (Elissa) sisters, respectively. The two knights begin to attack each other, but they turn and instead attack Guyon when he tries to stop them. Medina begs the knights to stop fighting, and they ultimately do so. Later, at the banquet, Guyon tells how the Faerie Queen charged him with finding and destroying Acrasia's Bower of Bliss. Guyon and the Palmer stay the night. In the morning, they depart, leaving the baby Ruddymane with Medina.

Canto 3 begins by relating how a peasant named Braggadocchio (braggart) has stolen Guyon's horse. Braggadocchio meets Trompart (trickster) and convinces him to become his servant. Archimago overhears the exchange and approaches the two peasants to convince them to attack Guyon and Redcrosse. Archimago promises to give Braggadocchio King ARTHUR's sword and flies off. This scares Trompart and Braggadocchio, and they leave. While traveling through the woods, Trompart and Braggadocchio meet a beautiful huntress named Belphoebe. After bragging about his accomplishments, Braggadocchio asks why Belphoebe does not dedicate herself to a life at court. Belphoebe denounces life at court and says that she prefers the life of a hunter. Braggadocchio makes advances on her, but the canto concludes as she runs away.

At the outset of Canto 4, Guyon and the Palmer encounter a madman named Furor and his mother, Occasion. Furor attacks a young man while his mother watches, but Guyon tries to stop the attack, Furor turns his attack on him. The Palmer tells Guyon that he must first stop Occasion. Guyon conquers both Furor and Occasion and binds both of them. After this encounter, a man named Atin (strife) arrives and tells Guyon he must leave the area; if his master, Pyrochles (fiery temper), arrives, Guyon will be attacked because he defeated Occasion.

Atin soon leaves, and Pyrochles arrives to attack Guyon. Guyon wins the battle but does not kill Pyrochles; instead, he agrees to free Furor and Occasion. As soon as he does this, Furor attacks Pyrochles and defeats him, dragging him through the "durt and mire" (2.5.23.4).

Atin thinks his master is dead and runs off to tell Pyrochles' brother, Cymochles (ware), who lives with his mistress, Acrasia, in the Bower of Bliss. Acrasia is an enchantress who "Does charme her louers, and the feeble sprightes, / can call out of the bodies of fraile wightes" (2.5.27.4–5). Spenser offers a cursory description of the Bower of Bliss upon Atin's arrival, describing Cymochles as unarmed and surrounded by beautiful women. Upon hearing of his brother's death, Cymochles becomes enraged, swears revenge, and sets out to take it.

After Cymochles sets out, he finds a lake where a beautiful woman named Phaedria (frivolous) waits in a boat. He persuades her to take him across the lake to a beautiful island. Phaedria begins speaking, and Cymochles falls asleep. Phaedria returns to the shore and agrees to take Guyon to the island but not the Palmer. When Guyon reaches the island, Cymochles, now awake, begins to fight him, but Phaedria stops them from battle. She returns Guyon to the shore, and Cymochles stays on the island. Atin appears on the shore and begins to berate Cymochles, but Cymochles does not try to fight him.

Atin sees an armored knight jump into the water and soon recognizes him as his master, Pyrochles. Atin calls upon Archimago to help him, and the magician appears to restore Pyrochles to health.

Now without his guide, the Palmer, Guyon continues his journey. Guyon travels through a wasteland and meets a dirty man called Mammon (riches), who leads Guyon to his underworld lair. Mammon lives in the House of Riches and tempts Guyon with wealth many times. In one area of Mammon's underworld domain, Guyon meets Philotime, Mammon's daughter. Mammon offers Philotime to Guyon in marriage, but Guyon claims to be betrothed. Mammon next leads Guyon to the Garden of Proserpina, where Guyon sees a tree with golden apples growing on it. The river Cocytus surrounds the tree. Mammon tries to tempt Guyon with the golden apple, but Guyon resists. Mammon then leads Guyon back up to the surface, where Guyon faints at the breath of fresh air.

Guyon's squire, the Palmer, finds him unconscious and guarded by an angel, who then returns Guyon to the Palmer. Pyrochles and Cymochles arrive with Archimago and begin to strip Guyon of his armor despite the Palmer's objections. Arthur arrives and kills Pyrochles and Cymochles. Guyon wakes and thanks Arthur, and the two become friends.

Arthur joins Guyon in his journey. Shortly thereafter, they see a besieged castle. Arthur and Guyon drive off the attackers, and the castle's mistress, Alma, opens the gates for them. They enter a room in which courtiers flatter ladies with Cupid in their midst. Alma leads the three to a tower to meet three new men, Phantastes (melancholic imagination), Judgement, and Eumnestes (good memory). Eumnestes dwells in a library. Arthur enters and finds a CHRONICLE of Britain's history. It lists all the kings, but when it reaches Uther Pendragon, the book ends abruptly. Guyon finds a chronicle history of the Faerie, and reads avidly because he is part Faerie. Once they finish reading, Alma invites them to dine.

The next morning, a band of men attack the castle once again, led by Maleger ("wretchedly thin"). Arthur eventually comes to the rescue and fights off the attackers. When Arthur turns to fight Maleger, Maleger rides off, but his two hags, Impotence and Impatience, hold down Arthur. Arthur's squire rescues him from the hags, and in the chaos of the fight, Arthur wounds Maleger. Maleger continues to attack Arthur, but eventually Arthur kills him and throws him into a lake.

After the fight with Maleger and his men, Guyon and the Palmer take a three-day ferry ride to the island domain of Acrasia. Guyon and the Palmer find dangerous obstacles along the way, including fog, the Gulf of Greediness, and sea monsters. The Palmer leads them through these obstacles successfully. Once they reach the island, the Palmer must fight off several wild beasts with his magic staff. They eventually find Acrasia's lair, the Bower of Bliss.

The ivory gate of the Bower tells the story of Jason and Medea as Genius stands guard. Guyon insults Genius and breaks his staff. Guyon and the Palmer travel through a meadow and meet a dame named Excess. Guyon refuses to drink the wine she makes and crushes her cup. The two continue on their way and find a fountain in a lake where two naked women play. Guyon becomes interested in watching them, but the Palmer reminds him of his mission. Upon reaching Acrasia's lair, they hear people singing and find Acrasia lounging with her barely dressed lover, Verdant (lush). Guyon and the Palmer catch the two in a net and bind Acrasia in chains before Guyon destroys the Bower. When the Palmer and Guyon return to their ferry, the beasts they met upon their arrival menace them once again. They learn that Acrasia had turned these men into beasts, so Guyon orders the Palmer to turn them back to men, and the book ends.

Two main critical debates surround Book 2 of *The Faerie Queene*: whether Guyon remains temperate or chaste, and whether the book as a whole supports the order of nature or supports the order of grace. Guyon appears to resist temptation numerous times throughout Book 2, but when he reaches the ultimate realm of temptation, he fails to control himself: He looks longingly on the nymphs bathing in the fountain as he approaches Acrasia's lair, and he clearly fails to hold himself together when he decides to utterly destroy the Bower itself. This may lead the reader to believe that Guyon's assigned virtue is not possible in a pragmatic sense, and that only wanton violence and lack of temperance defeats lascivious practices. It seems as if Guyon merely keeps himself in line with his assigned virtue until he reaches the realm where he discovers what he truly misses, and he cannot further deny himself emotional release.

The scholar Stephen Greenblatt devotes a chapter of his highly influential *Renaissance Self-Fashioning* to Book 2 of *The Faerie Queene*. In this chapter, Greenblatt argues that in Spenser's world, temperance must be, paradoxically, produced by wanton excess and that the knights in *The Faerie Queene* seek release vehemently while fearing it at the same time. Greenblatt titles his chapter after the phrase in the "Letter to Raleigh" that reads, "to fashion a gentleman." Guyon, more than any other knight in *The Faerie Queene*, represents a knight who has attempted to "self-fashion" himself in his continual denial of pleasure.

In this denial of pleasure, Guyon initially appears to privilege grace over nature; human nature, after all, wishes to seek pleasure, and only through grace can humanity become Christ-like, overcoming temptation and sin. When Guyon destroys the Bower, however, he favors nature, as he violently attacks that which represents everything that stands against his assigned virtue. This constitutes the paradoxical nature of Book 2's conclusion: Guyon must behave in a way that counteracts his assigned virtue to destroy the possibility of others living in opposition to his assigned virtue.

Other critics contend that Guyon remains a man and is reliant on God's grace to get through his journey. Indeed, God's grace is what allows Guyon to even reach the Bower of Bliss, completing numerous trials and surviving several near-death experiences along his journey to the witch Acrasia's lair. Faced with the human excesses of the Bower, Guyon shows his true colors, and he cannot escape his destiny as a flesh-and-blood man with the complex emotional makeup that allows for his ultimate destructive act at the close of Book 2.

Other scholarship has focused on philological concerns of the book's thematic units, with special attention paid to individual episodes, particularly the relationship between temperance and the allegorical vision of Spenser's work. Critics have also established the relationship between Spenser and his Italian sources, with emphasis on the connection between "temperance" and epic ROMANCE. New directions further include the establishment of an early modern sensibility of temperance, contextualizing *The Faerie Queene* within the tradition of early printed materials on the subject and early modern commentary on Biblical notions of temperance.

See also ALLEGORY; CHIVALRY; *FAERIE QUEENE, THE* (OVERVIEW).

FURTHER READING

Berger, Harry, Jr. *The Allegorical Temper: Vision and Reality in Book II of The Faerie Queene.* New Haven, Conn.: Yale University Press, 1957.

Gohlke, Madelon S. "Embattled Allegory: Book II of *The Faerie Queene*." ELR 8 (1978): 123–140.

Dan Mills

***The Faerie Queene*: Book 3** EDMUND SPENSER **(1590)** The third book of EDMUND SPENSER's *The FAERIE QUEENE* tells the tale of Britomart, a princess who links Britain's mythical origins in Troy to Queen ELIZABETH I. Britomart is the embodiment of chastity—not in the sense of virginity, but in the sense of chaste love sanctified by marriage, wherein it can be productive. Britomart's character and quests bridge the archetypes of virgin and matron in a way that invites a parallel to the biblical Mary, but Spenser achieves this by means of non-Christian associations, and Britomart's quests revolve around earthly love. It is significant, too, that Britomart is absent from much of Book 3, leaving readers to learn from the examples of chaste and unchaste lovers who populate the tale, rather than solely from her example.

The tale begins in media res in Canto 1, with the hero from Book 2, Guyon, the knight of temperance, traveling with Arthur and his squire Timias. They encounter a knight who unhorses Guyon—Britomart. Guyon's pride is badly hurt—not so badly as it would have been had he known Britomart was a woman, of course—but he is reconciled to his conqueror, and the three knights travel together for a time.

As they wander through the forest, a beautiful woman rides by, apparently fleeing a would-be rapist. Arthur and Guyon chase the lady Florimell; Timias chases the ruffian who threatens her; Britomart, "whose constant mind / Would not so lightly follow beauties chace" (st. 19, ll. 1–2) stays behind and finds another adventure. She reaches a castle and sees a knight being attacked by six others. She defends the lone knight, swiftly defeating three of the attackers. The lone knight, revealed to be Redcrosse from Book 1, then defeats a fourth knight, and the remaining two yield and escort them to the lady of Castle Joyous, Malecasta (unchaste). Her custom is to sleep with every knight who seeks lodging with her. Since Redcrosse has a betrothed, he resists and is attacked by Malecasta's minions. Soon, however, Malecasta's attention shifts to Britomart, and she sneaks into Britomart's bed to seduce her, assuming the knight is a man. Britomart leaps out of bed. Malecasta realizes her error and faints, and the six knights appear to defend their lady. In the fracas, Britomart is wounded, grazed by an arrow from Gardante (looking), the first of the six brothers whose names indicate the six stages of lechery. Redcrosse rushes to her defense, and the two flee the castle together. In this first canto, then, chastity conquers temperance and, strengthened by holiness, escapes lechery.

Canto 2 sees Britomart and Redcrosse travel together. She reveals her history and her quest: Artegall (Arthur's equal). Britomart gently insults Artegall in order to hear him defended and praised by Redcrosse, and she indulges in sweet memories of how she fell in love with him—at first sight, in a magic mirror made by Merlin himself. Britomart had been hit by Cupid's arrow "so slyly that she did not feel the wound" (st. 26, l. 8), and her nurse set about curing her of her LOVESICKNESS by any means possible—potions, spells, and charms. She failed.

Canto 3 continues the story. In a last-ditch effort to cure Britomart, her nurse Glauce led her to Merlin, whose mirror produced the image of Artegall. Though Merlin was revealed to be a bad lover, he gave sound advice: Britomart should give in to her love, for she was destined to marry Artegall and produce a line of rulers of unparalleled glory. So Britomart struck out on her quest. Her story told, Britomart and Redcrosse separate amicably.

In Canto 4, Britomart laments her state of disquiet, pointing out the connections between Love and FOR- TUNE—bold and blind, and fickle masters, both. While she muses, Marinell, a knight who scorns good love because of his mother's fear, approaches, and they battle. Britomart hurts him, and his mother fetches his wounded body, taking him away to heal. Meanwhile, his beloved, Florimell, is still being chased by the grisly forester, and by Arthur and Timias. Echoing Britomart's opening COMPLAINT in this canto, Arthur laments his own unconsummated love, and he spends the night alone in the forest thinking of his love.

Canto 5 opens the next morning, and Arthur learns from Florimell's dwarf that Florimell is running in search of her beloved Marinell, whom she believes dead, so the two travel together to find her. Timias, Arthur's squire, had followed the forester, not Florimell, and he finds himself ambushed by the forester and his two brothers. He defeats them all but is wounded in the thigh and faints from fatigue and blood loss. Belphoebe, a virginal huntress, finds and heals Timias, and he falls wildly (but chastely!) in love with her. Then he laments the fortune that leads him to fall in love with someone so high above him that he cannot insult her with his suit.

Canto 6 reveals Belphoebe's background. A noble faerie maid, Chrysogonee, was impregnated by dancing sunbeams as she slept in a glade; she bore the twins, Belphoebe and her sister, Amoretta, also while asleep. The babies were found by two nymphs of the goddess Diana. Diana kept one, Belphoebe, and Venus took the other, Amoretta, to live with her in the garden of Adonis. Therefore Belphoebe was reared as a huntress with the nymphs of Diana, and Amoretta as a mother for the infant souls who inhabit the garden of Adonis. The myths are used to show two archetypal roles of women—the virgin and the mother—which Britomart will reconcile.

In Canto 7, Florimell's adventures continue. She flees until her horse collapses, upon which she seeks refuge at a witch's cottage in a glen, where the witch's son is consumed by lust for her. Florimell holds him off and then sneaks away. Failing to cure her son's lovesickness, the witch sends a beast to devour Florimell, who narrowly escapes. The beast eats her horse, and when the remains are found, Florimell is assumed to be dead. Meanwhile, Arganta the giantess—symbolizing unchecked female lust—tries to kidnap the Squire of Dames, but she is chased by Palladine, a knight.

Canto 8 opens back at the witch's house, where the son still pines for Florimell. His mother, unable to cure him, creates a false Florimell from snow and wax instead. Her son is appeased and lives happily with her for some time, until Braggadocchio (braggart), accompanied by his squire Trompart (trickster), steals her, but then subsequently loses her to another knight. The real Florimell continues her perilous journey on the water. She is accosted by a sailor but rescued by Proteus, the sea god, who then courts her himself. The canto ends with her resisting Proteus, while Satyrane and the newly liberated Squire of Dames meet Paridell, another knight chasing Florimell.

In Canto 9, Satyrane, Paridell, and the Squire of Dames arrive at the castle of Malbecco (evil goat; cuckold), but they are not granted entrance. Britomart arrives soon after and battles Paridell, until Satyrane intercedes and reconciles them. Together they plot to burn Malbecco's castle, but Malbecco relents, grudgingly, and admits them. Paridell flirts with Hellenore, the lady of the castle, over dinner, and he and Britomart tell the stories of their Trojan lineage.

In Canto 10, Paridell woos Hellenore and entices her to run away with him. She agrees, steals some of Malbecco's money, and throws the rest into the fire. As they flee, Hellenore cries out melodramatically for help, and Malbecco is paralyzed by the decision to save his wife or his money. Finally he follows the lovers, but instead he stumbles across Braggadocchio and Trompart, and he asks them to chase Hellenore. When they find Paridell, he is alone, having abandoned Hellenore in the forest. Braggadocchio dodges the fight; Trompart tricks Malbecco into burying his remaining money for safekeeping but steals it himself later. Malbecco continues his search for Hellenore. When he finds her, she has taken up residence with the satyrs, and he watches her wantonness with them with seething envy. When night falls, he entreats her to return with him, and she refuses. Malbecco runs wildly into the night, so consumed by his passion that his body wastes away; he is reduced to the incorporeal spirit of jealousy.

As Canto 11 opens, Britomart and Satyrane leave Malbecco's castle together. They encounter Ollyphant, the incestuous brother of the giantess Argante, chasing a youth. The two knights give chase and are separated in the woods. Britomart encounters a moaning knight, Sir Scudamour (love's shield), who is distraught because he cannot rescue his beloved Amoretta from the wizard Busirane. Britomart vows to aid him, and they approach the castle together. Britomart charges through the flaming porch and, evidently because of her pure intent, comes through unscathed, but Scudamour is repulsed. Inside the stronghold, Britomart perceives the tapestries and statuary all depicting Cupid's conquests.

In Canto 12, Britomart waits in a chamber, and Cupid's mask passes before her. He is accompanied by his servants—Fancy, Desire, Hope, Doubt, and others—and followed by Amoretta, who paces behind, carrying her beating heart on a silver salver. Britomart watches in anguish and waits until the next nightfall, then follows the procession into the chamber where Busirane sits, mumbling spells and writing charms with Amoretta's blood. Britomart flies at him, felling him with one blow and raising her arm to strike again, when Amoretta entreats her to wait until he reverses his spells. Britomart and Amoretta return to find Scudamour, and the lovers embrace so completely that they seem to merge into a single body. Britomart looks on, reminded of her own love and wishing for a similar meeting with Artegall.

The Faerie Queene consists of a series of books devoted to defining courtly virtues. Readers encounter various knights who embody a single virtue and who can be read allegorically as working out the problems and rewards of their virtue. This book explores the ways humans love. Britomart is a female hero, so Spenser has been both praised and castigated for inti-

mating that chastity is the highest or essential feminine virtue. The book contains many examples of good and bad love—so many in fact, that Britomart is absent from over half of the narrative, and her lover, Artegall, never appears at all. What populates the book in addition to Britomart is a fairly exhaustive list of male and female lovers and archetypes. Britomart, Florimell, and Amoretta are chaste; Malecasta is not. Arthur is tempted by Florimell but ultimately is faithful to his beloved. Timias is chaste and self-sacrificing; the Squire of Dames and Paridell are rakish and promiscuous. Argante and Ollyphant are monstrous and deviant, Merlin is foolish in love, and Busirane and Malbecco are selfish and controlling.

Spenser also explores the continuum of female chastity, as discussed by a number of feminist critics. He ultimately upholds chaste monogamy and productive, conjugal love as positive, without leaving room for female desire outside these avenues.

See also ALLEGORY; CHIVALRY; *FAERIE QUEENE, THE* (OVERVIEW).

FURTHER READING
Cavanagh, Sheila. *Wanton Eyes and Chaste Desires: Female Sexuality in The Faerie Queene.* Bloomington: Indiana University Press, 1994.

Gregerson, Linda. "Protestant Erotics: Idolatry and Interpretation in Spenser's *Faerie Queene. ELH* 58 (1991): 1–34.

Morgan, Gerald. "The Meaning of Spenser's Chastity as the Fairest of Virtues." In *Noble and Joyous Histories: English Romances, 1375–1650,* edited by Eilén Ní Cuilleanáin and J. D. Pheifer, 245–263. Dublin: Irish Academic Press, 1993.

Alison Baker

FALL OF PRINCES, THE JOHN LYDGATE (ca. 1430)
At over 36,000 lines long, *The Fall of Princes* is JOHN LYDGATE's longest work. Lydgate was commissioned to translate this text in the early 1430s by Humphrey, duke of Gloucester. Completed by 1438 or 1439, Lydgate's English text is an adaptation of the French *Des Cas des nobles hommes et femmes* (About the falls of great men and women, 1409) by Laurent de Premierfait, which was in turn a translation of Giovanni Boccaccio's Latin text, *De casibus virorum illustrium* (Concerning the fall of famous men, 1355–60). Lydgate's *The Fall of*

Princes was a very popular work and survives in a number of manuscripts.

The Fall is a collection of narratives about famous, powerful, and noble men and women who fall from positions of greatness to positions of despair, poverty, and even death. Their falls are brought about either through their own vices or sins, or by FORTUNE, whose capricious nature no person can control. Lydgate's biographical encyclopedia includes almost 500 biblical, mythological, and historical figures, beginning with the Fall of Adam and Eve and ending with the 14th-century King John II of France. *The Fall* is divided into nine loosely organized books; each book begins with a prologue, and after many of the narratives, Lydgate offers a moralizing ENVOI addressed to princes who are exhorted to remember the uncertainty of earthly happiness, the ever-changing nature of Fortune, and the necessity of avoiding sins and vices.

This text is a collection of "tragedies," which Lydgate defines as a story that "Gynneth with joie, endith with adversite" ("Begins with joy, ends with adversity," l. 3118). Stories of the downfalls of powerful people were quite popular in the Middle Ages. For instance, GEOFFREY CHAUCER included his own collection of tragedies in *The Monk's Tale*. *The Fall* also serves as a "mirror for princes," or a text that offers examples for leaders to avoid or to follow. Lydgate's envois remind the leader of the moral that he or she was supposed to learn from each narrative, and they offer guidelines for how to govern justly and effectively. The poem itself is iambic pentameter or decasyllabic (10-beat) lines. The STANZAS are in RHYME ROYAL form.

A number of scholars have examined how Lydgate adapted and revised his source material in order to emphasize different aspects of the narratives, as well as how much attention he allots to the role of sin versus that of Fortune in the poem. Many have commented on how Lydgate's envois develop the MIRROR FOR PRINCES aspect of the stories. Scholars have also examined Lydgate's treatment of less obvious sources, including Chaucer, OVID, and PETRARCH.

Recent scholarship has also examined the relationship between Lydgate and his Lancastrian patron Humphrey, duke of Gloucester, focusing on how Lydgate's narratives imagine church and state relationships, in the context of his monastic vocation. This latter idea was particularly important to early modern imitators.

See also MIRROR FOR MAGISTRATES, A.

FURTHER READING

Mortimer, Nigel. *John Lydgate's Fall of Princes: Narrative Tragedy in its Literary and Political Contexts*. Oxford: Clarendon Press, 2005.

Christine F. Cooper

"FAREWELL FALSE LOVE" SIR WALTER RALEIGH (ca. 1582–1585)

This highly stylized poem is a negative definition of love, emphasizing its irrationality. The poem is, essentially, a catalogue of images exemplifying love's harmful and irrational nature, including a temple of treason; a poisonous, flower-covered serpent (l. 7); a "gilded hooke that holds a poysoned bate" (l. 12); and a maze (l. 15). Many of the lines begin with "A . . . ," and the repetition increases the feeling of inescapability. The beginning and ending are somewhat circular, though the final goodbye in line 29 links false love with desire and beauty, whereas the initial rejection cites only love. Overall, the catalogue seems to be an exercise in stylistic virtuosity rather than the expression of any real emotion.

Six contemporary manuscripts indicate that SIR WALTER RALEIGH circulated the poem widely. William Byrd set it to music in his *Psalms, Sonets, and Songs* (1588), and Sir Thomas Heneage composed a poetic counterpart, "Most Welcome Love," praising love and turning Raleigh's language and images to positive ones. Recent critics have attempted to determine which poem was composed first, but no authoritative answer has been established. Raleigh's poem also resembles two 16th-century continental poems, the French "Contr' amour" (first printed in 1573), and the Italian "La've l'aurora" (first published in 1553). Although there is no evidence of Raleigh's familiarity with either of these poems, five of his images are common to the two earlier poems.

FURTHER READING

Gibson, Jonathan. "French and Italian Sources for Raleigh's 'Farewell False Love.'" *RES* (1999): 155–165.

Leah Larson

"FAREWELL LOVE, AND ALL THY LAWS FOR EVER!" Sir Thomas Wyatt (ca. 1535)

Although this SONNET by Sir THOMAS WYATT exists in two differing manuscript forms, it was first published posthumously in 1557 as a part of *TOTTEL'S MISCELLANY* under the simple heading "A renouncing of love." This simplicity belies complexity, as one of Love's "laws" is precisely its renouncement. "Love" here is also tripartite: Love as an abstract emotion, Love as referring to the poet's lady, and Love as Eros or Cupid. This three-way division is reinforced by the pun running throughout the first three lines. The "laws" of line 1 signify the rules of love as codified by classical authors such as OVID and medieval writers such as ANDREAS CAPELLANUS. The "baited hooks" of the second line constitute a lure, physical bait personified by the lady, whilst the apocryphal "lore" of line 3 represents the classical PERSONIFICATION. Furthermore, both "Senec and Plato" (l. 3) also represent Love simply by being philosophers (*philosophy* literally meaning "love of knowledge").

The second QUATRAIN's opening on the stock image of "blind" Love maintains the classical representation of the first quatrain and implies the present clarity of hindsight, which continues until the poem's end. However, the experience of Love's "sharp repulse" and its petty "trifles" cannot be regretted as they are essential to maturity; they "Hath taught me" (l. 7) and in doing so provide the experiential evidence of that which the speaker reads about in "Senec and Plato." One of the central tenets of early modern or Renaissance thought is that the active life (*vita activa*) must be pursued in correlation with book learning (*vita contemplativa*).

Following the VOLTA, the concluding SESTET, in accordance with the "laws" of the sonnet, effectively restarts the poem, but it does so with the knowledge provided by the OCTAVE: "Therefore farewell!" Here the spurning of Cupid's "brittle darts" is bound up with a sense of regret that "Love" has wasted the poet's "time," representing meter, and therefore the sonnet itself. It should be "younger hearts" who compose love poetry, "authority" in this sense referring both to power and author-status, it is inappropriate that the mature speaker should do so, as "property" likewise incorporates both ownership and a sense of what is (im)proper.

The final line ensures its victory by reducing the opening line's "Love" to lust—"Me lusteth no longer"—and by reducing the formerly beloved to an unchaste body rather than a person, constituted by "rotten boughs." The act of climbing these "rotten boughs" produces the biblical fall into lust as the branches inevitably break.

The sonnet displays a dexterous use of a reduced vocabulary rich in ambiguity. Words such as *Love* and *authority* divide and subdivide into meanings dependent on the reader's willingness to read further as part of a process that would peak in the ENGLISH SONNETs of SIR PHILIP SIDNEY and WILLIAM SHAKESPEARE. For example, the duality of mind (represented by "Senec and Plato") and body (represented by such physical phrases as "sharp repulse, that pricketh aye so sore" [l. 6], "brittle darts," and "rotten boughs") recall the insistence on an early modern outlook. "Love" at the court of HENRY VIII is revealed to be a fusion of expectation, experience, and reflection. The "laws" and the "lore" are read, the "sharp repulse" is felt, and the "time" is "lost" a second time through relating the matter in verse.

FURTHER READING

Daalder, Joost, ed. *Sir Thomas Wyatt: Collected Poems*. Oxford: Oxford University Press, 1975.

William T. Rossiter

FEUDAL OATHS

In the Middle Ages, when the basic political organization was founded on a contract between a lord and his retainers, men took oaths of fealty to their lords in return for protection and support. The retainer (vassal) was bound to defend his lord in military campaigns, and the lord was bound to protect the interests of his men. For example:

> Robert count of Flanders pledges to king Henry by faith and oath . . . that he will help him to hold and defend the kingdom of England against all men who can live and die . . . The king promises to protect count Robert in life and limb, . . . and to assure him against the loss of his land . . . as long as the count shall hold to these agreements. And in return for these agreements and this service king Henry will give as a fief to count Robert 500 pounds of English money every year. . . . (Strayer, pp. 144–145)

This agreement, dated 1103 between King Henry I of England and Count Robert of Flanders, clearly sets out the obligations of both parties. As CHIVALRY grew more important, feudal oaths became part of chivalric ideals. When vassals swore fealty to their lords, they also, by extension, swore loyalty to God. The lord or king was a stand-in for God, so a vassal became morally bound to remain loyal to one's earthly lord. This system of loyalties could get quite elaborate, as chivalry required one also to defend and honor women as well, which caused Gawain's dilemma in SIR GAWAIN AND THE GREEN KNIGHT. Gawain is above all interested in being a good Christian—that is, loyal to God. But he is also ARTHUR's knight, housed on his quest by Lord Bertilak and tempted by Lady Bertilak. When he is propositioned by the Lady, then, his oath to God to be chaste, his oath to Bertilak as his new host, and his oath to serve and obey ladies conflict with one another, and Gawain must negotiate his loyalties without breaking any oaths.

FURTHER READING

Strayer, Joseph R. *Feudalism*. Princeton, N.J.: Van Nostrand, 1965.

Alison Baker

FLORIS AND BLAUNCHEFLUR (FLORIS AND BLANCHEFLOUR) ANONYMOUS (ca. 1250–1300)

Floris and Blauncheflur, an anonymous Middle English ROMANCE written in the southeast Midlands dialect, exists in four manuscripts, all missing the first several leaves of the text. It is set in Spain, where Floris, the son of the Muslim king Fenix, and Blauncheflur, the daughter of a Christian servant, grow up together and are inseparable. Afraid that Floris will marry Blauncheflur when he comes of age, the king desires to kill the girl, but the queen convinces him to send Floris away and to sell the girl to a merchant, who then sells Blauncheflur to the emir of Babylon. Floris returns, and the king tells him that Blauncheflur has died. Distraught, Floris attempts suicide, so his parents tell him the truth. They help him disguise himself as a merchant, and then, armed with a magical ring, he sets out to rescue Blauncheflur.

Floris soon arrives in the emir's city and learns of the local custom: Each year the emir chooses a new queen from among the maidens he keeps in a tower. This year's choice is Blauncheflur. Floris gains entry into the tower by hiding in a basket of flowers, and the lovers are reunited. Soon after, the emir catches them and brings them to judgment before his council. Moved by the children's mutual love, the emir's men convince him to pardon them in exchange for their story. Floris then recounts their history, at which point the emir dubs Floris a knight and releases the lovers, who then marry in a church. The emir marries Claris, and the tale ends with Floris learning of his father's death and returning with Blauncheflur to claim his kingdom of Spain.

Along with *KING HORN* and *Havelok the Dane, Floris and Blauncheflur* is among the earliest of the MIDDLE ENGLISH romances. Its source, the Old French aristocratic romance *Floire et Blancheflor,* was composed about a century prior. The Middle English version deviates widely. The shortened tale, about one-third the length of its analogue, is dynamic, with an emphasis on action, adventure, and dialogue. The result is a straightforward poetic narrative with a tightly constructed plot.

Floris and Blauncheflur was a very popular medieval narrative that was recounted in several VERNACULAR (non-Latin) languages in addition to Middle English. The Middle English version is written in short COUPLETS and features several popular romance motifs, including the donning of disguises, the possession of magical objects, the emphasis on love, and a happy ending. While no eastern analogue has been found, the romance's Arabic themes and images, including the emir's harem and his enchanted garden, indicate a definite eastern influence, and scholars have noted similarities in plot between *Floris and Blauncheflur* and some of the tales found in the anonymous *Arabian Nights.*

Several plot points make *Floris and Blauncheflur* an interesting example of its genre. For instance, it neglects the conventional subject of knightly behavior in favor of the idyllic love of its protagonists, which, with their overcoming parental and governmental authority, culminates in a dominant theme of *amor omnia vincit* (love conquers all). That the lovers are children and not adolescents (as in the Old French versions) underscores the purity of the characters' emotions. It has been observed that their similarity in names (*Floris* meaning "of the flower" and *Blauncheflur* meaning "white flower"), ages, and looks emphasizes their being two parts of one whole. The romance is also notable for its sympathetic portrait of the SARACENS, itself unusual in medieval Western tradition. The entire action takes place in non-Christian countries (Spain, Babylon), and most of the central characters—Floris, his parents, the emir, and the helpful figures Floris encounters on his quest—are all Muslims who are likable, dynamic characters. This positive representation lends to the narrative's social, religious, and political dimensions, whereby the personal union of the lovers represents a healing of the west/east, Christian/Muslim dichotomy.

Postcolonial and feminist theories have informed more recent readings of the romance that examine its darker elements. While secondary to the overarching love motif, the topics of incest and slavery nonetheless run through the romance. Women like Blauncheflur, the child of a Christian slave in a Muslim world, are commodities to be bartered and sold, and the similarities between the children, coupled with the questionable identity of Blaucheflur's father, point to a possible incestuous relationship. Finally, scholars have begun to explore the linguistic, thematic, and narrative junctures in the romance, where east-meets-west topics reflect historical medieval events.

See also CHIVALRY.

FURTHER READING

de Vries, Franciscus Catharina, ed. *Floris and Blauncheflur. A Middle English Romance.* Groningen, Netherlands: Drukkerij V.R.B., 1966.

Heffernan, Carol. *The Orient in Chaucer and Medieval Romance.* Cambridge: D.S. Brewer, 2003.

Kelly, Kathleen Coyle. "The Bartering of Blauncheflur in the Middle English *Floris and Blauncheflur.*" *Modern Philology* 91, no. 2 (1994): 101–110.

Metlitzki, Dorothee. *The Matter of Araby in Medieval England.* New Haven, Conn.: Yale University Press, 1977.

Kimberly K. Bell

FLYTING

Flyting is a literary contest of abuse in which the participants strive to out-insult each other in verse. Flyting as a genre originated in 16th-century Scotland, where *to flyte* meant to scold or argue with an opponent, often publicly in a scurrilous manner, and noisy flyters were punishable by law. Originally, however, these contests may have begun at the behest of the monarch. The most famous surviving example is "The Flyting of Dunbar and Kennedy," composed sometime between 1490 and 1505, which stages a quarrel between WILLIAM DUNBAR and Walter Kennedy, a poet from the highlands. It is a triumph of satirical wit and poetic virtuosity, and the audience is asked to decide who gets the worst of the encounter.

The usual practice in a flyting seems to have been for two opponents to attack each other in successive rounds of combative verse, sometimes with other poets in the background as seconds or deputies. The number of rounds varies in the surviving examples, but in each case flytings tended to progress from the naming of one's opponent and the formal statement of challenges to a more developed battery of invective in the main body of the attack. The abuse could become personal in the extreme: A poet's appearance, morals, family history, and social background were frequent targets alongside the disparagement of his poetic skills, providing a natural outlet for obscenity and earthy humor. Critical debate has arisen over the degree of real versus imaginary animosity in flytings and how far they were intended for public performance.

The flytyng technique could also be adapted to other poetic forms. Some critics, for instance, see JOHN SKELTON's "Mannerly Margery" as an amorous flyting, and "GET UP AND BAR THE DOOR" has been viewed as a commoner's flyting.

FURTHER READING

Bawcutt, Patricia. "The Art of Flyting." *Scottish Literary Journal* 10, no. 2 (1983): 5–24.

Gray, Douglas. "Rough Music: Some Early Invectives and Flytings." In *English Satire and the Satiric Tradition,* edited by Claude Rawson, 21–43. Oxford: Blackwell, 1984.

Elizabeth Evershed

FORTUNE

Based on the Roman goddess Fortuna, Fortune appears in BOETHIUS's *The CONSOLATION OF PHILOSOPHY* as a device used to illustrate the untrustworthiness of temporal happiness. In the medieval tradition,

Fortune is more malevolent. "Dame" Fortune is typically presented as bearing a wheel that is in constant motion. Humans "travel" along the wheel, and as they do so, their "fortune"—status in life—rises and falls, and they may eventually be crushed underneath the ever-spinning wheel. There is no way an individual can tell how fast the wheel is turning; therefore, life is always uncertain—a person may be king or queen one day, and a peasant the next. GEOFFREY CHAUCER's "The Monk's Tale" and JOHN LYDGATE's *The FALL OF PRINCES* both consist of a series of tales about prominent people betrayed by Fortune.

See also *MIRROR FOR MAGISTRATES, A.*

FURTHER READING
Frakes, Jerold C. *The Fate of Fortune in the Early Middle Ages: The Boethian Tradition.* Boston: E. J. Brill, 1988.

FORTUNES STABILNES CHARLES D'ORLÉANS (1420–1440)
Born on November 24, 1394, Charles d'Orléans was imprisoned by the English after the Battle of Agincourt in 1415. During his captivity, he learned English, wrote poetry, and read widely, including works by GEOFFREY CHAUCER and JOHN GOWER. Freed in 1440, the twice-widowed Charles married Marie de Clèves and fathered the future King Louis XII. Charles retired to Asti, Italy, dying in January 1465.

Written over a period of 20 years, *Fortunes Stabilnes* includes many different types of poetry, but primarily relies on BALLADEs and rondels within a DREAM VISION framework. Composed during Charles's imprisonment in England, it is written in both French and English. It features numerous plays on words—particularly their sounds, spellings, and meanings—in the shifts between languages. The story combines COURTLY LOVE and authorship. A lovesick narrator, servant to the God of Love, writes love letters to his lady, who first denies but later accepts his love, and then dies. Mourning deeply, the narrator falls asleep and dreams about meeting Age, who convinces him to regain ownership of his own heart. The narrator awakens, works exhaustively on poetry, and then falls asleep again, dreaming that Venus appears, demanding that he choose a new lady. He refuses. Then he glimpses the lady FORTUNE. Alarmed by the height of her wheel, he cries out and awakens to see the woman from his dream. He confesses his love to her, and they commence an affair.

Charles's ballades consist of three STANZAS and an ENVOI, which use a central image to convey emotion. In Ballade 26, for example, the narrator's "burning heart" expresses his desire; in the envoi, he feels that fire bringing death closer. Early scholarship focused on biographical connections and imagery, but modern studies have begun looking at Charles's work in terms of nationalist identity formation.

FURTHER READING
Fein, David A. *Charles d'Orléans.* Boston: Twayne, 1983.
Charles d'Orléans. *Fortunes Stabilnes: Charles of Orleans's English Book of Love.* Edited by Mary-Jo Arn. Binghamton, N.Y.: Medieval/Renaissance Texts and Studies, 1994.
Spearing, A. C. "Prison, Writing, and Absence: Representing the Subject in the English Poems of Charles d'Orléans." In *Chaucer to Spenser: A Critical Reader,* edited by Derek Pearsall, 297–311. Oxford: Blackwell, 1999.

Susan Crisafulli

FOUR HUMORS
Medieval medicine taught that the human body contained four fluids—blood, phlegm, black bile, and yellow bile. When all of these are in balance (*eucrasia*), the individual is healthy; imbalance indicates infirmity. These fluids also determine a person's personality traits, depending on which is predominant, and are related to the astrological four elements as well as the four seasons. The complete schema of these was set out in Galen's *On the Temperaments.*

These could be interconnected to make more complex personality assessments (e.g., choleric-sanguine).

Humor	Temperament	Character	Temperature	Season	Element
Blood	Sanguine	Optimistic, cheerful, fun-loving	Warm and moist	Spring	Air
Phlegm	Phlegmatic	Calm, unemotional, shy	Cold and wet	Winter	Water
Black bile	Melancholic	Considerate, creative, perfectionist	Cold and dry	Autumn	Earth
Yellow bile	Choleric	Ambitious, dominant	Warm and dry	Summer	Fire

For instance, in the GENERAL PROLOGUE TO THE CANTER-
BURY TALES, GEOFFREY CHAUCER relies on the four
humors to reveal characteristic about the Pilgrims.

See also PHYSIOGNOMY.

FOURTEENERS

A fourteener is a line of 14 syl-
lables, usually consisting of seven iambic feet; it is synonymous with heptameter. But while heptameter
describes a line of seven metrical feet, the use of the
term *fourteener* seems to have begun in the 16th century; thus, its use as a critical term is often historically
specific, while the use of *heptameter* is not. Generally,
verse written in fourteeners consisted of unremarkable
rhymed COUPLETS.

Narrative verse in fourteeners flourished during the
later Middle Ages and the early Tudor period, enjoying
a brief vogue that roughly coincided with the initial
translation of a large number of Latin works into English. This has led to conjecture that the fourteener was
a response to the exigencies of such translation, the
longer line being useful to the translator since English
does not have Latin's gift for brevity, and the seven-
foot line having some precedent in Archilochian heptameter (iambic heptameter) and other classical verse
that translators would have taken as prose models.
This conjecture is borne out in the frequent use of
fourteeners in Tudor translations from the Latin—for
instance, in Jasper Heywood's *Troas, Thyestes,* and *Her-
cules Furens;* Alexander Neville's *Oedipus;* and John
Studley's *Agamemnon, Medea,* and *Hippolytus.* These
translations' long-winded verse did not, however, set a
precedent for the revival of classical tragedy on the
English stage, which was dominated by BLANK VERSE.

The fourteener proved more durable in poetry,
where it was combined with other lines (such as hexameter in HENRY HOWARD, EARL OF SURREY's "Complaint
of a Dying Lover,") or its rhymed couplets broken into
four lines, becoming the eight-and-six meter of the
common BALLAD STANZA.

Nathaniel Z. Eastman

"FOWELES IN THE FRITH" ANONYMOUS
(ca. 1270)   This short, enigmatic lyric appears, with
musical accompaniment, in one manuscript found at
the Bodleian Library in Oxford. In the opening two-
line "section" of the poem, the speaker looks outward
and notes that the creatures of the natural world are
where they ought to be: "Foweles in the Frith, / The
fisses in the flod . . ." (ll. 1–2)—birds are in the woods,
the fishes in the stream. The speaker then turns inward
and finds that harmonious nature contrasts with his
own, disordered state: "And I mon waxe wod. / Mulch
sorw I walke with . . ." (ll. 3–4)—literally, "And I must
grow mad. I walk with much sorrow . . ." What is the
nature of the "sorw" that separates the speaker from
nature? The answer comes in line 5: "For beste of bon
and blod" (l. 5). A corporeal being is the source of his
pain, and the opposition with the natural world seems
to heighten his suffering.

The fundamental critical debate surrounding this
lyric concerns genre: Is "Foweles in the Frith" a secular
or a religious lyric? Many critics assume that the poem
borrows conventions from the discourse of COURTLY
LOVE and find the pained, subjective emotion typical of
the Provençal and Middle English love lyrics of the
12th and 13th centuries, as well as reminiscent of
LOVESICKNESS. However, others argue that the poem is
religious, either a meditation on the fallen state of
humanity or a lamentation over Christ's sacrifice. This
particular lyric, though, refuses to fall unambiguously
into either camp—even the manuscript context offers
no clues—and continues to tantalize readers, making it
an often anthologized piece.

"Foweles in the Frith" draws upon a number of recognizable commonplaces and poetic traditions, but
even these do not help to settle the debate over its
nature. Most obvious is the notion of courtly love; the
"beste of bon and blod" is apparently a secular lover
who has rejected the speaker and occasioned the lyric.
Also, the *natureingang,* or "nature walk," that opens
the poem is a conventional way to begin a medieval
love song and ties the poem to the REVERDIE tradition—the world is greening in springtime and teems
with life and joy. However, *natureingang* also recalls
the biblical Creation theme. Birds and fish were both
created on the fifth day, and Adam would classify and
name them, establishing *lex aeterna,* or eternal law,
which alienates human beings from nature. Further,
frith can mean not only "woods" but also "divine law."

Biblical analogues to the first three lines of the lyric (Matthew 8.19–20 and Psalms 8.5–9, for example) argue powerfully that this is, in fact, a poem with a strong religious orientation.

The poet's use of paronomasia (punning), however, confounds any reader looking for an easy interpretation. The obvious pun in line four is on *wod,* most commonly translated "mad," with a play on "woods." In the last line of the lyric, though, the linguistic paronomasia has a profound effect. The speaker suffers because of the "beste of bon and blod." The ambiguous word here is *beste.* Does the "I" suffer because of the "best of bone and blood" or for the "beast of bon and blod"? The "best of bone and blood" would seem to suggest Christ. *Beast,* though, suggests a human being. There are two different poems contained in this lyric, depending on the reading of a single word. And because of the overlapping orthography (spelling) of *beste* in the 13th century and the lack of context provided by either the poet or the manuscript, *beste* could be either. Finally, could the speaker be Christ, suffering for as long as humanity continues to sin?

This lyric responds well to an exegetical reading, and critics have speculated on its reception—for instance, was it sung in court or in the monastery? However, the most fruitful direction for future study could lie in what this short song reveals about medieval hermeneutics, since its essential meaning always lies just beyond solution. The central figure that problematizes the poem—paronomasia—is a common mannerism of medieval hermeneutic writing.

See also EXEGESIS, MIDDLE ENGLISH LYRICS AND BALLADS.

FURTHER READING

Chickering, Howell D., Jr. "'Foweles in the Frith': A Religious Art Song." *PQ* 50 (1971): 115–120.

Moser, Thomas C., Jr. "'And I mon waxe wode': The Middle English 'Foweles in the Frith.'" *PMLA* 102 (1987): 326–337.

Osberg, Richard H. "Collocation and Theme in the Middle English Lyric 'Foweles in the Frith.'" *MLQ* 46 (1985): 115–127.

Tony Perrello

FRAME NARRATIVE

A frame narrative is the sum of a linear narrative and a story or series of stories embedded within it. The primary narrative provides an introduction or justification for the tales it supports; the embedded tales, however, can usually stand on their own, enriched rather than defined by the primary narrative. In some cases, the embedded stories are themselves frames, so that the whole becomes a series of stories within stories within a story. In all cases, the continued engagement of the reader or listener depends on the writer's ability to integrate all these stories into a single organic form.

The primary narrative, or frame, introduces the narrator and the occasion for telling the tales. In *1001 Arabian Nights,* for example, the reader learns that the virgin Scheherazade must keep the king captivated by weaving ever more elaborate stories. In the *Decameron,* GIOVANNI BOCCACCIO's narrator introduces a group of 10 who flee plague-ridden Florence for a rural villa. The 17th-century Spanish author María de Zayas has women connect on the complexities of love. Similarly, GEOFFREY CHAUCER's *The CANTERBURY TALES,* perhaps the most famous of all English frame narratives, begins with a prologue which introduces each of a group of pilgrims on their way to Canterbury.

The shorter stories vary in content and genre. They range from the frivolous and fanciful to the bawdiest of tales to political or religious ALLEGORY. Many of the tales combine the entertaining and the didactic, thus reflecting their folkloric roots. They also vary in their relationship to the narrator and the frame. The frame may also encourage the reader to distinguish the narrator from the author, who may include his or her own views as those of one of the other characters in the work.

FURTHER READING

Gittes, Katherine S. *Framing the Canterbury Tales: Chaucer and the Medieval Frame Narrative Tradition.* Westport, Conn.: Greenwood, 1991.

J. A. White

"FRANKLIN'S TALE, THE" GEOFFREY CHAUCER (ca. 1395)

In the opening of "The Franklin's Tale" from GEOFFREY CHAUCER's *The Canterbury Tales,* the knight Arveragus falls in love with a lady, Dorigen. He confesses his love to her at length, and because of his "worthynesse" and "obeysaunce" (ll.

738–739), she agrees to marry him. Each agrees to give obedience to the other, and the Franklin (a medieval landowner, not of noble birth) follows with a comment on the ideal state of marriage in which each partner honors and obeys the other. They go to his home and live in harmony for more than a year, until Arveragus decides to go and seek his fortune in "worshipe and honour" (l. 811) for a year or two in England.

Dorigen is heartbroken. In an attempt to distract her from her grief, her friends persuade her to go out walking near her castle, which overlooks the ocean. She looks down from the high cliffs to the rocks below, and her fear is intensified because Arveragus might be slain in the attempt to land a ship here. Again, her friends intervene, finding other places to walk, playing chess and backgammon, and taking her dancing.

While she is out one day in May, the squire Aurelius catches sight of Dorigen. Unbeknownst to her, he has been desperately in love with her for two years. On this day, they talk, and he reveals his love to her. "Have mercy, sweet, or ye wol do me deye!" he tells her (l. 978). She says she is sorry he is so miserable, but "Ne shal I nevere ben untrewe wyf" (l. 984), adding that if he will "remoeve alle the rokkes, stoon by stoon" (l. 993) from the coastline, she will give him her physical love, but "wel I woot [know] that it shal never betyde" (l. 1001).

Aurelius feels his heart grow cold, and "for verray wo out of his wit he brayde" ("out of true misery went out of his mind," l. 1027). Unknowingly, he prays to Apollo for a flood to cover all the rocks on the coast of Brittany and then falls down in a swoon. His brother carries him to his bed. Meanwhile, Arveragus comes home. He has no suspicions that anyone has wooed Dorigen in his absence, and they are once again blissful together.

Aurelius lies wretched in bed for two years, with his brother keeping him alive and keeping his secret. Eventually the brother remembers that during his years as a student in Orleans, he had seen a book about magic—"swich folye," comments the Franklin, "as in our days is nat [not] worth a flye" (ll. 1131–32). Aurelius's brother resolves to find a clerk or "philosopher"—that is, a magician—who can make it appear for a week or two that all of the rocks have vanished,

so that Dorigen would have to make good on her promise and cure Aurelius.

Aurelius gets out of bed and, with his brother, sets off for Orleans in search of such a philosopher. Just before they reach a town, they meet a clerk who tells them he knows of their mission and describes it to them in detail; he invites them to his home, where he shows them a series of magically created scenes and then gives them supper. This philosopher demands a thousand pounds to make all of the rocks disappear, and Aurelius promises it; together, they journey back to Brittany. Aurelius waits while the philosopher seeks the right conjunction of moon and planets; when the rocks appear to be absent, he falls to the magician's feet in thanks and then hurries off to find Dorigen. He reminds her of her long-ago promise, tells her that the rocks are all gone, and demands she meets him in a particular garden in the town to fulfill her promise.

Dorigen is horrified. Arveragus is once again out of town, and she considers killing herself rather than being forced to honor a rash promise to Aurelius at the expense of her marriage vows to Arveragus, but decides to wait until he comes home. When he does, she tells all. "Is ther oght [anything] elles, Dorigen, but this?" he asks, and she replies, "Nay, nay . . . this is to muche" (ll. 1469–71). He instructs her to uphold her promise but then, breaking into tears, forbids her from telling anyone else.

Dorigen goes out to meet Aurelius, who has been spying on her. He meets her in the street and asks where she is going. She replies: "Unto the garden, as myn housbounde bad [commanded], / My trouthe [vow] for to holde—allas, allas!" (ll. 1511–12). Aurelius is amazed, develops sudden compassion for both Dorigen and Arveragus, and decides to desist from satisfying his lust rather than assault "franchise and alle gentilesse" (l. 1524): both terms refer to nobility of character. He releases Dorigen from his bond, saying he would rather live in misery for the rest of his life than disturb the love between Dorigen and Arveragus. She thanks him on her knees and hurries home to Arveragus.

Aurelius brings 500 pounds to the philosopher and asks for two or three years to save up the rest, rather than having to sell off his estate so he can pay the remainder of the fee. The philosopher is angered by this and asks, "Hastow nat had thy lady as thee liketh?" (l. 1588). Aurelius tells the philosopher that he developed pity when he understood Dorigen's grief at the idea of being "a wikked wyf" (l. 1599). The philosopher answers that if a squire and a knight can act nobly, so can a clerk, and he releases Aurelius from the entire fee. "Thy hast ypayed wel for my vitaille [provisions]. / It is ynogh" (ll. 1618–19).

The Franklin concludes the tale with a question for his fellow pilgrims: "Which was the moste fre, [generous] as thinketh yow?" (l. 1622). Rather than giving his tale a fixed conclusion or moral interpretation, he opens it up for discussion and varied interpretation among the other pilgrims of The Canterbury Tales.

"The Franklin's Tale" is one of five varied ROMANCES in The Canterbury Tales. Chaucer frequently writes tales that disrupt or challenge expectations about generic forms. Here he has the Franklin state in the prologue to his tale that it is a Breton lai (LAY). However, stylistic and thematic characteristics make it a better example of romance than of lai. These include the emphasis on gentilesse—nobility of character, generosity, honor, honesty—as well as the careful rhetorical texture of the tale.

Though the Franklin claims he "lerned nevere rethorik" (l. 719), his tale is rhetorically complex, using repetition, digression, and recitation of proverb-like bits of wisdom about life, all rhetorical strategies common in Chaucer's works as well as in other medieval literature, though not in the lai. The Franklin uses other unusual rhetorical techniques that characterize the tale as especially rhetorically complex. For example, Dorigen lists exempla (see EXEMPLUM) of women who have committed suicide rather than lose their chastity. While one or a few such exempla are frequently employed, such a long list is uncommon. The use of periphrasis, or a long-winded way of referring to a common occurrence, is also infrequent in medieval literature, but it occurs here.

Some readers have taken "The Franklin's Tale" as a noble story in which the characters all act honorably. Others read all of the characters as behaving badly: Aurelius by extracting a promise of physical satisfaction from a married women, Dorigen by promising rashly to give in to Aurelius's lust if he makes all the rocks disappear, Arveragus by sending his wife to satisfy another man's sexual demands, and the magician by demanding an extravagant fee for his labors.

Gentilesse is a concept crucial to "The Franklin's Tale" and involves not simply nobility of character but also the idea of a model of behavior expected of members of the aristocracy or the "gentil" social class. "The WIFE OF BATH'S TALE" shows that members of the aristocracy do not always behave nobly; "The Franklin's Tale," in contrast, makes the argument that nobility of character is not limited to members of the aristocracy but may also be practiced by members of "lower" social classes. Such blurring of class distinctions also points back to the GENERAL PROLOGUE TO THE CANTERBURY TALES, in which any firm demarcations of social class are shown to be very difficult to maintain in England by the 14th century.

The tale investigates the theme of "trouthe," the requirement to uphold one's vows. Dorigen's promise of "trouthe" in marriage to Arveragus is threatened by her promise of sexual intercourse with Aurelius if he makes all the rocks disappear. However, she makes this promise believing it is an empty one. Moreover, Arveragus tells her she should keep this vow to Aurelius yet not tell anyone she has done so, apparently holding appearance to be more important than actual morality, as when he promised to obey Dorigen in marriage as long as she gave the appearance of obeying him. The privileging of appearances also occurs in the magician's demonstration of his skill, when he makes Aurelius and his brother see a forest full of deer and a pair of jousting knights within his study. The rocks which Dorigen fears are never actually removed; due to the magician's labors, "it semed that alle the rokkes were away" (l. 1296).

In choosing life over suicide, the Franklin's Dorigen provides a more moderate alternative to "The Physician's Tale" of a father who determines to kill his daughter rather than allow her to be raped by a corrupt public official. She also contrasts with but is nonetheless aligned in interesting ways with Criseyde of Chaucer's TROILUS AND CRISEYDE, who agrees to a sexual relationship with Troilus although she refuses marriage. She is then sent as a hostage into the Greek camp, where she gives in to Diomede's wooing and thus breaks her promise to wait until she can be reunited with Troilus.

The tale has long been considered the last in the "marriage group" of The Canterbury Tales, and the Franklin's tale of a marriage of mutual respect has been read as an answer both to the Wife of Bath's insistence on the sovereignty of women and to the Clerk's brutal Walter, who subjects his Custance to unremitting torture for the sake of demonstrating his mastery over her. The "love triangle" of "The Merchant's Tale," in which a woman agrees to sleep with her husband's friend for money, has an analogue in the love triangle of "The Franklin's Tale," though Dorigen's reluctance to break her marriage vow is in direct contrast to the Merchant's wife's willing infidelity. The generosity of the magician in giving up his fee is also in contrast to the mercenary greed of the husband, wife, and lover of "The Merchant's Tale." But if she is idealized as a wife, Dorigen is also passive, submitting to the demands of Aurelius (instead of challenging his interpretation of her flippant promise) and of her husband to submit to Aurelius's lust.

Chaucer provides another alternative in "The Tale of Melibee," in which a wife is a patient and wise counselor to a sometimes rash husband. Chaucer ascribes "The Tale of Melibee" to the character of "Chaucer," the one tale teller with a link to the real world outside the Canterbury pilgrimage. If any of the tales can be read as a touchstone or moral center for The Canterbury Tales as a whole, "Melibee" is a good candidate. The narrative and thematic links between "Melibee" and "Franklin," then, provide additional weight to an argument that sees in "The Franklin's Tale" an answer to the other tales about marriage, a suggestion that marital equality is a desirable goal rather than a threat to social structures.

Recent scholarship has turned toward readings of tales in their context within The Canterbury Tales. This can be difficult since there are different versions of the Tales' sequence in the early manuscripts. However, scholars have long identified "fragments" consisting of groups of tales that occur in sequence in all or almost all of the manuscripts. "The Franklin's Tale" and "The Squire's Tale" form one such fragment, and recent criticism has read these as a single narrative unit with thematic links, such as concepts of wealth and gift giving, between the two tales and their respective tellers. Moreover, scholars have recently given renewed attention to the relationships between tales and their tellers.

FURTHER READING
Cooper, Helen. The Canterbury Tales. Oxford Guides to Chaucer. Oxford: Clarendon Press, 1989.
Mann, Jill. Geoffrey Chaucer: Feminist Readings. New York and London: Harvester Wheatsheaf, 1991.
Harwood, Britton J. "Chaucer and the Gift (If There Is Any)." Studies in Philology 103, no. 1 (2006): 26–47.

Heide Estes

FRENCH HISTORY, THE ANNE EDGECUMBE DOWRICHE (1589)

Published in the year following the defeat of the SPANISH ARMADA, ANNE EDGECUMBE DOWRICHE's narrative poem relates three incidents in which French Protestants (Huguenots) were martyred and divine justice exacted on their persecutors, a timely reminder to the English about the dangers of Catholicism. In part one, titled "The taking of St. James his street," Dowriche describes an incident from 1557 that occurred in Paris. A private home, where a small Protestant worship service is taking place, is suddenly surrounded by angry Catholics. The Protestants who do not escape are quickly arrested and burned at the stake if they choose not to recant their beliefs. In part two, Dowriche relates the arrest and execution of Annas Burgeus (Anne du Bourg) in 1559. As a member of the French Parliament, Burgeus urged the king to reject Catholicism. King Henry II has him immediately arrested and executed. Dowriche concludes her work by narrating the St. Bartholomew's Day Massacre of August 1572, describing the assassinations of Admiral Cologny and several other prominent Protestant leaders, as well as the massacre in Paris itself.

In each section of the narrative, Dowriche stresses the honor, nobility, and piety of the Protestant victims; the treachery and savagery of the Catholic perpetrators; and the sudden, violent deaths of the persecuted. When contextualized through Dowriche's numerous biblical citations, persecuted Protestants become the mirror image of the Israelites in the Old Testament, whose faith was tested and proven by their suffering. The connection is further reinforced by Dowriche's closing EMBLEM, "Verity as purtraied by the French pilgrim." The woodcut depicts a crowned, naked woman with a scourge tied to her back, standing over flames. The accompanying verse describes how God's truth is strengthened rather than destroyed by Satan's tortures.

Dowriche frames her narrative within the context of what many Protestants believed was a multinational Catholic conspiracy to crush Protestantism. This context drives the poem's political implications. As citizens of the sole European nation headed by a stable, militarily powerful, Protestant monarch (ELIZABETH I), radical Protestant reformers believed that England had a responsibility to withstand this conspiracy, both by actively supporting European Protestants, and by instituting further church reforms at home. Perhaps because of its use of poulter's measure (COUPLETs that rely on alternating hexameter and heptameter lines), the poem was earlier dismissed as simplistic. Its heavy-handed portrayal of the Protestant-Catholic conflict reinforces this impression. Recently, however, feminist critics have reexamined this view of early modern women writers, and Dowriche's poem is now examined more favorably. She is particularly adroit in utilizing multiple poetic expressions, woven into a complete view. The narrative of the martyrs from St. James Street becomes a condemnation of the English government's prohibition of private religious meetings by Nonconformists. The narrative of Annas Burgeus becomes an indictment of the prohibition against discussing religious reforms in Parliament.

Such criticisms become even more pointed in light of Dowriche's opening dedication of her work to her brother, Pearse Edgecumbe, a six-term member of Parliament. This dedication includes both a letter and an ACROSTIC poem that spells out Edgecumbe's name. In this dedication, Dowriche exhorts her brother to greater piety, and in the letter ("To the right worshipfull her loving brother"), she refers to an apparent breech in their relationship, blaming it on "the contrarie crossings of those politique affections that hinder the working" of their natural affection.

Within this context, Dowriche's poem shrewdly navigates the dangerous waters of political speech. She blankets her political message within an uncontroversial condemnation of French Catholicism, yet she still conveys her underlying position to those who may be in a position to influence English parliamentary actions—the argument that Parliament should be permitted to openly debate matters of religious reform.

FURTHER READING

Beilin, Elaine. "'Some Freely Spake Their Mind': Resistance in Anne Dowriche's *French Historie*." In *Women Writing and the Reproduction of Culture in Tudor and Stuart Britain,* edited by Mary Burke, et al., 119–140. Syracuse, N.Y.: Syracuse University Press, 2000.

Dowriche, Anne. *The French Historie: That Is, A Lamentable Discourse of Three of the Chiefe, and Most Famous Bloodie Broiles that Have Happened in France for the Gospell of Jesus Christ.* Women Writers Online. Brown University Women Writer's Project. Available online. URL: http://textbase.wwp.brown.edu. Downloaded on February 14, 2006.

Lysbeth Em Benkert

FUTHARK ALPHABET (FUTHORC, FUTHORK, RUNES)

Runes date to the time before Christianity arrived in northern Europe, and because of this, they became associated in later times with non-Christian religions. The runic alphabet is called futhark after the first six letters of the alphabet— *f, u, th, a, r,* and *k.* The futhark alphabet consists of 24 letters, 18 consonants, and six vowels. Traditionally, these are divided into three groups of eight, called *ættir* (singular ætt). Some scholars believe that futhark is related to other early inscription systems, such as OGHAM, but no direct evidence connects these. Like other runic languages, the runes stood both for individual letters and for individual words.

The earliest extant runic inscriptions date to ca. 200 C.E. Most are found on hard surfaces—stone, wood, metal—which explains the angular nature of the letters. For some time, futhark coexisted with the Latin alphabet, though in England it began to decline around the ninth century. It did not survive the NORMAN CONQUEST.

The futhark alphabet provided an important grapheme, the thorn (þ), as an addition to the Latin alphabet. Since Latin does not contain the sound combination *th,* early representations of Old English used the thorn to represent the sound. Old English poetry also reflects the usage of runes. BEOWULF, for instance, contains several instances of the rune *ethel* ("homeland"). The RUTHWELL CROSS preserves a large portion of the DREAM VISION poem *The DREAM OF THE ROOD* in runes, lending a glimpse into early graphic systems and poetic composition.

FURTHER READING

Page, R. I. *An Introduction to English Runes.* 2nd ed. Woodbridge, U.K.: Boydell, 2006.

G

GARLAND OF LAUREL (OVERVIEW)

JOHN SKELTON (ca. 1495)   The centerpiece poems of
Garland of Laurel—those that describe the ladies of the
embroidery circle of Elizabeth Tylney Howard, countess of Surrey—were probably composed by JOHN SKEL-
TON about 1495 when he was a guest of the Howard
family at Sheriff Hutton Castle near York. The entire
work did not reach print until its publication by Richard Fakes on October 3, 1523. The second printed edition appeared in 1568 in the *Pithy, Plesaunt, and
Profitable Workes of Maister Skelton, Poet Laureate,* a collection edited by John Stow, and there is one extant
manuscript.

Garland of Laurel summarizes Skelton's accomplishments in his bid to become lionized at the court of
Fame. The work is framed as a DREAM VISION in which
the poet/narrator encounters Fame, who accuses him
of writing SATIRES and other scurrilous poems but not
poems of love, in which endeavor the poet "is wonder
slak" (l. 68). To prove his worth as a love poet, Skelton
proceeds in 11 verses to praise each of the aristocratic
ladies who are making him a garland, or chaplet of laurel, the poet's laureate crown. The astronomical data
and locale cited in the poem identifies these ladies as
the daughters and gentlewoman in the circle of Elizabeth, countess of Surrey (née Tylney), first wife of
Thomas Howard, earl of Surrey and eventually duke of
Norfolk.

The poet declaims to the ladies within a courtly
chamber, first addressing his noble patroness and then
her ladies by rank. In the manuscript, the short poems
are rendered one to a page, which gives the impression
of reading intimate personal letters, though in the
printed editions this layout has not been retained. The
dream-narrator is then shown into the presence of the
Queen of Fame. She is given Skelton's book of writings, which is adorned in the Flemish style with realistic depictions of insects, flowers, "and slymy snaylis" (l.
1154) in the margins; every other line is written in
aurum musicum ("gold," l. 1161). From this book,
Occupation then recites a lengthy list of Skelton's publications, not all of them surviving (and some, like "The
Balade of the Mustarde Tarte," possibly invented).
Thousands of orators and poets shout "Triumpha, triumpha!" and trumpets and clarions sound as Skelton
is admitted to the ranks of other eminent English poets
such as GEOFFREY CHAUCER, JOHN GOWER, and JOHN
LYDGATE, who themselves appear in the poem as Skelton's sponsors. The loud acclaim wakes the sleeping
poet-narrator, and the poem concludes with a series of
Latin, French, and English verses, showing Skelton's
wit and virtuosity at translation.

Skelton invented SKELTONICS, a verse form generally
characterized by short, rhythmic lines and variable,
often unusual rhyming. This form allowed Skelton to
write a range of poetry, from scathing satire to realistic
scenes of lower-class life to comic verse, as is found in
Garland of Laurel. Among Skelton's sources for *Garland
of Laurel* are Chaucer's *The HOUSE OF FAME* and the prologue to *The LEGEND OF GOOD WOMEN.* But the verses of

the *Garland* are also entirely original and performative; the reader seems to be one of the audience as the poet addresses the ladies in the countess's chamber. Many critics have pointed out that Skelton's poetry is concerned mainly with Skelton, including Alexander Dyce, Skelton's earliest editor, who remarked that "*Garland* consists of sixteen hundred lines written in honor of Skelton himself." A great comic poet, Skelton stands at the transition between the Middle Ages and the early modern period. There is no poet quite like him, and in his *Garland of Laurel,* the greatest of all Skelton's poems, we literally witness the poet celebrate and simultaneously mock his own accomplishments.

FURTHER READING

Boffey, Julia. "'Withdrawe Your Hande': The Lyrics of 'The Garland of Laurel' from Manuscript to Print." *Trivium* 31 (1999): 73–85.

Brownlow, F. S. *The Book of the Laurel: John Skelton.* Newark: University of Delaware Press, 1990.

Gingerich, Owen, and Melvin J. Tucker. "The Astronomical Dating of Skelton's *Garland of Laurel.*" *Huntington Library Quarterly* 32 (1969): 207–220.

Scattergood, John, ed. *John Skelton: The Complete English Poems.* Harmondsworth. Middlesex, U.K.: Penguin, 1983.

Tucker, M. J. "The Ladies in Skelton's 'Garland of Laurel.'" *Renaissance Quarterly* 22, no. 4 (1969): 333–345.

Martha W. Driver

Garland of Laurel: "To Margery Wentworthe" JOHN SKELTON (ca. 1495)

This poem, composed of five QUATRAINS rhyming *abab,* describes a young woman in the sewing circle of Elizabeth Tylney Howard, countess of Surrey. Margery Wentworthe (d. 1550) has been identified as Howard's niece and the daughter of Anne Say, the countess's half sister, and Henry Wentworthe of Nettlestead, Suffolk. Margery would later marry Sir John Seymour of Wolf Hall and bear him 10 children, one of whom was Jane Seymour, third wife of HENRY VIII and mother of Edward VI.

The performative element is particularly marked in these verses, with a repetition of three of the five STANZAS, suggesting a sung REFRAIN. In this refrain, the poet refers to the lady's "mantel of maydenhode"—presumably emblematic of her person—that has been embroidered with "mageran jantel" (l. 907). As various commentators note, this is not only a pun on the name *Margery* but also refers to the best kind of marjoram. The *Tacuinum sanitatis,* a medieval hardbook on wellness, describes sweet marjoram as valuable medicinally for the stomach and brain and as a purifier of the blood, which may suggest some further significance of this metaphor—or perhaps Skelton is simply invoking the herb's sweet aromatic qualities. Some scholars have noticed that the basic properties of marjoram—prettiness and usefulness—parallel Margery Wentworthe's virtues. She is further compared to the primrose and columbine, colorful perennial flowers that may adorn a garden or grow wild, but are always enduringly beautiful.

See also *GARLAND OF LAUREL* (OVERVIEW); SKELTON, JOHN.

Martha W. Driver

Garland of Laurel: "To Mistress Isabell Pennel" JOHN SKELTON (ca. 1495)

Among the liveliest of the lyrics dedicated to aristocratic ladies in JOHN SKELTON's *Garland of Laurel,* this poem celebrates its subject in a number of rapid-fire rhymes. In the opening lines, Skelton rhymes the words *lady, dady,* and *baby* ("By Seynte Mary my lady / Youre mammy and your dady / Browght forthe a goodely baby," ll. 974–976), thereby encapsulating the poet's inability to put his affection into verse. "Innocent" rhymes abound in this little poem, which seems as if spoken to a young girl. She is compared in a gentle yet teasing tone to spring flowers, fruits, and Venus as the morning star. Among the comic coinages are "rosabell" (to rhyme with "Isabell" and "camamel") from the Latin *rosa bella,* or beautiful rose, perhaps drawn from Italian love song tradition. There is also apparently a reference to Isabell's singing, which to hear, says the poet hyperbolically, is "A lif for God hym selfe" (l. 996). Isabell is compared with the nightingale, a symbol of both earthly and spiritual love, who sings with other harmonious birds.

The poem ends somewhat unceremoniously, but certainly comically, with "Dug dug / Jug jug / Goode yere and goode luk / Wyth chuk chuk, chuk chuk" (ll. 1000–1003). The reference to the "good year," or luck in the new year, may be an indication that Skelton's fictive *Garland of Laurel* records a real occasion: the laureation of Skelton as celebrated by the ladies of Elizabeth Tylney Howard's embroidery circle at Sheriff Hutton Castle, Yorkshire.

Though a firm identification of Isabell Pennel has not been made, the scholar M. J. Tucker has found an Isabel Paynell who married Thomas Dereham, who was born about 1472. Their son, Francis Dereham, would later become Catherine Howard's lover, executed by Henry VIII for his illicit sexual behavior with Catherine.

See also GARLAND OF LAUREL (OVERVIEW).

Martha W. Driver

Garland of Laurel: "To Mistress Jane Blennerhasset" JOHN SKELTON (ca. 1495)

This poem is one of the central verses in JOHN SKELTON's *Garland of Laurel,* composed about 1495, celebrating the ladies of the embroidery circle of Elizabeth Tylney Howard, countess of Surrey. In his DREAM VISION, the poet encounters a group of ladies in the countess's chamber who are engaged in making him a laurel crown, or chaplet. The identification of Jane Hasset (as she is called in the sole extant manuscript) or Blenner-Haiset (as she is named in the printed editions) is uncertain. The scholar M. J. Tucker suggests that Jane was probably the wife of Ralph Blennerhasset and grandmother of Thomas Blennerhasset, Howard's executor. She died in 1501 at the age of 97, so at the time of Skelton's original composition, which may have been drawn from an actual occasion (the poet was laureated three times—by Oxford in 1488, Louvain in 1492, and Cambridge in 1493), Jane Hasset would have been quite elderly.

There are three STANZAS praising Jane, written in SKELTONICS, the verse form invented by the poet. Though the poet claims to be tiring ("my pen wax faynte," l. 956), he says he will praise this lady's "goodely name" (l. 960). The poet then says he will intently apply himself "to stellify" (l. 964) Jane so that she will deserve entrance into the Court of Fame. This comic coinage, which means "to place among the Olympian gods," also occurs in GEOFFREY CHAUCER's *The HOUSE OF FAME.* In thanks for her setting "Smale flowris" into his poet's "chapelet," Skelton compares Jane to "fayre Laodomy," or Laodamia, a classical example of wifely fidelity. According to legend, she followed her husband, Protesilaus, to Hades out of love. Chaucer also cites Laodamia in love in *The LEGEND OF GOOD WOMEN.* The comparison with Laodamia here seems to imply that Jane is a widow.

The lyrics celebrating Jane seem to be overheard as they are declaimed by Skelton in the noble chamber of the countess of Surrey. The reader feels privileged to observe the courtly scene, yet remains puzzled by several references that have now become obscure.

In the larger context of *Garland of Laurel,* it is Skelton himself who wishes entrance into Fame's court, and the allusion to the small flowers that Jane has added to the poet's laureate garland may be literally to her embroidery, to flowers of rhetoric, or even more generally to the role of women as inspiration for courtly verse.

See also GARLAND OF LAUREL (OVERVIEW).

Martha W. Driver

Garland of Laurel: "To Mistress Margarete Hussey" JOHN SKELTON (ca. 1495)

The most anthologized of all the lyrics in JOHN SKELTON's *Garland of Laurel,* the poem to Mistress Margarete Hussey, celebrates the joyful character of a young woman. In the opening lines of the poem, which also serve as a REFRAIN, she is described as "Merry Margaret" and compared first with the "mydsomer floure," or daisy, which is also a pun on her name. In French, Margarete means daisy, a common summer flower. The next line of the refrain compares her with aristocratic birds of prey, the falcon and hawk ("Jantylle as fawkon or hauke of the towre," ll. 1006, 1018, 1031). The word *Jantylle,* or *gentle* in modern English, is employed in its older sense; in MIDDLE ENGLISH, *gentil* means both "nobly born" and "virtuous," terms that might be applied equally to the noble bird of prey, trained to hunt and serve the falconer, and to a strong, virtuous, yet gently bred woman. A "hauke of the towre," or high-flying hawk, was especially prized. Falconry was an aristocratic art in the medieval and early modern periods, practiced by both women and men as a sport requiring focus and skill.

After the opening COUPLET, the rhymes are tercets (units of three lines of verse), with short, irregularly rhythmic lines, a good example of the verse form devised by Skelton called SKELTONICS. The lady is described "as fulle of good wille / As the fayre Isyphill" (ll. 1020–1021), or Hypsipyle, a character who appears in GEOFFREY CHAUCER's *The LEGEND OF GOOD WOMEN*. Abandoned by Jason after their marriage, Hypsipyle, the daughter of King Thoas of Lemnos, composes a famous letter to her husband. In Chaucer's story, Hypsipyle remains faithful to Jason, then dies for love of him. In *De mulieribus claris* (Of Famous Women), GIOVANNI BOCCACCIO explains that Hypsipyle resists when the women of Lemnos decide to murder all men, saving the life of her father and later of her twin sons. Hypsipyle was seen as a type of loyal daughter, which has led to speculation that Margarete may have been a young woman who supported her own father through a difficult time.

In the next tercet, Skelton compares Margarete to "Colyaunder / Swete pomaunder / Good Cassander" (ll. 1022–1025). The lady is sweet as coriander, an aromatic herb sometimes employed in medicines or used in a pomander, a ball filled with aromatic spices used to sweeten the air or ward off plague. The meaning of "Cassander" has been much debated. Two classical allusions suggest a tragic interpretation: Cassandra, daughter of Priam, king of Troy, who has the unfortunate gift of prophecy; and Cassander, successor to Alexander the Great, who executed Alexander's mother, wife, and son. Herbal suggestions include cassava, or tapioca starch, as well as the herb cassawder. Skelton may also mean cassia or cinnamon, which, like coriander and pomanders, was used to perfume the air and for medicinal purposes.

Some have suggested that Margarete Hussey was the wife of Sir John Hussey, sheriff of Lincolnshire from 1493 to 1494, who was later controller of the household of Henry VII and the honorary court position of chief butler of England. This Margarete Hussey, however, died in 1492, some three years prior to the presumed date of the *Garland*'s composition. The lyrics may have been written prior to Margarete Hussey's marriage and then appended by Skelton to the series, though others insist that Skeleton would not have portrayed Margarete

so vibrantly to her friends if she were already dead. While the identity of the lady remains uncertain, her lively character is aptly described in Skelton's verses.

See also *GARLAND OF LAUREL* (OVERVIEW).

Martha W. Driver

GASCOIGNE, GEORGE (1539–1577) George Gascoigne was born a country gentleman in the village of Cardington in Bedfordshire, England. He attended Cambridge University, undertaking the study and practice of law at Gray's Inn in 1555, but also took the time to develop his literary talents. In 1557, he took his first seat in Parliament. A year later, while attending Queen ELIZABETH I's coronation, Gascoigne became entranced by courtly life, and thereafter, courtly ambitions dominated his life, while his poetry constantly endangered these hopes. However, today he is often referred to as an "ice-breaker" for later poets because he attempted so many literary forms.

To keep pace with court life, Gascoigne began to spend lavishly, and he went deep into debt. In 1562, he landed in prison for fighting with his wife Elizabeth's former husband over both her and her property. In 1570, he was jailed for debt, and two years later, continuing financial troubles resulted in the nullification of his second election to Parliament. By 1572, even his poetry had begun to darken Gascoigne's reputation, and he was brought before the Privy Council on charges of slander.

That same year, in the hope of paying his debts and salvaging his reputation, Gascoigne volunteered for military service. While he was abroad, in 1573, a scandalous anthology of poems, *A Hundreth Sundrie Flowres*, began to circulate at court, and while all the entries were anonymous, several clearly had been authored by Gascoigne. Before he could again hope for courtly favor, he had to distance himself from this somehow. In spite of this, and though no better off financially when he returned to England in 1574, his overall reputation was repaired to such a degree through his military adventures that in 1575 he received a commission to compose entertainment for the Queen, and he was recommended (unsuccessfully) for poet laureate.

See also COURT CULTURE, "LULLABIE," "WOODMANSHIP."

FURTHER READING

Gascoigne, George. *The Complete Works of George Gascoigne.* 2 vols. Edited by J. W. Cunliffe. 1907. Reprint, New York: Greenwood Press, 1969.

Johnson, Ronald. *George Gascoigne.* New York: Twayne, 1972.

Robert E. Kibler

GAWAIN-POET (PEARL-POET) (fl. ca. 1390)

Scholars assign the name "the *Gawain*-poet" (sometimes "the *Pearl*-poet") to the anonymous author of four poems in the MANUSCRIPT Cotton Nero A.x now housed at the British Library: PEARL, CLEANNESS, *Patience,* and SIR GAWAIN AND THE GREEN KNIGHT. Earlier scholars attributed the poem ST. ERKENWALD, found in a different manuscript, to this author, but that remains disputed.

Since the Cotton Nero poems give no firm indication of their author's identity, scholars have explored the poet's background through careful attention to the poems and the manuscript. Based on the date of the manuscript and on references within the poems, it appears that the *Gawain*-poet was writing around the last decade of the 14th century. Additionally, linguists have identified the dialect of the poems as English Northwest Midlands, around Cheshire. Highly learned references indicate a thorough grounding in biblical studies and familiarity with Latin literature, suggesting the poet may have been a clerk (member of a minor order). A focus on genteel manners and a familiarity with aristocratic traditions and values in the poems suggest that the poet may have been a retainer in a noble household. These characteristics and the self-presentation of the poems' speakers evince a male author, but there is no proof of this.

The intertwining of Christian themes with CHIVALRY and courtly values is a key characteristic of the *Gawain*-poet's work. The poems imagine God as the ideal form of a king or aristocratic lord, and *Gawain's* protagonist struggles with the frailty of the flesh as well as his knightly quest. The poems explore the contrast between the perfection demanded by chivalric-Christian virtue and the limits of human frailty—sympathetically, through the befuddled speaker of *Pearl* or the reluctant Jonah in *Patience,* or damningly, through the negative examples in *Cleanness.* Symbols of perfection and purity recur throughout the poems, two key examples being the immaculate pearl and the pentangle symbolizing virtue on Gawain's shield. Critics have also noted the poems' interest in exploring sexual mores—for example, the nuanced treatment of dangerous flirtation and potentially erotic male bonding in *Gawain.* *Cleanness* includes both exuberant praise of heterosexual relationships and condemnation of male-male homosexual intercourse.

Three of the poems are written in alliterative verse (and *Pearl,* though not in alliterative verse, shows strong alliterative elements). The combination of the poet's Northwest Midlands dialect and use of ALLITERATION might seem to suggest a provincial, old-fashioned writer; however, it is only the subsequent triumph of London English and of stressed-syllable rhyming verse that gives us this impression of the *Gawain*-poet's isolation, as the mid- to late 14th century saw an outburst of verse sometimes referred to as the ALLITERATIVE REVIVAL, and such verse was popular in gentry households. Moreover, close connections existed between the metropolitan centers of London and Westminster and the poet's likely homeland of Cheshire during this period, primarily because King Richard II had close connections there.

FURTHER READING

Brewer, Derek, and Jonathan Gibson, eds. *A Companion to the Gawain Poet.* Cambridge: D.S. Brewer, 1997.

Finch, Casey, trans. *The Complete Works of the Pearl Poet.* Berkeley: University of California Press, 1993.

Putter, Ad. *An Introduction to the Gawain-Poet.* London: Longman, 1996.

Brantley L. Bryant

GENERAL PROLOGUE TO THE CANTERBURY TALES GEOFFREY CHAUCER (ca. 1390)

The opening 18 lines of the *General Prologue* to the CANTERBURY TALES comprise the most famous sentence in medieval literature. Aside from setting forth one of the main themes of the entire collection—secular versus sacred love—these lines also provide temporal and geographic context for the tales to come: In spring, a group of pilgrims are on their way to Canterbury to visit the tomb of St. Thomas à Becket, martyr and miracle worker. Although ostensibly a religious journey, it quickly becomes clear that this eclectic group has more on its mind than saving souls. It is here that GEOFFREY CHAUCER develops the initial portraits of each pilgrim, providing the basis of their personality and of the rivalries that will later appear within the tales themselves.

The *Canterbury Tales* is structured as a FRAME NARRATIVE, like the *Decameron* by GIOVANNI BOCCACCIO and the *CONFESIO AMANTIS* by JOHN GOWER. However, the *Canterbury Tales* provides several unique additions to the frame narrative tradition. Whereas the introductory piece in most frame narratives serves solely as the setup for the subsequent stories, the *General Prologue* is a unique stand-alone poem. As well, the *Prologue* and all the tales are deftly interlinked—and meant to be that way. The interaction among the various pilgrims revealed in later tales is often dependent upon the initial relationships set forth in the *General Prologue* and revealed there by the singular Narrator, himself a pilgrim on the journey. Indeed, some of the Tales are so well suited to their teller that without the character development in the *General Prologue,* the audience could not appreciate all the story's nuances. The addition of a narrator character is unique to Chaucer, too, and likely has roots in another genre in which Chaucer excelled, the DREAM-VISION tradition. Finally, in his frame narrative, incomplete though it may be, Chaucer offers an example of every major medieval literary genre (e.g., FABLIAU, HAGIOGRAPHY, ROMANCE, BEAST FABLE, etc.) instead of relying solely on one or two story forms, or even a set of themes such as found in the *Decameron.*

Unlike many of the tales, the *General Prologue* has no direct source, though portions of it have analogues. Presumably, it was composed before the majority of the tales, although no exact date can be assigned. It begins in a manner reminiscent of a dream-vision poem, with a springtime setting and a chance encounter. However, instead of an allegorical setting, the Narrator enters a real-life establishment— the Tabard Inn in Southwark—and instead of describing allegorical characters, the Narrator depicts "real" people.

The *General Prologue* is set up to introduce the "portraits" (descriptions) of the pilgrims through narration, symbolism, and context. They are a "compaignye/ of sundry folk" (l. 24–25) who form a group by chance and circumstance—all of them just happen to be traveling to Canterbury at the same time. Chaucer the Narrator becomes a part of this group—"I was of hir felaweshipe anon" (l. 32)—and undertakes the task of describing the group: "me thynketh it acordaunt to resoun/ to telle yow al the condicioun/ of ech of hem, so as it semed me,/ and whiche they weren, and of what degree" (l. 36–40). Through his eyes, the audience will learn about each pilgrim's circumstances, clothing, and social rank. As well, the connection and clash of literal and symbolic is set up immediately with the idea of pilgrimage, which is both physical and spiritual, a journey of the body and the soul.

The Narrator is the main character of the *General Prologue,* as he does all the talking except for a few lines at the end by the Host, a character who never tells a tale but interacts in the liminal spaces between them. An outsider, the Narrator seems to be the ideal observer, yet he is naive and so holds a high opinion of many of the pilgrims whom he should not hold in esteem. Most of the portraits end up being SATIRICAL, although they are presented in a completely different manner because the Narrator overlooks many, though not all, of the pilgrims' shortcomings. The Narrator is also materialistic. He concentrates on the pilgrims' wealth and status as indicated by their possessions, and openly admires the wealth of the middle-class characters.

Scholars have often noted that there are three basic types of characters in the *General Prologue*: those merely mentioned (e.g., the three priests and the guildsmen), stereotypes (e.g., the Monk), and full characters (e.g., the Wife of Bath). Having individualized and stereotypical pilgrims is crucial to the success of the *General Prologue,* as the imagery, whether it works with the moral comment or against it, enhances it. Illusion, often presented by the Narrator, must be seen through to be successful—but it also must be presented without being seen through for this success to be possible.

Unlike the tales, the pilgrim portraits appear in an order that would have been expected by medieval society. The Knight serves as a figurehead, coming first, followed by his retinue, small though it may be. The ecclesiastic personages come next, followed by the "middle class" in various degrees. Where the rank becomes less clear, the pilgrims are then grouped in terms of social interaction. For instance, the Summoner and the Pardoner are riding together, and are described together. Only some pilgrims are described in terms of their physical appearance, but in these cases, the description is crucial to the character's development. The Pardoner, for example, is rendered more effeminate by his physical appearance, while the Clerk's scholarly arrogance is conveyed effectively through circumstance, not looks.

The collection of portraits therefore begins with the highest ranked pilgrim, the Knight. The Narrator deems him a "worthy man" (l. 43) who loved chivalry and justice and protected Christianity against heathens. The Crusades took him to many foreign places, such as Prussia, Lithuania, Turkey, Spain, and Morocco. The Knight is one of the few ideal pilgrims; he is "a verray, parfit gentil knight" (l. 72)—true, perfect, and noble. The Knight's retinue includes his son, the Squire, and his servant, the Yeoman. Unlike his father, the Squire is the epitome of a courtly lover. He is handsome and well dressed and rides along singing and playing the flute. He is more interested in poetry and love than in war; nevertheless, he is "curteis [. . .] lowely, and servysable" [courteous, humble, and attentive] (l. 99). The Yeoman, a forester dressed in green and carrying a bow, follows the Squire.

The Narrator next turns his attention to the Prioress, whom he describes in terms more applicable to a romance heroine than a nun. Her smile is "symple and coy" (l. 119). Her "nose tretys [well formed], hir eyen greye as glas/ hir mouth ful small, and therto softe and reed" (ll. 152–153). She dresses elegantly, has excellent manners, and is named "madame Eglentyne" (l. 121). The naive Narrator reports details about the Prioress that are seemingly incongruous with a religious life. Instead of having sympathy for poor, suffering humans, for example, she reserves all of her compassion for "a mous/ kaught in a trappe" (ll. 44–45), and while people starve, she feeds her lapdogs white bread and milk. The Prioress clearly belongs to the gentry, as

indicated by her name, attire, and education. She speaks French, wears a wimple of fine quality, and carries a rosary made of coral with a gold brooch attached. With the Prioress rides her retinue, including another nun and three priests. Although none of these Pilgrims is described, two of them—the Second Nun and the Nun's Priest—will tell tales.

The Monk rides after the Prioress. He loves to ride and hunt, and avoids prayer and manual labor: "What sholde he studie and make hymselven wood [mad],/ upon a book in a cloystre alwey to poure/ or swynken with his handes, and laboure,/ as Austyn [Augustine] bit? How shal the world be served?" (ll. 184–187). Though the Narrator is clearly impressed by this "manly man" (l. 167), his naive revelations allow the audience to condemn the Monk as a false cleric. A medieval reader would understand that a monk should remain in his cloister, studying and praying, should accept labor cheerfully, should follow the Rule of his order—and most certainly should ask how God (not the world) should be served.

Similarly, the Friar impresses the Narrator. The Friar, who follows the Monk, is "wantowne and merye" (l. 208), well dressed, well spoken, and clearly from the gentry class. According to the Narrator, the Friar is also generous: "he haade maad ful many a marriage/ of yonge wommen at his owne cost" (ll. 212–213), though once again the audience should catch the implication the Narrator seemingly misses—that the Friar has dallied with these women and now must find husbands for them. The Narrator's cheerful admiration of the Friar's popularity belies the cleric's falseness: "ful wel beloved and familier was he/ with frankeleyns over al in his contree/ and eek with worthy wommen of the toun/ for he hadde power of confessioun" (ll. 215–218). By noting his power of confession, the Narrator inadvertently reveals the nature of the Friar's popularity—he is willing to trade absolution for money or other favors.

The stylish Merchant, who has a forked beard and wears motley and beaver, rides after the Friar. Though praised by the Narrator for his astute business sense, it becomes clear that the Merchant is really a usurer. The Clerk follows, a poor student who is extremely thin and wears threadbare clothing because he spends all of his money on books. Though the narrator believes the

Clerk would willingly teach others, the overall portrait implies he is more concerned with theory than application. Riding alongside these two Pilgrims are the Sergeant of Law (Man of Law) and the Franklin, a wealthy landowner. The Man of Law's portrait is brief, but revealing: "nowher so bisy a man as he ther nas/ and yet he semed bisier than he was" (ll. 321–322). Appearances are deceiving. The Franklin is an older man with a long white beard, renowned for his gourmet appetites. One of the few Pilgrims to be described in terms of the FOUR HUMORS, the narrator notes, "of his complexioun he was sangwyn" (l. 323), meaning the Franklin is generally good humored.

Five Guildsmen follow: the Haberdasher, the Carpenter, the Weaver, the Dyer, and the Tapester (tapestry and rug weaver). None is described individually, but all are noted to be wearing opulent clothing and carrying silver knives in clear violation of medieval SUMPTUARY LAWS. The Guildsmen are accompanied by their Cook, whose culinary skills are highly praised by the Narrator despite the "mormal" ('ulcer,' l. 386) on his shin that drips into his pot.

The Shipman follows. Deemed a "good felawe" (l. 395) by the Narrator, the Shipman—festooned with daggers and drunk on wine—is a violent drunkard. However, he is also a skilled navigator who relies upon the heavens to guide him. The next pilgrim, The Doctor of Phisik (the Physician), also relies upon the stars. The Physician is known for his astrological skills: "wel koude he fortunen the ascendent/ of his ymages for his pacient," (ll. 417–418); however, he is also well versed in classical medical texts, such as Hippocrates and Galen, and excels at interpreting the body's humorial balance.

Following these two pilgrims is the Wife of Bath, the third woman of the group and the only one traveling alone. A weaver, the Wife has her own money and spends it as she pleases. She enjoys going on pilgrimages and has been to the major sites—Rome, Cologne, Boulogne, Jerusalem (three times), and St. James of Compostella in Galicia, Spain. The sense is, however, that she goes on pilgrimages to socialize, not for religious reasons. The Wife is bold, outspoken, forthright, and, above all, passionate. Not only has she been married five times, but also she wears red and is "gattothed" (I. 468)—which, according to PHYSIOGNOMY, indicates a lustful nature. Even the Narrator recognizes her zest for sex, as he observes: "Of remedies of love she knew per chaunce,/ for she koude of that art the olde daunce" (ll. 475–476).

The portraits of the two other idealized pilgrims—the Parson and the Plowman—follow. The Parson is the ideal priest—monetarily poor but spiritually rich. He is learned and enjoys teaching. He is patient, kind, and forgiving, a true "noble ensample to his sheep [congregation]" (l. 496). About him, the Narrator proclaims, "A better preest I trowe that nowher noon ys" (l. 524). The Plowman is the Parson's brother. He is not described physically, but it is noted that he is a "trewe swynkere" ("hard worker"; l. 531) and tithes regularly.

Following these two pilgrims, the Narrator lists the remaining group: "ther was also a Reve, and a Millere,/ a Somnour, and a Pardoner also,/ a Maunciple, and myself—ther were namo" (ll. 542–544). The Miller is ugly in nature as well as appearance. He is short and stout with a red beard and big mouth. Most noticeable, however, is the huge wart that grows on the end of his nose, from which grows a bristly patch of hair. He is also a cheat, who holds his side of the scale down with his thumb in order to acquire more wheat for less money. The Manciple (business agent) is also a cheat, which even the Narrator notes: "and yet this Manciple sette hir aller cappe" ("still this Manciple deceived them all"; l. 586). The Reeve follows. He is described as a "sclendre colerik man" (l. 587), with close-cropped hair, and a wiry body. The prevalence of the humor choler indicates a ruthless nature. Like the Miller and Manciple, the Reeve is a cheat: "His lord wel koude he plesen subtilly,/ to yeve and lene hym of his owene good,/ and have a thank, and yet a cote and hood" (l. 610–612). Through lending his lord the man's own goods, previously stolen by the Reeve, the Reeve earns himself additional praise and profit.

The next two Pilgrims, the Summoner and the Pardoner, appear as a pair. The Summoner is loathsome, and his mere appearance scares children. A drunk, he reeks of garlic and onions. His face is fire-red, with scabby brows and a patchy beard, and is covered with pustules. The Summoner is "hot" and "lecherous as a sparwe [sparrow]" (l. 626), and claims to have numerous concubines. He, too, is a cheat, and will release offenders from their ecclesiastical summons for a bribe. Riding with him is a Pardoner, who is equally repugnant in appearance. He has a smooth face, a high voice, and long yellow hair hanging in greasy ringlets. All of these are feminine attributes. According to physiognomy, the Pardoner's eyes, "glarynge [. . .] as an hare" (l. 684) reveal homosexual tendencies. His sexuality is definitely ambiguous, and even the Narrator is forced to concede: "I trowe he were a geldyng or a mare" (l. 691). The relationship between the Summoner and the Pardoner is equally ambiguous. The Pardoner is singing a love song, and the Summoner "bar to hym a stif burdoun" (l. 673)—musically a strong bass accompaniment, but certainly a phrase with strong sexual implications. The Pardoner, like his fellows, is a cheat. He carries with him a bag full of fake relics and a series of false indulgences for which he charges inordinate sums of money.

The Pardoner is the final pilgrim the Narrator describes fully. Of himself he says only "my wit is short" (l. 746). After the list of portraits, the Host, "a large man he was with eyen stepe" (l. 753), serves food and becomes enthralled with the company of pilgrims. He impulsively decides to travel with them, and he also proposes a contest: Each Pilgrim will tell two tales on the way to Canterbury and two on the return journey, with the winner earning a meal. The Host, who will serve as judge, sets forth the rules: "and which of yow that bereth hym best of alle—/ that is to seyn, that telleth in this caas/ tales of best sentence and moost solaas—/ shal have a soper at oure aller cost" (ll. 796–799). Sentence and solaas—meaning and pleasure—the basis of teaching through entertainment, were prominent in medieval pedagogy.

Comic irony and satire are the two most prevalent literary devices of the *General Prologue*. Quite often these effects are achieved through the Narrator's hearty agreement with the pilgrims' obviously incorrect perceptions, such as the Monk's casual dismissal of the Rule of St. Augustine. As well, the Narrator often undercuts himself without (apparently) meaning to. For instance, in the Prioress's portrait, he notes: "Frenssh she spak ful faire and fetisly,/after the scole of Stratford

at Bowe,/for Frenssh of Parys was to hire unknowe" (ll. 124–126). Although the Narrator's admiring tone does not change, the additional information he provides reveals that she speaks provincial, not aristocratic, French. Nevertheless, this constant irony is itself undercut somewhat because the Narrator never actually says that the pilgrims are inaccurate in their estimations of themselves. The Prioress, for example, thinks of herself as a fine lady, not a model nun, while the Monk clearly believes himself to be a country gentleman, not a cleric. Thus, the audience can trust the details that the Narrator reports, if not their presentation.

Scholars, particularly Jill Mann, have noted that the *General Prologue* is related to a neglected medieval genre, the estates satire. This literary genre is a satiric examination of all classes of society—the so-called THREE ESTATES. As well, such texts tend to concentrate on people's functions within a society as a whole, rather than on individual contributions. As a whole, there is an inordinate amount of time in the *General Prologue* devoted to "work," that is, dealing with what the pilgrims actually do as opposed to who they are. They tend to be sharply critical of characters that cheat others out of rightfully earned money or goods, such as the Miller and the Pardoner, both of whom are depicted in scathing terms. Estates satires are also typically anticlerical, often presenting religious characters as drains on an otherwise economically functioning society. The Friar's expensive habit of marrying off young women that he has dallied with and the Monk's stable of fine horses both typify this attitude.

Thus, the *General Prologue* provides a serious moral analysis of an entire society, which is, in turn, an essential setup for the whole tableau of the *Canterbury Tales*. The major themes, such as the nature of love and friendship, and the role of FORTUNE, are all introduced here. The idea of chance is particularly interesting in this regard. Beginning with line 19, "Bifil that in that seson on a day," the idea of chance permeates the Prologue, as it will the later Tales. *Bifil*, meaning "it happened," or "it chanced," seems to indicate that the Narrator simply stumbles into this grand opportunity to travel with a motley assortment of pilgrims and record their tales. Other references to chance abound, with the pilgrims randomly meeting, the Host impulsively joining the group, the contest springing from nowhere, with even the tale-telling order left to chance (the Pilgrims drew straws). Indeed, the Narrator ends the *Prologue* with a final tribute to chance: "and shortly for to tellen as it was,/were it by aventure, or sort, or cas" (ll. 843–844)—that is, by chance, luck, or destiny. Despite these great lengths taken to instill a sense of fortune into the *Prologue,* it is clear that the entire text has gone according to design and has not fallen according to chance.

The *General Prologue* also introduces the theme of ecclesiastical critique, which will return time and again in the tales. The satiric portraits of the ecclesiastical pilgrims are obvious examples, but more subtle critiques are present as well. For instance, the Physician is highly educated and well read, but "his studie was but litel on the Bible" (l. 438). Similarly, connections to LOLLARD beliefs have been attributed to the Parson, who resembles a Lollard "poor priest," and the Plowman, who may recall WILLIAM LANGLAND's *PIERS PLOWMAN.* Several allusions to Lollard beliefs—disparaging the mendicants, stressing the vernacular, and questioning authority, in particular—are found throughout *The Canterbury Tales,* but more orthodox beliefs (including the idea of pilgrimage) prevail consistently, and scholarly debates continue in this regard.

Finally, the *General Prologue* is also sometimes referred to as Chaucer's "London work," as it takes place at the Tabard Inn in Southwark, which was just across London Bridge. A number of the pilgrims are either from London (e.g., the Cook) or have clear connections to the city (e.g., the Manciple). Chaucer the Narrator may also be assumed to be a Londoner, as the poet clearly composed his masterpiece upon his return to the city. However, city life and city values do not pervade the work as a whole, and London serves as yet another piece of the frame on which the entire collection rests, which is, ultimately, the function of the *General Prologue* to the *Canterbury Tales.*

See also FRAME NARRATIVE; "FRANKLIN'S TALE, THE"; "MAN OF LAW'S TALE, THE"; "MILLER'S TALE, THE"; "NUN'S PRIEST'S TALE, THE"; "PARDONER'S TALE, THE"; "PRIORESS' TALE, THE"; "REEVE'S TALE, THE"; "WIFE OF BATH'S TALE, THE."

FURTHER READING

Benson, C. David. "The *Canterbury Tales*: Personal Drama or Experiments in Poetic Variety?" In *The Blackwell Guides to Criticism: Chaucer,* edited by Corinne Saunders, 127–142. Oxford: Blackwell, 2001.

———. "Historical Contexts: London." In *Chaucer: An Oxford Guide,* edited by Steve Ellis, 66–80. Oxford: Oxford University Press, 2005.

Cookson, Linda, and Bryan Loughrey, eds. *Critical Essays on the* General Prologue *to the* Canterbury Tales. London: Longman, 1989.

Mann, Jill. *Chaucer and Medieval Estates Satire: The Literature of Social Classes and the* General Prologue *to the* Canterbury Tales. Cambridge: Cambridge University Press, 1973.

GEST OF ROBYN HODE, A ANONYMOUS (ca. 1508)

Variously described as a folk BALLAD, tale, *ryme,* or *talking, A Gest of Robyn Hode* was, in its original form, orally recited or chanted by a minstrel. The poem survives in seven printed editions of the late 15th and 16th centuries, the most famous of which is the London edition by WYNKYN DE WORDE (ca. 1508). No manuscript survives, if one existed at all, and some scholars speculate that one of the early printers (perhaps RICHARD PYNSON) may have composed the present text from preexisting literary and historical materials, including a miracle of the Virgin Mary, CHRONICLES, ROMANCES, and other ballads. Also uncertain is the historical time depicted in the poem. Although the king in the last two parts is identified as "Edward our comly king," four different King Edwards reigned between 1272 and 1483. Some of the sources and analogues suggest the time of Edward II (1307–27), while others point to Edward III (1327–77) and possibly even to Edward IV (1461–83).

The 1,824-line poem is composed of 456 four-line STANZAS, rhyming *abcb,* arranged in eight parts, or *fyttes.* The tale consists of three interwoven episodes of Robin Hood: the protagonist with a knight, with the sheriff of Nottingham, and with the king. A short epilogue describing Robin's murder by a prioress concludes the poem.

In the first episode, Robin helps a knight, later called Sir Richard at the Lee, to recover his mortgaged lands by lending him 400 pounds. After redeeming his lands from the scheming abbot of St. Mary's York, Sir Richard returns home to gather the money to repay Robin. He sets off a year later for Barnsdale in Yorkshire, but is delayed when he stops to rescue a yeoman at a wrestling match. While Robin is impatiently waiting for the knight to arrive, members of his band, Little John and Much, waylay a monk from the abbey that tried to steal the knight's lands and take him to Robin. After failing to tell the truth about how much money he is carrying, the monk is robbed of 800 pounds, twice the amount owed to Robin, who believes that the Virgin has repaid the debt twice over. When the knight finally arrives, Robin refuses the knight's payment and gives him half of the money taken from the monk. While the exact source has not been found, a miracle story about the Virgin Mary aiding a knight likely influenced this adventure, which is cleverly interlaced among three of the eight *fyttes*.

In the second episode, Little John, disguised as Reynold Greenleaf, takes service with the sheriff, and, together with the sheriff's cook, robs the sheriff of 300 pounds while he is hunting. Upon meeting the sheriff in the forest, Little John entices him into a trap by promising him a stag and a herd of deer. After being captured, the sheriff swears an oath that he will not harm Robin or his men if they release him, but later he attacks them following an archery tournament in Nottingham, and Little John is wounded. They escape to Sir Richard's castle, where they are offered sanctuary. Sir Richard is subsequently captured by the sheriff while he is out hawking; his wife pleads for Robin's help. Robin goes into town, shoots the sheriff with an arrow, and frees the knight. Since the first half of this section focuses on Little John, some scholars suggest that it was derived from a separate cycle of Little John tales, now lost.

In the third episode, the king, upon hearing of Robin's outlawry, goes to Nottingham to capture him and Sir Richard, but he searches in vain for six months. Upon the advice of a forester, he disguises himself as an abbot and is soon captured by Robin, who robs him of 40 pounds. When the disguised monarch shows Robin the king's seal, Robin exclaims that he loves no man in all the world as well as his king. After feasting together, Robin loses an archery game and receives a buffet or blow from the king, whom Robin finally recognizes and begs for a pardon. The king agrees on the condition that Robin and his men will enter his service and give up their outlawry. Robin serves the king for 15 months at court; then, on the pretext of visiting his chapel in Barnsdale, he returns to Yorkshire, where he spends the rest of his life until he is treacherously murdered by the prioress of Kirklees abbey. This section was likely adapted from a popular cycle of tales known as the "King and the Subject," in which the monarch tours his domain in disguise in order to find out what the commoners think of him.

A Gest of Robyn Hode marks a crucial stage in the social and economic transformation of late 15th-century England, when the urban yeomanry began to eclipse the lesser aristocracy in power, prestige, and wealth. As the designated hero of this emerging social class, Robin Hood proves his superiority to the knightly class, as represented by Sir Richard, by lending him the money to redeem his property; he also exposes and punishes the corrupt abbot and scheming sheriff.

See also "BIRTH OF ROBIN HOOD, THE"; ROBIN HOOD BALLADS; "ROBIN HOOD'S DEATH AND BURIAL."

FURTHER READING

Knight, Stephen, and Thomas Ohlgren, eds. *Robin Hood and Other Outlaw Tales.* Kalamazoo, Mich.: Medieval Institute Publications, 1997.

Ohlgren Thomas H., ed. *Medieval Outlaws: Twelve Tales in Modern English Translation. Revised and Expanded Edition.* West Lafayette, Ind.: Parlor Press, 2005.

Thomas H. Ohlgren

"GET UP AND BAR THE DOOR" ANONYMOUS (16th century)

This traditional, humorous Scottish folk BALLAD is known throughout Europe and Asia and has many variations, both in verse and prose form. At Martinmas time (November 11, the feast of St. Martin), a housewife is boiling puddings (sausages) at night. A cold wind is blowing under the door, and the husband asks his wife to close the door. Since she is busy, she says no, and they strike up a bargain: Whoever is first to speak the next word must get up and bar the door. At midnight, two gentlemen (in other variations they are "thieves" or "strangers") ask whether the inhabitants of the house are rich or poor, but neither the wife nor the husband says a word. The gentlemen eat the puddings, then one of them tells the other to take his knife and "tak off the auld man's beard, / And I'll kiss the goodwife" (ll. 31–32). Since there is no hot water to shave the husband, they threaten to use the pudding broth, which causes the husband to shout his outrage. Because he has spoken first, the wife skips across the floor, saying, "Goodman, you've spoke the foremost word, / Get up and bar the door" (ll. 43–44). Of course, it is too late.

The ballad follows standard form and is divided into 11 four-line BALLAD STANZAS, rhyming abcb. Some scholars have related it to the FABLIAU, though it lacks certain elements. Others have examined it as a commoner's version of FLYTYNG.

FURTHER READING
Bronson, Bertrand Harris. *The Traditional Tunes of the Child Ballads, with Their Texts, According to the Extant Records of Great Britain and America.* Vol. 4. Princeton: Princeton University Press, 1992.

Gary Kerley

GNOMIC VERSE   See ANGLO-SAXON RIDDLES.

GOWER, JOHN (ca. 1330–1408)   John Gower was born into a prosperous Kentish family. It is almost certain that he lived in Kent throughout the first half of his life and later held properties in Suffolk and Kent. Though details of his education and personal life are scarce, there is speculation that he trained in law and was married, possibly for the second time, to Agnes Groundolf in 1398. Gower was a court poet during the reigns of Richard II and Henry IV, devoting his time to writing while living at the priory of St Mary Overie's in Southwark from 1377 until his death.

Although a considerably learned man whose moral and philosophical works are admirable in their own right, it is almost impossible to refer to Gower or his work without mentioning GEOFFREY CHAUCER, with whom he was close friends. In Chaucer's dedication of TROILUS AND CRISEYDE to his good friend, he coined the nickname "moral Gower." There is speculation, however, that the two authors eventually became estranged because a tribute to Chaucer in the first version of Gower's COURTLY LOVE poem CONFESSIO AMANTIS (*The Lover's Confession*) is removed in a later version. While Gower was greatly admired by his peers, his status as a poet declined from his late-medieval position alongside Chaucer and JOHN LYDGATE. Over time, he was reduced to "dull Gower," an unflattering epithet bestowed as a result of superficial critical attention in the 19th century. However, renewed interest in Gower in the late 20th century and early 21st century has prompted critics to recognize the value of his poems and rekindle admiration for them on their own merits.

Gower's principal works are three long poems written in three different languages. His first large-scale work, the *Mirour de l'Omme* (*The Mirror of Man*) an ALLEGORY written in French (1376–78), is concerned with humanity following the Fall of Adam and Eve, virtues, and vices. Gower later Latinized the poem's title to *Speculum Hominis* and made a final name change to *Speculum Meditantis*. His second major work, an essay in Latin elegiac verse, *Vox Clamantis* (*The Voice of One Crying*), written ca. 1379–81, is an apocalyptic poem of seven books that deals with politics and kingship while containing reflections of the disturbances of the early years of Richard II and the PEASANTS' REVOLT in 1381.

Gower's most acclaimed work, *Confessio Amantis*, existed in three manuscript versions by the 1390s. Written at the command of Richard II, *Confessio* is a collection of tales illustrating the vices that may accompany love, expressed by a lover to a priest of Venus. The poem is a superb contribution to courtly love literature in English.

In addition to the three major poems, Gower wrote several minor poems in English, French, and Latin throughout his lifetime. Blind by the time of his death in 1408, he left a considerable estate. John Gower was buried in St. Mary Overie's, now the cathedral of St. Savior's, in Southwark.

FURTHER READING
Echard, Siân, ed. *A Companion to Gower.* Cambridge: D.S. Brewer, 2004.

Mary R. Rambaran-Olm

"GRAVE MARKED WITH OGHAM, A" ("GRAVE MARKED WITH OGAM, A")

ANONYMOUS (12th century) The anonymous poem now called "A Grave Marked with Ogam" was originally untitled. It has seven four-line STANZAS, with the second and fourth line of each stanza rhyming. As OGHAM stones so often mark graves, the stone in the poem is no exception. Scholars attribute the poem to Oisín. It focuses on the deaths of Oscar, son of the author, and Cairbre, or Caipre, who kill each other at the battle of Gabhra. Finn MacCool (Irish war leader) and the Fenian clan, of which Oscar and his father are members, demand tribute from Cairbre when the latter announces the marriage of his daughter. Cairbre refuses, and a battle ensues. The poet Oisín fought in the battle and claims to have killed twice 50 warriors. The power of Finn and the Fenians was broken following their defeat in battle and the death of Oscar. The poem ends with the claim that the Ogham stone would be remembered better if Finn had lived. While the poem comes from the 12th century in Irish, it remains one of our best insights into Ogham stones and their use in early Irish culture.

See also EARLY IRISH VERSE.

FURTHER READING

Book of Leinster. Edited by R. I. Best and M. A. O'Brien. 5 vols. Dublin: Dublin Institute for Advanced Studies, 1954–67.

Lehmann, Ruth P. M. "'The Calendar of the Birds' and 'A Grave Marked with Ogam': Two Problem Poems from the *Book of Leinster.*" *Etudes Celtiques* 17 (1980): 197–203.

Mark DiCicco

GREVILLE, SIR FULKE, BARON BROOKE

(1554–1628) Born on October 3, 1554, Sir Fulke Greville became friends with SIR PHILIP SIDNEY while at school in Shrewsbury. He later studied at Jesus College, Cambridge University, but left without taking a degree. Greville's friendship with Sidney continued at court, where he also aligned himself with Robert Dudley, Sidney's uncle, and Robert Devereux, earl of Essex. In 1597, Queen ELIZABETH I knighted Greville, and the following year he was named treasurer of the navy. Though he retired briefly upon the ascension of JAMES VI/I, Greville returned to court in 1612, earning the offices of privy counselor and chancellor of the exchequer. Named Baron Brooke in 1621, Greville then served in the House of Lords until his death. Ralph Haywood, a dissatisfied servant, murdered Greville on September 30, 1628.

Unlike many other Renaissance authors, Greville did not begin writing early in his life; the majority of sources indicate that he only began composing after Sidney's death. His best-known work is CAELICA, a collection of 109 love poems. Although linked with the SONNET SEQUENCE tradition, only 41 of the poems are actually SONNETS. The majority of his other works reflect political philosophy (e.g., *A Treatise of Monarchy,* 1609), religious concerns (*A Treatise of Religion,* 1609), and ethical considerations (*A Treatise of Humane Learning,* 1633). He also wrote three plays: *The Tragedy of Mustapha* (ca. 1595), *Alaham* (ca. 1599), and *Antony and Cleopatra* (ca. 1601), which Greville destroyed after Essex's execution. He also completed a biography of Sidney entitled *The Life of the Renowned Sir Philip Sydney* in 1610, though it remained unpublished until 1652. This work is precocious in its combination of authorial biography with critical interpretation of Sidney's poems, as well as its discussions about Sidney's influence on English poetry and on the current political circumstances prevalent in Renaissance England.

FURTHER READING

Hansen, Matthew C., and Matthew Woodcock, eds. "Fulke Greville: A Special Double Issue." *Sidney Journal* 19, nos. 1 & 2 (2001): 1–182.

Steggle, Matthew. "Fulke Greville: Life and Works." *Sidney Journal* 19, nos. 1 & 2 (2001): 1–9.

Wilkes, G. A. "'Left . . . to Play the Ill Poet in My Own Part': The Literary Relationship of Sidney and Fulke Greville." *Review of English Studies* 57, no. 230 (2006): 291–309.

"GUIGEMAR" MARIE DE FRANCE (late 12th century)

MARIE DE FRANCE's first *lai* (LAI) is about Guigemar, son of Oridial, vassal of King Hoel of Britanny. Guigemar is a typical courtly knight, but he does not display the customary interest in love that a knight should. While hunting, he tries to kill a white deer, but the arrow ricochets and ends up wounding him instead. The deer places a curse upon him to remain wounded until cured by a woman's love. The injured knight journeys to a remote land where an old king is married to a lovely woman whom he guards jealously. She treats Guigemar's wound, and the two end up falling in love and exchanging tokens (a knotted shirt and a chastity belt). However, the lady's husband discovers their clandestine affair and sends Guigemar away. Eventually the lady goes in search of him but ends up being taken captive by Lord Meriaduc. When Guigemar chances upon Lord Meriaduc's castle, he recognizes the lady by her possession of his love token. He then engages Meriaduc in battle and kills him. The *lai* concludes with Guigemar being reunited with his beloved.

The *lai* contains a strong fairy-tale motif (the enchanted animal) and constitutes a type of story common in the medieval period: the unhappily married woman, usually of an older and possessive/jealous husband, who falls in love with a knight errant. The poem celebrates "true" love—based on the individuals' compatibility and emotional attachment—over duty. A number of scholars have seen this as indicative of the triumph of the individual heart over the dictates of society and the strictures of arranged marriages. Others have examined the seemingly Celtic concepts of the story, attempting to contextualize ANGLO-NORMAN society.

FURTHER READING

Burgess, Glyn S., and Keith Busby, trans. *Lais of Marie de France*. 2nd ed. New York: Penguin, 1999.
———. *The Lais of Marie De France: Text and Context*. Athens: University of Georgia Press, 1987.

Joseph Becker

GULLINGE SONNETS SIR JOHN DAVIES (1590s)

Though difficult to date with precision, the *Gullinge Sonnets* of SIR JOHN DAVIES were fashioned as a direct commentary on the saccharine SONNET SEQUENCES in vogue during the 1590s. The *Sonnets* consist of nine poems and a dedicatory verse to Sir Anthony Cooke.

In the dedicatory poem, Davies warns that throughout this sequence, his "camelion Muse" will assume "divers shapes of gross absurdities," such that "if some rich, rash gull these Rimes commend, / Thus you may sett his for all witt to schoole, . . . / and beg him for a fool" (ll. 12–14). The purpose of these poems thus was to both satirize the writers of bad SONNETs and expose those readers who pretend to have good taste by commending technically proficient but fundamentally flawed sonnets.

The wit of the opening two sonnets is contained in the sudden transition of the terminal COUPLET away from the expected—and overused—CONCEITs and metaphors regarding love to a comic resolution. The first sonnet is written in the third person, which allows Davies to criticize an external object. Here he is the lover whose endurance of his mistress's love is transformed "Into a patiente burden-bearinge Asse" (l. 14). In the second sonnet, Davies compares the "poysonous beauty" of a lover to a "contagious yll" that decimates a flock of sheep (ll. 7–8).

Sonnet 3 is a SATIRE on the rhetorical trope of reduplication, where the end of one phrase is repeated at the beginning of the next. Though technically proficient, the sonnet says very little and shows no progress of narrative or thought, which is the point. The octave of Sonnet 4 compares love to the workings of a gun, only to change the overarching metaphor at the VOLTA to that of a lamp, as though the SESTET and the OCTAVE were from different poems.

Sonnet 5 mocks trick poetry and list poetry, which relied on the poet's ability to find synonyms rather than create good verse. Sonnet 6 clothes a personified "love" in the attire of an Elizabethan gentleman rather than that of a mistress. Sonnets 7–9 are heavily laced with legal conceits and jargons, which is perhaps unsurprising from a man who later became a great lawyer. These three sonnets, though, are a direct attack on the writings of students at the Inns of Court that were laced with legal terminology quite foreign to a love poem.

As much of the humor is drawn from a very narrow historical and legal context, the satirical wit of the *Gullinge Sonnets* can be difficult for readers today to recognize. Nevertheless, they stand as a self-conscious reflection on the poetic standards and fashions of the late Elizabethan period.

FURTHER READING

Sanderson, James L. "Bérenger de La Tour and Sir John Davies: Two Poets Who Set the Planets Dancing." *Library Chronicle* 37, no. 2 (1971): 116–125.

Andrew Bretz

H

HAGIOGRAPHY　Derived from the Greek *hagio* (saint, holy one), hagiography is literally writing about saints. More specifically, hagiographies are usually the stories of saints' lives. Though connected to the Latin *legenda,* there is a slight difference. *Legenda* are not necessarily stories of the saints' lives; rather, they may more generally include anecdotal tales grouped into themes (e.g., miracles of the Virgin).

Scholars often cite the connections between ROMANCE and hagiography, and many hagiographies exhibit COURTLY LOVE characteristics. Commonly, Jesus is depicted as the courtly lover-knight who ardently pursues his beloved—a person or a soul—wooing him or her with gentle phrases, gifts, and so forth. Hagiographies are found in both poetry and prose, as well as in both sacred and secular literary collections. For instance, GEOFFREY CHAUCER wrote a hagiography of St. Cecilia for his "Second Nun's Tale" in THE CANTERBURY TALES.

FURTHER READING
Heffernan, Thomas J. *Sacred Biography: Saints and Their Biographers in the Middle Ages.* Oxford and New York: Oxford University Press, 1988.

HALF-LINE　Literally a half-line of poetry, in ANGLO-SAXON POETRY the half-line is the normal metrical unit, with two half-lines that alliterate forming a complete alliterative line. These half-lines are separated by a CAESURA (pause), often represented by a blank space. Each half-line has at least four syllables, but the pattern of stress and ALLITERATION vary, depending on the length of the syllable, phonetic stress, and the number of syllables. Each half-line also has two stressed syllables, and those syllables alliterate. In the most common pattern found in Old English, two alliterating words in the first half-line link with one in the second.

The poems of the 14th-century ALLITERATIVE REVIVAL, such as SIR GAWAIN AND THE GREEN KNIGHT, follow this same basic pattern: Each alliterative line contains two half-lines, wherein at least one stressed syllable in the first half alliterates with one or two syllables in the other half-line.

FURTHER READING
Fulk, Robert D. *A History of Old English Meter.* Philadelphia: University of Pennsylvania Press, 1992.

Larry J. Swain

HANDLYNG SYNNE. ROBERT MANNYNG OF BRUNNE (ca. 1303–ca. 1338)　Unusual for a work of Middle English religious poetry, *Handlyng Synne,* an early 14th-century penitential poem, clearly announces the identity of its author, ROBERT MANNYNG OF BRUNNE. The poem numbers almost 12,600 lines of East Midlands Middle English. Three complete copies and six fragments survive.

Handlyng Synne is a free and fluid translation of the French poem *Manuel des Pechiez* (ca. 1270s). Like the original, it clearly states its intent as being the religious education of the "lewd" [common] person. The poem successively focuses on each of the Ten Commandments, the SEVEN DEADLY SINS, and the Seven Sacraments, relying primarily on a series of amusing and edifying exempla (see EXEMPLUM). Mannyng omits many of the original's tales, however, substituting local ones or his own additions. The result is a poem 50 percent longer than its French model, containing considerably more didactic commentary.

Mannyng's greatest skill as a writer lies in his narrative technique, wherein he demonstrates a particular ability to manipulate his audience's emotions, especially by vividly detailing the torments of hell. For example, a backbiting (gossiping) English monk is sentenced to perpetually gnaw his own tongue, while a proud lady is continually reduced to ashes by a burning wheel, only to be restored again in order for the cycle to continue.

While Mannyng covers numerous spiritual infractions, he reserves particularly hostile treatment for the rich who oppress the poor. Similarly condemned are those who attend church for social intercourse rather than for spiritual improvement. As is typical of monastic literature of the period, women are often selected for especially harsh treatment. Inevitably, they are cast as providing a primary source of temptation, sin, and damnation, luring men away from salvation. Finally, clerics and monks are closely scrutinized. For these Mannyng offers unflinchingly acerbic criticism and punishment for sins that include receiving bribes, coveting worldly reward, and general moral hypocrisy. His compassion tends to be reserved for the poor and for children, although he advocates the need for strict corporal punishment.

Metrically, *Handlyng Synne* generally conforms to that of the French original. It is written in rhyming COUPLETs, using an octosyllabic iambic meter. However, within this framework there is considerable irregularity, due in part to the transitional, nonstandardized nature of Middle English, but also to the liberties Mannyng takes with his model. The poem is remarkable for its direct, lively narrative, its accessible simplicity, and its insightful use of vivid metaphor and exempla, as well as for its use of the VERNACULAR and local identity.

FURTHER READING

Ho, Cynthia. "Dichotomise and Conquer: 'Womman Handlyling' in *Handlyng Synne*." *PQ* 72, no. 4 (1993): 383–401.

Mannyng of Brunne, Robert. *Handlyng Synne*. Edited by Idelle Sullens. Binghamton, N.Y. Center for Medieval and Early Renaissance Studies, 1983.

Robertson, C. W., Jr. "The Cultural Tradition of *Handlyng Synne*." *Speculum* 22, no. 2 (1947): 162–185.

Schaaf, B. Marie van der. "The Manuscript Tradition of *Handlyng Synne*." *Manuscripta* 24 (1980): 119–126.

Liz Herbert McAvoy

HENRY VIII (1491–1547) *king of England*

Henry Tudor was born on June 28, 1491, the second son of Henry VII and Elizabeth of York. After his older brother, Arthur, died, Henry became Prince of Wales, and he inherited the throne in 1509. His first act was to marry his brother's widow, Catherine of Aragon, daughter of Ferdinand and Isabella of Spain. They had received a special dispensation to marry, predicated on the supposed nonconsummation of Catherine's first marriage. On June 24, 1509, Henry and Catherine enjoyed a joint coronation.

The young king's happiness was complete when Prince Henry was born on January 1, 1511, but devastation followed as the prince died 52 days later. Following this, Catherine had a miscarriage and then another son who died at an early age before giving birth to a healthy daughter, Mary (later MARY I). Henry felt unfulfilled by the lack of a male heir, despite having an illegitimate son with his mistress, Bessie Blount. This son, Henry Fitzroy, duke of Richmond, was friends with HENRY HOWARD, EARL OF SURREY, providing inspiration for at least two of his poems.

The licentious Henry had a number of mistresses, but by 1526 he had fallen in love with one of Catherine's ladies-in-waiting, Anne Boleyn (ca. 1500–36). The canny Anne, however, refused to give into the king's desires until he promised to make her queen. In exchange, she promised to give him a male heir. Henry burned with desire for both, and he began trying to rid himself of Catherine. He asked Pope Clement VII for an annulment; however, Clement was afraid to anger Catherine's powerful family, which included Holy

Roman Emperor Charles V. Anne and Henry were secretly married in January 1533. When Henry's hopes for an annulment did not materialize, he broke ties with the Roman Catholic Church, and Thomas Cranmer, archbishop of Canterbury, annulled his marriage to Catherine. Unfortunately for Anne, her promise to give Henry a son went unfulfilled. In September 1533, Anne gave birth to their daughter Elizabeth, the future Queen ELIZABETH I. A miscarriage and a stillbirth followed.

Anne's days as queen were numbered. In May 1536, she was imprisoned in the TOWER OF LONDON on charges of adultery (which translate into treason for the queen) with several men, including her own brother. Though the charges coincided with Henry's own desires, it is probable that the general charge of adultery was true; even Anne's father and uncle testified against her. Only 10 days after Anne's execution, Henry took a third wife—Jane Seymour, one of Anne's ladies-in-waiting. She provided the 45-year-old King Henry with his longed-for heir, giving birth to the future Edward VI on October 12, but died two weeks later. Henry VIII's fourth wife was the German princess, Anne of Cleves (1515–57). The marriage was famously annulled only a few months later. His fifth wife was Anne Boleyn's cousin, Catherine Howard (1521–42), who met her cousin's doom not even two years into the marriage. Henry's last wife was the twice-widowed Catharine Parr (1512–48), who outlived him.

Though most famous, perhaps, for his many wives, Henry also changed England irrevocably by breaking from the Roman church. At one time declared "Defender of the Faith" by the pope, Henry was formally excommunicated in 1533. This not only affected the country financially and politically, but also in a literary sense. Poetry became a medium through which support for Protestantism was expressed (e.g., *The FRENCH HISTORY*), criticism of Catholic relations was leveled (e.g., *The SHEPHEARDES CALENDER*), and martyrdom was upheld (see ROBERT SOUTHWELL).

Henry was the first English monarch to be educated under the influence of the Renaissance. Because of his interest in classical culture, fostered in part by his tutor, JOHN SKELTON, Henry was considered by the humanists of his time to be an ideal monarch. He achieved recognition as a scholar, linguist, musician, and poet. He was particularly known for his lyrical compositions, several of which remain popular today. The Henrican court was also home to a great number of courtier poets, including Sir THOMAS WYATT, among others.

Before King Henry died, he prepared a will stating that Edward would be his heir, but that Mary was to follow him if Edward were to die childless, with Elizabeth taking the throne if Mary were to die without an heir. In this will, Henry seems to be a bit of a prophet, as each of his three children ruled after him in succession.

FURTHER READING

Marshall, Peter. *Religious Identities in Henry VIII's England.* Burlington, Vt.: Ashgate, 2006.

Mayer, Thomas F. *Thomas Starkey and the Commonweal: Humanist Politics and Religion in the Reign of Henry VIII* New York: Cambridge University Press, 1989.

Ridley, Jasper. *Henry VIII: Politics of Tyranny.* New York: Fromm International, 1985.

Melissa A. Harris

HENRY THE MINSTREL   See BLIND HARY.

HENRYSON, ROBERT (ca. 1425–ca. 1500)

By the 20th century, Robert Henryson was considered the most well-known and critically important of the MIDDLE SCOTS poets, a group which usually contains Henryson, JAMES I of Scotland, WILLIAM DUNBAR, and GAVIN DOUGLAS, along with some other minor names. However, Henryson's birth and death dates are unclear mainly because he was neither a well-known nor a popular writer while alive. Indeed, while most scholars' best guess is that his major period of production was around 1475, it can only be said with certainty that his work was in circulation sometime during the last half of the 15th century. Henryson lived in Dunfermline, in Fife, and he was master of the grammar school in the Benedictine abbey there. Dunbar's "LAMENT FOR THE MAKARIS" was published in 1508 and refers to Henryson's death, causing scholars to estimate it to around 1506.

During his life, three of Henryson's major poems— *The MORALL FABILLIS OF ESOPE THE PHRYGIAN* (a collection of fables demonstrating his facility with both ALLEGORY and realism), *The TESTAMENT OF CRESSEID* (a response to GEOFFREY CHAUCER's work on the same subject), and *Orpheus and Eurydice* (a unique contribution to the Orpheus tradition)—were certainly in circulation and known outside of the small group of Scottish poets. But even these were not always attributed to Henryson himself—*The Testament of Cresseid,* for example, was often mistakenly ascribed to Chaucer. In the 18th and 19th centuries, Henryson's reputation grew considerably with the publication (for the first time) of the rest of his poems, including one of his most studied oeuvres, "ROBENE AND MAKYNE" (a love poem, influenced by the pastourelle).

Along with William Dunbar, Henryson is considered the most heavily influenced by Geoffrey Chaucer of the Middle Scots poets and hence is one of the SCOTTISH CHAUCERIANS. In addition, Henryson's work is often compared to Chaucer's because of his use of iambic pentameter and RHYME ROYAL in his three long poems (*Morall Fabillis, Cresseid,* and *Orpheus*), as well as his "Chaucerian" use of irony in his narratives. But Henryson also shows facility with other techniques, such as ALLITERATION, throughout his poetry. The extent of Chaucer's influence on Henryson and his poetry has been and continues to be a point of debate among critics.

Henryson's influences clearly include, in addition to Chaucer, religious EXEGESIS, the notion of COURTLY LOVE and CHIVALRY, and the new ideas of the Renaissance being imported from Italy and France. His educated background is reflected in his use of different poetic styles as well as his sophisticated use of Latin in the *Morall Fabillis,* his direct allusions to Chaucer's *Troilus and Criseyde* in his own *Cresseid,* and his use of BOETHIUS in *Orpheus.* He is also clearly influenced by the Scots literary tradition and language, and his poetry reflects an understanding of local Scottish dialect and how that can intermingle with AUREATION and educated diction.

While literary criticism of Henryson's poetry really only began to flourish at the end of the 19th century, it has continued to grow exponentially. Early Henryson scholarship barely looked critically at *Morall Fabillis* and *Cresseid,* focusing instead on his short poems and their relationship to Scottish history or to Chaucer. Indeed, early 20th-century scholarship considered

Henryson mainly a humorist who presented a naïve outlook on everyday life in the Middle Ages. But the 1950s signaled a turning point where critics began to look at Henryson's work as multifaceted and more literary than had previously been considered. By the early 21st century, Henryson was often cited as the greatest of the Middle Scots poets. With every year, it seems that more and more scholars are evaluating Henryson and his work, revealing at each step how truly complex this Middle Scots poet actually is.

FURTHER READING

Fox, Denton. "Middle Scots Poets and Patrons." In *English Court Culture in the Later Middle Ages,* edited by V. J. Scattergood and J. W. Sherborne, 109–127. London: Duckworth, 1983.

Kindrick, Robert L. *Robert Henryson.* Boston: Twayne Publishers, 1979.

Scheps, Walter. "Chaucer and the Middle Scots Poets." *Studies in Scottish Literature* 22 (1987): 44–59.

Jennifer N. Brown

HERBERT, MARY SIDNEY, COUNTESS OF PEMBROKE (1561–1621)

The daughter of Sir Henry Sidney, sister of Sir ROBERT SIDNEY, EARL OF LEICESTER, and sister of SIR PHILIP SIDNEY, Mary Sidney was born on October 27, 1561, at Ticknall Place, Bewdley, Worcestershire. She was finely educated in Greek, Latin, French, Italian, and music. A favorite of ELIZABETH I, Mary was invited to court early, in 1575. In 1577, she married Henry Herbert, earl of Pembroke, with whom she had four children, including Philip, a patron of WILLIAM SHAKESPEARE. Soon after her marriage, Mary began a literary circle, to which she invited many learned individuals, including EDMUND SPENSER, MICHAEL DRAYTON, SAMUEL DANIEL, and SIR JOHN DAVIES. Widely celebrated for her PATRONAGE of the arts, she also achieved a reputation as an author.

After Philip Sidney's death in 1586, Mary Herbert devoted many of her writing projects to his memory, including *The Doleful Lay of Clorinda* and "TO THEE PURE SPRITE." She also completed the *SIDNEAN PSALMS* that Philip had begun before his demise. Mary Herbert was a prolific and skilled translator. For instance, in her translation of PETRARCH's *The Triumph of Death,* she is the first writer to echo Petrarch's terza rima scheme in English. (Terza rima usually consists of tercets in iambic pentameter.) However, when her husband died in 1601, Mary retired from public life and from writing. By the time JAMES VI/I ascended the English throne, Mary's sons had taken over her role as literary patron, and she retired to her estate in Wiltshire. There she commissioned an "architecturally innovative" house, and carried on a flirtation with Sir Matthew Lister. Mary died of smallpox on September 25, 1621, and was buried in Salisbury Cathedral.

Besides her obvious literary patronage, Mary Herbert served as a inspiration for aspiring female writers, including her niece, also Mary Sidney, later Lady Wroth (author of *Urania*), and Aemilia Lanyer, who dedicated her poem *Salve Deus Rex Judaeorum* (1611) to Mary Herbert. However, she also inspired male poets, such as John Donne and George Herbert, particularly through her skillful renditions of the Psalms.

See also "EVEN NOW THAT CARE," "TO THE THRICE-SACRED QUEEN ELIZABETH."

FURTHER READING

Hannay, Margaret P. *Philip's Phoenix: Mary Sidney, Countess of Pembroke*. New York: Oxford University Press, 1990.

Waller, Gary. *Mary Sidney, Countess of Pembroke: A Critical Study of Her Writings and Literary Milieu*. Salzburg: University of Salzburg Press, 1979.

Young, Frances B. *Mary Sidney, Countess of Pembroke*. London: David Nutt, 1912.

HEREBERT, WILLIAM See "WHAT IS HE, THIS LORDLING, THAT COMETH FROM THE FYHT."

HERO AND LEANDER CHRISTOPHER MARLOWE (1598) *Hero and Leander* is English literature's finest EPYLLION, or minor epic, a genre that became popular in the 1590s. Most scholars date its composition to 1593, the year of CHRISTOPHER MARLOWE's death, though it was not published until 1598, when two editions appeared. The first edition, published by Edward Blount, described *Hero and Leander* as an "unfinished tragedy" and printed it with no subdivisions. In the second edition, George Chapman divided Marlowe's poem into two parts, which he called Sestiads (from the poem's setting in Sestos), and added "arguments" (introductory summaries) to each. Chapman then added an additional four Sestiads of his own, which completed the traditional story of Hero and Leander. Both early editions thus indicate that Marlowe's poem was unfinished, though this view has been recently disputed.

Marlowe's poem is based on Musaeus's *Hero and Leander* (fifth century), although Marlowe has expanded greatly on his source. Marlowe also used the versions of the story in OVID's *Heroides* and the reference to it in Ovid's *Amores*, which he had translated. The meter of *Hero and Leander* is the HEROIC COUPLET that Marlowe had pioneered for *All Ovid's Elegies*.

The plot of *Hero and Leander* is simple. Hero is an extremely beautiful priestess who attracts many admirers. However, because of her vow of chastity, she has spurned all lovers. The equally beautiful Leander, who lives across the Hellespont in Abydos, is a young man who has not yet known love. When he attends a religious festival in Sestos, it is love at first sight for both of them. He speaks to her, declaring both his love and the foolishness of her preservation of her virginity. Due to her modesty and her religious vows, Hero is extremely confused; nonetheless, she invites Leander to her dwelling, a small tower by the sea. The action is interrupted at this point by a lengthy digression: Cupid's desire that the couple's love be blessed by the fates leads into an elaborate "myth" of Marlowe's own making, which begins with Mercury's love for a country maiden and ends with an explanation of scholarly poverty.

Following Hero's invitation, the lovers exchange letters, and Leander then visits Hero at her tower and stays the night. However, because of Leander's inexperience and Hero's concern for her chastity, their love play does not extend beyond kissing. Leander leaves in the morning, but his wearing of myrtle together with Hero's ribbon and ring makes their love apparent throughout Sestos and Abydos. His father tries to discourage their love, which only makes Leander more determined. Spying Hero's tower from across the Hellespont, he resolves to swim to her. As he swims, he encounters Neptune, who is attracted to him. The naïve Leander assumes that Neptune has mistaken him for a woman, until the god attempts seduction by relating the tale of a shepherd who loved a boy. Impatient to see Hero, Leander abruptly leaves, which angers the god into throwing his mace at Leander, which he regrets and calls back.

Leander arrives cold and naked at Hero's door, where he begs to rest upon her bed and bosom. When he lies down, she is embarrassed and hides beneath the covers. However, Leander's hands ensnare her. He speaks beguilingly to her, and then becomes more forceful. Still conflicted, she resists, but with only half her strength. Afterward she is ashamed and wants to leave Leander in the bed alone, but he grabs her and triumphantly admires her naked body while her blushing cheeks light up the room. Morning is now coming, and the poem (or fragment) ends with an elaborate mythological allusion in which night is mocked by the light of day and retreats to hell filled with anguish, shame, and rage, the emotions that Hero is feeling.

The magic of *Hero and Leander* lies not in its plot but in its tone and wit. It is at once comic and erotic, ironic and tender, satirical and sad. It recalls the CLASSICAL TRADITION but also includes "myths" of Marlowe's own creation. Events happen quickly, but Marlowe lingers over detailed descriptions and digressions. The focus is on sex and the tension between desire and innocence. For instance, Leander first seems to be an experienced and sophisticated seducer: "Who taught thee rhetoric to deceive a maid?" asks Hero (l. 338). Nonetheless, at other times he seems inexperienced and ignorant: He fails to recognize flirtatious overtures such as Hero's dropped fan, and when he and Hero are first together, he has no idea of what "else was to be done" beyond hugging and kissing (l. 536). Moreover, he is completely confounded by Neptune's attempt at seduction, despite the god's obvious intent.

The poem displays intriguing perspectives on human sexuality. The narrator has a number of stereotypical and even cynical comments on female sexuality: "All women are ambitious naturally" (l. 428) and "In such wars women use but half their strength" (l. 780). Other aspects of the poem reverse gendered conventions. Critics often comment about the mock BLAZON, which creates an image of Hero's beauty and erotic appeal through a description of her clothing rather than her body. Leander's beauty, however, is evoked through the traditional blazon, typically reserved for women. The poem lingers on his neck, shoulder, breast, belly, back, and eyes, ending with the assertion that it is men who are moved by such beauty: "For in his looks were all that men desire" (l. 84) explains Neptune's homoerotic attentions. Other scholars have noted the disparity between Hero's profession—priestess of Venus, goddess of love—and her apparent chastity. Feminist critics have also explored the violence of Hero and Leander's sexual encounter, particularly as a misogynist comment.

FURTHER READING

Brown, Georgia E. "Breaking the Canon: Marlowe's Challenge to the Literary Status Quo in *Hero and Leander.*" In *Marlowe, History, and Sexuality: New Critical Essays on Christopher Marlowe,* edited by Paul Whitfield White, 59–75. New York: AMS Press, 1998.

———. "Marlowe's Poems and Classicism." In *The Cambridge Companion to Christopher Marlowe,* edited by Patrick Cheney, 106–126. Cambridge: Cambridge University Press, 2004.

Cheney, Patrick, and Brian J. Striar. *The Collected Poems of Christopher Marlowe.* New York: Oxford University Press, 2006.

Martz, Louis L., ed. *Hero and Leander by Christopher Marlowe: A Facsimile of the First Edition.* London 1598. New York: Johnson Reprint Organization; Washington: The Folger Shakespeare Library, 1972.

Bruce E. Brandt

HEROIC COUPLET

This is a rhyming COUPLET written in iambic pentameter, a common poetic device used in EPICS and other heroic-themed poems.

HEYWOOD, JOHN

See "BALLAD ON THE MARRIAGE OF PHILIP AND MARY, A."

HOCCLEVE, THOMAS (THOMAS OCCLEVE) (ca. 1367–1426)

Little is known of Thomas Hoccleve's early life, although it has been suggested that his family originated from the village of Hockliffe in Bedfordshire. From 1387, we have records of his employment as a clerk at the Privy Seal office in Westminster, where he was employed to copy writs, petitions, grants, and other official documents. In his free time, he pursued a career as a poet, although he never obtained the quasi-laureate status of his contemporary,

JOHN LYDGATE. Hoccleve claimed to have known GEOFFREY CHAUCER personally, which is plausible considering the older poet retired to Westminster in 1399.

Hoccleve shared lodgings with other clerks at the Chancery Inns before he was married, and he humorously recounted this period in his mock-penitential confession, *LA MALE RÈGLE* (1405–06). The marriage, which he claims was a love match, probably occurred between 1399 and 1411. Although the position of a Privy Seal clerk was relatively secure in the later Middle Ages, Hoccleve frequently described himself as short of money, and a number of his poems included petitions to the king and other influential figures to ensure the clerks received their backdated annuity payments. He solicited aristocratic PATRONAGE for some of his poetry, a strategy that seems to have succeeded with his most popular poem, *The Regiment of Princes* (*De Regimine Principum,* 1411–12) a book of advice for the future Henry V, which survives in more than 40 manuscript copies. He may also have found occasional work as a scribe for the London book trade, judging by the appearance of his scribal hand in a production of JOHN GOWER's *CONFESSIO AMANTIS.*

Sometime around 1414, Hoccleve suffered some kind of mental breakdown, which he refers to in a collection of poems, which his editors have titled the *Series.* The *Series* describes the poet's efforts to come to terms with his illness and its aftermath, and movingly details how the crowd turns away from him in London, still doubting whether he has recovered his sanity. The *Series* is Hoccleve's most remarkable achievement and an extraordinarily self-reflective commentary on the act of poetic composition.

Thomas Hoccleve died in 1426, probably shortly after his retirement. His last years saw an increase in his literary activities as he copied out many of his poems and compiled his *Formulary* (1423–25), a set of scribal templates for the use of Privy Seal clerks, which has now become an invaluable resource for students of English administrative history.

Hoccleve's poetry has attracted scholarly attention because of the unusual extent to which he utilizes material from his own life in the presentation of his author-narrators. Unfortunately, this led some scholars to assume a straightforward correspondence between Hoccleve the writer and his poetic persona, an anxious, inept, and rather pitiful figure. While they have been more sensitive to the complexities of literary invention at work in Hoccleve's self-portrait, later critics have generally centered on the topics of madness, autobiography, and subjectivity when exploring his influence on the world of letters. This has tended to reinforce the image of the poet as a victim or misfit, either as a strangely self-conscious writer in a medieval world (although this presupposes that self-consciousness is an early modern development) or as a man sidelined from society by mental illness. Recent work, however, has sought to redress the balance through a revaluation of Hoccleve's literary talents.

FURTHER READING

Burrow, J. A. "Thomas Hoccleve." In *English Writers of the Late Middle Ages,* edited by M. C. Seymour, no. 1. Aldershot, Hampshire, U.K.: Varorium, 1994.

Knapp, Ethan. *The Bureaucratic Muse: Thomas Hoccleve and the Literature of Late Medieval England.* University Park: Pennsylvania State University Press, 2001.

Elizabeth Evershed

HOUSE OF FAME, THE GEOFFREY CHAUCER (ca. 1378–1380)

The House of Fame is GEOFFREY CHAUCER's second DREAM VISION poem, written many years after his first, *The BOOK OF THE DUCHESS.* Probably written after Chaucer's travels in Italy, it reflects his interest in the works of the Italian authors Dante and GIOVANNI BOCCACCIO, as well as the wide range of his reading, from VIRGIL and OVID to the Bible, as well as other authors of French and Latin texts.

The House of Fame shares elements of Chaucer's other dream visions: The narrator dreams after reading a book, and there is much interest in dream theory and the nature of love. Written in octosyllabic COUPLETS, the poem is composed of three books, all of which begin with either a proem (preface) or invocation—an address to a deity for aid, a classical literary convention followed in many of the works that are discussed in the poem. The original manuscripts of this text are lost, and the later three remaining copies are all incomplete, leaving scholars with some speculation as to whether Chaucer had finished the work or had intentionally left it incomplete.

Book 1 of *The House of Fame* opens with a proem discussing dreams and dream theory; this leads into an invocation to the god of sleep to help him tell the tale of his dream. The dream begins with the narrator, Geffrey, finding himself in a glass temple, its walls lined with paintings of the gods and with brass tablets engraved with the text of Virgil's *Aeneid.* Through this, Chaucer retells the tale, with great attention paid to Dido's plight. Geffrey contemplates the many loves lost and betrayed in classic literature and leaves the temple to find a beautiful golden eagle soaring above him.

In book 2, after pleading to Venus to assist him in telling his tale, Geffrey resumes the story. The golden eagle swoops down and picks up Geffrey in "hys grymme pawes stronge" (l. 541) and tells him that he is to be taken to the House of Fame as a reward for his hermit-like life of reading and writing late into the night after a long day's work. As they travel, they embark on a long discussion of philosophy and the meaning of sound and language; ultimately, they tour the cosmos, discussing the sun, stars, and galaxies. They soon arrive at the house and hear the cacophony of voices within the house, both of "feir speche and chidynges" (l. 1028).

Book 3 begins with the narrator's appeal to Apollo, god of light, to grant him abilities in the "art poetical" (l. 1095), so that he may describe the House of Fame. The dream begins again, and the narrator climbs a high rock to reach the house, which is built on a feeble foundation of ice. The house is an ornately decorated castle, carved with the names of the many who have achieved fame. It is filled with music, talking, crowds, and magicians, lending it a carnival-like atmosphere. Geffrey then enters a court of royalty and the wealthy as Fame arrives: a goddess with many eyes, changing in size and shape, with winged feet. The walls of the hall are lined with portraits of writers, poets, and historians, representing their famous subjects. The crowds within beg the goddess for fame, which is granted arbitrarily by the fickle deity.

Speaking to Aeolus, the god of the winds, Geffrey admits that he does not seek fame but wishes to find tidings, or tales of love, for his books. He leaves the House of Fame and comes to the House of Daedalus, a cage-like house of twigs, seemingly full of the tidings

that Geffrey was looking for. But all that is passed on is gossip and lies, blown about by the winds. Frustrated, he finds a group of men talking of love but is left unfulfilled as they run away when he approaches. Geffrey finally finds a man who seems to be of "gret auctoritee" (l. 2158), leading the reader to believe that he has finally come upon someone who can offer "some good to lernen" (l. 1088), but as soon as the man is found, the text ends, left unfinished. It is not known if the work was ever finished, if it was finished and lost, or if Chaucer intentionally left this incomplete ending to prove just how unreliable a text can be.

The House of Fame is a self-conscious literary text, concerned with the poet and the poetic tradition, where even the narrator, Geffrey, dreams after reading late into the night. The dream is about literature and fame, specifically about how to achieve it as an author, and whether fame and renown can be trusted. While adopting the traditional dream-vision forms, Chaucer uses this poem to turn many literary traditions on their heads. Many aspects of the poem parody the revered works of men "of gret auctoritee" (l. 2158), such as Virgil's *Aeneid,* Ovid's *Metamorphoses,* and Dante's *Divine Comedy.* Chaucer also pokes fun at himself through Geffrey, portraying him as a bookworm who lives like a hermit, reading into the late hours of the night until he is dazed and as "domb as any stoon" (l. 656).

Analysis of the poem over the years has discussed Chaucer's use of other EPIC poems and their authors, such as his possible parody of the *Divine Comedy,* and the significance of the many epic and literary texts that Chaucer acknowledges with *The House of Fame.* Recent criticism also focuses on discourse, language, and the "voice"—Chaucer's narrative voice and subversive voices within the text, such as the voice of the eagle, an unusual mouthpiece for their debate on discourse, and Chaucer's attention to Dido, giving her a freedom in speech that she never had in the *Aeneid.*

FURTHER READING

Kordecki, Lesley. "Subversive Voices in Chaucer's *House of Fame." Exemplaria* 11, no. 1 (1999): 53–77.

Steinberg, Glenn A. "Chaucer in the Field of Cultural Production: Humanism, Dante, and the *House of Fame." The Chaucer Review* 35, no. 2 (2000): 182–203.

Catherine Ann Perkins

HUNDRED YEARS' WAR (1337–1453)

This misleadingly named episode in history featured violent struggle that drew families, empires, and economic interests into a series of wars between 1337 and 1453. The war owes its origins to a history of conflict between the French and English that dates to at least the NORMAN CONQUEST in 1066. In the intervening centuries, English and French interests mixed frequently on the continent, and by the early 14th century Edward III of England enjoyed control of extensive holdings in France. When King Charles IV of France died without leaving a male heir to the French throne, the closest potential successor to the throne was Edward III of England, son of Charles IV's sister. French nobility invoked ancient laws in order to avoid this, and eventually crowned Philip of Valois, a cousin of previous Capetian kings, Philip VI.

Both Edward and Philip were acutely aware of the monetary importance of controlling commercial trade in the neighboring cloth-making region of Flanders, which depended on imported English wool and had a history of rebellion against their French rulers. A similar feudal conflict occurred over Edward's control of Aquitaine, where wine exports had become a valuable part of the English economy. Philip insisted that Edward pay him extensive and formal homage for these valuable fiefdoms, but Edward, a king in his own right in England, refused to agree to an act that would make him subservient to the French king. Instead, Edward used the dispute as an opportunity to ally himself with an artisan rebellion in Flanders against the French and ultimately to declare war.

The ensuing war pitted two very differently armed and trained forces against one another in a struggle driven by economic interests, chivalric ideals, and dynastic ambitions. Edward, whose knights were seasoned by long experience fighting in Scotland and Wales, took a practical approach. He raised money through Parliament, drew on international loans, and organized an army that combined armed knights with large companies of footsoldiers armed with pikes and longbows. By contrast, Philip took his rhetoric about CHIVALRY seriously. He expected to defeat the English with an army of heavily armored knights, each backed up by further ranks of lightly armored vassals.

The English enjoyed early successes at sea and at Crécy (1346), then later at Poitiers (1356), which ended with the capture of the Philip's successor, King John II. As the spread of the BLACK DEATH compounded the social and economic toll of the war, both sides sought a settlement in 1360. The English renounced their claims to the French throne but were granted control over a much larger territory in and around Aquitaine.

Literary scholars will recognize many of the actors of the final period of the Hundred Years' War from WILLIAM SHAKESPEARE's work, as well as from contemporary BALLADS such as "The AGINCOURT CAROL." The war(s) also allowed for the further development of a uniquely English identity and set the stage for British imperialism.

See also WARS OF THE ROSES.

FURTHER READING
Seward, Desmond. *The Hundred Years War: The English in France, 1337–1453.* London: Atheneum, 1978.

Daniel Ringrose

HYPERBOLE

From the Latin term meaning "excess," this is figurative language that depends on deliberate use of exaggeration or extravagant language; intentional overstatement. Used in both literary and nonliterary texts, both poetry and prose, hyperbole is a staple of rhetoric. In poetry, hyperbole is found in numerous genres, from ROMANCES to love poems to SONNETS. For instance, CHAUCER relies upon hyperbole to emphasize his position in "To ROSAMUNDE," and in Sonnet 94 from *ASTROPHIL AND STELLA*, hyperbole and APOSTROPHE combine for a dramatic effect.

See also SONNET.

FURTHER READING
Stanivukovic, Goran V. "'Mounting Above The Truthe': On Hyperbole in English Renaissance Literature." *Forum for Modern Language Studies* 41, no. 1 (2007): 9–33.

I

IAMBIC PENTAMETER The most common meter of English poetry, iambic pentameter is an unrhymed line containing five iambs (feet), alternating unstressed and stressed syllables. This terminology is derived from the quantitative meter of classical Greek poetry, which consists of a short syllable followed by a long syllable. In English, it is the basis of many major poetic forms, such as BLANK VERSE and HEROIC COUPLETS, among numerous others.

Although traditional iambic pentameter consists solely of iambs and has 10 syllables, this does not need to be the case. Many poets, especially skilled ones such as WILLIAM SHAKESPEARE, vary the rhythm of their lines while still maintaining the overall scheme of iambic pentameter.

See also SONNET.

FURTHER READING
Halle, Morris, and Samuel Jay Keyser. *English Stress: Its Forms, Its Growth, and Its Role in Verse.* New York: Harper and Row, 1971.

"I CARE NOT FOR THESE LADIES"
THOMAS CAMPION (1601) This bawdy song was first printed with music by THOMAS CAMPION himself in *A BOOKE OF AYRES*. The first STANZA sets up an opposition between courtly "Ladies" and Amarillis, described as a "wanton countrey maide" (l. 4), an obscene pun that establishes from the beginning the lewd tone that characterizes this poem. This innuendo is continued in the REFRAIN, particularly in the line "when we come where comfort is" (l. 9), where the ALLITERATION helps to recall the "countrey maide" of the first stanza. The refrain also asserts that Amarillis has an inexhaustible sexual appetite, and that, despite her feigned struggle against the poet's advances, "she never will say no" (l. 10), reflecting 16th-century attitudes to sexuality in a way that may prove uncomfortable for a modern reader.

The poet asserts that "nature art disdaineth" (l. 4), and this implies an opposition between the artifice traditionally associated with the court and the simplicity and "naturalness" of the country, which is continued throughout the poem. The second stanza figures the willingness of Amarillis to engage in sexual activity as a gift of "fruit and flowers" (l. 12). This is presented as a model of reciprocality in contrast with the one-sidedness of relationships with courtly "Ladies," where the lover has effectively bought love with "gold" (l. 15). The third stanza portrays the location of lovemaking as among "mosse and leaves unbought" (l. 24) in contrast to the "beds by strangers wrought," where courtly assignations take place. This recalls the expense that the poet complained of in the second stanza, but it also suggests the unnecessary complexity of formal courtship alluded to by its association with "art." The opposition between the artifice of the court and the "naturalness" of the country thus serves as a way of invoking an ideally honest space, where human relationships can operate free from stifling social conventions.

FURTHER READING

Lindley, David. *Thomas Campion.* Leiden: E. J. Brill, 1986.

Susan L. Anderson

IDEAS MIRROUR (OVERVIEW) MICHAEL DRAYTON (1594–1619)

MICHAEL DRAYTON's *Ideas Mirrour* first appeared in 1594 as a series of 51 SONNETS with two dedicatory poems: one to Anthony Cooke and the other to MARY SIDNEY HERBERT, countess of Pembroke. By the time of its final version in 1619, *Ideas Mirrour* contained 63 sonnets.

Along with SIR PHILIP SIDNEY, EDMUND SPENSER, and SAMUEL DANIEL, Drayton was a pioneer of the sonneteering craze in Elizabethan England. His work was long considered to have been one of the most significant influences on WILLIAM SHAKESPEARE's sonnets, though more recently this influence has been called into question.

Drayton's sonnets, called *amours,* are written largely in the ENGLISH SONNET form, with each poem consisting of three QUATRAINS written in an *abab* rhyme scheme and ending in one final, rhymed COUPLET. However, Drayton does vary this formula in some of his poems; in two of them, for example, he includes an extra quatrain, while in others the rhyme scheme for the quatrain is *abba* and not *abab.*

The entire SONNET SEQUENCE is inspired by a woman that Drayton labels Idea, a name he utilized in some of his other poems; it probably comes from a French sonnet sequence called *L'Idée* by Claude de Pontoux. Idea herself, whom Drayton alludes to throughout the piece, has been identified by critics as Lady Anne Rainsford, née Goodere. Anne Goodere was the daughter of Sir Henry Goodere, Drayton's patron during his youth, and the two young people likely shared a friendship. Though Anne married within her social circle, Drayton remained faithful to his poetic love, and referred to her in several of his works, including *IDEA THE SHEPHEARDS GARLAND, The Barons Wars,* and his magnum opus, *Poly-Olbion.* Critics have often speculated about the exact nature of the relationship between Drayton and Lady Rainsford, but there is no evidence to indicate whether or not they were lovers.

The poems in the sonnet collection vary in their excellence: While critics note that several are worthy examples of Elizabethan sonneteering and Sonnet 61 is a veritable masterpiece, many are also pedestrian and common. Nonetheless, *Ideas Mirrour* was popular from its release. Drayton, who constantly revised and reissued his earlier works, made numerous alterations to the text between 1594 and his death in 1631. He issued wholly new versions of the sonnet sequence in 1599, 1600, 1602, 1605, and 1619. Changes included alterations within the poems themselves, the addition of new sonnets, the omission of others, and ultimately the rearrangement of the entire sequence. Critics contend that Drayton's changes wholly altered the scope of his work, and that the *Ideas Mirrour* of 1594 is not the same text that was released in 1619 (which was reissued under the simpler title of *Idea*). The individual sonnets that follow here are the numbers of the 1619 edition, but the text of the 1599 version.

FURTHER READING
Brink, Jean R. *Michael Drayton Revisited.* Boston: Twayne, 1990.

Buxton, John, ed. *The Poems of Michael Drayton.* Cambridge, Mass.: Harvard University Press, 1953.

Elton, Oliver. *Michael Drayton: A Critical Study.* New York: Russell & Russell, 1966.

Whitaker, Lemuel. "The Sonnets of Michael Drayton." *Modern Philology* 1, no. 4 (1904): 563–567.

Michael Cornelius

Ideas Mirrour: Sonnet 12 ("To nothing fitter can I thee compare") MICHAEL DRAYTON (1599)

Sonnet 12, also known as "Amour XII," first appeared in the 1599 edition of *Ideas Mirrour* as Sonnet 14 before being renumbered for the final 1619 edition. The entire SONNET SEQUENCE concerns the poet's love for and unswerving dedication to a woman he calls Idea, who has been identified by critics as Lady Anne Rainsford, a childhood friend of the author's.

In Sonnet 12, which MICHAEL DRAYTON dedicates "To the soul" (something he also does for Sonnet 13), the author interweaves a complex CONCEIT wherein Idea, his love, is considered to be a physical manifestation of such divine gifts as will, reason, memory, sense, conscience, and love, while conversely personifying these traits through the guise of Idea: "In judging, Reason only is her name; / In speedy apprehension it is

Sense; / In right or wrong they call her Conscience" (ll. 9–11). In extending the conceit around his unnamed (at least in this sonnet) "she," Drayton concludes by bringing to the poem back to himself: "These of the Soul the several functions be / Which my Heart, lightened by thy love, doth see" (ll. 13–14). Sonnet 12 reflects the author's desire to utilize the metaphysical genre of poetry, later popularized by John Donne, which emphasized spiritual and intellectual pieces over lighter, love-inspired works.

The poem is written in the ENGLISH SONNET form, but its three quatrains rhyme in an *abba* scheme rather than the more common *abab* pattern before ending in a rhyming COUPLET. It utilizes iambic pentameter, though the meter is not as strong as in Drayton's other SONNETS. Still, as an early example of metaphysical poetry, Sonnet 12 remains one of Drayton's more introspective and thus interesting works.

See also *IDEAS MIRROUR* (OVERVIEW), PERSONIFICATION.

Michael Cornelius

Ideas Mirrour: Sonnet 13 ("You're not alone when you are still alone") MICHAEL DRAYTON (1594)

Sonnet 13, also known as "Amour XIII," was part of the original 1594 collection called *Ideas Mirrour,* but it was the 21st poem in the sequence, being renumbered to the 13th piece by the final edition of 1619. The entire SONNET SEQUENCE concerns the poet's love for and unswerving dedication to a woman he calls Idea, who has been identified by critics as Lady Anne Rainsford, a childhood friend of the author's.

In Sonnet 13, which MICHAEL DRAYTON dedicates "To the soul" (something he also does for Sonnet 12), the author utilizes the same metaphysical genre he used in the 12th SONNET. Yet while the subject matter of Sonnet 12 is inspiring and hopeful, Sonnet 13 reflects the grim tone of Sonnet 8. The poems use the metaphor of decay, but in Sonnet 13, the decay is focused on inanimate objects: "Metals do waste and fret with canker's rust, / The diamond shall once consume to dust, / And freshest colours with foul stains disgraced" (ll. 2–4). Even the author's words, immortal in Sonnet 6, are now fallible to decay: "Letters and lines we see are soon defaced" (l. 1). In some ways, the sonnet reads as a response to Dray-

ton's critics: "Paper and ink can paint but naked words, / To write with blood of force offends the sight" (ll. 5–6). It is also, however, a rumination on the act of writing itself and the frivolous nature of fame. The "shadow" of Drayton's lady Idea encourages him to continue writing, despite the harshest criticism or the fleeting wanes of fame: "That everything whence shadow doth proceed / May in my shadow my love's story read" (ll. 13–14). Drayton concludes, somewhat triumphantly, that his work will live on after his death, if only as a reflection of his great love.

Sonnet 13 is written in the ENGLISH SONNET form, but its three quatrains rhyme in an *abba* scheme rather than the more common *abab* pattern before ending in a rhyming COUPLET. The subject of his own writing appeared consistently throughout Drayton's works, and Sonnet 13 remains a key example of this aspect of the poet's oeuvre.

See also *IDEAS MIRROUR* (OVERVIEW).

Michael Cornelius

Ideas Mirrour: Sonnet 61 ("Since there's no help, come, let us kiss and part") MICHAEL DRAYTON (1594)

Sonnet 61, also known as "Amour LXI," is MICHAEL DRAYTON's most famous SONNET. It held the same place in all versions of *Ideas Mirrour.* The opening line is remarkable: "Since there's no help, come, let us kiss and part" (l. 1). Drayton has realized the futility of pursuing his lady love and asks only for one final kiss before eternally giving up the chase. Yet in the second line, he changes his mind: "Nay, I have done, you get no more of me" (l. 2). Drayton has resolved to end this love forever: "Shake hands for ever, cancel all our vows, / And when we meet at any time again / Be it not seen in either of our brows / That we one jot of former love retain" (ll. 5–8). The rest of the sonnet concerns the effects losing his love has on the poet and on passion: "Passion speechless lies, / When Faith is kneeling by his bed of death / And Innocence is closing up his eyes" (ll. 10–12). The use of PERSONIFICATION emphasizes the poet's personal devastation. Though the speaker recovers in the final COUPLET, the poem remains a devastatingly simple treatise on the potential woes that are in wooing, and it has long been considered one of the finest poems in any genre that deals with the heartbreak of lost love.

Sonnet 61 is written in the ENGLISH SONNET form, with three QUATRAINS rhyming in an *abab* scheme and a final rhyming couplet. It is universally hailed as the masterpiece achievement of Drayton's poetic career and is often considered the best sonnet produced in Elizabethan times.

See also *IDEAS MIRROUR* (OVERVIEW).

Michael Cornelius

Ideas Mirrour: Sonnet 63 ("Truce, gentle Love, a parley now I crave") MICHAEL DRAYTON (1594)

Sonnet 63, also known as "Amour LXIII," was the 55th poem in the 1599 collection called *Ideas Mirrour,* but it was renumbered to the 63rd and last piece by the final edition of 1619. The entire SONNET SEQUENCE concerns the poet's love for and unswerving dedication to a woman he calls Idea, a woman who has been identified by critics as Lady Anne Rainsford, a childhood friend of the author's.

In Sonnet 63, the final SONNET in the sequence, MICHAEL DRAYTON compares love to war and offers a "truce" to "gentle Love"—"a parley now I crave, / Methinks 'tis long since first these wars begun" (ll. 1–2). Though Drayton has failed in his amorous endeavors, he declares the conflict a draw: "Nor thou nor I the better yet can have; / Bad is the match where neither party won" (ll. 4–5). Drayton's suggestion that neither party was the winner in the affair offers critics interesting speculation on the exact nature of his relationship with Lady Anne Rainsford—the Idea of the title—suggesting perhaps that his lady returns to her husband only out of wifely duty. Still, it is more likely that Drayton is rationalizing a draw out of defeat: Having been rejected by Idea, he cannot face the heartbreak he now must endure. The point is almost moot, since the sonnet is written not to Idea but to Love itself, and Drayton's gently jocular proposal for a truce with Love resembles a defiant cry for Love to release the author from his bonds: ". . . if no thing but death will serve thy turn" (l. 9). "Gentle Love" has become an enemy to the author: "Do what thou canst, rase, massacre, and burn, / Let the world see the utmost of thy hate" (ll. 11–12). Drayton's final message of defiance suggests that,

though the sonnet sequence is over, the author's battle with Love will never be complete.

Sonnet 63 is written in the ENGLISH SONNET form, with three QUATRAINS rhyming in an *abab* scheme, followed by a final rhyming COUPLET. The poem represents a strong and apt ending to the author's ruminations about the nature of love.

See also *IDEAS MIRROUR* (OVERVIEW).

Michael Cornelius

IDEA THE SHEPHEARDS GARLAND (AMOURS) MICHAEL DRAYTON (1593, revised 1606)

Idea the Shepheards Garland is a series of nine ECLOGUES, or PASTORAL poems. The nine poems represent the nine Muses, and MICHAEL DRAYTON organized his piece so that the first four eclogues are joined with the last four, causing the text to come full circle and thus resemble, in spirit, a garland adorning a lover's neck. The individual poems also represent different genres within the pastoral tradition, including pastoral ELEGY, eulogy, and debate.

Idea the Shepheards Garland was inspired by EDMUND SPENSER's *The SHEPHEARDES CALENDER* (1579), but the piece eschews the typical Renaissance moralizing often found in pastorals and instead focuses on the author's own woes with love, interspersed with praise to other noted figures. For instance, the third eclogue is in praise of Queen ELIZABETH I, while the fourth is a lament for SIR PHILIP SIDNEY, and the sixth laments several departed worthies of England, including MARY SIDNEY HERBERT, countess of Pembroke.

FURTHER READING

Brink, Jean R. *Michael Drayton Revisited.* Boston: Twayne, 1990.

Buxton, John, ed. *The Poems of Michael Drayton.* Cambridge, Mass.: Harvard University Press, 1953.

Elton, Oliver. *Michael Drayton: A Critical Study.* New York: Russell & Russell, 1966.

Michael Cornelius

"I FIND NO PEACE, AND ALL MY WAR IS DONE" ("DESCRIPTIONS OF THE CONTRARIOUS PASSIONS IN A LOVER") SIR THOMAS WYATT (1557) This SONNET,

one of SIR THOMAS WYATT's most well-known, appears in two manuscript versions and was also printed in *TOTTEL'S MISCELLANY* in 1557 with the title "Description of the contrarious passions in a lover." The poem is a translation of a sonnet by the Italian poet laureate PETRARCH, upon whom Wyatt relied for the vast majority of his Italian sources.

The structural principle governing this poem is a sustained use of antitheses, a process that later became known as Petrarchan paradox. Thus, when we read "peace," we can expect "war" as a counterpoint; "hope" will echo "fear"; a "laugh" will follow "pain"; and, of course, "love" becomes inextricable from "hate." It may be argued that what begins as a means of expressing internal division is reduced to a formulaic litany of oppositions that dissipate any sense of genuine feeling that may or may not have been the poem's impetus. However, the closing line makes the cumulative effect of these antitheses powerful.

The sonnet's antithetical dynamics work on at least two levels of interpretation. The first signifies the pain over the inability to achieve resolution, whilst the second displays an obvious pleasure in the organization of the extremes into poetic form. These two factors taken together produce a speaker who takes a somewhat masochistic delight in his misery, which underlines and circumscribes the antithetical framework of the sonnet: Pain is pleasure, or "my delight is causer of this strife" (l. 14), and vice versa. This reading is reinforced by the ITALIAN (PETRARCHAN) SONNET form's tendency to discuss its own process. Thus, the "prison" of line 5 refers both to the psychological state of the "I" who appears in almost every line, and also to the sonnet itself, while the "device" that follows two lines later points toward the rhetorical "device" of antithesis. It is almost, then, the voice of the sonnet itself that opens the concluding section (the SESTET): "Without eyen I see, and without tongue I plain" (l. 9).

The sonnet is a faithful translation of Petrarch, and part of its fidelity lies in the transportation of the original author's "delight" in writing it. All of "this strife," symbolized antithetically, is produced by a pleasure in structuring. Wyatt's version exemplifies the bringing of order to chaos through writing, and the feeling of catharsis through telling.

FURTHER READING
Daalder, Joost, ed. *Sir Thomas Wyatt: Collected Poems.* Oxford and New York: Oxford University Press, 1975.
Kirkpatrick, Robin. *English and Italian Literature from Dante to Shakespeare: A Study of Source, Analogue and Divergence.* London and New York: Longman, 1995.

William T. Rossiter

"I HAVE A GENTIL COK" ANONYMOUS (14th century)

This medieval lyric is composed in the standard BALLAD STANZA, a QUATRAIN with the rhyme scheme *abcb*. Unlike many other BALLADS, however, it does not feature a consistent REFRAIN. The first three STANZAS begin with "I have a gentil cok," but the last two start with "His legges ben of asor" (l. 13) and "His eynen arn of cristal" (l. 17), respectively. It also features an interlocking stanza system, particularly among the first three. "I have a gentil cok," is, of course, repeated. As well, the third line in stanza 2—"His comb is of red corel" (l. 7)—is repeated in stanza three (l. 11). Additionally, there are structural repetitions: "Comen he is of gret" (l. 6) pairs with "Comen he is of kinde" (l. 10); "His tayel is of jet" (l. 8) matches with "His tail is of inde" (l. 12). The final two stanzas also display parallel structures, but not as overtly. Lines 13, 15, and 17 begin "His legges ben . . . ," "His spores arn . . . ," and "His eynen arn . . . ," The interlacing serves to reinforce the double entendre on which the lyric rests.

Essentially, this lyric is an extended bawdy pun, with "cok" standing for "rooster" and "penis." Every attribute and action is applicable to both cocks. Additional wordplays further enhance the effect. For instance, "tail" is a posterior appendage on an animal, but it is also slang for genitals. There are also a number of implied references to penetration. For example, the narrator describes the cock's spurs, which are used in mating. The final two lines signify consummation: "And every night he percheth him / in min ladyes chaumber" (ll. 18–19), while also alluding to alertness—presumably the cock is there to serve as an alarm clock, thus returning to the image in the opening stanza ("He doth me risen erly," l. 3).

See also MIDDLE ENGLISH LYRICS AND BALLADS.

FURTHER READING

Baird-Lange, Lorrayne Y. "Symbolic Ambivalence in 'I Haue a Gentil Cok.'" *Fifteenth-Century Studies* 11 (1985): 1–5.

Roscow, Gregory. "'Of Red Scorel' in 'I Haue a Gentil Cok.'" *English Studies* 83, no. 1 (2002): 6–8.

INGLIS, ESTHER   See TUDOR WOMEN POETS.

"IN PRAISE OF MARY" ANONYMOUS (late 13th century)

The majority of Middle English lyrics dealing with religious themes were composed anonymously. This French-influenced religious lyric in praise of the Virgin Mary employs the same erotic language as secular lyrics. The text is written in the Southeast Midlands dialect of MIDDLE ENGLISH. The narrator, presented as Mary's "knight" suffering from LOVESICKNESS, begs her mercy and compliments her by contrasting her with her antitype, Eve.

The first five stanzas contain numerous phrases and metrical forms from Latin hymns as well as conventions from secular love poetry. Mary is "My swete Levedy" (l. 7) as well as "Hevene Quene" (l. 1) who must hear and "rew" (l. 8), or take pity on him. There is no other lady more "fair, "shene" (beautiful), "rudy" (bright), "softe," or "swote." Yet Mary's praise is attached to the "new light" (l. 11) that will spring from her when the Holy Ghost "reste[s] upon" (l. 18) her. Her child will bring humanity's healing "monkunnes bote" (l. 19), and "alesen" (l. 20) or delivery of the soul. In alignment with COURTLY LOVE, the narrator pledges himself to Mary's service both "to honde and to fote" (l. 23). These first five stanzas conclude in a prayer. The lover's voice declares that all his "drauct" (draught) (leaning, l. 36) is "lovebende"—that is, bound by love to Mary, who is his shield from Satan. The use of the word *drauct*, which also creates connotations of desire, attraction, inclination, education, and drink, like a love potion with Mary as the full vessel, was included in many secular lyrics.

Scholars debate whether the last three STANZAS were part of the original text because they are more impersonal and formal than the preceding stanzas. Stanza 6 elaborates on what has occurred before: "Thy love us broughte eche [eternal] wunne [bliss]" (l. 47) because she bore "thine Helere" (the Savior, l. 56). Stanzas 7 and 8 are more doctrinal and do not continue the courtly love conventions. Stanza 7 focuses on Mary's pregnancy and delivery without labor pains, while the prayer that ends stanza 8 requests Mary's assistance from hell's "wrake," or vengeance.

The main theme of this lyric is to depict Mary's role as intercessor. The lyric begins by addressing Mary as queen of heaven and ends with her protecting supplicants from hell, an image largely spread through the *Ave Maria* in which Mary's prayers for sinners at the hour of their death can keep them from punishment. In addition, this lyric begins with a VERNACULAR antiphon (verse from Scripture) and draws on the typological significance of the "blossom from one root" from Isaiah 11 (the coming of Christ) and Gideon's fleece in Judges 6 (the soaking of the fleece by dew figuring Mary's impregnation by the Holy Spirit) to present her as a contrast to Eve, who led humanity away from Heaven.

See also MIDDLE ENGLISH LYRICS AND BALLADS, VIRGIN LYRICS.

FURTHER READING

Saupe, Karen. *Middle English Marian Lyrics*. Kalamazoo: Western Michigan University, 1998.

R. L. Smith

"I SING OF A MAIDEN" ANONYMOUS (15th century)

Though this brief religious lyric is simple, many scholars have deemed it among the best of the medieval English lyrics for its effortless elegance and beauty. The subject of the poem is the Blessed Virgin Mary, Mother of God. She is introduced in the first STANZA as a woman who is "makeles" and who chose the king of kings for her son. The poet puns on the word *makeles*, which means spotless, matchless, and mateless. In other words, she is perfect and without blemishes; there is no one in the world like her, and she has no husband (that is, she is a virgin). The following three stanzas describe the immaculate conception, each likening Christ's approach to his mother's womb to dew in April. The final stanza reminds the reader that there was never another like Mary and asserts that she was a fitting mother for God.

Many scholars have noted that the first stanza is unusual in that it emphasizes that Mary chose Christ as her son, rather than focusing on why God might have chosen Mary. This mention of Mary's choice underscores the reciprocal nature of the conception; God was willing for Mary to bear Christ as a son, and she was willing to do it. The union of the human and divine depicted here is both mutual and gentle, as the subsequent images of dew and stillness, or silence, indicate.

The following three stanzas, which deal with the Immaculate Conception itself, contain a great deal of religious symbolism. Dew was a common medieval symbol for the Holy Ghost, and April signifies the rebirth and regeneration that occur in springtime, and, correspondingly, the new beginning for humankind that Christ's birth brought about. Throughout the three stanzas, the dew falls in three different places. Just as Christ is characterized as dew in these lines, Mary is symbolized in turn as the grass, the flower, and the spray. The grass might refer to Mary's humility; the flower was a medieval symbol for virginity, and Mary was often associated in medieval literature with the rose; the spray can be taken as a reference to the outcome of the union between the human and divine. The spray seems to refer to the rod of Jesse—a flowering branch symbolically representing the birth of Christ to Mary. More than just three different representations of Mary, these symbols are also steps in a progression: The dew creates growth from grass to flower to tree.

The structure of the poem is also significant. There are five stanzas in the poem, and five is a number associated strongly with Mary in medieval literature. Two of the most important associations are her five joys and the fact that her name in Latin is Maria, which has five letters. Additionally, the rhyme scheme is noteworthy. The final words in the second and fourth HALF-LINES of each stanza rhyme, but in the middle three stanzas the first and third half-lines also rhyme "stylle" and "aprille." This repetition underscores the importance of those terms to the poem, thereby emphasizing the idea of the Immaculate Conception as a peaceful new beginning.

This particular work was designed to be sung as a CAROL, and as such it has enjoyed continued popularity into the modern era. "I Sing of a Maiden" is still often reprinted in collections of carols to be sung at Christmas.

See also MIDDLE ENGLISH LYRICS AND BALLADS, VIRGIN LYRICS.

FURTHER READING

Brown, Carleton, ed. *Religious Lyrics of the 15th Century.* Oxford: Clarendon, 1939.

Manning, Stephen. "I Syng of a Myden." *PMLA* 75 (1960): 8–12.

Kathryn C. Wymer

ITALIAN (PETRARCHAN) SONNET

Considered the traditional SONNET (14-line poem) form, the Italian, or Petrarchan, sonnet arises from the Italian literary tradition but was popularized in the 14th century by PETRARCH (Francesco Petrarca), thus giving rise to its distinctive name. The form usually consists of an OCTAVE and a SESTET. The octave, or octet, presents a narrative, a proposition, or a question, while the sestet provides the conclusion, response, or answer. The rhyme scheme of the octave is typically *abbaabba*. The sestet is generally more flexible, following one of three rhyme schemes: *cdecde, cdcdcd,* or *cdedce*. Of course, some sonnets utilize other variants.

SIR THOMAS WYATT and HENRY HOWARD, EARL OF SURREY are credited with introducing Italian sonnets to England through translations of Petrarch's works. The adaptation into a SONNET SEQUENCE was popularized by SIR PHILIP SIDNEY's *ASTROPHIL AND STELLA,* which was composed mostly of Italian-form sonnets.

See also ENGLISH SONNET.

"I. W. TO HER UNCONSTANT LOVER" ISABELLA WHITNEY (1567)

This is the first poem in ISABELLA WHITNEY's first book of poetry, *The Copy of a Letter.* As the title of this poem suggests, the speaker is I. W., or Isabella Whitney, and she is writing a letter to an unfaithful, or "unconstant," lover. She begins by telling her faithless lover that she has heard he is going to be married, in spite of his attempts to keep the fact secret, or "close" (l. 1). Whitney then begins to alternate between speaking as a jilted woman who reminds her lover of what he is giving up by abandoning her and speaking as a counselor offering her former lover advice.

First she says that she always wished him well and always will, and that if he is determined to be a husband, she hopes God will send him a good wife. But then she reminds him that he will always be able to boast about how faithful she was, and she suggests that her love could be his again if he wanted it. She gives up this hope since he is going to marry; however, she suggests that if he needs to marry, he could marry her and so keep the promises he made.

At this point Whitney makes the first of many classical allusions. She tells her love to choose between honesty or "Sinon's trade" (l. 28). Sinon, the Greek soldier who allowed himself to be captured by the Trojans and then persuaded them to take the Trojan Horse into their city, was a symbol of deception and treachery. Whitney also mentions many other treacherous men from classical mythology, such as Aeneas, who abandoned his lover Dido; Theseus, who deserted Ariadne; and Jason, who betrayed Medea after she had saved his life several times. She notes the shame attached to such people, and she advises her lover not to follow such examples, nor to be like Paris, who brought about the destruction of Troy by betraying his host, Agamemnon, and running away with Agamemnon's wife, Helen. Instead, she counsels her paramour to be her Troilus, or her faithful lover, since Troilus, a brother of Paris, died faithful to his lover, Cressida, and became a symbol of constancy.

After this list of unfaithful men, Whitney lists the virtues that she hopes her lover's wife will have so that he will not regret his decision. Again she takes her examples from classical figures, and she hopes that his wife will have the beauty of Helen, the faithfulness of Penelope, the constancy of Lucrece, and the true love of Thisbe. In case he thinks it unlikely for one woman to have all of these qualities, she reminds him that she had all of them except Helen's beauty. She then quickly notes that she is not saying this to turn him from his new love, as he already knows from experience what she, I. W., deserves. She only wishes that she possessed the gift of prophecy, like Cassandra, so that she could foresee the future and prevent either her own misfortune or his, but since she cannot have this, she resigns herself to her fate and prays for God to guide her. She then closes with a few more classical allusions, wishing her inconstant lover the long life of King Nestor, the wealth of King Xerxes, and the gold of King Crœsus, along with as much "rest and quietness" as any man on earth may have.

By writing this poem in the form of a letter from an abandoned woman, Whitney is working, as she often does, in the tradition of OVID's *Heroides,* which were verse epistles written from the point of view of an abandoned woman speaking to the man who had betrayed her. Whitney's many allusions to classical figures that appear in Ovid's *Heroides* emphasizes this connection. However, as critics have often noted, Whitney does not confine herself to the traditional role of an abandoned woman. She does not simply lament being abandoned; rather, she offers advice to her lover about what he is losing and how he should behave. In offering this advice, Whitney is taking the moral high ground. She not only attempts to correct his mistakes and guide him in a better direction, but she also does not criticize him or the woman for whom he has left her. Rather than portraying herself as a victim, she is portraying herself as a virtuous woman and a morally superior individual who can instruct her weak and inconstant lover. Her wavering back and forth between the role of adviser and the role of the abandoned woman at once mirrors his fickleness and, ironically, emphasizes her own constancy, since she remains faithful and true enough to offer him good advice even when he has abandoned her. Some critics have examined Whitney's work in relation to GEOFFREY CHAUCER'S *The LEGEND OF GOOD WOMEN,* which is also based on the *Heroides,* particularly in light of the difference between the male and female perspective on faithfulness.

See also "ADMONITION, BY THE AUTHOR, THE."

FURTHER READING

Jones, Ann Rosalind. "Nets and Bridles: Early Modern Conduct Books and Sixteenth-Century Women's Lyrics." In *The Ideology of Conduct: Essays on Literature and the History of Sexuality,* edited by Nancy Armstrong and Leonard Tennenhouse, 39–72. New York: Methuen, 1987.

Marquis, Paul A. "Oppositional Ideologies of Gender in Isabella Whitney's *Copy of a Letter.*" *The Modern Language Review* 90, no. 2 (1995): 314–324.

Donna C. Woodford

J

JAMES I (1394–1437) *king of Scotland*   James I was born in Dunfermline in late July 1394 to Robert III (d. 1406) and Annabella Drummond (d. 1401) during a time of political conflict. Captured en route to France, James was in English custody from age 12 to 30 in a number of places, including the TOWER OF LONDON, Nottingham Castle, and Windsor Castle. James was educated in the households of English kings Henry IV and Henry V, even serving in France with English armies from 1420 to 1422.

James married Joan Beaufort (d. 1445), the second cousin of Henry VI, in February 1424 and returned to Scotland in April of that year. He was immediately compelled to face two major opponents: his uncle, Robert Stewart, and Alexander MacDonald, Lord of the Isles. He eventually defeated both.

In foreign policy, James I kept up the French alliance against England but also worked out a five-year truce with the English in 1431. Domestically, James carried out taxation in the English style, causing the Scottish nobles to bristle at his attempts to centralize power. Fighting with the English broke out in the spring of 1436, and James suffered defeat at Roxburgh as many of his nobles deserted him. Rebels captured and assassinated James I on February 21, 1437, at Perth. His son, James II, was six at the time.

James I endures as a literary figure. He is author of *The KINGIS QUAIR*, a DREAM VISION written during his captivity, as well as a number of SONNETs and other poems. He is often classified with the SCOTTISH CHAUCERIANS.

FURTHER READING

Balfour-Melville, E. M. W. *James I, King of Scots: 1406–1437.* London: Metheun, 1936.

Brown, Michael. *James I.* Edinburgh: Canongate Academic, 1994.

Duncan, A. A. M. *James I, King of Scots: 1424–1437.* Glasgow: University of Glasgow Press, 1984.

Mark DiCicco

JAMES VI/I (1566–1625) *king of Scotland [as James VI] and England [as James I]*   The first monarch of England from the House of Stuart, and the first to unite the crowns of the three kingdoms (England, Ireland, and Scotland), James Stuart was born in June 1566 to MARY, QUEEN OF SCOTS. Following his mother's forced abdication, the 13-month-old "cradle king" was crowned sovereign and baptized in July 1567. James ruled Scotland as James VI from 1567 on, and England and Ireland as James I beginning in 1603, following the death of England's queen ELIZABETH I.

James married Anne of Denmark by proxy in 1589, and between 1594 and 1607, they had seven children, three of whom survived to adulthood. Throughout his reign, James maintained a querulous relationship with Parliament, as he was a firm adherent to the divine right of kingship, believing the monarch to be a direct extension of God on earth.

An educated and learned man, James authored several works on a wide variety of subjects: *The Essays of a Prentice in the Divine Art of Poesy* (1584) addresses

English literary theory; *Daemonologie* (1597) covers the occult; *Basilikon Doron* (1599) and *The True Law of Free Monarchies* (1598) articulate his theories of kingship. Involvement in contemporary theological culture and political debates was a hallmark of James's intellectual acuity throughout his tenure as monarch.

See also "SONNET ON TICHO BRAHE, A."

FURTHER READING

Croft, Pauline. *King James*. New York: Palgrave, 2003.

Stewart, Alan. *The Cradle King: The Life of James VI & I, the First Monarch of a United Great Britain*. New York: St. Martin's, 2003.

Willson, David Harris. *King James VI and I*. London: Jonathan Cape, 1956.

Mardy Philippian, Jr.

"JESUS, MY SWEET LOVER" ANONYMOUS (14th century)

Though short, the lyric "Jesus, My Sweet Lover" is powerful. Through its devotion to Jesus and his "woundes two and three" (l. 4), the poem reads much like a prayer, and its religious significance is clear: The poem is directed to Jesus in order to have his love "fixed" in the narrator's "herte." Christ's death (ll. 2/8) is mentioned twice, once in the beginning and once at the end, creating a frame, and the five wounds that Christ suffered are mentioned within the body of the poem, as they were inflicted upon his body. These wounds evoke violent images of Christ's crucified body on the "Rode Tree" which are then linked to the beseeched (l. 3) (though gentle and loving) piercing of the narrator's own heart, where love is to be held fast.

Simple on its surface level, the poem has intriguing secular undertones. MIDDLE ENGLISH LYRICS AND BALLADS frequently explored the parallelism between sacred and secular, erotic love, a tradition based on the vocabulary of love found in the Song of Songs (Song of Solomon in the Bible). In particular, the symptoms of LOVESICKNESS described in the biblical song became a prime source of material for COURTLY LOVE as well as mystical love. Moreover, medieval theology interpreted the Bride in the Song of Songs as an ALLEGORY of the soul's desire for God, who was the absent beloved.

Situated in this context, this title "Jesus, My Sweet Lover" manifests the language of both sacred and secular love. Like many of the secular lyrics whose narrators address their lady, this piece is a direct address to "Iesu." Unlike the beloved in other lyrics, Christ is not a cruel lover who allows the lovesick to wither away and die from unfulfilled love. Jesus is the narrator's sweet lover, who has already proved his devotion through the five wounds suffered on the cross.

Although a tender invocation to Jesus and a desire for love, this poem is also mixed with violent images of Christ's death, which are portrayed in language similar to descriptions of courtly love. Courtly love was thought to pierce the eyes through Cupid's arrow and then enter the heart. Here, however, love pierces not the lover's eyes but rather his heart, directly. The narrator emphasizes the sacred using the language of the secular: Pierce my heart with love, as your "herte" was pierced at the crucifixion. The effect is to link the narrator, now a lover, so firmly with Christ, that Jesus can be called a "lemmon swete" "sweet beloved" (l. 1), who is clearly unlike the unmoved beloved women in secular lyrics such as "ALISOUN" and "Spring."

FURTHER READING

Brook, G. L. *The Harley Lyrics: Old and Middle English MS. 2253*. 4th ed. Manchester, U.K.: Manchester University Press, 1968.

Gray, Douglas. *Themes and Images in the Medieval English Religious Lyric*. London: Routledge, 1972.

James M. Palmer

"JOLLY JANKYN" ANONYMOUS (ca. 1450)

Recounting the tale of a clerical seduction, this anonymous medieval CAROL is written in a woman's voice and is remarkably light in tone, despite its rather serious conclusion—an unwanted pregnancy. The cleric—probably a priest—is named Jankyn, and the unfortunate, seduced woman is presumably called Alisoun. The poem recounts how Alisoun first notices Jankyn at Christmas mass, and although the details of her seduction are sparse, the poem follows the course of the mass, during which Alisoun becomes more and more attracted to Jankyn. The cleric has an especially fine voice, which he displays when marching in procession, reading the epistle, and singing a particularly elaborate melody for the Sanctus, a key part of the mass. The only direct indication in the poem that Jankyn notices Alisoun is that in the second-to-last STANZA, he winks at her and then steps on her foot. The final stanza reveals the secret that a bold dalliance has had serious consequences. In the concluding line, the persona dramatically cries: "Cryst fro schame me schylde [shield] . . . Alas, I go with schylde [child]!"

As with many carols, "Jolly Jankyn" is set in the yuletide season, as indicated by its first line: "As I went on Yol Day." Furthermore, the poem may convey a parodic reflection of the pregnancy of the Blessed Virgin. The stanzas are comprised of four lively three-beat lines in MIDDLE ENGLISH, with an occasional four-beat line mixed in. The fifth line of each stanza is the same: "Kyrieleyson," a Greek phrase taken from the mass, meaning "Lord have mercy on us." The last stanza also contains Latin liturgical phrases. "Benedicamus Domino" means "Let us bless the Lord," and "Deo gracias" means "Thanks be to God."

The poem's wit comes primarily from a pun on "Kyrie Eleison." Because of this, some scholars have viewed it as a type of KYRIELLE, though it is not written in *quatrains*. To the persona, "Eleison" sounds like Alisoun, and therefore she is cheered each time Jankyn sings the phrase because she pretends (or is it true?) that he is slyly calling out to her while saying mass. Indeed, the BURDEN—"Kyrie, so Kyrie / Iankyn syngyt mirie [sings merrily] / With aleyson"—emphasizes the resemblance of the words. Although the word *singen* meant to sing a song and also to sing a mass, it seems to take on a sexual connotation in the burden because Jankyn "sings" *with* Alisoun.

Each stanza ends with the phrase *Kyrieleyson,* but the persona's joy in the phrase dramatically turns to sorrow in the last stanza, when she confesses that she is pregnant. Here the repetition of the phrase is finally revealed as religiously appropriate, for Alisoun and for her handsome cleric, both of whom have sinned. The phrase adds a surprisingly moralistic finish to a worldly and witty dance song.

See also MIDDLE ENGLISH LYRICS AND BALLADS.

FURTHER READING

Crowther, J. D. W. "The Middle English Lyric: 'Joly Jankyn.'" *Annuale Mediaevale* 12 (1971): 123–125.

Deyermond, Alan. "Sexual Initiation in the Woman's Voice Court Lyric." In *Courtly Literature: Culture and Context: Selected Papers from the 5th Triennial Congress of the International Courtly Literature Society,* edited by Keith Busby and Erik Kooper, 125–58. Utrecht Publications in General and Comparative Literature 25. Amsterdam: John Benjamins, 1990.

Reichl, Karl. "The Middle English Carol." In *A Companion to the Middle English Lyric,* edited by Thomas G. Duncan, 150–70. Woodbridge, Suffolk: D. S. Brewer, 2005.

Gregory M. Sadlek

JUDITH ANONYMOUS (before 1072)

The Old English *Judith* is a verse interpretation of an episode from the biblical Book of Judith from what is now called the Apocrypha, but was then a canonical book of the Bible. The one surviving copy of the poem, found in MS COTTON VITELLIUS A.XV, is incomplete, beginning in mid-sentence. Modern scholars generally believe, however, that no more than 100 lines of introductory material are missing.

The events depicted in the 349-line poem are taken largely from chapters 12 through 16 of its biblical source. The Jewish city of Bethulia is besieged by the Assyrian army under the fierce general Holofernes, so the beautiful widow Judith resolves to save her city and sets out for the Assyrian camp, accompanied only by a handmaid. Captivated by her beauty, Holofernes invites Judith to a banquet, at which he and his men become insensibly drunk. Judith is then led to the general's bed, where he presumably intends to defile her. Finding him incapacitated with drink, Judith beheads him with his own sword and slips out of the camp. When she returns to Bethulia and displays the severed head, the Jewish army rejoices and easily routes the stunned and leaderless Assyrians.

In adapting the biblical material, the *Judith* poet condensed the plot and omitted secondary characters, such as Holofernes' officer Achior, who converts to Judaism in the original story. The poet instead focuses primarily on the two main characters, who are in even more extreme opposition than in the source. Judith, described in terms usually reserved for virgin saints (*eadigan mægð,* blessed maid, l. 35; *scyppendes mægð,* the Creator's maid, l. 78), lacks the sexual manipulativeness of the biblical heroine. Here, her innocence and total reliance on God are contrasted with Holofernes' utter debasement and hostility toward God. Describing him in terms such as *heathen warrior* (l. 179) and *hateful to the Savior* (l. 45) and removing all examples of his direct speech, the poet makes Holofernes an almost inhuman enemy.

The violent clash between a holy woman and a demonic opponent would have been a familiar motif to an Anglo-Saxon audience through popular HAGIOGRAPHY, such as those of the virgin martyrs Juliana and Margaret. Although Judith is not a martyr, her story has a number of hagiographical elements, including her prayer for strength just before slaying Holofernes. (In the poem, she prays to the Trinity; in the Bible, to God.) Yet *Judith* also resonates with the conventions of Anglo-Saxon heroic poetry. The sections of the poem that deal with the Hebrew army's preparation for battle and the conflict itself (ll. 199–241) have little correspondence with the biblical source but are typical of Old English battle narratives. The poem also highlights the supremacy of heroic values: Judith's courage and faith enable her victory, while Holofernes is doomed by his antiheroic debauchery and failure to lead his warriors well. The reversal of usual gender roles is necessitated by the source, but again it finds parallels in the lives of numerous female saints. Judith's status as one of the few active women protagonists in Old English poetry (along with *Elene* and *Juliana*) has attracted a great deal of interest from feminist scholars.

Judith has also been studied in relation to its manuscript companion, *BEOWULF*. Though the poems differ in many respects, there are significant parallels between Beowulf's confrontation with Grendel and Judith's slaying of Holofernes. These similarities—both victors face their adversaries alone following a feast, and both display a severed body part as evidence of victory—have even lent support to a Christian interpretation of the ostensibly pre-Christian *Beowulf*.

See also ANGLO-SAXON POETRY.

FURTHER READING

Belanoff, Patricia A. "Judith: Sacred and Secular Heroine." In *Heroic Poetry in the Anglo-Saxon Period: Studies in Honor of Jess B. Bessinger Jr.,* edited by Helen Damico and John Leyerle, 247–264. Kalamazoo, Mich.: Medieval Institute Publications, 1993.

Griffith, Mark. ed. *Judith.* Exeter, U.K.: University of Exeter Press, 1997.

Lochrie, Karma. "Gender, Sexual Violence, and the Politics of War in the Old English *Judith.*" In *Class and Gender in Early English Literature: Intersections,* edited by Britton J. Harwood and Gillian R. Overing, 1–20. Bloomington: Indiana University Press, 1994.

Orchard, Andy. *Pride and Prodigies: Studies in the Monsters of the Beowulf-Manuscript.* Cambridge: D.S. Brewer, 1995.

Lori A. Wallach

K

KENNING   The word *kenning* is derived from the Old Norse expression *kenna eitt við* ("to express relationally" or "to make known by"). As a literary device, kenning is found predominantly in ANGLO-SAXON POETRY, particularly heroic verse, as well as OLD NORSE/ICELANDIC EDDAS AND SAGAS. The technique is used abundantly in *BEOWULF,* from which all these examples are drawn.

The simple definition of *kenning* is a metaphorical compound word or short phrase that replaces a name or noun, in which the object of the metaphor is implied but not stated. These compounds may consist of noun/noun combinations ("whale-road" or "swan-way" for the sea), or noun/verb combinations ("heath-stepper" for deer). Some scholars believe that a pure kenning must involve a simile, implied or stated, and not mere description. Thus, "battle-friend" would be a kenning for sword, but "battle-iron" would not. Other scholars allow for phrasal kennings as well as compound ones (e.g., "storm of swords" for "battle").

Kennings were particularly important to a culture with a limited lexicon. As embedded metaphorical devices, kennings have the potential to create multilayered effects. For example, they may be used to convey irony or humor ("shield-play" for "battle") or to assign honor and prestige ("gold-friend" for "lord"). In Old Norse poetry, kennings themselves can be used in layers (e.g., "storm of battle-friends" meaning "storm of swords" or "battle"), a technique employed only rarely in Old English.

FURTHER READING

Gardner, Thomas. "The Old English Kenning: A Characteristic Feature of Germanic Poetical Diction?" *Modern Philology* 67, no. 2 (1969): 109–117.

Godden, Malcolm R. "Literary Language." In *The Cambridge History of the English Language,* edited by Richard M. Hogg, 490–535. Cambridge: Cambridge University Press, 1992.

Ogilvy, J. D. A., and Donald C. Baker. *Reading Beowulf: An Introduction to the Poem, Its Background, and Its Style.* Norman: University of Oklahoma Press, 1983.

KING HORN ANONYMOUS (ca. 1275)   *King Horn,* written by an unknown author, is probably the oldest extant English ROMANCE. It may derive from an earlier and longer ANGLO-NORMAN poem, *Horn et Rimenhild,* although some scholars have argued that both works instead draw on a common source. *King Horn* exists in three manuscripts that contain significantly different textual variations. The poem consists of over 1,500 lines that tend to have two or three stresses, are paired in rhymed COUPLETS, and often use ALLITERATION. Originally it was probably sung or chanted when performed.

The plot takes place in four separate kingdoms that are connected by sea journeys. The poem opens in Suddene, the location of which is uncertain, ruled by King Murry. His son, Horn, is 15 and the fairest in the land: "Fairer nis non thane he was" (l. 13). Murry is killed by invading SARACENs whom he discovers landing on the beach; they proceed to overrun the kingdom and slaughter all its inhabitants who do not renounce Christianity. The Saracens are reluctant to kill Horn outright because of his fairness, so they set him and his companions adrift at sea in a galley.

The boat fortuitously comes ashore in Westernesse (probably the western coast of England), where Horn and his companions are befriended by King Aylmar. Rymenhild, the king's daughter, falls in love with Horn, but he, having kept the fact of his royal birth a secret, declares himself too lowborn to wed her. However, he suggests that she persuade her father to knight him and his companions, which would elevate his social status and make him eligible to marry her. This being accomplished, Rymenhild gives him a gold ring that she says will protect his life. He then proves his knighthood by single-handedly killing an invading band of Saracens. However, Fikenhild, an evil companion of Horn's who is "the wurste moder child" (l. 652), deceives the king into thinking that Horn is plotting to usurp his throne. Aylmar then angrily banishes Horn, who asks Rymenhild to wait for him seven years before he departs.

Horn then travels to Ireland, where, concealing his identity again, he enters the service of King Thurston and saves the kingdom from invading Saracens, slaying the giant who had previously had killed his father. In Horn's absence, Rymenhild's father arranges a marriage between her and King Modi of Reynes. She sends a desperate plea for Horn to return by a messenger who, after wandering from land to land, by chance encounters Horn and gives him the message. On his way back to Rymenhild, however, the messenger is drowned in a storm. Rymenhild finds his body and despairs.

In the meantime, Horn reveals his true identity to King Thurston and enlists his aid in rescuing Rymenhild. Reaching Westernesse on the morning of the wedding, Horn conceals his identity by exchanging clothes with a palmer (pilgrim) and gains entry into the hall. He gets the attention of Rymenhild, who does not recognize him, by asking her for drink, mentioning Horn's name and throwing his ring into the drinking horn. At first he pretends Horn gave him the ring before dying, but finally he reveals his true identity to her. He and his companions then kill Modi and all of his men.

Before wedding Rymenhild, however, Horn travels back to Suddene and wins his rightful throne by defeating the Saracens. In his absence, the evil Fikenhild, desiring to marry Rymenhild, carries her off to a castle surrounded by water. Dreaming that Rymenhild is in danger, Horn rushes back to Westernesse, where he and his companions gain entry into the castle disguised as minstrels. In the end, he kills Fikenhild and his men, rewards his loyal friends, and marries Rymenhild.

King Horn is a coming-of-age story that, like most other romances, follows the pattern of exile and return. However, compared to later English romances, its descriptions seem meager, characterizations are underdeveloped, and chivalric and courtly themes are less evident. Some critics have emphasized its affinity with folktales and pointed out folkloric motifs, such as the disguises and portentous dreams, while others have commented on its ballad-like features. While some have observed that the Saracens probably represent memories of the Viking incursions, at least one scholar has suggested that the Saracen invasions, although historically inaccurate, reflect the actual social and political tensions and fears of 13th-century England. The poem contains archaic features in language and was once commonly dated to around 1225. However, Rosamund Allen has convincingly argued that it was more probably composed in the 1270s, probably by an author in the London area, and that the original audience may have been fish merchants, given the importance of fish and sea journeys in the poem.

See also BALLAD (FOLK BALLADS), CHIVALRY.

FURTHER READING

Allen, Rosamund, ed. *King Horn: An Edition Based on Cambridge University Library MS Gg. 4.27(2)*. New York and London: Garland, 1984.

———. "The Date and Provenance of *King Horn*: Some Interim Reassessments." In *Medieval English Studies Presented to George Kane,* edited by Edward Donald Kennedy, Ronald Waldron, and Joseph S. Wittig, 99–125. Wolfeboro, N.H.: Brewer, 1988.

Herzman, Ronald B., Graham Drake, and Eve Salisbury, eds. *Four Romances of England: King Horn, Havelok the Dane, Bevis of Hampton, and Athelston.* Kalamazoo, Mich.: Medieval Institute, 1999.

Kelvin A. Massey

KINGIS QUAIR, THE JAMES I (ca. 1424)

The Kingis Quair by JAMES I, king of Scotland, opens with an image of the heavens that serves to introduce the narrator's account of his own experience. One night, he began to read BOETHIUS's *The CONSOLATION OF PHILOSOPHY*. Rather than soothing him, however, the narrative of Boethius's misfortune and the remedy of philosophy leads him to consider the unstable nature of FORTUNE's wheel, his own youthful experience of adversity, and how he overcame it. Rising at the sound of the matins bell, he is overcome by the "fantasye" that it is commanding him to describe this fate, and so he begins to write.

James uses the image of a rudderless ship to represent and link the subjects of the vulnerability of youth, the problems of the present task of literary composition, and the beginning of his past troubles. Voyaging in youth, he was taken by enemies and imprisoned in a foreign land, where he suffered until he caught a glimpse of a beautiful woman walking in the garden beneath his window. Her departure drove him to despair, and at length he fell into a trance. In a dream, he was transported to the celestial home of Venus, where, in a scene that alludes to the literary genre of the vision of the afterlife, he saw departed lovers whose fates reflected their conduct in love. Petitioning the goddess, he was advised to seek the aid of Minerva, goddess of wisdom, which evokes an ideal of love that complements reason rather than undermining it. This theme is reinforced in Minerva's insistence that she might aid the dreamer only if his love were founded on virtue rather than lust. From Minerva, the poet learned that Fortune's power is strongest where forethought and wisdom are lacking. Descending to the earthly paradise, he witnessed the nature of Fortune's wheel for himself and woke as the goddess set him to climb on it.

The narrator's doubts as to the meaning of his vision are resolved by the appearance of a dove bearing a message, and its promise of good fortune is fulfilled in the restoration of his liberty and his success in love. The poem closes with a litany of thanks and prayers.

The Kingis Quair survives in a single manuscript dating from the late 15th or early 16th century housed at Oxford's Bodleian Library, which gives the work its title and identifies the poet as James I of Scotland (1394–1437). Although this claim has been questioned, the weight of evidence is on the side of James's authorship, and the narrator's account of his early life presents significant parallels with the king's.

James spent his youth as a prisoner in England, and this captivity gave him ample opportunity to read authors such as GEOFFREY CHAUCER and JOHN GOWER, acknowledged as "poetis laureate" in the *Quair's* final STANZA. This contact with VERNACULAR court culture is reflected in the poem's substitution of the RHYME ROYAL stanza for the metrical form of the octosyllabic COUPLET favoured in Scots EPIC poetry, and the *Quair* is a landmark in the development of lyrical and allegorical writing in Scotland. Thematically and linguistically, James is considered one of the MIDDLE SCOTS poets (SCOTTISH CHAUCERIANS). In locating its origins in an act of reading, the *Quair* also alludes to the DREAM VISION form employed in Chaucer's *The BOOK OF THE DUCHESS* and *The PARLIAMENT OF FOWLS*. However, rather than provoking a dream, here reading leads the narrator to perceive similarities between his own experience and that of Boethius, bringing him to a new understanding of a past vision. The role of memory gives the poem a circular structure like that of the dream vision. This underlines its focus on questions such as the role of fortune in the divine order, since the form of the circle was perceived as a reflection of God's eternal being and so was often used to indicate a concern with theological matters.

Once dismissed as an imitation of Chaucer's poetry, *The Quair* has since been recognized as a sophisticated engagement with the philosophical ideas and methods of its source materials. In recent years, the work's rendering of James's personal history has attracted attention as an early form of autobiography.

See also ALLEGORY.

FURTHER READING

McDiarmid, Matthew P., ed. *The Kingis Quair of James Stewart.* London: Heinemann, 1973.

Mapstone, Sally. "Kingship and the *Kingis Quair.*" In *The Long Fifteenth Century: Essays for Douglas Gray,* edited by Helen Cooper and Sally Mapstone, 51–69. Oxford: Clarendon, 1997.

Elizabeth Elliott

"KNOLEGE, AQUAYNTANCE, RESORT, FAUOUR WITH GRACE" JOHN SKELTON
(1527) This is the third of five poems collectively given the title *Dyvers Balettys and Dyties Solacyous*. The collection was probably printed in 1527, but the composition date may be significantly earlier. The poem is composed of seven STANZAS, each seven lines long, except for the final one, which ends with the tag line, "Quod Skelton laureat" (Says Skelton, laureate). This tag line is a concluding line common to four of the lines in the collection and many other JOHN SKELTON poems. The rhyme scheme is *ababbcc,* also known as RHYME ROYAL. The concluding COUPLET at the end of each rhyme royal stanza might suggest that each stanza is a self-contained unit, when in fact the first five stanzas comprise one long sentence of praise to a woman. Because of that initial, very long sentence, the poem reads much like a list.

Each of the first five stanzas focuses on a different type of praise for the beloved woman. In the first, a series of the woman's mainly public virtues come tumbling forth. She has "knolege, aquayntance, resort, and fauour with grace" (l. 1), which might be rendered as "knowledge, acquaintances, places she is welcomed at, and graceful beauty." The second stanza notes the beloved's ability to soothe hearts filled with woe, pain, and distress. The third stanza is highly Petrarchan, offering comparisons of the beloved to topaz, rubies, and pearls, among other gems. The fourth stanza associates the woman with safety and light, comparing her to a clear image in a mirror; the evening star, Hesperides, which guides sailors; and an anchor. The fifth and final stanza of the initial sentence addresses the woman's effect upon the speaker, who is awed by her many wondrous qualities and rues her absence.

Although this poem uses Petrarchan CONCEITS, it is unusual in that the speaker does not accuse the woman of cruelty in making the speaker suffer for love. The beloved can soothe pain, but she does not cause it. Instead, the blame is placed on "absens" (absence), which assails the speaker with "fere and drede" that "abashyth" him, although, he is careful to note, "I haue no need" (ll. 34–35). The persona recognizes that he has no definite need to worry without his beloved, but he cannot help it.

The tone of the speaker is somewhat impersonal in the first four stanzas; it is not at all clear for a long time that the speaker is speaking of his own love for the woman, although his heart does "oft lepe and sprynge" when contemplating her behavior, goodness, and womanhood (ll. 29–32). The speaker calls her the "Lodestar to lyght these louers to theyr porte" (l. 25) although it is not clear at first whether "these lovers" are the speaker and the woman, another couple, or lovers in general. By the sixth stanza, the speaker reveals his personal feelings for the woman. The speaker declares that if she wants to know why absence is his foe: "Open myne hart, beholde my mynde expres: / I wold you coud!" In these lines, there is the sense that the breathless, fragmented stanzas before are just what the speaker here proposes: an unabashed, wholly exposed, opening up of himself.

Skelton says in the final stanza that he has "grauyd" (engraved) her "wythin the secret wall / Of my trew hart" (ll. 48–49). He may have also "engraved" this woman elsewhere: The first letter of each stanza spells out KATERYN, which may well be the name of the otherwise unnamed woman so thoroughly blazoned forth in this poem.

FURTHER READING
Fish, Stanley. *John Skelton's Poetry.* New Haven, Conn., and London: Yale University Press, 1965.
Halpern, Richard. *The Poetics of Primitive Accumulation.* Ithaca, N.Y.: Cornell University Press, 1991.
Scattergood, John, ed. *John Skelton: The Complete English Poems.* New Haven, Conn., and London: Yale University Press, 1983.

Kreg Segall

KYRIELLE
A popular poetic form of the Middle Ages, the kyrielle is derived from the *kyrie eleison* (lord have mercy)—an element of the pre-Reformation liturgy. Kyrielles are usually written in QUATRAINS, with the refrain as the last line. The most common rhyme scheme is: *aabB, ccbB, ddbB, eebB,* etc., with *B* being the refrain. Despite its liturgical origins, the kyrielle is not limited in subject to religious works. For instance, WILLIAM DUNBAR's "LAMENT FOR THE MAKARIS" is a secular kyrielle. THOMAS CAMPION also wrote in the kyrielle form, such as his poem "A Lenten Hymn."

See also "JOLLY JANKYN."

L

LAI See LAY.

LA MALE RÈGLE THOMAS HOCCLEVE (ca. 1405) THOMAS HOCCLEVE's *La Male Règle* is a 448-line poem divided into 56 eight-line STANZAS employing the rhyme scheme *abab, bcbc*; a suitable title translation might be misrule, since this poem is a confession of a misspent youth. Hoccleve begins with an APOSTROPHE to Health—here a combination of physical wellness and material prosperity—and claims to have once possessed both but to have squandered them while working at the Privy Seal office where the king's official paperwork was processed. After several opening stanzas setting forth his miserable state, Hoccleve goes on to chastise his "unwar yowthe," condemning his rejection of Reason and grieving his subjection to Sickness.

In subsequent stanzas (16–25), Hoccleve is more specific about his faults: He was a too-frequent patron of the Paul's Head Tavern, indulging in both wine and women. Hoccleve maintains that he never had intercourse with these women, but he confesses that his abstinence was mainly due to an embarrassment concerning sexual matters: "Whan that men speke of it in my presence, / For shame I wexe as reed as is the gleede" (ll. 158–159). Hoccleve admits to overtipping the tavern keepers who called him "gentleman," and to squandering his Privy Seal pay by taking boats down the Thames when it was inconvenient to walk. The flattery of shopkeepers, boatmen, and other beneficiaries of his largesse contributed to his profligate existence.

The final 20 stanzas are less cohesive than foregoing ones, as Hoccleve ranges widely over a number of subjects: the demonic influence of excess, the fickleness of friends, and the importance of a good reputation. In stanza 50, he begins to bring his poem to a close by asking himself, "Ey what is me that to my self, thus longe, / Clappid have I . . .[?]" (ll. 393–394). Hoccleve attributes his ranting speech to his straitened circumstances—especially financial. He concludes by turning his confession of misrule into a request for payment, asking Lord Fourneval, the treasurer, to pay his annual salary of 10 pounds. Hoccleve acknowledges that he does not want to be seen begging for his salary, but since begging is the custom, he fears that if he does not speak up, he will get nothing, so in the end the ailing poet maintains that coin is all the medicine he really needs.

Hoccleve's poem bears affinities with his other works such as the *Regiment of Princes, Hoccleve's Complaint,* and *Dialogue with a Friend* in offering autobiographical details. Scholars have attempted to ascertain whether or not these details relate to a persona or to Hoccleve himself. Studies have also attempted to define the "begging poem" genre, or the confessional poem. With this confessional petition, Hoccleve may be following his acquaintance, GEOFFREY CHAUCER, whose "COMPLAINT OF CHAUCER TO HIS PURSE" shares a similar function, though without the penitential tone which marks *La Male Règle*.

FURTHER READING
Burrow, J. A. *Thomas Hoccleve.* Aldershot, U.K.: Variorum, 1994.

Knapp, Ethan. *The Bureaucratic Muse: Thomas Hoccleve and the Literature of Late Medieval England.* University Park: Penn State University Press, 2001.

Mitchell, Jerome. *Thomas Hoccleve: A Study in Early Fifteenth-Century English Poetic.* Urbana: University of Illinois Press, 1968.

Gavin Richardson

LAMENT

A lament is a personal expression of sorrow over loss. This lyric impulse pervades poetry and song in secular and religious works throughout the Middle Ages and forms the foundation for its later use in EDMUND SPENSER and WILLIAM SHAKESPEARE. One of the most influential works expressing lament is the poetry in BOETHIUS's CONSOLATION OF PHILOSOPHY from the sixth century. Boethian lyrics of loss echo in several of GEOFFREY CHAUCER's works, such as "The Knight's Tale" and The BOOK OF THE DUCHESS. Themes of mourning over the loss of innocence and the transience of the fallen world occur in monophonic songs such as the popular 13th-century English song "Worldes blis." In the Old English period, the most famous expressions of lament are found in the elegiac poetry of the EXETER BOOK, written before 1072: "The WIFE's LAMENT," "WULF AND EADWACER," The WANDERER, The SEAFARER, DEOR, and "The RUIN." In addition to these shorter works, laments characterize the later sections of BEOWULF and shape the tone of the "Storm Riddles" of the Exeter Book. In the later Middle Ages, the lament appears in English and Scottish BALLADs and in MIDDLE ENGLISH LYRICS.

See also COMPLAINT, ELEGY.

FURTHER READING

Cross, James E. *Latin Themes in Old English Poetry.* Lund, Sweden: University of Lund, 1962.

Frey, Leonard. "Exile and Elegy in Anglo-Saxon Christian Epic Poetry." *Journal of English and Germanic Philology* 62 (1963): 293–302.

Karmen Lenz

"LAMENT FOR THE MAKARIS" WILLIAM DUNBAR (before 1508)

The 25 STANZAS and 100 lines of WILLIAM DUNBAR's KYRIELLE comprise a complex meditation on death. This is accomplished through adept and touching praise of the "makaris," great poets, that have passed on. The opening stanza and the final two stanzas are personal, and from a note in an early printed version of the text, some scholars believe that he was gravely ill at the time of its composition. Others feel that the theme is common and that the biographical note serves as a poetic convention.

Whatever the impetus, the poem moves from the personal to the universal: Stanzas 2–10 offer a universal reflection on the mutability of the world and the mortality of human life. This section names classes of people from high and low positions whose end is death and provides the segue to the next set of verses, as the speaker realizes that poets, too, share this fate. Stanzas 11–23 catalogue those poets who have gone to the grave before Dunbar. Some, like GEOFFREY CHAUCER, are well remembered; others, like Roull of Aberdeen, are lost to human memory. The argument of the work returns to the personal as the speaker realizes that death will take him as surely as it has overcome his colleagues and his fellow mortals.

Commentators present different interpretations of the final stanza, in which the speaker tells the audience and reminds himself that humans must live in this world in such a way as to live beyond it. A number see this verse as an expression of the usual medieval concern about life after death: The way people live now determines how their souls will fare in the afterlife. Some, however, see this QUATRAIN as remarkably free from concern with the afterlife; rather, they see hope for living on in human memory as the import of this final stanza, which would seem to point to the Renaissance belief in the eternizing quality of poetry.

The poem's BURDEN suggests a religious reading; it comes from the response in the seventh lesson of the Office for the Dead, which priests said nightly. The REFRAIN is also found in eight of JOHN LYDGATE's poems, as well as in several medieval CAROLS. Within Dunbar's poem, the Latin refrain unifies the work thematically and universalizes the speaker's reflections. In addition to having a metric form, the kyrielle, the composition can be characterized by its theme, and critics have called it a *danse macabre* (dance of death), a *memento mori* (reminder of death), a *vado mori* (I go to death), or an *UBI SUNT* (where are they?) poem. The list of people who die brings to mind the visual image of the *danse macabre,* in which Death leads or hauls people away from their earthly life; the personal and universal in the poem remind the speaker and the reader that death comes for all. The enumeration of social ranks who pass away is reminiscent of other medieval poems in which people of all stations meet Death, and the roll of 24 poets asks where they have gone, to which the poem gives the conventional answer.

For all its dwelling on mutability and death, "Lament for the Makaris" has a delightfully human tone, and many scholars consider this complex metric meditation Dunbar's finest piece of poetry.

FURTHER READING

Conlee, William W., ed. *William Dunbar: The Complete Works.* Kalamazoo, MI: Medieval Institute Publications, 2004.

Drexler, R. D. "Dunbar's 'Lament for the Makaris' and the Dance of Death." *Studies in Scottish Literature* 13 (1978): 144–158.

Kinghorn, A. M. "Death and the *Makaris*: Timor Mortis in Scottish Poetry to 1600." *English Studies* 60 (1979): 2–13.

Scott, Tom. *Dunbar: A Critical Exposition of the Poems.* New York: Barnes and Noble, 1966.

Karen Rae Keck

LANGLAND, WILLIAM (ca. 1332–ca. 1400)

The only biographical details that exist about William Langland have been gleaned from two versions of PIERS PLOWMAN. Born near the Welsh border, Langland may have been educated at Great Malvern Priory. He apparently took minor orders but was never ordained, leaving him free to marry. In London, he worked as a clerk, singing masses and copying documents, and also wrote the popular alliterative poem, *Piers Plowman,* an extensive, allegorical social SATIRE, which was revised a number of times.

See also ALLEGORY, ALLITERATION.

"LANVAL" MARIE DE FRANCE (ca. 1165)

"Lanval" is the fifth *lai* (LAY) of MARIE DE FRANCE's collection, *Les Lais.* It consists of 646 lines of Old French and is significant because it is the source for the 538-line Middle English poem "Sir Landevale," which, in turn, provides the basis for THOMAS CHESTRE's 14th-century SIR LAUNFAL.

Marie's "Lanval" contributes to the rich corpus of medieval ARTHURIAN LITERATURE. The poet claims to present the story "just as it happens." ARTHUR and his court are at Carlisle because of a war with the Scots and Picts. Arthur is presented as a "worthy and courtly king" (l. 6), who distributes presents, women, and land to his followers. The phrase "women [or wives] and lands" (*femmes et tere,* l. 17), equating women with property, reflects the common view of noble women during the 12th century: They are commodities used to strengthen feudal or business ties, who must produce male heirs for their husbands.

Amid all the gift-giving, Arthur forgets to reward one of his knights, Lanval, the hero of Marie's tale. He has served the king well and has many noble qualities: "valour, generosity, beauty, and prowess" (l. 21–22). These qualities are envied, so none will speak for him. Envy is a common theme in the *Lais,* as well as a personal concern of Marie's: elsewhere, she states that she has been the victim of envy. Marie and Lanval share another connection as well: They are both strangers in a foreign land. In his loneliness, Lanval wanders away from the court and into the wilderness. As he takes his ease, "disconsolate because of his troubles" (l. 51), two beautiful maidens approach him. They are messengers who have come to bring him to their mistress. He follows them to her richly decorated tent. This sumptuous richness presents a striking contrast to Lanval's relative poverty.

The maiden inside the tent is extraordinarily beautiful, and Marie compares her to the lily and the rose—two flowers that invoke love and purity. Wearing only a shift, she is lying on a bed. The maiden calls Lanval to her and declares that she has come in search of him, for she loves him "above all else" (l. 116). Lanval admires her beauty. In true OVID-like fashion, "Love's spark pricked him" (l. 118), and he offers his service to her, pledging himself to her in the manner of a FEUDAL OATH, saying, "I shall do as you bid" (l. 127). She, in her turn, grants him "her love and her body" and "a boon that henceforth he could wish for nothing which he could not have" (ll. 133, 135–137). The maiden only has one condition: Lanval must swear to tell no one of their love. If he does, she will vanish, and he will never have her again. He eagerly agrees, and the two lovers spend the afternoon together. She clothes him richly, and when Lanval returns to Arthur's court, he shares his newfound wealth with others, entertaining many knights and performing good deeds. As the days go by, Lanval is full of joy at his newfound love, who comes to him anywhere, anytime he wants to see her.

This sequence of events is key to understanding several different themes in "Lanval." The lady (presumably a fairy) is the complete opposite of the "femmes" Arthur gives to his men at the opening of the story. The fairy lady is clearly in control of her own life; she has made the decision to seek out Lanval, and it is she who has vast amounts of wealth to bestow upon him. Marie reverses the typical gender paradigm by having this extraordinary woman wield power over her own life. Lanval is her vassal, in keeping with the tradition of COURTLY LOVE, yet she does not maintain her distance from Lanval, instead rewarding him as Arthur failed to do.

Lanval's pleasure in his beloved continues until sometime "in that same year . . . after St. John's Day" (ll. 219–220). A group of knights, led by the "noble and worthy" Gauvain (Gawain), invites Lanval to go with them to a garden near the queen's tower. Guinevere watches them from above. When she sees Lanval, she summons her ladies to go down to the garden. This is another of Marie's gender reversals, as it is usually the woman who is the object of desire for the man.

Guinevere approaches Lanval privately (he is alone, wishing for his love) and addresses him: "Lanval, I have honored, cherished and loved you much. You may have all my love: just tell me what you desire! I grant you my love and you should be glad to have me" (ll. 263–268). Lanval refuses her invitation, saying that he does not want to betray his lord. The queen's wounded pride makes her spiteful, and she accuses Lanval of homosexuality. Lanval is driven over the edge by her jibe and replies "in spite" (l. 289) that he has a lover whose lowest handmaid is more beautiful and more worthy to be loved than the queen. In tears, the queen flees to her chamber and later tells Arthur that Lanval had attempted to seduce her, then boasted of having a superior woman. Infuriated, Arthur swears that Lanval must defend himself in court or suffer death. Lanval agrees to a trial, though he knows he cannot prove his claims to be true: Having revealed his secret, he has lost his lover forever. Alone in his lodgings, he laments his rash words.

On the day of the trial, before this verdict is announced, the proceedings are interrupted by the appearance of beautiful, richly dressed maidens who tell Arthur to make ready to receive their mistress. Twice the court falls back to deliberation—which angers Guinevere—until the majestic entrance of Lanval's beloved astounds everyone. She announces: "King [Arthur], I have loved one of your vassals, Lanval. . . . You should know that the queen was wrong, as he never sought her love. As regards the boast he made, if he can be acquitted by me, let your barons release him!" (ll. 615–624). Lanval is promptly freed. As the maiden leaves the hall on her white palfrey, he jumps onto the horse behind her, never to return.

With these final lines, Marie brings the central message of "Lanval" to fulfillment: that true love cannot exist within the confines of feudal society. Marie contrasts its conventions and rules with the parameters of love set out by the fairy woman. The queen, as the fairy's foil, is a sad example of the effects of such a society: She is manipulative, jealous, and seemingly unaware of the true meaning of love.

See also "GUIGEMAR."

FURTHER READING

Bloch, R. Howard. *The Anonymous Marie de France.* Chicago: University of Chicago Press, 2003.

Burgess, Glyn S., and Keith Busby, trans. *The Lais of Marie de France.* 2nd ed. New York: Penguin Books, 1999.

Eccles, Jacqueline. "Feminist Criticism and the Lay of *Lanval*: A Reply." *Romance Notes* 38, no. 3 (1998): 281–285.

Whitfield, Pam. "Power Plays: Relationships in Marie de France's *Lanval* and *ElIduc*." *Medieval Perspectives* 14 (1999): 242–254.

Sierra M. Wilson and K. Sarah-Jane Murray

"LAÜSTIC" MARIE DE FRANCE (ca. 1165)   One of MARIE DE FRANCE's shorter *lais*, "Laüstic" tells the story of a *malmariée* (unfortunately married woman), her lover, and the husband that comes between them. Like all of Marie's *lais*, "Laüstic" is written in octosyllabic COUPLETS.

At the beginning of the poem, Marie refers to the multicultural literary tradition in which she is operating. She tells us that this *lai* (LAY) was named *laüstic* by the Bretons but is called *rossignol* in French and nightingale in English. She then proceeds to the story. At Saint-Malo live two knights who had brought honor to the city. One knight is married to a beautiful wife; the second, a bachelor, is in love with the wife of the first (who has granted her love in return). As the two knights are neighbors, the lovers, separated by a wall, speak to each other nightly at an adjoining window. To evade her jealous husband, the lady claims that she gets up during the night because she loves to hear the song of the nightingale. The angry husband has the bird trapped and shows it to his wife. When she pleads for him to release it, he instead kills it and throws it on her, staining her garment. The lady wraps the bird in a cloth and sends it to her lover. He makes a little golden, jeweled casket for the bird, and thenceforth he carries it around with him at all times.

Typically enough for Marie's *lais,* "Laüstic" serves as a scholarly vortex for opposing views on love. Some feel that "Laüstic" does not chart a tale of true love at all. The wife agrees to the pleas of the bachelor knight because he is good, but also simply because he lives near her. The tale is devoid of the quest for love that we encounter, for example, in Marie's "GUIGEMAR," or the magical transformation of "Yonec," in which a man metamorphoses into a bird in order to enter the room of his lover. Furthermore, while in "Yonec" the husband's fatal wounding of the bird/man ultimately leads to an ennobling of the love (the lady jumps out her window and goes off to find her beloved) and to a revenge against the jealous husband (the son born of the love affair later cuts off the husband's head), in "Laüstic" there is no sense that the lovers make any effort to pursue their relationship after the bird is killed.

On the other hand, the husband in "Laüstic" acts excessively, and his character builds sympathy for the frustrated lovers. Moreover, the unmarried knight's continuing devotion, manifested in his carrying of the casket, suggests the meaningfulness of what existed between himself and his neighbor's wife. Although the nightingale has been crushed as a vehicle for their relationship, it still serves as a memorial, as does the *lai* itself. The enclosure of the bird evokes the context of a spiritual reliquary (although this imagery has also been interpreted as an ironic comment on the lovers unspiritual love).

The association between the casket and the poem—two artistic constructions that hold potential meaning within—raises the central issue of love in a different way. Clearly Marie is interested in the imagery of entrapment in "Laüstic." The wife is held within her own home, and the bird is first ensnared by the husband's servants, then encased in its little coffin. Does the *lai* become a sort of beautifully adorned mausoleum for a love that was never really alive; or, conversely, does it reveal that what is inside, although static (the written form of the tale, the dead bird), still has movement through the symbolic and interpretive messages it conveys?

FURTHER READING

Burgess, Glyn S. *The Lais of Marie de France: Text and Context.* Athens: University of Georgia Press, 1987.

McCash, June Hall. "Philomena's Window"; "Issues of Intertextuality and Influence in Works of Marie de France and Chrétien de Troyes." In *"De sens rassis": Essays in Honor of Rupert T. Pickens,* edited by Keith Busby, et al., 415–430. Amsterdam: Rodopi, 2005.

Tudor, A. P. "The Religious Symbolism of the 'Reliquary of Love' in *Laüstic.*" *French Studies Bulletin: A Quarterly Supplement* 46 (1993): 1–3.

John Kerr

LAY (BRETON *LAI, LAI*)

A lay (or *lai*) is a short narrative poem, often performed aloud to music (e.g., the strumming of a harp). Although a few of the surviving texts draw from the CLASSICAL TRADITION— such as the 14th-century SIR ORFEO—the genre typically includes subjects of Celtic origin (the "matter of Britain").

The ANGLO-NORMAN poet MARIE DE FRANCE composed the earliest surviving *lais* ca. 1165. Her collection includes 12 stories, composed in rhyming octosyllabic COUPLETS, and which she claims to have heard sung by storytellers in Britain and in Brittany. In the general prologue, Marie explains that she wrote her *lais* down because they are worthy of remembrance and must not be forgotten (ll. 35–40). Women occupy a central role in all of the narratives, which portray the complexities of human love and often focus on an illicit love affair.

In the 14th century, the lay—which became known in England as the Breton *lai*—gained popularity among authors writing in MIDDLE ENGLISH LANGUAGE. The explicit insistence on the Breton origin of these stories is due to the widespread belief, corroborated by Marie de France, that the professional storytellers of ancient Brittany performed such pieces in front of courtly audiences. None of the ancient Breton sources have survived, probably because they belonged to the oral tradition.

Throughout the later Middle Ages, the Breton *lai* enjoyed ongoing popularity among English audiences. Thus, the anonymous authors of the *Erle of Tolous* and *Emaré* identify their own narratives as "lays" in order to emphasize their authority. In *The* CANTERBURY TALES, GEOFFREY CHAUCER's Franklin also narrates a Breton *lai* (ll. 709–714); and in many ways, "The Clerk's Tale" recalls the tradition, too. Other well-known English lays include *Sir Dégaré, Sir Gowther,* and *Sir Cleges,* all ARTHURIAN LITERATURE.

Allusions to music, which constitutes an integral part of the genre, appear frequently in medieval *lais*. Hence, in Marie's "*Chevrefoil,*" Tristan composes a *lai* on his harp to commemorate his forbidden love for Queen Iseult (ll. 111–113). The Middle English *Freine* refers to similar performances of "layes that ben in harping" (l. 3). Nowhere, however, is the theme of music more central than in *Sir Orfeo,* which recasts the classical legend of Orpheus and Euridyce within a Celtic setting. Such allusions are not limited, however, to French and English literature. In his German romance *Tristan,* Gottfried von Strassburg describes how the eponymous hero performs a "Breton *lai*" (l. 3557) in front of King Mark.

See also "FRANKLIN'S TALE, THE."

FURTHER READING

Laskaya, Anne, and Eve Salisbury, eds. *The Middle English Breton Lays.* Kalamazoo, Mich.: Medieval Institute Publications, 1995.

K. Sarah-Jane Murray

LAYAMON (late 12th century)

In the opening of *The* BRUT, Layamon names himself and says that he is a priest. He gives his father's name—Leouenathes—and says he lived by a church on the bank of the Severn in Areley near Redstone (now Stourport in Worcestershire) where he read the books that inspired him to write the history of the English. He further claims to have then traveled extensively. He concludes by asking the reader to pray for his soul and those of his mother and father.

Evidence points to the likelihood of Layamon having been in holy orders. He was apparently well-educated, and in one manuscript he identifies himself as a priest, though in another he claims to live in a knight's household (possibly as a chaplain). As to his origins, the manuscripts both suggest, through dialectal analysis, composition in the Worcestershire area.

Layamon styles himself as a translator or compiler, claiming three principal sources: Bede's *Historia Ecclesiastica,* a book by Sts. Albin and Austin, and the ANGLO-NORMAN *ROMAN DE BRUT* by the Jersey poet WACE. In reality, he relies almost exclusively on Wace, and he provides more than a simple translation: his *Brut* is more than double the length of *Roman de Brut.*

FURTHER READING

Bryan, Elizabeth J. *Collaborative Meaning in Medieval Scribal Culture: The Otho Layamon.* Ann Arbor: University of Michigan Press, 1999.
Given-Wilson, Chris. *Chronicles: The Writing of History in Medieval England.* London and New York: Hambledon and London, 2004.
Layamon. *The Brut.* Edited by W. R. J. Barron, and S. C. Weinberg. New York: Longman Group, 1995.

David A. Roberts

LEGEND OF GOOD WOMEN, THE GEOFFREY CHAUCER (ca. 1386–87)

GEOFFREY CHAUCER's *The Legend of Good Women* is a collection of stories about 10 "good women" (Cleopatra, Thisbe, Dido, Hypsipyle, Medea, Lucrece, Ariadne, Philomela, Phyllis, and Hypermnestra) written by the narrator following a DREAM VISION request by Alceste, the consort of the God of Love. The Poem is composed in COUPLETs of iambic pentameter (HEROIC COUPLETS). The prologue to the *Legend* exists in two forms: the Bodlean Fairfax 16 MANUSCRIPT (called manuscript F) and Cambridge's Gg 4.27 manuscript (called manuscript G). Scholars regard these two versions as distinct: F is praised for its warmth and G for its better structure. The legends themselves are self-contained in that they are perfectly comprehensible without having any prior knowledge of the stories or contexts. While such a structure worked well for writers such as JOHN GOWER, BOCCAC-CIO, and Christine de Pizan, scholars reveal that Chaucer found it uninspiring and limiting.

In the poem, the narrator is summoned by the God of Love to answer, under pain of death, why he spread disparaging tales about love and true lovers in his earlier English translation of *Le Roman de la Rose* (*The Romance of the Rose*) and his *Troilus and Criseyde*. Defending him, Alceste argues that the narrator did not fully comprehend what he was writing in these works since he has other works that praise love and lovers. Rather than executing him, Alceste asks that the narrator's penance involve "makynge of a gloryous legende / of goode women, maydenes and wyves, / That were trewe in lovynge al here lyves" (G. 473–475) and so the God of Love charges him with this task. He awakes from the dream and writes the unfinished collection of legends. The irony is that while the women of the legends are "trewe," the men are not.

Chaucer opens with the story of Cleopatra and Antony. Antony, a senator, is also "a ful worthy gentil werreyour [warrior]" (F. 597) who falls in love with Cleopatra. She returns his sentiments, and the two marry. After their wedding, Octavius plots the destruction of Antony through a great battle. Cleopatra must flee the area, and Antony is left to fight, which leads to his despair and suicide. Hearing of her husband's death, Cleopatra instructs her servants to build a shrine and, next to it, dig a pit to be filled with serpents. Cleopatra walks naked into the pit, killing herself.

The second legend is that of Thisbe and Pyramus, whose love for each other is blocked by a wall separating their city. The two devise a plan to meet outside of the city limits. Wearing a wimple, Thisbe leaves first and encounters a ferocious lioness. Seeking refuge, Thisbe loses her headpiece, returning later to find it bloodied and torn by the lioness. Pyramus arrives late, sees the wimple, and believes his beloved to be murdered. He despairs and stabs himself. Thisbe finds him mortally wounded. Grieved by his death, Thisbe kills herself with Pyramus's own sword.

Dido's story, the third in the collection, is the longest at 443 lines. Dido dreams of Aeneas, a man who is "lyk a knyght" (F. 1066) and staying in her court. The two are part of a hunting expedition that gets caught in a storm. Seeking refuge, they discover their mutual affection and agree to marry. Once their marriage is consummated, Aeneas secretly plans to steal away in the night. Dido announces she is with child. He leaves but does not take his sword. Before killing herself with Aeneas' word, Dido writes him a letter.

The fourth story comprises the legend of Hypsipyle and Medea, both spurned by Jason. Hypsipyle married Jason and had two children by him. Following these births, Jason sailed away and never came back. Hypsipyle writes him, saying that she will live truly and chastely as his wife. She later dies of "sorwes smerte" (F. 1579). Jason sails straight to Colcos, where he meets and marries Medea "as trewe knyght" (F. 1336). Medea is also left by Jason, who has moved on to marry yet another woman. Like Hypsipyle, Medea writes him a letter that upbraids him for his behavior.

The fifth legend is that of Lucrece, who is praised by her husband Colatyn for her faithfulness. Upon hearing of her goodness, Tarquinius, the king's son, becomes enchanted with Lucrece's reputation. He visits Lucrece's home, where he is welcomed as Colatyn's friend. At night, Tarquinius rapes Lucrece, and threatens to cut her throat if she makes noise. Throughout his assault, she remains silent. Overcome with shame, Lucrece takes a knife and kills herself, making her a martyr.

The sixth legend is of Ariadne, who helps Theseus, a troubled knight. With her sister Phaedra, Ariadne plots a way for Theseus to fight and defeat the Minotaur, and then escape. In return, he asks to serve Ariadne. She refuses, saying she will be his wife, as they are each of noble degree. After Theseus defeats the monster, all three escape, and Theseus marries Ariadne. During the voyage, the group spends the night on an island. While Ariadne sleeps, Theseus leaves, taking the fairer Phaedra. Upon wakening, Ariadne realizes she has been betrayed and begins a long lament of woe, which Chaucer abbreviates.

Philomela's legend is the seventh of the collection. Philomela, the sister of Procne, is raped by her brother-in-law, Tereus. Afterward, he shuts her up in a castle and cuts out her tongue. Tereus returns to Procne, saying that Philomela is dead. Meanwhile, Philomela weaves a tapestry that spells out Tereus's crime. A servant brings it to Procne, who finds her sister and rescues her from the castle.

The eighth legend tells of Phyllis and Demophon, the son of Theseus, who are betrothed. Despite his promise, Demophon leaves and never comes back. When he does not return, Phyllis, full of sorrow, kills herself. Before she does, however, she writes Demophon a letter expressing her desire to have him return, and outlining the woe she suffers because of his loss.

The final legend is that of Hypermnestra's love for her husband and her father. Hypermnestra is to marry Lyno, but her father believes that only ill will come of such a union. He instructs Hypermnestra to murder Lyno while he sleeps. Hypermnestra decides not to murder her husband, and instead helps him escape. He does, but she is caught, imprisoned, and sentenced to death.

The main critical discussion of the *Legend* is whether it actually endorses the types of female behavior that it describes. The best-known source for such a collection is OVID's *Heroides,* a series of letter-poems composed as if written by women lamenting their betrayal by men. However, the legend is not all about women and their troubles, as the men, overall, fare rather well. Each legend contains as many lines about the errant men as it does about their female subjects. Composed in this way, the narrative leaves open the possibility for textual and narrative misogyny, making *The Legend of Good Women* really the "Legend of men who got away with boorish behavior." Another interesting avenue of scholarship examines the role of LOVESICKNESS in the *Legend,* as the women in the poem suffer from this affliction. Finally, another body of criticism looks at the violent implications in the relentless deaths of the female protagonists.

FURTHER READING

Lerer, Seth. *The Yale Companion to Chaucer.* New Haven, Conn., and London: Yale University Press, 2006.

Pearsall, Derek. *The Life of Geoffrey Chaucer.* Oxford: Blackwell, 1994.

Quinn, William A. *Chaucer's Dream Visions and Shorter Poems.* New York and London: Garland Publishing, 1999.

Kimberly A. Racon

LEICESTER, ROBERT SIDNEY, EARL OF (VISCOUNT DE L'ISLE) (1563–1626) A long-serving politician and soldier, Robert Sidney was governor of Flushing in the occupied Protestant Netherlands and eventually retired to the family estate at Penshurst, in Kent, becoming viscount de l'Isle in 1605 and earl of Leicester in 1618. Sidney was not known as a poet until recently. In 1973, a manuscript at Warwick Castle was identified as Robert's own manuscript of poems. It is the largest collection from the period in its author's own hand.

Modeled loosely (though with a less obvious sequential structure) on his brother SIR PHILIP SIDNEY's *ASTROPHIL AND STELLA,* Robert Sidney's collection of poems was mainly written in a short burst in the 1590s, after Philip's death and while Robert was serving in the Low Countries. It is full of nostalgia and loss that has personal origins—his brother's death, his separation from family, and his political frustrations—and is permeated by a melancholy brooding derived from the popular Petrarchan model. His verse includes poems where his life as a soldier, "the hardy captain, unused to retire" (Sonnet 7.1) is directly addressed; others where he looks nostalgically westward toward Penshurst, where "love holds fast his heart" (Song 6.18). Other poems are less personalized love plaints and SONNETs addressed to the typical Petrarchan beloved, who is at once elevated and complained against as "you that take pleasure in your cruelty" (Sonnet 25.1), and happiness is balanced by the pain of "my true mishaps in your betraying love" (Sonnet 16.11).

Robert's verse is careful and sometimes plodding, but it is metrically versatile, showing an interest in experimenting with a variety of metrical and stanzaic forms. The emotions of his poems are expressed in broad sweeps—generalized but poignant feelings about time, disillusion, absence, and death. Like SIR WALTER RALEIGH, another courtier-poet who felt the uncertainties of fortune on his career, Sidney uses the lyric both to escape from the world's pressures and to brood over the pressures that made him seek that solace.

Perhaps his most impressive poem is Song 6, which is based on the traditional BALLAD about a pilgrim returning from the shrine of Our Lady of Walsingham. It is a 136-line dialogue between a pilgrim and a lady who seems to represent Sidney's wife, Barbara, while "the knight that loves me best" (l. 8) and who "griefs livery wears" (l. 16) is clearly a projection of himself, described as an abandoned pilgrim, exiled in the Low Countries away from "the lady that doth rest near Medway's sandy bed" (l. 74), a reference to the river near Penshurst. Sidney's is a more personal adaptation of the ballad than Raleigh's. Like most of his poetry, it is melancholic, focusing on the awareness that "love no perpetuity / Grants of days or of joys" (ll. 39–40). It shares with Raleigh's poetry something of the same haunting quality of a nostalgia that is more than just personal but conveys something of the whole age's loss of shared meaning in a world of unpredictability and changing political and religious meanings. Ultimately the poem conveys a broader sense of loss and silence as it bids farewell to the medieval world.

See also HERBERT, MARY SIDNEY, COUNTESS OF PEM-BROKE.

FURTHER READING

Croft, P. J., ed. *The Poems of Robert Sidney*. Oxford: Oxford University Press, 1984.

Hay, Millicent V. *The Life of Robert Sidney, Earl of Leicester.* Cranbury, N.J.: Associated University Presses, 1984.

Waller, Gary. *English Poetry of the Sixteenth Century*. 2nd ed. London: Longman, 1994.

Gary Waller

"LENTEN YS COME WITH LOVE TO TOUNE" ("SPRING HAS ARRIVED WITH LOVE") ANONYMOUS (1300)

As printed in modern editions, "Lenten is come" comprises three 12-line STANZAs rhyming *aabccbddbeeb*. In the generally accepted three-stanza poem, the *b*-rhyme lines contain three metrical feet, while the other lines contain four. The structure therefore separates each stanza into four discrete three-line sections, loosely connected by the *b* rhyme. Like many MIDDLE ENGLISH LYRICS AND BALLADS, the poem's first stanza celebrates the coming of spring, praising the blossoming flowers and the birds' songs. As the stanza ends, the poet begins to project his own emotions onto the birds, whom he represents as rejoicing over their good luck so that all the wood rings with their song.

In stanza 2, this pathetic fallacy (concept of celebrating spring) continues as all of nature rejoices at the coming of spring, but in such human terms that it is clear the speaker is projecting his emotions into the natural scene. The poet depicts the rose deliberately donning her red face, the leaves in the bright wood beginning to grow with desire, and the animals cheering their mates. But as the second stanza ends, a new note is sounded as the speaker complains of his own unrequited love.

The poem's third stanza is structured much like the second: It opens with further description of the secret songs of the birds and animals, then shifts to the human world. In a striking juxtaposition, the speaker says that worms make love under the ground, but that women simply grow inordinately proud. Women, therefore, are depicted as unnatural, out of step with the natural impulses of spring in which even the worms, God's lowest creatures, participate. Clearly his mistress's rejection has caused the speaker to make this judgment, and he ends the poem declaring that if his lady continues her disdain, he will run off to live in the woods.

The poem has been called the most artistic REVERDIE in MIDDLE ENGLISH LANGUAGE, but some have criticized it for including the conventional "love longing" in a "nature poem" where it does not seem to belong. The scholar Andrew Howell, however, notes that such a nature opening would have led the medieval reader to expect the lover to reveal himself after the opening stanza, and notes that the beginning of the poem may allude to the Middle English poem "The Thrush and the Nightingale." The point of the work seems to be the deliberate contrast between the harmonious natural world and the human conflict caused by unrequited love. The critic Edmund Reis sees the speaker of the poem as being out of step with the natural world, because his love longing makes it impossible for him to participate in the joy of the spring (l. 67). The speaker's vow to leave the world of humans and join the natural world of the woods seems appropriate as well, until one remembers that in medieval literature, the wild man of the woods who abandons human society was a conventional image of madness, or of an unnatural man. Thus, the poem ends with the speaker and his lady both acting inappropriately, and with the implication that they would be wiser to act in sympathy with nature and come together.

FURTHER READING

Dane, Joseph A. "Page Layout and Textual Autonomy in Marley MS 2253 'Lenten ys come with love to toune.'" *Medium Aevum* 68 (1999): 32–41.

Moore, Arthur K. *The Secular Lyric in Middle English*. Lexington: University of Kentucky Press, 1951.

Reis, Edmund. *The Art of the Middle English Lyric: Essays in Criticism*. Athens: University of Georgia Press, 1972.

Jay Ruud

"LIE, THE" Sir Walter Raleigh (ca. 1592)

This poem is typical of Sir Walter Raleigh's combination of moral commonplaces and strong direct moral assertions. It takes as its initial premise the traditional religious dualism of body and soul—the soul is described merely as the "body's guest"—and from that he builds a mounting rejection of the world in which he spent most of his career as politician, soldier, and courtier. Raleigh's personal ambitions and the recklessness with which he pursued them found the glittering surfaces and unpredictability of the court an alluring place to try to fashion himself. "The Lie" is written in the voice of an embittered courtier—rejected by the court and acknowledging his own mortality—who chooses to "give the lie"—that is, openly defy an enemy, even at the risk of death—to it and all its members and fashions. He accuses the court of "glow"ing, not with gold or glory, but like "rotten wood" (ll. 7–8); he accuses "potentates" and "men of high condition" (ll. 13, 19) and all the apparent impressive aspects of the court, even those apparent glories—like the arts, medicine, love, and religious devotion—of being corrupt and deceiving. The poem concludes with an acknowledgement that "giving the lie" is such an insulting rejection of the court, it deserves a response "no less than stabbing," but nevertheless he affirms that stabbing would kill only the body, not the soul, since "no stab the soul can kill" (ll. 76, 78).

"The Lie" can be read as a direct ejaculation of masculine anger, as Raleigh—never one to avoid confrontation—saw his career at Elizabeth I's court thwarted by his enemies. It is a statement of deep frustration, as

if no other way of living is possible. It is also a violent expression of nihilism, offering nothing positive as an alternative. In "The Lie's" direct diction, simple verse form, its style reflects the simplicity of its sentiments.

See also COURT CULTURE.

FURTHER READING

Dodsworth, Martin, ed. *Sir Walter Raleigh: The Poems*. London: Everyman, 1999.

Rudick, Michael. *Poems of Sir Walter Raleigh: A Historical Edition*. Ithaca, N.Y.: Cornell University Press, 2000.

Waller, Gary. *English Poetry of the Sixteenth Century*. London: Longman, 1994.

Gary Waller

"LITANY IN TIME OF PLAGUE, A" ("ADIEU, FAREWELL EARTH'S BLISS")

Thomas Nashe (1592) Thomas Nashe probably wrote *Summer's Last Will and Testament*, the play from which "A Litany in Time of Plague" comes, in early autumn 1592. The occasion of the play's performance was the entertainment of Nashe's patron, John Whitgift, archbishop of Canterbury, as well as the employees and guests in Whitgift's country home at Croydon. An outbreak of plague had prevented the archbishop and his company from returning to London at the end of summer. Nashe's allegorical show incorporates this contemporary threat of disease into timeless festive themes such as the celebration of a harvest, the ebb and flow of the seasons, and the natural processes of growth and decay.

The sixth of the play's seven songs, "Litany" responds to the ailing Summer's request for "some dolefull ditty" to "complaine my neere approaching death" (ll. 1572–73). Its tone, reminiscent of the memento mori (reminder of death) idea, is mournful and solemn, even ceremonial; each STANZA addresses the transitory, "uncertaine" nature of life and the immediacy and inevitability of Death, which is personified in a traditional manner as wielding darts. But while the subject matter remains constant throughout, examples are employed to illustrate the hollowness of "lifes lustfull joyes" (l. 1576). The middle four stanzas address the different "joyes" ultimately emptied out by Death, and they order these from least to seemingly most permanent: wealth, beauty, strength, and wit (or intelligence). All get exposed as hopelessly insubstantial; in the case of beauty, for instance, we are provided the classical example of Helen of Troy, reputed to be the most beautiful woman in the world but now obscured by the "dust" of the grave.

Each stanza concludes with a REFRAIN drawn directly out of the Elizabethan Book of Common Prayer: "I am sick, I must dye: / Lord, have mercy on us" is a response to the litany of saints and was a phrase often posted on the doors of plague-infected homes. Such direct, topical reference to the disease ravaging London, a descendent of the BLACK DEATH, localizes the poem's broad concluding statement about the necessity of preparing spiritually for the afterlife: "Haste therefore eche degree, / To welcome destiny: / Heaven is our heritage" (ll. 1609–11). Universal concerns are accommodated to the particular individuals for whom the song was first performed—namely, those being sheltered from plague in Whitgift's country home. In this way, the somber religious overtones of the "Litany" encourage a sense of spiritual community—a community of sufferers and worshippers, regardless of "degree," or station in life—that differs from the secular versions of community in the play, which result from participation in holiday pastimes and life-affirming celebrations.

Over the course of the last century, "A Litany in Time of Plague" has fostered considerable critical debate focusing on the meaning of the line "Brightnesse falls from the ayre" (l. 1590). While some critics took the line to be purposely ambiguous, others contended that "ayre" was meant to be "hayre," and that the line was thus a straightforward commentary on the passing nature of beauty. It has also been suggested that this line refers to the lightning and comets that were thought to foreshadow the plague deaths of late summer. More recent commentary accommodates Nashe's demonstrated anti-Puritan feeling by reading the poem's concern with representing the natural, universal human condition of suffering as a refutation of the Puritan idea that plague resulted from unnatural social abuses.

FURTHER READING
Hilliard, Stephen S. *The Singularity of Thomas Nashe.* Lincoln: University of Nebraska Press, 1986.

Nashe, Thomas. *Summer's Last Will and Testament: The Works of Thomas Nashe,* edited by Ronald B. McKerrow, Vol. 3. Oxford: Basil Blackwell, 1958.

Trimpi, Wesley. "The Practice of Historical Interpretation and Nashe's 'Brightnesse falls from the ayre.'" *JEPG* 66 (1967): 501–518.

Jamie Johnston

LOCK, ANNE VAUGHAN   See TUDOR WOMEN POETS.

LOCUS AMOENUS   One of the most ancient of all nature descriptions, the *locus amoenus* (Latin for "beautiful place") contains all that is necessary (shade, running water, and greenness) for humans to enjoy a summer's afternoon. It is an entirely separate landscape from the *sylva* (wild wood) and the *hortus inclusus* (enclosed garden).

The *locus amoenus* is the traditional setting of the PASTORAL and of love—lost, found, or sought. VIRGIL embedded it in the western psyche through his *Eclogues.* It remained the preeminent literary landscape, until the rise of the sublime (nature as distinct from beauty) in the 18th century. Because the use of the *locus amoenus* become so commonplace, only the briefest shorthand description in the lyric became necessary.

See also ARCADIA, EKPHRASIS.

FURTHER READING
Curtius, Ernst. *European Literature and the Latin Middle Ages.* Translated by W. R. Trask. Princeton, N.J.: Princeton University Press, 1953.

Helen Conrad-O'Briain

LOLLARDISM (LOLLARDY, WYCLIFFISM) (ca. 1382–1430)   The Lollards were a heretical sect whose ideas were based on the principles of Oxford theologian John Wycliffe (ca. 1330–1384) Lollardism is the only heresy to have flourished in medieval England. It is often said to be the only native heresy, though that viewpoint has been challenged recently.

Frustrated in his career, Wycliffe began advocating radical church reform, including an insistence on the Bible as the source of grace and ultimate authority, as well as a renunciation of priestly tithes and ecclesiastical holdings. He also supported the right of the Crown to levy taxes on church holdings. This garnered him powerful court supporters, including Richard II, the Black Prince, and John of Gaunt. Wycliffe also promoted lay education, particularly citing the need for a VERNACULAR translation of the Bible. He began a translation in 1381 and had most of the Old Testament and the Gospels completed before his death in 1384. Lollardism grew apart from Wycliffe's positions after his death. In particular, practitioners came to reject all spiritual practices not found in the Bible, including the sacraments, and to sanction the priesthood of all believers.

Lollardism was political from its inception, having its basis in Wycliffe's discontent with his career, and its initial alignment was with state funding. As Wycliffe grew more radical—for example, rejecting the doctrine of transubstantiation (the belief that bread and wine become the actual body and blood of Christ)—the aristocracy distanced themselves from Lollards, while the gentry and artisan classes moved to embrace it. Many of the anticlerical points raised during the PEASANTS' REVOLT of 1381 were attributed to Lollardism, and it became feared as a synonym for anarchy and a basis for rebellion. Henry IV was particularly vigorous in his efforts to suppress Lollardism, though it continued to be prosecuted into the 16th century.

Lollardism deeply affected English literature. In particular, the first complete translation of the Bible into English was a major accomplishment that kindled the laity's desire to be educated. The widespread influence of the movement is also noticeable in popular literature, such as WILLIAM LANGLAND'S PIERS PLOWMAN, as well as other works within the PIERS PLOWMAN TRADITION or related to it, including PIERCE THE PLOWMAN'S CREDE, MUM AND THE SOTHSEGGER, and Richard the Redeless. Another Lollard text, Jack up Lande, was erroneously attributed to GEOFFREY CHAUCER in the 16th century, even being published as a "lost" Canterbury Tale. Though that was disproved, Chaucer's works contain allusions to Lollardism, such as the Host's exclamation in the epilogue to "The MAN OF LAW'S TALE: "'I smelle a Lollere in the wynd', quod he . . . This Lollere heer wil prechen us somewhat" (ll. 1173, 1177).

FURTHER READING

Aston, Margaret E. Lollards and Reformers. London: Hambledon, 1984.

Lollard Society, The. Homepage. Available online. URL: www.lollardsociety.org. Downloaded on February 2, 2007.

McSheffrey, Shannon. Gender and Heresy: Women and Men in Lollard Communities. 1420–1530. Philadelphia: University of Pennsylvania Press, 1995.

Rex, Richard. The Lollards. New York: Palgrave, 2002.

"LONDON, HAST THOU ACCUSED ME" HENRY HOWARD, EARL OF SURREY (1543)

HENRY HOWARD, EARL OF SURREY wrote "London, hast though accused me" while inside London's notorious Fleet prison. In this 68-line poem, the 26-year-old earl attempts to justify the actions that had resulted in his being locked up: breaking Lenten fast, running riot with a group of companions through the streets of London, and assaulting its citizens.

The poem, which begins, "London, hast thou accused me / Of breech of laws, the root of strife" asserts that the poet was not really breaking the laws of city, but was attempting to warn its populace of the coming wrath of God for their own lawlessness. The next lines contain an allusion in which Surrey claims that he had become "A figure of the Lord's behest" (l. 21), a type of Jeremiah sent to reprove his people of their dissolute ways. The poem features an enumeration (ll. 28–41) of the SEVEN DEADLY SINS (pride, envy, wrath, sloth, covetousness, lechery, gluttony), indicating how the poet wished his late-night rampage to have been a curative to London's "proud people that dread no fall, / Clothed with falsehood and unright" (ll. 45–46). The poem's other major structural feature comes as a kind of climax in the form of a series of BIBLICAL ALLUSIONS (ll. 56–64) that predict London's apocalyptic fall. In the end, Surrey predicts "none thy ruin shall bemoan" (l. 65), because no one except the righteous shall remain.

Critics of the poem come in two varieties: those who see it as a lark and those who see it as something serious. The former often claim that Surrey wrote the poem to reflect the mood with which he had enjoyed his revels; the latter point to its intricate and sophisticated poetic qualities, even likening its structure to the rhetoric of a courtroom defense oration. Still, others, because of its reliance on the Bible, see the poem as a serious avowal of Protestantism and a statement about a wicked urban population.

FURTHER READING

Brigden, Susan. "Henry Howard, Earl of Surrey, and the 'Conjured League.'" *The Historical Journal* 37 (1994): 507–537.

Jentoft, C. W. "Surrey's Four 'Orations' and the Influence of Rhetoric on Dramatic Effect." *Papers on Language and Literature* 9 (1973): 250–262.

Sessions, W. A. *Henry Howard the Poet Earl of Surrey: A Life.* Oxford: Oxford University Press, 1999.

Doug Eskew

"LONG LOVE THAT IN MY THOUGHT DOTH HARBOR, THE" Sir Thomas Wyatt

(1557) By most accounts, Sir Thomas Wyatt's visit to Italy in 1527 gave him the incentive to translate several of Petrarch's sonnets into English, including this version of Sonnet 140, which was also translated by Wyatt's contemporary, Henry Howard, earl of Surrey. Wyatt's confidence both in the suitability of English and in his competence as a poet may account for the freedom with which he reinterpreted, rather than slavishly translated, the Petrarchan poems. For example, in this sonnet, line 12 in the original poem alludes to the lover's fear of his master, Love, whereas Wyatt changes the poem to mean that his master, Love, is afraid of the beloved.

Wyatt followed the form of the traditional Italian (Petrarchan) sonnet. He also incorporated many of the common Petrarchan themes derived from the conventions of courtly love. These include an obsessed lover who must endure great hardship in the service of love and a fickle beloved whose indifference causes severe pain to her noble lover. Ultimately, this is a poem about a lover who is in love with a woman, but whose fundamental allegiance is to love itself.

In the first four lines of this poem, Love is personified as a lonely knight who takes shelter in the speaker's thoughts and keeps his home in the speaker's heart. From there, the knight makes bold incursions into the speaker's face, where he displays his insignia in the form of blushes, "spreading his banner" (l. 4). By portraying Love as a separate entity from the lover, the speaker conveys the idea that the lover is a victim who is held hostage by love—whose thoughts, feelings, and outward expressions of love are entirely involuntary.

The next four lines focus on Love's object, known only as "She" (l. 5). The beloved is displeased with Love's boldness, preferring that her lover rein in his unruly passions by the threefold approach of right thinking, emotional control, and spiritual reverence. The beloved holds a position of authority over the lover in that she teaches him how to love, "me learneth to love and suffer" (l. 5), as well as imposes her standards as to which expressions of love are appropriate, "with his hardiness taketh displeasure" (l. 8). Consequently, the lover is torn between the vagaries of love's whims and his beloved's censure of love's boldness.

Whereas the first eight lines set forth the lover's situation, the final six focus on the resolution of his dilemma. In response to the beloved's displeasure, Love flees into the heart's forest (with the common pun on *hart,* meaning deer, suggesting that Love is preyed upon by the beloved), where he hides unseen, no longer showing himself in the lover's face. In the final three lines, the lover acknowledges that banished love is his master and concludes that he must be Love's faithful servant, going with him into battle, willing to die there for him, "for good is the life ending faithfully" (l. 14).

See also Love that doth reign and live within my thought, personification.

FURTHER READING

Foley, Stephen M. *Sir Thomas Wyatt.* Boston: Twayne Publishers, 1990.

Heale, Elizabeth. *Wyatt, Surrey, and Early Tudor Poetry.* London and New York: Longman, 1998.

Margaret H. Dupuis

"LORD RANDAL" (15th century)

Like most folk ballads, "Lord Randal" enjoyed a lengthy oral tradition until it was recorded in the 17th century, and it focuses on action and dialogue. Lord Randal, a "handsome young man" (ll. 2–3), is confronted by his mother, asking where he has been. His answer is that he has been hunting in the greenwood, but then he says he is weary and wants to lie down. In the next

STANZA, the mother asks whom he met there. The response is "my true-love" (l. 7), and again he says he is weary and wants to lie down. When his mother asks Lord Randal what his true love gave him to eat, he replies "eels fried in a pan" (l. 11). (In other variations, the meal is fish or snakes). Through a series of questions and answers, Lord Randal reveals that his hawks and hunting hounds have been poisoned: "They swelle and they died, mother" (l. 29).

After the revelation that his hawks and hounds have been poisoned, Lord Randal's mother says she fears he, too, has been poisoned, which Lord Randal readily admits. He wants to lie down, but his mother asks what he leaves. He says he leaves her 24 cows, his sister his gold and silver, and his brother his houses and his lands. Finally, his mother asks what Randal will leave his true love, and he answers, "I leave her hell and fire" (l. 39). The poem ends with the same plaintive wish that ends each of its eight stanzas: "For I am sick at heart, and I fain wad lie down" (l. 40).

Traditional scholarship links this ballad to the death of Thomas Randall, earl of Murray, who was poisoned in 1332 by his sweetheart, an English spy who fed him black eel broth. It is a narrative song whose structuring principle is incremental repetition leading up to its final, deathbed curse for the murderer. The dramatic tension in the poem is its question-and-answer intensity, where each question leads to further, more heartrending revelations. As a victim of fate, the young and handsome Lord Randal must deal with betrayal and jealousy, and the ballad's structure adds to its impending sense of shattered illusions.

See also MIDDLE ENGLISH LYRICS AND BALLADS.

FURTHER READING
Leach, MacEdward. *The Ballad Book.* New York: Harper & Brothers, 1955.
"Lord Randall." In *Poetry for Students,* Vol. 6, edited by Mary K. Ruby, 104–117. Detroit: Gale Group, 1999.

Gary Kerley

LOVELY BOY (FAIR YOUTH, FAIR LORD)
The Lovely Boy—also called the Fair Youth or Fair Lord—is the ambiguous young man to whom the first 126 of *SHAKESPEARE'S SONNETS* are dedicated. The term derives from the first line of sonnet 126: "O thou my lovely boy who in thy power . . ." Scholars continue to debate the identity of the young man, with the main two contenders being Henry Wriothesley, earl of Southampton, and William Herbert, earl of Pembroke. Both were WILLIAM SHAKESPEARE's patrons at one time, and Wriothesley in particular was considered good-looking. However, a host of other candidates have been suggested, including William himself, or a false persona devised solely as a publicity trick.

See also DARK LADY.

LOVER'S COMPLAINT, A WILLIAM SHAKESPEARE (1591?)
The date of actual composition of *A Lover's Complaint* is debatable, with scholarly opinions ranging from 1591 to 1604. Complicating the matter is its publication date of 1609 as an appendage to *SHAKESPEARE'S SONNETS* and the persistent belief that the poem is only spuriously attributable to WILLIAM SHAKESPEARE. Consequently, the poem has long been marginalized both in the Shakespeare canon and in Shakespearean criticism.

A Lover's Complaint comprises 329 lines of IAMBIC PENTAMETER verse composed in 47 STANZAS of RHYME ROYAL. It is thought by some scholars to be stylistically and thematically reminiscent of EDMUND SPENSER's *Prothalamion* (1596), which was written in honor of the approaching double marriage of the ladies Elizabeth and Katherine Somerset. However, *A Lover's Complaint* is a much darker tale of a woeful young woman who has been seduced and abandoned by a charming and ruthless male suitor, rather than a celebratory commemoration of marriage.

The poem employs a series of increasingly inset narrators and layered narratives to tell its story. In the opening stanza, the poet begins by explaining that this "plaintful story" has come to him "[f]rom off a hill," the "concave womb" of which has "reworded" it "from a sist'ring vale" (ll. 1–2). The natural world is thus complicit in the storytelling, and the narrator stops to listen to its "double voice," whereupon he sees a distraught girl—a "fickle maid full pale" (l. 5)—destroying love tokens and disposing of them in a river.

Stanzas 2–8 offer a detailed description of the maid's appearance and behavior. She wears a "platted hive of straw" upon her head which confirms the PASTORAL setting. Using agrarian language, the narrator observes that while her beauty at first appears to be "spent and done," a closer inspection reveals that "[t]ime had not scythed all that youth begun" (l. 12). She cries into a handkerchief that has "conceited characters"—i.e., letters or images—embroidered upon it in silk. Her eyes shift their gaze from earth to sky, signaling her emotional distress by showing her "mind and sight" to be "distractedly commix'd" (l. 28). Her "slackly braided" hair falls out from her straw hat and hangs next to her "pale and pined cheek." One by one she removes "favors" from a basket—tearing letters ("folded schedules") and cracking rings before throwing them into the water along with her tears. Enraged, she curses the "false blood" with which some of the missives were written.

The ninth stanza introduces another character to this scene—a former courtier and now aged and "reverend man"—who also spots the maid and offers to listen to her tale to help "assuage" her "suffering ecstasy" (l. 69). In response to him, the girl assumes the role of narrator, and in stanzas 11–22 she describes the handsome looks and appealing nature of the seducer to whom she gave "all [her] flower" (l. 147). She details the "browny locks" of his curly hair and the "phoenix down" on his young face; his free-spirited demeanor and expert horsemanship; and, most crucially, the persuasive force of his "subduing tongue" (l. 120). He is so alluring, in fact, that he manages to enchant all types of people and bend them to his will, including a number of young women who have surrendered themselves to him. Thus, the narrator initially chooses to distance herself from him.

Nonetheless, the maid's passion and curiosity quickly prevail over her good judgment (stanzas 23–25), and when he "besiege[s]" her "city," she gives the young man an audience. His becomes the new narrative voice here as the cad declares his devotion for the maid and pleads his case to her. Skillfully he hinges his argument on honest admissions of his own charisma and irresistibility. Women, he claims, have given their hearts and bodies to him freely, and so they bear the responsibility for their own, and indeed for his, actions. Having been given a multitude of "fair gems enrich'd" and "deep-brain'd SONNETS" (which symbolize more carnal

and emotional female treasures), he will now unselfishly yield this entire fortune to the maid—as an obedient "minister" does to a deity (l. 229).

The young man's adoption of religious rhetoric at this point facilitates his segue into a story about a nun—a "sister sanctified, of holiest note" (l. 233)—whom he managed to "subdue" and to seduce out of her chosen seclusion, but whom he admires as a "valiant" woman among the "broken bosoms" that belong to him. The young man's narration ends there, and the maid resumes speaking. She explains to the old man that her "reason" was ultimately "poisoned" by the young man's show of tears and ornate speech, and that she was moved to tears herself—those which served only to "restore" him (l. 301). In the final stanzas, the maid laments her undoing at the hands of this artful scoundrel who "preach'd pure maid" to her (l. 315), but sorrowfully admits that she would probably be "new pervert[ed]" by him if he ever came around again (l. 329).

With its male-authored, female-voiced paradigm, *A Lover's Complaint* represents in its own right a popular and sophisticated variation on the early modern COMPLAINT. Presenting something of a straightforward storyline, *A Lover's Complaint* rather defies multifarious interpretations of its meaning and structure. Consequently, critical approaches toward the poem itself tend to focus on linking and comparing it to other Shakespearean works, to other works of the same genre, and to the rhetorical and confessional literary and cultural trends of the period. Primarily, the question of authorship remains central to the small body of criticism on this poem. Scholars who argue in favor of Shakespeare having penned *A Lover's Complaint* call for the need to read the poem as a direct response and a literary complement to his sonnets—which on the whole reflect its themes of nature and sexual desire and of idolatrous love and agonizing loss, and most of which describe the poet's affection for a young gentleman of great beauty and high social rank. It was, after all, not uncommon in the period for longer poems, and specifically complaints, to accompany groups of sonnets. Conversely, scholars who doubt Shakespeare's authorship of this poem often cite as proof its presentation of too many words rarely used or not found at all in other Shakespearean works. Moreover, they declare its more labored and challenging verse to be decidedly "un-Shakespearean" in style and tone.

FURTHER READING

Burrow, Colin, ed. *Shakespeare: The Complete Sonnets and Poems.* Oxford and New York: Oxford University Press, 2002.

Jackson, MacDonald P. "A Lover's Complaint Revisited." *Shakespeare Studies* 32 (2004): 267–294.

Sharon-Zisser, Shirley, ed. *Suffering Ecstasy: Critical Essays on Shakespeare's A Lover's Complaint.* Aldershot, U.K., and Burlington, Vt.: Ashgate, 2006.

Katie Musgrave

"LOVER SHOWETH HOW HE IS FOR-SAKEN OF SUCH AS HE SOMETIME ENJOYED, THE" THOMAS WYATT (1557)

This poem appears in the 1557 collection TOTTEL'S MISCEL-LANY. It is an edited version of SIR THOMAS WYATT's untitled poem known as "THEY FLEE FROM ME." Reading Tottel's version of Wyatt's poem is instructive, not only because it demonstrates a surprising amount of editorial control over early modern poetic texts, but also because it provides a deeper appreciation for the expressive quality of Wyatt's irregular metrical line, a quality that is absent in Tottel's version.

In preparing Wyatt's original 161-word poem for publication, a title was added, 18 words and punctuation marks were changed or moved, and the last line was completely rewritten. Most of these changes were made to regularize Wyatt's rugged and powerful (but uneven) IAMBIC PENTAMETER.

A comparison of Wyatt's and Tottel's versions of line 13 provides a representative example of Tottel's changes. Wyatt's original reads:

Therewithal sweetly did me kiss.
/ x x / x x x /

While Tottel's version reads:

And therewithal so sweetly did me kiss.
x / x x x / x / x /

Wyatt's line, irregularly metered, feels more like speech and echoes the previous line: "And she me caught in her arms long and small, / Therewithal sweetly did me kiss" (ll. 12–13). Tottel's revision is less speechlike and has a relentless, sing-song quality, including three consecutive lines that begin with *And*: "And she me caught . . . And therewithal . . . / And softly said." Tottel's addition of two filler words to Wyatt's line revision not only makes a 10-syllable line, the line itself is much more iambic—that is, containing a preponderance of groups of one unstressed syllable followed by a stressed syllable.

Tottel's intervention is most significant in the last two lines:

Wyatt:
But since that I so kindely am served,
   I would fain know what she hath deserved.

(ll. 20–21)

Tottel:
But since that I unkindely so am served,
   How like you this? What hath she now
      deserved?

(ll. 20–21)

Wyatt's closing lines are biting and cynical; there is venom just under the surface of the persona's closing comment. Wyatt's persona knows perfectly well what "she hath deserved," and it's nothing good. He puns on the word *kindely,* which here means both the modern "gently or friendly"—rather sarcastic in this context—but also the directly angry "according to her kind."

In changing Wyatt's comment into a pair of questions, Tottel's version is less complex and less acidic. Tottel's edit transforms Wyatt's sarcastic and ambiguous "so kindely" into the simple "unkindly." Finally, Tottel's final two questions directly address the reader, creating a shrill and angry tone. Tottel's changes, as in line 13 above, were made in order to preserve the regularity of the iambic pentameter. Wyatt's COUPLET has nine syllables in each line; Tottel adds an extra syllable to each to make up the full 10-syllable iambic pentameter line. Wyatt's couplet is highly metrically irregular, especially the final line, while Tottel's couplet is composed of 20 syllables of flawless iambic pentameter.

Part of the beauty of the Wyatt poem is that the persona's bitterness is not made explicit, but kept barely restrained under a polished veneer. Tottel's edits make that bitterness more obvious. Tottel directly calls the departure of one of the women "a bitter fashion of forsaking," instead of Wyatt's more ambiguous "strange fashion of forsaking."

FURTHER READING

Greenblatt, Stephen. *Renaissance Self-Fashioning from More to Shakespeare.* Chicago and London: University of Chicago Press, 1980.

Kreg Segall

LOVESICKNESS Lovesickness, termed *amor hereos* in the medieval medical tradition, is a psychosomatic disease, a physical manifestation of emotional distress caused by love. In the medieval and early Renaissance periods, the phenomenon of lovesickness crossed boundaries between science and the arts. It was a much-discussed medical condition as well as a literary theme, particularly in conjunction with the COURTLY LOVE tradition.

The primary symptoms of lovesickness are sunken eyes, jaundiced (yellow) color, insomnia, anorexia, and depression. Medieval contributions to the medical tradition of lovesickness also associate it with the body's humors. It was thus classified as being a step toward or similar to melancholia, which involved an increase in black bile and was a type of depression. Cures and treatments for the disease were baths, wine, song, and sexual intercourse (preferably with the beloved, but also with substitutes). However, curative intercourse, although often considered the best remedy, conflicted with the dominant Christian moral code of the day.

Some thought lovesickness was caused by love philters, both charms and potions. ANDREAS CAPELLANUS's *De amore,* a treatise on love (the basis of courtly love) connects love first and foremost with the sight of the beloved. His tract connects love with several of the physical symptoms in the medical tradition of lovesickness. His work is closely associated with the French ROMANCE tradition that heavily influenced English literature, in which examples of lovesickness abound. Popular conceptions of lovesickness indicate a true crosspollination of ideas from the medical and literary traditions.

Recorded medical history of lovesickness began with the well-known Greek physician Galen (ca. 130–200), whose influence persevered through the Renaissance. In *Prognostics of Hippocrates* (2nd century), Galen discussed lovesickness not as a bodily affliction, but rather as a passion of the soul. Notably, his study looks at the case of a woman, known only as the wife of Justus, whose symptoms increased upon hearing the beloved's name. This is one of the few recorded instances of a woman being diagnosed with lovesickness. From antiquity through much of the Middle Ages, the medical institution focused its discussions of lovesickness on males. Women are largely neglected despite their greater proclivity for the disease because patriarchal medieval culture finds men's affliction more problematic and harder to cure. In the Renaissance, it becomes associated with women, considered the lustier of the sexes.

Several other physician-scientists made significant contributions to a medical understanding of lovesickness trough the Middle Ages. The seventh-century encyclopedist Isidore of Seville called the disease *femineus amor,* or womanly love. It is this thinking that makes lovesickness so problematic to the male population. A series of Arabic physicians, Rhazes (860–932), ibn al-Jazz'r (d. 979), Haly Abbas (d. 994), and Avicenna (980–1070), also paid considerable attention to the disorder. For his 1124 *Viaticum,* Constantine the African translated into Latin ibn al-Jazz'r's *Zad almus'fir.* The *Viaticum,* which includes a chapter on lovesickness, was considered a major and authoritative medical text, and along with its several glosses, it was a source for information on lovesickness for years. Perter of Spain (ca. 1205–77) notably includes women in his commentary, *Questions on the Viaticum.* In the Renaissance, lovesickness became primarily associated with women, as Jacques Ferrand's treatise, "Melancholie Erotique" (Lovesickness) attests.

The disease pervades much of the poetry of the medieval and early Renaissance periods. GEOFFREY CHAUCER's "The Knight's Tale" from THE CANTERBURY TALES provides an excellent example of lovesickness in literature. Arcite exhibits many of the key symptoms, among other physical signs of emotional distress (ll. 1361–71). The physical and mental discomforts associated with the disease are all illuminated in Arcite's love for Emilye. He has the sunken eyes ("eyen holwe"), the jaundiced coloration ("hewe falow"), the insomnia ("His slep . . . is hym biraft"), anorexia ("his mete, his drynke, is hym biraft"), the depression ("wolde he wepe"; "So feble eek were his spiritz, and so lowe"), among other ailments, such as paleness and weight loss. Chaucer even uses the medical terms, showing the close relationship between the medical and literary discussions of lovesickness. He names the medical condition: "Nat oonly lik the loveris maladye / Of Hereos, but rather lyk manye, / Engendred of humour malencolik / Biforen, in his celle fantastic" (ll. 1372–76). This is but one of many examples.

Throughout Chaucer's *Troilus and Criseyde,* for instance, one can find in Troilus's behavior further example of lovesickness in medieval poetry. It is very prevalent in the romance tradition. In *SIR ORFEO,* the hero weeps, moans, and feels woe. Floris of *FLORIS AND BLAUNCHEFLUR* sighs and bemoans the absence of his beloved. Unlike the medical tradition, the literature did not present lovesickness as an exclusively male disorder. Blauncheflur indeed goes pale at the sight of Floris. In *The LEGEND OF GOOD WOMEN,* Chaucer follows the ancient tradition of Dido's lovesick reaction to Aeneas's departure: "[S]he hath lost hire hewe and ek her hele" (l. 1159). Her symptoms then increase: "She siketh sore, and gan hyreself turmente; / She walketh, walweth, maketh many a breyd / As don these lovers, as I have herd sayd" (ll. 1165–67).

The disease, or at least the expression of its symptoms, becomes the sign of true love, of devotion to the beloved. For this reason there are instances of feigned symptoms in an attempt to prove one's love. The Middle Ages, as well as the early Renaissance period, show a marked interest in the way in which this medical condition translates into literature. Lovesickness becomes part of the poetry and the popular culture of the time. For this reason it has also sparked academic interest in the past two decades. Two trends dominate modern literary criticism's attentions to lovesickness. One is to use literary examples of the disease to define it medically and to argue the prevalence of the medical tradition. The second trend discusses the disease's implications for gender identity. Lovesickness in the Middle Ages is often connected to emasculation. This current critical debate mirrors the manner in which medieval physicians depicted the disease.

FURTHER READING

Lowes, John Livingston. "The Loveres Malady of Hereos." *Modern Philology* 11 (1914): 491–546.

Wack, Mary Frances. *Lovesickness in the Middle Ages: The Viaticum and Its Commentaries.* Philadelphia: University of Pennsylvania Press, 1990.

Molly A. Martin

"LOVE THAT DOTH REIGN AND LIVE WITHIN MY THOUGHT" HENRY HOWARD, EARL OF SURREY (ca. 1543)

Surrey's "Love that doth reign and live within my thought" is a translation of PETRARCH's sonnet 140 of *Canzoniere*. In translating Petrarch's SONNET, Surrey has changed the rhyme to take the ENGLISH SONNET form.

In the first QUATRAIN, the speaker declares how the personified Love has conquered and consumed his body. Now Love, quite physically, lives in the speaker's thought and breast. Love has erected a banner on the speaker's face. In the second quatrain, the female beloved objects to such open display of love on the speaker's face, and she looks angrily at the speaker and Love. In the SESTET, Love retreats from the speaker's face and hides in his heart. The speaker notes that he is suffering because of Love's boldness, yet he will not leave his fallen lord, Love, but, instead, is happy to die at his master's side.

Surrey's translation uses several Petrarchan images that became fashionable in poetic representations of love. The simile of "love as a battlefield," is central to Petrarchanism. Words like *captive, arms, banner,* and *coward* create a military confrontation between Love and the beloved woman in which the speaker suffers. The beloved as "cruel fair" is a related Petrarchan idea. The object of affection inspires both desire and terror with her gaze. The lover may feel desire but must refrain from any outward show of it; here, the speaker unfairly suffers the withering gaze of his beloved when in fact it is the personified Love who is boldly showing himself, although the beloved is not likely to accept that excuse.

Surrey uses fairly regular IAMBIC PENTAMETER in this poem, although some lines begin with a trochee before returning to iambs: "Clad in the arms . . ."; "Sweet is the death" (ll. 3 and 14). Most lines are smooth, predictable, and composed of 10 syllables, especially when compared to SIR THOMAS WYATT's "The LONG LOVE THAT IN MY THOUGHT DOTH HARBOR," which is a translation of the same Petrarch sonnet. Surrey's translation puts a greater emphasis on Love as martial conqueror. His Love "reign[s] and live[s]" in the speaker's thought, while Wyatt's Love merely "harbors" in his thought; Surrey's Love has a "seat" in the speaker's "captive breast," while Wyatt's Love keeps "his residence" in the speaker's "heart."

The Petrarchan ideal of the lover languishing in and reveling in unswerving service to a cruel mistress is well illustrated in the final line of Surrey's sonnet: "Sweet is the death that taketh end by love." Wyatt's translation uses *life* as the operative word in the final line, and he uses the more neutral *good* instead of *sweet*: "For good is the life ending faithfully." Surrey's translation puts a somewhat greater emphasis on the pain and pleasure of the Petrarchan lover's pose, even as his more regular pentameter lines may suggest more artifice than emotion.

See also PERSONIFICATION; SURREY, HENRY HOWARD, EARL OF.

FURTHER READING
Jones, Emrys, ed. *Poems*. Clarendon Medieval and Tudor Series. Oxford: Clarendon Press, 1964.
Woods, Susanne. *Natural Emphasis: English Versification from Chaucer to Dryden*. San Marino, Calif.: Huntington Library Press, 1984.

Kreg Segall

"LULLABIE" GEORGE GASCOIGNE (1573)

GASCOIGNE's "Lullabie" appears as one of the poems attributed to him in the 1573 anthology *A Hundreth Sundrie Flowres* and again in the same work revised and attributed exclusively to him in 1575, entitled *Posies*. In the latter volume, the poem appears among the "Flowers" section, which Gascoigne notes as reserved for those poems "invented upon a verie light occasion" and having in them "some rare invention." Yet "Lullabie" only seems light on the surface, while conveying to the reader a very dark understanding of human mutability and loss. It connects the nurturing notion of mothers singing their babies to sleep with the stark and fretful one of losing to old age and the grave a personal sense of youth, beauty, imagination, and even sexual virility.

The poem is comprised of six eight-line STANZAS, rendered in iambic tetrameter, and in its content it resembles a LAMENT, echoing the lamentations of the biblical Job and the classical Roman BOETHIUS, without offering any of the spiritual consolation they received. Moreover, because Gascoigne maintains the hushed tones of a soothing lullaby used to lull babies to sleep, the poem grows increasingly cynical with each additional loss the poet describes. This cynicism is furthered through the haunting repetition of "lullabie" from the beginning to the end, where the moralizing poet extols the reader to "welcome payne" and "let pleasure pass," because all must recognize the inevitability of old age and loss in a world where lullabies of the gentler kind deceive even dreams.

Gascoigne's use of soft tones and soothing repetition contribute to this poem's cynical effect, in addition to suggesting the gloomy state of the poet himself. Gascoigne had spent much of his adult life playing the spendthrift dandy at Queen ELIZABETH I's court, only to realize his folly later in life, when he was cast off by the court. The poem thus also serves as a vehicle for the kind of emotionally dark honesty that critics have long recognized as a signature of his work.

FURTHER READING
Cunliffe, J. W. *The Complete Works of George Gascoigne*. 2 vols. Cambridge: Cambridge University Press, 1907–10.

Robert E. Kibler

"LULLAY, LULLAY, LIKE A CHILD" JOHN SKELTON (1528)

The available evidence suggests that "Lullay Lullay, Like a Child" was composed during JOHN SKELTON's first period at court (1485–1504), though it was published in 1528 in a collection entitled *Dyvers balettys and dyties solacyous* (Diverse Ballads and Salacious Ditties). The title of this collection (of "balettys" and "dyties") and the poem's regular tetrameter and REFRAINS both suggest that "Lullay" was a lyric. If so, the music it was set to has been lost.

The poem begins with a conversation between a man and a woman: He asks her if he may lie in her lap, and she invites him to nap. The man is so "drowsy . . . That of hys love he toke no kepe," (ll. 8–9) the speaker tells us, before directly addressing the man with a two-line refrain—"With, Lullay, lullay, lyke a chylde, / Thou slepyst to long, thou art begyled" (ll. 1–2)—which follows all STANZAS except the fourth.

The second stanza begins with the woman kissing the man into drowsiness and confusion, so that "he wyst [knew] never where he was" and forgot "all dedely syn" (ll. 13–14)—that is, his sexual desire. The next lines couch the woman's approaching deceit and infidelity in metaphor: Were sexual fidelity money, the man is expecting a "payment" he will never receive.

The third stanza sees the woman crossing a river to meet a second man, who "halsyd [held] her hartely and kyst her swete" (l. 22). She tells him that her "lefe [lover] rowtyth [snores] in hys bed" (l. 24) and that she thinks her sleeping lover has a "hevy hed" (l. 25), doubly suggestive of drowsiness and impotence.

In the fourth stanza, the speaker forgets the woman's situation entirely and roundly abuses the man for drinking himself into drowsiness, forgetting his "lust and lykyng," and ultimately for discovering her infidelity by waking up alone.

"Lullay" combines the language of a courtly lyric with an infidelity plot and formally echoes 15th-century religious lyrics in which the Virgin Mary rocks the Christ child to sleep (see VIRGIN LYRICS). Skelton's combination of these traditions lends the poem its motive ironies: The woman singing the man to sleep is some distance from her virginity, and the man, who falls asleep instead of having sex with her, saves himself from "dedely syn" at the cost of being cuckolded. This tension is emblematic of both Skelton and his poetry.

FURTHER READING

Dent, J. M. *John Skelton*. London: Orion Publishing Group, 1997.
Fish, Stanley Eugene. *John Skelton's Poetry*. New Haven, Conn.: Yale University Press, 1967.
Gordon, Ian A. *John Skelton*. New York: Octagon Books, 1970.

Nathaniel Z. Eastman

LUTE SONG See AYRE.

LYDGATE, JOHN (ca. 1370–ca. 1450) Along with GEOFFREY CHAUCER and JOHN GOWER, John Lydgate was one of the most widely read and highly esteemed poets of the 15th century. Born in the village of Lydgate (or Lidgate) in Suffolk, he entered a Benedictine abbey at Bury St. Edmunds around 1386 and was ordained in 1397. At some point he attended Gloucester Hall, the Benedictine college at Oxford. There he studied rhetoric and composed his first verses, a translation of Aesop's *Fables*. In 1423, Lydgate was appointed prior of Hatfield Broadoak in Essex, a post he subsequently relinquished in 1432. Absent from England from 1426 to 1429 as a member of the duke of Bedford's retinue in France, Lydgate returned to England, and in 1433 he moved to the abbey of St. Edmunds, where he remained until his death.

Lydgate's canon is remarkably diverse and expansive. It has been estimated that he wrote about 145,000 lines of verse over the course of his lifetime, covering many genres, including short didactic poems, devotional poetry, HAGIOGRAPHY, ROMANCES, DREAM VISIONS, and historiography. He also acquired a variety of patrons, among whom were members of royalty and nobility as well as rural gentry, members of religious orders, and craft guilds.

Among Lydgate's first significant works is the *Troy Book,* a translation in COUPLETS of Guido delle Colonne's *Historia destructionis Troiae,* which supplements the original poem in order to produce a full narrative of the fall of Troy. *The Siege of Thebes,* Lydgate's next major work, is framed as a Canterbury tale and functions as a precursor to GEOFFREY CHAUCER's "The Knight's Tale." While abroad in France, Lydgate composed *Pilgrimage of the Life of Man* (1428) and the *Danse Macabre* (ca. 1430), a translation of a French text inscribed on the cloister walls of the Church of the Holy Innocents in Paris.

Upon returning to England, Lydgate wrote a number of highly dramatic occasional works, including mummer plays for the guilds of the Goldsmiths and the Mercers and poems celebrating the coronation of Henry VI. It was also during this period that he was commissioned by Humphrey, duke of Gloucester, to translate GIOVANNI BOCCACCIO's *De casibus virorum illustrium* from Laurent de Premierfait's French rendition. *The FALL OF PRINCES,* completed in 1438, is Lydgate's lengthiest work at 36,365 lines and expands Boccaccio's compilation of historical figures oppressed by misfortune into a universal history and encyclopedia of mythology. During this period, Lydgate also composed, among other works, the *Lives of St. Edmund and St. Fremund* (1434) and the *Debate of the Horse, Goose and Sheep* (ca. 1436). Among Lydgate's last significant compositions are *Lives of St. Albon and St. Amphabell* (1439), *Testament of Dan John Lydgate* (ca. 1440–49), and *Secrees of old Philisoffres* (ca. 1449), unfinished at the time of his death.

Aside from his prolific poetic output, Lydgate is also well known for his aureate poetic language (see AUREATION) as well as his contributions to the development of the English vocabulary through the introduction of new words and repeated use of rare ones. Finally, Lydgate's deference to Chaucer (his poetic "master") and his persistent eulogizing helped cement Chaucer's poetic reputation in the 15th century and beyond.

FURTHER READING

Pearsall, Derek. *John Lydgate (1371–1449): A Bio-bibliography.* Victoria, B.C.: English Literary Studies, 1997.
———. *John Lydgate.* Charlottesville: University Press of Virginia, 1970.
Schirmer, Walter F. *John Lydgate: A Study in the Culture of the 15th Century.* Translated by Anne Keep. London: Methuen and Company, 1961.

Brandon Alakas

"MADAM, WITHOUTEN MANY WORDS"

SIR THOMAS WYATT (1503–1542) The speaker of this lyric presents his proposition up front and succinctly: "'I am sure ye will or no" (l. 2), which captures the essence of romantic relationships. Wyatt is tired of waiting for the answer—he has "burneth alway" (l. 6). He requests her "pity," the typical gift bestowed upon the COURTLY LOVE lover by his lady. He then immediately follows this with a reassurance: "If it be yea, I shall be fain / If it be nay, friends as before" (ll. 9–10). Even if the relationship is not consummated, the speaker will not hate his lady; rather, they will remain friends. Even more importantly, he reassures her that she will find another man—and that he will move on, too, and not bother her anymore. Where the assurances of continued friendship may not have motivated her, the assurances of freedom may have.

This poem suggests that the speaker feels a sense of urgency that is not particularly shared by the subject of the poem. In a manner that carries with it a sense of CARPE DIEM (seize the day), the speaker attempts to wheedle an immediate answer—a "yea or nay"—from the lady. This goes directly against the courtly love tradition, which places the man in a submissive position before his lady, allowing her to make all of the choices on her own schedule. Despite his passionate burning, Wyatt also assumes a more reasonable and rational position than many courtly lovers, as demonstrated by his reassurances.

The source of this poem is Dragonetto Bonifacio's *Madonna Non So Dir Tante Parole,* which Wyatt follows but, in his typical style, also adapts. It is a 12-line lyric, broken into three quatrains rhyming *abab, cdcd, efef.* The structure of the poem adds to its overall sense of rationalism: Each quatrain is a self-contained rhyming unit and has two lines that share parallel structures ("And . . ." at lines 3 & 4, 5 & 6; "If . . ." at lines 9 & 10); each stanza contains a direct address ("Madam" at line 1, "Ye" at lines 7 & 11); and, each "yea" is balanced with a "nay," maintaining the sense of proportionality.

FURTHER READING
Levine, Robert T. "Madame, Withouten Many Wordes." *Explicator* 38, no. 3 (1980): 46–49.

MADRIGAL

Madrigals originated in Italy in the early 14th century as short love poems set to music. More specifically, madrigals are lyrics ranging from one to four three-line STROPHES followed by a two-line REFRAIN (called a *ritornello*). Sixteenth-century madrigals are directly inspired by the early originals, though they exhibit entirely different music. Sometimes madrigals are referred to as PASTORAL songs, though the subject matter does not have to reflect this.

See also CAMPION, THOMAS; CANZONE; DOWLAND, JOHN.

FURTHER READING
Kerman, Joseph. *The Elizabethan Madrigal.* New York: American Musicological Society, 1962.

"MAIDEN IN THE MOR LAY" ANONYMOUS (14th century)

This enigmatic 14th-century Middle English lyric has delighted and perplexed critics for years. Its opening STANZA quickly establishes a pattern of repetition that is followed throughout the lyric. The maiden is introduced, and the reader learns that she lay on the moor for a full week. The phrase "in the mor lay" appears in four of the six lines (ll. 1, 2, 4, 5). Technically, then, these lines rhyme only because they end with the same word. The final line of the stanza, however, ends with "day," which rhymes with "lay." This first stanza is the only one that is six lines long; the others are seven.

The remainder of the lyric focuses on how she lived in the wilderness, addressing, in turn, her food, drink, and residence. This information is imparted as if the curious reader were inquiring into the maiden's habits. Each stanza begins with an announcement concerning the subject: "Welle was hire mete [good was her food]" (l. 7); "Welle was hire dring [good was her drink]" (l. 14); "Welle was hire bour [good was her bower]" (l. 21). This statement is followed by an echoic question effectively asking, "In the wilderness of the moors, what items could furnish the necessary comforts of life?" In turn, these questions are followed by aborted answers, all of which break off with "the," which lead into a repeat of both statement and question, finally followed by a "complete" answer. Through this rhythmic linguistic dance, where statements are made, questions are asked, and answers are hesitantly supplied, tentatively withdrawn, and then reproffered, the reader learns that the maiden eats "primeroles" (primroses) and violets, drinks "chelde" (cold) water from the wellspring, and sleeps in a bed made from red roses and lilies. As in the first stanza, the only true rhyme links the repeated phrase with the final word of each stanza.

No matter their approach, most critics agree that the poem is hauntingly beautiful. The majority of critical inquiries attempt to answer the question, "Who is this maiden?" These investigations end up falling into two basic categories. One camp believes that the lyric can and should be interpreted using a Christian perspective; the other holds out for "popular" sources of the poem. Christian readings usually focus on the maiden as representative of Jesus' mother, the Virgin Mary. A few, however, have suggested either Mary Magdalene or Mary of Egypt as the template for the maiden in the poem. In this case, the maiden's exile to the moor is a self-imposed ascetic practice, undertaken to expurgate her sins of the flesh. Cultural readings generally insist on folkloric sources for the text, although at least one has suggested that the lyric was a drinking song, and another has posited its importance as a ritual dance. Whatever the origins, the multiplicity of meanings found within and around it serve only to make it a more valuable poem to read.

The most common Christian reading of this lyric aligns the maiden with the Virgin Mary. This interpretation relies on conventional symbolism and biblical EXEGESIS. Seven, the number of nights that the maiden lay on the moor, represents life on earth, which was shrouded in darkness before the light of Christ dawned. The moor, a wild and untamed place, represents earth under the old law (Old Testament). The world awaits the coming of the new law (New Testament). The time span also suggests the seven days of creation, with the greatest creation of all, Jesus, promised to arrive when needed the most. In the meantime, the maiden is prepared for her role by consuming violets (the sign of humility) and primroses (which represent human beauty), and drinking from the cool well waters (God's grace). Moreover, eating primroses, a flower as common as it is beautiful, recalls God's generosity to humanity, and the maiden is a part of his gifts of grace and bearer of his ultimate generosity (Christ). The maiden reclines on a bed of lilies and roses, which symbolize purity and martyrdom (and/or charity), respectively. Again, this is evocative of the Virgin Mary. In pre-Reformation theology, the mother of Jesus is eternally virginal, the supreme example of purity. By welcoming her son's disciples into her home and caring for them as her own children, she embodies charity. Mary also suffered a "bloodless" martyrdom as she watched her son being arrested, beaten, and crucified.

The folkloric interpretation suggests that the maiden is either a human involved in magic rituals or a fairy. This analysis relies on the tone of the poem as well as its words. The lyric is suggestive of a trance-inducing chanted ritual (it has often been called a *characteristic lilt*). This effect is achieved through the constant repetition of phrases. Otherwise, the maiden's actions reveal her involvement with the fairy realm. She is unified with nature through eating flowers, sleeping on the moor, and drinking from the wellspring. The wellspring may refer to "well-wakes," which was the pre-Christian practice of worshipping wells. This type of ceremony is well documented in historical sources and remaining architectural evidence, and it even overlapped with the coming of Christianity. Numerous saints were said to have blessed "holy springs," the waters of which were said to possess healing powers. The pre-Christian well-wakes mainly took place during Midsummer festivals and are thus connected with fertility, making the well-maiden a fertility symbol herself.

Germanic legends contain a number of references to water sprites known as moor-maidens. In these stories, the moor-maidens appear at village dances and enchant the young men. This lyric, written in the form of a dance, suggests this type of activity. Often the moor-maidens appear in villages bearing gifts of wild flowers such as violets. In each of these legends, the moor-maiden is allowed to mingle with humans only on certain occasions and, when she does so, must return to the wilds of her moor by dusk or she will die. Attempts to restrain the maiden always fail, and even if she is persuaded to remain for a while, she will eventually fade into the darkness, perhaps returning on the next feast day.

See also MIDDLE ENGLISH LYRICS AND BALLADS, VIRGIN LYRICS.

FURTHER READING
Greene, R. L. "The Maid of the Moor in the *Red Book of Ossory*." *Speculum* 27, no. 4 (1952): 504–506.
Manzalaoui, Mahmoud. "*Maiden in the Mor Lay* and the Apocrypha." *N&Q* 210 (1965): 91–92.
Waldron, Ronald. "'Maiden in the Mor Lay' and the Religious Imagination." *Unisa English Studies* 29 (1991): 8–12.
Wenzel, Siegfried. "The Moor Maiden—A Contemporary View." *Speculum* 49, no. 1 (1974): 69–74.

MANNYNG, ROBERT, OF BRUNNE (ca. 1265–after 1338)
Robert Mannyng of Brunne, a Gilbertine lay brother, also studied at Cambridge University, where he met and befriended ROBERT I THE BRUCE. He wrote two poems, both based on ANGLO-NORMAN originals: *HANDLYNG SYNNE*, an exposition on the SEVEN DEADLY SINS and the sacraments; and *A Chronicle of England* based on WACE'S *ROMAN DE BRUT*. His work is often considered somewhat plodding, but it marked an important step toward reestablishing the VERNACULAR literary tradition in England.

See also CHRONICLE.

FURTHER READING
Taylor, Andrew. "Manual to Miscellany: Stages in the Commercial Copying of Vernacular Literature in England." *Yearbook of English Studies.* (January 3, 2003).

"MAN OF LAW'S TALE, THE" GEOFFREY CHAUCER (ca. 1390)
"The Man of Law's Tale," along with its introduction and epilogue, constitute Fragment 2 of *The CANTERBURY TALES* by GEOFFREY CHAUCER. The introduction begins with the most precise description of the date and time of events in the *Tales*: The narrator tells us that it is exactly 10 A.M. on the 18th of April. His method of describing the time is a highly sophisticated one involving the use of astronomical devices and tables, and the narrator's observation that at this time every tree's shadow was as long as the tree itself (ll. 7–9) comes directly from the *Kalendarium* of Nicholas of Lynn. Since the *Kalendarium* was written in 1386, we can be confident that at least the prologue to "The Man of Law's Tale" was written afterward.

Noticing that it is already 10 A.M., the Host eloquently urges the pilgrims not to waste time and suggests, with an apt and possibly ironic use of legalistic terminology, that the Man of Law tell his tale. The Man of Law, or "Sergeant of the Lawe" as identified in the GENERAL PROLOGUE TO THE CANTERBURY TALES (GP l. 309), acquiesces, but with the caveat that the range of tales available to him is limited since: "Chaucer, . . . / Hath seyd hem in swich Englissh as he kan . . . / as knoweth many a man. (ll. 45–52). This is an interesting self-reference that presents Chaucer as an established and well-known poet, even if he does not meet the Man of Law's standards; he is crude and immoral.

The Man of Law's criticism of Chaucer's immoral stories includes his observation that Chaucer never wrote a word about the wicked Canacee, who fell in love with her brother and bore his child. Because this story is told by JOHN GOWER (in book 3, part 1 of his

CONFESSIO AMANTIS), it has been suggested that Chaucer here criticizes Gower's version of the story, and this is why Gower removed a flattering reference to Chaucer in book 8 of his *Confessio Amantis,* though recent research has discredited this theory. Because authors are not accountable for the perspectives of their characters, this description has been understood as a betrayal of the Man of Law's rigid moral code.

Understanding the Man of Law's character is essential to understanding his tale. His deliberate obtuseness makes his own tale that much harder to accept as a serious and instructive story. The story instead uncovers the Man of Law's own moral code, which has more to do with appearing righteous than with doing the right thing, although some recent scholarship has challenged this general view, pointing out that in the tale Chaucer asks serious questions about how evil can remain in a world created by a powerful and righteous God.

The Man of Law's tale begins with a prologue (told in RHYME ROYAL) against poverty, which deprives a person of respect and affection, before proceeding on to the narrative. In part 1 (ll. 34–385), a company of merchants travel from Syria to Rome both to trade their wares and to find entertainments. They catch sight of Custance, the Roman emperor's daughter, whose beauty has been the talk of the Romans. After their return, the merchants tell the sultan of Syria of her beauty; he immediately falls in love with this beautiful woman and wishes to wed her. The sultan sends for his private council and tells them of his intentions. When they warn him that no Christian prince would let one of his children be allowed to marry under Muslim law, the sultan responds with a simple solution: He will convert to Christianity to have her. When word of this reaches the Roman emperor, he quickly agrees and sends Custance, who then goes "with sorwe al overcome" (l. 264) to Syria to marry the sultan. Several Romans accompany her.

The sultan's mother, whom the Man of Law calls a "welle of vices" (l. 323), hears of her son's intentions and convinces her councillors not to give up the Muslim faith or the "hooly lawes of our Alkaron [Al-Koran, or the Koran with its Arabic definite article] / Yeven by Goddes message Makomete [Mohammed]" (ll. 332–

333). She suggests they go through the Christian rituals in any case and pretend to be Christians, while she also schemes to do away with her son's Christian bride.

In the second part (ll. 386–875), the sultan's mother succeeds in killing the Roman Christians and the sultan, because "she hirself wolde al the contree lede" (l. 434). Custance is put on a rudderless boat and set adrift. Her boat carries her from the eastern Mediterranean to the Strait of Gibraltar and then continues northward all the way to Northumberland, where she is finally cast ashore. She is discovered by King Alla's constable, who with his wife Hermengild promises to care for her. They are converted from their native religion, and Custance lives pleasantly with them until Satan causes a young knight to fall in love with her, "so hoote, of foul affeccioun, / That verraily hym thoughte he sholde spille," (ll. 586–587) with a pun on *spille* as meaning both "ejaculate," and "die," which of course were elided medicinally anyway. Custance "wolde do no synne" (l. 590) and so rejects the knight. He is infuriated and retaliates by cutting Hermengild's throat and putting the bloody knife by Custance, and then accusing her of the murder in court. However, the knight is miraculously stricken down, inspiring the king "and many another in that place" (l. 685) to convert to Christianity.

King Alla then marries Custance, which displeases his mother, Donegild. When Alla goes to war in Scotland, Custance returns to the constable's care and bears a son who is baptized Mauricius. A messenger is sent to tell King Alla of his son's birth, but Donegild makes him drunk, steals his letters, and substitutes one with a letter which announces that Custance's baby was a monster, and she herself was a sorcerous whore. Though upset, Alla writes back insisting on mercy for Custance, whereupon Donegild again gets the messenger drunk and replaces the letter with another counterfeit ordering Custance's banishment. Custance is once again set adrift, this time with her baby "wepyng in her arm" (l. 834).

In part three (ll. 876–1162), Alla returns, discovers his mother's treachery, and kills her. This does not help Custance, who drifts at sea until her ship returns to the Mediterranean. At this point the story shifts focus to the Roman emperor, who had learned of the slaughter of his Christian retinue in Syria and the dishonor done to his daughter, and sent his senator and other lords to Syria to exact vengeance. The senator is on his way back to Rome when he chances upon Custance's ship. He entrusts her and her son to his wife. This state of affairs remains for some time, until King Alla comes to Rome to receive penance from the pope for killing his mother.

Word spreads in Rome that Alla has arrived, and when the senator hears of this, he insists on showing the Northumbrian king reverence. Custance's son attends the feast and stares at Alla, who "hath of this child greet wonder" (l. 1016) and asks the senator who the boy is. The senator proceeds to tell the story of how he and his mother were found at sea. Alla begins to wonder if this is his son and goes with the senator to his house to see if the boy's mother is his wife. Alla and Custance are soon reunited. Then Alla invites the emperor to dinner, and Custance reveals herself and is reunited with her father. Her son is made emperor, and Custance returns to England with Alla, where she lives until his death, after which she returns to Rome to live with her father until death separates them.

This tale's genre is difficult to define, demonstrating characteristics of HAGIOGRAPHY and ROMANCE, but conforming to neither. "The Man of Law's Tale" is also a highly rhetorical work. Unlike his sources, Nicholas Trivet's CHRONICLE written in ANGLO-NORMAN and Gower's rendition of Trivet's story, Chaucer embellishes the style of his version with the ornate rhetorical figures recommended by medieval rhetoricians. The poem is particularly self-conscious, constantly referring to the storytelling with narratorial interjections (e.g., "I dar sey yow na moore," l. 273).

Thematically, the poem emphasizes that Custance's strength of faith empowers her in the face of adversity. Her passivity makes her piety more reverent; she does not respond with violence to the threats presented by the two royal mothers of the story because she entrusts her fate to God. It is her constant faith in the eyes of inconstant FORTUNE that allows for her eventual happy ending, although this, too, is ultimately transient, which is reinforced by the tale's final emphasis on death. Some have argued that the tale focuses on the

manifestations of her belief and not the faith behind it, making it more interested in propriety than in virtue.

The tale ends with a problematic epilogue. In it, the Host praises the Man of Law's tale and accuses the Parson of being a Lollard (see LOLLARDISM). Parallelling Custance's stolid nature, the Parson does not reply—an ambiguous response at best. Another pilgrim speaks up to insist that she or he will not hear a sermon, and offers to tell a tale lacking in philosophy, legal terminology, and Latin instead. This passage proves a challenge, since the name of the pilgrim varies in the different manuscripts, being variously named the Shipman, the Summoner, the Squire, and the Wife of Bath. To make matters worse, it appears that these names were scribal or editorial inventions based on whose tale appears next in the manuscript. Even the epilogue is questionable, as it does not appear in all manuscripts.

Recent feminist scholarship has further explored the tale's obvious misogyny, displayed both in Custance's extreme passivity and silence and in the monstrosity of the mothers-in-law, both of whom further demonize themselves by desiring authority. Other critics have examined Chaucer's portrayal of the SARACENS, including his knowledge of the Koran. Still, this tale has not undergone the frenzy of scholarly examination that others have, and there is room for more work to be done.

FURTHER READING
Allen, Elizabeth. "Chaucer Answers Gower: Constance and the Trouble with Reading." *ELH* 64 (1997): 627–655.
Clogan, Paul M. "The Narrative Style of the Man of Law's Tale." *Medievaliuet Humanistica* N.S. 8 (1977): 217–233.
Cooper, Helen. *Oxford Guides to Chaucer: The Canterbury Tales.* 2nd ed. Oxford: Oxford University Press, 1996. 123–138.
Delsanta, Rodney. "And of Great Reverence: Chaucer's Man of Law." *Chaucer Review* 5 (1971): 288–310.
Spearing, A. C. *Textual Subjectivity: The Encoding of Subjectivity in Medieval Narratives and Lyrics.* Oxford: Oxford University Press, 2005: 101–136.
Sullivan, William L. "Chaucer's Man of Law as a Literary Critic." *MLN* 68 (1953): 1–8.

Michael Foster

MANUSCRIPT From the Latin *manu scriptus,* "written by hand," a manuscript is a document that has been written by hand and not printed. Before the invention of the printing press, all texts were so written; thus, the majority of medieval works (with the exception of some 15th century texts) are manuscripts. As printing took some time to become widely available, a great many early modern texts exist only in manuscript form as well. Moreover, some authors, such as SIR THOMAS WYATT, preferred that their work be only available in manuscript even when the printing press was available for use.

Most medieval manuscripts were written on parchment, made of low-quality calfskin or sheepskin, though some were composed on vellum (thicker, high quality sheep or calf skin). Late Middle Ages texts were occasionally written on paper. Some, though not all, contained pictures called illuminations. These may have been simple decorations, or may have been related to the content of the manuscript; for instance, the manuscript that contains SIR GAWAIN AND THE GREEN KNIGHT contains elaborate illuminations that reflect the contents of the poem.

Today, British medieval manuscripts follow a consistent cataloguing system for the most part. Documents are labeled by city, library name, and then manuscript name. Thus, a work found in London, Lambeth Palace, MS 92 would be housed at the Lambeth Palace Library in London, and be labeled "Manuscript 92" on the shelf. There are some obvious exceptions to this standard practice (for instance, the EXETER BOOK), but this is, for the most part, standard practice.

See also COTTON VITELLIUS A.XV.

FURTHER READING
Ker, Neil Ripley, A. J. Piper, and Ian Campbell Cunningham. *Medieval Manuscripts in British Libraries.* Oxford: Oxford University Press, 2002.

British Library Catalogue of Illuminated Manuscripts. Available online. URL: http://www.bl.ukcatalogues/illuminatedmanuscripts/welcome.htm.

MARIE DE FRANCE (late 12th century) All

we know of Marie de France is that her name was Marie, that she came from France, as she self-identifies—"Marie ai nun, si sui de France" (My name is Marie, I am from France)—and she wrote in ANGLO-NORMAN for the enjoyment of the French-speaking English court. Marie was one of the few well-known female authors of the Middle Ages. She is best known as the author of 12 short narrative ROMANCES, also known as *lais* (LAYS): "BISCLAVRET" (The Werewolf), "Chaitivel," "CHEVREFOIL" (The Honeysuckle), "Les Deux Amanz," "ELIDUC," "Equitan," "Le Fresne" (The Ash Tree), "GUIGEMAR," "LANVAL," "LAÜSTIC" (The Nightingale), "Milun," and "Yonec." Her other texts include 103 FABLES, translated from Henry Beauclerc under the titles of *Ysopet,* the *Purgatoire de St. Patrice,* and the recently attributed *La Vie Seinte Audree.* The *lais,* their prologue, and *Ysopet,* are preserved collectively in a mid-13th-century manuscript, MS Harley 978, though various *lais* appear in other manuscripts as well.

Establishing an identity for Marie is complicated and uncertain. Scholars have suggested a number of candidates: Marie, abbess of Shaftesbury; Marie, countess of Boulogne, daughter of King Stephen of England and Matilda of Boulogne; Marie, daughter of Waleran II, count of Meulan; and Marie, abbess of Reading. However, none of these candidates has been universally accepted.

Marie's works are important contributions both to ARTHURIAN LITERATURE and to the romance tradition, as well as to the establishment of the VERNACULAR. While her work is not particularly feminist, her writing does provide a medieval feminine perspective missing from other popular literature of the time.

See also ANGLO-NORMAN POETRY.

FURTHER READING
Barban, Judith Clark, and June Hall McCash, eds. *The Life of Saint Audrey: A Text by Marie De France.* Jefferson, N.C.: McFarland, 2006.

Burgess, Glyn S. *The Lais of Marie de France: Text and Context.* Athens, Ga.: University of Georgia Press, 1987.

Marechal, Chantal A, ed. *The Reception and Transmission of the Works of Marie De France, 1774–1974.* Lewiston, N.Y.: Edwin Mellen, 2003.

Shoaf, Judith, trans. "The Lais of Marie de France." University of Florida, Gainesville. Available online. URL: http://web.english.ufl.edu/exemplaria/intro.html. Downloaded on January 7, 2007.

Susannah Mary Chewning

MARLOWE, CHRISTOPHER (1564–1593)

Born in Canterbury in 1564, Christopher Marlowe was the son of a shoemaker. In January 1579, he was awarded a scholarship to the King's School in Canterbury. Near the end of 1580, he enrolled at Corpus Christi College, Cambridge University, where he had received a scholarship intended for students who planned to become clergymen. He received his B.A. in July 1584 and his M.A. in July 1587. The award of the latter degree has left a tantalizing biographical mystery. The university was going to deny the M.A. to Marlowe because of a rumor that he was planning to enter the English seminary at Rheims (that is, convert to Roman Catholicism). However, the Privy Council intervened on Marlowe's behalf in June, writing that "he had done her majesty good service" and that his degree should not be hindered. Precisely what service Marlowe had provided is not known, though it is usually thought to have involved some kind of undercover work, perhaps as a courier or spy.

After graduation, Marlowe embarked on a literary career in London. Several of his works are commonly attributed to his years in Cambridge, though without hard evidence: *All Ovid's Elegies*; "The PASSIONATE SHEPHERD TO HIS LOVE"; and his tragedy *Dido, Queen of Carthage*. The first part of *Tamburlaine the Great* must have been written in Cambridge as well, since part 2 of the play was already being performed by fall 1587. Between 1588 and 1592, Marlowe authored four more plays: *Doctor Faustus, The Jew of Malta, The Massacre at Paris,* and *Edward II*. Their order and precise dating are uncertain. His poem "On the Death of Sir Roger Manwood" was written sometime after Sir Roger's death in December 1592, with HERO AND LEANDER and Marlowe's translation of *Lucan's First Book* probably following in 1593.

This brief career encompasses extraordinary accomplishment, influence, and innovation. Marlowe's much-imitated lyric "The Passionate Shepherd to His Love" established the classical "invitation" poem in English literature, and his translations of OVID's *Amores* and the first book of Lucan's *Pharsalia* are the first in English. *All Ovid's Elegies* revitalized the use of the HEROIC COUPLET in early modern England; and *Tamburlaine,* together with Thomas Kyd's *The Spanish Tragedy,* made BLANK VERSE into the standard meter of English Renaissance drama. His *Hero and Leander* is the finest EPYLLION in English, approached only by WILLIAM SHAKESPEARE's *VENUS AND ADONIS*. Marlowe and Shakespeare clearly imitated and learned from each other in their drama as well, and while Shakespeare's plays would soon transcend Marlowe's, Marlowe was the more prominent playwright at the time.

Marlowe's life in London was not simply the life of a sedate and scholarly writer. It is commonly assumed that he continued to perform at least occasional undercover services for the government. Records also exist of several violent or criminal acts in which he was involved. In 1589, he was involved in a swordfight with one William Bradley. The poet Thomas Watson intervened and killed Bradley. Marlowe was arrested and released; Watson pled self-defense and was pardoned. In 1592, Marlowe and Richard Baines were arrested in Flushing, the Netherlands, for counterfeiting. He was returned to England and apparently suffered no legal consequences. Baines later accused Marlowe of atheism and sodomy.

In 1593, Thomas Kyd, with whom Marlowe once roomed, was arrested and tortured on suspicion of authoring a libel against immigrants. A document found in Kyd's possession was deemed heretical, and he claimed that it belonged to Marlowe. Shortly thereafter, Marlowe was arrested by the Privy Council, who received additional reports of Marlowe's atheism, including the note from Baines. Released on his own cognizance, four days later, on May 30, Marlowe was killed in a tavern brawl at Eleanor Bull's house in Deptford, a suburb of London. Ingram Frizer stabbed Marlowe over the bill, and one of the greatest geniuses of English literature was dead at the age of 29.

FURTHER READING

Honan, Park. *Christopher Marlowe: Poet and Spy*. Oxford: Oxford University Press, 2005.

Hopkins, Lisa. *Christopher Marlowe: A Literary Life*. Houndmills, U.K.: Palgrave, 2000.

Kuriyama, Constance Brown. *Christopher Marlowe: A Renaissance Life*. Ithaca, N.Y.: Cornell University Press, 2002.

Riggs, David. *The World of Christopher Marlowe*. New York: Henry Holt, 2004.

Bruce E. Brandt

MARY I (1516–1558) *queen of England* Mary Tudor was born in 1516 to King HENRY VIII and his first wife, Catherine of Aragon, whom Henry divorced after breaking from the Roman Catholic Church. Thereafter, Mary was declared illegitimate by Parliament. Despite this turn of events, however, Mary eventually assumed the throne in 1553, after the death of her young half brother, King Edward VI, and after defeating, with strong support, the claim made by the Protestant Lady Jane Grey ("the nine day queen"). In doing so, she became, in the summer of 1553, the first undisputed queen to rule England. As queen, Mary's overriding concern was to reconcile her country with Rome and bring back the Catholic faith.

In 1554, the 37-year-old queen married her younger cousin, Philip of Spain, son of Holy Roman Emperor Charles V (King Charles I of Spain). Mary was besotted with Philip; unfortunately, her affection was not returned to the same degree. Even more unfortunately, Mary's subjects resented Philip, seeing in him a symbol of their great rival, Spain. Two false pregnancies, likely caused by the disease that would eventually kill her (ovarian cancer), did nothing to secure her position. As her health deteriorated, Mary was forced to consider the question of succession, and eventually agreed to pass the crown to her half sister, who became Queen ELIZABETH I. On November 16, 1558, Mary died.

Despite their personal difficulties, both Mary and Philip enjoyed poetry, music, and the arts, so witty and intelligent individuals populated their court. Though the great writing of Mary's reign tended to be ecclesiastical and political rather than poetic, a number of poets, mostly those who were Catholic or had Catholic sympathies, rose to prominence or began their careers under Mary, including JOHN HEYWOOD, Nicholas Grimauld (1519–62), Thomas Tusser (1524–80), George Cavendish (1494–ca.1562), and Thomas Sackville, earl of Dorset (1536–1608). The most important poetic developments of Mary's reign, however, were not compositions, but rather the assembly of two key anthologies: *A MIRROR FOR MAGISTRATES*, under the auspices of the Roman Catholic John Wayland, and *TOTTEL'S MISCELLANY*.

FURTHER READING

Loach, Jennifer. *Parliament and the Crown in the Reign of Mary Tudor*. Oxford: Clarendon Press, 1986.
Loades, D. M. *Mary Tudor: A Life*. Oxford: Blackwell, 1990.
———. *The Reign of Mary Tudor: Politics, Government, and Religion in England, 1553–1558*. New York: St. Martin's Press, 1979.

Melissa A. Harris and Michelle M. Sauer

MARY, QUEEN OF SCOTS (MARY STUART) (1542–1587)

Mary Stuart was born to James V of Scotland and Marie de Guise at Linlithgow Palace; she was crowned Queen of Scots six days later, following her father's death. In 1548, she married the French dauphin, and she remained in France for the next 12 years. Her husband ascended the French throne as King Francis II in 1559 but died the following year. Power passed to his mother, Catherine de'Medici, who sent Mary home to Scotland.

The Catholic Mary returned to Scotland in 1561 only to find that John Knox, the Presbyterian preacher, had created religious instability there. Mary's troubles only increased when she married Henry, Lord Darnley, in 1564. Darnley was pompous, politically unskilled, and fond of taverns. Furthermore, he arranged for the murder of her secretary, David Rizzio. The relationship became irreparable.

Mary gave birth to a son, James Stuart, later James VI of Scotland (1566) and James I of England (1603), in 1566. In 1567, Lord Darnley was killed in an explosion south of Edinburgh's Royal Mile (Kirk of Field). Many thought that James Hepburn, earl of Bothwell, Mary's new paramour, was responsible, and soon her enemies accused Mary as well. Nevertheless, Mary and Bothwell married, which outraged Scotland. The newlyweds attempted an armed conflict, but the queen was defeated and forced to renounce her title. One year later, Mary escaped prison and attempted to retake her throne. She was defeated again by Protestant forces, and in 1568 fled to England, seeking the protection of her cousin Queen ELIZABETH I.

In 1587, Mary's Catholic supporters attempted to murder Elizabeth and place her on the throne. Elizabeth reluctantly decided to execute her cousin, a deed that was accomplished at Fotheringay Castle on the morning of February 8, 1587.

Mary is the undisputed author of a number of letters that are increasingly studied as fine examples of the epistolary genre. She corresponded with numerous people, including popes and rulers. Her status as a poet, however, is a contentious one. The authenticity of the so-called CASKET LETTERS has long been in dispute. The eight letters, 12 SONNETS, and two marriage contracts contained in them were used as the main pieces of evidence against Mary in her trial for complicity in Darnley's murder. The originals, however, disappeared in 1584, and only copies (in French, English, and Scots) remain. Nevertheless, the sonnets themselves are interesting, and even if not authentic, certainly served their political purpose, and they are commonly anthologized today.

See also JAMES VI/I.

FURTHER READING
Donaldson, Gordon. *Mary Queen of Scots*. London: English University Press, 1974.
Fraser, Antonia. *Mary Queen of Scots*. London: Weidenfield/ Nicolson, 1969.
MacRobert, A. E. *Mary, Queen of Scots and the Casket Letters*. London and New York: I. B. Tauris Publishers, 2002.

Melissa A. Harris and Michelle M. Sauer

MEDITATIONS ON SIN ANNE VAUGHAN LOCK (1560)
This SONNET SEQUENCE, consisting of "The Preface, Expressing the Passioned Minde of the Penitent Sinner" and "A Meditation of a Penitent Sinner, upon the 51st Psalme," was published in 1560, appended to Anne Vaughan Lock's English translation of the French *Sermons of John Calvin, upon the songe that Ezechias made after he had been sicke, and afflicted by the hand of God*. The 19 verses of the "51st Psalm" reflect on the need for sinners to confess their sins so that they can receive God's forgiveness. Lock's devotional *Meditations* elaborate and contemporize each verse of the "Psalme" to emphasize Calvinist theology, particularly the idea of repentance. The "Preface," which contains five SONNETS, begins a lament about "The loathsome filth of my distained life" (l. 5). Twenty-one sonnets—rhyming *abab, cdcd, efef, gg*—follow this opening lament in the primary *Meditation*. The verses of the psalm are printed as marginalia, and the words

of the verses are incorporated, repeatedly, into the corresponding sonnets as part of the paraphrasing to emphasize the penitential aspects that the devout must meditate upon.

Lock was a Protestant and a longtime friend and correspondent of John Knox and other Calvinists. Her writings and translations, under her various married surnames, including Dering and Prowse, reinforce her political and religious support of the Reformation. Lock's recent recognition as the translator "A. L." of the Calvin sermons and as author of the sonnet sequence, in spite of a textual note claiming that a friend gave the *Meditations* to her, has refocused scholarly attention on Lock and the sonnets. The sonnet sequence is now acknowledged to be the first in English. Its female authorship challenges the canon and the traditional lines of influence on sonneteers such as SIR PHILIP SIDNEY and WILLIAM SHAKESPEARE. Additionally, the religious nature of Lock's poems is leading scholars to reconsider women's devotional writing and its place within the literary and polemical traditions.

See also TUDOR WOMEN POETS.

FURTHER READING
Lock, Anne Vaughan. *The Collected Works of Anne Vaughan Lock*. Edited by Susan M. Felch. Tempe: Arizona Center for Medieval and Renaissance Studies, 1999.

Jennifer L. Ailles

METERS OF BOETHIUS ALFRED THE GREAT (ca. ninth century)
Two different versions of BOETHIUS's *CONSOLATION OF PHILOSOPHY* exist in OLD ENGLISH, both dated to the ninth century. One renders all of the *Consolation* into Old English prose. The other treats only the verse sections of the *Consolation* and is an adaptation of the corresponding sections of the Old English prose version into Old English poetry. This version is known as *Meters of Boethius*, and both have been attributed to ALFRED THE GREAT.

Perhaps the most noteworthy aspect of both Old English versions of the *Consolation* is the way Alfred has recast Boethius's original work, framed as a conversation between Boethius and Lady Philosophy, into more explicitly Christian terms. For example, the narrator (referred to simply as Mind for most of the work) is speaking to Wisdom, rather than Philosophy, and the subject matter of the verses often deals directly with the greatness of God. At the same time, Alfred sometimes calls upon the traditions of Germanic heroic poetry, such as when he replaces Boethius's discussion of the Roman politician Fabricius with a reference to Weland, a figure from Germanic mythology. Alfred seems to be at his best when he departs from Boethius. The first of the *Meters,* for example, represents his attempt to place Boethius and his work into a historical context. In it, Alfred recounts the sack of Rome by the Goths, using the language of Anglo-Saxon heroic narratives.

FURTHER READING

Krapp, George Philip. *The Paris Psalter and the Meters of Boethius.* New York: Columbia University Press, 1932.

Monnin, Pierre Eric. "Poetic Improvements in the Old English *Meters of Boethius.*" *English Studies* 60 (1979): 346–360.

William H. Smith

"METHOUGHT I SAW THE GRAVE, WHERE LAURA LAY" ("A VISION UPON THE CONCEIPT OF THE FAERY QUEENE") Sir Walter Raleigh (ca. 1589)

When EDMUND SPENSER's great EPIC poem, *The FAERIE QUEENE,* first appeared in print in 1590, seven short commendatory poems followed at the end. The adventurer, courtier, soldier, and poet SIR WALTER RALEIGH wrote the first two of these poems, which praise Spenser and his literary achievement. The first one, beginning "Methought I saw the grave, where Laura lay," is considered by many critics to be among the best lyric poems of the Elizabethan era, particularly due to its vividly dramatic content, Raleigh's accomplished use of the fashionable SONNET form, and the relationship it suggests between his poem and Spenser's epic on which it comments, as well as between the two authors themselves. To encounter such a memorable poem is unusual in this context; commendatory verses were typically artless "blurbs" by like-minded poets or acquaintances who hoped to benefit from a little flattery.

The position of all seven poems is also unusual: Often preceding the main work to act as a preview or even advertisement, the verse commendations in the case of *The Faerie Queene* become a kind of epilogue. This placement may simply reflect their late arrival at the printer, or they may have been consciously intended to create an impression-forming, sympathetic first reception of Spenser's ambitious poem. In this context, Raleigh offers in his sonnet the first literary criticism on Spenser's epic.

"Methought I saw" is specifically an ENGLISH SONNET, with its three quatrains followed by a concluding COUPLET. The speaker begins by describing a vision he or she has received of the grave of Laura, the idealized, unobtainable subject of PETRARCH's poems. Whereas the real Laura purportedly died in Avignon, Raleigh imagines her grave within the Temple of Vesta, in the Roman Forum (ll. 1–3). The first quatrain ends with a statement of purpose: The speaker has passed by her grave to see "that buried dust of living fame" (l. 4). The motivation initially seems positive: Petrarch has immortalized Laura in his poetry, despite her physical death. Yet the very presence of Laura's "dust" compromises that fame: Petrarch ultimately can commemorate, but not save, her. The "buried" dust refers to Laura entombed, but more figuratively it foreshadows the death of her "living fame," subtly personified here. Raleigh also personifies "faire love" and "fairer vertue" (l. 5). These "graces" maintain Laura's grave, even as vestal virgins once kept the sacred fire of Rome continuously lit in Vesta's temple. The climax of the narration occurs next: "All suddeinly I saw the Faery Queene" (l. 6). This revelation constitutes the central action of Raleigh's vision.

The sonnet's formal title is "A Vision upon the Conceipt of the *Faery Queene.*" For years, Raleigh's editors did not preserve the title's italics, but this change causes a significant shift in emphasis. The original title clearly speaks of Spenser's epic poem, though in Raleigh's sonnet itself the phrase appears without italics, suggesting instead the *character* the Faerie Queene. Spenser further complicates the matter in a "Letter to Raleigh," printed just before the sonnet. There he explains how the character of the Faerie Queene represents glory generally and Queen ELIZABETH I in particular. In this way Spenser honors by imitation Raleigh's court poetry, which allowed for effusive praise of the queen. Raleigh, in turn, employs these multiple identifications. He emphasizes the Faery Queene's "approch" (l. 7), which causes Petrarch's soul to weep. This initial focus on the Italian author directs Raleigh's praise toward Spenser as a superior poet. However, this focus then turns to the queen herself; "those graces" (l. 8), love and "vertue," abandon Laura's tomb to join the Faery Queene's court. In other words, the graces acknowledge that Queen Elizabeth is more worthy than Laura, and that Spenser has idealized his heroine more memorably than Petrarch. The third quatrain underscores the consequences: stones bleed, ghosts groan, and, even more strikingly, Oblivion replaces the graces at Laura's "herse" (l. 10). In the final couplet, Homer's spirit also appears, trembling and cursing Spenser, "that celestiall theife" (l. 14), for excelling earlier poets and stealing their fame. These last lines concentrate Raleigh's praise of Spenser as an *epic* poet, not just as a love poet such as Petrarch.

Critics continue to disagree about the exact relationship between Raleigh and Spenser in this sonnet. The two poets were friends and owned adjacent properties in Ireland, and it was Raleigh who used his influence at court to introduce Spenser to the queen. Raleigh, then, may simply be proud of his protégé. However, others have inferred from these lines anxiety or even passive aggression on the part of Raleigh, whose favor with the queen was waning. Perhaps he was jealous of Spenser's immense achievement. Still, Spenser speaks of Raleigh and represents him as the character Timias in *The Faerie Queene,* and even at times adopts his poetic style. Whatever the reason, Raleigh crafts a dramatic sonnet of praise in the poetic mode of his gifted friend.

FURTHER READING

Raleigh, Walter. *The Poems of Sir Walter Raleigh*. Edited by Agnes Latham. Cambridge, Mass.: Harvard University Press, 1951.

Bednarz, James P. "The Collaborator as Thief: Raleigh's (Re)Vision of *The Faerie Queene*." *ELH* 63, no. 2 (1996): 279–307.

Cousins, A. D. "Raleigh's 'A Vision upon the Conceipt of the Faery Queen.'" *Explicator* 41 (1983): 14–16.

Koller, Katherine. "Spenser and Raleigh." *ELH* 1, no. 1 (1934): 37–60.

Oram, William A. "Spenser's Raleighs." *Studies in Philology* 87 (1990): 341–362.

Brett Foster

METONYMY A poetic device, commonly employed in SONNETs, wherein a detail or a noteworthy characteristic of someone or something is used to represent the whole. Occasionally, metonymy involves the use of something closely related to the person or object to represent it. For instance, "wood" is a common use of metonymy for cross in religious lyrics such as "NOW GOTH SONNE UNDER WOD."

See also SYNECDOCHE.

R. Jane Laskowski

METRICAL PREFACE TO THE *PASTORAL CARE* (ca. 890)

Near the end of the ninth century, ALFRED THE GREAT completed a translation into Old English of Saint Gregory's *Regula Pastoralis* (*Pastoral Care*), a treatise concerning the duties and qualities appropriate to ecclesiastical leaders. Alfred affixed two prefaces to his translation: a lengthy preface in Old English prose, describing the poor state of learning in England at the time and Alfred's motivations for providing the translation, and a very brief (only 17 lines long) preface in Old English verse.

The metrical preface briefly details the history of the *Regula Pastoralis,* describing how Gregory directed Augustine of Canterbury to bring the work to England in order to spread the ideas of Christianity to the "island-dwellers." The preface goes on to say that Alfred translated the work and had copies made of his translation in order to send it to English bishops, some of whom were unable to read the Latin original. Throughout, the poem employs the persona of the book itself, stating, for example that "King Alfred translated *me.*" In this way, the poem is reminiscent of ANGLO-SAXON RIDDLES that often speak in the voice of the object being described.

Unlike the prose preface, which precedes it, the metrical preface has received very little scholarly attention. Many early studies of ANGLO-SAXON POETRY, in fact, treated the verse preface as a poorly written poem of little historical or literary interest. Recently, however, a few scholars have begun to reconsider it, and current studies have focused on the way Alfred mixes traditional poetic language and motifs with specific words and phrases more typical of learned Old English prose. By doing so, Alfred demonstrates his facility with both styles of writing and highlights his own abilities as an author and a translator. The content of the preface may also be important in understanding key aspects of Alfred's reign as king. By placing himself in the same category as Saint Gregory and Augustine of Canterbury, Alfred blurs the line between secular and religious power and strengthens his own authority over the bishops who received copies of the translated work.

FURTHER READING

Discenza, Nicole Guenther. "Alfred's Verse Preface to the *Pastoral Care* and the Chain of Authority." *Neophilologus* 85 (2001): 625–633.
Dobbie, Elliott Van Kirk, ed. *The Anglo-Saxon Minor Poems.* New York: Columbia University Press, 1942.

William H. Smith

MIDDLE ENGLISH LANGUAGE   Prior to the arrival of William the Conqueror, the common English language was OLD ENGLISH, which reflected its Germanic roots more distinctly than Middle English. The NORMAN CONQUEST, however, changed this. The Norman French influence, and the subsequent development of an ANGLO-NORMAN culture, deeply affected the way English was spoken and written. English went into a decline, and when it reemerged, it was permanently changed.

Scholars agree there were at least five dialects of Middle English: Southern, West Midlands, Northern, East Midlands, and Kentish. Many believe, however, that there were many more dialects than these five, and scholarly debates continue. Eventually, the East Midlands dialect—the one spoken in London—emerged as the strongest of these, becoming the standard for spoken and written language. This dialect was not a direct descendant of West Saxon, the Old English dialect with the most surviving materials. Moreover, English was rarely written down during the Anglo-Norman period, so by the time it became regularly written down again, there was an even poorer match between written and spoken language than in Old English. French scribes introduced additional spelling errors. Many of these became frozen when the printing press arrived, leaving a language today that does not match phonetically and graphemically.

Phonologically, the consonant inventory was much like Present Day English with a few exceptions, most notably in final syllables. All Old English diphthongs became pure vowels, but the French influence provided several new diphthongs. Middle English retained two of the graphemes not used in the Latin alphabet, the thorn (þ) and the yogh (ȝ). Occasional use of the ash (æ) and eth (ð) remained. The consonant inventory was very similar to Present Day English, with the French influence making the occurrence of letters rarely used in Old English (j, v, q, and z) more common.

The most significant change between Old English and Middle English was the loss of the inflectional system. No longer a synthetic, inflected language, Middle English became an analytic language dependent upon word order to create syntactical structure. Nouns were reduced from five cases to two (possessive and nonpossessive), just as they are in Present Day English. Adjectives lost all inflections. Syntax became the determining factor of sentence meaning.

Forms of the first and second pronouns remained relatively unchanged, but the dual pronoun found in Old English was lost. The use of *ye* as a polite form of address is found from the late 13th century, and is modeled on French practice. In general, you or þou was used between equals and to inferiors, while ye was used to address a superior. Indefinite and relative pronouns became more defined, and late Middle English witnessed the beginnings of reflexive and reciprocal pronouns.

Like Old English and Present Day English, Middle English verbs had only two tenses: past and present. The present tense was used to express habitual actions and general truths as well as current activities and, occasionally, the future. By late Middle English (the 14th century), the historical present was developed and regularly used in literature, especially ROMANCEs. Historic present allows the narrative of past events to place the audience in the midst of the action. Middle English verbs also had the same three moods as those in Old English and Present Day English: indicative, subjunctive, and imperative.

Finally, Middle English had a much larger lexicon than Old English. Aside from the huge infusion of French loanwords, Middle English also absorbed words from the Scandinavian languages, Latin, Celtic languages, Dutch, and other Continental languages.

Compounding was still used to create new words, as was affixing, blending (combinations of two existing words), and clipping (removing pieces of words).

FURTHER READING

Burrow, J. A., and Thorlac Turville-Petre. *A Book of Middle English*. 3rd edition. Oxford: Blackwell Publishing, 2005.

Mossé, Fernand. *A Handbook of Middle English*. Translated by James A. Walker. Baltimore, Md.: Johns Hopkins University Press, 1952.

Jordan, R. *Handbook of Middle English Grammar: Phonology*. Translated and revised by E. J. Crook. The Hague: Mouton, 1974.

MIDDLE ENGLISH LYRICS AND BAL-LADS

These genres belong to the popular literature of this era, and most BALLADS, but not all lyrics, are songs. A ballad is a dramatic, narrative work, a folk poem with no single author, but a lyric is generally an expression of one poet's feelings, presenting the poet's voice. Thus the lyric belongs to the poet and the ballad to the people.

Ballads were passed on like rumors, composed and transmitted orally long before they were written down, gaining and losing details as a leader sang new lines and a chorus repeated the BURDEN. Comparisons of old and current forms of ballads and of versions from different sources show the variations of repeated performances, each one fixed in its time and place. They describe stock characters in formulaic terms and predictable situations, yet each retelling enthralls the audience with its striking vigor, linking the familiarity of well-loved tales and the freshness of striking accounts. Their familiarity allows dramatic brevity, without the need for detailed description. Imagination completes pictures that begin with such ballad motifs as young warriors (for example Lochinvar), riderless horses (as in "BONNIE GEORGE CAMPBELL"), abandoned maidens (too numerous to mention), revenants (as in "The Unquiet Grave"), and flowers growing from the graves of parted lovers (another very widespread ballad motif).

Early gatherers of English and Scottish ballads were Bishop Thomas Percy (1729–1811) and Sir Walter Scott (1771–1832), both of whom amended the works, unlike their contemporary, Joseph Ritson (1752–1803). Their works are still prized and have frequently been reprinted. A more recent foundation of ballad scholarship is Francis James Child's collection. He faithfully recorded variant forms of the ballads in five volumes published between 1882 and 1898, and many later works of criticism refer to "Child ballads," citing the numbers he gave to the ballads as points of reference. Helen Child Sargent and George Lyman Kittredge reduced this work to one volume in their edition of 1904.

The poems now called lyrics did not have this name when they were written. The term *medieval lyric* as it is used now generally means no more than a short poem. These explore all aspects and moods of medieval life, embracing meditations, prayers, hymns, mnemonic poems, and love poems, and only occasionally imply a narrative. Some lyrics convey the poet's emotions; some songs are found with their music, and many CAROLS display their connection with dance in their rhythms and patterns. In such ways they resemble the lyrics of later eras, but many other poems we now call medieval lyrics are quite unlike them.

Religious meditations, for instance "NOW GOTH SONNE UNDER WOD" ("Sunset on Calvary") and "YE THAT PASEN BY THE WEYE," are designed to inspire an individual's silent thoughts, as do the prayers for various occasions. There are many hymns. "Stand wel Moder, vnder Rode" and "Iesu Cristes Milde Moder" are among those which recall the Latin hymn "Stabat iuxta Christi Crucem," by translation or inspiration. The latter are only two of the English lyrics that show a debt to other European languages, in particular to Latin and French.

Many lyrics told of the passing of the seasons, expressing the exuberance of the coming of spring and love after the deprivations of winter, as in "LENTEN YS COME WITH LOVE TO TOUNE." The love that inspires lyrics may be divine, as in "I Syke When I Syng" and "I SING OF A MAIDEN," or earthly; some of the latter, such as "JOLLY JANKYN" and "The WILY CLERK" suggest the stories of betrayed maidens and their clerical seducers. Mnemonic poems arranged information so that it could easily be remembered, with no thought of feelings or emotion. A few works, including "Judas," which clearly tells a story, and the enigmatic "CORPUS CHRISTI CAROL" have been seen both as lyrics and ballads.

The varied assortment of the lyrics includes the most concentrated poetry of the period, and brevity intensifies the emotions expressed in poems such as "Foweles in the Frith" and "Western Wind" and the compression of the lines intensifies their ambiguities. Although some works appear to be slight, this impression is deceptive, since much meaning may be packed within a few lines. For example, the rich implications of its imagery and sophisticated structure belie the apparent artlessness of "I Sing of a Maiden," and even the briefest lyrics repay close study. The most enduring of all the Middle English lyrics is "Thirty dayes hath November," one of many mnemonic short poems which shaped and preserved worldly information, religious doctrine, and social mores and so influenced and enforced attitudes in an era when many people could not read.

General anthologies of medieval poems usually include lyrics of love written to earthly mistresses and lyrics to the Virgin Mary (often in very similar terms), religious meditations, and carols such as "Adam Lay Bound" and "Bring us in Good Ale." Specialized collections show more of the range of the style and material found in these works. Seeking to study medieval lyrics and ballads may seem to mean consulting forbidding texts with words that are difficult to understand. It is possible, though, to begin with editions in standardized form, to avoid the problem of varying dialects; many modern editions also give helpful notes on the same page as the text. Familiarity with these more encouraging forms will show that difficulties are more apparent than real, and a reader is soon prepared to consult and enjoy collections such as Child's, Brown's, and Robbin's, which use original dialects, allowing us contact with the literature, customs, faith, joys, and sorrows of those who spoke our language in the past and the tales they treasured.

See also BALLAD, REVERDIE, VIRGIN LYRICS.

FURTHER READING

Brook, G. L., ed. *The Harley Lyrics: The Middle English Lyrics of MS Harley 2253.* 4th ed. Manchester, U.K.: Manchester University Press, 1968.

Buchan, David. *The Ballad and the Folk.* London: Routledge, 1972.

Child, Francis James, ed. *The English and Scottish Popular Ballads.* 5 vols. Boston: Houghton, 1882–98. Reprint, New York: Dover, 1965.

Davies, R. T., ed. *Medieval English Lyrics: A Critical Anthology.* Evanston, Ill.: Northwestern University Press, 1964.

Fowler, David C. *A Literary History of the Popular Ballad.* Durham, N.C.: Duke University Press, 1968.

Rosemary Greentree

MIDDLE ENGLISH POETRY   There were two traditions that influenced the poetry of the Middle English period, which lasted roughly from the time of the NORMAN CONQUEST in 1066 to around 1500, both of which had a major impact on the poetry that would follow. The first tradition came from ANGLO-SAXON POETRY, a hard-driving and alliterative style that consisted of no rhyme scheme or accentual structure, only stressing alliterative beats (see ALLITERATION). The second tradition came from French poetry, which contained rhymes, COUPLETS, STANZAS, and a fixed number of syllables (as opposed to a fixed number of *stressed* syllables found in Anglo-Saxon poetry). Thus, from these two influences, Middle English poetry began as poetry that should be heard, not read quietly alone, and it grew chiefly in the 13th century as English began to overtake French as the dominant language in all levels of society.

From its divergent beginnings, Middle English poetry blossomed, branching into a number of subgenres, including lyric poetry, ROMANCES, DREAM VISIONS and allegorical poetry, FABLIAU and burlesque, and verse history. However, while a variety of genres arose within Middle English poetry, it remains important to note that not every poem can be placed neatly into one specific genre. In some cases, poems exhibit characteristics of more than one genre, while others, such as lyric poetry, fit fairly nicely in one category. And while scholars tend to classify Middle English poetry into two general periods—the early Middle English period and 14th-century poetry—these lines are often crossed as well.

Generally speaking, we can outline the varieties of poetry appearing in the Middle English period that culminate in the poetry of GEOFFREY CHAUCER. During the early period, lyric poetry arose. There are two basic types of Middle English lyric poetry: the secular and the sacred. While the great bulk of this type of poetry is sacred, there exist a number of secular poems, which have as their themes COURTLY LOVE, drinking songs, and popular customs. Sacred poetry comes in a variety of forms, relying largely on religious Latin texts, the Bible, and other patristic writings. The basic thrust is some form of appeal to Christ or the Virgin Mary for redemption. Middle English lyricists remained somewhat anonymous in voice, meaning they emphasize a more shared experience as opposed to a subjective or personal one. Another form of sacred poetry was the versification of popular hagiographies (saint's lives; see HAGIOGRAPHY).

In the romance poetry of the 13th century, we find one of the best-represented genres of Middle English poetry. Romances in verse often evolved from Anglo-Saxon heroic poetry, usually involving knightly exploits and adventures. The heroes in each style, however, differ slightly. While Anglo-Saxon heroics emphasized an allegiance to men and duty, Middle English romance heroes are devoted more to a lady and to God. There are often elaborate settings and descriptions, and the message is very didactic. There are also a variety of rhyme schemes and metrical patterns, most notably the octosyllabic couplet and a tail rhyme scheme. The most famous of these poems are the cycle poems, such as Arthurian poems (see ARTHURIAN LITERATURE) and *SIR GAWAIN AND THE GREEN KNIGHT* and the rest of the Gawain Cycle, but noncycle romances also exist. A subgenre of the romance is the verse CHRONICLE, which contains a short history of verse, often involving the founding of England—these include Arthurian histories—and possessing a theme of national pride.

A later form, Middle English dream visions and ALLEGORY poems, differ from the previous two genres in that these poems invent tangible objects as representations of immaterial objects or reality. These visions are usually encountered in a dream in which the dreamer is cast into a rustic setting—a dream world—that replaces the real world. Usually, the dreamer acquires some prevision of the future, and he is often led by a guide who helps interpret the dream. *PIERS PLOWMAN* by WILLIAM LANGLAND is one example of a dream vision in alliterative verse. Another is JOHN GOWER's (1327–1408) *CONFESSIO AMANTIS*. Some of Chaucer's most famous minor poems are dream poems, including *The PARLIAMENT OF FOWLS, The BOOK OF THE DUCHESS,* and *The HOUSE OF FAME.*

Of course, Chaucer is well known for his fabliau poems (of which there exist seven in *The CANTERBURY TALES*). These poems, along with the burlesque, are mostly verse tales written for the purpose of amusement. Fabliau was popular in France before the 13th century and is said to have come to England about that time. Contrary to romances, they are not didactic, and they were often written for the upper class. Fabliaus are often coarse and descriptive; they involve a realistic setting and generally are written from a comic point of view. Similarly, burlesques are hyperbolic imitations of characters or events intended to effect laughter. Chaucer's "Tale of Sir Topas" is an excellent example of a burlesque of courtly romance.

Another genre of Middle English poetry, BEAST FABLES, probably derived from Aesop. These are didactic poems that involve beasts acting in an anthropomorphic manner, often at odds with their characteristic nature (for example, a wolf might be portrayed as dimwitted). Frequently, beasts represent human social or political groups. Middle English beast literature was thought of as good for SATIRE, since the animals masked any references to identity. Some examples of this genre include REYNARD LITERATURE and Chaucer's *The Parliament of Fowls.* The Reynard tales, which probably came from France or Germany, involve a wily fox and center on biting criticism of the upper class. Chaucer's *Parliament* combines a beast tale with a dream vision, critiquing government and courtly love.

Around 1350–1400, England enjoyed an ALLITERATIVE REVIVAL, or resurgence in the use of alliteration by poets. Langland's *Piers Plowman, PEARL,* and *Sir Gawain and the Green Knight* all share this characteristic, among other traits. In the second half of the 14th century, alliterative poetry became more involved with political and social protest (and *Piers,* with its three visions, is a good example). Again, as in much Middle English poetry, no one category can fully do justice to these poems, so it remains best to look at them as the divergent base of what would blossom into Renaissance poetry, where some genres would flourish while others would disappear.

FURTHER READING

Chism, Christine. *Alliterative Revivals*. Philadelphia: University of Pennsylvania Press, 2002.
Duncan, Thomas G., ed. *A Companion to the Middle English Lyric*. Cambridge and Rochester, N.Y.: Brewer, 2005.
Pearsall, Derek. *Old English and Middle English Poetry*. London: Routledge & K. Paul, 1977.

Michael Modarelli

MIDDLE SCOTS *literary language*

Early academic critics of the makars (Scottish court poets) argued that *Middle Scots* (a term first used in the Victorian era) was purely a written construction and not a genuine spoken language in Scotland. More recently, however, scholars have argued that the Middle Scots dialect was indeed a living speech, and that the poets' genius was the incorporation of the rhythm and syntax of this local speech into high poetic verse drawing on a Chaucerian, French, and Latin tradition simultaneously. The Middle Scots poets themselves referred to their language as *Inglis,* or English, mainly to distinguish themselves from Gaelic dialects rather than linking themselves with English. Middle Scots developed directly from Old English and is in effect a northern dialect of Middle English. The vocabulary of the Middle Scots poems reflect a heavy drawing on Latin and French terms, and some poems such as WILLIAM DUNBAR's *The Tretis of the Twa Mariit Wemen and the Wedo* reflect the common speech of the Scots people.

Even a casual reader of Middle Scots poetry will immediately notice the orthography as markedly different from the more familiar Middle English spelling. Many of the colloquial terms probably did not have written counterparts at all, so the poets' spelling of some of these terms is arbitrary (such as *widow* rendered as *weido* and *wiedo*). However, the truly distinctive features of the Middle Scots forms are the use of *quh* for *wh* (as in *quhose* and *quhat*), the use of *sch* for *sh* (as in "schowris"), and the plural form *is* rather than *es* ("lassis" and "rokkis"). Like nearly all medieval poetry, Middle Scots poems are ultimately meant to be read aloud, and the orthography is secondary to the rhythm and rhyme of the words.

See also SCOTTISH CHAUCERIANS.

FURTHER READING

Corbett, John. *Written in the Language of the Scottish Nation*: *A History of Literary Translation into Scots*. Somerset, U.K.: Multilingual Matters, 1999.

Mark DiCicco

"MILLER'S TALE, THE" GEOFFREY CHAUCER (ca. 1388–1395)

One of the most frequently studied of *The CANTERBURY TALES,* "The Miller's Tale" is often considered one of the most entertaining tales as well. The action begins, however, in "The Miller's Prologue." The Knight has just finished telling his tale, and according to the dictates of social class, the Host invites the Monk to go next. However, the drunk Miller interrupts and offers to tell a tale that will "quite" (repay, l. 3126) the Knight's. Thus, the traditional hierarchy is disrupted, and the pilgrimage thrown into disarray. The Reeve protests the proposed tale on three grounds: It will be insulting to carpenters (he is a carpenter), it will be "harlotrie" (bawdy), and it will slander wives—the latter two characteristics being true of "The REEVE'S TALE" as well.

The story opens with an introduction to wealthy but old John the Carpenter and his poor young lodger, Nicholas, a student, who is handsome and charming. John is married to an 18-year-old woman named Alisoun, of whom he is quite jealous and protective. As the Miller notes, he kept her "narwe in cage" (l. 3224), or closely guarded. Alisoun is attractive, well-dressed, jolly, and clean—no suitable match for an old man.

Nicholas is attracted to Alisoun, and one day while John is out, "prively he caughte hire by the queynte" (discreetly he grabbed her by the cunt, l. 3276), making known his desire. Alisoun protests, but Nicholas pleads with her, and eventually she agrees to an affair as long as her husband never finds out. The pair await an opportunity.

Meanwhile, a prissy clerk named Absolon has encountered Alisoun and fallen in love with her. Absolon is a fastidious fop but schooled in the arts of COURTLY LOVE. One night he serenades Alisoun under her bedroom wndow, inciting John's wrath and Alisoun's disdain. Despite her obvious dislike, Absolon continues in the throes of LOVESICKNESS.

One Saturday while John is out of town, Nicholas and Alisoun finally put their plan into action. Nicholas hides in his room over the weekend, and when John finally seeks him out on Monday, he finds Nicholas apparently passed out in his room. Upon reviving, Nicholas reports his findings from the stars: The following Monday will witness a flood similar in proportion to Noah's Flood in the Bible. Nicholas instructs John to save himself by constructing three tubs in which to hide and fastening them to the roof. The three of them will then lie inside the tubs awaiting the flood—perfectly silent so as not to disrupt prayers.

Dutifully, John secures and provisions the tubs, and on Monday night, all three participants—Nicholas, Alisoun, and John—climb in. As soon as John is asleep, however, Nicholas and Alisoun sneak down to the bedroom, where they sport all night.

The next morning finds Absolon thinking of Alisoun. Boldly, he decides to approach her house. She castigates him, but he is so persistent that she agrees to give him a kiss if he agrees to leave her alone afterwards. Planning a practical joke, Alisoun "at the wyndow out she putte hir hole" (l. 3732). Absolon realizes that he has kissed Alisoun's nether region and not her mouth when he encounters a beard (pubic hair) and, instantly furious, plans revenge. Running across the street, he borrows a hot poker from the local smith. Returning to the window, he calls up to Alisoun, begging another kiss. This time, Nicholas sticks his behind out the window, and when Absolon calls out, Nicholas releases a tremendous fart. In retaliation, Absolon "Nicholas amydde the ers he smoot" (l. 3810). In pain, Nicholas shrieks and yells for water. John wakes up, hears the shouts for water, and, thinking the flood is beginning, cuts the ropes of his tub. The tub crashes to the floor, breaking John's arm. The neighbors all come running. Nicholas and Alisoun convince everyone that John has gone mad, and so his reputation remains.

"The Miller's Tale" is a FABLIAU in form. It is told by the Miller to "quite"—that is, match—the Knight's Tale, which is a ROMANCE. As a fabliau, it is heavily dependent on plotting and staging. It features a typical fabliau love triangle—an older husband (John), a young wife (Alisoun), and a young suitor (Nicholas)—with the addition of a fourth party, Absolon, who is portrayed as a

"courtly lover." The characters are, for the most part, stock types: John, the cuckolded husband, is a wealthy would-be social climber who is ridiculed at the end; Alison is an attractive and lusty young wife; Nicholas is a scheming student; Absolon is a squeamish fop. Contextually, it perfectly offsets "The Knight's Tale." Both feature two men in love with one woman, dreams (prophetic and unprophetic), love versus sex, seeking beyond one's means, and rash promises.

A number of analogues for "The Miller's Tale" have been identified, though no direct source has been uncovered. The earliest of these is the Flemish fabliau *Dits van Heilan van Beersele,* in which similar adventures (ass-kissing, fake flooding, limbs breaking) befall a woman's three lovers. The Tale also features a number of BIBLICAL ALLUSIONS, although Nicholas is the only character to quote it accurately. GEOFFREY CHAUCER also firmly grounds his tale in its local setting of Oxford through location details, as well as the invocation of local saints (e.g., Saint Frideswide and Saint Neot).

Early criticism of the Tale focused, typically, on its sources, analogues, and textual variants, but a number of critics also sought to establish its moral code. However, like many fabliaux, it metes out its own warped sense of justice, not standard morality. The punishments seem disproportionate, and the Tale as a whole seems generally amoral. Is it, then, a celebration of adultery?

Recent criticism has examined the economics of exchange in the Tale, the treatment of Alisoun, and the various interactions between the men. There are a number of references to exchanges, monetary comparisons, and reprisal. In fact, the Miller sets up the principle of exchange—of women and their sexuality—in the Prologue, and the idea carries through the narrative. Marxist critics have also suggested that the varying degrees of social classes presented in the Tale—considered more nuanced than in many fabliaux—also reflect historical imbalances and shifting economic relations among and within the classes.

Feminist critics have examined the role and presentation of the only woman in the Tale, Alisoun. Though she escapes relatively unscathed, Alisoun's life is not unproblematic. She is depicted in nonhuman terms, being kept "narwe in cage" like a bird, but also as various barnyard animals—a weasel, colt, kid, calf, mouse, etc. She is described only externally, even more of a "flat" character than the men, and also has the fewest lines to speak. Moreover, she is treated rather brutally by all the men: Her husband is mentally cruel, if not physically; Nicholas grabs her by the genitals; Absolon intends to burn her behind with a hot poker. To all of them, she is merely an object and a sexual plaything. Finally, queer and gender critics have begun examining the interconnected relationships among the men in the Tale. In particular, the scene between Absolon and Nicholas reveals an underlying homoeroticism, between the kissing of the "nether eye" and the thrusting of the red-hot poker, itself borrowed from Gerveys the Smith, a "freend so dere" to Absolon he would lend the clerk anything. These recent avenues of criticism have provided insight not only into "The Miller's Tale" itself, but also into the fabliau genre, particularly as it is rendered into MIDDLE ENGLISH LANGUAGE.

FURTHER READING

Laskaya, Anne. *Chaucer's Approaches to Gender in The Canterbury Tales.* Cambridge: Cambridge University Press, 1995.

Schweitzer, Edward C. "The Misdirected Kiss and the Lover's Malady in Chaucer's *Miller's Tale*." In *Chaucer in the Eighties,* edited by Julian N. Wasserman and Robert J. Blanch, 223–233. Syracuse, N.Y.: Syracuse University Press, 1986.

"MINE OWN JOHN POINS" SIR THOMAS WYATT (1536–1537)

This poem is one of three epistolary SATIRES—satirical poems written as letters—attributed to SIR THOMAS WYATT. It is addressed to John Poynz (Poins), a fellow courtier and friendly correspondent from Gloucestershire. The poem is a rough translation of Luigi Alamanni's (1495–1556) "Tenth Satire," and follows the Italian poem in several particulars though it also focuses more specifically on Wyatt's own *de facto* house arrest on his family's estate during 1536. It is a long answer to the implied question of why he is absent from the court—why he "draws" homeward rather than following the "press of courts" (ll. 2–3). He first assures Poins that it is not a matter of contempt for royal power and influence, though he does reserve for himself a deeper-piercing judgment

than to blindly adore the great and powerful as the more common sort might (ll. 7–13).

As the poem proceeds, Wyatt is willing to admit that he would like preferment and honor as much as the next person; however, he is not willing to part with his honesty to do so (ll. 17–18). Here the satire reaches a fuller voice by repeating the motif of what he "cannot" do. Each behavior enumerated, each brand of dishonesty and injustice, helps him do the work of the satirist by exposing the vices of a court that by its nature looks magnificent. First, he cannot flatter; he cannot offer praise to those who deserve censure (ll. 19–21). Second, he cannot honor those whose lives are given over to vice—"Venus" representing lust and "Bacchus" representing drunkenness—even if he hurts himself by his refusal (ll. 22–24). Third, he cannot "crouch" to "worship" those who prey on the innocent like wolves among lambs—those who abuse their political and economic power (ll. 25–27). After this inventory of sins, the poet proceeds to qualify his earlier complaints by reaffirming his commitment to hold to honesty even at great personal cost (ll. 28–30). He continues with this theme of honesty and forthrightness, emphasizing that he cannot use "wiles" or "deceit" for his own advancement (ll. 31–33) and that he cannot use injustice for personal gain (ll. 34–36).

What follows is more satirical protest in a like vein, but this time the specifics are enumerated in much quicker succession. They still focus on the poet's obligation to hold to truth, emphasizing that he cannot pretend that vice is virtue, and that he will not live thrall to the whims of another, no matter how powerful (ll. 37–55). This is the central assertion in the poem, and it is crucial: The fact that he "cannot learn the way" to do the things he condemns frames his moral stance as involuntary and natural rather than as the outgrowth of misanthropy or pride. More examples follow, showing how he will not cloak vice with the "nearest virtue" (l. 61)—drunkenness as good fellowship, duplicity as eloquence, and so forth. The complaint rises to a crescendo with his refusal to grant the right of "tyranny" to the prince, reiterating yet again the phrase "I cannot" (l. 76).

The remainder of the poem provides the contrast, a declaration of independence from courtly life and a

PAEAN to the simple country life—hunting, hawking, study, and a kind of freedom (though he is constrained to admit the "clog" at his heel—the involuntary nature of his retirement to the country [l. 86]). Finally, he is in England—"Kent and Christendom" (l. 100)—a far better place than any glamorous but morally tainted foreign land such as France, Italy, or Spain.

The poem may be profitably read through three perspectives. The first is biographical. The poem shows influence from Wyatt's intimate knowledge of court life and his customary stance of disaffection and complaint. His relationship with the throne was rocky, so the relief shown in the poem at being far from the centers of power is unfeigned. The second perspective is closely related to the first. Wyatt's greatest contributions to English poetics came in his importation of Continental (French and Italian) verse forms and topics. This poem, like many of Wyatt's poems, is a translation, and it even adopts terza rima, an interlocking rhyming structure common in Italian Renaissance poetry and found in the Alamanni poem from which this poem is adapted.

The third perspective has to do with the genre of the poem. Generally, the satirist is seen as one whose piercing vision exposes folly and evil. Such is obviously a major concern of this poem, as it consists primarily in an inventory of the wrongs that our speaker will not engage in. The royal court was a ripe target for this kind of unflattering exposure, both by literary tradition and in reality. As we see in this poem, though, the poet's trustworthiness is just as crucial as his discovery of the alleged abuses. He must be seen as a credible voice and reliable critic—hence his repeated assertions that he is neither able to engage in court vices nor willing to excuse or explain them away. Since he is an honest, plain-speaking man who likes nothing more than to be left alone to hunt at his estate, the poet is compelled only to speak truth. This is neither the first nor the most prominent example of satire in English poetry, but it is a notable achievement if only for the penetrating voice of frustration we find in it.

See also COURT CULTURE.

FURTHER READING
Gleckman, Jason. "Thomas Wyatt's Epistolary Satire: Parody and the Limitations of Rhetorical Humanism." *Texas Studies in Literature and Language* 43, no. 1 (2001): 29–45.

Graham, Kenneth. *The Performance of Conviction.* Ithaca, N.Y., and London: Cornell University Press, 1994.

Christopher A. Hill

MINOT, LAURENCE (ca. 1300–ca. 1352)
Nothing is known for certain about Laurence Minot other than he was a poet who lived in northern England and wrote political poems that refer to events dating from 1333 to 1352, during the HUNDRED YEARS' WAR. As these poems staunchly support Edward III (r. 1327–57), it has been suggested by a number of scholars that he was attached to the court in some way, though no evidence of that remains.

Minot's poetry is distinctive for its strong use of ALLITERATION, as well as its fierce patriotism, and has been hailed by some as a landmark of the political poem genre. He is one of the first to model short poems about battles after ROMANCES rather than BALLADS.

See also "SIEGE OF CALAIS, THE."

FURTHER READING
James, Thomas Beaumont, and John Simons, eds. *The Poems of Laurence Minot: 1333–1352.* Exeter: University of Exeter Press, 1989.
Moore, Samuel. "Lawrence Minot." *MLN* 35 (1920): 78–81.

MIRROR FOR MAGISTRATES, A (1559–1610)
This collection, written by various Tudor poets, is a continuation of JOHN LYDGATE's *The FALL OF PRINCES,* itself a translation/nationalization of GIOVANNI BOCCACCIO's *De Casibus Virorum Illustrium* (*On the Downfall of Famous Men*). Though there is evidence that an edition was compiled as early as 1555 (only the title page remains), the first complete edition was published by Thomas Marsh in 1559. William Baldwin was the editor and primary author, though he assembled a group of writers to assist him, including George Ferrers, Thomas Phaer, and Thomas Churchyard. This first edition contained 19 biographical poems; subsequent editions (1563, 1574, 1578, 1587, and 1610) added more biographies and involved new authors, such as MICHAEL DRAYTON and Thomas Sackville. Not all entries were signed.

The term *mirror* derives from the Latin *mirare,* "to look at," and a magistrate is any ruler. Since antiquity, literary mirrors have typically presented positive examples for readers to follow, but *A Mirror for Magistrates's* title relies on a second meaning for *mirror*—warning (ca. 1325–1610)—and thus demonstrates conduct to be avoided.

Most of the stories are told in first person by the "fallen prince." In every version, the vignettes are written in RHYME ROYAL, and prose bridges connect the poems. The common verse form provides uniformity, while seven authorial styles give variety.

This collection of tragedies rendered in verse reinforces Renaissance views of morality and teaches English history with a Tudor political inflection. One of the overarching themes is lust of varying sorts: The lives of Henry Percy, Owen Glendower, and Jack Cade caution against lust for power; Richard II tells readers that his lust for admiration allowed him to be easily deceived; Eleanor Cobham lusted after power (she wanted her husband, Duke Humphrey, to be king so badly that she conspired with witches); Jane Shore, mistress to Edward IV, describes the effects of physical lust on her life.

Another common strain throughout *A Mirror for Magistrates* is the inevitability of punishment for vice: Neither position nor secrecy can protect those who behave immorally. FORTUNE's wheel turns and throws the one on top to the bottom. Just as Lady Philosophy in BOETHIUS's *The CONSOLATION OF PHILOSOPHY* is the servant of God, so, too, is Fortune in *A Mirror for Magistrates,* dispensing God's justice in earthly life.

See also WARS OF THE ROSES.

FURTHER READING

Budra, Paul. *A Mirror for Magistrates* and the *de casibus* Tradition. Toronto: University of Toronto Press, 2000.

Kiefer, Frederick. "Fortune and Providence in the *Mirror for Magistrates.*" *Studies in Philology* 74 (1977): 146–164.

Winston, Jessica. "*A Mirror for Magistrates* and Public Political Discourse in Elizabethan England." *Studies in Philology* 101 (2004): 381–400.

Karen Rae Keck

MIRRORS FOR PRINCES

MIRRORS FOR PRINCES A genre of political writing popular during the Middle Ages and the Renaissance. Poems and prose treatises in this genre were, essentially, instruction manuals for rulers. As literary works, they often include historical or literary examples designed to illustrate positive or negative examples of rulers.

Perhaps the most famous example is Niccolò Machiavelli's *The Prince* (1532), but numerous other examples exist from a wide variety of cultures. The early 16th century text *A MIRROR FOR MAGISTRATES,* a continuation of JOHN LYDGATE's *The FALL OF PRINCES,* was particularly popular in England.

FURTHER READING

Meens, Rob. "Politics, Mirrors of Princes and the Bible: Sins, Kings and the Well-Being of the Realm." *Early Medieval Europe* 7, no. 3 (1998): 345–358.

MORALL FABILLIS OF ESOPE THE PHRYGIAN, THE (OVERVIEW)

MORALL FABILLIS OF ESOPE THE PHRYGIAN, THE (OVERVIEW) ROBERT HENRYSON (ca. 1485) Robert Henryson's collection of BEAST FABLES is generally considered the finest medieval example of the genre and was widely read in late-medieval Scotland. However, no editions of the work survive from Henryson's lifetime. In fact, all texts date from at least 75 years after his death, so determining the date and order of composition of the 13 FABLES, their accompanying morals (see ALLEGORY), and the Prologue is a difficult task. Some work has been done to assign priority based on source study, but fables were such a popular genre in the Middle Ages that it is nearly impossible to determine source relationships with the precision necessary to date individual fables. In the most general terms, Henryson's sources fall into two categories: the Aesop tradition and the Old French REYNARD LITERATURE. Aesop's fables were a staple of medieval pedagogy, and if Henryson had not been exposed to them in oral recitations, he certainly would have been familiar with them in his role as schoolmaster. The tales of Reynard the fox, on the other hand, were generally considered strictly entertainment. By adapting them for didactic purposes and providing each with an allegorical interpretation, Henryson made an original contribution to the beast fable genre.

Within the text itself, this didactic emphasis appears in the very first lines as Henryson stresses that fables, despite their status as fictions, are useful in teaching moral lessons. He conveys this point through several traditional figures for reading as a morally edifying activity. First, he compares the diligent reader who can glean "ane morall sweit sentence" (one pleasant, instructive moral; l. 11) from a fable to a gardener laboring to grow flowers and corn. Second, he invokes the common metaphor of the text as a nut waiting to be cracked to reveal the kernel of meaning within. Finally, he justifies the pleasure one obtains from reading fables by reminding his readers that a bow that is always bent soon becomes warped and useless. Like the proverbial bow, readers need relaxation, and fables can provide it, while not losing sight of their moral teaching. These repeated meditations on the fable as a genre suggest that along with moral instruction, Henryson uses the collection to explore the subject of poetics.

The fables of *Morall Fabillis* are themselves quite diverse in their register, encompassing both the comic and the tragic, the realistic and the fanciful. In their diversity, Henryson's fables have been compared to Geoffrey Chaucer's *The Canterbury Tales,* and there is a note of a typically Chaucerian humor at the expense of the animals' pretensions. This connection between the two works is reinforced by Henryson's condensed retelling of the same fable that is recounted in "The Nun's Priest's Tale." However, because of the limitations of the fable genre, none of the animals in any of the fables reaches the level of detailed characterization of the Canterbury pilgrims.

In a similar vein, the narrator of the *Morall Fabillis* is not nearly as clearly defined a character as the narrator of *The Canterbury Tales,* but he is a presence throughout the text, describing how he learned certain fables by eavesdropping on the animals, or even, in the case of "The Lion and the Mouse," meeting Aesop and asking the master to teach him. Critics have focused on the narrator's developing character as key to understanding the didactic strategy behind the tales. Some have argued that as the fables progress, the narrator (and by extension the reader) learns different lessons. This line of reasoning, however, is complicated by the lack of agreement among the witnesses as to the correct order of the fables. Only three fables, "The Cock and the Fox," "The Fox and the Wolf," and "The Trial of the Fox," demonstrate explicit internal links. Beyond these three, the narrative thread linking individual fables is quite thin, a situation that has led some critics to posit that the tales of the *Morall Fabillis* should be read less as a unified collection that as a series of independent poems.

The issue that has most engaged critics is the degree to which the fables are connected to their morals. To a modern reader, these allegorical explanations often seem quite farfetched, suggesting that the moral is a vestigial appendage that can be ignored. Perhaps the most startling example of this apparent gap between fable and moral comes in the first fable, "The Cock and the Jasp." The fable recounts the story of a cock who, while scratching for food, comes across a jasp (a jasper, a semiprecious stone) and ignores the jewel since, he sensibly points out, he cannot eat it, and therefore, it is of no use to him. The moral roundly condemns the cock for ignoring the stone since, the narrator explains, the jewel represents wisdom and in rejecting it in favor of worms and snails, the cock represents those humans who reject the spiritual in favor of more immediate pleasures. The idea that the cock is simply trying to survive is not even broached. Other fables suggest a similar disconnect between the story and its explanation, although perhaps not to this degree. Critics have approached this problem in several ways. One strategy treats the perceived distance between fable and interpretation as part of the author's didactic strategy; that is, in making the path between fable and meaning somewhat convoluted, Henryson forces his readers to examine their own reasoning on these moral issues. A second strategy maintains that for a medieval audience, there would be no disconnect between fable and *morals,* arguing that such allegorical interpretations were a common feature of both scholastic discourse and fraternal sermons and thus would have been familiar to the educated and uneducated alike.

The most promising recent readings of the *Morall Fabillis* focus on this last approach and place the text in a larger cultural context. In doing so, these critics seem to be returning to an older mode of criticism that also examined the text in its historical context. However, where the older criticism mined the poems for biographical or political allusions, current contextual readings recognize that the allegorical method Henryson employs in the *Morall Fabillis* precludes drawing such conclusions with any certainty, and instead focus on discursive aspects, such as the allegorical method itself or the realistic natural description. This suggests that in the *Morall Fabillis,* Henryson presents a compelling mixture of traditional medieval doctrine with the newly emerging humanism of the 15th century, and as such, this collection of beast fables can be read as an important transitional text between the Middle Ages and the Renaissance.

See also ALLEGORY.

FURTHER READING

Fox, Denton, ed. *The Poems of Robert Henryson.* Oxford: Clarendon Press, 1981.

Gopen, George, ed. *Moral Fables of Aesop by Robert Henryson.* South Bend, Ind.: University of Notre Dame Press, 1987.

Kindrick, Robert L. *Robert Henryson.* Boston: Twayne Publishers, 1979.

———. *Henryson and the Medieval Arts of Rhetoric.* New York: Garland, 1993.

Wheatley, Edward. *Mastering Aesop: Medieval Education, Chaucer, and His Followers.* Gainesville: University Press of Florida, 2000.

Christian Sheridan

Morall Fabillis: **"The Cock and the Fox"** ROBERT HENRYSON **(1485)**   The third tale of the *Morall Fabillis,* "The Cock and the Fox," is a condensed version of the same BEAST FABLE presented in GEOFFREY CHAUCER'S "The Nun's Priest's Tale" and recounts how a fox (identified as Lowrence by ROBERT HENRYSON) beguiles a cock (Chantecleir) by flattering him into closing his eyes, turning around three times, and crowing. The fox, of course, uses that interlude to snatch the cock and escape. This escape proves shortlived as the widow and her dogs are quickly on his trail. Inspired by "some good spirit" (l. 558) Chantecleir escapes by advising the fox to tell the dogs that he and the fox have been friends for a year so that they will cease their pursuit. When the fox opens his mouth to do so, the cock flies into a tree. The fox tries one last time to cajole the cock into joining him on the ground by offering to be his servant for a year, but the cock has learned his lesson and flies home. The lesson the reader ought to learn, according to the moral accompanying the poem, is to

flee the twin sins of flattery (represented by the fox) and pride (the cock).

The most interesting sections of the text are digressions from the main narrative. Henryson devotes seven STANZAS to a discussion between three hens, Pertok, Sprutok, and Coppok, about the character of their former lover. Pertok begins with a fairly conventional show of mourning, remembering Chantecleir as both a capable lover and as a provider. Sprutok responds with a much less flattering memorial, casting doubt on the cock's lovemaking and noting that he was afflicted with jealousy. Pertok, who the text tells us was only feigning faith before, quickly agrees and reveals her lustful nature. Coppok then delivers a mini-sermon connecting Chantecleir's fate to his promiscuous lifestyle. One assumes that the humor of this hen involved in a polygamous marriage condemning adultery would not have been lost on Henryson's audience.

Critics have focused mostly on the relationship between this FABLE and its Chaucerian source, noting similarities and differences, and examining Henryson's concise writing style. Beyond the fable's relation to "The Nun's Priest's Tale" and its humor, "The Cock and the Fox" deserves attention because of the light it sheds on Henryson's method in his collection of fables. The beginning of the *Morall* emphasizes that in order to interpret the fables correctly, the audience must employ a allegorical method so that each character represents a different vice. As with the other fables, an edifying meaning can be found through diligent reading. In another self-conscious moment, the opening two stanzas of the text as a whole discuss the beast fable as a genre and note that despite lacking judgment, animals' temperaments are so diverse that it exceeds the poet's ability to describe them. After this cursory modest introduction, Henryson begins the narrative proper by noting that the story he is about to recount is a recent event (it happened "this other year," l. 409) and not something he has drawn out of an older work. These two moments, one in which he asserts the authenticity of his story and the other in which he indicates that his story is merely chaff to be discarded in favor of the moral, suggest the extent to which Henryson is a transitional figure invoking both the traditional medieval way of interpreting stories and a more modern conception of authorship.

See also ALLEGORY, *MORALL FABILLIS* (OVERVIEW).

FURTHER READING

Macdonald, Donald. "Henryson and Chaucer: Cock and Fox." *Texas Studies in Literature and Language* 8, no. 4 (1967): 451–461.

Christian Sheridan

***Morall Fabillis*: "The Fox and the Wolf"** ROBERT HENRYSON (ca. 1485)   This BEAST FABLE is internally linked to the one that appears before it, "The Cock and the Fox," as it relates the further adventures of the fox who missed his chance to devour Chantecleir.

As the tale opens, the fox (Lowrence) realizes he is a sinner and needs to confess. Conveniently, he encounters Freir Volff Waitskaith [Friar Wolf Do-harm] (ll. 667–69). The fox falls on his knees and begs the wolf to hear his confession. Dutifully, the wolf asks the fox if he is sorry for his crimes and will no longer commit them. The fox answers negatively to both questions, claiming the taste of hens and lambs is too delicious and that he has no other means of providing food for himself. Though the wolf correctly points out that the fox "wantis pointis twa / Belangand to perfyte confessioun [lacks two points belonging to a perfect confession]" (ll. 712–23), this lack does not overly concern him, and he proceeds to issue the fox penance: Lowrence must refrain from eating meat until Easter. The fox protests, and the wolf agrees to allow meat twice a week, because "need has no law" (l. 731).

Soon afterward, Lowrence tries to fish but is frightened by the tempestuous waves. Instead, he seizes a goat from a nearby herd, drags it to the water, and dunks it in, proclaiming, "'Ga down, schir Kid, cum up, schir Salmond, agane'" ['go down sir Kid, come up [as] sir Salmon'] (l. 751). After feasting on this newly christened "salmon," the fox curls up in the sun and "recklessly" asserts that it would be appropriate for an arrow to pierce his belly (ll. 758, 760). The goatherd from whom the fox stole the kid sees him, shoots him with his bow, and takes his pelt as recompense.

The *morals* that accompanies the FABLE interprets it as a warning for the sinful to mend their ways lest they be killed unshriven like the fox. Indeed, most criticism on this fable has focused on the issue of sacramental abuse. Also, the narrator is surprisingly present in this text, a departure from traditional fables and a technique that allows for slippages between fantasy and reality, as well as an insistence that its readers to be aware of their interpretive processes.

See also ALLEGORY, *MORALL FABILLIS* (OVERVIEW), REYNARD LITERATURE.

Christian Sheridan

***Morall Fabillis*: "The Lion and the Mouse"** ROBERT HENRYSON (1483)   "The Lion and the Mouse," the seventh BEAST FABLE in ROBERT HENRYSON's *Morall Fabillis,* has a number of unique features: It is the only fable with a prologue, the only DREAM VISION, the only tale that has a happy ending, and the only one in which the characters follow suggested advice.

In the prologue, the narrator dreams about Aesop and begs his master to tell a fable. So the tale begins. A lion is basking in the sun when a group of mice appear and dance across his body. The lion seizes the chief mouse. She readily admits guilt but says that she acted out of negligence, not spite. Nevertheless, the lion accuses her of treason, as he is king of the beasts, for which the punishment is death. The mouse begs for mercy and appeals to his reason, arguing that he will gain no glory by killing a harmless mouse and may, instead, lose renown. Mercy and reason overcome anger, and the lion releases the mouse. The lion then goes on a rampage, killing tame and wild beasts alike, and is captured by hunters. As the lion mourns his situation, the mouse hears his cries, calls on her kin, and frees him. The moral then indicates that mercy, pity, justice, and temperance are the qualities of a good king and inspire loyalty.

The FABLE has clear connections to contemporary Scottish politics. The lion moves from being a slothful, indolent king of the beasts to a just, merciful one, and this benevolence inspires faithful service from his subjects. James III's subjects, clearly not inspired by loyalty, censured him through Parliament on six different occasions for his failures. Similarly, the hunters represent Scottish nobles: James III was kidnapped and held prisoner during the Lauder Rebellion (1482).

See also ALLEGORY, *MORALL FABILLIS* (OVERVIEW).

Mark DiCicco

MORE, SIR THOMAS (1478–1535) Sir

Thomas More was born in London on February 7, 1478, to John and Agnes More. The second of four surviving children, it is believed that More studied at St. Anthony's School in London, which was well known for producing scholars. He excelled in his studies, learning Latin grammar, logic, and debating skills. In 1490, his father sent him to study under John Morton, the archbishop of Canterbury and soon-to-be cardinal, who likely influenced the young man's decision to study at Oxford, where he enrolled in 1492. More spent only two years at Oxford, supposedly being pulled out of his studies and away from the "liberal university life" by his father, who wanted him to become a lawyer. More studied at the Inns of Court, and by 1501 he was a barrister.

In 1504, More married Jane Colt, the daughter of a family friend, with whom he had four children (Margaret, Elizabeth, Cecily, and John) before her death in 1511. He then married a widow, Alice Middleton, a mere month later. Scholars attribute his haste in remarrying to his desire that his children have a mother.

Aside from having a private law practice, More began writing patriotic EPIGRAMS and epigraphs as support for HENRY VIII's wars. He served as undersheriff of London between 1510 and 1518 and undertook a number of royal diplomatic commissions as well. During this time, it is believed that More began work on his unfinished historiography, *History of King Richard III,* which was WILLIAM SHAKESPEARE's main source of inspiration for his play on the controversial king. It is also believed that while visiting Bruges in 1515, More finished what would become part two of *Utopia,* his treatise on a perfect society and how such a place would be governed. Enlisting the help of his friend Desiridius Erasmus, More finished the book, and *Utopia* was published in 1516. While the book was not particularly successful during More's lifetime, it is now recognized as undeniably influential in its sardonic

(*utopia* in Greek literally means "no place"), markedly humanist description of the ideal society and the politics, laws, religion, and daily lives of its citizens.

During the last years of his life, More served as lord chancellor under Henry VIII; however, he resigned the position in May 1532, in disagreement with Henry's divorce from Catherine of Aragon and separation from the Roman Catholic Church. When More refused to swear an oath upholding Henry's marriage to Anne Boleyn and, later, to support the Act of Supremacy, Henry had him imprisoned in the TOWER OF LONDON. On July 6, 1535, Sir Thomas More was beheaded for high treason. His steadfast adherence to the tenets of his religion, even when facing certain death, earned him canonization in 1935.

Though not particularly well known as a poet, More did try his hand at Latin verse, such as "Quis Optimus Reipublicae Status," and "DE PRINCIPE BONO ET MALO." The majority of his verse relied on the COUPLET and revolved around political interests, as did most of his adult life.

FURTHER READING
Marius, Richard. *Thomas More.* New York: Alfred A. Knopf, 1984.

Tyler Hancock

MUM AND THE SOTHSEGGER ANONY-

MOUS (15th century) *Mum and the Sothsegger* is an alliterative social SATIRE inspired by WILLIAM LANGLAND's popular *PIERS PLOWMAN.* Only one manuscript of the poem exists (London, British Library, MS Additional 41666), and the poem is missing its beginning and conclusion, but its main body of 1,751 lines survives. Because the poem refers to events in 1409, during Henry IV's reign, scholars have dated it to the early 15th century.

The poem's title is that offered by the manuscript's scribe, who named it after the two main speakers in the poem: Mum (one who holds his/her tongue out of self-interest) and Sothsegger ("truthteller"—one who speaks the truth despite the consequences). The text of the poem begins with a debate between these two personified abstractions, wherein Sothsegger insists that it is necessary to tell the truth in the commonwealth, so that those in power can hear honest criticism. Mum, however, argues that flattering those in power is far more practical—and lucrative. Although the reader clearly recognizes Mum's hypocrisy and self-interest, the poem's narrator is unable to choose between the two opinions and so decides to look into the matter further by a closer look at the world. In a section recalling the estates satire genre (see SATIRE, THREE ESTATES) of Langland's opening vision (or of GEOFFREY CHAUCER's *GENERAL PROLOGUE TO THE CANTERBURY TALES*), the narrator visits a university and speaks with personified Liberal Arts, with friars, with townspeople, and with a parish priest. In his satire of the ecclesiastical status quo, the poet reveals what some scholars have seen as sympathy for LOLLARDISM (a heretical movement).

As he wanders, the narrator is able to find Mum everywhere he looks, but he has a much more difficult time finding anyone who will tell the truth. Finally, like *Piers Plowman* itself, the poem turns into a DREAM VISION, in which the narrator sees a hive of bees representing the ideal commonwealth. A beekeeper (the wise king) stamps out those bees that do not contribute to the common good of the hive.

In the end, or the end as we have it, the speaker of the poem becomes, through telling his or her own story, the kind of Sothsegger that is necessary for the kingdom to flourish. A good king, the poem asserts, must be willing to listen to open constructive criticism in order for the kingdom to thrive.

See also ALLITERATION, MIDDLE ENGLISH POETRY, PERSONIFICATION.

FURTHER READING
Barr, Helen, ed. *The Piers Plowman Tradition: A Critical Edition of Pierce the Ploughman's Crede, Richard the Redeless, Mum and the Sothsegger, and The Crowned King.* London: J. M. Dent, 1993.
Dean, James M., ed. *Richard the Redeless and Mum and the Sothsegger.* Kalamazoo: Western Michigan University for TEAMS, 2000.

Jay Ruud

"MY GALLEY CHARG'D WITH FORGETFULNESS" SIR THOMAS WYATT (1557)
"My Galley Charg'd with Forgetfulness" is a translation and adaptation of PETRARCH's *Rima* 189, as is Sonnet 34 from EDMUND SPENCER's *AMORETTI*. Arranged in the ENGLISH SONNET form, the first two QUATRAINS interlock through a shared rhyme: *abba, acca, deed, ff.* The final quatrain and concluding COUPLET feature all new rhymes, driving the poem's rhythm forward with an almost brute force, perhaps mirroring the onward motion of the relentless oars (l. 5).

The poem is built upon an extended (and traditional) CONCEIT of a ship as vessel of love and highlights the suffering the lover must endure in the face of unrequited love. Physical and psychological separation are conflated, all controlled by the cruel lord of love who delights in the speaker's suffering. The poem is an ALLEGORY of LOVESICKNESS: Rain stands for tears, clouds for disdain, stars for the beloved's eyes, and so forth. The situation is encapsulated in the couplet: "Drowned is reason that should me consort, / And I remain despairing of the port" (ll. 13–14). Though logic should be guiding the speaker, instead he is being guided by his unreachable beloved's eyes, leaving him forever lost at sea, tossed on the tempestuous waves of love. His ship will never berth, a clearly erotic image of penetration.

A number of critics have suggested that this poem reflects SIR THOMAS WYATT's despair over the loss of his mistress, Anne Boleyn, to King HENRY VIII, though there is no direct evidence the two were lovers. Recent psychoanalytic views suggest that Wyatt's despair preceded the poem, making the seascape bleaker and darker than the Petrarchan original. Most agree overall, that "My Galley" is an excellent example of stylized emotional verse.

FURTHER READING
Thomson, Patricia. *Sir Thomas Wyatt and His Background.* Stanford, Calif.: Stanford University Press, 1964.

"MY LIEF IS FAREN IN LONDE" ANONYMOUS (14th century)
This brief Middle English lyric has seven lines, rhymed *ababcbc*. It was apparently meant to be sung, but, as with many secular lyrics, specific music for it has not survived. The poem expresses the lament of a lover for his beloved, who has departed to a place where the speaker cannot go. The speaker's heart, however, is in the beloved's possession wherever she travels; it accompanies her on her journey with "trew love a thousand fold."

Although its theme is quite conventional, the poem is notable for the subtle treatment of the speaker's position, which is expressed in the middle line of the STANZA: "I may nat com her to" (I cannot come to her). The lines just above and below, literally surrounding the middle line, reinforce the speaker's immobility. Line 3 refers to his being "sore bounde," but the reader does not know whether he is bound by obligation, physical constraint, or perhaps the command of the beloved. In line 5, the lover's heart is described as "in hold"—that is, imprisoned. This phrase suggests that his confinement is at least partially metaphorical: he is a prisoner of, and for, love.

The lyric is best known for its appearance in GEOFFREY CHAUCER's "The NUN'S PRIEST'S TALE" as the song that the rooster Chanticleer and his mate Pertelote are in the habit of singing together at sunrise. There is a mild irony in this lyric's serving as the birds' song, for the tale relates how Chanticleer is stolen away by the fox. Chanticleer is the one who must "faren in londe," while Pertelote becomes the lover who cannot follow him.

Because the poem appears in "The Nun's Priest's Tale," which was written about 1396, it is more than a century older than the single MANUSCRIPT in which it appears, a collection of courtly short poems and verse tales, including two by Chaucer and several by JOHN LYDGATE, compiled about 1480. The poem is appended to a longer, similarly themed lyric, which ends "And for your love, evermore weeping I sing this song." "My Lief" can thus be read as a coda (ending) to the longer poem.

The poem is frequently anthologized, and editors vary in using the phrase "in a londe," which appears in the manuscript, or "in londe," which scans more smoothly and appears in most manuscripts of "The Nun's Priest's Tale." There is a slight difference in meaning, however. "In a londe" suggests a journey to a specific place, while "in londe" could mean simply "far away." "In londe" can also function as meaningless filler to finish out a line.

See also MIDDLE ENGLISH LYRICS AND BALLADS.

FURTHER READING

Mooney, Linne R. "'A Woman's Reply to Her Lover' and Four Other New Courtly Love Lyrics in Cambridge, Trinity College MS R.3.19." *Medium Aevum* 67 (1998): 235–256.

Robbins, Rossell Hope. *Secular Lyrics of the XIVth and XVth Centuries.* 2nd ed. Oxford: Clarendon Press, 1955.

Susan Yager

"MY LUTE AWAKE!" SIR THOMAS WYATT (1557) This lyric poem by SIR THOMAS WYATT is composed of eight five-line STANZAS. It also features a modified refrain: The final line of each stanza ends with ". . . for I have done," although the first half of the lines varies.

The poem opens with an APOSTROPHE to the poet's personified lute, calling for it to awake, apparently one last time, so that he and it can complete their last mutual task before they die. The subsequent stanzas describe, through various metaphors, the way the poet has been repulsed by his lady. The beginning of the fifth stanza signals a violent turn in the poem, which until this point has been bitter but now becomes savage. "Vengeance shall fall on thy disdain," warns the poet (l. 21). This revenge is warranted not because she has shown disdain—to some extent that would be expected—but rather because she "makest but a game on earnest pain" (l. 22). It is her cruelty that must be punished. His viciousness continues as he predicts her future: "Perchance thee lie withered and old / The winter nights that are so cold" (ll. 26–27). Because she has been so extraordinarily heartless, the poet predicts that no one will ever love her for long, and that she will end her days alone. When it is too late, "then may chance thee to repent" (l. 31), but no one will care. The final stanza witnesses the silencing of both the lute and the poet.

Scholars often note the impassioned and embittered tone, which is sustained throughout. The sense is almost one of a CARPE DIEM (seize the day) poem: The lady is warned that because she failed to accept love, she will end up cold and alone, regretting her wasted time. The continual connections between the lady and the moon, as well as with coldness and stillness, invokes a sense of barrenness; indeed, if she remains alone, she will also remain barren. Other scholars have commented on the musical references in the lyric ("sing," "ear," etc.), which progressively fade, just as the woman fades. She becomes the lute in still life, like a painting, instead of the lively lute in music. Overall, this is a dark and gloomy work, relating the death of love, love poetry, and artistry. Ironically, through the poem's initial line calls for the lute to awake, the final result is utter stillness.

See also PERSONIFICATION.

FURTHER READING

Jentoft, Clyde W. *Sir Thomas Wyatt and Henry Howard, Earl of Surrey: A Reference Guide*. Boston: G. K. Hall, 1980.

Thomson, Patricia. *Sir Thomas Wyatt and His Background*. Stanford, Calif.: Stanford University Press, 1964.

"MY RADCLIFFE" HENRY HOWARD, EARL OF SURREY (ca. 1544)   Presumably written to the poet's first cousin, the 18-year-old Thomas Radcliffe, whose brother had recently died under HENRY HOWARD, EARL OF SURREY's command fighting in Scotland, "My Radcliffe" cautions the youth on the need for self-control in the face of violence, a subject with which Surrey was intimately acquainted. Both Surrey's military career and his social interactions demonstrate that he frequently found himself caught up in the intrigues of the Tudor court.

The poem, published in TOTTEL'S MISCELLANY in 1557, is an adaptation of an Italian STRAMBOTTO. While the strambotto form is usually elegiac in nature and consists of eight lines with a rhyme scheme of *abababcc*, Surrey's poem is admonitory and relies on a six-line structure with a rhyme scheme of *ababcc*. The verse is in iambic pentameter. As indicated by its subheading when published by Tottel, the poem's moral is an "Exhortacion to learne by others trouble." Surrey warns that if his advice is ignored, the nameless offense Ratcliffe has committed can lead to the calling down of unheralded "plages" (l. 4). Tread carefully, writes the poet, some 10 years older than his addressee. Though it is pleasant to think that a punished man can once again become whole with the passage of time, that he may "recure" (l. 5), it is more realistic that such an offender must come to understand that the effects of these wrongs can last forever. The poem's final COUPLET contrasts Solomon's wisdom, from Ecclesiasticus 27:21, with that of Surrey's friend, SIR THOMAS WYATT. Wyatt had apparently been writing about his own imprisonment by Henry

VIII, and the very use of such a juxtaposition between the holy text and Surrey's contemporary demonstrates the high regard Surrey clearly felt for Wyatt as both a writer and a thinker.

See also COURT CULTURE.

FURTHER READING

Jones, Emrys, ed. *Henry Howard Earl of Surrey: Poems*. Oxford: Clarendon Press, 1970.

Sessions, William A. *Henry Howard, Earl of Surrey*. Boston: Twayne Publishers, 1986.

———. *Henry Howard The Poet Earl of Surrey: A Life*. Oxford: Oxford University Press, 1999.

David Houston Wood

"MY SWEETEST LESBIA" THOMAS CAMPION (1601)   Published as the first AYRE in THOMAS CAMPION's *A BOOKE OF AYRES*, for which he composed the music as well as the lyrics, this is a translation of Catullus's famous poem *Vivamus, mea Lesbia*. It develops the original's CARPE DIEM (seize the day) theme into an assertion of the triumph of love over death. The first STANZA endeavors to persuade Lesbia to give in to the poet's sexual advances by highlighting the comparative shortness and insignificance of human existence. This is emphasized by the comparison of the "little light" of human life (l. 5) with the rising and setting of "heav'ns great lampes"—the sun and stars (l. 3). The CAESURA in line 3 also gives a sense of finality and importance to the command "Let us not way [weigh] them."

The second stanza develops the argument further by questioning the principle of militaristic honor, exposing it as a shortsighted "wast" of life. In contrast, the poet playfully invokes the metaphorical "wars" of love, an image that is also sexually suggestive in its proposal that only an "alar'me . . . from the campe of love" should disturb "peaceful sleepes" (ll. 9–10).

The third stanza continues this opposition to traditional heroism, imagining the poet's own funeral as a time of celebration and affirmation, rather than mourning and misery. The reference to "timely death" (l. 13) suggests that the poet accepts the inevitability of death, and that fate must be allowed to take its course. This continues the idea that the poet will not hasten death by rushing into battle, like the "fooles" described in the second stanza.

The final COUPLET of each stanza forms a REFRAIN of the light/night image, which echoes the sense of rising and falling in the original image in the first stanza. This and the oxymoronic "happie tombe" contribute to the poignancy of the poem's bittersweet conclusion, where the poet asks Lesbia to "crowne with love my ever-during night."

FURTHER READING
Lindley, David. *Thomas Campion.* Leiden: E. J. Brill, 1986.

Susan L. Anderson

NASHE, THOMAS (1561–ca. 1601)

Thomas Nashe was born in Lowestolt in 1561. He attended St. John's College, Cambridge, graduating in 1586 with a B.A. Primarily known as a satirist and a playwright, Nashe was part of the "University Wits" group that included men such as CHRISTOPHER MARLOWE and Thomas Kyd. He is especially remembered for a series of public (and vicious) debates with the poet Gabriel Harvey and his brother Richard that are reminiscent of the medieval FLYTING tradition and of the literary debates between Thomas Churchyard and Thomas Camel in the late 1500s. Nashe's best-known work is *The Life of Jack Wilton* (1594), considered by some to be the first picaresque novel in English. Nashe, like most of the University Wits, also dabbled in poetry. Many of these poems were incorporated into other works. For instance, "A LITANY IN TIME OF PLAGUE" was published as part of the play *Summer's Last Will and Testament*. Nashe died in 1600 or 1601, of unknown causes.

See also "LITANY IN TIME OF PLAGUE, A."

FURTHER READING

Hibbard, G. R. *Thomas Nashe: A Critical Introduction.* Cambridge: Harvard University Press, 1962.

McGinn, Donald J. *Thomas Nashe.* Boston: Twayne, 1981.

Nashe, Thomas. *The Works of Thomas Nashe.* 5 vols. Edited by R. B. McKerrow. London, 1904, 1910.

"NATURE THAT WASHED HER HANDS IN MILK" SIR WALTER RALEIGH (1590)

This poem is a combination of a BLAZON—a systematic listing of a beloved's physical charms—and a COMPLAINT about the shortness of life and the inevitability of time's decay and death. Each STANZA in the first half sets out some miraculous beauty created by Nature, only to find it destroyed by Time. The "mistress" that Nature creates from pure and dazzling ingredients such as snow, silk, and milk (instead of earth and water) is beautiful but fragile: While she presents herself in "her inside," to her lover as having "wantonness and wit" (l. 12), he complains that on her outside, she is unresponsive to him. In a typically Petrarchan approach, the speaker contrasts her seductive presentation of self with her coldness in their relations. The tone of the poem then changes as the speaker ruthlessly points out the lesson of human beauty—that it decays and is destroyed by Time, which "dims, discolors, and destroys" the beauty of Nature's creation. Her outside beauty decays; her sexual energy, conveyed in metaphors of liquidity and liveliness, will be "dull"ed and "dried" up (ll. 29–30). And like beauty and sexual desire, human life itself, "the story of our days" (l. 36) is destroyed. Like everything else in Nature, we die, unknown and alone.

The poem's grim message is appropriately conveyed in relentlessly plain verse. Direct, almost proverbial, sayings replace Petrarchan metaphor: Slow lines of single syllable words force a sense of solemnity upon a reader, culminating in the emotional appeal at the conclusion as the speaker looks around hopelessly for an answer that neither Nature nor Time, which overcomes all things, can provide him: "Oh, cruel Time! which takes in trust / Our youth, our joys, and all we have" (ll. 31–32). The conclusion is seemingly inevitable as Time, "When we have wandered all our ways / Shuts up the story of our days" (ll. 35–36). It is a grim and seemingly inescapable ending to what starts as a cheerful, celebratory love compliment.

See also RALEIGH, SIR WALTER.

Gary Waller

NEW WORLD

The notion of a "New World" loomed large in the medieval and early modern imagination. As represented in works such as John Mandeville's *Travels* and Marco Polo's *Travels,* notions of people with mysterious bodies and unusual tribal rituals shaped the expectations of early modern explorers and writers. Columbus, having read the work of Marco Polo, knew what he should expect when he reached the land of India. For the early modern writer, the New World represented an opportunity to begin civilization anew. Some even believed in the New World that they would find the Old World, a kind of Eden-like state. In his first encounters with indigenous peoples, Christopher Columbus recalled images of the naked Adam and Eve in the Garden of Eden. In a highly romanticized view of this New World, others longed for a return to this setting.

The PASTORAL celebrates the simplicity of this New World, but it is in the exploration narratives produced by Spanish, Italian, Portuguese, French, and English discoverers that the myth of the New World was born. Cultural explorations, based on comparisons with European practices, dominate the texts. SIR WALTER RALEIGH's *Discovery of Guiana* (1595) details his findings in the New World in terms the monarchy wanted to hear. Poems also celebrated the New World. For instance, MICHAEL DRAYTON wrote "Ode to the Virginian Voyage" (1606) using many of the standard images and ideologies, providing impetus for further explorations. In general, poems of this ilk celebrate the possibilities the New World offered, both financially and politically.

FURTHER READING

Greenblatt, Stephen J. *Marvelous Possessions: The Wonders of the New World.* Chicago: University of Chicago Press, 1991.

Hadfield, Andrew. *Literature, Travel, and Colonial Writing in the English Renaissance 1545–1625.* Oxford: Oxford University Press, 1998.

Daniel F. Pigg

"NIGHTINGALE, THE" ("PHILOMELA") SIR PHILIP SIDNEY (1595)

"The Nightingale," widely considered one of the best of SIR PHILIP SIDNEY's short poems, appears in the second part of his DEFENSE OF POESY. It is based on a popular song of the time, "Non Credo Gia Che Piu Infelice Amante." Also known by the title "Philomela," the poem is based on the story of Philomela in book 6 of OVID's *Metamorphoses.* Philomela and Procne were the daughters of King Pandion of Attica. Procne married Tereus of Thrace, though he lusted after Philomela. Eventually, Tereus raped Philomela and cut out her tongue to silence her. She, however, wove the story into a tapestry that she sent to her sister. Procne then killed her son and served him for dinner to Tereus. The women fled, pursued by Tereus, but the gods turned them all into birds: Procne became a nightingale, Philomela a swallow, and Tereus a hoopoe.

The richness of the rhyme in this poem is indicative of its basis on an Italian piece, as are the musicality and continuity of the phrases. The innovation in this piece lies in Sidney's comparison of himself to Philomela as he explores sexual dynamics, voice, self-expression, and the English tradition of male stoicism. This is accomplished through both words and rhythm.

Sidney establishes the mood instantly: "The nightingale, as soon as April bringeth / Unto her rested sense a perfect waking . . . / Sings out her woes" (ll. 1–4). April is a month of juxtapositions: Winter has ended and summer is approaching; destructive rain falls alongside generative sunshine; life is beginning even as some ends. Similarly, Philomela's rape features juxtapositions, too—death of the girl and birth of the woman; end of innocence and beginning of experience—as demonstrated: "Her throat in tunes expresseth / What grief her breast oppresseth" (ll. 6–7). Acknowledging the terrible act that has led to this moment—"For Tereus' force on her chaste will prevailing" (l. 8)—Sidney then promptly inverts the tale. The audience should not feel pity for Philomela; rather, they should feel sorry for Sidney: "O Philomela fair, O take some gladness, / That here is juster cause of plaintful sadness" (ll. 9–10).

Initially commiserating with Philomela, Sidney then berates her for vocalizing her pain when he himself cannot. Philomela, Sidney claims, at least can express her sadness through song and thus purge herself of it, but he, as a man, must suffer in silence. With her song, he claims, "Thine earth now springs," but as he can say nothing in his situation, "mine fadeth" (l. 11). He ends the first STANZA by underscoring her emotional release through song and his own emotional strain in silence: "Thy thorn without, my thorn my heart invadeth" (l. 12). At this point, it becomes clear that this poem is not only a retelling of the Philomela myth and a clever parody of a popular song, but is also in part a criticism of the social mores dictating that a woman may express her emotions openly while a man may not. It also refers to the popular belief that certain songbirds sang their most beautiful song immediately before their death, caused by plunging their breast onto a thorn.

In the second stanza, Sidney continues his diatribe against Philomela's vocalization of her experience, flippantly observing that "Alas, she has no other cause of anguish / But Tereus' love, on her by strong hand wroken, / Wherein she suffering, all her spirits languish; / Full womanlike complains her will was broken" (ll. 13–16). Indeed, Sidney almost seems to be implying here that Philomela did not mind things as much as she claims, but rather is making use of her position as a woman to claim she has been wronged, therefore maintaining her own innocence and chastity in the face of the act committed. In other words, she could enjoy physical love without social consequences, something permitted to no man in polite society.

Sidney then continues on with his own side of things, claiming, "I, who daily craving, / Cannot have to content me, / Have more cause to lament me, / Since wanting is more woe than too much having" (ll. 17–20). These lines clearly reveal the difference between the sexes: Women see sexuality as an onerous duty forced upon them, while men see it as something desired but rarely achieved.

Sidney embraces the male perspective: Women are cruel torturers who tease men with their allure but then protest when men pursue them, unfairly exploiting the woman's generally acknowledged right to voice her emotions and causing men to suffer in agonized silence at their cruel behavior. By making use of the classic Philomela myth, he indicates that this sort of behavior and these tensions between the sexes have been going on since the beginnings of civilization, and the tongue-in-cheek parody of a contemporary Italian love song allows him to express this highly vitriolic point of view in a fashionable and nonthreatening manner via a recognizable, enjoyable form that allows the whole thing to appear innocuous. He is able to air his views safely in the guise of a poetry-writing exercise. Sidney may claim again in the second stanza that Philomela has a voice and he has none, that "Thine earth now springs, mine fadeth; / Thy thorn without, my thorn my heart invadeth" (ll. 23–24), but the poem itself is his song, and Philomela, a mere myth now dead and gone, has nothing more to say on the matter. Sidney has therefore cleverly won his argument and had the last word.

Recent gender criticism has examined the implications of Sidney's gender role swapping—something he occasionally does in the SONNETS as well, while feminist critics have looked at his views of rape. Contextualized within early modern society, Sidney's views are not surprising; however, they still validate the false perception of women as commodities and lustful.

FURTHER READING
Duncan-Jones, Katherine, ed. *Sir Philip Sidney: The Major Works*. Oxford University Press, 2002.
Kay, Dennis, ed. *Sir Philip Sidney: An Anthology of Modern Criticism*. Oxford University Press, 1988.

Melissa A. Elmes

NORMAN CONQUEST, THE (1066)

The Norman Conquest of England began on September 27, 1066, when the forces of William the Bastard, duke of Normandy, later known as William the Conqueror, landed on the southern coast of England at Pevensey, but it continued throughout the formative years of the English nation. William completed military conquest of England when he successfully defeated the last Anglo-Saxon king of England, Harold Godwinson, on

October 14, 1066, at the Battle of Hastings. William's coronation as William I, king of England, on December 25, 1066, firmly established the Norman dynasty as the new royal family of England. The sociocultural conquest of the English people would continue over the next century.

One of William's first goals was to change the social structure of English society. He rewarded faithful followers at the expense of English nobles, reassigning lands and titles. His earliest efforts to realize this ambition involved the disruption of traditional Anglo-Saxon rulership by election and the foundation of a strong centralized monarchy based on patriarchal lines of inheritance, including primogeniture (oldest son as heir). The new Norman nobility assisted with this agenda. Other sociocultural changes followed.

One of the most drastic shifts in English culture was the subversion of the English language. Members of William's court spoke Norman French. Despite the fact that individuals who spoke English were viewed as inferior and commonplace, the majority of the individuals who were not part of the royal court refused to adopt a new language. As a result, a dual linguistic system emerged where many members of the nobility spoke Norman French while the language of the common people remained English. In 1086, a massive survey of the English countryside and its population entitled *The Domesday Book* was completed at William's insistence. *The Domesday Book* contained detailed census information about every shire and its tenants in England. This survey helped William to implement in England the continental Norman practice of feudalism. Traditionally defined as a military arrangement made between lords and their vassals (see FEUDAL OATHS), feudalism did not exist in Anglo-Saxon England. The military relationship between the Anglo-Saxon kings and their nobles was similar to that portrayed in the OLD ENGLISH poem BEOWULF. William bolstered the spread of feudalism in England by embarking on a massive castle-building project. The TOWER OF LONDON is one of the most famous castles built during his reign.

The English people initially resisted William's efforts. They resented the dominance of the new Norman aristocracy, the ascendancy of the Norman-French language, and the heavy taxation they were forced to pay in order to finance the king's Continental military expeditions. However, the Norman dynasty ruled England until the reign of Henry II, William the Conqueror's great-grandson, in 1154. Henry II was a product of the hybrid ANGLO-NORMAN society that developed as the Norman Conquest of England came to a close during the 12th century. He established a new royal dynasty known as the Norman-Angevins, or Plantagenets. Troubadours (singer-poets) from southern France who accompanied Eleanor of Aquitaine, Henry's queen, introduced the ideas of CHIVALRY and COURTLY LOVE to the English populace. These motifs were two of the biggest influences on medieval English poetry. By the time GEOFFREY CHAUCER wrote the The CANTERBURY TALES in the 14th century, the effects of the Norman Conquest had long been absorbed.

FURTHER READING

Barlow, Frank. "The Effects of the Norman Conquest." In *The Norman Conquest: Its Setting and Impact,* edited by Dorothy Whitelock et al., 125–161. London: Eyre & Spottiswoode, 1966.

Brown, R. Allen. *The Normans and the Norman Conquest.* New York, N.Y.: Thomas Y. Crowell Company, 1968.

Deborah L. Bauer

"NOW GOTH SONNE UNDER WOD" ("SUNSET ON CALVARY") ANONYMOUS (ca. 1240)

The earliest version of this meditative poem exists in the ANGLO-NORMAN version of the *Speculum ecclesiae* of St. Edmund of Abingdon, archbishop of Canterbury. With serene yet powerful imagery, the poet paints a picture of Christ's crucifixion. The speaker seems to describe the sun sinking beneath a line of trees on the horizon, then perhaps the cross, finally focusing on the sorrow and pity evoked by the face of Mary.

Like a BALLAD, the lyric is a QUATRAIN, or set of four lines; some speculate that it may be the REFRAIN of a longer composition. It borrows other techniques from the ballad, including incremental repetition and end-rhyme (though *aabb* rather than *abab*). Also, it reverses the traditional ballad meter (trimeter line followed by a tetrameter line rather than the other way around). Easily memorized, the poem circulated widely, surviving in many manuscripts. Probably recited by clerics at the close of the day, the lyric conjures images of nature, but also pity for Mary, the sorrowing mother.

"Now Goth Sonne Under Wod" is unique among 13th-century lyrics in its borrowing of strategies from both genres of religious lyrics—those on the passion of Christ and those on the Virgin. An important commonplace in the lyric is a focus on the beauty of the Virgin and a compassion for her that borders on Mariolatry, or excessive praise of Mary.

The poem is evocative and somber. The suggestive nature of the verse derives not only from the immediacy of the imagery but also from the poet's skillful use of paronomasia (wordplay). Key secular words become imbued with religious significance: "Now goth sonne under wod," the poem begins. In one possible reading, the sun is sinking beneath the trees. However, the "son" is also sinking beneath the wood ("wod"), or cross—a common use of METONYMY. "Wod" also carries an association with madness, a manifestation of excessive grief, which prepares the reader for the next line: "Me reweth, Marye, thy faire rode" (l. 2). "Rode" is a key pun in the poem. It could mean "cross," but it could also mean "face," which signals pity for Mary herself through SYNECDOCHE. The polysemous nature of "rode" links Mary to the cross and her dying son.

Line 3 reiterates the image in line one: "Now goth sonne under tree." Through metonymy, again, "tree" may be read not only as a tree in the distance but as "cross" (a conventional poeticism). Line 4 returns to the two figures, mother and son, movingly isolated: "Me reweth, Marye, thy sone and thee."

Among the debates that have surrounded this poem is the nature of Mary's face. Does the speaker pity Mary's face because it has been marred, reddened, by the sun, or is the poem an example of Franciscan piety, where human emotion is shifted from the worldly to the sacred? The latter seems more likely; certainly, though, the tone, voice, and evocative images in this poem make it one that will continue to be anthologized and studied.

See also MIDDLE ENGLISH LYRICS AND BALLADS, VIRGIN LYRICS.

FURTHER READING
Gray, Douglas. *Themes and Images in the Medieval English Religious Lyric.* Boston: Routledge & Kegan Paul, 1972.

Manning, Stephen. "Nou goth Sonne vnder wod." *MLN* 74, no. 7 (1959): 578–581.

Woolf, Rosemary. *The English Religious Lyric in the Middle Ages.* Oxford: Clarendon Press, 1968.

Tony Perrello

"NUN'S PRIEST'S TALE, THE" GEOFFREY CHAUCER (ca. 1395)

"The Nun's Priest's Tale" opens in a barnyard owned by a poor widow. She owns only a few animals; among them is her prize rooster named Chanticleer. He has seven wives, the prettiest of which is Pertelote. One night, Chanticleer has a nightmare. Pertelote, hearing his groaning, wakes him, and Chanticleer relates his dream, in which a vile beast invaded their yard. Pertelote mocks Chanticleer, telling him she cannot love a coward. Dreams mean nothing; they are caused by overindulgence and an overabundance of one of the FOUR HUMORS—in this case, too much choler. Citing Cato, whom she claims to have counseled ignoring dreams, Pertelote suggests a purge (consisting of a laxative and an enema), and offers to concoct one herself. Chanticleer retorts with a claim that many authorities believe dreams are powerful, and he proceeds to tell two stories about dreams being useful. After this, however, he proclaims that Pertelote's beauty and his desire for her outweighs his reason. With that, Chanticleer flies down from the perch and awakens the hens.

More than a month later, on May 3, Chanticleer and his wives are in the yard enjoying the sun when a fox appears. Biding his time, the fox eventually engages Chanticleer in conversation, flattering him about his renowned singing and comparing him to BOETHIUS. Chanticleer is tickled and agrees to sing for the fox. When his neck is stretched to the fullest, however, the fox seizes the rooster by the throat and flees. The hens raise a clamor, and the widow, her daughters, servants, and dogs all run after the fox and cock. The narrator laments that these events occurred on a Friday, and at one point he even compares this clamorous crowd to "Jack Straw and his followers" (ll. 4191–94), a direct reference to the PEASANTS' REVOLT. The narrator then reminds his audience that "Dame FORTUNE" changes sides quickly. Indeed, Chanticleer, having regained his wits, suggests to the fox that he shout at their pursuers.

The fox foolishly does so, and the nimble rooster escapes. The fox and cock then exchange morals: "beware of flattery" and "hold your tongue."

One of the most brilliant and witty stories in The CANTERBURY TALES, "The Nun's Priest's Tale," GEOFFREY CHAUCER's only BEAST FABLE, is widely anthologized. It retells the story of the cock and the fox, a FABLE that goes as far back as Aesop. Chaucer's sources for his tale are largely French and ANGLO-NORMAN redactions: MARIE DE FRANCE's fable "Del cok e del grupil," and REYNARD LITERATURE, especially the Renart le Contrefait. (ca. 1319–1342). Chaucer's tale, however, is somewhat longer and more complex than many of his sources, owing to the characterizations of his chickens and the descriptive talents of the pilgrim narrator. Moreover, the Tale also contains elements from the ROMANCE and sermon traditions, such as courtly manners (parodied by chickens), exempla (see EXEMPLUM), and a moral. The moral of "The Nun's Priest's Tale" remains far less clear than those of its sources or its modern adapted forms, leaving a tale that deals more with moralizing than any one particular moral. Overall, however, "The Nun's Priest's Tale" does not lack the moral typically found in fables of the cock and fox—admonitions regarding pride or false flattery. Instead, it offers a hyper-abundance of morals, both throughout the tale and in a crescendo at the story's close.

The wit and sophistication of "The Nun's Priest's Tale" lies in its telling, especially the highly self-conscious mode of narration that combines simplicity and irony. That style appears in a number of incongruous and lengthy passages discoursing on various subjects typically of no concern to barn fowl: COURTLY LOVE, digestion, free will, predestination, tragedy, antifeminism, and the nature of dreams. The tale's characters, as well as the narrator, invoke numerous authorities on these subjects, from the homespun wisdom of Cato on the physiology of dreams and digestion to the book of Lancelot, "That wommen holde in ful gret reverence." The protagonist rooster, Chanticleer, cites what he claims to be biblical wisdom to quell the disturbance with his wife caused by his dream: "In principio, / mulier est hominis confusio" [In the beginning, / Woman is man's confounding], which Chanticleer intentionally mistranslates in such a way as to regain his authority over Pertelote intellectually and sexually. Authorities such as Geoffrey of Vinsauf and Thomas Bradwardine are also cited in the raucous comedy of the Nun's Priest's beast fable. Meditating on the largest issues such a tale-telling pilgrimage might engage, "The Nun's Priest's Tale" makes its claim to being the most self-conscious of Chaucer's literary productions. Largely for this reason, scholars attribute a late date to the tale's composition, after the idea of The Canterbury Tales had firmly taken hold of Chaucer's imagination. Moreover, the reference to the Peasants' Revolt of 1381 dictates composition after that, and only two occurrences of Friday, May 3—1392 and 1398—occur afterward. Thus, most scholars date the tale to the mid- to late 1390s.

The narrator's modest protestations of his tale's simplicity and his polite deferrals to the authority of other books are everywhere overwritten by the formal and structural qualities of his story. This is a tale in which a talking rooster admonishes his wife about the prophetic powers of dreams by recounting the narrative in a book (by "Oon of the gretteste auctour that men rede") in which the protagonist recounts a dream in which yet another figure arrives to tell a story of murder and a dung cart that foretells his own death. These receding, inset narratives contain other narratives around which various textual authorities are assembled. The multilayered structure of the tale thus reflects the multilayered structure of the tale collection as a whole, in which pilgrim figures are invented to voice various inset narratives, and where the speaker's voice recedes in the wake of the inset levels of fiction he creates, all of which are overlaid by Chaucer's own "authoritative" position outside the frame.

The superlative self-conscious situation and narrative exposition in "The Nun's Priest's Tale" leads us to a consideration of its narrator, a shadowy figure who recedes so seamlessly into the background that we may be tempted to identify with Chaucer himself. This may be an effect of his facelessness in the GENERAL PROLOGUE TO THE CANTERBURY TALES, where he is simply one of the "preestes three" traveling with the Prioress. The blank characterization allows for, and perhaps cultivates, this kind of authorial projection. But it is most certainly the quintessentially Chaucerian nature of his tale that makes the Nun's Priest capable of bearing such close comparison to the figure of his author.

See also MORALL FABILLIS OF ESOPE THE PHRYGIAN: "COCK AND THE FOX, THE."

FURTHER READING

Cooper, Helen. *Oxford Guides to Chaucer: The Canterbury Tales.* 2nd ed. Oxford: Oxford University Press, 1996.

Howard, Donald. *The Idea of the Canterbury Tales.* Berkeley: University of California Press, 1976.

Pearsall, Derek, ed. *A Variorum Edition of the Works of Geoffrey Chaucer. Part II: The Canterbury Tales. Part Nine: The Nun's Priest's Tale.* Norman, Okla.: Pilgrim Books, 1983.

Elizabeth Scala and Michelle M. Sauer

"NYMPH'S REPLY TO THE SHEPHERD, THE" SIR WALTER RALEIGH (1599)

This poem is a response to CHRISTOPHER MARLOWE's "The PASSIONATE SHEPHERD TO HIS LOVE." Out of the many answers and imitations Marlowe's poem provoked, "The Nymph's Reply to the Shepherd" is the most celebrated, the two poems appearing together from their earliest printings. The full texts of both poems were first published in the collection *England's Helicon* (1599), where "The Nymph's Reply" was signed "Ignoto," or anonymous. Not until more than half a century later do we find an attribution to SIR WALTER RALEIGH, in *The Compleat Angler* by Izaak Walton (1653). We do not know what evidence Walton was using, and some scholars see no compelling reason to assume Raleigh wrote the poem, grouping it instead with the many lyrics spuriously credited to the famous courtier during and after his lifetime.

Other readers hear in the nymph's voice a distinctive blend of feisty wit and dark realism characteristic of Raleigh's poetry. This nymph, or maiden, is no easy mark for the shepherd's attempts to persuade her to "live with [him], and be [his] love." She counters his pretty promises with clear-eyed reason, exposing their fragility in a world where time passes and objects, bodies, and feelings decay. The delightful garments and "beds of Roses" the shepherd offers "Soone breake, soone wither," and are "soone forgotten" in such a world (l. 15). The nymph meticulously takes up and dismisses each detail of the shepherd's golden vision, from the rocks he imagines them relaxing on, which in

her world "grow cold," to the "Melodious byrds" singing "Madrigalls," here replaced by "dombe," tragic "Philomell" and other songbirds who "[complaine] of cares to come" (ll. 7–8). The nymph's lines track the shepherd's every move, wittily echoing the language, sound effects, and form of Marlowe's verse.

The poem's most thorough critic, S. K. Heninger, notes that until the shepherd's final lines, he focuses on sensual pleasures, only belatedly questioning whether these will "move" the nymph's "minde." The nymph, by contrast, dwells on abstract issues of time, love, and truth. Where he is literal and concrete, she is figurative and philosophical. In her poem, his homely shepherd becomes a figure for Time, driving "the flocks from field to fold" as the world grows chill (l. 5). Several of her STANZAS culminate in what sound like moral EPIGRAMS. Beyond remarking the transience of the shepherd's offerings, she declares them "In follie ripe, in reason rotten" (l. 16). She likewise condemns the shepherd's deceptions: "A honny tongue, a hart of gall, / Is fancies spring, but sorrowes fall" (ll. 11–12). Both judgments employ the imagery of passing seasons that dominates the poem. In denouncing the shepherd's "honny tongue," the nymph may also be criticizing poetry whose fictions idealize harsh truths. The "poesies" that wither with the rest of his fleeting enticements are both posies, or flowers, and poesies, poems.

Critics disagree about the tone of the nymph's critique. She appears to end up where she began, describing the impossible conditions under which she would succumb to the shepherd's seductions. If she and the shepherd and love and the world's delights were young, and could stay fresh and vital, then, she concedes, his offerings might move her. Somewhere between the first stanza and the last, however, her insistence on "truth" seems to fade. Although the two stanzas are almost alike, in the last, the line disparaging the truth of the shepherd's tongue is replaced by details of the utopia she envisions. Is she parodying the shepherd's fantasies, or implicitly granting the worth of imagination? Perhaps both, at once mocking and wistful.

Ambivalence toward an imaginary rural ideal often attends the PASTORAL mode, in which complex philosophical and social questions are explored under the guise of the simple life of shepherds. Heninger and others observe that even Marlowe's poem betrays ambivalence, with sophisticated details like gold buckles and amber studs revealing the unavoidable contamination of the pastoral ideal by the worldly. Defiantly, the so-called shepherd insists on the ideal regardless. His self-conscious strain in maintaining the illusion suggests that he is less naive than the skeptical nymph implies. Their shared awareness of the ideal's vulnerability complicates the relationship between their poems.

FURTHER READING

Heninger, S. K. "The Passionate Shepherd and the Philosophical Nymph." *Renaissance Papers* (1962): 63–70.

Latham, Agnes M. C., ed. *The Poems of Sir Walter Raleigh.* Cambridge, Mass.: Harvard University Press, 1951.

Christine Coch

"OCEAN TO CYNTHIA, THE" See RALEIGH, SIR WALTER.

OCTAVE (OCTET)
In English, an octave (also called an octet) consists of eight lines of IAMBIC PENTAMETER (five syllables), though in Italian, it is comprised of hendecasyllables (11 syllable). ITALIAN (PETRARCHAN) SONNETS, both in English and Italian, utilize an octave as the initial part of the poem, which is then followed by a SESTET. Traditionally, the octave concludes one idea, paving the way for another, although ENGLISH SONNETS tend to alter this tradition radically.

See also SONNET.

"ODE, AN" See CYNTHIA, WITH CERTAIN SONNETS.

OFERMOD
In The BATTLE OF MALDON, BYRTHNOTH makes a tactical error allowing the Vikings to cross on to the mainland: "Þa se eorl ongan for his ofermode / alyfan landes to fela laþere þeode" ("Then the lord began, on account of his ofermod, to grant too much territory to the hateful people," ll. 89–90). The Old English noun/adjective ofermod (ofer [excessive] + mod [mental quality, negatively, arrogance]) translates into the Latin term supurbia (pride).

The poem was long considered an example of heroic praise poetry, and that the poet should take a critical stance to the hero Brythnoth was an irritation to many readers. In the 1960s, scholars claimed that ofermod could have a positive meaning such as "high-spirited-ness" or "exceeding courage"; however, general consensus now holds that ofermod can only be used in the negative sense of "pride" or "arrogance," and that interpretations of the poem must take this criticism of Byrthnoth into consideration.

Synonymous with ofermod in the meaning of "pride" or "arrogance" is oferhygd (ofer [excessive] + gehygd [mental quality, consideration]). In BEOWULF, Hrothgar says "oferhygda dæl" ("a portion of prideful thoughts," l. 1741) causes a ruler to begin to neglect his responsibilities. He enjoins Beowulf that he "oferhyda ne gymeþ" ("pay no attention to prideful thoughts," l. 1760).

FURTHER READING
Cavill, Paul. "Interpretation of The Battle of Maldon, Lines 84–90: A Review and Reassessment." Studia Neophilologica 67 (1995). 149–164.

Scragg, Donald, ed. The Battle of Maldon AD 991. Oxford: Blackwell, 1991

Shaun F. D. Hughes

"OF UNSACIABLE PURCHASERS" ROBERT CROWLEY (1550)
ROBERT CROWLEY, a clergyman, poet, prose polemicist, and publisher, was dedicated to the Protestant cause, but he argued vociferously that the Reformation must be managed so that it benefited the poor in particular. Most of his writing was contrived to argue against the exploitation of the poor, and his poems, such as "Of Unsaciable Purchasers," present moral tales delivered with acerbic sharpness, attacking

the greedy mismanagement of resources by the wealthy. One such abuse is the unnecessary accumulation of land.

In "Of Unsaciable Purchasers," Crowley relates a presumably fictional anecdote about a man who acquires property but fails to use it to the wider community's advantage. The poem is built upon a BIBLICAL ALLUSION to a parable in the Gospel of Luke, wherein a wealthy man feeds the poor because they are more grateful than the rich. The generosity of the rich biblical figure is presented as a negative mirror image of the uncharitable rich man in Crowley's 20-line EPIGRAM. This tightfisted, "unreasonable ryche manne" represents the antisocial, selfish, "unsaciable" people Crowley argued against—the greedy land devourers who are never happy.

The rich man boasts to his servant that he has purchased some nearby land. His cheeky servant, rather than praising his vain master, states that local people are perplexed by the man's desire to buy more land, because his "housholde is smal"—that is, he does not share. The rich man replies with rhetorical sarcasm, to which the lad then simply states that it is thought that the man buys "the Devill, his dame and all" (l. 20). This last line encapsulates the crux of Crowley's withering social and religious SATIRE. The man is obsessed with worldly ownership of land but will not improve his community. To acquire land pointlessly is to buy only an association with the Devil. In other words, Crowley argues that the unnecessary accumulation of land by self-interested, ungenerous, wealthy men is bad not only for the worldly welfare of the poor, but also for the souls of the inevitably hell-bound rich "purchasers."

FURTHER READING

Martin, J. W. "The Publishing Career of Robert Crowley." *Publishing History* 14 (1983): 85–98.

———. *Religious Radicals in Tudor England*. London: Hambledon Press, 1989: 147–170.

McRae, Andrew. *God Speed the Plough: The Representation of Agrarian England, 1500–1660.* Cambridge: Cambridge University Press, 2002, 40–42, 61–63.

Kevin de Ornellas

OGHAM Ogham, the ancient runic script of Ireland, was named after the Celtic god of eloquence and persuasion, Ogmios (Oghma). Developed in Ireland around the 2nd century, ogham script made its way to Pictland (Scotland), Wales, and Cornwall, presumably through trade and conquest.

Ogham does not represent a native Celtic language; instead, its characters correspond to vowels and consonants of the Roman alphabet. The 20 ogham runes are signified by one or more horizontal and slanting strokes, although sometimes notches are used for vowels. Like other runic alphabets, ogham letters have names. Most of these refer to trees, which is why ogham is often called the *tree alphabet*. For example, the first letter in ogham is *b,* which is represented by a single vertical stroke [|], but also stands for "beith" (beech tree).

Ogham was primarily used for monumental inscription. The bars were carved into grave markers, and are read starting at the bottom and progressing upward, with no word division or punctuation of any kind. A typical Ogham inscription includes a personal name in the genitive (possessive) case, and so translates into "of [name]," meaning "the grave of [name]." Many inscriptions also include the Celtic appellation *mac (meqq),* which means "son of." In this way, ogham stones also recorded family genealogies. Indeed, some stones recording genealogies tracing back several generations have been found, particularly in the southwest of Ireland. A number of the ogham stones found in Britain also have a side-by-side Latin inscription as well.

Ogham stones have inspired poems such as the anonymous "A GRAVE MARKED IN OGHAM," and feature in the EARLY IRISH SAGAS. Moreover, as genealogical repositories, the ollaves (Irish court poets) would have relied upon these markers in composing heroic songs. Their locations have also assisted in mapping the trade routes of the early Celtic tribes.

See also "CHEVREFOIL," FUTHARK ALPHABET.

FURTHER READING

Barrett, John, and David Iredale. *Discovering Old Handwriting*. Princes Risborough, Buckinghamshire, U.K.: Shire Publishing, 1995.

Mag Fhearaigh, Críostóir, and Tim Stampton. *Ogham.*
Indreabhán, Ireland: Cló Iar-Chonnachta, 1996.

Mark DiCicco and Michelle M. Sauer

"O HAPPY DAMES" HENRY HOWARD, EARL OF SURREY (1545)

This poem, written while HENRY HOWARD, EARL OF SURREY, was fighting in France, is one of the earliest examples in English of a major male poet writing in the voice of a woman. Eventually set to music, it originally circulated in the Tudor court in the Devonshire Manuscript, a manuscript verse collection that was compiled by Surrey's sister Mary (Howard) Fitzroy, duchess of Richmond; Mary Shelton, a friend of the duchess; and Margaret Douglas, niece of HENRY VIII. While critics have disagreed over which Mary actually copied the poem into the manuscript, the poem's authorship has not been questioned. Indeed, the poem seems to give voice to Surrey's personal anguish at being separated from his beloved wife Frances, countess of Surrey.

In both its tone and the treatment of its subject, the poem departs from the courtly poetic conventions that characterize many of the other verses in the Devonshire Manuscript and TOTTEL'S MISCELLANY. The female speaker, who laments the separation from her beloved, uses the common Petrarchan image of a "ship, fraught with remembrance / Of words and pleasures past" (ll. 8–9). Such an image alludes to her lover's departure across stormy seas, but it also stands as a symbol of her fidelity and devotion: "He sails that hath in governance / My life, while it will last" (ll. 10–11). The language is Petrarchan, but the relationship between lover and beloved is warm and close. Furthermore, her constancy sets this portrayal of woman apart from SIR THOMAS WYATT's satiric depiction of courtly women, who change lovers as fashion and their own fickleness dictate.

Surrey's status in general and this poem in particular seem to have contributed to the popularity of "ventriloquized poems" throughout the English Renaissance. Even more importantly, however, "O Happy Dames" may signal a new shift in the treatment of Petrarchan lyric conventions. Although the poem was authored by a male poet, its honest and painful treatment of female longing may have opened the door for later female poets such as MARY SIDNEY HERBERT to voice the experience of COURTLY LOVE from *their* perspective.

See also WYATT, SIR THOMAS.

FURTHER READING

Sessions. W. A. *Henry Howard, the Poet Earl of Surrey: A Life.* Oxford: Oxford University Press, 1999.
Southall, Raymond. "Mary Fitzroy and 'O Happy Dames' in the Devonshire Manuscript." *Review of English Studies* 45, no. 179 (1994): 316–318.

Carol D. Blosser

OLD ENGLISH LANGUAGE (OVERVIEW)

Germanic peoples came to England in the fifth century, subsequently establishing a series of kingdoms that in one form or another lasted until the NORMAN CONQUEST. It became popular during the 16th century to refer to both the people and their language as *Anglo-Saxon.* Current usage restricts *Anglo-Saxon* to refer to the people and their culture, while the language is called Old English. These Germanic peoples came from the Elbe-Weser region of Lower Saxony and from Schleswig-Holstein. The language that they spoke was a development of Proto-Germanic called North-West Germanic, attested to in the earliest runic inscriptions. With the settlement of England, North-West Germanic split into North Germanic in Scandinavia and West Germanic elsewhere. West Germanic began to diverge into North Sea Germanic (Old Saxon [> Low German], Old Frisian, and Old English) and Upper-German (> High German)–Franconian (> Dutch, which, however, also shows significant influence from North-Sea Germanic).

The fairly uniform language of the Germanic settlers began to diverge in its new environment so that when Bede writes his *History of the English Church and People* in the early eighth century, he claims that the English descend from three separate continental peoples corresponding to the then current dialect divisions, Anglian (Northumbrian and Mercian), Saxon, and Kentish (Bede's Jutes). Nevertheless, Bede recognizes only a single language, which all three dialects refer to as *englisc.*

Old English is a typical West Germanic language. Nouns and adjectives have three numbers, although dual and plural are only distinguished in the first and second person singular pronouns and in a special form of the adjective (comparative and superlative). They show three grammatical "genders," conventionally designated masculine, feminine, and neuter and are inflected in four cases, nominative (subject), accusative (direct object), genitive (possessive), and dative (indirect object), although the masculine and neuter demonstrative article preserves the form of a fifth case, the instrumental ("by means of").

The verb system is simplistic. There are three persons and only two formal tenses, present and past. There are "strong" verbs, which show predictable vocalic patterns (known as ablaut—vowel changes) in the present and past tenses and the past participle. "Weak" verbs are a Germanic innovation, and they make their past tense by means of a dental suffix, d or t.

The settlers brought with them a writing system, the 24 item runic alphabet (FUTHARK), which they expanded to up to 33 characters, although its use can hardly have been very widespread. After Christianity began to spread, a vibrant monastic culture developed in Northumbria under Irish influence in the early seventh century that was soon involved in the production of manuscript materials both in Latin and the vernacular. This later was written in the Insular script-system used by the Irish, modified by the introduction of characters from the runic alphabet to accommodate English sounds not in Irish or Latin.

Most of the surviving material in Old English postdates the reign of King ALFRED THE GREAT and is written in a West-Saxon dialect. Even though this language is called Old English, it is not the direct ancestor of Modern English, which derives from an Anglian dialect (South-East Midland) that has been heavily influenced by Old Norse.

See also ALLITERATION, ANGLO-SAXON POETRY.

FURTHER READING

Hogg, Richard M., ed. *The Cambridge History of the English Language*. Vol. 1, *The Beginnings to 1066*. Cambridge: Cambridge University Press, 1992.

Nielsen, Hans Frede. *The Continental Backgrounds of English and Its Insular Development until 1154*. North-Western

European Language Evolution, Supplement 10. Odense, Denmark: Odense University Press, 1998.

Townend, Matthew. *Language and History in Viking Age England: Linguistic Relations between Speakers of Old Norse and Old English*. Studies in the Early Middle Ages, 6. Turnhout, Belgium: Brepols, 2002.

Shaun F. D. Hughes

"OLD MAN'S PRAYER, AN" (14th century)

"An Old Man's Prayer" is a poignant poem of 107 lines presenting an elderly sinner's reflections upon life and mortality in the face of approaching death. The piece can be considered "lyrical" in the sense that the writer is at pains to create and sustain the voice of the speaker. As he discloses the nature of his transgressions, the reader gains a strong sense of his remorse and inner torment.

"An Old Man's Prayer" begins with a heartfelt appeal to the "High Lord" whose laws the speaker has abused. He asks to be absolved of his sins, claiming that his cheeks are now wet with tears. The Old Man recalls how he once rode proudly upon a steed but must now lean upon a walking cane, assailed by the twin penalties of "euel ant elde" ("evil and old age," l. 46). The seventh STANZA reveals how he has succumbed to each of the SEVEN DEADLY SINS: "Lecherie" has been his mistress, "Lyer" his translator, and so forth.

In the 11th stanza, the speaker directly addresses death, lamenting that his body must fade like a flower (l. 86). His prayer increasingly has the feel of a *memento mori* (reminder of death); however, there is optimism as the speaker determines to approach the Lord begging for salvation.

The text is broadly demonstrative of the medieval *timor mortis,* or the fear of death, associated with CONTEMPT FOR THE WORLD. It is also notable for its ALLITERATION and complex vocabulary, especially where the speaker recalls the insults that have been heaped upon him. In his time, the Old Man has been branded a "fulleflet" (l. 15; space waster) and a "waynoun wayteglede" (l. 16; good-for-nothing).

FURTHER READING

Brook, G. L., ed. *The Harley Lyrics*. Manchester, U.K.: Manchester University Press, 1940.

Duncan, Thomas G., ed. *A Companion to the Middle English Lyric.* Woodbridge, Suffolk, U.K.: D. S. Brewer, 2005.

Woolf, Rosemary. *The English Religious Lyric in the Middle Ages.* Oxford: Clarendon Press, 1968.

Robin Gilbank

OLD NORSE/ICELANDIC EDDAS AND SAGAS

Scholars since the 17th century have made substantial use of Old Norse/Icelandic literature as they have attempted to interpret medieval English literature. Nowhere has this tendency been more prominent than in the discussions of Anglo-Saxon pre-Christian religion. Almost all that we know about Anglo-Saxon religion prior to Christianity comes from place names, archeological evidence, and a small amount of written evidence, but almost all we understand about it comes from Old Norse sources. These written sources are themselves not without problems as the forms in which they survive date from more than two centuries after Iceland's conversion to Christianity. Chief among them are two very different texts known as the Eddas.

The Poetic Edda (also known as the Elder Edda or Sæmundar Edda) is a collection of 29 poems found in one manuscript known as the Codex Regius, written in the late 13th century. The manuscript contains 12 poems that deal with a pre-Christian belief system. Most of these poems are narratives concerning the pre-Christian gods, but "Hávamál" (The Sayings of Hávi) is a poem of 164 STANZAS containing gnomic wisdom, wise counsel, runic ritual, and the function of spells, all attributed to "the High One," or Óðin. Perhaps the most famous of the mythological poems is *Voluspa* (The Prophecy of the Sybil), which recounts the final battle between gods, giants, and wolves, which will destroy the world. The heroic (EPIC) poems deal with heroes and heroines whose exploits are also found outside Old Norse in works such as *BEOWULF*.

The Prose Edda (also known as the Younger Edda or Snorra Edda) is the work of Snorri Sturluson (1178/9–1241). A handbook for poets, it is divided into four parts. The first, a brief prologue, is an euhemeristic account of the pagan pantheon. Part 2 presents a non-Christian account of the creation and destruction of the world along with narratives involving the pagan gods, all copiously illustrated with quotations from the Elder Edda and Old Norse skaldic poetry. Part 3 is mainly concerned with explaining the meaning of the *kenningar* (KENNING, compound metaphors) and the *heiti* (synonyms) which were a feature of skaldic poetry. Part 4 is a 102-stanza poem in praise of king Hákon Hákonarson of Norway (1217–63) and the earl Skúli Bárøarson (1188/9–1240). Each stanza is in a slightly different meter which is introduced and commented upon if necessary. Like the Poetic Edda, the Prose Edda, particularly parts 2 and 3, has been ransacked for information that might elucidate pre-Christian references in Old English texts, forgetting at times that the Eddas themselves are not unproblematic documents and that they have been significantly affected by the ideology and practice of Christianity.

Beginning in the 12th century, a tradition of prose narrative or saga came into being, which tradition has been conventionally divided into numerous "genres": *konungasögur* (kings' sagas); *biskupasögur* (bishops' sagas), *Íslendingasögur* (saga of the Icelanders), *samtíðarsögur* (sagas of contemporary events), *heiligramanna-* and *postulasögur* (sagas of saints and apostles), *fornaldarsögur Norðurlanda* (sagas of ancient times in the northern lands), and *riddarasögur* (sagas of knights). The 40 sagas of the Icelanders have historically been best served by translation into English. Some of these sagas, such as *Egils saga Skalla-Grímssonar* and *Gunnlaugs saga ormstungu*, have significant sections that are set in England during Anglo-Saxon times.

Perhaps the best-known claim for a link between Old English literature and the *Íslendingasögur* are the parallels found between *Beowulf* and *Ásmundarsonar* from the Grettis saga. Of particular note are the similarities in the fight between Beowulf and Grendel and that between Grettir and Glámur, and in Beowulf's encounter with Grendel's mother at the bottom of the mere and Grettir's one with the giant (*jötun*) behind the waterfall at Sandhaugar. While it might not be possible to determine the relationship between the two works to everybody's satisfaction, it seems incontrovertible that there is a relationship.

Other scholars who have investigated Norse–English literary relationships have looked at Norse links to the English Gawain Cycle, Sir Thomas Malory's "Tale of Sir Gareth," and GEOFFREY CHAUCER's "The PARDONER'S

TALE," and "The WIFE OF BATH'S TALE." Claims have also been made for a link between *Áns saga bogsveigis,* a *fornaldarsögur Norðurlanda* saga surviving from the 15th century and the Middle English ROBIN HOOD BALLADS. While these are inconclusive, other investigations have revealed possible connections between the stanzaic form and parts of *PIERS PLOWMAN.*

The lack of surviving information about the belief system of pre-Christian England means that the Eddas and the sagas will continue to be used as resources to make up the deficiency, but in some ways the work that is being done to find links between this material and Middle English literature promises to open up more fruitful avenues of inquiry.

FURTHER READING

Clover, Carol, and John Lindow, eds. *Old Norse-Icelandic Literature: A Critical Guide.* Toronto: University of Toronto Press and Medieval Academy of America, 2005.

Fjalldal, Magnús. *Anglo-Saxon England in Icelandic Medieval Texts.* Toronto: University of Toronto Press, 2005.

Hollander, Lee M., trans. *The Poetic Edda.* 2nd ed. Austin: University of Texas Press, 1962.

Hreinsson, Viðar, gen. ed. *The Complete Sagas of Icelanders.* 5 vols. Reykjavík: Leifur Eiríksson, 1997.

Hughes, Shaun F. D., trans. "The Saga of Án bowbender." In *Medieval Outlaws: Twelve Tales in Modern Translation,* edited by Thomas H. Ohlgren, 290–337. West Lafayette, Ind.: Parlor Press, 2005.

McTurk, Rory. *Chaucer and the Norse and Celtic Worlds.* Burlington, Vt.: Ashgate, 2005.

Taylor, Paul Beekman. *Sharing Story: Medieval Norse-English Literary Relationships.* New York: AMS Press, 1998.

Shaun F. D. Hughes

"OLD WOMAN OF BEARE, THE" ANONYMOUS (800 C.E.)

"The Old Woman of Beare" is untitled and anonymous in the five manuscripts in which it survives. The length of the poem varies in the manuscripts with the longest being 35 STANZAS. In all versions, the stanzas are four lines long. The poet employs the Celtic meter *deibide,* in which a stressed syllable rhymes with an unstressed syllable. The poem is a LAMENT and, perhaps, the best and certainly the most famous of the early Irish lyrics that have survived.

In Irish, the titular character is *Cailleach Bhéarra.* No doubt exists that *Beare* is a place name for a peninsula in County Cork. *Cailleach,* however, may be translated as "hag," "old woman," or, in a Christian setting, as "nun." In Irish and Scottish Gaelic mythology, Cailleach Bhéarra is a female divinity, goddess of the land and of sovereignty, who has seen seven ages of youth and old age. This role has some bearing on the poem, but the character primarily functions as an ancient nun who has endured endless cycles of youth and age. She repeatedly mentions the ebb and flow of the tide. The old woman also uses the name *Bui;* it could be her own name or another place name.

Whatever the character's name, she laments her lost youth, her long-gone friends, and her former life. Like the Wanderer in the Old English ELEGY, the narrator of this lament becomes religious after having outlived earthly friends and lovers. Thus, we can see the age-old theme of transience. Unlike BOETHIUS, who turned to philosophy, the nun has turned to religion to provide her consolation. She contrasts her youth with its glories and passion with the suffering and hardships of old age. She had relationships with kings and lords in days gone by spent conversing and drinking in the mead hall. Now she lives in a dark and lonely cell. Fine clothes, high station, and good looks have been replaced by a threadbare shift and gray hair. Her eyes are failing her, if she is not blind already. The poem repeatedly mentions her drinking ale, beer, and wine in her youth; now she has a cup of whey. Thus, we see her mingling the sacred with the profane. She recounts her sins and regrets the loss of the circumstances that had given rise to them.

Nevertheless, the narrator still has one thing remaining to her—the Irish virtue of generosity. Here the lament gains its true staying power over the ages. The nun welcomes her new lord Christ to visit her. She cannot offer Christ anything else but her body. In making this offer, she weaves together aestheticism and sensuality when, as a "Bride of Christ," she invites Christ to enter her bed chamber. And she readily admits that she has not said "no" to any man before. This sexual element fits in with Cailleach Bhéarra's mythological role of vegetative fertility. This offer provides a sly and subtle turn, the connotations of which add life and dynamism to the poem. While the Old Woman of the lament may be a nun, she is still a woman with the needs of any woman, or man, for that matter. Having made the offer, the nun then closes the poem by referring back to the turning of the tides and the passing of time. She does not expect to outlive the next tide. This oft-anthologized Irish lament remains popular to this day and easily rivals any other early Irish or English poem of its kind.

See also EARLY IRISH VERSE.

FURTHER READING

Kato, Eileen. "A Comparative Look at 'Ono no Komachi' and 'The Old Woman of Beare.'" *Transactions of the Asiatic Society of Japan* 11 (1996): 135–149.

MacCana, Proinsias. "Mythology in Early Irish Literature." In *Celtic Consciousness,* edited by Robert O'Driscoll, 143–154. New York: George Braziller, 1982.

Mark DiCicco

"ON MONSIEUR'S DEPARTURE" ELIZABETH I (ca. 1582)

This poem was written about 1582 at the conclusion of the marriage negotiations between England and France regarding the potential marriage of Queen ELIZABETH I and Francis, duc d'Alençon, whom she called "Monsieur." Elizabeth, as a single queen, was very circumspect on the issue of marriage, as she realized that a consort would necessarily weaken her own authority. Negotiations for the marriage with the duc d'Alençon were the last engaged in by the queen, as she was 49 by the time they concluded and presumably past childbearing age. However, the language in the poem suggests that the queen did have a certain amount of affection for the man who was many years her junior.

The poem has three STANZAS, each with an *ababcc* rhyme scheme. It is organized around a series of contradictions between the queen's private and public bodies. Her private, inner, woman's body feels sad at the various implications surrounding the end of the "betrothal," while her public, queen's body needs to hide all her personal feelings and act for the good of the country. In the first stanza, the queen indicates that inwardly she grieves, loves, wants to say what she means, talks incessantly, and suffers the pains of LOVESICKNESS: "I am, and not; I freeze and yet am burned, / Since from myself another self I turned" (ll. 5–6). Out-

wardly, however, she "dare not" (l. 1) show how upset she is or what she really feels about the situation. She is "forced to seem to hate" (l. 2) the man who was part of the marriage deal.

In the second stanza, Elizabeth talks about how her "care" (l. 7), what or who she cares about, is "like my shadow in the sun" (l. 7). Just as our shadows are part of us—following us or going before us, depending on the time of day—her "care" is always with her just as her shadow is. He has, in a sense, become so much a part of her that she finds "No means . . . to rid him from my breast [or heart], / Till by the end of things it be suppressed" (ll. 11–12). Again, like the person suffering from lovesickness, only death will end the queen's pain.

The third stanza allows the queen's private, womanly body to be revealed. She wishes a "gentler passion to slide into" (l. 13) her mind, perhaps one that does not cause her to freeze and burn as this one does. She wishes this because, as a woman, she sees herself as "soft, and made of melting snow" (l. 14). Now she switches to address Love itself, to ask it to be, paradoxically, more cruel to be more kind. This is sort of a wish to be put out of her misery, as the stanza moves back to the kind of opposition displayed in stanza 1. She asks to either "float or sink" or "be high or low" (l. 16), a request either to swim or drown, to be happy or sad. The poem's final COUPLET puts things in an even starker form: "Or let me live with some more sweet content, / Or die and so forget what love e'er meant" (ll. 17–18). The queen asks Love to grant her either a life that contains some sort of pleasant comfort, or let her die so that she can forget what love meant. Interestingly, the poem ends with the Latin phrase *Eliza betha Regina,* "Elizabeth the Queen," making us wonder whether the queen finally decides to do what her public body needs to do, despite the pain in her private body.

FURTHER READING

Hopkins, Lisa. *Writing Renaissance Queens: Texts by and about Elizabeth I and Mary, Queen of Scots.* Newark: University of Delaware Press; London: Associated University Presses, 2002.

Marcus, Leah S. "Queen Elizabeth I as Public and Private Poet: Notes toward a New Edition." In *Reading Monarch's*

Writing: *The Poetry of Henry VIII, Mary Stuart, Elizabeth I, and James VI/I,* edited by Peter C. Herman, 135–153. Tempe: Arizona Center for Medieval and Renaissance Studies, 2002.

OVID (PUBLIUS OVIDIUS NASO) (43 B.C.E.–CA. 17 C.E.)

Ovid was born in Sulmo, Italy. With VIRGIL, he is considered one of the foremost Latin authors. Not much is known about his personal life. As a young man, Ovid traveled to Rome to study law, becoming a pupil of Porcius Latro and Arelius Fuscus, both master rhetoricians. He then embarked on an administrative career, working at the mint and in the prison system before becoming a judge. He was married three times.

Ovid wrote *Amores* (a collection of love poetry), *Heroides* (letters from/about female heroes), *Remedia Amoris* (*The Cure for Love*), *Ars Amatoria* (*Art of Love*), *Medicamina Facici Feminae* (a treatise about cosmetics), *Metamorphoses* (a collection of mythological legends), *Fasti* (a book on the months), and a number of other works, now lost. In 8 C.E., Ovid was exiled to Tomi on the Black Sea, where he remained until his death. No specific reason for his exile has been found. Scholars speculate that the emperor Augustus, who had recently undertaken a campaign to clean up Rome's debauchery, was offended by Ovid's *Art of Love*. The volume, which contains frank descriptions of love and actions inspired by love, likely made the conservative government uncomfortable.

Ovid is known for his preservation and elevation of Roman mythology, as well as for his love poetry. His verse forms vary, but he favored the elegiac COUPLET (alternating lines of dactylic hexameter and dactylic pentameter).

Ovid's influence on medieval and Renaissance poetry was substantial. For instance, GEOFFREY CHAUCER relied on Ovid's *Metamorphoses* for both *The LEGEND OF GOOD WOMEN* and *The BOOK OF THE DUCHESS,* both for inspiration and for source materials. Likewise, JOHN GOWER drew on Ovid's works, especially his letters and *Art of Love,* for the *CONFESIO AMANTIS. The Art of Love* served as inspiration for the later work *The ART OF COURTLY LOVE* by ANDREAS CAPELLANUS.

During the Tudor era, English translations of Ovid's works only served to increase his visibility as inspiration for poets. Arthur Golding is credited with the first English translation of Ovid's *Metamorphoses,* in 1567. Similarly, CHRISTOPHER MARLOWE translated the *Amores* before his death in 1593, though the work was published posthumously in 1599 and subsequently banned as "offensive." Ovid's works were particularly fertile ground for the sonneteers. Numerous SONNET SEQUENCES, including Sir PHILIP SIDNEY's *ASTROPHIL AND STELLA* and WILLIAM SHAKESPEARE's, owe a debt to his works. ISABELLA WHITNEY's works, especially her "ADMONITION BY THE AUTHOR," directly reference Ovid's works. These are but a few examples—Ovid's influence continued to be felt strongly in British poetry throughout the early modern period and well into the modern era.

See also CLASSICAL TRADITION, TRANSLATION TRADITION.

FURTHER READING

Davis, Peter J. *Ovid and Augustus: A Political Reading of Ovid's Erotic Poems.* London: Duckworth, 2006.

Desmond, Marilynn. *Ovid's Art and the Wife of Bath: The Ethics of Erotic Violence.* Ithaca, N.Y.: Cornell University Press, 2006.

Oakley-Brown, Liz. *Ovid and the Cultural Politics of Translation in Early Modern England.* Aldershot, U.K., and Burlington, Vt.: Ashgate, 2006.

Rimell, Victoria. *Ovid's Lovers: Desire, Difference and the Poetic Imagination.* Cambridge and New York: Cambridge University Press, 2006.

OWL AND THE NIGHTINGALE, THE

ANONYMOUS (ca. 1189–1216) *The Owl and the Nightingale* is a Middle English poem (see MIDDLE ENGLISH POETRY) of 1,794 lines, written in the late 12th or early 13th century. There are two extant manuscripts containing the poem, both from the late 13th century, but internal evidence suggest it was written a good deal earlier, since references in the text to the late King Henry suggest it must have been written between Henry II's death in 1189 and Henry III's taking the throne in 1216. It is a debate poem in which the solemn Owl disputes with the spirited Nightingale over their relative value to humankind.

The poem is comic, depicting the self-important Owl as melancholy, severe, and quick-tempered, and the lighthearted Nightingale as sanguine but shallow. The two argue about a variety of random subjects, though they never probe very deeply. It is possible that the poem is an allegory in which the Owl represents the contemplative life and the Nightingale the active life; or perhaps, as some scholars have suggested, the birds represent philosophy and art, or the preacher and the minstrel, or (the most popular interpretation) love poetry and religious poetry. Indeed, the characters touch on all of these subjects in the poem, but never with any depth or apparent seriousness.

What stands out more than any particular theme is the character of the two debaters. They are more interested in self-aggrandizement and in personal attacks against each other than in any serious ideas. The Nightingale calls the Owl ugly, and the Owl accuses the Nightingale of being scrawny. Each attacks the other's sanity and cleanliness. The Owl complains that all the Nightingale can do is sing, while she, the Owl, can do many things. In particular, she boasts of her practical contribution of exterminating mice in barns. The poem's narrator seems to come down ultimately on the side of the Owl, though it is just as possible that he, like the Nightingale herself in the end, is simply impressed by the Owl's egoism and self-importance. In that case, the poem may simply be a satire of human contentiousness.

The debate concludes without a clear victor, and the birds fly off to present their case to someone named Nicholas of Guildford to judge. Some readers have assumed that Nicholas was the author of the poem, others that he was the author's patron (which would explain his flattering characterization in the poem as a man of learning and accomplishment). Still others have suggested that the poem was written in order to be presented to Nicholas by an anonymous clerical friend of the poet's, or by the nuns of Shaftesbury Abbey, a possibility that would be consistent with the poem's southwest dialect. But there is no critical consensus about Nicholas of Guildford's connection to the text, or about the poem's authorship in general. We do know that the bird debate was to become a popular subgenre of MIDDLE ENGLISH POETRY, so that the inspiration for the later *Thrush and the Nightingale* (late 12th c.), Thomas Clanvowe's *Cuckoo and the Nightingale* (ca. 1400), and perhaps GEOFFREY CHAUCER's *The PARLIAMENT OF FOWLS*, probably came ultimately from *The Owl and the Nightingale*.

FURTHER READING

Cartlidge, Neil, ed. *The Owl and the Nightingale.* Exeter, U.K.: University of Exeter Press, 2001.

Hume, Kathryn. *The Owl and the Nightingale: The Poem and its Critics.* Toronto: Toronto University Press, 1975.

Stone, Brian, trans. *The Owl and the Nightingale, Cleanness, and St Erkenwald.* 2nd ed. London: Penguin Classics, 1988.

Jay Ruud

P

PAEAN In English literature, a paean is a formal song of joy, praise, or triumph. The tradition derives from the ancient Greek practice of singing hymns of thanksgiving to (or invocation of) Apollo for protection against disease and defeat in battle. Paean is one of Apollo's names, referring to his role as healer. Occasionally, paeans were sung to other gods, especially Dionysus, Asclepius, and Helios.

See also ENCOMIUM, PANEGYRIC.

PANEGYRIC A panegyric in the Greek tradition was a laudatory speech delivered at a public assembly (*panegyris*), such as an Olympic or other religious festival. The oration often focused on past civic or personal glories and was couched in flowery language. It became associated with eulogy, the praise of famous or eminent individuals, which in Roman society was restricted to living persons. Panegyrics dominated the OLD NORSE/ICELANDIC EDDAS AND SAGAS and were the main product of skalds (ancient Scandinavian bards). The form was later Christianized to include praise of God and the saints, as a complement to HAGIOGRAPHY. In English literature, the terms *panegyric* and ENCOMIUM are often used interchangeably.

During the Renaissance, a common form of panegyric was the "mirrors for princes," a genre of political writing instructing kings how to behave. One of the implicit principles underlying the "mirror" was that praiseworthy princely behavior demonstrated God's plan was working as it should, that the prince (King)

was a legitimate ruler. Numerous panegyric offerings were produced for Queen ELIZABETH I.

See also MIRRORS FOR PRINCES.

FURTHER READING:
Noreña, Carlos F. "The Communication of the Emperor's Virtues." *The Journal of Roman Studies* 91 (2001): 146–168.
Vickers, Brian. "Epideictic and Epic in the Renaissance." *New Literary History* 14, no. 3 (1983): 497–537.

Carol E. Harding

"PANGUR BÁN" ANONYMOUS (ninth century) "Pangur Bán" is contained in the margin of a ninth-century manuscript containing Greek and Latin literature found in the monastery of St. Paul at Unterdrauberg in Carinthia, Austria. The poem is untitled and anonymous. It has eight four-line STANZAS in a Celtic meter called *deibide,* in which a stressed syllable rhymes with an unstressed syllable. It derives its title from the white (*bán*) cat named Pangur. The cat's name, Pangur, is an early Welsh form of *pannwr* ("a fuller").

This is not simply a poem about a cat. It is about the monk-author comparing his search for meaning while commenting on texts with his cat chasing—and catching—mice. The poem's cozy domesticity creates a world modern readers can easily imagine. The monk-poet may have adopted the white cat in Wales. The poet and the cat live in harmony and happiness; neither is bored. The poet pursues learning, and the cat pursues mice, a witty ZEUGMA, or ironic linking of two words. The cat traps mice in its "net" or paws; the scholar "nets" abstruse argument—another zeugma. The catching of mice counterbalances the monk's scholarship as he attempts to illuminate complex problems with his clear, though feeble, eyes. The poet does not take himself too seriously; his academic endeavors are little more than a mouse hunt. This sophisticated humor and subtle turns of phrasing result in "Pangur Bán" being an often-anthologized poem.

FURTHER READING

MacCana, Proinsias, ed. and trans. "Pangur Bán." In *Field Day Anthology of Irish Writing,* edited by Seamus Deane, 44–45. Derry: Field Day Publications, 1991.

McCormick, Malachi, ed. and trans. *Pangur Bawn.* Staten Island, N.Y.: Stone Street, 1992.

Mark DiCicco

"PARDONER'S TALE, THE" GEOFFREY CHAUCER (ca. 1390)

"The Pardoner's Tale" on the consequences of greed and deviousness is one of the best stories in *The CANTERBURY TALES* collection, although the storyteller is, as he acknowledges to the pilgrims, "a ful vicious man." It is one of two tales in GEOFFREY CHAUCER's work that resembles a sermon, the other being the Parson's treatise on penance and the SEVEN DEADLY SINS. Chaucer seems to have composed the Pardoner's allegorical story, which has widespread folktale origins, specifically for *The Canterbury Tales;* it dates from about 1390 to 1400. A late date may be inferred from the close matching of the Pardoner's "voice" and his story's content. It is uncertain where Chaucer might ultimately have intended to place "The Pardoner's Tale" in the scheme of the Canterbury collection, but it usually appears midway through the *Tales* in both manuscript compilations and in modern editions.

Before his sermon-like tale, the Pardoner displays and explains his preaching techniques. The Pardoner, the spiritual and ethical antithesis of the ideal Parson, details his rhetorical skillfulness in relating his sermons, which, he says, are always organized around the theme of "Greed is the root of evil" (*Radix malorum est cupiditas*). He has perfected this sermon not only from frequent repetition but also because, as he acknowledges, he is himself the epitome of avarice, so he understands the sin from within, so to speak. "The Pardoner's Tale" incorporates features of the typical late medieval sermon, including a sermon theme, three subtopics (gluttony, gambling, and oaths or swearing), and an exemplary story (EXEMPLUM) that illustrates the sermon theme and weaves in the three subtopics. The Pardoner relates the story in a highly rhetorical manner, framing his denunciations of sin in ANAPHORA (the repetition of the same word at the beginning of adjacent lines) and exclamatio (an exclamation or APOSTROPHE, often beginning with "O!"). His message is simple yet chilling: The wages of sin are death.

The Pardoner's story features three young Flemish men who frequent the tavern, eat and drink to excess, engage in gambling and whoring, and swear violently, tearing apart the body of Christ, which constitutes the worst kind of cursing, since those who swear in this way take God's name in vain and participate in Christ's death. They embody the typical medieval "tavern sins." The Pardoner himself engages in this conduct, swearing "by Seint Ronyon" (l. 320) and pausing, before his story, to indulge in a "draughte of corny ale" (l. 456). The three tavern-goers, whose names we never come to know but who are consistently characterized as *riotours* (profligates), learn that "Deeth" has claimed a friend of theirs, a man who was "fordronke" (exceedingly drunk) while he was sitting on a tavern bench, and "he hath a thousand slayn this pestilence along with a thousand others" (ll. 672–679). The taverner confirms this, adding that "Deeth" has carried off many in the nearby village. "Deeth" has the allegorical value of the fate that awaits all mortals, but here it has a specific meaning as well: the bubonic plague, or BLACK DEATH, the pandemic that ravaged Flanders and England in 1349 and western Europe in general from 1347 until 1351. The riotours decide to seek out "Deeth" and kill him. They even form a fellowship, pledging their "trouthes"—their sacred words—"To lyve and dyen ech of hem for oother, / As though he were his owene ybore brother" (ll. 702–704).

The bond between and among the three *riotours* may inspire reflection on the fellowship of the Canterbury pilgrims; but whereas the goal of the pilgrims is pilgrimage and atonement for sins, the goal of the riotours is sinful revenge. They set out on their murderous quest in a drunken rage. Before they have gone far, they encounter a mysterious old man, completely muffled except for his face, who tells the young men that he seeks death. Although the old man is polite to the riotours, they menace him and demand more information about the whereabouts of "Deeth." The almost mythical old man directs the riotours to a special route: "If that yow be so leef / To fynde Deeth, turne up this croked wey" (ll. 760–761). He explains that he left Death there under the oak tree.

The "croked wey" is the appropriate metaphor for the course of the three riotours, who have been on the wrong path, it seems, all their lives, for they have lived their lives in sin. This sinful route, which the riotours eagerly pursue in their quest for Death, takes them to heaps "of florins fyne of gold ycoyned rounde" (l. 770). The three worry about transporting the gold back to their homes during the day, so they decide to send one to town for provisions (food and drink) while the other two remain with the gold to guard it. They draw straws to determine who will go to town—a variant of the gambling subtopic of the sermon—and that task falls to the youngest *riotour*. As soon as he departs, one of the remaining "sworn brothers" suggests that the two of them cut the youngest out of the deal by killing him. He sums up:

> And thanne shal al this gold departed be,
> My deere freend, bitwixen me and thee.
> Thanne may we bothe oure lustes all fulfille,
> And pleye at dees right at oure owene wille
> (ll. 831–834)

In town, the youngest purchases food but also rat poison with which he spikes *one* of the three wine bottles. When he returns, the other brothers slay him and, as the Pardoner puts it, they just happen "To take the botel ther the poyson was" (a final instance of the "gambling" subtopic) (l. 886). As a conclusion to his exemplum, the Pardoner returns to his rhetorical denunciations of greed, gluttony, lust, gambling, and cursing (ll. 895–903). The Pardoner can sermonize so well on the subject of greed because he has himself followed the "croked wey" all his professional life.

As corrupt as he admits he is, the Pardoner says he can still help others to the true Christian path and sal-

vation. Although he does not care if his parishioners go to hell and "pick blackberries," his artful storytelling may yet, he claims, inspire them to repentance: "Yet kan I maken oother folk to twynne / From avarice and soore to repente" (ll. 431–432). The Pardoner exposes an underlying theme for *The Canterbury Tales*: the purpose of storytelling, especially on a pilgrimage. Should stories always and only have a moral purpose? Can moral stories be related by corrupt sinners? This issue may have been important to Chaucer, the master poet, who introduced new and sometimes controversial European modes of storytelling to the English court.

The exemplary tale of the three *riotours* has been told by a pilgrim who freely and even proudly admits that he is greedy and false. Chaucer modeled the Pardoner in part on Faus Semblant (False Seeming), a notorious character in Jean de Meun's portion of *Le Roman de la Rose* (The *Romaunt* of the Rose), a 13th-century work that Chaucer studied closely and claimed to have translated. Faus Semblant is depicted as one of "Antecristes men," those who affect holiness and appear to be virtuous but who are quite other than they seem. The Pardoner is one such man but is even more dangerous since he pledges help toward salvation with his relics and absolution, while his supposed efforts on behalf of his congregations are based entirely on bad faith. As he explains to the pilgrims:

> I wol have moneie, wolle, chese, and whete,
> Al were it yeven of the povereste page,
> Or of the povereste wydwe in a village,
> Al sholde hir children sterve for famyne.
> Nay, I wol drynke licour of the vyne
> And have a joly wenche in every toun.
> (ll. 448–453)

Unlike the pilgrim Parson, who shares his meager wealth with his impoverished parishioners, the Pardoner selfishly takes from the poorest widow and her hungry children; he seeks an abundance of food and drink and a "wench" with whom he can fornicate. Or so he claims.

In the GENERAL PROLOGUE TO THE CANTERBURY TALES, Chaucer describes the Pardoner as of dubious sexuality whose sexual partner (such is the implication) is the

Summoner. He says the Pardoner has a high voice like a goat's, no beard, and long, thin, flaxen-colored hair. Of his sexuality the narrator muses, "I trowe he were a geldyng or a mare" (l. 691). These are two quite different beasts, of course: A gelding is a castrated male horse and a mare is a female horse; the gelding would suggest a eunuch, and the mare a male with female characteristics. The issue of the Pardoner's sexuality is important for two reasons: First, his sexuality is connected to the falseness of his relics; second, the Host attacks the Pardoner with regard to his sexuality at the close of the tale. The Pardoner is not what he seems; he cannot deliver what he promises. Impotent himself, he offers "relics" that would cheat expectations for salvation from hell's fire. He seems to embody all that was wrong with the late medieval church, including the marketing of indulgences.

After his exemplary story of the *riotours*, the Pardoner ends his sermon demonstration by saying, "And lo, sires, thus I preche" (l. 915). This closes off his revelation to the Canterbury pilgrims of how he usually preaches back home at St. Mary Rouncivall, a hospital at Charing Cross, London, that created a scandal when it tried to raise money through selling indulgences. The Pardoner has delivered a gripping sermon on the root of evil, and he has integrated his subtopics of gluttony, gambling, and swearing very effectively. But now he invites the Canterbury pilgrims to purchase the relics he has earlier exposed as fraudulent, calling upon Harry Bailly, Host of the pilgrimage, to be the first to offer up his money and to kiss the sham relics. The Host takes great offense at this invitation, shouting, among other things, that he wishes he had the Pardoner's testicles in his hands so he could cut them off and enshrine them "in a hogges toord" (l. 955). The Host's implication is that the Pardoner does not possess testicles to cut off; the Pardoner's response is fury ("wroth," l. 957).

The Canterbury fellowship threatens to unravel because of this verbal altercation. The Knight, socially the highest-ranking pilgrim, steps in to restore order and repair the fellowship, getting the Host and the Pardoner to kiss and make up. So much in "The Pardoner's Tale" speaks to the aims of pilgrimage: the true Christian path (as opposed to the "croked wey"); fellowship (as opposed to the false "brotherhood" of the *riotours*); the spiritual goal of the journey to Canterbury (as opposed to the tavern and tavern sins of the *riotours*); moral storytelling (as opposed to some of the more "entertaining" stories told along the way); Christian charity (as opposed to the angry exchange between Host and Pardoner). Ironically, the Knight, a good man but a crusader and warrior, must step in to keep the peace, thus testifying to the importance of secular figures on the road to the cathedral at Canterbury.

Modern scholars, especially queer theorists, have examined the Pardoner as a potential reclamation of gay history. For instance, in the Prologue and Tale, the female is excluded but parodied by men, creating a homosocial society. In this way, Chaucer seemingly admits a homosexual possibility. Others believe that the Pardoner is written out of homophobia, citing the overt heterosexist remarks, as well as the violence (e.g., the Host's desire to cut off the Pardoner's testicles) and corruption (e.g., the Pardoner's falseness) as evidence.

See also ALLEGORY.

FURTHER READING

Cooper, Helen. *The Canterbury Tales: Oxford Guides to Chaucer.* 2nd ed. Oxford: Oxford University Press, 1996.

Faulkner, Dewey R., ed. *Twentieth Century Interpretations of the Pardoner's Tale: A Collection of Critical Essays.* Englewood Cliffs, N.J.: Prentice-Hall, 1973.

Gray, Douglas, ed. *The Oxford Companion to Chaucer.* Oxford: Oxford University Press, 2003.

Hamel, Mary. "The Pardoner's Prologue and Tale." In *Sources and Analogues of The Canterbury Tales,* Vol. 1, edited by Robert M. Correale and Mary Hamel, 267–319. Cambridge: D.S. Brewer, 2003.

Mann, Jill. *Chaucer and Medieval Estates Satire.* Cambridge: Cambridge University Press, 1973.

McAlpine, Monica E. "The Pardoner's Homosexuality and How It Matters." *PMLA* 95, no. 1 (1980): 8–22.

Patterson, Lee. "Chaucerian Confession: Penitential Literature and the Pardoner." *Medievalia et Humanistica* 7 (1976): 153–173.

Pearsall, Derek. *The Canterbury Tales.* London: Allen/Unwin, 1985.

James Dean

PARLIAMENT OF FOWLS, THE GEOFFREY CHAUCER (ca. 1380)   *The Parliament of Fowls* is one of GEOFFREY CHAUCER's major DREAM VISIONS. Traditionally,

there has been an assumption that the poem was written for an engagement (perhaps that of Richard II and Anne of Bohemia), but no consensus has been achieved regarding which betrothal, if any, the poem seeks to comment on. The action of the *Parliament* takes place on Saint Valentine's Day; the poem may, in fact, have inaugurated the tradition of Valentine's Day love poems. Chaucer wrote the *Parliament* in RHYME ROYAL, a STANZA form consisting of an *ababbcc* rhyme scheme in iambic pentameter.

The Parliament of Fowls can be broken into three primary divisions: (1) the narrator's comments on himself and his reading; (2) the first part of the dream, in which the narrator enters a seductive but also sinister garden; and (3) the second part of the dream, in which the narrator witnesses a bird debate regarding which male eagle should be chosen as a mate for a female eagle. While none of these sections is particularly long, each is quite complex in itself, and the attempt to determine the significance of the relationship between the three has been a major focus of scholarship.

The poem's narrator introduces himself as a typical Chaucerian persona: self-deprecating, bookish, and inexperienced in love. He tells of reading Cicero's *Dream of Scipio* (really Macrobius's *Commentary on the Dream of Scipio*), in which the deceased Roman general, Scipio the Elder, appears to his grandson so that he may show him the cosmos and charge him to live for "commune profyt" ("the common good," ll. 47, 75). While reading the book, the narrator falls asleep; Scipio then appears in a dream and promises to reward him for his labor.

Transitioning to the second part, the dreaming narrator finds himself before a gate modeled after Hell's gate in Dante's *Inferno*. Unlike Dante's gate, though, which promises only eternal sorrow, the gate in the *Parliament* offers two possibilities, bliss or pain. Scipio pushes the narrator through the entrance with the assurance that the gate's terms apply only to those who are servants of Love. Once inside, the narrator finds himself in a beautiful forest with a garden, streams, and singing birds. He sees Cupid and a host of allegorical figures (such as "Delyt" and "Desyr") that suggest both the wonderful and terrible nature of Love. The narrator enters a temple of Venus, which is filled with sighs of desire and adorned with images of famous figures who suffered for love. He sees Venus there, scantily clothed, but leaves her alone and exits the temple.

In the poem's final section, the narrator sees Nature herself surrounded by birds "of every kinde that men thynke may" ("of every kind one could imagine," l. 311). Under Nature's governance, the birds are having a debate to decide which eagle deserves to marry the *formel* (female) eagle. Three *tercels* (males) present their suits, after which the other species of birds begin to chatter and dispute over which eagle is most worthy. Ultimately, the decision is left with the female eagle, who decides to defer selection for a year. The remaining birds take their mates and then sing a song to welcome the spring season. The narrator awakes at this point and begins to read more books.

One major problem in understanding *The Parliament of Fowls* involves its main theme. On one hand, the poem would seem to be an examination of love. The introduction presents love as the narrator's central concern—indeed, as his crisis, since he is inexperienced and only knows about amorous affairs through books. Certainly the erotic garden and the temple of Venus deepen this theme, as does the birds' squabbling over mating selection. On the other hand, within the discussion of the *Dream of Scipio,* the narrator emphasizes the importance of "commune profyt" (common good), and so it is has been typical to see the *Parliament* as a social commentary. Pursuing this track, the class hierarchy of the bird debate is of especial importance.

Taking love as the *Parliament*'s primary concern, we encounter a highly contradictory presentation. Given the cosmic perspective of the *Dream of Scipio* in the opening, Nature's attempt to preserve order during the spring mating can be linked to an overall order under divine governance—the earthly world reflecting in microcosm what is orchestrated on the much larger universal level. The birds' concluding song would thus serve as a celebration of the harmony that permeates creation. Several elements of the poem, however, work against such an interpretation, including the bickering during the birds' deliberation, the lack of any decision regarding the *formel* eagle's mate, and the return at the end of the poem to the narrator, who does not devote himself to love but instead commits himself voraciously to further reading.

Focusing on the common good as the poem's core leads to a similar impasse. While it is clear that Scipio the Elder advises his grandson to work for "commune profyt" in the *Dream of Scipio* itself, Scipio does not explicitly address this idea when he appears in the narrator's dream. Furthermore, the opening universal view in which the poem advances the notion of "commune profyt" as a model for human behavior is undermined by the fighting amongst and within species during the debate. This is particularly the case since the one bird that refers to the "commune spede" (common good, l. 507) is the cuckoo, who is looked down upon by the other birds and who has no higher purpose than simply wanting to get the debate over with. It is also difficult to discern how the second part of the poem (the garden and Venus's temple) serves the common good.

More and more, the *Parliament*'s inconclusiveness has come to be seen as crucial to unlocking the poem. The poem offers its audience a variety of choices as it resists a notion of objective truth. One aspect of this interpretive openness involves Chaucer's use of previous writers. The conflicting worldviews of Macrobius's *Commentary on the Dream of Scipio*, Dante's *Commedia*, GIOVANNI BOCCACCIO's *Teseida,* Alan of Lille's *De planctu Naturae,* and Guillaume de Lorris and Jean de Meun's *Roman de la Rose*—to pick but the most important examples—are all woven into the *Parliament*'s odd tapestry. Commentary on these texts prior to Chaucer (such as the commentaries on Dante's *Commedia* or Boccaccio's own glosses on his *Teseida*) already suggests their interpretive complexity; Chaucer puts these fertile texts in tension with one another and further complicates matters by reinterpreting each one to suit his own purposes. The result is a somewhat bizarre hybrid of styles, poetic registers, and viewpoints.

Chaucer's refusal to provide clarity for the reader may serve to put the responsibility upon the reader's own judgment. Reading the poem would thereby become an act of the will. Alternately, Chaucer may be responding to philosophical debates of his time over how we know the world, and the *Parliament* would then not be centered so much on will as on knowledge, particularly our inability to acquire determinate meaning. Whether Chaucer was equally concerned with love or the good of society (or other matters suggested in recent discussion on the poem, such as homoerotic desire, or nature and the feminine), it seems clear that Chaucer was fundamentally meditating on the human condition of trying to understand a vast world that is always filtered through a variety of authorities.

FURTHER READING

Aers, David. "The *Parliament of Fowls*: Authority, the Knower and the Known." *Chaucer Review* 16 (1982): 1–17.

Leicester, H. M., Jr. "The Harmony of Chaucer's *Parliament*: A Dissonant Voice." *Chaucer Review* 9 (1974): 15–39.

Pinti, Daniel. "Commentary and Comedic Reception: Dante and the Subject of Reading in *The Parliament of Fowls.*" *Studies in the Age of Chaucer: The Yearbook of the New Chaucer Society* 22 (2000): 311–340.

Ruud, Jay. "Realism, Nominalism, and the Inconclusive Ending of the *Parliament of Fowls.*" In *Geardagum: Essays on Old and Middle English Language and Literature* 23 (2002): 1–28.

John Kerr

"PASSIONATE SHEPHERD TO HIS LOVE, THE" CHRISTOPHER MARLOWE (1599)

Though contemporary allusions to "The Passionate Shepherd to His Love" suggest that it was composed during the middle to late 1580s, it was first printed in 1599, six years after CHRISTOPHER MARLOWE's death, when an untitled and anonymous four-stanza version of the poem appeared in the poetry anthology *The Passionate Pilgrim.* A year later, a six-stanza version appeared in the poetic anthology *England's Helicon.* This anthology supplied the title "The Passionate Shepherd to His Love" and identified the author as "Chr. Marlow." This longer and textually superior version is normally used for modern editions of the poem.

The "his" of the title identifies the shepherd as male. Some recent critics have noted that this title may have been an editorial addition when *England's Helicon* was published, and argue that if one looks only at the text of the poem, there is nothing to indicate whether a man or woman is speaking, or indeed whether the one being spoken to is a man or woman. A key point in the argument is that "kirtle" (l. 11) could refer to either a woman's gown or a man's tunic. However, Marlowe uses the first sense in HERO AND LEANDER, and the second would have been in decline by his time. Moreover, among them, Sir WALTER RALEIGH's "THE NYMPH'S REPLY TO THE SHEPHERD" and John Donne's "Bait" poem, without exception, depict the speaker as male and the one to whom the invitation is extended as female.

The lyric's opening line, "Come live with me and be my love," places it within a tradition of "invitation" poems that extends back at least as far as Theocritus and VIRGIL. The speaker indicates that by living together, the pair will be able to enjoy all of the pleasures that country living can provide. The following four STANZAS describe a series of these rural delights. First, the pair will sit on the banks of a river where they can watch the shepherds feeding their flocks and hear birds singing along with the sound of a waterfall. Next, the speaker offers to provide beds of roses and other fragrant flowers, a flower-bedecked cap and shepherd's smock embroidered with a myrtle pattern, a lambs-wool gown, warm slippers with gold buckles, and a belt of straw and ivy with coral clasps and amber studs. The initial invitation is then repeated: If you find such pleasures moving, "Come live with me and be my love." The final stanza adds one more pleasure, that of being entertained by the singing and dancing of the shepherds on May mornings, and it again repeats the invitation to "live with me, and be my love." The repetition of the invitation in stanzas 5 and 6 is often seen as a textual problem, perhaps indicating that the text in England's Helicon incorporates alternate endings. However, it has also been suggested that while stanza 5 makes the invitation contingent on being moved by the pleasure of actually having or experiencing the things described, stanza 6 focuses on enjoying the very idea of such delights ("thy mind may move"). In this interpretation, what will be shared is a way of looking at life.

Marlowe leaves open the question of his shepherd's attitude and intentions. The poem may be read as a love poem, with the speaker attempting to persuade someone he hopes to live with to live with him. Or one may see it as it a seduction poem. Such is the argument of Raleigh's "The Nymph's Reply to the Shepherd" (first printed immediately after Marlowe's poem in England's

Helicon), whose female speaker points out that "every shepherd's tongue" may not speak the truth. The initial verb come may also be read as a command. Allusions to the poem in Elizabethan drama plays almost invariably suggest that the threat of force lies behind the invitation to "come live with me." The wealthy and powerful speaker of the invitation will offer wealth and pleasure, but it is an offer that one cannot refuse. However, this veiled threat is not found in the early poetry that alludes to or imitates Marlowe's poem, and it is not evident within "The Passionate Shepherd" itself.

During the late 16th century, PASTORAL had become primarily a way of figuratively talking about the values and tensions of courtly society. The language of Marlowe's poem reflects this convention. The clothing described is more ornate and costly than what real shepherds would wear, and while "madrigals" might be used merely to mean "songs," an actual MADRIGAL as sung at court is far more elaborate than the natural songs of birds. The speaker's language thus embodies the perspective of courtly society. It may also suggest that the simplicity of rural life and even of nature itself is improved by art, an idea frequently argued during the Renaissance.

FURTHER READING

Brown, Georgia E. "Marlowe's Poems and Classicism." In The Cambridge Companion to Christopher Marlowe, edited by Patrick Cheney, 106–126. Cambridge: Cambridge University Press, 2004.

Cheney, Patrick, and Brian J. Striar. The Collected Poems of Christopher Marlowe. New York: Oxford University Press, 2006.

Forsythe, R. S. "'The Passionate Shepherd' and English Poetry." PMLA 40 (1925): 693–742.

Kinney, Arthur F. "Reading Marlowe's Lyric." In Approaches to Teaching Shorter Elizabethan Poetry, edited by Patrick Cheney and Anne Lake Prescott, 220–225. New York: MLA, 2000.

Sternfeld, Frederick W., and Mary Joiner Chan. "Come Live with Me and Be My Love." Comparative Literature 22 (1970): 173–187.

Bruce E. Brandt

PASSUS　Most commonly associated with WILLIAM LANGLAND's medieval DREAM VISION PIERS PLOWMAN, the passus is a portion of or a division within a literary work. *Passus* comes from the Latin word of the same spelling, meaning "step" or "pace." The use of the term in English literature first appeared in conjunction with Langland's work, and it is similar in style to that of the canto (a major division in a long poem), which enjoys a wider usage among early English poets.

FURTHER READING

Simpson, James. "From Reason to Affective Knowledge: Modes of Thought and Poetic Form in *Piers Plowman*." *Medium Aevum* 55, no. 1 (1986): 1–23.

Erin N. Mount

PASTORAL

PASTORAL The word *pastoral* evokes images of lush greenery, secluded retreat, carefree idealism, and the occasional stray sheep. But the essential observation about the pastoral is that it is not a genre but a mode—that is, one can create or read pastoral lyric poetry, but one can also create or read pastoral drama or pastoral novels. Renaissance poets certainly demonstrated this adaptability, but they also stuck close to convention. The Greek poet Theocritus and the Roman poet VIRGIL serve as the significant classical practitioners of pastoral. Following Virgil's lead, Renaissance poets often began their careers with pastoral to prepare them for writing an elevated EPIC, and they wrote primarily classical lyric pastoral. They adhered to pastoral conventions and topics such as innocence, happiness, and the simplicity of the bucolic lifestyle, often opposing this lifestyle—with its shepherds, landscapes, singing matches, and purity—to the corruption, ceremony, and superficiality of the city or the court.

There are two major types of pastoral. It can often be sentimental and even sensational, with an idyllic longing for leisure and escape to a fictional and pastoral world; CHRISTOPHER MARLOWE's "The PASSIONATE SHEPHERD TO HIS LOVE" offers an excellent example of this aesthetic and idealized pastoral. The response by SIR WALTER RALEIGH, "The NYMPH'S REPLY TO THE SHEPHERD," on the other hand, is often called an antipastoral for its open denigration of the conventions of the genre. Pastoral can also address social issues, using rustic elements to discuss larger and more complex conflicts. Either way, the lives of shepherds and herdsmen can generalize across all tiers of society, and a pastoral poet can address didactic, amorous, or social themes, to name a few. As George Puttenham writes in *The ARTE OF ENGLISH POESIE* (1589), "under the veil of homely persons, and in rude speeches" a pastoral poet can "insinuate and glance at greater matters."

See also LOCUS AMOENUS.

FURTHER READING

Alpers, Paul. *What is Pastoral?* Chicago: University of Chicago Press, 1996.
Empson, William. *Some Versions of Pastoral.* New York: New Directions, 1968.

Craig T. Fehrman

PASTOURELLE From the French, meaning "shepherdess," a pastourelle is a medieval lyric in a bucolic context. It is a short lyric dialogue in which a gallant, knight, or (sometimes) clerk (often coinciding with the narrating voice) attempts to seduce a shepherdess. The outcome varies, sometimes even veering toward rape. The pastourelle was popular because of the battle of wits between the two characters and the mixture of narrative poetry, *contrasto,* and amorous COMPLAINT, with some borrowings from popular art forms such as the BALLAD. It is often an enjoyment at the expense of the shepherds, whose role is usually comic.

The origin of the pastourelle is uncertain, though it flourished in Provençal between the 12th and 14th centuries. The genre includes some notable examples in English and Welsh, but was most popular in late-medieval Scotland. An outstanding 15th-century example is *ROBENE AND MAKYNE* by ROBERT HENRYSON.

See also PASTORAL.

FURTHER READING

Jones, William Powell. *The Pastourelle. A Study of the Origin and Tradition of a Lyric Type.* 1931. Reprint, New York: Octagon Books, 1973.
Paden, William D., ed. *The Medieval Pastourelle.* New York: Garland, 1987.

Alessandra Petrina

PATRONAGE Patronage defines the relationship between an influential and powerful person/institution and an artist. The parties agree to exchange one's protection or money for the other's talent or intellectual work, usually on terms set by the patron. In historical periods such as classical antiquity or the High Middle Ages, in which there was little or no recognition of intellectual labor and no direct contact between the artist and potential buyers of the work of art, such exchanges monetarily supported artists, while secondarily enhancing a community's cultural development. Art of this time was typically shaped by the desires, spoken or unspoken, of patrons rather than the desires of the artists. Literary patronage was even more directed, where patrons would commission works to further their political views or enhance their status in society and the court.

There are obvious limitations and constrictions created when patronage becomes involved with the act of writing. The writer, by accepting the patronage, becomes a part of the patron's "family," which provides the support the artist seeks but also demands the allegiance of the artist to the patron. The patron's dominance over the writer, created by the underlying economic dependence of the writer to the patron, creates the ideal climate for the furthering of the patron's own politics. These views thus influence the subject matter, forms, and genres of the works created. In the case of English literature, this becomes patently clear in observing the vying between Protestant and Catholic sympathies expressed in Tudor writing.

The arrival of the printing press (1474) reduced the demand for literary patronage and altered the basic nature of commissioned literature. The production of literature now had the potential to be profitable for the author and to reach a wider audience. This facilitated the creation of two separate literatures, popular literature for the common people and commissioned literature for the elite. There was now opportunity for opinions and ideas of dissent, not only those of the wealthy patrons. One of the paradoxes of literary production within Tudor COURT CULTURE was that many writers, particularly those in the court circle, such as Sir THOMAS WYATT and HENRY HOWARD, EARL OF SURREY, did not want to have their works published and preferred a restricted manuscript circulation.

See also SCOP.

FURTHER READING

Holzknecht, Karl Julius. *Literary Patronage in the Middle Ages.* 1923. Reprint, New York: The Collegiate Press, 1966.

Lefevere, André. "The System: Patronage." In *Translation, Rewriting, and the Manipulation of Literary Fame.* London: Routledge, 1992, 11–25.

Alessandra Petrina and Adam Bures

PEARL ANONYMOUS (late 14th century) *Pearl* is the first of four exceptional poems in MIDDLE ENGLISH that have survived in one single manuscript, housed at the British library, MS Cotton Nero A.x. It is followed by CLEANNESS, Patience, and SIR GAWAIN AND THE GREEN KNIGHT. These poems all appear to be written by the same author, who is not identified and whose name has simply become either the PEARL-POET or the GAWAIN-POET.

The poem is divided into 20 parts, with five STANZAS per part. In the first part, the first-person narrator of the poem mourns the loss of a "perle wythouten spot" (l. 12) in a garden. We are told that the unblemished, valuable jewel was perfectly formed: "so rounde, so reken in uche araye, / So small, so smothe her sides were" (ll. 5–6). The narrator also describes the garden and its flora as he searches for the pearl. The speaker falls asleep in part 2, and the remainder of the poem proceeds as a DREAM VISION. Soon after falling asleep, the narrator finds himself in a second garden, a celestial one, where even the gravel is made of "precious perles of orient" (l. 82).

In part 3, the narrator sees a young woman dressed in blinding white and decorated with pearls standing across a stream under a "crystal clyffe" (l. 159). The narrator recognizes her; indeed, the longer he looks at her, he "knew hyr more and more" (l. 168). Transfixed, the dreamer wants to stay with the maiden. The description of the maiden continues in part 4, where she is described in similar terms to the lost pearl in part 1 as "so smothe, so smal, so seme slyght" (l. 190). Soon this similarity is explained: This maiden *is* the dreamer's lost pearl; she is closer to him than "aunte or nece" (l. 233), which nearly all scholars have interpreted as meaning that the maiden is the speaker's daughter. It is here that it becomes clear that the poem is about the narrator's grief and bereavement at the death of a child. The woman removes her crown of "grete tresore" (l. 237) and bows to the narrator, who is overcome with joy at seeing his pearl.

In the dramatic fifth part of the poem, the dreamer addresses the pearl, asking her, "art thou my perle that I have playned, / regretted by myn one on nyghte?" (ll. 242–243). He asks her if they are in the land of Paradise and tells her that he has been a "joyles jueler" (l. 252) and torn with grief since she had been lost. The maiden speaks by responding that he is "mysetente" (misconceived, l. 257) in believing that his pearl is lost. Replacing her crown, the maiden tells him that it is not lost but kept in the casket ("cofer," l. 259) of the beautiful garden, and she rebukes him for blaming his fate for the loss of the jewel. She tells him he really only lost a rose "that flowred and fauled" as flowers do (l. 270). The speaker answers that he is now happy at the return of his pearl and that her gentle words are a comfort to him. He claims he plans to live with her and "love [his] Lorde and al his lawes" (l. 285), living as a "joyfol jueler" (l. 288) in contrast to the "joyles" one he had been before.

The maiden responds to his words almost angrily, wondering "wy borde ye men? So madde ye be!" (l. 290). She tells him that he has spoken three "unavysed" (l. 292), or ill-considered, things: that he believes her to be in the valley because he has seen her there, that he will come and live with her in this place, and finally that no "joyfol jueler" could cross the water before her. This speech transitions to the next part of the poem, a debate between the maiden and the dreamer, where she—as a messenger of God—can instruct and teach him as to things he clearly does not understand.

In part 6, the maiden expands on the three points she rebutted in part 5. She begins by telling him that he should not believe what he sees because that is a mark of sinful pride. Second, she continues, only God can grant him permission to live with her, and only then after he has died. The dreamer asks sorrowfully whether he will now lose his "precios perle" (l. 330) again. She tells him that he does not profit by his anger and that he needs to praise God always, in both joy and sorrow.

The narrator apologizes in part 7, claiming that his grief has clouded his judgment, and that he meant no offense to his Lord. He tells her his pain is softened now that he knows where his pearl has gone, but that he had been sad and dejected. He asks her what kind of life she leads now. She responds that his words please her for their humility, and that the Lord loves meekness. She tells him that even though his pearl was "young and tender of age" (l. 412) when it "con schede" (fell down, l. 411), she has been taken into marriage with the "Lorde the Lombe" (l. 413) and is crowned as his queen in heaven.

The maiden continues to instruct the speaker in part 8, where he shows his confusion at her words by asking "may thys be trew?" (l. 421) and wonders if she has taken the place of the Virgin Mary as the queen of heaven. The dreamer's question causes the maiden to kneel and praise Mary as a "makeles moder" (matchless mother, l. 435), and assures the speaker that Mary is the empress of the heavens and has been usurped by nobody. She teaches him that in God's kingdom, everybody is equal in courtesy to their heavenly king and queen.

In part 9, the dreamer demonstrates his need for further instruction from the maiden by trying to apply a model of an earthly court to the heavenly one. He argues that she had died at less than two years old before she could earn her place with God, barely knowing her prayers, and could not be a queen. She responds by reiterating that all are kings or queens in God's kingdom.

The maiden turns to the parable of the vineyard from the Gospel of Matthew (20:1–16), continuing to recount it in section 10, where laborers who worked long hours are rewarded equally as those who work only one. She tells him that this is divine justice, and though she worked but a little, she received the same reward. The dreamer continues to demonstrate his need for instruction by persisting with an earthly reason, arguing that the system is "unresounable" (l. 590) where one could receive the same payment as a laborer who had worked all day for working less: "Now he that stod the long day stable, / And thou to payment com hym before, / Thenne the lasse in werke to take more able, / And ever the lenger the lasse, the more" (ll. 597–600).

Parts 11 and 12 continue elaborating the heavenly system, focusing on the importance of God's grace. Five stanzas end with the phrase "For the grace of God is gret inoghe," emphasizing God's justice and redemption.

Section 13 expounds on the concept of innocence; everyone must enter the kingdom of heaven "as a chylde" (l. 723), guiltless and humble. Invoking Christ's parable of the pearl in which a merchant sells everything to gain it, where it represents the kingdom of heaven, she then points out the pearl she wears on her breast and tells him that it is "lyke the reme of heavenesse clere" (like the realm of heaven, l. 735), and that the Lord had placed it there as an emblem of his peace. The dreamer expounds on the beauty of the pearl "of prys" (l. 746) and the maiden (the "perle in perles pure," l. 745) who wears it. He asks her who formed her "fayre figure" (l. 746) and what sort of "offys" (l. 755) does the pearl she wears hold? The maiden reiterates that she is a bride of Christ, who called to her: "Cum hyder to me, my lemman [beloved] swete, / For mote ne spot is non in the" (there is no spot on you, ll. 763–764), then washed her in his blood, crowned her, and dressed her in pearls. The dreamer, however, is still confused: How was she chosen above so many women to be the bride of Christ? Is she the only "a makeles may and maskelles" (both a matchless [peerless] and spotless maiden in the eyes of God, l. 780)?

In part 14, the maiden answers that she is, indeed, "maskelles" (l. 781), "unblemyst" and "wythouten blot" (l. 782), as the dreamer has suggested, but she is not a "makeles quene" (l. 784) as he also said. She again reminds the dreamer that she is not the only heavenly queen, but says that she is one of 140,000 in heaven as "in the Apocalyppes hit is sene" (l. 787). She continues with this explanation in part 15, telling the dreamer that the queens of heaven wear the pearls on their breasts, spotless like their Lord. Even though their bodies are rotting in the earth, they are unblemished and rejoicing in heaven. The dreamer, more humble now in his questions, persists in asking for explanations.

In part 16, the dreamer wonders about the maiden's dwelling place, sure it is Jerusalem. He is speaking of the "old Jerusalem" (l. 941), however, which the maiden points out—she dwells in the new, celestial Jerusalem referenced in Bible's Book of Revelation. He cannot enter, though she has permission to show it to him.

Parts 17 and 18 reveal the heavenly city to the dreamer as if it is coming down from heaven to the other side of the stream. It has 12 types of gems, each outlined and explained, and 12 steps, and it is 12 furlongs long, reinforcing the numerological significance of Revelation and its descriptions. The city is exactly square and has streets of gold. There is no sun: "God was her lambe-lyght" (l. 1046). A river runs from his throne "bryghter than bothe the sunne and mone" (l. 1056).

In part 19, the dreamer sees a procession of maidens—at least 100,000 crowned with clothes of pearls. The Lamb is there, too, but the dreamer notices that he has a wound in his side from which "blod outsprent" (l. 1137). The dreamer wonders: "[W]ho did that spyt?" (l. 1138), but then he notices his pearl in the procession. He longs to join her across the water, and in the final section, part 20, the dreamer prepares to throw himself into the stream, even though he recognizes it may be his death, so that he can join the maiden in the celestial city. This displeases the Lord, however, and he is awakened, finding himself once more in the garden. This time there is no maiden to rebuke him for not heeding the lessons. He rebukes himself for attempting to go against God's will and reflects that at least he knows the maiden is saved in heaven, even though he is left in sorrow on earth. He realizes that by doing God's will and accepting Christ's blessings, everyone may become a pearl of God: "He gef uus to be his homly hyne / Ande precious perles unto his pay" (ll. 1211–12).

This poem encompasses two genres of medieval poetry, the dream vision and the debate poem, but is more generally considered part of the ALLITERATIVE REVIVAL. As such, it imitates Anglo-Saxon conventions with alliterated consonants on either side of a CAESURA, usually two before and one afterward. This structure is clearly evident throughout *Pearl* from its first two lines: "Perle, plesaunte to prynces paye / To clanly clos in golde so clere" (ll. 1–2). Structurally, the poem is also concerned with numerology as its subject, particularly in the description of the celestial city, but is also interested in representing that numerological perfection within its lines. As a result, the poem has 101 stanzas of 12 lines each, making it 1,212 lines long, reiterating the importance of the biblical number 12. Each of the 20 parts is five stanzas long, except part 15, which has six.

The rhyme scheme for the 12-line stanza is *abababab-bcbc*. In addition, the poet uses *concatenatio,* or concatenation, in which a word from the last line of a stanza is repeated it in the first line of the next one. For example, the last line of the first stanza in part one reads "Of that pryvy perle wythouten spot" (l. 12), and the first line of the second stanza reads "Sythen in that spote hit fro me sprange" (l. 13). The word *spot* has been reiterated as *spote*. The effect of the *concatenatio* is to link the stanzas together like a necklace, or, as many scholars have pointed out, like a string of pearls. This effect is underscored by the last line of the poem, "Ande precious perles unto his pay" (l. 1212), which echoes the very first line, "Perle, plesaunte to prynces paye" (l. 1). Thus, the last line is linked to the first, creating the circular structure of the poem.

The central image of the poem is the pearl; however, it is not a static image, and its meaning constantly shifts. Originally, it seems to be a literal jewel, lost in the garden, but soon it is clear that the maiden is the narrator's pearl, his daughter who died in childhood. The pearl then changes to the "pearl of price," or salvation, simultaneously representing purity and materialism, heavenly immortality and earthly perfection. The pearl is also the perfectly innocent, the souls who have been baptized and cleaned of sin through penance. It becomes the reward of life in the celestial city. Accordingly, the image of the "jeweler" shifts from the narrator to Christ. This is a poem about transformation. It traces the narrator's initial ignorance and rejection of God through to an understanding and embracing of his human condition.

Likewise, the idea of the garden changes with the poem. It is a literal garden in the beginning, moves to an Edenic celestial garden, and finally becomes the new Jerusalem, the city of God. The dreamer's journey parallels this. He begins absorbed by the earthly material world, receives heavenly instruction, and finally wakes up back in the earthly garden, but with new knowledge. Thus, the location of the poem, like the words and structure, is returned to the starting point.

The poem is an explication of Christian beliefs and doctrines. His misconceptions and ignorance are carefully refuted by the maiden, whose lessons are marked by important biblical passages, notably the parable of the vineyard, the parable of the merchant and the pearl of great price, and the apocalyptic descriptions of the celestial city. The dreamer is not stupid; he is merely human and has trouble understanding the divine. The reader can empathize with the speaker and likewise be educated by the maiden. As well, the dreamer's starting point of grief and loss is common to humanity—an effect magnified by the fact that the narrator never actually names his lost pearl as his daughter but merely implies this particular relationship.

The poet uses worldly metaphors to describe heaven but uses the maiden to point out that a simple comparison is inadequate. Although the company of maidens is, indeed, courtly and subject to Mary, the "empress," and their spouse, the Lamb of God, there is no other hierarchy in the heavenly court. In the majestic splendor of the procession toward the church elders, the Lamb—although proudly leading his queens—is marked by the blood pouring out of his side. It is only after the dreamer sees this image, and his maiden following the Lamb, that he tries to cross the stream. It is through these juxtapositions of heavenly and earthly images and items that the poet ultimately instructs his audience as the dreamer is instructed.

See also ALLEGORY, ALLITERATION.

FURTHER READING

Andrew, Malcolm, and Ronald Waldron, eds. *The Poems of the Pearl Manuscript.* Exeter, U.K.: University of Exeter Press, 1999.

Conley, John, ed. *The Middle English 'Pearl': Critical Essays.* Notre Dame, Ind.: University of Notre Dame Press, 1970.

Fein, Susanna Greer. "Twelve-Line Stanza Forms in Middle English and the Date of *Pearl*." *Speculum* 72, no. 2 (1997): 367–398.

Robertson, D. W. "The Pearl as a Symbol." *MLN* 65, no. 3 (1950): 155–161.

Jennifer N. Brown

PEARL-POET   See *GAWAIN*-POET.

PEASANTS' REVOLT (GREAT RISING; GREAT REVOLT) (1381)

The Peasants' Revolt was a violent uprising of the lower strata of society, primarily throughout the southeast of England. Historians often prefer the contemporary terms—"The Great Revolt" or "Great Rising"—since the class composition of the revolt was more varied than its popular title suggests.

The rebels were, in the main, laborers, peasants, and serfs, but their number included craftspeople and even some relatively prosperous landowners.

The revolt's origins go back to the BLACK DEATH (1348–49), which created labor shortages, allowing the laborers and workers to demand larger wages. This "seller's market" for labor led to greater geographical mobility among the lower classes. In response, wealthy landowners produced a series of laws fixing wages and restricting the movement of laborers. This class tension was aggravated by the extensive taxation financing the HUNDRED YEARS WAR; a poll tax instituted by Parliament in November 1380 directly sparked the revolt. Falling disproportionately on the poor, the tax inspired many to evade it, resulting in punitive investigations.

Riots broke out in Essex and Kent in early June 1381, quickly spreading throughout the counties. Led by Wat Tyler, large bands of the rebels marched toward London to demand reform. Professing loyalty to the king, Richard II, the rebels directed their anger against great lords, ministers, and the day-to-day administrators of government. The king met with the rebels on June 14 and agreed to their demand for the manumission of all serfs. The rebels had already attacked lawyers and engaged in vandalism; after the meeting with the king, they broke into the TOWER OF LONDON and beheaded, among others, the treasurer and the archbishop of Canterbury. During the king's next meeting with the rebels on June 15, Wat Tyler was killed in a scuffle, and the king persuaded the rebels to move away from the city, effectively dispersing them. The government, revoking the royal agreement to the rebels' demands, used armed force to pacify the counties and executed those considered to be instigators of the revolt.

The rising not only appears in literature but is also evidence of attitudes about written culture among the classes who left few records of their own. The 1381 rebels seemed to view the written word as a tool of their oppressors, and also had a canny grip on how it functioned. They destroyed documents that held records of their obligations to landholders and executed the lawyers, clerks, and officials who produced them. Some cryptic letters associated with the rebels have survived in CHRONICLES, suggesting that they may have spread their ideas through circulating poem-like texts. These texts seem to refer to WILLIAM LANGLAND's PIERS PLOWMAN, prompting the hypothesis that a shocked Langland may have removed inflammatory social statements from his poem for the post-1381 text.

Despite (or because of) these signs of literacy in the rebels, contemporary chroniclers depict them as animalistic, irrational, and debased. It is their denigration of the rebels as yokels that contributed to the eventual popularity of the term Peasants' Revolt. JOHN GOWER literalizes the chroniclers' animal metaphors by depicting the rebels as an army of beasts in his Vox clamantis.

Chaucer treats the event less directly. He makes only one precise allusion to the rising, in "The NUN'S PRIEST'S TALE," but critics have suggested that the rising is reflected in his view of the interaction among different social classes, especially his depiction of a peasant mocking aristocratic values in "The MILLER'S PROLOGUE AND TALE's" parodic inversion of elements of "The Knight's Tale."

See also PIERS PLOWMAN TRADITION.

FURTHER READING

Dobson, R. B., ed. The Peasants' Revolt of 1381. 2nd ed. London: Macmillan, 1983.

Hilton, Rodney. Bond Men Made Free: Medieval Peasant Movements and the English Rising of 1381. Introduced by Christopher Dyer. London: Routledge, 1983.

Justice, Steven. Writing and Rebellion: England in 1381. Berkeley: University of California Press, 1994.

Brantley L. Bryant

PEMBROKE, COUNTESS OF   See HERBERT, MARY SIDNEY, COUNTESS OF PEMBROKE.

PERSONIFICATION   Personification is a figure of speech that attributes human abilities and responses to things that are not human. In many languages, personification is unavoidable due to the linguistic practice of attaching a feminine or masculine gender to proper nouns. Personification is widespread in the poetry of even those cultures whose language is comparatively nongendered, since, long before the invention of print, poets spoke and sung of nature in ways that embodied it with human qualities. GEOFFREY CHAUCER's GENERAL PROLOGUE TO THE CANTERBURY TALES

contains many famous instances of personification. Within eight lines, its narrator attributes sweetness to rain, forcefulness to drought, a vascular system to plants, breath (and inspiration) to the wind, age to the sun, and animal form to the stars. As these examples indicate, personification is basically an attempt to use metaphor to understand the mysteries of nature and human-nature interactions. Despite its frequent use, personification poses problems for poets, since granting nature a kind of sentience may make for good verse, but it misrepresents the nonhuman world. This problem would later be characterized by John Ruskin as "pathetic fallacy."

Larry T. Shillock

PETRARCH (FRANCESCO PETRARCA) (1304–1374) Francesco Petrarca, better known simply as Petrarch, spent his early years at Avignon where his father, a lawyer, worked at the papal court. Petrarch also studied law, but he eventually devoted himself fully to literary pursuits. He spent most of his life, until 1361, in Avignon and Vaucluse, although he retired to Padua, where he enjoyed the friendship of GIOVANNI BOCCACCIO. Credited as one of the fathers of humanism, Petrarch not only studied the classical authors but also avidly sought lost manuscripts. His most famous discovery, made in 1345, was of Cicero's letters to Atticus, Brutus, and Quintus, at the cathedral library in Verona.

Petrarch's large literary output is mostly in Latin, including the unfinished epic L'Africa, though he is now best known for a VERNACULAR collection of carefully constructed and ceaselessly revised love poems, popularly called the Canzoniere but formally named Rerum vulgarium fragmenta (Song Book). Most of these poems focus on the poet's unrequited love for a woman he calls Laura. These are divided into two main sections: poems 1–263, written while Laura was alive, and poems 264–366, written after her death on April 6, 1348, exactly 21 years after he first saw her.

It is hard to overestimate Petrarch's influence and importance in the history of European poetry. GEOFFREY CHAUCER translated one of the SONNETS (number 132 of the Song Book) in his Troilus and Criseyde, and he used Petrarch's Latin translation of a tale in Boccaccio's Decameron as the basis for "The Clerk's Tale" in The CANTERBURY TALES. SIR THOMAS WYATT and HENRY HOWARD, EARL OF SURREY, both translated Petrarchan sonnets. SIR PHILIP SIDNEY's collection ASTROPHIL AND STELLA was strongly influenced by Petrarchan models, as was EDMUND SPENSER's AMORETTI. Indeed, all of the numerous and popular SONNET SEQUENCES owe a debt to Petrarch's work.

FURTHER READING
Foster, Kenelm. Petrarch: Poet and Humanist. Edinburgh: Edinburgh University Press, 1984.
Mann, Nicholas. Petrarch. Oxford: Oxford University Press, 1984.
Wilkins, E. H. Life of Petrarch. Chicago: University of Chicago Press, 1961.

K. P. Clarke

PETRARCHAN PARADOX Sustained use of ANTITHESES within a SONNET or SONNET SEQUENCE. A paradox, in general, is a statement that contains two seemingly oppositional parts. These appear contradictory or incompatible on the surface but, upon deeper consideration, make sense. Similar to this is an oxymoron, which is essentially a compact paradox in which two successive words seemingly contradict each another yet provide a complete description. The Petrarchan paradox combines these two approaches, which are used to describe the object of the poet's desire, the unobtainable lady. She is both fire and ice, both free and trapped, both love and hate. Particularly common Petrarchan paradoxes describe lovers burning in seas of ice and melting under icy glares. Another common theme focuses on self-annihilation, which is accomplished through loving.

FURTHER READING
Berdan, John M. "A Definition of Petrarchismo." PMLA 24, no. 4 (1909): 699–710.

PETRARCHAN SONNET See ITALIAN (PETRARCHAN) SONNET.

"PHILIP SPARROW" ("PHYLLYP SPAROWE") JOHN SKELTON (1505) JOHN SKELTON's poem "Philip Sparrow" is divided into three clearly

distinct parts. The first is a young girl's lament for the death of her pet sparrow, Philip, who was killed by a cat. Her character is based on Jane Scrope, who was educated by Benedictine nuns. This background shows in the way her ELEGY is interspersed with Latin phrases from various offices for the dead, albeit in a garbled form. In short, rhyming trimeter lines (SKELTONICS), Jane evokes in simple words the sparrow's activities while still alive: His tricks and clever ways, including his appetite and his fondness for his mistress, are described in a very vivid manner, so as to make Jane's deep feeling of loss comprehensible. This is followed by a section in which the other birds are called to Philip's funeral, and each is assigned a particular task. Finally, Jane attempts to compose an epitaph for Philip, exhibiting an astoundingly wide, though not very deep, knowledge of classical mythology and philosophy as well as of English literature. By these means, the reader is made to empathize with Jane's sorrow for the death of her sparrow, and she emerges as a very engaging personality.

This is clearly also the view taken by the adult male speaker of the second part of the poem who praises the maid and her elegy. He specifically extols her beauty by giving detailed descriptions of her physical attractions, and he does not hesitate to express bodily desire for her, although allegedly only in his imagination. The language of this part is more sophisticated, especially in its rhetorical devices, than the preceding one. The third part is a later addition (1523) and is evidently a reaction to adverse criticism of the poem. The speaker, "Maister Skelton" himself, defends what he has written by accusing his critics of envy because they are not able to do what he has done.

There is indeed a known denigrating reference to "Philip Sparrow" by Alexander Barclay in his translation of Sebastian Brant's *Ship of Fools* (1509), but it is not clear what exactly he (and probably others) objected to. The quotations from the burial service may have been deemed blasphemous in this context, or possibly the lascivious attitude of the second part was regarded as offensive. The seemingly innocent first part is perhaps not free of sexual innuendo either, since in medieval iconography the sparrow stood for lechery.

Later critics found the poem badly structured and incoherent, but, concentrating mainly on the first part, also applauded its specificity of detail and its evocation of childhood. More recent criticism has, in contrast, tried to show the unity of the poem in its providing complementary perspectives on life and death on the one side, and its empowerment of the feminine outlook on the other. In this view, Jane appropriates the male-dominated literary tradition and rewrites it to give her mourning a female voice. Later gender critics, however, have pointed out that the words are still written by a man adopting the persona of a woman. These diverse positions show that the modern reader may still make surprising discoveries in this outstanding poem.

FURTHER READING
Schibanoff, Susan. "Taking Jane's Cue: Phyllyp Sparrowe as a Primer for Women Readers." *PMLA* 101, no. 5 (1986): 832–847.

Herbert G. Klein

"PHOENIX AND TURTLE, THE" WILLIAM SHAKESPEARE (before 1601)

"The Phoenix and Turtle" begins with a call to neighboring birds to join a funeral procession honoring the death of the Phoenix and the Turtledove, then "commences an anthem" for the passionate love between the title characters. The thematic persona Reason, however, cannot comprehend the bond that existed between the Phoenix (a symbol of uniqueness) and the Turtledove (a symbol of constancy), nor can Reason understand the narrator's reassurance these two birds continue to love even in death. The poem concludes with Reason's lament for the dead lovers and observation that with the death of the Phoenix and the Turtledove, "Truth and Beauty buried be" (l. 64).

"The Phoenix and Turtle" was originally appended to Robert Chester's *Love's Martyr* (1601), which included other commendatory poems by John Marston, George Chapman, and Ben Jonson. It is written in tetrameter and contains quatrains that rhyme *abba, cdcd,* etc., but concludes with rhyming triplets that make up a threnos, or funeral song—outdated by WILLIAM SHAKESPEARE's day but still recognizable to an Elizabethan audience.

"The Phoenix and Turtle" does not fit any particular genre, though the narrator's rhetoric on love alludes at times to a BEAST FABLE, wherein animal characters connect to allegorical representations of people known to Shakespeare. Most critics acknowledge the poem's tribute to love, and most agree that the Phoenix represents Queen ELIZABETH I, but few agree about the allegorical identity of the Turtledove. Suggestions include the earl of Essex, the duke of Anjou, Sir John Salisbury, and Anne Lyne (executed for harboring Catholic priests). The poem attracts scholarly debates over allegorical identities, and recent studies situate "The Phoenix and Turtle" against the context of the entire collection of *Love's Martyr* poems. Other studies have studied the influence of earlier authors such as JOHN SKELTON or examined the poem for what it reveals about religion and burial rites in Elizabethan England.

See also ALLEGORY.

FURTHER READING

Asquith, Clare. "The Phoenix and the Turtle." *Shakespeare Newsletter* 50, no. 1 (2000): 3, 10, 24, 26.

Tipton, Alzada. "The Transformation of the Earl of Essex: Poet-Execution Ballads and 'The Phoenix and the Turtle.'" *Studies in Philology* 99 (2002): 57–80.

James N. Ortego II

PHYSIOGNOMY

Physiognomy is the medieval belief that the physical appearance of the body reflected the purity (or impurity) of one's soul, or at least insight into an individual's character. Physiognomy was a common university subject, and its tropes were almost universally understood—so much so that they were used throughout British literature. It is particularly important in GEOFFREY CHAUCER'S GENERAL PROLOGUE TO THE CANTERBURY TALES, wherein the pilgrims' true natures are revealed through their physical descriptions. For instance, the Pardoner's yellow ringlets, beardless face, and high voice (like a goat's), indicate he is effeminate, and the Wife of Bath's gapped teeth indicate that she is lustful.

See also FOUR HUMORS.

FURTHER READING

Brasswell-Means, Laurel. "A New Look at an Old Patient: Chaucer's Summoner and Medieval Physiognomia." *The Chaucer Review* 25, no. 3 (1991): 266–275.

Friedman, John Block. "Another Look at Chaucer and the Physiognomists." *Studies in Philology* 78, no. 2 (1981): 138–152.

Stimilli, Davide. *The Face of Immortality: Physiognomy and Criticism.* Albany: State University of New York Press, 2005.

PIERCE THE PLOUGHMAN'S CREDE

ANONYMOUS (1393–1401)   The early 15th-century Middle English alliterative poem *Pierce the Ploughman's Crede* is a social and religious SATIRE of 850 lines in the tradition of WILLIAM LANGLAND's PIERS PLOWMAN. The poem survives in a printed edition from 1553 and two 16th-century manuscripts, as well as a fragment dating from the 15th century. It is remarkable for its vigorous satire of mendicant friars (begging orders) and for the sympathies to LOLLARDISM that the poet displays.

The poem depicts a narrator who starts off on a spiritual quest to learn the Apostles' Creed (statement of Christian faith). Searching for someone to teach him, he visits each of the four orders of friars in turn, beginning with a Franciscan. He tells the Franciscan that a Carmelite has promised to teach him the creed; the Franciscan condemns all Carmelites as whoremongers and liars who have no rule at all, unlike the Franciscans, who live like the first apostles. For a contribution, the Franciscan promises to absolve the narrator of his sins, creed or no creed. Next the narrator visits a Dominican, who is "fat as a barrel" and dressed in rich robes. The narrator tells the Dominican that an Austin (Augustinian) friar promised to teach him the creed, and the Dominican complains that Austins do nothing but associate with prostitutes and thieves. When the Dominican goes on to boast about the virtues of his own order, the narrator muses on the sin of pride, one of the SEVEN DEADLY SINS, and leaves to find an Austin friar.

When he tells the Austin that a Franciscan has offered to teach him the creed, the Austin berates the Franciscans for their wealth, their avarice, and their hypocrisy. The Austin then asks the narrator to donate to his order and become a "lay brother," after which the Austins will absolve his sins whether he knows the creed or not. Concluding that the Austins' only creed is greed, the narrator finds a Carmelite. He says that a Dominican has promised to help him, but the Carmelite condemns the pride of the Dominicans, claiming that Carmelites were founded by Elijah himself. For a contribution to the order, the Carmelite promises to help the narrator. When the narrator suggests that the Carmelite teach him the creed simply for the sake of God's love, the Carmelite calls him a fool and rushes off to visit a woman preparing to leave money to his order.

Finally the narrator comes across Piers, a poor plowman with three hungry children and a shoeless wife. Piers, who accepts God's will without question despite his hard life, teaches the narrator the creed in straightforward, simple language. In passing, he praises the virtues of Saint Dominic and Saint Francis, at the same time berating the contemporary adherents of their orders. In the end, the poet says that his only purpose in writing is to reform those he satirizes. He prays God to forgive him if he has said anything wrong, and he asks God to save all friars who are truly faithful, while causing other friars to repent.

Antifraternal satire was abundant in the late Middle Ages—one need only look as far as GEOFFREY CHAUCER'S GENERAL PROLOGUE TO THE CANTERBURY TALES, where the conventional complaints about the friars' easy penance, lechery, greed, and vanity are personified in the figure of Huberd the Monk. The theologian John Wycliffe had gone farther, calling for the pope to revoke the friars' privileges. In *Pierce the Ploughman's Crede,* the poet has Piers cite Wycliffe's views sympathetically. He also has Piers express support for Walter Brut, a Welsh Lollard (follower of Wycliffe) whom friars had condemned as a heretic in 1393. The poet seems to be on dangerous footing in his sympathy for the heretical Lollard sect, though he does uphold the doctrine of transubstantiation in Piers' description of the Apostles' Creed, a doctrine Wycliffe had rejected in his late writings. In general, however, he is far more sympathetic to the Lollard cause than Langland had been, or than the authors of poems like MUM AND THE SOTHSEGGER in the satirical PIERS PLOWMAN tradition. The poet's antifraternal satire and Lollard sympathies have been the focus of most critical studies of the poem, although some have focused on the poem as a part of the ALLITERATIVE REVIVAL of the 14th century, noting that, like its inspiration, *Piers Plowman,* this poem makes no use of the specialized diction that characterized the heroic kinds of texts that typified poems in that alliterative tradition.

FURTHER READING

Barr, Helen, ed. *The Piers Plowman Tradition: A Critical Edition of Pierce the Ploughman's Crede, Richard the Redeless, Mum and the Sothsegger, and The Crowned King.* London: Dent, 1993.

Lampe, David. "The Satiric Strategy of *Peres the Ploughmans Crede.*" In *The Alliterative Tradition in the Fourteenth Century,* edited by Bernard S. Levy and Paul E. Szarmach, 69–80. Kent, Ohio: Kent State University Press, 1981.

Lawton, David. "Lollardy and the Piers Plowman Tradition." *Modern Language Review* 76 (1981): 780–793.

Szittya, Penn. *The Antifraternal Tradition in Medieval Literature.* Princeton, N.J.: Princeton University Press, 1987.

von Nolcken, Christina. "Piers Plowman, the Wycliffites, and *Pierce the Plowman's Creed.*" *The Yearbook of Langland Studies* 2 (1988): 71–102.

Jay Ruud

PIERS PLOWMAN (OVERVIEW) (WILLIAM'S VISION OF *PIERS PLOWMAN*) WILLIAM LANGLAND (ca. 1362–1386)

Piers Plowman is an extensive and complex DREAM VISION that relies heavily on ALLEGORY in order to instruct its readers. It is a combination of political/social commentary, religious history, and salvation manual—the main question of the text is "How can I save my soul?" Other literary forms incorporated throughout include debate and dialogue, as well as the use of parable and exempla (see EXEMPLUM). Very little is known about the work's purported author, WILLIAM LANGLAND, though *Piers* was popular during its day. It is likely that Langland was a clerk in minor orders, which explains his familiarity with religious tenets and works. The main character is the naive and humble Will, a plowman who has fallen asleep in a field.

There are at least 53 extant manuscripts of *Piers Plowman,* and three (complete) versions, referred to as the A-, B- and C-texts. The A-text is the shortest and earliest, as well as being unfinished. It was probably written during the 1360s, though continually revised. The B-text is dated between 1377 and 1381, and it is the version cited by John Ball and other leaders of the PEASANTS' REVOLT. The C-text is believed to have been completed by 1387, as Thomas Usk, who was executed in 1388, cites it in his *Testament of Love*. Recently, two scholars have posited the existence of a so-called Z-text, which is a short fragment predating all three other versions but containing elements of each. This finding is, however, very much disputed.

In all three versions, the text is divided into two distinct parts: *Visio Willelmi de Petrus Plowman* (*William's Vision of Piers the Plowman*) and the *Vita de Dowel, Dobet et Dobest* (*Life of Dowell, Do-better, and Do-best*). Modern editions almost universally retain the title *Piers Plowman* for both parts. The first part concerns the dreamer's search for the answer to humanity's salvation, presented as an allegory, with personified (see PERSONIFICATION) characters. The second part concerns the search for individual faith. All versions begin with a prologue and proceed to the various PASSUS.

In its most complete form, *Piers Plowman* encompasses eight visions and 20 passus. Vision 1 (Prologue and Passus 1–4) determines the course of the narrative and introduces Will, the Dreamer, to the "fair field of folk" (society). The prologue sets the tone—though people's sins are many, the worst offense is greed and obsession with wealth. The passus set out to undo this by demonstrating the true purpose of life: Christian love. Passus 1 provides explanation. Holy Church answers Will's initial questions and criticizes humanity for pursuing transitory earthly treasure while ignoring spiritual treasure (truth). Passus 2–4 are set up as a trial. Lady Meed (false reward) is on trial with Holy Church prosecuting. Holy Church wins a provisional victory over Lady Meed with the assistance of Reason and Conscience. Thus, this vision is shaped as a debate.

Vision 2 (Passus 5–7) considers the broader picture of humanity as a whole and the concept of justice. This is accomplished through four distinct actions: the sermon, the confession, the pilgrimage, and the pardon. Although this vision opens with Will's repentance, he is not the main character; instead, Piers Plowman is. He is presented as an ideal Christian, who avidly desires truth (not Meed). He proceeds to show everyone how to work well and earn heaven—actions that earn him Truth's pardon. He promptly tears this up, however, in an action that has incited much scholarly debate.

Vision 3 (Passus 8–12) shows Will, a clerk, choosing the intellectual path towards *dowel*, or "salvation." He meets Knowledge, Wit, Clergy, and Scripture but is continuously appalled by the hypocrisy he encounters. Clergy even foretells the church's reform at the hands of rulers. Voicing his concerns, Will is rebuked by Scripture and sent into an inner dream (a dream within a dream). There he witnesses the emperor Trajan, who avoided hell by living in truth, and thus begins to see God's justice. Still, Will questions the workings of God, earning him another rebuke—this one from Reason—and he returns to the outer dream. There he learns from Imaginative and finally comes to realize that he has been conflating knowing truth with living it, and once this distinction is made, Will becomes more settled.

Vision 4 (Passus 13–14) is more action-filled. A prologue that summarizes the third vision precedes Passus 13. In the passus itself, Will encounters Doctor of Divinity and Active Man, both gluttons, who are set in constant opposition to Patience, who lives a balance between activity and contemplation. Everyone has dinner with Conscience, where it is revealed that dowel is an active virtue (charity) achieved through a passive approach (patience). Active Man feels he offsets the Doctor of Divinity through virtue of his humility; however, he must then learn true humility, and he is introduced to Confession, the remedy for sin.

Vision 5 (Passus 15–17) contains another inner dream. It opens with Will encountering Anima (soul), who demonstrates how God's grace operates. Anima first reproaches Will for loving science more than holiness. Next, she attacks the institution of the church (not the church itself), especially as evidenced through corrupt and hypocritical clergy. In order to clarify her point, Anima uses an image of a tree (Passus 15)—a bad root spreads poison throughout the branches. Will asks Anima if charity is possible for the wealthy. She answers in the affirmative, though she also emphasizes the necessity of being detached from the world. Passus 16 introduces the inner dream of Vision 5 in response to Will's question, "what does charity mean?" The ensuing discussion gives way to two central images of the poem, the Tree of Charity and Christ as jousting knight. By Passus 18, Jesus' quest for Hope and Faith becomes fused with Will's quest for Piers. Both quests connect through the personage of the Good Samaritan, who describes his active charity and demonstrates how it alone can heal the soul.

Vision 6 (Passus 18) is short and closely connected to Visions 7 and 8. The hero wins his joust, but Conscience and his followers receive a temporary setback. Scattered throughout are Langland's attempts at recreating the contemporary church service. Vision 7 (Passus 19) contextualizes the Christian community within history. Will sees Piers carrying a cross and bleeding—not taking Christ's place but, rather, demonstrating the merging of actual and mystical. Vision 8 (Passus 20) returns Will to the forefront. He meets Need and almost falls prey. He is afflicted by age and must choose between the world and the spirit. Conscience, who here assumes a role similar to Piers's earlier one, calls for an end to punishment, and the Dreamer is thus caught up in a world entranced by "pride of life"—sheer relief from having survived the BLACK DEATH. Will then awakens with the name Piers Plowman ringing in his ears.

Overall, the PIERS PLOWMAN tradition became an important part of English VERNACULAR literature. However, this history is a controversial one. Early on, *Piers Plowman* became associated with LOLLARD-ISM, particularly because of the dreamer's active role in determining his own salvation and the anticlerical statements it contains (e.g., the greedy Orders). Later on, Protestant reformers and poets, such as ROBERT CROWLEY and Thomas Churchyard, heralded *Piers* as inspiring and wrote literature based on it. Indeed, Robert Crowley published an edition of the poem in 1550, hailing it as a proto-Protestant reform text. Scholars have determined that Crowley altered his version of the text by deleting and adding lines and altering others.

Though seized upon by reformers of both religion and social systems, Langland's position throughout the poem is conservative and orthodox. He supports the traditional THREE ESTATES, and while scathing towards the rich and indolent, he is equally derisive towards all who fail to live up to their expectations. Greed is a sin of the rich, the church, and the poor equally. Simply by calling attention to needed reforms, however, *Piers* became labeled as revolutionary.

FURTHER READING

Aers, David. *Piers Plowman and Christian Allegory*. London: Arnold, 1975.

Alford, John A., ed. *A Companion to Piers Plowman*. Berkeley and Los Angeles: University of California Press, 1988.

Baldwin, Anna P. *The Theme of Government in Piers Plowman*. Cambridge: Brewer, 1981.

Bloomfield, Morton. *Piers Plowman as a Fourteenth-Century Apocalypse*. New Brunswick, N.J.: Rutgers University Press, 1962.

Brewer, Charlotte, and A. G. Rigg, eds. *Piers Plowman: A Fascimile of the Z-Text in Bodelian Library, Oxford MS Bodley 851*. Woodbridge, U.K.: Boydell & Brewer, 1994.

Griffiths, Lavinia. *Personification in Piers Plowman*. Cambridge: Brewer, 1985.

Pearsall, Derek, ed. *William Langland's* Piers Plowman: *The C-Text*. 2nd ed. Exeter: University of Exeter Press, 1994.

Schmidt, A. V. C., ed. *William Langland: Piers Plowman: A Critical Edition of the B-Text based on Trinity College Cambridge MS B.15.17*. 2nd ed. London: Dent, 1995.

Simpson, James. *Piers Plowman: An Introduction to the B-Text*. London: Longman, 1990.

Piers Plowman: Prologue WILLIAM LANGLAND (ca. 1362–1386)

The prologue to *Piers Plowman* opens with the narrator wandering in the Malvern Hills, where he lies down by a stream, falls asleep, and has a dream. Dressed in sheep-like garments that suggest he is an errant sinner and a penitent, he is tired, having gone astray, implying he is a lost soul. He has been preoccupied with the things of this world. In his dream, he sees "a fair feeld ful of folk" (B-text, l. 17) overlooked by two castles; there is a tower on a hill and a dungeon in a valley, representing heaven and hell. In the A-text, the rest of the Prologue consists of little more than a catalogue of the people present and observations on whether they do or do not fulfill their duties. It discusses those who work and those who laze around, consuming the efforts of others. There is a strong moralizing note, unlike the geniality of GEOFFREY CHAUCER. In the B-text, lines 31–32, there is a harsh note against cupidity, the desire to acquire riches. Lines 35–36 note that those who lie make fools of themselves.

There is no obvious order in the portraits. There are large numbers of people milling about, good and bad people intermingling. Underlying these seemingly haphazard portraits is the Parable of the Tares from Matthew 13: 24–30, which advocates the urgency to work, accumulate righteous treasure, and grow in goodness. At the heart of WILLIAM LANGLAND's vision of society and religion is their corruption by the desire to accumulate wealth. The reader is invited to see all this confusion of people in relation to the tower and the dungeon. The Palmer is a pilgrim who comes back from the Holy Land with a palm. There is no merit in going on pilgrimages unless it stems from an inner impulse. Lines 46–86 in the B-text Prologue provides more examples of money-grubbing by religious orders. This concern with wealth disrupts the possibility of penitence for mankind. Langland uses invective language such as "losels" (wretches) in line 77 and "boy" (rogue) in line 80 to convey this. Cupidity is the route of all evils.

Langland appears to turn the traditional model of society, the THREE ESTATES (peasants, knights, and clergy) upside down. Ploughmen appear to be placed to the fore, created by Kynde Wit (natural understanding) to benefit the community. This is because Langland is interested in each individual's contribution and soul rather than an attempt to promote an alternative social model. He shares the general anticlericism of the time, referring to the schism in the papacy of September 1378 in B-text lines 107–111 and C-text lines 134–188. This has led earlier critics and contemporary readers to associate him with LOLLARDISM and John Wycliffe. In the C-text, Langland tempers his criticism of clerics and condemns vagrants and those who pervert the traditional order of society, possibly in response to such a reception.

In the latter B- and C- texts, there are two additional episodes, a coronation scene and the Rat or "Belling of the Cat" tale, which raise political and historical issues. The coronation scene deals with the question of counsel, who should advise the king. The king is offered various forms of counsel, but only in the B-text is the common populace allowed to proffer advice (B-text, l. 122, 139–142). In the C-text, the monarch relies on Kynde Wit and Conscience (C-text, l. 147, 151). The B-text was written shortly after Richard II's coronation. In the Rat fable, Langland censors the community's attempts to prevent the cat exercising its authority and

hindering some of their desires. The cat has been compared to Edward III, Richard II, and John of Gaunt, but it is not definitively linked to any of them.

The poem, particularly the Prologue, has been used extensively as a source of information about social, political, and ecclesiastical history. Earlier studies tend to be limited and to overlook what Langland was trying to achieve. They have also tended to try and reduce everything in the poem to a simple mirror of late 14th-century society.

Piers Plowman has been considered a vision for reform. Critics have investigated its generic influences—SATIRE, prophecy, vision—and tried to establish what it is exhorting us to do. Alternatively, one can take an exegetical approach and access its use of Scripture and theology. *Piers Plowman* is such a complex poem that debates over its text, sources, and the concepts it puts forward are still far from achieving consensus. Current thinking favors looking at Langland's handling of literary, theological, political, and historical sources as well as genres and forms, rather than defining what they are. It is now accepted that *Piers Plowman* is not merely a compendium of late 14th-century British life and thought; rather, it is an intricate and enigmatic literary masterpiece.

See also "CROWNED KING, THE"; *PIERS PLOWMAN* (OVERVIEW); *PIERS PLOWMAN* TRADITION.

FURTHER READING
Cooper, Helen. "Langland's and Chaucer's Prologues." *Yearbook of Langland Studies* 1 (1987): 71–81.

Bonnie S. Millar

Piers Plowman: **Passus 1** WILLIAM LANGLAND (ca. 1362–1386) Passus 1 from *Piers Plowman* expands on the nature of truth. Truth was at the heart of medieval feudalism. It referred to loyalty and the keeping of faith, exhibited in the duties and obligations of one's estate, and was dependent on the honesty and justice of all parties. A lovely lady comes down from the castle on the hill to instruct the dreamer. She is dressed in linen, which is a reference to Revelation 15:6, where fine white linen is linked to the righteousness of saints. She explains that the lord of the castle on the hill is Truth, who is the father of faith, and that the other lord is Wrong, father of falsehood. Humans owe Truth loyalty and Wrong nothing. He is faithless, and those who trust in him are betrayed. Truth is obviously God, and Wrong is the devil.

The choice seems easy, but it is rendered difficult by cupidity. God has given humans all the requisites of life "in mesurable manere" (B-text, l. 19), but most want more. Underlying this is the exhortation in Matthew 6:19–21 not to accumulate treasures on the earth but to store them in heaven. The dreamer realizes that his guide is Lady Holy Church and duly falls to his knees and asks her how he may save his soul. She replies that when treasure is tested, "Treuthe is the beste" (B-text, l. 85). This is the central point of the poem, with the rest of it constituting an exploration of its implications. The fact that the dreamer's spiritual question is answered with a political axiom shows that both spheres are linked. Lady Holy Church expands on this relationship. She cites the examples of David and his knights and Christ and his nine orders of angels as examples of Truth. The Holy Trinity is the model of perfect harmony and the source of truth, while Lucifer is the source of its lack. In *Piers Plowman*, each answer leads to another question or series of questions. Thus, the dreamer duly asks, how does one know about Truth? Lady Holy Church explains that the natural understanding present in human hearts leads to loving the Lord above all else. Truth is expressed most fully through love, which is a state of will combined with matching outward behavior. Genuine truth is manifested in charitable actions, an outpouring of love, and such charity leads to grace.

Lady Holy Church's speech is structured like a medieval sermon, using devices to be found in the aids for preaching. For instance, she takes her starting point from quotations and develops her matter from them. Her speech shapes how the rest of the poem examines the meaning of truth and the problems surrounding it. Truth is the supreme principle for social behavior as heaven itself is based upon it. In this section, Langland's theology is influenced by concepts in Saint Augustine's *City of God*. The world is doomed, and although both love and loyalty exist in this corrupt earthly society, they do so without expectation. Social virtues reap their rewards, as do all other virtues, in heaven.

Lady Holy Church is not only a PERSONIFICATION and a figure of authority who helps the dreamer interpret what he sees; she is also part of a tradition that stems back to the Bible. All the elements of ALLEGORY and dream visions found in *Piers Plowman* are ultimately derived from biblical tradition, where prophets have dreams and visions that frequently feature an angel or other figure of authority who explains what has been seen.

Debate still rages over how to interpret the satirical and allegorical elements in Passus 1. Recent scholarship has contextualized it within the medieval preaching and pastorship tradition. Another avenue of exploration is the tension between politics and religion.

See also PASSUS, *PIERS PLOWMAN* (OVERVIEW).

FURTHER READING

Kaske, R. E. "Holy Church's Speech and the Structure of *Piers Plowman*." In *Middle English Studies in Honor of Rossell Hope Robbins,* edited by Beryl Bowland, 320–327. London: Allen and Unwin, 1974.

Bonnie S. Millar

Piers Plowman: **Passus 2** WILLIAM LANGLAND (ca. **1362–1386)** Passus 2–4 elaborate on the initial part of Lady Holy Church's speech. The first part of her theme—"when alle treasure arn tried" (B-text, l. 85)—is turned into a drama. Treasure is personified as Meed the Maid. Meed is about to wed Fals (False), who appears to be her father, an alliance to which Theology objects on the grounds that God has granted her to Truth. They decide that the matter should be tried at the king's court. Meed rides on a sheriff, while Fals settles for the back of a juror.

Meed arrives dressed in ostentatious attire, red scarlet dripping with gold jewels and fur, dazzling the dreamer. She is contrasted to Lady Holy Church. Meed is not simply wealth; she is also reward, implying a relationship: the acquiring of wages for work—bribery or spiritual treasure for penitence and virtuousness. Meed is not covetousness, but rather the object of it. In the B-text, Fals is her father, while in the A-text it is Wrong and in the C-text it is Favel. WILLIAM LANGLAND tries different fathers for her as he wishes to predicate two kinds of falseness by birth or parentage (not conscious) and by marriage (conscious). The first set of meanings for falseness encompasses wrong or error—that is, falseness in the perception of something or falseness in knowledge, which is subjective. The second range covers mendaciousness, deceitfulness, treachery (objective falseness), and falseness in the thing itself. Two characters for falseness represent each semantic set. The parentage of Meed is a metaphor for falseness in the conception of a thing, the thought of Meed as a material good. Meed is an attractive figure, one whom people desire. The point of her being a whore is that she represents whoring after money in indiscriminate fashion.

Favel, according to the Middle English Dictionary, is duplicity or guile, and in the Oxford English Dictionary it is cunning. Favel is thus evil no matter what the end is. He rides on flattery, as the hallmark of cunning is that you do not recognize it until it is too late. Flattery aids cunning (Favel) in obtaining Meed. Favel himself always appears with Fals. Both are involved in Meed's marriage scheme, and both are thanked for their bribes. They accompany her to Westminster for her trial, where the king promises to exact vengeance on them both. Meed is to marry Fals, so he is objective rather subjective. Thus, Favel is cunning and False refers to deceit. Favel initiates the process, and Fals is the result.

Favel is supported by other PERSONIFICATIONS. Liar is a separate but related character. It is a lie whether you want to deceive or not. Cunning implies the intention to deceive. Liar is turned into a cart supporting the activities of all those he transports. Guile, dressed as an apprentice by the merchants, carries out the scheme devised by Favel. He delivers the charter endowed by Favel, distributes his bribes, and acts as a guide on the journey. Symony and Civil Law are intimate with Meed, and they receive the charter. It gives her free reign to indulge all the SEVEN DEADLY SINS. Theology rebukes Civil Law and Symony, telling them to beware of Fals. He proposes that the case of Meed's marriage be tried by the king. All assembled journey to Westminster, where Fals, Favel, and their followers meet with a hostile reception from the king.

In this PASSUS, Theology takes over from Lady Holy Church. He appears to personify her doctrine, systematized and applied to society. Conscience, in fact, systematizes Lady Holy Church, as we learn later. Lady Holy Church describes Meed (B-text, l. 24) as illegitimate, while Theology states (B-text, ll. 132–133) that she is legitimate and of noble lineage. If we accept Lady Holy Church's account that there is no justification for Meed in the sense of material goods, why does Theology give her partial legitimacy. He is motivated by the similar desires to the corrupt members of society, and hence he provides a more complicated argument. He finds a theory which seems to make her acceptable, and thus begins the process of accommodating Meed.

Scholars tend to explore the semantic range of meanings for the concepts in Passus 2. In addition, they look at the theological principles that are intertwined with them; discuss the techniques Langland uses in trying to tease out these ideas; and frequently compare the A, B, and C redactions.

See also ALLEGORY, *PIERS PLOWMAN* (OVERVIEW).

FURTHER READING

Benson, C. David. "The Function of Lady Meed in Piers Plowman." *English Studies* 6 (1980): 193–301.

Yunck, John A. *The Lineage of Lady Meed: The Development of Venality Satire.* Notre Dame, Ind.: University of Notre Dame Press, 1963.

Bonnie S. Millar

Piers Plowman: **Passus 6** WILLIAM LANGLAND (ca. 1381–1382)   Passus 6 of the B-text (Passus 7 in the A-text) presents WILLIAM LANGLAND's experiment in solving the problems created by human action and inaction, by human need and greed, and by social forces and social disillusionment. In Passus 5, Piers explains the route through obedience to the Ten Commandments that a person must follow in order to reach Saint Truth. Passus 6 presents a further unfolding of the pilgrimage motif in a nontraditional mode. The scholar J. A. Burrow says the "half-acre episode" of Passus 6 has been called "a kind of pilgrimage" because work, which is given a new status of value in the poem, takes the place of a literal pilgrimage. Though Langland is not opposed to pilgrimage entirely, it is clear that he views it as an intensely personal activity with corporate dimensions.

Passus 6 is rooted in the social problems surrounding the BLACK DEATH (1348–49) and the wages paid to the remaining laborers in the initial years following the catastrophic event (the Statutes of Laborers of 1351). The events in this PASSUS display one of the central conflicts at the heart of the poem: the individual versus society. In the poem, Langland asks the essential question about the nature of reform: Can one reform society itself, or can one reform the individual as a key to larger social and spiritual change? As several scholars have noted, Langland appears to endorse the view that social reform can only follow ecclesiastical change.

Passus 6 opens with the pilgrims who are seeking St. Truth in a quandary about Piers's allegorical directions using the Ten Commandments as a road map for travel, as featured in Passus 5. Piers offers to lead them after the planting of his half-acre and the harvest. A faithful member of the feudal order of the manor, Piers must fulfill his obligations, and he engages others in the reestablishment of "truth," which serves as a symbolic image of the feudal order. "Truth," identified with God in Passus 1, is here imaged in the threefold order of society (those who fight, pray, and work). The "noble experiment" of the half-acre continues with Piers putting all people to work, according to their abilities and class pursuits. Noble women sew vestments for clergy; middle-class married women and widows weave cloth. A knight who volunteers to learn aspects of plowing is instructed to "kepe Holy Kirke and myselve (Piers) / Fro wastours and fro wikked men that this world destuyeth" (l. 27–28) instead. The knight becomes, for Piers, the representation of order in its most clearly manifested form. In the midst of this activity, Piers adopts "pilgrimages wise" (l. 57)—that is, actual clothing that he wears for planting. Piers next writes his will, a practice common before going on a pilgrimage, in which he leaves his soul to God, his body to the church for burial, and his goods to his wife and children. As he begins his plowing of the half-acre, all seems to be going well, until he stops to survey the work.

At "heigh prime" (l. 112), or 9:00 A.M., Piers stops to survey his half-acre and notices that some have already stopped working and are singing idle songs ("How trolly lolly," l. 116). Their decadent songs and idleness reinforce the images of destruction apparent in society at large. Piers angrily rebukes them and says he will not support anyone who is physically able to work to earn sustenance. Surveying those who pretend to have various disabilities, Piers rebukes their fraudulence. The workers remain indignant toward Piers, especially the Breton Bragger, who tells Piers to "go pissen with his plowgh" (l. 155). Not even the knight, who speaks in mild and ineffectual tones, can get the peasants back to work on the half-acre that Piers holds in trust from Truth. Piers then summons Hunger, who is quite successful in getting the peasant workers to reengage their labor, both out of want and fear. Hunger reduces many to the state of starvation and malnutrition—common images throughout England after the Black Death. Yet summoning Hunger brings its own set of problems. Langland the poet, through Piers, asks Hunger about how to keep people working. Fundamentally, Langland is asking one of the challenging questions about the use of force to maintain social control: What is the appropriate level of force to be applied to make society work?

Hunger suggests to Piers that it is important to distinguish those who are in need from whose who should be punished for their falseness. The truly poor deserve charity, while those who shirk their duties, according to Hunger, may be hit hard with adversity. Hunger's method, however, results in people only working to avoid starvation. In fact, Piers and others must offer a gluttonous amount of food to send Hunger away, only to discover that when Hunger/hunger is satisfied, the people have again become lazy. The passus ends with a warning that in five years, hunger, famine, and flood will return to judge the people.

Readers of this passus will notice a confusing sense of failure and success. Piers has been able to get a new understanding of the social order reestablished, the feudal model. Truth in the form of productive activity reigns for a moment, but it is maintained not by mutual consent, but by force. Scholars continue to debate this ending. Some see Piers as a failed leader, while others view the scene as a whole as a commentary on why corporate failure occurs. Still others see elements of a conflict between Piers as a representation of Old Testament law and New Testament grace. Work alone cannot save, nor can obedience to the Law. If society cannot be reformed from the top down, as noted in earlier passus of the poem, can it be reformed from the bottom up here? Some good, however, has been accomplished because a general lawlessness has been held in check, even if it is only momentarily.

Human needs, wants, desires, and motivations are at the center of Langland's contemplation of society in *Piers Plowman,* and the plowing of the half-acre episode presents the first installment of that question with its potential answer. Human need can blind people to personal actions and ethics; human need can thwart social responsibility. Reactivity can provide only partial answers. Herein lies Piers's problem in not being able to anticipate the problems of various social schemes. He remains an enigma that demonstrates lack of comprehension.

See also ALLEGORY, *PIERS PLOWMAN* (OVERVIEW).

FURTHER READING
Alford, John. A. "The Design of the Poem." In *A Companion to Piers Plowman,* edited by John A. Alford, 29–65. Berkeley: University of California Press, 1988.

Daniel F. Pigg

Piers Plowman: Passus 7 WILLIAM LANGLAND (ca. 1381–1382)
As Passus 7 opens, Truth decides to give a pardon to Piers and his heirs. Kings, bishops, merchants, laborers, and even lawyers and beggars have the opportunity to receive the pardon, if they have lived justly. A priest demands to read the pardon because he is familiar with them; however, the priest fails to recognize the exact words as a pardon, after which Piers tears up the document out of "pure tene" (l. 115). Piers and the priest start arguing, which in turn awakes the Dreamer, Will

Passus 7 is the last PASSUS of the second vision, which started with Reason's sermon to the "field full of folk," the confession of the SEVEN DEADLY SINS (Passus 5) and was followed by the attempt to go on pilgrimage to "Saint Truth," leading the pilgrims to the plowing of the half-acre under Piers Plowman's guidance (Passus 6). Some critics have interpreted this vision as the logical pre-Reformation Christian sequence of sermon, confession, repentance, pilgrimage, and pardon.

The climax of this passus occurs when Piers tears up the pardon, a dramatic scene that has led to an overflow of interpretations. The B-text shows subtle changes from the A-text; however, the C-text has a significant change: It omits the tearing of the pardon. Most agree that WILLIAM LANGLAND feared the misinterpretation of this scene, especially after the PEASANTS' REVOLT, and because of LOLLARDISM, which found inspiration in Langland's work.

Pre-Reformation Christianity taught that sins were forgiven through sacramental confession—only canonical temporal punishment could be remitted through a pardon; however, most people believed that a pardon could do both. The pardon reads as follows: *Et qui bona egerunt ibunt in vitam eternam; / Qui vero mala, in ignem eternum.* (And those who have done well shall go into eternal life, but those who have done evil will go into eternal fire, ll. 110–111.) Scholars have debated who is going to be saved: The pilgrims confess and work hard; the Sins confess, but insincerely; the "wastours" are indolent about both. Most scholars accept the pardon's validity because it comes from Truth, who represents God, making its tearing even more confusing. Is it Langland's way of showing his contempt for the corrupt selling of papal indulgences? Does Piers recognize himself as a failure and throw himself on God's mercy? Or does he tear the pardon because he realizes that it lacks mercy? Whatever the case, the tearing brings the connection between good works and mercy into question.

See also *PIERS PLOWMAN* (OVERVIEW).

FURTHER READING
Woolf, Rosemary. "The Tearing of the Pardon." *Piers Plowman: Critical Approaches.* Edited by S. S. Hussey. London: Methuen, 1969.

Annemarie Thijms

Piers Plowman: Passus 17 WILLIAM LANGLAND (1377–1379?)
PASSUS 17 (from the B-text of *Piers Plowman*) concludes the fifth DREAM VISION that began in Passus 15. This three-part section of the poem centers on the meaning of charity (or love), the greatest of the three Christian VIRTUES. Charity first appears in Passus 15 as the virtue the dreamer finds most absent in a world of self-interested individuals. The true nature and meaning of charity as a redemptive force then becomes the object of his quest. It is identified with the church, the Gospel, the Trinity, and Christ in particular. Passus 17

explores the meanings of these last two identifications, emphasizing what each teaches about charity.

Passus 17 begins with the figure of Spes (Hope) searching for Christ and carrying a letter that says "love God and your neighbor." As Faith was identified in Passus 16 with Abraham who teaches the dreamer about the Trinity, Spes is identified with Moses. His letter represents the law or covenant between God and Israel given to Moses. In the Ten Commandments. "Love God and your neighbor" is a summary of that law endorsed by Christ in the Gospel of Luke in response to the question from a scholar of the law, "What must I do to be saved?" But if this law is sufficient for salvation, it raises the question of why Christ introduced a new law. At this point, perhaps comically, the dreamer seems to interpret Abraham/the Trinity and Moses/"Love God and your neighbor" as two different, mutually exclusive means of salvation. This observation alludes to the question raised in Luke 10:29—"And who is my neighbor?"—which Christ answers with the parable of the Good Samaritan, the next and most important character to appear in Passus 17. The point of the parable and Passus 17 is that everyone is one's neighbor, and loving others enough to suffer for their benefit is the highest expression of love for God, as it imitates Christ's suffering for humanity's salvation.

The Samaritan appears riding a mule to Jerusalem, allegorically aligning him with Christ. He is on his way to "joust" in Jerusalem with the "outlaw" (Satan) who robbed and injured a man the Samaritan encounters (fallen humanity). Faith (Abraham) and Hope (Moses) are unable to help the injured man; only the Samaritan can save the wounded man in an act of charity that comes at considerable personal cost. Described as riding a horse called Caro (Flesh)—that is, the humanity assumed by Christ—the Samaritan brings the injured man to a farmhouse called Lex Christi (the law of Christ), an allusion to Galatians 6:2—"Bear one another's burdens, and so fulfill the law of Christ." Here the injured man can have his wounds washed ("baptized as it were") in the blood of a baby born of a virgin and "plastered with the penance and passion [i.e., suffering] of that baby." His full health can only be restored by eating the baby and drinking his blood—that is,

receiving the sacrament of Holy Communion. For those outside the church, the Samaritan says that until he returns, Faith will guide them safely to Jerusalem (Heaven), and Hope will lead those who cannot be taught by Faith.

From this point to the end of the PASSUS, the Samaritan explains how the meaning of the Trinity can be understood analogically through the image of a hand. Another extended analogy follows where the Trinity is likened to a torch or a candle where the flame (the Holy Spirit) comes from the unity of the wax and wick (the Father and the Son), bringing grace and mercy to sinners—but only when the Spirit is present. The torch is also compared to a good man who believes in the Trinity and whose life is illuminated by Charity and the Holy Spirit.

In this long theological excursus, the poet seems to be struggling to reconcile God's power, grace, and mercy with human agency and merit. God's ability to save or damn people is absolute, but what humans do must also be consequential in determining their fate. WILLIAM LANGLAND wants to emphasize and also qualify the disturbing idea that without Spirit, Christian beliefs and practices are not salvific but damning. In the words of the Samaritan, he makes a stern moral and social critique by naming acts of popular piety that are often performed without charity and consequently have no spiritual benefit. The Samaritan ascribes the worst lapses of and offenses against charity to rich people whose avarice and envy lead them to physically kill or murder the reputations of others. These acts are identified with the unpardonable sin against the Holy Spirit, but somewhat paradoxically the Samaritan says that even grave sins of this nature—for which there is no possible restitution—are not necessarily unpardonable.

This observation brings Passus 17 to its conclusion as the Samaritan warns of three things that drive a person from his home, i.e., conditions conducive to sin. The first, likened to an intractably hostile wife who drives off her husband, is the flesh, meaning a willful rejection of legitimate correction and the tendency to make excuses for one's own failure. This instance has been subject to recent feminist criticism that also addresses Langland's misogyny holistically. The second, likened to a roof that leaks in one's bed, is sickness and sorrow that one should accept and suffer without complaint or anger. Historicists have contextualized this image within the framework of the BLACK DEATH. The third, likened to a smoky fire that blurs one's vision, is covetousness and unkindness that inhibit God's mercy. After all these dire warnings, the Samaritan departs, reassuring the dreamer that no one is so corrupt that he may not learn charity and reform himself.

See also ALLEGORY, *PIERS PLOWMAN* (OVERVIEW).

FURTHER READING

Davlin, Mary Clemente. "Piers Plowman as Biblical Commentary." *Essays in Medieval Studies* 20 (2003): 85–94.

Godden, Malcolm. *The Making of Piers Plowman.* London and New York: Longman, 1990.

Waldron, R. A. "Langland's Originality: The Christ-Knight and the Harrowing of Hell." In *Medieval English Religious and Ethical Literature,* edited by Gregory Kratzman and James Simpson, 66–81. Cambridge: D.S. Brewer, 1986.

Warner, Lawrence. "Jesus the Jouster: The Christ-Knight and Medieval Theories of the Atonement in *Piers Plowman* and the 'Round Table' Sermons." *The Yearbook of Langland Studies* 10 (1996): 129–143.

Daniel P. Knauss

Piers Plowman: Passus 19 and 20 WILLIAM LANGLAND (ca. 1381–1382)

The last two sections of the B-text of *Piers Plowman* extend the commentary on salvation history and at the same time bring this monumental work to a frenetic, apocalyptic close. Passus 19 begins with the Dreamer awaking and then immediately falling asleep again in the middle of mass. In this new dream, he sees what he believes to be Piers Plowman covered in blood and asks Conscience whether or not this image is really Piers or if it is Jesus. Conscience reiterates a previous lesson: Jesus donned Piers's armor in order to joust with the Devil. Conscience teaches the Dreamer that the title *Christ* signifies Jesus' role as conqueror and explains that he fulfilled this role by using Dowel, Dobet, and Dobest, symbolizing the different types of miracles performed by Jesus. Dowel, for example, represents the minor miracle of turning water into wine; Dobet, the healing miracles and the feeding of the 5,000; and Dobest, the ultimate miracles of resurrection and redemption. Sig-

nificantly, this is the last time WILLIAM LANGLAND employs the three-part motif that has served him so well throughout the poem.

Christ then grants a pardon to Piers that reads *Redde quod debes* ("pay what you owe," l. 188). This pardon is contrasted with the vague pardon issued to Piers in Passus 7, which he destroyed out of frustration. This true pardon simply involves confession and contrition. Conscience then calls on Grace, who organizes humanity into different occupations in order to defend themselves against the coming onslaught of Antichrist. As another means of defense, Grace constructs the church of Unity out of the mortar of Christ's blood. Conscience then pleads for all Christians to enter Unity, and, shortly thereafter, the Dreamer awakens.

Passus 20 deals with chaos of the Apocalypse. Awake, the Dreamer is verbally attacked by Need. The Dreamer then falls asleep and immediately sees Antichrist, in the shape of a man, cut down "truthe." The minions of Antichrist, such as Pride, begin to overtake humanity and fight against Conscience. Conscience, sensing the danger, tries to gather everyone into Unity for protection, but instead must call on Kind (who brings with him Old Age and Death) in an attempt to convince others to join him in Unity. The ravages of Kind affect the Dreamer by making him old, bald, deaf, and impotent. Faced with the ends of their lives, many turn back to Conscience and Unity, until Health returns and Life forgets the lessons learned from Kind.

Langland's SATIRE here is immediately apparent: People are most contrite when death is near. So few, in fact, are left after all of the disease and death that many scholars believe Passus 20 to be a symbolic account of the Last Days. Indeed, Conscience finally gathers the remaining Christians into Unity, and Antichrist's army bitterly attacks them, gradually weakening their defenses to the point where Unity is penetrated by evil and all begins to fall apart. Conscience, declaring that he will "bicome a pilgrym" (l. 381), sets out to find Piers Plowman. The poem then ends, rather suddenly many feel, with Conscience shouting for Grace and the Dreamer finally awakening. The sense of doom felt at the conclusion of the poem, however, is tempered by the expectation of Piers's return. Indeed, the ending of *Piers Plowman* rings with the hope of the Second Coming and the dawn of the millennial era of the heavenly kingdom.

See also ALLEGORY, PIERS PLOWMAN (OVERVIEW).

FURTHER READING
Bloomfield, Morton. *Piers Plowman as a Fourteenth-Century Apocalypse.* New Brunswick, N.J.: Rutgers University Press, 1962.

Joshua R. Eyler

PIERS PLOWMAN TRADITION   The *PIERS PLOWMAN* tradition comprises a large body of mostly anonymous, pseudepigraphic, and often hybrid texts produced over more than 200 years in which fiction and history, text and context cannot be easily differentiated. Its defining feature is the political appropriation of the figure and ethos of Piers Plowman—the character and the poem—as a voice for political and religious dissent during and after the PEASANTS' REVOLT and throughout the English Reformation in the 16th and 17th centuries.

One of the leaders of the Peasants' Revolt, a priest named John Ball, put Piers and other characters from *Piers Plowman* into cryptic verses and speeches that were circulated in letters among the rebels. Consequently, the *Dieulacres Abbey Chronicle* named Piers as one of the leaders of the rising, as if he were a real person. This view of Piers was encouraged early in the history of the poem's scribal transmission, as the character Piers was often taken as an authorial persona, if not the name of the actual author whose name and identity was obscured, remaining a subject of some debate to this day.

In some contemporary CHRONICLES of the Peasants' Revolt, Ball and the Lollards (see LOLLARDISM) were blamed for the revolt, and Piers began to be associated with heresy and rebellion. The earliest literary works comprising the Piers Plowman tradition follow in the wake of these events, although they and their 16th-century successors are not antimonarchical or supportive of rebellion. Like WILLIAM LANGLAND, who may have written the C-text version of *Piers Plowman* to disassociate himself from the revolt, they look for the reform of the English church and society by the removal of abuses in what the authors deem a restorative, rather than an innovative, project.

The Piers Plowman tradition proper begins with a body of anonymous poetic and prose compositions circulated by manuscript that have an explicit or attributed kinship with *Piers Plowman.* They are politically charged, sometimes allegorical social complaints with elements of SATIRE and polemic. These chiefly include PIERCE THE PLOUGHMAN'S CREDE (1395), *The Complaynte of the Ploughman/The Plowman's Tale* (1400), *The Praier and Complaynte of the Ploweman unto Christe* (1400), *Richard the Redeless* (1405), MUM AND THE SOTHSEGGER (1405), and "The CROWNED KING" (1415). Many of these texts have a more or less evident Lollard message and provenance. *Richard the Redeless* and *Mum and the Sothsegger* are probably by the same author and may be two parts of a single work.

The *Piers Plowman* tradition was revived and transformed in the 16th century by the appearance of printed, and somewhat altered, pro-Protestant versions of *The Praier and Complaynte of the Ploweman unto Christe* (1531/32), *The Plowman's Tale* (1533–36, 1548), *Piers Plowman* (1550, 1561), and *Pierce the Ploughman's Crede* (1553, 1561). The purpose of these books was to support Protestantism, in part by establishing its antiquity and thus its authority. Notably, *The Praier and Complaynte* was printed with a preface possibly by the reformer William Tyndale. It was attacked by SIR THOMAS MORE, and it appeared in four editions of John Foxe's *Actes and Monuments* from 1570 to 1610. *The Plowman's Tale* appeared in four editions of GEOFFREY CHAUCER's *Works* from 1542 to 1602. At that time Chaucer was widely considered to have been a Lollard, largely because of his association with poems he did not write, especially *The Plowman's Tale,* which was thought to correspond to Chaucer's Lollard Plowman in the GENERAL PROLOGUE TO THE CANTERBURY TALES.

There is a considerable body of original 16th-century texts that might be included in the Piers Plowman tradition by dint of their use of plowmen figures or truth-telling characters named Piers in a satirical or critical fashion. For example, EDMUND SPENSER's *The SHEPHEARDES CALENDER* has a character named Piers and borrows directly from *The Plowman's Tale.* Considering only the texts that contain or refer to a "Piers Plowman," the following stand out: *A Godly Dyalogue and Dysputacyion Betwene Pyers Plowman and a Popysh Pre-*

est (1550); THOMAS CHURCHYARD's *The Contention . . . upon David Dycers Dreame* (1551–52); *Pyers Plowmans Exhortation unto the Lordes, Knightes, and Burgoysses of the Parlyamenthouse* (1550), possibly by ROBERT CROWLEY; GEORGE GASCOIGNE's *The Steele Glas* (1576); *Newes from the North Otherwise called the Conference between Simon Certain and Pierce Plowman* (1579), possibly by Francis Thynne; and the play *A Merry Knack to Know a Knave* (1594), possibly by William Kempe and Edward Alleyn. There is also *I Playne Piers which Cannot Flatter*—an amalgam of material from *The Plowman's Tale* and new topical matter added after the 1540s. Unique among these pro-Protestant texts, *The Banquet of John the Reeve unto Piers Plowman* (1532) is an anti-Protestant work in which Piers defends Catholic Eucharistic doctrine.

FURTHER READING

Aston, Margaret. *Lollards and Reformers: Images and Literacy in Late Medieval Religion.* London: Hambledon Press, 2003.
Barr, Helen, ed. *The Piers Plowman Tradition.* London: Everyman's Library, 1993.
Hudson, Anne. "Epilogue: The Legacy of *Piers Plowman.*" In *A Companion to Piers Plowman,* edited by John A. Alford, 251–266. Berkeley: University of California Press, 1988.
Rydzeski, Justine. *Radical Nostalgia in the Age of Piers Plowman: Economics, Apocalypticism, and Discontent.* New York: Peter Lang, 1999.

Daniel P. Knauss

"PILLAR PERISHED IS WHERETO I LEANT, THE" SIR THOMAS WYATT (1557)

This translation of a SONNET by PETRARCH, which is ascribed to SIR THOMAS WYATT both in its manuscript form (the Arundel manuscript) and in TOTTEL'S MISCELLANY (1557), carries with it a certain amount of circumstantial evidence that not only points toward Wyatt's authorship but also suggests a possible period of composition.

The title which Tottel provides, "The lover lamentes the death of his love," is now universally acknowledged to be an act of misreading, possibly deliberate. In Petrarch's original sonnet, the "pillar perished" refers to the death of the poet's great friend and patron, Giovanni Colonna, whose surname is the Italian for column, or "pillar." Wyatt, in turn, is thought to have composed his translation following the death of his great friend and patron, Thomas Cromwell, who was executed on July 28, 1540.

Such an autobiographical context loads the sonnet with implied meanings. The opening declaration becomes a potentially dangerous admission of dependence on a man executed for treason: "whereto I leant" (l. 1). This admission extends into the second line's "strongest stay of mine unquiet mind," a possible reference to Wyatt's 1527 work *The Quiet of Mind,* which was originally commissioned by Queen Catherine of Aragon as a translation of Petrarch's *Remedies against Good and Evil Fortune* (1358?–60?). Indeed, an emphasis on FORTUNE recurs throughout: "hap away hath rent" (l. 5); "I alas by chance am thus assigned" (l. 7); "it is by destiny" (l. 9). This recurrent Boethian stress on providence serves as a safety net: Wyatt could not very well criticize the king, despite one of the reasons for Cromwell's downfall having been arranging the marriage between Henry VIII and Anne of Cleves, whom Henry loathed.

Wyatt continues to disassociate himself in the SESTET, whereby the sonnet lapses into the kind of Petrarchan antitheses which we encounter in poems such as "I FIND NO PEACE, AND ALL MY WAR IS DONE": "pen" counters "voice" and "mind" balances "body," resulting in the internal division of "I myself always to hate" (l. 13). The rhetorical question that constitutes the sestet—if we were to consider the poem without its political context—effectively adds nothing; the anticipation of the "dreadful death" that will "cease my doleful state" simply reiterates the OCTAVE's closing line, "Dearly to mourn till death do it relent" (l. 8). Read in correspondence with events at court, the capitulation to received poetical formula allows Wyatt to covertly voice dissent in the octave, as personal unhappiness extends to unhappiness over its cause, while maintaining what one critic has termed an air of deniability. The sestet's rhetorical question thereby achieves a certain gravitas as it gives voice to a sense of frustration felt by those who serve a capricious and tyrannical monarch. By their nature, rhetorical questions expect no answer; in this instance it is also because the real question—that of responsibility—has not been, indeed could not be, asked.

"The Pillar Perished" thus provides an exemplary model of Wyatt's translation, skills which not only entail linguistic transposition, but also incorporate semantic and contextual metamorphosis. What appears to be a straightforward reproduction of an ITALIAN (PETRARCHAN) SONNET harbors an implicit critique of a sovereign's power that could never have been made explicitly; thus, the oblique language of poetry enables freedom of speech.

FURTHER READING

Daalder, Joost, ed. *Sir Thomas Wyatt: Collected Poems.* Oxford and New York: Oxford University Press, 1975.

Greenblatt, Stephen. *Renaissance Self-Fashioning: From More to Shakespeare.* Chicago: University of Chicago Press, 1980.

POETS OF THE NOBILITY (fl. 1282–1526)

The Poets of the Nobility flourished after the fall of independent Wales (1282–84). Metric and thematic innovation, engagement with outside (particularly French) literary influences, and the element of entertainment characterize this poetry. The best-known among these poets, DAFYDD AP GWILYM, is credited with developing the distinctive CYWYDD meter, initially used exclusively for love poems but eventually applied to formal poetry. Other notable Poets of the Nobility include Gruffudd Llwyd (d. 1335), Gwerful Mechain (fl. 1462–1510), and Llywelyn Bren (d. 1318).

See also POETS OF THE PRINCES; WELSH WOMEN POETS.

FURTHER READING

Loomis, Richard, and Dafydd Johnston, eds. and trans. *Medieval Welsh Poems.* Binghamton, N.Y.: Medieval & Renaissance Texts & Studies, 1992.

Kathleen H. Formosa

POETS OF THE PRINCES (fl. ca. 1100–1282)

The Poets of the Princes sang in the courts of the independent Welsh princes. They held official court positions since poetic recitals served a ceremonial function, and their duties, status, and rights were defined and protected by law. Thematically, their poetry is deliberately nostalgic, celebrating ancient Welsh heroes and featuring elaborate genealogies. Common poetic conventions included hyperbolic praise, ornate metric forms, and complex ALLITERATION, as well as internal and end rhyme. These poets were the direct inheritors of a venerable, distinctly Welsh tradition founded by Aneirin and TALIESIN, and include such writers as Cynddelw and Cuhelyn of Cemais.

See also POETS OF THE NOBILITY; WELSH WOMEN POETS.

FURTHER READING

Lewis, Ceri W. "The Court Poets: Their Function, Status and Craft." In *A Guide to Welsh Literature,* Vol. 1, edited by A. O. H. Jarman and Gwilym Rees Hughes, 123–156. Swansea: Christopher Davies, 1976.

Kathleen H. Formosa

"PRIORESS'S TALE, THE" GEOFFREY CHAUCER (ca. 1385)

"The Prioress's Tale" is part of GEOFFREY CHAUCER's *The CANTERBURY TALES.* Written in stately RHYME ROYAL, the tale is 238 lines long and the shortest of the completed tales. The shortness of the poem suggests that it had been recited during a visit on March 26, 1387, by King Richard II and Queen Anne to Lincoln Cathedral, which houses the shrine of St. Hugh, the young Christian martyr mentioned at the end of this tale. "The Prioress's Tale" belongs to the narrative grouping called the Miracles of the Virgin, which is a subgenre of the greater group known by its Latin term *legenda* (saints' legends); it is related to HAGIOGRAPHY. "The Prioress's Tale" is based on these stories in which, upon hearing the pleas from her devotees, the Virgin Mary rescues them from danger or harm. These stories of miraculous rescue and protection by the Virgin Mary became highly popular between the 12th and 15th centuries and were disseminated throughout Europe in a variety of narrative forms, both written and oral.

The tale's prologue is a devotional prayer to the Virgin Mary. The five STANZAS mark an allusion to the five joys and five sorrows of the Virgin Mary. Praising the Virgin Mary's power and goodness, the Prioress pleads for her aid in telling the story of the little Christian boy who becomes a martyr in the service of the Virgin Mary. This devotion is a masterful interweaving by Chaucer of echoes and allusions from a variety of religious sources, such as Psalm 8, the biblical story of Herod's slaughter of the innocents, the Mass of the Holy Innocents, and the Little Office of the Virgin Mary. Emphasis is placed heavily in the tale on the theme of innocence, thereby providing the stark and brutal contrast to the realities of earthly and material affairs. Words such as *yong, tendre,* and *smale* permeate the story in order to underscore the meek and mild nature—two traits highly valued in the medieval Christian culture—of the little Christian boy, who presses forward through life each day, blissfully unaware of the worldly dangers that constantly surround him.

Chaucer sets the boy's story in the exotic locale of Asia, and there, in the midst of a nondescript Jewish ghetto, is a Christian school. Each day the seven-year-old boy, a widow's son, walks through the ghetto to the school. During his short journey, he sings the antiphon *Alma redemptoris mater* as proof of his deep devotion for the Virgin Mary. Hearing this child's song, Satan stirs up the Jewish community to plot and kill the Christian boy. The Jews hire a murderer to slit the boy's throat and throw him into a latrine filled with waste and sewage. When the boy fails to return home after school, his mother begins a frantic search for him, all the while praying to the Virgin Mary, whom the widow believes will understand her desperate plight.

Not finding her little boy anywhere, the widow enters the Jewish ghetto and begs and pleads with each Jew for any news of her son. The Jews reject her pleas, but help comes through Christ, who leads the widow to the site where her boy's body is lying. The boy once again begins to sing the *Alma redemptoris mater* in a loud, clear voice. Upon hearing the antiphon, Christians from the community appear at the site and marvel at this miracle. The boy is then lifted out of the latrine and taken to the nearest abbey for proper burial.

Chaucer wastes little time with the punishment of the Jews for their crimes. In stark and matter-of-fact language, they are summarily put to death as prescribed by law—hanged and drawn by horses. In the medieval period, this act of punishment is usually reserved for those who committed treasonous acts. Chaucer's description of the Jews' punishment as a treasonous act may tie back to the New Testament story of the treasonous act of Judas against Christ, which led to his crucifixion.

Meanwhile, the little Christian boy explains to the abbot that at the time of his death, the Virgin Mary appeared and placed a seed on his tongue so that he could sing and promised to take him to her when the seed was removed. The abbot then removes the seed, and the boy "softly gave up his soul," after which his body is placed in a marble tomb. Chaucer ends the tale with an invocation, a plea through prayer, to Little St. Hugh of Lincoln, asking the saint to pray for sinful folk and that God grant his mercy in honor of the Virgin Mary.

"The Prioress's Tale" is not only connected to Virgin Miracle tales but is also more directly based on the myth of "blood libel," which involves the depiction of Jews as soldiers of Satan, and the ritualistic act of murder, particularly of Christian children, as a commonplace, and perhaps enjoyable, undertaking. The myth extended to the idea that the blood of a Christian child was used to make Passover matzohs. Little St. Hugh of Lincoln, who is invoked at the end of the tale (ll. 684–686), and St. William of Norwich were both considered part of this tradition. Blood libel saints were all boys, though more general stories sometimes included girls. This division based on sex was directly linked to the Christian fear of circumcision and the belief that it would "convert" a Christian male.

The violent and anti-Semitic nature of "The Prioress's Tale" has proven problematic for modern readers. In general, anti-Semitism was part of the social fabric of medieval Christian Europe, and Chaucer, as many other writers of the medieval period, used stereotypes as a means to heighten the pathos of a predominantly Christian audience. For instance, the reference to "Hugh of Lyncoln, slayn also / with cursed Jewes . . ." is a deliberate device. Hugh (d. 1255) was not actually murdered by Jews, and that was known even in Chaucer's day; however, it was widely believed to be the case since 19 Jews were executed for the crime. It is difficult to address the nature of anti-Semitism within such a cultural context; nevertheless, it is egregious and pervasive. Chaucer was, at minimum, an insightful observer of human nature, and "The Prioress's Tale" can be perceived as an investigation into a society's capability for violence and cruelty in contrast to an individual's innate ability for compassion and pity.

The narrative layout of "The Prioress's Tale" follows three major Christian themes that can be found in many other religious tales of the 14th century. These include several Canterbury tales, such as "The MAN OF LAW'S TALE," "The Clerk's Tale," "The Second Nun's Tale," and, to some extent, "The PARDONER'S TALE." Each of these tales highlights the themes of travel, suffering, and reward. In "The Prioress' Tale," for example, the theme of travel is reflected in the boy's journey through the Jewish ghetto to his school; the theme of suffering is underscored by his death and the agony experienced by his mother; the reward is brought when the seed is removed and the boy goes to heaven. It can also be linked to the genre of EXEMPLUM, particularly illustrating the moral "mordre wol out" (l. 576)— murder will be revealed. The tale's religious affiliations are further strengthened by its continual reference to prayer: It opens with an invocation, refers to a hymn throughout, and also contains several instances of prayer-like interruptions by the narrator (e.g., "O martir sowded to virginitee . . .," l. 579).

"The Prioress's Tale" also shares other important themes with the tales of the Clerk and Physician, such as parenthood and children, for example. The social turmoil following the BLACK DEATH—including the increase in child mortality rates—is revealing in "The Prioress's Tale," rendered even more poignant through the widow's extreme grief and her social class. She is often compared to the Virgin Mary, as a humble earthly representation of the *mater dolorosa* (grieving mother). Reading "The Prioress's Tale" with these themes in mind reveals the greater complex nature of medieval society and Chaucer's attempt at tackling stark realities.

FURTHER READING

Gies, Frances and Joseph. *Marriage and the Family in the Middle Ages.* New York: HarperRow Publishers, 1989.

Rubin, Miri. *Gentile Tales: The Narrative Assault on Late Medieval Jews.* New Haven, Conn.: Yale University Press, 1999.

Schildgen, Brenda Deen. *Pagans, Tartars, Moslems, and Jews in Chaucer's Canterbury Tales.* Gainesville: University Press of Florida, 2001.

Carola Mattord

PUTTENHAM, GEORGE (ca. 1520–1590)

George Puttenham, purported author of the highly influential treatise *The Art of English Poesie,* was born into a genry family from Hampshire. Little is known of his life. He married the twice-widowed Elizabeth Coudray with whom he had at least one daughter. He may also have been involved in a plot against Lord Burleigh in 1570, as he was imprisoned in 1578, though released in 1585. He died in 1590.

FURTHER READING

Nash, Walter. "George Puttenham." *The Dictionary of Literary Biography, Volume 281: British Rhetoricians and Logicians, 1500–1660,* 229–248. Detroit, Mich.: Gale, 2003.

PYNSON, RICHARD (ca. 1449–1529) *printer*

An important figure in the early years of English printing, Richard Pynson was Norman by birth but lived and worked in England. He began his printing career around 1490 out of a shop located in the Strand, outside the Temple Bar. He produced his first book late in 1492 and received his patent of naturalization in the following year. Within a decade, Pynson moved to the City of London. In 1506, Pynson succeeded William Faques as printer to the king; he served under both Henry VII and HENRY VIII.

In the four decades of his career as a printer, Pynson produced about 400 books; between them, Pynson and WYNKYN DE WORDE printed two-thirds of all English books from 1490 to 1530. One of Pynson's main publishing interests was in law books, for which he held the sales monopoly. He was also involved in the production of popular literary works, including GEOFFREY CHAUCER's *The CANTERBURY TALES* (1492), as well as devotional texts and hagiographies. Overall, Pynson successfully balanced his official status with commercial considerations and, in so doing, helped to firmly establish the printing press in England.

See also CAXTON, WILLIAM; HAGIOGRAPHY.

FURTHER READING

Duff, E. Gordon. *A Century of the English Book Trade.* . . . Folcroft, Pa.: Folcroft Library Editions, 1972.

Steinberg, S. H. *Five Hundred Years of Printing.* Rev. ed. London: British Library, 1996.

Christine F. Cooper

QUATORZAIN   From the French *quatorze* (fourteen), a quatorzain is a poem similar to the SONNET. It consists of 14 rhymed iambic lines divided into two tercets (a group of three lines of verse) and two quatrains (a group of four lines of verse), and always ending in a COUPLET (unlike sonnets, which do not always do so). Technically, most of the Elizabethan SONNET SEQUENCES were truly composed of quatorzains, not sonnets, but few 16th-century poets made the distinction (an exception being MICHAEL DRAYTON). Some critics also believe that SIR PHILIP SIDNEY employed the form deliberately in his collection *CERTAIN SONNETS,* which contains a miscellany of forms. Later poets, such as John Donne, clarified the two forms.

QUATRAIN   A four-line STANZA composed of rhyming lines. The quatrain is the most common stanzaic form used in English poetry. The sets of lines that make up the first four or eight lines of a SONNET are also referred to as quatrains.

The most common rhyme schemes include: *abac* or *abcb* (BALLAD STANZA, used also for hymns), *aabb* (double COUPLET), and *abab* (heroic quatrain, usually in IAMBIC PENTAMETER).

R

RALEIGH, SIR WALTER (SIR WALTER RALEGH) (ca. 1552–1618)

Sir Walter Raleigh lived a varied and adventurous life—soldier, privateer, explorer, prisoner, and author. Born into a prosperous family at Hayes, a farmhouse in Barton, Devonshire, Raleigh attended Oriel College, Oxford, briefly before leaving to distinguish himself early in the French civil wars. A staunch Protestant, he fought on behalf of the Huguenots from 1569 until his return to England in 1572. In 1578, he began his naval career, joining his half brother, Sir Humphrey Gilbert, on an expedition. Soon afterward, Raleigh earned a command and distinguished himself in the Irish Wars. Returning to England in 1581, he quickly became a part of Queen ELIZABETH I's inner circle.

The next years of Raleigh's life read like a catalogue of political success. He was elected to Parliament in 1584 and appointed captain of the Queen's Guard in 1587. As queen's adviser, he supported expeditions in 1585 and 1587 to the NEW WORLD. However, his power and influence were greatly diminished in 1592 when his secret affair with and subsequent clandestine marriage to Elizabeth Throckmorton, one of Elizabeth's ladies-in-waiting, was discovered. Both were immediately imprisoned in the TOWER OF LONDON, an occasion Raleigh examines in "The Ocean To Cynthia."

The queen never forgave Raleigh completely, but she did need his naval skills. In 1593, Raleigh was released in order to pursue Spanish pirates and protect the interests of the English Crown. He also embarked on an expedition to Guiana, an account of which he published in 1596.

When Elizabeth died in 1603, Raleigh's prospects diminished, as he had a poor relationship with JAMES I. Soon after James's ascension, Raleigh was accused of conspiring with Spain against the king, and he was once again imprisoned in the Tower. He remained there until 1617, when he persuaded James to allow him to captain a return expedition to Guiana. The voyage was a complete disaster—his son died, and Raleigh was disgraced. Fearing royal reprisal, Raleigh attempted to flee to France, but he was caught and, on October 29, 1618, executed for treason.

Raleigh is an interesting author. His early works include commendatory verses for GEORGE GASCOIGNE's *The Steele Glas,* composed while he was at Oxford. These show precocious development not only of poetic skill but also of political prowess. His other poetic works include a number of short pieces, an ELEGY for his son, and the PANYGERIC "The Ocean to Cynthia," written to placate the queen. Raleigh was more prolific in prose, undertaking the ambitious *History of the World* as well as his *Travels to Guiana* and an "apology" for his return to Guiana.

For quite some time, critical reception of Raleigh's poetry was devoted to establishing definitive authorship for his works. Another area of critical debate involves the completeness of "The Ocean to Cynthia," fragments of which were found with the titles "The 21st [sic] and last booke of the Ocean to Scinthia" and

"The end of the 22 Boock, entreatinge of Sorrow," leading to speculation that an immense EPIC had originally existed. Recent studies, however, have demonstrated that the titles were a ploy by Raleigh intended to please the queen. Otherwise, most critical studies focus on political interpretations of Raleigh's poems, as well as its contribution to the studies of PATRONAGE.

See also "LIE, THE"; "NYMPH'S REPLY TO THE SHEPHERD, THE;" "SIR WALTER RALEIGH TO HIS SON"; "WHAT IS OUR LIFE?".

FURTHER READING
Lacey, Robert. *Sir Walter Ralegh*. 1973. Reprint, London: Phoenix Press, 2000.

Raleigh, Sir Walter. *The Letters of Sir Walter Raleigh*. Edited and translated by Agnes M. C. Latham and Joyce A. Youings. Exeter, U.K.: University of Exeter Press, 1999.

RAPE OF LUCRECE, THE WILLIAM SHAKE-SPEARE (ca. 1593)
This is a long narrative poem composed of seven-line STANZAS in RHYME ROYAL, with the rhyme scheme of *ababbcc*. Although the poem comes complete with its own plot summary ("The Argument"), virtually every educated person of the 16th century knew the story of the virtuous Roman wife Lucretia (Lucrece). In "Publishing Shame: *The Rape of Lucrece*," Coppelia Kahn even calls it "a founding myth of patriarchy," a social structure in which men had virtually total control over women. The Roman social structure was patriarchal, and patriarchy existed, in a somewhat modified form, in early modern England.

The poem's action centers on events that occurred around 509 B.C.E., when Rome was still only a city-state ruled by a tyrant named Tarquinius Superbus (Tarquin the Proud). His son, Tarquinius Sixtus, raped Lucretia, the wife of Collatinus (Collatine in Shakespeare), who was his friend and kinsman. Lucretia revealed her rape to her family, demanded they revenge her honor, named Tarquin the rapist, and committed suicide. Lucrece's kinsmen brought her body to the Roman Forum to show the citizens, and Lucius Junius Brutus, a nephew of the king and friend of Collatinus, led a revolt against the Tarquins. They were exiled, and the Roman people began a republican government, ruled by a senate and elected consuls.

This story was important in early modern England for two reasons: It provided historical justification for the expulsion of an unjust ruler and the foundation of a new government (in this case the Roman republic), and, it provided an EXEMPLUM (example) of the correct, chaste behavior all wives in a patriarchal society should practice. WILLIAM SHAKESPEARE's concise version of the tale, however, focuses primarily on the rape and its aftermath, as well as on Lucrece's behavior.

The poem can be broken down into the following sections: (1) Tarquin's journey to Rome, his reflection upon Lucrece's beauty and chastity, the decription of events after he arrives (ll. 1–189); (2) Tarquin's thoughts before the rape, his entering Lucrece's bedchamber, and his view of the beautiful, sleeping Lucrece (ll. 190–448); (3) Lucrece's discovery of Tarquin, her pleas to be spared, Tarquin's theoretical justification of his actions, the rape, and his departure (ll. 449–749); (4) Lucrece's lament, her blaming of Night, Time, and Opportunity for the crime, and her reflection on whether her honor has been compromised (ll. 750–1211); (5) Lucrece's writing to Collatine to demand his immediate return (ll. 1212–1365); (6) Lucrece's reflection upon the painting of the fall of Troy (ll. 1366–1582); (7) Collatine's arrival, Lucrece telling her tale and committing suicide, her kinsmen avenging her death, and the exile of the Tarquins (ll. 1583–1855). Despite the focused nature of the tale, it does raise many issues regarding what constitutes chastity and how and when a woman's honor is compromised.

To understand these issues, we need to consider the nature of the society Shakespeare presents in *Lucrece*. While ancient Rome was clearly not 16th-century England—and we therefore cannot assume Roman cultural mores were English ones—Rome was often used as a metaphor for England. Early modern English writers could be arrested for sedition if the government decided their political critiques were too harsh. As a result, they often set poems or plays in a country other than England so as not to risk arrest. A generic "Rome" was often chosen to symbolize England, so we can consider the "vision" of Rome presented in literary works to be actually a picture of England. Since both ancient Rome and early modern England were patriarchal social structures that legally considered women to be property—owned by their fathers until they married and by their husbands after—it is easy to see how Lucrece's behavior could, or should, suggest the correct behavior of an English wife.

English women were expected to remain virginal until marriage and to be "chaste" after marriage. This meant that they were to engage in sexual relations *only* with their husbands and behave at all times as though they *were* chaste. Such behavior meant they were to remain at home, enclosed and protected within the walls of their home. They were also to be virtually silent, speaking only when necessary and only on serious subjects. If their doors and mouths were *literally* closed, people—including their husbands—assumed that their vaginas were equally "closed." Chaste sexual behavior, therefore, was reinforced by chaste social behavior.

The Rape of Lucrece begins with Collatine, Tarquin, and their comrades camped outside Ardea, where they amuse themselves by bragging about their wives' beauty and chastity. Anxious to see whose boasts are true, they ride off to Rome to check on each wife. Not surprisingly, Lucrece is the only one engaged in chaste activity; she is sitting at home spinning with her servants. This discovery not only allows Collatine to win the competition but indicates how women were viewed in patriarchal society: as objects consistently in need of control. This scene also calls to mind the end of the poem after Lucrece's suicide. Her father and her husband each declare he suffers more grief. But in the course of this "grieving," they both dwell upon their "ownership" of Lucrece: one as the man who "gave her birth," the other as the man who "owned" her after marriage. According to their arguments, Lucrece does not "own" her own body. As a woman, she is denied a self (agency) in patriarchal society. The only power women retain is the power to kill themselves, and when they do that, their right is challenged by the men who own them.

The idea of male ownership of women permeates all patriarchal societies, and is the impetus for reading rape as a crime of power, not passion—and in premodern England, as a property crime too. Thus, even a man who does not have legal ownership of Lucrece—Tarquin—feels that he can rape her with impunity. Despite the rhetoric of *Lucrece,* which seems to indicate that Tarquin raped Lucrece because her beauty and chastity inflamed his lust, in truth, he rapes her simply because he can. Moreover, by raping Lucrece, Tarquin not only proves his (physical) male dominance over her but also demonstrates his (social/political) power over Collatine.

Her rape places Lucrece in a strange social position. She knows that her society equates her chastity with Collatine's and their family's honor. If she is "stained" by Tarquin's rape, she equally stains her husband's honor. Motivated by this, she would rather die than dishonor her family, yet Tarquin has devised a way to make her live with her shame. He threatens to kill her and then an innocent servant whom he will place in bed with her, swearing to her husband that he found the two engaged in sexual intercourse. This is an ingenious and ironic plan: If Lucrece is raped, the violation stains Collatine's honor; if she has voluntarily slept with a servant, the act primarily stains *her* honor. Interestingly, Lucrece does not consider that her husband might believe in the chastity that he has so proudly boasted about—and proved—to his friends. This bizarre situation regarding women in patriarchal Roman society damns them not only if they are really sexually loose, but also if a man says they are. Lucrece reflects on this when she ponders that, even though she did not consent to Tarquin's attack, she still feels "stained" by it. Granted that women do feel "dirtied" by the physicality of rape, Lucrece is obsessed by the metaphorical "stain" upon her honor—and Collatine's. The only way she can remove the stain is to get her husband to agree to avenge their honor and then kill herself, the physical representation of dishonor, even though she never consented to the dishonorable event. Literally and socially, then, a totally chaste woman is a totally dead one.

Shakespeare uses the colors red, white, and black as images to describe Lucrece's and Tarquin's physical and emotional states. Red and white allude to the early modern period's standard of female beauty: pale white complexion and red lips and cheeks. Gems like rubies and coral could double for the red color, while silver, ivory, alabaster, and pearl for the white. Hair was gold, and the truly beautiful and virtuous woman seemed to actually shine. As the scholar Nancy Vickers points out, Shakespeare uses a BLAZON when describing Lucrece's beauty. The blazon was a figure that was used to describe the device on a hero's shield. Shakespeare describes Lucrece using this figure as though she were an object, the shield with which to defend her virtue against Tarquin's attack.

As the attacker, Tarquin is described as dark and black (evil), the opposite of the light and white (pure) Lucrece. It is important to remember that, during the early modern period, devils were perceived to be black. The normal arrangement of red and white on Lucrece's face would confine the red to her lips and cheeks and the white to the rest of her complexion. Yet in the course of her negotiations with her rapist, the act itself, and her subsequent behavior, the colors exceed their normal bounds and her face becomes completely white with fear or red with shame. The color coding appears even as Tarquin uncovers Lucrece's body just prior to the rape. In addition to commenting on her face, he looks at her white breasts, like globes, with blue veins running around them like rivers. Here begins the metaphor of Lucrece's body as a land newly discovered by Tarquin, soon to be its conqueror. The woman is again an object, one that is designed to be conquered by men, just as the NEW WORLD was being explored and conquered by England. Tarquin's hand on Lucrece's breast is a sign of the power of his conquest of her body as though it were a new piece of real estate. This idea of conquest reinforces how the Tarquins came to power in Rome and acts as a precursor to how they lost power.

While waiting for her husband to return to Rome, Lucrece meditates on a picture of the fall of Troy, which serves to call attention to both her rape and the forthcoming change in Roman government. The Trojan War began because Paris, a son of Priam, king of Troy, "raped" Helen, wife of Menelaus, king of Sparta. In this sense, rape means "carried off." The kings of the Grecian city-states supported Menelaus in his war to regain Helen, and many died on both sides. The Greeks won by using a wooden horse to enter Troy and burning the city to the ground. According to Roman myth—recounted by Virgil in The Aeneid—the Trojan prince

Aeneas escaped the burning city and eventually founded Rome. Thus, Helen's "rape" foreshadowed the founding of Rome itself, while Lucrece's rape foreshadows the expulsion of the tyrant Tarquin and the founding of the Roman Republic. Perhaps not as many will die in this endeavor as did in the Trojan War, but Lucrece presciently connects herself with Helen as a "cause," while rejecting any connection between herself and the "strumpet" Helen. While Tarquin claimed a new land in Lucrece's body, that very body will be used to claim a new body politic in the Roman republic to come.

Lucrece is also concerned with other possible consequences of her rape, especially how to protect her husband's honor as regards any children she has or might have. According to early modern law, any child born to a woman while she was married was legally her husband's child. If Lucrece became pregnant by Tarquin, people would scorn Collatine for raising his wife's rapist's child as his own. And if Lucrece were in the early stages of pregnancy before the rape—or became pregnant by her husband after the rape—people would still believe the child to be Tarquin's, thus again compromising her husband's honor. The paternity of any existing children would also be suspect: If Lucrece were raped by Tarquin, she may have been raped earlier by someone else, a standard perception for a culture that saw women as basically dishonorable and lustful.

Suicide was an honorable way for Romans to end their lives or protect their honor. Thus, even though Collatine and Lucretius, her father, mourn Lucrece's death, they laud her for protecting their collective honor in the ultimate way. Despite the Rome-England connection in this poem, suicide in early modern England was not viewed in the same way; it was a major sin. Indeed, those who committed it were guilty of the cardinal sin of despair. Similarly, the Christian view held Lucrece sinless—blameless—for the rape, although socially she was condemned. By Roman law, she was guilty because she invited Tarquin in.

Thus, some sort of stain can be perceived in Lucrece. After her death, when her blood pours out of her body, it separates into the red of true blood and the black matter of a stain, finally leaving her now-bloodless body chaste. Thus, the last red and white dichotomy in *The Rape of Lucrece* is the red of her honorable blood contrasted to the white of her bloodless and chaste body.

FURTHER READING

Augustine, St. *The City of God.* Translated by D. Knowles. Harmondsworth, U.K.: Penguin, 1972.

Donaldson, Ian. *The Rapes of Lucretia: A Myth and Its Transformations.* Oxford: Oxford University Press, 1982.

Dubrow, Heather. *Captive Victors: Shakespeare's Narrative Poems and Sonnets.* Ithaca, N.Y.: Cornell University Press, 1987.

Hendricks, Margo. "'A Word, Sweet Lucrece': Confession, Feminism, and *The Rape of Lucrece.*" In *A Feminist Companion to Shakespeare,* edited by Dympna Callaghan, 103–118. Oxford: Blackwell, 2003.

Jed, Stephanie. *Chaste Thinking: The Rape of Lucretia and the Birth of Humanism.* Bloomington: Indiana University Press, 1989.

Kahn, Coppelia. "Publishing Shame: *The Rape of Lucrece.*" In *A Companion to Shakespeare's Works. Volume IV: The Poems, Problem Comedies, and Late Plays,* edited by Richard Dutton and Jean E. Howard, 259–274. Oxford: Blackwell, 2003.

———. "The Rape in Shakespeare's *Lucrece.*" *Shakespeare Studies* 9 (1976): 45–72.

MacDonald, Joyce Green. "Speech, Silence, and History in *The Rape of Lucrece.*" *Shakespeare Studies* 22 (1994): 77–103.

Shakespeare, William. *The Rape of Lucrece.* In *The Norton Shakespeare,* edited by Stephen Greenblatt, et al., 635–682. New York and London: W.W. Norton, 1997.

Stallybrass, Peter. "Patriarchal Territories: The Body Enclosed." In *Rewriting the Renaissance: The Discourses of Sexual Difference in Early Modern Europe,* edited by Margaret W. Ferguson, Maureen Quilligan, and Nancy Vickers, 123–142. Chicago: University of Chicago Press, 1986..

Theodora A. Jankowski

"REEVE'S TALE, THE" GEOFFREY CHAUCER (ca. 1390)

"The Reeve's Tale" appears in the first fragment (or group A) of "*The CANTERBURY TALES,*" after the General Prologue, "The Knight's Tale," and "THE MILLER'S PROLOGUE AND TALE." It is followed by the extremely short, and obviously incomplete, Cook's Tale. This first group forms a tightly knit unit, in which the various tellers respond to each other, under the attempted orchestration of Harry Bailly, the Host. In the GENERAL PROLOGUE TO THE CANTERBURY TALES, the Reeve and the Miller, as is socially appropriate, are to be found in the last group, together with the Summoner, the Pardoner, the Manciple, and Chaucer the Narrator. As the Miller disrupts the orderly, class-based sequence of narrations suggested by the Host by intervening directly after the Knight, so does the Reeve speak deliberately after the Miller, and his motives in doing so are made clear in his long Prologue.

Here the Reeve (a word indicating the Steward of a manor), a man of choleric disposition and one of the less likeable among Chaucer's pilgrims, laments the infirmities associated with old age and reveals his animus against the drunken and overbearing Miller, who has spoken before him and has allegedly offended him. His harangue is rudely interrupted by the Host, who reminds him that "The devel made a reve for to preche" (l. 3903) and urges him to begin his story. The tale proper begins, and it is clear from the start that it is conceived as a riposte to the Miller, since the Reeve fancies himself parodied in the portrait of the old and gullible carpenter in the previous tale.

The narrative is set at Trumpington, near Cambridge. Symkyn, a grasping and bold miller, lives there, and he is equally in love with money and with his (mostly imagined) social position. The long description of this character emphasizes his apelike face and body, his boastful bearing, the excessive weaponry he always wears, his outrageous thievery, and his family pride. He fancies himself well-connected since his wife is the illegitimate daughter of the parson, and the two of them project their ambitions on their 20-year-old daughter, Malyne (whose quick physical description marks her as far from the conventional beauty of the type), and on their small baby, who, though only six months old, is already "a propre page" (l. 3972).

Having been sent by the master of their college to have their corn ground, Aleyn and John, two poor scholars of Cambridge, visit the mill. While the miller foresees another opportunity to steal on the correct measure of flour, the two scholars are fatuously certain that they will not be cheated, as they think their learning far outshines the miller's native ingenuity. They are determined to watch the miller's every move, but he proves more than a match for them: Not only does he steal their flour and give it to his wife to knead into a cake, but he also makes their horse bolt, forcing them into an undignified scramble across the fields to recapture the animal; thus the miller proves that "The gretteste clerkes been noght wisest men" (l. 4054).

By the time the scholars manage to detach their horse from its company of wild mares, night has fallen and they are forced to ask for Symkyn's hospitality. The provisions and ale they send for become the occasion for an impromptu feast at which both the Miller and his wife get drunk, and when they all go to bed (in the same room, as was the custom), the two older people's (and their daughter's) snores are a sonorous accompaniment to the scholars' rueful nightly meditations. But they also provide the cover under which the two students undertake their revenge by "swyving"— that is, having sex with, the Miller's wife and daughter. First, Aleyn slips quietly into Malyne's bed and rapes her before she has a chance to cry out; then John, shamed by his friend's boldness, moves the cot where the baby sleeps from the proximity of the parents' bed to his own, so that when the miller's wife has to get up, she mistakes the bed in the pitch-dark room and ends in John's arms, enjoying his enthusiastic lovemaking in the drunken conviction that it is her husband's.

Dawn arrives, and the denouement begins with a mock AUBAUDE: Malyne's tearful adieus to her "lemman" ("sweetheart," l. 4240), who in his turn swears, "I is thyn awen clerk" (l. 4239). This is soon forgotten, however, as Aleyn, equally tricked by the displaced cot, enters the miller's bed and boasts of his success. The uproar caused by the miller's discovery of his daughter's undoing causes a furious fight with Aleyn, which is abruptly ended when the wife, persevering in her mistake, deals her husband a stunning blow. With dishonor upon both women and the recapture of the stolen flour, the students' revenge is completed, and they can go back to Cambridge victorious.

"The Reeve's Tale" is a FABLIAU, a short, comic, and scurrilous tale in verse, generally dealing with low-born characters, set in the present or in a not-too-distant past, so as to make the setting and characters (however generic or stereotyped) immediately recognizable to the audience. Born of the Reeve's bitter desire for revenge, however, this tale is less light and humorous than its companion piece, "The Miller's Tale," and the fate it metes out to innocent characters such as the miller's daughter helps us understand the fabliau's darker side. Yet the comedy is far from sacrificed, and the tightly constructed plot turns the final scene into a triumph of slapstick comedy, a farce of clock-like inevitability. Faithful to the spirit of the genre, Chaucer does not pass judgement on any of his characters, nor do any of the pilgrims comment on the scholars' outrageous revenge. However, Chaucer avoids the transformation of the comedy into mechanical farce and the representation of the miller and his rival as mere puppets by preserving the individuality of each character, giving most of them a name, often unforgettable physical traits (such as the "camuse nose" marking the kinship between the miller and his daughter), and a distinctive personality, while these characteristics preserve evident links with the types of the genre tradition.

Critical attention to "The Reeve's Tale" has tended to focus on individual characters, as they are distinctive enough to warrant in-depth analysis and may suggest literary analogues and echoes beyond the fabliau tradition. The miller, for instance, has suggested analogies with Simon the Magician as represented in Dante's *Inferno*; he has also evoked outright analogies with the devil or, given his name and simian appearance, with the ape. The two students, with their association with one of the most famous and ancient universities in Europe, have prompted analyses of their role in medieval scholarly tradition, suggesting derivations from Richard de Bury's *Philobiblon* (1473) or other conventional treatises on scholarly life. More generally, biblical analogies are suggested by the Reeve's declaration, in his Prologue, that his rival the Miller "kan wel in myn eye seen a stalke, But in his owene he kan nat seen a balke [beam]" (ll. 3919–20), and recent studies have used the biblical analogy as a possible interpretative key for the tale. Some attention has also been dedicated to the animal imagery in the tale, and to its associations with allegorical images of pride, wrath, and lust.

A number of parallels in French, Italian, German, and Flemish literature have been identified for this tale, and a number of studies have concentrated on its relation to its sources and analogues. The most important are two anonymous French fabliaux, *Le Meunier et les II Clers* and *De Gombert et des II clers,* and GIOVANNI BOCCACCIO's *Decameron* Book 9, Tale 6, along with another Italian novella and two German tales. In all cases, the plot is substantially the same, especially in regard to the bed trick, although the characters' social status and the motivations differ. This might make the reader think that Chaucer's tale is too constrained by the tradition to which it belongs, but "The Reeve's Tale" demonstrates the poet's ability in handling and renovating traditional material. It is also unique in the "bed-trick" tradition in its almost complete absence of romantic overtones. This motif, in which two characters unknowingly have sex with each other because of mistaken identity, was particularly popular in fabliaux. The mock aubade concluding Malyne's and Aleyn's "night of love" is also unique to Chaucer's text.

Another aspect that has attracted critical attention is Chaucer's use of dialect, as he offers the first extensive representation of a dialect in English literature. Critical studies have lately focused on linguistic details in an attempt to pinpoint the exact dialect Chaucer used and his accuracy in reproducing it.

More recently, the use of space in the tale's final scene—a use anticipated by the miller's ironic consideration that the scholars may consider themselves welcome in his house, since, though it is narrow, they can "by argumentes make a place/A mile brood of twenty foot of space" (ll. 4123–24)—has triggered critical discussion on the use of space and place in the tale, and on the concept of sight and its association with knowledge. It has also helped to put the miller's pride in a new perspective, linking it with his "greet sokene" (l. 3987)—that is, his monopoly on grain-grinding and his dreams of his great estate, which he wants to enlarge through marital alliances, thus effectively founding an imaginary dynasty. The ambition of this character is thus not simply a comical trait predetermining his downfall, but a marker of social unrest. Chaucer may also have hidden in his description of the miller's pride a satirical note against holy orders and the abuse of church privilege. For instance, the parson in the Tale diverts church goods for his own use. At the same time, the rivalry between the miller and the scholars has been reassessed in terms of a competition between university and country wits, transcending the usual class war inherent in fabliaux to suggest how the expansion of the universities in the 14th century might create new social problems. The expansion challenged the traditionally established class structure by inserting a new order, that of the clerks, who, while conscious of their intellectual superiority and their financial disadvantages, were made aggressive and perhaps violent by the uncertainty of their status.

Finally, feminist scholarship has investigated the "comic" treatment of rape and deception within the tale, focusing primarily on the "no really means yes" aspect of Malyne's and Aleyn's sexual encounter. Another avenue of investigation involves the use of innocent women to punish men.

FURTHER READING

Friedman, John B. "A Reading of Chaucer's Reeve's Tale." *The Chaucer Review* 2 (1967): 8–19.

Greentree, Rosemary, and T. L. Burton, eds. *Chaucer's Miller's, Reeve's, and Cook's Tales: An Annotated Bibliography 1900 to 1992.* Toronto: University of Toronto Press, 1997.

Yager, Susan. "'A Whit Thyng in Hir Ye': Perception and Error in the *Reeve's Tale.*" *The Chaucer Review* 28 (1994): 393–404.

Alessandra Petrina

REFRAIN In poetry, a refrain is a word, phrase, or complete line of verse repeated at the end of each STANZA. The refrain usually refers to the main topic or theme, but occasionally it comprises nonsensical "filler" words (e.g., "tra la la"). It is often used in poems related to musical compositions, such as CAROLS or folk BALLADS.

See also BURDEN.

RENAISSANCE See EARLY MODERN V. RENAISSANCE.

REVERDIE From the French *reverdir,* meaning "to become green again," reverdie is a genre that thematizes the arrival of spring and all of the emotive associations that accompany the end of winter, especially love and gaiety. It emerged out of troubadour songs that often began by evoking springtime (the "springtime opening"). The genre is often marked by narrativity—for example, in an idyllic setting the singer meets a young woman on his path, and after describing her, he engages her in conversation. Reverdie became popular during the course of the 13th and 14th centuries in England. Examples include "SUMER IS ICUMEN IN" and "LENTEN YS COME WITH LOVE TO TOUNE."

See also MIDDLE ENGLISH LYRICS AND BALLADS.

FURTHER READING

Greentree, Rosemary. *The Middle English Lyric and Short Poem*. Cambridge and Rochester, N.Y.: D.S. Brewer, 2001.

Daniel O'Sullivan

REYNARD LITERATURE

The origins of the story of the wily, rebellious, and usually badly behaved fox name Reynard, also known as Renart and Renard, have long been in dispute. Like much of medieval literature, stories about Reynard are often seen as either the result of long folkloric tradition or written works composed in a particular time and place with influences from other traditions. For Reynard literature, similar stories can be found in the Indian *Panchatantra* and the Arabic *Kalila wa Dimna*, both of which predate the fox's appearance in European literature. The *Ysengrimus*, a Latin verse epic, was written in Flanders around 1150, with its eponymous hero being the wolf, who is beleaguered by a crafty fox. In the 1170s, Pierre de Saint Cloud penned the earliest French tales centered on Renart the fox, and the tales became so popular that the word *renart* eclipsed the Old French word *goupil* for fox.

Much of Reynard's popularity can be attributed to the undoubtedly funny and yet deeply ironic situations in which the fox finds himself. For instance, the COURTLY LOVE triangle among Reynard, the wolf, and the wolf's wife is a satiric send-up of literature of the period, while Reynard's participation in a crusade has profound political importance for a society embroiled in conflict. Because of their animal status, Reynard and his friends allowed authors to poke fun at existing social conventions and structures, cloaking their meaning behind the "innocent" BEAST FABLES.

Tales of Reynard's escapades flourished in Germany, Flanders, and France, and spread to England, written in ANGLO-NORMAN French. MARIE DE FRANCE's 12th-century *Fables* contain a story taken from the Reynard cycle, telling of a rooster who outwits a fox. GEOFFREY CHAUCER reworks and expands this FABLE in "The NUN'S PRIEST'S TALE." Reynard stories were retold into the early modern era in England, as well, including the WILLIAM CAXTON version of the cycle published in 1485, and some scholars have postulated connections to the ROBIN HOOD BALLADS.

FURTHER READING

Blake, Norman F. "English Versions of Reynard the Fox in the Fifteenth and Sixteenth Centuries." *Studies in Philology* 62 (1965): 63–77.

Varty, Kenneth. *Reynard, Renart, Reinaert, and Other Foxes in Medieval England: The Iconographic Evidence*. Amsterdam: Amsterdam University Press, 1999.

Lynn Ramey

RHYME ROYAL (CHAUCERIAN STANZA, TROILUS STANZA)

This STANZA form consists of seven lines of 10 syllables each, or pentameters, with a rhyme scheme of *ababbcc*. GEOFFREY CHAUCER was one of the first to use rhyme royal in "Complaint unto Pity," *The PARLIAMENT OF FOWLS*, and *Troilus and Criseyde*. In *The CANTERBURY TALES*, he used rhyme royal for "The MAN OF LAW'S TALE," "The Clerk's Tale, "The PRIORESS'S TALE," and "The Second Nun's Tale," all of which focus on the suffering of a virtuous Christian. Because Chaucer was the first to use rhyme royal in English, it is sometimes, albeit rarely, called the Chaucerian stanza or the Troilus Stanza because of *Troilus and Criseyde*. The form remained popular in the 15th and 16th centuries and was used by WILLIAM DUNBAR, ROBERT HENRYSON, WILLIAM SHAKESPEARE, EDMUND SPENSER, and SIR THOMAS WYATT. Whereas it had been thought that rhyme royal took its name from the fact that JAMES VI/I used it in *The KINGIS QUAIR*, it has also been suggested that the name derives from the term *ballad royal*, which was used to denote the same verse form in the 14th century.

FURTHER READING

Stevens, Martin. "The Royal Stanza in Early English Literature." *PMLA* 94 (1979): 67–76.

Michael Foster

RIDDLES See ANGLO-SAXON RIDDLES.

RIME COUÉE (TAIL RHYME) *Rime couée,* or tail rhyme, is a type of STANZA where rhyming short lines are separated by one or more longer lines. Early forms are prevalent in satirical verse. In the Middle Ages, however, it was commonly used for ROMANCES, such as *SIR LAUNFAL, Emaré,* and *Sir Cleges.*

FURTHER READING

Freeman-Regalado, Nancy. *Poetic Patterns in Rutebeuf.* New Haven, Conn., and London: Yale University Press, 1970.

Daniel O'Sullivan

"ROBENE AND MAKYNE" ROBERT HENRYSON (ca. 1470) Together with much of ROBERT HENRYSON's work, "Robene and Makyne" is preserved in the Bannatyne manuscript now in the National Library of Scotland. No source is known for this poem, though it contains allusions to French and Scottish BALLADS. It is a clear parody of courtly ROMANCE and also, perhaps, of other modes of poetry, such as the ELEGY and the CARPE DIEM genre. The names of the two title characters are typical of literary shepherds and country girls, though in the latter case a bawdy overtone may be intended.

Robene, a young shepherd, sits on a hill tending his flock; Makyne comes to him confessing her love in passionate tones, but she is rudely rejected, as the shepherd knows nothing of love. Makyne tries to teach him, offering him both her heart and her maidenhood, but to no avail; Robene is only concerned with the well-being of his flock and even suggests that Makyne might come back on the next day, as now his sheep seem disposed to wander. The spirited dialogue between the two occupies more than half the poem, evoking and parodying images familiar to COURTLY LOVE literature and contrasting Makyne's high-flown aspirations with Robene's earthly concerns. The latter concludes this first part of the poem by going abruptly away and leaving Makyne to her lament, but as he gathers his sheep, he feels Makyne's malady assailing him; this time it is his turn to go to the girl and plead. But the man who does not want when he may, shall have nothing when he wants: This is Makyne's bitter retort, and the moral meaning of the poem, as this second, symmetrical debate of love concludes with a grieving shepherd sighing with his flock under the hillside.

The poem belongs to the late medieval genre of the PASTOURELLE—that is, a PASTORAL lyric that here takes the form of a lovers' debate. Unlike the French instances of the genre, its characters are all lowly born (there is no knight or clerk pleading with a shepherdess for love) and the setting unequivocally realistic. Part of the comedy resides in the reversal of roles, but we should also underline the contrast between the homely characters and their everyday occupation as well as the courtly tone Makyne would like to establish. This effect is obtained through very simple means: Robene contrasts Makyne's pleading with a very healthy concern for the well-being of his flock and never forgets his duty, whether he is tempted by Makyne's offers or consumed by love himself.

It is difficult to find a place for this poem within the Henryson canon, as its light, comic tone and sheer readability contrast with the serious, occasionally moralistic tone employed by him elsewhere. But typical of Henryson is the creative transformation of an established tradition and the insight he gives us into human nature as he turns his characters from simple rustic children to knowledgeable adults, thanks to no external influence but simply to the power of love. Such a transformation is highlighted by the language used by the two characters in their debates; in particular, Makyne surprises the reader for the psychological subtlety of her portrait, while her speech, didactic and impassionate, prevents her falling into the stereotype of the mannered shepherdess and makes her plastic and vibrant—one of the memorable female characters created by this unexpectedly modern poet.

FURTHER READING

Cornelius, Michael G. "Robert Henryson's Pastoral Burlesque 'Robene and Makyne' (1470)." *Fifteenth-Century Studies* 28 (2003): 80–96.

Greentree, Rosemary. "Literate in Love: Makyne's Lesson for Robene." In *Older Scots Literature,* edited by Sally Mapstone, 61–69. Edinburgh: John Donald, 2005.

Petrina, Alessandra. "Deviations from Genre in Robert Henryson's *Robene and Makyne.*" *Studies in Scottish Literature* 31 (1999): 107–120.

Alessandra Petrina

ROBERT I THE BRUCE (1274–1329) *king of Scotland*

Robert the Bruce—later Robert I, king of Scotland—was the son of Robert de Brus (d. 1304), the sixth lord of Annandale, and Marjory, countess of Carrick (d. 1290). He was born on July 11, 1274, at Turnberry Castle in Ayrshire. JOHN BARBOUR's poem *The BRUCE* (1375) provides one version of Robert the Bruce's story.

The Bruce family laid claim to the Scottish throne through its relation to David I of Scotland, but their claim was rejected in 1292. Robert then sought to make himself more appealing by aligning himself with WILLIAM WALLACE in the Rebellion of 1297, and by identifying himself with Scottish independence.

On March 25, 1306, Robert seized the Scottish throne. After England's Edward I died on July 7, 1307, Robert began the reclamation of Scotland, including waging a civil war against opposing Scottish nobles, and consolidated his power. On June 23–24, 1314, Scottish forces met and defeated English forces under Edward II at Bannockburn, though Edward II escaped. Bruce continued raiding in the north of England until 1328, when Edward II recognized Scotland as independent in the Treaty of Edinburgh.

FURTHER READING

Barrow, G. W. S. *Robert Bruce and the Community of the Realm of Scotland.* 3rd ed. Edinburgh: Edinburgh University Press, 1988.

Mackenzie, Agnes Mure. *Robert Bruce, King of Scots.* 1934. Reprint, Edinburgh: Oliver/Boyd, 1956.

Scott, Ranald McNair. *Robert Bruce, King of Scots.* London: Hutchinson, 1982.

Mark DiCicco

ROBIN HOOD BALLADS

A distinct subgenre of the outlaw tale, the Robin Hood ballads trace their roots back to the Middle Ages. As with many BALLADS, they were told or sung many years before being recorded beginning in the 15th century. The first reference to them in English literature is found in WILLIAM LANGLAND's *PIERS PLOWMAN,* where Sloth, who cannot remember his paternoster (Our Father), can easily recall the "rymes of Robyn hood" (B-text, Passus 5, l. 402). Another sermon from the same time period admonishes people in a similar fashion.

Through the tales were popular, the Robin Hood of these early medieval ballads is not the Robin Hood of today. He is not concerned with social justice; he is concerned with self-preservation, mockery of others, and self-gratification. He is also violent and selfish. He fled into the forest because he killed the king's foresters, not because he was cheated of his legacy. He is also not egalitarian: His men kneel to him. The medieval Robin is neither a peasant fighting for rights nor a displaced noble—he is a yeoman (a farmer who owns his own farm). In a number of the ballads, Robin is set against the church, and by the 16th century, the "steal from the rich, give to the poor" theme began to emerge as Robin steals from abbots and distributes the gains. The name became associated with treason, and in 1605, Guy Fawkes and his conspirators were branded "Robin Hoods" by Robert Cecil.

See also "BIRTH OF ROBIN HOOD, THE"; *GEST OF ROBYN HODE, A;* "ROBIN HOOD'S DEATH AND BURIAL"; *TALE OF GAMELYN, THE.*

FURTHER READING

Knight, Stephen, ed. *Robin Hood: An Anthology of Scholarship and Criticism.* Cambridge: Brewer, 1999.

———. *Robin Hood: A Complete Study of the English Outlaw.* Oxford and Cambridge, Mass.: Blackwell, 1994.

Knight, Stephen, and Thomas Ohlgren, eds. *Robin Hood and Other Outlaw Tales.* Kalamazoo, Mich.: Medieval Institute Publications, 1997.

Ohlgren, Thomas H. "Teaching Robin Hood at the University: A Practical Guide." In *Robin Hood: The Many Faces of that Celebrated English Outlaw,* edited by Kevin Carpenter, 145–154. Oldenburg, Germany: Bibliotheks-und Informationssystem der Universität Oldenburg, 1995.

"ROBIN HOOD'S DEATH AND BURIAL" ("THE DEATH OF ROBIN HOOD," "ROBIN HOOD'S DEATH") ANONYMOUS (15th century)

This later BALLAD is sometimes referred to as "The Death of Robin Hood" or simply "Robin Hood's Death." While neither of the two surviving manuscripts date to the Middle Ages, the content of the poem resembles such early ROBIN HOOD BALLADS as *A GEST OF ROBYN HODE,* and most scholars accept a medieval composition date. The surviving texts differ slightly, leading some early editors to present both versions; however, most scholars today agree that combining the two is most warranted.

In this version, Robin, feeling ill during a shooting match with Little John, decides to visit his cousin, a prioress at Kirklees Abbey, so she can bleed him. Both John and Will Scarlet advise against this, but Robin insists. During the procedure, Robin notices that his blood, which was thick at first, is quickly thinning. Realizing he has been betrayed, Robin blows three horn blasts, calling on John for assistance. John arrives, but before Robin can escape, Red Roger, a ruffian, stabs him. Using the last of his strength, Robin manages to behead Red Roger. He asks Little John to hear his confession and then shoots an arrow out the window, requesting burial wherever it lands. His wish is carried out.

Recent scholarly discussion has examined the relevance of the prioress as the agent of Robin's death and the anticlerical ramifications thereof. Others have looked into the connections between Robin Hood and the unnamed outlaw in *The Hermit and the Outlaw,* both of whom suffered similar fates.

FURTHER READING

"The Death of Robin Hood." In *Robin Hood and Other Outlaw Tales,* edited by Stephen Knight and Thomas Ohlgren, 592–601. Kalamazoo, Mich.: Medieval Institute Publications, 1997.

Hepworth, David. "A Grave Tale." In *Robin Hood: Medieval and Post-Medieval,* edited by Helen Philips, 91–112. Dublin: Four Courts Press, 2005.

Alexander L. Kaufman

ROMANCE As a genre, romance is notoriously difficult to define. Romances usually, but not invariably, feature a hero who embarks on a quest or seeks adventures to prove his chivalric values and discover his own identity. Generally, in order to accomplish these goals, the hero has to leave home, sometimes symbolized by the court. Often, the romance hero must fight dragons or oppose vicious giants; it has been suggested that almost all of the "identity romances" (for example, *Lybeaus Desconus, Guy of Warwick, BEVIS OF HAMPTON, Sir Degaré, KING HORN*) feature belligerent monsters which the hero has to quell. Instead of or as well as confronting a monster, the hero must sometimes submit to extraordinary tests before being able return home and live happily ever after (see, for example, Sir Gawain in *SIR GAWAIN AND THE GREEN KNIGHT*). The tests may be obstacles that have to be overcome in order for the hero to win the lady, although occasionally the hero is female, as in *Emaré.* The genre combines naturalistic touches with elements of the marvellous: romance geography is sometimes vague; and time is often unreal (though characters may age as in *SIR ORFEO*).

English romances may be divided into two groups: EPIC romance and lyric romance. Poems such as *The Siege of Thebes* and *The Siege of Troy* fall into the first category, being more realistic, historical, and martial. The second group includes poems such as *FLORIS AND BLAUNCHEFLUR.* These romances are more emotive and more concerned with love, faith, constancy, and the marvellous. The audience is privy to the hero's thoughts and feelings as he or she undertakes feats of arms. The hero has an inner consciousness, and very often he is in love. In the earlier French versions of the genre, these two types of romance came as successive waves, but in English these types coexisted. Even after collecting together characteristics that may be present in a prototypical romance text, medieval romance is still hard to pin down. The slipperiness of the genre means that the corpus of romance is not fixed. Some romances are centrally typical, containing a hero, a quest, and a happy ending, while others are categorized as romances simply because they seem closer to romance than to any other genre. Some romances seem to blur into history, while others appear to merge into epic: *The Siege of Troy* is a romance epic, but JOHN LYDGATE's *Troy-Book* is a straight epic. There are also didactic romances and hagiographies (see HAGIOGRAPHY) that resemble romances.

The earliest extant MIDDLE ENGLISH LANGUAGE romances are *King Horn* and *Floris and Blauncheflur,* both found in a single manuscript. Early Middle English romances (those written between 1280 and 1380) are somewhat homogenous, reflecting the same plot patterns, situations, and phrases; this probably relates to the social context of Middle English itself as a popular language. Romance was unquestionably medieval England's most popular genre. The number of surviving texts is unmatched by any other secular genre (there are more than 100 extant romances). The manuscript evidence shows the social and geographical diversity of the medieval audience of romance. Romances written in the 13th century continued to be copied into the 15th century, and the persistent demand for more and more romance meant that new texts were still being produced well into the early modern period. In the modern period, medieval romance has been credited with having been the originator of the novel and the ancestor of almost all contemporary popular fiction in print and on the screen.

Early criticism suggested that the readers of Middle English romances were primarily lower-class or lower-middle-class, an emergent bourgeoisie who wanted to hear narratives that they thought were the same as those that the aristocracy were enjoying in French, rendered in English. By the end of the 14th century, this audience became more sophisticated, partly through reading GEOFFREY CHAUCER's subtle and subversive versions of romances and *lais* (see LAY). Fifteenth-century romance was directed at a more sophisticated bourgeois audience that was conscious of social tone and criticism, such as in Sir Thomas Malory's prose work *Morte d'Arthur*. More recent scholarship argues that the meaning of the term *popular*, as attributed to Middle English romance by early critics of the genre, is largely negative in that it is used to denote a textual genre that was not courtly or aristocratic. Some argued that the romances read by the English aristocracy of the Middle Ages were predominantly in French, so all Middle English romances could be described as "popular." However, this raises the suspicion that "popular" and "courtly" are disguised value judgments.

There has been a great deal of scholarly debate about the kind of audience and the mode of composition and reception of these romances. One view suggests that romances in the Middle English period were the improvised compositions of minstrels. According to this argument, romances were recited orally at feasts and festivals and were intended "for the people" (hence the designation *popular romances*). The counterargument is that so-called popular romances were composed and copied for the amusement and edification of the newly literate classes. This does not mean the lower orders, but rather the minor gentry and the prosperous middle classes who formed the market for VERNACULAR books in the later medieval period.

The question of gender has dominated recent scholarship in romances. It has increasingly been recognized, for instance, that the courtly ideology voiced in romance texts did women little service. One clear indication of this is the preponderance of male heroes in Middle English romance, as the titles indicate: *Sir Gawain and the Green Knight, Sir Orfeo, Sir Isumbras, Sir Gowther, Amis and Amiloun, King Horn, Kyng Alisaunder, Sir Tristrem, Sir Degaré,* and so on. With very few exceptions, Middle English romance is a genre that deals almost exclusively with male concerns and puts male experience at the center of its universe. Women almost always play a secondary or supporting role: They are mothers, mothers-in-law, lovers, wives, and sisters. The genre itself, as indicated above, deals with young men and their passage into maturity, their emergence from a state of dependence on authoritative, parental figures into autonomy and independence.

It is nevertheless generally believed that women formed a large part of romance audiences at all levels of medieval society, and it has recently been argued that conventional interpretations of romance have been partial and male-centered. Critics have begun to try to reconstruct what may have been the experience of the women in the audience, offering a new, female-centered "implied reader." Such readings can, of course, adduce little conclusive historical evidence in their cause; even so, scholarship cannot dismiss audiences we know existed simply because they have left few traces and are therefore extremely difficult to access.

See also CHIVALRY, MIDDLE ENGLISH POETRY.

FURTHER READING

Brewer, Derek, ed. *Studies in Medieval English Romances: Some New Approaches.* Cambridge: D.S. Brewer, 1988.

Jewers, Caroline. *Chivalric Fiction and the History of the Novel.* Gainesville: University Press of Florida, 2000.

McDonald, Nicola. *Pulp Fictions of Medieval England: Essays in Popular Romance.* Manchester, U.K.: Manchester University Press, 2004.

Putter, Ad, and Jane Gilbert, eds. *The Spirit of Medieval English Popular Romance.* Harlow, U.K.: Pearson Education, 2000.

Louise Sylvester

ROMAN DE BRUT (*GESTE DES BRET-ONS*) WACE (1155)

This poem by the ANGLO-NOR-MAN poet WACE consists of 14,866 lines in rhymed octosyllabic COUPLETS written in VERNACULAR French. Probably begun in 1150, it was completed in 1155, when it was dedicated to Eleanor of Aquitaine (1122–1204). It is also sometimes known by the alternative title, *Geste des Bretons* (Song of the Britons), and as its author's most popular work, it survives in 22 manuscripts. Most likely its intended audience was an Anglo-Norman one, curious about the history and legends of the British territories. The *Roman de Brut* itself is largely an adaptation of the *Historia Regum Britanniae* (History of the Kings of Britain) of Geoffrey of Monmouth (1135–38), and in it, Wace gives particular emphasis to the ARTHURIAN LITERATURE derived from Geoffrey's prose narrative. As Wace was a scholarly and unusually critical poet, his decision to amplify his source's recounting of King ARTHUR's legendary court contributed significantly to the development of the *matière de Bretagne,* or "matters of Britain," as a subject for poetry in succeeding generations of authors and ROMANCEs. Wace's compositional mode of detailed matter-of-factness also proved to be influential. The *Roman de Brut* is also significant in the development of the Arthurian legends. It contains the first mention of Arthur's Round Table and is the first source to name Arthur's sword Excalibur. Apart from its role in introducing Arthur to French vernacular literature, the poem's other important contribution is to credit Arthur and his court with a highly developed code of CHIVALRY. Wace describes the splendor and refinement of Arthur's realm, likening him to Charlemagne, who presided over a golden age in British history.

The *Roman de Brut* begins with the founding of Britain by the Trojan warrior Brutus, a companion of the Trojan hero Aeneas. The story then follows the chronology of factual and legendary circumstances of British history, and for the most part Wace adheres to the chain of events sketched by his predecessors. He also recalls the lives of both mythical and historical figures such as the following: Corineus (companion of Brutus and founder of Cornwall), "Old King Cole" (Coel Hen, a Welsh king who ruled during the Roman withdrawal, ca. 350–420 C.E.), Cymbeline (king of Britain, thought to have reigned during the first century C.E.), Leir (a pre-Christian warrior king who became WILLIAM SHAKESPEARE's "Lear"), Cassibelanus (or Cassivellaunus, historical king of the Britons who led the defense against Julius Caesar's second invasion in 54 B.C.E.), Caradocus (titular king of the Britons in the absence of Emperor Magnus Maximus, who had left to campaign in Gaul), Aurelius Ambrosius (victorious war leader against the Saxons and supposed builder of Stonehenge and uncle of King Arthur), Uther Pendragon (supposed father of King Arthur), and Cadwallader (last Welsh king to wear the crown of Britain and the leader of the Celtic resistance against the Saxons). In each portrait, Wace imbues the story with a sense of vitality and drama. For example, in Corineus's story, beyond describing the legendary founding of Cornwall, Wace gives special attention to a fatal wrestling match between Corineus and the giant Gogmagog. Similarly, in almost every case where Wace differs significantly from his sources, he does so either to dwell on details capable of contributing to the emotional intensity of his tale or to dwell on those in which he evidently took a special interest. Among the latter are such details as the derivation of place-names, the description of nautical practices, and all manner of entertainment, especially music.

More important, however, it was Wace's skill in interpreting the meaning of events as rooted deeply in their human participants that gives his writing its special quality. For instance, early in the poem he reminds the audience that Julius Caesar's invasion of Britain succeeded because of a dispute between Cassibelanus and his nephews. Later, Wace's exploration of the complex motives and responses of those characters inhabiting King Arthur's Britain is particularly seen. Far more than in Geoffrey's recounting of Arthur's downfall, Wace locates the source of decay in Arthur's idealized world within the moral turpitude of Arthur's nephew Mordred and his corruption of Guinevere. Apart from its many other innovations, it was this capacity to infuse the deeds of these figures with plausible motives that earned Wace's *Roman de Brut* a place as a transitional text between the fragmentary retellings of British legends and the highly developed Arthurian romances of succeeding centuries.

FURTHER READING

Weiss, Judith, ed. *Wace's* Roman de Brut: A History of the British. *Text and Translation.* Exeter: University of Exeter Press, 2002.

J. D. Ballam

ROUNDEL (RONDEAU)

A short type of lyric composition, initially developed in France, that grew in popularity from the 13th to the 16th centuries with the BALLADE and the VIRELAI. The seven- or eight-line form is built upon a REFRAIN sung at the outset and close of the song. The first line of the refrain is then taken up in the fourth verse.

The form evolved considerably over time, growing to encompass 12 and 15 line versions. In English language poetry, the form is composed typically of 13 lines of eight syllables, also over three STANZAS, rhyming either *a* or *b*, plus two shorter refrains, rhyming *c*. In GEOFFREY CHAUCER's *PARLIAMENT OF FOWLES,* for example, the birds sing an interlaced roundel with their mates at Nature's departure.

FURTHER READING

Butterfield, Ardis. *Poetry and Music in Medieval France: From Jean Renart to Guillaume de Machaut.* Cambridge: Cambridge University Press, 2002.

Daniel O'Sullivan

"RUIN, THE" ANONYMOUS (before 1072)

"The Ruin" appears in the EXETER BOOK, a late 10th-century manuscript, which is severely damaged in several places. Because of this, the existing text of "The Ruin" is difficult to read, with several missing lines.

The narrator of this ELEGY describes what he or she sees, an inexplicable and confusing ruined town or settlement whose builders were from a different time and culture. The speaker notes the unbarred gate and the unprotected town—a stronghold made vulnerable because its inhabitants, warriors "joyful-hearted and bright with gold" (l. 33), are all dead, probably due to some pestilence, and there remains no one who can repair or rebuild the "mutilated" towers and walls.

The text reveals Anglo-Saxon attitudes toward loss, helplessness, and loneliness. Echoing other elegies, particularly "THE WANDERER," the narrator of "The Ruin" notes the emptiness of a former mead hall, once filled with sound and celebration, but now quiet because of WYRD, or fate (ll. 22–24). Mourning a community he or she cannot interpret, the speaker considers social and natural disasters while pondering the former inhabitants. Based on his or her own culture, the speaker assumes it must have been nature that destroyed this society. The potential for natural disaster (disease, bad weather, destruction of crops) and the threat of annihilation was frequently embodied in Anglo-Saxon literature as an attack by a physical force, such as the monster Grendel in *BEOWULF.*

Some readers assume the ruin being described in the poem is the Roman city of Aquae Sulis (now known as Bath), which was protected by an outer wall and contained bathhouses (*burnsele*), large temples, and great halls. Such a place might have been confusing to an Anglo-Saxon. If the city is Bath, then the poem may date as early as the mid-seventh century, when King Osric of the Hwicce occupied the area. The ruins would have been at least two centuries old and similar to those described in the poem.

Other scholars view the poem as an ALLEGORY of the destructive nature of fate. In either case, the ruins depicted in the poem and the narrator's comments evoke the fear of human and cultural annihilation through natural or other means.

FURTHER READING

Magennis, Hugh. *Images of Community in Old English Poetry.* Cambridge Studies in Anglo-Saxon England. Cambridge: Cambridge University Press, 1996.

Treharne, Elaine, ed. and trans. "The Ruin." In *Old and Middle English: An Anthology,* 84–87. Malden, Mass.: Blackwell, 2000.

Susannah Mary Chewning

RUNES   See FUTHARK ALPHABET.

RUTHWELL CROSS (ca. seventh century)

A large stone cross standing 17 feet, 4 inches tall, now housed in the town of Ruthwell (near Dumfries), Scotland, this artifact is highly significant to English history. Its intricately engraved faces feature biblical scenes as well as verse fragments in Latin. Most significantly, 156 lines of The DREAM OF THE ROOD, a DREAM VISION, appear on the east and west faces in the FUTHARK ALPHABET. Though evidence is scanty, most scholars believe the cross was constructed around 650–850 C.E.

See also BRUSSELS CROSS.

FURTHER READING

Cassidy, Brendan. *The Ruthwell Cross: Papers from a Colloquium Sponsored by the Index of Christian Art, Princeton University, 8 December 1989.* Princeton, N.J.: Princeton University Press, 1992.

Hilmo, Maide. *Medieval Images, Icons, and Illustrated English Literary Texts: From Ruthwell Cross to the Ellesmere Chaucer.* Burlington, Vt.: Ashgate, 2004.

S

SARACEN The word *Saracen* is an English adaptation of the Greek word *sarakenos* (easterner). It was used commonly in medieval and early modern British literature to refer to any non-Christian, non-Jewish person, usually from the Middle East but also possibly from North Africa or even Spain; *Arab* or *Muslim* are rough synonyms. The use of the term is usually pejorative and indicates an opponent of Christianity. It is seldom attached to actual cultural knowledge; instead, most literary depictions of Saracens involve simple behavioral stereotypes (treachery, greed, cowardice), either for comic effect or as part pro-Christian propaganda.

Saracens are almost always simple villains in ROMANCES, where for the most part Christianity triumphs, and they either die or are converted. However, there are exceptions to this ethnocentrism. For instance, in the Charlemagne romance *The SULTAN OF BABYLONE* (ca. 1450), the Saracens are more multifaceted and thoughtful. As travel and ethnic encounters increased in the later 15th and 16th centuries, the word began to be replaced—in literature as well as in nonliterary texts of many kinds—by more precise cultural nomenclature.

See also *BEVIS OF HAMPTON*; *FLORIS AND BLAUNCHEFLUR*; "MAN OF LAW'S TALE, THE."

FURTHER READING

Cohen, Jeffrey Jerome. "On Saracen Enjoyment: Some Fantasies of Race in Late Medieval France and England." *Journal of Medieval and Early Modern Studies* 31, no. 1 (2001): 113–146.

Neill, Michael. "'Mulattos,' 'Blacks,' and 'Indian Moors': *Othello* and Early Modern Constructions of Human Difference." *SQ* 49, no. 4 (1998): 361–374.

Fred Porcheddu

SATIRE Satire is a mode of literature that ridicules vice and folly. The satirist employs humor, irony, and exaggeration to describe and criticize contemporary people and mores. The term *satire* originated with ancient Roman poets such as Horace (65–8 B.C.E.) and Juvenal (late first to early second century C.E.), who attacked Roman corruption and vice. However, satire was not confined to the Greco-Roman world; medieval Celts believed that the satire of their bards had the magical power to harm its victims.

No evidence survives of satire in English before the NORMAN CONQUEST of 1066. While Roman (and possibly Celtic) satire influenced the development of English satire, Latin and Old French sources were closer to hand. From the seventh century onward, churchmen wrote Latin satires to attack ecclesiastical corruption and hypocrisy. In the 1100s and 1200s, *estates satire* emerged when satirists expanded their targets to include nobility, tradesmen, peasants, and women. Estates satire criticized in turn the faults of all THREE ESTATES, or social classes, of medieval society: clergy, nobility, and laborers. Sophisticated and celebrated examples of the genre include works by JOHN GOWER and especially the *GENERAL PROLOGUE TO THE CANTERBURY TALES* by GEOFFREY CHAUCER.

351

Estates satire continued into the 15th century with ALEXANDER BARCLAY's popular *Ship of Fools* (1509), a translation of a German original, and anticlerical satire likewise long remained popular. The anonymous *Land of Cockaygne* (1330) depicts the immoral fantasies of a common monk. Both WILLIAM LANGLAND's PIERS PLOWMAN and Chaucer's "The PARDONER'S TALE" attack simony (the selling of ecclesiastical appointments or offices). Satires about flattery and corruption in royal courts accompanied the expansion of royal power in the 15th and 16th centuries. These include the works of THOMAS HOCCLEVE; the Scottish poet WILLIAM DUNBAR; and JOHN SKELTON, whose satires caused him to be periodically exiled from HENRY VIII's court. During the Elizabethan period, THOMAS NASHE satirized literary and political rivals through pseudonymous pamphlets. In the late 17th and early 18th century, usually considered the golden age of English satire, satirists rejected the influence of these earlier English satires in favor of Roman models. Nevertheless, the creative and diverse body of English satire written before 1600 has proven a lasting, if often unacknowledged, influence on English literature.

FURTHER READING

Mann, Jill. *Chaucer and the Medieval Estates Satire: The Literature of Social Classes and the General Prologue to the Canterbury Tales.* London: Cambridge University Press, 1973.

Yunck, John A. *The Lineage of Lady Meed: The Development of Medieval Venality Satire.* Notre Dame, Ind.: University of Notre Dame Press, 1963.

Jonathan M. Newman

SCOP An Anglo-Saxon poet and storyteller, the *scop* could be a traveler or part of a lord's personal retinue. If he was a permanent attendant, the *scop* was usually treated with honor and respect and accorded a place of honor at the lord's side in the mead hall. ANGLO-SAXON POETRY itself illustrates the cultural significance of the *scops*. In the poem "WIDSITH," a traveling *scop* is called the "guardian of fame" and heaped with honor. The lyric "DEOR" similarly illustrates the glory that a *scop* can find, but also laments its loss:

I will say that of myself, that I was once a scop
of the Heodeningas, dear to my lord; Deor was

my name. For many years I had an excellent following. (ll. 6–7)

The poet goes on to grieve over the loss of his position and coveted privilege to another man who was "skilled in song."

Scops were masters of oral-formulaic poetry and expert storytellers who memorized EPIC tales and skillfully wove new episodes into traditional stories. Sometimes the stories were historical, but more often they were entertaining and (seemingly) carefully crafted to suit the particular audience. In reality, the *scops* were familiar with a number of formulas that they could adapt to suit their needs. *Scops* were particularly important during feasts, where they entertained the crowd, promoted the king, glorified the warriors, and led the drinking games.

The etymology of the word *scop* is unclear. Although it seems to be related to the verb *sceppan/scyppan* (to shape, to create), the *Oxford English Dictionary* finds that connection "unlikely." More likely connections might be found in the Old High German word *scoph* (poetry), and the Old Norse term *skop* (mocking, scoffing). Whatever the case, the word *scop* itself became a part of many compounds, including *sceop-craeft* (poetry, the poet's art), *sceop-gereord* (the language of poetry), and *scop-leofl* (a poetic composition).

There were many other cultural figures similar to the Anglo-Saxon *scop,* such as the Old Icelandic skald, the welsh bard, the early Irish *ollave,* the Scottish makar, and the French *trouvere,* although Middle English society had no equivalent.

FURTHER READING

Cassidy, Frederic G. "How Free Was the Anglo-Saxon Scop?" In *Franciplegius,* edited by J. B. Bessinger and Robert P. Creed, 75–85. New York: New York University Press, 1965.

French, W. H. "*Widsith* and the Scop." *PMLA* 60, no. 3 (1945): 623–630.

Hollowell, Ida Masters. "Scop and Wodbora in OE Poetry." *JEGP* 77 (1978): 317–329.

SCOTTISH CHAUCERIANS The term *Scottish Chaucerians*—given to ROBERT HENRYSON, WILLIAM DUNBAR, GAVIN DOUGLAS, JAMES I of Scotland, and others—though long used, is somewhat of a misnomer. These poets wrote in a different time and place than GEOFFREY CHAUCER, and while they generally followed him in meter and subject, they were not slavish imitators. Like Chaucer, however, they played an important part in establishing the VERNACULAR tradition in literary pursuits. Further, they wrote for a varied audience in the high, middle, and low styles. There are also direct connections in subject matter. For instance, Henryson wrote a version of the Troilus and Cressida story called The TESTAMENT OF CRESSEID. William Dunbar's "Tua Mariit Wemen and the Wedo" can be compared to "The WIFE OF BATH'S TALE" because both works feature women talking candidly about sex, and in the spirit of Chaucer's The LEGEND OF GOOD WOMEN, Gavin Douglas wrote about Dido and Aeneas. These poets also specifically praise Chaucer for his rhetoric and style: Dunbar, for example, lists him in "LAMENT FOR THE MAKARIS."

Recent critics prefer the term *makar* to Scottish Chaucerian. *Makar* is a direct translation of the Greek word for poet into Middle Scots, and Henryson, Dunbar, and Douglas all used it to describe themselves. These poets are also part of a larger movement of MIDDLE SCOTS poetry.

FURTHER READING
Fox, Denton. "The Scottish Chaucerians." In *Chaucer and Chaucerians,* edited by D. S. Brewer, 164–200. London: Nelson, 1966.
Ridley, Florence. "A Plea for the Middle Scots." In *The Learned and the Lewed,* edited by Larry D. Benson, 175–196. Cambridge: Harvard University Press, 1974.

Mark DiCicco

"SEAFARER, THE" ANONYMOUS (before 1072)
"The Seafarer" is an Old English ELEGY that is found in the EXETER BOOK. Like other poems in this tradition, "The Seafarer" features an *anhaga* (solitary) figure, and employs ALLITERATION as the rhyme scheme.

The speaker introduces his tale by describing the hardships a seafarer has to deal with when he is out alone at sea: hunger, loneliness, coldness, frost, and stormy waters. He contrasts himself with the man who lives happily on land and has no idea of the suffering the seafarer has to undergo. Accordingly, the first part of the first half of the poem (ll. 1–33a) is very negative about seafaring. In the second part of the first half (ll. 33b–58), the seafarer, despite his sufferings, contemplates undertaking another, very different sea journey. This time, he has a clear goal: to look for the "home of the exiles" (l. 38). His heart longs for the tumbling of the waves, and the signs of spring are urging him to undertake his journey. The comfortable life on land is dead to the seafarer, who prefers the joys of the Lord ["Dryhtnes dreamas" (l. 65)], which he can find in seafaring.

Lines 58–66a form a transition to the second half of the poem (ll. 66b–124). In these lines, it seems that the seafarer's heart or spirit, his "hyge" (l. 58), flies away over the earth across the sea and comes back, encouraging the speaker to embark on his journey. However, seafaring is no longer mentioned; instead, the poet writes about the transience of earthly life and the permanence of heavenly life. Further, only humility will help humans; arrogant and boastful people will meet death unexpectedly. Material gain is useless. The poem closes with the poet praising God.

Most critics agree that "The Seafarer" is an elegy. As such, there is a sense of UBI SUNT—the speaker expresses nostalgia for his happier days. The poem includes a personal element, denoted by the first-person singular pronoun. Finally, the theme of exile is a standard elegiac element.

Many critics, however, argue that the poem also shows characteristics of other genres. For instance, the second half of the poem reads like a verse homily in which the speaker preaches about the fleeting quality of worldly riches. The speaker's description of his sufferings as a seafarer in the first half of the poem shows similarities to the lament or COMPLAINT. The latter half of the poem contains several gnomic statements—wise but subtly obscure sayings about life. This part has a lot in common with other Old English wisdom poetry (see GNOMIC VERSE). Because of the very different nature between the two halves of the poem, it has been suggested that the sea journey in the first half should be read as an ALLEGORY for something more spiritual.

"The Seafarer" has often been connected to "THE WANDERER," both in style and content. "The Wanderer," too, is an elegy that displays elements of other genres and demonstrates the transience of earthly prosperity, finding true happiness in Christian values. However, "The Seafarer" insists on a more active pursuit of these Christian values. In the attempt to unite two sets of tradition, the Germanic heroic tradition and the Christian tradition, the author has often been praised for his or her original use of diction. The word *dryhten* (lord) can refer to the Germanic use of the word that denotes the Anglo-Saxon lord/retainer relationship, or it can refer to the Heavenly Lord (see, for example, ll. 39–42). *Lof* means the earthly praise that a person can obtain by doing heroic deeds, or it can refer to the heavenly glory that a person can obtain by doing good deeds (ll. 72–80). Other examples include *dream* (joy), *blæd* (glory), and *duguð* (noble host). The poet freely uses idiom, which is common in heroic literature, to express homiletic ideas, thus uniting the first and second halves of the poem. By using ambiguous diction, the author tries to move away from the temporary secular world to the everlasting heavenly sphere, without alienating the Anglo-Saxon audience.

Perhaps because of this ambiguous diction, modern critics cannot agree on the poem's interpretation. For instance, debates abound as to whether or not the sea journey is actual or metaphorical (spiritual). Further difficulties arise from the two very different and seemingly unrelated parts of the poem. Although most critics—today, anyway—agree that both parts form a whole, methods of uniting the seafaring and the homily are under debate.

The standard allegorical interpretation connects the exile to Adam and his descendants who were cast out of Paradise. Good Christians who belong to the "city of God" are exiles in this sinful earthly world. The seafarer's journey is therefore a spiritual journey toward his heavenly home, as his life on earth has been an exile among Germanic non-Christians.

Another critical stance sees the seafarer's journey as a pilgrimage for the love of God. There are many examples in early Anglo-Saxon literature that refer to a voluntary exile or pilgrimage to strange countries, often by sea, in order to improve his or her state in the afterlife. The speaker thus decides to undertake such a sea journey to reach the land of the exiles because he realizes that the pleasures of earthly life can steer him away from a heavenly reward. This stance is slightly different from the allegorical reading in that the journey is both literal and spiritual, and it is voluntary and necessary.

Still other scholars view the poem as a linear narrative, with the first part relating the past, the transition describing the present, and the second part projecting the future. The story progresses as the seafarer develops a positive and Christian insight into his experiences. Thus, the seafaring, the exile, and the so-called homily are seamlessly interwoven into a journey of salvation and conversion.

FURTHER READING
Gordon, I. L., ed. *The Seafarer.* London: Methuen & Co, 1960.

Orton, Peter. "The Form and Structure of *The Seafarer.*" *Studia Neophilologica* 63, no. 1 (1991): 37–55.

Whitelock, Dorothy. "The Interpretation of *The Seafarer.*" In *The Early Cultures of Northwest Europe,* edited by Cyril Fox and Bruce Dickens, 259–272. Cambridge, 1950.

Annemarie Thijms

SEAGER, JANE See TUDOR WOMEN POETS.

SESTET The sestet is either a six-line poem or poem STANZA (e.g., the SESTINA is built of six sestet stanzas), or it is the last six lines of an ITALIAN (PETRARCHAN) SONNET. As part of the SONNET, the sestet follows the OCTAVE, or first eight lines, and develops a resolution to the poetic situation presented in the octave. It is distinguished from the octave by a new set of rhymes; the octave is usually *abba, abba,* and the sestet will then follow with *cde, cde,* though many variants (*ccd, ccd; cdc, ede*; etc.) are used.

FURTHER READING
Dasenbrock, Reed Way. "Wyatt's Transformation of Petrarch." *Comparative Literature* 40, no. 2 (1988): 122–133.

Oppenheimer, Paul. "The Origin of the Sonnet." *Comparative Literature* 34, no. 4 (1982): 289–304.

Carol E. Harding

SESTINA A sestina is a very strictly structured poem of six SESTETS and a three-line ENVOI, which summarizes or dedicates the poem. The specific structure

of a sestina focuses on the repetition, in all its STANZAS, of the same six words at the ends of the lines, with the last word of one stanza becoming the end of the first line in the next, and no word occupying the same number line-end in more than one stanza. The envoi also uses the six stanza end-words (two in each line).

The earliest surviving examples of sestinas were produced by French troubadours, which were ably imitated by Dante and PETRARCH. In English literature, the sestina enjoyed brief popularity in the Tudor era. SIR PHILIP SIDNEY produced a double sestina, "Ye Goat-herd Gods," in *The Old Arcadia,* among other examples.

FURTHER READING

Spanos, Margaret. "The Sestina: An Exploration of the Dynamics of Poetic Structure." *Speculum* 53, no. 3 (1978): 545–557.

Carol E. Harding

"SET ME WHEREAS THE SONNE DOTH PERCHE THE GRENE" HENRY HOWARD, EARL OF SURREY (1557)

A translation of PETRARCH's *Rime* 145, this SONNET by HENRY HOWARD, EARL OF SURREY, was included in *TOTTEL'S MISCELLANY* in 1557. Surrey finesses the poem, however, into a new form of his own creation, subsequently called the ENGLISH SONNET. While Surrey certainly had Petrarch's sonnet before him, it is likely that he was also familiar with Petrarch's principal Latin source for his poem, Horace's Ode 1.22, and he is largely faithful to both sources.

The poem's overall effect is contrast and balance, which Surrey achieves through a range of situational antitheses. The pattern of the poem advances this concept quatrain by quatrain, as each begins with "Set me" and builds to the final COUPLET in a way that ultimately effaces landscape altogether and emphasizes the relationship of the lover with the beloved. But this pattern, which GEORGE PUTTENHAM, author of the ART OF POESY, calls *merismus* or *amplificatio* (amplification), is made still more subtle in Surrey's hands. Within the technical structure of the sonnet form, Surrey's poem further retains metrical elements of ACCENTUAL VERSE, incorporating CAESURAe—or midline pauses—that further highlight the antitheses Surrey presents. Thus, the poem's frequent pauses, marked by commas in lines 3–13, isolate discrete phrasal units that balance one another. Scholars have also noted that in striking such a balance, Surrey appears to make use of the marriage ceremony of the Roman Catholic Church—which would have been used in Surrey's own wedding in 1532—whose English vows were inserted in an otherwise Latin service: "I N. take the[e] N. to my weded wife to haue and to hold from this day forwarde for bettere for wers for richere for pouerer: in sykeness and in hel[th]e tyl dethe vs departe . . ." Drawing on these contrasts, Surrey successfully maintains that geography, condition, and circumstance are ultimately irrelevant in the affairs of the heart: what matters most is simply the individual freedom to love.

FURTHER READING

Jones, Emrys, ed. *Henry Howard Earl of Surrey: Poems.* Oxford: Clarendon Press, 1970.

Sessions, William A. *Henry Howard, The Poet Earl of Surrey: A Life.* Oxford: Oxford University Press, 1999.

David Houston Wood

SEVEN DEADLY SINS (CARDINAL SINS, CAPITAL VICES)

The "cardinal sins" were considered the most serious sins in pre-Reformation Christianity and generally included all mortal (major) sins. These were relatively abstract terms under which the medieval church categorized other more specific sins for the purpose of eliciting confession. Technically, the terms *deadly sins* and *cardinal sins* are not interchangeable; indeed, the phrase *deadly sins* did not start to come into common use until the 14th century. However, these have been elided over the years. The number of deadly sins—seven—has its own significance in medieval theology. Seven was thought to represent completion, based on the precedent set by the seven days of the Creation.

Though the idea of a list of the most serious sins has a long pre-Christian history, the cardinal sins have their basis in the Bible. This would seem to suggest that the idea of a list of major sins originated in the Bible, though it does have history before the Judeo-Christian era. The fourth-century theologian John Cassian proposed the first list of sins, which Pope Gregory revised into the list most commonly recognized throughout the Middle Ages: *superbia, ira, invidia, avaritia, acedia, gula, luxuria* (pride, wrath or anger, envy, avarice or greed, sloth, gluttony, lust). Gregory even suggested the mnemonic acronym SIIAAGL as an aid for devout Christians.

Gregory's list was intended to rank the sins according to their severity. Pride, for example, was thought such a direct affront to God that it merited the top position on the list. It is the sin of excessive self-love, or extreme confidence in personal ability, thus denying the grace and assistance of God. It is related to the pre-Christian concept of hubris (overbearing, godlike pride). Wrath, more commonly known as anger, refers to the failure to accept love and the embracing of conflict. Envy involves all-consuming desire—in this case, the desire to be someone else (or at least to have their position, possessions, and characteristics). Gluttony is similarly all-consuming, as it is the desire to consume beyond one's means and necessity. Avarice goes beyond simple greed, or lust for material possessions; it also involves the desire to possess everything. Sloth is the avoidance of both physical and spiritual work, while lust is the desire to indulge in the pleasures of the flesh. Occasionally one or more of the following terms is substituted on the list: *vana gloria,* or vainglory, which is related to pride; *tristitia,* or the sin of despair/hoplesness; and *cupiditas,* or covetousness, which is related to both avarice and lust.

One very popular representation of the deadly sins is the ubiquitous model of the "Tree of Vice," usually portrayed with its counterpart, the "Tree of Virtue." The seven cardinal sins are also popular in literature, with the more famous examples including "The Parson's Tale" from GEOFFREY CHAUCER's The CANTERBURY TALES, WILLIAM LANGLAND's PIERS PLOWMAN (Passus 5), EDMUND SPENSER's The FAERIE QUEENE (book 1), and the pageant in CHRISTOPHER MARLOWE's play Dr. Faustus.

See also CONFESSIO AMANTIS, VIRTUES.

FURTHER READING

Bloomfield, Morton W. *The Seven Deadly Sins: An Introduction to the History of a Religious Concept.* East Lansing: Michigan State College Press, 1967.

Newhauser, Richard. *In the Garden of Evil: The Vices and Culture in the Middle Ages.* Toronto: Pontifical Institute, 2005.

Wenzel, Siegfried. "The Source of Chaucer's Seven Deadly Sins." *Traditio* 30 (1974): 351–378.

Kathryn R. Vulic and Michelle M. Sauer

"SEVEN SONNETS FOR ALEXANDER NEVILLE" GEORGE GASCOIGNE (1573, 1575)

"Seven Sonnets for Alexander Neville" is the fourth in a series of five poems written by GEORGE GASCOIGNE as he returned from the war. The SONNET appears in both *A Hundreth Sundrie Flowres* (1573) and in the "Flowers" section of *Posies* (1575). As is the case with all five poems in the series, "Seven Sonnets" takes its theme in response to a maxim, each suggested by a different friend. Alexander Neville suggested the theme "If it be done quickly, let it be done well," to which Gascoigne responded with seven sonnets explicating the theme "if done too quickly, hardly done well." He uses his own recent experience of court life as the exemplar of his theme.

The poem describes the first time Gascoigne's "gazing eye" (l. 2) beheld the "stately pompe of princes and their peeres" (l. 5) who seemed to "swimme in floudes of beaten goulde" (l. 6) amid all sorts of young and beautiful people, especially women, "so faire of hue, so freshe of their attire" (l. 10). The sight made the country boy ("seemely swayne") Gascoigne think he had stumbled into a kind of heaven. Thereafter, with "puffte up" heart and full of "peevish pride," he desperately sought to "playe his parte" in courtly life (ll. 37, 39). The rest of the poem explains the high cost of that decision for him. Seeking to maintain a lavish lifestyle while attempting to become ever "higher plaste" at court, he runs out of funds and is compelled to lease all of his inherited farmlands for more. Soon enough, merchants demand his assets as payment on his debts, and with all his wealth lost, he leaves court having experienced very little gain at very heavy cost.

Gascoigne composed all five of the poems in the series containing the SONNET SEQUENCE written for Neville because his friends at Gray's Inn wished him to write some worthy verse before rejoining them. Gray's Inn had long fostered the literary and dramatic arts, and like many of the works produced by students there, Gascoigne's "Seven Sonnets" have about them an awareness and use of literary tradition combined with the awkwardness of an academic exercise. Having his "gazing eye" bedazzled by courtly life shows Gascoigne making sly use of the medieval tradition of love entering first through the eye by shifting its traditional focus from a love interest to an alluring political culture in order to morally condemn both its object and its effect. At the same time, each sonnet in the sequence begins with a pedantic repetition of the moralizing line ending the last, until the lines of the final sonnet conclude that all haste is good, so long as "wisdom makes the way" (l. 98)—a lesson his biography suggests Gascoigne was still too slowly learning when he wrote the poem.

See also COURT CULTURE.

FURTHER READING

Cunliffe, J. W. *The Complete Works of George Gascoigne*. 2 vols. Cambridge: Cambridge University Press, 1907.

Prouty, C. T. *George Gascoigne, Courtier, Soldier, and Poet*. New York: Columbia University Press, 1942.

Robert E. Kibler

SHAKESPEARE, WILLIAM (1564–1616)

William Shakespeare was born on April 23, 1564. His father, John Shakespeare, was a glove maker who owned a leather shop. Shakespeare's mother, Mary Arden, was a farmer's daughter related to minor gentry. At age seven, William Shakespeare entered grammar school with other boys of his social class, studying Latin among other things. In 1582, at age 18, he married 26-year-old Anne Hathaway, with whom he had three children, Susanna, Hamnet, and Judith.

There is little known about Shakespeare's life during two major spans of time, commonly referred to as the "lost years": 1578–82 and 1585–92. The first covers the time after Shakespeare left grammar school until his marriage; the second covers the seven years of Shakespeare's life when he was probably perfecting his dramatic skills.

Around 1592, Shakespeare traveled to London to begin a writing career. Most critics conclude that he spent time as both a writer and an actor with Lord Pembroke's Men before 1592. Some time after 1593, a group of seven men, including Shakespeare, started a theater company called Lord Chamberlain's Men; later, after 1603, they became the King's Men under JAMES VI/I. Shakespeare wrote most of the plays for the company, averaging two plays per year. Many of these were produced during his lifetime.

Shakespeare's career spanned the reigns of both ELIZABETH I (1558–1603) and James I (1603–25). He died in Stratford-upon-Avon on April 23, 1616, at the age of 52 and was buried in the Church of the Holy Trinity.

Though he is best known as a playwright, Shakespeare also wrote a variety of poems. In 1593, Henry Wriothesley, earl of Southampton, became his patron; Shakespeare's VENUS AND ADONIS and The RAPE OF LUCRECE were dedicated to Southampton. SHAKESPEARE'S SONNETS, written during the late 1590s but published in 1609, were dedicated to a mysterious "W.H." who has never been definitively identified. William Herbert, earl of Pembroke, was another of Shakespeare's patrons; the First Folio (1623) was dedicated to him. This text, edited by John Heminge and Henry Condell, was published seven years after Shakespeare's death and contained 36 plays as well as the famous Droeshout portrait of Shakespeare and various commendatory verses by contemporaries.

In the 18th century, Shakespeare's reputation increased, and he became an iconic figure. Still, some critics conclude from his simple education that his plays were written by someone else—Francis Bacon and the earl of Oxford are the two most popular candidates—through support for these theories is minimal.

Shakespeare contributed a great deal to the development of the English language. Many words and phrases from his plays and poems have become a common part of everyday speech. His ideas on subjects such as romantic love, heroism, comedy, and tragedy have shaped the attitudes of millions of people. As well, Shakespeare's portrayal of historical figures and events have influenced the way people think about written history.

See also LOVER'S COMPLAINT, A.

FURTHER READING

Rosenblum, Joseph. *The Greenwood Companion to Shakespeare*. Westport, Conn.: Greenwood Press, 2005.

Melissa A. Harris

SHAKESPEAREAN SONNET See ENGLISH SONNET.

SHAKESPEARE'S SONNETS (OVERVIEW)

WILLIAM SHAKESPEARE (1599) Often given less attention than Shakespeare's plays, his SONNETS and poems form a complete body of work. Because they seem so complete within themselves and because Shakespeare hints at such interesting characters, the sonnets, especially, have elicited many questions to which they provide few, if any, answers. Critics have questioned almost everything about the sonnets, from their authorship and arrangement to their references to Shakespeare's personal life to the identities of the LOVELY BOY, the DARK LADY, and the rival poet to whom they refer.

Although the sonnets form a roughly coherent body, no autograph copy of them exists, but there is no doubt that Shakespeare wrote sonnets. Francis Meres, a cleric who recorded pithy sayings and interesting works, comments about Shakespeare's "sugred Sonnets among his private friends" in *Palladis Tamia, Wit's Treasury* (1598), and two Shakespeare sonnets (138 and 144) appear in William Jaggard's *Passionate Pilgrim* (1599). Shakespeare's contemporaries record that he did not approve Jaggard's publication. Shakespeare probably wrote sonnets during theater closures generated by the plague, and thus prior to their publication. In fact, publication of the sonnets occurred during the theater closure between 1608 and 1609. All 154 sonnets, including the two that previously appeared in *Passionate Pilgrim*, appeared in 1609, published by Thomas Thorpe. Scholarly debates abound as to whether or not Shakespeare authorized this printing, and it is still unknown if the dedication to "Mr. W. H." reflects Shakespeare's or Thorpe's views. There are only references to the sonnets before they appeared as a sequence, but some of the event references and parallels to early plays suggest their earlier composition. The final arrangement of the SONNET SEQUENCE, however, seems to have been set in this printing, even though critics still question whether or not Shakespeare authorized the 1609 printing. Some attempts at rearrangement have been made, but none seem more satisfactory than that of the original.

Although often treated as a sequence, Shakespeare's sonnets do not seem to follow a typical sequence pattern. Usually, the poems in a sequence progress through a particular experience or emotion and reflect a theme, often one of unrequited love. In contrast, Shakespeare's sonnets seem to break into two smaller sequences. The first subsequence, from sonnets 1 to 126, expresses love for a young man sometimes referred to as the "lovely boy" or the "fair lord." The second subsequence, from 127 to 154, expresses love for an anti-Petrarchan "Dark Lady." The final part of Shakespeare's poetic sequence is *A LOVER'S COMPLAINT,* a single, longer poem that mirrors the sonnets in tone but records the voice of a female, rather than male, lover. Readers may also find two minisequences within the first subsequence: Sonnets 1–17 focus on urging the young man to marry and to beget children (the "procreation sonnets"); sonnets 76–86 focus on competition with a rival poet. All but three of the sonnets (99, 126, 145) maintain the traditional length—14 lines—and traditional English meter—IAMBIC PENTAMETER. (This is a pattern of an unstressed syllable followed by a stressed syllable. An unstressed syllable followed by a stressed syllable comprises one iamb. Five iambs make one line of iambic pentameter.) Shakespeare's sonnets follow the Elizabethan or Shakespearean rhyme scheme—*abab, cdcd, efef, gg.* Usually a VOLTA, or turn, appears at the end of the eighth line, a shift frequently marked with a period ending the line and a word at the beginning of the ninth line indicating contrast or conclusion. This move subtly reinforces the octave and sestet divisions, which distinguish PETRARCH's sonnets and those of his imitators.

In addition to the two subsequences, many of the sonnets, regardless of their position in the sequence itself, are arranged around certain themes or image patterns, including time, death, writing, and fame, though many sonnets reference multiple themes and use multiple images. Most of the images are strongly anti-Petrarchan. For instance, the address of a sequence to a young man represents a significant inversion of the Petrarchan tradition, and Shakespeare never names his beloved. However, the poet also uses images that are essentially Petrarchan, but inversely applied. For example, the sonnets to the Dark Lady address a beloved woman who is dark, not fair; sexually experienced, not virginal.

Critics have often attempted to identify the mysterious Master W. H. to whom the whole volume was dedicated, the lovely boy, and the Dark Lady. Early interpretations of the sonnets, including reactions by such Shakespeare's contemporaries as Ben Jonson, indicate that many readers found the address to a young man particularly problematic. The inability to identify the speaker conclusively as Shakespeare himself complicates these reactions and readings that derive from them. Following their publication, however, the sonnets were mostly ignored until 1790, when Edmond Malone reprinted the 1609 Quarto edition of the sonnets. As they thus gained critical attention, interpreters tempered both their regard for Shakespeare and their critical stances.

Some interpreters, including the Romantic poets Samuel Taylor Coleridge and William Wordsworth, sought to diminish or to explain the fact that some of the sonnets written by Shakespeare clearly address a man. Some critics simply avoided the issue, focusing on the sonnets as an expression of Shakespeare's creativity. Late 19th- and early 20th-century writers such as Oscar Wilde and W. H. Auden, while recognizing the homoerotic implications of the sonnets, did not publicly discuss their opinions, believing that the public would not accept such a reading. Many earlier readers who ignored this homoerotic potential explained the eroticism by suggesting that expressions of friendship in the early modern era differed considerably from expressions of friendship now, and that readers can hear Shakespeare's erotic language simply as verbalizing feelings of friendship for the young man rather than expressions of homoerotic affection.

The clear, strong affection that the speaker feels for the young man, however, continued to present problems for later critics who were unable to escape the sense that these sonnets, written by a man, expressed a degree of affection that surpassed friendship. With the New Critics (1950s), scholars began to treat the poems with regard to form and word choice without regard to the author who wrote the texts. By studying the sonnets as the speech of a person who is a creation of the writer and not Shakespeare himself, these critics avoided the question of personal address altogether and examined the sonnets exclusively as poetry. In the late 20th century, critics became more willing to recognize publicly the multiple meanings present in Shakespeare's language. Some critics now examine the ways in which the sonnets illuminate class, race, and gender as perceived by Shakespeare's era. Psychoanalytic critics investigate the way in which the sonnets treat subjectivity, the human mind, and human emotion. Still other critics explore the homoerotic and bisexual implications of the sonnets more fully. In the future, more religiously focused criticism is expected to emerge, as critics examine the entrenched tensions between Roman Catholicism and Protestantism in general and Puritanism in particular.

FURTHER READING

Alexander, Catherine M. S., and Stanley Wells. *Shakespeare and Sexuality*. Cambridge and New York: Cambridge University Press, 2001.

Blakemore Evans, G. *The Sonnets*. Cambridge: Cambridge University Press, 1996.

Booth, Stephen. *An Essay on Shakespeare's Sonnets*. New Haven, Conn.: Yale University Press, 1969.

———, ed. *Shakespeare's Sonnets*. New Haven, Conn.: Yale University Press, 1977.

Dubrow, Heather. *Captive Victors: Shakespeare's Narrative Poems and Sonnets*. Ithaca, N.Y.: Cornell University Press, 1987.

Duncan-Jones, Katherine. "Playing Fields or Killing Fields: Shakespeare's Poems and Sonnets." *SQ* 54, no. 2 (2003): 127–141.

———. *Shakespeare's Sonnets*. London: Arden, 1997.

Edmondson, Paul, and Stanley Wells. *Shakespeare's Sonnets*. Oxford: Oxford University Press, 2004.

Fineman, Joel. *Shakespeare's Perjured Eye: The Invention of Poetic Subjectivity in the Sonnets*. Berkeley: University of California Press, 1986.

Hammond, Gerald. *The Reader and Shakespeare's Young Man Sonnets*. Totowa, N.J.: Barnes and Noble, 1981.

Herrnstein, Barbara, ed. *Discussions of Shakespeare's Sonnets*. Boston: Heath, 1964.

Hubler, Edward. "Shakespeare's Sonnets and the Commentators." In *The Riddle of Shakespeare's Sonnets*, 1–21. New York: Basic Books, 1962.

Kay, Dennis. *William Shakespeare: Sonnets and Poems*. New York: Twayne, 1998.

Pequigney, Joseph. *Such Is My Love: A Study of Shakespeare's Sonnets*. Chicago: University of Chicago Press, 1985.

Rosenblum, Joseph. *The Greenwood Companion to Shakespeare*. Westport, Conn.: Greenwood Press, 2005.

Schiffer, James, ed. *Shakespeare's Sonnets: Critical Essays*. New York: Garland, 1999.

Traub, Valerie. "The Sonnets: Sequence, Sexuality, and Shakespeare's Two Loves." In *A Companion to Shakespeare*, Vol. 4, *The Poems, Problem Comedies, Late Plays*, edited by

Richard Dutton and Jean E. Howard, 275–301. Malden, Mass.: Blackwell, 2003.

Vendler, Helen. *The Art of Shakespeare's Sonnets.* Cambridge, Mass., and London: Belknap/Harvard, 1997.

Wells, Stanley. *The Cambridge Companion to Shakespeare Studies.* Cambridge: Cambridge University Press, 1986.

———. *Looking for Sex in Shakespeare.* Cambridge and New York: Cambridge University Press, 2004.

Martha Kalnin Diede

Shakespeare's sonnets: Sonnet 1 ("From fairest creatures we desire increase") WILLIAM SHAKESPEARE (1599)

The general themes of WILLIAM SHAKESPEARE's Sonnet 1 is the topic of parenthood, despite ostensibly being addressed to a young male friend. What is extraordinary is his subversive use of the Petrarchan tradition popular in the period—a tradition of poetry in which a highly idealized person, most often a woman, was praised and the poet declared his unworthiness to praise that person. Shakespeare proves his mastery of the tradition while using it nontraditionally. In Sonnet 1, the poet addresses the male figure as though he were a woman, thus demonstrating that men not only enjoyed receiving the same flattery as women of the period, they also shared many of the same concerns about aging, procreative ability, and death. Shakespeare argues that his subject is the "fairest," the most "ornament[al]," person that ever lived. He argues that that the entirety of humanity will suffer if his subject fails to engender an "heir" (have a child). Unchanged through time, according to this SONNET, is the argument that a man lives on through his children. Shakespeare's argument also supports the social, economic, and religious strictures of his time, but does so artistically.

In the first quatrain, Shakespeare's subtlety lies in the reminder to his friend that a man is no different than any born thing—it must die. He then declares that his friend is narcissistic because he loves only himself, not the world or the woman necessary to engender a child. And just as the rose dies because of the natural run of time, so in lines 5 and 6 do we find that there is "famine" in the world because his friend refuses to "feed" any person but himself with the "self-substantial" abundance that he represents.

Some critics maintain that Sonnet 1, because of its foreshadowing of topics to come later in the SONNET SEQUENCE, was actually composed later in the series, and that either Thomas Thorpe (the publisher) saw how well it worked as an introductory piece, or that Shakespeare wrote it as an afterthought to tie his various topics and imagery together, just as one writes the table of contents after writing the chapters of a book. Even if the sonnet is of later date, that does not affect the mastery of the form, imagery, or selection of exactly the right word. This sonnet's very placement as first sets more weight on it, although perhaps, as some critics claim, it is inferior to some later in the series. But it is difficult to tie such opposites as *increase* and *decrease,* or *famine* and *abundance,* together cohesively. The very topics struggle against each other for mastery, yet Shakespeare manages to hold them together artistically.

See also ITALIAN (PETRARCHAN) SONNETS, SHAKESPEARE'S SONNETS (OVERVIEW).

Leslie J. Ormandy

Shakespeare's sonnets: Sonnet 2 ("When forty winters shall besiege thy brow") WILLIAM SHAKESPEARE (1599)

Given that human physical beauty is transitory, this SONNET considers how fleeting beauty is best used and offers a strategy to prolong it. In the beginning, the persona addresses a handsome young man and asks him to imagine himself at 40. At that age, the friend will be asked where his beauty, represented here as a kind of clothing ("proud livery" or a "tattered weed"), lies. If, on the one hand, he replies that his beauty still resides in his own "deep-sunken eyes," he would be making a shameful reply—shameful not only because little beauty would be left in those eyes but also because the friend would be confessing to the wasteful hoarding of beauty. If, on the other hand, the friend could point to a "fair child" whom he had engendered, he would have successfully invested his own beauty and proven himself worthy of praise. The "fair child" would "sum his count," an accounting metaphor which means that the child would render the friend's financial accounts balanced. The poem concludes with a COUPLET stating that to engender a child is to remake oneself when one is old, for the child has the ability to reheat the blood made cold through age.

Sonnet 2 fits in with the overarching theme of the first 17 sonnets of WILLIAM SHAKESPEARE'S SONNET SEQUENCE, all of which concern procreation as a way of defeating death and achieving a kind of immortality. In form, it is an ENGLISH SONNET, with the typical rhyme scheme of *abab, cdcd, efef, gg.*

Thematically, Sonnet 2 treats beauty as a commodity in which to invest. In line 6, for example, beauty is called the "treasure of thy lusty days." The poem argues that a beautiful young person who does not procreate wastes this precious resource. In significant ways, the poem harkens back to Matthew 25:14–30, the parable of the talents. In that parable, Jesus praises "good and faithful servants" who invest their master's money and make a profit, but he condemns a "wicked and lazy servant" who, out of fear, buries his master's money and then returns it without interest. For Shakespeare, the handsome young man who does not procreate is a kind of bad servant because he does not use beauty to produce additional income (i.e., children) for his master. This, says Shakespeare, is a "thriftless" way to act.

Sonnet 2 begins with an ironic inversion of a conventional image of the sexual act being described as "plowing." Instead of a man plowing a woman's field in order to seed it, here the man's body becomes the plowed field, and time itself is the plowman. Forty winters plow deep trenches—wrinkles—in his forehead. This plowing is sterile, producing only ugly tatters in the "proud livery" of the friend's good looks. The poem's message is that the friend should get to his own productive "plowing" before time reverses the gender roles and "plows" his face. If he does so, the friend will then be able to look back at the product of his efforts, and the resulting pride will warm his old, tired blood because the "fair child" will be the bearer of his own beauty and blood line. The friend will, thus, be newly remade metaphorically.

See also SHAKESPEARE'S SONNETS (OVERVIEW).

FURTHER READING

Crosman, Robert. "Making Love out of Nothing at All: The *Issue of Story* in Shakespeare's Procreation Sonnets." *SQ*, no. 4 (1990): 470–488.

Gregory M. Sadlek

Shakespeare's sonnets: Sonnet 3 ("Look in thy glass and tell the face thou viewest") WILLIAM SHAKESPEARE (1599)

Of the 154 sonnets written by WILLIAM SHAKESPEARE, the first 17 form what is known as the procreation SONNET set. These poems urge the reader to have sex both for enjoyment and for procreation. They also emphasize marriage as the fulfillment of social obligations and the underlying structure of society. Part of the encouragement to procreate is a desire for preservation (of family, humanity, and English society), and Sonnet 3 emphasizes this idea of continuation.

In the poem, the speaker urges the audience, in this case, the "LOVELY BOY," to begin considering producing offspring. The idea is that the lovely boy is so attractive that if he does not produce an heir, the world will be cheated forever when his image is lost. Finding a willing woman should not be very difficult, either, since few women exist who would deny the lovely boy. The speaker goes on to remind his audience that he is the mirror for his parents, as his child would be for him. The poem concludes with a dire warning: If you die without reproducing, you will be forgotten and your image will go to the grave with you.

Sonnet 3 is fairly unique among the procreation set. Unlike its companions, which focus primarily on images of life, Sonnet 3 contains paradoxical alternatives that combine life and death. For instance, bleak images such as an unblessed womb (l. 4), disdained husbandry (l. 5), and stopped posterity (l. 8) are paired with corresponding images of life, such as replication (l. 2), the accepting woman (ll. 5–6), and the not-foolish man (ll. 7–8). This series of complications is connected to the notion of *dédoublement,* which is an integral part of all of Shakespeare's sonnets. In literature, *dédoublement* (French for "split") is the process of aesthetic self-doubling, or double consciousness. It can occur within a single character or within a literary construct. A character might be involved in an unexpected situation, which results in a sudden escape from his or her self-conception, and thus be forced to reevaluate his or her fundamental identity. Textually, *dédoublement* is a simultaneous fragmentation and binding through writing and images. Linking constructive and destructive ideas within a text leads to a cycle of division and repetition that both informs and interprets the world surrounding and created through the text.

Despite the name of the subset, *procreation sonnets,* the focus is predominately on the male reproductive role and not on motherhood. However, Sonnet 3 introduces the idea of woman-as-womb, suggesting that no woman would refuse her womb to the young man. Moreover, the phrase "unbless some mother" (l. 4) has been connected to maternal guidance books, a new genre developed in the early modern era. These advice books suggested that mothers contributed more to their children's existence than simply incubation and later nurturing. They advocated a prominent role in childhood education and instruction for mothers. These books also assumed that all women wanted to be mothers and implied that the refusal to reproduce, by either men or women, was a real social evil and denied women their biological destiny.

Sonnet 3 is written in iambic pentameter, has three cross-rhymed quatrains, and ends with a COUPLET. Sonnet 3 is the only one of Shakespeare's 154 sonnets to have five rhymes: *abab, cdcd* followed by *dede, dd.* Although this structure, technically an OCTAVE followed by a SESTET, seems closer to the ITALIAN (PETRARCHAN) SONNET form, in theme the sonnet remains aligned with ENGLISH SONNET structure. Sonnet 3 also features a series of internal rhymes (couplet ties). In particular, the repetition of *-re* (or re-) both connects the poem internally and recalls the "theme" of regeneration and renewal. Words featuring *-re* include: fresh, repair, renewest, where, unear'[e]d, remember'[e]d. Another internal connecting rhyme is *-age*: tillage, age, image.

The first two lines of the poem form a SYNECDOCHE, in which "face" represents the lovely boy whom the speaker addresses. His fundamental goal is to persuade the youth of the advantages of producing a child. He begins rather directly by imperatively instructing the youth that "now is the time" that he "should form another" (l. 2). He follows up this charge with flattery and then with a series of rhetorical questions. By asking open-ended questions, the speaker distances himself from the final decision but guides the lovely boy toward making the "right" choice by presenting logical scenarios. All of these rhetorical strategies are contained within the octave. The sestet, on the other hand,

witnesses a return to flattery of a sort, although this adulation is tempered by a quiet admiration and a sincere regret. The speaker wistfully closes the poem with the solemn reminder, "die single, and thine image dies with thee" (l. 14).

There is no singular controlling image found within Sonnet 3; however, there are consistent ideas. With the governing objective being procreation, Shakespeare employs a number of agricultural metaphors. Like the fertile field waiting to be planted, all attractive, virginal women are waiting to be approached by the lovely young man. This idea is emphasized through *uneared* (l. 5), *tillage* (l. 5), and *husbandry* (l. 5). Agricultural images, particularly the plowing metaphor, can also be traced throughout some of Sonnet 3's allusions to classical works. Besides the clear reference to the Narcissus legend from OVID's *Metamorphoses,* the poem contains a number of additional Ovidian references. These include book 15 of *Metamorphoses, Medicamina Faciei,* and *Ars amatoria.* All include a connection between age and wrinkles, which are created through plowing.

Besides agricultural metaphors, the sonnet depends on a number of references to *glass* to convey the message of procreation. In early modern English, *glass* often means "mirror." In Sonnet 3, the youth's image is replicated in the mirror, as it would be in his children—an idea confirmed by his mother's use of him as a "glass" of her youth (l. 9). People can be copied both by looking in a mirror and by procreating.

However, in Shakespeare's sonnets, the word *glass* sometimes refers to an hourglass instead of a mirror. Although "mirror" makes the most sense in Sonnet 3, if the dual meaning is explored, there are temporal implications. *Glass* is used in the first line, and the second contains *time.* Line 10 combines *glass* with *calls back,* implying a function of time. All of these subtle reminders serve to underscore the main message of the poem's speaker, who is urging the lovely boy to produce offspring before it is too late and he runs out of time.

See also SHAKESPEARE'S SONNETS (OVERVIEW).

FURTHER READING
Burrow, Colin. "Shakespeare's Wrinkled Eye: Sonnet 3, Lines 11–12." *N&Q* 245, no. 1 (2000): 90–91.

Crosman, Robert. "Making Love out of Nothing at All: The Issue of Story in Shakespeare's Procreation Sonnets." *SQ*, no. 4 (1990): 470–488.

Miller, Naomi J. "Playing the 'Mother's Part': Shakespeare's Sonnets and Early Modern Codes of Maternity." In *Shakespeare's Sonnets: Critical Essays,* edited by James Schiffer, 347–347. New York and London: Garland, 1999.

Shakespeare's sonnets: Sonnet 12 ("When I do count the clock that tells the time") WILLIAM SHAKESPEARE (1599)

This SONNET, part of WILLIAM SHAKESPEARE's procreation sonnet set, is organized into two sections by its rhyme and its content, and although it follows the standard ENGLISH SONNET form of three quatrains followed by a COUPLET, its syntax is more true to the ITALIAN (PETRARCHAN) SONNET structure. The first dozen lines, with three sets of alternative rhymes, establish that the speaker is worried about time and death. Indeed, this is the first sonnet in which the subject pronoun *I* governs the action. The last two lines give an answer, though it may not be seem very romantic. The speaker finds neither a spiritual nor an emotional answer; only creating new life can challenge time. Repetition of images of time and ALLITERATION within the lines unifies the sonnet into a cohesive message.

The first quatrain uses many images of ominous colors and different parts of the day to express the speaker's feeling about the incessant movement of time. In line 1, the speaker says that he "counts the clock." But since a single clock is counted only once, the implied repetition creates a feeling of being trapped within time. In the second line, the speaker uses two images that are counterpoints, contrasting the "brave day" with its bright impression to the "hideous night," an evil dark image. We learn that the day has "sunk," an active verb that also describes the sun's action at twilight. Overall, we see the progression of an entire day from joy to horror, which echoes in later sections. Lines 3 and 4 emphasize a series of brooding colors— "violet past prime" probably signifies twilight, with prime indicating the ninth hour of the day, and "sable" recalls the darkness, perhaps with "silvered" stars. Similarly, as a man's life progresses, he begins bravely, but after his prime he sinks into his twilight years, wherein his beard contains silver hairs.

The second quatrain continues to rely on images from nature, but begins to connect them to humanity. The "lofty trees . . . barren of leaves" illustrate the natural cycle of death. Death's counterpart is the promise of the following spring's rebirth with the "summer's green," particularly noted as wheat. After the summer, however, the once-green sheaves of wheat turn brown and are harvested. This image continues in the sonnet's clever metaphor found in line 8: "Borne on the bier with white and bristly beard." *Borne,* which means carried or birthed, is followed by *bier,* a type of cart used at harvest time but also a funerary coffin-stand. The juxtaposition of words parallels the life/death cycle with the growth and harvest of wheat. Extending this image, "the white and black beards" (l. 8) could be middle-aged male pallbearers or the dried husks of the wheat heads. Some scholars have suggested that this is further reminiscent of a funeral procession.

In the final quatrain, there is a major shift in tone as the speaker begins to use second person with "thy," most likely addressing the LOVELY BOY. Line 10 clearly states, "thou among the wastes of time must go," meaning there is no escape from decay and death. It is the speaker's most deliberate statement yet of the inevitability of death and feeling of absence for the survivors. Lines 11 and 12 combine into a single, supporting image of the "sweet and beauties," which, like flowers or crops, must "die" and "see others grow."

The final turn is in the concluding couplet. Time is no longer a concept; it is now a proper noun. Its "scythe" is the long handled and bladed tool used for harvesting and part of the Grim Reaper's stereotype, and to "make defense" is to attempt fighting off Time. *Breed* literally means to have offspring, or children, and *brave* can mean to "deny," so Time will be denied only if one reproduces. This connects back to the end of line 12 when those that pass on "see others grow," with the others suggesting a new generation. The speaker is proposing that their children being born (and so a possible pun with *borne*) is the only way to fight against Time and Death's inevitable march.

See also SHAKESPEARE'S SONNETS (OVERVIEW).

FURTHER READING

Forker, Charles R. "Sonnet 12." In *The Greenwood Companion to Shakespeare,* vol. 4, edited by Joseph Rosenblum, 1089–1095. Westport, Conn.: Greenwood, 2005.

Michael Young

Shakespeare's sonnets: Sonnet 15 ("When I consider every thing that grows") WILLIAM SHAKESPEARE (1599)

In this SONNET, the poet begins to immortalize his patron in verse since it seems that Time is going to take him away before any worldly offspring can be born to preserve his heritage upon the earth. The first quatrain (ll. 1–4) presents the poet pondering existence and the shortness of mortal life, even likening the brevity of life to a play on the stage (l. 3). The second quatrain (ll. 5–8) introduces an elaborate simile comparing the stages of plant growth to the stages of human life: youthful vigor, adult decline, and oblivion in old age. The last quatrain (ll. 9–12) emphasizes how the speaker views the addressee—as one who risks squandering their brief youth to the ravages of unrelenting time. In the concluding COUPLET, the speaker declares himself at war with time: He will assuage the temporal ravages inevitably suffered by the addressee by grafting the immortal verses of the poem to his memory.

This sonnet extends the poet's continuous request: that his patron produce an heir so that his beauty will not be forever lost. Until such time, however, the speaker adopts the tactic of immortalizing the addressee in verse. This situation builds up to a climax in the famous lines of Sonnet 18.

See also SHAKESPEARE, WILLIAM; SHAKESPEARE'S SONNETS (OVERVIEW).

Joseph E. Becker

Shakespeare's sonnets: Sonnet 18 ("Shall I compare thee to a summer's day?") WILLIAM SHAKESPEARE (1599)

Sonnet 18 is an ENGLISH SONNET structured around three arguments—or parts of arguments—in three quatrains followed by a concluding COUPLET. It begins with the speaker searching for appropriately beautiful things to which to compare the beloved. The speaker questions whether one might be "a summer's day?" (l. 1), but then realizes that the lover is not only "more lovely" but "more temperate" (l. 2), more even in personality and temper. The flower buds that appear in May can be destroyed by a strong wind, and summer itself does not really last that long.

The second quatrain leaves the lover to consider the natural progression of nature. Summer, lovely as it can be, is sometimes too hot; the "eye of heaven" (l. 5)—the sun—shines too brightly. Alternatively, though, the sun is dimmed, and summer lacks the expected brightness. In fact, too-hot or bright summers—or too-dim and cloudy ones—have an inevitable, negative effect on nature, causing that which began as "fair" or beautiful to "decline" in fairness (l. 7). In other words, things we expected to be beautiful in nature during the summer—flowers, shrubs, the landscape as a whole—can sometimes be unattractive because of an overly hot summer that burns plants and flowers, or because of an overly dim, cool, or rainy summer that either prevents flowers from blooming or washes away their beautiful petals as soon as they appear. This decline of beauty usually happens by chance: It was too hot or too cold. Or, as the poet points out in the metaphor of the sailing ship, decline in beauty can happen because Nature changed her course and did not bother to trim her sail in the process. In order to change course while sailing, the captain needs to be sure to trim his sail carefully so that the ship does not wander all over or, worse, capsize. The poet indicates that those unhappy and unbeautiful summers can come about either "by chance" or because Nature, for some reason, is not paying attention to her sailing and allows extreme weather to happen.

The third quatrain returns to the beloved while continuing the comparison to nature. The speaker indicates that the beloved is superior to nature because his or her "eternal summer" (l. 9) will not fade. In addition to being the victim of sun or rain, the beauty of summer is also the victim of time. No matter how beautiful a summer is, it will still turn to autumn. No one, not even Nature, can make it be summer always. The speaker of this SONNET, however, is implying that the beloved's "summer" (his or her time of especial beauty)—unlike that of nature—will not fade nor will the "fair" (the beauty that is part of the beloved) be lost. How is this possible? Summer cannot last forever, but neither can spring, autumn, or winter. Humans may be beautiful, but all humans grow old, lose their beauty, and die; they are subject to time. So why is the speaker implying that the beloved can escape the effects of time on his or her beauty? The speaker goes even farther by saying that Death cannot brag that he holds the beloved in his domain. Why? Because the beloved will continue to live in the poet's lines. But more than that, she or he will grow "in eternal lines to time" (l. 12) as though engrafted onto time. One way of allowing certain plants to grow better or last longer is to graft a branch (scion) of the weaker plant onto the roots or main stem (stock) of a much stronger plant, as roses were grafted onto lilac or privet stock. Or, as the critic Stephen Booth indicates, *lines* can also refer to the cords used to fix the scion to the stock or to the threads of one's life, spun, measured, and cut by the Fates. In this way Time is cheated, since the stronger stock allows the weaker rose to live much longer than it would "naturally." The speaker is indicating here that he has grafted the weaker scion of the beloved onto the stronger stock of the poet's verse, which will allow the beloved to cheat time and be beautiful—and alive—long past the beloved's natural death.

Overall, the speaker, being rather prideful about his own poetic abilities, indicates in the couplet that as long as this sonnet lives—which is, as the speaker states, as long as people are alive to breathe and see (read)—the beloved will live because the sonnet gives life to a person long dead by the time later readers discover it.

See also SHAKESPEARE, WILLIAM; SHAKESPEARE'S SONNETS (OVERVIEW).

Theodora A. Jankowski

Shakespeare's sonnets: Sonnet 19 ("Devouring Time, blunt thou the lion's paws") WILLIAM SHAKESPEARE (1599)   Sonnet 19 expands upon the imagery found in OVID's *Metamorphoses* of time as "the devourer of all things" (book 15, l. 234). Some critics consider Sonnet 19 to be the ending sonnet of the so-called procreation sonnets, in which the speaker suggests procreation as a defense against the ravages of time, though most end that set with Sonnet 17.

The poem's unidentified speaker begins Sonnet 19 by noting in the first QUATRAIN that "Devouring Time" (l. 1) may blunt the lion's claws, make the earth devour her children, cause the fierce tiger's sharp teeth to fall out of its jaws, and allow the phoenix to burn up instead of being born again, as tradition would have happen to the creature. All of these images point to the ferocity of time in this world. In addition, in the first three lines of the second quatrain, the speaker observes that "swift-footed Time" (l. 6) may manage to bring happiness and sadness to the whole world according to its whims as it swiftly passes. The final line of the second quatrain joins the third quatrain to complete the poem's primary concern, as the speaker forbids a personified Time to commit what the speaker considers to be the "most heinous crime" (l. 8) of all: to carve a record of Time's passage into the beloved's brow, or to draw any lines at all upon the loved one's brow with Time's magical pen; instead, Time must allow the beloved to remain "untainted" (l. 11) for men to admire in the future. Nonetheless, the speaker concludes in the final COUPLET, should Time do what comes naturally to it and etch the lines of age upon the beloved's face, the loved one will stay forever young in this verse.

Each quatrain is built around a governing metaphor: Time as ravager, its poignant effects, and its transformative abilities. The paradox of dying beauty is celebrated in the second quatrain: The seasons are both "glad" and "sorry" (l. 5) about the passage of time. Time is also likened to an artist—but an artist who preserves ugliness not beauty, a situation the speaker cannot abide.

Other critics view the images as aligning Time with Death, while also depicting Time as an entity who would be breaking the law if it were to touch the face of the friend in the course of its normal legal action, which ultimately "arrests" all men in death. An alternate meaning of the word *untainted* (l. 11) appears to be "not arrested" or "not impeached," so that the speaker is ultimately asking that Time neither arrest nor impeach his friend. Instead of Time doing what comes naturally, the poet's verse will "arrest" the friend by providing a permanent record of the friend's beauty. More recently, critics have pointed out that the speaker and Time pose similar threats to the young man: Both seek to prevent his development.

See also ENGLISH SONNET; PERSONIFICATION; SHAKE-SPEARE, WILLIAM; SHAKESPEARE'S SONNETS (OVERVIEW).

FURTHER READING

Jungman, Robert E. "'Untainted' Crime in Shakespeare's Sonnet 19." *ANQ* 16, no. 2 (2003): 19–21.

Peggy J. Huey

Shakespeare's sonnets: Sonnet 20 ("A woman's face with Nature's own hand painted") WILLIAM SHAKESPEARE (1599)

While this SONNET may appear at first to make a straightforward statement regarding the beloved, a closer look shows just how confusing is the gender situation presented here. To begin with, the speaker never identifies him/herself by gender. Therefore, the speaker can be either male or female. The identification of the lover as the Master Mistress of the speaker's "passion" confuses the issue as to whether the beloved is male or female. There is also the question of what exactly Nature "added" to the beloved that "defeated" the speaker's "purpose" in regard to the lover. This poem may very well have been designed purposely to be confusing, to make a statement that love itself is stronger and more important than the individual bodies of the lovers themselves.

Throughout the poem, the speaker refers to the personified "Nature" as the creator of the beloved. While we may assume that if Nature did it, it is "natural," and the way things *should* be, as the poem progresses we can see that the speaker believes that Nature is capable of making mistakes, mistakes that deny him or her pleasure in love. Lines 1 and 2 describe the lover as having "A woman's face" (l. 1) "painted" by Nature. This phrase suggests that the beloved is as beautiful as someone wearing cosmetics, but this beauty is totally natural. But does this image mean that the beloved is a woman whose face Nature painted, or does it mean that the lover is a man upon whom Nature has painted a face that looks like a woman's? Line 2 does not help us figure this out because it describes the beloved as being the speaker's "master-mistress." How are we to interpret that phrase? Does it mean the beloved is a dominating, masterful woman, or a man who looks like a woman or has other womanly characteristics? The speaker does not identify his or her own gender, leav-ing the following possibilities for interpreting the scenario of these two lines: A male lover has a woman beloved who is manly or masterful; a male lover has a male beloved who looks like a woman; a woman lover has a woman beloved who is manly or masterful; a woman lover has a male beloved who looks like a woman. Several critics suggest that this poem is androg-ynous or hermaphroditic, while others argue for one reading or another based on what they believe to be Shakespeare's "sexual orientation" (a phrase and a concept unknown in the early modern period). A close reading of these lines allows *all four* to be possibilities.

Lines 3 and 4 do not help untangle this problem. The lines refer to early modern ideas of women as having both positive and negative qualities, often in the same individual. A woman was expected to be gentle but also fickle. Thus, the beloved has a "woman's gen-tle heart" either because she has been born with one or because he is unusual in having this characteristic. Whether man or woman, the beloved's heart is not fickle or changeable, a negative characteristic a woman may be born with that a man may avoid because of his gender. Cultural attitudes also suggested that women's eyes were supposed to be bright. Line 5 tells us that the beloved's eyes are "more bright" than most women's, so bright that the light from them make the person gazed upon seem to be covered with gold ("gilded," l. 6). The eyes of the beloved are also "less false in roll-ing" (l. 5)—that is, less prone to wander and gaze long-ingly, or lecherously, at other potential love objects. Again, the lover's sex is ambiguous. If a woman, she displays all positive aspects and contains no negative ones; if male, he possesses all the good female qualities and none of the bad. The word *hue* (l. 7) can mean either "looks," "complexion," or "appearance." Thus, the beloved either looks like a man—or is a man—whose beauty is greater than that of all other men or women. As a result, this beauty "steals men's eyes" and amazes "women's souls" (l. 8). This dominating, manly beauty, or the male or female beloved, has a powerful effect on both men and women.

The final QUATRAIN reveals the problem that the speaker encounters in the beloved. Line 9 tells us that the beloved was created first, or primarily, "for a woman" (l. 9). This could mean that the lover is male, having been created for a woman's sexual use, or the beloved could have been created to be a woman. Unfortunately, while she was creating the beloved, Nature "fell a-doting" (l. 10), or did not pay close attention, or behaved foolishly. Consequently, she added "one thing" (l. 12) that removed the beloved from the lover. That thing was "nothing" (l. 12) that the lover needed or wanted. The COUPLET attempts to explain the "one thing." It states that Nature "pricked thee out for women's pleasure" (l. 13). On one level that line can simply indicate that nature "chose" the beloved to provide women with pleasure. But how was that to happen? If the thing added to the beloved was a "penis"—and the word *prick* was also slang for the penis in the early modern period—then we can say that nature gave a womanly beautiful man a sex organ that was designed for a woman and not the male speaker. But there is another possibility. Since *nothing* could also be slang for a woman's vagina, the addition referred to could also be a clitoris, a woman's organ of pleasure. Again this presents a number of possible readings: A heterosexual male lover is upset because the beautiful person he loves has a penis, something he wishes his lover did not have; a homosexual male lover is upset because the beautiful person he loves has a clitoris, something he wishes his lover did not have; a heterosexual female lover is upset because the beautiful person she loves has a clitoris, something she wishes her lover did not have; a homosexual female lover is upset because the beautiful person she loves has a penis, something she wishes her lover did not have. The sad final line indicates that the speaker will always love the beloved, but in a nonsexual way. The beloved's sexual activity ("use," l. 14) will be the "treasure" (l. 14) of the others who want a lover of the beloved's biological sex.

See also SHAKESPEARE, WILLIAM; SHAKESPEARE'S SONNETS (OVERVIEW).

FURTHER READING
Mahood, M. M. *Shakespeare's Wordplay*. 1957. Reprint, London: Methuen, 1968.

Theodora A. Jankowski

Shakespeare's sonnets: Sonnet 23 ("As an unperfect actor on the stage") WILLIAM SHAKESPEARE (1599)
WILLIAM SHAKESPEARE's Sonnet 23, one of those addressed to the LOVELY BOY, describes the poet's awkwardness; it is one of several sonnets to do so. This awkwardness is sometimes due to the speaker's social status, which is lower than that of the young man, and at other times is a result of a transgression committed by one of them. In Sonnet 23, however, the awkwardness is due to the strength of the speaker's love for the young man. His intense emotions prevent him from speaking with his accustomed eloquence, and he pleads with the young man to read "what silent love hath writ" (l. 13) in the more controlled medium of the poet's books.

Like most of Shakespeare's SONNETS, Sonnet 23 is divided into three QUATRAINS and a COUPLET. The first quatrain works by antithesis: The poet compares himself first to an actor, a person whose words and actions are carefully scripted, and then to "some fierce thing" (l. 3), a wordless being whose actions are driven by uncontrolled appetites. The "unperfect actor on the stage"—that is, an inexperienced or inept actor who "with his fear is put besides his part" (ll. 1–2)—is unable to speak the lines written for him. The "fierce thing replete with too much rage" may be a wild animal, but "thing" is a common Renaissance slang term for penis. This thing is strong, but his "strength's abundance weakens his own heart" (l. 4) and depletes what was once replete. Thus, the timid actor and the fierce thing arrive at the same speechless conclusion.

The poet then moves to the first person, explaining that his "fear of trust" causes him to "forget to say, / The perfect ceremony of loves [rite]" (ll. 5–6). Grammatically, it is not clear whether the speaker fears to trust himself or the young man, but like the actor or the fierce thing, he also forgets what to say, because he too is "unperfect" or "replete with too much rage." The "perfect ceremony," the right set of words that will complete "love's rite" and permit the union of the young man and the speaker, consists of words the speaker cannot remember when he is in the young man's presence. Like the fierce thing, the poet finds "in mine own love's strength [I] seem to decay" (l. 7), and that self-destruction is the result of his being "O'ercharg'd with burthen of mine own love's might" (l. 8). *O'ercharg'd,* like many images in the sonnets, has multiple meanings: commercial (the beloved is too costly); military (like a cannon replete with too much gunpowder); emotional (fearing that he has been entrusted with too much responsibility in the relationship). *Burthen,* now spelled *burden,* is similarly ambiguous, encompassing song (a REFRAIN), pregnancy (a common Renaissance term for the fetus), and the weight imposed by love's power. The poet, like the actor and the fierce thing, is rendered speechless by a combination of fear and overwhelming desire.

The third quatrain offers a solution to this speechlessness: The speaker pleads with the young man to "let my books be then the eloquence, / And dumb presagers of my speaking breast" (ll. 9–10), where "books" may refer to theatrical playbooks, the books of Shakespeare's erotic poetry already in print (VENUS AND ADONIS and The RAPE OF LUCRECE), any collection of writings, or the book containing the sonnets themselves. The "dumb presagers"—with *dumb* meaning silent, not stupid—may refer back to the unperfect actor: Some Renaissance dramas were preceded by a "dumb show," a silent reenactment of the main action of the play to help audience members follow a complex plot, but a later sonnet, number 83, claims that the young man's beauty has caused the speaker to go dumb, and that the young man has misinterpreted the silence as the speaker's "sin" (l. 9). In Sonnet 23, the speaker explains that the "dumb presagers" "plead for love, and look for recompense, / More than that tongue that more hath more express'd" (ll. 11–12), telling the young man that the books will say what the speaker, terrified or in the throes of passion, is unable to express. As with *o'ercharg'd,* the word *recompense* has a commercial application: The narrator may be expecting a reward, financial or physical, for the eloquent pleas in his books.

The couplets that end Shakespeare's sonnets often change the meaning of what has gone before, or complicate it in some way. Here, however, the couplet intensifies the emotion as the speaker begs, "O, learn to read what silent love hath writ" (l. 13). Confessing that his writings convey his love silently, perhaps meaning secretly or privately, he then introduces a paradox: "To hear with eyes belongs to love's fine wit" (l. 14). Love's intensity allows one sense (sight) to do the work of another (hearing); Shakespeare may here

refer to one of his early comedies, *A Midsummer Night's Dream,* in which a most unperfect actor, Bottom the Weaver, awakens from what he thinks must have been a dream about a transgressive love affair with the Queen of Fairies and announces, "The eye of man hath not heard, the ear of man hath not seen, man's hand is not able to taste, his tongue to conceive, nor his heart to report, what my dream was" (4.1.211–14). Bottom and his friends then perform a play to celebrate the three weddings that end Shakespeare's comedy, and their courtly audience, like the young man the sonnet's speaker addresses, must see beyond the halting and imperfect performances to the profound narrative of love and fidelity the company is trying to enact.

FURTHER READING

Cheney, Patrick. "'O, Let My Books Be . . . Dumb Presagers': Poetry and Theater in Shakespeare's Sonnets." *SQ* 52, no. 2 (2001): 222–254.

Catherine Loomis

Shakespeare's sonnets: Sonnet 29 ("When, in disgrace with Fortune and men's eyes") WILLIAM SHAKESPEARE (1599)

This SONNET begins with the speaker wallowing in a pit of depression, disgraced both in terms of fortune—he has had a lot of bad luck—and in the world's view of him. Consequently, the speaker views himself as a weeping, lonely outcast who prays to heaven constantly. But heaven is deaf and never hears these useless cries. All that is left is to look at his pitiful self and curse fate. We know the speaker is very unhappy, but the first quatrain does not tell us of the cause of this upset.

The second quatrain gives us more detail. The speaker wishes to be like someone who is more hopeful, has better prospects, someone who believes that things will eventually work out well. He wishes to look like someone else, presumably someone more good-looking, and he wishes for friends like someone else—either more friends or better ones. He also wishes for the artistic abilities of someone else, though these abilities could be in writing and not necessarily painting or drawing. He wishes to have the scope, the range, or generally grand abilities of some other person. The speaker sums up this longing by indicating that he is least content with his own talents which he once presumably enjoyed.

It seems as though there is nothing that can remove the speaker from this black pit of despair. In fact, the third quatrain reminds the reader again that these thoughts of the speaker's own inadequacies make him almost self-despising. But then, suddenly, things change. The speaker uses the word *haply* (l. 10) to indicate that this change is "by chance." Also, however, *haply* puns on *happily,* what this chance reflection makes him feel. The speaker is able to change this depressed "state," or mood, by thinking of "thee," who is clearly identified as the speaker's beloved. This person can change the speaker's mood amazingly and completely.

The rest of the quatrain demonstrates this newfound happiness by focusing on one image that signifies the speaker's new state: a lark singing at the gate of heaven, the place that was previously deaf to the speaker's cries. The speaker probably chooses the lark to indicate his extreme happiness and change of mood because of the lark's habit of flying straight up in the air in the early morning singing all the time. The direction the lark flies—up—is opposite the direction in which the speaker was living—down. This word can refer to depression—or to the direction of human life "down" on the "sullen" earth. Since the speaker was hardly in the mood to sing earlier in the sonnet, the image of the small bird pouring out its song becomes a blissful alternative to the speaker's unhappy state.

The speaker's depression calls to mind the Christian sin of despair. Given all that he laments in life, we might consider that he is very close to experiencing this sin, which can be viewed by the depressed person as a feeling that he is being denied the love of God. Thus, while a despairing soul might be "cured" of despair through feeling and acknowledging the love of God, for the speaker, the beloved's love replaces that of God. This substitution can be regarded as blasphemous on one level, but also as platonic in that the beloved becomes the means by which the speaker is directed toward a personal acknowledgment of God's love. Additionally, the "disappearance" of the bird in the air as it is viewed could make one believe that the lark has flown up to heaven. The beauty of its song thus surely indicates that

it must be singing hymns "at heaven's gate" (l. 12), hymns God would certainly want to hear, even if God was deaf to the cries of the speaker.

The final COUPLET reinforces the speaker's reliance on the beloved to provide happiness. While he had previously wished to trade everything in his life, from his abilities to his looks, with any number of persons, he now acknowledges that the mere remembrance, the thought, of this beloved brings such a wealth of happiness that he now would scorn to change his particular status in life with anyone, even a king.

See also SHAKESPEARE, WILLIAM; SHAKESPEARE'S SONNETS (OVERVIEW).

Theodora A. Jankowski

Shakespeare's sonnets: Sonnet 30 ("When to the sessions of sweet silent thought") WILLIAM SHAKESPEARE (1599)

In this SONNET, WILLIAM SHAKESPEARE uses metaphors connected to the law courts to help describe the speaker's feelings about his beloved, recalling both guilt and punishment. The sonnet also considers how time can affect friendship and love. Possibly the slowness with which English court cases preceded in the past suggested this combination of images to the poet. The speaker begins by talking about the periods—using the term that refers to the sittings of law courts, "sessions"—when he pleasantly muses upon the past and the changes that have occurred in his life. He uses the word *summon* (l. 2)—which refers to the legal document that calls a person to appear at a court proceeding—to describe how the beloved calls up past memories. Pondering these memories, the speaker mourns the loss of things that he tried to obtain but did not, and he laments again all the precious time wasted in the past.

The second quatrain indicates that, even though these periods of reminiscence are sweet, they are also sad because of the thoughts they call up. A good way to describe these memories would be "bittersweet," because they recall both good and bad moments. They cause the speaker, who sees himself as an unemotional type, to "drown" eyes that are not used to weeping in a flood of tears. What specifically causes these tears are memories of precious friends now hidden in the perpetual dark night of death, the sadness of past love affairs, and pleasant memories of the past. The speaker uses the legal phrase *long-since-cancelled* (l. 7) to indicate that all of the aspects of the love affair are over; like a bill or a loan, they have been marked "paid" and cancelled from the account of what is owed.

The third quatrain continues the speaker's grieving over incidents in the past and employs additional legal metaphors. He mourns over past grievances and sadly counts them up, as a lawyer might count up details of a case. This is a sad account—or story—of what has gone from his life, but the word *account* can also refer to finances. Lines 11 and 12 suggest that the loss of so many things in the speaker's past seems to bankrupt him, because each incident of grief causes a payout of grief and sadness as though he has not suffered it before. Thus, the remembrance of grief "charges" the speaker again and again for the sorrow.

The COUPLET summarizes the incidents described above by recalling the remembrance of a "dear friend" whose closeness and importance to the speaker has the effect of not only ending his sorrows but of restoring all the losses previous remembrances of others have taken from him. Despite the vast power of a country's legal establishment, the memory of a loved friend or lover can overcome that power in such a way that the speaker no longer feels victimized by circumstances beyond his—or anyone else's—control.

See also SHAKESPEARE'S SONNETS (OVERVIEW).

Theodora A. Jankowski

Shakespeare's sonnets: Sonnet 31 ("Thy bosom is endeared with all hearts") WILLIAM SHAKE-SPEARE (1599)

Sonnet 31 continues WILLIAM SHAKE-SPEARE's meditation on the theme introduced in the previous poem—memory and recollection. The sonnet opens wistfully: The poet states that many of his friends are absent or deceased and live on only in his heart. However, the most important figure that dwells there is the LOVELY BOY whose memory drives away the melancholy caused by his other losses. Fittingly, line 3 contains a homoerotic pun on "loving parts." The second QUATRAIN (ll. 5–8) develops the idea that the young man is the focus of the speaker's emotions. Indeed, he need only think of his friend to experience the joy of all his other relationships. The third quatrain is, perhaps, the most erotic. It proposes that the young man possesses all the qualities the poet has admired in his other acquaintances. The imagery plays on sexual innuendo: The addressee possesses all the "trophies" (l. 10) of the poet's old lovers, while the young man has received the "parts" (l. 11), an allusion to the "loving parts" of line 3. The concluding COUPLET summarizes the poem's central theme succinctly: Everything that the speaker likes in his other lovers/acquaintances is embodied and enshrined in his friend's heart—including his own.

This SONNET is particularly charged with metaphoric nuance and is a good example of how language play could engender a strong sexual element in the poetry. Indeed, though modern scholars are sometimes quick to point out that same-sex relations were not uncommon during the Renaissance, at the same time the use of sexually charged language was also used in platonic relationships in many Renaissance poems by various authors. Thus, it is difficult to ascertain whether or not Shakespeare intends the material to be taken as a conventional, hyperbolic poem that emphasizes the depth of his respect for his patron, or if it is, indeed, a love poem. Nonetheless, the sonnet powerfully illustrates the emotional impact that grew from the speaker's relationship with the young man to whom he addresses his poem.

See also SHAKESPEARE'S SONNETS (OVERVIEW).

Shakespeare's sonnets: Sonnet 33 ("Full many a glorious morning have I seen") WILLIAM SHAKESPEARE (1599)

In this SONNET, WILLIAM SHAKESPEARE uses the poetic voice, the "I" (l. 1), to express the lament of a lover for the loss of a brief romantic relationship. The lover, whose gender is not declared, is now separated from the male beloved who "was but one hour mine" (l. 11). The poem uses both meteorological and alchemical imagery to describe the love affair. Specifically, the beloved is equated with the sun, which, in the first QUATRAIN, "one early morn did shine / With all triumphant splendour on my brow" (ll. 9–10) and which is also found "Gilding pale streams with heavenly alchemy" (l. 4). In the early modern period, it was commonplace that the sun symbolized masculinity, in opposition to the feminine moon, and it was often tied to the hierarchy of the monarchy. Shakespeare follows this convention by having the lover note how the "sovereign eye" (l. 2) of the "heavenly" (l. 4) beloved "Flatter[s] the mountain tops" (l. 2). Alchemy, which was also a frequent topic in the early modern period, involves the protoscientific quest to transform base materials into gold.

In the second quatrain the "golden" (l. 3) sun, rather than creating more gold and sharing his love with the lover, "permit[s] the basest clouds to ride / With ugly rack on his celestial face" (ll. 5–6). The beloved "hide[s]" (l. 7) from the lover behind the clouds, "Stealing unseen to west with this disgrace" (l. 8). The exact form of the "disgrace" that the beloved is suffering from, which led to the end of the relationship, is not mentioned in this sonnet. The third quatrain celebrates the actual relationship when the beloved did focus his attention on the lover before being "masked" by "The region cloud" (l. 12). The final COUPLET concludes the lament by stating that in spite of the beloved's actions the lover still loves the beloved.

Sonnet 33 is thematically linked with Sonnet 34 ("Why didst thou promise such a beauteous day"), which continues to lament the lost relationship through the use of meteorological imagery. A number of critics read Sonnet 33 as Shakespeare's poetic lament over the ending of his homoerotic relationship with his beloved, who may have been the earl of Southampton, one of Shakespeare's patrons.

See also SHAKESPEARE'S SONNETS (OVERVIEW).

Jennifer L. Ailles

Shakespeare's sonnets: Sonnet 35 ("No more be grieved at that which thou hast done") WILLIAM SHAKESPEARE (1599)

Sonnets 1–126 of WILLIAM SHAKESPEARE'S SONNET SEQUENCE are addressed to a beautiful young man with whom the speaker has a relationship. Scholars continue to debate the nature of the relationship—a passionate friendship? a love affair? a poetic fiction?—but not its intensity. Sonnet 35 documents a difficult point in the relationship: The young man has committed a serious transgression, introduced in Sonnet 34, and followed up in Sonnet 36. Sonnet 35 describes the painful position of a betrayed lover who remains willing to forgive, but not forget, the offense, yet who realizes that extending this forgiveness is a self-betrayal.

Sonnet 35 begins with the reassuring command "No more be griev'd at that which thou hast done" and goes on to justify this seeming pardon by showing that faults are natural: "Roses have thorns, and silver fountains mud, / Clouds and eclipses stain both moon and sun" (ll. 2–3). We can still take pleasure in a rose or a fountain if we are careful to avoid the thorns and mud; we can enjoy the benefits of the sun and the moon while keeping in mind that clouds and eclipses temporarily mar their beauty. But the quatrain ends with a menacing shift, noting that "loathsome canker lives in sweetest bud" (l. 4). A beautiful outward show, which the young man has in abundance, is capable of hiding a pernicious disease that destroys from within.

The second quatrain repeats the assurance of the SONNET's opening line: All men make faults, the narrator generously claims, but then he suddenly twists the meaning by shifting the fault from the transgressive young man to the speaker himself: "and even I [have made a fault] in this, / Authorizing thy trespass with compare . . ." (ll. 5–6). The speaker has "authorized"—allowed by his authority, or written as an author—the young man's trespass by comparing it to natural elements such as thorns and clouds. Rather than identifying the trespass as unnatural behavior—the young man has the power to hurt and does so willingly—the speaker has made the sin acceptable by making it as natural as mud in a fountain or an eclipse of the sun. In doing so, the speaker has himself been contaminated by what the transgression really is: a sin, a disease, the "canker" in the sweet bud. By "salving" (applying a healing balm, or granting salvation to), the young man is "amiss," and by "Excusing [thy] sins more than [thy] sins are" (ll. 7–8), the speaker has corrupted himself. The young man's sins are evil, or perhaps just sleazy—Sonnet 96 attributes them in part to "youth" and "wantonness" (l. 1)—and the poet, by putting them into sonnet form and using elegant comparisons, has elevated the trespasses into art.

The third quatrain shifts into legal terms. To the "sensual fault" of the young man, the speaker "bring[s] in sense" (l. 9), a punning phrase that may refer to incense, the holy smoke sometimes used to expiate sins. The phrase also illustrates how the carefully controlled sonnet form helps make sense of the young man's senseless betrayal of the speaker. It may also mean the speaker is now incensed—in a rage—about the trespass he has just authorized. The sonnet represents a terrible paradox for the speaker: He should be the adverse party or complainant in an action against the transgressor, but by generously offering forgiveness in the first quatrain, he has instead become the young man's "advocate" (l. 10). This, the speaker realizes, perhaps to his shame, means that he is commencing a "lawful plea" against himself and has gone to court as both the prosecutor and defense attorney. Like the natural images that move from thorns to canker, the legal image becomes much larger in the final line of the third quatrain as the speaker's conflicting emotions, his "love and hate," blossom into "civil war" (l. 12). The war is "civil" in several senses: It is conducted in legal terms, it is internal (within the speaker; within the relationship), it is conducted in civilized terms (the elegant rhetoric of the sonnet), and it is self-destructive.

The legal language continues in the sonnet's COUPLET: The civil war between the speaker's love and hate has made him an "accessory," a coconspirator in the trespass rather than its victim, and this, sadly, is a position that his love for the young man makes necessary: He "needs must be" an accomplice "To that sweet thief which sourly robs from me." The label "sweet thief" links the beloved to the "sweetest bud" in which the "loathsome canker" lives, and shows the speaker's awareness that the young man is treacherous company. In an unusual use of punctuation in the 1609 edition of the poems, the final line of Sonnet 35 ends with a comma rather than a period. This allows Sonnet 36 to continue the story of the young man's transgression and its aftermath, and to deliver a verdict on the "sweet thief."

See also SHAKESPEARE'S SONNETS (OVERVIEW).

Catherine Loomis

Shakespeare's sonnets: Sonnet 60 ("Like as the waves make towards the pebbled shore") WILLIAM SHAKESPEARE (1599) Though Sonnet 60 is written in the SONNET format of three QUATRAINS and a COUPLET traditionally associated with WILLIAM SHAKESPEARE, this poem has its roots in book 15 of OVID's *Metamorphoses*. Tradition places this sonnet in a group of "immortality" sonnets that runs from Sonnet 54 to Sonnet 65. The person addressed in Sonnet 60 is traditionally considered to be a young man, known as the LOVELY BOY.

The poem begins with the unidentified speaker making an analogy between the undulation of waves and people's movement through time. The speaker observes that just as the ocean's waves move toward the pebble-covered shore, the minutes of our lives hurry toward their end (functioning, for example, like the sands of time slipping through the hourglass). Each wave changes places with the wave that goes before it, all of them struggling to press forward, one after the other, in order to reach the shore. Similarly, the bright light of birth, and all of its inherent possibilities, gives way to maturity, which eclipses the bright light of possibilities, allowing time, which is so generous to us in our youth, to take back its gifts. Time, the eternal reaper, removes the bloom of youth and digs furrows into beauty's brow, feeding on what is rare in "nature's truth" (l. 11), leaving nothing standing for time's scythe to mow down. The couplet concludes the poem by suggesting a solution to the problem of resisting throughout the future: This verse will still stand, praising the beloved's worth even through the havoc that has been caused by the ravages of time, thereby resisting time's movement with its stasis.

Critics often address the tentativeness of the promise of immortality as it appears in this sonnet. The possibility of defying death is less secure here than in previous poems in the sequence, such as in Sonnet 19. In the process of developing the idea of immortality, the CONCEIT has become almost an afterthought to the statement the poet has been making throughout the sequence about just how universal the progress of time really is. All of humanity starts from the same place and progresses through the same stages to reach the same place, yet some people will be immortalized while others are forgotten.

See also ENGLISH SONNET, SHAKESPEARE'S SONNETS (OVERVIEW).

FURTHER READING

Dingley, R. J. "Time Transfixing Youth's Flourish: A Note on Sonnet 60." *Shakespeare Bulletin* 12, no. 3 (1994): 41–42.

Peggy J. Huey

Shakespeare's sonnets: Sonnet 64 ("When I have seen by Time's fell hand defaced") WILLIAM SHAKESPEARE (1599)   In Sonnet 64, an older poet broods about a young man's vulnerability. The poem is burdened by a dark future and mourns a romantic commitment that cannot be as steadfast as desired. It follows the standard ENGLISH SONNET form, and the tripartite structure of the first 11 lines strikingly reinforces the chosen SONNET form. Each of the three QUATRAINS begins with a repeated opening clause—"When I have seen . . ." (ll. 1, 5, 9). The following images of decline and change diversely bring to mind the theme of "Ruin" (l. 11). This contemplation leads to a devastating realization: The beloved's own decline (and death) is equally inescapable.

The opening quatrain broods on the destruction of earthly things, with the speaker signifying his emotional alarm through the PERSONIFICATION of Time. Although the quatrain ends with grand architectural images, it seems to begin on more personal terms: "defaced" and "age" suggest the physical body of the young man, as does the "rich proud cost" that may refer to the opulent fashions of a nobleman. The words *outworn* and *buried* on one level simply mean that young age is long forgotten—and old fashions are made threadbare—by the time the speaker sees Time's defacement, yet the words also introduce visions of ancient buildings, such as those in Rome, half buried in earth. The next lines act as confirmation: The speaker describes once-lofty towers that have fallen or monumental brasses enslaved (their inscriptions obliterated?) by "mortal rage."

The second quatrain is obsessed with incessant change. The poet figures the ocean and land as rival military powers, neither of which dominates: The ocean gains position ("advantage") on the land, only to see the land "win" back territory from the ocean. The eighth line wonderfully imitates this oscillating by using CHIASMUS: "Increasing store with loss and loss with store[.]" This line also insinuates that loss will grow in either case. WILLIAM SHAKESPEARE borrows these images of flux from Arthur Golding's translation of OVID's *Metamorphoses,* a Latin poem influential on Renaissance writers.

The third quatrain is more general and subtly shifts to summary: Its lament at seeing "interchange of state" refers to the preceding quatrain, and "state" here continues the earlier political connotations (e.g., "kingdom of the shore"). Similarly, "state itself"—whose meaning is now closer to "condition" or essence—looks back to the opening lines in its being "confounded to decay." Having seen this, the speaker arrives at the poem's central, punning statement: "Ruin hath taught me thus to ruminate / That Time will come and take my love way" (ll. 11–12). The critic Helen Vendler has emphasized how the Latinate word *ruminate* makes possible the powerful tonal contrast of the 12th line, whose almost childlike simplicity—"Time will come and take my love away"—constitutes a powerful climax to the prior images. Moreover, the word *ruin* is literally present in "ruminate" later in the line, a resemblance heightened by Renaissance printing. The specter of ruin, then, haunts the poet's ruminations.

This use of dense wordplay is typical of Shakespeare, and its poetic meaning informs the disconsolate COUPLET. Here, thought equates to death because it pains the speaker so much it feels like death, but also because no thought of the beloved is now without fears of death. The last line also features a dual meaning: Either the speaker weeps at having a beloved who will eventually die, or, despite the beloved's vulnerability, the enthralled speaker will nevertheless "weep to have" him—that is, emotionally entreat the young man for his love.

Sonnet 64 is also steeped in the CLASSICAL TRADITION. In the fourth line, "And brass eternal slave to mortal rage," a first glance might suggest that brass is forever a slave; however, the notion that "brass eternal" is enthralled to a mortal thing is a paradox made valid by the phrase's clear echo of the *Odes* by the Roman poet

Horace. Similarly, Renaissance "ruins poetry," by EDMUND SPENSER and others, provides "mortal rage" with connotations of civic strife. This less-obvious meaning foreshadows the political and military metaphors that follow.

See also "RUIN, THE"; SHAKESPEARE, WILLIAM; SHAKESPEARE'S SONNETS (OVERVIEW).

FURTHER READING

Hieatt, A. Kent. "The Genesis of Shakespeare's *Sonnets:* Spenser's *Ruines of Rome:* by Bellay." *PMLA* 98, no. 5 (1983): 800–814.

Brett Foster

Shakespeare's sonnets: Sonnet 65 ("Since brass, nor stone, nor earth, nor boundless sea") WILLIAM SHAKESPEARE (1599)

In Sonnet 65, the speaker ponders how his beloved can survive the destructive effects of time, since nothing or no one on earth can do so. Most of the imagery in this SONNET derives from nature and natural objects and how they react to the changes caused by time and aging. This kind of change is often referred to as *mutability,* a word that means "change," but in literary studies it usually refers to the destructive changes that are wrought by time and are inescapable.

The first quatrain begins with the observation that things we usually think of as very strong—the metal brass, stones, earth, and the sea—cannot escape the power of "sad mortality" (l. 2). This last phrase is used here to indicate the power of mutability and the sadness it causes humans because of its destructive power. Critic Stephen Booth reminds us that "to hold a plea" (l. 3) is a legal term meaning to successfully argue an "action" (l. 4) or a law case. Thus, if all these very strong things cannot hold out against mortality, then how can beauty? After all, beauty is "no stronger than a flower" (l. 4).

The second quatrain works in a similar way. The speaker lists some additional strong things—rocks and steel gates—that are "decayed" by mutability, referred to as "the wreckful siege of battering days" (l. 6). If these things are "not so stout" (l. 7) against the attacks of time, how can "summer's honey breath" (l. 5)—a beautiful but transient time in our life—hold out? In the third quatrain, we see how these thoughts scare the speaker. He feels the fear that all humans feel as beings trapped in time: Everyone grows older because there is no choice. Close friends, lovers, family members, and pets will die. Even possessions will decay: flowers from a lover, clothes, and so on.

Once he realizes this, the speaker tries to think of a way that mutability can be defeated, especially in terms of his lover. The speaker refers to the beloved as "time's best jewel" (l. 10), an acknowledgement that the beloved lives within time and can also be seen as a gift of time. The speaker, however, does not seem to think about the possibility of his own decay, only that of the beloved. In this way, the speaker is like all lovers, caring more about the survival and happiness of the lover than about himself. In fact, the speaker wishes to find a place to hide the beloved from "time's chest" (l. 10). This could be a treasure chest where time keeps those especially precious things like its "best jewel," the beloved. Or the word *chest* could refer to a "coffin," the ultimate destiny of all humans.

The speaker also asks two impossible questions about controlling time, which is now imaged as human. Who has a hand strong enough to hold back time's foot, asks the speaker. The image here is of time running after the beloved to capture him or her. Or who, asks the speaker, can "forbid," or prevent, time from "spoiling" beauty, as in destruction by an invader. Again the speaker shows time to be invulnerable to the puny attempts by a flower or a sweet breeze—which are the only strengths of the speaker or the beloved—to control it.

Even though the speaker has spent 12 lines describing a very uneven struggle between himself and his beloved against the almost supernatural powers of time or mutability, he shows in the COUPLET that the poet/writer ultimately has more power than time. The speaker states that, given time's power, only a miracle can overcome it. Yet the miracle he indicates is somehow smaller than we might expect. The speaker does not need magical or futuristic weapons to deflect the force of time. He only needs a pen and paper. For "in black ink" (l. 14), the lines describing the beloved that the poet writes on paper, the love and the beloved (as well as the poet as lover/writer) may "shine bright" (l.

14) or continue to exist in the future. This couplet contains two verbal paradoxes. The first—that black may be bright—is an especially interesting one, as Stephen Booth points out, in a culture that viewed "black" as "ugly" or the direct opposite of "beautiful." The second—the philosophical paradox—is that, even though no human is powerless to stop or destroy time, a human's writings can outlast the lives of lover and beloved to reveal the love as well as the beauty of the beloved to future generations as yet undreamed of. Thus, despite the power of time and mutability that has aged and killed the lover and the beloved, we are reading of that love and those people over 400 years after their deaths.

See also SHAKESPEARE, WILLIAM; SHAKESPEARE'S SONNETS (OVERVIEW).

Theodora A. Jankowski

Shakespeare's sonnets: Sonnet 73 ("That time of year thou mayest in me behold") WILLIAM SHAKESPEARE (1599)

Sonnet 73 describes the speaker's feelings as he describes his aging to the beloved. Each quatrain contains a developed image of just how the speaker views himself as the result of the aging process. The images also describe the older lover to the beloved in terms of both the lover's approaching death as well as the lover's approaching old age.

In the first quatrain, the speaker describes himself as autumn. Since it is difficult to picture a season of the year by itself, the speaker focuses on one specific image of autumn, a tree. In looking at the lover, the beloved might see a tree in autumn whose leaves have turned yellow. He might also see a tree that has no leaves left on, or only a few leaves. The leaves have succumbed to the shaking of the tree's boughs caused by the cold winds of autumn that remind us of the coming of winter. As a result, the speaker looks like a "bare ruined choir" (l. 4) that is missing all its birds. This image is a bit complex. Birds live in trees and certainly do sing in the summer, but more so in the spring, when they are calling for mates. If a tree is particularly large and desirable, many birds may choose to nest and sing in it, so many that we hear a group—or "choir"—of birds singing, not just one or two. Poets are also sometimes

referred to as "singers," so the birds could also refer to the speaker as poet/singer. But a "choir" also refers to that part of a church where the choir sings. If the choir is good, they may sound like "sweet birds." In Gothic architecture, columns of stone that supported the church look like bundles of sticks which soar up to the roof splitting into "branches" that allow stained glass windows to be inserted. A tree in winter could look as though it had blue sky stained glass between its branches.

In the second quatrain, the speaker likens himself to the twilight of a day. Sunset has faded, and the sky is dark. Curiously, though, the speaker does not indicate that this sunset has any color. The light of day is being taken away by a "black night" (l. 7). Such a night seems to cause an absence of color or light. Using *black* to describe the night also calls up the image of night as "death's second self" (l. 8). An unmoving sleeper and a dead person look alike from a distance. And when elderly people sleep soundly, there is always the question of whether they are just asleep or dead. While the speaker here is obviously not dead, the image indicates the progression of age to death.

The third quatrain presents the image of the speaker as a dying fire. As a fire burns down, the flaming logs—the fuel of the fire—are consumed, and what is left are burning embers on the ash that results from the logs that started the fire. Thus, "such fire" (l. 9) that the speaker describes is the old fire, consisting mostly of "glowing" (l. 9) embers. This fire lies upon "the ashes of his youth" (l. 10)—that is, the ashes produced by burning the logs, the "youth." Eventually these embers will die on the "death-bed" (l. 11) of the ashes. Paradoxically then, the embers will die because they are "consumed" by that which originally "nourished" (l. 12) them—that is, embers in a fire will eventually be choked by the ashes which cut off the embers' oxygen source. And like the embers, the speaker will eventually die.

The speaker sums up his lesson to the beloved by indicating that, also paradoxically, the beloved's love will grow stronger as the lover ages because it is natural to "love that well which thou must leave ere long" (l. 14). The speaker hopes the beloved will love him more strongly because he will eventually die, most likely before the beloved since he is older. Additionally, the speaker suggests that the beloved's love will grow stronger since she or he also is caught in the cycle of time and will eventually die.

See also SHAKESPEARE, WILLIAM; SHAKESPEARE'S SONNETS (OVERVIEW).

Theodora A. Jankowski

Shakespeare's sonnets: Sonnet 74 ("But be contented; when that fell arrest") WILLIAM SHAKESPEARE (1599)

Sonnet 74 is one of several sonnets in which the poet imagines dying before the young man does, and he expresses his hope that both of them will find a kind of immortality through the sonnets that document their relationship.

Sonnet 74 opens with a conjunction, *But,* perhaps implying that the lines that follow are a continuation of Sonnet 73's closing couplet: "This thou perceiv'st, which makes thy love more strong, / To love that well which thou must leave ere long" (ll. 13–14). Sonnet 74 modifies the romance of that COUPLET by giving the young man a way out: "But be contented when that fell arrest / Without all bail shall carry me away" (ll. 1–2) the narrator commands, repeating the sentiment that opens Sonnet 71 ("No longer mourn for me when I am dead"), but doing so in legal language: Death will "arrest" him, meaning it will stop him as well as confine him, and there is no hope of bailing himself out of the grave. The first QUATRAIN ends on a more hopeful note, however: "My life hath in this line some interest / Which for memorial still with thee shall stay" (ll. 3–4), a wonderfully ambiguous statement in which "this line" can refer to the speaker's poetry (as in the "eternal lines" of Sonnet 18, l. 12) and where "interest" promises a return on the young man's investment in the relationship (as well as a reward for readers' continuing attention to the sonnets).

When the young man looks at the poems again and reviews the lines, he is once again seeing "The very part [that] was consecrate to thee" (l. 6), a line that combines the sacred act of consecration with the profane sexual connotation of *part,* a common slang term for the genitals. The speaker's body will, as the *Book of Common Prayer*'s funeral service reminds the congrega-

tion, go to earth, but the corpse is the only thing the earth is entitled to claim: "The earth can have but earth, which is his due, / My spirit is thine, the better part of me" (ll. 7–8). The word *part* now takes on an additional meaning: the speaker's spirit or soul. This spirit belongs to his beloved, and it finds expression in the sonnets.

In the third quatrain, what the young man will lose when the narrator dies is merely "the dregs of life" (l. 9), something to be discarded and forgotten. The speaker's body will become, in a common sentiment, "The prey of worms" (l. 10) as it decays in the grave. His corpse will be "The coward conquest of a wretch's knife" (l. 11) because the speaker is unable to fight back, or because the wretch holding the knife—the embalmer preparing the corpse for burial, or, Time with his scythe—would not be brave enough to confront a living man with his weapon. The corpse, and perhaps the speaker himself, will be "Too base" (l. 12) to be remembered by the young man: The corpse is "base," or disgusting, because it is rots; the speaker is "base" because, as he has claimed in other sonnets, he is of a lower social status than the young man. The speaker's despairing realization that he will be "soon ripe, soon rotten, and soon forgotten," demonstrates that the young man seems to have the upper hand in the relationship.

As is often the case in Shakespeare's sonnets, though, the COUPLET changes everything. It appears to be a mere platitude: "The worth of that is that which it contains" (l. 13), a reminder that "it's what's inside that counts." More seriously, it reminds the young man that, while a dead body is worthless, that which it was the vessel for—a spirit, a soul, an intelligence, a poet, a lover—is invaluable. The speaker concludes, "And that is this, and this with thee remains" (l. 14). His spirit lives in this poem, and the sonnet remains with the young man, and with us, to bring the speaker, the young man, and the relationship back to life each time the poem is read. The poet ultimately triumphs over death and, in his immortal declaration of his love and fidelity, over the young man as well.

See also SHAKESPEARE'S SONNETS (OVERVIEW).

Catherine Loomis

Shakespeare's sonnets: Sonnet 80 ("O, how I faint when I of you do write") WILLIAM SHAKESPEARE (1599)   In Sonnet 80, the speaker accepts the challenge of producing higher praise and greater verse than his rival produces. The first QUATRAIN finds the poet acknowledging the difficulty of rising to meet his rival's challenge, which has left the speaker "tongue-tied" (l. 4) in trying to best him in this war of words. The second quatrain introduces a simile into the poem that elaborates the image of the friend as the ocean and the two rival poets as boats sailing upon it. The rival poet possesses the more worthy vessel (i.e., poetic form) and is held up by the "soundless" (l. 10) depths of the friend's magnanimity. However, the speaker, with a lesser boat, is held up by the friend's slightest help or acknowledgement. In the final quatrain, the speaker continues the simile of the poets as sailing vessels and notes that the rival is strong and prideful whereas the speaker has relied upon his friend's charity. The final COUPLET has the speaker stating that, even if his friend does not want his praise anymore, the speaker will at least know that it was his own desire to praise his friend that lead to his downfall.

This sonnet vividly describes the competition poets underwent in trying to secure PATRONAGE and also provides a good example of the use of elaborate imagery—in this case, nautical allusions—to create a richly developed poem.

See also SHAKESPEARE, WILLIAM; SHAKESPEARE'S SONNETS (OVERVIEW).

Joseph E. Becker

Shakespeare's sonnets: Sonnet 85 ("My tongue-tied muse in manners holds her still") WILLIAM SHAKESPEARE (1599)   In this SONNET, the speaker paradoxically writes about being unable to write and speaks about being silent, providing many images of illiteracy and muteness. The first QUATRAIN in this ENGLISH SONNET contrasts the speaker's muse with the Classical Muses as they praise the subject, the anonymous youth. The speaker's muse is "tongue-tied" and holds herself silent ("still," l. 1), while all the other muses praise the youth in written ("character" and "precious phrase") treatises ("comments") (ll. 2–4).

The associated words *reserve, golden,* and *precious* have the effect of further contrasting the quality of the others' muses with the speaker's. They have access to all the splendor of written words, as opposed to the speaker's muse, who can only produce "manners," the courtesy to keep silent in the company of her betters. Scholars agree that line 3 may be corrupt; many emendations have been suggested, such as *thy* for *thei* and *Preserve* in place of *Reserve,* but none makes a line that is entirely compelling.

In the second quatrain, the speaker stands forth without the mask of the muse: "I" think good thoughts while the other poets ("other") write good words (l. 5). All he can do is speak the "amen" to their praises, in the way that any illiterate monk would do in a worship service where another, who could read, would say the prayers from the book. The speaker recognizes the quality of the praise the others write, realizes he cannot equal their efforts, and prefers silence to embarrassment.

The speaker becomes more specific in the third quatrain: When he hears the youth praised, he says "'Tis so, 'tis true" (l. 9) and adds his own, higher, praises—but only within his thoughts, where, he asserts, his love is greater than any other man's ("holds his rank before"), even though his "words come hindmost" (l. 12). Through the three quatrains, the speaker's tone is respectful of his rivals' achievements; they are consistently presented as having superior talent and greater eminence. Only the COUPLET offers a challenge to this analysis.

The couplet asks the youth to respect the others for what they have said aloud ("the breath of words," l. 13), and also to recognize the speaker's "dumb thoughts" as being spoken "in effect" (l. 14), as if they were spoken aloud and as effective as any words spoken aloud could be. Thus, even though the speaker has been unable to say—or write—a single word, the youth should recognize the inestimable value of the love he has imagined.

The very existence of Sonnet 85 destabilizes its point: To write about being unable to write creates the kind of paradox WILLIAM SHAKESPEARE relies on time and again to present the myriad complexities of feeling and expression. While all the other muses produce impressive-looking "comments"; he produces a sonnet.

See also SHAKESPEARE'S SONNETS (OVERVIEW).

Marjory E. Lange

Shakespeare's sonnets: Sonnet 86 ("Was it the proud full sail of his great verse") WILLIAM SHAKESPEARE (1599)

Sonnet 86, like several of the SONNETs immediately before and after it, presents elements of a poetic rivalry between the speaker and another, anonymous poet—neither of them ever fully identified—for the favor of the equally anonymous youth. In this SONNET, the speaker proposes three questions to explore why he has been unable to speak or write when the rival poet is around. These questions and the speaker's rejection of each explanation occupy the first 12 lines. He concludes in the COUPLET that the youth's infidelity has rendered him speechless.

In the first QUATRAIN, the speaker asks if it was the power of the rival's poetry (l. 1) that killed his own ability to write, leaving the speaker's ripe thoughts "inhearse[d]" (l. 3)—that is, placed on a hearse, buried in the speaker's brain. The image is of stillbirth ("their tomb the womb wherein they grew," l. 4). The tone of this quatrain is ambivalent: The speaker could be praising the rival's poetry in terms of a great galleon, or even of a fleet, but he could equally be describing it in terms that make it appear pretentious and grandiloquent. Either way, "bound for" (l. 2) is a nautical term referring to a ship approaching another with the clear intent of capture. Coupled with the images of stillbirth, this is a violent quatrain.

The second quatrain suggests that the rival poet gets a great deal of his inspiration from "spirits" or "ghosts" (ll. 5, 7, 9). It is important to note these choices in diction: WILLIAM SHAKESPEARE does not use *muse,* the more conventional term for inspiring spirits, but *spirit,* which is altogether ambiguous. In the middle of this quatrain, Shakespeare begins to answer the questions he has asked: No, neither the poet himself nor any extraterrestrial help he gets has silenced the speaker. This insistence continues into the third quatrain, where the speaker reiterates his insistence that neither the poet nor the ghost can claim to have silenced him: They "as

victors of my silence cannot boast; / I was not sick of any fear from thence" (ll. 11–12).

Only the couplet, where the VOLTA occurs, resolves the issue: When the youth deserted the speaker in favor of the rival, the speaker no longer had any subject to write about. The youth's presence in the rival's verse, "when your countenance fill'd up his line" (l. 13), demonstrates that, as far as the speaker is concerned, he has been deserted, and as a result, he lacked "matter" (l. 14), or a subject. The pun on "filling the lines" is subtle but pointed, particularly if the first quatrain is read ironically: The rival poet needed the youth's physical qualities to make his lines scan even, while the speaker crafted his lines to enhance the youth's beauties with their praise.

During the first 12 lines, the speaker's attention remains on the rival and the possibility that he has affected the speaker's writing. The speaker inserts himself into the discussion only when he rejects each explanation, reminding us that, in fact, he himself is the sonnet's subject. Inverting the syntax in lines 10 and 11 returns the rival (and the ghost) to prominence, putting the focus back on the rival so that the couplet, clarifying the beloved youth's responsibility, assumes even greater force. The strategy is designed to put the youth—and the reader—off guard so that when the responsibility for the poet's inability to write is finally assigned, we are all surprised.

Among Shakespeare's sonnets, this one is syntactically unusual because it is written entirely in past tense. Even at the end, no reason is given for the fact that apparently the rival no longer figures in the poet's landscape. In addition, Sonnet 86 features a 12-2 pattern of development, where the couplet bears the BURDEN of the turn. However, the substantial shift of focus in line 7 gives the sonnet an inverted Italian logic. For six lines, the focus remains on the rival poet, who is proposed as the reason for the speaker's enforced silence. At that point, the speaker reappears and, for another six lines, rejects the charges. A second inversion in lines 11 and 12, this time syntactic, places the speaker squarely against both the youth (for his disloyalty) and the rival poet in the couplet. Sonnet 86 raises more questions than it answers—chief among them, what happened to the rival poet?—and the sonnet teases its audience with a surface that cannot be penetrated.

See also SHAKESPEARE'S SONNETS (OVERVIEW).

Marjory E. Lange

Shakespeare's sonnets: Sonnet 87 ("Farewell: thou art too dear for my possessing") WILLIAM SHAKESPEARE (1599)

In format, Sonnet 87 follows the three QUATRAINS and a COUPLET pattern traditionally associated with the ENGLISH SONNET form. Similar to Sonnet 20, Sonnet 87 relies on feminine rhyme for most of the poem (lines 2 and 4 are an exception). Feminine rhymes pair two-syllable words in a stressed/unstressed pattern reminiscent of the rhyme schemes found in medieval ROMANCES; they were usually saved for comical poems, whereas this SONNET is solemn in tone. The poem is filled with financial and legal imagery designed to support the patently trivial metaphor of a beloved too expensive to love, which becomes the poem's ruling CONCEIT. In this case, the beloved is usually considered to be the LOVELY BOY.

The sonnet opens with the unidentified speaker telling the young man goodbye because he is too "dear" (expensive, with the pun on *dear* also meaning precious) for the speaker to keep around. The young man, in all his vanity, undoubtedly knows his own worth. His worth releases him from the speaker's hold, which has expired, just as bids to purchase stocks or bonds expire at a certain point in time. The speaker recognizes that, like the butterfly that must be free to be appreciated, the only way that he can hold the young man is by allowing him the freedom to make the choice to stay or go. For that generosity, the speaker deserves to be treated better. However, the reason for the speaker's generosity is unclear even to him, so in the poem, he is leaning toward reversing his decision. Either the young man gave himself to the speaker (whether sexually or in friendship) not knowing his own worth, or the speaker, to whom the young man gave himself, made a mistake in accepting the gift; so the young man's generous gift is, in hindsight, even more generous, and it is being returned to him after the speaker has had second thoughts on the matter. In this way, the speaker has had the wealth of the young man's

companionship in his dreams, like a king, but that is no longer the case when the speaker awakes, and he becomes poor again.

This poem is part of a group of sonnets in which the poet expresses concern about his originality of expression and his own worth. Also considered an estrangement sonnet, it demonstrates the poet's struggles saying goodbye.

See also SHAKESPEARE, WILLIAM; SHAKESPEARE'S SONNETS (OVERVIEW).

Peggy J. Huey

Shakespeare's sonnets: Sonnet 90 ("Then hate me when thou wilt, if ever, now") WILLIAM SHAKESPEARE (1599)

Sonnet 90 continues the thought developed in Sonnet 89. The speaker asks that, if the beloved young man plans to hate him, he do it now, so that this most disastrous blow will mitigate all later pain. If the hatred comes later, after lesser setbacks have occurred, it will strike an already grieving man as catastrophe. The sonnet is built around elements of time's contrasts—then/when, now/then, first/last—and comparisons. All of these elements blend to make a poignant statement of the speaker's lack of confidence in the beloved's reliability.

The first word of this ENGLISH SONNET, *Then,* sets up the relation with *when* and the paired *now* (ll. 1–2), and connects with Sonnet 89 when understood as "therefore." The speaker is not certain the young man ever will hate him, but if he is going to, the speaker asks that he show it now. Already "the world is bent my deeds to cross" (l. 2)—that is, everyone is determined to frustrate the speaker's goals. If the beloved joins "with the spite of fortune" (l. 3), the speaker must bow only once, whereas if the beloved "drop[s] in for an after-loss" (l. 4), the speaker's suffering is extended. "After-loss" is colored by expressions such as "after-thought," which emphasizes the casual, incidental nature of the deed.

The second quatrain rephrases and reiterates the plea: Do not come to beat down a defeated man, begs the speaker. "Give not a windy night a rainy morrow, / To linger out a purpos'd overthrow" (l. 7) adds a meteorological image to the military metaphor in which it is embedded. It also incorporates a bit of weather-wise folk wisdom: It was common to assert that a windy night promised a calm day, or that the coming of rain would calm blustering winds. In any event, the speaker begs the beloved not to prolong his agony.

The third quatrain shows again the conditional nature of the speaker's preoccupation: "If thou wilt leave me . . ." (l. 9). Here his concern is that he not be abandoned by the young man "last," after "petty griefs have done their spite" (l. 10), because this would not be a petty grief, but "the very worst" (l. 12). The COUPLET underscores the message: If you leave me, any other disaster will not seem disastrous by comparison.

Sonnet 90 pays the young man quite a compliment by yielding to him absolute influence over the speaker, who does not portray himself in a very positive light. Throughout this SONNET, the speaker's uneasiness remains unsupported by any facts. He offers no evidence in this poem that there is a reason for the projected desertion; it seems to be all in his mind. His only, and reiterated, concern is that, if the beloved leaves him, it should be at a time when it will dwarf all other disasters: "But in the onset come, so shall I taste / At first the very worst of fortune's might" (ll. 11–12). This second reference to "fortune" (also in l. 3) suggests that the speaker is unaware of having done anything to deserve his friend's departure, but he fears it anyway. This anxiety links Sonnet 90 thematically with the sonnets around it.

See also SHAKESPEARE, WILLIAM; SHAKESPEARE'S SONNETS (OVERVIEW).

Marjory E. Lange

Shakespeare's sonnets: Sonnet 91 ("Some glory in their birth, some in their skill") WILLIAM SHAKESPEARE (1599)

Sonnet 91 is a classic ENGLISH SONNET. In this poem, the speaker characterizes his love of the aristocratic object of desire in terms of the aristocratic pursuits and passions that the LOVELY BOY would understand, and then intimates the possibility of the young man rejecting him.

The SONNET begins with a direct appeal to the hierarchical nature of society, underscoring the difference in positions that the speaker and his object of desire

occupy. "Some glory in their birth" (l. 1) is at once a direct appeal to the young man of the sonnets, who does "glory" in his birth at a higher status in society than the speaking voice of the sonnets, and it is also, more generally, a description of the hierarchical system of which both are a part. The first QUATRAIN is a list of aristocratic and courtly pursuits and interests. Courtiers were expected to be, of course, wealthy (l. 2) and well-dressed (l. 3), but they were also expected to have some skills in equitation, falconry, and hunting (l. 4). Indeed, the sonnet's speaker even comments on the perennial subject of the English court's interest in new French and Italian fashions in line 3 "though newfangled ill."

The second quatrain acts as a pivot for the sonnet, allowing the third quatrain to return to the ground covered by the first with a different approach. The second quatrain is even divided easily into two grammatical units. The first unit is the sentence that grammatically completes list of dependent clauses of the first quatrain. This unit, lines 5–6, draws on the theory of the FOUR HUMORS, a theory of medicine, psychology, and physics whereby each individual thing or person is attracted to, or repelled by, another thing or person based on its humor (predominant bodily fluid). A phlegmatic person, by this theory, would not be drawn to falconry, because the primary element of the phlegmatic person is water. Thus, according to the theory of the humors, "every humour hath his adjunct pleasure" (l. 5) is quite literally true, as certain types of people will be drawn to certain types of activities and social alliances. The second unit of the second quatrain begins the turn back to the beginning of the poem by stating that the sonnet's speaker finds "one general best" (l. 8)—that is, the young man, who is better than "these particulars" (l. 7).

The third quatrain revisits the same list that the first quatrain did, but prefaces it with "Thy love is better than . . ." (l. 8), inverting the stratified system that the first quatrain points to and placing the young man at the apex of a new hierarchy of desire. Wealth, fashion, and the gentlemanly pursuits stand in a pale shadow to the love that the speaker has for the young man. The final line of the third quatrain even goes so far as to upset the humorial theory that the second quatrain had relied on, by claiming the young man is singularly loved by "all men," regardless of their humor.

The consequences of this reversal of the hierarchy is not recognized until the COUPLET, when the speaker notes that to put such an emphasis on the affections of one person subjects him to the possibility of devastating rejection. While he has the affections of the young man, the speaker is totally happy with only one exception— that the possibility remains of the young man rejecting him, taking "all this away" (l. 14) and leaving him utterly wretched. It is the doubt of others, the possibility that the one whom the speaker loves would reject him so callously, that is at the heart of the sonnet.

See also SHAKESPEARE, WILLIAM; SHAKESPEARE'S SON-NETS (OVERVIEW).

Andrew Bretz

Shakespeare's sonnets: Sonnet 93 ("So shall I live supposing thou art true") WILLIAM SHAKE-SPEARE (1599)

As is common in the structure of many SONNETS by WILLIAM SHAKESPEARE, this is a series of four sets of rhyming lines. The first three sets are each four lines long, with the first and third lines of each QUATRAIN rhyming, as do the second and fourth lines. The last two lines of the sonnet form a rhyming COUPLET. Often, in what is called a Shakespearean sonnet, or ENGLISH SONNET, the last two lines deliver a final twist in the message.

The speaker of the poem expresses his great affection for his lover, especially for his or her physical beauty. But this is the irony of this very melancholy poem—the speaker knows that the beloved's beauty hides the fact that he or she has actually found someone else who they now love, making this sonnet distinct from the famously romantic ones.

In the second half of line 1, the word choice of *supposing* shows that, at best, the relationship is going on as if they are pretending. The portrayal, like that by a performer on stage, is as if their love is "true," which does not simply mean it to be factual but also to be faithful to a pledge or vow. The state of the relationship is revealed when the speaker describes himself as being "Like a deceived husband" (l. 2). This use of the conditional establishes that while the speaker is not the lover's husband, their relationship is as profound (and probably as public) as that of a married couple. While a cuckold was often seen as a bawdy, humorous figure, this speaker holds hope for a reconciliation.

The first quatrain is actually one sentence, but its beginning, "so shall I live," potentially makes it an interrogative even though there is no question mark at its end, depending on how "shall" is read. The second quatrain continues the internal, and possible public, conflict of emotions. While the lover's eye shows "no hatred" (l. 5), which is usually a good thing in a relationship, the speaker's torture has not ended because the lover's expression is false. So the common virtue of a lack of hatred is, in Shakespeare's poem, an uncommon sign of the vice of unfaithfulness.

The beginning of the next line presents an interesting technical puzzle. The word *many's* (l. 7) is written as if a possessive, which means it would be read as a noun, not an adjective, as is its normal use. There seems to be a noun missing from the line's syntax that is being replaced by this unique possessive, such as "many people," "many hearts," or "many relationships." Until now, this anguish may have simply been in the speaker's imagination or a momentary falling-out with the lover, but once the accusation escalates to the beloved's own "false heart's history" (l. 7), it seems the speaker has evidence of a record of unfaithfulness. History also carries the added pain, for the speaker, of something that is known and acknowledged publicly. If so, then the missing word is something like *people* or *friends*.

Line 8 lists signs of this false affection. The first is "moods," or emotions, but the next two are physical qualities of the face: "frowns," and therefore sadness, and "wrinkles," which would appear with a frown but also can be an echo of advancing age. This may show the speaker fears the fate of living within a heartless facade of a marriage until death.

The third quatrain brings the first implication of God and Christianity through the use of "heaven" (l. 9). To the speaker, God "did decree" (l. 9), either to be taken as announced or ordered, that the lover's "sweet" (l. 10) face belies its true meaning of falseness. If that is so, then God wanted apparent sincerity to be a sign of sin, though why God would wish for such a masquerade is an unasked question. Thus, it is only the image of love that "dwell(s)," in the beautiful face (l. 10), and those "looks" produce "nothing . . . but sweetness tell" (l. 12), with *tell* pointing to perception, not fact. The speaker may seem to be complimenting the lover's beauty, but it is by an indirect negation—in other words, by reminding us what is not there.

The couplet at the very end again focuses on religious imagery, with a reference to the very well-known biblical story of Eve, the first woman—and first temptress—who was unfaithful to God. The lover's "beauty" is now finally compared to "Eve's apple" (l. 13), the original forbidden fruit that the lover has metaphorically copied by finding a different romantic companion. Like Eve's original sin, the infidelity does not represent or "answer" (l. 14) the lover's beauty, and the lover's sin will continue to "grow" (l. 13) if there is not true "virtue" (l. 14) to match the appearance of love. Despite all the previous despair, in this last line the speaker seems to be holding onto the faintest hope for their own renewed happiness and the lover's redemption.

See also SHAKESPEARE'S SONNETS (OVERVIEW).

Michael W. Young

Shakespeare's sonnets: Sonnet 94 ("They that have power to hurt and will do none") WILLIAM SHAKESPEARE (1599)

Sonnet 94 plays on the Petrarchan convention common to many other Elizabethan SONNET SEQUENCEs, that of the beloved as a coldhearted mistress. Starting with the basic ITALIAN (PETRARCHAN) SONNET form of setting up the problem in the initial OCTAVE before resolving it in the final SESTET, WILLIAM SHAKESPEARE spends the first eight lines talking about people and then the next four lines talking about flora before, in a uniquely Shakespearean twist on the topic, comparing people and flora in the final COUPLET, to the former's disadvantage.

The SONNET begins by explaining that people who have the power to hurt others, yet do not hurt them, are not doing what would be the most natural thing for them to do. Though capable of moving others, whether through their words or actions, they are themselves like stone—unmoved, cold, not easily tempted. These people fittingly inherit heaven's graces and do not

squander their gifts; they own their own images while others can only serve them. Similarly, the summer flower makes the summer sweet, though the flower merely lives and dies. However, if the flower is infected, then the basest weed outlives it. In this manner, sweet things (and people) can be turned sour by the things they do, just as dying lilies smell worse than weeds.

Reworking the floral imagery that previously appeared in Sonnet 54, the poem places an ironic twist on the topic of estrangement. Using a BIBLICAL ALLUSION to the parable of the talents, the speaker justifies severing his connection with the young man because he is "cold" and has been "unmoved" (l. 4) by the speaker's proffered friendship. Editorial choice results in variations in the punctuation at the end of line 12, rendered as either a period or a colon. This choice shifts the emphasis placed on the final two lines as the poem ends with either a complete sestet or a QUATRAIN and a couplet.

See also SHAKESPEARE'S SONNETS (OVERVIEW).

FURTHER READING
Easthope, Anthony. "Same Text, Different Readings: Shakespeare's Sonnet 94." *Critical Quarterly* 28, no. 1–2 (1986): 53–60.

Peggy J. Huey

Shakespeare's sonnets: Sonnet 97 ("How like a winter hath my absence been") WILLIAM SHAKESPEARE (1599)

Scholars have long held that this poem is addressed to the LOVELY BOY, a beautiful young aristocrat whose presence dominates most of WILLIAM SHAKESPEARE's SONNET. It begins with the speaker-poet reflecting on a time when the two men were apart. The poet likens this period of separation to winter and laments, "What freezings have I felt, what dark days seen!" (l. 3). As an extended metaphor, winter is a season as well as a state of being. By contrast, the young aristocrat is decidedly unwinter-like and described, appositionally, as "the pleasure of the fleeting year" (l. 2). The poet and the young aristocrat are thus separated by space, season, and mood.

Estranged, the poet feels time pass slowly, as it does during periods of self-absorbed melancholy. His memories of the young aristocrat only worsen matters, for they recall the embodied pleasures that seem, by contrast, to make time go by so quickly. Early on, Sonnet 97 marks this temporal problem in its sound effects by juxtaposing the lengthy *e* sounds—associated with the aristocrat—of "thee," "fleeting," and "seen," with the alliterative *d* sounds—associated with the poet—of "dark," "days," and "December's." To emphasize how "old December's bareness" is "everywhere" (l. 4) perceived as painful, each of the sentences in the first QUATRAIN ends with an exclamation mark.

That use of hyperbole prepares us for its qualification. As the second quatrain begins, readers learn that the true time of year is just before the harvest. The unexpected shift in season pits the poet's imaginary winter against the world as it exists. Here the world wins out, for the poet now looks beyond his emotions to the abundance of fall. Within two lines, he refers to its fertility six times; three of these references occur in his observation that the fields are "big with rich increase" (l. 6). Autumn is here personified as a pregnant woman.

Sonnet 97 insists that spring and summer are responsible for autumn's abundance. What is now "teeming" thus derives from the "wanton" past—specifically, from the fathering effects of spring. That abundance is a condition of possibility, a harvest yet to come. The poet sees these seasons immediately, but readers must struggle to comprehend this compressed, multiseasonal temporality. Complicating matters, the second quatrain then ends with the unsettling assertion that growth is informed by death, since what the poet sees of the earth reminds him of "widowed wombs after their lords' decease" (l. 8). It is therefore premature to think that the sonnet has moved from describing the poet's melancholy to treating the world.

The third quatrain expands this despondent sense of pregnancy without birth by returning to the poet's perspective. Now, looking on agriculture, he does not anticipate its eventual harvest. Rather, its very abundance reminds him of the "hope of orphans, and unfathered fruit" (l. 10). Hope, in this metaphorical sense, is orphaned, unrealized, split off. The fruit is "unfathered" and therefore separated from its parentage. Time is poised, almost unmoving. The third quatrain offers these counterintuitive metaphors of arrested fertility to recall the problem of yearning with which the poem began. The poet is waiting, looking ahead, with the very sense of time to come that underscores hope. Matters will not improve for him until he and the beautiful young aristocrat are reunited, since "summer and his pleasures wait on thee" (l. 11).

The concluding COUPLET begins where the third quatrain ends—with the conjunction of the poet's feelings and his views of nature. Now, in his eyes, the young aristocrat's absence has made "the very birds" be silent (l. 12). Correcting himself, the poet allows that if the birds do sing, they do so with little "cheer." A SYNECDOCHE for nature, the birds are thus as woeful as our poet. The PERSONIFICATION then becomes even stronger as their dispirited singing somehow causes leaves on the trees to "look pale" (l. 14), itself a harbinger of decline and death. Sonnet 97 emphasizes absence and therefore is best linked to Sonnets 43–51. It ends by passing over the period of celebration associated with harvest and instead setting its sights on barren winter.

See also SHAKESPEARE'S SONNETS (OVERVIEW).

Larry T. Shillock

Shakespeare's sonnets: Sonnet 98 ("From you have I been absent in the spring") WILLIAM SHAKESPEARE (1599)

Sonnet 98 continues the romantic themes of Sonnet 97, in which the narrator grieves the absence of his beloved during the "barrenness" of winter and finds it impossible to bear spring or summer without the object of his affection. Pining for his beloved during spring—a time of birdsongs (l. 5), flowers (ll. 6, 9, 10), and delight (l. 11)—the poet of Sonnet 98 yearns for his lover and cannot enjoy the season's gifts of birth, regrowth, and beauty. While new life and beauty are evident, even spurring "heavy Saturn" (associated with old age and Father Time, 1.4) to rejoice, the woeful speaker finds foul company in "April, dressed in all his trim" (l. 2). Although he speaks of "the lily's white," "the deep vermillion of the rose," and of "the sweet smell"—poetically "playing" with spring—several contradictory conjunctions, such as *yet, or, nor,* and *but,* reveal that the speaker loves and misses his beloved, and they possibly point to an awareness that his feelings are selfish. Clearly these words reveal his contradictory state of mind and echo and emphasize the winter-spring binary in this and the SONNET before it.

The object of affection is not revealed in Sonnet 98—or in the previous and following sonnets. Not only is the gender of the beloved unclear, so is the precise nature of the relationship between the poet and his loved one. Nevertheless, the repeated use of the word *you* and its variations, including *your, youth,* and *hue,* gives attention to and exposes the poet's fascination with the absent beloved. Written in past tense, this sonnet perhaps indicates that the lovers are no longer separated, or that he is passing judgment and assigning guilt to the beloved, or the narrator could simply be selfish and dramatic in the absence of love and lack of time, two themes found in many of Shakespeare's sonnets. Sonnet 98 also relies on a number of obvious erotic wordplays. The most obvious of the sexual references in Sonnet 98 is the "lily" (l. 9) and the "rose" (l. 10), both expressions of female sexuality. A closer look gives way to phallic reference as well: the ALLITERATION of line 8's "proud lap pluck."

See also SHAKESPEARE, WILLIAM; SHAKESPEARE'S SONNETS (OVERVIEW).

Kristen N. Heintz

Shakespeare's sonnets: Sonnet 99 ("The forward violet thus did I chide") WILLIAM SHAKESPEARE (1599)

Sonnet 99 is one of a pair of sonnets (with Sonnet 98) whose unexploited insinuations about sexual love give it an unusual illusive dimension. WILLIAM SHAKESPEARE sets out to answer two unspoken questions about origins: How did certain plants get their aromas? And how did certain plants get their color? In the process, he takes full advantage of traditional Petrarchan CONCEITs. In the COUPLET, the poet concludes that every flower he has seen has stolen odor or color from his beloved.

This is a 15-line sonnet, the only one Shakespeare wrote. Line 1 is introductory, resulting in a five-line first "QUATRAIN" with an *ababa* rhyme scheme. Apart from this anomaly, Sonnet 99 is a structurally normal ENGLISH SONNET, although there is a turn after line 7 as well as at the couplet. If the reader treats the first five lines as a "quatrain," this VOLTA indicates that there is an inverted Italian logic at work here, providing a kind of structural ambiguity echoing the many linguistic ambiguities.

The first line sets up an embedded speech, where the speaker says he scolded the early ("forward") violet. *Forward* can also mean presumptuous; this ambiguity provides the poet with the basic contrasts that play out through the SONNET. In lines 2–5, the speaker addresses the violet oxymoronically as "sweet thief" (l. 2). This is a traditional CONCEIT, but on this occasion *sweet* does not describe a mistress, and *thief* is not the hyperbolic characterization of an attractive person. Violets are flowers, "sweet" by nature, and this one is being whimsically accused of a real theft—of stealing "that sweet that smells" (l. 2) from the beloved's breath. The rest of the quatrain, and indeed, the eight-and-one-half lines, shift from aroma to color. The violet, says the poet, gets its color from the beloved's complexion. As with *forward, purple* (l. 3) has two connotations, red and violet, so the violet is accused of stealing its rich purple from the red blush of the beloved.

In the second quatrain, the speaker shifts so that the rest of the sonnet addresses the beloved: When the speaker says he "condemned" the lily "for thy hand" (l. 6), he is blaming this whitest of flowers for stealing its color from the beloved's fairness. Similarly, the "marjerom" (marjoram) is accused of stealing its color from the beloved's hair, which thus would seem to be dark auburn—or brown-haired. Alternatively, the marjoram could be guilty of having taken the waviness of the beloved's hair; the ambiguity could be resolved only by identifying the beloved.

Lines 8–12 detail the much more serious and thoroughgoing thefts perpetrated by the roses. These are discovered standing fearfully on thorns (l. 8); the phrase is proverbial, describing a person in a state of painful anxiety. Roses also, of course, stand on the ends of their thorny stems, and "thorns" also traditionally can replace "rose bush" in a SYNECDOCHE. The poet personifies the colors of the first two roses: One is "blushing shame," that is, bright red; the other "white despair" (l. 9). The third rose is "nor red nor white" (l. 10), presumably because it has passed its prime and its petals have fallen. The poet exploits this state to indicate the fate of any flower presumptuous enough to have appropriated not only the beloved's color but also the fragrance ("to his robb'ry had annex'd thy breath," l. 11); it has been eaten by "a vengeful canker" (l. 12), the cankerworm. What makes this fate particularly gruesome for this rose is that canker generally attacks buds, not full-blown roses. The heinous crime has produced a shocking outcome. Thus, the poet has built a crescendo up through the levels of felony until he has reached the worst theft and the only explicit punishment.

The couplet moves away from the destruction of the thieves to praise the beloved by asserting that the speaker found no flower "But sweet or color it had stol'n from thee" (l. 14). Every flower in the garden obtained either its aroma or its beautiful hue—or, as in the case of the canker-infested rose, both—from the beloved.

See also SHAKESPEARE'S SONNETS (OVERVIEW).

Marjory E. Lange

Shakespeare's sonnets: Sonnet 104 ("To me, fair friend, you can never be old") WILLIAM SHAKESPEARE (1599)

Sonnet 104 is one of WILLIAM SHAKESPEARE'S SONNETS dedicated to his young male friend, the LOVELY BOY. As in many of this sequence, the idea of aging as a prod to reproduction is employed. Shakespeare's metaphor is that of the time and the seasons, which come and go in a circular pattern, one being born as another dies. The speaker begins by declaring that his friend "never can be old" (l. 1) in his eyes, because time stands still when he looks at his friend. He undercuts this position by discussing how much time has passed since they met—"three years" (l. 3)—how the cold of winter supplants the warmth of spring, and how autumn—middle age—is come. However, he states once more, directly addressing the friend, you have not changed at all. You have not been touched by time—although if you look out the window, you can see all of nature is touched by time. Shakespeare furthers the metaphor with "dial hand" (a watch) with which the passing time is marked, without seeing the motion of it. While the speaker's friend may seem to him unchanged by time, he has experienced it himself. In the final COUPLET, he brings his

premise and the extended metaphor to its logical conclusion: his friend hasn't "bred." Before his birth, "beauty" was not born, so after his autumn will come his winter, and he must engender a new "spring" before that comes. In form, this is an ITALIAN (PETRARCHIAN) SONNET.

See also SHAKESPEARE'S SONNETS (OVERVIEW).

Leslie J. Ormandy

Shakespeare's sonnets: Sonnet 105 ("Let not my love be called idolatry") WILLIAM SHAKESPEARE (1599)

Unlike the two SONNETs that surround it, Sonnet 105 is not directly addressed to the young male beloved. It is, however, about him, and the poet walks a fine line between playful wit and outright sacrilege as he refutes the prior unspoken reproach that his worshipping of the young male is idolatrous in a religious sense. The sonnet makes its case that to love one god—in this case the youth—is not idolatry since in fact loving and worshipping two or more is. The poet's religion, he goes on to say, is not very different from Christianity: His praises are to one divine being who is "ever so" (l. 4), the object of his worship is triune, being fair, kind, and true (ll. 9, 10, 13), like the Christian God. Critics have noted, however, that the rhetoric of Christian allusion used in the sonnet convicts the poet of the very sin he defends himself against.

Sonnet 105 hinges on the recognition that the accusation of idolatry comes from a Christian who believes the Trinity is comprised of three persons (Father, Son, and Holy Spirit) in one eternal God. Line 4 ("To one, of one, still such, and ever so") echoes the Christian doxology recited in church: "Glory be to the Father, and to the Son, and to the Holy Spirit; as it was in the beginning, is now and ever shall be, world without end. Amen." The poet claims here that his beloved is also triune, not unlike the God of his accuser, and he is "still such, and ever so." Similarly, the three-time repetition of the words *fair, kind,* and *true,* in lines 9, 10, and 13, reiterate the three-in-one theme, and the poet goes so far as to claim that these qualities never "kept seat in one" (l. 13) until they did so in his own beloved.

As the sonnet progresses, emphasis is increasingly placed on the word *one* as it occurs in the last line of each QUATRAIN (ll. 4, 8, 12) and in the final line of the COUPLET (l. 14). However, "one" also occurs phonetically or graphically in the words *wondrous* (ll. 6, 12) and *alone* (l. 13). Taken together, these repetitions and allusions clearly situate the sonnet as a song of praise and a pledge of loyalty to the beloved. The sonnet also clearly employs Neoplatonic devices, too. The poet identifies the beloved's three qualities (fair, kind, and true) as those of the Platonic Triad (the Beautiful, the Good, the True), thereby opposing the Christian Trinity with the classical emblem of the divine.

Overlooked and undervalued for its lack of a central metaphor, image, and clear interpretation, this sonnet, as the critic Helen Vendler and others have noted, is frequently "dull," "tautologous," or "repetitive," though others clearly appreciate the poem, referring to it as "witty," "playful," and even "charming." Such differing responses to the sonnet reflect how difficult it has proven to be for interpreters. Is it a serious defense aimed at overcoming the accusation of idolatry? Or is it a playful refutation meant to highlight poetic craft through allusions to the doxology, Christian Trinitarian theology, and the Platonic Triad? Although these two interpretations are dichotomous, they are both contingent on the reader's ability to recognize the poetic allusion to Christian doctrine and devotion in the sonnet.

See also SHAKESPEARE, WILLIAM; SHAKESPEARE'S SONNETS (OVERVIEW).

James M. Palmer

Shakespeare's sonnets: Sonnet 106 ("When in the chronicle of wasted time") WILLIAM SHAKESPEARE (1599)

Sonnet 106 describes what contemporary critics would call "the anxiety of influence." In addition to the many English SONNET SEQUENCES, WILLIAM SHAKESPEARE was familiar with classical, medieval, and Renaissance ROMANCEs, many of them extremely accomplished. As he did in Sonnet 53, in Sonnet 106 he responds in a witty way to the pressure exerted by these literary forbears. In acknowledging the literary past, Shakespeare almost reverts to an older SONNET form, the ITALIAN (PETRARCHAN) SONNET, which, instead of three QUATRAINS and a COUPLET, is made up of an OCTAVE (the first eight lines), which establishes a situation, and a SESTET (the final six lines), which resolves it. But Shakespeare manages to make it through only seven lines before the topic shifts from love poetry of the past to love of the young man in the present tense. In terms of sense, if not of punctuation, Sonnet 106 can be divided into quatrains and a couplet, and it employs the "when/then" structure Shakespeare uses in Sonnets 2, 12, 15, 29, 30, 43, and elsewhere.

The SONNET opens with an ambiguous image of old books, which the speaker calls "the chronicle of wasted time" (l. 1). A CHRONICLE is an orderly chronological record of past events; "wasted time" might mean time that has passed, or it might refer to the decaying condition of the book containing the chronicle, but the words also imply that there might be better ways to spend time than pursuing unattainable lovers. In the chronicle of wasted time, the speaker finds "descriptions of the fairest wights" (l. 2), where *wights* means people of either gender, and where the superlative shows the limitations of history: it describes not everything that happened, but only the best or most noteworthy events, and not even the fairest wights can survive time's ravages. The speaker also finds "beauty making beautiful old rhyme" (l. 3) in the literature of the past, a function that the narrator has asserted the young man's beauty performs for these sonnets. The old rhymes were written "In praise of ladies dead and lovely knights" (l. 4), a line that neatly encapsulates the sonnets' misogyny: there are no living ladies addressed in the first 126, and the emphasis is on the lovely and aristocratic young man, sometimes referred to as the LOVELY BOY.

The "When" of the first quatrain is answered by the "Then" of the second: when reading old love poetry, the poet finds "in the blazon of sweet beauty's best" (l. 5) a prefiguration of the beauty of his subject. BLAZON is a term adopted from heraldry, referring to the coat of arms by which a knight is identified, but for Elizabethan poets it meant a descriptive list of body parts. In Sonnet 106, the narrator reads the descriptions other poets wrote "Of hand, of foot, of lip, of eye, of brow" (l. 6) and decides what the poets of the past were trying to capture, what "their antique pen would have expressed" (l. 7), is the perfect beauty of the young man—"such beauty as you master now" (l. 8). Poets were often credited with the ability to prophesy, and poets who wrote of beauties of the past were merely "prefiguring" the young man because they were unable to see him as clearly as the speaker can. Like the characters in Plato's ALLEGORY of the Cave in book 7 of Plato's *The Republic,* the antique poets can only sense the transcendent beauty embodied in the young man through their contact with less worthy objects. Because they saw him only in their imagination, "with divining eyes" (l. 11), they were unable to do the young man justice. Despite their gifts as poets, "They had not still enough your worth to sing" (l. 12). Many editors change the word *still* in this line to *skill,* but "still enough" allows for a greater range of meaning: Enough inspiration? Enough wisdom? Enough time? Enough skill?

In the couplet, as in Sonnet 23 and elsewhere, the speaker then confesses that the young man's beauty has left him not just tongue-tied but tongue-less: "For we, which now behold these present days, / Have eyes to wonder, but lack tongues to praise" (ll. 13–14). Living in the present, in the presence of the young man, the poet can be amazed by his beauty but cannot find words to describe it adequately. The explanation the narrator offers for his silence is, in part, that other poets have already written some of the best lines. But Shakespeare is here playing a rhetorical trick as well: At least some readers of his sonnets would be familiar with the love poetry this sonnet describes, and by promising that the young man exceeds all existing descriptions of beauty, the poet describes that beauty in the highest possible terms without himself having to find the right words for it. He claims to lack the ability to speak in tongues, or to be inspired to speak, as were the New Testament's apostles, by tongues of flame, and yet he has managed to make an eloquent plea that conveys the young man's extraordinary beauty.

See also ENGLISH SONNET, SHAKESPEARE'S SONNETS (OVERVIEW).

FURTHER READING
Go, Kenji. "Unemending the Emendation of 'Still' in Shakespeare's Sonnet 106." *Studies in Philology* 98, no. 1 (2001): 114–142.

Catherine Loomis

Shakespeare's sonnets: Sonnet 109 ("O, never say that I was false of heart") WILLIAM SHAKESPEARE (1599)   Sonnet 109 commences a number of SONNETS that use travel as a reason for the poet's waning attention to his patron. The first QUATRAIN emphasizes that he is not being unfaithful or indifferent, though it may seem that the flame of his interest has diminished (l. 2). Indeed, he points out that his very soul resides in his friend's heart. The poet further proclaims, in the second quatrain, that even if he travels (seeks other sources of PATRONAGE), he returns with all his fervor for his patron intact. At the same time, the poet seems to take offense at the implication that he is being disloyal to his addressee, and in the third quatrain, he points out that he would never "leave for nothing all thy sum of good" (l. 12). The final COUPLET summarizes the speaker's sentiments by complimenting the friend (likening him to a rose) and declaring that the speaker's entire universe is found in his friend. As the sonnets progress, it seems that the speaker has begun to distance himself from his patron, and the closeness detailed in earlier poems seems to be diminishing as time and interest alter for the speaker.

See also SHAKESPEARE, WILLIAM; SHAKESPEARE'S SONNETS (OVERVIEW).

Joseph E. Becker

Shakespeare's sonnets: Sonnet 115 ("Those lines that I have writ before do lie") WILLIAM SHAKESPEARE (1599)   Though many of WILLIAM SHAKESPEARE's SONNETS engage in the *monumentum aere perennius* (from the poet Horace, a monument more lasting than bronze) trope, this poem does so in a novel and unique manner, combining two themes of the SONNET SEQUENCE: immortality through procreation and immortality through artistic creation. The trope figures the poem as a verbal or textual monument, which will outlast both the sonnet's speaker and the object of desire. In other cases in the sequence, the speaker has encouraged the young man to beget children and thereby create a lasting monument to himself in the images of his own children, but here the love that the speaker has for the young man, exemplified through the poem itself, is described as an immortal and ever-growing child.

The poem begins with an appeal to the past, wherein the speaker claims that all previous monumental poems he has written to the young man, which said that "I could not love you dearer" (l. 2), "do lie" (l. 1). The love the speaker feels for the young man increases as time goes on, yet there is no reason for the speaker to believe that his love "should afterwards burn clearer" (l. 4).

The poem moves into a self-referential register in the second QUATRAIN. Grammatically, the second quatrain is simply a description of the activities or "accidents" of PERSONIFIED Time. King's decrees change, beauty fades, and vows are broken, all by time. The self-referential move comes at the end of the quatrain, anticipating the traditional VOLTA between lines 8 and 9. Line 8, "[Time's accidents] Divert strong minds to th' course of altering things," thematically reflects the purpose of a volta, as the accidents of time change the course of the poem. However, the actual volta does not come between lines 8 and 9; rather, it occurs immediately before the final COUPLET, in line 12. By referencing the "proper" place for the volta within the fiction of the poem, Shakespeare shows his awareness of the ITALIAN (PETRARCHAN) SONNET convention that he is breaking, but he is also drawing the audience out of the sonnet's fiction. By making the audience aware of the poem as a poem, he highlights the artificial and monumental nature of the sonnet, which itself refers back to the idea of immortality through artistic creation.

The first quatrain deals with the past, showing that any statements of monumental love from the past are false, and the second quatrain shows that the future cannot be decided because all things, even the most certain, eventually fall prey to time. The third quatrain focuses wholly on the present and is wholly in the form of a question about the legitimacy of saying "Now I love you best" (l. 9). The present moment is not the final or ultimate expression of the speaker's love for the LOVELY BOY, for the hanging doubt of the first two quatrains is embodied in the fact that the present is questioned. The answer to the question comes in the couplet.

"Love is a babe" (l. 13) is a phrase that works on at least three levels: It points to the CONCEIT that the love between the speaker and the young man is still in its infancy, it appeals to the traditional image of Cupid as

Love, and it implicitly references the procreative urge found in the rest of the sequence. The speaker's love, like a child, "Still doth grow" (l. 14), and with the love the speaker's ability to create a monument in verse will grow as well.

See also SHAKESPEARE'S SONNETS (OVERVIEW).

Andrew Bretz

Shakespeare's sonnets: Sonnet 116 ("Let me not to the marriage of true minds") WILLIAM SHAKESPEARE (1599)

In this SONNET, the speaker tries to describe a love that is so strong that it can act as a model for true married love. Interestingly, the description begins with an acknowledgment that real love exists in "the marriage of true minds" (l. 1), and in order for the speaker to acknowledge this kind of love, he refuses to allow "impediments" (l. 2). This last word is one used in the marriage ceremony at the point where the minister asks if anyone knows of any reason to prevent the marriage from happening—for example, one of the parties may already be married. Both the cleric and the speaker are concerned with truth, then, in the legal sense of allowing the marriage to occur as well as in the truth of the love between the two partners in the union. The phrase "let me not" (l. 1) indicates that the speaker is taking a vow or promising truthfully. But here the speaker is more concerned with the marriage of the couple's "minds" than with their bodies. This kind of love is truly an unusual sort. The love the speaker writes of is immutable (unchangeable), no matter what it encounters. It does not alter "when it alteration finds" (l. 3), nor does it accept the influence of time—"the remover" (l. 4)—to change the love in any way for the worse.

The love described in this poem is definitely not changeable; it is "an ever fixed mark" (l. 5), an immutable, fixed point in the changeable ocean, like a lighthouse or a beacon, which is never "shaken" (l. 6) but guides sailors to safety, even during huge storms, or "tempests" (l. 6). This love is also like a particular star—perhaps Polaris, the pole star or North Star—by which ships ("barques," l. 7) that have wandered from their course can adjust it. The actual composition ("worth," l. 8) of the star may not be known, but its height above the horizon has been charted ("taken," l. 8) with a quadrant or sextant so that the captain of the ship can plot a safe course and cease wandering.

In the third QUATRAIN, the speaker brings the poem back to an examination of love and time, and he states that true love is not the "fool" (l. 9) or plaything, of time, even though lips and cheeks—once rosy in youth—are the victim of Time's "sickle" (l. 10). Here the poet conjures up an image of Father Time with a sickle (rather than a scythe) that he uses figuratively to indicate the power of Time, who works like a harvester to cut down not only the youth or the aged, but especially lovers. The word *compass* (l. 10) refers to the range of the sickle, but it can also call to mind the nautical imagery in the second quatrain, for a compass allows a sailor to plot a safe course for the vessel. Even though time may have a negative effect on the youth and beauty of the lovers, their love "alters not" (l. 11) over the passage of time and continues until "the edge of doom" (l. 12), or "doomsday," the last day of the world. The speaker then indicates that if he is in error about this description of love, then his writing is untrue and no one has ever loved. What is recorded is deemed true not only in terms of the speaker's skill in description, but in all lovers' experiences throughout time.

See also SHAKESPEARE, WILLIAM; SHAKESPEARE'S SONNETS (OVERVIEW).

Theodora A. Jankowski

Shakespeare's sonnets: Sonnet 124 ("If my dear love were but the child of state") WILLIAM SHAKESPEARE (1599)

Sonnet 124 brings the reader near the conclusion of the speaker's passion for the young man, sometimes called the LOVELY BOY, expressed in a mixture of social, religious, mercantile, and gardening metaphors. He proclaims his love's organic and self-sustaining nature until the final COUPLET, when he calls on rather suspect witnesses to his natural sentiments.

In the sonnet's first QUATRAIN, the speaker reveals that his love is not motivated by the beloved's position in society and, therefore, is not a passing fancy or a self-serving passion. It matters not whether "[w]eeds among weeds or flowers with flowers [are] gathered"

(l. 4). The gardener cannot keep the weeds out from among the flowers no matter how hard he tries. Love, like the English garden, is subject more to nature than nurture. The speaker has come into his love naturally, without regard to human-created distinctions that call some "weeds" and others "flowers." Human intrusion will not undo his love.

In the second quatrain, the speaker asserts that his feeling of love does not come or go by chance or by "fashion" (l. 8). Society's whims do not affect his love. The contrived expectations or dictates of "th'inviting time" which enslaves people has no power over his love (l. 8).

The third quatrain immediately declares the strength of his love in terms both religious and mercantile. His love is not a "heretic / Which works on leases of short-numbered hours" (ll. 9–10). It is not a product of recanting cowardice, a quick and sure means to possessing his beloved. Rather, his love grows from its own prudent nature, "all alone and hugely politic," without artifice or fear of any external interference (l. 11). The last line of the quatrain reinforces its natural state once again. In the garden, love grows in a natural harmonious balance, neither too hot nor too moist, the perfect balance of the humors.

The concluding COUPLET calls this natural state of his love's engendering and its self-nourishing quality into question, again using the language of both religion and mercantilism. These final lines conjure up false religious conversions. Here the speaker summons to "witness" those who have feigned religious conversions at the end of their life and, by so doing, he turns his revelation of naturally balanced, unimpeded, self-sustaining love on its head (l. 13). The speaker's love, which grew naturally from within, undeterred and peerless, can be recognized and verified only by those questionable converts.

The nature of his love has, in the end, left the speaker in dangerous company at the end of the 16th century. Queen ELIZABETH I, though hardly a religious zealot or a rigid enforcer as was her half sister, MARY I, did assert her position as head of the infant Church of England. Recusants would and could be punished, and unrepentant Catholics were executed, especially in the last decades of her reign. Is the speaker then saying that his love is, in the end, easily converted, or, in the language of the market, easily exchanged?

See also SHAKESPEARE, WILLIAM; SHAKESPEARE'S SONNETS (OVERVIEW).

FURTHER READING

Starkey, David. *Elizabeth: The Struggle for the Throne.* New York: Harper Perennial, 2000.

Julie A. Chappell

Shakespeare's sonnets: Sonnet 126 ("O thou, my lovely boy, who in thy power") WILLIAM SHAKESPEARE (1599) Sonnet 144 opens with a famous declaration: "Two loves I have, of comfort and despair"; one love is "a man right fair" (l. 3), to whom the first 126 of the sonnets are directed, and the other "a woman color'd ill" (l. 4), sometimes referred to as the DARK LADY, to whom sonnets 127 through 152 are addressed. Sonnet 126 is the last sonnet to the fair young man, and it is unusual in many ways.

Unlike the majority of WILLIAM SHAKESPEARE'S SONNETS, Sonnet 126 does not follow what has come to be called the Shakespearean form (see ENGLISH SONNET). Instead, it has only 12 lines: The rhyme scheme is *aabbccddeeff*; the narrative is presented in COUPLETS; and what should be the final couplet, lines 13 and 14, is, in the original 1609 edition of the sonnets, represented by two sets of empty parentheses spaced as if to mark missing lines. At least in poetic terms, the relationship with the LOVELY BOY does not end well.

The opening lines of Sonnet 126 recall the first 17 sonnets, sometimes referred to as the procreation set, in which the narrator urges the beautiful young man to marry so that he can leave a copy of himself to the world before time destroys his beauty. Now, however, the young man seems to be in control of time rather than at time's mercy. Using the intimate pronoun *thou,* the narrator reminds his "lovely boy" that the young man holds in his power "Time's fickle glass, his sickle hour" (ll. 1–2). Time's "glass" refers to the hourglass that an allegorical figure of Time would hold, but *glass* also means looking glass, or mirror. Many of the sonnets mention that the young man's beauty does not seem to fade over time. The "sickle hour" refers to the hour of death, when Time will mow the young man down with his scythe.

The second couplet introduces a paradox: The young man has "by waning grown" (l. 3). To *wane* usually means to lose size and strength, but the young man seems to have become more beautiful as he ages; as the poet promised in Sonnet 18, his eternal summer really has not faded. His lovers have not been so fortunate. In direct address, the speaker reminds the young man of this harsh truth: By not seeming to grow older, "[thou] showest / Thy lovers withering as thy sweet self grow'st" (ll. 3–4). Throughout the sonnets, the word *sweet* is frequently and sometimes ironically applied to the young man: His "sweet love" saves the poet from despair in Sonnet 29; his transgression against the poet makes him a "sweet thief" in Sonnet 35; his "sweet hue" is untouched by time in Sonnet 104. The words *sweet self* also appear not only in the final sonnet addressed to the young man, but also in the first one (Sonnet 1, l. 8), and by reusing the phrase, Shakespeare links the beginning of the relationship to its end.

The next pair of couplets forms a unit in which the narrator asserts that Nature is preventing the young man from aging in order to show off the skill she employed in making him in the first place. Nature is declared the "sovereign mistress over wrack" (l. 5), a reminder that all natural beings eventually die and decay. As Time passes, the young man is plucked back by Nature in order that she may show her superiority to Time. Proud of her work in creating the young man, Nature disgraces Time and kills the "wretched [minutes]" (l. 8) before they can destroy his beauty.

There follows a shift in the sonnet's tone. As in the first 17 poems in the sequence, the speaker issues a warning to the young man: This cannot last forever. He must fear Nature; he is merely her "minion"—an inferior servant or a male prostitute—and exists at and for "her pleasure" (l. 9). When she is finished with him, Time will claim him. Nature may "detain" him—a legal term meaning she can hold him temporarily—but the older, wiser speaker knows that Nature cannot "keep her treasure" (l. 10); the young man will eventually become an old man and die. Nature's "audit," another legal or commercial term meaning a review of accounts, a way of establishing what one owes to whom, has been postponed in the young man's case, but Nature "answered must be" (l. 11). Her "quietus," another legal term meaning the settlement of an obligation, is to "render" the young man (l. 14). *Render* is a fluid word: In culinary terms it means to melt fat, to turn something solid into something liquid, as will happen when a corpse decays. The word also has legal and commercial associations: To render what is due is to pay what one owes. The young man must render himself to Nature, and Nature must render the death he is owed. Another young man who imagines making a "quietus" with Nature is Shakespeare's Hamlet, who proposes to do so "with a bare bodkin" as he debates the merits of suicide in his "To be or not to be" soliloquy (*Hamlet*, 3.2.55–87).

Something is missing from the end of Sonnet 126: Obviously, there is no closing couplet. In the 1609 edition, and in some modern editions, there are two sets of parentheses at the end of the poem to indicate the absence. But something seems to be missing in a grammatical sense as well: The verb *render* is often transitive (one that takes an object), and here it seems to have no object. However, the empty lines indicated by the parentheses, like the incomplete relationship the first 126 sonnets document, signify nothing, and the poem's final sentence can be read bleakly: "And her quietus is to render thee / Nothing / Nothing." The sonnet replicates the relationship's unhappy ending: There is no further coupling among the lines of poetry or between the men who are their subject. By leaving the sonnet unfinished, the poet leaves open the possibility of a different, more satisfying ending, but also, more sadly, implies that there is really nothing left to say.

See also SHAKESPEARE'S SONNETS (OVERVIEW).

FURTHER READING

Graves, Roy Neil. "Shakespeare's 'Sonnet 126.'" *Explicator* 54, no. 4 (1996): 203–207.

Catherine Loomis

Shakespeare's sonnets: Sonnet 127 ("In the old age black was not counted fair") WILLIAM SHAKESPEARE (1599)

This and the next few SONNETS in WILLIAM SHAKESPEARE's SONNET SEQUENCE comment on the early modern concept of female beauty and how the speaker views his mistress, or female beloved, who possesses a different type of beauty. The accepted standard of female beauty for early modern women was blond hair, blue eyes, fair (almost white) complexion, pink or red cheeks, and red lips. Many sonnets by poets such as SIR PHILIP SIDNEY describe beloveds who possess these particular qualities. Shakespeare's sonnets celebrate a beloved who does not adhere to early modern notions of beauty, so they are sometimes referred to as the DARK LADY sonnets, even though the beloved is never actually identified as a "lady."

The speaker begins by indicating that long ago ("in the old age," l. 1) "black" was not counted fair. However, the Song of Songs in the Bible celebrates black beauty, so the idea does have precedent, and some scholars have even posited that the woman in question was African or at least a darker European. The first quatrain argues that if there were those who considered black to be "fair"—and there is a pun here between "fair" as good-looking or attractive and "fair" as pale—they did not consider it to be "beautiful." Now, however, black is the heir of "fair" and takes over, while beauty as "fairness" is "slandered with a bastard shame" (l. 4). Bastards, or illegitimate children born out of legal wedlock, cannot be heirs and inherit property. "Fairness" becomes slandered with the shame of bastardy through the use of cosmetics that unnaturally make skin whiter and cheeks and lips redder. (Interestingly, these cosmetics were made of white and red lead, which destroyed the skin.) Thus, black becomes "beautiful" primarily because fair is adulterated, no longer pure or honest.

The second quatrain continues the examination of false beauty, especially in terms of women cheating men by using cosmetics to make them artificially beautiful. Women's hands have taken over Nature's power to create a beautiful face by using cosmetics. This kind of alteration means that a fair woman's beauty can no longer be trusted. The hand that wields cosmetics can very well have made a "foul"—or ugly—face "fair" with the borrowed skills of "art," here meaning artifice, or falseness. Thus, beauty has lost its "reputation" (name) through the unnatural creation of "beautiful" women from ones who are truly ugly. Beauty is no longer holy; it is "profaned," or violated, and "lives in disgrace" (ll. 7–8).

The speaker then reminds us that the sonnet's female subject has eyes that are "raven-black" (l. 9) and eyebrows to match. While such features would previously have rendered this woman plain or ugly, she is now considered beautiful because the black is natural. There has been so much false use of cosmetics to make unattractive women conform to the standards of fair beauty that a very natural beauty—one who does not use cosmetics—is perceived to be beautiful even though she does not conform to existing social criteria for "fair" beauty. A "natural" black woman may be more desirable than an "unnatural" fair one. As a result, the falsely fair women mourn the fact that they are not as beautiful as this natural, though black, beauty who is praised for what she is without cosmetics.

Many puns are active in this sonnet, and they act as ways not only to convey the poet's ideas but to comment on social values and ideas. Beauty for women meant having a fair complexion and being blond. *Fair* also means "beautiful" as its opposite, *foul*, means "ugly." Thus, to call a woman "fair" is to comment not only on her coloring but on her beauty. A woman who is "blond" can also be referred to as "light," as in the color of her hair relative to darker shades like brown or black. But "light" can also have other meanings. "Light" recalls "fair" and leads us to consider "beautiful." "Light" also calls to mind its opposite, "dark," both in color and in lack of light (darkness). So we can see the development of a binary, an opposition of two words, phrases, or concepts. On one side is "fair, light, and beautiful." On the other is "foul, dark, and ugly." Adding the colors, "white" is attached to the "fair" side of the binary and "black" to the "dark" side. It is only a step away to add "good" to the "fair" side and "bad" to the "dark" side. Thus we have the potential for black-white racism encoded in the English language, which, in the early modern period, signified that "light" and "white" were good, and "dark" and "black" were bad. In medieval and early modern religious art, angels were always white and devils black.

See also SHAKESPEARE'S SONNETS (OVERVIEW).

Theodora A. Jankowski

Shakespeare's sonnets: Sonnet 128 ("How oft when thou, my music, music play'st") WILLIAM SHAKESPEARE (1599)

In this SONNET, the speaker reflects on the many times when the beloved has played upon the virginal, a very early version of the piano. Its keys were called *jacks,* and they were made of wood. In line 1, "my music" refers to the beloved, who *is* music and who simultaneously produces music, and using "music" twice emphasizes the beloved's importance. The effect is somewhat magical for the speaker, who hears the mechanism that causes the jacks to coax music from the "blessed wood" (l. 2) of the instrument animated by the beloved's "sweet fingers" (l. 3). The speaker's ear is confounded, or amazed, by the "wiry concord" (l. 4) that comes from the interaction of the lover's fingers and the mechanism of the jacks that causes them to pluck the virginal's wires and call up musical sound.

The sonnet then moves from a long shot to a close-up of the beloved's fingers. The speaker focuses on the jacks that are touched by the beloved in the act of playing the instrument. While the wood jacks are completely inanimate and moved solely by the motion of the beloved's fingers, the lover, perhaps feeling slighted by the beloved, hyperbolically imagines that the jacks are leaping up of their own free will "to kiss the tender inward" (l. 6) of the beloved's hand. The speaker somewhat ridiculously envies "those jacks" (l. 5), speaking of them as human and bold. His "poor lips" should reap the "harvest" of kisses that the jacks reap. And while all this musical kissing goes on, the speaker sits by and "blushes," embarrassed by the "wood's boldness" (l. 8).

The third QUATRAIN continues this image and plaintively presents the outlandish wish that the speaker's "poor lips" would gladly undergo a complete change to become wooden jacks if they could be assured of being "kissed" by the beloved's fingers, which "walk with all gentle gait" (l. 11) over them. In fact, the jacks, being touched by the beloved, become "more blessed" (l. 12) than the speaker's living lips. In the COUPLET, the speaker moves back from the position of being envious of the inanimate jacks to tell the lover to "give thy fingers" (l. 14) to them, but give "me thy lips to kiss" (l. 14). This sonnet presents a picture of a lover so insecure, yet so enamored of the beloved, that he would do anything to attract her attention, even going so far as to become a thing, rather than a person.

See also SHAKESPEARE, WILLIAM; SHAKESPEARE'S SONNETS (OVERVIEW).

Theodora A. Jankowski

Shakespeare's sonnets: Sonnet 129 ("Th' expense of spirit in a waste of shame") WILLIAM SHAKESPEARE (1599)

SONNETS of the early modern period often focus on love and are beautifully phrased with gentle tempos. However, Sonnet 129 is something completely different both in meter, tempo, and subject. It is a poem that is passionate, angry, and bitter, with a jarring, rough tempo. It is not difficult to discover the reason for this shift in tone. The other sonnets may be about love; this one is about lust.

The first QUATRAIN begins by defining lust in its active mode: "Th'expense of spirit in a waste of shame / Is lust in action; . . ." (ll. 1–2). "Spirit" here refers to "vital energy," or sperm. The belief at this time was that each man had a limited amount of vital energy in his body. Each time he ejaculated, he released some of that energy and reduced his life by some span of time, usually a day. Therefore, each ejaculation, whether caused by sexual intercourse, masturbation, or a nocturnal emission, cost a man some of his life. So the belief was that a man could literally ejaculate himself to death if he engaged in too much sexual intercourse. The speaker of this sonnet feels shame because he has wasted some of his vital energy—"spirit"—in lust rather than in something worthwhile, like fathering a child with his wife.

Lust was also believed to have a bad effect on men's personalities and bodies. Lust is "perjured, murd'rous, bloody, full of blame, / Savage, extreme, rude, cruel, not to trust" (ll. 3–4) and, as such, causes men to lie and to be cruel, rude, savage, bloody, and murderous. If this preintercourse behavior was not bad enough, the actual experiencing of sexual intercourse can do nothing to stop it. Once the man has "enjoyed" sexual intercourse, it is "despised" (l. 5) because lust is unreasonable. There is shame involved in being dominated by an emotion and not reason, being at the mercy of a body part rather than the thought processes of a brain that is able to control one's urges. The speaker "hunts" sexual activity "past reason" (l. 6), but once he has

obtained it, he hates it equally unreasonably, as though he has been made mad by some sort of poison, such as the "poison" of lust. He is mad when he goes after intercourse and mad once he has achieved it: "Had, having, and in quest to have, extreme" (l. 10). Sexual intercourse may be "bliss" (l. 11) or "joy" (l. 12) when thought about or during the act, but afterward it is a "woe" (l. 11) or a "dream" (l. 12), probably a bad one. The COUPLET ends with a truism: Everyone knows how bad it is to be controlled by lust and constantly chase after sex, yet nobody knows how to avoid the "heaven" of sexual intercourse that leads to the "hell" of madness, irrationality, and shame that constant sexual activity causes.

Sonnet 129 reflects the uncontrolled passion of the speaker. There are no beautiful words, soft phrases, or tuneful lines. The lines of Sonnet 129 are harsh and jarring. Lines 3 and 4 present a list of characteristics of the lust-possessed person in sharp, repetitive spondees (a metrical foot with two long or stressed syllables). Paired words do not explore the good and bad of a subject, but focus on the bad and worse: "enjoyed . . . But despised" (l. 5); "Past reason hunted . . . Past reason hated . . ." (ll. 6–7); "Mad in pursuit and in possession" (l. 9); "Had, having, and in quest to have, extreme" (l. 10); "A bliss in proof and proved a very woe" (l. 11). Thus, the rhythms of this sonnet reflect the tortured feelings examined within it.

See also SHAKESPEARE, WILLIAM; SHAKESPEARE'S SONNETS (OVERVIEW).

Theodora A. Jankowski

Shakespeare's sonnets: Sonnet 130 ("My mistress' eyes are nothing like the sun") WILLIAM SHAKESPEARE (1599)

This SONNET is a response to the prevailing ideas of English beauty from the medieval to the early modern period. Ideals of beauty demanded that the woman be blond, blue-eyed, pale of complexion, pink or red of cheek, and red of lips. She should also seem to glow as though illuminated by an inner light. Poets competed with each other to see who had the most beautiful—or most beautifully described—beloved. However, Sonnet 130 is, in many ways, an anti-BLAZON (unflattering description). But it is also something else.

The three QUATRAINS of Sonnet 130 focus on what the speaker's mistress is *not*. In the first quatrain we learn that her eyes are "nothing like the sun" (l. 1). While women's eyes were ideally blue, it was more important that they shone like the sun. Sea coral is "far more red" (l. 2) than her lips. While a woman's complexion should be as fair and as white as snow, the speaker's beloved's breasts are "dun" (l. 3), a grayish tan color. While it would be ideal for the woman to have hair like thin, spun golden wire, the speaker's mistress seems to have black wires growing out of her head. The fact that her hair is described as being black and wiry and her skin as dun has suggested to some critics that the mistress might be an African.

In the second quatrain, the speaker describes beautiful damask roses. This kind of rose has petals that are both red and white. Likening a woman's cheek to damask roses would be flattering because it would suggest that the woman's skin is white and her cheeks are red. Unfortunately, though, the speaker has seen "no such roses" (l. 6)—that is, none of this lovely color—in the mistress's cheeks. During the early modern period, dental hygiene and dental care was not very advanced. People brushed their teeth—if they even bothered to do so—with twigs whose ends were chewed to make something like bristles, or they wiped them with a tooth cloth. There was no way to fill teeth that had cavities, so they either were pulled or, worse, just rotted out. Unfortunately, the speaker's mistress may have been a victim of these dental limitations, because her breath "reeks" (l. 8). It is so foul that perfume smells much better.

Women were also expected to be very graceful and soft-spoken. While the speaker loves to hear the mistress speak, her voice must not sound very sweet—"music hath a far more pleasing sound" (l. 10). And though her walk should be graceful, making her glide softly over the ground as though she were a goddess, the mistress actually "treads on the ground" (l. 12), probably indicating that she is very heavy-footed and clumps along. Yet while the mistress is clearly not a stereotypical beauty, the speaker presents her unflattering features in a calm, straightforward way. He does not actually say that she is plain or ugly, just that she is completely unlike the cultural ideal of beauty. Even though the speaker tells us all the ways in which the mistress fails to live up to conventional ideals of beauty, he does not seem to be bothered by this. The fact that the speaker makes no value judgment about the mistress's looks, and the fact that she is referred to as "my love" (l. 13) reinforces the speaker's opinion that she is "rare" and unusual, though in a very special way, in her difference from the standard run of "beauties."

See also DARK LADY; SHAKESPEARE, WILLIAM; SHAKESPEARE'S SONNETS (OVERVIEW).

Theodora A. Jankowski

Shakespeare's sonnets: Sonnet 138 ("When my love swears that she is made for truth") WILLIAM SHAKESPEARE (1599)

Sonnet 138 is unique among WILLIAM SHAKESPEARE'S SONNETS in that, like number 144, it exists in two moderately different forms: the 1599 collection *The Passionate Pilgrim* and the 1609 Quarto edition of 154 sonnets. There is critical disagreement about the nature of the 1599 version of Sonnet 138. Some believe it is an inferior, early draft later revised by Shakespeare for the 1609 edition, while others claim it is a pirated, memorial reconstruction of the poem, taken from early sonnet readings exchanged informally with Shakespeare's friends and colleagues.

In Sonnet 138, the speaker admits to his mistress's lies and infidelity, his knowledge of these transgressions, his coexistent faith in her and disbelief of her lies, and his culpability in sustaining such a relationship. He brings up his age in relation to the younger mistress and the fact that they both admit and deliberately deny this difference in age. This coexistent belief and distrust is contradictory, and yet it describes the speaker's emotional state.

The first QUATRAIN introduces the sonnet's main idea that the mistress swears she speaks and behaves honestly, and that the speaker believes her even though he knows she lies (ll. 1–2). He then admits she must think him naïve to accept her lies as truth (ll. 3–4). In the second quatrain (ll. 5–8), the speaker, apparently anxious about his age, notes that she believes he is young (while in this very act admitting they both know this to be false). He accepts her flattering statements that support this lie, demonstrating a collusion wherein they both tell this lie while knowing perfectly well it is untrue. The third quatrain (ll. 9–12) explains the reason for the deception: "Why not tell the truth?" he asks. Because "love's best habit"—works toward a "seeming" rather than a realistic appraisal of the two lovers, with habit referring both to dress and to actions.

The relationship of the speaker and the mistress in Sonnet 138 is demonstrated in the almost wistful punning on the word *lie* that ends the sonnet: "Therefore I lie with her, and she with me, / And in our faults by lies we flattered be" (ll. 13–14). The dual meanings of *lie*—falsehood and sexual intercourse—sum up the nature of the speaker's concerns throughout the sequence. The preposition *with* demonstrates their cooperation in the "flattering" lies they tell each other (and those the speaker tells himself) and the intimacy and passion of their sexual activity (as well as, one suspects, the lack of any emotional connection beyond their lust and the consequent bitterness and confusion experienced by the speaker). The central significance of these meanings of *lie* in their relationship is further demonstrated in one of the most insidious lines in all the Dark Lady sonnets: "O, love's best habit is in seeming trust" (l. 11). Apparently, the appearance of trust is all that the speaker, or perhaps any lover, can hope for in a relationship. This dearth of real love and affection is what the speaker ultimately comes to accept by the end of the sequence, as he recognizes his responsibility in the deception central to this relationship.

See also SHAKESPEARE'S SONNETS (OVERVIEW).

Michael Petersen

Shakespeare's sonnets: Sonnet 139 ("O, call not me to justify the wrong") WILLIAM SHAKESPEARE (ca. 1599)

Scholars and readers alike have long been unable to resist reading WILLIAM SHAKESPEARE'S SONNETS addressed to the DARK LADY as a narrative. Traditional scholarship has the narrative begin with Sonnet 127 and run to Sonnet 152. By Sonnet 139, the putative narrative's midpoint, the speaker-poet is past his initial attraction to the Dark Lady, past falling in love with her, past debasing himself erotically, past even the point when he realized that he is being cuckolded. Now he is angry—with himself and with her—and the result is an unstable poem.

The sonnet begins as a refusal. Using the imperative, the poet rejects the implied, offstage suggestion that he must explain her actions: "O, call not me to justify the wrong / That thy unkindness lays upon my heart" (ll. 1–2). Beginning in a tone of onomatopoetic woe ("O") and shifting to one of understated blame ("thy unkindness"), this assertion is marked by disbelief. The initial rejoinder—"call not me"—is emphatic, clear, and addresses four groups: the sonnet tradition, which contains a subgenre of poems wherein a speaker justifies a beloved's infidelity; the Dark Lady; the poet; and readers. Sonnet 139 will be unable to satisfy all of these parties.

Dissatisfaction is precisely the problem the first QUATRAIN addresses. The Dark Lady clearly has power over the poet. Complicating matters, he lacks control of himself, especially in matters of the heart. The poet has little choice but to recognize her authority, but he does not capitulate to it outright. Rather, he learns from his beloved / adversary and answers deception with deception. His goal is to forestall his inevitable debasement.

The first instance of this strategy occurs as the opening quatrain nears its close. Speaking imperatively again, the poet instructs his beloved, "Wound me not with thine eye, but with thy tongue" (l. 3). Here the telling is a kind of asking. The poet wants his dark mistress to use language, rather than her cunning gaze, to hurt him. That gaze is directed at others, and he sees it as a sign of infidelity. Language is his domain; speaking and interpreting words are what poets do best. In effect, he asks that she meet him on his terms, not hers, and he does so by distinguishing language from artifice, a distinction that does not survive scrutiny. The poet masks his sophistry by challenging her to "Use power with power" (l. 4) rather than deploy lowly cunning.

The second quatrain begins with a concession. If you must, the poet says, "Tell me thou lov'st elsewhere" (l. 5), but when we are together, look at me. Here he asks directly for directness. His request is also a lover's stratagem. What hurts the poet most is not the dark lady's infidelity but being reminded of it. He fears that her glances signify future betrayals. To placate his beloved, the poet calls her "Dear heart," a phrase that speaks his love as it indicates the price such love extracts. He continues in this deceptively submissive vein by recognizing that the dark lady's "might / Is more than my o'er-pressed defence can bide" (ll. 7–8). This recognition is posed as a question, however, which undercuts its power.

The most difficult quatrain to believe is the last one, because in it, the poet does what he has refused to do earlier: "excuse" the Dark Lady. He does so by reinterpreting the very looking that has been so hurtful to him. Her glances remain his "enemies," but if turned elsewhere, he remarks, they will only injure others. This concession is an act of self-deception. Apparently the poet has failed to persuade the Dark Lady to alter her behavior, and he faces a dilemma—either to rationalize her gaze as harmful to others or to ask that she wound him with it, and undercut his earlier refusal. Unhappily, the COUPLET ends as it must—with the overmatched and no longer angry lover acknowledging his powerlessness before his beloved. Metaphorically dead at heart, he asks to be killed by the very gaze he has struggled to surmount. Despite his considerable mastery of language, then, his cunning is no match for his adversary's dark and fluid desirability.

See also SHAKESPEARE'S SONNETS (OVERVIEW).

Larry T. Shillock

Shakespeare's sonnets: Sonnet 140 ("Be wise as thou art cruel, do not press") WILLIAM SHAKESPEARE (1599)

Tradition holds that Sonnet 140 takes up where Sonnet 139 leaves off, and there is much to recommend this view. Both address the DARK LADY imperatively, link the poet's decline to her infidelity, and seek, through verbal stratagems, to control her gaze. However, Sonnet 140 does more: It replaces the powerlessness of a lover's anger with voiced, if unrealized, threats of retaliation.

The SONNET begins with the poet addressing the Dark Lady. Readers quickly sense that they have blundered into a quarrel, and it is now the lover's turn to speak. His reply takes his beloved's cruelty to be accomplished and, in a cruel retort, recommends that she become equally wise. Ostensibly, the sonnet is to educate her, yet it teaches through a reasoned threat. Should the Dark Lady treat him disdainfully, the poet says, and should his resulting pain become overwhelm-

ing, he will end his "tongue-tied patience" (l. 2) and tell what she has done. Rhetorically speaking, the QUATRAINS first three lines list the causes that will compel the lover's response. The quatrain climaxes with a promise to reveal "The manner of my pity-wanting pain" (l. 4).

This threat borrows from the language of logic, but its metaphors come from the domain of torture. Prisoners who were accused of a felony but would not speak underwent *peine forte et dure*. Pressed under heavy weights, they offered a plea or "patiently" died silent. Here, the Dark Lady is the torturer, and the poet's silence a kind of tortured "patience." But matters between the lovers are not that simple. He is speaking, not she. Moreover, the phrase "pity-wanting pain" means pain that her behavior has caused, his desire to be pitied, and a pitiful desire to feel pain. The poet's patience is strained and holds on only for impure reasons.

The second quatrain reasserts the poet's teaching role. However, the teacher now instructs the pupil to lie. As a lover, she should say she loves him, an instruction that recalls Sonnet 138 and its lovers' flattering lies. Like a physician, she should give her dying patient "No news but health" (l. 8), an untrue diagnosis. To this point, Sonnet 140 has likened the poet to a prisoner undergoing torture, a lover who is being deceived, and a dying—understandably impatient—patient. These analogous cases share poor ends: The prisoner is likely to remain imprisoned or die; the lover, to realize that deception has occurred; and the patient, to see that death is near.

The poet acknowledges his plight by returning to the rhetoric of threats. The causal chain that will inform the third quatrain starts with despair, shifts to the insanity such despair causes, and concludes with the poet—now out of control—telling all. Aptly, the key words in this quatrain are *mad,* repeated three times, and its variant, *madness.* Should I be made mad by you, the poet reasons, "And in my madness might speak ill of thee" (l. 10), it is likely in our "ill-wresting world" (l. 11) that I will be heard. Madness moves the poet beyond powerless anger and, paradoxically, confers linguistic authority, signaled by the alliterative phrase "my madness might." This ambiguous phrase could signify that the power of madness could compel speech. It also implies that madness is "might" in a distorted world where mad "slanderers by mad ears believed be" (l. 12).

The COUPLET carries over the alliterative *b* sounds of "bad," "by," "believed," and "be." It then concludes with an implied threat that is offered so that the poet and the Dark Lady may be reconciled. The threat emerges when the couplet's lines are read in reverse order. So long as you "Bear thine eyes straight" (l. 12), the poet says, I will not descend into madness, and madness will not cause me to say things that will lead to your being "belied" (l. 11). The poet would benefit from such a threat-induced understanding. But the Dark Lady would, too, since her reputation provides a cover that would enable—in an archery-derived metaphor—for her "proud heart [to] go wide" (l. 12). Hence the poet will accept her infidelities as long as, in public, she looks "straight" at him and not at others.

See also ALLITERATION; SHAKESPEARE, WILLIAM; SHAKESPEARE'S SONNETS (OVERVIEW).

Larry T. Shillock

Shakespeare's sonnets: Sonnet 141 ("In faith, I do not love thee with mine eyes") WILLIAM SHAKESPEARE (1599) This SONNET forms a coda (conclusion) to Sonnet 130, with the poet stressing that his lover is anything but typical as regards her beauty. It is usually considered to be one of the DARK LADY sonnets (which comprise Sonnets 127–152) in which the poet addresses a mysterious lover—one whose historical identity has never been satisfactorily ascertained. As the sonnet commences (following typical ENGLISH SONNET rhyme structure: *abab, cdcd, efef, gg*), the speaker notes that his lover does not possess any remarkable physical features that attract his attention, and indeed, he is more likely to find flaws. Still, he goes on to emphasize (l. 3) that he loves her emotionally despite any physical defects that others may observe. Indeed, she possesses nothing that would make a lover aspire to be her paramour, and in the third QUATRAIN, the speaker acknowledges that he is a slave of his heart (ll. 10–11). A hint of masochistic tendencies are reflected in the final COUPLET, in which the speaker indicates that his only source of suffering is in

the knowledge that it is illicit and he is thereby pained in the soul for his breach of societal and religious mores. At the same time, the speaker seems to relish the thought of suffering such anguish. This theme of suffering for the sake of love is expanded in Sonnet 142, which follows in the sequence.

See also SHAKESPEARE, WILLIAM; SHAKESPEARE'S SONNETS (OVERVIEW).

Joseph E. Becker

Shakespeare's sonnets: Sonnet 144 ("Two loves I have of comfort and despair") WILLIAM SHAKESPEARE (1599) The scenario of this SONNET is a love triangle, and the speaker is the lover who is getting the worst deal. He has two loves, "of comfort and despair" (l. 1), who have the power to "suggest" (or "entice") him like "spirits" (l. 2). Calling the two loves spirits implies that they have supernatural powers over the speaker, though as the sonnet progresses, it will become obvious that these powers are both good as well as evil. The good spirit is identified as a "fair" man who is an "angel" (l. 3), while the "worser spirit" is "a woman coloured ill" (l. 4). The juxtaposition of fair and ill-colored recalls Sonnets 127 and 129, which focused on a beloved who was a dark-haired, perhaps even dark-skinned, woman. Since the opposition of fair/light to ugly/dark was ingrained in early modern culture, it is not surprising that the "ill-colored" woman would be described as evil.

In the second quatrain, the speaker expands on the vile nature of the "female evil" (l. 5). He indicates that the woman's aim is to "win" the speaker "to hell" (l. 5). But this is not a hell in which the speaker will suffer. That hell is to watch the woman tempt the male beloved—the speaker's "better angel"—from his side and "corrupt" him so that this "saint" becomes a "devil" (l. 7). Thus, the woman becomes a devil figure who tempts good souls to evil and, ultimately, damnation. Referring to the male lover as an angel who is tempted to fall also recalls the Christian creation story in which evil entered heaven through Lucifer, who challenged God's authority. In the subsequent battle, Lucifer was defeated by the not-yet-incarnated Christ and forced out of heaven with all his followers. Thus, according to

Christian thought, devils are fallen angels. The woman corrupts the angel beloved by "wooing" (l. 8) him with her "foul pride" (l. 8). This is not a casual choice of phrase. "Foul" echoes the ugliness of the woman's ill color mentioned in line 4, and pride is the first and worst of the SEVEN DEADLY SINS. This is the sin that caused Lucifer to rebel against God and be cast down to hell and renamed Satan. It is also the sin that caused Adam to eat the forbidden fruit and be cast out of paradise.

The poem's final six lines present the speaker as caught in time, unable to do anything about the situation until some definite action occurs. He does not definitely know, at this point, whether the angel beloved has already been "turned fiend" (l. 9), although he suspects that he has (l. 10). The speaker cannot know the truth because both the man and the woman are away from him and they are "both to each friend" (l. 11). This means that both the man and the woman have left the speaker and become lovers themselves. In fact, the speaker suspects that "one angel [is] in another's hell" (l. 12). That is, the woman could have succeeded in tempting the angel man to hell, though in this line the description probably means that the man is having sexual intercourse with the woman; he is in her "hell," or vagina. Although this is an image that torments the speaker, he can never know for sure what has occurred. He will "live in doubt" (l. 13) until "my bad angel fires my good one out" (l. 14). Probably, the angel man will remain with the woman until she throws him out, or until he catches a venereal disease from her. Syphilis, which was indicated through a terrible burning sensation, was endemic in early modern England and there was no cure. The speaker, then, is in "limbo" until the liaison between the woman and the angel man is over.

See also SHAKESPEARE, WILLIAM; SHAKESPEARE'S SONNETS (OVERVIEW).

Theodora A. Jankowski

Shakespeare's sonnets: Sonnet 146 ("Poor soul, the center of my sinful earth") WILLIAM SHAKESPEARE (ca. 1599)

Sonnet 146 is a poem in the ancient tradition of the body-and-soul dialogue or debate, a subject that was common for writers in WILLIAM SHAKESPEARE's time (see SIR PHILIP SIDNEY's *Arcadia* [1590] and *ASTROPHIL AND STELLA* [1591] and Bartholomew Griffin's *Fidessa* [1596]). However, this SONNET demonstrates a broadening of the debate in showing the interreliance and importance of both body and soul. Sonnet 146 is unique in that unlike the other DARK LADY sonnets, which advance the narrative in some way, this poem, like Sonnet 129, does not concern the mistress or the friend, but instead discusses the speaker's generally negative mental state in relation to the sins of the body and fate of his soul.

In Sonnet 146, the speaker addresses the soul, enclosed in the sinful body, which permits the body to indulge itself while the soul pines and suffers. Why does the soul expend so much energy on a body, a "fading mansion" (l. 6) whose time on earth is so short? Will the body, weakened by sinful excess, merely be left for worms? The soul should instead prepare itself for heaven ("buy terms divine," l. 11) by feeding itself and letting the body starve. The soul will feed on death, and death will feed on the body. Eventually the soul will kill death itself, and there will be no more death (i.e., eternal life, ll. 13–14).

The body-and-soul debate or dialogue can be found in one form or another in most ancient literatures, including Egyptian, Greek, and Hebrew, as well as medieval English literature, and it generally traces its roots back to St. Paul's letters in the New Testament. This debate was also thought an effective way to frighten people with the prospect of eternal damnation. Typically, the address is praise or complaint from the body to the soul or the soul to the body, or an argument about which is most responsible for their fate. However, for Shakespeare the conflict between body and soul is a more complex interaction between the body and soul, one that implicitly allows for the individuality and autonomy of self-governance and responsibility. Unlike in many other debates, Sonnet 146 shows that the body and soul are codependent and equally responsible for a person's general spiritual health. The speaker's problem is apparent, but it is, by and large, solved internally. The absence of an implicit condemnation of the body, which is so common in medieval discussion, indicates an elevation of the body to an autonomous and therefore responsible and valuable position.

In Sonnet 146, arguably Shakespeare's most directly Christian work, there is an absence of God. Although the poem is clearly in the religious tradition of the struggle between the pleasures of this life and the happiness of the next, this theological and philosophical difference separates this late Renaissance poem from other body/soul debates. Still, in many ways, the poem seems like a prayer, albeit one in which the speaker attempts to fortify his soul at the expense of the body, bringing him closer to God. In this case, the soul acts as an intermediary with God in that it can establish terms to save itself.

See also SHAKESPEARE'S SONNETS (OVERVIEW).

Michael Peterson

Shakespeare's sonnets: Sonnet 147 ("My love is as a fever, longing still") WILLIAM SHAKE-SPEARE (1599)

One of the darkest among the later WILLIAM SHAKESPEARE'S SONNETS, the speaker in Sonnet 147 proceeds through simile, proverbs, paradox, and inversions to utterly condemn the corruption of his beloved and, coincidentally, his own fevered, fervently positive previous estimation of her.

The first three QUATRAINS describe the speaker's LOVE-SICKNESS—passionate feelings of love as disease, a fever that the physician, Reason, has tried to treat appropriately. The sufferer has rejected Reason's treatments, preferring to dwell on love, and has been abandoned by Reason. With Reason gone, the patient is past cure and can anticipate only death. As he lies raving, he unexpectedly addresses the woman he has lavished his love on, in an APOSTROPHE declaring that all his past praise for her has been wrong, the one he has sworn to be beautiful, true, and honest he now admits is evil and ugly.

In the first line, a simile, "love is as a fever," sets the dramatic situation. The speaker's love affects him as sickness, but he would prefer to remain sick ("longing still / For that which longer nurseth the disease," ll. 1–2) than to take his medicine. Before this context is established by means of the simile, the first two words, *My love,* could refer to the woman who has inspired the passion, even though they clearly denote the infatuation, or passion of love in context. This ambivalence thickens the poetic texture and makes the COUPLET's apostrophe more shocking. *Nurseth* can mean to feed, as a mother nurses her child, or it can mean to care for or attend to, the action of a patient's nurse. The second meaning is the expected one—a fever sufferer needs nursing. Because the disease is being nursed, not the patient, clearly the speaker wants to evoke the "Feeding" that appears as the first word in line three. Much of the meaning is carried by paradoxes, as when the speaker wants to preserve the disease, not his health (l. 3) and please the "uncertain, sickly appetite" (l. 4). "Appetite" can refer to "love" or "disease"; in either case, it has a pejorative connotation because this is not a healthy love to begin with.

In Renaissance medicine, disease was treated most often by application of opposites. Thus, fever was treated with cold and by abstinence from solid food because its nature was hot and dry. The speaker longs for whatever might sustain the fever, not what would break it.

The second quatrain introduces the speaker's reason as the physician who can ameliorate the condition. Reason was traditionally placed in opposition to passion; reason was supposed to rule the character. Here, because "his prescriptions are not kept" (l. 6), Reason has abandoned the patient altogether. Lines 7 and 8 have many possible nuances of meaning, although the general sense remains consistent: Without Reason, the speaker comes to know that the only outcome for unreasonable desire is death. "Approve" (l. 7) can mean "test" or "prove" by experience; it can also carry its modern meaning of "endorse" or "commend." "[That] which physic did except" can refer either to the patient having refused (excepted) medical treatment (physic), or to the fact that medicine would (if utilized) destroy desire. The antecedent can be either death or desire.

As a way of underscoring the intentional ambivalence and multivalence, the poet inverts a popular proverb in the start of the third quatrain. The proverb is "past cure past care"; by inserting "now reason is," the poet gives a specific, delimiting cause for being past cure. The sufferer is "past cure" *because* Reason has stopped caring, has abandoned him for refusing Reason's prescriptions. This leads toward the couplet: "And frantic-mad with evermore unrest" (l. 10), both completes the situation in line 9 and prepares for the thoughts in line 11. Most modern editions end line 10 with a semicolon; the 1609 edition has the more appropriate comma, which emphasizes the linking function of line 10. If all of the third quatrain is connected with commas, the tone supports the syntax, highlighting the repeated element of madness (ll. 10, 11). "Randon" (l. 12) connotes both "random" in the modern sense of disconnected and evokes the French *randon,* or "headlong rush" with which it is linguistically associated.

The couplet pulls diseased ravings into the service of "truth vainly express'd" (l. 13). Addressing the woman for whom he suffers this fever, the speaker asserts that, although he has (in the past) "sworn thee fair" (with both "blonde" and "just" or "fine" as connotations) and "thought thee bright," i.e., illuminating and intelligent, he now knows she is "black as hell, as dark as night" (l. 14). All four adjectives—*fair, bright, black,* and *dark*—represent both physical and moral conditions.

Although it appears that Sonnet 147 ends in unequivocal condemnation of the lady, the third quatrain's emphasis on the speaker's "mad" thoughts and words also condemns him. This subsidiary thread of self-denunciation is picked up in the next sonnet, "O me! what eyes hath Love put in my head" (Sonnet 148). Thus, the immediate conclusion and the longer-range conclusion are quite different, and the poet remains primarily concerned with his own feelings, even more than with any betrayal by a lover.

See also SHAKESPEARE'S SONNETS (OVERVIEW).

Marjory E. Lange

Shakespeare's sonnets: Sonnet 152 ("In loving thee thou know'st I am forsworn") WILLIAM SHAKESPEARE (1599)

Sonnet 152 is the last of what critics commonly call WILLIAM SHAKESPEARE'S DARK LADY poems. Throughout the sequence (127–152), the speaker has praised and condemned his mistress. He has also questioned his own foolishness and wondered about his overpowering sexual attraction to a woman whom he knows to be deceitful and promiscuous. Sonnet 152 contains a rather comprehensive discussion of many issues addressed throughout the Dark Lady sonnets, including his unsettling sexual attraction to a promiscuous woman whose very promiscuity is what excites his lustful feelings. Here he finally realizes his own culpability in the inevitable failure of such a relationship. More importantly, he admits that the sincerity of his vows and his oaths of her kindness, love, truth, and constancy (ll. 9–10) have been undermined by their real purpose: "to misuse" her (l. 7).

The speaker is guilty of lust, deception, and betrayal, to be sure, but also of misusing language, a serious artistic transgression for a poet. In order to praise his mistress, he has blinded his eyes, "made them swear against the thing they see" (l. 12) and to "swear against the truth so foul a lie" (l. 14). Also, all of his "honest faith . . . is lost" (l. 8)—faith not only in the mistress, but perhaps also in himself. Importantly, however, his attention has shifted from the mistress to himself. This refocusing of attention will, one might believe, lead to greater self-understanding and a closing of the emotionally (and now artistically) harmful relationship with the Dark Lady. If nothing else, he seems to be seeing things more clearly.

The speaker first admits that he is "forsworn" (l. 1), a statement that can mean that he is unfaithful to his lover or that he has lied or both. He then complains that the mistress is "twice forsworn" (l. 2)—that she is guilty of adultery to her husband ("thy bed-vow broke," l. 3; see also Sonnet 142, ll. 5–8) and of breaking her oath to the speaker, professing hatred when she previously had professed love (ll. 4–5). He further reveals that he has broken "twenty" oaths (l. 6) in deliberately blinding himself to her true nature, stubbornly swearing that she is righteous despite what is clearly evident (ll. 7–12). The first line of the COUPLET features a line— "For I have sworn thee fair" (l. 13)—also used in Sonnet 147. This line allows for some revealing connections between the passionate sickness the speaker feels in both sonnets. The second half of line 13 contains a pun—"more perjured eye"—that might simultaneously be read as "more perjured I" to indicate not only his deliberate blindness, but also that he is "more" self-deceived here than ever before (and that he is coming to terms with this self-deception). The "fair"/"foul" dichotomy is common in the Dark Lady sonnets, describing his *perception* of the Dark Lady and her behavior ("fair") and the *reality* ("foul").

See also SHAKESPEARE'S SONNETS (OVERVIEW).

Michael Peterson

Shakespeare's sonnets: Sonnets 153 and 154 ("Cupid lay by his brand and fell asleep" and "The little Love-god, lying once asleep") WIL-LIAM SHAKESPEARE (1599) These two SONNETs form the bridge between the rest of the SONNET SEQUENCE and the narrative poem *A LOVER'S COMPLAINT*. Both concern Cupid and Diana, the god of love and the virgin goddess of the hunt. In Sonnet 153, Cupid sets down his torch (replaced in modern times by a bow and arrow), which is snatched up by a virgin nymph after he falls asleep. She attempts to quench it, but only succeeds in turning the water into a boiling fountain. In Sonnet 154, Cupid falls asleep, leaving his torch unguarded, and as a group of nymphs pass by, the most beautiful one takes it. She attempts to extinguish it in a nearby well, with the same results as before. Both sonnets leave the speaker with a message: Water cannot quench love.

These are the only sonnets to use mythological allusions, but they are thematically consistent with the others in their defense of human desire. A number of critics have also noted the use of hot springs as a cure (ineffective) for venereal diseases in the 16th century, lending an additional air of speculation about the speaker's parting from the DARK LADY.

Both sonnets follow the ENGLISH SONNET form, but Sonnet 153 follows the ITALIAN (PETRARCHAN) SONNET narrative form, while Sonnet 154 matches semantics with form. Bawdy references abound. The torches are clearly phallic symbols, while the well and fountain are vaginal images. Love and disease are also linked. Besides the "inevitability" of venereal disease, love itself is a sickness that overtakes reason and action, forcing humans to act (and react) in curious manners. Overall, the universality of love and sexuality are clearly displayed.

See also SHAKESPEARE, WILLIAM; SHAKESPEARE'S SONNETS (OVERVIEW).

FURTHER READING

Hutton, James. "Analogues of Shakespeare's Sonnets 153–154: Contributions to the History of a Theme." *Modern Philology* 38, no. 4 (1941): 385–403.

SHEPHEARDES CALENDER, THE (OVERVIEW) EDMUND SPENSER (1579) *The Shepheardes Calender* was first published, anonymously, in 1579; it

was republished five times between 1579 and 1597, with EDMUND SPENSER named as author. The *Shepheardes Calender* is a collection of 12 ECLOGUEs, or conversations among shepherds (PASTORAL dialogue poems), dedicated to Sir PHILIP SIDNEY, later earning Spenser a mention in Sidney's *DEFENSE OF POESY* (1595). Though steeped in the CLASSICAL TRADITION and pointedly linked to the work of VIRGIL and Mantuan (1447–1516), Spenser's *Calender* also recalls the medieval calendar tradition through its incorporation of illustrative woodcuts. Moreover, Spenser deliberately used archaic language in order to point to a connection with an English poetic tradition, specifically recalling the work of GEOFFREY CHAUCER.

Spenser's eclogues are rhetorically complex and, in typical Spenserian style, exhibit archaic phrasing and a complex rhyme scheme. The pastoral genre gave critical writers of the city a chance to praise the quality of the simple life. The main character is Colin Clout, a character originally found in the works of JOHN SKELTON, who is introduced in January. Each eclogue traces another of his adventures, the primary being the pursuit of his lady-love, Rosalind. Each eclogue represents a month of the year, and as a whole they form a "calendar," symbolic of an entire human life. A woodcut and an EMBLEM that reveals the speaker's attitude precedes each eclogue. They can be grouped commonly into themes (e.g., love, religion, politics, etc.); indeed, the work's first publisher, identified only as "E.K.," divided the eclogues into smaller series of "plaintive" (four), "moral" (five), and "recreative" (three). Spenser incorporates multiple modes of the pastoral into his work, including debate, singing matches, love complaints, and ELEGY, with incidental personal and political allusions.

Overall, the *Shepheardes Calender* is read mainly as a political allegory, published just in time to be a response to Queen ELIZABETH I's proposed marriage to the duc d'Alençon, a young, Catholic Frenchman. Its originally anonymous publication supports this, for a general anti-Catholic work would have been embraced, but a work specifically criticizing the queen would have been punishable. Through it, Spenser also seeks to recover a native English voice and to secure England's primacy by warning his queen against the dangers of a French alliance.

The scholar Paul E. McLane sought to identify dozens of Spenser's allegorical figures and topical allusions and has pinned down several: Colin Clout is Spenser himself or the English people as a whole; Rosalind is usually Queen Elizabeth. The forms of the various eclogues also vary. "Januarye," for instance, features a six-line STANZA, which reappears again in "October" and "December." "Aprill" offers a marvelously lyrical "laye" [LAY] in honor of the Queen composed of linked QUATRAINS made to frame the emblematic ode at the center.

FURTHER READING

Brennan, M. G. "Foxes and Wolves in Elizabethan Episcopal Propaganda." *Cahiers Elizabéthains* 29 (1986): 83–86.

Hamilton, A. C. "The Argument of Spenser's Shepheardes Calender." *ELH* 23, no. 3 (1956): 171–182.

Herman, Peter C. "*The Shepheardes Calender* and Renaissance Antipoetic Sentiment." *SEL* 32 (1992): 15–33.

Maley, Willy. *A Spenser Chronology.* London: Macmillan, 1994.

McLane, Paul E. *Spenser's Shepheardes Calender: A Study in Elizabethan Allegory.* Notre Dame, Ind.: University of Notre Dame Press, 1961.

Spenser, Edmund. *Shepheardes Calender.* Edited by S. K. Heninger, Jr. Delmar, N.Y.: Scholars' Facsimiles & Reprints, 1979.

Melissa A. Harris and Michelle M. Sauer

The Shepheard's Calender: "Maye Eclogue"

EDMUND SPENSER (1579)   "Maye" is the first ECLOGUE in EDMUND SPENSER's *The SHEPHEARDES CALENDER* to focus on the politics of the Elizabethan church. (The other ecclesiastical eclogues are "Julye" and "September.") It is an allegorical dialogue between the two shepherds, Piers and Palinode, who are identified in the Argument as representations of Protestant and Catholic clerics. In this context, *Catholic* means priests who are considered superficially or insufficiently reformed by the more zealous Protestants whom Piers represents. Piers is not a Puritan, however.

Piers's name and speech evokes the PIERS PLOWMAN TRADITION, and especially *The Plowman's Tale,* which is connected to "Februarie." These other texts are as concerned as Piers is in "Maye" with "faytours" (i.e., "fakers"), or corrupt priests. *Faytours* is the term Piers uses

to condemn the shepherds who are celebrating the season after Palinode describes them admiringly in sensuous detail. In Piers's view, these shepherds should be tending to their flocks, meaning those in their spiritual care. Palinode then accuses Piers of envy and argues against austerity: One must enjoy what is good in life while it lasts. Piers counters that shepherds must live for others, not themselves. Then he makes an appeal for returning to the practices of the early church when he suggests that inheritable lands and wealth have corrupted many shepherds and injured their flocks. Palinode is deeply angered by this last criticism, which he rejects as an absurd and divisive exaggeration. In his view, things are as they are and cannot be otherwise. Piers insists that the situation is inherently divisive: There are true and false shepherds, and they are as different as day and night. Piers's arguments are more intellectually developed and persuasive than Palinode's, but his cold, stoic temperament contrasts negatively with Palinode's colorful praise and enjoyment of the late spring landscape and festivities.

The eclogue concludes with Piers telling a variation of a traditional FABLE about a disguised fox who tricks and catches a young goat. This is intended as an ALLEGORY of the various foreign and domestic Roman Catholic threats to English Protestantism. Palinode seems to agree about the threat, but since he wants to tell the story in church to a potentially Roman Catholic priest or sympathizer, it is unlikely he has been persuaded to think as Piers does.

FURTHER READING

Hume, Anthea. "Spenser, Puritanism, and the 'Maye' Eclogue." *RES* 20 (1969): 155–167.

Daniel P. Knauss

SIDNEIAN PSALMS (THE SIDNEY PSALMS) (OVERVIEW) SIR PHILIP SIDNEY AND MARY SIDNEY HERBERT, COUNTESS OF PEMBROKE

(1599)   Begun by Sir PHILIP SIDNEY but completed by his sister, MARY SIDNEY HERBERT, COUNTESS OF PEMBROKE, the collection contains 150 translations of the biblical psalms. Herbert contributed 107 of the 150. She also wrote two poems that preface the psalms themselves: "TO THEE, PURE SPRITE," an ELEGY for her brother, and

"EVEN NOW THAT CARE," which dedicates the collection to Queen ELIZABETH I.

The TRANSLATION TRADITION was strong in the 16th century, and translating the Psalms was particularly popular. The Psalms have traditionally been ascribed to king David of Israel as a series of ejaculatory poems praising God, though they include a variety of forms: praise poems, supplications, hymns, and liturgy. Historically, of course, David could not have been the author of the Psalms, but that traditional belief has shaped the way people have approached them for centuries. For instance, Protestant theologians believed that through David's lineage they could be traced forward to Jesus. Moreover, during the Reformation and the years following, the Psalms held particular political significance for the Protestant community. Like David, they felt afraid and overwhelmed and cried out to God for political and spiritual assistance. Translations and versions of the Psalms were so popular that by the mid-17th century, more than 300 versions existed.

The *Sidneian Psalms* are considered a superior example for a variety of reasons. First, they manage to both capture the spirit of the original Psalms, often using almost literal translations of the Hebrew while simultaneously creating unique and memorable imagery. Scholars continue to debate whether Mary Sidney knew Hebrew or received outside assistance (it is generally assumed that Philip did not know Hebrew). At minimum, both Sidneys used a variety of sources—the Geneva Bible, the Vulgate, various commentaries, Hebrew texts (perhaps)—for their translation. In completing the collection, Herbert used 126 verse variants, displaying incredible literary prowess. In at least one case, for example, she changes the Psalm into a SONNET.

The Psalms themselves are considered a monumental achievement in the establishment of Protestant religious discourse and influenced John Donne and George Herbert, among others. While a few critics have looked into the possible crypto-Catholicism of Sir Philip Sidney and the possible ramifications for the Psalms, a great deal of scholarship has examined the *Sidneian Psalms* as reflecting a Calvinist sprit, wherein humanity is incomplete and ineffectual without the grace of God for assistance. The dedication to Queen Elizabeth takes on political dimensions in this light—she becomes "David," defender of the true faith. The *Sidneian Psalms* also had an impact on later British literature, not only on other psalm collections, but also on general poetry: John Donne wrote a poem in celebration of them, for example.

See also "TO THE THRICE-SACRED QUEEN ELIZABETH," *WHOLE BOOK OF PSALMS COLLECTED INTO ENGLISH METER, THE.*

FURTHER READING

Clarke, Danielle, ed. *Isabella Whitney, Mary Sidney, and Aemilia Lanyer: Renaissance Women Poets.* New York: Penguin Books, 2000.

Hamlin, Hannibal. *Psalm Culture and Early Modern English Literature.* Cambridge: Cambridge University Press, 2007.

Hannay, Margaret P. "'Wisdome the Wordes': Psalm Translation and Elizabethan Women's Spirituality." *Religion and Literature* 23, no. 3 (1991): 65–81.

———, ed. *Philip's Phoenix: Mary Sidney, Countess of Pembroke.* Oxford: Oxford University Press, 1990.

———, ed. *Silent But for the Word: Tudor Women as Patrons, Translators, and Writers of Religious Works.* Kent, Ohio: Kent State University Press, 1985.

———, Noel J. Kinnamon, and Michael G. Brennan, eds. *The Collected Works of Mary Sidney Herbert, Countess of Pembroke.* 2 vols. Oxford: Clarendon Press, 1998.

Rathmell, J. C. A. *The Psalms of Sir Philip Sidney and the Countess of Pembroke.* New York: New York University Press, 1963.

Rienstra, Debra K. "Mary Sidney, Countess of Pembroke, Psalmes." In *A Companion to Early Modern Women's Writing,* edited by Anita Pacheco, 110–124. Malden, Mass. and Oxford: Blackwell, 2002.

Sidney, Mary, Countess of Pembroke. *The Sidney Psalms.* Edited by R. E. Pritchard. Manchester: Carcanet, 1992.

Slavitt, David R. "Shine in the dreadful dark: The Sidnean Psalms." *Hudson Review* 52, no. 4 (2000): 563–576.

Steinberg, Theodore L. "The Sidneys and the Psalms." *Studies in Philology* 92, no. 1 (1995): 1–17.

Swaim, Kathleen M. "Contextualizing Mary Sidney's *Psalms.*" *Christianity and Literature* 48, no. 3 (1999): 253–273.

Sidneian Psalms: Psalm 50 ("Deus Deorum," "The ever living God the mighty lord") MARY SIDNEY HERBERT, COUNTESS OF PEMBROKE (1599)

MARY SIDNEY HERBERT's version of Psalm 50 addresses both the Protestant spirit of reformation and the emphasis on faith rather than works. Her version of Psalm 50 emphasizes the contrast between idolatry and true faith. Rather than earthly sacrifices, the psalm explains, the most appropriate gift to God is praise. Significantly, substantially different versions of Herbert's Psalm 50 exist; that found in Text A, commonly used by editors, contain notable differences in wording and structure than that found in Text B, a variant collection. Unless otherwise designated, quotations refer to Text A.

Herbert uses the spread of God's word throughout all of the earth to recall the proliferation of Protestantism, but by the second stanza she moves from describing God to invoking his voice directly. The remainder of the psalm conveys God's message to his people. His people are not at fault, he says, because of a lack of sacrifices or offerings; rather, Psalm 50 suggests the ultimate inappropriateness of such actions. God refuses gifts of bullocks, beasts, or birds because all creatures on earth are his; he knows all, and all know him. God's possession of all things living on earth suggests the paradox of animal sacrifice; owning "all that the earth doth beare" (l. 28), he has no need, or hunger, for his own possessions to be returned to him in the form of sacrifice.

God demands a different sacrifice, one of "praise" (l. 33), which is more valuable and everlasting than a material sacrifice. In exchange for "peace" granted in response to "the knott that anguish tyes" (l. 37), God requests true faith—not merely actions or deeds, but belief. The behavior of the faithful stands in sharp contrast to the deceptive conduct of the "godlesse" (l. 40). These unreformed people may publicly follow religious statutes, but in private and in their hearts they fail to follow God's commandments. Notably, Herbert associates the "reformed religion" with perfect righteousness.

Of particular interest is the language Herbert uses to describe the unrighteous; in versions of the Psalm found in both Texts A and B, Herbert focuses on the mouths of sinners. Text A describes "thie mouth is slaunders ever-open porte, / and from thie tounge doth nought, but treason, flow" (ll. 47–48), while Text B observes, "Thy mouth a denn where Serpent slaunder lyes / Thy tongue a stamp that coines but fraud and lyes" (ll. 51–52). In the Text A version, Herbert equates treason against God—slander—to betrayal of the state. The image of the Serpent is an unsurprising and tradi-

tional choice to suggest the ills of evil; more interesting is the word choice of "coines," equating language with money. Both, in Herbert's analogy, are currency; both are used to communicate different types of value. Notably, both versions ultimately express the same concept: Betrayal of God must also infect the secular state. The psalm ends with both an implicit threat and a promise: To the unfaithful, God promises to clutch with "griping fingers," (l. 60) which none can escape. In contrast, those whose offerings consists of the "sweete perfume of offred praise" (l. 52) will "see gods saving grace" (l. 64).

See also SIDNEAN PSALMS (OVERVIEW).

Winter Elliott

Sidneian Psalms: Psalm 58 ("Si Vere Utique," "And call ye this to utter what is just") MARY SIDNEY HERBERT, COUNTESS OF PEMBROKE (1599)

The Biblical psalm presents a plea for justice by David, Israel's King, which MARY SIDNEY HERBERT and her contemporaries linked to the Protestant situation in England and the Continent. Therefore, the language of this psalm may be interpreted as both justification and encouragement for the Protestant faith. The psalm opens with a direct address to those who sit in judgment—rulers—and the first lines question the justice of sentencing the "wronged" (l. 4). The psalm contrasts the honored status and positions of judges with their own mortality; no matter how privileged they may be, they are still descended from Adam and created from the same earthly dust as he. Significantly, Herbert's translation of the Psalms opened with a dedicatory poem to Queen ELIZABETH I, "EVEN NOW THAT CARE," which itself underscored the need to continue to advance the Protestant cause in England and elsewhere. The rulers suggested in the opening lines of Psalm 58 thus subtly recall Herbert's address to Elizabeth.

Herbert consistently uses strong and politically charged language throughout the psalm. From the suggestions of legal issues and public policy implied in the opening lines, she shifts to problems of justice and oppression. The speaker notes that his oppressors, who now sit in judgment of him, have long harbored wrong in their hearts—a prejudice that, from a position of power, they now reveal to the world. However, this injustice is not entirely unexpected, as the oppressors have consistently declined to follow truth and right. Indeed, the accusers have serpent poison lodged in them; both their words and thoughts, the poem suggests, are tainted.

The psalm moves from directly addressing David's response to his accusers (and, more implicitly, the enemies of the contemporary Protestant faith) to invoking the Lord's protection. The psalm asks the Lord to crush the teeth—and thus the voice—of the speaker's enemies, to drown them and to break their weapons. The psalm then asks that all of the oppressors' actions, ("Springing thorns," l. 25) thoughts, and deeds die a stillborn death, decaying into nonexistence before they can fully mature.

Herbert concludes that when the just person witnesses this divine treatment of injustice, he or she shall rejoice and "bath his feet in bloud of wicked one" (l. 30). Finally, the psalm concludes with a clear definition of equal and unbiased justice. God will mete out to each his or her deserved good or ill: All shall observe that "there is a god that carves to each his own" (l. 32).

See also SIDNEAN PSALMS (OVERVIEW).

Winter Elliott

Sidneian Psalms: Psalm 59 ("Deliver me from my enemies") MARY SIDNEY HERBERT, COUNTESS OF PEMBROKE (1599)

Like many of her other translations, MARY SIDNEY HERBERT's treatment of Psalm 59 maintains the essence of her sources while also incorporating her own sense of style and imagery. Psalm 59 revolves around several contrasting images of the faithful speaker and his enemies; his voice is juxtaposed with their voiceless howling, and his faith contrasts their enmity.

The central theme, repeated throughout the psalm, is a fairly typical prayer for aid and strength in the face of apparently invincible enemies. "Save mee from such as me assaile" (l. 1) the psalm begins, and the preoccupied speaker reiterates this phrase throughout the poem. More interesting is the speaker's depiction of the foes from which he requests deliverance: They "make a trade of cursed wrong / and bredd in bloud for bloud doe long" (ll. 4–5). In other words, the speaker's enemies are

professional murderers; worse still, they pass their vile trade from generation to generation. The speaker effectively dehumanizes these foes, emphasizing the apparently inherited nature of their evil. The recurring dog imagery throughout the poem underscores this distinction between the humanity of the speaker and the inhumanity of those who seek his overthrow.

By line 25, the speaker has begun to expand his characterization of his enemies. When the sun sets,

> as houndes that howle their food to gett
> they runn amaine
> the cittie through from street to street
> with hungry maw . . . (ll. 27–30)

Herbert uses these images of dogs to further dehumanize the speaker's enemies; consequently, she links humanity to righteousness. In order to be human, the poem implies, one must also be faithful to God. In contrast to the loyal speaker, oppressed but still hopeful, his enemies descend upon the world, a perpetually hungry plague determined to devour the weak and the vulnerable. "Babling" (l. 32), these dogs jabber their desire to consume the life of the speaker, who explains that this inimitable food "extinguish may / their deadly hate" (l. 33). Throughout the poem, the babbling jibberish of the dog-enemies contrasts with the speaker's clear voice and his promise to sing praise to God.

The speaker requests that his enemies' ravenous rage consume them entirely. Repeating almost exactly the stanza in which she introduces the hound metaphor, Herbert shifts the emphasis from one of destruction to one of victory. With God's help, the hounds will not succeed in their hungry march from city to city; instead, hunted themselves by famine, they bay, refusing to return to their kennels (ll. 67–78). The remainder of the psalm depicts the speaker's song, uniting his limited strength and will to God's omnipotent will. Through God's "free grace" (l. 89), the speaker receives his own "freedom" (l. 97). Thus, Herbert links obedience and faith in God to freedom, while the speaker's enemies are relegated to a painful subservience to their own endless hate and hunger.

See also SIDNEAN PSALMS (OVERVIEW).

Winter Elliott

Sidneian Psalms: Psalm 71 ("In Te Domini Speravi," "On thee my trust is grounded") MARY SIDNEY HERBERT, COUNTESS OF PEMBROKE (1599) Psalm 71 is typically regarded as David's prayer to God for deliverance from his son Absalom. The poem is also a particularly touching appeal for aid and comfort in old age, when previous strength, power, and social status have been lost.

Psalm 71 opens with an emphatic statement of trust in the Lord, and this concept recurs repeatedly throughout the entire poem. The speaker appeals to the Lord for freedom and justice, stressing his own faith in God's willingness and ability to defend him. In God alone, the poem affirms, the speaker finds stability and safety. Subtly, he suggests his present insecure position in the world. The speaker underscores his lengthy relationship with God: "Since imprison'd in my mother" (l. 19), the speaker has trusted in God. The line recalls not just the speaker's embryonic existence in his mother's womb but also the transmission of sin from mother to child, and the speaker's own inevitable participation in that inheritance.

Midway through the poem, the speaker has begun to suggest his own advanced age (l. 55) and his mistreatment at the hands of his fellow men. His mature years, he admits, have left him bereft of any other comfort or strength besides that which he finds in the Lord. Deprived of almost every worldly good, then, he pleads that the Lord not abandon him as well. Because his earthly enemies have gathered against him, he can turn to no one but the Lord. The speaker hopes that his enemies' own spite and hate will work against them, destroying them from within; since the speaker places his own hopes in the hands of God, though, he ultimately sees his age as an advantage rather than a weakness. His snowy head bears witness to his years—time in which he may demonstrate the power and might of the Lord to the ages and every other living person. He acknowledges that while he may have experienced great sorrow and woe, God's power may again revive and exalt him. The psalm ends with the speaker's promise to continue raising his voice in song and music; with that harmony, he implies, his enemies will be vanquished.

See also HERBERT, MARY SIDNEY; *SIDNEAN PSALMS* (OVERVIEW).

Winter Elliott

Sidneian Psalms: Psalm 120 ("Ad Dominum," "As to th'Eternal often in anguishes") MARY SIDNEY HERBERT, COUNTESS OF PEMBROKE (1599) MARY SIDNEY HERBERT modeled Psalm 120 on her composite readings of multiple translated versions of the Psalms. Written in unrhymed quantitative meter, Psalm 120 showcases her attention to poetic variety and allows her to experiment with a verse form that her brother, SIR PHILIP SIDNEY, had also attempted to utilize in his psalm paraphrases.

Herbert identifies the speaker of Psalm 120 as a Babylonian exile rather than David, King of the Israelites. In the first four lines of the poem, the anguished psalmist describes how he has repeatedly called out for God without ever receiving an answer. In the second STANZA, the speaker entreats God to help him recognize eloquent but treasonous language for what it is. What good, the speaker asks in the third stanza, results from wronging, forgery, and deceit?

Stanza 4 is crafted of an elegant series of similes that build upon one another:

> Though like an arrow strongly delivered
> It deeply pierce, though like to Juniper
> It coales doe cast, which quickly fired,
> Flame very hott, very hardly quenching?
>   (ll. 13–16)

The words of the "filthy forgers" described in stanzas 2 and 3 pierce deeply and burn fast like juniper—a highly flammable wood.

The poem's final two stanzas heighten the psalmist's exilic, nomadic lifestyle. The psalmist has lived in Kedar and Mesech, lands in Arabia and Asia Minor, far from his homeland. During his exile, he frequently has lived in a tent or a "howslesse harbour" (l. 20). For too long, he concludes, he has led a nomadic lifestyle. "With frendly peaces furious enemies" (l. 22) he has dwelled—that is, he has lived with furious enemies in times of peace, and he finds that when he calls them to peace, these enemies respond by being quick to arm themselves for war.

Psalm 120 is a tightly crafted exercise in metrical precision, allusiveness, and imagery. Beyond its careful composition, what makes this psalm paraphrase remarkable is the raw yet controlled emotion, the careful yet earnest political coding, and the succinct yet expansive religious sentiment that Herbert expresses so confidently.

See also SIDNEAN PSALMS (OVERVIEW).

Emily Smith

Sidneian Psalms: Psalm 121 ("Levavi Oculos," "Unto the hills, I now will bend") MARY SIDNEY HERBERT, COUNTESS OF PEMBROKE (1599)   Both the theme and diction of Psalm 121 combine to produce a tone of celebration. The people rejoice as they see the hills of Judaea; their praise and thanksgiving, however, may be extended to all of God's people—contemporary Protestants as well as Old Testament exiles. Psalm 121 underscores the dangers of travel, using repetition and questions to contrast the mortal problems God's people face with their eternal expectation of divine assistance. "What? and doe I behold the lovely mountaines, / whence comes all my reliefe, my aid, my comfort?" (ll. 1–2) begins the poem. Line 4 repeats the second line, suggesting that God's divine support is both near and far—something that the speaker can see and believe in, but not something immediately present. "March, march, lustily on, redoubt no falling" (l. 5), the speaker encourages. God needs no sleep or rest, and is never absent when his people face perils.

Then people should march on by day, despite the heat of the sun. By night, he repeats, the people should continue to journey, despite the "Moony vapors" (l. 16). Journey by night or day is identified as dangerous; neither the sun nor the moon look upon travelers with kindness; both day and night are fraught with peril. Despite the evident danger, though, God remains constant, offering protection from every hazard. Still, the psalm ends with confident joy. Through God, each traveler will be "safe in all thy goings, in all thy comings, / now thou shalt by his hand, yea still be guarded" (ll. 19–20). Though the travelers have not yet reached their destination, they may still expect God's continued comfort and protection as they continue their journey.

See also HERBERT, MARY SIDNEY; SIDNEAN PSALMS (OVERVIEW).

Winter Elliott

Sidneian Psalms: Psalm 139 ("Domine Probasti," "O Lord, in me there lieth nought") MARY SIDNEY HERBERT, COUNTESS OF PEMBROKE (1599)   In the biblical version of Psalm 139, the pattern of stark contrasts of beginning and ends, before and after, and high and low is intended to show God's absolute knowledge and protection. In MARY SIDNEY HERBERT's translation, there is a smoothing out of the contrasts. She replaces them with puns and jangling wordplay—a characteristic found in Hebrew poetry, but also a favorite Elizabethan practice.

The wordplay itself becomes a way of deeply knowing, a kind of secret probing that seems to hide its intentions just as it is at work. Both eye and ear are important to the rhyme that Herbert imposes on the verse. As the psalm develops, she follows closely the subject of the biblical psalm, choosing not to inject herself or typical imagery from her time period. God is both creator and knower, and cursing against God's enemies reveals devotion to God.

Psalm 139 is representative of Herbert's method in the translation of the Psalms: Her work shows the triumph of the Protestant vision of the world, especially in its reliance upon personal reading of the Bible, coupled with religious and political triumph.

See also SIDNEAN PSALMS (OVERVIEW).

Daniel F. Pigg

SIDNEY, SIR PHILIP (1554–1586)   Born to Sir Henry Sidney, lord deputy of Ireland, and Lady Mary Dudley Sidney, sister of Robert Dudley, earl of Leicester, Sir Philip Sidney was a celebrity during his own lifetime. At age 10, he entered Shrewsbury School, where he met his lifelong friend and biographer, SIR FULKE GREVILLE. Though he later attended Oxford University, Sidney did not take a degree; rather, he supplemented his formal education with three years of extensive

traveling throughout the Continent (1572–75). The journey left ineffable impressions on him. For instance, he witnessed the Massacre of St. Bartholomew's Day, a gory event resulting in the deaths of numerous Huguenots (French Protestants), which strengthened his Protestant resolve.

Sidney was greatly admired by his contemporaries as both an author and a patron. His literary circle included Greville, Thomas Drant, Edward Dyer, and EDMUND SPENSER, who went so far as to dedicate *The* SHEPHEARD'S CALENDER (1579) to him. Sidney's own works include *Lady of May* (1578), an entertaining piece composed in honor of Queen ELIZABETH I; the SONNET SEQUENCE entitled *ASTROPHIL AND STELLA,* which is credited with establishing the genre's popularity; *Arcadia,* a PASTORAL prose ROMANCE, revised later into the *New Arcadia* (1590); CERTAIN SONNETS (1598); and the magisterial DEFENSE OF POESY (1595).

Though Sidney's literary life seemed charmed, his political and romantic entanglements were complicated. In 1580, he was dismissed from court for publicly opposing Queen Elizabeth's proposed marriage to the Catholic duke of Anjou. Soon afterward, in 1581, his beloved Penelope Devereux, the daughter of the earl of Essex, married Lord Rich, though she had supposedly been engaged to Sidney in 1576. Two years later, Sidney married Frances Walsingham, the daughter of Sir Francis Walsingham, and was knighted.

Four years later, in the Battle of Zutphen on September 22, 1586, Sidney was mortally wounded in the left thigh. He succumbed to a gangrenous infection at the age of 32 on October 17, 1586. Virtually the entire country mourned Sidney's death. His sister, MARY SIDNEY HERBERT, COUNTESS OF PEMBROKE, became the custodian of Sidney's prolific writings and kept his memory alive. Sidney retained his status even after death, and he continues to be admired today.

See also QUATORZAIN; SIDNEIAN PSALMS; SHEPHEARDES CALENDER, THE.

FURTHER READING

Duncan-Jones, Katherine. *Sir Philip Sidney.* Oxford and New York: Oxford University Press, 1989.

Stewart, Alan. "Philip Sidney: A Double Life." *The New Criterion* 20 (2002): 28.

Christopher D. Lozensky

"SIEGE OF CALAIS, THE" LAURENCE MINOT (1347?)

The seventh in the collection of 11 political poems attributed to Laurence Minot (fl. 1333–52) describing a series of English victories against the Scots and on the Continent. Minot concentrates on an episode of the HUNDRED YEARS' WAR in which King Edward III defeated the French, successfully besieging the port of Calais (where he had arrived in September 1346) and making it an English possession for the following 200 years.

Minot gives a fairly accurate, if patriotic, retelling of events, presenting the siege as a retribution for the men of Calais and their piracy on the channel. He mentions how Edward had a wooden encampment built in order to shelter his troops in the winter and rather sarcastically alludes to Philip VI and his son, John of France, who vainly assembled a force to relieve Calais in April 1347; with equal hostility, he mentions the pope's attempt to arrive at a negotiation. In both cases, the poet echoes popular English sentiments.

The second part of the poem is more moving. It describes the plight of the people of Calais, forced by starvation to eat their cats and dogs, and then to surrender to the English in August 1347. The last figure to appear on the scene is John de Vienne, warden of Calais, who gives King Edward the keys of the city.

In the opening lines, Minot uses the word *romance* to refer to the record of history, and the tone of the poem maintains the balance between the sober accounts of fact and the enchantment of oral retelling. This is achieved through the sustained use of ALLITERATION and other devices typical of oral poetry such as the use of formulaic phrases, or the interconnection between STANZAS. Also typical of this poet is his focus on individual heroes or villains (King Edward, the French king) as the true protagonists of the action, elevating the narrative and giving it lyrical overtones.

See also CHRONICLES; HUNDRED YEARS' WAR.

FURTHER READING

Osberg, Richard H., ed. *The Poems of Laurence Minot: 1333–1352.* Kalamazoo, MI: Medieval Institute Publications, 1996.

Alessandra Petrina

SIR GAWAIN AND THE GREEN KNIGHT

ANONYMOUS (14th century)   Part of the 14th century's ALLITERATIVE REVIVAL, *Sir Gawain and the Green Knight* is perhaps the best-known and most studied Arthurian ROMANCE. It is the last poem in the manuscript MS Cotton Nero A.x in London's British Library. It is preceded by three other alliterative poems: *PEARL, CLEANNESS* (Purity), and *PATIENCE*. All of these poems are written in the same scribal hand, in the Northwest Midlands dialect of Middle English, leading to the speculation that they share a common author, known as the *GAWAIN*-POET or the *PEARL*-POET. This manuscript is lavishly illuminated (decorated), with four-color drawings corresponding with each poem. Many scholars agree that evidence points to a Cheshire author, but that assumption has been challenged in recent scholarship. Internal evidence further points to composition during the reign of Richard II (1377–99).

Sir Gawain and the Green Knight totals 2,530 long alliterative lines divided into 101 STANZAS. There is no uniformity in stanza length; however, each ends with a BOB-AND-WHEEL structure. The long alliterative line is descended directly from Old English poetry, particularly in carrying the stress within the first half of the line. However, Middle English alliterative poems, and *Sir Gawain* in particular, tend to incorporate other elements—such as ASSONANCE, consonance (repetition of consonant sounds), and binding repetition (linked words)—into the rhyme scheme, too, which alleviate alliterative tensions caused by syntactical changes within the language. Further, although *Sir Gawain* relies primarily on rising rhythm (initial unstressed syllables), a number of initial stress lines show deliberate variation.

The poem opens with a reference to the mythical founding of Britain by Brutus, a descendent of Aeneas, thus assuring Britain's dominance. The true story opens at King ARTHUR's court during the Christmas season, where lords and ladies are dancing, singing, feasting, and playing games. Gawain, Morgan le Fey's son and Arthur's nephew, is one of the knights at the table. Arthur oversees all the activities, though he petulantly craves more excitement. This soon arrives in the person of the Green Knight, who is huge, powerful, and completely green. A number of lines are devoted to the particulars of the Green Knight's appearance, detailing not only his unusual coloring but also his large size, oddly coupled with a slim waist and delicate features. He is dressed in green (with a few gold pieces) and has green hair and green skin, although his eyes are red. Even his horse is green. He is not wearing war gear—he has no helmet or hauberk (chain mail tunic)—and bears a holly branch (a Celtic peace symbol) in one hand and an enormous axe in the other.

Speaking directly to Arthur, the Green Knight claims to have heard of the Round Table's fame, which he now, looking around at "beardless children" (l. 280), doubts. Despite this lack of confidence, the Green Knight requests a Christmas game: He will lend his axe to any knight brave enough to accept his challenge and allow him to take the first blow. The Green Knight will not flinch from the swing and will quitclaim (release unconditionally) his claim on the axe, provided the chosen knight agrees to seek him out at the Green Chapel in a year and a day (the standard duration of a medieval contract) in order to receive a blow in exchange. The stunned court sits in silence, until, provoked by the Green Knight's taunts, Arthur feels compelled to accept the challenge himself. Gawain, however, cannot sit idly by and allow his king and uncle to accept such an undertaking. Claiming to be the most unworthy member of the court, and courteously requesting Queen Guinevere's permission, Gawain rises and accepts the challenge. The Green Knight reviews the terms with him and gives directions to his abode. Grasping the axe, Gawain deals a mighty blow to the unflinching Green Knight's neck, striking off his head. To the surprise of everyone, the Green Knight picks up his head, reminds Gawain not to be a coward, gets on his horse, and rides away. Gawain, though amazed, returns to the party.

The next several months, which pass in two stanzas, witness Gawain enjoying courtly life, not preparing for his journey spiritually or mentally or even determining the location of the castle. On Michaelmas (September 29), Gawain suddenly realizes that he will soon have to undertake his quest or risk damaging his reputation. However, he remains in the court, still without preparations, until All Saint's Day (November 1), before requesting leave of Arthur. The king and court mournfully agree that he must leave, and the following morning,

Gawain rises and (finally) prepares for his journey. Unlike the Green Knight, Gawain is clothed primarily in gold and dons full war gear. When dressed, Gawain and his horse, Gringolet ("white hard"), make a stunning picture. Both glitter with gold and rustle with silk, and the ladies of the court sigh at their departure. Gawain's helmet is encrusted with diamonds, and he is finally presented with a magnificent shield. This shield is made of *gules*—pure red gold—and emblazoned with a pentangle (five-pointed star) on the outside and a picture of the Virgin Mary on the inside. The pentangle is carefully explained in the poem as an important symbol. Dubbed the "endless knot" in Celtic cultures, the pentangle symbolizes perpetual loyalty. Moreover, each of its five points stands for another set of five, creating an interlocking network of "five fives." The first set of five stands for Gawain's five senses; the second for his five fingers; the third for the five wounds of Christ; the fourth for the five joys (Annunciation, Nativity, Resurrection, Ascension, and Assumption); and the fifth for the five aspects of CHIV-ALRY (generosity, chastity, loyalty, courtesy, and piety). Finally securing his leave, Gawain rides off throughout the realm, seeking the location of the Green Chapel. Similar to the passage of seasons, two stanzas compress this task, providing a general commentary on Gawain's exploits: He climbs cliffs; fords waters; slays beasts; endures cold, hunger, and hardship; and prays for Mary's help.

Finally, on Christmas Eve, weary to the bone, and nearly out of time to achieve his goal, Gawain spots a formidable-looking castle. He approaches, seeking rest and shelter, and is welcomed by the porter. After crossing the drawbridge, Gawain is met by the lord of the castle, who welcomes him heartily. The lord is a fit and handsome man who immediately settles Gawain in a luxurious chamber. After resting and washing, Gawain proceeds to a feast, where he is a model of courtesy. He converses about the court, flirts with the ladies, and courteously consumes his meal. After dinner, the lord invites Gawain to his study. There he has a chance to observe the lady of the castle more clearly. She is "more beautiful than Guinevere" (l. 945) and accompanied by a foul older woman. However, Gawain notes the great deference all pay to the elder woman and con-

cludes (rightfully so, as he will discover) that she is powerful. Everyone plays games until bedtime.

In the morning, a Christmas feast is prepared, and the household spends the day in merriment. Gawain and the lady converse intimately together on a number of occasions, as they do the following day, St. Stephen's Day, during still more feasts. St. John's Day (December 27) witnesses the final day of feasting and games. In the evening, Gawain courteously thanks his host for the hospitality and declares his intent to leave. The lord attempts to persuade Gawain to stay longer, but Gawain insists that he must leave. When pressed, Gawain finally reveals that he is on a quest and that he must find the Green Chapel within four days. The lord laughs in relief—his castle, he says, is only two miles away from that chapel, and if Gawain will stay until New Year's, the lord will then arrange for him to be guided to the chapel the following day. A relieved Gawain readily agrees. The lord then proposes a further arrangement: Gawain, he says, is not well rested; therefore, he should remain in the castle resting while the lord goes out hunting. At the end of each day, the two men will meet and exchange whatever they gain during the day with each other. Gawain accepts the host's proposition, and a bargain is struck.

The following morning, the lord and his men rise early to hunt. Quickly they set upon the deer, letting both the bucks and the fertile does pass at the lord's command. The scene then shifts to Gawain's chamber, as the lady slips into the room. The noise wakes Gawain, but he pretends to remain asleep until the lady approaches. As he blinks sleepily, the lady accosts him, calling Gawain an "unwary sleeper" ("sleper unslyȝe," l. 1209) who is easily caught—not typical behavior for a knight. She threatens to bind him to his bed unless they can achieve a truce. Though clearly uncomfortable, especially after she reminds him that they are alone, Gawain manages courteous discourse with the lady. Though she tries to cajole him into further intimacy, Gawain reminds the lady of God and her marriage and manages to divert her attentions. Nonetheless, the lady manages to acquire a kiss from Gawain as she takes her leave.

The scene then shifts back to the hunt, where the lord and his men have just killed several fat, barren does. The grisly butchering scene is described in detail, with particular emphasis placed on splitting the deer. The day ends with the lord and Gawain meeting in the study, where they exchange their day's winnings. The lord presents Gawain with fresh venison, while Gawain courteously kisses the lord once. They proceed to dinner, and each agrees the exchange was worthy.

The next morning, the lord and his men once again wake early and proceed to the hunt. This time their quarry is a wild boar, more vigorous and violent than their previous prey. Three men are downed by the boar, which then rushes off with the others in pursuit, its thick hide repelling arrows as it flees. The scene shifts, once again, to Gawain's bedroom, as the lady creeps in. This time, however, Gawain is awake and waiting for her. She teases him, especially about his reputation for courtesy and chivalry. Stung, Gawain angrily defends himself. The lady responds by reminding him that he is strong enough to force her ("Ye ar stif innoghe to constrayne wyth strenkþe," l. 1496), but also that he would never have to. Having said this, she kisses him. Afterward, she begs Gawain to teach her about true love. Gawain realizes he has been outwitted, and they spend the rest of the afternoon laughing together. The lady kisses Gawain and takes her leave.

The story then shifts back to the hunt, as the lord continues the chase after the boar. Finally, the boar is cornered, and the lord himself leaps off his horse, sword in hand, to dispatch it. He strikes the beast in the heart, and although it escapes temporarily, floating downstream, the dogs converge, tearing it to pieces. As the head is triumphantly returned to the lord, the scene shifts back to the castle. He meets Gawain and presents him with the boar's head; in return, Gawain kisses the lord twice. They feast, and plans are made for a final exchange on the morrow. The evening ends with the lord praising Gawain, whom he has tested twice during their exchanges, and whose faithfulness has proved true.

On the third morning, the lord once again rises early and hears mass before leaving for the hunt. He and his men are soon in pursuit of a wily fox, who flinches from the baying hounds and runs in terror. The scene then shifts to Gawain's bedroom, where the lady has once again come to visit. Dressed provocatively, she

enters while Gawain wrestles with a dream about his impending death. She wakes him with a kiss, and he is enthralled. Gawain's chastity is in peril ("Nif Mare hir knygt mynne," l. 1769)—that is, unless the Virgin Mary guards him against temptation. Gawain has decided that he has been discourteous to the lady, and he now sets out to charm her. He succeeds to some extent, though she understands he is deceiving her. Before she leaves, she kisses him and then begs a token of him. Gawain demurs, fearing to enter into another gift exchange and its accompanying obligations. The lady then insists on giving him a gift instead. First, she offers Gawain a red gold ring, which he declines because it is too expensive. The lady then suggests that he accept her "girdle" (a belt or sash) instead, as it "gaynes [him] lasse" (l. 1829). Again, Gawain attempts to refuse. This time, however, the lady insists he hear her out. It seems that this is no ordinary girdle—it is magical. Anyone who wears it cannot be harmed. Gawain is immediately tempted, as he will soon be facing the Green Knight's axe. Eventually he allows himself to be coaxed into taking the girdle. Moreover, the lady beseeches him never to reveal it, "bot to lelly layne for hir lorde" (l. 1863), keeping it even from her husband. Despite his agreement with the lord of the castle, Gawain agrees to the lady's terms. She kisses him and leaves. Gawain, feeling relieved, rises, bathes, dresses, and seeks a priest. He confesses his sins—except that he fails to reveal that he accepted the girdle—and receives penance.

The scene then returns to the lord's hunt. He has cornered the fox, and skinned it. He returns to the castle, where he is met by Gawain. Gawain, for the first time, takes the lead in the gift exchange and kisses the lord three times. The host declares that Gawain's profits far outstrip his own, and he tosses the fox's pelt down. The two go in to a grand feast, where Gawain laughs and relaxes as he has not before.

In the morning, the lord sends a servant to conduct Gawain to the Green Chapel. Leaving before daylight, Gawain sets out into a gloomy storm, wearing the girdle underneath his armor. As Gawain descends toward the chapel, the terrain gets bleaker, the air fouler, and the atmosphere wilder. As a final temptation, the lord's servant suggests to Gawain that he flee this awful place, offering to keep the secret for him. Gawain faces this final temptation successfully, however, and continues towards the chapel.

When he arrives, Gawain bemoans his fate but continues ahead. The Green Knight greets him courteously, and Gawain kneels down, baring his neck. The Green Knight raises the axe high above his head, and brings it down in a crashing blow—into a snow bank. Gawain has flinched, revealing his cowardice. The Green Knight mocks Gawain, who swears he will not flinch again. The Green Knight raises his axe for a second mighty blow, which he begins, but pulls at the final moment. This time, Gawain does not flinch, and the Green Knight praises him for his bravery. On the third try, the Green Knight's axe nicks Gawain's neck but does him no real harm. Seeing this, Gawain springs up, grabs his helmet, and cries "bede [bait] me no mo!" (l. 2322). The Green Knight laughs and tells Gawain not to worry—he is the most nearly faultless knight on foot. Of course, he realizes that Gawain has the garter; indeed, it is his wife's girdle. The Green Knight and the lord of the castle—Lord Bercilak—are the same person. He rules through the power of Morgan le Fey, the old woman Gawain noticed with the lady of the castle, who desires revenge against Guinevere for Christianizing Arthur's court. The Green Knight commends Gawain for loving his life and for making a "clean confession" (l. 2391) and sends him away with the girdle. Gawain humbly accepts it—and his faults—and ties the garter to the outside of his armor as a sign of his humility. He rides away, returning to Arthur's court to share all he has learned about faith and courtesy. The court, however, ignores his words—but adopts the girdle as a fashion statement.

There are a number of interesting elements at work in *Sir Gawain*. It is a romance with numerous antiromance aspects. For instance, it praises court life and courtly manners while simultaneously satirizing them. Early scholars also examined the text for its "Englishness." Many of the tales in the Gawain Cycle were French; critics sought to establish a particularly British spirit in this poem. These scholars cited the emphasis on native traditions—Celtic religions, Brutus founding London, and so forth—and native poetic devices—ALLITERATION in particular—to justify this position. As well, traditional scholarship examined the work in the context of being a "handbook" of chivalry.

Some see *Sir Gawain* as a conflict between courtesy and purity. Other scholars have examined the role of penance and confession in *Sir Gawain*. For instance, Gawain skips necessary steps (no remorse, insufficient disclosure) and makes a false confession—until he confesses to the Green Knight, a non-Christian. A similar stance examines the shame/guilt dichotomy, contextualized within early English society.

Feminist and gender critics have examined the relative power structures present in *Sir Gawain,* in particular what it means that Bercilak rules through Morgan's power, the aggressiveness of the lady toward Gawain, and the influence of the Virgin Mary. Queer theorists, on the other hand, have focused on the exchanges between Gawain and Bercilak and the potential desires underlying the game. The men both agree to exchange their "winnings"—in each case, kisses and animals. However, what if Gawain had given in to temptation and slept with the lady? Would he then have to sleep with Bercilak? A similar viewpoint suggests that lesbian desire underlies the poem, since all the events were caused by Morgan in order to strike at Guinevere.

See also ARTHURIAN LITERATURE.

FURTHER READING

Dinshaw, Carol. "A Kiss Is Just a Kiss: Heterosexuality and Its Consolations in Sir Gawain and the Green Knight." *Diacritics* 24, no. 2 (1994): 205–226.

Spearing, A. C. *The Gawain-Poet: A Critical Study.* New York: Cambridge University Press, 1970.

SIR LAUNFAL THOMAS CHESTRE (14th century)

THOMAS CHESTRE's poem *Sir Launfal* has been dated to the 14th century. About the author, nothing is known for certain beyond his name. Because of the poem's dialect, it seems likely he came from Chester, which is in northwest England. Although it is preserved in only one manuscript, there are a number of medieval versions of the story. Chestre's *Sir Launfal* is based primarily on *Landevale,* an earlier English version of MARIE DE FRANCE's "LANVAL"; it also draws heavily on a version of the Old French ROMANCE *Graelent,* primarily for the account of the queen's enmity toward the hero, the episode of the mayor's daughter, the depiction of the arrival of the gifts at Launfal's lodging, and the account of the disappearance of Gyfre and Blaunchard. Other episodes may have been made up by Chestre or may have other sources; there is, for example, an analogue to the Sir Valentyne episode in a story told by ANDREAS CAPELLANUS in *The Art of Courtly Love,* and this anecdote has been accepted as the third source of Chestre's poem.

The eponymous hero of *Sir Launfal* is an extremely generous knight who is made the king's steward. Ten years later, King ARTHUR marries Guinevere, whom Launfal and all the other knights dislike because she is reputed to behave wantonly. There is a sumptuous wedding, and then, in order to show off her courteousness, the queen gives out gold, silver, and jewels to all the knights except Sir Launfal. Launfal then asks Arthur's permission to leave and is offered costly gifts and two of Arthur's nephews as escort.

Launfal and his party journey as far as Karlyoun, to the mayor's house. When Launfal makes it known that he and the king are estranged, the mayor refuses him lodging. Launfal makes to ride off, but the mayor asks him to stay, offering to put him up in his orchard. After a year, Arthur's nephews leave Launfal, complaining that all his wealth is gone. He asks them not to tell anyone about his poverty, and they agree. At Trinity, a feast is held, but Launfal is not invited on account of his poverty. The mayor's daughter goes to Launfal and invites him to dine with her that day. He refuses, citing his poverty, and rides off to seek solace in the country side. Launfal becomes the object of derision when his horse slips in mud.

Launfal dismounts in a forest, and as he rests under a tree, he sees two expensively dressed maidens carrying vessels of gold and silk. They come toward him, and he greets them courteously. They tell him that their mistress, Tryamour, has sent them to speak to him in secret. They lead him further into the forest, where he sees an amazingly wrought pavilion. Inside is Tryamour, daughter of the king of faeries, lying on a bed canopied with purple linen. She is astonishingly beautiful, charmingly disrobed because of the heat, and announces that she loves him. After Launfal kisses her, she tells him that if he will be her lover, she will make him rich. She offers him a purse, which will always contain a gold mark wherever he is. She also offers him her horse, servant, and coat of arms. She wines and dines Launfal, and then they go to bed together. In the morning, she tells him that if ever he wishes to speak to her, he should go somewhere private, and she will come to him secretly. She warns him not to brag about her, however. If he does, she will be lost to him.

The servant, Gyfre, brings Launfal his horse, and he journeys to Karlyoun in his poor clothes. Later, 10 men ride through the city, their horses loaded with gold, silver, rich clothes, and bright armour, and, to the chagrin of the mayor, they ask for Launfal. With his new wealth, Launfal holds feasts for the poor and distressed and buys horses, clothing, and gifts for priests, prisoners, and minstrels. A tournament is arranged in his honor, which Launfal wins. Every night Tryamour comes to him in secret.

A giant knight named Valentyne issues a challenge to Launfal. As the two knights fight, Launfal's helmet is knocked off. Valentyne laughs and Launfal is shamed. At this point, an invisible Gyfre leaps onto Launfal's horse and helps Launfal defeat Valentyne. Launfal then kills all the knights of Atalye who had sworn vengeance.

Arthur hears about Launfal's prowess and summons him to a feast at which he will be the steward. Following the feast there is dancing, and Launfal catches the queen's eye. She tells Launfal that she has loved him for more than seven years, and that if he does not return her feelings, she will die. Launfal responds that he will not betray the king. Guinevere then implies that Launfal is not interested in women. At this, Launfal can no longer keep quiet. He says that for more than seven years, he has loved a woman more beautiful than Guinevere has ever seen; this lady's ugliest maid would make a better queen than Guinevere. The queen is furious and plots vengeance.

When Arthur returns from hunting, Guinevere tells him that Launfal shamefully propositioned her and insulted her beauty, and she begs Arthur to avenge her honor. Arthur swears to kill Launfal and summons his knights. Meanwhile, Launfal has gone to his room and found that, true to her word, his lover has vanished. There is now no money in his purse, Gyfre has left, and his white armour has turned black. Launfal faints through grief and chagrin at having broken his promise. Arthur's knights catch up with him and he is bound and brought to the court.

Twelve knights are sworn in to act as jurors at the trial, but everyone knows the queen's reputation for infidelity, so Launfal is acquitted of the first charge. The court says that if Launfal can produce his lover, he will be judged innocent of the second charge, but if he cannot, all agree that he should be hanged. Launfal must give himself as a pledge, and the queen says her eyes may be put out if Launfal produces someone more beautiful than she. Sir Percevall and Sir Gawain stand surety for the period of a year and two weeks.

On the appointed day, Arthur orders Launfal to produce his lover. Launfal says that he cannot, so he is condemned to death. The earl of Cornwall speaks out against the sentence and suggests that it be commuted to banishment. As he is speaking, the barons see 10 beautiful maidens riding toward them, and the ugliest could certainly be a queen. Gawain tells Launfal that he does not need to be afraid because his beloved is coming, but Launfal replies that none of the maidens is she. The women ride to the castle and ask Arthur to prepare a beautiful room for their lady, who is on her way. Arthur agrees and then orders the barons to pronounce judgment. Having seen the maidens, some want to acquit Launfal, while others are convinced of his guilt.

Everyone wants to see these beautiful women, but Launfal observes wretchedly that he does not know them. They go to the palace and again ask Arthur to prepare a room. The queen suspects that Launfal will be acquitted by Tryamour's appearance and tells Arthur that if he cares for her honor, she will be avenged. As the queen is speaking, the barons see a beautiful grey-eyed woman with hair like gold approaching on a white palfrey. As soon as Launfal sees her, he cries out that this is his beloved. Tryamour goes into the hall, her maidens help her to dismount, and she removes her mantel so that everyone can see her better. Tryamour tells Arthur that she has come to liberate Launfal because he never propositioned the queen. She warns Arthur to look to his reputation, saying that it was Guinevere who begged Launfal to be her lover. Tryamour then blows at Guinevere, blinding her, and

leaps onto her palfrey. Gyfre appears with Launfal's horse, onto which Launfal springs, and he rides away into the land of faery with his lover, never to be seen again.

Sir Launfal is a RIME COUÉE romance and shares the form with more than 20 other 14th-century romances. Along with these, *Sir Launfal* has been seen by scholars as a popular, rather than an aristocratic poem, which contains a streak of unmistakeable bloodthirstiness. This is especially noticeable in the episode involving the killing of all the lords of Atalye. Several motifs, such as the spendthrift knight, the fairy lover, combat with a giant, the magical dwarf-servant, magical gifts, a secret oath that is broken, and the cyclic return of the knight's spirit to this world each year, suggest a connection to folklore. Chestre's poem also fits into the ARTHURIAN LITERATURE tradition, most notably in its unquestioning acceptance of the king's authority, although, as in some other Middle English romances, Arthur is depicted as somewhat inept and easily manipulated, and the queen as promiscuous with his knights. The blinding of Guinevere in fulfilment of her own careless words has no parallel in other Arthurian materials, however, and seems rather to connect with the folklore traditions present in the poem. The poem has most commonly been read as an entirely secular fantasy of wish fulfillment.

See also MIDDLE ENGLISH POETRY.

FURTHER READING

Ramsey, L. C. *Chivalric Romances: Popular Literature in Medieval England.* Bloomington: Indiana University Press, 1983.

Spearing, A. C. "The Lanval Story." In *The Medieval Poet as Voyeur: Looking and Listening in Medieval Love-Narratives,* 97–119. Cambridge: Cambridge University Press, 1993.

Louise Sylvester

SIR ORFEO ANONYMOUS (ca. late 13th–early 14th century) *Sir Orfeo,* a Breton LAY written in Middle English during the late 13th or early 14th century, imaginatively retells the familiar Greek myth of Orpheus and Eurydice as medieval ROMANCE. In the poem's first 24 lines, the narrator establishes both its genre and its specific origins in the narrative traditions of the Bretons, as the delivery of this tale is framed with a suggestive reference to the *lai*'s original oral performance, accompanied by harp music.

Orpheus of classical antiquity morphs into the consummate harp-playing medieval king, Sir Orfeo, whose skill is so great that his music has paradisiacal qualities. Through this initial focus on the restorative powers of this medieval minstrel king's harp playing (ll. 25–38), the poem foregrounds its dynamic narrative shift from a focus on tragic loss to human restoration and redemption through the power of art. Whereas the Orpheus and Eurydice narrative of the CLASSICAL TRADITION ends with the irrevocable loss of Eurydice and ultimately the complete destruction of Orpheus, this medieval romance restructures King Orfeo's loss of his queen, Heurodis, as temporary—an event that initiates a move into exile, a quest to the Otherworld, and ultimately the recovery of both his queen and the kingdom he abandons.

Heurodis's abduction takes place almost immediately, in a typical romance setting—the cultivated medieval orchard that regularly serves not only as a topography that expresses culture, community, and aesthetic self-consciousness, but also, with its garden-like qualities, as a potential locus for a fall from grace. During a May morning stroll with two of her ladies, Heurodis falls asleep on the green under "a fair ympe-tree" (a grafted fruit or ornamental tree, l. 70). She wakes up screaming, rubbing her face and hands and scratching her "visage" until it bleeds (l. 80). With the help of knights from the castle who have heard that their queen may be going mad, Heurodis's ladies return her to the castle and bring her to her bed. A troubled King Orfeo joins Heurodis at her bedside to find out what has been disturbing her. Heurodis narrates her dream from the orchard—a nightmarish visitation from a dark lord who took her forcibly from the castle garden, showed her his parallel realms, and insisted, in complete disregard of her objections to this *raptus* (abduction), that he will return on the following day and that Heurodis should be ready to accompany him. Orfeo and 1,000 of his best knights prepare a valiant defense for the next day but fail to prevent the dark lord from snatching Heurodis from their midst and taking her to the Otherworld (ll. 192–193).

In response to his overwhelming grief, Orfeo gathers his lords and explains that he will leave the kingdom to live out his sorrow in isolation as a hermit in the forest. He appoints his steward to rule in his place and indicates that his subjects should convene "a parlement" to select a new king once he is dead (ll. 215–218). He puts on a pilgrim's mantle and leaves his hall to the general mourning and weeping of all.

While living out his despair in the forest, Orfeo still manages to charm its beasts with his harp playing. At one point, he recognizes Dame Heurodis as part of the hunting party of "the king of fairy and his rout" (l. 284) and follows her as she disappears with the fairy retinue "in at a roche" (l. 347). He discovers a dramatic realm, beyond that of the living, occupied by fantastic folk. The glimmering quality of this kingdom recalls a Christian paradise even as its torsos with severed heads and strangled, drowned, and burned occupants summon up a Dantean Christian hell. Contiguous fields of plenty and locales for suffering recall classical Hades. Royally arrayed battlements, burnished castle architecture, and occupants who seem fixed in circumstances identical to those at the moment of their abduction into "fairi" finally recall the Celtic Otherworld of medieval romance. It is here that Orfeo, disguised as a poor minstrel, discovers Heurodis, plays his harp for the Otherworld's king, and impresses him with his art so thoroughly that he wins the boon of returning to the realm of the living with Heurodis literally in hand.

There is no tragic separation of the lovers at the edge of Hades; rather, with their departure from the Otherworld, the *Orfeo*-poet initiates a sequence of events that builds to Orfeo's return to his kingdom. In his poor minstrel disguise, he continues to test the honesty of the steward he has left in charge. He discovers from his faithful steward that "everich gode harpour" ["every good harper"] is welcome in his abandoned kingdom "for mi lordes love, Sir Orfeo" (ll. 517–518). It is, in fact, Orfeo's magnificent harp playing combined with the moving speculative narrative he tells of King Orfeo's death (ll. 538–539) and his quick offer of an alternative Orfeo-resurrection narrative that ultimately allows the steward and his entire court not only to recognize Orfeo but to restore him to his throne.

The narrator opens *Sir Orfeo* with an extended discussion of the tale's genre, describing the poem as a Breton *lai*—one of a series of "aventours" that explore marvelous subject matter ("ferli thing," 1.4). The narrator's relatively detailed description provides a medieval perspective on the Breton *lai*. They cover a rich emotional range of subjects: narratives of war and sorrow, joy and mirth, treachery and guile (ll. 5–7) as well as ribald narratives (l. 9). These tales of "aventours that fel bidayes" (adventures that happened in olden times, ll. 8, 15) draw on an archaic or fictive cultural past that often includes an encounter or exchange with a "fairy" (l. 10) or the Otherworld. A lyrically compressed form of romance, the Breton *lai* foregrounds love as its subject matter. The narrator's closing emphasis in these introductory lines on oral performance as an essential characteristic of the Breton *lai* proves especially intriguing given the function of Orfeo's harp within this poem as the central symbol of resurrection and restoration of community. The harp serves literally as the vehicle for Orfeo's restoration of Heurodis from the Celtic Otherworld to the world of the living and Orfeo's subsequent restoration, healed through the power of his own art, to his rightful position as minstrel king.

The text of *Sir Orfeo* has been preserved in three manuscripts, which range in date from the 14th to 15th centuries. Some evidence indicates that GEOFFREY CHAUCER may have had access to one of these before writing his own Breton *lai,* "The FRANKLIN'S TALE."

While there are no known extant sources for *Sir Orfeo,* some critics argue that the narrator of the poem hints at an Old French/Breton Ur-text (source text that no longer exists) for the lai in his opening discussion of genre (ll. 13–20). Several Old French texts include references to a musical *lai* of Orpheus. Late 13th and early 14th-century educated readers and listening audiences for *Sir Orfeo* would have been familiar with the Orpheus legend from a variety of classical and medieval sources. The most readily available classical sources include OVID's *Metamorphoses,* book 10, and VIRGIL's *Georgics,* book 4, as well as related commentaries on these volumes. Familiar medieval venues for material on Orpheus include BOETHIUS's *The CONSOLATION OF PHILOSOPHY,* the *Ovide Moralisé* (late 13th–early 14th century), and Pierre Bersuire's *Reductorium Morale* (ca. 1325–37).

Established critical tradition for this poem draws its energy from the competing influences that shape the trifold face of the Otherworld: classical, Christian, and Celtic. The crosscultural comparative dynamic of criticism for this poem has always been especially rich, particularly as a nuanced response to Christian allegorizations of Orpheus as Christ. Explorations of the poem's Celtic substrata have provided the foundation for exploring intercultural influences between Celtic folklore and its Christian sociopolitical counterparts. Recent work on Christian music—especially the significance of the *lai*'s central symbol, Orfeo's harp—has introduced intriguing discussions of this poem's manipulation of cultural boundaries between textuality and orality and its claim for the restorative power of narrative artistry in a chaotic world. Such readings have opened up a vein of criticism that, beneath the master narrative of the restoration of love and concomitant restoration of the bonds of human society, looks at the poem's reflection of troubling uncertainties and cultural fragmentation, its juxtaposition of the chaotic and harmonic qualities of the Otherworld at best uneasily reconciled.

See also ALLEGORY, MIDDLE ENGLISH LANGUAGE.

FURTHER READING
Bliss, A. J., ed. *Sir Orfeo.* 2nd ed. Oxford: Clarendon Press, 1966.

Cartlidge, Neil. "Sir Orfeo in the Otherworld: Courting Chaos?" *Studies in the Age of Chaucer* 26 (2004): 195–226.

Friedman, John Block. *Orpheus in the Middle Ages.* Cambridge, Mass.: Harvard University Press, 1970.

Lerer, Seth. "Artifice and Artistry in *Sir Orfeo.*" *Speculum* 60, no. 1 (1985): 92–109.

Regula Meyer Evitt

"SIR WALTER RALEIGH TO HIS SON" ("THREE THINGS THERE BE") SIR WALTER RALEIGH (ca. 1600)

Although there is no certainty that SIR WALTER RALEIGH wrote this poem, it does complement his prose "Instructions to his Son." The first QUATRAIN of this clever ENGLISH SONNET poses the riddle: What three things that flourish when they are apart, hurt each other when they meet? The answer, provided in line 5, is the wood, the weed, and the wag. The second quatrain goes on to elaborate this connection. Wood is used to make the gallows. The weed, or hemp, is used to make the noose. The wag, Raleigh states, is his son "my pretty knave" (l.8). The third quatrain warns the boy to make sure that the three never meet, because a meeting would result in the timber rotting, the rope fraying, and the child choking. The ending COUPLET repeats this warning and offers the hope that such a dire meeting will never occur.

There are two main interpretations of this poem. Some critics believe that Raleigh is being seriously threatening, while others believe that the tone of the poem points to a much less serious interpretation. The riddling format combined with the heavy use of ALLITERATION and terms of endearment for young Walter (Wat) Raleigh certainly indicate that even though Raleigh senior knew firsthand about the dangers of being on the wrong side of the law or government, he chose to couch his serious warning in this clever SONNET.

FURTHER READING

May, Stephen R. *Sir Walter Raleigh.* Twayne's English Authors Series. Boston: Twayne, 1989.

Leah Larson

SKELTON, JOHN (ca. 1460–1529)

It may surprise some readers to learn that John Skelton, whose poems sometimes seem irreverent if not downright bawdy, was a serious courtier and a priest. Skelton attended Cambridge University, and shortly before entering service at court, Oxford University gave him the title *poet laureate;* the University of Louvain and Cambridge followed suit a few years later. Although the title did not carry the weight it now does, Skelton was praised early in life by the likes of WILLIAM CAXTON and Desiderius Erasmus. He took holy orders in 1498 and was promptly appointed tutor and chaplain to Prince Henry, son of King Henry VII. A year later *The Bowge of Courte* (1498) became Skelton's first published poem.

Despite his renown as a scholar, Skelton's position at court was disrupted by the death of Prince Arthur, the heir apparent. Skelton's pupil, Prince Henry, became heir apparent, and positions in the service of the young Henry were highly sought after by those hoping to maintain their influence in affairs of state.

Skelton was dismissed from tutoring the prince and appointed rector of Diss in Norfolk, a prosperous town far from court.

When Henry VII died, Skelton immediately began offering verses to his former pupil, King HENRY VIII. By 1512, he had attracted the new king's attention, returned to court, and was given the title *orator regius* (the king's orator). Biographers tend to view this return as somewhat ironic since Skelton's poem *Why Come Ye Nat to Courte* (1522) criticizes those who abandon their clerical duties, as Skelton had apparently done, in favor of a court appointment.

Despite the new title, Skelton's function in court and his relation to the king is not at all clear. Several of Skelton's most famous satirical poems—*Collyn Clout* (1519); *Speke, Parrot* (1521); and *Why Come Ye Nat to Courte* (1522)—attack Cardinal Wolsey when the influential Wolsey was closest to the king. In a surprising reversal, Skelton later dedicated GARLAND OF LAUREL (1523) and *Howe the Douty Duke of Albany* (1523) to Wolsey. What conditions led to this complete change of attitude have provided scholars with an apparently endless debate about Skelton's politics, poetic aspirations, and PATRONAGE.

In addition to satirical poems, Skelton wrote several plays, only one of which survives, *Magnificence* (1515). Framed as a morality play, *Magnificence* provides a political ALLEGORY about the monarch's choice of advisors.

However, Skelton is remembered primarily as a poet. Occasionally described as antiquated or merely transitional, he should be read as an early modern poet. What has come to be known as SKELTONICS, poems heavily rhymed but with no set rhyme scheme and lines containing beats that range from two to five, is not an indication of Skelton's inability to write in regularized meter. Skeltonics show that the poet was an experimentalist, consciously breaking with set rhyme schemes, playing with colloquial speech, and working with various metrical patterns derived from ballads and sacred chants. Through his poetic experiments, Skelton pushed the limits of conventional poetry and created a lively form for his social and political commentary.

See also KNOLOGE, AQUAYNTANCE, RESORT, FAUOUR WITH GRACE; "PHILIP SPARROW"; SATIRE; "TUNNING OF ELINOUR RUMMING, THE"; WOMANHOOD, WANTON."

FURTHER READING

Edwards, Anthony S. G., ed. *Skelton, the Critical Heritage*. London and Boston: Routledge/Kegan Paul Press, 1981.

Kinney, Arthur. *John Skelton, Priest as Poet*. Chapel Hill, N.C. and London: University of North Carolina Press, 1987.

Walker, Greg. *John Skelton and the Politics of the 1520's*. Cambridge and New York: Cambridge University Press, 1988.

SKELTONICS As the term suggests, Skeltonics is a verse form associated with the court poet and satirist JOHN SKELTON (ca. 1460–1529). Consisting of two accented syllables and an irregular number of unaccented syllables, the short lines proceed rapidly, almost breathlessly. This hurried effect is compounded by the frequent presence of ALLITERATION and rhyming COUPLETs and triplets; sometimes as many as a dozen consecutive lines end on the same rhyme. When used to interrupt other metrical forms, Skeltonic passages often feature catalogues similar to a BLAZON, emphasizing the comic, even grotesque, features of the verse's subjects. Though rejected by GEORGE PUTTENHAM in his ART OF ENGLISH POESY as "short measures pleasing onely the popular eare," the simple meter was praised by Auden as wonderfully akin to the rhythm of natural speech.

See also GARLAND OF LAUREL; "PHILIP SPARROW."

Candace Barrington

"SO CRUEL PRISON" ("WINDSOR ELEGY," "ELEGY ON THE DUKE OF RICHMOND," "PRISONED IN WINDSOR, HE RECOUNTETH HIS PLEASURE THERE") HENRY HOWARD, EARL OF SURREY (1537)

This poem by HENRY HOWARD, EARL OF SURREY concerns his imprisonment at Windsor Castle in 1537, probably for striking Sir Edward Seymour, the new queen's brother. Surrey, a member of the powerful Howard family, had spent his youth at Windsor Castle in the company of HENRY VIII's illegitimate son, Henry Fitzroy, duke of Richmond. With the king's marriage to Jane Seymour, the Howard family's influence had waned while the Seymour family's influence had grown. Additionally, Surrey's friend Richmond had died the year before. Surrey thus expressed his double bereavement, personal and political, through this poem.

Although not a SONNET, the form of this poem grows out of the sonnet model. It has 14 STANZAS, echoing the sonnet's 14 lines. Like an ENGLISH SONNET, all the stanzas are QUATRAINS, except for the closing COUPLET. Surrey would place his sonnets' VOLTA in line 9, and in "So Cruel Prison" the volta is in the ninth stanza. This expanded sonnet form indicates that this poem may be connected to "WHEN WINDSOR WALLS," a sonnet also concerning his 1537 imprisonment.

"So Cruel Prison" may be read simultaneously as an ELEGY, a statement on the political climate, and, to some scholars, a love poem. The poem begins with a personal cry lamenting Surrey's situation. He recalls his youth at Windsor as passed "In greater feast than Priam's sons of Troy" (l. 4). In the next seven quatrains, Surrey focuses on the activities he and Richmond participated in during their youth—hunting, wrestling, jousting, playing games, riding, courting—and describes the places connected with each activity. All these activities emphasize the stark contrast between Surrey's experience as the friend of the king's son and that of prisoner. His depiction of his earlier experience highlights the courtliness of the youthful activities and perhaps indicates that such a noble era has passed, along with Richmond and the influence of the venerable Howard family, and been replaced by the upstart Seymour family. Thus, this poem of personal loss is also a reflection of the changes in English society.

"So Cruel Prison" does not include the elegiac concern that the audience should not only lament the dead subject of the poem, but also emulate his or her virtue. Surrey's aim is solely to lament Richmond's death and the loss of the way of life he represented. In this, the poem is in line with the PASTORAL elegy, which proposes no solutions but instead proposes a concrete setting for posing questions and diffusing grief. This connection between the setting of Windsor and the loss of Richmond emphasizes that to Surrey the two are inseparable.

Recently, "So Cruel Prison" has been interpreted as a love poem. The catalogue of pursuits recounted in the first eight stanzas also provides insight into the nature of Surrey and Richmond's relationship. All of these physical contests serve as an acceptable way for two young males to demonstrate their love for each other.

Starting with the volta in stanza 9, the poem takes a more personal turn from describing diurnal chivalric activities in a stylized way to expressing personal grief. Mentioning the nights the two spent together in "sweet accord" (l. 35), Surrey goes on to describe "The secret thoughts imparted with such trust, / The wanton talk, the divers change of play, / The friendship sworn, each promise sworn . . ." (ll. 37–39). The closeness of the personal relationship is emphasized, as well as the inviolable world that has passed with Richmond's death.

Stanza 12 marks a shift in the poem's language and is Surrey's APOSTROPHE to Windsor Castle. The abrupt change in diction results in an unsatisfactory ending to an elegy but can also reinforce the love poem reading. The final stanzas echo the lament of GEOFFREY CHAUCER's Troilus for the lost Criseyde with its connection between place and person. This echo both connects the end of the poem to the allusion to Troy in line 4 and indicates the depth of the relationship between Surrey and Richmond.

At the end Surrey fully recognizes the horrible reality of his condition. The final couplet offers comfort that is no comfort at all: His pain at the loss of his dear friend and possible lover and the loss of a way of life will offer relief from the much lesser grief of his incarceration.

FURTHER READING

Guy-Bray, Stephen. "'We Two Boys Together Clinging': The Earl of Surrey and the Duke of Richmond." English Studies in Canada 21, no. 2 (1995): 138–150.

Sessions, William A. Henry Howard, Earl of Surrey. Twayne's English Authors Series. Boston: Twayne, 1986.

Leah Larson

"SOMETIME I FLED THE FIRE" SIR THOMAS WYATT (ca. 1532–1533)

In this EPIGRAM, the speaker celebrates his freedom from a lady he once loved. While he claims that he now "follow[s] the coals that be quent" (l. 3) and that "desire is both sprung and spent" (l. 5), SIR THOMAS WYATT's characteristic bitterness does not entirely let the former object of his affections off the hook. The ambiguous final COUPLET, "And all his labor now he laugh to scorn, / Meshed in the briars that erst was all to-torn," (ll. 7–8) can be read two ways. The speaker may either be declaring his release from the "briars" that once injured him, or he may be ironically observing that he is still caught in her snares, although this time without even the cold comfort of unrequited love, as his feelings for her have died.

Critics may disagree about the exact nature of the relationship depicted in the poem, but they largely agree that the lady in question is Anne Boleyn. As a diplomat, Wyatt was probably in HENRY VIII's or Anne's retinue when the couple met with Francis I of France at Calais in 1532. The speaker's insistence that he has followed the ashes of his former fire "from Dover to Calais, against my mind" makes this reading attractive (l. 4). Neither historians nor literary critics have ever been able to prove a romantic relationship between Wyatt and Anne, but circumstantial evidence suggests that it may have at least been possible. Their background as childhood neighbors, their proximity at Henry's court, and Wyatt's imprisonment with Anne's alleged lovers all provide an intriguing backdrop for poems such as "WHOSO LIST TO HUNT" and "Sometime I Fled the Fire." Certainly Wyatt's poetic skill would have assured him a place in the ranks of esteemed Tudor poets without Anne Boleyn. However, the biographical narrative of lost love and courtly ambition will most likely always be a favorite with readers and critics, and it may even generate an interest in poems such as "Sometime I Fled the Fire" that they might not otherwise have received.

FURTHER READING

Southall, Raymond. The Courtly Maker: An Essay on the Poems of Wyatt and His Contemporaries. New York: Barnes & Noble, 1964.

Carol D. Blosser

SONNET

From Italian Sonetto for "little song," a sonnet is a 14-line poem, usually in IAMBIC PENTAMETER, that follows various rhyme schemes. The sonnet was developed in 12th or 13th-century Italy, but reached its zenith in the 14th century in the works of PETRARCH. Conventional sonnets deal with the subject of idealized, unrequited love. As well, typical sonnet devices include antithesis, CONCEITS, and the BLAZON. Many sonnets also employ the use of a persona—an assumed identity not necessarily shared by the poet—in order to present renditions of idealized COURTLY LOVE. Sonnets may be linked together in order to form a complete narrative in what has become known as a SONNET SEQUENCE.

There are three basic forms of sonnets: the traditional form, called the ITALIAN (PETRARCHAN) SONNET; the ENGLISH SONNET, sometimes referred to as the Elizabethan or Shakespearean sonnet; and the rare SPENSERIAN SONNET (named for EDMUND SPENSER). In England, sonnets became popular in the 16th century, reaching a peak in the 1590s, although the form remained popular well into the 17th century. SIR THOMAS WYATT and HENRY HOWARD, EARL OF SURREY, are credited with introducing the sonnet to English literature.

See also QUATORZAIN, STRAMBOTTO.

FURTHER READING

Oppenheimer, Paul. "The Origin of the Sonnet." *Comparative Literature* 34, no. 4 (1982): 289–304.

Wilkins, Ernest Hatch. "The Invention of the Sonnet." *Modern Philology* 13 (1915): 463–494.

"SONNET ON TICHO BRAHE, A" JAMES VI/I (ca. 1590)

In October 1589, Scotland's James VI (King James I of England) sailed for Norway to marry Anne of Denmark. During the couple's stay in Denmark, James visited astronomer Tycho Brahe on March 20, 1590. On the island of Hven, between Denmark and Sweden, Tycho had built an observatory named Uraniborg, after Urania, the astronomers' muse. Tycho Brahe's work, undertaken before the discovery of the telescope, is of great significance for Renaissance astronomy, influencing Johannes Kepler and, through him, Isaac Newton.

After the visit, James composed "A Sonnet on Ticho Brahe" as well as two more poems, each entitled "Another on the same." The second is also a SONNET, while the third is a hexastich (poem consisting of six verses or lines). Editors today sometimes print the poems as separate entries but more often treat them as a series.

"A Sonnet on Ticho Brahe" traces the creation of the universe: God, "he [who] in ordour everie thing hade brought" (l. 3), fashions the earth, humanity, and the beasts. The planets were traditionally believed to govern life on earth, "as heavenlie impes to governe bodies basse" (l. 11). The sonnet is elegantly concluded in the closing COUPLET: "The great is Ticho who by this his booke / Commandement doth ouer these commanders brooke" (ll. 13–14). "Commandement," or understanding of the workings of the planets (and by extension of the works of God) is Brahe's great accomplishment.

The notion of the heavenly spheres in the first sonnet, "eache Planet in his place" (l. 9), is continued in the second, where "euerie planet hath his owen repaire" (l. 19). The poem stresses the beauty of divine order and praises "Tichoes tooles" (l. 25), his instruments, and possibly the planetary model at Uraniborg, reflecting all heaven's "ordour" (l. 24) in miniature. The syntax of the final hexastich (six-line poem) is complex and ambiguous. It appears to argue that Brahe, in guiding or tracking the course of the sun, is wiser than the mythic character Phaeton, who died attempting the same, or even the sun god Apollo, Urania's "eldest fostre dear" (l. 34). The lines juxtapose modern scientific understanding with non-Christian notions of the workings of the universe, favoring Brahe's insights.

It should be noted that James's depiction of the heavens is rather old-fashioned, following the Ptolemaic system rather than the Copernican model that Brahe followed and revised. Although James's poems are flattering, scientific discovery had not yet replaced poetic commonplaces: The king's work does not reflect Brahe's astronomical discoveries. Nonetheless, they are a fine tribute to a significant scientist.

See also JAMES VI/I.

FURTHER READING

Westcott, Allan F., ed. *New Poems by James I of England.* New York: Columbia University Press, 1911.

Craigie, James, ed. *The Poems of James VI of Scotland.* 2 vols. Edinburgh: Scottish Text Society, 1955, 1958.

Sebastiaan Verweij

SONNET SEQUENCE

The term *sonnet sequence* refers to a collection of related SONNETs. A sonnet is a poem that consists of 14 lines and can take different forms: the ITALIAN (PETRARCHAN) SONNET, The ENGLISH

SONNET (also known as the Shakespearean or Elizabethan sonnet) or the SPENSERIAN SONNET. The term *Italian,* or *Petrarchan, sonnet* is derived from the 14th-century poet PETRARCH, who refined the sonnet and the sonnet sequence in Italy. SIR THOMAS WYATT and HENRY HOWARD, EARL OF SURREY, brought the sonnet into England, and Wyatt translated many of Petrarch's poems. While the first English sonnet sequence was by ANNE VAUGHAN LOCK (reflections of Psalm 51 in 1560), SIR PHILIP SIDNEY's *ASTROPHIL AND STELLA* (published in 1591 and again in 1598) represents the first Petrarchan sonnet sequence in England. *Astrophil and Stella* offers typical Petrarchan CONCEITS: the poet's unrequited love, the unrelenting lady, images of Cupid, descriptions of the beloved's beauty (the BLAZON), and the poet's failure to win the lady's love.

Atypical sequences also appeared in the 16th century. WILLIAM SHAKESPEARE's sonnets (published in 1609) take some of these Petrarchan motifs and make drastic changes to the typical scenario. He addresses Sonnets 1–126 to a young man, known as the LOVELY BOY, and Sonnets 127–154 talk about the woman commonly known as the DARK LADY. SHAKESPEARE'S SONNETS tend to be reflective or nostalgic rather than longing. Shakespeare also utilizes a different sonnet structure than his predecessors, the English sonnet (also called the Shakespearean sonnet because of his influence on this form). EDMUND SPENSER's sonnet sequence *AMORETTI* (1595), dedicated to his bride, Elizabeth Boyle, differs from Sidney's and Shakespeare's sequences in both form and content. *Amoretti* does have the typical Petrarchan motif of the lover trying to win the lady's hand, but in this sequence he actually succeeds. A collection of poems called *EPITHALAMION* accompanied *Amoretti* in publication and enforce the difference between typical Petrarchan sequences and Spenser's (*epithalamion* means wedding song).

The sonnet sequence is a very significant poetic feature for several reasons. First, as some scholars and critics argue, poets used their sonnets for political or monetary reasons. For example, there is the argument that Shakespeare's poems portray his relationship with his patron Henry Wriothesley, earl of Southampton, and during this time writers commonly sought the PATRONAGE of those who could support them financially.

Critics have also argued that Sidney's *Astrophil and Stella* expresses his political frustrations with Queen ELIZABETH I, and therefore she is Stella. They suggest that Sidney wanted to demonstrate her power over him politically, and he therefore used this language to flatter the queen in an attempt to advance his status at court.

In addition, an argument exists that sonnets reveal important biographical insights into authors' personal lives. The "Dark Lady" of Shakespeare's Sonnets 127–154 could be, as some have suggested, his mistress (poet Aemelia Lanyer has been suggested), while the rival poet in other Shakespeare sonnets could refer to Ben Jonson. Some argue that Stella in Sidney's *Astrophil and Stella* is Penelope Devereaux, the woman whom Sidney had once entertained marrying, and that his sonnets display his disappointment over losing her to Lord Rich in 1581. Edmund Spenser also seems to present biographical details in Sonnet 74 of *Amoretti*. He references his mother, the queen, and his wife Elizabeth in one of his sonnets, and some have said that both *Amoretti* and *Epithalamion* refer to his courtship and marriage.

The sonnet and the sonnet sequence had become tired by the early 17th century, but poets later continued the tradition with some alterations. Lady Mary Wroth wrote *Pamphilia to Amphilanthus* (1621) and imitated conventions that her uncle, Sir Philip Sidney, had used in *Astrophil and Stella.* However, she did alter a significant detail: The beloved becomes male and the pining lover female. John Donne wrote his *Holy Sonnets* before his death in 1633. Instead of a lover complaining about his unrelenting beloved, these sonnets discuss his relationship with God.

FURTHER READING

Dubrow, Heather. *Echoes of Desire: English Petrarchism and Its Counter-Discourses.* Ithaca, N.Y., and London: Cornell University Press, 1995.

Lever, J. W. *The Elizabethan Love Sonnet.* London: Methuen, 1966.

Kerri Lynn Allen

"SOOTE SEASON, THE" ("DESCRIPTION OF SPRING, WHEREIN EVERY THING RENEWS, SAVE ONLY THE LOVER") HENRY HOWARD, EARL OF SURREY **(1547)** This SONNET, along with HENRY HOWARD,

EARL OF SURREY's other lyric poetry, was published post-humously in 1547 in TOTTEL'S MISCELLANY, thus making it impossible to date accurately. The publisher took the liberty of giving it a title, "Description of Spring, Wherein Every Thing Renews, Save Only the Lover," but modern editions prefer the above.

The poem combines medieval English constructions found in ACCENTUAL VERSE with its original Petrarchan verse, while still rendering a thoroughly early modern desiring subject. Adapted from the 310th sonnet of PETRARCH's *Canzoniere,* the poem takes the setting of the original and replaces it with an English rather than Italian summertime scene. In its depiction of an English summer scene, the ideal LOCUS AMOENUS has more in common with medieval lyric poetry such as "SUMER IS ICUMEN IN" and GEOFFREY CHAUCER's GENERAL PROLOGUE TO THE CANTERBURY TALES than the Italian summer of Petrarch's creation. The simplicity of the rhyme scheme is appropriated from medieval sources and forced into the 14-line sonnet format—*abab, abab, abab, aa.*

The poem is formally a list-sonnet, with each line of the first 12 representing some new part of the list to be described. It relies heavily on ALLITERATION in its description of spring: "bud and bloom forth brings" (l. 1), "The hart hath hung his old head" (l. 6), "adder all her slough away she slings" (l. 9). The heavy accentual rhythm of lines like "The buck in brake his winter coat he slings," (l. 7) is reminiscent of the driving rhythms of MIDDLE ENGLISH LYRICS AND BALLADS. Also, the use of word forms that were already becoming outdated such as *soote, eke,* and the adjective *smale,* conjures a sense of nostalgia. Even the use of the often overlooked pun in "mings" is reliant on an older, almost forgotten meaning which was "to remember" as well as "to mix." It is ironic that Surrey employs these archaic poetic devices to describe the spring wherein all that is old is renewed.

The oscillation between present and past tense of the verbs in the sonnet ("brings," "clad," "sings," "told," etc.) is indicative of the subject's inability to deal with the absence of his object of desire, as expressed in the COUPLET. The isolated subject is able to observe the change and growth that spring suggests but is unable to join in it himself. As time moves forward, so his

"sorrow springs" (l. 14), which marks the end of the alternating pattern as well as a verb and a pun that sums up the sonnet's enterprise. The final couplet, whose verbs are in the present tense, locates the subject desires in the past, for the renewal of all things means the loss of all things of old. Surrey's deliberate use of archaic vocabulary intensifies these changes and emphasizes the sense of loss while refocusing the emotion inward.

Andrew Bretz

SOUTHWELL, ROBERT (ca. 1561–1595)

Hailing from a gentry family, Robert Southwell was born in Norfolk, one of the places where Catholicism prevailed even under ELIZABETH I. The exact date of his birth is unknown, but he claimed that he was 33 when he stood trial in February 1595. In 1576, Southwell was sent to school in Douai, France, a refuge for exiled English Catholics. From here he went to the Jesuit college of Clermont in Paris. In 1577 he applied to enter the Jesuit order, and in 1578 he went to Rome, where he remained for several years.

In 1585, an Act of Parliament barred those English citizens who had been abroad since Elizabeth's accession to the throne from returning to England, and Catholicism was formally outlawed in England. It was illegal to attend mass or go to confession, to be a priest or to assist a priest. As all of these actions constituted treason, they were punishable by death. Nevertheless, in 1586 Southwell embarked on a secret mission to England with another Jesuit, Henry Garnet. The two priests remained at large for several years, acquiring a certain reputation for missionary zeal. Richard Topcliff, one of Queen Elizabeth's priest hunters, was particularly eager to capture Southwell, which he did on June 25, 1592. Southwell endured torture, deprivation, and imprisonment in the TOWER OF LONDON, but he never betrayed any of his fellow Catholics. He was finally executed on February 21, 1595. Southwell was beatified by Pope Pius XI in 1929.

Southwell's poetry tends toward the didactic and meditative. It dates from the period of July 1586, his return to England, until his arrest in 1592. His only long poem, *Saint Peter's Complaint,* is a monologue in which Saint Peter laments betraying Christ. Critics have noted that WILLIAM SHAKESPEARE's later poem *The RAPE OF LUCRECE* (1593–94) shows the influence of Southwell's earlier work. The poem represents the sum of Southwell's priestly and poetic insights, and it is geared to a variety of audiences: practicing Catholics, lapsed Catholics, and other poets.

Southwell's poetry deals with spiritual maturity and the intent of teaching the way to love God through suffering; it covers topics such as the nativity of Christ, the Virgin Mary, and Christ's ministry. "The Virgin Mary's Conception" is perhaps the best known of the Mary poems, while "The BURNING BABE" commands the most attention overall. It has force and simplicity and was much admired by contemporaries. Printing and possessing Southwell's work was illegal during the reign of Elizabeth I; nevertheless, his poetry surreptitiously enjoyed wide circulation.

FURTHER READING

Brownlow, F. W. *Robert Southwell*. New York: Twayne, 1996.

McDonald, James H., and Nancy Pollard Brown, eds. *The Poems of Robert Southwell, SJ.* Oxford: Clarendon, 1967.

Pilarz, Scott R. *Robert Southwell and the Mission of Literature, 1561–1595*. Aldershot, U.K.: Ashgate, 2004.

Mark DiCicco

SPANISH ARMADA (1588)

In 1588, a large fleet (armada) of 130 Spanish vessels sailed through the English Channel with the objective of occupying England. The duke of Parma's troops in the southern Netherlands were to embark on the fleet, and the Spanish troops would be set on English soil. The armada's objectives failed miserably: Before it even reached Parma's soldiers, the Spanish ships suffered heavy damage from the English navy, and many vessels were lost on their return voyage off the West Irish coast. The expedition was a human and financial disaster for the Spanish Crown, which became increasingly destitute by financing its wars in the Low Countries (today's Belgium, Luxembourg, and Netherlands). Moreover, the armada's demise was a sign of the Spanish navy's decreasing power, freeing up their English, French, and Dutch competitors to challenge Iberian authority over its overseas possessions in the Americas, Africa, and Asia.

Moreover, this victory proclaimed the Protestant deliverance over Catholic tyranny during the 16th century's religious wars, and set the stage for English imperialism.

The outcome of the religious and political warfare made its way into pamphlets, memorial medals, and literature. For instance, EDMUND SPENSER's *The FAERIE QUEENE* and THOMAS CAMPION's "Ad Thamesin" both directly reference the armada. WILLIAM SHAKESPEARE's Sonnet 107 (see SHAKESPEARE'S SONNETS) also boasts cryptic references to this event. Historians have taken the armada's defeat as the ultimate sign of "Spanish decline" and English "rise to glory." Though perhaps not quite so definitive as this, the English victory did encourage the budding nationalists, and later literature referenced it often.

FURTHER READING

Mattingly, Garrett. *The Defeat of the Spanish Armada*. Harmondsworth, U.K.: Penguin Books, 1962.

Whitehead, Bertrand T. *Brags and Boasts: Propaganda in the Year of the Armada*. Dover, N.H.: Alan Sutton Publishers, 1994.

Ernst Pijning

SPENSER, EDMUND (ca. 1552–1599)

Edmund Spenser was an important figure of the English Renaissance who succeeded in inventing his own verse form, style, and vocabulary. Spenser not only stimulated a whole contemporary PASTORAL tradition with the publication of his first major work, *The SHEPHEARDES CALENDER* (1579), but also, posthumously, exerted a powerful influence on a series of major canonical authors, most notably John Milton, William Blake, and T. S. Eliot.

Edmund Spenser was born around 1552 to a family of modest means and earned his education through academic prowess. In 1561, Spenser entered the Merchant Taylors' School as a "poor scholar." There he came under the tutelage of Richard Mulcaster, a noted humanist scholar and writer, who emphasized equally the CLASSICAL TRADITION and studies in the VERNACULAR. Spenser continued his education in 1569 by entering

Pembroke College, Cambridge University, as a sizar, a student who earns his tuition by acting as a servant to wealthy students. He earned his B.A. in 1573 and his M.A. in 1576.

While at Cambridge, and later in London, Spenser cultivated important acquaintances, such as Gabriel Harvey and Robert Dudley, earl of Leicester, and noted poet and courtier SIR PHILIP SIDNEY. Through these connections, Spenser entered the social circle at Queen ELIZABETH I's court, and secured a career in government, being appointed secretary to Arthur, Lord Grey de Wilton, in 1580. Spenser remained in Ireland for the rest of his life.

In Ireland, Spenser began his masterpiece, The FAERIE QUEENE. By 1589, he had finished the first three books of his projected 12-book EPIC. After reading these, SIR WALTER RALEIGH encouraged Spenser to return with him to England, where he arranged an audience with Queen Elizabeth. In 1590, with court PATRONAGE, his work was published and deemed an immediate success. Impressed, the queen promised Spenser a large pension, which was later reduced due to political machinations. He returned to Ireland, and on June 11, 1594, married Elizabeth Boyle, his second wife, commemorating the event with the SONNET SEQUENCE AMORETTI and his poem EPITHALAMION.

Living in Kilcolman Castle with his family, Spenser composed the last six books of The Faerie Queene and was appointed sheriff of Cork in the fall of 1598. Tragedy struck only weeks later when rebellion broke out among the Irish in Munster and mobs set fire to his castle. The family escaped with their lives, but the fire claimed most of Spenser's recent writing. Only two CANTOS of Book 7 of The Faerie Queene survived (published in 1609); consequently, Spenser's ambitious masterwork was never completed. In December 1598, Spenser was recalled to England. Weakened by the winter journey, Spenser died in London on January 16, 1599. He was buried near GEOFFREY CHAUCER in Westminster Abbey.

FURTHER READING

Cheney, Patrick. Spenser's Famous Flight: A Renaissance Idea of a Literary Career. Toronto: University of Toronto Press, 1993.

Maley, Willy. A Spenser Chronology. Lanham, Md.: Barnes and Noble, 1994.

Waller, Gary F. Edmund Spenser: A Literary Life. New York: St. Martin's Press, 1994.

Melissa Femino

SPENSERIAN SONNET   A variation, developed by EDMUND SPENSER, of the SONNET (14-line poem), this form is quite rare. Considered a complication of the ENGLISH SONNET form, the Spenserian sonnet also exhibits three QUATRAINS and a concluding COUPLET, but features a more complex, interlinking rhyme scheme: abab bcbc cdcd ee. The repetition of rhymes bridging quatrains creates a tight, focused narrative structure. Spenser's AMORETTI is the most prominent example of this sonnet type.

See also ITALIAN (PETRARCHAN) SONNET.

"STAND WHOSO LIST" SIR THOMAS WYATT (1557)   This short poem is a translation from Seneca's Thyestes (lines 391–403). Like some of SIR THOMAS WYATT's other political laments, it is a declaration that life at the centers of political power—here described as "the slipper top / Of court's estates" (ll. 1–2)—is far too uncertain. Its joys are "brackish" (l. 4), meaning that even at its best, the courtly life offers pleasures that only partially mitigate the dangers. Indeed, to ingest them may be poisonous. Instead, says the speaker, he wishes to live apart, in quiet and peace, and to die an old man in relative anonymity. The alternative is to live always in the grip of death (l. 8), meeting an unwelcome and unforseen end (l. 10). The final line of the poem uses ALLITERATION ("Doth die," "dazed," "dreadful") to emphasize the frightening picture. The manners of the two deaths (lines 6–7 and 10, respectively), when compared, make the point most dramatically: Better to die old, happy, and anonymous than young and (implicitly) an easy target.

As is the case with so many of Wyatt's poems, an autobiographical reading is hard to avoid. His career at the court of HENRY VIII was fraught with danger and conflict. This also shows how important the work of translation was in the new poetics Wyatt introduced into England. It is of a piece with several of Wyatt's other poems that also express mistrust of the court and its values, particularly "WHO LIST HIS WEALTH AND EASE RETAIN," and the epistolary SATIRES including "MINE OWN JOHN POINS."

See also COURT CULTURE.

FURTHER READING

Muir, Kenneth. *Life and Letters of Sir Thomas Wyatt.* Liverpool: Liverpool University Press, 1963.

Rebholz, R. A., ed. *Sir Thomas Wyatt: The Complete Poems.* New Haven, and Conn., and London: Yale University Press, 1978.

Christopher A. Hill

STANZA From the Italian for "room" or "stopping place," a stanza is a group of verse lines, usually set off in print by space between the stanzas. The structure of any given stanza is determined by its rhyme scheme, meter, and/or number of lines; poems will generally maintain the same stanza structure throughout. Standard English stanza forms include the COUPLET (two lines ending in the same rhyme), heroic couplet (IAMBIC PENTAMETER meter, same rhyme), tercet (three lines with the same rhyme), QUATRAIN (four lines), BALLAD (a quatrain with an *abab* or *abcb* rhyme), heroic quatrain (iambic pentameter, *abab*), RHYME ROYAL (iambic pentameter, *ababbcc*), and Spenserian (based on *The FAERIE QUEENE,* eight lines of iambic pentameter plus one of iambic hexameter). SIR THOMAS WYATT is credited with introducing several Italian stanzaic forms, such as terza rima and ottava rima, into English practice. Stanza is often used interchangeably with STROPHE.

FURTHER READING

Addison, Catherine. "Little Boxes: The Effects of the Stanza on Poetic Narrative." *Style* 37, no. 2 (2003): 124–143.

Solopova, Elizabeth. "Layout, Punctuation, and Stanza Patterns in the English Verse." In *Studies in the Harley Manuscript: The Scribes, Contents, and Social Contexts of British Library MS Harley 2253,* edited by Susanna Fein, 377–389. Kalamazoo, Mich.: Medieval Institute, Western Michigan University, 2000.

Carol E. Harding

ST. ERKENWALD ANONYMOUS (1380–1420)

This 352-line poem relates the discovery of a rosy-cheeked, fresh-faced, talking corpse buried in the foundation of St. Paul's Cathedral in London. The poem begins with a brief account of how all the ancient heathen temples of London were destroyed and then rebuilt as early Christian churches under the direction of Augustine of Canterbury in the late sixth century. After this short history, the poem jumps forward in time by 100 years. The bishop of London, Saint Erkenwald, is continuing the work of his predecessor and has ordered a foundation dug for St. Paul's Cathedral. The workers dig so deep that they unearth an elaborately carved, marble sarcophagus, ringed by illegible, gilded, runic letters. Word of the discovery quickly spreads, and Londoners gather around the workmen as they pry the lid off the casket. Inside they find the perfectly preserved body of man who is dressed like a king, wearing a crown, and holding a scepter. No record is found of his rule, however, and the city buzzes with speculation about just who the unusual stranger might have been while he was alive. London's bishop, Erkenwald, is visiting an abbey in a neighboring town as these events unfold, but as soon as he hears what is going on, he immediately returns to London on horseback.

Erkenwald does not go straight to see the body when he arrives in the city, however. He shuts himself in a room in his palace instead and spends the night weeping and praying for guidance. The Holy Spirit responds to his pleas, and Erkenwald, dressed in his priestly robes, sings High Mass as dawn breaks. Only after he has finished leading mass does Erkenwald approach the tomb. One of the other church officials explains that even after seven days of scouring the city records, they are still not able to identify the man lying before them. The church official marvels at how such an obviously important figure could slip so completely out of public memory. Bishop Erkenwald reminds him that what men find remarkable pales in comparison to the wonders of Christ; then he turns his attention to the tomb. He lifts up the corpse's eyelids and commands him, in the name of Christ, to identify himself. The body begins to speak, saying it must obey the will of God. The dead man explains that he is neither a king nor a noble, but a judge. He says he was always even-handed in the administration of the law and that his temperance healed a bitter feud between the king of his time and the king's brother. When the judge died, the people of the city expressed their gratitude by burying him with a crown, robe, and scepter.

Bishop Erkenwald then presses him for details about his perfectly preserved body and clothes. He wonders aloud if the man has been embalmed, but the talking corpse explains that God alone is responsible for his uncorrupted state. Erkenwald then asks about the man's soul. The body groans and concedes that despite his unusual postmortem appearance, his soul suffers in Hell. Although God allowed the man's body and clothes to sustain a perfected material state because of his righteousness in life, the judge lived before Christ and so was denied baptism and final salvation after death. Erkenwald is moved to tears by the man's plight and prays aloud, wishing God would provide an opportunity for him to baptize the "virtuous heathen." As the bishop bows over the body in sympathy, a tear falls on the dead man's face. Suddenly the body sighs with happiness and explains that the prayer and tears have baptized him as a Christian and that his soul has just ascended to Heaven. The body has just enough time to thank and bless Erkenwald before his corpse blackens and crumbles to dust. The assembled give thanks to God, and the poem ends with the local church bells all ringing in harmony.

St. Erkenwald does not fit into a single stylistic category. The story is too focused on a single event to fully function as a HAGIOGRAPHY, but it does mimic the genre. The poem also displays many of the attributes of a legend. The author probably drew his inspiration from assorted versions of the Trajan legend, some of which date from as far back as the eighth century. These tales all recount the same basic story, in which the soul of the just, non-Christian Roman emperor Trajan is saved after death by the prayers of Pope Gregory the Great. The Trajan story gained popularity in the 14th century, and versions from this period are most famously present in the works of Dante Alighieri and WILLIAM LANGLAND.

St. Erkenwald is written in alliterative verse. This poetic form is characteristic of works that belong to the ALLITERATIVE REVIVAL movement of the late 14th and early 15th centuries. *St. Erkenwald* is composed in a dialect common to the Northwest Midlands at a time when the alliterative verse form was closely identified with this area. The dialect in which the poem is written has fueled speculation about the identity of its unknown author. One significant theory names the GAWAIN-POET as the author of *St. Erkenwald*. Based on marginal notations (glosses), anagrams, and ACROSTICS in some of the poems that appear to spell out a surname, some critics have attempted to attribute authorship of all five poems to a poet whose last name was some variation of "Massey." However, this attribution has never been conclusively proven. Other theories attempt to link the poet to the court of Richard II or infer clerical training.

The poem's meaning is also contested. Some critics read *St. Erkenwald* as an affirmation of the necessity of ecclesiastical intercession in personal salvation. Even though the non-Christian judge was extraordinarily virtuous while he was alive, he lived before Christ and so was never baptized as a Christian. The righteous actions of the dead man while he was alive on earth prove insufficient to save him from the damnation of Hell after death. Bishop Erkenwald represents the power and authority of the church, and it is his tear that ultimately baptizes the body and saves the man's soul. Thus, Erkenwald (representing the Catholic Church) is the poem's central protagonist. Other critics however, deemphasize the role of the bishop and focus on the good works of the judge. They suggest that he is largely responsible for his own salvation, since his just actions are directly responsible for his miraculous preservation. Despite the difference in critical opinion, most agree that *St. Erkenwald* is admirable for its dramatic narration.

See also ALLITERATION.

FURTHER READING

Peterson, Clifford. *Saint Erkenwald.* Philadelphia: University of Pennsylvania Press, 1977.

Whatley, Gordon. "Heathens and Saints: *St. Erkenwald* in its Legendary Context." *Speculum* 61, no. 2 (1986): 330–363.

Anne Salo

STRAMBOTTO An early verse form found in Italian poems, primarily in Tuscan and Sicilian works, strambotto is considered one of the forerunners of the

SONNET. This form utilized either six or eight hendeca-syllable lines (11 syllable lines of alternating stress), with a standard rhyme scheme of *ababccdd*. English examples include SIR THOMAS WYATT's "VULCAN BEGAT ME" and EDMUND SPENSER's *The Ruins of Rome*.

STROPHE

From the Greek for "act of turning," strophe refers to the movement of an ancient Greek dramatic chorus to the left while reciting the lines assigned; movement to the right was labeled *antistrophe*. The Greek poet Pindar adapted this idea into the performance of his odes, and in the regular Pindaric ode, the sections of strophe and antistrophe are presented in the same meter, while the epode (final section) uses another.

The term *strophe* is also used interchangeably with STANZA to identify a distinct unit within a poem. When the two are differentiated, the stanza will usually refer to rhymed, identically structured, repeated groupings, while the strophe is irregular and either unrhymed or using varied rhymes. A number of the Middle English ROMANCES are written using a strophic format.

FURTHER READING
Duggan, Hoyt N. "Strophic Patterns in Middle English Alliterative Poetry." *Modern Philology* 74, no. 3 (1977): 223–247.

Carol E. Harding

SULTAN OF BABYLONE, THE ANONYMOUS (before 1450)

The Sultan of Babylone is a 15th-century ROMANCE concerned with the exploits of the Frankish king Charlemagne and his 12 Peers of the Realm. Stories of these figures, and especially their battles with the SARACENS, were immensely popular throughout Europe.

This poem opens with the sultan Laban hunting in Spain. Stopping to rest, he discovers that a ship, meant for him, has been pillaged in Rome. Swearing vengeance, Laban attacks Rome. The pope retaliates, and so it continues.

The pope enlists Charlemagne's help. Laban instructs Ferumbras, his son, to kill all the Christians save Charlemagne, to whom he wishes to teach courtesy, and the knights Roland and Oliver, if they will convert to the heathen faith. Ferumbras approaches Charlemagne and requests a fight, but he is defeated. He agrees to be baptized as his gods have proved false, but hidden Saracen forces rush out, capturing Roland and Oliver.

Floripas, Laban's daughter, persuades her father to imprison the knights, including Roland, Oliver, and Guy of Burgundy, instead of executing them. They are held in appalling conditions. Floripas, moved by their plight, determines to help them. She pushes Maragound, her governess, out of a window and murders the jailer, thus gaining responsibility for the prisoners. Meanwhile, Laban sends messengers to Charlemagne seeking Ferumbras's release. The Christians instead chop off their heads and send them to Laban. Enraged, Laban wants to take revenge on his prisoners, but Floripas intervenes. She is in love with Guy of Burgundy, so Roland and Oliver persuade Guy to agree to marry her. Floripas helps them escape. They capture a castle, and hold out until Charlemagne arrives. Laban is captured, and at Ferumbras's behest, he is offered baptism. The sultan refuses and is executed. Floripas marries Guy, and Spain is divided between Guy and Ferumbras.

Most of the critical attention this romance has received has focused on the relationships between the extant versions of the story, particularly the French and English, and their sources. As well, this text is interesting for its attitudes toward Saracens. It places more emphasis on the emotions, motivation, and characterization of Saracens than most other contemporary texts.

FURTHER READING
Crane, Susan. *Insular Romance: Politics, Faith, and Culture in Anglo-Norman and Middle English Literature*. Berkeley: University of California Press, 1986.

Lupack, Alan, ed. *Three Middle English Charlemagne Romances*. Kalamazoo, Mich.: Medieval Institute Publications, 1990.

Millar-Heggie, Bonnie. "The Performance of Masculinity and Femininity: Gender Transformation in *The Sowdone of Babylone*." *Mirator* (2004). Available online. URL: http://www.ccjyu.fi/mirator/artikkelit.htm. Downloaded on July 10, 2005.

Bonnie S. Millar

"SUMER IS ICUMEN IN" ANONYMOUS (ca. 1250)

A traditional English rota (round), this secular lyric is sometimes considered the earliest example of a canon (a six-part musical composition). It is rather short, consisting of a celebration of summer, with a repeated directive to the cuckoo to sing. A few animals—cows and ewes—are keeping watch over their offspring. The cuckoo is enjoined to sing again.

The poem is found in one manuscript: London, British Library, MS Harley 978, which can be traced to Reading Abbey. The lyric appears on the page alongside an alternate Latin text, which is a lyric on the Passion of Christ. Thus, many of the critical discussions surrounding this lyric involve identification of its genre, particularly in context with its companion piece. Some scholars connect this lyric with the REVERDIE tradition, citing the images of birth and growth. Others suggest it is a contrafactum (parody), in which secular words were adapted to sacred verse.

More recently, scholars have begun looking at other aspects of the lyric, including its treatment of adultery. The cuckoo was a common symbol for adultery—called *cuckoldry* in the Middle Ages—based on the cuckoo's practice of stealing other birds' nests.

FURTHER READING

Fischer, A. "'Sumer is icumen in': The Seasons of the Year in Middle English and Early Modern English." *Topics in English Linguistics* 13 (1994): 79–96.

Obst, W. "'Svmer is icumen in': A Contrafactum?' *Music and Letters* 64 (1983): 151–161.

Roscow, G. H. "What Is 'Sumer is Icumen in?'" *Review of English Studies* 50, no. 198 (1999): 188–196.

"SUNSET ON CALVARY" See "NOW GOTH SONNE UNDER WOD."

SURREY, HENRY HOWARD, EARL OF (ca. 1517–1547)

Henry Howard was the eldest son of Thomas Howard, earl of Surrey, who became the third duke of Norfolk in 1524, and Elizabeth Stafford, daughter of Edward Stafford, duke of Buckingham. No birth record or christening record exists, but Henry Howard seems to have been born early in 1517. When his father was elevated to the dukedom, Henry received the courtesy title of earl of Surrey. His father was a leader of the conservative nobles who opposed HENRY VIII's Reformation. The Howards as a family had earlier resisted the Tudor claims to the English throne. Nevertheless, in 1530 Surrey and Henry Fitzroy, duke of Richmond and illegitimate son of Henry VIII, became close friends. They traveled with the king to France in 1532 and spent a year in the court of King Francis I. That same year, Surrey married Lady Frances Vere, the daughter of the earl of Oxford. During this period, Surrey was exposed to Italian humanism.

These carefree days were soon to end. In 1535 Surrey was back in England to witness his father preside over the trial of Anne Boleyn, his cousin, and Henry VIII's second queen. The following year, 1536, saw the death of Surrey's good friend Henry Fitzroy and the rise of Edward Seymour, brother of Henry VIII's new queen, Jane Seymour. The two men became instant enemies, and Surrey was jailed in 1537 for assaulting Seymour at Hampton Court.

When Surrey's cousin, Catherine Howard, became Henry VIII's fifth wife, he was made a knight of the Garter. He was also jailed twice more for public violence but was released in spring 1543 to fight on the continent against France. For Surrey's excellent military service, Henry VIII named him marshal of the field in 1543 at age 27, and in 1545 he was named lieutenant general of the king on sea and land. These honors were short-lived, however. The great success that Surrey achieved at such a young age led to Seymour and many of the new Tudor men becoming jealous, and Seymour plotted his revenge. Surrey was demoted and recalled to England in March 1546 after his outnumbered, insufficiently funded, and poorly supplied troops were routed at Boulogne in January that year.

In December 1546, Surrey was jailed in the TOWER OF LONDON for treason. He was brought up on trumped-up charges, one of which was including the royal coat of arms of King Edward the Confessor in the first quarter of his shield. Edward the Confessor was the only Catholic saint not defiled by Henry VIII and his adviser Thomas Cromwell. Thus, this was both a political and religious matter. Seymour claimed that Surrey did not have the right to the royal arms. Surrey did; however, he did not first receive Henry VIII's permission, which was required for the change. Being a commoner and not a peer of the realm like his father, Surrey was quickly tried in common court with no objective evidence and no cross-examination. He was found guilty and beheaded just before his 30th birthday on January 19, 1547, nine days before the king himself died. Surrey was the last man executed by Henry VIII.

Henry Howard, earl of Surrey, was much more than a political figure. He was also an excellent poet who left behind 60 poems, all unpublished at his death except for his tribute to SIR THOMAS WYATT, which appeared in 1542. He wrote 15 SONNETs, some of which are a direct translation of PETRARCH and others that are imitations, although all of his sonnets are composed in the ENGLISH SONNET form. Surrey also composed elegies, songs, verse letters, a SATIRE ("LONDON, HAST THOU ACCUSED ME"), and translations. His translation of books 2 and 4 of VIRGIL's *Aeneid* also arguably introduced BLANK VERSE poetry into the English canon. This may be his greatest poetic achievement. He cast off the archaic forms and aureate language of his predecessors to write in a fresh poetic diction.

See also "ALAS SO ALL THINGS NOW DO HOLD THEIR PEACE . . ."; "LOVE THAT DOTH REIGN AND LIVE WITHIN MY THOUGHT"; "SO CRUEL PRISON"; "TH' ASSYRIANS' KING IN PEACE WITH FOUL DESIRE"; "SOOTE SEASON, THE"; "WHEN WINDSOR WALLS."

FURTHER READING
Casady, Edwin. *Henry Howard, Earl of Surrey.* 1938. Reprint, Millwood, N.Y.: Kraus, 1975.
Jones, Emrys, ed. *Henry Howard, Earl of Surrey Poems.* Oxford: Clarendon, 1964.
Sessions, William A. *Henry Howard, Earl of Surrey.* Boston: Twayne, 1986.

Mark DiCicco

SYNECDOCHE   Synecdoche is a figure of speech in which a part of something is used in place of the whole. It is a commonly employed poetic device in the SONNET, especially the love sonnets, where a portion of the beloved's anatomy stands in for her entirety. Synecdoche is related closely to METONYMY.

R. Jane Laskowski

T

"TAGUS, FAREWELL" ("OF HIS RETURNE FROM SPAIN") Sir Thomas Wyatt (1539)

Sir Thomas Wyatt probably wrote this poem in 1539, when Henry VIII finally granted him permission to return home to England after a long diplomatic sojourn in Spain. The only manuscript version of this poem is believed to be in Wyatt's own hand. The poem, which is titled "In Spain" in the manuscript, appeared in print for the first time in Tottel's Miscellany as "Of his returne from Spain" (1557), but it is called "Tagus, Farewell" in most modern collections.

In this poem, an almost dreamy quality replaces the biting humor and sharp political commentary typical of Wyatt's earlier lyrics and satires. The speaker, like the river Tagus's "grains of gold already tried" (l. 1), has been honed by his experiences in the courts of Henry VIII and the continental monarchs. He seems able now to integrate his identities of poet and courtier, a balance that is reflected in the poem's structure. His wish to "go seek the Thames / Gainward the sun that shew'th her wealthy pride" (ll. 3–4) stands in counterpoint to his description of London, curving around the Thames in a crescent, as "the town that Brutus sought by dreams, / Like bended moon doth lend her lusty side" (ll. 5–6). The complementary images of sun and moon, gold and silver suggest an acceptance of the complexity inherent in Wyatt's dual role as poet and courtier. The mention of Brutus recalls the rich Roman heritage of Britain but also recalls the brutality of Rome's rule.

The balance and the symmetry of the poem, however, do not always help to clarify Wyatt's characteristic ambiguity, nor do they mean that the poem is without tension. The publisher Richard Tottel made changes to the poem that merely draw attention to that tension, the most significant being a rearrangement of the final COUPLET. In Wyatt's original, these lines read, "My king, my country, alone for whom I live / O mighty love the wings for this me give" (ll. 7–8), suggesting that Wyatt's patriotism is his sole motivation. A number of critics have noted the startling omission of God from the list. Tottel's revision of these lines rectifies this oversight: "My king, my country, I seek for whom I live, / O mighty Jove, the winds for this me give." This alteration provides the added impetus of religion—but also adds a questing note. The substitution of "I seek" for "alone" recalls the Wyatt of the SATIRES and lyrics, always restlessly seeking and questioning, constantly trying to reconcile the demands of political service with the dictates of his conscience.

FURTHER READING

Mason, H. A. *Humanism and Poetry in the Early Tudor Period.* London: Routledge/Paul, 1959.

Carol D. Blosser

TAIL RHYME (CAUDATE RHYME)

A tail rhyme is a scheme in which rhyming lines are followed by a tail—a line of shorter length with a different rhyme. The tails then rhyme with each other to form a tail-rhyme STANZA. The initial rhyming lines are usually a COUPLET or tercet. This form is also called caudate rhyme and is closely related to RIME COUÉE.

TÁIN BÓ CULAIGNE   See EARLY IRISH SAGAS.

TALE OF GAMELYN, THE ANONYMOUS (ca. 1350)

We owe the survival of this poem to GEOFFREY CHAUCER, who apparently included it among his papers, intending to use it as the source of a tale that was never composed. Upon Chaucer's death in 1400, early 15th-century copyists added it in one group of 25 manuscripts to the unfinished "Cook's Tale" as part of The CANTERBURY TALES. The poem also indirectly influenced WILLIAM SHAKESPEARE's As You Like It (1598–1600) through Thomas Lodge's poem Rosalynde: Euphues Golden Legacie (1590).

The Tale of Gamelyn consists of 898 long and occasionally alliterative lines of rhymed COUPLETs with generally three stresses before and after the CAESURA: "To telle hym tydinge / the wynde was wente" (l. 699). Each of the six parts or "fyttes" opens with the poet's command to the audience to listen and be quiet, suggesting oral performance at some point in its evolution.

Part 1 opens with the impending death of Sir John of Boundes, who wishes to divide his property equally among his three sons: John the Younger, Ote, and Gamelyn. Though Sir John instructs the knights of the shire to honor his request, they ignore his wishes and decide to deliver all the lands to the two eldest sons, giving none to Gamelyn. Accordingly, John seizes Gamelyn's lands, tenants, and horses, but he lets them go to ruin. Upon reaching his maturity, Gamelyn confronts his brother about his stolen inheritance, and his brother counters by accusing him of being low-born and a bastard, ordering his servants to beat him. Gamelyn retaliates, and John retreats, fearing for his life. He cunningly tells Gamelyn that he arranged the attack as a test of strength. Gamelyn then offers to reconcile if John returns his inheritance to him, and his brother falsely agrees.

In part 2, Gamelyn goes to a wrestling match to win honor for the family. As soon as he leaves, his brother locks the gate against him. At the match, Gamelyn challenges the champion and eventually emerges vic-

torious. Declared the champion, Gamelyn returns home with his prizes—a ram and a ring—and a large company, only to discover that his treacherous brother has locked the gate.

In part 3, Gamelyn breaks open the gate, chases the porter who refused him entry, then breaks the porter's neck and throws him into the well. Once inside, Gamelyn and his friends celebrate his victory by consuming his brother's food and drink for seven days. Hiding in a turret, John observes the drunken revelry and plots his revenge.

Part 4 opens with John capturing Gamelyn. Gamelyn maintains that he spent only what was owed to him from his inheritance, whereupon John, who has no heir, offers to make Gamelyn his heir. Naively, Gamelyn is lured into believing his brother, who then binds him hand and foot and tells everyone that Gamelyn is insane. Gamelyn begs Adam, the household servant, to release him, promising him a share of his lands, and he does so. The two embark on a plan: At a Sunday banquet, to which John has invited the local clergy, Gamelyn pretends to be bound to a post in the hall. After the "men of Holy Church" refuse to help him, Gamelyn and Adam "absolve them of their sins" by beating them with staves. Gamelyn then strikes his brother, breaking his back.

In part 5, the sheriff's men come to the manor to capture Gamelyn. The porter refuses to admit them and warns Gamelyn, who escapes into the woods with Adam. There they encounter a band of outlaws. After explaining their plight, they are given food and drink, and soon after, Gamelyn is made second in command under the "crowned king of the outlaws." After three weeks, the master outlaw is pardoned, and Gamelyn assumes the title. Meanwhile, his false brother John is appointed sheriff, and he declares Gamelyn an outlaw, or "wolf's head." When he is informed about his indictment by his faithful tenants, Gamelyn goes to the shire court to proclaim his innocence, but his brother has him arrested and thrown into prison. Upon hearing of his arrest, Sir Ote, Gamelyn's middle brother, demands that Gamelyn be released on bail until the next sitting of the shire court. John agrees, providing that Ote bear the judgment if Gamelyn fails to appear. Once released into Ote's custody, Gamelyn, against his brother's advice, departs for the forest to rejoin his outlaw band.

Part 6 opens with Gamelyn's return to the forest, where he resumes his robbery of "abbots, priors, monks, and canons." While he is gone, his evil brother John bribes the jury to render a death sentence for him, and when he is late for his court appearance, Sir Ote is arrested and condemned to death. Upon hearing this, Gamelyn, Adam, and the outlaws rescue Ote. Gamelyn then overthrows John and takes his place. Acting as judge, Gamelyn holds an inquest and sentences the justice, the jury, and John to death by hanging. After the executions, Gamelyn goes to the king and receives his pardon. Sir Ote is appointed the new justice, and Gamelyn is made the "chief justice of his free forest." Thus, Gamelyn wins back his land and tenants and avenges himself on his enemies. Afterward, he marries a "fair and good" wife.

The poem contains some strikingly original imagery. When the local clerics refuse Gamelyn's pleas for help, Gamelyn and Adam beat them with staves, parodying the asperges, or sprinkling of the congregation with holy water—"speyeth holy watere with an oken spire" (l. 499). After the sheriff raises the hue and cry, Adam swears that some of the sheriff's men "shal make her beddes in the fenne" (l. 584), or "make their graves in the mud." Later, when the sheriff arrives, he finds a nest but no eggs: "Tho fonde the scherreve nyst but non aye" (l. 606).

The Tale of Gamelyn marks an important transitional stage in the evolution of the medieval outlaw tale due to the change in the social status of the hero. Unlike earlier aristocratic protagonists, such as Hereward the Wake, Eustace the Monk, and Fouke fitz Waryn, Gamelyn is the youngest son of a knight, and he acts more like a farmer, engaging in wrestling and rough horseplay with staves, a pestle, and a cart axle. The depiction of the band of outlaws in the forest with its mention of archery and the unnamed master outlaw anticipates the early ROBIN HOOD BALLADS, and the tales are often connected in scholarship.

FURTHER READING

Knight, Stephen, and Thomas Ohlgren, eds. *Robin Hood and Other Outlaw Tales*. Kalamazoo, Mich.: Medieval Institute Publications, 1997.

Ohlgren, Thomas H., ed. *Medieval Outlaws: Twelve Tales in Modern English Translation*. Rev. ed. West Lafayette, Ind.: Parlor Press, 2005.

Thomas H. Ohlgren

TALIESIN (534–599) Taliesin is one of the earliest poets whose writings in Old Welsh have survived; all are contained in the Peniarth MS 2 at the National Library of Wales, known as the *Book of Taliesin*. Though this manuscript dates to the 14th century, it is generally assumed that the poems were orally transmitted from the sixth century through generations of bards to a monk of Glamorgan.

Taliesin is mentioned by the Welsh historian Nennius in the "Northern History" section of his *Historia Brittonum* (ninth century) as one of the five poets of renown, but what little is known about Taliesin's life is found in his poems. He was chief bard in the courts of at least three kings in northern Wales: King Brochfael of Powys in the mid-sixth century, then his successor Cynan Garwyn, and finally King Urien of Rheged and his son Owain mab Urien.

Based on a variety of linguistic and historical evidence, the 12 poems contained in the *Book of Taliesin* can be placed in the late sixth century. Taliesin's patrons are mentioned in the *Historia Brittonium*, Gwallawg and Urien specifically as having participated in the siege of Lindisfarne in the late sixth century. Taliesin lists the Bernicians as the enemies of his patrons, who were known to be a major threat to northern British kingdoms in the late sixth century. The English ruler named Fflamddwyn (Flamebearer) in "The BATTLE OF ARGOED LLWYFAIN" has been identified as Urien's contemporary and adversary, Theodric of Anglia (r. 572–579).

The *Book of Taliesin* records some of Taliesin's rewards for his service. For instance, Cynan Garwyn gave him over a hundred horses with silver trappings and mantles, a hundred bracelets, and a beautiful sword and scabbard for his service. Urien of Rheged also provided Taliesin with many presents, including gold, mead, and many other treasures. Taliesin's reputation in British folklore would eventually see him included in later stories related to King ARTHUR and his court, and he figures prominently in the modern science fiction and fantasy genre as well.

See also POETS OF THE PRINCES; "URIEN OF YRECHWYDD"; "WAR-BAND'S RETURN, THE."

FURTHER READING

Evans, Stephen S. *The Heroic Poetry of Dark-Age Britain: An Introduction to Its Dating, Composition, and Use as a Historical Source.* Lanham, Md.: University Press of America, 1997.

Huws, Daniel. *Medieval Welsh Manuscripts.* Cardiff: University of Wales Press, 2000.

Bradford Lee Eden

TESTAMENT OF CRESSEID, THE ROBERT HENRYSON (ca. 1492)

The MIDDLE SCOTS poem *The Testament of Cresseid* is the best-known work by ROBERT HENRYSON. Though commonly considered one of the SCOTTISH CHAUCERIANS, in this work Henryson clearly rejects material GEOFFREY CHAUCER included in his version of the story, *Troilus and Criseyde.*

The story of *The Testament of Cresseid* is set during the Trojan War and is based on a brief incident from Homer's *Iliad.* Cresseid's character is based on two women, both prisoners of war in the Greek camp: Chryseis, the captured daughter of a Trojan priest of Apollo, and Briseis, a slave. When Chryseis's father calls down a plague, Agamemnon returns her. In exchange, he takes Briseis from Achilles, who sulkily withdraws from battle. Over time, these two women merged into one, Briseida (later Criseida), who is beautiful and pleasant, but unconstant of heart. Her name became Criseyde in Chaucer's poem, Cressida in WILLIAM SHAKESPEARE's play, and Cresseid in Henryson's poem. Most tales have her becoming involved with Troilus before being sent from Troy in a prisoner exchange, and then submitting sexually to Diomedes, a Greek hero. In most versions, Criseida realizes nothing positive will ever be written about her.

The Testament of Cresseid does not include the love story with Troilus. Instead, it picks up with Cresseid's expulsion from the Trojan camp, and Troilus's sorrow over her failure to return as promised. Cresseid is soon faced with a dilemma after Diomedes rejects her. Returning to her father Calchas, a priest of Cupid, she

is welcomed home. Entering the temple, Cresseid falls asleep. Before doing so, however, the embittered woman rails against Cupid and his mother Venus. In response, Cupid curses Cresseid, and she is infected with leprosy. Cresseid awakens to a ruined life, and, crying, she joins a leper colony. One day, while begging for alms at the roadside, she encounters Troilus. Though neither recognizes the other, Troilus is reminded of his lost mistress, so he gives the leper woman gold before riding away. Afterward, another leper reveals the warrior's identity, and Cresseid is devastated. Realizing how far she has fallen, Cresseid repents, asks that her ring be returned to Troilus, and dies. Upon learning of her death, Troilus builds a monument and buries her honorably. The poem ends with a warning to female readers not to be deceitful in love, and to remember Cresseid's sad end.

Henryson's version of the tale is misogynist and disturbing. For instance, Cresseid consistently refers to herself as licentious: "My mynd in flescehlie foull affectioun / Was inclynit to lustis lecherous" (ll. 558–559). This discrepancy speaks to the central question of the tale: Is Cresseid a wronged victim or a promiscuous, unprincipled whore? Neither Chaucer nor GIOVANNI BOCCACCIO fully decides, but Henryson does—she is an agonized (but repentant) whore. In particular, his use of leprosy, commonly associated with prostitution in the Middle Ages, confirms her as a lustful, willing participant in her own disgrace. He creates, in Cresseid, a figure of desire and feminine changeability, demonstrating an alternate view of a figure made sympathetic by others.

FURTHER READING

Fox, Denton. *The Poems of Robert Henryson.* Oxford: Oxford University Press, 1987.

Macqueen, John. *The Narrative Poetry of Robert Henryson.* Scottish Cultural Review of Language and Literature. Amsterdam: Rodopi, 2006.

Susannah Mary Chewning

"THEY FLEE FROM ME" ("THE LOVER SHOWETH HOW HE IS FORSAKEN OF SUCH AS HE SOMETIME ENJOYED") SIR THOMAS WYATT (1557)

Like all of SIR THOMAS

WYATT's poetry, the date of composition of this poem is uncertain since none of Wyatt's poetry was published during his lifetime. Fifteen years after his death, 97 poems attributed to Wyatt appeared in the collection *Songs and Sonnets* (better known as TOTTEL'S MISCELLANY) gathered and published by Richard Tottel in 1557. Although Wyatt deliberately wrote in a rough, plain style that was more concerned with expression than with smooth meters, by the time the poems were published, that style was considered unsophisticated; thus, Tottel, or perhaps one of his assistants, "smoothed out" Wyatt's poems. In this case, Tottel even renamed it: "The Lover Showeth How He Is Forsaken of Such as He Sometime Enjoyed." The original text of this poem can be found in London's British Library MS 2711, known as the Edgerton manuscript. Both Wyatt's original and Tottel's "improved" version are composed in RHYME ROYAL.

Wyatt chose the words in this poem deliberately and carefully. In the first seven-line STANZA, he begins by describing his amorous conquests in HENRY VIII's court. He seeks out many mistresses who often become vulnerable and attached to him. The timid women approach his chamber apprehensively, knowing that they put themselves "in danger," certainly emotionally and possibly physically, by being there. Still, he manages to tame them, so that they become "gentle" and "take bread" from his hand. He gentles them by being gentle to them, but he will not remain constant; instead, he seeks out the "continual change" of new sexual adventures. They also, apparently, learn the delights of love from him and go away to "range," seeking their own new affairs.

In the second stanza, however, the seducer becomes the seduced. A delicate woman seeks him out, and they become lovers at her initiative. However, the unthinkable happens—he is "caught" by her, as the other "wild ones" were caught by him before. She takes his power and his love. The once-virile man lies in his chamber as a beautifully dressed woman approaches, disrobes before him, and bends down to kiss him. Afterward, she asks, softly, "Dear heart, how like you this?" (l. 14). She is sexually knowledgeable and knows where his pleasure lies. She has taken over his role of demonstrating pleasure to a lover.

The third stanza highlights the speaker's betrayal. He lies awake wondering if the situation is even real, and just when he decides it is, the lady gives him "leave to go." In doing so, she grants both of them permission to practice "newfangleness," which he has done himself many times in the past. No longer "caught," the speaker should be relieved. Instead, he is bitter: "But since that I so kindely am served," he writes (l. 20). In these ironic words, the speaker acknowledges that he has been as considerately served as his past lovers, but that still does nothing to soothe his ego. He is left wondering how to deal with this role reversal, as the abandoner becomes the abandoned.

The imagery Wyatt employs also recalls the animal world. In the first stanza, the women the speaker dallies with are referred to simply as "they" and "them," grouping them together into a generic mass that is barely human. The women's human qualities become further depleted by the other words applied to them such as *tame* and *wild*. Even their actions are those of the animal world—they "take bread at my hand," "stalk," and "range." More specifically, several of the images can be connected to falconry, one of the popular aristocratic sports in early modern England. Falcons were controlled through the use of jesses, or strips of leather tied around their legs and feet, which were called *stalks*. A bird with a "naked leg," such as the women in the first stanza had, was considered tame.

Other images can be connected with hunting as well. The verb *seek* implies looking for game, and "caught" in the second stanza signals the result of the hunt. The lady's phrase "dear heart" may also be read as a play on "hart," meaning a stag, the grandest prize of the hunt. A recent critic has suggested that this particular pun suggests the overlapping of gender: As female deer and male hart, the poet is both the passive recipient of love and the active model for the lover. The sense of activity and passivity is heightened by the repetition of images of freeing and binding. In the initial stanza, the speaker is free while the women are "tame" (bound), but in the next stanza, he is "caught" by the free woman in her loose gown. He becomes more ensnared as the affair progresses, but she soon gives him "leave to go." The poem ends with both of them having freedom, although only one party desires it.

Often called Wyatt's most original poem, "They Flee from Me" constructs a sexually aggressive woman and a nervous, hesitant male poet. The passive male is pursued, teased, and mocked by the woman, who ultimately rejects him after having had her way with him. In undertaking the role of the pursuer, the woman assumes the traditional male sexual role and symbolically appropriates his penis, the symbol of his sexual and social power. In doing so, she thus causes her lover to be powerless and incapable of action—in a sense, impotent.

Another hint about the speaker's impotence can be found in the second stanza, as the affair begins. Some critics have pointed out that the question, "Dear heart, how like you this?" contains not only a pun on *heart/hart* but also a pun on *dear/dire*. In this case, *dear* refers to a "romantic companion," while *dire* recalls "language art" or a "talker" (Italian). As a poet, the speaker is an expert wordsmith, and in writing about his escapades, his release of words has come to be aligned with sexual release. However, at the end of this affair, the poet becomes inarticulate, unable even to fashion a response to his abandonment: "I fain would know what she doth deserve" (l. 21). As a "dire" man, when the poet is out of words, he is out of the sexual game and rendered impotent.

The speaker, a 16th-century man, would have been used to having power. When he loses control of the love affair, he is left in complete confusion and disarray. Her aggression cancels his dreams (he lays "broad waking") and his manliness (he is gentled). She is indifferent to his feelings. When she lets him go to move on, he remains "stuck." He does understand that he was "served," but her service was rendered only for her pleasure, not just for his, or even for their mutual pleasure. In his mind, his service deserves and ought to receive its reward, but the lady has reminded him, quite forthrightly, that in the COURTLY LOVE game, the lover is supposed to be lady's servant and subject to her whims. Thus, she has not only beaten him at his own game, but has also shown him how he has been playing the game incorrectly. Perhaps this is what makes Wyatt's poem so original and so memorable.

See also "WHOSO LIST TO HUNT."

FURTHER READING

Daalder, Joost, ed. *Sir Thomas Wyatt: Collected Poems.* Oxford: Oxford University Press, 1975.

Estrin, Barbara L. *Laura: Uncovering Gender and Genre in Wyatt, Donne, and Marvell.* Durham, N.C.: Duke University Press, 1994.

LeVay, John P. "Wyatt's 'They Flee from Me.'" *Explicator* 41, no. 1 (1982): 3–4.

THREE ESTATES　The traditional social classes of feudal society were commonly referred to as the Three Estates. The First Estate—*bellatores,* or "those who fight"—included the aristocrats and knights; the Second Estate—*oratores,* or "those who pray"—included members of the clergy and monastic orders; the Third Estate—*laboratores,* or "those who work"—included everyone else. This classification separated people based on their function in society. This tripartite stratification is different from the traditional two social classes found in Anglo-Saxon culture: *eorls* (nobles) and *ceorls* (everyone else). Some scholars classify women as being outside the three-estate system and call them the "fourth estate." Others recognize that women had a separate system, the so-called three feminine estates of virgin (first estate), widow (second estate), and wife (third estate). These divisions are also based on social function, though they are more specifically related to sexual function.

This traditional view, never completely definitive anyway, began to break down seriously as the Middle Ages drew to a close, the merchant classes grew wealthier and more influential, and clerks—educated men possibly in minor orders, but not true clergy—grew more common. GEOFFREY CHAUCER'S The CANTERBURY TALES is sometimes referred to as an estates satire because it mockingly challenges the rigidity of the class system. Nevertheless, all three estates are represented within the narrative as a whole, and the order of pilgrims in the GENERAL PROLOGUE TO THE CANTERBURY TALES reflects the traditional divisions.

"THREE RAVENS, THE" ("THERE WERE THREE RAVENS") ANONYMOUS (before 1600)
A popular folk BALLAD first published in 1611 by Thomas Ravencroft, (ca. 1582–1633) in his songbook

compilation *Melisata,* the contents of "The Three Ravens" suggest composition long before that. It follows the standard BALLAD STANZA form with four-line STANZAS and a REFRAIN, and it relates a poignant narrative. Three ravens are sitting in a tree. When one asks about breakfast, another reports that while there is a potential meal in the field—the body of a dead knight—the corpse is too heavily guarded by faithful animal retainers (a hawk and a hound). As this tale is being told, a pregnant doe comes up to the knight's body, licks his wounds clean, and then bears away his body for burial. Afterward, she lies next to his grave and dies. The ballad does not return to the ravens; instead, it closes with a "prayer" of sorts, asking God to send to send every man "Such haukes, such hounds, and such a Leman [sweetheart]."

Most critical debates about the ballad have focused on the "fallow doe" in the poem. To assume the figure is literally a deer presents physical problems (how might a doe lift up a man?), ethical concerns (why would a doe assist a hunter?), and moral complexities (why would the doe be a man's sweetheart?). Many scholars suggest that the doe is a supernatural creature, perhaps a wood-wife from Teutonic mythology—a wood fairy that takes human lovers. As a supernatural creature, the fairy could shape-shift into animal form.

Other scholars have suggested that the ballad may have had Celtic origins, particularly because of the spelling of the word *derrie.* In this case, the doe may represent the knight's attendant spirit, a personal animal guide unseen by the individual until death approaches. Ravens serve as a symbol of death, being carrion eaters, but also as a symbol of potential evil forces—black birds that feast on eyes, traditional "windows of the soul." The animal spirits protect and surround the honorable knight, depriving evil of its opportunity to take him. That there are three ravens also finds a parallel in Celtic mythology: the Morrigan, a goddess of death who took the form of a raven, appeared with her sister Fates as a trio and consumed the heads of slain warriors. Scholars also note the connection to the ballad "The TWA CORBIES," which is often considered a parody of this one.

FURTHER READING

Chatman, Vernon. "The Three Ravens Explicated." *Midwest Folklore* 13, no. 3 (1963): 177–186.

"TO ADAM, HIS SCRIBE" GEOFFREY CHAUCER (1385)   GEOFFREY CHAUCER's briefest poem, "To Adam, His Scribe" details the frustrations of a poet who must rely on a careless scribe to copy and transmit his words to the world. Adam, Chaucer's scribe, is accused of "negligence" and "rape" [haste], making many mistakes while copying the manuscripts that Chaucer must later correct. In venting his frustrations, Chaucer wishes "scalle," an itchy, scabby scalp, upon the scribe for making the author constantly "scrape" out Adam's copying and editing errors.

This amusing, seemingly lighthearted epigraph reveals much about the relationships and troubles of publication in the 14th century. Scholars have associated Chaucer's concerns with those of Dante and other contemporaries who feared losing control of their work once it was sent out to the world.

Analysis of this poem has varied, presenting it as a broad COMPLAINT that is not directed at any one scribe in particular, or presenting "Adam" as an allusion to the biblical Adam, connecting creation through an author's textual work with God's power to create life. The possibility of "Adam" being one of Chaucer's more authoritative scribes is also of interest, and recent scholarship has focused on identifying the scribe through analysis of historical records and manuscripts.

FURTHER READING

Ruud, Jay. *"Many a Song and Many a Leccherous Lay": Tradition and Individuality in Chaucer's Lyric Poetry.* New York: Garland, 1992.

Catherine A. Perkins

"TO ST MARY MAGDALEN" HENRY CONSTABLE (early 1590s)   HENRY CONSTABLE wrote two important SONNET SEQUENCES. The first, *Diana,* published in 1592, is a pioneering collection of carnal and romantic love SONNETS. By contrast, his 17 *Spirituall Sonnettes*—not published until 1815—are devotional poems that celebrate an intense relationship with God. The *Spirituall Sonnettes* were almost certainly written

just after Constable converted to Roman Catholicism in 1590 or 1591. The poem beginning with a direct address to the "Sweete Saynt," Mary Magdalen, is one of a number of sonnets in the sequence that are addressed to the saint who, according to popular tradition, had lived an immoral life before turning to Christ.

"To St Mary Magdalen" is an ENGLISH SONNET, consisting of three quatrains and a rhyming COUPLET. The first quatrain asserts the speaker's modesty: He converses with St Mary directly and respectfully, suggesting that she, better than he, can account for the superiority of "heavenly love" over any other sort of love. In the second quatrain, the speaker implies that he sees himself as a sort of Mary Magdalen figure. It is imagined that he will behave like a chaste woman: The soft "s" sounds of the fifth line convey the gentleness of his newly meek disposition—"lyke a woman spowse my sowle shalbee," he states. Once base and earthy, the speaker has redeemed himself, as Mary did, because now he too is "enamored" with Christ when he was previously motivated by "lust" and "synfull passions."

In the third quatrain, the speaker looks forward to death. It is anticipated that death will lift the mortal burden of life's "labors" and the liberation of "my spryght"—his soul or spirit. The concluding couplet appropriates language from erotic love poetry but uses it in a profoundly religious manner. As devoted to God as Mary Magdalen was to Jesus, the speaker's spirit will be "clasped in the armes of God" and forever wedded in a "sweete conjunction." As a recusant—a campaigner for England's reversion back to Catholicism—Constable was an outsider in 1590s' England, one whose religion was denigrated and forbidden by law. But in this poem the speaker can anticipate only eternal, heavenly victory for all moral beings who follow the example of saints such as Magdalen: The poem ends with a rousing prediction of "everlasting joye."

FURTHER READING

Grundy, Joan, ed. *The Poems of Henry Constable.* Liverpool, U.K.: Liverpool University Press, 1960.

Salmon, F. "Mary Magdalen, Frederico Borremeo, and Henry Constable's *Spirituall Sonnettes.*" *Recusant History* 18 (1986–87): 227–236.

Wickes, G. "Henry Constable, Poet and Courtier, 1562–1613." *Biographical Studies* 2 (1953–54): 272–300.

Kevin de Ornellas

"TO THEE PURE SPRITE" ("TO THE ANGEL SPIRIT OF THE MOST EXCELLENT SIR PHILIP SIDNEY") MARY SIDNEY HERBERT, COUNTESS OF PEMBROKE (1623)

Upon the death of her brother, SIR PHILIP SIDNEY, MARY SIDNEY HERBERT decided to complete his unfinished project, a translation of the Bible's Psalms, herself. She dedicates the SIDNEAN PSALMS to his memory in the poem "To Thee Pure Sprite," a poem that also serves as an ELEGY for her brother. The poem exhibits the tension inherent in this moment, a tension between Herbert's pleasure, pride, and excitement at completing the work and her guilt in finishing the project without her brother.

The poem is written as a direct address to Sidney. Herbert's writing, with interjections, questions, and parenthetical statements, displays an informal yet controlled style, appropriate for a poem spoken to a sibling. For example, in the lines "Yet here behold (oh, wert thou to behold!) / This finished now" (ll. 22–23), Herbert interrupts herself to address Sidney parenthetically. The line reads as a sincere exclamation and expression of Herbert's desire to have her brother present.

The poem expresses Sidney's genius while understating Herbert's own contributions. Herbert begins by stating that the subsequent poems are, "by double interest," truly his. Sidney wrote the initial poems, and Herbert credits the later poems she wrote herself to Sidney as well, for he was her inspiration. Throughout the collection, Herbert reinforces the idea that the poems belong to both her brother and herself. In the first STANZA, "So dared my muse with thine itself combine" (l. 5), asserts that Herbert attempted to marry her muse to her brother's. This line, suggesting a form of marriage between the two siblings, is echoed in the end of the poem when she writes, "If any mark of thy sweet sprite appear / Well are they born" (ll. 86–87). In this sense, the poems are the children of Herbert and Sidney.

In addition to making clear her debt to Sidney, Herbert also openly praises him, at times exalting her work and at other times claiming her inadequacies in relation to him. Herbert writes, "There lives no wit that may thy praise become" (l. 49), claiming that she is not fit to extol Sidney's talents. At the same time, Herbert claims that the psalms are "immortal monuments" to Sidney's fame (l. 71). She assures Sidney, and herself, that through the poems Sidney will be remembered: "Yet there will live thy ever-praised name" (l. 77).

Herbert also defends the larger project itself. As a translation of the Psalms, the poems are translations of holy poems written by King David and sung by the angels. Herbert makes it clear that neither she nor Sidney were attempting to improve upon God's work, but rather, sought "to praise, not to aspire / To those high tones" (ll. 10–11).

Recent critical discussions of Herbert's work consider the ways that her self-deprecation and her exaltation of Sidney provide cover for Herbert's own goals and ambitions. For instance, reading this poem alongside another dedicatory poem of Herbert's, "To the Thrice-Sacred Queen Elizabeth," might exalt Sidney as a type of Protestant saint who is encouraging Queen Elizabeth to support the Protestant cause in England and throughout Europe. Others have noted the complicated position Herbert was in as a woman writer circulating her own work in early modern England, where women were discouraged from speaking or writing publicly. In this light, this poem provides Herbert's means of defending—and praising—her own work while also eulogizing her brother.

FURTHER READING

Fisken, Beth Wynne. "'To the Angell Spirit . . .' Mary Sidney's entry into the 'World of Words.'" In *The Renaissance Englishwoman in Print: Counterbalancing the Canon*, edited by Anne M. Haselkorn and Betty S. Travitsky, 263–275. Amherst: University of Massachusetts Press, 1990.

Hannay, Margaret P. "'Doo What Men May Sing': Mary Sidney and the Tradition of Admonitory Dedication." In *Silent But for the Word: Tudor Women as Patrons, Translators, and Writers of Religious Works*, edited by Margaret P. Hannay, 151–165. Kent: Ohio State University Press, 1985.

Kathleen Kalpin

"TO THE THRICE-SACRED QUEEN ELIZABETH" Mary Sidney Herbert, countess of Pembroke (1599)

This dedicatory poem by Mary Sidney Herbert prefaced her translations of the Psalms in 1599, along with "To Thee Pure Sprite." "To the Thrice-Sacred Queen Elizabeth" reflects the political tensions between the Sidney family and Queen Elizabeth. Herbert begins her poem in a traditional fashion by flattering Elizabeth with appeals to the queen's "happy greatness" and her able mind. The poet describes Elizabeth's position, strength, and goodness as divinely granted, and intimates that her will affects the entirety of Europe. The tone of the poem changes, however, as Herbert moves from praise of Queen Elizabeth to a lament for her late brother, Sir Philip Sidney. She mourns her loss and says that she cannot "name whom sighing signs extend" (l. 25). She tells Elizabeth that her brother started the translation of the Psalms (now known as the Sidnean Psalms), and that she now finishes what he started. Herbert's and Sidney's work is a "livery robe" that she now presents to the queen, and she asks, "For in our work what bring we but thine own?" (l. 41).

Herbert next compares the biblical David's "great conquests" with Elizabeth's "greater blessed." She emphasizes Elizabeth's great power in stanza 11: Men obey a woman, and "Kings on a Queene enforst their states to lay" (l. 81). This comparison to David is quite typical, and many poets dedicated translations of the Psalms to Elizabeth. This dedicatory poem therefore has a seemingly typical tone: Herbert praises Queen Elizabeth through a comparison to David and hopes that her writing may be worthy of the queen. However, as critics have pointed out, Herbert's dedication addresses Elizabeth politically and does not engage in the typical praise of her beauty and chastity.

Other critics suggest that despite her praise of the queen, Herbert reveals her frustration with what she views as Elizabeth's lack of support for the English army in its fight against Catholic Spain. Herbert writes that what is English is "Where wit, where art, where all that is divine / Conceived best, and best defended lies" (ll. 47–48). She praises her brother's defense of the Protestant cause and England and believes that because he fought bravely and gave his life for his country, Elizabeth should "do what men may sing" (l. 96) by providing more financial support to the Protestant cause.

See also Even now that Care.

FURTHER READING

The Collected Works of Mary Sidney Herbert, Countess of Pembroke, Vol. 1, edited by Michael G. Brennan, Margaret P. Hannay, and Noel J. Kinnamon, 92–101. Oxford: Clarendon Press, 1998.

Hannay, Margaret P. "Doo What Men May Sing: Mary Sidney and the Tradition of Admonitory Dedication." In *Silent but for the Word,* edited by Margaret P. Hannay, 149–165. Kent, Ohio: Kent State University Press, 1985.

Kerri Lynn Allen

TOTTEL'S MISCELLANY (*SONGES AND SONNETTES*) (1557)

In 1557, English publisher Richard Tottel (ca. 1530–ca. 1594) published a collection of 213 poems under the title SONGES AND SONNETTES. This collection, which we now know as *Tottel's Miscellany,* is significant for the study of 16th-century poetry because of the vast corpus of poems that it contains. Many of SIR THOMAS WYATT's poetry posthumously appeared in this volume, a fact that ensures the continual relevance of *Tottel's Miscellany.* In addition to preserving and disseminating many poems that had previously circulated only in manuscript, *Tottel's Miscellany* had a remarkable impact on the print marketplace and generated huge waves of interest in compiling, printing, and reading miscellanies over the next 50 years.

Although the title page labels HENRY HOWARD, EARL OF SURREY as its author, *Tottel's Miscellany* can hardly be described as having a single author—and in fact Surrey wrote only about one-fifth of the poems. Scattered throughout *Tottel's Miscellany* are poems by Howard, Thomas Wyatt, Nicholas Grimald, and many anonymous or "uncertain" authors. Like the many manuscript compilations, miscellanies, commonplace books, and anthologies that circulated throughout the century, *Tottel's Miscellany* showcases the writings of a large network of writers, and the poems included reflect vital cultural practices as well as exemplifying literary merits.

Of course, the key difference between such manuscript texts and *Tottel's Miscellany* is a material one: *Tottel's Miscellany* appeared in print. As mentioned above, many of the poems published in *Tottel's Miscellany* were available in manuscript form. In fact, quite a few of the poems were written during the 1530s—nearly 30 years before the publication of *Tottel's Miscellany.* This temporal gap meant that the poems acquired new material, ideological, and literary contexts when they were presented in the volume.

It is difficult to overestimate the popularity of *Tottel's Miscellany.* After seven weeks, the book had already gone through three editions. During the next 30 years, it was issued seven more times. Because of the number of poems complied in *Tottel's Miscellany,* it might be described as the most significant published collection of verses that appeared during the mid-16th century. The miscellany gives us a sense of the wide variety of verse forms, themes, and subjects that were popular during this period. Moreover, *Tottel's Miscellany* was crucial to the wide dissemination of poetry written in the Petrarchan tradition (see PETRARCH).

FURTHER READING

Hamrick, Stephen. "Tottel's Miscellany and the English Reformation." *Criticism: A Quarterly for Literature and the Arts* 44, no. 4 (2002): 329–361.

Pomeroy, Elizabeth. *The Elizabethan Miscellanies: Their Development and Conventions.* Berkeley: University of California Press, 1973.

Wall, Wendy. *The Imprint of Gender: Authorship and Publication in the English Renaissance.* Ithaca, N.Y.: Cornell University Press, 1993.

Emily Smith

TOWER OF LONDON

Begun by William the Conqueror shortly after the NORMAN CONQUEST, the Tower of London has served as royal residence, armory, treasury, fortress, and barracks. It is situated on the north shore of the Thames, a site that takes advantage of defensive construction dating back to Roman times, and it is probably best known for its function as a jailhouse for important prisoners. The Tower has also been associated with the composition of numerous poems, many written within its walls, including some by ROBERT SOUTHWELL, SIR WALTER RALEIGH, Princess Elizabeth (later Queen ELIZABETH I), and many others.

The original 1066/67 castle was sited on one and a quarter acres, with the central White Tower as the focal point. Over the years, the Tower was more than doubled in size. During Edward I's reign (1272–1307), a luxurious royal suite was added. In the Tudor era, political and social trends contributed to the decline of the Tower as a royal residence; instead, it became the home to government departments and continued as an infamous royal jail.

Some important historical events connected to the Tower include Richard II's retreat there in 1381 during the PEASANTS' REVOLT and his abdication in 1399; Henry VI's murder in 1471; and the imprisonment and execution of SIR THOMAS MORE in 1534–35 and of Anne Boleyn, HENRY VIII's second queen, in 1536.

FURTHER READING

Impey, Edward, and Geoffrey Parnell. *The Tower of London: The Official Illustrated History*. London: Merrell Publishers with Historic Royal Palaces, 2001.

Lapper, Ivan, and Geoffrey Parnell. *The Tower of London: A 2000-Year History*. Botley: Osprey Publishing, 2000.

Carol E. Harding

TRANSLATION TRADITION Translation was an important literary, cultural, political, and intellectual activity in the Renaissance. It was how the majority of English readers came into contact with and appropriated ideas from the much-admired literature and culture of classical Greece and Rome. It was also a way of acknowledging their deference and indebtedness to this past, while simultaneously claiming that they and their society were worthy of that inheritance, and that their language was capable of embodying the ideas contained therein. Additionally, translation was a cornerstone of the school curriculum. Students learned style, eloquence, and morality through translation exercises. Moreover, in this era where imitation was the dominant mode of composition—where texts were, in many ways, valued and judged according to how they built on their sources and allowed earlier styles and ideas to resonate in their texts—translation played a significant role in literary composition.

The Renaissance humanist movement led to the wide-scale valorization of the language, culture, literature, philosophy, art, and science of the Greeks and Romans. Translators embraced the important task of making such seminal classical works available to the English public. They were likewise preoccupied with translating many of the most popular French, Italian, and Spanish texts. It was by virtue of these translations that the majority of English people first came into contact with the writings of Cicero, Aristotle, OVID, VIRGIL, Dante, PETRARCH, and Montaigne. The demand for texts extended beyond the humanist curriculum and far beyond literature. Readers desired, for instance, scientific treatises, medical texts, and manuals of warfare, cookery, and hunting. These demands were usually initially sated by translations, and the translations were then followed by the production and publication of native English texts. Printing also played a large role in the translation tradition, particularly by giving more readers access to more texts. The blurring of class distinctions is connected to the translation tradition, too, as individuals without a classical education could now read classical texts.

Accuracy and fidelity to the source text was not a universally accepted theory of translation in all modes and genres or amongst all translators. Attitudes and practices ranging from literal (word-for-word) translation to free translation (a preservation of the text's ideas) are discernible. The different translation policies adopted are matched only by the sheer generic variety of translations that circulated. Equally varied was the group of people who devoted themselves to translation: nobles, professionals, merchants, and students practiced the art, and a significant proportion of this group comprised women.

In this period, women's educational opportunities and reading material were heavily circumscribed in an attempt to mould them to the ideals of chastity, silence, and obedience. It was deemed indecorous for a woman to speak out or to express her ideas in writing. Such restrictions prevented literate women from participating wholeheartedly in the male-dominated intellectual and literary culture that surrounded them. Translation, however, provided women with an acceptable way into the realm of writing. As the female translator was not deemed to be writing in her own voice or expressing her own ideas, translation was regarded as a suitable female literary activity. As a result, it was often through translations that women became writers. Far from sublimating their voices to those of their source texts, female translators used the translated text as a forum to express personal and original ideas. This practice, of course, was not unique to women. Translators of both sexes recognized the usefulness of the cover that translation provided: Radical, controversial, or touchingly personal thoughts could be expressed in translations, and if ever confronted, translators could profess innocence, ascribing the offending material to their sources.

See also CLASSICAL TRADITION, EARLY MODERN V. RENAISSANCE.

FURTHER READING

Barber, Charles. *Early Modern English*. Edinburgh: Edinburgh University Press, 1976.

France, Peter, ed. *The Oxford Guide to Literature in English Translation*. Oxford: Oxford University Press, 2000.

Krontiris, Tina. *Oppositional Voices: Women as Writers and Translators of Literature in the English Renaissance*. London and New York: Routledge, 1992.

Joyce Boro

TROILUS AND CRISEYDE GEOFFREY CHAUCER (1382–1386)

GEOFFREY CHAUCER's *Troilus and Criseyde* provides one of the richest, most lyrical versions of a much larger intertextual tradition detailing the love story of Troilus, younger son of King Priam of Troy, and Criseyde, daughter of the Trojan seer Calkas. In Chaucer's version of the narrative, Troilus, younger brother to Hector, Paris, and Deiphoebus (of the epic warrior legends of Troy), falls in love with Criseyde, a young widow whose father has just defected from the Trojan to the Greek camp. Troilus's efforts to court Criseyde are negotiated by Pandarus, Troilus's friend and Criseyde's uncle (Calkas's brother). Although the two lovers consummate their love, ultimately an exchange of prisoners results in Criseyde's transfer to the Greek camp, where she and Troilus can no longer arrange for their secret trysts.

Chaucer's poem survives in 16 manuscripts and a number of fragments. He chose IAMBIC PENTAMETER in RHYME ROYAL for its meter. Chaucer drew on various sources for his version of this narrative, including most prominently Benoît de Sainte-Maure's *Roman de Troie* (late 1150s), Guido delle Colonne's *History of the Destruction of Troy* (1287), and GIOVANNI BOCCACCIO's Boccaccio's *Il Filostrato* (late 1330s). Chaucer's chief source is dramatic narrative. Chaucer adapts *Il Filostrato* freely, distilling Boccaccio's nine-book structure into five books and, in the process, inventing new scenes, developing his main characters more fully, demonstrating more empathy for Criseyde than previous versions demonstrate, and deepening the philosophical vision of the poem. Some critics argue that Chaucer's new five-book structure and the poem's larger focus on exile versus return to the divinity point to the influence of his reading of BOETHIUS's *The CONSOLATION OF PHILOSOPHY* (*Boece,* which Chaucer was known to be translating from Latin into Middle English during the years he worked on *Troilus and Criseyde*). The narrative develops as follows:

Book 1

Troilus sees Criseyde in the temple, is smitten by her beauty (and Cupid's arrow), makes a long, anguished complaint about how to catch her attention.

Book 2

Pandarus goes to visit Criseyde to convince her to consider Troilus as a lover. He urges friendship, though his clear design is to see Troilus and Criseyde consummate their love. This book is famous for Criseyde's interior monologue in which she contemplates the pros and cons of loving Troilus only to be interrupted in her musings by his return from battle in full marshal valor. Her subsequent dream of the eagle suggests the combination of terror and ecstasy she feels at the prospect of loving Troilus. At the end of this book, Troilus and Criseyde eventually meet at a dinner party at the home of Deiphoebus, Troilus's brother.

Book 3

After the dinner party, Pandarus schemes about how he will arrange a meeting time and place for their consummation. He brings the lovers together at his house (where Troilus is hiding in a small alcove) after prevailing upon Criseyde to stay the night because of an unusually powerful "smoky reyn" (smoky rain). Troilus and Criseyde consummate their love. Dawn comes and the lovers can barely part.

Book 4

Criseyde is traded to the Greeks in exchange for Antenor's return to Troy. Chaucer explores the various levels of irony attending the "chaungynge of Criseyde": the exchange is a less than auspicious exchange politically (since Antenor is, in part, responsible for the acceptance of the Trojan Horse within the walls of Troy). As Troilus and Criseyde take their leave from one another, Criseyde swears she will return on the 10th day.

Book 5

Upon her departure from Troy, Diomede arrives to lead Criseyde into the Greek camp. She never returns to Troy (in spite of an exchange of letters in which she and Troilus discuss schemes for doing so), becoming instead Diomede's paramour to assure her safety in the Greek camp. Distraught over the "chaungynge of Criseyde" and disturbed by his inability to construe his dream of a Criseyde lying in the arms of a boar, Troilus seeks out Diomede in battle but is not successful in avenging himself. He is killed by Achilles, and his soul ascends to the eighth sphere. The poem ends with a prayer to God and the Trinity.

Troilus and Criseyde has been described as fulfilling the expectations of many different genres. (To this extent, it anticipates Chaucer's later more explicit experiments with genre in *The Canterbury Tales*.) An extended narrative poem, it includes vivid dramatic scenes with lively dialogue exchanges. As a result, some critics emphasize its dramatic qualities most. In addition, it shares in the characteristics of the following genres:

Epic

Chaucer's narrative has its origins in medieval versions of Homeric epic, and he invokes epic at the start of the poem.

History

For many of his details, Chaucer draws on the historical narrative of Guido delle Colonne's *History of the Destruction of Troy,* and relies, as well, on Joseph of Exeter's explanation of supposed histories for the details he includes in his literary account.

Lyric

The poem is replete with lyrical moments that recall sub-genres of the lyric, such as lamentation and AUBADE.

Fabliau

Pandarus's behavior as entremetteur, his voyeuristic involvement in the lover's exchanges, and forthright naughty behavior all call to mind the fabliau.

Romance

Chaucer uses the love story as an extended meditation on the conventions of romance, in particular: private versus public morality; the chivalric code; the value and definitions of honor and truth. Modern readers have also sometimes compared the poem to a novel because of its psychological realism. Chaucer himself called his poem "litel myn tragedgye," and probably had in mind the *de casibus* tradition (rise and fall of princes), connecting it to the MIRRORS FOR PRINCES genre.

Recent critical approaches have explored, quite thoroughly, the poem's tangled gender structure (e.g., examining Chaucer's remaking of Criseyde within the tradition of Troilus and Criseyde intertexts). Queer readings have focused on Pandarus's triangulated relation with Troilus and Criseyde, as well as on Troilus's masculinity, particularly in relation to LOVESICKNESS. Feminist critics have been divided into two main camps—those who attempt to redeem Criseyde, deploring the misogynistic tradition behind more traditional readings, and those who attempt to disavow her as a creation meant to satirize. Still other readings have examined the poem's anticipation of "postmodern" concerns in its complex construction of narrative voice.

See also CHIVALRY, "TESTAMENT OF CRESSEID."

FURTHER READING

Chaucer, Geoffrey. *Troilus and Criseyde.* Edited by Stephen A. Barney. New York: W. W. Norton, 2006.

Windeatt, Barry. *The Oxford Guides to Chaucer: Troilus and Criseyde.* Oxford: Clarendon Press, 1992.

Regula Meyer Evitt

"TROUBLE IN A TAVERN" ("TRAF-FERTH MEWN TAFARN," "TALE OF A WAYSIDE INN") DAFYDD AP GWILYM (14th century)   Possibly DAFYDD AP GWILYM's most famous poem, this CYWYDD describes the poet's encounter with a girl in an inn. Entering a tavern, he sees an attractive young woman, buys the girl food and drink, and sets up a tryst with her. Later in the night, he will visit her

bed once all the other occupants are asleep. However, feeling his way in the dark, he trips over a stool and hurts his shin, cracks his forehead on a table on getting up, and causes a large bronze basin to fall off the table with a huge clang. This wakes the dogs and disturbs three English merchants who think he is a thief after their packs. A host is raised to hunt for him. Dafydd hides under a table, and prays to God for forgiveness.

Modern scholarship has examined the extent of Continental literary traditions on Dafydd ap Gwilym, as well as the ways he plays with the COURTLY LOVE tradition. For instance, a number of his poems, like this one, involve the character Dafydd going to his lover's house or setting up an amorous adventure at night in order to maintain secrecy; however, the trysts fail, and secrecy is blown. In these, Dafydd is the central, comic figure who rarely succeeds in finding the girl. Some scholars suggest that these poems are deliberate parodies of ROMANCE texts, while others believe that this lightheartedness indicates reliance upon OVID, not an attempt to undermine another tradition.

FURTHER READING

Bromwich, Rachel. *Aspects of the Poetry of Dafydd ap Gwilym. Collected Papers.* Cardiff: University of Wales Press, 1986.

Edwards, Huw Meirion. *Dafydd ap Gwilym: Influences and Analogues.* Oxford: Oxford University Press, 1996.

Johnston, David. "The Serenade and the Image of the House in the Poems of Dafydd ap Gwilym." *Cambridge Medieval Celtic Studies* 5 (1983): 1–19.

Sara Elin Roberts

"TRUTH" ("BALADE DE BON CONSEYL")

GEOFFREY CHAUCER (1386) Judging by manuscript evidence, GEOFFREY CHAUCER's short poem "Truth" was the most popular of his lyric poems in the late Middle Ages, surviving in 22 manuscripts and two editions. The poem belongs to a group of Chaucerian lyrics that also include the poems "Gentilesse," "Lak of Stedfastnesse," "The Former Age," and "Fortune," and which, because of their tone and subject matter, are often called his "Boethian" poems. This group of moral and philosophical lyrics was probably written in the 1380s, when Chaucer was translating BOETHIUS's *The CONSOLATION OF PHILOSOPHY* into Middle English. Boethius's views colored Chaucer's literary output throughout this decade, particularly in "The Knight's Tale," (see *The CANTERBURY TALES*) *TROILUS AND CRISEYDE,* and in these Boethian short poems.

"Truth," also called the "Balade de Bon Conseyl" ("Ballad of Good Counsel") in some manuscripts, is composed in the French poetic form called the *ballade* and includes three RHYME ROYAL stanzas (*ababbcc*). In it, Chaucer explores the ethical principle of *truth,* which in Chaucer's day was defined as a personal integrity that included fidelity to one's word, one's lord, and one's God, and by extension involved right moral conduct in one's relationships with others. The speaker of Chaucer's poem advises his reader to flee from the crowd, and not to seek the rewards of FORTUNE and the world. Our true home, he says, is in heaven, and we are only pilgrims passing through this life. Alluding to John 8:32 ("the truth shall set you free"), Chaucer ends each STANZA with the REFRAIN "And trouthe thee shal delivere, it is no drede" ("And truth shall deliver you, there is no doubt").

Modern editions of the poem invariably include a final ENVOI, also in rhyme royal, that is attached to the poem in one manuscript. It is a direct address to "thou Vache," presumably Sir Philip de la Vache, a courtier and acquaintance of Chaucer in the court of the English king Richard II. This stanza has been used by many critics to date the poem to the years 1386–89—the period when both Chaucer and Vache, as well as other supporters of the king, were in disfavor under the ascendancy of Richard's uncle, the duke of Gloucester. It is possible that the poem had been composed earlier and that the envoy was added later, when Vache needed Chaucer's special counsel. However, since the poem contains several apparent puns on the name *Vache* (French for "cow")—puns such as "Forth, beste, out of thy stal!" in line 18—it seems quite feasible that the poem was written with Vache in mind.

See also MIDDLE ENGLISH POETRY.

FURTHER READING

Minnis, A. J., V. J. Scattergood, and J. J. Smith. *Oxford Guides to Chaucer: The Shorter Poems.* Oxford: Clarendon Press, 1995.

Ruud, Jay. *"Many a Song and Many a Leccherous Lay": Tradition and Individuality in Chaucer's Lyric Poetry.* New York: Garland, 1992.

Jay Ruud

TUDOR WOMEN POETS   In *A Room of One's Own* (1929), Virginia Woolf (1882–1941) invented a fictional character—Judith Shakespeare—to remedy what she imagined to be the absence of early modern women writers. But, as the work of many recent scholars suggests, women did write during the 16th century. In fact, women produced works in every major literary genre used by male authors. The designation of *Tudor women poets* therefore reflects a vast range of female literary output. Women were far more prolific, both in manuscript and print, during the early modern period than was once believed.

Some Tudor women poets include ISABELLA WHITNEY (fl. 1567–73), ANNE VAUGHAN LOCK, MARY SIDNEY HERBERT (1561–1621), Jane Seager (fl. ca. 1589), ANNE DOWRICHE, Elizabeth Melville (ca. 1582–1640), and Elizabeth Jane Weston (ca. 1581–1612). Much of the writing produced by women between the years of 1550 and 1600 was religious; in particular, writers like Elizabeth Tyrwhit, Mary Sidney Herbert, and Anne Lock produced poetry that endorsed Protestant values. Religious poetry often took shape as prayers, psalms, and meditations.

The most striking exemplar for female authorship during the period was Queen ELIZABETH I. Although only two of Elizabeth's poems survive in autograph copies, she produced a range of poems throughout her life. Some of her earliest verses were written while she was imprisoned at Woodstock from 1554 to 1555. These two poems, "WRITTEN ON A WINDOW FRAME [OR WALL] AT WOODSTOCK" AND "WRITTEN WITH A DIAMOND," give us an indication of the ductility and inventiveness of women's writing: even when lacking quills and paper, women chose materials such as chalk or instruments such as writing rings that allowed them to scratch their words onto walls, windows, and other unexpected surfaces. Elizabeth's education, her status, and her centrality to 16th-century literary culture is everywhere evident, both in her own writings and in such texts as EDMUND SPENSER's The FAERIE QUEENE (1596). Moreover, the queen's impressive accomplishments in effect encouraged many women to write, and religious movements also catalyzed female writers with energetic literary zeal.

Mary Sidney Herbert and Jane Seager both composed poems for Elizabeth. Herbert's SIDNEAN PSALMS, a continuation of a project that her brother SIR PHILIP SIDNEY began before his death, disseminate Elizabeth's Protestant ideals and include a dedicatory poem to Elizabeth, "EVEN NOW THAT CARE," in which Herbert asserts that "Kings on a Queene enforst their states to lay" and enforces a comparison between Elizabeth and the biblical David.

Scribally circulated in manuscript, Herbert's *Psalms* included some words written in gold, reflecting the elaborate care that was taken in manuscript texts intended for royal audiences. Jane Seager's translation of the 10 sibyls' prophecies of the birth of Christ similarly acquires value through its material production. Ruled in gilt and with gilt capital letters, the 10-leaf manuscript is carefully held together by a glass binding probably painted by Seager and trimmed in velvet. The volume comprises poems written in calligraphy. Facing each poem is a version of the same poem written in character, a form of shorthand invented by the physician and writer Timothy Bright. The manuscript begins with a dedicatory epistle to Elizabeth in which Seager asks for "your Majesties most gracious acceptaunce" of her manuscript, although there is no evidence of whether Elizabeth received the text.

The most famous calligraphic artist of the early modern period was Esther Inglis (1571–1624). Inglis produced a series of 50 poems, her *Octonaries*. Although Inglis did not write the eight-line poems and possibly was not even their translator, her sumptuous text showcases the interactivities between poems and their contexts. Women such as Inglis and Seager could use skills like painting and calligraphy to insert their own authorial identities into literary culture.

Unlike women who circulated their writings in beautiful manuscript presentation copies, Isabella Whitney printed two volumes of poetry in cheap editions. Whitney's poetry stands as a unique example of secular, printed poetry by a 16th-century woman. Her first volume, *The Copy of a letter by a yonge Gentilwoman to her unconstant Lover* (1567), calls on Ovidian source materials and displays Whitney's insightful wit. Her later volume, *A Sweet Nosegay* (1573), is a series of translated aphorisms framed by original epistolary verses. Whitney skillfully employs ballad meter, and she engineers a space for herself within the discourse of lovers' COMPLAINT poems by creating a female complaint.

For women writing outside of the scope of the court and the print marketplace, the ELEGY was a popular genre. Elizabeth Cooke Russell, Lady Hoby (1528–1609), and Anne de Vere, countess of Oxford (1556–1588), both wrote elegies for family members. Other women experimented with ways of incorporating poetry into their religious, domestic, and social worlds by keeping household books or by interspersing their own poems along with copies of other authors' poems in their domestic papers. Because poetry was often used as a mnemonic device, new studies of lower-class women's writing may reveal that women produced poetry as a device for remembering (and teaching) rules germane to agriculture, cooking, or midwifery, among the various other domestic tasks taken on by women.

See also MARY, QUEEN OF SCOTS.

FURTHER READING

Beilin, Elaine. *Redeeming Eve: Women Writers of the English Renaissance.* Princeton, N.J.: Princeton University Press, 1987.

Demers, Patricia. *Women's Writing in English: Early Modern England.* Toronto, Buffalo, and London: University of Toronto Press, 2005.

Pacheco, Anita, ed. *A Companion to Early Modern Women's Writing.* Oxford and Malden, Mass.: Blackwell, 2002.

Emily Smith

"TUNNING OF ELINOR RUMMING, THE" JOHN SKELTON (ca. 1517)

"The Tunning of Elinour Rumming," is one of the best known poems by JOHN SKELTON, poet laureate and former tutor to the young Prince Henry, later HENRY VIII. Skelton, famous and infamous in his day for his scandalous satirical verses, was a cleric and noted scholar who also wrote allegories, morality plays, and poems celebrating noble patrons. While the exact date of this poem's composition is uncertain, its probable reference to a London alewife named Alianora Romyng and internal details about the brewing trade place it somewhere around 1517. *Tunning* refers to the pouring of ale into casks for storing.

The poem's loose structure mirrors the openness of the women's bodies it depicts. Composed in SKELTONIC meter—short lines of two or three stresses ending in rhyming COUPLETS—the poem gallops through a catalogue of lowly women ravaged by drinking Elinor's magical brew. The "comely dame" (l. 91) of the title is in fact quite ugly: "Comely crinkled, / Wondrously wrinkled, / Like a roast pig's ear / Bristled with hair" (ll. 18–21). Her lips "slaver, men sain, / Like a ropy rain" (ll. 23–24). Likewise, her customers come dripping with tears and snot, "With their heels dagged, / Their kirtles all to-jagged" and their corsets unlaced (ll. 123–124). They are a drunken, lusty, and brawling lot, completely unrestrained by the hierarchical and gender rules of their society.

Critics in the early part of this century followed Skelton's contemporaries in regarding the poem as artless at best, and disgustingly vulgar at worst, often terming it a "novelty." More recently, however, critics interested in Rabelais and the grotesque have applied the philosopher Mikhail Bakhtin's theories of carnival to reclaim "Elinor Rumming" as a poem that celebrates female companionship in a society that increasingly deprived women of the means to make a living. Elinor and her crew colorfully and gloriously burst through the boundaries in which their culture tried to contain them and provide a vivid glimpse of London street life at the turn of the 16th century.

See also ALLEGORY, PATRONAGE, SATIRE.

FURTHER READING

Herman, Peter C. "Leaky Ladies and Droopy Dames: The Grotesque Realism of Skelton's *The Tunnynge of Elynor Rummynge.*" *Rethinking the Henrician Era: Essays on Early Tudor Texts and Contexts,* edited by Peter C. Herman. Urbana / Chicago: University of Illinois Press, 1994.

Carol D. Blosser

"TWA CORBIES, THE" ANONYMOUS (before 1600)

Often considered a parody of "The THREE RAVENS," *The Twa Corbies* is a BORDER BALLAD about despair. An unnamed narrator overhears two ravens ("corbies") discussing their next meal. Their plan is to feast on the abandoned body of a dead knight, plucking out his eyes, and then using his hair to make a nest within his bones.

Most scholarship on this poem compares it to "The Three Ravens," pronouncing "The Twa Corbies" shallow, cynical, and even gruesome; a few have suggested that the faithless lady has murdered her lover. However, other scholars have demonstrated that the PERSONIFICATION of the ravens makes this ballad more complex than a simple parody. Though scavengers, the ravens are polite and dignified. As a married couple, they are a success—the husband provides, the wife sweetly follows, and they work together to build a nest and raise their young— while the slain human is completely alone: His hound hunts without him, his falcon flies free, and his wife has "ta'en another mate" (l. 11). Whichever the case, the ballad poignantly demonstrates the fleeting quality of human life and human relationships.

See also BALLAD (FOLK BALLADS).

FURTHER READING
Wiatt, William H. "'The Twa Corbies' Again." *Keystone Folklore Quarterly* (1965): 116–126.

U

UBI SUNT   *Ubi sunt* was a common poetic motif employed in the Middle Ages. The term derives from the Latin phrase *Ubi sunt qui ante nos fuerunt* (Where are the ones who came before us?) and evokes a sense of loss, longing, and nostalgia. Poems utilizing the theme often lament the transience of youth, beauty, and life.

In commenting on the brevity of human existence, the *ubi sunt* theme is somewhat related to the CARPE DIEM (seize the day) topos popularized by the classical poet Horace. However, the *ubi sunt* motif does not urge the audience to embrace worldly pleasures; instead, it cautions the reader or listener to prepare for the inevitable loss of these pleasures. One of the distinguishing features of the *ubi sunt* theme is its melancholic tone, which longs for the "good old days" that will never come again; the present can never measure up to the glories of the past due to the poet's or speaker's circumstances.

One of the best-known Old English examples of the *ubi sunt* motif is "The WANDERER," in which a solitary exile questions where the former joys of his life have gone. The answer, of course, which serves as a memento mori, a remembrance of death, is that they are dead and gone, as we all shall be someday. The MIDDLE SCOTS poem, *The TESTAMENT OF CRESSEID* by ROBERT HENRYSON, provides a later example of this motif, which is also found in many MIDDLE ENGLISH LYRICS AND BALLADS.

See also CONTEMPT FOR THE WORLD.

Clinton Atchley and Michelle M. Sauer

"URIEN OF YRECHWYDD" TALIESIN (sixth century)   This poem, contained in the *Book of Taliesin*, is one of the oldest poems in Welsh. It is attributed to the poet TALIESIN, who was active at the end of the sixth century. The poem itself is a tribute to Urien, king of Rheged (590 C.E.), one of Taliesin's patrons. Bards of kings in Celtic and Germanic medieval societies were expected to praise their lords in order to publicize their fame within the community as well as to other neighboring tribes and enemies; the poems and songs also preserved their memory into future generations. Urien is described as a generous Christian man whom many poets rejoice and praise. A paramount leader and ruler by whom the Lloegrians have suffered defeat, he is Rheged's defender and a great battle-lord, one that Yrechwydd can be proud of. Because of this poem, his reputation will live on.

See also POETS OF THE PRINCES.

FURTHER READING
Evans, Stephen S. *The Heroic Poetry of Dark-Age Britain: An Introduction to its Dating, Composition, and use as a Historical Source*. Lanham, Md.: University Press of America, 1997.

Bradford Lee Eden

V

VENUS AND ADONIS WILLIAM SHAKESPEARE

(ca. 1592)   The lengthy narrative poem *Venus and Adonis* begins with the goddess's supplications to Adonis to grant her amorous desires; however, Venus's entreaties soon turn to frustration and questions regarding his masculinity. The two then engage in a rhetorical discourse on love, and after a great deal of pleading, Adonis grants Venus a farewell kiss that inflames her passion. Her desire quickly turns to fears for his safety when she learns that he plans to hunt boar the next day. Adonis ignores her suggestion to pursue tamer beasts such as the hare. The next day, hearing the furious baying of the hounds, Venus runs out to discover Adonis's lifeless, bloody body. She laments his death but soon observes his body "melt" and marvels that from his blood, "A purple flow'r sprung up, check'red with white" (l. 1168). Plucking the flower and wearing it near her heart to observe her lover's memory, Venus then departs dejectedly for her home in Paphos.

Venus and Adonis is an Ovidian mythological love poem, a style popular in Elizabethan England and well known by WILLIAM SHAKESPEARE and Henry Wriothesley, earl of Southhampton, Shakespeare's patron to whom the poem is dedicated. It is written in six-line verse STANZAs rhyming *ababcc*. Several other Tudor poets wrote versions of the Venus and Adonis story. Thomas Lodge completed *Scilla's Metamorphosis, Interlaced with the Unfortunate Love of Glaucus* (1589), a work that comments briefly on the love between Venus

and Adonis but centers on a maiden's courtship of a reluctant young man. In *The FAERIE QUEENE,* EDMUND SPENSER also briefly treats the legend of Venus and Adonis. Scholars continue to debate whether either or both of these influenced Shakespeare's poem. As well, some critics believe that Shakespeare read CHRISTOPHER MARLOWE's *HERO AND LEANDER* in draft form before its publication after Marlowe's death. Though not directly about the same subject, Marlowe's poem details the erotic love between the title characters and may have served as an inspiring model.

In 1593, Richard Field, son of a Stratford tanner and probably Shakespeare's friend, printed the first edition of *Venus and Adonis*. The Stationers' Register records the poem in April 1593, which means that it was probably composed sometime between August 1592 and April 1593, when the theaters were closed due to the plague. *Venus and Adonis* was the first poem Shakespeare published and one of the few he saw through the entire publication process, probably because of its dedication to a noble patron. It was quite popular in its own time and immediately thereafter, and by 1636, *Venus and Adonis* had gone through at least 20 editions.

Despite its contemporary popularity, *Venus and Adonis* was long overlooked critically. Like A *LOVER's COMPLAINT,* its place within the Shakespeare canon was often doubted based on its unique subject matter and verse form. However, most scholars now accept this poem as Shakespeare's, and its reputation has been rehabilitated. Indeed, it is now seen as a valuable glimpse into Shakespeare's early development as a poet.

Traditional critical interpretations of *Venus and Adonis* address Shakespeare's use of classical myth to depict Elizabethan thoughts about love, situate the context of the poem in relation to Shakespeare's efforts to secure noble PATRONAGE, or compare Shakespeare's poem to others of the same genre and era. Although modern scholars have not abandoned allegorical studies of *Venus and Adonis*—that is, its possible references to Queen Elizabeth—or its comparison to Shakespeare's other works, recent criticism has emphasized the *Venice and Adonis*'s highly stylistic verse and what it reveals about Shakespeare's culture during his formative years. Some recent studies have, for instance, emphasized the importance of hunting in *Venus and Adonis* in relation to the context of Elizabethan England. Other studies have explored ALLEGORY outside the political, concentrating primarily on the abundant bestial imagery and allusions to numerous animals. Though the narrative presents itself as a tragedy on the surface, some recent criticism has examined the comedic overtones of the narrative. Feminist and gender critics have also found rich subject matter within this poem, especially in examining Venus's aggressive pursuit of Adonis, who seems uninterested in pursuing an affair with the beautiful goddess of love and more interested in pursuing masculine activities within a homosocial environment, and who preferred death to sexual consummation. Contextually placed within the Shakespeare canon in this manner, it provides an important view of Shakespeare's initial perspectives on relations between the sexes.

See also OVID.

FURTHER READING

Bush, Douglas. *Mythology and the Renaissance Tradition*. New York: Norton, 1963.

Duncan-Jones, Katherine. "Playing Fields or Killing Fields: Shakespeare's Poems and Sonnets." *Shakespeare Quarterly* 54, no. 2 (2003): 127–141.

Kolin, Philip C. *Venus and Adonis: Critical Essays*. New York: Garland, 1997.

James N. Ortego II

VERNACULAR

Two senses of this term are relevant to literary studies. First, *vernacular* generally refers to a common manner of speaking and the natural and informal figures of speech that people use in their local, everyday lives. In this sense, the term is usually employed in direct contrast to formal, polysyllabic forms of expression, sometimes for comic effect.

The other sense of vernacular refers to differences between languages and is best represented by comparing Latin and other languages. When Latin began fading after the collapse of the Roman Empire, it grew into new local languages: Italian, Catalan, Spanish, Portuguese, French, Provençal, and Romanian. From this, the term *vernacular* broadened to include "any language that is not Latin"—but it also has connotations of folk and popular culture.

This last point is important because most vernacular languages held little or no authority or prestige during the early Middle Ages (from the fifth through the 11th centuries). Despite Latin being a "dead" language, it continued to be the only one taught in schools and was used as the official international language of church, state, law, and history throughout Europe. Occasionally, a monarch or educational reformer might try to encourage the use of a vernacular language. ALFRED THE GREAT, for example, himself translated many Latin works into Old English in the second half of the ninth century. But Latin's supreme authority as a written language did not become questioned in a widespread way until the 14th century, when a number of political and intellectual changes, quickened by the upward social mobility available to survivors of the BLACK DEATH, caused people to assert their vernacular language at Latin's expense. One of the strongest allies in the rise of vernacular languages was religious reform. The Protestant Reformation in the early 1500s involved a mistrust of a Bible that very few people (including, more and more often, priests themselves) could read accurately.

See also CHAUCER, GEOFFREY.

FURTHER READING

Bassnett, Susan. *Translation Studies*. New York: Routledge, 2002.

Clanchy, Michael T. *From Memory to Written Record: England 1066–1307*. Oxford: Blackwell Press, 1993

Fred Porcheddu

VIRELAI (VIRELAY)

The virelai is a fixed verse form established by the 14th century in French poetry, and often set to music. The poem begins with the REFRAIN, followed by three STANZAS, with the refrain occurring between each stanza and at the end. Each stanza also has three sections: Sections one and two share the same rhyme (and music), and section three shares its rhyme sound with the refrain. The structure is similar to other fixed forms such as the CAROL(E), BALLADE, and cantiga (monomorphic song). Among those English poets influenced by the pattern was SIR THOMAS WYATT.

FURTHER READING

Françon, Marcel. "On the Nature of the Virelai." *Symposium* 9 (1955): 348–352.

Carol E. Harding

VIRGIL (PUBLIUS VIRGILIUS MARO) (70 B.C.E.–19 B.C.E.)

Virgil was born on October 25, 70 B.C.E. into a wealthy farming family. He was an adept student. Although he leaned towards medicine and mathematics at first, his pursuit of rhetoric, Greek, and literary arts led him to the Academy of Epidius in Rome, ca. 54 B.C.E., where he studied law. While there, he became friends with a classmate, Octavian, later Emperor Augustus and Virgil's patron (see PATRONAGE). Virgil graduated and practiced law, but he soon gave that up in pursuit of philosophy. Civil disturbances led him to flee Rome in 49 B.C.E. Arriving in Naples, Virgil continued his studies and began writing poetry. He remained primarily in Naples for the remainder of his life, occasionally traveling to Rome or Greece. It was on one such trip, in 19 B.C.E., that he grew ill and died.

Contemporary accounts describe Virgil as intelligent, pleasant, friendly, and somewhat sickly. He never married. Many scholars believe he was predominantly same-sex oriented, as he frequently wrote about a relationship with a man named Alexander ("Alexis").

Virgil produced only three works: the *Eclogues* (sometimes called the *Bucolics*), the *Georgics,* and the *Aeneid.* Though Virgil was greatly admired during his lifetime, his influence on later poetry was tremendous.

He is directly referenced by Chaucer in numerous poems, including "THE HOUSE OF FAME," *The BOOK OF THE DUCHESS,* and *TROILUS AND CRISEYDE.* The *Aeneid,* translated fully by GAVIN DOUGLAS, immortalized Rome as an ideal of perfection, a theme that pervaded works ranging from ARTHURIAN LITERATURE to WILLIAM SHAKESPEARE's plays. A later partial translation by HENRY HOWARD, EARLY OF SURREY, led to the development of English BLANK VERSE. Virgil's work also directly inspired almost every poetic genre, especially the PASTORAL and the EPIC. EDMUND SPENSER, for instance, cited him as a direct predecessor for *THE SHEPHEARDES CALDENDER.* It also became fashionable during the Tudor era to write in the style of his *Eclogues* in spite of their homosexual themes (see, for example, RICHARD BARNFIELD's *THE AFFECTIONATE SHEPHERD*).

See also ECLOGUE, TRANSLATION TRADITION.

FURTHER READING

Levi, Peter. *Virgil: His Life and Times.* New York: St. Martin's Press, 1999.

Reed, J. D. *Virgil's Gaze: Nation and Poetry in the Aeneid.* Princeton, N.J.: Princeton University Press, 2007.

VIRGIN LYRICS

Lyric is a broad term whose definition has changed over time. When modern readers encounter "lyric poetry," they tend to expect intense personal emotion. However, medieval lyrics are usually rather conventional and lack the individual voice of a personal speaker. As a result, critics are sometimes apologetic of the form. Lyrics to the Virgin are no exception.

Devotion to Mary was an extremely popular form of piety throughout the Middle Ages. Medieval legends and artwork demonstrate an interest in the life of Virgin; they create and draw upon the Apocrypha (noncanonical biblical texts) to fill in the blanks of the sparse Gospel narratives. However, the lyrics diverge from such legends in that they usually either describe biblical events from Mary's point of view or they praise and revere the Virgin as the mother of Christ, the mother of all humanity, the queen of heaven, and the second Eve, who redeems original sin and through whom all of humanity is redeemed. Many lyrics are anonymous, but we also find lyrics written by such illustrious writers as GEOFFREY CHAUCER and, later, JOHN LYDGATE.

There is some debate as to how much influence the Franciscan and Dominican orders had on the origins of lyrics to Mary. Some scholars suggest that the earliest lyrics were actually verse translations of basic Latin prayers, such as the "Ave Maria." Tropes such as the Joys and Sorrows of the Virgin have been traced back to the *Meditationes* of John of Fécamp (1078), and in the mid-12th century St. Godric composed his well-known lyrics to the Virgin, which at one time earned him the title of the "first English lyricist." In the 12th and 13th centuries, the Franciscans and Cistercians certainly contributed to the genre's popularity.

Virgin lyrics are found in Latin and the VERNACULAR, as well as a combination of both, often with the REFRAIN written in Latin. Some lyrics draw upon scriptural and liturgical themes and may have been used in homilies or sermons, while others, based on the manuscript's context, seem to have been used for contemplation and mystical purposes.

The imagery, allusions, and titles used in lyrics to describe Mary are remarkably conventional. They often draw from the natural world and from Old Testament biblical images that the Christian church reads as "prefigurations" of Mary and Christ's birth. For example, the Virgin is accompanied by or aligned with the dawn, a dove, a rose without thorns, a lily among thorns, a fountain, or a sealed door or garden. The lyric "Marye, mayde mylde and fre" is particularly rich in BIBLICAL ALLUSIONS, with Mary as the Burning Bush, as dew, and as other common prefigurations. The epithets most frequently used for the Virgin refer to her role as maid, mother, queen, or, at times, all of these at once.

Lyrics from the 12th and 13th centuries are marked by what has been called a "restrained" style. They seem didactic, fashioned to be used as guides for devotion. This period reflects an emphasis on Mary as merciful mediator. Audiences would have found in Mary a sympathetic mother to whom they could plead for intercession with her Son the Judge. Such lyrics will often feature legalistic imagery.

During this period, which saw an increase in affective (emotional) piety, we also find lyricists describing events such as the Crucifixion from Mary's perspective. Affective piety encouraged empathy in the believer and focused on Christ's manhood rather than his divinity.

Mary's point of view both allows the audience to witness divine events through human eyes and encourages identification between the audience member and Mary. These lyrics use homely and tender imagery, as in the lyric "Stond wel modor under rode."

In the 14th and 15th centuries, the lyrics take on courtly language, and they feature Mary as a ROMANCE heroine, where often sin is a disease and Mary is the physician. Indeed, the romance genre and the language of religious devotion influence one another so heavily that it is sometimes difficult to classify a particular lyric as secular (to a maiden) or religious (to Mary). "MAIDEN IN THE MOR LAY" and "I SING OF A MAIDEN" are two popular examples of such ambiguous lyrics. The 14th century also saw lyrics in which Mary is cast as a model of perfect courtesy: a meek, mild, and dutiful maiden to be imitated by medieval women.

The lyrics of the 15th century and later contrast the "restrained" style of the earlier works as they express devotion rather than instruct. These lyrics do not encourage identification with Mary as mother and maid but express admiration for Mary as queen of heaven. Rather than featuring the Nativity and Crucifixion as earthly narrative foci, these later lyrics describe Mary's heavenly Assumption and coronation. There is an aesthetic self-consciousness among these later lyrics, which are marked by an ornate, aureate style (see AUREATION). This is particularly true of those with named authors, as it was believed that the more elaborate the lyric, the more lavish the praise it would send to Mary.

While there seems to be great variation over time in this genre, lyrics to the Virgin are conventional enough that thematic categories can be established, including: the Annunciation, the Nativity, Mary at the foot of the Cross, the Assumption and Mary as Queen of Heaven, Mary Mediatrix and penitential poems, and Meditations of the Joys of Mary.

See also "CHERRY-TREE CAROL, THE"; "IN PRAISE OF MARY"; MIDDLE ENGLISH LYRICS AND BALLADS.

FURTHER READING

Dronke, Peter. *The Medieval Lyric*. 3rd ed. Suffolk: D.S. Brewer, 1996.

Saupe, Karen. *Middle English Marian Lyrics*. Kalamazoo: Medieval Institute Publications, Western Michigan University, 1998.

Whitehead, Christiania. "Middle English Religious Lyrics." In *A Companion to the Middle English Lyric,* edited by Thomas G. Duncan, 96–119. Woodbridge: Brewer, 2005.

Karolyn Kinane

VIRTUES

There are two sets of virtues that are important to medieval culture: the cardinal virtues, which are complemented by and often combined with the theological virtues; and the capital virtues, which stand in opposition to the SEVEN DEADLY SINS.

The four cardinal virtues—prudence/wisdom, temperance, justice, and fortitude/courage—are "natural" virtues that can be achieved through human effort. These virtues as specific concepts can be traced all the way back to Plato's *Republic,* but in the Middle Ages they were further developed by Christian theologians, particularly St. Thomas Aquinas, and associated with the three theological virtues—faith, hope, and charity—which can only be achieved through the intervention of Grace. According to Thomas Aquinas, Prudence, the faculty that helps determine what is best and how best to achieve it, arises from the intellect; it serves as a guide with respect to the other cardinal virtues. Justice represents the desire to provide both to God and to humans what is their due. Temperance helps the will control human instinct, moderating the attraction or temptation of pleasures. Fortitude, or courage, helps humans strengthen their resolve to resist temptation and to conquer fear.

The second set of medieval virtues, the capital virtues, are directly opposed to the seven deadly sins. Thus, in this list, humility stands opposite pride, liberality against avarice, fellowship versus envy, meekness in opposition to wrath, chastity in conflict with lust, temperance as counter to gluttony, and diligence against sloth. In the Middle Ages, the virtues and vices were common figures of ALLEGORY in such texts as the morality play *Everyman* and EDMUND SPENSER's *The FAERIE QUEENE.*

FURTHER READING

Houser, R. E., trans. *The Cardinal Virtues: Aquinas, Albert and Philip the Chancellor.* Toronto: Pontifical Institute of Mediaeval Studies, 2004.

Woodford, Archer. "Medieval Iconography of the Virtues: A Poetic Portraiture." *Speculum* 28, no. 3 (1953): 521–524.

Carol E. Harding

VISION OF PIERS PLOWMAN, THE

See *PIERS PLOWMAN.*

VOLTA

Volta means "turn" in a number of Italic languages, and in poetry the volta is the place where a distinct turn of thought occurs. A common characteristic of ITALIAN (PETRARCHAN) SONNETS, the volta in these usually occurs in line 9, between the OCTAVE and the SESTET, marking both the rhyme change and the move toward resolution. ENGLISH SONNETS often exhibit a volta as well, though it may occur between any quatrain.

"VULCAN BEGAT ME" SIR THOMAS WYATT (1557)

The answer to this translation by SIR THOMAS WYATT of a Latin riddle is handily provided in *TOTTEL'S MISCELLANY,* as it bears the legend "discripcion of a gonne [gun]." However, this poem is more than merely descriptive; it is also contemplative regarding the explosive nature of firearms—and of love.

The poem begins with the gun's parentage: Vulcan, the divine Roman blacksmith and god of fire, is named as the father, while Wyatt's pun on Mother Nature ("Nature my mother," l. 2) confirms maternity. However, interposing between the father and mother is the gun's tutor, Minerva, the Roman goddess of wisdom and war. Thus, the gun is crafted by the blacksmith out of natural materials and put to use not only by the user's knowledge of its handling but also by the context of warfare.

As with any infant, the amount of nutritional input is disproportionate to the waste output, and so the "Three bodies" which "are my food" (l. 3)—namely, the sulphur, charcoal, and saltpeter which together make gunpowder—produce four "children dear" of the weapon's own: "Slaughter, wrath, waste and noise" (l. 4). The reference to the gun's "strength" being "in nought" by extension must refer to the gaping mouth of the barrel, which consumes and produces the above. The introduction to this "infant" is followed by a question (ll. 5–6): Who would wish to be friends with a monster? The closing COUPLET answers this by giving the reader power: We may be either "friend," in which case "I may thee defend," or "enemy," whereby "I may thy life end" (l. 8).

Structurally, the poem is a Tuscan STRAMBOTTO (eight lines, rhyming *abababcc*), the brevity of which form greatly appealed to Wyatt, who used it often. The sing-song rhyme of the strambotto form lends itself to flippancy, as do riddles, yet here that lightheartedness sits alongside a sense of gravity which stems from the poem's reminding the reader of their own mortality: the choice between taking a life or losing one's own hangs in the balance of a couplet. Such a balance would have been a daily occurrence to Wyatt as a courtier in the scene of HENRY VIII, whose jealousy and temper were both easily provoked.

Critics have also noted that the early Tudor perception of women as potential adulterers is also evident in the poem's organization. As "Vulcan" noticeably precedes both the goddess "Minerva" and feminized "Nature," so masculinity symbolically precedes femininity in the poem, just as it did in actuality. Henry VIII's brutality in part stemmed from his desire for a male heir (or, rather, his disappointment at producing female heirs). From this perspective, the poem signifies success: the gun's voice is unmistakably male, as is its environment (the battlefield), and it produces "children dear" of its own. Ironically, this instrument of death produces life, which is a reproduction of itself, and therefore death. Life and death, represented by levity and gravity, do not exchange places so much as fuse into a unity that Wyatt declares inseparable.

FURTHER READING

Daalder, Joost, ed. *Sir Thomas Wyatt: Collected Poems.* Oxford: Oxford University Press, 1975.
Rebholz, R. A., ed. *Sir Thomas Wyatt: The Complete Poems.* Harmondsworth, U.K., and New York: Penguin, 1978.

William T. Rossiter

W

WACE (1115–1183) Most of what is known about Wace is drawn from information supplied in his poems. He was born on the island of Jersey, and he was taken as a boy to mainland Normandy. He claims to have studied for many years in the Ile de France, but circumstantial evidence suggests he was back in Normandy while still a young man. He was a *clerc lisant* (an ecclesiastical official with duties including writing and reading aloud) in Caen from the 1130s. It was here that he earned the title *Maistre,* a title he attaches to his name 10 times in his own work. Some time later, he was also made a canon of Bayeux by Henry II. Various attempts have been made to ascribe additional names to Wace, including Robert, Richard, and Matthieu, but these rest on little authority.

Wace is the author of five surviving ANGLO-NORMAN poems, two of which are very substantial in scale. His earliest known pieces are three devotional poems, including hagiographies of St. Margaret and St. Nicholas and a poem entitled *La Conception Notre Dame.* These were followed by his best-remembered poem, *ROMAN DE BRUT* (1155), which was the first major translation of the Arthurian legends into French verse, and which had a strong influence on Arthurian ROMANCE for nearly two centuries. Nearly 15,000 lines long, it is notable for introducing many new features to ARTHURIAN LITERATURE.

Around 1160, Wace began work on a chronicle of the dukes of Normandy, entitled *Le Roman de Rou.* He continued to work on this poem until the mid-1170s, when he abandoned it. While the *Roman de Brut* has remained popular to this day, the ambitious *Roman de Rou* began to lose a wide readership relatively early. Nevertheless, Wace's innovative narrative style focusing on dramatic scenes and limited psychological realism were very influential, particularly among French authors of romance.

See also HAGIOGRAPHY.

FURTHER READING
Le Saux, Francoise H. M. *A Companion to Wace.* Cambridge: D.S. Brewer, 2005.

J. D. Ballam

WALLACE, THE BLIND HARY (ca. 1475) The beginning of *The Wallace,* composed in MIDDLE SCOTS by BLIND HARY around 1475, introduces an exclusivist nationalistic discourse in which the English are represented as the traditional enemy of Scotland. Blind Hary reflects the contemporary political situation at a time when James III was interested in securing alliances with England to strengthen his position with other powerful noble rulers. He stirs nationalistic blood with a reminder that the Scots will honor their "ald enemy," those of Saxon blood (the English), and that God is punishing them for their pride by making "thar mycht to par" ("power diminish," l. 14). It is as much a reaffirmation of Scottish independence as a manifesto against the English. Blind Hary bases his argument on the Scottish experience in the Wars of Independence

(1296–1328 and 1332–57) and applies it to the time in which he was writing. The past serves to explain the present. WILLIAM WALLACE becomes the voice of Scottish nationalism through his combativeness and hatred for the English.

From the very beginning, Hary merges the protagonist's thirst for revenge with the national cause. Wallace is represented as a tragic hero who endures the loss of most members of his family at the hands of the English. His personal sorrow is equated with his suffering for Scotland (ll. 181–184). The personal and the national will form an inseparable goal in the hero's mind. From then on, his words and his behaviour do not correspond to that of a youthful warrior but to that of an experienced leader, an indispensable requisite to lead his nation against Edward I. Wallace's nonnaturalistic representation is closer to HAGIOGRAPHY than to a ROMANCE hero.

Wallace's knightly deeds are dependent on the national cause as well. The main reason to fight is personal vendettas, yet, this is integrated within Scotland's struggle for freedom, which is an essential feature of Blind Hary's ideological discourse. In the battlefield, the Scottish leader is depicted as a very strong and revengeful knight. As in JOHN BARBOUR's *The Bruce* (ca. 1375), to which Blind Hary is indebted, the hero's personal ambitions are subservient to the national cause.

When treating female characters, Wallace's conduct is profoundly altered. In book 4, Wallace's lover betrays him after the English offer her a reward. Up to this point, the hero killed English enemies and Scottish traitors mercilessly—but he forgives his lover. Blind Hary creates a complete image of the protagonist not only during combat but also in social interchanges with ladies. Wallace dissociates the EPIC world of war from the courtly world of social relationships to emerge as the perfect romance hero.

Wallace's image is also reshaped along the lines of the European courtly tradition when he meets his future wife. Her description follows the conventions of COURTLY LOVE. At the same time, however, a reference to her Scottish origin accentuates the nationalistic dialectics once again (Book 5, ll. 604–609). When the English kill her, Wallace's revenge acquires political connotations. Not only does he avenge himself, but he also expels the English from Lanark in Lanarkshire. Blind Hary presents a lover's tragic story as a suitable tool for the liberation of Scotland. Even the most explicitly courtly scenes are integrated within the nationalistic literary project.

The employment of DREAM VISIONS and prophecies offers an allegorical framework. Wallace's personal quest after revenge dilutes within the collective defence of the country. His face-to-face combats and sporadic skirmishes are politically and allegorically redefined in the milieu of Scotland's fight for freedom. God himself supports and approves of Wallace's bloodthirsty way of action, which elevates the Wars of Independence to the realm of ALLEGORY—so much so that when Wallace is thought to be dead (Book 2, l. 252) and his body is washed (Book 2, l. 267), biblical typology is inescapable. Blind Hary imagines his hero as a Christ-like figure with his passion and resurrection. William Wallace the man dies, and the legendary liberator of Scotland is born. Christological symbolism relocates the narrative in the domain of religious iconography.

Blind Hary structures the allegorical pattern of the text according to his nationalistic beliefs. The pseudo-mythical figure of Thomas of Erceldoune tells the audience that Wallace is the elect to liberate Scotland when he was believed to be dead (Book 2, ll. 346–350). The Scottish authority of Thomas supplants the customary classical *auctoritas* (authorities) of the past. After this, it is Saint Andrew, the patron saint of Scotland, who confirms his role as a national leader in book 7. The holy figure also takes the warrior to the presence of the Virgin Mary, who explicitly designates him as her chosen one (Book 7, ll. 95–97). While the intervention of Saint Andrew synthesizes political issues and allegorical significance, Mary elevates Wallace's mission to the domain of ANAGOGY. As a Christ-like incarnation, his quest to set his country free will typologically bring to the audience's mind Jesus Christ's sacrificial death to save humankind to the extent that the protagonist's death follows the pattern of hagiographies and the passion of Christ.

In Book 12, when Wallace goes back to Scotland, the arch Scottish traitor Sir John Menteth, like Judas, sells him to the English. Blind Hary refuses to relate the knight's torture, stating merely that Wallace's end was "displesans" [distressing], so he would not relate it. The dramatic effect of this rhetorical device is successful: The audience is left to imagine the brutality of the English actions. Yet the sense of sadness and defeat will suddenly change. Mimicking the structural disposition of saints' legends, Wallace's death is reconstructed as a joyful tribute to his accomplishments. Torture and death precede the hero's real victory in the other world, culminating with his entrance in heaven (Book 12, ll. 1285–1288).

FURTHER READING

Goldstein, R. J. *The Matter of Scotland.* Lincoln and London: University of Nebraska Press, 1993.

Jack, R. D. S. "Discoursing at Cross Purposes. *Braveheart* and *The Wallace.*" In *Renaissance Humanism—Modern Humanisms,* edited by W. Göbel and B. Ross, 41–54. Heidelberg: Universitätsverlag, 2001.

Walsh, Elizabeth. "Hary's *Wallace*: The Evolution of a Hero." *Scottish Literary Journal* 11, no. 1 (1984): 5–19.

Sergi Mainer

WALLACE, WILLIAM (ca. 1270–1305) William Wallace was the most important early patriot in the fight for Scottish independence, and was immortalized in the 15th century poem The WALLACE. The first record of William Wallace appears in May 1297, where he is listed as killing William Heselrig, the English sheriff of Lanark (Lanarkshire), an episode that sparked the Rebellion of 1297. Wallace and his followers raided far and wide, attacking the English on sight. On September 11, 1297, Wallace engaged the British army at the Battle of Stirling Bridge, winning a great victory. He then spent the winter raiding across the border in Northumbria.

In 1298 the English king Edward I returned from war in France to personally lead an invasion of Scotland. On July 22, 1298 at the Battle of Falkirk, the British heavy cavalry and archers devastated Wallace's ranks of schiltroms (spearmen). Wallace survived with only a small contingent. The following year he went to France seeking aid from Philip IV, but instead he endured captivity. Upon his release in 1303, Wallace returned to Scotland and resumed raiding.

William Wallace was finally captured in or near Glasgow on August 3, 1305. He was tried three weeks later in London and found guilty of treason. Wallace received the traditional sentence: He was drawn, hanged, and quartered, with portions of his body sent to Newcastle, Berwick, Stirling, and Perth. He immediately became a national hero, a reputation sealed by Blind Hary's poem.

See also BLIND HARY, ROBERT I THE BRUCE.

FURTHER READING

Fisher, Andrew. *William Wallace.* Edinburgh: John Donald, 1986.

Gray, D. J. *William Wallace: The King's Enemy.* London: Robert Hale, 1991.

Mackay, James. *William Wallace: Braveheart.* Edinburgh: Mainstream, 1995.

Mark DiCicco

"WANDERER, THE" ANONYMOUS (before 1072) "The Wanderer" is recorded on folios 76b–78a of the EXETER BOOK and consists of 115 lines of Old English alliterative verse. It is generally considered an ELEGY, as it focuses on the wanderer's sadness and loneliness as well as his mourning of a lost life or, in this case, a lost way of life.

The poem tells the story of a former warrior, called an *eardstapa* (wanderer), who has lost his lord and comrades—no longer part of the COMITATUS—and is now wandering alone. In vain, he tried to find comfort in another lord. The wanderer, who achieved a form of stoic wisdom after his many years of loneliness, first describes the feeling of his solitary journey, only to mourn the transitory nature of the world and humans. Ultimately, he concludes, everything is destined to decay except for the heavenly kingdom, humanity's only hope of eternal shelter, in which security stands.

The poem can roughly be divided into two parts. One part describes the fate of a solitary wanderer, first focusing on this wanderer's personal experience and then moving to a general statement concerning all lonely wanderers. The second part depicts humanity's entire existence. This deep concern with the fundamentals of human existence and experience is a typical feature of wisdom literature with which the second half of the poem is often associated.

The poem begins with a generalization of a wanderer's situation, reflecting the speaker's own circumstances; this continues until he speaks for the first time.

He tells of the sorrow he has to endure due to his solitary state, though he keeps his sad thoughts inside. Lines 19–29a give the wanderer's personal history. Since he lost his friends and his lord a long time ago, he tried to seek another lord.

The text continues with a description of the experiences of all lonely voyagers. Realizing his loss, the wanderer recalls all the joys that have vanished. He falls asleep and dreams of the times when he was still in the service of his lord, but awakens to the realization that only sea birds keep him company. At this point the wanderer expands the theme to the whole of existence. Some scholars argue that with the change of subject, a new speaker is introduced. Since the poem shifts into the area of wisdom literature, it is often assumed that the following passage is spoken by an anonymous wise man. Apart from the change of tone, the reappearance of the personal pronoun *I* is the only piece of evidence to support this assumption.

The speaker goes on to define a wise person, but he does so through the negative—that is, listing what a wise one's characteristics should *not* be. The wanderer next speaks about the destruction of human artifacts, recalling the style found in *The RUIN*. Some scholars suggest this passage refers to doomsday, but the non-Christian motifs, such as the Beasts of Battle who carry away the nobles, indicate otherwise. The next speech starts with an UBI SUNT motif, asking where past joys have gone. The speaker reminds the audience that nature will endure while human-made creations fall; only the person who seeks the grace of God will find security. The second part of the poem implies a strong contrast between this world and the heavenly kingdom.

One of the major concerns of past scholarship has been the number of speakers. It is now generally accepted, though not unchallenged, that the first seven lines of the poem serve as an introduction. The wanderer's monologue would therefore begin in line 8 with the first mention of the personal pronoun ic [I]. A second monologue begins in line 92, after the introduction of one who has "thought wisely." Whether this is a new speech or a speech within the speech of the wanderer, who might have become a wise man himself, is still subject to debate. The end of the speeches is in line 110, followed by a conclusion that sees the heavenly kingdom as the only place of security. Another possibility is to see the whole poem as the wanderer's monologue.

A great deal of scholarship has considered the question of religion in connection with "The Wanderer." The poem shows elements of both the Christian and non-Christian. The lord-retainer relationship, especially in the dream sequence, and elements such as the Beasts of Battle are typical features of Germanic poetry. Yet many of the stylistic elements give the poem a Christian tone. Passages like the one in which the poet states that wisdom comes with years of experience are reminiscent of homiletic works (e.g., ll. 64–72). So does the *ubi sunt* motif, which is widely used in homilies. Many scholars conclude that "The Wanderer," like BEOWULF or *The BATTLE OF MALDON*, is a blend of Germanic and Christian elements.

Due to the poem's theme, scholars often associated it with the works of BOETHIUS. The poet's descriptions of the decaying world and the hardship that humans have to endure are typical elements of a Boethian poem, as is the confidence that God will lead everyone to a good end.

"The Wanderer" is often related to the poem "The SEAFARER," with which it has several features in common. Like "The Wanderer," "The Seafarer" is divided into two main parts. One refers to the life of the speaker, in this case the seafarer, and the other refers to life in general. The decay of the world of men as well as the search for bliss and joy in God are also themes of that poem. Thus, similar to "The Wanderer," the poem's second part is to be regarded as a part of the genre of wisdom literature. It is these aspects that make both these poems into typical representatives of the elegy genre.

FURTHER READING

Beaston, Lawrence. "The Wanderer's Courage." *Neophilologus* 89, no. 1 (2005): 119–137.

Cross, J. E. "On the Genre of *The Wanderer*." *Neophilologus* 45 (1961): 63–75.

Dunning, Thomas P., and Alan J. Bliss, eds. *The Wanderer*. London: Methuen, 1969.

Fowler, Roger. "A Theme in *The Wanderer*." *Medium Aevum* 36 (1967): 1–14.

Leslie, Roy F., ed. *The Wanderer*. Manchester, U.K.: Manchester University Press, 1966.

Prins, A. A. "The Wanderer and The Seafarer." Neophilologus 48 (1964): 237–251.

Torben R. Gebhardt

"WAR-BAND'S RETURN, THE" TALIESIN (sixth century)

This poem, contained in the *Book of Taliesin*, is one of the oldest poems in Welsh. It is attributed to the poet TALIESIN, who was active at the end of the sixth century and was chief bard in the courts of at least three Welsh princes of that time period. While the manuscript itself is from the 14th century, it is generally assumed that the poems were orally transmitted through generations of bards to a monk of Glamorgan and are thus authentic.

The poem itself is a reflection by the poet about what would happen if his patron, Urien, did not return from battle. The poem not only praises Urien's heroism but also comments on the importance of the poet and the king in society. He further contemplates the possible loss of a way of life and exile. Urien was king of Rheged, a northern Welsh kingdom, at the end of the sixth century. Bards of kings in Celtic and Germanic medieval societies were expected to praise their lords and, if he was killed in battle, eulogize him as well. In performing this duty, the bard was an essential part of the COMITATUS (warband) structure, able to publicize the honor and shame of warriors in battle, thus bringing fame or disgrace to one's family and community. Bards were often killed during battles along with their patron, but if they did survive, their preservation of the battle in poetry was highly regarded and transmitted orally for generations.

FURTHER READING

Evans, Stephen S. *The Heroic Poetry of Dark-Age Britain: An Introduction to its Dating, Composition, and Use as a Historical Source.* Lanham, Md.: University Press of America, 1997.

Bradford Lee Eden

WARS OF THE ROSES (1455–1485)

The Wars of the Roses comprised a series of conflicts and battles in England between two branches of the English royal family—the House of Lancaster and the House of York—and refers to the heraldic symbols associated with Lancaster (red rose) and York (white rose). Both houses asserted competing claims to the English throne.

The king in 1455, Henry VI, was ineffective, perhaps mentally challenged, and subject to months-long fits of insanity. Henry was a Lancastrian, but during his incapacity, the duke of York ruled as protector of England. This instability helped create an opening for the first battle of the wars, on the streets of St. Albans in 1455. Though the victorious Yorkists professed loyalty to the king, the queen, Margaret of Anjou, was not convinced, and to protect her young son's right of succession, she gathered her own troops and munitions. A few years later, the Yorkists defeated the king's loyalists at Northampton in 1460, and Henry VI returned to London a virtual prisoner. Parliament recognized the duke of York as Henry's heir, thus dispossessing Henry and Margaret's son.

The following decade saw York killed in battle at Wakefield, and the Lancastrians also won at the Second Battle of St. Albans. However, the duke of York's son was proclaimed King Edward IV in London, and before his coronation in June 1461, the Yorkists won a decisive victory at Towton, while Henry VI fled to the protection of the Scots.

Edward and his ally, the earl of Warwick (known in later centuries as Warwick the Kingmaker), soon disagreed over alliances with Burgundy versus France, and over Edward's secret marriage to Elizabeth Woodville. Warwick attempted to raise a rebellion with the help of the king's brother George, duke of Clarence. When the rebellion failed, Warwick and Clarence escaped to France. During his exile, Warwick secured a rapprochement with his onetime enemy, Queen Margaret. By autumn 1470, Warwick had invaded England, and this time it was Edward who fled, to Burgundy. Edward's departure ushered in the brief "Readeption" of Henry VI as king. But this was not to last: Edward returned to England in early 1471, winning at the Battle of Barnet, where Warwick was killed, and at Tewkesbury, where Margaret was defeated and her son killed. Henry VI, who had fled the capital, now returned to his last confinement in the TOWER OF LONDON and, in short order, his murder.

After Tewkesbury, Edward IV enjoyed over a decade of rule, but in 1483 he died following a brief illness (perhaps appendicitis). He was succeeded by his brother Richard, duke of Gloucester, who took the throne as Richard III. Richard ruled only two years before dying in battle against another claimant to the throne, Henry Tudor, a Lancastrian offshoot, at Bosworth in 1485. Upon ascending the throne as HENRY VII, he married Elizabeth of York, thus uniting the two houses.

Many poems and BALLADS are associated with the Wars of the Roses, some written during the period. Printed anthologies of such medieval ballads appear as early as 1612. Sixteenth-century poems about the Wars of the Roses appear in *A MIRROR FOR MAGISTRATES* (1559), with 18 tragedies in verse (for example, poems on Henry VI and the earl of Warwick, and a long entry on Anthony Woodville, Queen Elizabeth Woodville's brother).

See also HUNDRED YEARS' WAR.

FURTHER READING

Chambers, E. K. *English Literature at the Close of the Middle Ages.* Oxford: Clarendon, 1964.

Ross, Charles. *The Wars of the Roses: A Concise History.* New York and London: Thames/Hudson, 1986.

Graham N. Drake

WEDDYNGE OF SIR GAWEN AND DAME RAGNELL, THE (THE WEDDYNG OF SYR GAWEN AND DAME RAGNELL FOR HELPYNG OF KYNG ARTHOURE)

ANONYMOUS (ca. 1450–1500) Out hunting, King ARTHUR encounters Sir Gromer Somer Joure, who claims that Arthur has wrongfully given his lands to Sir Gawain (Gawen). He presents Arthur with a challenge: In one year's time, Arthur must return, alone, and reveal "whate wemen love best." If he cannot complete this challenge, Arthur will lose his head. Arthur agrees to the terms.

At court in Carlisle, Arthur tells Sir Gawain, one of his knights, what has happened. Gawain proposes that together they seek out the answer to the question, so the two ride out, stopping everyone they see and recording in books the various answers they receive. The answers vary widely and include such things as "to be welle arayd" (well dressed) and "a lusty man" (a strong man). None of the answers satisfies Arthur, who rides out again in desperation. This time, he encounters an ugly lady, Dame Ragnell, whose hideousness, or "lothynesse" (loathliness) is described at length. She purports to have the answer to the question but will only give it to Arthur if she marries Gawain. Arthur agrees, somewhat unwillingly, to ask Gawain.

Gawain readily agrees to marry her. Arthur meets her once more in the forest, and she tells him the answer: Women desire to have sovereignty, or authority and rule, over men. Arthur then returns to Gromer Somer Joure and gives him all the answers he has received, including the correct one. Gromer Somer Joure is infuriated that Arthur has found the correct answer; however, he is forced to concede that Arthur is right. As Arthur leaves, Gromer Somer Joure curses Dame Ragnell, who, it emerges, is his sister.

Ragnell accompanies Arthur back to the court, where she meets Gawain, and the wedding preparations begin. Guinevere tries to persuade Ragnell to marry in private, but she insists on a public celebration. Gawain fulfils his duties without complaint until the wedding night arrives. In bed, Ragnell asks Gawain for a kiss, whereupon he responds, "I wolle do more!" However, when he turns to face her, he discovers a beautiful lady instead of an ugly hag. Gawain is surprised but delighted. Then Ragnell offers him a choice: She can be fair by night and foul by day or the other way around. Instead of choosing, Gawain gives the choice over to her. In doing so, he breaks the enchantment Ragnell had been under, which could be broken only by marrying "the best of Englond" and winning sovereignty over him. Now she will be beautiful all the time.

The next day, a concerned Arthur seeks out Gawain, and is told the delightful truth. Ragnell then promises Gawain that she will be obedient to him for the rest of her life, and Arthur forgives Gromer Somer Joure. Gawain and Ragnell have a son together, Gyngolyn, but their marriage lasts only five years before Ragnell's death. Gawain marries many more times but never loves as well again. The narrator of the tale ends by asking for God's help, since he is imprisoned.

The Weddynge of Sir Gawen and Dame Ragnell is a late 15th-century ROMANCE written in an East Midlands dialect of the MIDDLE ENGLISH LANGUAGE. Although no author is named in the text, Sir Thomas Malory has been suggested as a possibility, partly on the basis of the poem's final references to imprisonment. It is composed in TAIL-RHYME STANZAs of six lines each, rhyming *aabccb,* but this frequently breaks down, indicating that many lines are likely missing.

The *Weddynge of Sir Gawen and Dame Ragnell* belongs to a group of late medieval texts that feature the motif of a loathly lady transformed into a beautiful one. Its narrative is very close to that of GEOFFREY CHAUCER's "The WIFE OF BATH'S PROLOGUE AND TALE," JOHN GOWER's "Tale of Florent" in his *CONFESSIO AMANTIS,* and the fragmentary BALLAD "The Marriage of Sir Gawain." No common source is known. There are two main differences between the *Weddynge of Sir Gawen* and "The Wife of Bath's Tale." First, the Wife's Tale features an unnamed knight who is forced to answer the question and to unwillingly marry the hag as punishment for a rape, whereas in the *Weddynge of Sir Gawen,* the transgression is Arthur's, and it is Gawain who (willingly) marries. Second, Chaucer presents the choice as having the wife be fair and unfaithful or foul and humble, not fair by night and foul by day.

Early critical commentary on the *Weddynge of Sir Gawen* disparaged its poetic quality and lack of moral and aesthetic complexity and compared it unfavorably to its more famous analogues. However, there has been a growing appreciation of its humor and liveliness, including the grotesque descriptions of Ragnell and the comedy of Arthur and Gawain riding the land to collect in their books the answers. Some argue that it is intended to be read as a satiric response to or a comic imitation of other late romances (see SATIRE).

Other recent criticism has centred on the text's handling of noble values. The land dispute that precipitates the action of the poem seems to be a commentary on contemporary practices of land inheritance. The *Weddynge of Sir Gawen and Dame Ragnell* also gives prominence to the values of courtesy, beauty, and fidelity. It has been seen as weighing the importance of such values and, simultaneously, examining the ability of the noble world to live up to them. Gawain emerges as a man of exemplary honor and loyalty, treating Ragnell with respect and remaining true to his word.

FURTHER READING

Hahn, Thomas, ed. *Sir Gawain: Eleven Romances and Tales.* Kalamazoo, Michigan: TEAMS, Medieval Institute Publications, 1995.

Shepherd, Stephen H. A. "No poet has his travesty alone: *The Weddynge of Sir Gawain and Dame Ragnell.*" In *Romance Reading on the Book: Essays on Medieval Narrative presented to Maldwyn Mills,* edited by Jennifer Fellows, 112–128. Cardiff: University of Wales Press, 1996.

Sumner, Laura, ed. *The Weddynge of Sir Gawen and Dame Ragnell.* Folcroft, Pa.: The Folcroft Press, 1924.

Cathy Hume

WELSH WOMEN POETS Early Welsh female poets faced a number of obstacles. Welsh poetic techniques were dominated by strict-meter verse (fixed metrical pattern), but access to appropriate training and membership in the poets' guild was denied to women. Moreover, Welsh bardic law even forbade women to hear strict-meter poetry declaimed publicly in court.

How, then, did women in Wales acquire their knowledge of the strict meters? Three possible channels seem likely: reliance on oral transmission; the influence of a poetically inclined father or husband; and, to a lesser degree in this period, the support of poetic circles. Once the bardic guild began to decline, court entertainments were accessible for women. It is also likely that many learned their craft from their fathers or husbands, a pattern that echoes the strong hereditary vein of the poetic guild as a whole. For instance, the 12th-century poet Gwenllïan ferch Rhirid Flaidd (fl. 1460s) is believed to be the daughter of the poets Tudur Penllyn and Gwerful Fychan. Alis ferch Gruffudd ab Ieuan (b. 1500) was the daughter of Gruffudd ab Ieuan ap Llywelyn Fychan (1485–1553), a celebrated amateur poet. Elsbeth Fychan (fl. 1530?) was also the daughter of a gentleman amateur poet, Siôn ap Hywel ap Llywelyn Fychan (fl. 1500–30). Bardic circles may have helped, though evidence is scarce. Other women, such as Jane Fychan of Caer-gai (b. ca. 1590s), Catherin Owen (d. 1602), and Elin Thomas (d. 1609) were married to amateur poets.

Not confined by the bardic guild's rules, women poets were free to choose their own themes and experiment with conventions. For example, Marged Harri (fl.

1550s) adapted the *llatai* (animal messenger) poem to her own purpose—the animal carries not a love letter but rather a message to her friend, Siân Griffith (née Owain), with whom she had lost touch. Gwerful Mechain's (1460–1502) erotic poems subvert the tradition medieval love lyric tradition. Her "Cywydd y gont" (Cywydd of the Cunt), for instance, issues a challenge to the traditional BLAZON that avoids the most prized part of a woman's body, her genitalia: "leaving the middle without praise / and the place where children are conceived" (ll. 21–22). Similarly introspective, though religious in nature, are poems by Catrin ferch Gruffudd ap Hywel (fl. 1500–55) and Elsbeth Fychan that provide personal responses to the Reformation.

See also CYWYDD, POETS OF THE PRINCES AND POETS OF THE NOBILITY.

FURTHER READING

Lloyd-Morgan, Ceridwen. "Women and their Poetry in Medieval Wales." In *Women and Literature in Britain 1150–1500,* edited by Meale Carole, 183–201. Cambridge: Cambridge University Press, 1993.

Powell, Nia M. W. "Women and Strict-Metre Poetry in Wales." In *Women and Gender in Early Modern Wales,* edited by Michael Roberts and Clarke Simone, 129–158. Cardiff, 2000.

Cathryn A. Charnell-White

WERGILD

In pre-Christian Anglo-Saxon society, satisfaction for the killing or maiming of family members by outsiders was exacted either by pursuit of a feud, which always risked spiraling out of control and causing enormous social disruption, or by demanding the appropriate *wergild* (*wer* [man] + *gild* [payment of money]), a sliding scale of substantial monetary equivalents to be paid by the offending family. In the laws of the Anglo-Saxon king Ine (r. 688–726), the *wergild* for killing a *thegn* (thane, or nobleman) was 1,200 shillings, and for killing a freeman it was 200 shillings. The killing of a slave was uncompensated. Although the coming of Christianity modified the system somewhat, it remained in place until the 12th century.

Problems arose when the rules were violated. A famous example may be found in BEOWULF. In this EPIC, Grendel pursues a feud against Hrothgar but violates his responsibilities as a "hall-thegn" (l. 142) by refus-

ing to offer monetary compensation (*wergild*) for any of his killings (ll. 151–158). In contrast, Hrothgar had paid a heavy *wergild* to the Wylfingas to settle a feud Beowulf's father had instigated (ll. 459–472). Part of Beowulf's responsibility is to deal with Grendel as an asocial element who threatens social stability. Yet the system has its flaws as Hrethel, Beowulf's maternal grandfather, experiences when he has to forgo any *wergild* for the accidental killing of his son Herebeald, slain by his brother Hæthcyn (ll. 2435–2442).

FURTHER READING

Hill, John M. *The Cultural World in Beowulf.* Toronto: University of Toronto Press, 1995.

Shaun F. D. Hughes

"WHAT IS HE, THIS LORDLING, THAT COMETH FROM THE FYHT" WILLIAM HEREBERT (before 1333)

A poetic paraphrase by William Herebert (d. 1333) of Isaiah 63:1–7 ("Quis est iste qui venit de Edom?"), this poem is a liturgical reading for Wednesday of Holy Week written in the West Midlands dialect of Middle English. A Franciscan friar, Herebert composed some 20 lyrics from French and Latin sources and copied them into own miscellany book, which also contains sermons, recipes and medicinal cures.

"What is he . . ." is a poem of divine retribution. In Herebert's first quatrain, the speaker is a prophet, one of the "watchmen on the walls of Jerusalem" (Isa. 62:6), who sees the approach of the "lordling." The watcher challenges the stranger here and in two further lines; the balance of the poem is a voicing of the response.

That response is vividly heroic and sanguinary. The avenger's clothes are red—"mined" with blood: He has trampled men like grapes in a wine press. Calling himself the "champion to heal mankind in fight" (l. 6), his work is not only the spilling of blood but also the visitation of shame on the transgressors. His clothes are splattered with blood "to their great shame" (l. 13); he has "drowned them all in shame" (l. 23). Furthermore, the avenger has done this all alone with none to aid him. It was his strength alone that brought about this "remedy" ("bote," l. 18), and in its aftermath it is God's mercy ("mylsfolnesse," l. 20) he will rely on.

The poem relies on both translation and EXEGESIS: The unnamed avenger of the Old Testament is refigured as the blood-bespattered Christ. This Christ-as-warrior motif is a cognate with the Old English *The Dream of the Rood*.

See also MIDDLE ENGLISH LYRICS AND BALLADS.

FURTHER READING

Pezzini, Domenico. "Versions of Latin Hymns in Medieval England: William Herebert and the English Hymnal." *Mediaevistik* 4 (1991): 297–315.

Reimer, Stephen R. *The Works of William Herebert, OFM.* Toronto: Pontifical Institute of Mediaeval Studies, 1987.

Thomas H. Crofts

"WHAT IS OUR LIFE?" SIR WALTER RALEIGH (ca. 1590)

This little poem is a witty stringing together of a number of moral commonplaces, held together by the cliché of life as a "play of passion" or "jest" (ll. 1, 10). SIR WALTER RALEIGH uses theatrical metaphors that were probably drawn from his experience of the public theater at the time: "tyring houses" (l. 3), the backstage areas where the actors prepare for their entrance onto stage, for the womb; costumes for life's various roles; judgmental spectators for neighbors and courtiers; and, finally, the curtain as death. The final lines are typical of Raleigh in that they move from a witty exploration of a commonplace, even clichéd, metaphor to a solemn, plainly spoken moral that is impressive in the powerful directness of its short syllables and ironic final phrase: "Thus march we playing to our latest rest, / Onely we dye in earnest, that's no jest" (ll. 9–10).

FURTHER READING

Rudick, Michael. "The Text of Raleigh's Lyric, 'What is our Life?'" *Studies in Philology* 83, no. 1 (1986): 76–87.

Gary Waller

"WHEN I WAS FAIR AND YOUNG" ELIZABETH I (16th century)

This poem cannot be directly linked to a specific biographical incident. It does reflect, in a general way, on the problems of a queen whose private woman's body might want a relationship with someone she loves, but whose public queen's body knows that, if she marries, she must agree to a political alliance with a man who might want to take royal power from her. In reading the poem, it is important to realize that the word *mistress* (l. 2) did not mean an adulteress; rather, "mistress" was a polite way of addressing married and unmarried women. It was also a polite way in which a man could refer to the woman with whom he was in love whether or not their relationship was sexual.

The poem consists of three STANZAS, each of which has a rhyme scheme of *aabb*. In addition, the last line of each stanza is the same, and the third line of each rhymes with the last word of the fourth, *more*. In the first stanza, ELIZABETH I talks about how she behaved as a young woman when "favor graced" her (l. 1). As a result of both her beauty and her personality, or talents, "many" (l. 2) tried to make her their mistress. Her reaction was to "scorn them all" (l. 3), perhaps out of pride in her worldly status, perhaps out of pride in her beauty and accomplishments. She apparently said something like what appears in the last line of all three stanzas, "Go, go, go seek some otherwhere; importune me no more" (ll. 4, 8, 12), to those who claimed they loved her. She chases them away by telling them to look for a partner somewhere else—that is, not with her—and commands them not to "importune"—pray or beg—her anymore. This is probably not an unusual stance for a rich, titled, talented, attractive young woman—or man. A certain kind of self-esteem can often make such people proud and unwilling to believe that there is anyone good enough for them.

Elizabeth receives her comeuppance from someone more powerful: Cupid (or Eros), the son of Venus (or Aphrodite), the goddess of love. The "victorious boy" (l. 5), who always wins at love, calls the queen a "scornful dame" who is too "coy" (l. 6). His plan is to "wound her heart," most likely with his golden arrow of love, so she will "learn" (l. 7) what she has been telling her suitors: "Go, go, go seek some otherwhere; importune me no more" (l. 8). In this case, however, it is Cupid who tells the queen not to bother him; she must look somewhere else for help.

Early modern literature often showed love victorious in all encounters. This one is no different. In stanza 3, Elizabeth reveals the change that came about as a result of Cupid's intervention: She "felt straightway a change within [her] breast," or heart, (l. 9). This change resulted in her days being "unquiet," or disturbed, and her nights allowing her no "rest" (l. 10). Tension and turmoil in days and nights, especially the inability to sleep or the occurrence of bad dreams, were characteristics of love problems. Cupid has his revenge on Elizabeth by infecting her with lovesickness. She suffers so terribly from the disease that she now "sore [very much] repents" (l. 11) having ever said, "Go, go, go seek some otherwhere; importune me no more" (l. 12). Thus, the poem seems to say that the scornful attitude toward love of the young Elizabeth was regretted as the queen grew older. It suggests that, on a personal level at least, the queen may have regretted living her private woman's life as a mirror of her public ruler's life as the "Virgin Queen." This powerful woman ruler may not have been threatened by a husband-consort who might think that he, as a man, could rule better than she could. Unfortunately, though, the private woman is left without the companionship of a loving life partner.

FURTHER READING

Elizabeth I. *Elizabeth I. Collected Works*. Edited by Leah S. Marcus, Janel Mueller, and Mary Beth Rise. Chicago and London: University of Chicago Press, 2000.

Hopkins, Lisa. *Writing Renaissance Queens: Texts by and about Elizabeth I and Mary, Queen of Scots*. Newark: University of Delaware Press, and London: Associated University Presses, 2002.

Marcus, Leah S. "Queen Elizabeth I as Public and Private Poet: Notes toward a New Edition." In *Reading Monarch's Writing: The Poetry of Henry VIII, Mary Stuart, Elizabeth I, and James VI/I*, edited by Peter C. Herman, 135–153. Tempe: Arizona Center for Medieval and Renaissance Studies, 2002.

Theodora A. Jankowski

"WHEN TO HER LUTE CORINNA SINGS" THOMAS CAMPION (ca. 1601)

This song was first printed with music by THOMAS CAMPION himself in *A BOOKE OF AYRES*. It describes the poet's lover, Corinna, singing "to her lute," a phrase that implies that she sings while accompanying herself and that she addresses her lute when she sings. The first STANZA asserts that Corinna's singing is powerful enough to revive the lute's "leaden stringes" (l. 2), punningly referring to the inanimate material of the strings while ascribing to the sing-

er's voice an enlivening and invigorating influence. This sense of the power of music is extended by the poet's assertion that when Corinna sings of mourning, the "strings do breake" (l. 3) in a sympathetic reaction to the song's gloomy subject matter.

The second stanza makes explicit the implied comparison between lute and poet, who also responds to the emotional expressiveness of Corinna's singing. The poet's heart, for instance, has "strings," just like the lute. There is also a sense of sexual suggestiveness in the second stanza. The "sodaine spring" (l. 10) of the poet's thoughts in response to a song of "pleasure" (l. 9) hints at sexual arousal, as does the assertion that Corinna's "passion" (l. 8) dictates whether the poet will "live or die" (l. 7). This last line puns on the concept of *la petit morte*, or death as sexual ecstasy. The poem testifies to the power that Corinna has over the poet's feelings by comparing it to music's power over the emotions of its listeners, an effect enhanced by Campion's musical setting of these lyrics.

FURTHER READING

Lindley, David. *Thomas Campion*. Leiden: E.J. Brill, 1986.

Susan L. Anderson

"WHEN WINDSOR WALLS" HENRY HOWARD, EARL OF SURREY (ca. 1537)

The uncertainty of the date for this poem, first published in *TOTTEL'S MISCELLANY* in 1557, is mitigated by clues it provides that correspond with incidents in the life of HENRY HOWARD, EARL OF SURREY. Two incidents particularly resonate within the emotional and geographical terrain offered in the poem. The first involves the 1536 death of Surrey's close friend, the duke of Richmond, also known as Henry Fitzroy, the illegitimate son of HENRY VIII who had been married to Surrey's sister. The second centers on Surrey's 1537 imprisonment in Windsor Castle for assaulting a powerful courtier in the proximity of Henry VIII. Such an assault threatened punishments: both the confiscation of the 21-year-old's extensive lands and goods, and, since the attack theoretically endangered the king, the loss of Surrey's right hand. While neither punishment transpired, Surrey was eventually beheaded by the king at the age of 30.

Surrey devised the SONNET form that came to be known as the ENGLISH SONNET. Here, however, instead of offering a poem with three quatrains and final COUPLET, he retains the ITALIAN (PETRARCHAN) SONNET model that SIR THOMAS WYATT had popularized in England, providing an OCTAVE, a VOLTA, and a SESTET. Surrey's second major innovation in the history of the sonnet, rather than simply structural, hinges on the subject matter he selects for this poem. Contrary to the poetic displays of VIRGIL, Dante, PETRARCH, GEOFFREY CHAUCER, and Wyatt, who generally wrote about unattainable women, Surrey here laments the loss of a man.

The poem itself serves as a meditation on this loss and demonstrates the speaker's wrestling with resultant suicidal impulses. Its first image is that of a "restless" (l. 2) head being held up by a hand—and, by extension, by the walls themselves—that enables the speaker to survey the unfolding of the spring season in a determinedly realistic setting: Blossoms flourish, the grass turns green again, "wedded" (l. 5) birds frolic. The CAESURA in line 6, the full pause midway through the line, compares this vitality with the speaker's reverie over a former companion—the "jolly woes" and the "hateless short debate" (l. 7) they shared, and the "rakehell [unconsidered] life" (l. 8) that belongs to the ease of love. But with those thoughts comes debilitating nostalgia; with the word *Wherewith,* the first of line 7, Surrey offers his volta, after which the speaker is overcome by a "heavy charge of care [sorrow] / Heaped in [his] breast" (ll. 9–10), a sorrow that forces itself from him in the form of "smoky sighs" (l. 11) that billow in the air. Such sighs cloud his eyes, distilling tears that, falling, startle into springs beneath him, and the poem concludes with the speaker "half bent" (l. 14).

FURTHER READING

Jones, Emrys, ed. *Henry Howard Earl of Surrey: Poems.* Oxford: Clarendon Press, 1970.

Sessions, William A. *Henry Howard, Earl of Surrey.* Boston: Twayne Publishers, 1986.

———. *Henry Howard, the Poet Earl of Surrey: A Life.* Oxford: Oxford University Press, 1999.

David Houston Wood

WHITNEY, ISABELLA (fl. 1567–1573)

Though Isabella Whitney is considered the first professional female poet in England, very little is known of her life.

Her brother, Geoffrey Whitney, was a well-known EMBLEM author who lived in London, and she probably had at least three other siblings. She was probably born in Cheshire in the 1540s and may have traveled to London to work as a servant for an aristocratic family.

Whitney was a pioneer in many respects: She was a lower-class woman who published secular verses addressing issues of gender, sexuality, and women's liberation. The London publisher Richard Jones printed her set of verse epistles, *The Copy of a Letter, Lately Written in Meter by a Young Gentlewoman: To Her Unconstant Lover* (1567), as well as *A Sweet Nosegay or Pleasant Posy: Containing a Hundred and Ten Philosophical Flowers* (1573).

See also "ADMONITION, BY THE AUTHOR," THE; "I. W. TO HER UNCONSTANT LOVER"; "WILL AND TESTAMENT"; TUDOR WOMEN POETS.

FURTHER READING

Ellinghausen, Laurie. "Literary Property and the Single Woman in Isabella Whitney's *A Sweet Nosegay.*" *SEL, 1500–1900* 45, no. 1 (2005): 1–22.

Marquis, Paul A. "Oppositional Ideologies of Gender in Isabella Whitney's Copy of a Letter." *Modern Language Review* 90, no. 2 (1995): 314–324.

Wall, Wendy. "Isabella Whitney and the Female Legacy." *ELH* 58, no. 1 (1991): 35–62.

WHOLE BOOK OF PSALMS COLLECTED INTO ENGLISH METER, THE ("STERNHOLD AND HOPKINS") (1562)

The Whole Book of Psalms Collected into English Meter went through more than 500 editions by 1700. Sometimes called "Sternhold and Hopkins" after its first two contributors, Thomas Sternhold and John Hopkins, *The Whole Book* contains poems by at least seven others. Its main contents are the 150 biblical Psalms in English verse with tunes for singing, but also included are English versions of hymns and verse paraphrases of the Ten Commandments and the Lord's Prayer. Most of the poetry is in QUATRAINS of alternating eight- and six-syllable lines known as BALLAD meter or, when referring to hymns, common meter.

ROBERT CROWLEY was the first to translate the entire Book of Psalms, but *The Whole Book of Psalms*' longevity demonstrates its adaptability. When first published, the psalms were praised and imitated; during MARY I's reign, they were adapted by Protestant exiles; afterward, they were developed into a complete edition for the public. Scholars often cite *The Whole Book*'s significance to the literature and culture of the period and its place in the development of popular devotional materials.

See also SIDNEAIN PSALMS.

FURTHER READING

Hamlin, Hannibal. *Psalm Culture and Early Modern English Literature.* Cambridge: Cambridge University Press, 2004.

Leaver, Robin. *Goostly Psalmes and Spiritual Songes: English and Dutch Metrical Psalms from Coverdale to Utenhove 1535–1566.* Oxford: Oxford University Press, 1991.

Beth Quitslund

"WHO LIST HIS WEALTH AND EASE RETAIN" SIR THOMAS WYATT (1536)

This is one of SIR THOMAS WYATT's several poems expanding on the theme of the dangers of court life. The poem starts with two STANZAS asserting the perhaps counter-intuitive idea that greater safety and security—the "wealth" and "ease" of the first line—is found far from the throne. The important image in the second of these stanzas opposes the harsh weather of the high mountain peaks against the low, mild valleys where the worst storms cannot penetrate. Seen in this light, to be low is a considerably happier position, especially since the worst falls ("grievous") are from great heights (l. 9). This attitude is reminiscent of the traditional view of FORTUNE.

In the third stanza, the poem seems to turn explicitly autobiographical as the poet shows his regret at the time and effort he has spent for such capricious and temporary returns as one finds in courtly circles; his youth and lust have given way to sore regret. His experience proves that ambition and the will to "climb" ends only in a "revert," meaning eventual failure (l. 14).

The final two stanzas are more specific, referring to Wyatt's imprisonment in the TOWER OF LONDON (1536) and his firsthand view "out of a grate" (l. 18) of Anne Boleyn's execution. He moralizes on the sight, or on its memory, lamenting that there is no innocence, virtue, or knowledge that can help or secure those caught in the machinations of royal power. The final three lines

of the poem are extraordinarily sour, counseling the reader not to "prate" of innocence (l. 23) and to "bear low" (l. 24), essentially realizing that there is no way to avoid or resist monarchial power.

The recurring motif in each stanza is the three-word Latin phrase (from Seneca) *circa regna tonat,* which translates roughly as "he thunders around thrones." Combined with the heading of the poem, which situates Wyatt's name ("Viat") amongst "Innocentia" (innocence), "Veritas" (truth), and "Fides" (Faith), a connection to the theological VIRTUES, the phrase serves as a commentary on the rest of the poem, contrasting the earthly pleasures in the heading with the raw use of power indicated in the Latin motto.

Read alongside Wyatt's epistolary SATIRES (including "MINE OWN JOHN POINS") and with other verse translations such as "STAND WHOSO LIST," this poem provides a clear look into the mind of a man whose close identification with the royal court has led to disaffection and mistrust. It is an autobiographical poem, probably more stridently so than most of his other anticourt lyrics.

See also COURT CULTURE.

FURTHER READING

Muir, Kenneth. *Life and Letters of Sir Thomas Wyatt.* Liverpool, U.K.: Liverpool University Press, 1963.

Rebholz, R. A., ed. *Sir Thomas Wyatt. The Complete Poems.* New Haven, Conn., and London: Yale University Press, 1978.

Christopher A. Hill

"WHOSO LIST TO HUNT" SIR THOMAS WYATT (1557)

In SIR THOMAS WYATT's poem, a lone hunter begins by stating, "Whoso list to hunt, I know where is an hind," (l. 1). He goes on to mourn the weariness of the chase, before imparting some advice to other men who might want to hunt: "Who list her hunt, I put him out of doubt, / As well as I may spend his time in vain" (ll. 9–10). The quarry—the deer (i.e., the woman)—is owned by another. She belongs to Caesar and is marked with the warning *Noli me tangere* ("Touch me not," l. 13).

This SONNET is technically a translation of PETRARCH's Sonnet 190 and, as such, generally follows the ITALIAN (PETRARCHAN) SONNET form. The most commonly accepted interpretation is a generally biographical reading wherein the hunter is Wyatt himself and the hind is Anne Boleyn, rumored mistress of Wyatt but definitely the mistress (and later queen) of HENRY VIII. Critics have examined Wyatt's changes to the original and his vocabulary choices. In particular, the focus has been on the motivation of the speaker. Wyatt's speaker, unlike Petrarch's, is weary of the chase: ". . . hélas, I may no more. / The vain travail hath wearied me so sore" (ll. 2–3). His "wearied mind" (l. 5) is expressed throughout the remainder of the OCTAVE, culminating with "Fainting I follow. I leave off therefore" (l. 7). The sense of exhaustion, weariness, and sadness is emphasized through the early repetition of an initial *h,* an aspiration, and akin to a sigh: "hunt" and "hind" (l. 1), "hélas" (l. 2), "hath" (l. 3). In particular, "hélas," an archaic form of "alas," not only echoes a lover's sigh but also tones down passion— "alas" is a common interjection, often followed by an exclamation point to emphasize alarm or extreme sorrow, but hélas is understated and tired.

Some critics have also noted that this sonnet works backwards, with the octave describing the effect (weary resignation) and the SESTET depicting the catalyst (seeing the hind). The hind herself differs from Petrarch's in a number of ways. His deer is a pure white doe with gold antlers, wearing a necklace of topaz and diamonds. The doe's purity, rarity, and worth are emphasized, as is her independence: Petrarch's deer wanders free because her Caesar has made her so. Wyatt's deer seems common; he suggests that any hunter might pursue her, and though she is "fair" (l. 12), she is neither pure nor rare. However, she is branded with ownership: Her collar firmly establishes that she cannot be touched. The provocative ending has caused some debate. The hind insists that she is "And wild for to hold, though I seem tame" (l. 14), leaving the impression that she merely appears to be trapped but is really free. This position imparts a measure of subjectivity to the otherwise constrained deer; indeed, through Petrarch's doe appears to wander farther and freer, she is free by her master's orders, while Wyatt's hind, though she appears to be completely possessed, is deceptively submissive while truly uncontrolled. Wyatt alludes to this earlier, in his metaphorical comparison of the hind to "the wind" (l. 8) and in the overall impossibility of the chase.

Finally, Wyatt's use of the phrase *noli me tangere* contains a BIBLICAL ALLUSION to John 20:17: Immediately post-Resurrection, Jesus appeared to Mary Magdalene, but when she tried to embrace him, he told her not to touch him. More literally, however, the phrase means "cease desiring to touch me"—a subtle difference, but one that imparts power to the hind: She is essentially ordering the speaker not to want to touch her, therefore controlling his feelings as well as his actions. However, she is only partially successful. Though Wyatt ends the chase, he cannot, by any means, draw his mind from the deer (ll. 5–6). He continues to want her, though he terminates the pursuit.

See also "THEY FLEE FROM ME."

FURTHER READING

Boyarin, Adrienne Williams. "Competing Biblical and Virgilian Allusions in *Wyatt's* 'Who so List to Hounte.'" *N&Q* 53, no. 4 (2006): 417–421.

Powell, Jason. "'For Caesar's I Am': Henrician Diplomacy and Representations of King and Country in *Thomas Wyatt's* Poetry." *Sixteenth Century Journal* 36, no. 2 (2005): 415–431.

"WIDSITH" ANONYMOUS (before 1072)

"Widsith," a 143-line poem found in the EXETER BOOK, is one of only two Old English (Anglo-Saxon) poems to focus on the life of the Anglo-Saxon poet-musician commonly called a *SCOP* (the other work is "DEOR"). As with most poems of this period, the authorship and date of composition of "Widsith" are unknown. Structurally, the poem is similar to "The WANDERER," with a brief prologue and epilogue by a third-person narrator framing the main portion, which is told from the perspective of the title character himself.

After being introduced by the narrator as a man who has visited many lands and received treasure from various leaders, Widsith ("Far-Traveler") recites three lengthy catalogs of the tribes, rulers, and nations he has seen. The names are mainly drawn from the Germanic heroic period of the fourth through the sixth centuries. The chronological and geographical range of these wanderings, however, makes it apparent that Widsith is no ordinary minstrel. He claims to have been with rulers including the third-century Eastgota (l. 113) and sixth-century Ælfwine (l. 70), and to have visited the Scandinavian tribes of the far north as well as the Middle Eastern homes of the Israelites and Persians. Clearly he is meant to be a representative figure, an idealized *scop* able to draw on a vast body of historic and legendary knowledge for his songs.

While much scholarship on *Widsith* has centered around its wealth of detail about early Germanic legends, the poem also gives an important description of the *scop*'s role in Anglo-Saxon society. Curiously, the term *scop* is never used in the poem, though the narrator refers to Widsith as one of the *gleomen*—minstrels—in the epilogue. Widsith claims to have received gifts such as gold collars in exchange for his services, much as warriors were given gold as reward for their bravery in battle. The *scop*'s importance to rulers lay in his ability to make or break reputations. As illustrated in *BEOWULF* and other poems, the songs sung by *scops* in the mead hall preserved the memories of heroic figures and events, and how a ruler was characterized by the singer had lasting effect on his or her fame (*dom*).

An interesting aspect of this reciprocal relationship is revealed in Widsith's tendency to whitewash the scandalous reputations of some of his patrons. Eormanric, for example, was known for his cruelty and especially for the murder of his wife Ealhhilde. The narrator alludes to this in the prologue by calling him a *wrafles wœrlogan* ("cruel troth-breaker," l. 9), yet Widsith himself only praises the great generosity of both Eormanric and his queen. Some earlier critics took this as evidence that the poem was intended as a "begging poem"—a device used by an actual *scop* to demonstrate his talent and ability to flatter, in hopes of gaining a new patron, much as GEOFFREY CHAUCER would do several centuries later in "The COMPLAINT OF CHAUCER TO HIS PURSE." More recent scholars, however, suggest that the poet is being intentionally ironic, satirizing the greed or naïveté of singers intent on pleasing their patrons. The poem's epilogue seems to support such an interpretation as the narrator hints at the political ambitiousness of rulers eager to build and sustain their reputations through the influential songs of the *scops*.

FURTHER READING
Bradley, S. A. J., ed. and trans. *Anglo-Saxon Poetry*. London: Dent, 1982.

Krapp, George Philip, and Elliott Van Kirk Dobbie, eds. *The Exeter Book*. New York: Columbia University Press, 1936.

Lori A. Wallach

"WIFE OF BATH'S PROLOGUE AND TALE, THE" GEOFFREY CHAUCER (ca. 1392–1395)
The Wife of Bath is one of the most memorable pilgrims in GEOFFREY CHAUCER's masterpiece, *The CANTERBURY TALES*. Her portrait in the GENERAL PROLOGUE TO THE *CANTERBURY TALES* reveals some interesting details: She is somewhat deaf, she is a weaver, she has had five husbands, she undertakes pilgrimages, and she is "gat-tothed" (gap-toothed), meaning she was very sexual (see PHYSIOGNOMY). Her prologue confirms all of these initial impressions as the Wife details the story of her life, especially her many marriages. Her first lines set out her premise: "Experience, though noon auctoritee / were in this world, is right ynogh for me" (ll. 1–2). Experience is more important than "authority," or studies, to the Wife, who is very experienced when it comes to marriage. She begins by challenging those who question her right to marry five times, citing biblical examples, including the Woman of Samaria, Solomon, Abraham, and Jacob—all of whom had more than one spouse.

The Wife's overwhelming reason for her multiple marriages, however, is her desire for sex, justifying her lustful nature by saying, "Bet is to be wedded than to brynne" (better to be married than to burn, i.e., be consumed with sexual desire, ll. 52), which is her version of Pauline doctrine. The Wife then proceeds to challenge the idealization of virginity, which was the Church's primary teaching in regard to women. Virgins were considered spiritually (as well as physically) pure. Similarly, widows who did not remarry proved themselves beyond physical desires. Wives, who were obligated to engage in sexual relations with their husbands, were the least sanctified as they regularly indulged in filth of the flesh. In particular, the Wife challenges St. Jerome, whose teachings about virginity had heavily influenced the Church. Her primary argument is that God created both sex and sexual organs, so they must be good and meant to be enjoyed. Her defense of sexuality culminates in an expression of personal enjoyment:

In wifhode I wol use mine instrument
As frely as my makere hath it sent.

. . .

Mine housbonde shal it have both eve and
    morwe,
Whan that him list com forth and paye his
    dette.

                (ll. 149–150, 152–153)

The Wife pledges to satisfy her husband completely, as long as he returns her regard, citing the "marital debt" (reciprocal sexual expectations) as her legal right.

At this point, the Pardoner, another pilgrim, interrupts the Wife's discourse. Claiming he is about to marry, he beseeches the Wife to share her vast knowledge, which she agrees to do. The prologue then continues with the story of her marriages.

Of her husbands, the Wife claims, "three of hem were goode and two were badde" (l. 196). Her first three husbands were older than she, kept her sexually satisfied, and left her their property when they died. She spends 144 lines paraphrasing speeches she gave her husbands, couched as advice to wives, all of which are based on traditional medieval antifeminist rhetoric. These culminate with her declaration, "We [wives] love no man that taketh kep or charge / wher that we goon . . ." (ll. 321–322). The Wife then continues, detailing how she controlled her husbands rhetorically, through accusations, drunken flattery, and deception—and of course through sex.

The Wife then turns to her two bad husbands. Her fourth kept a mistress and tried to stop her from drinking wine, neither of which pleased her. She repaid him by flirting outrageously with other men. The fifth husband she claims to have loved best, even though his love was "daungerous to me," (l. 514). In Middle English, *daungerous* meant both "standoffish" and, literally, "dangerous." Both meanings apply here. Jankyn was younger than she (20 to her 40) and poor. He was also handsome, and the Wife desired him sexually. After their marriage, however, Jankyn turned mean. He read to her each night from a book of "wicked wives." The Wife paraphrases the contents of this book, which include a list of selfish and unfaithful women throughout history. It is during this recitation that she asks her famous question: "Who peyntede the leon, tel me who?" (l. 692), referencing one of Aesop's FABLES in which a man paints a picture of a hunter killing a lion, whereupon a lion remarks that if he had painted the scene, he would have shown the lion as victorious. Similarly, the Wife dismisses Jankyn's antifeminist/ antimarriage rhetoric by implying that the stories would be much different if women had told them. Jankyn's book so infuriated the Wife that she punched him, grabbed the book, and burned it. He retaliated by hitting her in the head (the cause of her deafness). She collapsed. Jankyn, fearing she was dead, ran over and apologized. Eventually, the Wife says, the two came to some accord, and lived harmoniously until Jankyn died.

At this point, the Friar breaks in, declaring the prologue too long, to which the Summoner responds by cursing him. The Host ends the argument but urges the Wife to tell her tale.

"The Wife of Bath's Tale" echoes the ARTHURIAN LITERATURE tradition. It opens in the "dayes of King Arthour" (l. 857), with a knight riding through the forest. Spotting a beautiful young maiden, the knight is seized by lust and rapes her. When he is brought before the court, the queen begs the king for permission to decide his fate. This request is granted, and she renders his sentence: "I graunte thee lif if thou kanst tellen me / what thing is it that wommen moost desiren" (ll. 904–905).

Given a year and a day to complete his quest, the knight sets out. His quest is unsuccessful. Just as he begins his return to the court, however, he encounters a loathly old woman. She notices his sadness and offers to help, on the condition that he promises to grant an unspecified request. The bargain is struck, and the knight returns to court.

Appearing before the queen, the knight proclaims the answer to her question: "Wommen desiren to have sovereynetee / as well over hir housbond as hir love, / and for to been in maistrie hym above" (ll. 1039–1040). None of the women disputes this answer, so the knight is free to go. The old woman then approaches the knight, reminding him of his promise and demanding that he marry her. Repulsed, the knight begs her to "taak all my good and lat my body go" (l. 1061), but she refuses, and they wed.

In bed that night, the knight is distressed, though the old woman is merry. She asks why he is upset, and he replies, "thou art so loothly, and so oold also" (l. 1100). The old woman responds with a discussion in which she challenges the traditional notion of gentility being based on birth and wealth; rather, true gentility derives from one's actions. She concludes by offering the knight a choice: She will remain old, ugly, and faithful, or she will transform herself into being beautiful and young, but potentially unchaste. The knight considers his options and eventually declares: "I put me in youre wise governance; / Cheseth youreself which may be moost plesance" (ll. 1231–1232). Having acquired the mastery she desired all along, the old woman then chooses to be both beautiful and faithful, a decision the knight accepts happily.

"The Wife of Bath's Prologue and Tale" are commonly taught as one piece. The prologue combines elements of sermons and a confession. Like a sermon, it contains BIBLICAL ALLUSIONS and references, lessons, and an EXEMPLUM. In relating the personal details of her life and adventures, however, the Wife is also "confessing" to the other pilgrims in the sense of a modern talk show, not the medieval church. She is not seeking penance and redemption; rather, she is seeking validation and entertainment. The tale is a ROMANCE that contains the traditional elements but also includes unique variants such as the rather casual rape at the beginning.

The various characters described by the Wife are rarely individualized and instead are generally presented as a "type," or stock character. Her first three husbands are presented collectively, and even the fourth is not detailed, though he warrants special mention. The fifth, however, is not only discussed in depth but is also named and given a profession. Similarly, the knight, the maiden, and even the queen are not described beyond their standard roles. Only the old woman is given personality and true character.

"The Wife of Bath's Prologue and Tale" have been the subject of a great deal of critical attention and controversy over the years. Early critics concentrated on dating and manuscript variants as well as on determining source materials. For the prologue, Chaucer relied heavily on St. Jerome's letter *Adversus Jovinianum* and the French Romance *Roman de la Rose* by Guillaume de Lorris and Jean de Muin, of which Chaucer had completed a partial translation earlier in his career. For the tale, he drew on two sources: JOHN GOWER's "Tale of Florent," found in the *CONFESSIO AMANTIS*, and the anonymous romance *The WEDDYNGE OF SIR GAWEN AND DAME RAGNELL*.

Other early criticism sought to deemphasize the Wife's individuality and instead read her as a device, ALLEGORY, parody, or social type. For instance, the Wife is a secular professional woman in an era when that was rare. Allegorically, some critics have read the rape and the knight's subsequent gentility as a political message to Richard II, asking the king to stop "raping" his people and to treat them with gentility. Iconographically, some critics have viewed the Wife as a representation of femininity gone wild and/or lust. As a parody, the Wife is often seen as a "funny" portrait of a woman as portrayed by misogynists.

New Historicist and Marxist critics have taken different approaches than the traditional ones outlined above. For instance, situating the Wife in the context of 14th-century struggles between classes reveals commentary on the changing face of medieval social power structures, where wealth was increasingly not tied to aristocracy. Additionally, several critics have examined the Wife in terms of economics. She is a professional weaver, a guild member, and capable of earning capital. Moreover, through her marriages she has acquired capital, making her both merchant and commodity. Realizing this, the Wife then accumulates profit in the easiest and most efficient ways. She is a professional wife. Psychoanalytic critics have tended either to see the Wife as an extension of Chaucer and his conflicted views of women and marriage—complicated further by charges of *raptus*, which can indicate either rape or abduction or both, leveled against him—or to view her as an independent character complete with a unique psychological profile. These readings tend to view her prologue, and to a lesser extent her tale, as an autobiography rather than a sermon or confession. Coupled with the romance-fantasy tale, these narratives reveal the Wife's inner desires and pleasures.

The largest body of criticism on the Wife's prologue and tale, however, is feminist criticism, which often incorporates elements from other aspects as well. Numerous scholars have dubbed her a *proto-feminist,* sparking debates about the nature of that term. More problematically, the Wife is a character constructed by a male author—Chaucer. If she is a proto-feminist, does that, then, make him one? Along these lines is the idea that Chaucer, though a medieval man steeped in his own era, at least allows a glimpse of feminine desire and perspective. Another common approach sees the Wife as a subversive character but relies on her "pathetic" qualities to evoke sympathy and compassion. In this view, Chaucer is credited with a consciousness-raising effort, produced by demonstrating the monstrous qualities of misogyny.

Perhaps most intriguing is the tendency for critics to dismiss charges of misogyny and forgive Chaucer's lapses. Even many feminist critics who point out flaws in Chaucer's "feminism" or see limitations in his approach tend to excuse him somehow. Is this the hallmark of Chaucer's influence? Or is it a reluctance to give up the Wife as a symbol of early feminism?

More recently, feminist critics have begun questioning this complacency and the standard approaches. Elaine Tuttle Hansen, for example, effectively demonstrates how the Wife is actually silenced, though she speaks a great deal. Throughout most of her prologue and tale, the Wife says very little on her own and instead relies on the words of male authorities—reshaped, certainly, but nonetheless present. Moreover, the apparent rewarding of a rapist-knight is troubling and points to the overall ineffectiveness of the Wife's apparent feminism. In creating such an outrageous example of "feminism," Chaucer subtly and effectively undermines her apparent success, thus reinforcing the male status quo.

Other critics have begun examining the role of violence in the Wife's prologue and tale as a measure of misogyny, certainly, but also contextually as domestic violence and economic violence. In this way, too, the Wife only appears to be free from male control while actually serving to reinforce patriarchal standards.

FURTHER READING

Amsler, Mark. "The Wife of Bath and Women's Power." *Assays* 4 (1987): 67–83.

Colmer, Dorothy. "Character and Class in the *Wife of Bath's Tale.*" *JEGP* 72 (1973): 329–339.

Delany, Sheila. "Strategies of Silence in the Wife of Bath's Recital." *Exemplaria* 2 (1990): 49–69.

Dinshaw, Carolyn. *Chaucer's Sexual Poetics.* Madison: University of Wisconsin Press, 1989.

Hansen, Elaine Tuttle. *Chaucer and the Fictions of Gender.* Berkeley: University of California Press, 1992.

Justman, Stewart. "Trade as Pudendum: Chaucer's Wife of Bath." *Chaucer Review* 28 (1994): 344–352.

Martin, Priscilla. *Chaucer's Women: Nuns, Wives, and Amazons.* Iowa City: University of Iowa Press, 1990.

Straus, Barrie. "The Subversive Discourse of the Wife of Bath: Phallocentric Discourse and the Imprisonment of Criticism." *ELH* 55 (1988): 527–554.

"WIFE'S LAMENT, THE" ANONYMOUS (before 1072)

A short (53-line) poem in Old English, found in the EXETER BOOK, "The Wife's Lament" is generally treated as an ELEGY, though it is also referred to as a *Frauenlied* (women's song). However, since lamentation was women's responsibility, the two genres overlap.

As the poem opens, a lone female speaker is mourning her exile, which is the greatest trauma she has faced in her life. Her lord, perhaps her husband, sailed away. Worried, she decided to make her position more secure. Meanwhile, her lord's kinfolk plotted against her, conspiring to keep them apart. She has no friends where she dwells and remains only because her lord commanded that she do so. She has been alone before, but then she met her lord, and they had each other. Now she cannot bear the loneliness. She has been cast out of her home, sent to live in a cave. She looks out over the dark and friendless landscape, longing for her lord and mourning her losses.

Traditional scholarship has read the woman as a peace-weaver, sent to live among a hostile tribe and thus exiled from her friends and family, but also exiled within her new society. Based on this perspective, there has been a great deal of speculation about the nature of the husband-wife relationship. Clearly the wife misses her husband. Some scholars believe that the husband does not (or no longer does) reciprocate her feelings—he has turned against her, possibly because of his family's hostility. Another perspective is that she and her husband share the same feelings and that he is just as devastated as she is, though the poem reflects only her perspective. The general intimacy and tone of despair lend credence to this perspective. Linguistic support for a reciprocal relationship exists as well: The wife uses dual pronouns in her expression of grief to convey the relationship with her husband: *unc* (us two, l. 12b) and *wit* (we two, l. 13). The usage of these pronouns, which are no longer found in English, increase the private, inanimate nature of their relationship.

Another, less common, interpretation of the poem relies on ALLEGORY. In this reading, the wife is read as the church (the bride of Christ) who has been exiled from her lord (Christ in heaven). A similarly unusual reading sees the wife as someone speaking from beyond the grave, relying on her description of being sent to live in an underground cell, which might be a grave.

As an elegy, "The Wife's Lament" shares many characteristics with the other Old English poems of like construction such as "The SEAFARER" and "The WANDERER." There is a solitary figure speaking in the first person about being exiled, there is a sea journey, and the speaker faces hostile forces. Whether or not it is an elegy, most critics agree that the poem is an expression of mournful longing and female desire. Feminist critics have especially appreciated it as one of the only first person female authored (or at least female-voiced) poems to come out of early British literature.

FURTHER READING

Battles, Paul. "Of Graves, Caves, and Subterranean Dwellings: Eordscraef and Eordsele in the *Wife's Lament*." *PQ* 73, no. 3 (1994): 267–286.

Gameson, Fiona, and Richard Gameson. "Wulf and Eascwacer, the Wife's Lament and the Discovery of the Individual in Old English Verse." In *Studies in English Language and Literature: "Doubt Wisely,"* edited by M. J. Toswell and E. M. Tyler. London: Routledge, 1996.

Harris, Joseph. "A Note on Eoroscroefleorosele and Current Interpretations of the *Wife's Lament*." *ES* 58, no. 3 (1977): 204–208.

Straus Barrie, Ruth. "Women's Words as Weapons: Speech as Action in the Wife's Lament." *In Old English Shorter Poems: Basic Readings,* edited by Katherine O'Brien O'Keeffe, 335–356. New York: Garland, 1994.

"WILL AND TESTAMENT" ISABELLA WHITNEY (1573)

ISABELLA WHITNEY's "Will and Testament" is perhaps her best-known poem, and it forms the last section of her second book, *A Sweet Nosegay.*

Throughout the book, Whitney emphasizes her poverty as an unemployed maid, and in her "Will and Testament" she explains that she must leave London because she can no longer afford to live there. She compares the city to a cruel lover and says that she therefore has no reason to mourn her departure. Nevertheless, she admits that she, like many other women, loves those who are cruel to her. Having recalled that London has never helped Whitney when she needed assistance, she says farewell to the city and writes her final will, a mock testament in which she makes London her executor, bequest, and beneficiary; in other words, she asks London to supervise the distribution of London to London.

Whitney begins her will in an unusual manner, noting not, as writers of wills generally do, that she is of sound mind but ailing body, but rather that she is "whole in body, and in mind, / but very weak in purse" (ll. 37–38). Whitney's only illness, it seems, is financial, but this is a fatal failing in the commercial environment of 16th-century London. She then proceeds to will away to London all the things that London already contains and all the things that she must leave to London since she cannot afford to take them with her. Her will therefore becomes a map of London, but it is a map that focuses on the stores and the merchandise they sell and on the poorhouses and debtors' prisons in which those who are too poor to buy and sell are incarcerated. In fact, Whitney admits that she was saving one of these debtors' prisons for herself, but she decides to give it away when she realizes that she will never be in debt since she is so poor that nobody will lend her money. She thus describes London as an entirely commercial community in which one must have money to survive.

Whitney's map of the city points out both the great wealth of London and the inequity with which this wealth is distributed. Having left London all the things that "needful be" (l. 257), she asks that they "with conscience . . . disbursed be" when she is gone (ll. 259–260). It seems unlikely that this latter request will be fulfilled, however, since Whitney asks FORTUNE to be London's aid in distributing the goods, suggesting that it will, as usual, be a matter of luck that determines who gets what. She wryly admits that she has not left any money to cover the expenses of her own burial, but she observes that her body, if left above ground, will be an "annoyance" (l. 264). Even in matters such as the burial of a body, convenience and finances are considered before morals and ethics. Finally, Whitney asks to be commended to her friends, and she says that if those friends miss her, then they should have worked harder to help her when she was alive.

Whitney's "Will" is a witty condemnation of a city that places greater value on economic status than on a person's character. According to this economic value system, Whitney, being poor, is worthless. But her poem also gives her the opportunity to reverse this power dynamic. In willing away the contents of the city she cannot afford to live in, she imaginatively makes herself the owner of the entire city. Though she emphasizes her lack of material possessions, she takes possession of London and situates herself in a position of power from which she generously bestows gifts. At the same time, by using the form of a mock testament, Whitney deflects some of the criticism she might have received as a woman daring to publish her poems in print, an act that might have been seen as improper. A will was one moment in which a woman was empowered and able to speak without fear of censure, since it was her last chance to do so. By writing her poem in the form of a will, Whitney both escapes the criticism that might have been aimed at a woman writer and cleverly uses a legal document designed to distribute wealth as a means to comment on the unfair distribution of wealth in 16th-century London.

See also "I. W. To Her Unconstant Lover."

FURTHER READING
Travitsky, Betty. "The 'Wyll and Testament' of Isabella Whitney." *ELR* 10 (1980): 76–94.
Wall, Wendy. "Isabella Whitney and the Female Legacy." *ELH* 58, no. 1 (1991): 35–62.

Donna C. Woodford

"WILY CLERK, THE" Anonymous (15th century)
This short, secular lyric survives in a single manuscript, and although the author is unknown, scholars believe he or she hails from Norfolk.

There is some controversy in interpreting this poem. Traditionally, it has been viewed as a woman's lament over abandonment and pregnancy, but recent scholarship sees the speaker as a resourceful female pleased with her own cunning. The lyric begins with a COUPLET that repeats after each verse, and ends in the manner of a REFRAIN: "A, dere God, what I am fayn, / For I am madyn now gane!" (ll. 1–2). This has been translated as either "Ah, dear God, I am without worth, for I am no longer virgin" or "Ah, dear God, how well-pleased I am, for I am a maiden again!" In each verse, the speaker tells more of her tale: First, she meets a clever clergyman who tells her to listen to him but to also conceal his counsel. Next, she says he "had learning" (probably meaning he knew Latin), and that his knowledge gave him magical power, for she could not resist his will. In the third verse, she acknowledges he has seduced her, and now "will not my girdil met—" (l. 17), suggesting she is pregnant. In the final verse, she says she has been on pilgrimage and is now resolved not to allow any clergymen to toy with her. This can be read as a traditional repentance motif, but the alternative reading suggests the pilgrimage was a ploy to conceal the pregnancy and childbirth, allowing the speaker to return to life as though still a maiden—which is why she is "well-pleased."

In the poetic tradition, this poem is unusual because of its secularity (most Middle English lyrics are religious in nature) and because the female speaker marks it as a relatively rare "woman's song," similar to poems such as "The Wife's Lament."

Though the speaker is obviously female, many scholars believe this poem was written by a man—perhaps, like many Middle English lyrics, by a cleric. The wry, dramatic tone fits with known male authors, and the poem lacks the private, personal nature found in poems we can definitively attribute to female authors. The wiliness of the poem's clerk, attributed to his scholarly training, could suggest a clerical author engaged in both self-flattery and self-deprecation, especially since the poem plays on the popular motif of abuses within the church.

Regardless of which reading one chooses, it is important to note that women's virginity was highly prized in the Middle Ages, so much so that the woman in this poem either considers herself worthless for having given hers up before marriage or triumphant for having found a way to retain the appearance of virginity despite having lost it. Finally, the skilled rhetoric of the seducer is reminiscent of the cad in WILLIAM SHAKE-SPEARE's *A LOVER'S COMPLAINT*.

See also MIDDLE ENGLISH LYRICS AND BALLADS.

FURTHER READING

Cartlidge, Neil. "'Alas, I go With Chylde': Representations of Extra-Marital Pregnancy in the Middle English Lyric." *English Studies* 79, no. 5 (1998): 395–414.

Klinck, Anne L. and Ann Marie Rasmussen, eds. *Medieval Woman's Song*. Philadelphia: University of Pennsylvania Press, 2002.

Allegra C. Johnston

WISDOM POETRY See ANGLO-SAXON RIDDLES.

"WOMANHOOD, WANTON" JOHN SKEL-TON (1527)

It is possible to attach the date of composition for "Womanhood, Wanton" to JOHN SKELTON's first period at court (between 1485 and 1504), thanks to its dedication to "Anne" of "Temmys street" (presumably Thames Street in London), though the poem was first printed in 1527. Skelton wrote "Womanhood" in rough tetrameter, formally similar to his early lyrics and suggesting that it may have been set to music. If so, this music has been lost.

While the poem is often read as a monologue by a man berating his lover, Anne, reading it as a dialogue between lovers makes sense of otherwise baffling phallic imagery and weak transitions between STANZAS.

The poem begins with a male speaker cataloguing what are presumably his lover, Anne's, faults: her meddling, railing, and putting on of undeserved airs. Anne responds to him in kind, attributing his abuse to his fear that the price of her sexual favors will rise (ll. 9–10) and assuring him he will not have to pay for them (l. 11). This only further angers the male speaker, who compares Anne to a "pohen" (peahen) who spreads her tail proudly and is hence likely to chase away himself and "others"—simultaneously accusing Anne of pride and promiscuity (ll. 13–14). At the beginning of the third stanza, Anne appropriates the speaker's language for her retort, comparing the male speaker's tongue to both an adder's sting and a scorpion's tail (ll. 16–17).

At this point, the male speaker decides that the argument has gone on for long enough, and he tries to placate Anne with affectionate language and pet names ("What prate ye," he asks, "praty pyggysny?") (l. 20). The fourth stanza sees the lovers' reconciliation and a final deployment of sexual imagery: Keys and locks represent predictably situated male and female genitalia. The poem ends with a dedication to "Anne," who lives at the "Key" on "Temmys strete" (ll. 29–30).

This poem is typical of Skelton in that it combines the conventions of 15th-century COURTLY LOVE poetry (here, the berating of a proud and promiscuous woman) with those of the seduced-serving-maid class of popular lyrics (here, the frequent sexual imagery and innuendo)—reacting to medieval poetic conventions rather than anticipating the conventions of the early Renaissance.

FURTHER READING

Dent, J. M. *John Skelton*. London: Orion Publishing Group, 1997.

Fish, Stanley Eugene. *John Skelton's Poetry*. New Haven, Conn.: Yale University Press, 1967.

Gordon, Ian A. *John Skelton*. New York: Octagon Books, 1970.

Nathaniel Z. Eastman

"WOODMANSHIP" GEORGE GASCOIGNE (1572–1573)

"Woodmanship" is an autobiographical poem in a mildly satiric, self-deprecating vein. GEORGE GASCOIGNE uses the occasion of a hunt with Lord Grey of Wilton—and his own conspicuous lack of skill in the pastime—as a poetic CONCEIT, or extended metaphor, for his apparent ill fortune at every stage of life. The poem is an address to Lord Grey, and in it Gascoigne attempts to explain why he cannot hit a deer with an arrow, even at close range. The reason, the poet says, is that no matter what the target in life or learning, he always misses. The bulk of the remainder of the poem is a meditation on the failures he has experienced.

The cases Gascoigne expounds on are as follows: He tried "philosophy" (l. 18) but found his wits "awry," or insufficiently rigorous (l. 20). His attempt at the study of law, presumably at the Inns of Court, went similarly askew (ll. 21–32). The next "miss" recounts his attempts to gain favor and position at the royal court, where, instead of showing proper discretion (l. 40), he fell prey to prodigality, flattery, and foppishness—in short, he found that he could not afford it. He next describes his military career, which led him to fight against the Spanish in Flushing in 1572—and convinced him that he is no soldier.

From this point in the poem, Gascoigne adopts a tone more overtly indebted to the satirical tradition, as starting in line 73 he describes how he cannot wrest gain from the multiple forms of dishonesty that other men find so attractive (ll. 73–86). Typically for the tradition, he makes his lack of success a mark of simplicity and honesty—and goes on to assert that his lack of success is not attributable a lack of virtue. He shows that he does in fact know some worthwhile things, from Aristotle (ll. 100–102), Cicero (ll. 103–104), and various legal authorities from his time at the Inns of Court (ll. 105–106). Though he did not become a philosopher or lawyer, he did benefit in some way. This self-assurance, however, quickly retreats before renewed complaint about those whose successes come too easily or unworthily—those who know less or lack virtue, but somehow manage to gain position and wealth (ll. 109–124).

The last portion of the poem rehearses the self-pitying possibility that even were the poet to shoot a deer by some stroke of fate, she would prove a "carrion carcass" (l. 130), unfit for any use. It would not be a total loss, he adds: Divine providence could very well provide such a deer to reinforce the lesson that a gold exterior may very well hide "brass" innards (ll. 143–144). It is perhaps the case, then, that these kinds of misfortunes are meant to protect him from the moral blindness that equates show with substance.

In both its overall tone and its subject matter, Gascoigne's "Woodmanship" owes a lot to earlier satirical poems such as SIR JOHN WYATT's "MINE OWN JOHN POINS," especially in its conclusions that great position comes often at too high a cost—that simplicity in life and manners is preferable if it equates to honesty of soul. The poem is notable for its humorous, self-deprecating tone that strays only slightly into strenuous COMPLAINT—which may have something to do with the fact that it is more or less a litany of failure, not an explanation of a moral choice as in the case of Wyatt's poem.

In reading the poem, it is helpful to remember that many of Gascoigne's poems talk about a misspent youth and his subsequent desire to reform, so critics often see "Woodmanship" in particular as a type of Prodigal Son narrative. In addition to the poet's own travails, the poem illustrates that for a young man of limited means, the path to political or social improvement in Tudor England could be quite rocky.

See also COURT CULTURE, SATIRE, "SEVEN SONNETS FOR ALEXANDER NEVILLE."

FURTHER READING

Helgerson, Richard. *Elizabethan Prodigals.* Berkeley, Los Angeles, and London: University of California Press, 1976.

Prouty, C. T. *George Gascoigne: Elizabethan Courtier, Soldier, and Poet.* New York: Benjamin Blom, 1966.

———. *George Gascoigne's a Hundreth Sundrie Flowres.* Columbia: University of Missouri Press, 1970.

Christopher A. Hill

WORDE, WYNKYN DE (ca. 1455–1535)

Not much is known about the life of Wynkyn de Worde before his arrival in England. There is some question about his birthplace; although his 1496 letter of denization (a legal precursor to naturalization) states that he was from the duchy of Lorraine, neither of the locations that have been suggested as his birthplace (Woerth-sur-Sauer, Wörth am Rhein) were in the duchy at the time he was born.

It is probable that Worde met WILLIAM CAXTON in Cologne around 1471–72 and thereafter followed Caxton as his assistant, first to Bruges and, finally, to England in 1476. Worde worked with Caxton until the latter's death in 1492, when he took over the older printer's business. He lived in Westminster near Caxton's shop at the sign of the Red Pale; the records of Westminster Abbey note that Worde and his wife, Elizabeth, rented two tenements within its sanctuary, and the pair were members of the Fraternity of the Assumption at the church of St. Margaret's, Westminster, until her death in 1498.

Worde maintained Caxton's press in Westminster for a decade before moving the press to Fleet Street in the City of London, setting up shop at the sign of the Sun in 1501; he also maintained a stall in the churchyard of St. Paul's. At the turn of the 16th century, Fleet Street was already a center for the bookbinding and bookselling trades, and Worde was soon followed by other printers, including RICHARD PYNSON, Richard Redmond, and Julian Notary, establishing a tradition of publishing in Fleet Street, which has lasted for more than 500 years.

The move to Fleet Street was marked by a shift in printing focus for Worde, away from Caxton's interest in catering to readers from the court and government, to a more popular reading audience. Worde printed a wide variety of texts, including popular ROMANCES, works on household practice, and even children's books. While Caxton favored works of history and CHIVALRY, Worde specialized in religious works and educational books used in grammar schools. He cultivated relationships with religious houses and enjoyed the PATRONAGE of several important figures, most notably Margaret Beaufort, mother of Henry VII and grandmother of HENRY VIII.

While the print quality of Worde's work is frequently considered inferior to his master, Caxton, and his contemporary, Pynson, the value of his contribution to English printing cannot be overestimated. By the time of his death in 1535, Worde was responsible for roughly 800 publications. His vast output helped to popularize printed books in his own day and has led to more works surviving for scholars to study today.

FURTHER READING

Bennett, H. S. *English Books & Readers: 1475–1557.* Cambridge: Cambridge University Press, 1969.
Moran, James. *Wynkyn de Worde: Father of Fleet Street.* 3rd ed. London: British Library and Oak Knoll Press, 2003.

Christina M. Carlson

"WRITTEN ON A WINDOW FRAME [OR WALL] AT WOODSTOCK" AND "WRITTEN WITH A DIAMOND" QUEEN ELIZABETH I (1554–1555)

When she was a princess during the reign of her half sister MARY I, ELIZABETH I was imprisoned in a number of places, including the TOWER OF LONDON and a palace at Woodstock (1554–55). (Noble "Prisons" were places of confinement where they were isolated from contact with any-

one the ruler did not want them to see.) When Elizabeth finally ascended the throne in 1558, Protestants in England and throughout Europe were delighted, and in the years following made shrines of her former prisons. In describing his visit to one of them in 1600, Baron Waldstein of Moravia spoke of two poems written on a wall. He also alluded to some poems written with a diamond on a window. Others have spoken of the longer of these two poems as being written on a window frame or a shutter. The scholar Leah Marcus points out that the English "made an inveterate practice of writing messages, proverbs, and 'posies' on walls, shutters, and other public surfaces." Elizabeth may have written this longer poem on a wooden window frame or shutter initially in charcoal. This substance, however, is not very permanent and can easily be brushed off. Marcus speculates that the poem was later copied onto a wall so as to be more permanent and also to allow its being read more easily. Elizabeth probably carved the shorter poem into the window pane with a diamond.

It is not easy to write on glass with a diamond—especially if it is part of a ring, necklace, or earring—so "Written with a Diamond" is predictably short. It is a rhymed COUPLET that alludes to the causes of Elizabeth's imprisonment—her possible part in a rebellion against Mary and her possible affair with Thomas Seymour, her stepmother's husband: "Much is suspected by me, / Nothing proved can be" (ll. 1–2). The first line can be read two ways: that her accusers suspect Elizabeth of many things, or that Elizabeth suspects her accusers of many things. The second line is also open to two readings: the first, that the accusers cannot prove any of their suspicions, therefore Elizabeth is innocent; the second, only that no one can prove the suspicions. This circumstance does not necessarily assure Elizabeth's innocence. It merely states that nothing can be *proved* against her. The last line, with the Latin "Quod"—"said"—is the only completely unambiguous line in this poem: Elizabeth is a prisoner.

In the longer poem written on a window frame or wall, Elizabeth speaks with FORTUNE about her state. The medieval concept of Fortune as an uncaring goddess who turned the wheel of Fate was still extant in the early modern period. As a Protestant princess in a securely Protestant realm, Elizabeth had every reason to believe that she was "on top" and would remain there. During the reign of her Roman Catholic half sister, however, Elizabeth's position was precarious. Even though the "wresting, wavering state" (l. 1) of Fortune had caused Elizabeth's "wit"—mind or attitude—to be troubled and burdened with cares, she can now "bear" (l. 4) to be in a place where joy was once "quite flown" (l. 4). Line 3 has a lovely pun on the word *witness*. A witness is someone who sees an action and can attest to the circumstances surrounding that action. As a prisoner, Elizabeth can certainly "witness" her circumstances in the prison. But *witness* also plays on *wit,* the last word in line 2. *Mind* can be a synonym for *wit* in that line, and thus *witness* can be read as "mind-ness," or "quality of mind," so that the line can mean it is the prisoner's quality of mind that allows her now to be able to bear the confines of her prison.

The rest of the poem continues in couplets rather than the *abab* rhyme of the first four lines. Even though the prisoner may have told Fortune in the first four lines that she has found a way to accommodate herself to her imprisonment, the next four lines are the prisoner's accusations against Fortune for allowing her to be incarcerated while the guilty go free. Elizabeth accuses Fortune of "loosing" (l. 5)—letting go—the guilty from "lands where innocents were enclosed" (l. 6). The "lands" in this case would be England. However, "lands" may be a misprint for "bands," so the line would mean that Fortune loosed the bands—manacles or ropes—that bound the guilty. The next couplet accused Fortune of causing "the guiltless to be reserved" (l. 7) in prison while freeing "those" (l. 8), presumably the guilty, who "had well deserved" (l. 7) death.

In the final couplet, Elizabeth comes to a resolution of the situation in her own mind that involves God rather than a fickle, unpredictable fortune. She realizes that nothing can be done now, while she is confined (l. 9), "So God grant to my foes as they have thought" (l. 10). Again, these two lines can be read in various ways, especially given the fact that "thought" may actually have been "taught." Lines 9 and 10 can be read as "I cannot do anything here, but will wait until God gives my foes what they had planned on giving me." Or the line can be read slightly differently, and more despair-ingly, as "I cannot do anything here, so God must be granting my foes what they thought they would have by imprisoning me." One could argue that a person of strong faith, as Elizabeth's writings suggest her to have been, would think in terms of the first reading. However, being imprisoned, especially when one believes oneself to be innocent, can lead the most faithful people to despair.

FURTHER READING

Elizabeth. *Elizabeth I. Collected Works.* Edited by Leah S. Marcus, Janel Mueller, and Mary Beth Rise. Chicago and London: University of Chicago Press, 2000.

Hopkins, Lisa. *Writing Renaissance Queens: Texts by and about Elizabeth I and Mary, Queen of Scots.* Newark: University of Delaware, and London: Associated University Presses, 2002.

Theodora A. Jankowski

"WULF AND EADWACER" Anonymous (before 1072)

The Anglo-Saxon (Old English) poem "Wulf and Eadwacer" is found in the Exeter Book. A 19-line puzzle that is considered by scholars to be one of the most intriguing poems in the Anglo Saxon corpus, it has not yet been definitively interpreted. The most common reading is that it discusses a love triangle involving two men and one woman. The speaker is an unnamed woman who is lamenting over the loss of her lover. As the poem opens, the woman worries that if her lover returns, her people will destroy him. She mournfully cries out, "O, we are separated!" (l. 3), a refrain she repeats later in the poem. Her lover's name is Wulf, and he is far away from her on another island, although whether he has been exiled there or merely fled there is not clear. The speaker explains that she has grieved long and wept much over the loss of Wulf, who is no longer there to wrap his arms around her. Her constantly alternating feelings of fury at his absence and yearning for his presence have caused the speaker to become sick and weak. She calls out to the other man in her life, Eadwacer, most likely her husband, promising him that Wulf will bear their "whelp" (their child) away. The poem closes on a desolate note: The speaker acknowledges that her relationship with Wulf was never secure and so is easily destroyed.

Though it is difficult to pin down an exact genre for *Wulf and Eadwacer,* the most accepted interpretations place it as an ELEGY or call it a dramatic monologue, although it has also been suggested as being a riddle or a charm. This latter theory was suggested by the ambiguous dramatic action, but also because the space and the punctuation at the end of the selection do not clearly separate it from other riddles. However, for several reasons, critics have largely abandoned the riddle theory. First, if it were a riddle, it would be unsolvable. Moreover, no riddle subject is indicated—and even if a riddle is difficult to solve, it always refers to a physical subject, if obliquely.

As an elegy, "Wulf and Eadwacer" leaves something to be desired. Unlike the other elegies in the Exeter Book, such as "The WANDERER," "The SEAFARER," "Resignation," and "The Wife's Lament," there is no promise of hope or comfort at the end. Instead, the speaker sees only a bleak future, separated from one or both men and her child.

Many modern critics accept "Wulf and Eadwacer" as a dramatic monologue in which the speaker is a woman. Manuscript placement supports this interpretation as the poem directly follows "DEOR," which is universally accepted as such. Also like "Deor," "Wulf and Eadwacer" contains repetitive refrains. In fact, these are the only two Old English poems to have refrains of this sort.

Otherwise, 12 of its 19 lines display irregular verse patterns. Eight of the lines are quite short, consisting of HALF-LINES. These seemingly serve as STANZA dividers, and all are preceded by an exceptionally long line and followed by a line with irregular meter. Some editors have pointed out that the only manuscript punctuation, simple points at the ends of lines 3, 10, 12, and 13, also seem to indicate that stanzas might be divided in these places. However, since there are no actual divisions within the manuscript, this, too, is a matter of interpretation.

Not only has determining the poem's genre been a critical debate, but its meaning has been constantly reevaluated as well. The poem's lexical ambiguity essentially means that anyone who translates it automatically interprets it at the same time. For instance, the initial line reads as follows in Old English: "Leodnum is

minum swylce him mon lac gifte." *Lac* can be translated as "prey," "gift," "spoils," "sacrifice," "message," or "battle." Each of these translations bears its own implication: Something passive has been attacked and will be destroyed or consumed; something has been deliberately given (and possibly joyously received); something has been seized, but not necessarily with the intent to destroy; something has been willingly given to achieve a desired result; something is being passed as communication; two sides clash. Each of these interpretations, in turn, sets up a different mood for the speaker, and thus a different tone for the poem.

Similar lexical conundrums occur throughout the poem. Another major one concerns the word *hwelp* [whelp] in line 16, which literally translates into "pup" or "cub," although metaphorically often means human offspring. If it is taken literally, then the word *Wulf* in the following line may mean "wolf" (the animal) instead of Wulf (the lover). Yet another critic has suggested that *hwelp* means "outlaw," as it did in a parallel Old Norse saga and Old Icelandic linguistics, while still others suggest it is a metaphor for the relationship between the speaker and Eadwacer. Comparable ambiguity surrounds the name *Eadwacer.* This term can be read as an epithet instead of a proper name. As such, it translates into "property watcher," which does not necessarily indicate a spouse. In fact, if *eadwacer* is read in this manner, there may only be two characters in the poem—the speaker and her absent lover, Wulf. If Wulf were a wandering warrior, he would be forced to leave her behind on numerous occasions.

Critics continually question even the roles of the two men. While the most commonly accepted interpretation of the story identifies Wulf as the speaker's lover and Eadwacer as her husband, the poem itself does not clarify their respective roles. Some critics believe that the two men's roles should be switched. After all, the speaker acknowledges (ll. 10–12) that being with the "bold warrior" has brought her both pain and pleasure (emotional or physical). She may even be under the surveillance of a "property watcher." Others have suggested that Eadwacer is her father, who exiled her lover, Wulf, to an island after discovering the speaker's loss of virginity, and possibly a pregnancy. Wulf has alternately been read as the speaker's son, a SCOP telling her tale, and a figment of the speaker's overheated imagination.

The general subject matter has also been the subject of numerous investigations, and many different suggestions have been made. These have ranged from the standard (the poem is about a love triangle) to the unlikely (the poem is about a female dog's daydream) to the mundane (the poem is about a wart) to the bizarre (the poem is about a female zombie). The multiplicity of the available interpretations has resulted in years of lively discussions about the poem, if nothing else.

Because of the recent rise in feminist criticism, critical attention has been drawn back to "Wulf and Eadwacer." While the author's gender is unknown, the speaker's is not; therefore, the poem becomes an important artifact of the Anglo-Saxon feminine voice, perhaps even linked to the *Frauenlieder* tradition of Germanic women's songs. Most importantly, it preserves a feminine literary aspect that provides another viewpoint to the predominantly phallocentric, male-dominated Anglo-Saxon corpus. Feminist critics have further pointed out that many of the earlier interpretations and translations have, essentially, erased this feminine voice, subsuming it into the male heroic tradition, denying the inherent sexuality of the speaker herself. For example, while the poem bears no title in the manuscript, the one assigned to it reflects on the two men and says nothing about the speaker herself. More research in this direction is sure to be forthcoming and should provide even more intriguing possibilities about this enigmatic poem.

See also ANGLO-SAXON RIDDLES, CHARMS, OLD NORSE / ICELANIC EDDAS AND SAGAS.

FURTHER READING

Adams, John F. "Wulf and Eadwacer: An Interpretation." *MLN* 73, no. 1 (1958): 1–5.

Baker, Peter S. "The Ambiguity of *Wulf and Eadwacer*." *Studies in Philology* 78, no. 5 (1981): 39–51.

Davidson, Arnold E. "Interpreting *Wulf and Eadwacer*." *Annuale Mediaevale* 16 (1975): 24–32.

Giles, Richard R. "*Wulf and Eadwacer*: A New Reading." *Neophilologus* 65 (1981): 468–472.

Suzuki, Seiichi. "*Wulf and Eadwacer*: A Reinterpretation and Some Conjectures." *Neuphilologische Mitteilungen* 88, no. 2 (1987): 175–185.

WYATT, SIR THOMAS (1503–1542)

Thomas Wyatt was born in 1503 at Allington Castle in Kent. His father, Sir Henry Wyatt, was a faithful supporter of the Tudors, and his son benefited from this in his own career at court, which began early. Wyatt studied for a time at St. John's College, Cambridge, where he would have been exposed to the new humanist learning. As a gentleman poet and scholar, he probably wrote for his own and others' enjoyment in the hours he could spare from his duties as a courtier and ambassador.

Wyatt married Elizabeth Brooke around 1520, but it seems to have been an unhappy union, and the couple lived apart after the birth of their son, Thomas Wyatt the younger, in 1521. Wyatt's commissions and appointments show him to have been a favorite of both HENRY VIII and Thomas Cromwell. However, the uncertain machinations of court politics saw him imprisoned in the TOWER OF LONDON in May 1536 in a wave of arrests following the downfall of Henry's second queen, Anne Boleyn. Although he survived, Wyatt never again felt secure at court. His "epistolatory SATIRES" to Sir John Pointz and Sir Francis Bryan (probably composed between 1536 and 1542) examine the courtier's relationship to the court from a position of stoical detachment and personal alienation.

After 1536, Wyatt was sent on diplomatic missions to the emperor Charles V in an attempt to keep France and Spain from uniting politically against England. These were difficult years for the poet, who spent much time away from home and narrowly avoided death in the Tower again in January 1541. He died prematurely from fever in October 1542 in Sherborne, Dorset.

Wyatt's poems, which were never published during his lifetime, were preserved by his friends and contemporaries in several coterie collections. The chief of these are known as the Egerton, Devonshire, Blage, and Arundel-Harington manuscripts. Due to the manner in which his poems were transmitted, the extent of Wyatt's canon has frequently been disputed. The Egerton manuscript is generally taken to be the most authoritative source as it belonged to the poet himself and includes poems copied or edited by him. However, a number of poems of uncertain authorship have also been ascribed to Wyatt by some editors on the basis of probability.

An innovative experimenter with verse forms, Wyatt has been credited with introducing (or re-introducing) the ITALIAN (PETRARCHAN) SONNET into English verse. Although he has been accused of dry formalism in some of his lyrics, his best works—such as "THEY FLEE FROM ME," "MY LUTE AWAKE!," and "FAREWELL LOVE, AND ALL THY LAWS FOR EVER!"—bring a sense of vivid immediacy to the lover's experience. The majority of Wyatt's poems engage critically with the tradition of COURTLY LOVE, charting the psychological anguish of the unsatisfied lover and his search for intellectual and emotional stability. The relationship of Wyatt's biography to the personal "I" of his lyric poetry has often been explored.

Tradition holds that Wyatt was the lover of Anne Boleyn: "SOMETIME I FLED THE FIRE" and "WHOSO LIST TO HUNT" are often thought to refer to Anne, and she may also have been the "Brunet" mentioned in the sonnet "If Waker Care" (probably intended as a tribute to his mistress, Elizabeth Darrell), but there is no conclusive evidence either way. Wyatt's relationship to different Christian traditions has also been examined. His poetic paraphrases of the penitential Psalms were much admired by his contemporaries.

Historically, Wyatt has been linked with his younger contemporary, HENRY HOWARD, EARL OF SURREY. George Puttenham in *The Arte of English Poesie* (1589) saw these men as the chieftains of a new company of courtly makars (poets), a view which accords with the attention given to their poetry in Tottel's *Songes and Sonnettes* of 1557 (better known as *TOTTEL'S MISCELLANY*). Surrey's reputation overshadowed Wyatt's in the 19th century, but there has been a revival of interest in Wyatt since the 20th century as his psychological realism and bracing, choppy rhythms have generally been preferred to the smoother, more "artificial" lyrics of his counterpart.

FURTHER READING

Harrier, Richard. *The Canon of Sir Thomas Wyatt's Poetry.* Cambridge, Mass: Harvard University Press, 1975.

Jentoft, Clyde W. *Sir Thomas Wyatt and Henry Howard, Earl of Surrey: A Reference Guide.* Edited by Everett Emerson. Boston, Mass: Hall, 1980.

Muir, Kenneth. *Life and Letters of Sir Thomas Wyatt.* Liverpool, U.K.: Liverpool University Press, 1963.

Elizabeth Evershed

"WYATT RESTETH HERE" HENRY HOWARD, EARL OF SURREY (1542)   HENRY HOWARD, EARL OF SURREY composed this epitaph for SIR THOMAS WYATT the elder upon Wyatt's death in October 1542, and the poem appeared in print for the first time that autumn. It was the only one of Surrey's poems to be published during his lifetime; two other poems by Surrey on Wyatt ("The great Macedon" and "Diverse thy death do diversely moan") circulated in manuscript in the court of HENRY VIII. Richard Tottel printed all three poems with many of Wyatt's poems in his landmark poetic miscellany, *Songes and Sonnettes,* afterward known as *TOTTEL'S MISCELLANY* (1557). Although critics have long disputed the exact nature of the relationship between Surrey and Wyatt, the elegies indicate that the two poets were at least casually acquainted and that Surrey deeply admired the older poet's skill and reputation as a courtier and diplomat.

As several critics have noted, "Wyatt resteth here" differs significantly from Surrey's other poems and even from his other elegies, such as his tribute to his deceased squire and friend, Thomas Clere ("Norfolk sprang thee"). Instead of a statement of personal loss, the stanzas present a BLAZON, or catalogue, of Wyatt's physical traits and virtues. Surrey praises Wyatt's "hed" (l. 5), "hand" (l. 13), and "tongue" (l. 17) among other parts, arguing that the departed poet used his poetic skill, good judgment, and moral strength for the good of his king and country and to inspire England's young people "unto fame" (l. 20).

Only in the final STANZA and closing COUPLET does the speaker use first-person pronouns, and there they are plural: Wyatt was a witness "sent for our health, but not received so" (l. 36) and a "jewel we have lost" (l. 37). These lines and the opening mention of the "profit" Wyatt "by envy could obtain" (l. 4) refer obliquely to Wyatt's political enemies, some of whom seem to have been Surrey's opponents as well. By stating that Wyatt's "heavenly gifts increased by disdain" (l. 2), Surrey suggests that Wyatt was not defeated but instead made stronger by his experiences with these adversaries. However, the poem criticizes all of Wyatt's contemporaries, not only his foes, for not appreciating the poet or his poems enough.

The differences in style and tone between this and Surrey's other poems have led critics to a variety of interpretations. Earlier biographers and critics viewed the poem as a stiff and conventional tribute to a man Surrey knew only slightly or not at all. More recently, however, the poem has been praised for its elegant rhythms and imitation of Wyatt's own language and tropes. Most importantly, perhaps, in this poem Surrey argues that the figure of the poet is valuable to Tudor society as a voice of moral conscience and national memory. In a culture focused on social status, it is striking that Surrey the aristocrat was willing to publicly commemorate and honor a man who was his social inferior. For this reason, "Wyatt resteth here" marks an important moment in English poetry, one in which poetry becomes an important tool in altering the traditional bases of status and power.

See also ELEGY.

FURTHER READING

Jones, Emrys, ed. *Surrey: Poems.* Oxford: Clarendon Press, 1964.
Sessions, W. A. *Henry Howard, the Poet Earl of Surrey: A Life.* Oxford: Oxford University Press, 1999.
Tromly, Frederic B. "Surrey's Fidelity to Wyatt in 'Wyatt Resteth Here.'" *Studies in Philology* 78, no. 104 (1980): 376–387.

Carol D. Blosser

WYRD   *Wyrd* broadly means fate (i.e., destiny) in Old English. *Wyrd* carries both pre-Christian and Christian meaning. Its pagan meaning is linked to the Norns, the three fates in Scandinavian mythology, who execute *wyrd* as an all-powerful and impersonal force to which both gods and humans are subject. In its Christian context, *wyrd* is inextricably linked to the personal Christian God and signifies the temporal execution of divine plan, as discussed in the late ninth-century METERS OF BOETHIUS by ALFRED THE GREAT. Here, the omniscient teacher Wisdom defines *wyrd* as the temporal manifestation of providence. It regulates order and distributes changes evenly to create balance in nature as a material expression of commonplace divine justice: Fate is God's "everyday work."

See also BEOWULF, BOETHIUS' CONSOLATION OF PHILOSOPHY, EXETER BOOK, FORTUNE.

FURTHER READING

Lochrie, Karma. "*Wyrd* and the Limits of Human Understanding: A Thematic Sequence in the Exeter Book." *JEGP* 85 (1986): 323–331.
Payne, Anne F. "Three Aspects of *Wyrd* in Beowulf." In *Old English Studies in Honor of John C. Pope,* edited by Robert B. Burlin and Edward B. Irving, Jr., 15–35. Toronto: University of Toronto Press, 1974.

Karmen Lenz

Y

"YE THAT PASEN BY THE WEYE" ANONYMOUS (ca. 1372)

Taking as its starting point the biblical passage Lamentations 1:12, this poem imaginatively represents what Christ might have said to onlookers passing by and seeing him nailed on the cross. He begins by asking passersby to stop and look at him, and he then asks whether they have encountered anyone in a situation such as his, nailed to a cross, with a spear wound that has penetrated his side and heart.

Remarkable in this piece is that Christ as speaker is also making a direct appeal to the poem's contemporary audience. Those who "pasen be þe wey þe" are not only those who literally walked by Christ as he was being crucified, but also those hearers and readers of the poem who move through life without stopping to reflect on what Christ did for humankind. The poem asks that audience to pause for a moment and imagine themselves as witnesses to the Crucifixion. In so doing, it attempts to evoke sympathy for Christ's suffering, asking the audience to recognize the sacrifice that Christ made for them and spurring them to reflect on whether they have been deserving of that sacrifice.

There is a similar poem, which appears in more than one medieval manuscript, with the same theme and approach called "Abide, Ye Who Pass By." Analogous lines occur also in the play *The York Crucifixion of Christ.*

FURTHER READING

Brown, Carleton, ed. *Religious Lyrics of the XIVth Century.* Oxford: Clarendon, 1924.

Kathryn C. Wymer

Y GODODDIN ANEIRIN (ca. 600)

In his ninth-century *Historia Brittonum,* Nennius names a number of Welsh poets, including Aneirin, whom he describes as the "son of Dwywai," perhaps linking him with the chieftain families of the North. He is the named author of a long elegiac poem, *Y Gododdin,* one of the earliest surviving pieces of Welsh literature. The title refers to the Gododdin tribe, a Brythonic-speaking Celtic people inhabiting the southeastern corner of present-day Scotland. During the Romano-British era, their tribal center was at Din Eidyn (Edinburgh), which is why *Y Gododdin* is sometimes described as "the oldest Scottish poem."

Geography aside, the poem is set in an area that was culturally and linguistically Welsh, and the poem is composed in medieval Welsh. Most scholars agree that *Y Gododdin* was composed as an oral-formulaic piece shortly after the Battle of Catraeth (c. 600), today's Catterick, North Yorkshire. It consists of 99 alliterative and internally rhymed STANZAS, which record the bold deeds of the warriors who fought and fell fighting the Saxons. In the poem, Aneirin claims to be a survivor of the battle.

Y Gododdin is a celebratory poem, written explicitly to commemorate the bravery and virtue of the Briton warriors led into battle by their chieftain, Mynyddog. All pledge to fight either to victory or to death, and indeed, nearly all 300 of the Gododdin warriors are slain. Individual warriors or small, closely knit groups of warriors are eulogized separately in individual stanzas. In each,

Aneirin praises the virtues of death in battle and promotes the value of the eternal fame gained through loyalty and selfless valor in the face of ultimate defeat. For early Welsh societies, such texts served important historical and genealogical purposes while also clarifying a vision of insular unity and an explanatory preface to the isolated, separatist history later medieval historians often describe in their accounts of the Welsh people.

One of the most remarkable features of *Y Gododdin* is the appearance of the names of numerous warrior heroes who figure in later courtly ROMANCEs, both insular and continental. With particular reference to stanza 33, scholars often credit *Y Gododdin* as one of the earliest pieces of ARTHURIAN LITERATURE. Among the many heroes named in this stanza are Gwawrddur (Arthur) and Peredur (Perceval). There is a great deal of active debate on the nature of the connections between the heroes named in *Y Gododdin* and those appearing in the Arthurian romances. Some claim that the shared names indicate historic basis for King ARTHUR, but others see the appearance of names in common as coincidental. At the least, the textual linkages suggest some thematic parallels, and the names and references in *Y Gododdin* connect it with the later traditions of Welsh court poetry.

See also ELEGY, POETS OF THE PRINCES AND POETS OF THE NOBILITY.

FURTHER READING

Bromwich, Rachel. "Celtic Dynastic Themes and the Breton Lays." *Études Celtiques* 9 (1961): 439–471.

Jarman, A. O. H. "Aneirin: *The Gododdin.*" In *A Guide to Welsh Literature,* vol. 1, edited by A. O. H. Jarman and Gwilym Rees Hughes, 68–80. Swansea, Wales: Christopher Davies, 1976.

———, ed. and trans. *Y, Gododdin.* Llandysul, Wales: Gomer Press, 1988.

Kathleen H. Formosa

Z

ZEUGMA   From the Greek meaning "yoking," a zeugma is a rhetorical figure in which one word refers to or governs two or more, sometimes very different, terms. For example, in Sonnet 21 from ASTROPHIL AND STELLA, SIR PHILIP SIDNEY uses zeugma in the first quatrain to connect conflicting adjectives. The pairing of terms is often ironic. GEOFFREY CHAUCER's "The MILLER'S PROLOGUE AND TALE," for instance, warns that a husband should not be "inquisity / Of goddes pryvetee, nor of his wyf" (ll. 3163–3164). Here the yoking of divine mysteries, or "pryvetee," and a wife's private business (as well as "private parts") offers a shocking but humorous juxtaposition.

Zeugma is distinguished from syllepsis in that zeugma is sometimes considered a nongrammatical pairing of elements, whereas syllepsis is a grammatically correct pairing (and usually involves verbs). Many rhetoricians, however, use zeugma to refer to either kind of yoking.

Susan Yager

APPENDIX I

GLOSSARY

accent The STRESS on one or another syllable, especially when poetry is read aloud.

accentual verse A system of VERSE throughout at least a portion of a poem that depends on a certain fixed number of stresses in a line of poetry; this system, however, allows for any number of unstressed syllables.

allegory Extended metaphor or symbol with at least two levels of meaning, a literal level and an implied, figurative level; an allegorical narrative tells a story and at the same time suggests another level of meaning.

alliteration Repeating consonant sounds at the beginnings of words.

allusion Making reference to something or someone, usually in an indirect manner.

anapest A metrical foot consisting of two soft stresses followed by a hard stress. See METER.

anaphora A word or phrase that is repeated at the start of successive lines of poetry.

apostrophe A turn away from the reader to address another listener.

assonance Repetition of like vowel sounds, often in stressed syllables in close proximity to each other.

ballad A narrative in VERSE; the form derives from a narrative that was sung.

blank verse Unrhymed IAMBIC PENTAMETER.

cadence The rhythm in language, a pattern that can lend a musical order to a statement.

caesura A pause within a VERSE line, usually at approximately midpoint.

canon A term originally derived from the Roman Catholic Church having to do with church law, this term also refers to a body of literature that is generally accepted as exhibiting what is best or important in terms of literary art.

collagist poetry Poetry that employs the organizing element of collage or the bringing together of disparate material to create a new statement or vision.

conceit Not unrelated to the term *concept*, an unusual supposition, analogy, metaphor, or image, often clever.

connotation Meaning that is implied rather than stated directly as in DENOTATION.

consonance Repetition of identical consonant sounds, within the context of varying vowel sounds.

couplet Two VERSE lines in succession that have the same END RHYME. When the two lines contain a complete statement in themselves, they are called a closed couplet. See also HEROIC COUPLET.

dactyl A metrical FOOT consisting of a hard stress followed by two soft stresses.

denotation The literal meaning of a word or statement, the opposite of CONNOTATION.

diction Word choice, the actual language that a writer employs.

dimeter A VERSE line consisting of two metrical FEET.

dramatic monologue An address to an interlocutor (another potential speaker) who is not present; a dramatic monologue has only one actual speaker.

elegy   A poem mourning someone's death.

ellipsis   Part of a statement left out, unspoken.

end rhyme   A rhyme at the end of a VERSE line.

end-stopped   A VERSE line that pauses at its end, when no ENJAMBMENT is possible.

enjambment   A VERSE line whose momentum forbids a pause at its end, thus avoiding being END-STOPPED.

epic   A long poem that, typically, recounts the adventures of someone in a high style and diction; classically, the adventures include a hero who is at least partially superhuman in makeup or deed, and the events have special importance in terms of the fate of a people.

epigram   A brief, witty statement, often satiric or aphoristic.

epithet   A word or phrase that characterizes something or someone.

eye rhyme   Agreement of words according to their spelling but not their sound.

feet   See FOOT.

feminine ending   A VERSE line that ends with an extra soft stress.

feminine rhyme   The rhyming of two words in more than a single syllable.

figurative language   Language that employs figures of speech such as irony, HYPERBOLE, METAPHOR, SIMILE, SYMBOL, METONYMY, etc., in which the language connotes meaning.

foot   A configuration of syllables to form a METER, such as an IAMB, TROCHEE, ANAPEST, DACTYL, or SPONDEE. A line of one foot is called a MONOMETER line, of two feet a DIMETER line, of three feet TRIMETER, of four TETRAMETER, of five PENTAMETER, of six HEXAMETER, etc.

free verse   Poetry lacking a metrical pattern or patterns; poetic lines without any discernible meter.

haiku   A Japanese lyric form consisting of a certain number of syllables overall and in each line, most often in a five-seven-five syllabic line pattern.

half rhyme   A form of CONSONANCE in which final consonant sounds in neighboring stressed syllables agree.

heroic couplet   Two successive lines of end-rhyming (see END-RHYME) IAMBIC PENTAMETER.

hexameters   A VERSE line consisting of six metrical FEET.

hyperbole   An exaggeration meant to emphasize something.

iamb   A metrical FOOT consisting of a soft stress followed by a hard stress.

iambic pentameter   A five-FOOT line with a preponderance of iambic feet.

image   Language meant to represent objects, actions, feelings, or thoughts in vivid terms.

internal rhyme   A RHYME within a poetic line.

masculine rhyme   A RHYME depending on one hard-stressed syllable only.

metaphor   An implicit comparison, best when between unlike things, made without using the words *like* or *as*.

meter   An arrangement of syllables in units called FEET, such as IAMB or TROCHEE, and in numbers of feet to make a pattern, such as IAMBIC PENTAMETER; the syllables can be hard- or soft-stressed according to the type of FOOT or pattern to be employed.

metonymy   The substitution of a word that represents an association with, proximity to, or attribute of a thing for the thing itself; this figure of speech is not unlike SYNECHDOCHE.

monometer   A VERSE line consisting of a single metrical foot.

occasional verse   VERSE written to celebrate or to commemorate a particular event.

octave   An eight-line stanza of poetry, also the first and larger portion of a SONNET. See OCTET.

octet   An eight-line stanza of poetry. See OCTAVE.

ode   A lyric poem usually in a dignified style and addressing a serious subject.

onomatopoeia   A word or phrase whose sound resembles something the word or phrase is signifying.

oxymoron   A phrase or statement containing a self-contradiction.

paradox   A statement that seems to be self-contradictory but contains a truth that reconciles the contradiction.

pastoral   A poem that evokes a rural setting or rural values; the word itself derives from the Latin *pastor,* or "shepherd."

pentameter   A VERSE line consisting of five metrical FEET.

persona   The speaker in a poem, most often the narrator; the term is derived from the Latin word for "mask."

personification   Attributing human qualities to an inanimate entity.

prosody   The study of versification; the term is at times used as a synonym for METER.

quatrain   A four-line stanza of a poem, also a portion of a SONNET.

rhetorical figure   An arrangement of words for one or another emphasis or effect.

rhyme   Fundamentally, "agreement," the term specifically indicates the sameness or similarity of vowel sounds in an arrangement of words; there can be END-RHYME, INTERNAL RHYME, EYE RHYME, HALF RHYME, FEMININE RHYME, MASCULINE RHYME, SLANT RHYME.

rhyme scheme   The arrangement of END RHYMES in a poem, indicated when analyzing a poem with the letters of the alphabet, such as, for a poem in successive COUPLETS, *aa, bb, cc*, etc.

rhythm   A sense of movement created by arrangement of syllables in terms of stress and time.

sestet   A six-line stanza of poetry, also the final large portion of a SONNET.

sestina   A 36-line poem broken up into six SESTETS as well as a final stanza of three lines, the six words ending the first sestet's lines appearing at the conclusions of the remaining five sestets, in one or another order, and appearing in the final three lines; these repeated words usually convey key motifs of the poem.

simile   A comparison using the word *like* or *as*.

slant rhyme   A partial, incomplete RHYME, sometimes called a *half, imperfect, near* or *off rhyme*.

sonnet   A poem of 14 lines, traditionally in IAMBIC PENTAMETER, the RHYME SCHEME and structure of which can vary. There are two predominant types of sonnets: the English or Shakespearean, which consists of three QUATRAINS and a final COUPLET, usually with a rhyme scheme of *abab, cdcd, efef, gg*; and the Italian or Petrarchan sonnet, often with an initial OCTAVE rhyming *abba, abba* and a concluding SESTET rhyming *cdecde*. However, it is important to keep in mind that sonnet rhyme schemes can be very different from the above.

spondee   A metrical FOOT comprised of two hard stresses.

stanza   A group of lines of poetry.

stress   The emphasis when reading a poem accorded to a syllable.

strophe   A STANZA, or VERSE paragraph in a prose poem, derived from classical Greek drama.

syllabic verse   Poetry that employs a set number of syllables in a line, regardless of STRESS.

symbol   A figure of speech that means what it says literally but also connotes a secondary meaning or meanings, and which usually conveys a concept, motif, or idea.

synecdoche   A figure of speech in which a part of something is meant to signify the entirety of the thing, such as a hand that is meant to suggest a sailor whose hands are used in sailing a ship (as in "all hands on deck"). See METONYMY.

synesthesia   The mingling or substitution of the senses, such as when talking about a sound by mentioning a color.

tercet   A three-line STANZA grouping.

terza rima   Poetry comprised of TERCETS and an interlocking RHYME SCHEME: *aba, bcb, cdc*, etc.

tetrameter   A VERSE line of four metrical FEET.

tone   A poet's manifest attitude toward the subject expressed in the poem.

trimeter   A VERSE line of three metrical FEET.

trochee   A metrical FOOT consisting of a hard STRESS followed by a soft stress.

trope   A figurative or rhetorical mechanism, and at times a motif.

verse   A line of poetry or at times a synonym for *poetry* or *poem*.

vers libre   FREE VERSE.

voice   Not unlike the poem's PERSONA, a sense of a personality or speaker's diction, point of view or attitude in a poem; voice can also simply refer to a poem's speaker.

APPENDIX II

SELECTED BIBLIOGRAPHY

Borris, Kenneth. *Allegory and Epic in English Renaissance Literature: Heroic Form in Sidney, Spenser, and Milton.* Cambridge: Cambridge University Press, 2000.

Bronson, Bertrand Harris. *The Traditional Tunes of the Child Ballads, with Their Texts, According to the Extant Records of Great Britain and America.* Vol. 4. Princeton, N.J.: Princeton University Press, 1992.

Brook, G. L. *The Harley Lyrics: The Middle English Lyrics of MS. Harley 2253.* 4th ed. Manchester, U.K.: Manchester University Press, 1968.

Brown, Carleton, ed. *Religious Lyrics of the XVth Century.* Oxford: Clarendon Press, 1939.

Campbell, J. "Cynewulf's Multiple Revelations." *Medievalia et Humanistica* 3 (1971): 257–277.

Carlson, David R. "The 'Opicius' Poems and the Humanist Anti-Literature in Early Tudor England." *Renaissance Quarterly* 55, no. 3 (2002): 869–903.

Caviness, Madeline H. *Visualizing Women in the Middle Ages: Sight, Spectacle, and Scopic Economy.* Philadelphia: University Pennsylvania Press, 2001.

Child, Francis James, ed. *The English and Scottish Popular Ballads.* 5 vols. New York: Dover Publications, 1965.

Clarke, Danielle, ed. *Isabella Whitney, Mary Sidney, and Aemilia Lanyer: Renaissance Women Poets.* New York: Penguin Books, 2000.

Colie, Rosalie. *Paradoxia Epidemica: The Renaissance Tradition of Paradox.* Princeton, N.J.: Princeton University Press, 1966.

Cook, Albert S., and Chauncey B. Tinker. *Select Translations from Old English Poetry.* Boston: Ginn and Company, 1902.

Crawford, Patricia M. *Women and Religion in England 1500–1720.* New York: Routledge, 1993.

Damico, Helen, and Alexandra Hennessey Olsen, ed. *New Readings on Women in Old English Literature.* Bloomington: Indiana University Press, 1990.

Dillon, Myles. *Early Irish Literature.* Chicago: University of Chicago Press, 1948.

Donow, Herbert S. *A Concordance to the Sonnet Sequences of Daniel, Drayton, Shakespeare, Sidney, and Spenser.* London and Amsterdam: Feffer & Simons, 1969.

Fein, Susanna, ed. *Studies in the Harley Manuscript: The Scribes, Contents, and Social Contexts of British Library MS. Harley 2253.* Kalamazoo, Mich.: Medieval Institute Publications, 2000.

Gordon, R. K. *The Story of Troilus.* Toronto: University of Toronto Press, 1978.

Green, Martin, ed. In *The Old English Elegies: New Essays in Criticism and Research.* London and Toronto: Associated University Press, 1993.

Greenblatt, Stephen. *Renaissance Self-Fashioning: From More to Shakespeare.* Chicago: University of Chicago Press, 1980.

Greenfield, Stanley B., and Daniel C. Calder. "The Christian Saint as Hero." In *A New Critical History of Old English Literature.* New York: New York University Press, 1986, 158–182.

Guy, John. *Tudor England.* Oxford: Oxford University Press, 1991.

Hahn, Thomas, ed. *Sir Gawain: Eleven Romances and Tales.* Kalamazoo: Western Michigan University, 1995.

Hannay, Margaret P., Noel J. Kinnamon, and Michael G. Brennan, eds. *The Collected Works of Mary Sidney Herbert, Countess of Pembroke*. Oxford: Clarendon Press, 1998.

Hanson, Elizabeth. "Boredom and Whoredom: Reading Renaissance Women's Sonnet Sequences." *The Yale Journal of Criticism* 10, no. 1 (1997): 165–191.

Hardin, Richard F. "The Literary Conventions of Erasmus' Education of a Christian Prince: Advice and Aphorism." *Renaissance Quarterly* 35, no. 2 (1982): 151–163.

Hieatt, Constance B. *The Realism of Dream Visions: The Poetic Exploitation of the Dream Experience in Chaucer and his Contemporaries*. The Hague: Mouton, 1967.

Hoccleve, Thomas. *Hoccleve's Works: The Minor Poems*. Edited by F. J. Furnivall and I. Gollancz. Rev. ed. edited by Jerome Mitchell and A. I. Doyle. London: Oxford University Press for the Early English Text Society, 1970.

Horstmann, Carl, ed. *Yorkshire Writers: Richard Rolle of Hampole and his Followers*. 2 vols. London: Swan, Sonnenschein, 1895–96.

Howell, Andrew J. "Reading the *Harley Lyrics*: A Master Poet and the Language of Conventions." *ELH* 47, no. 4 (1980): 619–645.

Kinney, Arthur F. "Rhetoric as Poetic: Humanist Fiction in the Renaissance." *ELH* 43, no. 4 (1976): 413–443.

Klein, Lisa M. *The Exemplary Sidney and the Elizabethan Sonneteer*. Newark: University of Delaware Press, 1998.

Kristeller, Paul Oskar. *Renaissance Thought: The Classic, Scholastic, and Humanistic Strains*. New York: Harper, 1961.

Laskaya, Anne, and Eve Salisbury, eds. *The Middle English Breton Lays*. TEAMS Middle English Text Series. Kalamazoo: Medieval Institute Publications, 1995. Available online. URL: http://www.lib.rochester.edu/camelot/teams/salisbur.htm. Downloaded on February 10, 2007.

Lever, J. W. *The Elizabethan Love Sonnet*. London: Methuen and Co., 1956.

Marotti, Arthur F. "'Love Is Not Love': Elizabethan Sonnet Sequences and the Social Order" *ELH* 49, no. 2 (1982): 396–428.

May, Steven. *The Elizabethan Courtier Poets: The Poems and Their Contexts*. Asheville, N.C.: Pegasus, 1999.

Mehl, Dieter. *The Middle English Romances of the Thirteenth and Fourteenth Centuries*. London: Routledge, 1968.

Montrose, Louis Adrian. "Of Gentlemen and Shepherds: The Politics of Elizabethan Pastoral Form." *ELH* 30 (1983): 415–459.

Neely, Carol Thomas. "The Structure of English Sonnet Sequence." *ELH* 45, no. 3 (1978): 359–389.

Nelson, Deborah H. "Northern France." In *A Handbook of the Troubadours,* edited by F. R. P. Akehurst and Judith M. Davis, 255–261. Berkeley: University of California Press, 1995.

O'Curry, Eugene. *Manners and Customs of the Ancient Irish*. 3 vols. London: Williams/Norgate, 1873.

Parker, Tom. *Proportional Form in the Sonnets of the Sidney Circle: Loving in Truth*. Oxford: Clarendon Press, 1998.

Pearsall, Derek. *The Life of Geoffrey Chaucer: A Critical Biography*. Blackwell Critical Biographies. Oxford, U.K. and Cambridge, Mass.: Blackwell, 1992.

Reiss, Edmund. *The Art of the Middle English Lyric*. Athens: University of Georgia Press, 1972.

Richmond, Hugh M. *The School of Love: The Evolution of the Stuart Love Lyric*. Princeton, N.J.: Princeton University Press, 1964.

Roberts, Katherine J. *Fair Ladies: Sir Philip Sidney's Female Characters*. New York: Peter Lang Publishers, 1994.

Robinson, Forrest G. *The Shape of Things Known: Sidney's "Apology" in Its Philosophical Tradition*. Cambridge, Mass.: Harvard University Press, 1972.

Rollins, Hyder E., and Herschel Baker. *The Renaissance in England: Non-Dramatic Prose and Verse of the Sixteenth Century*. Boston: Heath, 1954.

Saunders, Corinne, ed. *A Concise Companion to Chaucer*. Malden, Mass.: Blackwell Publishing, 2006.

Saupe, Karen, ed. *Middle English Marian Lyrics*. Kalamazoo: Western Michigan University Press, 1998.

Scragg, Donald, ed. *The Battle of Maldon A.D. 991*. Oxford: Blackwell, 1991.

Smith, A. H., ed. *Three Northumbrian Poems: Cædmon's Hymn, Bede's Death Song, and the Leiden Riddle*. Rev. ed. Exeter, U.K.: University of Exeter Press, 1978.

Stevenson, Jane, and Peter Davidson, eds. *Early Modern Women Poets: An Anthology*. Oxford: Oxford University Press, 2001.

Strohm, Paul. *Social Chaucer*. Cambridge: Harvard University Press, 1989.

Swanton, Michael, ed. and trans. *The Anglo-Saxon Chronicle*. New York: Routledge, 1998.

Turville-Petre, Thorlac. *The Alliterative Revival*. Totowa, N.J.: D. S. Brewer, 1977.

APPENDIX III

CONTRIBUTORS LIST

Maia Adamina, M.A., teaches English at San Antonio College. Researches female writers and theater.

Karley K. Adney, Ph.D. candidate at Northern Illinois University, DeKalb, and instructor of English, Kishwaukee Community College, Malta, Illinois. Researches adaptations of Shakespeare for children.

Jennifer L. Ailles, Ph.D. candidate in English, University of Rochester, New York. Specializes in early modern literature, gender theory, and cultural studies.

Brandon Alakas, Ph.D. candidate, Queen's University (Kingston, Ontario). Researches monastic readings of John Lydgate and John Whethamstede.

Kerri Lynn Allen, graduate teaching assistant at Georgia State University. Researches Thomas More, Shakespeare, Aemelia Lanyer, and country-house poetry.

Susan L. Anderson, Ph.D. candidate, University of Leeds, Yorkshire. Researches Renaissance drama, poetry, and music's role in literature.

Clinton Atchley, Ph.D., associate professor of English and director of Master of Liberal Arts Program at Henderson State University, Arkadelphia, Arkansas. Specializes in the history of the English language.

Alison Baker, Ph.D., assistant professor of English, California State Polytechnic University, Pomona. Specializes in Chaucer and Arthurian literature.

J. D. Ballam, Ph.D., visiting fellow, Harris Manchester College, Oxford. Researches Victorian fiction and aesthetics in the English literary canon.

Candace Barrington, Ph.D., associate professor of English at Central Connecticut State University, New Britain. Publishes on Chaucer.

Deborah L. Bauer, M.A., postgraduate student at the University of Central Florida, Orlando. Researches political and gender issues in medieval British and Irish history.

Joseph E. Becker, Ph.D., assistant professor of English at the University of Maine, Fort Kent. Specializes in comparative literature and Jungian theory.

Kimberly K. Bell, Ph.D., assistant professor of English at Sam Houston State University, Huntsville, Texas. Researches medieval manuscript production, Middle English romance, and genre theory.

Lysbeth Em Benkert, Ph.D., associate professor of English at Northern State University, Aberdeen, South Dakota. Specializes in early modern women writers, Shakespeare, and Alexander Pope.

Andrew Bethune, Ph.D., assistant professor of English at Albion College, Michigan. Research interests in romance and the poetry of the 13th-century Barons' Wars.

Carol D. Blosser, Ph.D., teaches humanities at Regents School of Austin, Texas. Researches the Stationers Company and the English Reformation.

Janice M. Bogstad, Ph.D., professor and head collection development librarian at the University of Wisconsin, Eau Claire McIntyre Library. Researches comparative literature and religion.

Lisa L. Borden-King, Ph.D., assistant professor of education at Minot State University, North Dakota. Researches classical philosophy and semiotics.

Joyce Leslie Boro, Ph.D., assistant professor, medieval and Renaissance English literature, Département d'études anglaises, Université de Montréal. Published on *The Castell of Love* and specializes in romance, lyric poetry, and comparative literatures.

Matthieu Boyd, Ph.D. candidate in Celtic languages and literatures, Harvard University. Specializes in early Irish literature.

Bruce E. Brandt, Ph.D., professor of English at South Dakota State University, Brookings. President of the Marlowe Society; publishes on Marlowe and Elizabethan metaphysics.

Andrew Bretz, M.A. student at the University of Calgary, Alberta. Specializes in early modern drama and poetry, especially Bridewell and prostitution.

Jennifer N. Brown, Ph.D., assistant professor of English at the University of Hartford, Connecticut. Publishes in the area of medieval women's mysticism and vernacular hagiography.

Alexander M. Bruce, Ph.D., chair of the Department of English and Foreign Languages at the University of Montevallo, Alabama. Publishes on medieval studies, folklore, and pedagogy.

Brantley Lloyd Bryant, Ph.D., assistant professor of English at Sonoma State University, California. Investigates connections between trilingual poetry and political discourse in England.

Diane Cady, Ph.D., assistant professor of English at Mills College, Oakland, California. Specializes in gender, sexuality, and economics in late medieval and early modern culture.

Christina M. Carlson, Ph.D., assistant professor of English at Iona College, New Rochelle, New York. Investigates the effects of early publishing.

Julie A. Chappell, Ph.D., associate professor of English at Tarleton State University, Stephenville, Texas. Specializes in textual studies, mysticism, and early modern drama.

Cathryn A. Charnell-White, Ph.D., research fellow at Center for Advanced Welsh and Celtic Studies, Aberystwyth, Wales. Specializes in 18th-century Welsh literature.

Susannah Mary Chewning, Ph.D., associate professor of English at Union County College, Cranford, New Jersey. Specializes in medieval English anchoritism and feminist readings of medieval texts.

K. P. Clarke, D.Phil. candidate at Oxford University. Researches Chaucer and his Italian sources.

Christine Coch, Ph.D., assistant professor of English at College of the Holy Cross, Worcester, Massachusetts. Specializes in Elizabeth I and Edmund Spenser.

Helen Conrad-O'Briain, Ph.D., research associate at the School of English and the Center for Medieval and Renaissance Studies, Trinity College (Dublin). Publishes on the epic and early medieval theology.

Christine F. Cooper, Ph.D., assistant professor of English at Utah State University. Specializes in hagiography and late medieval English literature.

Raymond J. Cormier, Ph.D. Teaches literature at Longwood University, Virginia. Specializes in Old Irish and Celtic literature.

Michael G. Cornelius, Ph.D., professor of English and department chair at Wilson College (Pennsylvania). Specializes in Arthurian literture and film, monarchial identity, and sexuality studies.

John Micheal Crafton, Ph.D., professor of English at University of West Georgia, Corrollton. Specializes in medieval subjects, Christianity, and literature.

Susan Crisafulli, Ph.D., lecturer at Vanderbilt University. Scholarly interest is the intersection of the natural world and gender ideologies.

Thomas H. Crofts III, Ph.D., assistant professor of English at East Tennessee State University, Johnson City. Researches Malory and romances.

Joel B. Davis. Ph.D., assistant professor of English at Stetson University, DeLand, Florida. Specializes in Tudor poetry and prose with an emphasis on political poetics.

James Dean, Ph.D., professor of English at the University of Delaware, Newark. Publishes on Chaucer and medieval culture, especially biblical adaptations and Chaucerian language.

Kevin de Ornellas, Ph.D. Lectures on Renaissance literature at the University of Ulster. Recent publication on horses in early modern English culture.

Mark DiCicco, Ph.D., assistant professor of English literature at State University of New York, Cortland. Specializes in Scottish literature and film.

Martha Kalnin Diede, Ph.D., associate professor of English at Northwest University, Kirkland, Washington. Specializes in 15th- and 16th-century monarchs and religion.

Lauri S. Dietz, Ph.D., assistant professor at Angelo State University, San Angelo, Texas. Specializes in Renaissance literature, early modern poetics, and gender and sexuality.

Graham N. Drake, Ph.D., associate professor of English at the State University of New York at Geneseo. Research interests lie in Arthurian literature, scriptural texts, and gay and lesbian literature.

Martha W. Driver, Ph.D., distinguished professor of English and women's and gender studies at Pace University, New York City. Publishes on reception, text and illustration, and women's reading in the 15th and 16th centuries.

Margaret H. Dupuis, Ph.D., associate professor of English and director of Undergraduate Programs at Western Michigan University, Kalamazoo. Researches 16th-century poetry, particularly comic poetry.

Nathaniel Z. Eastman, Ph.D., assistant professor of English at Earlham College, Richmond, Indiana. Researches famine, economics, and problem morphology in Renaissance literature.

Bradford Lee Eden, Ph.D., head of Web and digitization services for the university libraries at the University of Nevada, Las Vegas. Scholarly interests include medieval musicology, Celtic literatures, and medievalisms.

Robert Einarsson, Ph.D, instructor of English at Grant MacEwan College, Edmonton, Alberta. He studies prosody and poetic language, especially in lyric poetry.

Elizabeth Elliott, Ph.D. candidate, University of Edinburgh. Specializes in English, French, and Scottish literature.

Winter Elliott, Ph.D., assistant professor of English at Brenau University, Gainesville, Georgia. Primary interests include early modern literature and gender studies.

Melissa A. Elmes, B.A., humanities instructor at Carlbrook School, Halifax, Virginia. Specializes in medieval, Renaissance, and French studies, English education, and writing.

Richard J. Erable, Ph.D., assistant professor of English at Franklin College, Indiana. Has written on Richard II.

Doug Eskew, Ph.D. candidate in English at the University of Texas, Austin. Specializes in Shakespeare's late tragedies.

Heide Estes, Ph.D., associate professor at Monmouth University, West Long Branch, New Jersey. Specializes in Jews in Anglo-Saxon poetry, Old and Middle English literature.

Elizabeth Evershed, Ph.D. candidate in English, University of Durham. Specializes in medievalisms as well as late medieval and early modern literature.

Regula Meyer Evitt, Ph.D., associate professor of English and comparative literature at Colorado College, Colorado Springs. Specializes in medieval women and medieval drama.

Joshua R. Eyler, Ph.D., assistant professor of English at Columbus State University (Georgia). Specializes in medieval sports and medieval disabilities.

Craig T. Fehrman, Ph.D. candidate at Yale, where he works on early modern and medieval literature.

Melissa Femino, Ph.D. candidate, University of New Hampshire. Specializes in 16th-century poetry.

Michael Foster, Ph.D. candidate at the University of Nottingham, England. Researches Middle English popular romances.

Kathleen H. Formosa, Ph.D., company secretary to the Architectural Association, Inc., a learned society and school of architecture. Publishes on medieval Welsh literature and higher-education administration.

Brett Foster, Ph.D., assistant professor of English at Wheaton College, Illinois. Specializes in Renaissance Rome as portrayed in early modern English texts.

Eric P. Furuseth, Ph.D., associate professor of English and Humanities, Minot State University, North Dakota. Researches Byron, especially *Don Juan.*

Torben R. Gebhardt, Ph.D. student, Ruhr-University-Bochum, Germany. Specializes in the Venerable Bede and *The Battle of Maldon.*

Michael W. George, Ph.D., assistant professor of English at Millikin University, Decatur, Illinois. Specializes in humor in the Middle Ages, medieval drama, and 14th-century Anglo-Irish literature.

Jamie Gianoutsos, M.A. candidate, Queen's University, Belfast (2007). Interest in early Irish literature.

Robin Gilbank, Ph.D. candidate, University of Wales, Aberystwyth, specializing in concepts of masculinity and Richard Rolle.

Christine Gilmore, Ph.D., independent scholar and editor. Researches and writes on Renaissance and medieval literature.

Rosemary Greentree, Ph.D., visiting research fellow, Department of English, University of Adelaide (Australia). She has published extensively on Middle English poetry, especially on lyrics and Henryson.

Candace Gregory-Abbott, Ph.D., assistant professor of history, California State University, Sacramento. Specializes in the history of medieval Europe.

Tyler Hancock, student, Minot State University, North Dakota. Pursuing a degree in Secondary English Education.

Carol E. Harding, Ph.D., associate professor of English and humanities at Western Oregon University, Monmouth. Specializes in German and comparative literature and researches Merlin in medieval romance.

Melissa A. Harris, editorial Assistant for this volume. Recent B.A. graduate of Minot State University in English (Lit.), with minors in gender studies, history, and humanities. Research interests in Christina of Markyate and early modern representations of gender.

Kristen N. Heintz. Teaches high school English while pursuing a degree in English education at Prairie View A&M University, Texas.

Christopher A. Hill, Ph.D., assistant professor of English, University of Tennessee at Martin. Specializes in Renaissance poetry, especially Sidney and Shakespeare.

Peggy J. Huey, Ph.D., associate professor of speech, theater, and dance at University of Tampa, Florida. Publishes on Breton *lais,* Chaucer, and Arthurian romances.

Shaun F. D. Hughes, Ph.D., professor of English at Purdue University, West Lafayette, Indiana. Interests in Old Norse and Old Icelandic texts.

Cathy Hume, Ph.D. candidate, University of Bristol, U.K. Researches advice literature and medieval reception of the Bible.

Theodora A. Jankowski, Ph.D., vice president of academic affairs and professor of English at Pennsylvania State University, Wilkes-Barre. Publishes on early modern drama and gender studies.

Allegra Johnston, Ph.D., instructor of English at University of Colorado, Colorado Springs. Specializes in early British literature, mythology, and medievalisms.

Jamie Johnston, Ph.D. candidate, University of Western Ontario, London, Ontario. Researches Elizabethan texts, religious otherness, and martyrological writings.

Kathleen M. Kalpin, Ph.D., assistant professor of English at the University of South Carolina, Aiken. Researches early modern texts, with an emphasis on feminist cultural studies.

Alexander L. Kaufman, Ph.D., assistant professor of English at Auburn University, Montgomery, Alabama. Specializes in medieval outlaw tales.

Karen Rae Keck, Ph.D., coeditor of the *St. Pachomius Library* and history of science editor of the *Net Advance of Physics.* Teaches English at Texas Tech University, Lubbock.

Gary Kerley, Ph.D., teaches language arts at North Hall High School, Gainesville, Georgia. Publishes on American literature and poetry.

John Kerr, Ph.D., assistant professor of English at Saint Mary's University of Minnesota, Winona. Publishes on Chaucer and Dante.

Robert E. Kibler, Ph.D., associate professor of English at Minot State University, North Dakota. Interests include Ezra Pound and the literature of Chinese antiquity.

Karolyn Kinane, Ph.D., assistant professor of English at Plymouth State University, New Hampshire. Specializes in Anglo-Saxon and medieval English hagiography, pedagogy, and contemporary medievalisms.

Herbert Klein, Ph.D., a lecturer in English literature at the Free University of Berlin. Research interests cover Skelton, Wyatt, and Surrey.

Daniel P. Knauss, Ph.D. candidate in English literature, Marquette University, Milwaukee, Wisconsin.

Kimberly Tony Korol, doctoral candidate in theater and drama at Northwestern University, Evanston, Illinois. Specializes in pre-Shakespearean Tudor drama and performance.

Marjory E. Lange, Ph.D., professor of English and humanities at Western Oregon University, Monmouth. Researches English Renaissance medicine and lyrics, Aelred of Rievaulx, and 20th-century women scholars.

Leah Larson, Ph.D., associate professor of English at Our Lady of the Lake University, San Antonio, Texas. Specializes in English, drama, and communication arts.

R. Jane Laskowski, M.A. candidate, North Dakota State University.

Karmen Lenz, Ph.D., assistant professor of Humanities at Macon State College, Georgia. Scholarly focus on Alfredian Boethius.

Catherine Loomis, Ph.D., associate professor of English and women's studies at University of New Orleans, Louisiana. Specializes in early modern literature.

Christopher D. Lozensky, English literature graduate of Minot State University, North Dakota. Researches Chaucer and gender studies.

Sergi Mainer, Ph.D., postdoctoral fellow at the Institute for Advanced Studies in the Humanities, University of Edinburgh. Specializes in the Scottish romance tradition and Arthurian literature.

Molly A. Martin, Ph.D. candidate, Purdue University, West Lafayette, Indiana. Researches gender and medieval romance.

Kelvin A. Massey, Ph.D. candidate, University of Tennessee, Knoxville. Interests in the crossover between the medieval and Victorian/modern eras.

Liz Herbert McAvoy, Ph.D., senior lecturer at University of Wales, Swansea. Specializes in medieval English anchoritism and Margery Kempe.

T. M. N. McCabe, Ph.D. candidate in medieval studies, University of Toronto, Ontario, specializing in John Gower.

Carola Mattord, Ph.D. candidate in English, with concentrations in Middle English and Middle High German literature, at Georgia State University.

Bonnie S. Millar, Ph.D., affiliate at University of Nottingham, U.K. Primarily publishes on alliterative poetry, medieval romances, and gender theory.

Dan Mills, Ph.D. candidate at Georgia State University. Specializes in Spenser's *The Faerie Queene*.

Michael Modarelli, Ph.D. candidate at the University of Tennessee, Knoxville. Interests include Chaucer and Spenser.

J. Hunter Morgan, Ph.D., assistant professor of English at Glenville State College, West Virginia. Researches figurative language and visual art in literature.

Erin N. Mount, M.A. candidate and graduate associate, University of Tennessee, Knoxville.

K. Sarah-Jane Murray, Ph.D., assistant professor of medieval literature and French in the Honors College at Baylor University, Waco, Texas. Researches the influence of Celtic and classical traditions on Old French literature.

Katie Musgrave, D.Phil. candidate, Corpus Christi College, Oxford University. Researches Shakespeare and rhetoric.

Lydia Newell, D.Phil. candidate, Balliol College, University of Oxford. Primary research area is theories of exegesis, authorship, and interpretation.

Jonathan M. Newman, Ph.D. candidate, Center for Medieval Studies, University of Toronto, Ontario. Researches satire and counsel in medieval literary discourse.

Richard Scott Nokes, Ph.D., professor of medieval literature at Troy University, Alabama. Research encompasses Anglo-Saxon magic and medicine and modern medievalism.

Thomas H. Ohlgren, Ph.D., professor of English at Purdue University, West Lafayette, Indiana. Publishes on medieval outlaw tales and Robin Hood ballads.

Rebecca Olson, Ph.D. candidate, Brandeis University, Waltham, Massachusetts. Examines the representation of tapestries in Tudor poetry and drama.

Leslie J. Ormandy, Ph.D., instructor of English at Clackamas Community College, Oregon City, Oregon. Specializes in early modern England and the British Victorian era.

James N. Ortego II, Ph.D., assistant professor of English at Troy University, Dothan, Alabama. Interested in poetry and literature by and about women, particularly women of color.

Daniel E. O'Sullivan, Ph.D., assistant professor of French at the University of Mississippi. Specializes in manuscripts and material culture, including historical linguistics, as well as medieval comparative literatures.

James M. Palmer, Ph.D., assistant professor of English at Prairie View A&M University, Texas. Publishes on Old and Middle English literature and composition.

Josie Panzuto, Ph.D. candidate in English, University of Montreal, Quebec. Specializes in early modern printing, bibliography, and romance.

Catherine Ann Perkins, Ph.D., assistant professor and reference/instruction librarian at City University of New York, Staten Island. Researches medieval and early modern English drama and poetry.

Tony Perrello, Ph.D., assistant professor of English at California State University, Stanislaus. Publishes on Renaissance drama and medieval literature and riddles.

Michael Peterson, Ph.D., instructor at Wright College, Chicago, Illinois. Specializes in early modern literature and film.

Alessandra Petrina, M.A., senior lecturer of English literature at Università di Padova, Italy. Publishes on late medieval and Renaissance literature.

Mardy Philippian, Jr., assistant professor of English at Simpson University, Redding, California.

Researches metaphysical poetry and the history of English devotional literature.

Daniel F. Pigg, Ph.D., professor of English, University of Tennessee at Martin. Researches sexuality and subjectivity in medieval literature, as well as pedagogical practices of higher education.

Ernst Pijning, Ph.D., associate professor of history at Minot State University, North Dakota. Specializes in Brazilian history, particularly 16th- and 17th-century smuggling.

Frederick Porcheddu, Ph.D., associate professor of English at Denison University, Granville, Ohio. Specializes in Middle English, Old French, and Old Norse texts, Arthurian and Charlemagne legends, and sexuality studies.

Beth Quitslund, Ph.D., assistant professor of English at Ohio University. Researches the English Renaissance and reformation, especially Spenser, Milton, and metrical psalmody.

Kimberly A. Racon, Ph.D. candidate and Teaching Fellow at Lehigh University, Bethlehem, Pennsylvania. Specializes in late medieval economic exchange and labor practices.

Mary R. Rambaran-Olm, Ph.D. candidate and teaching assistant, University of Glasgow, Scotland. Interest in Old and Middle English poetry and medieval military history.

A. Wade Razzi, Ph.D. candidate, Merton College, Oxford University. Researches the works of Robert Crowley.

Gavin Richardson, Ph.D., associate professor of English at Union University, Jackson, Tennessee. Publishes on medieval England and Anglo-Saxon literary culture.

Daniel Ringrose, Ph.D., associate professor of history at Minot State University, North Dakota. Researches post-Reformation France.

David A. Roberts, Ph.D. candidate, Ohio State University. Working on medieval English chronicles and the development of English national identity.

Sara Elin Roberts, Ph.D., lecturer at the University of Wales, Swansea. Specializes in medieval Welsh history, especially legal history, and the poetry of Dafydd ap Gwilym.

William T. Rossiter, Ph.D., instructor of late medieval literature at the University of Manchester, U.K. Researches Italian and English lyrics and the development of the English sonnet.

Robert Allen Rouse, Ph.D., professor of English at the University of British Columbia, Vancouver. Publishes on Arthurian literature and Anglo-Saxon culture.

Jay Ruud, Ph.D., chair of the English Department at the University of Central Arkansas, Conway. Publishes on Chaucerian lyrics and medieval culture, and is completing a critical companion to Dante for Facts on File.

Gregory M. Sadlek, Ph.D., professor of medieval English language and literature at Cleveland State University, Ohio. Publishes on Western literature of love, classical Rome, and late Middle Ages.

Anne Salo, M.A., graduate student in comparative literature, University of California, Davis. Interest in the politics of poetic vernaculars in 14th-century Spain and England.

Elizabeth Scala, Ph.D., associate professor of English and medieval studies at the University of Texas, Austin. Specialist in the field of Chaucer studies, currently working on the woodcut editions of the *Canterbury Tales* up to 1550.

Kreg Segall, Ph.D., assistant professor of English at Suffolk County Community College, Brentwood, New York. Researches Shakespeare, Spenser, and Skelton.

John P. Sexton, Ph.D., assistant professor of English at Bridgewater State College, Massachusetts. Researches intersections of literature and the law, and Anglo-Saxon and Anglo-Norman literature.

Christian Sheridan, Ph.D., assistant professor of English at Saint Xavier University, Chicago, Illinois. Publishes on Chaucer, Old French fabliaux, and Robert Henryson.

Larry T. Shillock, Ph.D., associate professor of English and Drusilla Stevens Mazur Research Professor at Wilson College, Chambersburg, Pennsylvania. Publishes on the history of the novel and critical theory.

Margaret M. Simon, Ph.D. candidate, University of Virginia, Charlottesville. Researches self-loss in 16th- and 17th-century lyric and prose romance.

Emily Smith, Ph.D. Publishes on Margaret Cavendish, Frances Brooke, domestic manuscript writing, and literary documents.

R. L. Smith, Ph.D., candidate at the University of Texas, Austin, working on women dramatists of the Tudor period.

William H. Smith, Ph.D. Teaches English at Weatherford College, Texas. Researches medieval scientific texts and Old English religious literature.

Larry J. Swain, Ph.D., instructor at the University of Illinois, Chicago. Interests in Hiberno-Latin literature, early Christian Ireland, and paleography.

Louise Sylvester, Ph.D., senior lecturer in English at the University of Westminster (UK). Publishes on pedagogy, Arthurian literature, and gender studies.

Annemarie Thijms, Ph.D. candidate, Trinity College, Dublin. Specializes in 16th-century Plowman texts and *St. Erkenwald*.

Sebastiaan Verweij, M.A. Teaches Scottish literature at Glasgow University, Scotland. Researches courtly culture, manuscript production, and circulation.

Kathryn R. Vulić, Ph.D., assistant professor of English at Western Washington University, Bellingham. Publishes on late medieval vernacular devotional literature and devotional writings.

Dianne Walbeck, senior English (Lit) major at Minot State University, North Dakota.

Lori A. Wallach, Ph.D. candidate, City University of New York Graduate Center. Specializes in teaching writing and literature courses.

Gary Waller, Ph.D., professor of literature, cultural studies, and drama at State University of New York, Purchase. Publishes in 16th-century poetry and examines the Virgin Mary and sexuality.

J. A. White, Ph.D., assistant professor of English at Morgan State University, Baltimore, Maryland. Specializes in medieval and Renaissance literature, psychology and literature, and popular culture.

Thomas Willard, Ph.D., associate professor of English at the University of Arizona, Tucson. Currently researching Northrop Frye's teaching of English literature.

Sierra M. Wilson, senior honors student in medieval studies. Baylor University, Waco, Texas. Research interest in Marie de France.

David Houston Wood, Ph.D., assistant professor of English at the University of Wisconsin, La Crosse. Publishes on Renaissance drama and prose.

Matthew Woodcock, D.Phil., lecturer in English at the University of East Anglia, Norwich, U.K. Publishes on Edmund Spenser's use of fairy mythology and early modern literature.

Donna C. Woodford, Ph.D., assistant professor of English at New Mexico Highlands University, Las Vegas. Specializes in motherhood in Renaissance literature and early modern women writers.

Kathryn C. Wymer, Ph.D., lecturer at University of North Carolina, Chapel Hill. Researches vernacular English preaching and medieval poetry and texts.

Susan Yager, Ph.D., associate professor of English and associate director of the Center for Excellence in Learning and Teaching at Iowa State University, Ames. Primarily researches Chaucer and the *Gawain*-poet.

Michael Young, Ph.D., senior lecturer in English at La Roche College, Pittsburgh, Pennsylvania, where he specializes in Shakespeare, writing, and pedagogy.

Hannah Zdansky, M.A. student at the National University of Ireland, Galway. Specializes in Old and Middle Irish.

INDEX